WITHDRAWN FROM
THE LIBRARY

UNIVERSITY OF
WINCHESTER

09

D0833792

KA 0292670 9

Advances in Sport Psychology

Second Edition

Thelma S. Horn, PhD

Miami University

Editor

UNIVERSITY COLLEGE WINCHESTER
LIBRARY

Human Kinetics

Library of Congress Cataloging-in-Publication Data

Advances in sport psychology / Thelma S. Horn, editor.--2nd ed.
    p. cm.
    Includes bibliographical references and index.
    ISBN 0-7360-3298-3
    1. Sports--Psychological aspects.   I. Horn, Thelma S., 1949-
GV706.4 .A38 2002
796'.01--dc21

                                                2002022912

ISBN: 0-7360-3298-3

Copyright © 2002, 1992 by Human Kinetics Publishers, Inc.

All rights reserved. Except for use in a review, the reproduction or utilization of this work in any form or by any electronic, mechanical, or other means, now known or hereafter invented, including xerography, photocopying, and recording, and in any information storage and retrieval system, is forbidden without the written permission of the publisher.

Acquisitions Editor: Michael S. Bahrke, PhD; **Developmental Editor:** Rebecca Crist; **Assistant Editor:** Mark E. Zulauf; **Copyeditor:** Julie Anderson; **Proofreader:** Sarah Wiseman; **Indexer:** Joan Griffitts; **Permission Manager:** Dalene Reeder; **Graphic Designer:** Fred Starbird; **Graphic Artist:** Kathleen Boudreau-Fuoss; **Photo Manager:** Les Woodrum; **Cover Designer:** Jack W. Davis; **Photographer (cover):** Tom Roberts; **Art Managers:** Carl D. Johnson and Kelly Hendren; **Illustrator:** Roberto Sabas; **Printer:** Edwards Brothers

Printed in the United States of America   10 9 8 7 6 5 4 3 2 1

Human Kinetics
Web site: www.HumanKinetics.com

United States: Human Kinetics, P.O. Box 5076, Champaign, IL 61825-5076
800-747-4457
e-mail: humank@hkusa.com

Canada: Human Kinetics, 475 Devonshire Road Unit 100, Windsor, ON N8Y 2L5
800-465-7301 (in Canada only)
e-mail: orders@hkcanada.com

Europe: Human Kinetics, 107 Bradford Road, Stanningley, Leeds LS28 6AT, United Kingdom
+44 (0) 113 255 5885
e-mail: hk@hkeurope.com

Australia: Human Kinetics, 57A Price Avenue, Lower Mitcham, South Australia 5062
08 8277 1555
e-mail: liahka@senet.com.au

New Zealand: Human Kinetics, P.O. Box 105-231, Auckland Central
09-523-3462
e-mail: hkp@ihug.co.nz

UNIVERSITY COLLEGE
WINCHESTER

796.015
HOR   02926709

This book is dedicated to . . .

. . . the memory of my father, Jerald John Sternberg,
whose life ended much too soon.
Although he had only an eighth-grade education,
my father's lifelong interest in reading and learning
is something I can only hope to have inherited.

. . . the future promise and potential of my daughters,
Jocelyn Lou and Karolyn Sternberg Horn.
Their interest in, passion for, and enjoyment of sports
of all sorts has continually refueled my desire
to study the sporting world within which they play.

Contents

Chapter 4   Self-Perceptions and Sport Behavior   83

Kenneth R. Fox

Chapter 5   Motivational Orientations and Sport Behavior   101

Maureen R. Weiss and Emilio Ferrer-Caja

Chapter 6   Self-Efficacy and Attributional Processes in Physical Activity   185

Edward McAuley and Bryan Blissmer

Part IV Psychological Skills, Intervention Techniques, and Sport Behavior   403

Chapter 16   Optimal Experience in Sport: A Flow Perspective   501
Jay C. Kimiecik and Susan A. Jackson

Chapter 17   Athletic Injury and Sport Behavior   529
Eileen Udry and Mark B. Andersen

Preface

In its most generic sense, sport psychology can be defined as the psychological study of human behavior in sport and physical activity. The literature in the field suggests that sport psychologists are particularly interested in the variation in individuals' behavior in such contexts. This includes the variation between individuals who are placed in the same situation as well as the variation in the behavior of the same individual across situations. To illustrate variation between individuals, consider the case of two athletes from the same team who are performing in a rather crucial athletic contest (e.g., league, state, or regional championship). Despite both athletes being placed in the same performance context, their behavior may well differ in this situation. That is, they may vary considerably in anxiety, confidence, motivation, and actual performance. Equally as interesting to sport psychologists is the behavioral variation that occurs when an individual athlete moves from one situation to another. For example, sport psychologists have noted consistently that the amount of anxiety an individual athlete experiences is highly dependent on the situation (e.g., practice vs. game, home vs. away contest). Similarly, an individual athlete may exhibit a high level of motivation in a soccer practice but then be considerably less motivated to achieve in a softball practice. Or an individual who coaches both cross-country and track-and-field teams at the same high school may exhibit significantly different leadership styles and behaviors across the two sporting contexts.

To explain such behavioral variation, sport psychologists have identified and examined a number of factors that can be categorized as either individual difference factors or socioenvironmental factors. Individual difference factors can refer to either (a) relatively stable traits, dispositions, or characteristics of the individual such as age, trait anxiety, motivational orientation, self-esteem, or other personality characteristics, or (b) differences between individuals in their subjective appraisals of the world around them and the events that occur in that world. That is, individuals may differ from each other not only in regard to relatively stable traits or dispositions but also in the way in which they perceive, analyze, interpret, and evaluate the events in their world. Sport psychologists have used these individual difference variables to explain and predict the behavior of individual participants in sport and physical activity contexts. From a related perspective, sport psychologists also have found that factors within the sport or social environment can affect the participants' behavior. Specifically, characteristics of the sport group (e.g., size, cohesion, composition) and the behaviors of the group leader (e.g., coach or exercise leader) have been found to affect the behavior of group members. In addition, the sociocultural or sociopolitical context within which sport occurs also can determine or strongly affect not only the behaviors exhibited by individual athletes, coaches, and others in the sport environment but also their attitudes, beliefs, cognitions, and orientations.

Although much of the research in sport psychology has examined the influence of individual difference and socioenvironmental factors separately, recent consensus in the field clearly suggests that these two entities exert an interactional effect. In other words, considerable evidence shows that the characteristics of the individual participant interact with factors in the social environment to determine the individual's behavior in specific sport or physical activity contexts.

Within the last three decades, we have accumulated much information concerning the individual and socioenvironmental factors that affect human behavior in sport and physical activity settings. However, we still have a considerable way to go before we will truly be able to understand, predict, and modify the behavior of individuals in sport and physical activity contexts.

The first edition of this text, *Advances in Sport Psychology*, was published in 1992 with the express purpose of summarizing the state of knowledge in sport psychology. Like its predecessor, this second edition of the text was written to provide a comprehensive and up-to-date review of the major issues that are of current research interest in sport psychology. This second edition emphasizes a discussion and critical analysis of the current state of knowledge in each topic area combined with recommendations concerning future research directions. The text is directed primarily toward graduate students enrolled in research-oriented sport psychology courses and toward individuals currently conducting research in sport psychology. Although the book is not intended to serve as a how-to text for practicing sport psychologists or to provide information about enhancing sport performance, the individual chapters should be useful to practitioners who need to understand the factors that affect the behavior of sport performers before they can effect behavioral change.

In contrast to the first edition of this text, which contained 13 chapters, the current edition contains 17 individual chapters organized into four parts. The two chapters in part I provide a comprehensive introduction to the field of sport psychology (e.g., definitions, history, research paradigms, research methodologies). The six chapters in part II examine the characteristics of individuals (i.e., individual difference factors) that affect their behavior in sport and physical activity contexts. These characteristics include personality, self-perceptions, motivational orientations, cognitions, arousal/anxiety, and moral reasoning levels. The four chapters in part III discuss various factors in the social environment that impinge on participants' behaviors. The first two chapters in part III discuss the impact of group dynamics and the behaviors of adult supervisors (e.g., coaches) on athletes' performance and behavior. The next two chapters in part III present perspectives that may be perceived to be outside of our traditional notions of sport psychology but which, nevertheless, constitute important socioenvironmental influences on the behavior of individual sport participants. Specifically, these two chapters discuss gender issues in sport and socialization processes within the sport context. Finally, the five chapters in part IV examine the research and theory concerning selected intervention techniques that have been used to enhance the performance or modify the behavior of athletes and other physical activity participants. Individual chapters discuss the research and theory pertaining to imagery and mental rehearsal, attentional processes, goal-setting, flow and peak performance, and athletic injuries.

The four new chapters that have been added to the second edition of this text cover topics related to self-perceptions, moral reasoning levels, flow and peak performance, and athletic injury. These chapters were added as a result of the rather extensive research base on these topics that has been accumulated since the first edition of this text was published. In addition, all of the original 13 chapters have been substantially or, in some cases, totally rewritten. This extensive revision of the 1992 edition of this text clearly and appropriately reflects the theoretical and empirical advances that have occurred in sport psychology within the last decade. Thus, returning readers will be able to see what we have, or have not yet, accomplished as a field in the past decade.

Although the chapters in this edited text were written by different authors, an attempt was made to use a consistent format. Specifically, each part begins with a fairly brief introduction to the topic area. This introduction includes an explanation of the scope of the part, and a clear outline of the chapters comprising the part. In the main body of each chapter, the authors review the available research and theory on the chapter topic. This review does not just summarize the research to date but rather analyzes and, in most cases, synthesizes the state of knowledge in the area. Finally, a section of each chapter is devoted to a discussion of future research directions.

The production of a textbook of this depth and breadth certainly requires the coordinated efforts of a number of individuals. It seems appropriate at this time to recognize the major contributors. First, it is important to acknowledge the contributions of the people at Human Kinetics Publishers. Michael Bahrke and Rebecca Crist were the developmental editors for this text. In this role, they provided the technical, administrative, and organizational support that was needed to move the second edition of the text from conceptualization to publication.

It is, of course, also essential to acknowledge the contributions of the authors who wrote the individual chapters for this text. All but one of the authors for the first edition of this text agreed to revise, update, and add to their original chapters. As editor of this second edition, I truly appreciate the willingness of these authors to rewrite and revise what were already high-quality summaries of the research in their respective topic areas. I also want to welcome to this second edition a new cadre of authors. Included are Robert Brustad, Kenneth Fox, Alan Smith, Jay Kimiecik, Sue Jackson, Eileen Udry, and Mark Andersen, who authored or coauthored the "new" chapters included in this edition. In addition, several new coauthors were recruited for this edition. These include Anthony Kontos, Emilio Ferrer-Caja, Bryan Blissmer, Christy Greenleaf, Kathleen Martin, and Sarah Naylor.

From my perspective as the book's editor, the 28 authors represented in this text are some of the most prolific researchers and scholars in the field. Despite their extremely busy schedules, these individuals invested considerable time and effort in writing their chapters. As several of them noted, it was not an easy task to condense the research and theory that has been accumulated in each particular topic area into a reasonable manuscript length. In addition, each author was specifically requested to go beyond just summarizing the available research and theory to critically review what we know and outline where we need

to go in the future. The idea in writing the individual chapters for this book was to push at the boundaries that have defined and, in many cases, limited our field since its inception. This was certainly a formidable task but one which each author has accomplished with distinction.

In soliciting authors for both editions of this book, I found that of the many arguments that I had marshaled to encourage their participation, the one that was consistently the most successful was the one that appealed to their commitment to the field of sport psychology. I am quite convinced that each author's primary motivation in writing her or his chapter was to advance the field and, perhaps more importantly, to stimulate the interest and enthusiasm of current and future researchers. It is our combined hope, then, that this text will not only further our readers' understanding of the field but also motivate all of us toward continued and qualitatively better research work. May our passion for sport psychology continue to burn brightly!

PART I

Introduction to Sport Psychology

Despite the early and relatively isolated work of such individuals as Coleman Griffith and Norman Triplett, sport psychology as an area of academic research within the sport sciences did not begin in earnest until the mid-1960s. As will become evident throughout this book, much has been accomplished over the last several decades. However, as with any area of academic study, many changes also have occurred with respect to the field of study itself. Thus, it seems appropriate for this text to begin with two chapters that introduce and survey the area of study known as sport psychology.

In chapter 1, Deborah Feltz and Anthony Kontos compare and contrast the various perspectives of sport psychology and link these perspectives to divergent research objectives and methodologies. They discuss the differing perspectives of sport psychology held by researchers both within and outside of North America as well as compare the divergent roles that sport psychologists can choose or can be expected to fulfill. Feltz and Kontos then offer a historical account of the last 50 years of research in sport psychology and conclude by identifying and discussing current issues and future trends in the field.

In chapter 2, Robert Brustad critically examines how knowledge has been defined and constructed in sport psychology. His chapter begins with an overview of the traditional bases of knowledge in sport psychology. This section includes a discussion of the assumptions and beliefs that underlie the positivist view of science. Brustad then presents the critiques concerning these dominant ways of knowing and uses this perspective to identify current limitations in our understanding of people's behavior in sport contexts. In discussing these varying perspectives on the pursuit of knowledge in sport psychology, Brustad clearly shows how our field's alliances with our parent discipline of psychology and with the other subdisciplines within the sport sciences have influenced the content of our knowledge base and the means by which we pursue this knowledge. Brustad concludes with an overview of alternate philosophies of knowledge development and with recommendations for future researchers in sport psychology. Although some readers of the first edition of this text have questioned the necessity and even the appropriateness of including such a "critical" analysis of knowledge construction in sport psychology, we believe that a chapter such as this is very necessary to our field because it should encourage all of us to reflect on our beliefs about what it means "to know" in our field of inquiry. In short, our research as a field cannot advance very quickly if we are unwilling to critically examine the assumptions, beliefs, values, and perspectives with which we approach our research studies. Thus, this chapter is offered not as a condemnatory critique of the field but rather as a challenge to researchers to critically reflect on the paths we choose to follow in our research work and on the methods we use to pursue knowledge about human behavior in sport contexts.

In combination, then, these two chapters provide an introduction to, and overview of, sport psychology as an area of academic study. As such, they establish a foundation on which the following more topically oriented chapters will rest.

CHAPTER 1

The Nature of Sport Psychology

Deborah L. Feltz and Anthony P. Kontos

Describing the nature of sport psychology is difficult because so many different perspectives on the field exist. Not only are there differences in definitions of the term itself, but there are also differences in the roles that psychologists are presumed to play. A content review of the definitions of sport psychology that appear in a number of recent books and articles shows that some writers view sport psychology as a subdiscipline of psychology, whereas others view it as a subdiscipline of sport and exercise science. A brief survey of these definitions is provided in table 1.1. In addition, sport psychology writers have differentiated between psychology focusing on athletics and psychology of physical activity encompassing all movement-related contexts (e.g., Cratty, 1989; Martens, 1974). Finally, some writers have created even more specialized terms, such as *developmental sport psychology* (Duda, 1987; Weiss & Bredemeier, 1983), *psychophysiological sport psychology* (Hatfield & Landers, 1983), and *cognitive sport psychology* (Straub & Williams, 1983). Given such diversity of opinion, it is no wonder that more than 15 years ago Dishman (1983) suggested that the field of sport psychology was suffering from an identity crisis.

In this chapter, we describe the nature of sport psychology, including different perspectives on the field of study and roles of sport psychologists, and present a historical overview of the research from 1950 to the present. Current issues in the field and future challenges also are presented.

PERSPECTIVES ON SPORT PSYCHOLOGY

Sport psychology, when viewed as a subdiscipline within the larger field of psychology, is defined as an applied psychology or as a field of study in which the principles of psychology are applied within a particular context. Although sport psychology traditionally has not been recognized as a subdiscipline within the field of academic psychology, Smith (1989) suggested that sport psychology was ready to be embraced by mainstream psychology. As evidence of this, sport psychology was approved as Division 47 within the American Psychological Association (APA) in 1986 and has long been recognized as a specialization within psychology throughout Europe. There are even some sport psychology specializations within graduate programs in clinical psychology (e.g., University of Washington) and educational/school psychology (e.g., Florida State University). The Association for the Advancement of Applied Sport Psychology (AAASP) publishes a directory of these "clinically oriented" sport psychology graduate

---

Table 1.1
Definitions of Sport Psychology

Sport psychology is

"the effect of sport itself on human behavior" (Alderman, 1980, p. 4)

"a field of study in which the principles of psychology are applied in a sports setting" (Cox, 1985, p. xiii)

"a subcategory of psychology focusing on athletes and athletics" (Cratty, 1989, p. 1)

"the branch of sport and exercise science that seeks to provide answers to questions about human behavior in sport" (Gill, 1986, p. 3)

"the educational, scientific, and professional contributions of psychology to the promotion, maintenance, and enhancement of sport-related behavior" (Rejeski & Brawley, 1983, p. 239)

"an applied psychology; the science of psychology applied to athletics and athletic situations" (Singer, 1978, p. 4)

"the scientific study of people and their behavior in sport and exercise activities" (Weinberg & Gould, 1995, p. 8)

---

programs (see Sachs, 1993, for more information). Still, sport psychology has not attained wide acceptance within the broader field of psychology.

The view of sport psychology as a subdiscipline of sport and exercise science comes mostly from researchers in physical education (or kinesiology). Henry (1981), for example, argued that the academic discipline of physical education consists of the study of certain aspects of fields such as psychology, physiology, anatomy, and sociology rather than the application of those disciplines to physical activity settings. Dishman (1983) and others (e.g., Gill, 1986; Morgan, 1989; Roberts, 1989) supported this view of sport psychology as a part of the broad area of sport science. Gill (1986) noted that although sport and exercise science is a multidisciplinary field that draws on knowledge from the broader parent disciplines, the subareas comprising sport and exercise science also draw on theories, constructs, and measures from each other. In fact, some sport psychology researchers (e.g., Brawley & Martin, 1995; Dishman, 1983; Feltz, 1989; Morgan, 1989) have suggested that sport psychology will need to include knowledge from other subdisciplines within sport and exercise science to explain phenomena specific to sport. McCullagh and Noble (1996) suggested that the emphasis placed on psychology or sport science will vary as a function of one's intended career goals (i.e., academic/research vs. practitioner/applied). They did contend, however, that knowledge in both sport psychology and sport science is necessary to address the issues facing academic and practicing sport psychologists.

These different perspectives concerning sport psychology parallel the situation in social psychology, where sociologists and psychologists differ in their definition of social psychology (House, 1977; McCall & Simmons, 1982; Perlman & Cozby, 1983; Stryker, 1977). Social psychology as seen from the psychological tradition emphasizes the individual, whereas social psychology viewed from the sociological tradition emphasizes group and social variables. Although recently the two traditions have converged somewhat, deep divisions are believed to remain regarding fundamentally different assumptions about the nature of human beings in society (McCall & Simmons, 1982). These divergent views pose different questions, which define the content of study in terms of topics, methods, and theoretical orientations.

Whether one views sport psychology as a subdiscipline of psychology or as a subdiscipline of sport and exercise science is an important issue, because the perspective chosen determines one's focus of study. For instance, if sport psychology is viewed as a subdiscipline of psychology, the focus of study generally would involve using activity as a setting to understand psychological theory and to apply psychological principles (see Goldstein, 1979; Martin & Hrycaiko, 1983). If, however, sport psychology is viewed as a subdiscipline of sport and exercise science, the focus of study would more likely involve trying to describe, explain, and predict behavior in sport contexts.

A third perspective is to view the relationship between sport psychology and psychology as an interface where there is an interchange of concepts and methodology (Brawley & Martin, 1995). Brawley and Martin viewed sport psychology as an extension of social psychology (the most influential force in sport psychology) into the sport context and also as a window into the nature of human society. Many of the current research themes in sport psychology (e.g., self-efficacy, anxiety, attitudes, and goal orientations) were adapted from or based on social psychology research and theory. Sport psychology, in turn, has influenced social psychology by contributing to its theoretical knowledge base and by contributing measurement and testing principles.

The perspective of this chapter is that Martens' (1974) concept of psychological kinesiology offers the most comprehensive view from which to study behavior in sport. Martens defined kinesiology as "the study of human movement, especially physical activity, in all forms and in all contexts" (1989, p. 101). Many departments of physical education and sport and exercise science have changed their names to kinesiology. When we use this term to define the overall field, psychological kinesiology (sport psychology and motor learning and control) becomes the study of the psychological aspects of human movement. The other areas of kinesiology then might be labeled physiological kinesiology (exercise physiology), biomechanical kinesiology (sport biomechanics), social–cultural kinesiology (sport

sociology), and developmental kinesiology (motor development).

Scholars typically specialize in one of these subdisciplines and may engage in research within their own specialty, multidisciplinary research, or cross-disciplinary research. In multidisciplinary research, various subdisciplinary specialists investigate a common problem from their own subdisciplinary perspective, whereas in cross-disciplinary research, specialists integrate their views and theories with those of others from different backgrounds into a consolidated viewpoint to try to understand a human movement problem (Abernathy, Kippers, Mackinnon, Neal, & Hanrahan, 1997). A cross-disciplinary approach to the study of kinesiology has greater potential to explain phenomena in human movement than a multidisciplinary or subdisciplinary perspective. As some sport psychologists (or psychological kinesiologists) have noted (e.g., Dishman, 1983; Feltz, 1989; Gill, 1986; Morgan, 1989), a thorough understanding of behavior in human movement settings requires the integration of knowledge from all the subdisciplines of kinesiology and from psychology. Figure 1.1 provides a schematic representation of kinesiology and some research problems with a psychological focus that can be studied from this cross-disciplinary perspective.

Figure 1.1 indicates the nature of potential interrelationships between sport psychology and

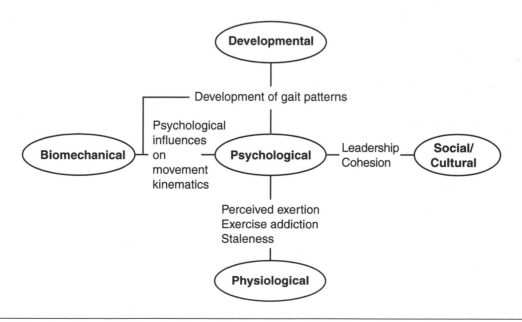

Figure 1.1   A schematic representation of kinesiology and some research problems with a psychological focus that can be studied from a cross-disciplinary perspective.

other disciplines within kinesiology. Developmental, biomechanical, psychological, social–cultural, and physiological subdisciplines represent the major perspectives in understanding human movement. The lines connecting these perspectives show where they might converge on a specific research problem. The location of the term *psychological* in the center of this figure is not meant to imply that sport psychology is the focal point of kinesiology. On the contrary, sport psychology is one of several equally important dimensions of kinesiology. Several examples are provided to illustrate this cross-disciplinary view.

For instance, in the first example, the study of the development of gait patterns could include biomechanical, developmental, and psychological factors. In the second example, a study of leadership and cohesion necessitates a knowledge of social, cultural, and psychological variables. In the third example, perceived exertion, exercise addiction, and staleness are research topics that involve physiological and psychological factors. In the last example, the psychological influences on movement kinematics were examined by Beuter and Duda (1985), who used a biomechanical approach (movement kinematics) to examine the effect of arousal on children's stepping movements.

Perspectives Outside North America

As has been the case for psychology in general, sport psychology has been examined primarily from a North American perspective. With this in mind, it is important to examine briefly the perspectives of sport psychology from outside of North America, in particular those from Europe.

The perspective of sport psychology in Europe, particularly Western Europe, is relatively similar to that in North America and, as Biddle (1995) suggested, "there are undoubtedly more similarities than there are differences [between European and North American sport psychology]" (p. xii). There are, however, different emphases in the research, theory, and application of sport psychology in Europe. In Germany, for instance, a holistic orientation to sport psychology has developed that includes both basic and applied research (Hackfort, 1993). Much of the basic research centers on action control theory (Kuhl, 1985) and includes work on the attentional demands of sport (e.g., Maxeiner, 1989) and motor memory (Janssen, Stoll, & Volkens, 1987). Most applied research in Germany has been designed specifically for integration into the training of elite athletes. In Eastern Europe and Russia, sport psychology has focused primarily on elite athletics. Recently, this research has begun to examine the development of psychological skills in youth sport participants as well (Kantor & Ryzonkin, 1993).

Another difference in sport psychology in Europe involves the emphasis placed on applied work with athletes. Evidence of this can be found in the *Directory of European Sport Psychologists* (Fédération Européene de Psychologie des Sports et des Activités Corporelles, 1993), where counseling was cited as a special skill more frequently than either teaching or research. In addition, many of the more common research themes in European sport psychology, including anxiety/stress reduction, mental training, and motivation, are applied in nature. In affirmation of this, Great Britain has seen a marked increase in applied research and work with athletes in the last decade (Biddle, 1995).

European perspectives in sport psychology, although not entirely different from mainstream North American sport psychology, are valuable in providing a culturally different perspective of the field. Perspectives from non-Western countries are also important in the development of sport psychology. In China, for instance, sport psychology researchers (who include coaches, psychologists, and kinesiologists) have examined the psychological selection of athletes into sport (Qiu & Qiu, 1993). In Japan, the focus has been primarily on achievement motivation, perceptual motor behaviors, and developmental aspects of sport psychology (Fujita & Ichimura, 1993). Unfortunately, much of this work has not been translated into English, which discourages many Western researchers from examining it. Hopefully, as we move toward a more global community within sport psychology, this barrier will be minimized.

Australia, although following similar research paradigms as North America and Europe, has been at the forefront in integrating sport psychology into mainstream psychology and university education. Examples of this include the creation of the Board of Sport Psychologists within the Australian Psychological Society in 1991 and a twofold increase in academic sport psychology positions within universities during 1993 (Morris, 1995; Morris & Summers, 1995). Sport psychology researchers and practitioners will need to incorporate the body of applied and basic knowledge from European, Asian, and other countries to best meet the challenges facing sport psychology.

ROLES OF SPORT PSYCHOLOGISTS

In the previous paragraphs, we discussed the increase of applied research and consulting with athletes outside of North America (e.g., Eastern Europe and Russia). Although there appears to be greater integration of applied and research roles outside North America, a schism between the two roles has developed primarily in the United States. Not only does the field have various perspectives on the academic study of sport psychology, but there also exist different views regarding the appropriate roles of sport psychologists.

Sport psychologists traditionally have worked from two perspectives: academic-oriented and practitioner-oriented. The academic sport psychologist focuses primarily on theoretical research and educational pursuits, whereas the practitioner emphasizes applied work and research. Although these two roles appear to differ considerably, some sport psychologists play both roles. Roberts (1989) expressed concern that a rapidly developing gulf was emerging between academic- and practitioner-oriented sport psychologists. Recently, in parallel with debates in psychology in general, sport psychology has struggled with the adoption of either a practitioner–academic- or academic–practitioner-oriented model of training and practice. This is a result of the expanding view that psychologists should have responsibility for both research and applied work, instead of working or learning in delineated academic or applied roles only. Furthermore, the research versus practice distinction is overly simplistic and unproductive. Applied work can provide questions, problems, observations, and issues that can guide research, which, in turn, should guide future practice.

Some sport psychologists have argued that professional services should not be sanctioned until we possess an applied body of knowledge and a reliable technology (Dishman, 1983; Morgan, 1989). Others have contended that professional services in sport psychology are needed now, and that those providing such service should not "sit idle until scientific evidence has validated their particular application or technique" (Landers, 1989, p. 477).

Throughout this debate, there has been a dilemma regarding who should be certified to "practice" sport psychology and what titles and roles a sport psychologist should fulfill. As a result of this quandary, AAASP developed a certification process for sport psychology practitioners in 1989. This resulted in the creation of the title "Certified Consultant, AAASP" rather than "certified sport psychologist," which is legally regulated by individual state psychology licensing boards. In 1995, AAASP, in conjunction with the United States Olympic Committee (USOC), formed a joint certification program for sport psychology professionals who were both APA members and AAASP certified (McCann & Scanlan, 1995). Similar certification processes have been instituted in Canada (Canadian Mental Training Registry) and Great Britain (British Association of Sport and Exercise Sciences–psychology section). Despite these apparent advances in certification, some researchers believe that the certification process excludes persons who come from an academic or kinesiology-based sport psychology background (Anshel, 1992, 1993). The members of the AAASP certification committee recently acknowledged this issue and plan to reexamine the certification process to possibly revise the requirements to include

Academic-oriented sport psychology has traditionally focused on theoretical research and educational pursuits.

© Terry Wild Studio

Box 1.1
Prominent Sport Psychology Journals and Organizations

Journals

International Journal of Sport Psychology (IJSP)
Journal of Applied Sport Psychology (JASP)
Journal of Sport Behavior
Journal of Sport and Exercise Psychology (JSEP)
Perceptual and Motor Skills
Research Quarterly for Exercise and Sport
The Sport Psychologist

Professional Organizations

Association for the Advancement of Applied Sport
    Psychology (AAASP)
British Association for Sports and Exercise Science
    (BASES)

Board of Sport Psychology, Australian Society of
    Psychology
Canadian Society of Psychomotor Learning and
    Sport Psychology (SCAPPS)
Division 47 of the American Psychological
    Association (Div. 47 APA)
European Congress for Sport Psychology
International Society for Sport Psychology
    (ISSP)
North American Society for the Psychology of
    Sport and Physical Activity (NASPSPA)

---

individuals from kinesiology backgrounds and individuals with master's degrees in sport psychology or related disciplines (Burton, 2000). The certification committee also is considering a certifying examination similar to those currently used in psychology and counseling certifications.

To further widen the gulf between academic- and practitioner-oriented sport psychologists, the field is witnessing a growing number of professional journals and organizations that have developed either along scientific research (e.g., *The Journal of Sport and Exercise Psychology*) or applied sport psychology lines (e.g., *The Sport Psychologist*). Refer to box 1.1 for a list of prominent sport psychology journals and organizations. A recent addition to the sport psychology journal field is *Psychology of Sport and Exercise*, which, according to Biddle (2001), will include academically rigorous articles that reflect both academic and applied research.

There is considerable controversy in the field today regarding the basic nature of sport psychology and the roles that sport psychologists can or should play. Roberts (1989) contended that the controversy in sport psychology is due primarily to the lack of a generally accepted conceptual paradigm to drive the research and applied efforts of sport psychologists. To understand the controversial issues in this field and why sport psychology lacks a generally accepted paradigm, it is necessary to examine where sport psychology has been in the past. Because several individuals have already written excellent historical overviews

(e.g., Cox, 1985; Landers, 1983; Ryan, 1981; Wiggins, 1984), we present only a brief overview of how the current paradigms in sport psychology evolved.

EVOLUTION TO THE CURRENT PARADIGMS IN SPORT PSYCHOLOGY

In any area of science, researchers' choices of topics to investigate, the methods they use, and the perspectives they take are not freely and logically determined. Rather, they are influenced heavily by sociological forces both within and outside the discipline (Keller, 1985; Shadish, 1985). Sport psychology is no exception, because trends in sport psychology have tended to parallel those in general psychology, which can be considered a major sociological force outside the discipline (Morgan, 1980). As Landers (1983) noted, the research that was conducted in sport psychology from 1950 to 1965 was characterized by empiricism, and most of the studies investigated personality. This perspective was consistent with the trait approach that was in vogue in the general area of psychology.

In contrast, 1966 to 1976 was characterized by a social analysis approach. Research during this decade consisted of selecting one theory at a time from mainstream psychology and testing that theory in the area of sport and motor performance (Landers, 1983). Topics such as social facilitation, achievement motivation, social reinforcement, and arousal and motor performance were investigated. Much of this research was influenced by Martens' (1970) recommendation of the social analysis approach. Research conducted from the late 1970s to the mid-1980s was influenced by leaders (i.e., sociological forces) in psychology and sport psychology. Wankel (1975) advocated the application of cognitive approaches to sport psychology issues. These approaches included causal attributions, intrinsic motivation, and self-efficacy/self-confidence.

During the late 1980s and into the 1990s, research in sport psychology became more sport-specific and measurement-driven. Evidence of this trend can be seen in the development and validation of several sport-specific measures for assessing psychological factors in sport during this time. Examples include the Group Environment Questionnaire (Carron, Widmeyer, & Brawley, 1985), Physical Self-Perception Profile (Fox & Corbin, 1989), Social Physique Anxiety Scale (Heart, Leary, & Rejeski, 1989), Sport Anxiety Scale (Smith, Smoll, & Schutz, 1991), and Task and Ego Orientation in Sport Questionnaire (TEOSQ; Duda & Nicholls, 1992). Advances in the statistical examination of data, including confirmatory factor analyses (e.g., Goode & Roth, 1993; Markland, Emberton, & Tallon, 1997), meta-analyses (Feltz, Landers, & Becker, 1988; Lirgg, 1991; Moritz, Feltz, Fahrbach, & Mack, 2000), and the acceptance of ethnographic research designs (e.g., Ming & Martin, 1996), further supported this claim. An increase in atheoretical and clinical research reflected the expanding interest in applied sport psychology research (Brewer, 1998; Krane, Greenleaf, & Snow, 1997; Moritz, Hall, Martin, & Vadocz, 1996; Murphy, Petipas, & Brewer, 1996). In contrast, sport-specific theoretical research also became more prominent, suggesting that sport psychology matured considerably from the 1980s through the 1990s.

We next examine in greater detail the research perspectives that characterized each of the four time periods in an effort to describe the evolution of sport psychology. Specifically, we describe a research topic from within each time period to illustrate the primary focus from that period.

Personality Research From 1950 to 1965

The relationship of personality to participation in sport and physical activity has been one of the most popular research areas in sport psychology. Much of the early research took a trait approach to studying personality profiles in athletes or athletic groups and has been described as "shotgun" research (Ryan, 1968). Researchers would gain access to a sample of athletes (from high school to Olympic caliber) and test them on the most convenient personality test. This research approach has been labeled as shotgun research because the researchers typically had no theoretical rationale for selecting the personality test used. Few conclusive answers resulted from the hundreds of studies conducted using this approach. This lack of consistency subsequently led to strong criticism of the area by a number of leaders in sport psychology (e.g., Kroll, 1970; Martens, 1975). Most of the criticisms were based on theoretical and methodological shortcomings of the research. The use of univariate instead of multivariate statistics, questionable sampling techniques, and lack of specificity in the operational-ization of variables were some of the major criticisms lodged against sport personality research. In addition, some questioned the applicability of general personality assessment techniques for sport and physical activity that may not have a logical link to participation or performance (Kroll, 1970).

This criticism of the personality research led to a general (if temporary) disenchantment with personality as an area of study in sport psychology. Martens (1970, 1975), one of the most vocal critics of this research approach, began advocating the use of a social analysis approach that combined empirical methods with theory. When Martens started testing psychological theories within a motor performance context, many other researchers followed. Most of this research was conducted in controlled laboratory settings and represents the second major stage in the history of sport psychology research.

Social Facilitation and the Arousal–Performance Relationship From 1966 to 1976

A considerable amount of sport psychology research was conducted during this decade. The typical research paradigm, which was laboratory-oriented, involved taking a social–psychological theory and testing its applicability to motor skill performance. The most popular topics of research during this social analysis period were social facilitation and the arousal–performance relationship. Much of the research in social facilitation and arousal in sport psychology was based on Zajonc's (1965) theory of social facilitation. Zajonc's hypothesis, based on drive theory, was that the presence of an audience creates arousal, which in turn enhances the emission of dominant responses. The dominant response of a complex task is the incorrect response in initial learning but the correct response when the skill is mastered. Martens (1969) initiated a series of laboratory studies on social facilitation by using motor skill tasks and found support for Zajonc's theory. A number of other investigators also attempted to extend this research to motor tasks by varying the task, audience, and subject characteristics (e.g., Carron & Bennett, 1976; Haas & Roberts, 1975). Their findings varied, depending on the variables studied. Reviewers of this research generally have concluded that the evidence for a drive theory explanation of social facilitation effects in motor performance has been mixed (Carron, 1980; Landers, 1980; Wankel, 1984). In addition, the size of social facilitation effects has been shown to be very small (Bond & Titus, 1983).

Another aspect of the social facilitation research that investigators found troublesome was the assessment of arousal. Regardless of the particular autonomic arousal measure used, no clear pattern of results was obtained. Some studies demonstrated increased arousal with the presence of others, and some reported no effect. Some reviewers believed the problem lay in the nature and assessment of arousal, because of its multidimensionality and individual specificity (Carron, 1980; Landers, 1980; Wankel, 1984). Landers (1989) also noted that one should not expect much change in physiological measures when the social facilitation effect is so small. Because of these measurement problems, inconsistent results, and the small percentage of variance accounted for by audience effects, many researchers abandoned the area of social facilitation in search of other psychological theories that might apply to sport.

The most frequently cited alternative to drive theory for social facilitation and arousal–performance research was the inverted-U hypothesis (Carron, 1980). This hypothesis predicted that there was a progressive enhancement in performance as a subject's arousal level increased up to some optimal point, beyond which further increases in arousal progressively decreased performance efficiency. Much of the arousal–motor performance literature of the 1970s also tested the inverted-U hypothesis (e.g., Klavora, 1978; Martens & Landers, 1970). However, just as in social

facilitation research, the measurement of arousal was problematic because it was not assessed in terms of its multidimensional nature.

Since this early work on arousal and performance began, many new conceptual models have been put forth, including reversal theory (Kerr, 1985, 1997), the catastrophe model (Hardy, 1990, 1996), and the individualized zones of optimal functioning (IZOF) model (Hanin, 1980, 1997). With the exception of IZOF, these conceptual models, although contributing to researchers' understanding of the arousal and performance relationship, have yet to yield consistent results. The catastrophe model also has proven to be difficult to assess (Hardy, 1996), whereas reversal theory has received only limited attention from researchers. Consequently, researchers' knowledge of the arousal–performance relationship in sport remains incomplete.

The research conducted during this time was characterized by use of psychological theories tested in the motor domain and in laboratory settings. However, Landers (1983) noted that the effects achieved with this type of research were small and of questionable generalizability to athletes and the sport setting. This state of affairs led researchers to become dissatisfied with the laboratory-oriented social psychological paradigm and to start looking to cognitive approaches and field methods to answer their research questions.

Cognitive Approaches and Field Methods From 1977 to the Mid-1980s

In the late 1970s and early 1980s, a variety of cognitive models in the sport personality, social facilitation, arousal–performance, and other motivation areas were proposed as a response to the general dissatisfaction with the simplistic and mechanistic drive theory perspective for explaining complex human behavior (Landers, 1980; Wankel, 1975, 1984). For example, Landers (1980) advocated a cognitive arousal–attention model based on Easterbrook's (1959) cue utilization theory. This model suggests that increased arousal narrows attentional focus and cue utilization, thus limiting performance. The concept of objective self-awareness (Duval & Wicklund, 1972) also has been used to interpret audience effects. This theory suggests that the presence of others leads to objective self-awareness (attention directed inward on the self), which affects task motivation. Baumeister (1984) suggested that audience-induced pressure increases conscious attention to the performer's own process of performance, which disrupts smooth execution.

Wankel (1975) outlined how attribution theory may be used to explain motivation in the presence of an audience. Wankel (1984) also advocated a closer look at Borden's (1980) model, which acknowledges the performer as a proactive, rather than a reactive, individual, who interprets information from the situation, makes predictions about the audience's reactions, and alters behavior accordingly.

Rejeski and Brawley (1983) called for innovative approaches and broader conceptual views to help us understand motivation in sport. The cognitive concepts of perceived ability, self-efficacy, and achievement orientation (Bandura, 1977; Harter, 1978; Maehr & Nicholls, 1980) were proposed to play a key role in mediating motivation. These concepts subsequently were incorporated into the sport psychology research in this area (Feltz, 1982, 1988; Roberts, Lueiber, & Duda, 1981; Weiss, Bredemeier, & Shewchuk, 1986).

At the same time that researchers were dissatisfied with mechanistic drive theory explanations for sport behavior, there was dissatisfaction with the laboratory-oriented social–psychological paradigm for sport psychology research that had characterized the research during the previous decade. This led some investigators to advocate the use of field research methodology. Martens (1980), in particular, pointed out the limitations of laboratory studies and suggested switching from laboratory settings to field settings to observe behavior more accurately and to understand the real world of sport. The publication of this article stimulated many researchers to switch to field research, resulting in a proliferation of field studies conducted during the last decade. However, as Landers (1983) noted, some investigators misinterpreted Martens' position and left theory testing behind, along with the laboratory, when they became field researchers. Some researchers conducted descriptive studies in field settings, but not much theory testing or theory construction (as Martens advocated) was initiated. Other researchers emphasized intervention studies on applied topics such as mental practice, imagery, "psych-up" strategies, stress management techniques, and biofeedback. The methodology used in these applied, nontheoretical studies was still based on a technology taken from mainstream (clinical) psychology (Dishman, 1983). In areas where theory testing was conducted, the cognitive approach

that had been developed in mainstream psychology was the focus.

Some of the leading researchers in the field were still frustrated at the slow pace at which sport psychology was developing. Landers (1983) suggested that the reason knowledge in sport psychology was not advancing more rapidly was its approach to testing theory. He contended that the field could no longer be content simply to test the relationships outlined by the creator of a theory. Rather, sport psychology must develop its own logically formulated alternative explanations and test them against the predictions of the theory. Dishman (1983) argued that sport psychology had been applying general psychology theories and trying to validate general psychology models in sport, rather than developing "applied theories" to answer sport-specific questions. Alderman (1980) noted that although psychology had increased our body of knowledge, this knowledge outside or apart from sport could carry us only so far in understanding behavior in sport. As more researchers began to view sport psychology as a subdiscipline within sport science rather than as a field of study in which psychological principles were tested and applied, they also began to advocate the development of theories or conceptual frameworks and measures within sport psychology to further explain sport behavior (Alderman, 1980; Dishman, 1983; Martens, 1980; Morgan, 1989).

Extension to Sport-Specific Theory and Advances in Measurement From the Late 1980s to the Present

Since the late 1980s, progress has been made in developing and extending the conceptual frameworks or models within sport that Alderman (1980) and Martens (1980) advocated. Examples include the development of concepts such as movement confidence (Griffin, Keogh, & Maybee, 1994), sport confidence (Vealey, 1986), sport enjoyment (Scanlan & Lewthwaite, 1986), sport motivation orientations (Duda & Nicholls, 1992; Gill & Deeter, 1988; Treasure & Roberts, 1994; Vealey, 1986), and sport leadership (Chelladurai, Haggerty, & Baxter, 1989; Smoll & Smith, 1989). Some researchers have echoed these suggestions that sport scientists test sport-specific theories but have suggested that these theories not be narrowly delineated within sport only (McCormack & Challip, 1988). They suggest that comparative analyses be made between sport and other social contexts to best determine the unique attributes of sport. Research using the TEOSQ, a measure of task and ego orientation in sport, is an example of work that has compared the influence of one's goal perspectives in sport and educational contexts (Duda & Nicholls, 1992).

Accompanying the development of conceptual frameworks specific to sport has been a call for the development of specific tests and questionnaires for specific sport and physical activity settings that are conceptually based (Gauvin & Russell, 1993). In response to this call, researchers have begun to develop sport-specific measures that are construct valid. This construct validation approach incorporates logical, correlational, and experimental analyses to assess the validity of a construct. The TEOSQ (Duda & Nicholls, 1992), the State–Trait Sport Confidence Inventory (Vealey, 1986), and the Group Environment Questionnaire (Carron et al., 1985) are three sport-specific measures that have used a construct validation approach and have strong links between concept and operational definition. As Brawley and Martin (1995) noted, these instruments have allowed sport psychologists to contribute to the broader field of psychology from a measurement perspective.

Although sport-specific measures are being developed through a construct validation approach, there is a concern regarding the possible mislabeling of these constructs (Marsh, 1994). Some researchers in sport psychology (e.g., Brawley, Martin, & Gyurcsik, 1998; Duda, 1998; Gauvin & Spence, 1998) have acknowledged the existence of this "jingle-jangle fallacy" (Marsh, 1994). The "jingle fallacy" refers to scales that have the same label but may not measure the same constructs. For instance, the Physical Self-Efficacy Scale (PSE; Ryckman, Robbins, Thornton, & Cantrell, 1982) is labeled as a self-efficacy scale but may represent more of a self-concept measure because the items (e.g., "I have excellent reflexes") were not constructed based on the tenets of self-efficacy theory, which places beliefs within a goal-striving context (Feltz & Chase, 1998; Maddux & Meier, 1995). The "jangle fallacy," on the other hand, pertains to scales that have different labels but may not represent different constructs. For example, Vealey's (1986) sport confidence scale has a different label than self-efficacy but still measures a person's capability to accomplish a certain level of performance. Sport confidence and self-efficacy represent the same construct, just with different degrees of specificity (Feltz & Chase, 1998). Marsh

(1994) emphasized the need to pursue construct validity studies more vigorously to test the interpretations of measures so as to help avoid jingle-jangle fallacies. In the jingle fallacy example with PSE, a construct validity study would test whether the scale held up when examined within the tenets of self-efficacy theory. That is, can people's PSE mediate their goal-striving behavior or be modified through mastery experiences?

In each of the first three time periods discussed (i.e., 1950 to 1965, 1966 to 1976, and 1977 to mid-1980s), researchers started with theories (e.g., personality traits, social facilitation, attribution) that were borrowed from psychology and applied to sport settings. These researchers often obtained mixed results because of theoretical or methodological shortcomings. Their discouragement and dissatisfaction led them to abandon either the research area or the methodology and search for a new approach. Until the mid-1980s, this historical pattern resulted in, or contributed to, three problems: few programs of sustained research, a lack of a generally accepted conceptual paradigm, and slow advancement of knowledge in sport psychology.

In the last time period discussed (late 1980s to present), researchers began to expand the realm of sport-specific, theoretical research. This has helped sport psychology begin to distinguish itself as a more theoretically driven science as opposed to a place where theories from other disciplines are tested. In addition, the increased and better use of statistics in validating and developing sport-specific measures has done much to further the legitimacy of the field. Still, many aspects of sport psychology are in their infancy (e.g., sustained research lines, accepted conceptual paradigms, systematic construct validation studies) or, more appropriately stated, are just entering into childhood and need to be continually advanced. These current issues and challenges are discussed in the remainder of this chapter.

CURRENT ISSUES

One of the most immediate issues facing sport psychology is the need for integrating applied and theoretical work. Currently, research studies and the journals that publish them are divided along applied or theoretical lines. Theoretical concepts often are not tested in applied settings, and applied concepts often do not serve as the basis for theory development. This lack of integration between applied work and theoretical research has slowed the growth of sport psychology and has created voids in the field.

Examples in which researchers have begun to address the theory/application issue include Hardy's (1996) reexamination of the cusp catastrophe model of anxiety (Fazey & Hardy, 1988) for its practical value to sport psychology. Williams and Andersen (1998) reviewed and critiqued their original model of stress and injury (Andersen & Williams, 1988) in relation to its use in applied and research settings. Gilbourne and Taylor (1998) made an initial foray into integrating goal perspective theory and injury rehabilitation. Their research suggests that this area holds potential, but it too needs further empirical validation.

The bidirectional flow of information between theory and practice is important to the growth of the field. A model adapted from Rivenes (1978; see figure 1.2) illustrates how a working relationship between researchers and practitioners in sport psychology can be mutually beneficial. This model can be a useful tool when trying to gain a new perspective on a research or professional problem. For instance, direct observation and clinical case studies may help create new constructs or explain conflicting findings in existing studies. Such was the case with the concept of relaxation-induced anxiety, which was first noted in anecdotal reports in clinical psychology (Heide & Borkovec, 1983). After documenting the occurrence of relaxation-

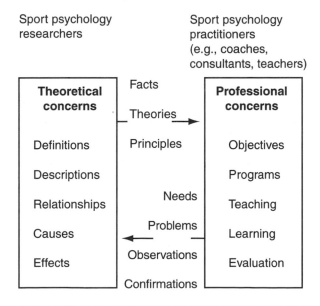

Figure 1.2 A model adapted from Rivenes (1978) illustrates how a working relationship between researchers and practitioners in sport psychology can be mutually beneficial.

R.S. Rivenes, *Foundations of Physical Education.* Copyright © 1978 by Houghton Mifflin Company. Adapted with permission.

induced anxiety (increases in anxiety as a consequence of relaxation training), Heide and Borkovec (1984) hypothesized several mechanisms to explain the phenomenon. They also proposed a theoretical model wherein relaxation-induced anxiety was viewed within a broader framework designed to explain the development and maintenance of the more generalized anxiety disorders.

Another issue pertains to whether we need a singular conceptual paradigm to drive our research and applied efforts. Roberts (1989) maintained that the slow growth is due to a lack of a generally accepted conceptual paradigm to drive our work. He advocated that we use cognitive models to understand behavior in sport and exercise and that we become better acquainted with the epistemological concerns of mainstream psychology, where the cognitive paradigm has dominated research since the late 1970s. However, Roberts also conceded that sport psychology researchers should be open to the work of those using other paradigms (e.g., psychobiological, social psychological). Other writers (Landers, 1989; Morgan, 1989) have suggested that it would be a mistake to shift to one conceptual paradigm. They advocate that broadening the prevailing zeitgeist may better elucidate problems in sport behavior.

We believe that the development of theoretical formulations within the context of sport and exercise should draw from multiple sources. As Landers (1989) suggested, theory cannot be developed in a vacuum. He contended that sport psychology researchers need to continue to borrow theories, methods, and approaches from academic psychology, examine their applicability, and modify them accordingly. However, as we stated in the beginning of this chapter, these models also may be inadequate to understand some of the psychological phenomena specific to sport unless researchers begin to integrate knowledge from other subdisciplines within sport and exercise science. Dishman (1983) advocated that researchers within kinesiology combine their talents across subdisciplines to answer questions of practical impact. Dishman termed this a "recycled suggestion," which has more frequently been ignored than followed.

For instance, in trying to explain why children drop out of youth sports, sport psychology researchers have looked for entirely psychological reasons (Feltz & Petlichkoff, 1983; Gould, Feltz, Horn, & Weiss, 1982; Klint & Weiss, 1986). As a result of such a narrow focus, training and conditioning or maturational explanations for dropping out often have been overlooked.

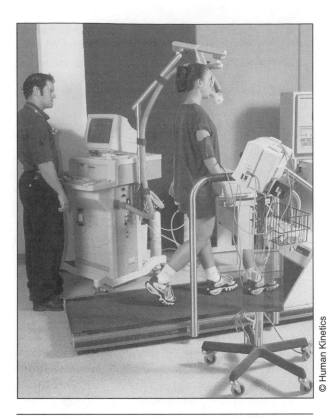

© Human Kinetics

Models of sport psychology could benefit from applied studies, such as those done in movement kinematics.

An example, previously illustrated in figure 1.1, of a cross-disciplinary approach to examining a sport-specific question is Beuter and Duda's (1985) analysis of the arousal–motor performance relationship. These researchers used movement kinematics (an assessment of the quality of performance) to examine the effect of arousal on motor performance. This approach allowed them to focus on the process by which arousal influences performance rather than simply focusing on the outcome or end products of performance. Cross-disciplinary studies may uncover explanations that a study based solely on psychological models could not provide.

A third issue has been the lack of response to the call for innovative approaches and broader conceptual views to understanding psychological phenomena in sport (Landers, 1983; Rejeski & Brawley, 1983). Broadening our conceptual views is not an easy task, given the human tendency to think recurring thoughts that tend to constrain our research efforts (Wicker, 1985). Wicker (1985) offered some strategies to help researchers get out of their conceptual ruts and stimulate new perspectives on familiar problems. One category of strategies was "playing with ideas," and another was "considering

contexts." Researchers and practitioners can play with ideas by working with metaphors, drawing graphic representations of ideas, and rethinking concepts in terms of process. For example, Selye's (1946) concept of stress and strain in the human body was taken from the domain of physics.

Consideration of contexts includes placing specific research problems in a larger domain, such as within the larger domain of kinesiology as mentioned earlier, and making comparisons to other domains. McCormack and Challip (1988) advocated making comparisons to social contexts outside the sport domain to help define the unique attributes of sport, but these comparisons also may generate new ideas. For instance, by examining the moral reasoning of athletes within and outside of a sport context, Bredemeier and Shields (1986) postulated that sport involves a "bracketed morality," a legitimated, temporary suspension of the usual moral obligations to consider the needs and desires of all persons equally.

These examples indicate the expanding nature of sport psychology beyond its own context. Theoretically driven research, cross-disciplinary approaches, and a broader conceptual framework will continue to be relevant issues in research and applied work in sport psychology. As these changes evolve and continue to shape the field, sport psychology practitioners and researchers will face a variety of new challenges.

FUTURE CHALLENGES

The field of sport psychology and the discipline of kinesiology are in exciting stages of development. Journals, professional societies, and graduate programs have proliferated, and the field of sport psychology has grown around the world. This growth poses challenges for the next generation of researchers and practitioners. We see four major challenges in sport psychology in the future: balancing specialization and integrative knowledge, keeping abreast of the knowledge expansion, learning new statistical methods, and funding research.

Researchers and graduate programs will need to balance specialization and integrative knowledge to develop the theoretical models that ultimately will answer sport and human movement questions (Alderman, 1980; Dishman, 1983; Martens, 1980). To achieve this integrated body of knowledge in kinesiology, departments may have to change their reward structure so that researchers are rewarded to a greater degree for publishing within kinesiology than in their parent discipline (Hoffman, 1985) and are not penalized for doing collaborative research (Mahoney, 1985). In addition, graduate curricular programs need to be modified to prepare students better for interdisciplinary research (Hoffman, 1985). However, an integrated knowledge of sport and exercise science does not eliminate intensive study in psychology. Both are necessary if students are to conduct state-of-the-art research.

A second challenge will be to keep abreast of the knowledge being generated in sport psychology. The incredible rate of information expansion has exceeded the capacity of sport psychologists to remain up-to-date in their own specialization, let alone in other subdisciplines. Technological knowledge in information management will be important to help one keep up with the literature. There also will be an even greater need for meta-analytical reviews of research studies to synthesize the research being generated.

A third challenge will be to keep current regarding the best statistical and research methods available to investigate the complex questions that are at the cutting edge of sport psychology and kinesiology research. There are many more tools available than there were just 20 years ago, such as hierarchical linear modeling, structural equation modeling, confirmatory factor analysis, simultaneous factor analysis, log-linear analysis of categorical data, and computer simulations of social interactions, to name just a few. Schutz and Gessaroli (1993) observed a gradual shift away from experimental analysis toward more complex statistical applications in the areas of inventory development, comprehensive model building, reliability and validity studies, survey analyses, and longitudinal intervention studies. They suggested that researchers will need to continually adapt and use the best tools available as our knowledge about a phenomenon increases. They also warned, however, against becoming method (or instrument) bound and ritualizing statistics instead of using them as tools to help answer questions that are well formulated and theoretically based. Helping researchers keep abreast of statistical advances in the field may require that leaders in the field devote more journal space and conference time to covering new methods and statistical techniques.

Last, we see the increased pressure to obtain external funding as a challenge for all researchers at institutions of higher education, including sport psychology professors, as the relative proportion of public support continues to decline and competition for other funds increases. Departments and individual faculty who want to succeed must demonstrate solid, extramurally funded research programs (Moore, 1998; Wilmore, 1998). Graduate students also will need to demonstrate their grant activity if they want faculty positions at research-intensive universities. In fact, if sport psychology as a field cannot demonstrate that its research is fundable, fewer sport psychology positions may be available at research universities in the future.

Garnering outside funding for research in sport psychology can positively influence the field, as Moore (1998) indicated, by enhancing a researcher's ability to answer important scientific questions and make significant scholarly contributions to the field. The availability of external grant money will also strongly influence research in sport psychology, by directing it toward those areas that funding sources deem worthwhile. For instance, there is presently more governmental funding for research on exercise behavior than sport behavior. Sport psychology has witnessed the results of this influence through the increasing number of research articles on issues of health and exercise and the change in the name of the *Journal of Sport Psychology* to the *Journal of Sport and Exercise Psychology*. The challenge will be not only to obtain funding for one's research but also to resist changing research orientations just to "chase money."

The issues surrounding sport psychology (e.g., its definition, roles, specialization, academic preparation, ecological validity, theoretical vs. applied emphasis) are not unique to this field, nor are the future challenges. Those fields that work to resolve these issues and embrace challenges will show continued growth and popularity. Those fields that polarize around the issues and whose members are more concerned with self-serving pursuits than with working together to advance the field will eventually dwindle and die. Sport psychology, within the broader field of kinesiology, has experienced increased growth and popularity. We believe it will continue to embrace its issues and challenges and show continued growth.

REFERENCES

Abernathy, B., Kippers, V., Mackinnon, N., Neal, L.T., & Hanrahan, S. (1997). *The biophysical foundations of human movement.* Champaign, IL: Human Kinetics.

Alderman, R.B. (1980). Sport psychology: Past, present, and future dilemmas. In P. Klavora & K.A.W. Wipper (Eds.),

Psychological and sociological factors in sport (pp. 3–19). Toronto, ON: University of Toronto.

Andersen, M.B., & Williams, J.W. (1988). A model of stress and athletic injury: Prediction and Prevention. *Journal of Sport and Exercise Psychology, 10,* 294–306.

Anshel, M.H. (1992). The case against the certification of sport psychologists: In search of the phantom expert. *The Sport Psychologist, 6,* 265–286.

Anshel, M.H. (1993). Against certification of sport psychology consultants: A response to Zaichowsky and Perna. *The Sport Psychologist, 7,* 344–353.

Bandura, A. (1977). Self-efficacy: Toward a unifying theory of behavioral change. *Psychological Review, 84,* 191–215.

Baumeister, R.F. (1984). Choking under pressure: Self-consciousness and paradoxical effects of incentives on skillful performance. *Journal of Personality and Social Psychology, 46,* 610–620.

Beuter, A., & Duda, J.L. (1985). Analysis of the arousal/motor performance relationship in children using movement kinematics. *Journal of Sport Psychology, 7,* 229–243.

Biddle, S.J. (1995). Introduction. In S.J. Biddle (Ed.), *European perspectives on sport and exercise psychology* (pp. xi–xviii). Champaign, IL: Human Kinetics.

Biddle, S.J. (2001). Psychology of sport and exercise: Present and future. *Psychology of Sport and Exercise, 1,* 1–5.

Bond, C.F., & Titus, L.J. (1983). Social facilitation: A meta-analysis of 241 studies. *Psychological Bulletin, 94,* 265–292.

Borden, R.J. (1980). Audience influence. In P.B. Paulus (Ed.), *Psychology of group influence* (pp. 99–131). Hillsdale, NJ: Erlbaum.

Brawley, L.R., & Martin, K.A. (1995). The interface between social and sport psychology. *The Sport Psychologist, 9,* 469–497.

Brawley, L.R., Martin, K.A., & Gyurcsik, N.C. (1998). Problems in assessing perceived barriers to exercise: Confusing obstacles with attributions and excuses. In J.L. Duda (Ed.), *Advances in sport and exercise psychology measurement* (pp. 337–350). Morgantown, WV: Fitness Information Technology.

Bredemeier, B.J., & Shields, D.L. (1986). Game reasoning and interactional morality. *Journal of Genetic Psychology, 147,* 257–275.

Brewer, B. (1998). Psychological applications in clinical sports medicine: Current status and future directions. *Journal of Clinical Psychology in Medical Settings, 5,* 91–102.

Burton, D.A. (2000). Fellows agree: Time is right to explore major certification changes. *AAASP Newsletter, 15,* 11–12.

Carron, A.V. (1980). *Social psychology of sport.* Ithaca, NY: Mouvement.

Carron, A.V., & Bennett, B. (1976). The effects of initial habit strength differences upon performance in a coaction situation. *Journal of Motor Behavior, 8,* 297–304.

Carron, A.V., Widmeyer, W.N., & Brawley, L.R. (1985). The development of an instrument to assess cohesion in sport teams: The Group Environment Questionnaire. *Journal of Sport Psychology, 7,* 244–266.

Chelladurai, P., Haggerty, T.R., & Baxter, P.R. (1989). Decision style choices of university basketball coaches and players. *Journal of Sport and Exercise Psychology, 11,* 201–215.

Cox, R.H. (1985). *Sport psychology: Concepts and applications.* Dubuque, IA: Brown.

Cratty, B.J. (1989). *Psychology in contemporary sport* (3rd ed.). Englewood Cliffs, NJ: Prentice Hall.

Dishman, R.K. (1983). Identity crises in North American sport psychology: Academics in professional issues. *Journal of Sport Psychology, 5,* 123–134.

Duda, J.L. (1987). Toward a developmental theory of children's motivation in sport. *Journal of Sport Psychology, 9,* 130–145.

Duda, J.L. (1998). *Advances in sport and exercise psychology measurement.* Morgantown, WV: Fitness Information Technology.

Duda, J.L., & Nicholls, J.G. (1992). Dimensions of achievement motivation in schoolwork and sport. *Journal of Educational Psychology, 84,* 290–299.

Duval, S., & Wickland, R.A. (1972). *A theory of objective self-awareness.* New York: Academic Press.

Easterbrook, J.A. (1959). The effect of emotion on cue utilization and the organization of behavior. *Psychological Review, 66,* 183–201.

Fazey, J.A., & Hardy, L. (1988). *The inverted-U hypothesis: A catastrophe for sport psychology* (British Association of Sport Sciences Monograph No. 1). Leeds, UK: National Coaching Foundation.

Fédération Européene de Psychologie des Sports et des Activités Corporelles. (1993). *Directory of European sport psychologists.* Lund, Sweden: Author.

Feltz, D.L. (1982). Path analysis of the causal elements in Bandura's theory of self-efficacy and an anxiety-based model of avoidance behavior. *Journal of Personality and Social Psychology, 42,* 764–781.

Feltz, D.L. (1988). Self-confidence and sports performance. *Exercise and Sport Sciences Review, 16,* 151–166.

Feltz, D.L. (1989). Theoretical research in sport psychology: From applied psychology toward sport science. In J.S. Skinner, C.B. Corbin, D.M. Landers, P.B. Martin, & C.L. Wells (Eds.), *Future directions in exercise and sport science research* (pp. 435–452). Champaign, IL: Human Kinetics.

Feltz, D.L., & Chase, M.A. (1998). The measurement of self-efficacy and confidence in sport. In J.L. Duda (Ed.), *Advancements in sport and exercise psychology measurement* (pp. 63–78). Morgantown, WV: Fitness Information Technology.

Feltz, D.L., Landers, D.M., & Becker, B.J. (1988). A revised meta-analysis of the mental practice literature on motor skill learning. In National Research Council (Ed.), *Enhancing human performance: Part III. Improving motor performance* (pp. 1–65). Washington, DC: National Academy Press.

Feltz, D.L., & Petlichkoff, L. (1983). Perceived competence among interscholastic sport participants and dropouts, *Canadian Journal of Applied Sport Sciences, 8,* 231–235.

Fox, K.R., & Corbin, C.B. (1989). The Physical Self-Perception Profile: Development and preliminary validation, *Journal of Sport and Exercise Psychology, 11,* 408–430.

Fujita, A.H., & Ichimura, S. (1993). Contemporary areas of research in sport psychology in Japan. In R.N. Singer, M. Murphey, & L.K. Tennant (Eds.), *Handbook of research on sport psychology* (pp. 52–57). New York: Macmillan.

Gauvin, L., & Russell, S.J. (1993). Sport-specific and culturally adapted measures in sport and exercise psychology. In R.N. Singer, M. Murphey, & L.K. Tennant (Eds.), *Handbook of research on sport psychology* (pp. 891–900). New York: Macmillan.

Gauvin, L., & Spence, J.C. (1998). Measurement of exercise-induced changes in feeling states, affect, mood, and emotions. In J.L. Duda (Ed.), *Advances in sport and exercise psychology measurement* (pp. 325–336). Morgantown, WV: Fitness Information Technology.

Gilbourne, D., & Taylor, A.H. (1998). From theory to practice: The integration of goal perspective theory and life development approaches within an injury-specific goal-setting program. *Journal of Applied Sport Psychology, 10,* 124–139.

Gill, D.L. (1986). *Psychological dynamics of sport.* Champaign, IL: Human Kinetics.

Gill, D.L., & Deeter, T.E. (1988). Development of the Sport Orientation Questionnaire. *Research Quarterly for Exercise and Sport, 59,* 191–202.

Goldstein, J.H. (1979). *Sports, games, and play: Social and psychological viewpoints.* Hillsdale, NJ: Erlbaum.

Goode, K.T., & Roth, D.L. (1993). Factor analysis of cognitions during running: Associations with mood changes. *Journal of Sport and Exercise Psychology, 15,* 375–389.

Gould, D., Feltz, D., Horn, T., & Weiss, M. (1982). Reasons for attrition in competitive swimming, *Journal of Sport Behavior, 5,* 155–165.

Griffin, N.S., Keogh, J.F., & Maybee, R. (1984). Performer perceptions of movement confidence. *Journal of Sport Psychology, 6,* 395–407.

Haas, J., & Roberts, G.C. (1975). Effect of evaluative others upon learning and performance of a complex motor task. *Journal of Motor Behavior, 7,* 81–90.

Hackfort, D. (1993). Contemporary areas of research in sport psychology in Germany. In R.M. Singer, M. Murphey, & L.K. Tennant (Eds.), *Handbook of research on sport psychology* (pp. 40–43). New York: Macmillan.

Hanin, Y.L. (1980). A study of anxiety in sports. In W.F. Straub (Ed.), *Sport psychology: An analysis of athlete behavior* (pp. 236–249). Ithaca, NY: Mouvement.

Hanin, Y.L. (1997). Emotions and athletic performance: Individual zones of optimal functioning. *European Yearbook of Sport Psychology, 1,* 29–72.

Hardy, L. (1990). A catastrophe model of performance in sport. In J.G. Jones & L. Hardy (Eds.), *Stress and performance in sport* (pp. 81–106). Chichester, UK: Wiley.

Hardy, L. (1996). Testing the predictions of the cusp catastrophe model of anxiety and performance. *The Sport Psychologist, 10,* 140–156.

Harter, S. (1978). Effectance motivation reconsidered: Toward a developmental model. *Human Development, 21,* 34–64.

Hatfield, B.D., & Landers, D.M. (1983). Psychophysiology— A new direction for sport psychology. *Journal of Sport Psychology, 5,* 243–259.

Heart, E.A., Leary, M.L., & Rejeski, J.W. (1989). The measurement of social physique anxiety. *Journal of Sport and Exercise Psychology, 11,* 94–104.

Heide, F.J., & Borkovec, T.D. (1983). Relaxation-induced anxiety: Paradoxical anxiety enhancement due to relaxation training. *Journal of Consulting and Clinical Psychology, 51,* 171–182.

Heide, F.J., & Borkovec, T.D. (1984). Relaxation-induced anxiety: Mechanisms and theoretical implications. *Behavior Research and Therapy, 22,* 1–12.

Henry, F.M. (1981). Physical education: An academic discipline. In G.A. Brooks (Ed.), *Perspectives on the academic discipline of physical education* (pp. 10–15). Champaign, IL: Human Kinetics.

Hoffman, S.J. (1985). Specialization + fragmentation = extermination: A formula for the demise of graduate education. *Journal of Physical Education, Recreation and Dance, 56*(6), 19–22.

House, J. (1977). The three faces of social psychology. *Sociometry, 40,* 161–177.

Janssen, J.P., Stoll, H., & Volkens, K. (1987). Short-term storage of power-time parameters: Studies with the rowing and bicycle ergometer for motor coding. *Psychologische Beitrage, 29,* 494–523.

Kantor, E., & Ryzonkin, J. (1993). Sport psychology in the former USSR. In R.N. Singer, M. Murphey, & L.K. Tennant (Eds.), *Handbook of research on sport psychology* (pp. 46–49). New York: Macmillan.

Keller, E.F. (1985). *Reflections on gender and science.* New Haven, CT: Yale University Press.

Kerr, J.H. (1985). The experience of arousal: A new basis for studying arousal effects in sport. *Journal of Sport Sciences, 3,* 169–179.

Kerr, J.H. (1997). *Motivation and emotion in sport: Reversal theory.* East Sussex, UK: Psychology Press.

Klavora, P. (1978). An attempt to derive inverted-U curves based on the relationship between anxiety and athletic performance. In D.M. Landers & R.W. Christina (Eds.), *Psychology of motor behavior and sport—1977* (pp. 369–377). Champaign, IL: Human Kinetics.

Klint, K.A., & Weiss, M.R. (1986). Dropping in and dropping out: Participation motives of current and former gymnasts. *Canadian Journal of Applied Sport Sciences, 11,* 106–114.

Krane, V., Greenleaf, C.A., & Snow, J. (1997). Reaching for gold and the price of glory: A motivational case study of an elite gymnast. *The Sport Psychologist, 11,* 53–71.

Kroll, W. (1970). Current strategies and problems in personality assessment of athletes. In L.E. Smith (Ed.), *Psychology of motor learning* (pp. 349–367). Chicago: Athletic Institute.

Kuhl, J. (1985). Volitional mediators of cognitive-behaviour consistency: Self-regulatory process and action versus state orientation. In J. Kuhl & J. Beckmann (Eds.), *Action control: From cognition to behaviour* (pp. 101–128). New York: Springer-Verlag.

Landers, D.M. (1980). The arousal-performance relationship revisited. *Research Quarterly for Exercise and Sport, 51,* 77–90.

Landers, D.M. (1983). Whatever happened to theory testing in sport psychology? *Journal of Sport Psychology, 5,* 135–151.

Landers, D.M. (1989). Sport psychology: A commentary. In J.S. Skinner, C.B. Corbin, D.M. Landers, P.E. Martin, & C.L. Wells (Eds.), *Future directions in exercise and sport science research* (pp. 475–486). Champaign, IL: Human Kinetics.

Lirgg, C.D. (1991). Gender differences in self-confidence in physical activity: A meta-analysis of recent studies. *Journal of Sport and Exercise Psychology, 13,* 294–310.

Maddux, J.E., & Meier, L.J. (1995). Self-efficacy and depression. In J.E. Maddux (Ed.), *Self-efficacy, adaptation, and adjustment: Theory, research, and application* (pp. 143–172). New York: Plenum Press.

Maehr, M.L., & Nicholls, J.G. (1980). Culture and achievement motivation: A second look. In N. Warr (Ed.), *Studies in cross-cultural psychology* (pp. 221–267). New York: Academic Press.

Mahoney, M. (1985). Open exchange and epistemic progress. *American Psychologist, 40,* 29–39.

Markland, D., Emberton, M., & Tallon, R. (1997). Confirmatory factor analysis of the Subjective Exercise Experience Scale among children. *Journal of Sport and Exercise Psychology, 19,* 418–433.

Marsh, H.W. (1994). Sport motivation orientations: Beware of the jingle-jangle fallacies. *Journal of Sport and Exercise Psychology, 16,* 365–380.

Martens, R. (1969). Effect of an audience on learning and performance of a complex motor skill. *Journal of Personality and Social Psychology, 12,* 252–260.

Martens, R. (1970). A social psychology of physical activity. *Quest, 14,* 8–17.

Martens, R. (1974, March). *Psychological kinesiology: An undisciplined subdiscipline.* Paper presented at the meeting of the North American Society for the Psychology of Sport and Physical Activity, Anaheim, CA.

Martens, R. (1975). The paradigmatic crisis in American sport personology. *Sportwissenschaft, 5,* 9–24.

Martens, R. (1980). From smocks to jocks: A new adventure for sport psychologists. In P. Klavora & K.A.W. Wipper (Eds.), *Psychological and sociological factors in sport* (pp. 20–26). Toronto: School of Physical and Health Education, University of Toronto.

Martens, R. (1989). Studying physical activity in context: Sport. In *Big Ten Leadership Conference Report, Chicago* (pp. 101–103). Champaign, IL: Human Kinetics.

Martens, R., & Landers, D.M. (1970). Motor performance under stress: A test of the inverted-U hypothesis. *Journal of Personality and Social Psychology, 16,* 29–37.

Martin, G.L., & Hrycaiko, D. (1983). *Behavior modification and coaching: Principles, procedures, and research.* Springfield, IL: Charles C Thomas.

Maxeiner, J. (1989). *Perception, attention, and memory in sports.* Schondorf, Germany: Hofmann.

McCall, G.J., & Simmons, J.L. (1982). *Social psychology: A sociological approach.* New York: Macmillan.

McCann, S.C., & Scanlan, T. (1995). A new USOC-AAASP partnership: Olympic world opens anew to interested certified consultants, AAASP. *AAASP Newsletter, 10*(3), 9.

McCormack, J.B., & Challip, L. (1988). Sport as socialization: A critique of methodological premises. *Social Science Journal, 25,* 83–92.

McCullagh, P., & Noble, J.M. (1996). Education and training in sport and exercise psychology. In J.L. Van Raalte & B. Brewer (Eds.), *Exploring sport and exercise psychology* (pp. 377–394). Washington, DC: American Psychological Association.

Ming, S., & Martin, G.L. (1996). Single-subject evaluation of a self-talk package for improving figure skating performance. *The Sport Psychologist, 10,* 227–238.

Moore, R.L. (1998). Building strong academic programs for the future: Practical experience at the University of Colorado-Boulder. *Quest, 50,* 198–205.

Morgan, W.P. (1980). The trait psychology controversy. *Research Quarterly for Exercise and Sport, 51,* 50–76.

Morgan, W.P. (1989). Sport psychology in its own context: A recommendation for the future. In J.S. Skinner, C.B. Corbin, D.M. Landers, P.E. Martin, & C.L. Wells (Eds.), *Future directions in exercise and sport science research* (pp. 97–110). Champaign, IL: Human Kinetics.

Moritz, S.E., Feltz, D.L., Fahrbach, K., & Mack, D.A. (2000). The relation of self-efficacy measures to sport performance: A meta-analytic review. *Research Quarterly for Exercise and Sport, 71,* 280–294.

Moritz, S.E., Hall, C.R., Martin, K.A., & Vadocz, E. (1996). What are confident athletes imaging? An examination of image content. *The Sport Psychologist, 10,* 171–179.

Morris, T. (1995). Introduction. In T. Morris & J. Summers (Eds.), *Sport psychology: Theory, applications, and issues* (pp. xxii–xxxv). Milton, QLD, Australia: Wiley.

Morris, T., & Summers, J. (1995). Future directions in sport and exercise psychology. In T. Morris & J. Summers (Eds.), *Sport psychology: Theory, applications, and issues* (pp. 592–604). Milton, QLD, Australia: Wiley.

Murphy, G.M., Petipas, A.J., & Brewer, B.W. (1996). Identity foreclosure, athletic identity, and career maturity in intercollegiate athletes. *The Sport Psychologist, 10,* 239–246.

Perlman, D., & Cozby, P.C. (1983). *Social psychology.* New York: CBS College.

Qiu, Y., & Qiu, Z. (1993). Contemporary areas of research in sport psychology in the People's Republic of China. In R.N. Singer, M. Murphey, & L.K. Tennant (Eds.), *Handbook of research on sport psychology* (pp. 50–51). New York: Macmillan.

Rejeski, W.J., & Brawley, L.R. (1983). Attribution theory in sports: Current status and new perspectives. *Journal of Sport Psychology, 5,* 77–99.

Rivenes, R.S. (1978). *Foundations of physical education.* Boston: Houghton Mifflin.

Roberts, G.C. (1989). When motivation matters: The need to expand the conceptual model. In J.S. Skinner, C.B. Corbin, D.M. Landers, P.E. Martin, & C.L. Wells (Eds.), *Future directions in exercise and sport science research* (pp. 71–84). Champaign, IL: Human Kinetics.

Roberts, G.C., Kleiber, D.A., & Duda, J.L. (1981). An analysis of motivation in children's sport: The role of perceived competence in participation. *Journal of Sport Psychology, 3,* 206–216.

Ryan, E.D. (1968). Reaction to "sport and personality dynamics." In *Proceedings of the National College Physical Education Assocaiton for Men* (pp. 70–75).

Ryan, E.D. (1981). The emergence of psychological research as related to performance in physical activity. In G.A.

Brooks (Ed.), *Perspectives on the academic discipline of physical education* (pp. 327–341). Champaign, IL: Human Kinetics.

Ryckman, R., Robbins, M., Thornton, B., & Cantrell, P. (1982). Development and validation of a physical self-efficacy scale. *Journal of Personality and Social Psychology, 42,* 891–900.

Sachs, M.L. (1993). Professional ethics in sport psychology. In R.N. Singer, M. Murphey, & L.K. Tennant (Eds.), *Handbook of research on sport psychology* (pp. 921–932). New York: Macmillan.

Scanlan, T., & Lewthwaite, R. (1986). Social psychological aspects of competition for male youth sport participants: Part 4. Predictors of enjoyment. *Journal of Sport Psychology, 8,* 25–35.

Schutz, R.W., & Gessaroli, M.E. (1993). Use, misuse, and disuse of psychometrics in sport psychology research. In R.N. Singer, M. Murphey, & L.K. Tennant (Eds.), *Handbook of research on sport psychology* (pp. 901–917). New York: Macmillan.

Selye, H. (1946). General adaptation syndrome and diseases adaptation. *Journal of Clinical Endocrinology, 6,* 117–230.

Shadish, W.R., Jr. (1985). Planned critical multiplism: Some elaborations. *Behavioral Assessment, 8,* 75–103.

Singer, R.N. (1978). Sport psychology: An overview. In W.F. Straub (Ed.), *Sport psychology: An analysis of athletic behavior* (pp. 3–14). Ithaca, NY: Mouvement.

Smith, R.E. (1989). Scientific issues and research trends in sport psychology. In J.S. Skinner, C.B. Corbin, D.M. Landers, P.E. Martin, & C.L. Wells (Eds.), *Future directions in exercise and sport science research* (pp. 23–38). Champaign, IL: Human Kinetics.

Smith, R.E., Smoll, F.L., & Schutz, R.W. (1991). Reactions to competition: Measurement and correlates of sport specific cognitive and somatic trait anxiety: The Sport Anxiety Scale. *Anxiety Research, 2,* 262–280.

Smoll, F.L., & Smith, R.E. (1989). Leadership behaviors in sport: A theoretical model and research paradigm. *Journal of Applied Psychology, 19,* 1522–1551.

Straub, W.F., & Williams, J.M. (Eds.). (1983). *Cognitive sport psychology.* Lansing, NY: Sport Science Associates.

Stryker, S. (1977). Developments in "two social psychologies": Toward an appreciation of mutual relevance. *Sociometry, 40,* 145–160.

Treasure, D.C., & Roberts, G.C. (1994). Perceptions of success questionnaire: Preliminary validation in an adolescent population. *Perceptual and Motor Skills, 79,* 607–610.

Vealey, R.S. (1986). Conceptualization of sport-confidence and competitive orientation: Preliminary investigation and instrument development. *Journal of Sport Psychology, 8,* 221–246.

Wankel, L.M. (1975). A new energy source for sport psychology research: Toward a conversion from D.C. (drive conceptualizations) to A.C. (attributional cognitions). In D.M. Landers (Ed.), *Psychology of sport and motor behavior* (Vol. 2, pp. 221–245). University Park: Pennsylvania State University.

Wankel, L.M. (1984). Audience effects in sport. In J.M. Silva & R.S. Weinberg (Eds.), *Psychological foundations of sport* (pp. 293–314). Champaign, IL: Human Kinetics.

Weinberg, R.S., & Gould, D. (1995). *Foundations of sport and exercise psychology.* Champaign, IL: Human Kinetics.

Weiss, M.R., & Bredemeier, B.J. (1983). Developmental sport psychology: A theoretical perspective for studying children in sport. *Journal of Sport Psychology, 5,* 216–230.

Weiss, M.R., Bredemeier, B.J., & Shewchuk, R.M. (1986). The dynamics of perceived competence, perceived control, and motivational orientation in youth sports. In M. Weiss & D. Gould (Eds.), *Sport for children and youth* (pp. 89–102). Champaign, IL: Human Kinetics.

Wicker, A.W. (1985). Getting out of our conceptual ruts: Strategies for expanding conceptual frameworks. *American Psychologist, 40,* 1094–1103.

Wiggins, D.K. (1984). The history of sport psychology in North America. In J.M. Silva & R.S. Weinberg (Eds.), *Psychological foundations of sport* (pp. 9–22). Champaign, IL: Human Kinetics.

Williams, J.W., & Andersen, M.B. (1998). Psychosocial antecedents of sport injury: Review and critique of the stress and injury model. *Journal of Applied Sport Psychology, 10,* 5–25.

Wilmore, J.H. (1998). Building strong academic programs for our future. *Quest, 50,* 103–107.

Zajonc, R.B. (1965). Social facilitation. *Science, 149,* 269–274.

CHAPTER 2

A Critical Analysis of Knowledge Construction in Sport Psychology

Robert Brustad

This chapter explores knowledge development in sport psychology and highlights the fundamental issues involved in this endeavor. Generating new knowledge in any scientific discipline may appear to be relatively straightforward and unproblematic and even may be regarded as an activity that is dictated primarily by methodologically based decisions, procedures, and rules. To the contrary, our research is fundamentally grounded in philosophically based assumptions about how best to study the world that we live in. Thus, philosophical, and not methodological, considerations are most relevant to our quest. This chapter examines the philosophical orientations and historical influences that have contributed most to shaping the course of knowledge development in sport psychology. Specifically, attention is directed to the positivist research tradition as the most influential paradigm of knowledge development in sport psychology and other fields of study. In addition, the natural link between sport psychology and the parent discipline of psychology, as well as the working alliance between sport psychology and the other sport sciences, is ex-

amined because these relationships have also shaped our research traditions. Alternative research traditions, specifically the hermeneutic/ interpretive perspective as well as critical and feminist approaches, are discussed to highlight some of the fundamental differences in philosophical assumptions about knowledge development that exist in social science research. The principal focus of the chapter is on recognizing the epistemological assumptions that guide various approaches to knowledge development and the historical and social influences that have shaped the current state of knowledge development in sport psychology.

By generating knowledge, we enhance our understanding of the world. The simplicity of this statement conceals the numerous philosophical, methodological, and social issues underlying the development of new knowledge. In fact, the means by which knowledge is produced in any area of inquiry reflects greatly on underlying epistemological assumptions and beliefs, accepted research traditions, sociocultural perspectives, and the shared beliefs and values of researchers. Knowledge development is inherently a social process and thus is not unproblematic (Dewar & Horn, 1992; Kuhn, 1970).

The purpose of this chapter is to critically evaluate the influences and traditions that have shaped research in sport psychology with the intent of encouraging greater reflection on our beliefs about what it means "to know" in our field of inquiry. A concurrent goal is to address how traditional, or orthodox (Martens, 1987), scientific approaches have shaped the types of questions that we ask and the processes by which we address these issues. For example, how have accepted scientific traditions within sport psychology affected the types of research questions that we pose? What sources of knowledge (e.g., experiential, observational, experimental) do we regard as appropriate for our use? Which methods (inductive or deductive) and forms of data analysis (quantitative or qualitative) provide us with the most trustworthy form of knowledge? Where should we conduct these studies (laboratory or field?) What are the purposes of our research, and whom does it benefit? Most importantly, how confident are we in the knowledge created by our own research?

As we address these concerns, it is important to distinguish between epistemological and methodological issues in relation to knowledge generation. Epistemology is the·branch of philosophy concerned specifically with knowledge development. Epistemological issues in any scientific discipline include concerns for the nature, sources, and validity of knowledge. A specific epistemological issue relates to which forms of knowledge we most trust. Methodological issues relate to the "how" of conducting research. Specifically, through what processes do we gain knowledge? In this case, we might think of differences between experimental, survey, and observational research. Logically, the methodology that we use is consistent with our underlying epistemological beliefs.

It might be helpful to provide one concrete example of a knowledge issue in sport psychology. This example relates to our knowledge about the relationship between self-confidence and sport performance. Do we know that higher self-confidence leads to better performance? If so, how do we know? Specifically, what sources of knowledge have we used in developing this belief? If we wish to test further the relationship between self-confidence and performance, how should we design our research to best address this issue? For example, would we use a controlled laboratory environment to manipulate self-confidence? Would

we rely on field research and gather information about self-confidence–performance relationships in natural settings? Would we use questionnaires, or would we interview athletes? Most importantly, what underlying assumptions would influence these decisions?

One major barrier to critical reflection on knowledge development in sport psychology is the expectation that the process of generating knowledge should be unproblematic. Knowledge development should never be regarded as unproblematic, because any approach to scientific inquiry itself rests on a particular set of philosophical assumptions that have been developed in relation to prevailing belief systems, historical traditions, and social conventions (Gergen, 1982; Giddens, 1978; Kuhn, 1970; Lather, 1986). Knowledge development in sport psychology research, which is a rapidly emerging field of study, faces the same sets of philosophical and methodological issues encountered by more mature disciplines (Dzewaltowski, 1997; Martens, 1987). Evidence of this struggle is apparent in controversies regarding the relative benefits of laboratory and field research, basic versus applied research, quantitative and qualitative forms of data utilization, and similar current issues. In sum, knowledge development in any field of study is not unproblematic, because it rests on a particular set of assumptions about the world and our means of studying it.

Due to the recent, rapid growth of sport psychology, most of our knowledge base has been generated within the last 20 years. The relatively recent emergence of this field of study might lead one to assume that sport psychology has developed its own unique research tradition during this time. In fact, the prevailing forms of knowledge development in our field have emanated from other established research traditions. It is helpful to conceptualize knowledge development in sport psychology as emerging from a "traditional" approach to conducting science that is grounded in the conventions of Western science and shaped by more recent traditions from psychology and the sport and exercise sciences.

TRADITIONAL BASES OF KNOWLEDGE IN SPORT PSYCHOLOGY

Although the knowledge base in sport psychology has been generated relatively recently, the empirical foundation of our knowledge rests largely on research carried out by using traditional scientific

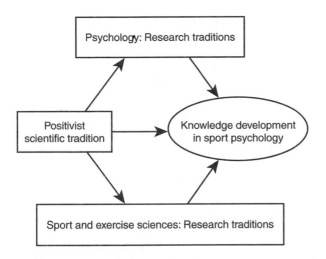

Figure 2.1 Influences on the knowledge base in sport psychology.

approaches (figure 2.1). As with other emerging scientific disciplines in search of acceptance, sport psychology researchers have relied on established scientific approaches, specifically positivism, to structure our approach to research. Furthermore, we have relied heavily on the research traditions of our parent discipline of psychology as well as the scientific conventions of our colleagues in the sport and exercise sciences. Collectively, these influences contributed to a very traditional approach to conducting research in the formative years of modern sport psychology.

The Positivist Scientific Legacy

The predominant influence on the Western scientific tradition has been the theory of knowledge known as positivism, or logical positivism. Positivism emerged out of the modernist era, which experienced its fullest expression during the Enlightenment of 18th-century Europe but which had been stimulated through the earlier writings of philosophers such as Auguste Comte, John Stuart Mill, and David Hume. A defining feature of modernism was the belief that the natural world follows systematic, orderly, and predictable laws. The belief in the lawful nature of the physical world inspired efforts to identify underlying causative mechanisms. A modernist conviction of importance for the growth of modern science was the belief that humans possess the requisite mental capacities to comprehend the laws that regulate the natural and social worlds. From a modernist perspective, the world was understandable by employing reason. Modernist thought thus dif-

fered substantially from all preceding worldviews, such as that of the romantic era, because for the first time humans were considered capable of understanding and, thus, shaping the world for their own benefit (Gergen, 1991). In fact, modernists believed that through systematic application of logical mental processes, ignorance and superstition could be replaced by progress, justice, and beauty (Dickens & Fontana, 1994). The tremendous optimism of the modernist era was accompanied by an unrelenting faith in both the epistemology and methodology of positivism.

The epistemological foundation of positivism was grounded in a mechanistic world view predicated on the assumption of predictable cause-and-effect patterns of relationships. Positivist philosophy strongly adhered to the "machinelike" explanations characteristic of Newtonian physics (Capra, 1982; Gergen, 1991). Furthermore, positivism was grounded in the belief that there exist immutable laws in the natural and social worlds that are unaffected by one's perspective and that can best be understood through reliance on objective scientific processes. In other words, this tradition adhered to the notion that there exists a singular, concrete reality that reasonable people using logical means can understand. The methodology of positivism relied heavily on the principles of reductionism and quantification for acquiring new knowledge and employed the hypothetico-deductive method of theory testing, which is best epitomized by controlled laboratory experimentation. Finally, positivists considered all reliance on subjective or unobservable processes, including emotional experiences, to be outside the realm of "good science." Thus, only that which is measurable, quantifiable, and objectifiable was appropriate for study from a positivist perspective. Although the scientific method that we are familiar with actually emerged gradually over many years, the core beliefs that drive orthodox science are directly attributable to positivist philosophy.

The assumption that there exist invariant, general laws of nature is an important dimension of positivist philosophy and has had a powerful influence on social science research. From this viewpoint, there exist concrete, universal laws that are unaffected by perspective or context. The idea that a cross-situational, universal reality exists contributes to the search for enduring causes or "determinants" of human behavior across contexts and cultures. Furthermore, this perspective results in the pursuit of nomothetic explanations of human behavior, or attempts to provide general laws across all individuals, rather than idiographic forms of explanation that direct attention toward the nature and extent of individual differences.

Belief in the possibility of objectivity is a core component of positivist philosophy and of the Western scientific tradition. Objectivity is the assumption that the researcher can engage in the scientific process without interjecting her views, beliefs, or biases in a way that might influence scientific conclusions and without affecting the object of study merely by her presence. As Martens (1987) noted, before the 20th century, it was also believed that "scientists' biases did not make any difference because nature's laws were impervious to influence by humankind" (p. 34). The concept of objectivity also is based on the premise that there exists a singular "absolute truth" on which reasonable people following systematic procedures can agree.

Reliance on reductionist practices is also an important component of positivist methodology. Reductionism is the belief that the best means of understanding reality is by analyzing the functioning of individual entities in isolation of other influences. Through the reductionist approach, the scientist attempts to understand the unique functioning of constituent parts but is less concerned with interactive relational patterns. Thus, reductionist practices are in direct contrast with "dynamic systems" and "systems theory" perspectives on the functioning of the physical and social worlds (Capra, 1996).

Dependence on quantifiable forms of knowledge is an additional characteristic of positivism. The reliance on quantifiable information was the result of an inherent distrust in the subjective and intuitive forms of knowledge that were characteristic of the premodernist era. From the positivist perspective on quantification, that which is not measurable is also not understandable and thus is not appropriate for study. Obviously, inductive approaches to knowledge development and the use of qualitative data have not been warmly embraced by positivists because of the perception that such approaches introduce subjective elements into the research process.

Inherent trust in the logic of the experimental method is another cornerstone of positivism. The experimental method is based on a hypothetico-deductive model of science in which testable hypotheses are derived from prevailing theories. Through the process of deduction, the scientist determines whether specific observations conform to hypothetical expectations that have been proposed a priori. The experimental method is based on implicit belief in cause-and-effect patterns of relationship in the world that can be accurately assessed only through controlled experimental procedures, typically in a laboratory setting.

Positivist philosophy has profoundly affected the course of Western science. Positivism represents just one philosophy of knowledge; however, given the widespread belief that this is the most trustworthy form of inquiry, philosophers of science have labeled this form of knowledge development as "orthodox science" (Martens, 1987) and "normal science" (Kuhn, 1970). In large part, the hegemony, or predominance, of the positivist philosophy of science is evident from the perception of most researchers that the positivist methodology is the only route to knowledge. Furthermore, other approaches to knowledge development are much less familiar to students because of a lack of exposure to alternate philosophies or because of their denigration by practitioners of orthodox

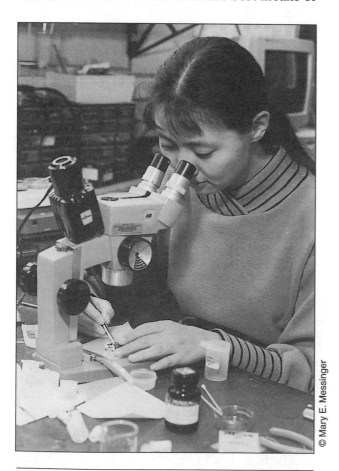

© Mary E. Messinger

Positivism holds as appropriate for study only that which is measurable, quantifiable, and objectifiable.

science. In Martens's (1987) words, the influence of the positivist paradigm cannot be underestimated because "orthodox science exerts a comprehensive power over most of us today, not unlike religion once did" (p. 36).

Critiques of Positivism

Until the 20th century, there were few challenges to positivism as the singular route to knowledge development in the sciences. However, limitations of the positivist worldview in the natural sciences became apparent early in the 20th century, particularly in theoretical physics, and sparked closer examination of positivist doctrine. Philosophers of science (e.g., Capra, 1982; Feyerabend, 1975; Hesse, 1980) also have strongly contested many of the fundamental beliefs about the world on which positivist epistemology is grounded. Within the social sciences, the merits of positivist philosophy for knowledge generation have been questioned further by those who argue that this paradigm of knowledge development is much less useful for understanding the complexities of human cognition and social behavior than for explaining natural phenomena (Giddens, 1978; Hoshmand, 1989). These perspectives on the limitations of positivist inquiry have resulted in the call for alternate paradigms for knowledge development, or at least the recognition that multiple approaches to knowledge development exist (e.g., Dewar & Horn, 1992; Harris, 1981, 1983a; Hoshmand, 1989; Martens, 1987; Sparkes, 1992).

Within the natural sciences, the foundational principles of positivism have been challenged by 20th-century research developments, particularly in physics. Within physics, the Newtonian cause-and-effect image of the physical world has been replaced by more complex explanations of physical phenomena characterized by quantum physics and relativity theory. Quantum physics diverges significantly from the mechanistic explanations of physical relationships that characterized classical mechanics. Based in part on Heisenberg's (1958/1997) experimentation, quantum physics deviates from the Newtonian model in that subatomic particles, the so-called basic building blocks of matter, are no longer regarded as "things" that cause other "things" to happen in a mechanistic fashion but rather as "wavelike patterns of probabilities" (Capra, 1996, p. 30) that reflect interconnections with other elements within a complex system. The significance of this knowledge is that the doctrine of reductionism fails at the ultimate level of reduction because the material properties of objects cannot be understood in isolation but only in reference to other material objects. The modernist worldview founded on a mechanistic, reductionist model was thus challenged. Capra (1996) suggested that the positivist metaphor of the machine be replaced by the image of the physical world as a dynamic system, or web, that focuses on the changing relational characteristics of system components. This challenge to the positivist "world as machine" model fueled further speculation about the limitations of positivist epistemology.

The epistemological foundations of positivism also are grounded in the belief that systematic, orderly, and immutable laws of nature exist. Within the social sciences, we might question how well a guiding belief in absolute, unchangeable laws serves our research interests. Specifically, do we really believe that universal laws of human behavior extend across all cultures and contexts? Is positivist philosophy too simplistic of a research model for the social sciences in the same way that classical mechanics did not hold up to the scrutiny of modern understandings in physics?

The complexities inherent in studying human behavior might argue further against a strict positivist perspective. Current cognitive psychology is based on the premise that individuals act with intention and in relation to situational interpretation and personal reflection, which highlights the intricacy and dynamic nature of human behavior (Nielsen, 1990). The recognition that humans are conscious of their behavior and thus capable of altering their behavior under observation contributes a dimension of complexity that is not present in the natural sciences and argues against a narrow deterministic model of social science. Human behavior also cannot be readily understood without reference to context. Social context provides the frame of reference from which any singular behavior takes on meaning. Context can be considered to include not only the objective characteristics of any situation but also individuals' previous experiences, their subjective interpretation of those experiences, and their expectancies for current encounters. Such a recognition suggests that viewing behavior in relation to a dynamic systems perspective may be more appropriate within the social sciences than the simpler mechanistic paradigm.

The principle of objectivity in research, which is a core foundation of positivist epistemology, represents an additional area of contention. Trust in objectivity rests on the belief that it is possible for any investigator to detach himself or herself from the subject matter of interest and thereby avoid influencing the interpretation of research outcomes. To illustrate the difficulty of maintaining objectivity in scientific research, Pagels (1982) provided the example of an anthropologist who visits a remote culture for study and, in so doing, cannot help but impact the course of village life and thus what is considered to be characteristic of that life. The objectivity assumption is further grounded in the belief that there exists a singular material reality unaffected by perspective. However, Einstein's relativity principle asserts that our understanding of time and motion is itself related to perspective. This conceptualization contributed to a relativist, rather than an absolutist, view of the physical world that conflicts with the positivist notion of a singular, absolute reality. In relation to the doctrine of objectivity, this recognition also has contributed to the view that "there is no basic unit of matter to be observed independent of those who make the observation. Subject and object are inextricably linked" (Gergen, 1991, p. 89).

Challenges to the objectivity assumption also have been voiced with regard to the process of theory testing. Theory testing is essential to the advancement of knowledge, but theories also serve as a priori frames of reference that structure our interpretation of subsequent outcomes. Thus, as researchers we do not approach our involvement as "blank slates" but rather as individuals who anticipate patterns of relationships and thus are more likely to find these hypothesized outcomes to be supported in contrast to competing, or unconsidered, explanations. As Nielsen (1990) noted, "Data are not detachable from theory. Theories are models of the way the facts themselves are seen" (p. 15). Maguire (1991) commented,

> Observations cannot simply be collected, stored, and presented as facts to be explained. Observations are always guided by some theory, no matter how simple or vague. On a continuum, there are no zero points, no absolute states of detachment or involvement, observation or theory formation. Rather it is a matter of balances and degrees. (p. 192)

Reductionism as a means of knowledge development in social science research is compromised by the recognition that the interaction of personal and social influences cannot be fully understood through a focus on singular entities in isolation.

Within sport psychology, many of the primary issues of interest inherently call for a "systems" perspective (Brustad & Ritter-Taylor, 1997; Foon, 1987). In particular, research in the social psychology of sport requires an interactionist perspective. For example, to study leadership effectiveness, group processes, or self-presentational influences in sport and exercise, we must direct our attention to the interactions that occur among individuals and the reciprocal forms of influence that take place over time. In our quest to understand the "whole" in social science research, it is important to identify and understand the functioning of constituent parts. However, the functioning of those parts in isolation is meaningless without reference to the other parts that make up the whole (Hesse, 1980). A systems view, rather than a mechanistic view, thus may be more appropriate in most sport psychology research.

The emphasis on quantification in orthodox science reflects both epistemological and meth-

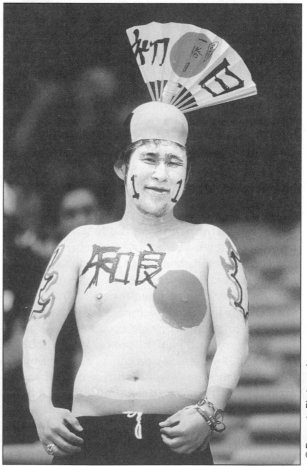

Can positivism adequately explain the rabid enthusiasm of the sports fanatic?

odological assumptions that constrain knowledge development. Because positivist philosophy only supported science that studied what was observable and measurable, subjective processes inherently fell outside the realm of "good science." For psychologists, however, the domain of study consists of those very subjective cognitive processes that the proponents of positivism did not consider worthy of study. Furthermore, the emphasis on quantification implies a false dichotomy between quantitative and qualitative approaches in psychological research. In reality, each form of data analysis relies heavily on human interpretive processes in assessing the dimensions of interest. For example, self-confidence levels may be quantified through the use of a research questionnaire. However, the questions and response options that make up the questionnaire require considerable interpretation on behalf of the respondent, and any response thus is mediated by interpretation, which we would consider to be a subjective process. Consequently, any numerical value assigned to a response is not a "pure" reflection of the extent of self-confidence but only an indirect estimate that has been obtained given the mediating influence of language and interpretation and the arbitrary nature of the measurement scale. When interview techniques are used as a form of qualitative methodology, these same issues of interpretation are present. Thus, the idea that quantitative and qualitative methodologies are fundamentally different is inaccurate.

Postpositivism

In response to 20th-century research developments and internally and externally generated forms of criticism, a scientific philosophy known as postpositivism has emerged. Overall, postpositivism is aligned closely with the worldview of its predecessor and, thus, will not be considered as a distinct philosophical tradition in its own right. In general, postpositivists have a much more restrained view of our capacity to ever "know" reality than do positivists. In recognizing limitations in humans' ability to fully know and understand the world, postpositivists recognize barriers to eventual understanding that result from these limitations (Guba & Lincoln, 1994). A second feature of postpositivism is the view that we should focus not on proving scientific theories but rather on disproving them through a variety of strong tests. The recognition that a single test may demonstrate that a theory or assertion is false

but that no single test can ever prove a theory or assertion to be true has led to the view that repeated challenges to theory are the best means of assessing the theory's validity. Third, postpositivists are much more open to a variety of methodologies than their predecessors. The methodology of postpositivism relies more heavily on "critical multiplism," which is similar to triangulation, in that the researcher uses a variety of methodological approaches to assess whether the phenomenon under study adheres to expectations. Thus, the postpositivist might use various forms of quantitative and qualitative methodologies. Although postpositivism represents an important departure from some of the traditions of positivism, the fundamental worldview of this approach does not differ substantially from its predecessor. Thus, for the remainder of this chapter, postpositivist work is considered to fall within the framework of positivist epistemology.

Although the limitations of positivist epistemology and methodology have been increasingly highlighted, positivism remains the primary route to knowledge development in the natural and social sciences. In this chapter, I am not attempting to discredit the positivist tradition, only to highlight the assumptions (and the limitations of these assumptions) that underlie this approach to knowledge development. Given that alternate forms of knowledge development have their own unique limitations, few critics of positivism would argue that orthodox science should be discarded. However, the dominance of orthodox science in the training of young researchers has been challenged because lack of exposure to alternate forms of knowledge development ignores current developments in the philosophy of science and provides the false impression that there is only one route to knowledge (Brustad, 1997; Hoshmand, 1989; Maguire, 1991; Sage, 1989; Sparkes, 1992). Thus, the predominance of this single research tradition on the course of knowledge development in our field is of greater issue than is the form of this research tradition.

Psychological Traditions and Influences on Knowledge Development in Sport Psychology

Although the positivist philosophy of science has had the greatest influence on our approach to knowledge development in sport psychology, research traditions within our parent discipline of psychology also have profoundly impacted the content and form of our inquiry. In fact, a common critique of sport psychology research has been that sport psychologists have been excessively reliant on the research conventions of psychology proper in generating questions for study and in our methodological approaches to studying these issues (Foon, 1987; Landers, 1983; Martens, 1979, 1987). An appreciation of the sociohistorical context within which North American psychology emerged is useful in understanding the influences that have shaped this tradition.

Compared with the natural sciences, psychology and the other social sciences are relatively young fields of study. A critical issue in the emergence of psychology as a social science was whether, as a new scientific discipline with human behavior as its subject matter, psychology would adhere to the strict positivist traditions of the natural sciences or would generate its own unique approaches to the study of human behavior. In contrast to other social sciences such as anthropology and sociology, psychological research has adhered very closely to the orthodox science traditions of positivism.

There are at least two reasons why psychological researchers in North America clung to the positivist scientific tradition of the natural sciences. First, before the late 1800s, recognition of psychology as a unique discipline of study was hindered by the perception that it was unsystematic and unscientific. This perception hindered the emergence of the social sciences (Collins, 1985). Use of the methodology of the natural sciences was an important step in gaining credibility as a science. Second, the successes of the positivist model in the natural sciences led to the unwarranted expectation that the use of this methodology would be similarly effective in explaining human behavior. Bertrand Russell commented that through a reliance on this methodology, social science research soon would be capable of producing "a mathematics of human behavior as precise as the mathematics of machines" (cited in Gergen, 1991, p. 30). However, little concern was expressed at the time about the unique problems inherent in attempting to explain human behavior through a scientific model developed for the natural sciences. As Gergen (1991) noted, the overwhelming belief in "truth through method" (p. 36) encouraged researchers to follow but a singular path to knowledge.

Because experimental psychology was built on an accepted methodological foundation, the his-torical context of the time supported the emergence of experimental psychology. Gergen (1982) described the social circumstances within which the "science" of psychology emerged:

It is no intellectual accident that psychology as a science was given birth at the close of the nineteenth century. One might indeed ask if it was not a sign of lassitude that its beginning was so late in arrival. The foundations had long been laid. The concept of an empirical science had been well developed since the time of Newton....There remained only the task of welding the belief in the palpability of mental entities with the experimental orientation of the natural sciences to give birth to the science of psychology. (p. 178)

In the United States, psychology researchers exhibited strong trust in the abilities of the experimental method to produce the purest form of knowledge about the mechanisms underlying human behavior. Although early research attempted to identify elemental cognitive and sensory mechanisms, this focus on unobservable processes eventually met with resistance, and the primary focus of study became behavior. The rise of behaviorism and its affiliation with the experimental methodology of positivism was directly attributable to a common mistrust of subjective and unobservable features (Collins, 1985; Gergen, 1982). During the decades when behaviorism ruled American psychology, the behavior of rats, pigeons, and other laboratory animals became the focus of study. As Gergen (1991) noted, "In retrospect, we find it disturbing that the scholarly world could believe that the fundamentals of human nature could be laid bare by the antics of a small number of laboratory animals" (p. 40). However, this outcome was directly attributable to an unquestioned acceptance of positivist methodology and the conviction that truth could be known through method.

The legacies of experimentalism and behaviorism within American psychology have had a lasting impact on the content and breadth of the knowledge base in psychology as well as on expectations about what is the appropriate way to gain knowledge. Because knowledge traditions in sport psychology have been influenced strongly by our parent discipline, these concerns extend to our field as well. The primary influence of experimentalism and behaviorism is that these traditions are so firmly grounded in the positivist heritage that alternate forms of knowledge development were able to contribute only minimally to the knowledge base within psychology. Second, because of a strong adherence to deterministic and reductionistic principles, psychological research has diverged considerably from related social sciences, such as sociology and anthropology, in its approach to research. Third, this research legacy severely retarded the development of U.S. social psychology because the study of humans in naturalistic social settings was not a primary focus of conventional psychological research (Gergen, 1982). Consequently, two distinct social psychological traditions are in evidence today (Saxton & Hall, 1987). Although the content of sociological social psychology and psychological social psychology is essentially the same, the research approaches of these two traditions differ substantially because they have traced much different historical and philosophical paths.

Because sport psychology research largely has reflected the research traditions within psychology proper, the history of our knowledge development is inextricably linked to the traditions of our parent discipline. Martens (1987, pp. 30–31) described the operative mindset when he began to pursue sport psychology research:

> I recall how we were enraptured with the American social psychological experimental paradigm, devoured the theories of the day, and charged into the laboratories to lift the field of sport psychology to a true science . . . we created unique, controlled, and artificial environments to observe people compete, imitate, be reinforced, cheat, and cope with stress. (We never once thought that these studies might in turn produce artificial, contrived behavior unique to the environment we created.) With strong convictions based on our ability to use the scientific method, we saw ourselves as the new generation of sport psychologists who were going to build a solid foundation of scientific facts for the field of sport psychology. Thus began the modern era of the academic discipline of sport psychology.

Knowledge development within psychology also reflects the prevailing theoretical paradigms popular within each era. The history of American psychology has been characterized as an ebb and flow between exogenic and endogenic theoretical perspectives in relation to the perceived causes of human behavior (Gergen, 1982). Exogenic perspectives are those such as behaviorism, which adhere to the notion that human behavior originates in response to forces external to the individual. In contrast, endogenic perspectives, including personality and contemporary cognitive theories, hold that individual dispositional or cognitive processes drive behavior. It has been rare in North American psychology that fully interactionist models of explanation have been used that account for behavior in relation to the simultaneous interaction of personal and situational influences (Bales, 1983; Gergen, 1985). In general, the exogenic perspective is much more compatible with the approaches of orthodox science because of its tendency to adhere to a lawful, deterministic model of human behavior with a strong trust in experimentalism. However, endogenic models also can be very compatible with orthodox science to the extent that they present a deterministic, cause-and-effect model of behavior. In contrast, interactionist perspectives are not at all compatible with these traditions because of the fundamental belief that human behavior is the manifestation of personal constructions in relation to a dynamic social context. The dynamic nature of this interaction is not well served by positivist tradition.

The "cognitive revolution" (Gardner, 1985) that has gained increasing prominence within North American psychology over the past several decades will have an important effect on the nature of knowledge development within psychology and, by implication, sport psychology. The strong endogenic focus of this perspective, with its concentration on individual differences in subjective appraisal processes, is not effectively served by the reductionist, experimentalist research tradition. From the cognitive theoretical worldview, the focus of knowledge development is on the world as it is known and the variability that exists among individuals in their subjective appraisals of the world. Such a perspective takes a relativist rather than an absolutist approach to understanding, because the focus of research is on understanding the nature of individual differences rather than identifying universal psychological laws. To the extent that cognitive theorists also examine context-specific cognitions, psychological research will use dynamic, relativistic, and context-bound approaches to knowledge development that are inconsistent with the determinism of orthodox science (Gergen, 1985).

Sport Science Sources of Influence on Knowledge Development

A third influential research tradition in sport psychology is the consequence of the traditionally close association between sport psychology and the other sport sciences. Although the theoretical foundations of most of our research were generated within psychology, the overwhelming majority of academic programs in sport psychology have been housed in departments of exercise and sport science, kinesiology, or physical education. Historically, it also has been more common for sport psychologists to be involved in intradisciplinary professional organizations such as NASPSPA and the American Alliance of Health, Physical Education, Recreation and Dance (AAHPERD) than in cross-disciplinary organizations such as the APA. With the growth of AAASP and the continued emergence of a division of sport and exercise psychology within APA (Division 47), this intradisciplinary allegiance is not currently as strong as in the past. However, our traditionally strong association with the other sport sciences has resulted in at least three forms of influence on the content of our knowledge and the means by which we pursue this knowledge.

First, sport psychologists have been strongly inclined to use the research methods of their sport science counterparts. Although the sport and exercise sciences represent an interesting mix of subdisciplines grounded in the natural sciences (exercise physiology, biomechanics) and social sciences (sport psychology, sport sociology), these subdisciplinary areas are not necessarily of similar size or status within most academic programs. In terms of status, number of academic positions, and program size, sport psychology historically has been relegated to a relatively minor role within sport science departments. Given the visibility and status accorded to exercise physiology within sport science departments, it is not surprising that sport psychology research has been prone to rely on the positivist scientific tradition characteristic of the physical sciences. Maguire (1991) summarized these influences:

> The current orthodoxy regarding science within sport science draws on ideas held by traditional realist philosophers of science. The scientific method is to be found in the procedures of the natural sciences (within sport sciences: biomechanics, exercise physiology, experimental psychology) and the exemplar of this is physics. Some naive positivists have tended to depict the social sciences (sociology, social psychology) as, at best, immature imitations of the natural sciences in which the "pure" and "eternal" scientific logic is contaminated by unscientific, socially determined ideological influences. Or, the focus has been on defining how the logic of the social sciences differs from the logic of the natural sciences. Sport scientists, untouched by developments within the philosophy of science, appear to have accepted this model in an unquestioning manner and have frozen out social scientific explanations from the curriculum and research agenda. (pp. 190–191)

A second form of influence on the growth of knowledge in sport psychology is the consequence of the strong historical association between sport psychology and motor learning. During the 1960s and 1970s, tremendous overlap existed between these two subdisciplines. The strength of this association is evident from the emergence of NASPSPA, which reflects the shared goals of motor behavior and sport psychology researchers. This relationship fostered a strong experimental orientation to sport psychology research such that "since its inception, the primary goal of NASPSPA has been to advance the knowledge base of sport psychology through experimental research" (Cox, Qiu, & Liu, 1992, p. 4). The early issues of the *Journal of Sport Psychology* contain a preponderance of tightly controlled, experimental studies that are more commonly associated with natural science methodology and that reflect an experimentalist orientation to sport psychology research. This link to the natural science methodology of motor learning maintained an association with the experimentalist tradition while distancing sport psychology research from the approaches to knowledge of its social science counterparts in the sport sciences.

A third major intradisciplinary form of influence on knowledge development in sport psychology relates to the focus and content of our inquiry. Specifically, this form of influence concerns the nature of the knowledge that we pursue and the goals and purposes of this knowledge development. The sport science research base, in general, has been characterized as reflecting an imbalanced focus on understanding and enhancing athletic performance for higher ability and elite performers with substantially less attention devoted to examining sport participation among nonelite populations (Hoberman, 1992; Tinning, 1997; Whitson & MacIntosh, 1990). Furthermore, it has been argued that sport science researchers avidly pursue issues related to the quality of sport performance while avoiding issues concerning the social and psychological consequences of sport participation (Coakley, 1997). Within sport psychology research, these arguments are supported by the disproportionate representation of research using elite athlete participants with particular focus on those psychological processes (e.g., concentration, imagery) underlying high-level performance. Conversely, a relatively limited amount of research exists on the psychological experiences of nonelite athletic populations and those areas of study most relevant to such populations, including the psychological and affective consequences of this participation. Within sport psychology, a tremendous growth also has occurred in the area of intervention. Although sport psychology interventions can occur with individuals of any ability or experience level, the clear focus of much of this research is elite athletic performance. In contrast, there has been much less interest in issues related to the psychological and social consequences of sport involvement (including moral and ethical issues), retirement and social readjustment issues, and psychological development through sport. The performance focus of our research also is represented by the reductionistic imagery of the "body as machine" (Hoberman, 1992; Whitson & MacIntosh, 1990) in which physiological, mechanical, neuromotor, and psychological processes are studied independently and without reference to the overall health and development of the individual.

A significant avenue of departure from the orthodox scientific traditions that have characterized sport psychology is the result of the increasing acceptance and use of qualitative methodology as a form of inquiry within our field. I consider Scanlan and colleagues' (Scanlan, Ravizza, & Stein, 1989; Scanlan, Stein, & Ravizza, 1989) investigations of elite figure skaters to be seminal in legitimizing this approach to knowledge development as a worthwhile and appropriate means of inquiry. This research was able to provide greater access to the underlying psychological and emotional meanings of sport involvement for these individuals that would not have been possible through traditional quantitative and deductive approaches. As researchers have recognized the benefits of inductive approaches to knowledge development, as well as the additional depth provided by qualitative approaches, an increasing proportion of published research in sport psychology has relied on qualitative methodology during the past decade. Although it is possible for qualitative methodology to emerge from a posi-

tivist perspective, this is unlikely given the qualitative researcher's typical reliance on inductive approaches and implicit distrust of the quantification doctrine. The increasing legitimation of qualitative research is an appropriate departure point to consider alternate philosophies of knowledge development in social science research.

ALTERNATE PHILOSOPHIES OF KNOWLEDGE DEVELOPMENT

Recurrent dissatisfaction with the limitations of orthodox science has resulted in the advancement of alternate approaches to knowledge development in the social sciences, including sport psychology. The hermeneutic/interpretive and the critical/feminist traditions represent two additional forms of inquiry. Each of these traditions deviates substantially from the underlying assumptions that guide the positivist philosophy of science. In fact, they share few commonalities with positivism, and thus each represents a unique paradigm or worldview in relation to knowledge development. A common feature of these approaches is their shared perspective that knowledge is socially generated. Furthermore, researchers within each tradition desire to gain much greater depth of understanding of human behavior in relation to personal, cultural, and social influences than is afforded by positivist science. In addition, the critical/feminist approach is characterized strongly by a concern for the value orientations of our research as reflected by the questions that we pose and the ultimate content of our knowledge base.

Hermeneutic/Interpretive Approaches

The paradigm that I refer to as the hermeneutic/interpretive tradition actually consists of a number of closely aligned perspectives, including the "naturalistic" and "constructivist" approaches to knowledge (Guba & Lincoln, 1989). This route to knowledge originated largely in response to the belief that positivist approaches did not satisfactorily explain human behavior. The term *hermeneutics* refers directly to the process of interpretation, and this tradition relies on interpretive methods, such as naturalistic and ethnographic approaches, to gain knowledge.

The epistemological foundation of the hermeneutic/interpretive tradition is grounded in the belief that human behavior is fundamentally related to individual perceptions of the meaning inherent within social contexts. Thus, human behavior is believed to occur in relation to the context-specific, dynamic meanings that we encounter and that have been formed in relation to our own life experiences and unique subjective appraisals. Consequently, this form of inquiry is more concerned with understanding the nature of individual differences in human behavior in relation to the interaction of personal and situational influences than in pursuing nomothetic generalizations about human behavior across contexts. The emphasis on humans interacting in relation to shared meaning systems also indicates a complete divergence from the reductionistic, nomothetic, and deterministic foundations of positivist philosophy. Whereas the metaphor of the machine is an appropriate characterization of positivist epistemology, an ecological network, or systems (Capra, 1982, 1996) image might better represent the hermeneutic/interpretive tradition. In this imagery, individual behavior can be understood only in relation to the broader social network within which one functions.

A key dimension of the hermeneutic/interpretive tradition is that it is based on a constructivist view of reality. From this perspective, humans construct meaning through experience and make sense of their world in interaction with others. As Hoshmand (1989) remarked, this tradition "views social reality as created by the participants in a given social context, essentially a construction based upon the actor's frame of reference" (p. 16). Language is the most important vehicle for developing and conveying this meaning to others. The hermeneutic research tradition is thus logically consistent with the symbolic interactionist theoretical perspective (Blumer, 1969) because each is concerned with the means by which our perception of reality is socially constructed, particularly through language. Whereas the positivist focus is on principles of reductionism and quantification and an implicit belief in direct cause-and-effect relationships, the hermeneutic tradition follows a much different path through its emphasis on socially generated and shared intersubjective meanings operative within dynamic social contexts.

The fundamental assumption that the reality which guides human behavior is socially constructed and emerges in interaction with others differs substantially from the image of an objective, external, physical reality coincident with positivism. Consequently, inductive research approaches are much more consistent with the hermeneutic/interpretive framework than are deductive approaches characterized by the testing of theoretically based hypotheses. Within the hermeneutic/interpretive paradigm, a grounded theory approach in which knowledge and perhaps theory are allowed to emerge from data is preferred over a priori theory testing (Erlandson, Harris, Skipper, & Allen, 1993). Furthermore, research findings are believed to be context-specific because patterns of relationships identified within one context are not necessarily anticipated to occur in differing contexts. Given the preference for inductive and contextual approaches to knowledge development, naturalistic and ethnographic research methods are preferred to remain consistent with these values. Qualitative forms of data (observations, interviews) also are relied on more typically than quantitative data, but neither qualitative nor quantitative data are inherently necessitated by this tradition. Because the purpose of knowledge development within this paradigm is to understand the meaningful nature of human behavior, no methodological approach is necessarily off limits.

Psychological research in sport from the hermeneutic/interpretive tradition is limited in quantity. Published research in this area has addressed athlete identity issues (Adler & Adler, 1987, 1991; Donnelly & Young, 1988), sport burnout (Coakley, 1992), retirement issues (Parker, 1994), and sport socialization processes (Harris, 1983b; Fine, 1987). A recent example of research from this paradigm is Faulkner and Sparkes' (1999) ethnographic study of exercise as therapy for schizophrenia. Unfortunately, virtually none of this research has been reported in sport psychology journals. I assume that this has occurred because sport psychology researchers are unfamiliar with this tradition. As previously noted, an increasing amount of sport psychology research has relied on qualitative methodology, but the authors of these studies rarely have been explicit regarding the epistemological foundation underlying their methodology (Krane, Andersen, & Strean, 1997). The hermeneutic/interpretive tradition can make a sizable contribution to our knowledge base; however, current researchers and students have little exposure to this form of knowledge development given the typical focus of our research training.

Critical/Feminist Research Traditions

A third paradigm for knowledge development is embodied in the critical and feminist forms of inquiry. Because these two traditions share some common roots and have many similar concerns with regard to the generation and use of knowledge, they are discussed together.

Three major commonalities link the critical and feminist research traditions and differentiate this worldview from the positivist and hermeneutic/interpretive paradigms. First, each focuses primarily on the nature and purpose of knowledge development. From either a critical or a feminist perspective, one questions why certain forms of knowledge have come to be valued above other forms and whom this knowledge serves. Neither the positivist nor hermeneutic/interpretive tradition is concerned principally with the eventual use of knowledge. Second, the critical and feminist perspectives discount the idea that truly objective knowledge can exist. Theorists from each perspective disavow the notion that it is possible to engage in science from a neutral, disinterested posture. Knowledge generation is not regarded as value-free but strongly value-laden, because it inherently reflects the beliefs and values of its practitioners and the scientific community. Third, each views the scientific enterprise as a social process in which the rules of science reflect the power relations that exist within the scientific community as well as within society as a whole. Thus, the scientific process is not divorced from its social context but actively reflects and perpetuates the same values and traditions.

It is more appropriate to consider the critical and feminist traditions as paradigms or perspectives on knowledge development (Krane, 1994; Nielsen, 1990) rather than as formalized research approaches in their own right. Each lacks the systemized set of rules that characterizes knowledge development in the positivist tradition, in particular. The primary area of divergence between critical and feminist work is their areas of focus. Within the critical tradition, researchers are concerned with understanding the nature of power and social relations within a society. And, as Nielsen (1990) expressed, "Criticism in this tradition means more than a negative judgment; it refers to the more positive act of detecting and unmasking, or exposing, existing forms of beliefs that restrict or limit human freedom" (p. 9). Similarly, feminist research is concerned with power relations within society but focuses primarily on uncovering gender-related patterns of influence. A feminist perspective thus places gender "at the center of the analysis, not on the periphery" (Krane, 1994, p. 397). Feminist research also has a strong contextualist orientation, similar in this respect to the hermeneutic/interpretive tradition,

in which situated social knowledge is preferred, particularly because it can contribute to our understanding of relational patterns within society (Gill, 1994; Krane, 1994). The critical and feminist traditions share the view that knowledge development should be a means for benefiting and transforming society.

Critical/feminist research directly addresses the content and purpose of knowledge development in our field. This concern commonly is manifested in relation to issues of value. From this standpoint, sport psychology research asks questions such as, Who do we study? Why is this research important? How will this knowledge benefit society? From this viewpoint, critical/feminist scholars are likely to challenge the elitist and performance outcome orientations of much of our research with regard to the eventual contribution of such knowledge to the betterment of society. Thus, the critical/feminist scholar would not argue that the knowledge we have gained in sport psychology is not valid but rather that it is limited in scope and social value.

Similarly, a critical/feminist perspective would argue that the psychological processes which we study in sport cannot be examined in isolation of the larger social system. For example, it is not possible to understand the psychological dimensions of female sport involvement while totally disregarding the history of sport opportunities for girls and women, as well as the stereotypes and socialization practices that currently impact this involvement. However, as Dewar and Horn (1992) commented, "Research in sport psychology has tended to treat sport as neutral and unproblematic" (p. 19). Because sport represents an increasingly important institution within our larger social system, it is difficult to consider sport as either neutral or unproblematic. I believe that sport psychology research has been late in recognizing that the personal and the social cannot be separated easily, in large part because of our historically closer scholarly alliance with natural science–based research (e.g., motor learning) than with the sport social sciences (sport sociology). Sage (1991) expressed this criticism in relation to sport science research overall:

With respect to research on human movement activities, especially in sport and exercise contexts, one implication is that these activities cannot be regarded as neutral practices devoid of wider social significance and free of specific cultural values. This suggests that any account of kinesiology—past, present, and future, must be rooted in an understanding that human movement activities are cultural practices embedded in the social, economic, political, and cultural contexts in which they are situated. Even some natural scientists are beginning to realize that the scientific process is socially constructed and embedded in the sociocultural milieu. (p. 158)

Perceived limitations of the objectivity doctrine are an additional bond linking the critical and feminist perspectives. Their shared view is simply that objectivity is rarely, if ever, possible in science. From this perspective, orthodox science is believed to reinforce inherent social biases largely because of the researcher's own immersion in the values and beliefs of a particular social system. In the same way that it is difficult to interpret data independently from preconceived theory or beliefs, so it would be argued from a critical/feminist position that it is virtually impossible to objectively understand human processes apart from the sociohistorical context and value systems within which we function. In their reviews of feminist theory and practice, Krane (1994) and Gill (1994) provided examples of sport psychology research issues that cannot be extracted and studied apart from social and cultural influences. As they noted, psychological characteristics such as personality, self-confidence, and leadership behavior are shaped in gender-related ways by a larger network of social practices. One hallmark of critical/feminist scholarship is that because it is grounded in the belief that knowledge development is inherently driven by underlying values, such research attempts to be direct in stating the underlying values that drive research rather than to hide these values in the guise of objectivity.

A further defining feature of the critical and feminist research traditions is that each views the process of science as reflective of power relations present within the scientific community and society as a whole. In this regard, the critical and feminist traditions are aligned strongly with Kuhn's (1970) perspective on the scientific social support networks that maintain a dominant scientific worldview during any era. In his highly influential account of the history of science, Kuhn argued that science does not advance in an incremental manner in which small bits of knowledge increasingly contribute to shaping our understanding of the world. Rather, Kuhn argued, scientific knowledge changes in relation to large-scale paradigm shifts

that support a particular scientific worldview because of the predominance of its adherents within the scientific community at that time.

In strong contrast to the positivist tradition, critical/feminist forms of inquiry do not consist of prescribed sets of rules about how knowledge should be generated. In actuality, general epistemological issues receive much greater attention from critical and feminist scholars than do methodological concerns. Although no singular methodology is necessarily associated with critical/feminist forms of inquiry, the shared distrust in the notion of "objective knowledge" steers this research away from the experimentalist and reductionist mindset of positivism and toward the social constructivist orientation of the hermeneutic/interpretive tradition. In particular, inductive, personalized, and highly contextualized approaches to knowledge are preferred (Nielsen, 1990), and thus interpretive and qualitative methodologies are used most frequently.

As with hermeneutic/interpretive forms of inquiry, there are relatively few examples of critical or feminist research in our literature. In her review, Krane (1994) identified the study by Bredemeier et al. (1991) as perhaps the best example of feminist research in sport and exercise psychology. Krane (1994) and Gill (1994) provided overviews of the fundamental guiding principles of feminist research and professional practice as applied to sport psychology.

The worldviews of the three major research traditions mentioned in this chapter diverge considerably in relation to their underlying beliefs and values regarding knowledge development. With regard to the purposes of knowledge generation within each tradition, Nielsen (1990) described the positivist tradition as inherently focused on prediction and control and the hermeneutic/interpretive tradition as concerned with the understanding of behavior, with the feminist/critical goal being emancipation. Given that three fundamentally different purposes characterize these research approaches, it is imperative to acknowledge the worldview that underlies each as we embark on research. Although particular methodological approaches are associated strongly with each tradition, it is possible to use multimethod approaches in addressing any research question. Furthermore, additional research paradigms that have not been mentioned in this chapter are appropriate to research in sport psychology. For example, the phenomenological (Fahlberg, Fahlberg, & Gates, 1992; Polkinghorne, 1989) research tradition is appropriate, particularly for issues related to individual change processes that might be of greatest interest in applied sport psychology.

RECOMMENDATIONS FOR FUTURE RESEARCHERS

In relation to the issues presented in this chapter, I have three recommendations to further knowledge development in sport psychology. The first recommendation is for researchers to consider a variety of routes for knowledge advancement in sport psychology. As much as we might wish it, there is not a single, direct, or unproblematic route to knowledge, and we need to acknowledge the strengths and limitations of any course. We also need to permit a diversity of approaches, even if we only follow one course in our own research. As Dewar and Horn (1992) commented in the previous version of this chapter, "We need to abandon the belief that there is only one legitimate way of knowing in sport psychology and begin to understand that it is both possible and desirable to examine behavior in different ways" (p. 17).

A second recommendation is to more closely consider and acknowledge the epistemological assumptions that guide our research. I have found that sport science research courses rarely direct attention to the underlying epistemological issues that should be the foundation of our research. In fact, most research courses provide students with methodological competence, but the methodology taught typically reflects an implicit positivistic perspective on the scientific process. Thus, there is an imbalance between epistemology and methodology. A parallel situation might be represented by the circumstance of an engineer who considers only the tools at his or her disposal rather than the conceptual issues involved in addressing a structural problem. Lack of attention to epistemological concerns also perpetuates the misperception that the positivist worldview is the only approach to knowledge development in sport psychology and implies that the orthodox approach to science is unproblematic and noncontroversial.

A final recommendation is to do research that counts. Sport psychologists study many important and relevant issues related to the personal and social development of individuals through sport. But we also study many trivial issues when considered in a larger human context. Knowledge issues don't concern just the process of doing re-

search but also the content of what we produce. What values and purposes will guide our research? As a field of inquiry, and as individual researchers, what will be our contribution?

SUMMARY

Knowledge development is inherently a social process in that humans collectively generate the rules and expectations about what is important to know and how this knowledge should be acquired. In this process, our prevailing philosophical beliefs, research traditions, social conventions, and scientific and personal values shape the course of our research and greatly impact the types of understanding that we will eventually derive. Knowledge development in sport psychology, as in all areas of study, has been influenced profoundly by the positivist research tradition, and the epistemological foundation of this tradition has been used as a reference point for highlighting the importance of philosophical beliefs about knowledge development. The sport psychology research tradition has been shaped further through its historical association with the discipline of psychology and through its close working relationship with the other sport sciences. Recent developments in sport psychology research, particularly the growing acceptance of qualitative and inductive forms of research, have contributed to a growing diversity of approaches to knowledge development that include the hermeneutic/interpretive and critical/feminist traditions. As with other forms of social science research, there is a growing awareness that a mechanistic approach to understanding human behavior is limited in its ability to explain behavior in dynamic social contexts. A systems or interactionist view thus may be more appropriate. It is essential that we recognize and value varied approaches to knowledge development and the differing purposes (prediction/control, understanding, social change/emancipation) that underlie these efforts. However, it is also essential that we critically evaluate the assumptions that underlie our own approaches to knowledge generation so that our chosen route will make a worthwhile contribution to sport psychology.

REFERENCES

Adler, P., & Adler, P.A. (1987). Role conflict and identity salience: College athletics and the academic role. *Social Science Journal, 24,* 443–455.

Adler, P.A., & Adler, P. (1991). *Backboards and blackboards: College athletes and role engulfment.* New York: Columbia University Press.

Bales, R.F. (1983). The integration of social psychology. *Social Psychology Quarterly, 47,* 98–101.

Blumer, H. (1969). *Symbolic interactionism.* Englewood Cliffs, NJ: Prentice Hall.

Bredemeier, B.J.L., Desertrain, G.S., Fisher, L.A., Getty, D., Slocum, N.E., Stephens, D.E., & Warren, J.M. (1991). Epistemological perspectives among women who participate in physical activity. *Journal of Applied Sport Psychology, 3,* 87–107.

Brustad, R. (1997). A critical-postmodern perspective on knowledge development in human movement. In J.M. Fernandez-Balboa (Ed.), *Critical postmodernism in human movement, physical education, and sport* (pp. 87–98). Albany, NY: SUNY Press.

Brustad, R.J., & Ritter-Taylor, M. (1997). Applying social psychological perspectives to the sport psychology consulting process. *The Sport Psychologist, 11,* 107–119.

Capra, F. (1982). *The turning point: Science, society, and the rising culture.* New York: Simon & Schuster.

Capra, F. (1996). *The web of life: A new scientific understanding of living systems.* New York: Doubleday.

Coakley, J. (1992). Burnout among adolescent athletes: A personal failure or social problem? *Sociology of Sport Journal, 9,* 271–285.

Coakley, J.J. (1997). *Sport in society: Issues and controversies* (6th ed.). Dubuque, IA: McGraw-Hill.

Collins, R. (1985). *Three sociological traditions.* New York: Oxford University Press.

Cox, R.H., Qiu, Y., & Liu, Z. (1992). Overview of sport psychology. In R.N. Singer, M. Murphey, & L.K. Tennant (Eds.), *Handbook of research on sport psychology: A project of the International Society of Sport Psychology* (pp. 3–31). New York: Macmillan.

Dewar, A.M., & Horn, T. (1992). A critical analysis of knowledge construction in sport psychology. In T. Horn (Ed.), *Advances in sport psychology* (pp. 13–22). Champaign, IL: Human Kinetics.

Dickens, D.R., & Fontana, A. (1994). Postmodernism in the social sciences. In D.R. Dickens & A. Fontana (Eds.), *Postmodernism and social inquiry* (pp. 1–22). New York: Guilford Press.

Donnelly, P., & Young, K. (1988). The construction and confirmation of identity in sport subcultures. *Sociology of Sport Journal, 5,* 223–240.

Dzewaltowski, D.A. (1997). The ecology of physical activity and sport: Merging science and practice. *Journal of Applied Sport Psychology, 9,* 254–276.

Erlandson, D.A., Harris, E.L., Skipper, B.L., & Allen, S.D. (1993). *Doing naturalistic inquiry.* Newbury Park, CA: Sage.

Fahlberg, L.L., Fahlberg, L.A., & Gates, W.K. (1992). Exercise and existence: Exercise behavior from an existential-phenomenological perspective. *The Sport Psychologist, 6,* 172–191.

Faulkner, G., & Sparkes, A. (1999). Exercise as therapy for schizophrenia. *Journal of Sport and Exercise Psychology, 21,* 52–69.

Feyerabend, P.K. (1975). *Against method.* London: Verso.

Fine, G.A. (1987). *With the boys.* Chicago: University of Chicago Press.

Foon, A.E. (1987). Reconstructing the social psychology of sport: An examination of issues. *Journal of Sport Behavior, 11,* 223–230.

Gardner, H. (1985). *The mind's new science: A history of the cognitive revolution.* New York: Basic Books.

Gergen, K.J. (1982). *Toward transformation in social knowledge.* New York: Springer-Verlag.

Gergen, K.J. (1985). The social constructionist movement in modern psychology. *American Psychologist, 40,* 266–275.

Gergen, K.J. (1991). *The saturated self: Dilemmas of identity in contemporary life.* New York: Basic Books.

Giddens, A. (1978). Positivism and its critics. In T. Bottomore & R. Nisbet (Eds.), *A history of sociological analysis* (pp. 237–286). New York: Basic Books.

Gill, D.L. (1994). A feminist perspective on sport psychology practice. *The Sport Psychologist, 8,* 411–426.

Guba, E.G., & Lincoln, Y.S. (1989). *Fourth generation evaluation.* Newbury Park, CA: Sage.

Guba, E.G., & Lincoln, Y.S. (1994). Competing paradigms in qualitative research. In N.K. Denzin & Y.S. Lincoln (Eds.), *Handbook of qualitative research* (pp. 105–117). Thousand Oaks, CA: Sage.

Harris, J.C. (1981). Hermeneutics, interpretive cultural research, and the study of sports. *Quest, 33,* 72–86.

Harris, J. (1983a). Broadening horizons: Interpretive cultural research, hermeneutics, and scholarly inquiry in physical education. *Quest, 35,* 82–96.

Harris, J.C. (1983b). Interpreting youth baseball: Players' understandings of attention, winning, and playing the game. *Research Quarterly for Exercise and Sport, 54,* 330–339.

Heisenberg, W. (1997). *The physicist's conception of nature.* In E.B. Bolles (Ed.), *Galileo's commandment: An anthology of great science writing* (pp. 345–354). New York: Freeman. (Original work published 1958.)

Hesse, M. (1980). *Revolutions and reconstructions in the philosophy of science.* Brighton, UK: Harvester Press.

Hoberman, J. (1992). *Mortal engines: The science of performance and the dehumanization of sport.* New York: Free Press.

Hoshmand, L.L.S.T. (1989). Alternative research paradigms: A review and teaching proposal. *The Counseling Psychologist, 17,* 3–79.

Krane, V. (1994). A feminist perspective on contemporary sport psychology research. *The Sport Psychologist, 8,* 393–410.

Krane, V., Andersen, M.B., & Strean, W.B. (1997). Issues in qualitative research methods and presentation. *Journal of Sport and Exercise Psychology, 19,* 213–218.

Kuhn, T.S. (1970). *The structure of scientific revolutions* (2nd ed.). Chicago: University of Chicago Press.

Landers, D.M. (1983). Whatever happened to theory testing in sport psychology? *Journal of Sport Psychology, 5,* 135–151.

Lather, P. (1986). Issues of validity in openly ideological research: Between a rock and a soft place. *Interchange, 17,* 63–84.

Maguire, J. (1991). Human sciences, sport sciences, and the need to study people "in the round." *Quest, 43,* 190–206.

Martens, R. (1979). About smocks and jocks. *Journal of Sport Psychology, 1,* 94–99.

Martens, R. (1987). Science, knowledge, and sport psychology. *The Sport Psychologist, 1,* 29–55.

Nielsen, J.M. (1990). Introduction. In J.M. Nielsen (Ed.), *Feminist research methods: Exemplary readings in the social sciences* (pp. 1–37). San Francisco: Westview Press.

Pagels, H.R. (1982). *The cosmic code: Quantum physics as the language of nature.* New York: Simon & Schuster.

Parker, K.B. (1994). "Has-beens" and "wanna-bes": Transition experiences of former major college football players. *The Sport Psychologist, 8,* 287–304.

Polkinghorne, D. (1989). Phenomenological research methods. In R. Valle & S. Halling (Eds.), *Existential-phenomenological perspectives in psychology* (pp. 41–60). New York: Plenum Press.

Sage, G.H. (1989). A commentary on qualitative research as a form of scientific inquiry in sport. *Research Quarterly for Exercise and Sport, 60,* 25–29.

Sage, G.H. (1991). Paradigms, paradoxes, and progress: Reflections and prophecy. In *New possibilities, new paradigms* (American Academy of Physical Education Papers, pp. 93–99). Champaign, IL: Human Kinetics.

Saxton, S.L., & Hall, P.M. (1987). Two social psychologies: New grounds for discussion. *Studies in Symbolic Interaction, 8,* 43–67.

Scanlan, T.K., Ravizza, K., & Stein, G.L. (1989). An in-depth study of former elite figure skaters: I. Introduction to the project. *Journal of Sport and Exercise Psychology, 11,* 54–64.

Scanlan, T.K., Stein, G.L., & Ravizza, K. (1989). An in-depth study of former elite figure skaters: II. Sources of enjoyment. *Journal of Sport and Exercise Psychology, 11,* 65–83.

Sparkes, A.C. (1992). *Research in physical education and sport: Exploring alternative visions.* Bristol, PA: Falmer Press.

Tinning, R. (1997). Performance and participation discourses in human movement: Toward a socially critical physical education. In J.M. Fernandez-Balboa (Ed.), *Critical postmodernism in human movement, physical education, and sport* (pp. 99–119). Albany, NY: SUNY Press.

Whitson, D., & MacIntosh, D. (1990). The scientization of physical education: Discourses of performance. *Quest, 42,* 40–51.

PART II

Individual Differences and Sport Behavior

Over the past 30 years, the sport psychology research literature has focused on identifying particular characteristics or traits of individuals that can be used to explain and predict their behavior in sport and physical activity contexts. As noted in the preface, such individual difference factors traditionally have been defined in our field to consist of relatively stable traits, dispositions, or characteristics of individuals that can be measured with varying degrees of ease and accuracy. More recently, however, researchers have begun investigating differences between individuals in their subjective appraisals of the world and of the events that occur within that world. These cognitive appraisal processes may be somewhat less stable in nature than traits, dispositions, or personality characteristics, but the research shows significant variability between individuals in the way they process, analyze, interpret, and evaluate events that occur in the sport environment. Furthermore, such interindividual variability in reasoning patterns, cognitive schemas, and subjective appraisal processes has been linked to subsequent differences in sport participants' performance and behavior. It is, of course, assumed that individuals' scores on all of these individual difference measures will vary on a continuum and that

this variability can explain at least a portion of the differences observed among individuals in sport and physical activity contexts.

The six chapters contained in part II examine the research that has been conducted to test the hypothesized relationship between selected individual difference factors and subsequent sport behavior and the theoretical frameworks that underlie that research. This section begins with a chapter by Robin Vealey, which provides an overall perspective on the reciprocal relationship between personality and sport behavior. Vealey begins chapter 3 by defining personality and outlining the corresponding theories that have been developed to explain the relationship between personality and behavior. She then critically reviews the research procedures that have been used both to measure personality and to examine the personality and sport behavior relationship. She concludes by summarizing the current status of knowledge in this area and outlining potential directions for future research. Because of this comprehensive overview, Vealey's chapter provides an excellent foundation for chapters 4 through 8, which focus on more specific aspects of personality.

In chapter 4, Kenneth Fox contributes a new chapter to this second edition that focuses on individuals' perceptions of themselves and their competencies, abilities, and worth in sport and physical activity contexts. Fox begins by detailing why self-esteem and its related self-perception constructs have attracted so much attention in both the academic literature and the popular press. He then reviews the theories that have been proposed to explain how self-concept is structured and, correspondingly, how it can best be assessed. Fox follows this theoretical discussion with a review of the research that has tested the bidirectional relationship between self-perceptions and sport and exercise behavior. As Fox concludes, this research clearly suggests that individuals' perceptions of themselves affect their performance and behavior in physical activity contexts. In addition, however, individuals' participation in physical activity has the potential to contribute to the shaping and refining of the self. Fox recommends that considerably more research is needed if we are to truly understand the mechanisms and processes involved in shaping the individuals' sense of self.

In chapter 5, Maureen Weiss and Emilio Ferrer-Caja provide a comprehensive review of the research and theory related to motivational orientations in the sport domain. These authors begin by summarizing the early descriptively based research on participation motivation and attrition in sport context. They use this early research as a basis for their discussion of five theoretical approaches to motivation in the sport domain. Within each of these areas, Weiss and Ferrer-Caja provide an overview of the theory with a particular focus on motivational aspects. They then summarize the research and conclude the section with a critical perspective on the current state of knowledge along with clear directions for future research work. As will be evident to readers, the chapter by Weiss and Ferrer-Caja is significantly longer than the others. This greater length is understandable and necessary given the salience of motivation to research within many areas of sport psychology and also given the importance that sport motivation has enjoyed in the popular press. In addition, perhaps no

area of research within sport psychology has received greater attention within the past decade than motivational orientation.

In chapter 6, Edward McAuley and Bryan Blissmer review the literature on self-referent thought in sport and exercise participants with particular attention directed toward self-efficacy perceptions and performance attributions. Their chapter begins with an explanation and critical review of the theory and research in both of these areas. They then synthesize the two approaches to illustrate how causal attributions and self-efficacy perceptions affect each other and how both are integrally related to behavior in sport and exercise contexts. McAuley and Blissmer argue that social cognitive theory should provide a particularly useful framework for researchers interested in studying human behavior in physical activity contexts.

In chapter 7, Dan Gould, Christy Greenleaf, and Vikki Krane examine individual differences in anxiety and arousal and again use this variability to explain subsequent differences in performance and behavior. Gould and his coauthors focus particularly on the research and theory pertaining to the arousal–performance relationship and critically review a number of hypotheses and theories that have been developed to explain this relationship. Noting that there has been considerable inconsistency in the sport psychology literature in the use of arousal-related terminology, Gould, Greenleaf, and Krane offer a conceptual model for integrating arousal construct terminology and then use this model to suggest directions for research on anxiety, arousal, and sport performance. Readers of the first edition of this text indicated that this chapter was particularly useful in clarifying confusion regarding the various terms that have been used to describe the anxiety–performance relationship and in identifying the critical questions that remain to be addressed by researchers examining the relationships among anxiety, arousal, and sport performance. This revised chapter aptly fulfills the same two roles.

As Maureen Weiss and Alan Smith note at the beginning of chapter 8, "morality in everyday life and sport is one of the hottest issues in contemporary society." Perhaps because of this "real-world" interest in morality, research on moral reasoning and moral development in relation to participation in competitive sport has burgeoned over the last two decades. Thus, it was deemed necessary and appropriate to add a chapter to the second edition of this text that explores individuals' variability in levels of moral reasoning and that links such interindividual variability to subsequent performance and behavior in sport contexts. Weiss and Smith begin their review of the scholarly literature with a historical perspective on the role of sport in contributing to morality in young athletes. They then review the theoretical and empirical research that has been conducted to examine moral reasoning levels in athletes and other physical activity participants. Much of this research is developmentally based and reflects a continuing interest among researchers and practitioners in identifying how sport participation affects children's and adolescents' moral growth and development. Weiss and Smith conclude by identifying obstacles that currently limit the pursuit of knowledge in regard to moral development but also offer clear suggestions for future research in this area.

Although the six chapters in part II are written from the perspective that individual difference factors can predict sport behavior, each author clearly recognizes that these individual difference factors must be used in combination with situational factors to obtain an adequate understanding of sport behavior. As Vealey, for example, notes in chapter 3, research has consistently shown that sport behavior is codetermined by intrapersonal and situational or environmental factors. Thus, although the individual chapters in part II focus on individual difference characteristics whereas the four chapters in part III focus on environmental or situational factors, the overriding theme of each chapter in parts II and III is the interactional approach to the study of behavior in sport and physical activity contexts.

CHAPTER 3

Personality and Sport Behavior

Robin S. Vealey

The human body is a machine;
it is a great chemical laboratory;
it is an achievement of engineering;
but it is also a self.
The ancients believed that the body
was merely the dwelling place
of a spiritual being
and that this being looked out
through the eyes as one would look
through a window to get knowledge
of the external world.
They believed that this soul
was responsible for all that the body did,
and that no matter how fatigued the body
or how great the obstacle, the soul could
by sheer "mental resolve" or "will power"
drive the body to further work
or to overcome any obstacle.
We now know that the ancients
were rather crude and unscientific
in many of their beliefs.
Although we cannot accept
their explanations of self or personality,
the facts that they sought to explain
are still before us and we must now
come to terms with them.

—Griffith, 1928

In the wake of Coleman Griffith's challenge, the relationship between personality and sport participation continues to intrigue researchers in sport psychology. It is popularly believed that personality contributes to success in sport. It is also popularly believed that valued personality attributes may be developed through sport participation. Ruffer (1975, 1976a, 1976b) identified 572 research studies that have examined the relationship between personality and sport. Fisher (1984) found that well over 1,000 studies have been conducted on personality and sport. However, does this plethora of research support the popular assumptions of the relationship between personality and sport behavior? Are there really "born winners" or personality profiles that relate to success in sport? Does sport "build character" or develop desirable personality characteristics in individuals?

The purpose of this chapter is to review theory and research concerning the relationship between personality and sport participation. Some people narrowly define the study of personality in sport based on the predominant trait research and descriptive personality profiling of the 1960s and 1970s. From this narrow perspective, it often is concluded that sport personality research is dead, because the trait approach has been replaced by newer theoretical approaches. However, the perspective taken in this chapter—a comprehensive view of sport personality—is that much of what we study in sport psychology today can be called the study of personality in sport. This comprehensive view supports the notion that personality psychology underlies much of what today is termed *social psychology* (Krahé, 1992; Pervin & John, 1997). In this sense, the study of personality is the study of why we are the way we are in terms of how we think, act, and feel as human beings.

The chapter is divided into three main sections. In the first section, I define personality and review the key issues surrounding theory and methodology in the study of personality in sport. In the second section, the major theoretical approaches to the study of personality are discussed in terms of conceptual underpinnings, assessment examples, and sport personality research. In the final section, I summarize the knowledge in sport personality and provide suggestions for future research.

THE STUDY OF PERSONALITY IN SPORT

Popular notions of personality typically involve value judgments based on observations of behavior such as "she has a good personality" or "he has lots of personality." However, understanding personality as a scientific area of study is much more complex. In this section, I define *personality* and explain its systematic study to provide a basic understanding of the research focus of personality in sport.

Even a cursory examination of the personality literature indicates little consensus as to the definition of personality. Allport (1961) defined personality as "the dynamic organization within the individual of those psychophysical systems that determine his characteristic behavior and thought" (p. 28). Guilford (1959) simply defined personality as "a person's unique pattern of traits" (p. 5). Maddi (1976) more extensively defined personality as "a stable set of characteristics and tendencies that determine those commonalities and differences in the psychological behavior (thoughts, feelings, and actions) of people that have continuity in time and that may or may not be easily understood in terms of the social and biological pressures of the immediate situation alone" (p. 9). Lazarus and Monat (1979)

defined personality as "the underlying, relatively stable, psychological structure and processes that organize human experience and shape a person's activities and reactions to the environment" (p. 1).

These definitions illustrate the diversity among theorists in their definitions of personality. This diversity makes it difficult to understand what personality is and may in part explain the contradictory findings and debates that have raged in the personality literature. Given the diversity among theorists in their definitions of personality, it seems useful to identify common features that pervade most definitions of personality. Basically, four characteristics are common to almost all specific definitions of personality. These characteristics may be thought of as the *four I's*, which typify personality as an area of scientific study:

1. **Identity.** Personality by nature involves behavior that is based on characteristics that define an important aspect of a person's identity. Psychologists may label these characteristics as *traits*, *styles*, *needs*, *motives*, or *cognitions*, but all of these terms represent a means by which the identity of an individual may be established. A popular question addressed in sport psychology research is whether there is a distinct athletic identity made up of specific personality characteristics.

2. **Individual differences.** Personality reflects individual uniqueness; thus, it is often said that personality is the study of individual differences. Although we recognize that all people are similar in some ways, personality researchers are particularly interested in the ways in which people differ. For example, why do some athletes persist in the face of all obstacles in their pursuit of sport achievement, compared with other athletes who give up easily? Why do some athletes perceive competitive stressors as exhilarating and challenging, whereas other athletes perceive competition as threatening and respond by choking?

3. **Internal determination.** Personality is concerned with behavior influenced by an internal locus of causation or behavior that cannot be explained entirely in terms of the external situation. For example, the startle reflex or the "fight or flight" response to danger would not be considered as areas of study in personality. Thus, personality is concerned with qualities inside the person that may account for consistent patterns of behavior, as opposed to characteristics of the external environment that may account for consistent behavior.

4. **Integrated self.** Personality focuses on the whole person in trying to understand how the different aspects of an individual's functioning are intricately related to each other. Human thought, feeling, and behavior possess some degree of organization or structure and fit together into meaningful patterns. Thus, personality focuses on the integrated whole or total person. Although human behavior is not perfectly consistent, the study of personality assumes that behavior is more than random and can be understood, if not totally predicted.

In summary, although personality is specifically defined in many ways, the four I's indicate the commonalities in these definitions. The scientific exploration of personality involves studying how thoughts, feelings, and behaviors are integrated within individuals to make them unique and distinctive. The next section presents the key theoretical issues surrounding the study of personality in sport.

THEORETICAL ISSUES IN THE STUDY OF PERSONALITY IN SPORT

Throughout the history of personality theory, a number of issues have confronted theorists and researchers repeatedly (e.g., Krahé, 1992; Pervin & John, 1997). Later in this chapter, the main theoretical approaches to studying personality are presented along with the sport research conducted within these approaches. What distinguish personality theories from each other are the ways in which each theory resolves the issues presented in this section.

To What Degree Is Behavior Internally or Externally Determined?

All theories of personality recognize that factors inside the person and events in the surrounding environment are important in determining behavior. However, personality theories differ in the level of importance given to internal and external determinants. This may be thought of as a be-

havioral determination continuum (see figure 3.1). At one extreme end of this continuum is the Freudian view that we are controlled by unconscious internal forces. Theories that fall toward this end of the continuum are known as *dispositional approaches*. Dispositional approaches focus on relatively stable, consistent internal attributes that exert generalized causal effects on behavior. At the other extreme end of the behavioral determination continuum is the Skinnerian view that individuals are largely passive and controlled by events in the environment. Theories that fall toward this end of the continuum are based on the *situational approach*, in which behavior is explained by examining environmental stimuli and individuals' responses to these stimuli. Theories that fall in the middle of the behavioral determination continuum are called *interactional approaches*. Interactionism posits that behavior is codetermined by intrapersonal and situational factors (Bowers, 1973; Magnusson & Endler, 1977).

The dispositional, situational, and interactional approaches may be thought of as paradigmatic trends in personality research. A paradigm is an accepted scientific practice that becomes a model for subsequent scientific inquiry in a particular area (Kuhn, 1970). The adoption of a particular paradigm is the most critical feature of research, because the paradigm defines the way in which the research question is structured and pursued. The so-called person–situation debate arose from tensions between paradigmatic trends in personality psychology.

The person–situation debate received its impetus from Walter Mischel's (1968) book *Personality and Assessment*, in which he reviewed 50 years of personality research and challenged the assumption that stable dispositions or traits could effectively predict behavior. Mischel coined the term "personality coefficient" to describe the weak relationship ($r = .30$) he found between self-report and behavioral measures. Mischel asserted that this weak personality coefficient indicated that behavior is situationally determined. Thus, he advocated a situational approach rather than a

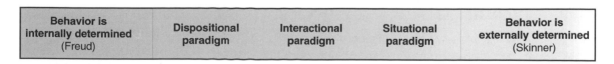

Behavior is internally determined (Freud)	Dispositional paradigm	Interactional paradigm	Situational paradigm	Behavior is externally determined (Skinner)

Figure 3.1 Continuum of behavioral determination.

dispositional approach. Mischel's book stimulated two decades of diverse reactions regarding what became known as the person–situation debate (see Kenrick & Funder, 1988, and Krahe, 1992, for reviews). The person–situation debate has appeared in the sport psychology literature as well (Fisher, 1976, 1984; Martens, 1975; Morgan, 1980a, 1980b; Silva, 1984). That is, sport psychologists have debated over which personality paradigm is the most efficacious approach to understand and predict behavior in sport.

Careful examination of the literature suggests that the person–situation debate is a "pseudo-issue" (Carlson, 1984; Houts, Cook, & Shadish, 1986). As Endler (1973) noted, this question is like asking whether air or blood is more essential to life. It is erroneous to think that dispositional theorists believe that people will behave the same way in all situations. In fact, Gordon Allport, a noted dispositional theorist, was an interactionist because he asserted that different traits are aroused to different degrees in different situations (Pervin, 1985). A provocative analogy was provided by Baron and Boudreau (1987) whereby dispositional characteristics are seen as "keys" in search of the right environmental or situational "locks." Clearly, understanding personality in sport requires the study of both locks and keys. Thus, most personality psychologists agree that behavior is best explained by accounting for both situational and personal characteristics (interactional perspective).

Almost all researchers today emphasize person–situation interactions. In reviewing sport personality research published in the 1970s and 1980s, I (Vealey, 1989) found an increasing trend in the adoption of the interactional paradigm and a decreasing trend in research within the trait paradigm. Yet even when persons, situations, and interactions are all accepted as important, the theories still differ in regard to what in the person interacts with what other things, how they interact, and which is most important at what times. Thus, the debate about internal versus external behavior determination remains an important issue when we consider various theoretical views of personality.

How Consistent Is Personality Over Time and Situations?

The second issue related to understanding theoretical perspectives about personality and sport has to do with the degree to which people believe personality is consistent over time and situations.

This issue is closely related to the person–situation debate just discussed. Some theorists state that people are consistent across situations, whereas others argue that people are totally variable from one situation to the other. Thus, theoretical approaches to the study of personality in sport vary in how they account for the consistency and variability of human behavior over time and situations.

Trait–State Distinction

A distinction made in personality research related to this consistency issue is the distinction between *personality dispositions* (popularly referred to as *traits* in this distinction) and *personality states*. Dispositional (trait) personality constructs are viewed as enduring over time and are abstract in that they must be inferred from behavior. Dispositions or traits may be thought of as tendencies to react in a certain way, or the "typical" or "usual" way that a person might act. For example, competitive trait anxiety is the tendency to view competitive situations as threatening and respond to these situations with apprehension and tension (Martens, Vealey, & Burton, 1990). State personality constructs are viewed as short-lived occurrences (something happening "right now") and are directly detectable and concrete in their manifestation. Thus, if personality dispositions/traits represent tendencies to respond in certain ways, then personality states are the actual responses that occur in specific situations.

Coleman Griffith (1926) made an early distinction between traits and states by describing personality in terms of persistency as well as insistency. Griffith stated that "habits" (his term for personality characteristics) are persistent in lasting over a period of time but also can be insistent as they are actively manifested in specific situations. Allport and Odbert (1936) differentiated personality traits from the more temporary and brief personality states. Spielberger formalized this distinction in 1966 with his state–trait theory of anxiety. In sport psychology, the theoretical conceptualizations of competitive anxiety (Martens et al., 1990) and sport confidence (Vealey, 1986) adopted the interactional perspective in which dispositional (trait) factors combine with situational factors to create a personality state that is predicted to influence sport behavior most directly.

The "trait" in trait–state conceptual approaches is clearly a dispositional construct. Traits and dispositions differ only by degree—degree of consistency—as opposed to kind. Dispositions are less rigid and enduring over time and situations than traits. Thus, although Martens (in Martens et al., 1990) spoke of competitive trait anxiety, he clearly viewed this construct as a disposition.

Cognitive Approach to Interactionism

The trait–state perspective is one way to account for consistency (dispositions) and variability (states) in behavior as influenced by personality. However, the "person" component in the person–situation interaction is not only represented by personality traits or dispositions. Many theorists believe that consistency in behavior across situations is better explained within a cognitive perspective of personality (D.J. Bem, 1983; Mischel, 1977a, 1977b; Snyder, 1983). Cognitive approaches are based on the premise that humans process information to appraise and interpret environmental stimuli before responding. The cognitive perspective is interactional because it is based on each sport performer's unique way of first interpreting, then responding to, different situations in competitive sport.

The cognitive approach has overshadowed the trait–state approach to interactionism because although the trait–state approach is conceptually logical, it is difficult to validate empirically (Mischel, 1968). In fact, the trait–state approach has been attacked as an "arbitrary" distinction with no conceptual or empirical viability (Allen & Potkay, 1981). Problems in predicting sport behavior (particularly performance) by using the trait–state approach have been discussed frequently in the literature (e.g., Burton, 1988; Gould, Petlichkoff, Simons, & Vevera, 1987; Sonstroem & Bernardo, 1982; Vealey, 1986) and usually have been attributed to inappropriate measurement and operationalization of variables. It seems fruitful for sport personality research to move beyond the arbitrary dichotomy of traits and states to

think about cognitive personality characteristics as being on a continuum from traitlike to statelike. In this way, consistency in personality and behavior over time and situations could be examined in many different ways across the continuum, as opposed to thinking of personality as being manifested statically in two dichotomous categories.

Conclusions

A major defining feature of different theories of personality is the degree to which they assert that human behavior is temporally and situationally consistent (see table 3.1).

However, to assert that there is absolute consistency in behavior, especially across persons, is unrealistic and naive. Conversely, it is counterintuitive to argue that human behavior is totally variable without any consistency. It seems much more appropriate to view consistency in relative terms, such as where dispositional theorists (e.g., Allport, 1937) assert the primacy of internal traits yet acknowledge behavioral variation as a function of the situation. This type of *relative consistency* is typical of the trait–state perspective on personality. Perhaps the most useful way of framing the issue of consistency in personality is to focus on *coherence* (Krahé, 1992), which allows for both stability and change in human behavior so long as they follow a systematic and understandable (and somewhat predictable) pattern. The cognitive approach to personality seems to emphasize coherence, because the focus is on understanding the reasoning patterns and schemas of individuals in an attempt to understand the integration of their thoughts, feelings, and behavior.

What Are the Roles of Affect, Behavior, and Cognitions in Personality?

The third issue related to understanding differences in theoretical perspectives about personality and

---

Table 3.1
Degree of Consistency in Approaches to the Study of Personality

Absolute consistency	Trait approaches (dispositional)
Relative consistency	Trait–state approaches (interactional)
Coherence	Cognitive approaches (interactional)
Variability (no consistency)	Situational approaches (situational)

sport is the relative primacy of—and relationship between—thoughts, feelings, and actions in human beings. Personality theorists and researchers are interested in the ABCs of individuals:

- Affect (emotions or feelings)
- Behavior (overt acts)
- Cognitions (thought processes)

Interest in the ABCs has varied throughout the history of psychology. For example, the radical behaviorism of Skinner (1938, 1953) led to a focus on overt behavior and a de-emphasis on research that investigated internal processes such as thoughts and feelings. However, the cognitive revolution that started in the 1950s led to the emphasis on internal thought processes in the study of personality. For much of this time, affect was largely ignored, although affect is increasing in prominence as an important component of personality.

Thus, the various theoretical approaches to the study of personality differ in the relative weight or attention they give to the ABCs. These differences greatly influence personality research in terms of how research is designed and what is measured. Scientific study in sport psychology has followed historical trends in psychology related to the ABCs. The social facilitation work of the 1960s emphasized behavior (Martens & Landers, 1972), motivation research in the 1960s and 1970s emphasized achievement motives (Roberts, 1974), and attribution research in the 1970s and 1980s emphasized information-processing cognitions (Roberts, 1984). Another interesting trend has been the focus on *negative affect* largely due to Martens' early conceptual work in competitive anxiety (in Martens et al., 1990) and popular fascination with "choking" in sport. Only within the last decade has *positive affect* come more into focus in sport psychology (e.g., Crocker, 1997; S. Jackson, 1992; Riemer & Chelladurai, 1998; Scanlan, Carpenter, Simons, Schmidt, & Keeler, 1993) even though Harter (1981) implored the field at the 1980 NASPSPA conference to "resurrect 'joy' as a legitimate construct and restore affect and emotion to its rightful place as central to the understanding of behavior" (p. 4). Harter's research demonstrated that children's affective reactions to their self-evaluation of competence were more influential on their motivation and subsequent achievement behavior than the cognitive self-evaluations themselves! Because participation in sport, at least initially, is typically motivated by affective reasons (fun, excitement, stimulation), this less studied component of the ABCs should receive more attention in sport personality research.

METHODOLOGICAL ISSUES IN THE STUDY OF PERSONALITY IN SPORT

Theoretical issues in personality have sparked continuous debate in the literature, and a similar debate has occurred over methodological approaches to the study of personality. Methodological issues refer to the ways in which the study of personality is designed and conducted. In this section, I examine various methodological approaches to the study of personality in sport. First, I outline the purposes of personality research and then discuss the context in which personality research is conducted.

Purposes of Personality Research

What methodological approach to the study of personality should be used? What are the reasons we engage in personality research? These questions seem important to address, as Mischel (1977b) stated that a source of confusion in personality psychology is the failure of researchers to clearly specify the goals or objectives of their research endeavors. Three categories of methodological approaches to the study of personality are discussed in this section:

- Idiographic versus nomothetic approaches to the study of personality
- Differences in experimental, correlational, and clinical methods of personality research
- Purposes of personality research in terms of description, prediction, and intervention

Idiographic Versus Nomothetic Approaches to Personality

The idiographic versus nomothetic issue raised by Allport (1937) asks, What should be the focus of personality research?

The *idiographic approach* to personality assessment

- studies the individual intensively and extensively to arrive at laws of behavior unique to that individual,

- assumes that a different set of descriptors is needed for each person, and

- is best suited for answering questions about within-person variation.

The *nomothetic approach* to personality assessment

- studies individuals by comparing them to each other to arrive at laws of behavior that hold for all individuals,

- assumes that a common set of descriptors, dispositions, or trait dimensions can be used to characterize all persons and that individual differences are to be identified with different locations on those dimensions, and

- is best suited for answering questions about central tendencies in the behavior of people in general.

Examples of nomothetic research in sport personality are abundant, with the typical purpose of differentiating subgroups of athletes (e.g., elite vs. nonelite, male vs. female, team vs. individual sports) on various personality characteristics (e.g., extraversion, self-confidence, aggressiveness). Examples of idiographic contributions to the sport personality literature are rare, but some examples include the analysis of personality in highly successful sport figures (Vealey & Walter, 1994; Wrisberg, 1990), case studies of athletes (Gould, Tuffey, Udry, & Loehr, 1997; Krane, Greenleaf, & Snow, 1997; Savoy, 1993), and the emergence of performance profiling as an idiographic research method (Butler, Smith, & Irwin, 1993; Jones, 1993). The nomothetic approach has dominated personality psychology in general and sport personality research in particular over the past three decades. One explanation for this domination by nomothetic work is that it is seen as the goal of science, whereas the idiographic approach has been labeled nonscientific (Martens, 1987).

The study of personality in sport should use both idiographic and nomothetic approaches and, in particular, should avoid the dichotomizing tendency to view them as antithetical. It is not imperative to search for a unique set of variables to characterize each person (the traditional idiographic approach), but the study of personality must be concerned with the unique salience and configuration of a common set of variables within the person rather than with the relative standing of persons across those variables. D.J. Bem (1983)

noted that this will result in more of a type theory of personality (as opposed to traditional trait theory) in which the focus of inquiry is on understanding "how certain *kinds* of persons behave in certain *kinds* of ways in certain *kinds* of situations" (p. 566). In this way, the structure or description of personality is studied idiographically, whereas the process or dynamics of personality is studied nomothetically.

Several examples of this idiographic–nomothetic combination approach in sport personality research have appeared in the literature. Scanlan and colleagues (Scanlan, Ravizza, & Stein, 1989; Scanlan, Stein, & Ravizza, 1989) interviewed elite figure skaters by using an idiographic approach to understand enduring sources of enjoyment that these athletes derived from their competitive experiences. Through content analysis, the skaters' responses were organized into thematic categories that represented various sources of enjoyment to provide a nomothetic picture of the data. Sadalla, Linder, and Jenkins (1988) combined idiographic and nomothetic research approaches to investigate the factors underlying preferences for participation in particular sports. The researchers used an idiographic phase in which participants generated personality descriptors related to sport preferences about hypothetical individuals. In a following nomothetic phase of the study, another sample of participants rated a hypothetical individual said to be a participant in a particular sport on the dimensions of personality generated in the idiographic phase. Sadalla et al.'s (1988) results indicated that specific personality characteristics are attributed consistently to individuals described as preferring certain sports.

Dunn (1994) compared a nomothetic profile of situational threat perceptions (based on the responses from 46 ice hockey players) with the idiographic stress perceptions of 3 individual ice hockey players. The group profile was valuable because it identified a broad range of psychological factors that influence hockey players' threat perceptions in competition, and the idiographic interview data revealed how and why these perceptions are configured uniquely within players as the result of specific playing roles within the team. An analysis by Gould and colleagues (Gould, Eklund, & Jackson, 1992a, 1992b; Eklund, Gould, & Jackson, 1993) of psychological factors related to Olympic success provides an example of advancing knowledge about personality in sport by using "the best of both worlds" in terms of nomothetic and idiographic inquiry. Gould and colleagues identified general principles about the influence of personality on the Olympic performance of wrestlers, yet the researchers also examined idiographic variation and uniqueness of athletes within the data as opposed to ignoring these characteristics by relegating them to measurement error. Doyle and Parfitt (1997) used an idiographic approach with 12 track-and-field athletes to develop individualized performance profiles for each athlete and then standardized scores for the athletes' responses to nomothetically test the construct validity of the profiles.

Clearly, the use of both forms of inquiry in sport personality research advances knowledge more effectively by identifying general principles of human behavior in sport yet also illuminating the variation of these principles within individual athletes. This should enhance not only the richness of our knowledge about personality in sport but also the social relevance of our findings. Hanin's (1997) groundbreaking research, which used stepwise idiographic methods to identify individually optimal and dysfunctional affective patterns related to sport performance, effectively integrates theory, research, and practice in elite sport. Hanin's work is based on the European personality research tradition, which has emphasized the applied needs of athletes and coaches, as opposed to the emphasis on the basic testing of theories developed in mainstream psychology that is prevalent in North America. The overemphasis on nomothetic research approaches (and marginalization of idiographic inquiry) in North American sport personality research has hampered the field of sport psychology in meeting the practical needs of athletes and coaches, and much more diversity in and acceptance of alternative research approaches are desperately needed.

Experimental, Correlational, and Clinical Methods

Another distinction between methodological approaches in the study of personality was developed by Carlson (1971). Drawing on the writing of Kluckhohn and Murray (1949), Carlson described the three major methods used in the study of personality:

- Experimental (an individual is like all other individuals)
- Correlational (an individual is like some other individuals)
- Clinical (an individual is like no other individuals)

Experimental methods seek to discover general laws of human behavior by manipulating social–environmental factors and de-emphasizing intrapersonal factors. Correlational methods seek to discover existing differences in personality characteristics among different kinds of individuals without any experimental manipulation. Thus, both experimental and correlational methods are nomothetic in nature because they strive to find generalities in human behavior. However, experimental studies attempt to control and manipulate environmental conditions to neutralize any individual differences in personality, whereas correlational studies seek to understand existing individual differences in various groups of people. Clinical methods are idiographic in nature—they seek to understand the uniqueness of personality characteristics or the organization of personality within individuals. Reviews have shown that correlational methods are the most prevalent in sport personality research and that very few clinical methods have been used (Martens, 1975; Vealey, 1989).

Description, Prediction, and Intervention

Personality researchers may adopt either idiographic or nomothetic approaches and use either experimental, correlational, or clinical methodology in their study of personality. What, then, are the reasons that they engage in personality research? Psychologists (Eysenck & Eysenck, 1985; Fiske, 1988; Mischel, 1977b) as well as sport psychologists (Silva, 1984; Singer, 1988) have identified several objectives of personality research that can be divided into three categories, each of which represent a particular purpose of personality research.

The first purpose of personality research is *description*—the static, noncausal description of personality. Descriptive studies focus on "what people are like" and examine elements of personality (e.g., traits, states, dispositions, cognitions, needs) and how they are related either within the individual or between groups. An example of a descriptive research objective in sport personality would be to identify the coping strategies used by successful athletes. The second purpose of personality research focuses on *prediction*, or "what people do." These studies are causal because they examine the dynamic relationship between personality and behavior. Predictive studies in sport psychology examine the influence of personality characteristics on sport behavior as well as the influence of sport participation on personality. An example of a predictive research objective in sport personality would be to determine if highly confident athletes persist longer when facing training obstacles compared with athletes who have less confidence. The third purpose of personality research is *intervention* to examine "how people change." Intervention studies examine how personality characteristics and behavior may be modified through various intervention strategies. This category differs from the prediction category in that some type of manipulation or treatment is induced and the effect is then measured as opposed to predicting the natural effects of sport participation on personality. An example of an intervention research objective in sport personality is to determine the effects of a seasonal psychological skills training program on athletes' self-confidence.

I (Vealey, 1989) found that 48% of the sport personality studies published between 1974 and 1988 focused on prediction, 44% focused on description, and 8% focused on intervention. However, in examining yearly trends, I found that predictive research has declined since 1982, intervention research has increased over the same time period, and descriptive research has remained fairly constant. The increase in intervention studies is the result of the upsurge of interest in applied sport psychology, whereas the decline in predictive studies suggests a lack of theory development and testing (Landers, 1983). I (Vealey, 1989) also noted difficulty in categorizing studies by objective, because the purpose of the research was often unclear or unstated. Thus, there is a need for clear definitions of, and congruence between, theoretical framework and purpose in sport personality research.

Context of Personality Research: Laboratory and Field Research Issues

Along with the issues of what methodological approaches and purposes are appropriate for sport personality research, a similar issue focuses on where sport personality research should be conducted. This issue has centered largely on whether the study of personality and sport is best accomplished in a tightly controlled laboratory or the naturally occurring sport setting in the field.

The laboratory–field debate, like other debates in psychology, has followed historical developments in the field. As a result of the publication of Campbell and Stanley's (1963) classic book on experimental design, the number of experimental personality research studies conducted in labo-

ratory settings increased in the 1960s and 1970s (West, 1986). This historical pattern also was reflected in sport personality research (Landers, 1983; Martens, 1979). However, probably as a reaction to Martens' (1979) plea for more external validity, field research in sport personality increased in the 1980s and 1990s. The strength of laboratory research is that it maximizes control and internal validity. However, the primary weakness of this approach is the lack of external validity, or generalizability of results, to situations outside the experimental setting. Researchers indicate that this is particularly a problem in personality research, because the prediction of behavior from dispositional variables is minimized when situational constraint is evident (Buss, 1989; West, 1986).

Design alternatives to the traditional laboratory–field dichotomy are needed. First, laboratory settings that minimize situational constraint could be used to facilitate the emergence of personality factors. For example, individuals' choices and modifications of situations could be investigated as dependent variables, in contrast to traditional designs in which situations are static variables that only affect individuals (Buss, 1989; Snyder, 1983). Examples might be to ask study participants to choose levels of competition, types of competitors, or methods of evaluation. Mischel (1977b) stated that the most striking differences between persons may be found not by studying their responses to the same situation but by analyzing their selection and construction of situational conditions.

A second design alternative could be the adoption of a quasi-experimental approach in field research to enhance internal validity within the real-world setting. As examples, field experiments proved useful in studying children's prosocial behaviors based on competitive conditions (Kleiber & Roberts, 1981) as well as in examining the relationship between competitive anxiety and performance (Gould et al., 1987). The field setting was used in these studies to simulate the evaluation potential of real-world competitive conditions, yet the investigators controlled critical aspects of the study to maximize internal validity.

Third, researchers need to engage in "full cycle social psychology" (Cialdini, 1980) in which personality research can move systematically back and forth between the "real world" and the laboratory by interweaving controlled laboratory methods, naturalistic field observation, personality inventories, and biographical and archival data. This has been argued similarly by Landers (1983) in the sport psychology literature.

© Dennis Light

The relationship between personality and sport behavior must take into account the sociocultural forces inherent in our society.

Fourth, and most important, personality researchers must examine more closely the contextual factors that influence the relationship between personality and sport behavior. Assessment of personality should take into account (or at least acknowledge) sociocultural and organizational influences. For example, the provocative issue of whether sport builds "character" could be examined by using an idiographic, clinical, longitudinal approach to study the personality development (e.g., identity formation and change, motivational orientations) of a young athlete as she moves through the sport feeder system from youth to college to elite sport. Joan Benoit Samuelson, the 1984 Olympic marathon gold medalist, has said, "When I first started running, I was so embarrassed when cars passed that I would pretend I was picking flowers." This quote emphasizes the significant impact of sociocultural factors on the sport behavior of girls and women. Similarly, it would be fruitful to understand the influence of typical sociocultural forces inherent in male sport, such as hegemonic masculinity and homophobia (Herek, 1984), on the personality development of male athletes.

Overall, the issue of context in the study of personality in sport has moved far beyond the oversimplified laboratory–field dichotomy. Breakthrough insight and meaningful understanding about the relationship between personality and sport await theory and research that are grounded more deeply in the sociocultural forces that pervade competitive sport.

ISSUES SURROUNDING THE USE OF PERSONALITY INVENTORIES IN SPORT

Besides the theoretical and methodological issues surrounding the study of personality in sport, the issue of personality assessment through the use of psychological inventories requires special attention. In particular, it is critical for sport psychology researchers and practitioners to understand the ethical and appropriate uses of personality inventories. In this section, I discuss the limitations and appropriate uses of inventories in assessing sport personality.

A psychological inventory, or test, is "an objective and standardized measure of a sample of behavior" (Anastasi, 1988, p. 23). The most important property of a psychological inventory is validity, or the degree to which a test actually measures what it purports to measure (Anastasi, 1988). A test is never valid in general—it is valid *for* something, such as heart rate, intelligence, or aggressiveness (Sundberg, 1977). That is, a test's validity must be established with reference to the particular use for which the test is being considered. Another important psychometric property of a test is reliability, which refers to the consistency, reproducibility, or accuracy of the results (Sundberg, 1977). The process of developing a reliable, valid measurement tool to assess personality requires rigorous and extensive psychometric procedures. Examples of this process in sport psychology were evaluated critically in the comprehensive measurement text edited by Duda (1998).

Limitations of Self-Report Techniques

The use of self-report psychological inventories in sport personality research has been criticized widely. Self-report assessment techniques have been criticized by researchers who believe that individuals do not know themselves well enough to give accurate assessments, that test items are open to misrepresentation, and that dispositional scales focus not on properties of individuals' personalities but on value judgments placed on them by the researchers (Hogan, DeSoto, & Solano, 1977). Another criticism of self-report measures is that they are susceptible to social desirability response bias (i.e., individuals falsify their responses to make themselves appear more socially desirable; Vane & Guarnaccia, 1989). Also, personality tests have been blamed for encouraging mindless research by marginally competent investigators who "discover" significant relationships without establishing any substantive a priori hypotheses (Hogan et al., 1977).

Need for Multiple Assessments

Despite the limitations of self-report personality inventories, they are an integral part of sport personality research. All research methods have limitations. The use of multiple assessment techniques in personality research is one strategy to overcome individual methodological weaknesses. The meaning of personality or behavior may not be the same in different measurement contexts, so multiple and repeated measures should be used. For example, research has lacked consistent agreement between self-report and physiological measures of anxiety (Karteroliotis & Gill, 1987; Yan Lan & Gill, 1984). However, this does not mean that physiological measures are more valid than self-report measures or vice versa. Self-report personality inventories that establish appropriate psychometric properties are no less valid than any other assessment method. The use of "anti-social desirability instructions" has been shown to lessen social desirability response bias in sport personality research (Martens et al., 1990), and the inclusion of scales to detect social desirability tendencies in research participants (Crowne & Marlowe, 1960) is also advocated in personality studies.

Multiple assessments also are needed to critically evaluate the construct validity of personality inventories that purport to measure the same or similar constructs. Marsh (1994) cautioned personality researchers to avoid what he termed the "jingle fallacy" (assuming that personality scales with the same name measure the same construct) as well as the "jangle fallacy" (assuming that scales with different names measure different constructs). Sport personality scales that claim to measure the same conceptual constructs have been shown to be orthogonal (Gill, Kelley, Martin, & Caruso, 1991; Marsh, 1994); thus, researchers are encouraged to carefully examine the construct validity of inventory scales to ensure accurate interpretations of the personality characteristics that they believe they are measuring. This is particularly critical in popular areas of personality research where multiple assessment instruments are available (e.g., achievement motivation, competitive anxiety, physical self-concept).

Beware of Tautologies

Although personality inventories may provide easy "weapons" for "mindless" research, perusal of the literature in any scientific area of study indicates that mindless research is not a phenomenon seen exclusively in those who use self-report personality inventories! However, there is some merit to the claim that predictive personality research at times is tautological, or characterized by "pseudo-explanations" of sport behavior (Bordens & Abbott, 1988). Consider the attempt to explain aggression, a popular topic in sport personality, with the concept of a trait (see figure 3.2). According to this position, people behave aggressively because of an aggressive trait. As shown in figure 3.2, the observed behavior (aggression) is used to prove the existence of the aggressive trait, and the concept of the trait is then used to explain the aggressive behavior. This form of circular reasoning is called a *tautology*, which is not a valid scientific explanation of human behavior. The example shown in figure 3.2 is a tautology because it states that humans are aggressive because they have a trait to behave aggressively. That is, the observed behavior is "explained" by a concept, but the behavior itself is used as proof of the existence of the explanatory concept. Sport personality research has been criticized as the "psychology of the obvious" when tautologies are used to explain behaviors.

It is important for sport personality researchers to use independent measures of the behavior of interest and the proposed explanatory concept to avoid falling into the pseudo-explanation trap of tautologies. To break the tautology in Figure 3.2, the researcher would have to find an independent measure of aggressive trait that does not involve the display of aggressive behaviors. As demonstrated in the aggression literature, one way to do this would be to measure level of arousal as an independent measure of aggressive drive theorized

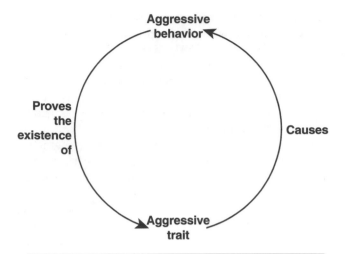

Figure 3.2 Circular explanation, or tautology. The observed behavior is explained by a concept, but the behavior itself is used as proof of the existence of the explanatory concept.

Adapted, by permission, from K.S. Bordens and B.B. Abbott, 1988, *Research design and methods: A process approach.* (Mountain View, CA: Mayfield), 10.

to arise from the aggressive trait and then examine its relationship to aggressive behavior as operationalized by administering electric shock to another person.

Although relationships between personality characteristics and other cognitions, feelings, and behaviors are of interest in sport psychology, true prediction and understanding of the complex nature of personality in sport await innovative assessment that avoids obvious tautologies in the use of personality inventories.

Toward Ipsative and Idiothetic Measures

Within the idiographic approach to personality assessment, researchers are encouraged to use interview and open-ended techniques to identify relevant and salient personality descriptions of individuals in sport (e.g., Sadalla et al., 1988; Scanlan et al., 1989). Hanin (1997) extended his original work in individual zones of optimal functioning (IZOF) to include an idiographic scaling procedure where athletes identified positive and negative emotions that were subjectively meaningful for each of them in relation to their sport performance. These athlete-generated items then were used to develop individualized inventories called Positive and Negative Affect (PNA) scales, which subsequently were refined and validated through continuous research. The reliability of the PNA scales was calculated intraindividually and ranged from .76 to .90. In comparing the content of the individualized PNA scales of 24 elite soccer

players with their respective scores on popular standardized personality measures of affect (Positive and Negative Affect Schedule, Watson & Tellegen, 1985; Profile of Mood States, McNair, Lorr, & Droppleman, 1981; State–Trait Anxiety Inventory, Spielberger, Gorsuch, & Lushene, 1970), Hanin found only a 14% to 23% overlap in terms of similarity in content. These results indicate that nomothetically based, standardized inventories may not assess the most relevant aspects of athletes' personalities that relate to their sport performance, and that sport personality researchers should consider Hanin's idiographic assessment models along with the widely used, nomothetically developed inventories.

Hanin's work (Hanin, 1997; Hanin & Syrjä, 1995) is based on the use of ipsative or idiothetic forms of self-report compared with normative self-report. Block (1957) proposed the ipsative approach to personality assessment in which an individual's responses on a rating scale are interpreted relative to his or her responses on other scales, under other conditions, or at other times. This is based on Allport's (1937, 1962) argument that personality characteristics are best studied in an intraindividual rather than interindividual context. Thus, if individuals rate themselves on a given characteristic above their average rating on other characteristics, they are viewed as possessing a high level of that characteristic, regardless of the value of the rating relative to those provided by others. Similarly, Lamiell (1981) proposed an idiothetic measurement model in which responses are interpreted with reference to the maximum and minimum possible responses that an individual could make in a given measurement situation.

Research has shown that ipsative and idiothetic personality scale ratings more closely resemble implicit personality ratings and use a wider range of response choices compared with normative scales (Chaplin & Buckner, 1988). This finding suggests that self-report ratings in personality assessment may be better represented by a model other than the traditional normative one. The ipsative self-rating method has been used by a few researchers in sport anxiety research (e.g., Gould et al., 1987, Sonstroem & Bernardo, 1982), and the results indicate that this assessment method may be of value for sport personality researchers. The emergence of performance profiling as a technique to study personality in sport is another example of ipsative assessment (Butler & Hardy, 1992; Doyle & Parfitt, 1997; Jones, 1993).

Ethical and Appropriate Uses of Personality Inventories

Personality inventories are validated for use *by* certain types of individuals *with* certain types of individuals *for* certain types of situations. Ethical and practical issues surrounding the use of inventories emanate from these validity questions in terms of, By whom? With whom? For what purpose? In what situation?

Inventories developed for licensed psychologists to use in clinical assessment are inappropriate for consultants to use outside of their area of expertise (American Psychological Association, 1985). Any personality inventory used in assessment should be completely understood by the consultant or researcher and clearly within that person's boundaries of professional training. The misuse of personality inventories based on a lack of competence or training is a severe breach of professional integrity, because it may harm athletes and damage the reputation of sport psychology (see Etzel, Yura, & Perna, 1998).

Personality inventories have been misused in the past to screen or select athletes for inclusion on sports teams. This misuse of personality inventories for sport selection is based on the general belief that desirable personality attributes are related to success in sport. The validity or accuracy of this proposed relationship is examined further in the next section of this chapter, but from an assessment perspective, the use of personality inventories for this reason is ethically questionable. As Singer (1988) stated, the ethical use of personality tests for team member selection assumes that we know the following:

- Which personality characteristics are relevant to success in that situation
- The ideal level of that characteristic
- How much athletes can compensate in some characteristics for the lack of others
- That the particular test being used provides a valid and reliable measure of these attributes

The early use of the Athletic Motivation Inventory (AMI; Tutko, Lyon, & Ogilvie, 1969) has been challenged based on ethical issues related to use of personality inventories. First, the AMI was marketed in a way that indicated that test scores predicted success in athletics, although no evidence of reliability and validity was published in the scientific literature. Second, the AMI is a trait scale and in no way considers the influence of situational factors on athletes' behavior. However, a book was published based on work with the AMI that identified "problem athletes" and provided guidelines about how to deal with these types of athletes without considering any environmental, social, or cultural characteristics (Ogilvie & Tutko, 1966). Third, even if the traits measured by the AMI are related to sport success, this still does not demonstrate causality. That is, these traits were not shown to cause success in sport. Overall, these points indicate that the AMI has limitations in its ability to predict sport behavior, as does any measurement technique, but what was problematic was that these limitations were not clearly identified. Research with potential professional ice hockey draftees showed that players' AMI scores were unrelated to on-ice behaviors as evaluated by National Hockey League scouts to represent psychological or motivational skills (Davis, 1991).

The use of personality inventories should not be discouraged in sport psychology; rather, their ethical and appropriate use should be encouraged. Guidelines for the development and appropriate use of psychological tests have been established by the American Psychological Association (1985). Appropriate use of personality tests means that tests should be used only in situations in which they are valid. Many psychological assessment techniques are used by clinical psychologists to diagnose psychopathology; these instruments have been validated for that purpose and the psychologists are trained, even licensed, to use these tests in clinical settings. However, most of the personality tests developed in sport psychology have been validated for research purposes only. For example, the Competitive State Anxiety Inventory (Martens et al., 1990) has been validated to predict competitive A-state but not clinical anxiety and certainly not success in sport.

Sport psychology consultants may ethically and appropriately use psychological inventories as part of their ongoing assessment with athletes to provide feedback to athletes regarding their specific thoughts, feelings, and behaviors and to encourage them to engage in the critical self-reflection that is necessary for psychobehavioral change (Vealey & Garner-Holman, 1998). But, as Nideffer (1981) emphasized, ethics dictate that consultants explain to athletes why they are being assessed, what conclusions are drawn from the assessment, and how the assessment information will be used. As with research, the multimethod approach seems to be useful in assessing athletes by combining personality inventories, interview techniques, behavioral observation, and self-monitoring to provide a more comprehensive perspective of athletes' personalities. Some sport psychology consultants believe that the use of personality inventories is detrimental to their style of intervention work (Halliwell, 1990; Orlick, 1989; Ravizza, 1990; Rotella, 1990), which is simply a practical decision based on each consultant's unique philosophy and experience.

Another issue regarding the use of personality inventories in sport research is the questionable use of inventories developed and validated for clinical populations (Kroll, 1976). Kroll contended that these types of tests emphasize a psychopathological view of personality that appraises normal personality in terms of susceptibility to maladjustment. For example, Holtzman (1965) argued that the Minnesota Multiphasic Personality Inventory (MMPI; Hathaway & McKinley, 1943), developed to identify psychiatric populations, is poorly suited to the examination of personality structure in normal populations. A similar criticism could be leveled against the use of the Profile of Mood States (POMS) in sport research, because this inventory was developed to assess mood in psychiatric patients (although it has been validated for use with normal college-age subjects).

Even if the validity of using tests such as the MMPI with athletes is not questioned, the information provided by these tests only examines the relationship between psychopathology (or lack of it) and sport behavior. Kroll (1976) stated, "Just as we recognize that health is more than the absence of disease, we must recognize that athletic personality is more than the absence of psychiatric deficiencies" (p. 379). Thus, sport personality should move beyond the use of clinically derived instrumentation, and even beyond general psychological inventories, to develop and use sport-specific personality assessment inventories based on the unique characteristics of the sport environment. Sport psychologists have demonstrated increased behavioral prediction when using valid, sport-specific personality measures as opposed to general psychological measures of the same attribute (e.g., Hanin, 1997; Martens et al., 1990; Smith & Christensen, 1995).

THEORIES OF PERSONALITY AND RELATED SPORT PERSONALITY RESEARCH

In the previous section, the theoretical and methodological issues related to the study of person-

ality in sport were reviewed. In the overview I attempted to provide a basic understanding of how personality in sport is studied. In this section, I present the specific theories of personality along with pertinent sport personality research to review what we know about personality as it relates to sport participation.

A main point of this chapter is that personality involves much more than just the trait approach. That is, research that is based on trait or dispositional theories represents only one part of the study of personality. As discussed at the beginning of the chapter, a comprehensive view of sport personality should include research conducted in all of the theoretical areas of personality. Much of the research discussed in chapters 4 through 8 of this book concerns specific aspects of personality (self-perceptions, motivational orientations, self-efficacy, attributions, anxiety, and moral reasoning). Thus, the results of this research are not extensively reviewed in this chapter. However, in this section I briefly discuss the specific areas of sport personality research related to each theoretical approach.

The goal of sport personality research is to explain the role of personality in sport in a way that is systematically understandable. To achieve this goal, a theoretical perspective is needed. *Theories* are systematic explanations of phenomena that are derived from the accumulation of empirical evidence. Because of the broad nature of personality psychology, numerous theories have been proposed. In this section, these theories are categorized broadly into four major theoretical approaches: psychodynamic, dispositional, phenomenological, and learning. I outline example theories and assessment techniques for each approach and review research conducted to test the applicability of these theories to sport.

Psychodynamic Approaches

Although psychodynamic approaches are very complex, only a cursory description of these theories is provided here. These theories have had little direct effect on sport personality research because of their clinical and psychopathological focus. However, psychodynamic theory has had an enormous influence on the field of psychology and is often used by clinical consultants in psychological intervention with athletes.

Conceptual Basis

Originating with the work of Sigmund Freud (1900/ 1953, 1901/1960), the psychodynamic approach is based on the premise that personality is a dynamic set of processes always in motion and often in conflict. This approach is called *deterministic* in that behavior is seen to be determined for individuals instead of by individuals. To psychodynamic theorists, personality is greatly influenced by early experiences, and behavior is viewed as being determined by unconscious processes. Freud's psychoanalytic theory is based on the continuous interaction and conflict between his proposed three parts of the psychic structure: id, ego, and superego. The adult personality is shaped by the resolution of these conflicts in early life as the ego mediates between the unconscious impulses of the id and the values and conscience of the superego. Several neo-Freudians (e.g., Alfred Adler, 1929; Erik Erikson, 1950; Erich Fromm, 1947; Karen Horney, 1924; Carl Jung, 1926) continued the psychodynamic approach by proposing various modifications in Freud's original theory. Generally, these neo-Freudians incorporated social and cultural forces into their psychodynamic theories as opposed to Freud's emphasis on instinctual drives.

Assessment and Sport Research

Many of the methods of assessing unconscious processes within the psychodynamic approach are termed *projective techniques*. These techniques are based on the assumption that significant aspects of personality are not open to conscious thought and thus cannot be reliably measured through self-report. These techniques are thought to let the subjects "project" their personality characteristics into interpretations of various kinds (Frank, 1939). Examples of projective techniques used in personality assessment are the Rorschach Inkblot Test, the Thematic Apperception Test, and various sentence completion or drawing tasks (Sundberg, 1977). Projective techniques were popular in the 1940s and 1950s when psychoanalysis was a predominant force in personality. These techniques are used very little in the study of sport personality. Other techniques used in the psychodynamic approach are life history or biographical data and various types of interviewing methods.

Specific and relevant hypotheses based on the psychodynamic perspective have not been generated and tested in the sport context. Although limited in its application to sport, the psychodynamic or deterministic approach may apply where sport personality researchers have suggested that individuals with certain personality types may

"gravitate" toward participation in certain sports (Bird, 1979; Kane, 1978; Kroll, 1970; Morgan, 1980b; Williams, 1978). No research has provided definitive evidence to support this suggestion.

Dispositional Approaches

Dispositional theories emphasize consistency in behavior over time and across situations. These theories contend that an individual's personality is essentially a collection of dispositional characteristics. Dispositional approaches represent most of the early research conducted in sport personality. Included in this category of theories are trait theories, dispositional–state approaches, biological theories, and motive–need theories.

Trait Theories

Trait theories of personality most clearly exemplify the dispositional approach and have generated a tremendous amount of research in psychology as well as sport psychology.

Conceptual Basis. Traits are relatively enduring and highly consistent internal attributes (Allport, 1937). That is, traits are intrapersonal characteristics that account for unique yet stable reactions to the environment. These theories emphasize the person as opposed to the situation; thus, personality is seen as a function of a set of enduring traits that make one person different from another. Trait theories emphasize consistent differences among individuals in their responses to the same situation.

Gordon Allport (1937) was an early influential trait theorist who emphasized individuality and uniqueness in each personality. According to Allport, traits never occur in different people in exactly the same way; rather, he suggested that traits operate in unique ways in each person. Allport believed that this unique pattern of traits or overall "personality structure" determined behavior. That is, each person's behavior is determined by his or her particular trait structure. However, Allport admitted that individuals tend to develop some types of common traits through social interaction.

Another proponent of trait theory was Raymond B. Cattell (1965), who also theorized that traits underlie human behavior. Similar to Allport, Cattell distinguished between common traits possessed by all people and unique traits that occur only in a particular person and cannot be found in another in exactly the same form. Through extensive factor analysis procedures, Cattell proposed that personality is composed of 16 dimensions or primary factors. Cattell parsimoniously reduced these 16 primary factors into four second-order factors that efficiently represented the primary factor components (high vs. low anxiety, introversion vs. extraversion, tough-minded vs. tender-minded, and independence vs. subduedness).

Like Cattell, J.P. Guilford (1959) subdivided traits into categories, but his categories represent different interests, aptitudes, needs, and attitudes. Guilford also distinguished between traits represented by behavior (behavior traits) and those represented by physical makeup (somatic traits). He defined personality as a unique pattern of traits and emphasized individual differences by stating that the best way to know personalities is to compare them with one another. Guilford's individual difference approach contrasts with Allport's position that personality is so unique that it cannot be studied by making comparisons among people.

Hans Eysenck (1967, 1970) extended the search for personality dimensions to the area of abnormal behavior and used factor analytic techniques similar to Cattell. Eysenck theorized that there are two superordinate type or trait dimensions in personality: introversion–extraversion and emotionality–stability. These superordinate types are further subdivided into component traits that lead to habitual responses (e.g., extraversion is broken down into sociability, impulsiveness, activity, liveliness, and excitability). Although Eysenck and Cattell derived their structures of personality quite differently, their theories have distinct similarities. Both theories include introversion versus extraversion, and Eysenck's emotional stability is similar to Cattell's anxiety dimension. Eysenck also included a third personality dimension called psychoticism, which relates to the development of psychopathologies, but this dimension is referred to far less in the literature than the other two dimensions.

Assessment.   Trait theorists traditionally have used objective personality inventories that involve direct quantification without any intervening interpretation of the subjects' responses as in projective techniques. Three trait inventories from general psychology were typically used in early sport personality research (1960s and 1970s):

- Minnesota Multiphasic Personality Inventory (MMPI; Hathaway & McKinley, 1943)
- 16 Personality Factor Questionnaire (16PF; Cattell, 1946)
- Eysenck Personality Inventory (EPI; Eysenck & Eysenck, 1975)

The MMPI was developed to differentiate among various psychiatric categories and contains 10 clinical scales (e.g., depression, hypochondria, paranoia) and four validity scales. The 16PF measures 16 factors (traits) that Cattell (1946) thought were descriptive of personality, and it was a particularly popular assessment choice in early sport personality research. The EPI measures the personality dimensions of neuroticism and introversion—extraversion.

Inventories such as the 16PF, the MMPI, and the EPI provide an overall assessment of an individual's personality. Other trait inventories have been developed to measure only selected personality characteristics. Examples of these types of inventories that have been used in sport personality research are the Mehrabian (1968) Measure of Achieving Tendency and the Taylor Manifest Anxiety Scale (J. Taylor, 1953).

The first sport-specific trait personality inventory, the AMI, was developed by Tutko and colleagues (1969) to provide an overall assessment of an athlete's personality. The AMI assesses 11 personality traits predicted to be related to athletic success: drive, aggressiveness, determination, guilt proneness, trust, self-confidence, emotional control, leadership, coachability, conscientiousness, and mental toughness. As discussed in a previous section, the AMI was an early source of controversy in sport personality research because of unsubstantiated claims of its ability to predict success in sport (Davis, 1991; Gill, 1986).

Sport Research.   Research on sport personality that is based on trait theory may be categorized into three groups:

- Studies attempting to identify trait-descriptive personality profiles of athletic subgroups
- Studies that have examined the relationship between personality traits and various sport behaviors
- Studies that have examined the effects of sport and physical activity on the development and change in personality traits

Most of the studies in the trait area have focused on the description of personality based on hypothesized differences between three comparison groups: athletes versus nonathletes, athletes of one sport type versus athletes of another sport type, and the comparison of athletes based on different ability or success levels. The basic premise underlying these studies is that these different groups of individuals possess unique and measurable personality traits. The prototypical study of this type used the 16PF or MMPI and compared the personality profiles of different groups to each other or against population norms for that particular inventory (see Fisher, 1976, or Morgan, 1980b, for examples of these studies). Although several types of personality differences (e.g., athletes are more extroverted and emotionally stable than nonathletes) have been found between various groups, no clear pattern can be discerned from this research.

This tendency to find "insignificant significant differences" in trait-descriptive sport personality research is illustrated in a study in which athletes from a variety of sports and schools were compared by using a standard personality inventory (Lakie, 1962). As expected, personality differences were found between different groups of athletes (e.g., between baseball and track-and-field athletes), but the differences between groups of athletes were not consistent across schools! Morgan (1980a, 1980b) argued that this failure to find consistent descriptive differences in personality traits is due to multiple problems including inadequate operationalization of variables, small samples and poor sampling procedures, misuse of theory, inappropriate statistical procedures, and disregard for response distortion.

Overall, the trait approach of attempting to identify personality differences among various groups in sport has not produced any consistent results. Much of the research in this area has been plagued by methodological, statistical, and theoretical problems. Furthermore, no consistent pattern of personality traits has been identified as representative of an "athletic personality." Vanek and Cratty (1970) summarized this area of personality research as follows:

> The findings of recent studies . . . indicate that the identification of a typical personality trait pattern expected to appear in an "athlete" is a tenuous undertaking. The trait patterns isolated in these investigations indicate that within certain sport groups, traits may often be identified. But the delineating of some ubiquitous "animal" called an athlete cannot be done with any degree of certainty. (p. 82)

The research described in the previous paragraphs was conducted to describe personality differences in existing groups of athletes and nonathletes. Other researchers have focused more on predicting sport behavior (particularly successful sport performance) by using personality traits as predictors. Debate over the ability of personality traits to predict sport behavior has been referred to as the "credulous–skeptical argument" (Morgan, 1980a). Proponents of the credulous argument believe that personality traits may predict success in sport, whereas proponents of the skeptical argument believe that traits do not predict sport success. Similar to the person–situation debate, this argument has been called a pseudo-issue (Morgan, 1980a), as Morgan (originally in the credulous camp) admits that traits alone do not predict sport behavior and success. However, Morgan argued that traits should not be abandoned but should be used for prediction purposes in conjunction with other types of data such as personality states, cognitions, and physiological measures.

The notion that sport builds character, or that valued personality attributes may be developed through sport participation, traditionally has been espoused in American society. The construct of "character" originally was referred to as personality structure (Freud, 1901/1960), but the term was subsequently modified to reflect culturally valued attributes that reflect morality as defined by society (Allport, 1961; Peck & Havighurst, 1960). However, the claim that sport builds character, as measured by personality traits, has not been substantiated in the research literature. Ogilvie and Tutko (1971) disputed the claim that sport builds character and contended that the personality characteristics associated with character in athletes are probably established before they begin involvement in sport (although their claim is unsubstantiated by research evidence). Two sets of researchers using the 16PF found no significant changes in personality characteristics of college athletes over four years (Werner & Gottheil, 1966) or over the course of a season (Rushall, 1976).

Similar to the idea that sport builds character, exercise or fitness training also has been popularly associated with positive personality change. However, with regard to changes on global trait measures of personality (e.g., 16PF), the research indicates rather modest changes or no changes after fitness training (Buccola & Stone, 1975; Ismail & Young, 1973, 1977; Tillman, 1965; Young & Ismail, 1976). Folkins and Sime (1981) stated that global personality traits as measured by the 16PF are probably not permeable enough to be modified through fitness training. They suggested that specific personality characteristics identified as target variables should be the focus of modification through physical training or exercise. For example, Duke, Johnson, and Nowicki (1977) found a significant increase in internal locus of control in children during an 8-week sport fitness camp.

Dispositional–State Approaches

The second category of theories within the dispositional approach to the study of personality involves dispositional–state approaches.

Conceptual Basis and Assessment Examples

Dispositional–state approaches to the study of personality in sport are based on the interactional paradigm in which personality dispositions and situational factors interact to create a personality state. This personality state is then predicted to influence behavior most directly. Dispositions, as referred to in this section, are traitlike constructs, yet they are commonly viewed as less rigid and absolute than traits.

Popular dispositional inventories used in sport personality research include the following:

- Sport Anxiety Scale (SAS; Smith, Smoll, & Schutz, 1990)
- Sport Competition Anxiety Test (Martens et al., 1990)
- Test of Attentional and Interpersonal Style (TAIS; Nideffer, 1976)
- Sport Orientation Questionnaire (Gill & Deeter, 1988)
- Trait Sport-Confidence Inventory (Vealey, 1986, 1988)

Several inventories have been developed to measure statelike qualities of personality, which often are used in conjunction with congruent dispositional inventories. For example, the State–Trait Anxiety Inventory, a general anxiety scale, contains a dispositional and a state scale of anxiety (Spielberger et al., 1970).

Sport-specific state personality measures include the following:

- Competitive State Anxiety Inventory-2 (CSAI-2; Martens et al., 1990)
- State Sport-Confidence Inventory (Vealey, 1986)

Several measures of affective mood states have been used in the sport literature. One of the most popular has been the POMS (McNair et al., 1981), which measures six dimensions of subjective mood states: tension–anxiety, depression–dejection, anger–hostility, vigor–activity, fatigue–inertia, and confusion–bewilderment. Although the initial intent of the POMS was to assess moods in psychiatric patients, it has been used extensively in sport personality research (LeUnes, Hayward, & Daiss, 1988). McNair et al. (1981) indicated that the POMS is designed to measure "typical and persistent mood reactions to current life situations" (p. 5), and they stated that the standard instructions of having research participants rate their moods during the past week may be modified to time sets such as "right now" or "today." Other emerging affective mood measures include the Positive Affect Negative Affect Schedule (Crocker, 1997; Watson, Clark, & Tellegen, 1988) and the individualized PNA scales developed by Hanin (1997).

Sport Research: The Mental Health Model

Other than Griffith's (1926) distinction between personality "persistency and insistency," the earliest study examining the influence of personality states on sport behavior was C.O. Jackson's (1933) analysis of the effects of fear on muscular coordination.[1] Jackson noted, "There seems to be some correlation between the mental and physical state of the performer, his performance, and his susceptibility to fear. A subject who is depressed, or who is tired or ill, can seldom perform as well as he will under more ideal conditions" (p. 79). Another early study by Johnson (1949) examined precontest emotion and concluded that this tension had "a decided deleterious effect in terms of performance and well-being during and after competition" (p. 77).

Related to this early work connecting mood states to sport performance, Morgan (1985b) proposed a "mental health model" in which the presence of positive mood states in athletes is associated with higher performance levels when compared with athletes who have less positive mood states. That is, the mental health model asserts that positive mental health and athletic success are directly related, whereas psychopathology and success are inversely related. The pattern of mood states associated with positive mental health was termed the "iceberg profile" by Morgan and is

---

1. This study was conducted at the University of Illinois Laboratory for Research in Athletics under the direction of Professor Coleman Griffith as partial fulfillment for the degree of Master of Arts in Education.

operationalized by scores on the six mood dimensions of the POMS (McNair et al., 1981). The iceberg profile is characterized by scores above the population norm on vigor and below the population norm on tension, depression, anger, fatigue, and confusion (see figure 3.3). This profile has been supported with various athletic samples, but the proliferation of research in this area has failed to substantiate the predicted relationship between mood and performance (see reviews by Renger, 1993; Rowley, Landers, Kyllo, & Etnier, 1995; Terry, 1995).

Morgan's (1985b) mental health model was an important contribution to the study of personality and sport because it spawned a significant line of research examining the relationship between state personality characteristics and performance. However, over time, research has supported the conclusion that the iceberg profile contributes little to predicting athletic performance. There are substantial individual differences in mood functioning, and many athletes perform well despite having theoretically "negative" profiles (e.g., Hanin, 1997; Terry, 1995). Research in competitive anxiety has corroborated that athletes differ in the degree to which state anxiety is viewed as facilitative or debilitative to performance (Jones & Swain, 1995). Also, research shows that there is substantial variation between sports in terms of the desirability of specific mood factors (Terry, 1995). Thus, the generalized nomothetic approach of using the iceberg profile of mood states to predict performance in sport is not viable. However, an idiographic approach to mood state profiling has been shown to be effective in understanding and predicting intraindividual performance fluctuations (Hanin, 1997; Terry, 1995).

Sport Research: The IZOF Model

As an alternative to the mental health model/iceberg profile, Hanin extended his early work on IZOF in precompetitive anxiety to the analysis of functionally optimal and dysfunctional patterns of positive and negative emotions (the PNA model) in athletes (Hanin, 1997; Hanin & Syrjä, 1995, 1996). These models were developed in the naturalistic setting of elite sport and combined within- and between-individual analyses to examine the emotion–performance relationship in athletes. For the IZOF anxiety model, athletes who were inside or close to their optimal zones of anxiety were found to perform better than those outside their optimal zones (Hanin, 1997; Prapavessis & Grove, 1991). The PNA model also has been supported as predictive of performance, and Hanin has con-

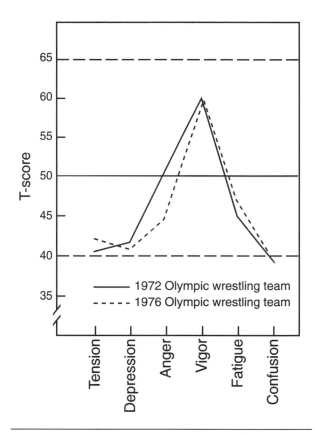

Figure 3.3 The iceberg profile is a pattern of mood states associated with good performance in sport.

Reprinted with permission from the *Research Quarterly for Exercise and Sport* vol. 51, no. 1, 1980, p. 64. The *Research Quarterly for Exercise and Sport* is a publication of the American Alliance for Health, Physical Education, Recreation and Dance, 1900 Association Drive, Reston, VA 22091.

ceptually interpreted these findings within a psychobiological theoretical perspective. For example, the PNA profile of the javelin thrower shown in figure 3.4 was developed based on recalls of previously successful and poor performances (Hanin, 1997). The individual zone of optimal intensity was identified for each functionally optimal (P+, N+) emotion, and the individual zone of dysfunctional intensity was identified for each dysfunctional emotion (see figure 3.4). Thus, there are zones of optimal function in some emotions (P+, N+) within which the probability of successful performance is the highest. Additionally, there are also dysfunctional zones in other emotions (P–, N–) within which the probability of poor performance is the highest. Positive and negative emotions associated with performance for individual athletes are considered both separately and jointly in terms of their unique and interactive optimal and dysfunctional effects. Hanin offered a research model for future work in this area that

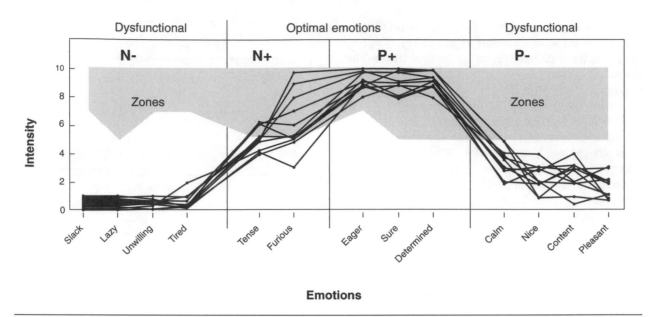

Figure 3.4 The individualized PNA profile of an elite Finnish javelin thrower.

Reprinted, by permission, from Y. Hanin, 1997, "Emotions and athletic performance: Individual zones of optimal functioning model," *European yearbook of sport psychology,* 1: 29–72. Copyright © Academia Verlag.

suggests integrating the study of cognitions, behavior, and affect to more holistically understand the influence of personality on sport performance.

Other Dispositional–State Research in Sport

Other noteworthy research within the dispositional–state approach to personality may be found in the sport-specific conceptualizations of competitive anxiety (Martens et al., 1990) and sport confidence (Vealey, 1986, 1988). In particular, the work of Martens and colleagues in modifying Spielberger's (1966) trait–state anxiety distinction for sport generated an enormous amount of research in sport personality with regard to the anxiety–behavior relationship (see Martens et al., 1990, for review). Gill and colleagues developed a sport-specific measure of the disposition of competitiveness that has been shown to predict achievement choices and behavior in sport (Gill & Deeter, 1988; Gill, Dzewaltowski, & Deeter, 1988). Vealey and Gill also included sport-specific goal orientation constructs in their respective conceptualizations of self-confidence and competitiveness to account for tendencies to strive for certain goals in sport. Nideffer's (1976, 1990) development of the TAIS as a measure of attentional and interpersonal styles sparked a great deal of research in sport psychology as well.

A common research theme within the dispositional–state approach is to examine the influence of various personality dispositions on the more statelike moods and affects that occur before and during competition (e.g., Martens et al., 1990; Prapavessis & Grove, 1994a, 1994b; Vealey, 1986; Willis, 1982). These studies are all based on conceptual models that propose that dispositional characteristics interact with situational factors to influence mood state responses within sport. The reported variance in mood states accounted for by dispositions has ranged from 3% to 30% across most studies. However, research in sport personality has not adequately examined the relative importance of dispositional characteristics in relation to situational or contextual factors. This was identified at the beginning of the chapter as a critical question in personality research. Thus, although the relationships between dispositions and various states often are significant, personality research must advance beyond describing these relationships to a more critical understanding of how dispositional and situational influences interact to influence mood states and other sport behaviors.

Another research area within the dispositional–state approach is examination of the effects of physical activity on changes in mood states. Most individuals admit that under normal circumstances, they "feel better" or "feel good" after vigorous physical activity. Research substantiates that state anxiety and tension reportedly are reduced after acute physical activity (McDonald & Hodgdon, 1991; Petruzzello, Landers, Hatfield, Kubitz, & Salazar, 1991). Chronic physical activity also is associated with significant decreases in depression in individuals who are clinically depressed as well as in nonclinical populations (Martinsen & Stephens, 1994; Mutrie & Biddle, 1995). Several hypotheses have been advanced to explain these changes. The *distraction hypothesis* maintains that the attentional distraction from stressful stimuli, as opposed to the actual effect of exercise, reduces anxiety and tension (Bahrke & Morgan, 1978). Other explanations (e.g., monoamine hypothesis, endorphin hypothesis) have focused on physiological parameters to explain the effects of exercise on affective states (see Morgan, 1985a).

Biological Theories

A third group of theories embracing the dispositional approach to the study of personality in sport are biological theories.

Conceptual Basis

Like trait theories, biological theories involve human dispositions that are predicted to influence behavior across situations. However, these theories postulate that human dispositions are related to biological processes. Ancient Greeks believed, based on the writings of Hippocrates and Galen, that there were four basic body fluids, or "humors," that all people possessed in varying proportions. Different temperaments, or personalities, of individuals were seen as reflecting the different proportions of these humors. For example, yellow bile was related to irritable behavior, whereas black bile was associated with sadness or melancholy.

Personality also has been related to body configuration. Sheldon (1942) built on the earlier work of Kretschmer (1925) to define three somatotypes that are theorized to genetically predispose individuals toward certain types of behaviors. Ectomorphy refers to a linear and lean body type and is associated with cerobrotonia, which is characterized as tenseness, inhibition, and introversion. Endomorphy describes a round or plump body type and it is associated with viscerotonia, which is characterized by sociability, warmth, and complacency. Mesomorphy is defined as a muscular body type and is associated with somatotonia, or assertiveness, risk taking, and high levels of energy. Although Sheldon found initial support for his theory, additional research proved equivocal, and the theory has never gained wide acceptance. Also, social expectancy effects based on stereotypes of body configurations have been offered as an alternative explanation to the genetic predisposition to behave a certain way based on somatotype (Carver & Scheier, 1988).

As discussed in the previous section, Eysenck's (1967, 1970) trait theory is based on two trait dimensions: extroversion–introversion and emotionality–stability. Eysenck also provided a biological analysis of these personality dimensions. First, he suggested that introverts and extroverts differ from each other in the brain functioning of the ascending reticular activating system (ARAS). The ARAS is responsible for activating or deactivating higher portions of the brain. When the ARAS is functioning at a high level, individuals feel alert, and when it is functioning at a low level, individuals feel drowsy. Eysenck (1981) proposed that the base levels of ARAS activation of introverts are higher than those of extroverts. Thus, because introverts have higher base levels of arousal, they avoid further stimulation, whereas the lower base level of extroverts may induce them to seek additional stimulation. Eysenck also proposed a neural basis for the emotionality–stability dimension. It is beyond the scope of this chapter to discuss nervous system functioning, but it is important to note that Eysenck anchored his trait theory in brain functions.

Like Eysenck, Zuckerman (1971, 1979, 1987) attempted to link the personality characteristic of sensation seeking with nervous system functioning. Individuals high in sensation seeking search for experiences that are exciting, risky, and novel. Zuckerman originally hypothesized that people differed from each other in levels of cortical arousal but refined the theory to suggest that sensation seekers possess stronger orienting responses than other individuals. The orienting response is an individual's first reaction to a new or unexpected stimulus. It is a tendency toward sensory intake and is contrasted to defense responses, which attempt to screen out stimuli. Research has substantiated stronger orienting responses among sensation seekers (Neary & Zuckerman, 1976) as well as a link between sensation seeking, brain-wave response (Zuckerman, Murtaugh, & Siegel, 1974), and the production of endorphins (Johansson, Almay, van Knorring, Terenius, & Astrom, 1979).

Sport Research

Two psychobiological approaches to understanding sport behavior appear in the sport literature. In the psychophysiological approach, inferences of psychological processes and emotional states are derived from the examination of psychophysiological measures such as heart rate and brain (electroencephalogram) or muscle (electromyogram) activity (e.g., Lawton, Min Hung, Saarela, & Hatfield, 1998). An example of this type of research approach is that which has examined the relationship between the Type A behavior pattern and psychophysiological responses to stress (e.g., Hardy, McMurray, & Roberts, 1989; Rejeski, Morley, & Miller, 1983).

The second biological approach to sport personality uses biological measures in conjunction with different types of personality measures to improve behavioral prediction in exercise (e.g., Dishman, 1982, 1984) and sport (e.g., Silva, Shultz, Haslam, & Murray, 1981) settings. This multivariate approach to understanding behavior is particularly pertinent for understanding how behavior in sport and exercise is influenced simultaneously by biological, psychological, and social factors.

Motive or Need Theories

A fourth class of dispositional theories consists of motive or need theories, which essentially propose that behavior is influenced by underlying needs.

Conceptual Basis

To motive or need theorists, personality differences are a function of individual differences in need patterns. The earliest and most influential need theorist was Murray (1938), who proposed that individuals possessed two types of needs: viscerogenic or primary needs, and psychogenic or secondary needs. Viscerogenic needs are primary because they are somatic in nature (e.g., food, sex, avoidance of pain). Murray proposed 28 psychogenic needs (e.g., achievement, autonomy, dominance, deference, affiliation) that each have characteristic desires and feelings that drive behavior. Although closely allied with psychoanalytic theory, Murray's need theory does not incorporate psychoanalytic assumptions about the instinctual origins of human behavior. Murray coined the term "environmental press" to emphasize that the environment plays an important role in behavior. Just as an internal need increases motivation, thus creating behavioral action, an environmental press can do the same thing. For example, being in an environment in which achievement is rewarded and modeled appropriately may increase an individual's desire to achieve. Sport psychologists have linked the importance of understanding and meeting individuals' needs to participation motivation and attri-

tion in sport (Gould & Petlichkoff, 1988).

Of Murray's original 28 needs, the need for achievement has received the most attention in the psychological literature. McClelland (1961) and Atkinson (1957) are well known for their theory and research using the need for achievement as the basis for understanding motivation. The need for control also has sparked interest in the psychological literature because of its proposed link to the Type A behavior pattern. Friedman and Rosenman (1974) defined the Type A personality as characterized by competitiveness, hostility, and time urgency. Glass (1977) proposed that the underlying basis for the Type A behavioral characteristics is the need for control over the environment. That is, competing is seen as controlling a situation, time urgency is related to the fear of losing control, and hostility may result when control of a situation is blocked.

Sport Research

The motive or need theory that has sparked the greatest amount of research in sport personality

© The Image Finders/Michael Evans

Participation in high-risk sports has been associated with the personality motive, or need, for sensation seeking.

is Atkinson's (1957) achievement motivation theory, which is interactional but contains a motive construct known as the need for achievement. Differences in risk-taking and performance behaviors have been examined based on differences in the need for achievement (e.g., Healey & Landers, 1973; Ostrow, 1976; Roberts, 1972, 1974; E.D. Ryan & Lakie, 1965).

Sensation seeking, or the need for adventure or risk, also has been examined in relationship to sport based on the work of Zuckerman (1971, 1979). Sensation seeking has been shown to describe participants in high-risk sports (Breivik, 1996; Fowler, von Knorring, & Oreland, 1980; Hymbaugh & Garrett, 1974; Rossi & Cereatti, 1993; Straub, 1982). Rowland, Franken, and Harrison (1986) extended the earlier descriptive studies of sensation seeking to demonstrate that sensation seeking predicts not only choice of sport but also degree of involvement in various sports.

Phenomenonological Approaches

Phenomenological approaches to personality focus on individuals' subjective experience and personal views of the world and self. That is, behavior is seen to be determined by the individual's understanding of self and environment rather than by predetermined or dispositional responses to external events.

Conceptual Basis and Assessment

Phenomenology developed from the writings of the philosopher Edmund Husserl (1911/1965), who believed that too much emphasis had been placed on interpreting and classifying human experience instead of studying what human experience actually is. Other sources for the emergence of this approach were the early writings of Jung and Allport, Gestalt psychology, Kurt Lewin's (1935) field theory, and existential philosophy. Phenomenological approaches to the study of personality in sport have become extremely popular as sport psychology follows psychology in moving away from the dispositional approach toward cognitive theory and measurement.

Phenomenological measurement involves the person as his or her own assessor. In this area of personality, subjects are asked directly how they feel or will behave. Phenomenological, or cognitive, assessment focuses on individuals' contextualized strategies and self-perceptions, which have been referred to as "personal action constructs" (Little, Lecci, & Watkinson, 1992). Phenomenologi-

cal constructs tend to be motivational and developmental in nature, focusing on what people are consciously trying to do during a particular period of their lives. This differs from trait or dispositional assessment, which attempts to measure more decontextualized, comparative dimensions of personality that represent typical behavior patterns. Trait measures get at what a person "has," whereas phenomenological measures speak to what a person "does" (Emmons, 1995).

Three categories of phenomenological approaches to personality are presented in this section: actualization/self-determination theories, cognitive information-processing theories, and social cognitive theories. All of these theoretical areas within the phenomenological approach have been popular areas of sport personality research.

Actualization/Self-Determination Theories

Actualization or self-determination theories focus on the striving of individuals to actualize, or to fulfill human potential and be self-determining. Carl Rogers' (1961) self theory and Abraham Maslow's (1968) hierarchy of needs are examples of phenomenological approaches that emphasize self-determinism and the human tendency toward growth and self-actualization. The central idea behind these theories is that all persons have the potential for positive growth and change, and behavior is the result of an individual's tendency toward growth or actualization. Although Maslow's hierarchy of needs theory would seem to fit under the motive/need theories of the dispositional approach, Maslow was not interested in categorizing individuals according to their dominant motives or needs. Maslow theorized that all people have the same kind of motives or needs, but they differ in how completely their various motives or needs are satisfied at a given time.

Most of the sport personality research grounded in actualization/self-determination theory is based on Deci and Ryan's (1985) cognitive evaluation theory of motivation. Cognitive evaluation theory focuses on self-determination in that people are viewed as having an intrinsic interest in actively engaging with their environment. To Deci, motivational behavior is a function not of internal motives, instinctual needs, or desired external reinforcement but rather the need for competence and self-determination. Much of the sport research in this area has used R.M. Ryan's (1982) Intrinsic Motivation Inventory (IMI) as an assessment tool, but the Sport Motivation Scale (SMS; Pelletier et al., 1995) provides researchers with a sport-specific conceptualization of degree of self-determination based on theoretical advances in self-determination theory. However, besides the use of self-report questionnaires, self-determining behavior also may be assessed via direct behavioral observation (e.g., Lepper, Greene, & Nisbett, 1973). Deci's cognitive evaluation theory has received a great deal of attention in the sport psychology literature (see reviews by Frederick & Ryan, 1995; Vallerand & Fortier, 1998). This research is discussed in greater detail in chapter 5 of this book.

Another actualization/self-determination theory of interest in sport personality is the concept of hardiness. Hardiness is related to Rogers' (1961) view that congruence between perceived self and actual experience leads to active engagement in life and thus to actualization or an integrated personality. Incongruence between self and experience (termed *alienation*) is believed to lead to psychological problems. Hardiness (the opposite of alienation) is used to describe this level of engagement with and commitment to life experiences resulting from the congruence between self and experience. Research has supported the relationship between hardiness and stress and illness susceptibility (Kobasa, 1979; Kobasa, Maddi, & Kahn, 1982) as well as a relationship between hardiness and sport performance (Maddi & Hess, 1992).

Cognitive Information-Processing Theories

The second group of theories within the phenomenological approach to the study of sport personality includes cognitive information-processing theories.

Conceptual Basis

Cognitive information-processing theories focus on how individuals actively process external events and their own behavior to make sense of things that take place around them. This approach emphasizes the uniqueness of each person's worldview and assumes that individuals actively construct reality for themselves. Cognitive theories view individuals as novice behavioral scientists attempting to understand, or construct, behavior and events in meaningful ways.

George Kelly's (1955) personal construct theory most clearly reflects cognitive theory. Whereas trait approaches attempt to explain personality by the individual's place on a personality dimension derived by the theorist, personal construct theory attempts to understand human behavior by studying what dimensions of personality individuals subjectively construct for themselves. Kelly believed that people do not experience the world directly or in the same way. Rather, personal constructs that we develop for ourselves serve as a lens, or filter, through which we view external events and our own behavior. People continuously evaluate the predictive efficiency of their personal constructs, and these constructs remain stable as long as they allow the person to interact successfully with the environment.

Schema theory also has emerged from the personal construct approach of Kelly. Schema theory is concerned with the influence of cognitive structures on the selection and organization of information in individuals (Markus, 1977, 1983). Self-schemas are used to organize new and incoming information; thus, they are guides to the processing of self-related information obtained through social interactions with the environment. These cognitive structures, or schema, are theorized to predict future behavior. Like schema theory, attribution theory is another example of behavioral explanation based on the processing of self-related information. Attribution theory posits that the ways in which individuals judge the causes of particular events or outcomes significantly affect future motivation and behavior (Kelley, 1973; Weiner, 1985).

Along with questionnaires (e.g., Causal Dimension Scale, Russell, 1982), cognitive assessment techniques include interviewing, self-monitoring, thought-sampling, and Q-sort techniques (Block, 1961), which provide a measure of how individuals organize their thoughts. Also, the Role Construct Repertory Test (or Rep test) was developed by Kelly (1955) to assess the cognitive construct systems of individuals.

Sport Research

Two studies used personal construct theory in the study of sport personality. Lerch (1976) used an idiographic approach to study four athletes' unique perspectives within their specific environmental context across the course of the competitive season. The results emphasized unique differences in personality functioning within an athletic context. As discussed previously in this chapter, Sadalla et al. (1988) used construct theory to examine factors that underlie preferences for participation in particular sports. Their results indicated that specific personality characteristics are associated with preferences for certain sports.

Cognitive consistency theory has been used to demonstrate that sport performance is positively associated with less conflict and the use of cognitive conflict reduction mechanisms, whereas sport dropouts are characterized by cognitive conflict (Volp & Keil, 1987). Cognitive attribution theory has generated a tremendous amount of research in sport psychology (see chapter 6).

Social Cognitive Theories

The third group of theories within the phenomenological approach to the study of personality consists of social cognitive theories.

Conceptual Basis

Social cognitive theory has its roots in traditional learning theory and originally was known as social learning theory. Social learning theories evolved as distinct from operant learning theories (e.g., Skinner, 1938) as theorists realized that unlike animals, humans may engage in social learning without any apparent direct reinforcement (Bandura, 1986; Mischel, 1968). These early social learning theories extended the concepts and principles of learning to interpersonal, social contexts that now are referred to as social cognitive approaches. Over time, theories in this area have evolved with an increasing emphasis on cognitions, or thought processes, so that the social cognitive approach is now viewed as separate from other learning approaches to personality (Pervin & John, 1997). Thus, social cognitive theory emphasizes the social origins of behavior; the importance of cognitive thought processes in human motivation, emotion, and action; and the learning of complex individualized patterns of behavior in the absence of rewards. Within social cognitive theory, behavior is situation-specific, and distinctive situation–behavior patterns are viewed as more defining of personality than the aggregate, cross-situational differences emphasized by dispositional theorists. For example, social cognitive theorists emphasize that it is more important to know about the kinds of situations that elicit anxiety in athletes as well as their strategies to cope with this anxiety, as opposed to assessing athletes' overall levels of competitive trait anxiety relative to others.

One of the oldest social cognitive personality theories was conceptualized by Rotter (1954). Rotter's social cognitive formulation contends that the probability that a particular pattern of behavior will occur depends on the individual's expectancies concerning the outcomes to which his or her behavior will lead and the perceived values of those outcomes. These generalized expectancies are assumed to be consistent and stable across situations; thus, they are similar to traits although they are construed as learned expectations. Rotter (1966) also conceptualized the term *locus of control* to describe the cause–effect connection between individuals' perceptions of their behavior and the reinforcement that occurs afterward. Rotter contended that people who expect their outcomes to be determined by their actions (internal locus of control) learn from reinforcers, and people who expect their outcomes to be unrelated to their actions (external locus of control) do not learn from reinforcers.

Another classic social cognitive theoretical perspective on personality is Bandura's (1986) self-efficacy theory. Self-efficacy theory is based on Rotter's theme of the importance of expectancy in influencing behavior. Drawing on his clinical experiences, Bandura asserted that a sense of personal efficacy is necessary for persistent behavioral striving. Self-efficacy is the self-perceived ability to carry out desired behaviors, and Bandura argued that this construct is central to human behavior. Self-efficacy is a prime example of a social cognitive personality construct, because it is the product of a complex process of self-persuasion that relies on the cognitive processing of diverse sources of efficacy information from within the individual and the external environment.

Assessment Examples

Numerous self-report measures have been used to assess the social cognitive aspects of personality in sport:

- Internal–External Locus of Control Scale (Rotter, 1966)
- Bem Sex-Role Inventory (S.L. Bem, 1974)
- Athletic Coping Skills Inventory-28 (ACSI-28; Smith, Schutz, Smoll, & Ptacek, 1995)
- Physical Self-Perception Profile (PSPP; Fox & Corbin, 1989)
- Athletic Identity Measurement Scale (AIM; Brewer, Van Raalte, & Linder, 1993)
- Self-Perception Profile for Children (Harter, 1985)
- Task and Ego Orientation in Sport Questionnaire (Duda, 1989)

Sport Research

Within the last two decades, the social cognitive approach to the study of sport personality has far overshadowed other theoretical approaches. Bandura's (1986) self-efficacy theory has been tested repeatedly in sport and has been shown to be an important mediator of sport behavior, cognitions, and affect (see chapter 6 and Schunk, 1995). Research on physical self-concept has substantiated the self-enhancement hypothesis (Baumeister, 1987) that is so central to social cognitive theory (see chapter 4 and Fox, 1997). Self-enhancement, a major social cognitive goal of human beings, involves individuals in a lifelong pursuit to validate their sense of self. The study of this self-validation goal seems to be especially salient in sport personality research based on the socially valued mastery and achievement-striving inherent in sport. Rotter's (1966) locus of control construct also has been included in many sport personality studies, typically as a hypothesized predictor of more statelike moods and cognitions. Also, there is evidence that performance is facilitated by an internal locus of control (Chalip, 1980). Based on the premise that one of the most powerful roles we learn in life is our gender role, the relationship between perceived gender role and behavior in sport is also a critical area of study within the social cognitive approach to personality (see chapter 11).

The social cognitive construct of perceived ability (Nicholls, 1984) emerged from the attribution literature and has been hailed by some as the personality construct that is the central mediator of behavior in sport (Roberts, 1992). Research has indicated that perceived ability is a significant predictor of persistence and attrition in sport. The increased focus on the achievement goal orientation of individuals has advanced our understanding of sport behavior from a nomothetic perspective of motivated behavior to an idiographic perspective, in which sport behavior is examined relative to personal goals or intent (see chapter 5).

Studies examining personality differences in athletes based on social cognitive constructs have taken the place of the trait-descriptive personality difference studies of the 1960s to determine if successful athletes differ from less successful athletes on various cognitive characteristics (see review in Williams & Krane, 1998). Overall, this research indicates that successful athletes have the following qualities:

- More self-confident
- Able to use more effective cognitive strategies and coping mechanisms to retain optimal competitive focus in the face of obstacles and distractions
- Able to self-regulate activation efficiently
- Positively preoccupied with sport, in terms of thoughts, images, and feelings
- Highly determined and committed to excellence in their sport

Research also supports that cognitive intervention strategies enhance performance behaviors and coping skills in sport (see reviews by Greenspan & Feltz, 1989; Vealey, 1994). Areas of social cognitive inquiry in sport personality that seem to be particularly significant in relation to the socially evaluative and inherently stressful context of competitive sport include coping (Anshel, Williams, & Hodge, 1997; Crocker & Isaac, 1997; Eklund, Grove, & Heard, 1998; Gould, Eklund, & Jackson, 1993; Grove & Heard, 1997; Smith & Christensen, 1995), perfectionism (Gould, Udry, Tuffey, & Loehr, 1996), burnout (Gould, Tuffey, Udry, & Loehr, 1996; Raedeke, 1997), self-presentational processes (James & Collins, 1997; Leary, 1992; Wilson & Eklund, 1998), and athletic identity (Murphy, Petitpas, & Brewer, 1996).

The influence of sport and physical activity on personality development and change has been examined within the social cognitive approach to see if participation has any facilitative effect on individuals' personalities. Laboratory research has shown that competition reduces prosocial behavioral tendencies such as helping and sharing (Barnett & Bryan, 1974; McGuire & Thomas, 1975) and increases antisocial tendencies (Estrada, Gelfand, & Hartmann, 1988; Rausch, 1965). Furthermore, both of these effects are magnified by losing. Kleiber and Roberts (1981) examined the effects of sport competition on the prosocial behaviors of cooperation and altruism in a field experiment with children. They found that sport competition had a negative effect on the occurrence of prosocial behavior in boys, and that children who were more experienced in competitive sports were significantly less altruistic than those who were less experienced. This is consistent with Webb's (1969) research indicating that fairness as a sport value becomes subordinate to competence and winning as age and experience in sport increase. However, contemporary research is needed within the social cognitive perspective to more fully understand the possible facilitative effect of sport participation on such personality characteristics as coping, attentional/cognitive strategies, and emotional adaptiveness to stress.

The personality characteristic that has been examined most frequently in this type of research is self-concept or self-esteem (see reviews by Biddle, 1995; McAuley, 1994; Sonstroem, 1984). Research generally has confirmed that fitness training improves self-concept in children, adolescents, and adults (Calfas & Taylor, 1994; Gruber, 1986; McDonald & Hodgdon, 1991). Interestingly, several researchers believe that these changes in self-concept may result from perceived as opposed to actual changes in physical fitness (Heaps, 1978; Leonardson, 1977; Sonstroem, 1984). This assertion has important implications for fitness training programs, in that mere involvement may not directly enhance self-esteem.

Learning Approaches

Theories of personality based on the learning approach emphasize that learning accomplished through interactions with the environment explains human behavior. Seen from this perspective, personality is an accumulation of learned behavior.

In conditioning approaches to personality, behaviors are "conditioned" by consequences that either strengthen or extinguish the behavior. Miller and Dollard (1941) were the first to describe personality in terms of conditioned behavior. They are often called "psychodynamic behavior theorists" (Mischel, 1971), because they included a motive or drive component in their theory. However, they represent the learning theory perspective because they attempted to account for psychoanalytic phenomena in learning theory terms (Carver & Scheier, 1988).

In his "radical behaviorism" approach, B.F. Skinner (1938, 1953) postulated that drives and motives are unnecessary to understanding behavior. Radical behaviorists such as Skinner describe behavior as one of two stimulus conditions: deprivation or satiation. Both of these phenomena are viewed as observable, measurable, and completely unrelated to internal personality components. Research based on conditioning theories has focused mainly on behavior modification. Although this area has important implications for influencing behavior in sport (Lee, 1993), it is not discussed here because it is not directly related to intraindividual characteristics of personality.

A Comprehensive View of Personality and Sport

The comprehensive view of personality assumed in this chapter reviews personality from several theoretical perspectives. Table 3.2 encapsulates the various ways personality is studied in sport. This table outlines the theoretical approaches to the study of personality by identifying brief characteristics of each theory, the paradigm with which that theory is associated, examples of sport research areas within that theoretical approach, and examples of assessment techniques used in these research areas. Placing theories in particular categories may be arguable, but the intent of the categorization is to provide a comprehensive overview of the study of personality particularly as it has been investigated in the sport context.

SUMMARY AND FUTURE DIRECTIONS IN SPORT PERSONALITY RESEARCH

Personality in relation to sport and physical activity has been studied by using a variety of approaches and methods to ask a variety of questions. In this section, I draw broad conclusions regarding what we know about personality and sport and offer possible directions for future research.

Summary of Knowledge

1. No distinguishable "athletic personality" has been shown to exist. There are no consistent research findings to support that athletes possess a general personality type or set of traits or dispositions that are distinct from the personalities of nonathletes.

2. No consistent trait personality differences between athletic subgroups have been shown to exist (athletes vs. nonathletes, athletes of one sport type vs. athletes of another sport type, athletes of different ability or success levels). Although methodological limitations have been cited as the reason for the lack of any consistent trait differences in athlete subgroups, it may be concluded that there are no meaningful or conceptually relevant differences in personality traits between subgroups of athletes.

3. Success in sport is facilitated by self-confidence, productive cognitive strategies and coping mechanisms, adherence to personally optimal patterns of precompetitive and competitive emo-

Table 3.2
Theoretical Approaches to the Study of Personality

Approach/ theory	Characteristics	Paradigm	Sport research	Assessment
Psychodynamic	Deterministic Instinctual Unconscious processes	Dispositional	"Gravitational theory"	—
Dispositional				
Trait	Consistent internal attributes Stable across time	Dispositional	Personality profiles	16PF, MMPI
Dispositional– state	Disposition, state, and situation influence behavior	Interactional	Mental health model	POMS
			Competitive anxiety IZOF model Attentional style	SAS/CSAI-2 Individual PNA TAIS
Biological	Physiology and personality related	Dispositional	Psychophysiology	Heart rate
Motive/need	Underlying motives Need patterns	Dispositional/ interactional	nACH Sensation-seeking	Mehrabian scale Zuckerman scale
Phenomenological				
Actualization/ self- determination	Self-fulfillment Self-determinism	Interactional	Intrinsic motivation Hardiness	Observation SMS IMI
Cognitive information- processing	Personal meaning Subjective construction	Interactional	Attribution theory Cognitive strategies	CDS Q-sort Rep test
Social cognitive	Social origins of behavior Learned cognitive thought processes/ patterns	Interactional	Locus of control Self-efficacy Coping	ACSI-28 PSPP AIM
Learning				
Conditioning	Working for reinforcement Observable behavior No intrapersonal construct	Situational	Behavior modification	Observation

tion, and extreme levels of commitment and determination. It is significant that personality differences between successful/elite and less successful/nonelite athletes have been found in cognitions and self-regulatory coping abilities, as opposed to more enduring personality traits and dispositions. For example, successful/elite athletes are better able to use anxiety as a means to stimulate performance than less successful/nonelite athletes, although traditional dispositional research could not establish any significant differences between successful and less successful athletes in trait or state anxiety levels (Jones, Hanton, & Swain, 1994; Jones & Swain, 1995; Jones, Swain, & Hardy, 1993;

Mahoney & Avener, 1977). Thus, although successful/elite and less successful/nonelite athletes may not differ at the dispositional level of anxiety, successful/elite athletes seem to be more cognitively skilled in controlling anxiety that is manifested in stressful competitive conditions.

4. Cognitive–behavioral intervention strategies enhance performance behaviors and cognitive coping skills in sport but are less effective in altering personality traits or dispositions. Social cognitive personality characteristics, as opposed to traits or dispositions, are more malleable in response to sport psychology interventions targeted to enhance athletes' affects, behaviors, and cognitions.

5. Participation in sport does not build "character," as viewed as developing or enhancing socially valued personality traits. Research indicates that sport participation increases rivalrous, antisocial behavior and does not alter socially valued personality traits.

6. Physical activity enhances self-concept and reduces negative affective states but has little influence on global personality traits. Although physical activity seems to influence personality with regard to self-perceptions and mood, stable personality traits are less adaptable to change via physical training.

7. The focus of sport personality research has changed from a broad assessment approach using multivariate trait inventories in the 1960s and 1970s (e.g., AMI, 16PF) to a more narrow approach focused on the study of specific personality content areas (e.g., competitive anxiety, self-efficacy) in the 1980s and 1990s. Areas of inquiry that are most active in sport personality research are those with solid theoretical underpinnings and valid measurement instrumentation (e.g., see chapter 4 on self-perceptions, chapter 5 on motivational orientations, chapter 6 on self-referent thought, chapter 7 on anxiety, and chapter 8 on moral development).

Future Directions in Sport Personality Research

Although many researchers in sport psychology believe that sport personality research has yielded no useful findings, this is not true. The conclusions stated in the previous section illustrate that the sport personality research of the last three decades has progressed across paradigms, theories, and assessment methods to provide sport psychologists with some definitive, albeit limited, findings. Pessimistic views about sport personality research are understandably based on the fact that a lot of research was conducted that basically supports the null hypothesis that no consistent, enduring (trait) differences exist between subgroups of athletes. Yet, it seems important to avoid criticizing early personality research for its lack of sophistication and realize that early attempts in all scientific areas involve less than precise theories and methods. The early work in sport personality, although lacking in scientific rigor, did in fact generate tremendous interest in sport psychology and was a major impetus for the emergence of the field as an academic subdiscipline of kinesiology. However, definitive knowledge that is conceptually useful and socially relevant is needed in sport personality research to significantly extend the knowledge base.

I hope that the discussion in this chapter will stimulate renewed conceptual and research ideas in sport personality. In this section, I present some additional directions for future research.

Answering the Hard Questions

Early in this chapter, I presented three key questions that represent the main theoretical issues in the study of personality in sport. These are the "hard questions" about personality, and these are the questions that we should attempt to answer.

To What Degree Is Behavior Internally or Externally Determined?

The interactional perspective in understanding behavior in sport is widely accepted, and most researchers in sport personality indicate that their work is based on this paradigm. Yet it often appears that we give lip service to the acknowledgment of contextual influences on the ABCs (affect, behavior, cognitions) of athletes. The study of burnout in sport psychology provides an example of this.

Three burnout models have been developed that all hypothesize complex relationships between personality characteristics and social–structural factors in sport that influence the development of burnout (Coakley, 1992; Silva, 1990; Smith, 1986). Coakley (1992) argued that the social–structural organization of high-performance sport constrains normal identity development in adolescent athletes and prevents them from having meaningful control over their lives. Coakley takes sport psychology to task for focusing too exclusively on intrapersonal stress-based antecedents of burnout and ignoring the inherent social–structural problems of sport, and then prescribing cognitive–behavioral strategies for athletes to "help them adjust to their conditions of dependency and powerlessness" (p. 283).

The popular sport media increasingly has voiced concern that young athletes are ripe for burnout and exploitation based on the money and prestige available at elite sport levels. Yet there is a paucity of research on athlete burnout, and research on burnout in coaches (Dale & Weinberg, 1989; Vealey, Udry, Zimmerman, & Soliday, 1992) and sport officials (A.H. Taylor, Daniel, Leith & Burke, 1990) has tended to focus on personality predictors of burnout without accounting for the inherent structural demands and social pressures of sport. More recent research has attempted to incorporate Coakley's ideas within a truer integrative–interactional perspective of burnout in sport (Gould, Tuffey, Udry, & Loehr, 1996; Gould, Udry, Tuffey, & Loehr, 1996; Gould et al., 1997; Raedeke, 1997). However, research perspectives on burnout should continue to work toward more meaningful contextual grounding.

Sport personality researchers across all areas should attempt to understand the relative importance of personal and contextual factors by asking such questions as, What specific contextual factors influence the development of various sport-related cognitions, affective responses, and range of behaviors? What types of contextual factors in sport override personality factors, and vice versa? Is this the same for all individuals, or are subgroups of people more influenced by one or the other? What social cognitive personality characteristics are especially relevant in light of the unique social culture of competitive sport? Recent research related to this last question is encouraging (e.g., self-presentational concerns, social physique anxiety, perfectionism, athletic identity) and should be extended to consider cognitive–behavioral–affective phenomena that have developed in the 1990s such as hyperconformity, which leads to burnout and the excessive behaviors of disordered eating and drug abuse, as well as the increasing professionalization of sport at youth levels.

The task of studying personality takes place within the confines of a social world—the unique world of competitive sport—that poses its own constraints on the manifestation of behavior exhibited in this world. Attempts to glean any conceptually or socially useful knowledge about personality in sport must account for these social constraints directly, as opposed to the cursory lip service given to research within the interactional paradigm.

How Consistent Is Personality Over Time and Situations?

The issue of personality consistency over time and situations typically has been studied in sport personality within the dispositional–state approach, with disappointing results. The artificial categorization of personality characteristics as traits or states has not enhanced the prediction of sport performance. Obviously, personality can be manifested as being more traitlike (consistent over time and situations) or statelike (variable over time and situations). Yet instead of arbitrarily conceptualizing personality constructs into traits and states, researchers could examine different personality characteristics to understand the factors that make them more or less consistent. For example, self-confidence could be studied by using a social cognitive perspective to see how enduring it is over time, how this might differ in different people, what social or competitive conditions tend to decrease its consistency or stability, how and why individuals rely on different sources of confidence in different situations, and how levels and sources of confidence develop and change longitudinally within athletes in relation to the social structure of sport. It seems important that future research on personality concepts in sport move from static one-time assessment to a more dynamic approach to assess the consistency or variability of relationships across time and situations. For example, Kingston and Hardy (1997) stated that athletes may perform most effectively by selectively using multiple goal orientations across various competition times and situations, as opposed to adopting a more stable goal orientation that is assumed to fit them well in all circumstances.

What Are the Roles of the ABCs in Sport Personality Research?

The study of personality involves the ABCs: affect, behavior, and cognition. The study of sport personality has emphasized the study of cognitions, which has been fruitful in understanding the ways that individuals process information in sport, self-regulate to cope with obstacles, and develop physical self-concepts. However, affect largely has been ignored except for extensive interest in competitive anxiety and mood state research based on the mental health model. Interest in the study of flow and peak experience in sport has increased in this decade (e.g., S. Jackson, 1992), yet systematic personality research needs to extend to the study of other positive emotions such as enjoyment and satisfaction. The provocative area of psychological reversals could be examined to more fully understand how and when factors in competitive sport shift or reverse the content and intensity of emotions (Apter, 1982; Kerr, 1993). Idiographic research on psychological reversals in emotional states could be linked to cognitive coping strategies and personalized intervention plans for athletes.

The study of performance behaviors in sport psychology research has been problematic, typically because of an emphasis on outcome behaviors that logically extend from sport outcomes (e.g., winning, batting average, 100-meter sprint time; Burton, 1988). Alternative behaviors other than outcomes need to be assessed to more precisely understand the link between the ABCs of sport personality. The ipsative assessments of performance that use PNA profile patterns (Hanin, 1997) and idiographic performance profiling (Butler & Hardy, 1992) are innovative ways to examine personalized performance behaviors, thoughts, and feelings. Other criterion variables of interest in sport personality include cognitive efficiency and emotional adaptiveness, which have been supported as important outcomes of self-efficacy (Maddux & Lewis, 1995).

Besides understanding the relative importance of the ABCs, sport personality researchers should consider the important interrelationships between them. Recent examples of this in the sport psychology literature include the adoption of a social cognitive perspective to examine the effects of specific motivational variables on the patterning of negative affect in sport (Hall & Kerr, 1998) as well as examining the influence of individual differences in information-processing perspectives on the efficacy of mental skills training with golfers (Thomas & Fogarty, 1997). Future research should not underestimate the powerful interactions between thoughts and feelings that affect behavior in sport.

Focus on the Neglected I's

At the beginning of the chapter, four I's were presented to represent important aspects of personality as an area of scientific study: identity, individual differences, internal determination, and integrated self. Although all four are important in understanding personality, it seems that the study of the integrated self and identity in personality has been neglected in favor of the study of individual differences and internal determination. Thus, future research should focus on the neglected I's: integrated self and identity.

Integrated Self

As our database of personality theory and research expands, we are inundated with large amounts of decontextualized information. We generate mini-theories that are, by definition, limited in scope, which contribute to a fragmented view of personality. Some of this is inevitable and typical of knowledge development. Yet, we should continue to search for ways to form coherent and integrative views of how personality works in sport.

McAdams (1994) proposed an integrative framework for the study of personality by asking, What do we know when we know a person? Understanding how personality "works" requires inquiry at three levels of analysis to "know the person." The first level is the relatively nonconditional, comparative, *decontextualized dimensions of personality* typically assessed in nomothetic personality research, such as traits, dispositions, states, and cognitive styles. The second level consists of *contextualized strategies and plans* that are typically motivational and developmental in focusing explicitly on achieving personally important life goals. The third level is the *life narrative* and consists of stories that people construct, which provide them with a sense of identity that lends a sense of meaning or purpose to their lives. The life narrative integrates all of one's Level 1 and 2 elements into a coherent and constantly evolving "self."

The study of personality in sport should involve assessment at all three levels, although the vast majority of research has focused on Level 1. Research has begun to move to Level 2, as seen by lines of research that pursue personality components by using multiple conceptual and methodological approaches to assess generalized nomothetic principles of thought, feeling, and emotion as well as more contextualized idiographic analyses of personal experiences and strategies (e.g., Gould, Tuffey, Udry, & Loehr, 1997; Gould, Udry, Tuffey, & Loehr, 1996). Personality research at Level 3 truly would be integrative, because retrospective life narratives of individuals with rich and complex biographies in sport could be examined to learn about the unique ways in which their personalities and sport identities developed in relation to significant life events and social influences.

Considering how personality is integrated in relation to sport requires thoughtful consideration. Although sport personality research has moved from the use of broad measures of personality (e.g., AMI, 16PF) to more specific conceptual models and instruments (e.g., competitive anxiety, self-efficacy), it might be interesting to consider returning to a broad perspective in seeking out new knowledge about personality in sport. The field of psychology, after decades of personality research and multiple replications, has proposed the existence of five basic personality dimensions called the *Big Five* (McRae & John, 1992). Through extensive factor analysis procedures, five factors repeatedly have been shown to subsume all other personality characteristics. The actual factors themselves are not of importance here; rather, the Big Five are significant because they are theorized to capture those personality characteristics that people consider most important in their lives. This clarifies personality researchers' attempts to understand human behavior, because although there is an endless array of individual differences, the particular individual differences represented by the Big Five are the ones viewed as most significant in peoples' daily interactions with each other.

Although it is doubtful that there is a Big Five (or other number) unique and specific to the study of personality in sport, perusal of the literature (and material in this book) indicates that several personality components could be considered together as particularly relevant personality dimensions related to the specific nature of sport. This list could include motivational orientation, physical self-concept, athletic identity, emotionality, moral developmental level, and coping patterns or abilities. Although this is a cursory list that crosses theoretical approaches to the study of personality, it is simply a template to stimulate sport psychologists to consider an integrative approach to examining personality in sport. And to enhance behavioral understanding, various social–structural components of sport (e.g., control, power, social and economic incentives) could be categorized to more explicitly examine the development, display, and interaction of personality characteristics within the unique context of sport.

Overall, to truly study the holistic, integrative nature of personality, our decontextualized, minitheoretical approaches must at some point start to become an overall picture of meaningful knowledge about how personality "happens" in sport. This may sound unrealistic when considered in relation to current, and sometimes limiting, approaches to conducting research in sport personality. But as our epistemological assumptions and methodological approaches mature and broaden, a truly integrative study of personality in sport may be possible.

Identity

The second neglected *I* of personality, identity, refers to an accrued confidence that the way one views oneself has a continuity with one's past and is matched by the perceptions of others (Erikson, 1950). Marcia (1994) identified four identity statuses that individuals achieve. *Identity achievement* occurs when individuals have established a sense of identity after exploration and when they function at a high psychological level capable of independent thought, complex moral reasoning, and commitment and intimacy. *Identity moratorium* occurs when individuals are in an identity crisis in which they struggle with who they are and are less prepared to make commitments. *Identity foreclosure* occurs when individuals become committed to an identity without having gone through the process of exploration, which leads to rigidity, conformity, and unstable self-esteem. *Identity diffusion* occurs when individuals lack any strong sense of identity or commitment.

Identity status has begun to be examined in relation to sport participation, as athletes have been found to be more identity foreclosed than nonathletes (see Murphy et al., 1996, for review). *Athletic identity* has been conceptualized as the cognitive, affective, behavioral, and social concomitants of identifying with the athlete role (Brewer et al., 1993), and it has been shown to be inversely related to postsport career planning, career maturity, and ease of adjustment after sport career termination (Murphy et al., 1996). Because a crucial task of personality development is identity development, and athletic identity is particularly salient in our society, research is needed to extend and expand our knowledge about how identity influences and is influenced by sport participation. In particular, a retrospective, idiographic life span approach to the study of athletic identity could further our understanding of personality development and change as the result of social and individually historical events that shape one's identity in sport. Because of the importance attached to moral development in Erikson's theory of identity development, the study of character development in sport could be renewed within identity theory to reveal how positive and negative identity cognitions and behaviors are learned and developed in relation to sport participation.

CONCLUSION

I advocate a comprehensive view of personality to stimulate research that increases our understanding of the structure and process of personality as it relates to sport and physical activity. It is time to ask the hard questions—to move beyond a trivial, narrow model of science to pursue creative and important questions that are socially relevant to the world of sport. To ask and answer these hard questions, researchers should be prepared to move beyond familiar and comfortable approaches in personality research to expand current epistemological, theoretical, and methodological ways of knowing.

REFERENCES

Adler, A. (1929). *The science of living.* New York: Greenberg.

Allen, B.P., & Potkay, C.R. (1981). On the arbitrary distinction between states and traits. *Journal of Personality and Social Psychology, 41,* 916–928.

Allport, G.W. (1937). *Personality: A psychological interpretation.* New York: Holt.

Allport, G.W. (1961). *Pattern and growth in personality.* New York: Holt.

Allport, G.W., & Odbert, H.S. (1936). Trait-names: A psycho-lexical study. *Psychological Monographs, 47*(Whole No. 211).

American Psychological Association. (1985). *Standards for educational and psychological testing.* Washington, DC: American Psychological Association.

Anastasi, A. (1988). *Psychological testing.* New York: Macmillan.

Anshel, M.H., Williams, L.R.T., & Hodge, K. (1997). Cross-cultural and gender differences on coping style in sport. *International Journal of Sport Psychology, 28,* 141–156.

Apter, M.J. (1982). *The experience of motivation: The theory of psychological reversals.* London: Academic Press.

Atkinson, J.W. (1957). Motivational determinants of risk-taking behaviors. *Psychological Review, 64,* 359–372.

Bahrke, M.S., & Morgan, W.P. (1978). Anxiety reduction following exercise and meditation. *Cognitive Therapy and Research, 2,* 323–333.

Bandura, A. (1986). *Social foundations of thought and action: A social cognitive theory.* Englewood Cliffs, NJ: Prentice Hall.

Barnett, M.A., & Bryan, J.H. (1974). Effects of competition with outcome feedback on children's helping behavior. *Developmental Psychology, 10,* 838–842.

Baron, R.M., & Boudreau, L.A. (1987). An ecological perspective on integrating personality and social psychology. *Journal of Personality and Social Psychology, 53,* 1222–1228.

Baumeister, R.F. (1987). How the self became a problem: A psychological review of historical research. *Journal of Personality and Social Psychology, 52,* 163–176.

Bem, D.J. (1983). Constructing a theory of the triple typology: Some (second) thoughts on nomothetic and idiographic approaches to personality. *Journal of Personality, 51,* 566–577.

Bem, S.L. (1974). The measurement of psychological androgyny. *Journal of Consulting and Clinical Psychology, 42,* 155–162.

Biddle, S. (1995). Exercise and psychosocial health. *Research Quarterly for Exercise and Sport, 66,* 292–297.

Bird, E.I. (1979). Multivariate personality analysis of two children's hockey teams. *Perceptual and Motor Skills, 48,* 967–973.

Block, J. (1957). A comparison between ipsative and normative ratings of personality. *Journal of Abnormal and Social Psychology, 54,* 50–54.

Block, J. (1961). *The Q-sort method in personality assessment and psychiatric research.* Springfield, IL.: Charles C Thomas.

Bordens, K.S., & Abbott, B.B. (1988). *Research design and methods: A process approach.* Mountain View, CA: Mayfield.

Bowers, K.S. (1973). Situationism in psychology: An analysis and a critique. *Psychological Review, 80,* 307–336.

Breivik, G. (1996). Personality, sensation seeking and risk taking among Everest climbers. *International Journal of Sport Psychology, 27,* 308–320.

Brewer, B.W., Van Raalte, J.L., & Linder, D.E. (1993). Athletic identity: Hercules' muscles or Achilles heel? *International Journal of Sport Psychology, 24,* 237–254.

Buccola, V.A., & Stone, W.J. (1975). Effects of jogging and cycling programs on physiological and personality variables in aged men. *Research Quarterly, 46,* 134–139.

Burton, D. (1988). Do anxious swimmers swim slower? Reexamining the elusive anxiety–performance relationship. *Journal of Sport and Exercise Psychology, 10,* 45–61.

Buss, A.H. (1989). Personality as traits. *American Psychologist, 44,* 1378–1388.

Butler, R.J., & Hardy, L. (1992). The performance profile: Theory and application. *The Sport Psychologist, 6,* 253–264.

Butler, R.J., Smith, M., & Irwin, I. (1993). The performance profile in practice. *Journal of Applied Sport Psychology, 5,* 48–63.

Calfas, K.J., & Taylor, W.C. (1994). Effects of physical activity on psychological variables in adolescents. *Pediatric Exercise Science, 6,* 406–423.

Campbell, D.T., & Stanley, J.C. (1963). *Experimental and quasi-experimental designs for research.* Chicago: Rand McNally.

Carlson, R. (1971). Where is the person in personality research? *Psychological Review, 75,* 203–219.

Carlson, R. (1984). What's social about social psychology? *Journal of Personality and Social Psychology, 47,* 1304–1309.

Carver, C.S., & Scheier, M.F. (1988). *Perspectives on personality*. Boston: Allyn & Bacon.

Cattell, R.B. (1946). *Description and measurement of personality*. Yonkers-on-Hudson, NY: World.

Cattell, R.B. (1965). *The scientific analysis of personality*. Baltimore: Penguin Books.

Chalip, L. (1980). Social learning theory and sport success: Evidence and implications. *Journal of Sport Behavior, 3,* 76–85.

Chaplin, W.F., & Buckner, K.E. (1988). Self-ratings of personality: A naturalistic comparison of normative, ipsative, and idiothetic standards. *Journal of Personality, 56,* 509–530.

Cialdini, R.B. (1980). Full-cycle social psychology. In L. Bickman (Ed.), *Applied social psychology annual* (pp. 69–102). Beverly Hills, CA: Sage.

Coakley, J. (1992). Burnout among adolescent athletes: A personal failure or social problem? *Sociology of Sport Journal, 9,* 271–285.

Crocker, P.R.E. (1997). A confirmatory factor analysis of the Positive Affect Negative Affect Schedule (PANAS) with a youth sport sample. *Journal of Sport and Exercise Psychology, 19,* 91–97.

Crocker, P.R.E., & Isaak, K. (1997). Coping during competitions and training sessions: Are youth swimmers consistent? *International Journal of Sport Psychology, 28,* 355–369.

Crowne, D.P., & Marlowe, D. (1960). A new scale of social desirability independent of psychopathology. *Journal of Consulting Psychology, 24,* 349–354.

Dale, J., & Weinberg, R.S. (1989). The relationship between coaches' leadership style and burnout. *The Sport Psychologist, 3,* 1–13.

Davis, H. (1991). Criterion validity of the athletic motivation inventory: Issues in professional sport. *Journal of Applied Sport Psychology, 3,* 176–182.

Deci, E.L., & Ryan, R.M. (1985). *Intrinsic motivation and self determination in human behavior*. New York: Plenum Press.

Dishman, R.K. (1982). Contemporary sport psychology. *Exercise and Sport Science Reviews, 10,* 120–159.

Dishman, R.K. (1984). Motivation and exercise adherence. In J.M. Silva & R.S. Weinberg (Eds.), *Psychological foundations of sport* (pp. 420–434). Champaign, IL: Human Kinetics.

Doyle, J., & Parfitt, G. (1997). Performance profiling and construct validity. *The Sport Psychologist, 11,* 411–425.

Duke, M., Johnson, T.C., & Nowicki, S., Jr. (1977). Effects of sports fitness camp experience on locus of control orientation in children. *Research Quarterly, 48,* 280–283.

Duda, J.L. (1989). Relationship between task and ego orientation and the perceived purpose of sport among high school athletes. *Journal of Sport and Exercise Psychology, 11,* 318–335.

Duda, J.L. (Ed.) (1998). *Advances in sport and exercise psychology measurement*. Morgantown, WV: Fitness Information Technologies.

Dunn, J.G.H. (1994). Toward the combined use of nomothetic and idiographic methodologies in sport psychology: An empirical example. *The Sport Psychologist, 8,* 376–392.

Eklund, R.C., Gould, D., & Jackson, S.A. (1993). Psychological foundations of Olympic wrestling excellence: Reconciling individual differences and nomothetic characterization. *Journal of Applied Sport Psychology, 5,* 35–47.

Eklund, R.C., Grove, J.R., & Heard, N.P. (1998). The measurement of slump-related coping: Factorial validity of the COPE and Modified-COPE inventories. *Journal of Sport and Exercise Psychology, 20,* 157–175.

Emmons, R.A. (1995). Levels and domains in personality: An introduction. *Journal of Personality, 63,* 341–364.

Endler, N.S. (1973). The person versus the situation—A pseudo issue? A response to Alker. *Journal of Personality, 41,* 287–303.

Erikson, E.H. (1950). *Childhood and society* (1st ed.). New York: Norton.

Estrada, A.M., Gelfand, D.M., & Hartmann, D.P. (1988). Children's sport and the development of social behaviors. In F. Smoll, R.A. Magill, & M.J. Ash (Eds.), *Children in sport* (3rd ed., pp. 251–262). Champaign, IL: Human Kinetics.

Etzel, E., Yura, M.T., & Perna, F. (1998). Ethics in assessment and testing in sport and exercise psychology. In J.L. Duda (Ed.), *Advances in sport and exercise psychology measurement* (pp. 423–432). Morgantown, WV: Fitness Information Technology.

Eysenck, H.J. (1967). *The biological basis of personality*. Springfield, IL: Charles C Thomas.

Eysenck, H.J. (1970). *The structure of human personality* (3rd ed.). London: Methuen.

Eysenck, H.J. (1981). *A model for personality*. Berlin: Springer-Verlag.

Eysenck, H.J., & Eysenck, M.W. (1985). *Personality and individual differences*. New York: Plenum Press.

Eysenck, H.J., & Eysenck, S.B.G. (1975). *Manual of the Eysenck Personality Inventory*. London: Hodder & Stoughton.

Fisher, A.C. (1976). *Psychology of sport: Issues and insights*. Palo Alto, CA: Mayfield.

Fisher, A.C. (1984). New directions in sport personality research. In J.M. Silva & R.S. Weinberg (Eds.), *Psychological foundations of sport* (pp. 70–80). Champaign, IL: Human Kinetics.

Fiske, D.W. (1988). From inferred personalities toward personality in action. *Journal of Personality, 56,* 815–833.

Folkins, C.H., & Sime, W.E. (1981). Physical fitness training and mental health. *American Psychologist, 36,* 373–389.

Fowler, C.J., von Knorring, L., & Oreland, L. (1980). Platelet monoamine oxidase activity in sensation seekers. *Psychiatric Research, 3,* 273–279.

Fox, K.R. (Ed.) (1997). *The physical self: From motivation to well-being*. Champaign, IL: Human Kinetics.

Fox, K.R., & Corbin C.B. (1989). The Physical Self-Perception Profile: Development and preliminary validation. *Journal of Sport and Exercise Psychology, 11,* 408–430.

Frank, L.K. (1939). Projective methods for the study of personality. *Journal of Psychology, 8,* 389–413.

Frederick, C.M., & Ryan, R.M. (1995). Self-determination in sport: A review using cognitive evaluation theory. *International Journal of Sport Psychology, 26,* 5–23.

Freud, S. (1953). The interpretation of dreams. In J. Strachey (Ed.), *The standard edition of the complete psychological works of Sigmund Freud* (Vols. 4, complete, and 5, pp. 1–627). London: Hogarth Press. (Original work published 1900.)

Freud, S. (1960). The psychopathology of everyday life. In J. Strachey (Ed.), *The standard edition of the complete psychological works of Sigmund Freud* (Vol. 6, complete). London: Hogarth Press. (Original work published 1901.)

Friedman, M., & Rosenman, R.H. (1974). *Type A behavior and your heart*. New York: Knopf.

Fromm, E. (1947). *Man for himself*. New York: Holt.

Gill, D.L. (1986). *Psychological dynamics of sport*. Champaign, IL: Human Kinetics.

Gill, D.L., & Deeter, T.E. (1988). Development of the Sport Orientation Questionnaire. *Research Quarterly for Exercise and Sport, 59,* 191–202.

Gill, D.L., Dzewaltowski, D.A., & Deeter, T.E. (1988). The relationship of competitiveness and achievement orientation to participation in sport and nonsport activities. *Journal of Sport and Exercise Psychology, 10,* 139–150.

Gill, D.L., Kelley, B.C., Martin, J.J., & Caruso, C.M. (1991). A comparison of competitive-orientation measures. *Journal of Sport and Exercise Psychology, 8,* 266–280.

Glass, D.C. (1977). *Behavior patterns, stress, and coronary disease*. Hillsdale, NJ: Erlbaum.

Gould, D., Eklund, R.C., & Jackson, S.A. (1992a). 1988 U.S. Olympic wrestling excellence: I. Mental preparation, precompetitive cognition, and affect. *The Sport Psychologist, 6,* 358–382.

Gould, D., Eklund, R.C., & Jackson, S.A. (1992b). 1988 U.S. Olympic wrestling excellence: II. Thoughts and affect occurring during competition. *The Sport Psychologist, 6,* 383–402.

Gould, D., Eklund, R.C., & Jackson, S.A. (1993). Coping strategies used by U.S. Olympic wrestlers. *Research Quarterly for Exercise and Sport, 64,* 83–93.

Gould, D., & Petlichkoff, L. (1988). Participation motivation and attrition in young athletes. In F. Smoll, R.A. Magill, & M.J. Ash (Eds.), *Children in sport* (3rd ed., pp. 251–262). Champaign, IL: Human Kinetics.

Gould, D., Petlichkoff, L., Simons, J., & Vevera, M. (1987). Relationship between competitive state anxiety inventory–2 subscale scores and pistol shooting performance. *Journal of Sport Psychology, 9,* 33–42.

Gould, D., Tuffey, S., Udry, E., & Loehr, J. (1996). Burnout in competitive junior tennis players: II. Qualitative analysis. *The Sport Psychologist, 10,* 341–366.

Gould, D., Tuffey, S., Udry, E., & Loehr, J. (1997). Burnout in competitive junior tennis players: III. Individual differences in the burnout experience. *The Sport Psychologist, 11,* 257–276.

Gould, D., Udry, E., Tuffey, S., & Loehr, J. (1996). Burnout in competitive junior tennis players: I. A quantitative psychological assessment. *The Sport Psychologist, 10,* 322–340.

Greenspan, M.J., & Feltz, D.L. (1989). Psychological interventions with athletes in competitive situations: A review. *The Sport Psychologist, 3,* 219–236.

Griffith, C.R. (1926). *Psychology of coaching*. New York: Scribner's.

Griffith, C.R. (1928). *Psychology and athletics*. New York: Scribner's.

Grove, J.R., & Heard, N.P. (1997). Optimism and sport confidence as correlates of slump-related coping among athletes. *The Sport Psychologist, 11,* 400–410.

Gruber, J.J. (1986). Physical activity and self-esteem development in children: A meta-analysis. In G. Stull & H. Eckert (Eds.), *Effects of physical activity on children* (American Academy of Physical Education Papers, pp. 30–48). Champaign, IL: Human Kinetics.

Guilford, J.P. (1959). *Personality*. New York: McGraw-Hill.

Hall, H.K., & Kerr, A.W. (1998). Predicting achievement anxiety: A social-cognitive perspective. *Journal of Sport and Exercise Psychology, 20,* 98–111.

Halliwell, W. (1990). Providing sport psychology consulting services in professional hockey. *The Sport Psychologist, 4,* 369–377.

Hanin, Y.L. (1997). Emotions and athletic performance: Individual zones of optimal functioning model. In R. Seiler (Ed.), *European yearbook of sport psychology* (pp. 29–70). Sankt Augustin, Germany: Academia Verlag.

Hanin, Y.L., & Syrjä, P. (1995). Performance affect in junior ice hockey players: An application of the individual zones of optimal functioning model. *The Sport Psychologist, 9,* 169–187.

Hanin, Y.L., & Syrjä, P. (1996). Predicted, actual and recalled affect in Olympic-level soccer players: Idiographic assessments on individualized scales. *Journal of Sport and Exercise Psychology, 18,* 325–335.

Hardy, C.J., McMurray, R.G., & Roberts, S. (1989). A/B types and psychophysiological responses to exercise stress. *Journal of Sport and Exercise Psychology, 11,* 141–151.

Harter, S. (1981). The development of competence motivation in the mastery of cognitive and physical skills: Is there still a place for joy? In G.C. Robert & D.M. Landers (Eds.), *Psychology of motor behavior and sport—1980* (pp. 3–29). Champaign, IL: Human Kinetics.

Harter, S. (1985). *Manual for the Self-Perception Profile for Children*. Denver: University of Denver.

Hathaway, S.R., & McKinley, J.C. (1943). *MMPI manual*. New York: Psychological Corporation.

Healey, R.R., & Landers, D.M. (1973). Effect of need achievement and task difficulty on competitive and noncompetitive motor performance. *Journal of Motor Behavior, 5,* 121–128.

Heaps, R.A. (1978). Relating physical and psychological fitness: A psychological point of view. *Journal of Sports Medicine, 18,* 399–408.

Herek, G.M. (1984). Beyond "homophobia": A social psychological perspective on attitudes towards lesbians and gay men. *Journal of Homosexuality, 10,* 1–21.

Hogan, R., DeSoto, C.B., & Solano, C. (1977). Traits, tests, and personality research. *American Psychologist, 32,* 255–264.

Holtzman, W.H. (1965). Personality structure. *Annual Review of Psychology, 16,* 119–156.

Horney, K. (1924). On the genesis of the castration complex in women. *International Journal of Psychoanalysis, 5,* 50–65.

Houts, A.C., Cook, T.D., & Shadish, W.R. (1986). The person-situation debate: A critical multiplist perspective. *Journal of Personality, 54,* 52–105.

Husserl, E. (1965). *Phenomenology and the crisis of philosophy* (Q. Lauer, Ed. and Trans.). New York: Harper Torchbooks. (Original work published 1911.)

Hymbaugh, K., & Garrett, J. (1974). Sensation seeking among skydivers. *Perceptual and Motor Skills, 38*, 118.

Ismail, A.H., & Young, R.J. (1973). The effect of chronic exercise on the personality of middle-age men by univariate and multivariate approaches. *Journal of Human Ergology, 2*, 47–57.

Ismail, A.H., & Young, R.J. (1977). Effect of chronic exercise on the personality of adults. *Annals of the New York Academy of Sciences, 301*, 958–969.

Jackson, C.O. (1933). An experimental study of the effect of fear on muscular coordination. *Research Quarterly, 4*, 71–80.

Jackson, S. (1992). Athletes in flow: A qualitative investigation of flow states in elite figure skaters. *Journal of Applied Sport Psychology, 4*, 161–180.

James, B., & Collins, D. (1997). Self-presentational sources of competitive stress during performance. *Journal of Sport and Exercise Psychology, 19*, 17–35.

Johansson, F., Almay, B.G.L., von Knorring, L., Terenius, L., & Astrom, M. (1979). Personality traits in chronic pain patients related to endorphin levels in cerebrospinal fluid. *Psychiatry Research, 1*, 231–239.

Johnson, W.R. (1949). A study of emotion revealed in two types of athletic sports contests. *Research Quarterly, 20*, 72–79.

Jones, G. (1993). The role of performance profiling in cognitive behavioral interventions in sport. *The Sport Psychologist, 7*, 160–172.

Jones, G., Hanton, S., & Swain, A.B.J. (1994). Intensity and interpretations of anxiety symptoms in elite and nonelite sports performers. *Personality and Individual Differences, 17*, 657–663.

Jones, G., & Swain, A. (1995). Predispositions to experience debilitative and facilitative anxiety in elite and nonelite performers. *The Sport Psychologist, 9*, 201–211.

Jones, G., Swain, A.B.J., & Hardy, L. (1993). Intensity and direction dimensions of competitive state anxiety and relationships with performance. *Journal of Sport Sciences, 11*, 533–542.

Jung, C.G. (1926). The structure and dynamics of the psyche. In H. Read, M. Fordham, & G. Adler (Eds.), *Collected works* (Vol. 8). Princeton, NJ: Princeton University Press.

Kane, J.E. (1978). Personality research: The current controversy and implications for sports studies. In W.F. Straub (Ed.), *Sport psychology: An analysis of athlete behavior* (pp. 228–240). Ithaca, NY: Mouvement.

Karteroliotis, C., & Gill, D.L. (1987). Temporal changes in psychological and physiological components of state anxiety. *Journal of Sport Psychology, 9*, 261–274.

Kelly, G. (1955). *The psychology of personal constructs*. New York: Norton.

Kelley, H. (1973). The process of causal attribution. *American Psychologist, 28*, 107–128.

Kenrick, D.T., & Funder, D.C. (1988). Profiting from controversy: Lessons from the person–situation debate. *American Psychologist, 43*, 23–34.

Kerr, J.H. (1993). An eclectic approach to psychological interventions in sport: Reversal theory. *The Sport Psychologist, 7*, 400–418.

Kingston, K.M., & Hardy, L. (1997). Effects of different types of goals on processes that support performance. *The Sport Psychologist, 11*, 277–293.

Kleiber, D.A., & Roberts, G.C. (1981). The effects of sport experience in the development of social character: An exploratory study. *Journal of Sport Psychology, 3*, 114–122.

Kluckhohn, C., & Murray, H.A. (1949). *Personality in nature, society, and culture*. New York: Holt.

Kobasa, S.C. (1979). Stressful life events, personality and health: An inquiry into hardiness. *Journal of Personality and Social Psychology, 37*, 1–11.

Kobasa, S.C., Maddi, S.R., & Kahn, S. (1982). Hardiness and health: A prospective study. *Journal of Personality and Social Psychology, 42*, 168–177.

Krahé, B. (1992). *Personality and social psychology: Towards a synthesis*. London: Sage.

Krane, V., Greenleaf, C.A., & Snow, J. (1997). Reaching for gold and the price of glory: A motivational case study of an elite gymnast. *The Sport Psychologist, 11*, 53–71.

Kretschmer, E. (1925). *Physique and character*. New York: Harcourt.

Kroll, W. (1970). Personality assessment of athletes. In L.E. Smith (Ed.), *Psychology of motor learning* (pp. 349–367). Chicago: Athletic Institute.

Kroll, W. (1976). Current strategies and problems in personality assessment of athletes. In A.C. Fisher (Ed.), *Psychology of sport* (pp. 371–390). Palo Alto, CA: Mayfield.

Kuhn, T.S. (1970). *The structure of scientific revolutions* (2nd ed.). Chicago: University of Chicago Press.

Lakie, W.L. (1962). Personality characteristics of certain groups of intercollegiate athletics. *Research Quarterly, 33*, 566–573.

Lamiell, J.T. (1981). Toward an idiothetic psychology of personality. *American Psychologist, 36*, 276–289.

Landers, D.M. (1983). Whatever happened to theory testing in sport psychology? *Journal of Sport Psychology, 5*, 135–151.

Lawton, G.W., Min Hung, T., Saarela, P., & Hatfield, B.D. (1998). Electroencephalography and mental states associated with elite performance. *Journal of Sport and Exercise Psychology, 20*, 35–53.

Lazarus, R.S., & Monat, A. (1979). *Personality* (3rd ed.). Englewood Cliffs, NJ: Prentice Hall.

Leary, M.R. (1992). Self-presentational processes in exercise and sport. *Journal of Sport and Exercise Psychology, 14*, 339–351.

Lee, C. (1993). Operant strategies in sport and exercise: Possibilities for theoretical development. *International Journal of Sport Psychology, 24*, 306–325.

Leonardson, G.R. (1977). Relationship between self-concept and perceived physical fitness. *Perceptual and Motor Skills, 44*, 62.

Lepper, M.R., Greene, D., & Nisbett, R.E. (1973). Undermining children's interest with extrinsic rewards: A test of the "overjustification effect." *Journal of Personality and Social Psychology, 28*, 129–137.

Lerch, H.A. (1976). Four female collegiate track athletes: An analysis of personal constructs. *Research Quarterly, 47*, 687–691.

LeUnes, A., Hayward, S.A., & Daiss, R. (1988). Annotated bibliography on the Profile of Mood States in sport. *Journal of Sport Behavior, 11,* 213–240.

Lewin, K. (1935). *A dynamic theory of personality.* New York: McGraw-Hill.

Little, B.R., Lecci, L., & Watkinson, B. (1992). Personality and personal projects: Linking Big Five and PAC units of analysis. *Journal of Personality, 60,* 501–525.

Maddi, S.R. (1976). *Personality theories: A comparative analysis.* Homewood, IL: Dorsey.

Maddi, S.R., & Hess, M.J. (1992). Personality hardiness and success in basketball. *International Journal of Sport Psychology, 23,* 360–368.

Maddux, J.E., & Lewis, J. (1995). Self-efficacy and adjustment: Basic principles and issues. In J.E. Maddux (Ed.), *Self-efficacy, adaptation, and adjustment: Theory, research, and application* (pp. 37–68). New York: Plenum Press.

Magnusson, D., & Endler, N.S. (1977). Interactional psychology: Present status and future prospects. In D. Magnusson & N.S. Endler (Eds.), *Personality at the crossroads: Current issues in interactional psychology* (pp. 3–31). Hillsdale, NJ: Erlbaum.

Mahoney, M.J., & Avener, M. (1977). Psychology of the elite athlete: An exploratory study. *Cognitive Therapy and Research, 2,* 135–141.

Marcia, J. (1994). Ego identity and object relations. In J.M. Masling & R.F. Bornstein (Eds.), *Empirical perspectives on object relations theory* (pp. 59–104). Washington, DC: American Psychological Association.

Markus, H. (1977). Self-schemata and processing information about the self. *Journal of Personality and Social Psychology, 35,* 63–78.

Markus, H. (1983). Self-knowledge: An expanded view. *Journal of Personality, 51,* 543–565.

Marsh, H.W. (1994). Sport motivation orientations: Beware of jingle-jangle fallacies. *Journal of Sport and Exercise Psychology, 16,* 365–380.

Martens, R. (1975). The paradigmatic crisis in American sport personology. *Sportwissenschaft, 1,* 9–24.

Martens, R. (1979). About smocks and jocks. *Journal of Sport Psychology, 1,* 94–99.

Martens, R. (1987). Science, knowledge, and sport psychology. *The Sport Psychologist, 1,* 29–55.

Martens, R., & Landers, D.M. (1972). Evaluation potential as a determinant of coaction effects. *Journal of Experimental Social Psychology, 8,* 347–359.

Martens, R., Vealey, R.S., & Burton, D. (1990). *Competitive anxiety in sport.* Champaign, IL: Human Kinetics.

Martinsen, E., & Stephens, T. (1994). Exercise and mental health in clinical and free-living populations. In R.K. Dishman (Ed.), *Advances in exercise adherence* (pp. 55–72). Champaign, IL: Human Kinetics.

Maslow, A.H. (1968). *Toward a psychology of being* (2nd ed.). Princeton, NJ: Van Nostrand.

McAdams, D.P. (1994). Can personality change? Levels of stability and growth in personality across the life span. In T.F. Heatherton & J.L. Weinberger (Eds.), *Can personality change?* (pp. 299–314). Washington, DC: American Psychological Association.

McAuley, E. (1994). Physical activity and psychosocial outcomes. In C. Bouchard, R.J. Shephard, & T. Stephens (Eds.), *Physical activity, fitness, and health* (pp. 551–568). Champaign, IL: Human Kinetics.

McClelland, D.C. (1961). *The achieving society.* Princeton, NJ: Van Nostrand.

McDonald, D.G., & Hodgdon, J.A. (1991). *Psychological effects of aerobic fitness training.* New York: Springer-Verlag.

McGuire, J., & Thomas, M.H. (1975). Effects of sex, competence and competition on sharing behavior in children. *Journal of Personality and Social Psychology, 32,* 490–494.

McNair, D.M., Lorr, M., & Droppleman, L.F. (1981). *Profile of Mood States.* San Diego: Educational and Industrial Testing Service.

McRae, R.R., & John, O.P. (1992). An introduction to the five-factor model and its applications. *Journal of Personality, 60,* 175–215.

Mehrabian, A. (1968). Male and female scales of the tendency to achieve. *Educational and Psychological Measurement, 28,* 493–502.

Miller, N.E., & Dollard, J. (1941). *Social learning and imitation.* New Haven, CT: Yale University Press.

Mischel, W. (1968). *Personality and assessment.* New York: Wiley.

Mischel, W. (1971). *Introduction to personality.* New York: Holt.

Mischel, W. (1977a). The interaction of person and situation. In D. Magnusson & N.S. Endler (Eds.), *Personality at the crossroads: Current issues in interactional psychology* (pp. 333–352). Hillsdale, NJ: Erlbaum.

Mischel, W. (1977b). On the future of personality measurement. *American Psychologist, 32,* 246–254.

Morgan, W.P. (1980a). Sport personology: The credulous-skeptical argument in perspective. In W. Straub (Ed.), *Sport psychology: An analysis of athlete behavior* (pp. 330–339). Ithaca, NY: Mouvement.

Morgan, W.P. (1980b). The trait psychology controversy. *Research Quarterly for Exercise and Sport, 51,* 50–76.

Morgan, W.P. (1985a). Affective beneficence of vigorous physical activity. *Medicine and Science in Sports and Exercise, 17,* 94–100.

Morgan, W.P. (1985b). Selected psychological factors limiting performance: A mental health model. In D.H. Clarke & H.M. Eckert (Eds.), *Limits of human performance* (American Academy of Physical Education Papers, pp. 70–80). Champaign, IL: Human Kinetics.

Murphy, G.M., Petitpas, A.J., & Brewer, B.W. (1996). Identity foreclosure, athletic identity, and career maturity in intercollegiate athletes. *The Sport Psychologist, 10,* 239–246.

Murray, H.A. (1938). *Explorations in personality: A clinical and experimental study of fifty men of college age.* New York: Oxford University Press.

Mutrie, N., & Biddle, S.J.H. (1995). The effects of exercise on mental health in nonclinical populations. In S.J.H. Biddle (Ed.), *European perspectives on exercise and sport psychology* (pp. 50–70). Champaign, IL: Human Kinetics.

Neary, R.S., & Zuckerman, M. (1976). Sensation seeking, trait and state anxiety, and the electrodermal orienting reflex. *Psychophysiology, 13,* 205–211.

Nicholls, J.G. (1984). Conceptions of ability and achievement motivation. In R. Ames & C. Ames (Eds.),

Research on motivation in education: Student motivation (Vol. 1, pp. 64–92). New York: Academic Press.

Nideffer, R.M. (1976). Test of Attentional and Interpersonal Style. *Journal of Personality and Social Psychology, 34,* 394–404.

Nideffer, R.M. (1981). *The ethics and practice of applied sport psychology.* Ithaca, NY: Mouvement.

Nideffer, R.M. (1990). Use of the Test of Attentional and Interpersonal Style. *The Sport Psychologist, 4,* 285–300.

Ogilvie, B.C., & Tutko, T.A. (1966). *Problem athletes and how to handle them.* London: Palham Books.

Ogilvie, B.C., & Tutko, T.A. (1971). Sport: If you want to build character, try something else. *Psychology Today, 5,* 60–63.

Orlick, T. (1989). Reflections on sportpsych consulting with individual and team sport athletes at summer and winter Olympic games. *The Sport Psychologist, 3,* 358–365.

Ostrow, A.C. (1976). Goal-setting behavior and need achievement in relation to competitive motor activity. *Research Quarterly, 47,* 174–183.

Peck, R.F., & Havighurst, R.J. (1960). *The psychology of character development.* New York: Wiley.

Pelletier, L.G., Fortier, M.S., Vallerand, R.J., Tuson, K.M., Briere, N.M., & Blais, M.R. (1995). Toward a new measure of intrinsic motivation, extrinsic motivation, and amotivation in sports: The Sport Motivation Scale (SMS). *Journal of Sport and Exercise Psychology, 17,* 35–53.

Pervin, L.A. (1985). Personality: Current controversies, issues, and directions. *Annual Review of Psychology, 36,* 83–114.

Pervin, L.A., & John, O.P. (1997). *Personality: Theory and research* (7th ed.). New York: Wiley.

Petruzzello, S.J., Landers, D.M., Hatfield, B.D., Kubitz, K.A., & Salazar, W. (1991). A meta-analysis on the anxiety-reducing effects of acute and chronic exercise. *Sports Medicine, 11,* 143–182.

Prapavessis, H., & Grove, J.R. (1991). Precompetitive emotions and shooting performance: The mental health and zone of optimal function models. *The Sport Psychologist, 5,* 223–234.

Prapavessis, H., & Grove, J.R. (1994a). Personality variables as antecedents of precompetitive mood state temporal patterning. *International Journal of Sport Psychology, 22,* 347–365.

Prapavessis, H., & Grove, J.R. (1994b). Personality variables as antecedents of precompetitive mood states. *International Journal of Sport Psychology, 25,* 81–99.

Raedeke, T.D. (1997). Is athlete burnout more than just stress? A sport commitment perspective. *Journal of Sport and Exercise Psychology, 19,* 396–417.

Rausch, H.L. (1965). Interaction sequences. *Journal of Personality and Social Psychology, 2,* 487–499.

Ravizza, K. (1990). Sportpsych consultation issues in professional baseball. *The Sport Psychologist, 4,* 330–340.

Rejeski, W.J., Morley, D., & Miller, H. (1983). Cardiac rehabilitation: Coronary-prone behavior as a moderator of graded exercise test performance. *Journal of Cardiac Rehabilitation, 3,* 339–343.

Renger, R. (1993). A review of the Profile of Mood States (POMS) in the prediction of athletic success. *Journal of Applied Sport Psychology, 5,* 78–84.

Riemer, H.A., & Chelladurai, P. (1998). Development of the athlete satisfaction questionnaire (ASQ). *Journal of Sport and Exercise Psychology, 20,* 127–156.

Roberts, G.C. (1972). Effect of achievement motivation and social environment on performance of a motor task. *Journal of Motor Behavior, 4,* 37–46.

Roberts, G.C. (1974). Effect of achievement motivation and social environment on risk taking. *Research Quarterly, 45,* 42–55.

Roberts, G.C. (1984). Children's achievement motivation in sport. In J.G. Nicholls (Ed.), *The development of achievement motivation* (pp. 251–281). Greenwich, CT: JAI Press.

Roberts, G.C. (1992). Motivation in sport and exercise: Conceptual constraints and conceptual convergence. In G.C. Roberts (Ed.), *Motivation in sport and exercise* (pp. 3–30). Champaign, IL: Human Kinetics.

Rogers, C.R. (1961). *On becoming a person.* Boston: Houghton Mifflin.

Rossi, B., & Cereatti, L. (1993). The sensation seeking in mountain athletes as assessed by Zuckerman's sensation seeking scale. *International Journal of Sport Psychology, 24,* 417–431.

Rotella, R.J. (1990). Providing sport psychology consulting services to professional athletes. *The Sport Psychologist, 4,* 409–417.

Rotter, J.B. (1954). *Social learning and clinical psychology.* Englewood Cliffs, NJ: Prentice Hall.

Rotter, J.B. (1966). Generalized expectancies for internal versus external control of reinforcement. *Psychological Monographs, 80*(1, Whole No. 609).

Rowland, G.L., Franken, R.E., & Harrison, K. (1986). Sensation seeking and participation in sporting activities. *Journal of Sport Psychology, 8,* 212–220.

Rowley, A.J., Landers, D.M., Kyllo, L.B., & Etnier, J.L. (1995). Does the iceberg profile discriminate between successful and less successful athletes? A meta-analysis. *Journal of Sport and Exercise Psychology, 17,* 185–199.

Ruffer, W.A. (1975). Personality traits in athletes. *Physical Educator, 32,* 105–109.

Ruffer, W.A. (1976a). Personality traits in athletes. *Physical Educator, 33,* 50–55.

Ruffer, W.A. (1976b). Personality traits in athletes. *Physical Educator, 33,* 211–214.

Rushall, B.S. (1976). Three studies relating personality variables to football performance. In A.C. Fisher (Ed.), *Psychology of sport* (pp. 391–399). Palo Alto, CA: Mayfield.

Russell, D. (1982). The causal dimension scale: A measure of how individuals perceive causes. *Journal of Personality and Social Psychology, 42,* 1137–1145.

Ryan, E.D., & Lakie, W.L. (1965). Competitive and noncompetitive performance in relation to achievement motive and manifest anxiety. *Journal of Personality and Social Psychology, 1,* 342–345.

Ryan, R.M. (1982). Control and information in the intrapersonal sphere: An extension of cognitive evaluation theory. *Journal of Personality and Social Psychology, 45,* 736–750.

Sadalla, E.K., Linder, D.E., & Jenkins, B.A. (1988). Sport preference: A self-presentational analysis. *Journal of Sport and Exercise Psychology, 10,* 214–222.

Savoy, C. (1993). A yearly mental training program for a college basketball player. *The Sport Psychologist, 7,* 173–190.

Scanlan, T.K., Carpenter, P.J., Simons, J.P., Schmidt, G.W., & Keeler, B. (1993). An introduction to the sport commitment model. *Journal of Sport and Exercise Psychology, 15,* 1–15.

Scanlan, T.K., Ravizza, K., & Stein, G.L. (1989). An in-depth study of former elite figure skaters: I. Introduction to the project. *Journal of Sport and Exercise Psychology, 11,* 54–64.

Scanlan, T.K., Stein, G.L., & Ravizza, K. (1989). An in-depth study of former elite figure skaters: II. Sources of enjoyment. *Journal of Sport and Exercise Psychology, 11,* 65–83.

Schunk, D.H. (1995). Self-efficacy, motivation, and performance. *Journal of Applied Sport Psychology, 7,* 112–137.

Sheldon, W.H. (1942). *The varieties of temperament: A psychology of constitutional differences.* New York: Harper.

Silva, J.M. (1984). Personality and sport performance: Controversy and challenge. In J.M. Silva & R.S. Weinberg (Eds.), *Psychological foundations of sport* (pp. 59–69). Champaign, IL: Human Kinetics.

Silva, J.M. (1990). An analysis of the training stress syndrome in competitive athletics. *Journal of Applied Sport Psychology, 2,* 5–20.

Silva, J.M., Shultz, B.B., Haslem, R.W., & Murray, D. (1981). A psychophysiological assessment of elite wrestlers. *Research Quarterly for Exercise and Sport, 52,* 348–358.

Singer, R.N. (1988). Psychological testing: What value to coaches and athletes. *International Journal of Sport Psychology, 19,* 87–106.

Skinner, B.F. (1938). *The behavior of organisms.* New York: Appleton.

Skinner, B.F. (1953). *Science and human behavior.* New York: Macmillan.

Smith, R.E. (1986). Toward a cognitive–affective model of athletic burnout. *Journal of Sport Psychology, 8,* 36–50.

Smith, R.E., & Christensen, D.S. (1995). Psychological skills as predictors of performance and survival in professional baseball. *Journal of Sport and Exercise Psychology, 17,* 399–415.

Smith, R.E., Schutz, R.W., Smoll, F.L., & Ptacek, J.T. (1995). Development and validation of a multidimensional measure of sport-specific psychological skills: The athletic coping skills inventory–28. *Journal of Sport and Exercise Psychology, 17,* 379–398.

Smith, R.E., Smoll, F.L., & Schutz, R.W. (1990). Measurement correlates of sport-specific cognitive and somatic trait anxiety: The Sport Anxiety Scale. *Anxiety Research, 2,* 263–280.

Snyder, M. (1983). The influence of individuals on situations: Implications for understanding the links between personality and social behavior. *Journal of Personality, 51,* 497–516.

Sonstroem, R.J. (1984). Exercise and self-esteem. *Exercise and Sport Sciences Reviews, 12,* 123–155.

Sonstroem, R.J., & Bernardo, P. (1982). Intraindividual pregame state anxiety and basketball performance: A re-examination of the inverted-U curve. *Journal of Sport Psychology, 4,* 235–245.

Spielberger, C.D. (1966). *Anxiety and behavior.* New York: Academic Press.

Spielberger, C.D., Gorsuch, R.L., & Lushene, R.L. (1970). *Manual for the State-Trait Anxiety Inventory.* Palo Alto, CA: Consulting Psychologists Press.

Straub, W.F. (1982). Sensation seeking among high and low-risk male athletes. *Journal of Sport Psychology, 4,* 246–253.

Sundberg, N.D. (1977). *Assessment of persons.* Englewood Cliffs, NJ: Prentice Hall.

Taylor, A.H., Daniel, J.V., Leith, L., & Burke, R.J. (1990). Perceived stress, psychological burnout and paths to turnover intentions among sport officials. *Journal of Applied Sport Psychology, 2,* 84–97.

Taylor, J. (1953). A personality scale of manifest anxiety. *Journal of Abnormal and Social Psychology, 48,* 285–290.

Terry, P. (1995). The efficacy of mood state profiling with elite performers: A review and synthesis. *The Sport Psychologist, 9,* 309–324.

Thomas, P.R., & Fogarty, G.J. (1997). Psychological skills training in golf: The role of individual differences in cognitive preferences. *The Sport Psychologist, 11,* 86–106.

Tillman, K. (1965). Relationship between physical fitness and selected personality traits. *Research Quarterly, 36,* 483–489.

Tutko, T.A., Lyon, L.P., & Ogilvie, B.C. (1969). *Athletic Motivation Inventory.* San Jose, CA: Institute for the Study of Athletic Motivation.

Vallerand, R.J., & Fortier, M.S. (1998). Measures of intrinsic and extrinsic motivation in sport and physical activity: A review and critique. In J.L. Duda (Ed.), *Advances in sport and exercise psychology measurement* (pp. 81–101). Morgantown, WV: Fitness Information Technology.

Vane, J.R., & Guarnaccia, V.J. (1989). Personality theory and personality assessment measures: How helpful to the client? *Journal of Clinical Psychology, 45,* 5–19.

Vanek, M., & Cratty, B.J. (1970). *Psychology and the superior athlete.* Toronto: Macmillan.

Vealey, R.S. (1986). Sport-confidence and competitive orientations: Preliminary investigation and instrument development. *Journal of Sport Psychology, 8,* 221–246.

Vealey, R.S. (1988). Sport-confidence and competitive orientation: An addendum on scoring procedures and gender differences. *Journal of Sport and Exercise Psychology, 10,* 471–478.

Vealey, R.S. (1989). Sport personology: A paradigmatic and methodological analysis. *Journal of Sport and Exercise Psychology, 11,* 216–235.

Vealey, R.S. (1994). Current status and prominent issues in sport psychology interventions. *Medicine and Science in Sport and Exercise, 26,* 495–502.

Vealey, R.S., & Garner-Holman, M. (1998). Applied sport psychology: Measurement issues. In J.L. Duda (Ed.), *Advances in sport and exercise psychology measurement* (pp. 433–446). Morgantown, WV: Fitness Information Technology.

Vealey, R.S., Udry, E.M., Zimmerman, V., & Soliday, J. (1992). Intrapersonal and situational predictors of coaching burnout. *Journal of Sport and Exercise Psychology, 14,* 40–58.

Vealey, R.S., & Walter, S.M. (1994). On target with mental skills: An interview with Darrell Pace. *The Sport Psychologist, 8,* 427–441.

Volp, A., & Keil, U. (1987). The relationship between performance, intention to drop out, and intrapersonal conflict in swimmers. *Journal of Sport Psychology, 9,* 358–375.

Watson, D., Clark, L.A., & Tellegen, A. (1988). Development and validation of brief measures of positive and negative affect: The PANAS scales. *Journal of Personality and Social Psychology, 54,* 1063–1070.

Watson, D., & Tellegen, A. (1985). Towards a consensual structure of mood. *Psychological Bulletin, 98,* 219–235.

Webb, H. (1969). Professionalization of attitudes toward play among adolescents. In G.S. Kenyon (Ed.), *Aspects of contemporary sport sociology* (pp. 141–167). Chicago: The Athletic Institute.

Weiner, B. (1985). An attributional theory of achievement motivation and emotion. *Psychological Review, 92,* 548–573.

Werner, A.C., & Gottheil, E. (1966). Personality development and participation in college athletics. *Research Quarterly, 37,* 126–131.

West, S.G. (1986). Methodological developments in personality research: An introduction. *Journal of Personality, 54,* 1–17.

Williams, J.M. (1978). Personality characteristics of the successful female athlete. In W.F. Straub (Ed.), *Sport psychology: An analysis of athlete behavior* (pp. 249–255). Ithaca, NY: Mouvement.

Williams, J.M., & Krane, V. (1998). Psychological characteristics of peak performance. In J.M. Williams (Ed.), *Applied sport psychology: Personal growth to peak performance* (3rd ed., pp. 158–170). Mountain View, CA: Mayfield.

Willis, J.D. (1982). Three scales to measure competition-related motives in sport. *Journal of Sport Psychology, 4,* 338–353.

Wilson, P., & Eklund, R.C. (1998). The relationship between competitive anxiety and self-presentational concerns. *Journal of Sport and Exercise Psychology, 20,* 81–97.

Wrisberg, C.A. (1990). An interview with Pat Summitt. *The Sport Psychologist, 4,* 180–191.

Yan Lan, L., & Gill, D.L. (1984). The relationships among self-efficacy, stress responses, and a cognitive feedback manipulation. *Journal of Sport Psychology, 6,* 227–238.

Young, R.J., & Ismail, A.H. (1976). Personality differences of adult men before and after a physical fitness program. *Research Quarterly, 47,* 513–519.

Zuckerman, M. (1971). Dimensions of sensation seeking. *Journal of Consulting and Clinical Psychology, 36,* 45–52.

Zuckerman, M. (1979). *Sensation seeking: Beyond the optimal level of arousal.* Hillsdale, NJ: Erlbaum.

Zuckerman, M. (1987). A critical look at three arousal constructs in personality theories: Optimal levels of arousal, strength of the nervous system, and sensitivities to signals of reward and punishment. In J. Strelau & H.J. Eysenck (Eds.), *Personality dimensions and arousal* (pp. 217–231). New York: Plenum Press.

Zuckerman, M., Murtaugh, T.M., & Siegel, J. (1974). Sensation seeking and cortical augmenting-reducing. *Psychophysiology, 11,* 535–542.

CHAPTER 4

Self-Perceptions and Sport Behavior

Kenneth R. Fox

Motivation is inevitably tied to the way the individual views the self. In this chapter I summarize key concepts and theories used to help us understand the complexity of the self and its ways of functioning. Specific attention is paid to the structure, content, and assessment of the physical self. Finally, the roles of the self and physical self-perceptions as both determinants and consequences of sport participation are addressed. I conclude the chapter with suggestions for future research.

It is difficult to find a topic that has generated more academic activity than the self and its related constructs of self-esteem, self-concept, and identity. It has attracted the interests of philosophers, sociologists, anthropologists, and theologists in addition to social, developmental, and clinical psychologists. Many theorists argue that the self is integral to our whole existence and, consequently, strongly influences our physical and mental health. Self-esteem is also one of the few psychological constructs to acquire meaning among the general public, and the term is seen regularly in the popular press and heard in incidental conversations. The promotion of self-esteem features in the policy documents of many organizations and corporations and often is listed as a primary program goal in education, health promotion, and therapeutic sports settings. It even has been seen as the key to economic and social success (California Task Force to Promote Self-Esteem and Personal and Social Responsibility, 1990). In the context of this chapter, sport traditionally has been seen as a potent vehicle for self-esteem or "character" development in children and youth. Also, the success of sport teams at regional and national levels often is seen as boosting civic pride and self-respect.

It is impressive that a phenomenon which remains essentially a mental construction, real only in the mind of the individual, has been assigned such significance. However, there are good reasons why self-esteem and its related self-perception constructs have attracted so much attention:

• For some time, self-esteem has been recognized widely as a key marker for mental well-being (Sonstroem, 1984). For example, it is strongly associated with such positive qualities as emotional stability, adjustment to life demands (coping with stress), happiness, and life satisfaction (Diener & Diener, 1995), at least in Western societies.

• Low self-esteem often accompanies mental disorders such as clinical depression, trait anxiety, neuroses, low assertiveness, sense of powerlessness, and suicidal tendencies (Brown, 1993). As a result, low self-esteem often has been identified as a key target for therapy (Rogers, 1951; Wylie, 1979).

• High self-esteem is associated with a range of positive qualities such as social adjustment, independence, adaptability, leadership, and a high level of achievement in education, work, and sport (Wylie, 1989).

• Self-esteem and more specific self-perceptions are tied closely to how we choose to invest our time and effort and whether we persist in or withdraw from the range of life arenas on offer (Harter, 1996). This includes which sports we might pursue and how well we perform and persevere in them. Also, our choices of health behaviors such as smoking, alcohol and drug use, and eating habits (which are all critical to sport performance) are associated with our self-perceptions.

In summary, where freedom of choice and expression have become increasingly possible, as in the developed world, the self has become critical to the explanation of human functioning and performance (Baumeister, 1987). The search for self-esteem is so strong that it was labeled by Campbell (1984) as the First Psychological Law of Human Nature, expressing how people invest a large amount of their mental and physical energy in a lifelong struggle to validate who they are or who they feel they should be. Certainly, if sport psychologists wish to understand individuals, their state of mind, their level of well-being, and how they function in settings such as sport and exercise, they cannot afford to ignore how individuals view themselves in general and in these specific life contexts. At the same time, sport is an increasingly common life experience, and because of its public nature, its function as an arena for demonstrating prowess, and the strong cultural values underpinning sport, it has particular potential to affect the individual and his or her sense of self.

This chapter sets out theory and research regarding the interaction of sport and exercise involvement and the self. Specifically, I outline views of how self-concept is structured, how it is assessed, how it influences sport participation and performance, and, conversely, how sport and exercise involvement can contribute to shaping the self. Throughout, I draw implications for future research.

THE SELF-SYSTEM

The self is best regarded as a complex system. Several relatively modern theories are consistent with this view, including a model of the self provided by Epstein (1973), self-schemata theory (Markus & Wurf, 1987), and organismic integration theory (Deci & Ryan, 1991). Harter (1996) provided an excellent summary of influential thinking on the self-system, some of which dates back many decades. There is general agreement that the self has an organizational function, which has been referred to as *self-direction*. It gathers and acts on the information that is constantly fed into the self through its interactions with the world. The notion of the *self-director* is reflected in the writings of James (1892), who distinguished between the "I" as the subject of self and the "Me" as the object of self. The "I" is the element of the self that is capable of knowing and making judgements about the "Me" of the self. The analogy of the function of the large corporation illustrates this distinction. The "I," the subjective self, or the self-director could be compared with the chief executive whose job it is to produce a managerial structure and a production strategy and to keep account of activities. The "Me" or objective self would be the structure of the company itself, its various departments, how they operate, and the activities they are involved with.

This comparison helps us sort out some of the confused terminology in the literature. The terms *self-concept* and *self-esteem* often have been used interchangeably, particularly in research before the 1990s. However, self-concept is best viewed as the self-description of the corporation and all it achieves. It is based on the abilities, activities, qualities, traits, personal philosophies, morals and values, and roles adopted by the self. When Murphy (1947) described the self-concept as "the individual as known to the individual" (p. 996), he meant the "Me" as known by the "I." The term *identity* is seen more frequently in the sociology or educational psychology literature (see Erikson, 1968; Marcia, 1980; Stryker, 1987) and overlaps considerably but usually implies more than the self-concept. It describes the self as a dynamic system that is in a constant state of reorganization in its attempt to integrate the various components into a consistent and coherent whole (seeking or developing identity).

The main outcome of the self, as with the corporation, is a healthy balance sheet. Self-esteem or *self-worth* is the equivalent of the annual financial report on how well this mission is being achieved. Whereas self-concept is essentially descriptive, self-esteem is evaluative, and Campbell (1984) defined it as "an awareness of good possessed by self " (p. 9). The criteria on which self-esteem is based vary among individuals. For the company director, certain factors such as profit and public relations cannot be ignored. Similarly, the dominant culture in which the individual exists will exert influences. In the developed Western world, for example, sporting prowess, educational attainment, job performance, physical appearance (particularly slimness), and financial success are particularly valued, and self-ratings in most of these areas are closely related to an individual's self-esteem (Harter, 1996). People also ascribe to subcultures and adopt their values. Sporting groups clearly emphasize physical abilities and status and perhaps personality characteristics such as competitiveness. Criminal subcultures or religious groups have their own priorities. Some people may be relatively free from cultural constraints and express "individualism" or even "quirkiness," whereas others may be viewed as more conformist and perhaps may be seen as submissive, "victims of fashion," or "influenced by peer pressure." In this latter sense, some theorists such as Cooley (1902) would argue that we adopt a *looking-glass self* that simply reflects how others see us. In other words, we are what we think we are simply because those around us see us that way. Symbolic interactionists (Hall, 1992) have followed this notion and believe that the self can be explained largely in terms of the fragmented set of social roles it has to play and that any central and stable core of self is either nonexistent or weak.

Regardless of the influences, the criteria by which self-esteem is determined ultimately reflect the value and priority system adopted by the individual, even if they originate from the culture or those close to the individual. Self-esteem is therefore based on being an "OK person" dependent on what the individual considers as OK. This underpinned the views of James (1892), who suggested that self-esteem could be expressed as a function of the degree to which an individual perceived that he or she was meeting personal aspirations. These points are critical, because they suggest that self-esteem cannot be understood without an accompanying analysis of (a) the cultures to which the individual ascribes, (b) the value systems of those cultures, and (c) the degree to which the individual adopts the values of those cultures. Frequently, these matters have not been considered in self-esteem research, and this needs to be kept in mind when exploring the literature.

The scope for individuality has increased as the constraints of social class, religion, and strong family ties have reduced (Baumeister, 1987), and as a result, the self has become more complex. It is not unusual in recent literature to see the self described as several self-concepts or identities linked together. In essence, the job of the self-director has become increasingly demanding, because it requires the integration of many elements of the self into an efficient and effective system or

© Human Kinetics

Sporting groups form subcultures that exert influences on an individual's self-worth.

identity. This traditionally has been seen as the main task of adolescence, but increasingly it seems to be a lifelong struggle as employment, family, and marriage have become less stable and predictable.

Self-Esteem Enhancement Strategies

The purpose of the self-director is to organize information and then determine where to invest time and energy in serving the mission of the company. This will involve directing choice and persistence in activities and it will require a range of public relations strategies for maximizing success and presenting the company in the best possible light. These strategies may be used internally to convince the self that it is doing well or externally to convince others. The following have been recognized as strategies used by individuals to promote or protect their sense of self:

• *Self-serving bias* is evident in the interpretation of incoming information. Negative information is more likely to be ignored and forgotten, and the most is made out of successes and acclaim. The self is more likely to attribute success to its own efforts and ability and failure to external factors such as luck and lack of control (Blaine & Crocker, 1993).

• To minimize the amount of negative information filtering through to self-esteem, individuals may actively reduce the importance of elements where they exhibit low competence. The term *discounting* has been used to explain the attachment of low importance value to inadequacies, which in effect removes them from the individual's self-esteem complex. However, some areas that carry a high cultural currency such as attractiveness may be too overpowering for an individual to discount, and studies have shown that this is particularly the case for girls (Harter, 1996) and young women (Fox, 1990). This element therefore often becomes detrimental to self-esteem.

• The self also uses external public relations techniques or *self-presentational strategies*, such as developing a confident style, to convince others that it is doing well (Leary, 1995). In return, it is more likely to receive positive responses such as smiles, compliments, or even preferential treatment by others.

Some of this processing may operate at the conscious level, whereas much will remain at the subconscious level and will be inaccessible to the in-

dividual (Guidano, 1986). To a point, self-serving strategies are beneficial and regarded as healthy because they help build confidence and provide a buffer in times of adversity. Absence of their use is one of the strongest predictors of low self-esteem (Blaine & Crocker, 1993).

However, there may be a potential for the self to become excessive in these strategies. For example, it is possible to become overprotective and exclude stimuli and challenges that might develop the self, as in the case of those with low self-esteem. On the other hand, it is possible to be deluded and develop an inflated self-view that is out of touch with the realities of the social world in which the self exists. Furthermore, self-presentation may be played too forcefully in an attempt to compensate for an underlying lack of self-belief. These types of self-protection or presentation strategies are likely to result in less effective social functioning and, in the long term, curtailed development. These notions have emerged through clinical and counseling psychology and remain underresearched at the normative level. In addition, discounting certain behaviors that are inherently important to health, such as exercise, also could be detrimental.

Establishing and maintaining self-esteem is a complex process. Although humans seem to have an intrinsic drive to explore and develop the self, there is also a need to establish and protect a coherent base from which to operate. Thus, stability across time and consistency across situations in patterns of behaviors and emotional reactions provide the sense of identity and predictability that ties the self together. This stability, in turn, equips the individual with the roots necessary for the challenges of personal learning and growth. The self, therefore, is left with a delicate balancing act of establishing a solid and recognizable core, while at the same time remaining open to the challenges of personal development and change, a process that is all too apparent in adolescence.

The Components of the Self-System

The importance of the self began to be recognized by contemporary psychologists with the decline of drive theory and behaviorism and the upsurge of interest in personality in the 1950s and 1960s. By the 1970s, self-esteem had become the construct of the day, and there was a rush of empirical activity. A simplistic unidimensional view of self-esteem was adopted, and this was reflected in instrument design. Items eliciting a diverse array of self-ratings of personal characteristics from facial features to social skills were thrown together and summed to produce self-esteem scores. Groups based on all sorts of factors, such as gender, age, or educational or sporting achievement, were then compared on self-esteem. Unfortunately, this era of research did not take us very far in understanding what the self is, how it operates, and how it might change (Wylie, 1979, 1989).

Epstein (1973), one of the first theorists to present the idea that the self was multidimensional, suggested that perceived competence, moral self-approval, power, and love-worthiness were key contributing components. Similarly, Coopersmith (1967) suggested that dimensions included competence, virtue, power, and significance. Fitts (1965) was probably the first to operationalize multidimensionality into an instrument. The Tennessee Self-Concept Scale attempts to assess physical, moral–ethical, family, personal, and social dimensions of self-concept, and this instrument has featured heavily in sport- and exercise-related research throughout the last 30 years, largely because of its inclusion of a separate physical self subscale.

Recently, the competence domain has been addressed more closely, and a *self-perception profiles* approach has been used which has clearly established that self-ratings are differentiated according to the domain of life being addressed. Notably, Harter (1985) developed the Self-Perception Profile for Children, which assesses self-ratings of academic, social, and behavioral conduct, athletic ability, and appearance. Profiles of increasing multidimensionality that assess a more complex set of competencies such as work, same-sex relationships, and opposite-sex relationships have been developed for adolescents (Harter, 1988), college students (Neemann & Harter, 1986), and adults (Messer & Harter, 1986). Marsh developed the Self-Description Questionnaire series along similar lines (Marsh, 1992).

Within these theoretical tenets, overall or global self-esteem or self-worth is seen to exist as an outcome of the range of self-ratings made by the individual. It is best measured by a separate subscale by using items that avoid domain-specific content such as job competence or physical attractiveness and that provide self-related summaries such as pride in oneself and general level of competence. Rosenberg's 10-item Global Self-Esteem Scale (Rosenberg, 1965) was designed with these principles in mind, and similar general self-worth subscales feature in the profiles of Harter and Marsh. The recent development of instrumentation that accommodates multidimensionality in this way has allowed the relationships between the subcomponents of competence and global self-esteem to be systematically investigated for the first time.

The Structure of the Self-System

After the development of multidimensionality in self-concept research came discussion on how the separate components were organized in relationship to each other. Marsh discussed the topic of self-concept structures in detail (Marsh, 1997; Marsh & Hattie, 1996), including multifaceted, taxonomic, and hierarchical models, and how this topic has mirrored developments in research on the content and structure of intelligence. The self-concept model that has captured most research attention to date is that of Shavelson, Hubner, and Stanton (1976; see figure 4.1). Their model was restricted in the sense that it focused on competencies, particularly those that might have relevance to education. Four life domains were specified—the physical, social, academic, and emotional selves—each of which was subdivided further into levels of increasing specificity. Thus, a rootlike hierarchical system was proposed with quite specific self-perceptions of ability at the base and global self at the apex. The view was that daily experiences would produce specific self-perceptions of ability that might eventually, with repetition, generalize to higher levels of perceived competence in the hierarchy. Subsequently, these might influence self-esteem. Specific self-perceptions are hypothesized to be more changeable, whereas global self-esteem is seen to be more stable and enduring. Marsh developed the Self-Description Questionnaire series around this structure and validated, through a series of advanced statistical techniques, its multidimensionality and to a lesser extent its hierarchical properties.

The Physical Self and the Self-System

Of particular relevance to sport participation and performance is the physical self, and this has been assigned an important role throughout the recent developments in self-concept theory. It consistently has emerged as a critical component of the overall self and is related to a range of important health and achievement behaviors and global

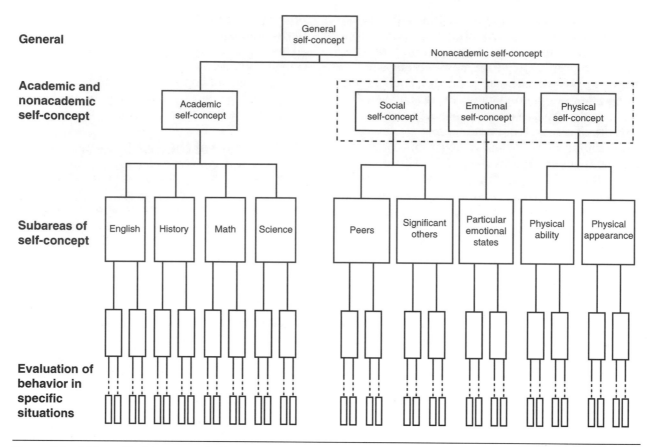

Figure 4.1 A hierarchical structure of self-concept.

Reprinted, by permission, from G.R. Shavelson, J.J. Hubner, and G.C. Stanton, 1976, "Self-concept: Validation of Construct Interpretations". *Review of Educational Research, 46*: 413. Copyright 1976 by the American Educational Research Association.

self-esteem. Instruments to measure specific aspects of the physical self have been around for some time. For example, Secord and Jourard's Body Cathexis Scale (1953), which measures self-perceptions of different body parts, has been used in many studies. In 1976, Sonstroem published results with the Physical Estimation Scale, designed as a unidimensional measure of perceived sports and physical abilities. There were also several other attempts at assessing perceived sports competence or ability. However, the existence of a physical self, which was assessed initially through appearance and physical ability components, was validated through factor analysis of comprehensive self-perception profiles that emerged in the 1980s. Low correlations between the physical self components and other elements of self-concept such as the academic or social self established the independence of the physical self. In addition, consistent, moderately strong relationships between the physical self components and global self-esteem confirmed the importance of self-perceptions in the physical domain to overall well-being. The correlation between physical appearance and self-esteem, for example, typically has been around *r* = .7 in populations throughout the life span. This has led some researchers to suggest that the physical self, because it represents the physical interface between the self and the world, is inevitably tied to self-presentation and is better regarded as the *public self*.

In the late 1980s, greater attention was drawn to systematically identifying the content and structure of the physical self. Ryckman, Robbins, Thornton, and Cantrell (1982) derived the three-subscale Physical Self-Efficacy Scale through factor analysis. Lintunen (1987) developed the Perceived Physical Competence Scale for Children, which features Physical Performance Capacity and Physical Appearance subscales. In 1989, Fox and Corbin published the Physical Self-Perception Profile (PSPP), which is a 30-item, five-subscale instrument assessing perceived sport competence, physical conditioning, physical strength, and body attractiveness. The content of these subscales was derived through analysis of open-ended interviews and questionnaire responses of college students. The fifth scale, which contains six items, provides a separate assessment of overall physical self-worth that is hypothesized to represent global feelings about self within the physical domain at a higher level in the self-perception hierarchy than the remaining subscales. More recently, Marsh, Richards, Johnson, Roche, and Tremayne (1994) developed the Physical Self-Description Questionnaire (PSDQ), a 70-item instrument that assesses nine elements of the physical self: strength, body fat, activity, endurance fitness, sports competence, coordination, appearance, flexibility, and health. The instrument also includes Physical Self-Concept and Global Self-Concept subscales.

In addition, the development of instruments that focus on specific elements of the physical self continues to increase. These tend to fall into three categories: physical and sports ability measures (see Feltz & Chase, 1998), body image and self-presentational measures (see Bane & McAuley, 1998), and self-efficacy for physical challenges (see McAuley & Mihalko, 1998).

It now seems clear that physical self-perceptions can be measured successfully at different levels of specificity. Self-perceptions of task competence or ability similar to self-efficacy statements are possible at the most specific levels. These might eventually, through sufficient repetition, produce generalized perceptions of competence or ability.

Perceived ability to successfully shoot a basketball free throw in the last minutes of a game eventually might produce high levels of perceived shooting competence. This, in turn, might generalize to perceived competence in basketball and sports in general. General physical competence might contribute to physical self-worth. Thus, self-perceptions can be conceptualized and assessed at various levels of hierarchical self-concept structures, such as that provided by Shavelson et al. (1976) featured in figure 4.1. The PSPP, for example, assesses content at the subdomain level in addition to providing the Physical Self-Worth subscale to measure overall perceptions at the domain level. Figure 4.2 provides examples of self-constructs at different levels of specificity within the physical self.

Further work that is highly significant to the study of the physical self has been conducted under the theoretical framework of identity development. Brettschneider and Heim (1997) described a typology of physical identities in German youth that is delineated by beliefs and self-perceptions regarding sport and lifestyles. Athletic identity, or the degree to which an individual described him- or herself as athletic, was studied by Brewer, Van Raalte, and Linder (1993), and the construct has demonstrated logical relationships with other physical self-perceptions. Kendzierski (1994) adopted self-schema theory (Markus, 1977) to investigate exercise identity. Specific identities

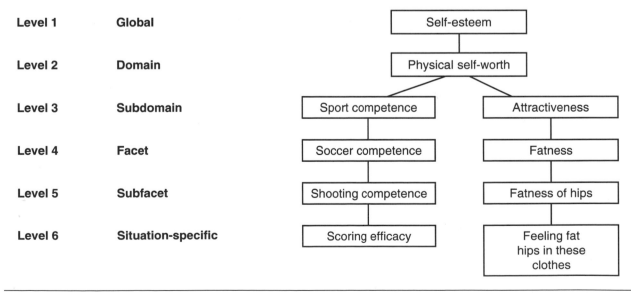

Figure 4.2 Levels of specificity of self-perceptions within the physical domain.

Reprinted from K.R. Fox, 1998, Advances in measurement of the physical self. In *Advances in sport and exercise psychology measurement*, edited by J.L. Duda (Morgantown, WV: Fitness Information Tech., Inc.), 298. Copyright 1998 by the American Educational Research Association. Reproduced with permission from the publisher.

or self-schemata are seen to be determined by self-descriptions, beliefs, and behaviors, and studies have examined the criteria that individuals use to self-define as an exerciser and also the correlates and consequences of such membership (Kendzierski, Furr, & Schiavoni, 1998). Thus, an integrated approach is taken to help describe how the physical self is psychologically and emotionally attached to behavioral roles. The study of identity and schema may be particularly insightful in furthering our understanding of the exercise adoption and maintenance process.

This wealth of theory and instrumentation, which has included profiles and individual scales, has provided a much-needed boost to research in this area of the self. With particular regard to the sport focus of this chapter, some important statements can now be made:

- The physical self is clearly multidimensional. This has been established consistently through confirmatory factor analysis of multidimensional instruments (Fox & Corbin, 1989; Marsh et al., 1994). Sports or athletic competence appears to be an integral part throughout the life span.

- There are several levels of specificity of self-perceptions within the physical domain, from state-like measures similar to self-efficacy statements, to general physical competence, to global physical self-worth.

- The physical self is, at least in part, hierarchically organized. The physical self-worth subscale of the PSPP has been shown in several studies (Fox & Corbin, 1989; Eklund, Whitehead, & Welk, 1997; Sonstroem, Harlow, & Josephs, 1994) to mediate relationships between the specific subdomains and global self-esteem.

- The physical self may develop as a set of specific identities, such as athlete, exerciser, bodybuilder, basketball player, and dancer, which are accompanied by supportive psychological and behavioral profiles. These may have strong motivational properties and provide a useful approach to understanding adoption and maintenance of sport and exercise (Brettschneider & Heim, 1997; Kendzierski, 1994).

Assessment of the Physical Self

Although important advances have been made in physical self instrumentation in the past decade, the array on offer has become somewhat daunting. However, several good volumes are available to guide the researcher. Most notable are Byrne's

Measuring Self-Concept Across the Lifespan (1996), Duda's *Advances in Sport and Exercise Psychology Measurement* (1998), and Ostrow's *Directory of Psychological Tests in the Sport and Exercise Sciences* (1996). Because of our better understanding of the content and structure of the physical domain and self-concept instrumentation in general, it is possible to suggest several general rules for instrumentation selection:

1. Choose well-validated, reliable instruments. Establishing instrument integrity is a long, complex process and has been discussed in more detail elsewhere (Fox, 1998; Marsh, 1997). If we are to move further with research, we must focus on instruments that we can trust. We are fortunate in having two comprehensive perception profiles (the PSPP and PSDQ) in the physical domain that have been critically appraised and achieved some acclaim (Byrne, 1996). These should be given careful consideration alongside other instruments that have established various forms of reliability and validity and that have content relevant to the research question.

2. Choose instruments that have a strong theoretical foundation. Without theoretical underpinnings, it is difficult to attach meaning to results or place findings in context with other studies. Research then remains at a superficially descriptive level, and little progress is made in understanding the mechanisms involved in the sport–self interface.

3. Determine the nature of self-related content addressed by the research question. This can be diverse, even within the physical domain, which includes content such as body image, sport competence, exercise or movement confidence, social physique anxiety, physical health, and physical independence. It is critical to seek out a selection of instruments or subscales that provide rich documentation of the mediating or outcome variables that operationalize the research question.

4. Determine the degree of focus of the research question. It is now possible to assess physical self-perceptions across a wide range of specificities from global to statelike constructs (see figure 4.2). A research question that is to assess the mechanisms of change in the self through soccer involvement might require the assessment of soccer-related self-efficacy ("I can do that" statements), perceptions of soccer-related abilities such as tackling and shooting, and more general self-measures such as sports competence and physical self-worth.

5. Consider other domains and mechanisms outside sport-related perceptions. Some research questions might require physical self-perceptions to be assessed alongside other elements of self such as those in the social domain, particularly if change in the social self is seen as a potential mechanism. Where well-being is the key issue, global measures of the self, alongside other indicators such as life satisfaction and emotional adjustment, would need consideration.

Instrument choice remains a critical challenge and requires careful preparation. Too frequently studies fail, not because they were designed or conducted badly, but because the instrumentation was inappropriate or insufficiently sensitive or reliable to reflect true findings.

THE SELF IN SPORT AND EXERCISE

The self interacts with many life domains daily. One reason why the physical domain is so critical is that the self is presented primarily through the body and is intimately involved with the physical environment. Some of this is incidental through the physical tasks of our daily routines, and some of it is formally organized such as in sport, exercise, or dance participation. These interactions can be viewed conceptually from two contrasting perspectives. *Self-enhancement* describes mechanisms by which the self dictates and drives its energies into increasing its worth. *Skill enhancement* describes processes by which involvement in activities can produce change that reshapes the self.

Self-Enhancement Motives and Sport and Exercise

The concept of self-enhancement draws on Campbell's notion that a basic drive in the individual is to maximize opportunities of feeling good and that this is reflected in choice and persistence in behaviors. This implies a flow of energy or motivational force from the individual that is manifested in how and where time and energy are invested. The general tenet of this approach is that individuals will gravitate to elements of life where there is a potentially high payoff (either in the short or long term) and will avoid situations that produce failure, threat, or embarrassment. Several theories that have been applied to sport have been built along these lines including achievement motivation (Nicholls, 1989), competence motiva-

tion (Harter, 1978), personal investment (Maehr & Braskamp, 1986), self-efficacy (Bandura, 1977), and expectancy-value (Biddle, 1997).

The Role of Perceived Competence and Ability

To confirm these theories in sport, it has to be shown that those who are involved in sport will have a higher level of perceived sport competence or ability and expectancy of success than those who are not. The self will be driven to demonstrate its high abilities and avoid the exposure of low abilities. The degree to which this can be an intrinsic motive directed out of curiosity or a drive to take charge of the physical world along the lines of White's (1959) effectance motivation theory (as in the infant who strives to walk or climb stairs) remains unclear. A more dominant motive may be the desire to seek an arena where competence can be displayed to others and where acclaim and recognition might be the reward. The conditions under which such mechanisms operate, particularly with regard to developmental stages in children,

© Human Kinetics

The concept of self-enhancement implies that an individual will choose to participate in activities that might offer a high payoff.

still present interesting research questions. Deci and Ryan's (1991, 1995) self-determination theory provides an opportunity to examine the relationship between such behavioral motives and the nature of self.

Sonstroem's Psychological Model of Physical Activity Participation, one of the first models in the field of the psychosociology of sport, was fundamentally a self-enhancement model. Sonstroem (1976) hypothesized that perceived physical ability (as assessed by the Physical Estimation Scale) led to attraction to physical activity, subsequent participation, improved physical ability, and improved physical estimation. Physical estimation then had the potential to improve global self-esteem. Of course, the reverse of this upward spiral is possible, with low physical estimation leading to avoidance of physical activity, little improvement in ability, and perhaps a reduction in estimation.

There is considerable support for an association between elements of physical competence and sport and exercise involvement. Research with the newer physical self-perception profiles such as the PSPP and the PSDQ, as well as with older instruments such as the Physical Self-Efficacy Scale (Ryckman et al., 1982), has clearly indicated this in children and adults. Those who have higher self-ratings of competence in subdomains such as sport competence, strength, and physical conditioning are more likely to be physically active. The PSPP alone, for example, has consistently classified between 70% and 80% of inactive and active college students (Fox & Corbin, 1989), middle-aged men (Sonstroem, Speliotis, & Fava, 1992), and older adults (Chase & Corbin, 1992). It also has predicted 26% of variance in female adult attendance at exercise classes (Sonstroem et al., 1994). Furthermore, in one study (Fox & Corbin, 1989) that used canonical correlation analyses to investigate the relationship between activity and self-perceptions, the PSPP competence subscales were closely related to the type of activity participation. Marsh and Redmayne (1994) also showed that elements of physical self-perceptions such as perceived strength and fatness are most closely related to the corresponding performance measure such as grip strength dynamometer or skinfold scores, respectively.

The association between perceived sport ability/competence and participation (Roberts, Kleiber, & Duda, 1981; Weiss & Petlichkoff, 1989) and dropout from sport in youngsters (Feltz & Brown, 1984; Feltz & Petlichkoff, 1983) also has been established for some time. Perceived

athleticism clearly is related to involvement in athletic pursuits by early adolescence, and this continues to predict involvement in sport throughout the life span.

Although there is theoretical and intuitive logic to this association, the evidence to support a *causal* role for the self as an instigator of behavioral decisions in the sport setting is limited. Logical competing hypotheses also are available, a simple example being that the competitive nature of sport causes low-competence participants to be eliminated through nonselection by coaches. However, a few studies have used longitudinal design to address the degree to which self-ratings determine degree of involvement. An early study by Sonstroem and Kampper (1980) showed that the physical self-concept of junior high school boys was predictive of a subsequent decision to enroll in a sports program. Lintunen and colleagues (1995), in a 4-year study, indicated that self-selection based on self-perceptions of physical ability was already taking place by age 11.

Even longitudinal analysis of groups does not fully elucidate causal ordering. The relationship between the individual and sport involvement is likely to be both subtle and reciprocal. More intense study is required, perhaps using within-subject design, which assesses the role of physical self-perceptions in the decision-making process around critical events such as recruitment, selection, and deselection in sport and transition from middle to high school. Also required is clearer documentation of the conditions under which coaches and teachers can produce high perceived competence in children of all levels of sport ability. Research into motivational climate in sport and exercise has developed rapidly. It has a lot to offer our understanding of the interaction between perceived competence, achievement predispositions, and how the experiences of sport, exercise, and physical education can be designed and delivered to promote motivation and self-esteem in children (Papaioannou & Goudas, 1999).

The impact of subcomponents of the physical self on sport behavior has been addressed to a greater extent than the influence of global self-esteem. Only one sport study has used a longitudinal design to specifically address the impact of self-esteem on future sport performance (Sonstroem, Harlow, & Salisbury, 1993). In this study, self-esteem was predictive of swimming achievements across a season. There are also many other interesting issues to address. High self-esteem, for example, may equip individuals with the courage to venture into unknown domains of competence or an area where they already have experienced low perceived competence. Such drive is likely to enhance development and learning. Conversely, low self-esteem may cause conservatism, overdefensiveness, caution, or an overreliance on those areas where competence is already established and a subsequent stifling of progress. These hypotheses have not been addressed within the sport and exercise domains.

Self-Presentational Motives

Because the body provides the most common way in which we deliver our self to the public, the way we judge our appearance and present our body becomes critical to understanding a range of behaviors. The need to look attractive and confident is likely to be as powerful as the need to be physically competent in sport and exercise. This may affect sport and exercise behavior in several ways. In the same way that those who are highly skilled in sport are attracted to demonstrate such prowess, situations where the body is on open access to the public gaze offer opportunities for body display. This is particularly true where the body is scantily clad, such as gymnastics, swimming, track and field, or various forms of dance, or where the body is actively shaped and molded through resistance or endurance training, as in some health clubs or power lifting gyms. Similarly, the salience of self-presentational motives may be stronger in individual than team sports, where attention of the coach and audience is more focused on the single player.

Conversely, self-presentational concerns may deter participation and hinder performance in sport. For example, Wilson and Eklund (1998) developed the Self-Presentation in Sport Scale and found that self-presentational concerns such as feeling as though performance was inadequate, not looking athletic, or appearing fatigued were moderately correlated to state competitive anxiety. It seems that many athletes are concerned about impression management during events, and this ultimately may affect performances. There is scope to develop this line of work alongside other factors that contribute to anxiety, such as perfectionism and neuroticism (Hall, Kerr, & Matthews, 1998).

Of interest to those concerned about promoting activity in the overweight or very unfit, such groups are likely to have an aversion to situations where the body is on public display. To date, this has been researched primarily through the study of *social physique anxiety* (Bane & McAuley, 1998; Eklund & Crawford, 1994; Hart, Leary, & Rejeski, 1989; Leary, 1992, 1995), which is defined as "a subtype of social anxiety that occurs as a result of the prospect or presence of interpersonal evaluation of one's physique" (Hart et al., 1989, p. 96). The Social Physique Anxiety Scale, originally developed by Hart et al., was used in several studies throughout the 1990s. Although there remains some debate regarding its unidimensional status, it has shown logical relationships with several constructs including a range of physical self-perceptions (Petrie, Diehl, Rogers, & Johnson, 1996). In addition, intervention studies (McAuley, Bane, & Mihalko, 1995; McAuley, Bane, Rudolph, & Lox, 1995) have indicated that social physique anxiety can be reduced through careful exercise program leadership and delivery. This area of research has strong theoretical underpinnings and holds considerable promise in aiding exercise and sport participation across the age groups.

Self-Deficiency Motives

There may be occasions where competence and self-presentational motives and anxieties, which provide positive associations with sport participation along the normal lines of self-enhancement, just do not apply. For example, there may be strong reasons for taking part in an activity in the absence of perceived competence or the presence of low perceived body attractiveness or high social physique anxiety. This is most likely to operate when the benefits of taking part in the related behavior are so important to the individual that any perceived inadequacy is overridden. In the exercise domain, this is most likely to occur where participation is driven through a desire for health improvement, such as a patient rehabilitating from a coronary incident or an obese person who needs to lose weight. There are also examples in sport where individuals take part because they are highly motivated to overcome their perceived and actual incompetence, such as the adult who never learned to swim as a youngster. There may be a need to prove worth by overcoming fears and difficulties. Similarly, other self-deficiency motives may be operating that emanate from outside the physical domain. The social motive of needing to feel affiliation or acceptance of a group, for example, may stimulate a youngster to turn out regularly for the soccer team, even if it means remaining on the bench and even if perceived soccer competence remains low.

Self-deficiency motives such as these have not been considered systematically in the sport domain. However, if they are found to occur, they will weaken the generally moderate positive associations observed between perceived competence/adequacy and participation. They are particularly evident in settings involved in exercise for weight loss or weight management. The relationship between constructs such as body image and perceived body attractiveness and exercise participation has been weak in males and often insignificant in females. This is probably explained by large numbers reacting to culture-driven pressures to be slim and toned. Although many use exercise and sport to display their attractiveness (as in self-enhancement motive), this may be offset by many who are motivated to remove the source of their feelings of low attractiveness (as in the self-deficiency motive), which in this case is perceived overfatness. This confounds and weakens the self-behavior relationship. This kind of anomaly needs careful consideration by researchers, and it calls for greater efforts to identify participation motives alongside self-perceptions. Perhaps it is time to revisit personal investment (Maehr & Braskamp, 1986), popular in the late 1980s, where the self and the motives and barriers to exercise are combined in a single model to define the meaning of sport or exercise to the individual.

Perceived Importance and Self-Enhancement

There is a logic to the concept that personal skills and characteristics that are not important to an individual will have no effect on the person's sense of worth. An extension of this view is that individuals will actively seek to reduce the importance of those areas of life in which they demonstrate low competence. This has attracted considerable attention by a range of theorists as far back as James (1892) and including Rosenberg (1965) and Harter (1996). Harter advocated the calculation of a discrepancy index that represents the difference between perceived competence and importance for those particular domains or subdomains of life experience that are deemed important. These ideas have been applied to the physical self by using the Physical Importance Profile that accompanies the PSPP (Fox, 1990). Consistent findings have been achieved across samples from children (Whitehead, 1995) to older adults (Chase, 1991) that show a moderate, negative dose–response relationship between discrepancy indexes and both physical and global self-worth. Those whose aspirations are not matched by their competencies have a lower sense of worth. This is further supported by evidence showing that correlations between importance and competence are lower in those with lower physical self-worth (Fox, 1997). This suggests that those who have higher self-esteem are more easily able to discount their inadequacies in the physical domain and match their good points with high importance. This is apparent in young adolescent girls who perceive low sports competence but who also attach a low importance to it. This is in direct contrast to the combination of high importance of appearance and poor body image, which is related to lower self-esteem in females. Once again, we return to the importance of understanding values and the impact of culture when studying self-perceptions and their impact on well-being and behaviors.

Unfortunately, this empirical line has not been supported by findings from the regression modeling approach used by Marsh and Sonstroem (1995). Their models failed to show that perceived importance ratings explained added variance to the prediction of self-worth above and beyond perceived competence scores. On the other hand, perceived importance ratings have added to the explanation of physical activity participation. It remains puzzling why these two approaches have not yielded compatible findings. However, current perceived importance instrumentation has not proved to be psychometrically robust, and further work is required to test the importance hypothesis, perhaps by using identity and schema theories. The supportive evidence and its intuitive appeal make it difficult to ignore.

ENHANCING THE SELF THROUGH SPORT AND EXERCISE INTERVENTIONS

The converse perspective of self-enhancement is skill enhancement (Marsh & Hattie, 1996). Here, it is suggested that improvement of aspects of physical skill or fitness will improve the individual's sense of self. Because a wider range of physical changes than motor and sports skills might be targeted, such as weight loss, muscle gain, and improvements in cardiovascular fitness, strength, and flexibility, the term *intervention hypothesis* has been used (Fox, 1997). With this hypothesis, the direction of energy flow is seen to be from the behavior (in this case sport or exercise performance, practice, or participation) and elements of self. Initially, impact on self-esteem was addressed. More recently, the effects of participation on specific aspects of the self such as physical self-worth, body image, or perceived sports competence have been studied. Through this work, it has become clear that improvements in the self may be driven by perceptual change rather than actual physical change.

The intervention hypothesis has underpinned physical education curriculum design around the world and frequently has been used as the basis for involving youth in sport, as in the much-voiced premise that "sport builds character." It also frames the many studies in the field of exercise and mental well-being that have examined the effect of exercise on self-esteem.

The Effectiveness of Sport and Exercise to Enhance Self

Although there has been rapid growth in the number of studies investigating the effect of exercise on psychological disorders such as depression and anxiety, along with many meta-analyses to establish overall effect sizes, progress with exercise and self-esteem research has been slow. Cross-sectional research has (a) compared those taking part in specific sports or exercise modes with those who do not take part, (b) compared those who are fit or normal weight with those who are unfit or overweight, and (c) calculated correlation coefficients between degree of involvement in sport or exercise and self-esteem. At best, these studies provide weak and inconsistent evidence that participation is related to higher levels of self-esteem. However, cross-sectional evidence of this nature does not allow us to eliminate the likelihood of selection bias or establish a causal relationship. It is likely that those who choose to participate in sport are already more confident and achievement-driven and have higher self-esteem on entry.

Self-esteem intervention studies with adults have been reviewed by Sonstroem (1984), and with children by Gruber (1986), and Leith (1994). The most recent review was by Fox (2000), who summarized the outcomes of randomized controlled studies and nonrandomized studies conducted between 1970 and 1999. Both sport and exercise programs were included. Thirty-six randomized controlled studies were reported, and these included nine unpublished theses or dissertations. Randomized controlled studies are particularly important given the susceptibility to socially de-

sirable responding, expectancy effects, self-presentational strategies, and temporary versus lasting effects in self-esteem research (Sonstroem, 1984). In addition, a further 44 non-randomized controlled studies were considered.

Of the 36 randomized controlled studies, 28 (78%) indicated positive changes in some aspects of physical self-esteem or self-perception. This is a robust and significant finding which provides clear evidence that exercise and sport stimulate more positive self-referent thoughts. The results appear strongest for aspects of the physical self (particularly aspects of body image). This is important because such constructs are consistently related to global self-esteem throughout the life span. Furthermore, an important recent study has indicated that *physical self-worth* (from the PSPP), which is the global summary of all perceptions in the physical domain, carries important emotional adjustment qualities. This has been established independently of self-esteem and socially desirable responding on questionnaires (Sonstroem & Potts, 1996). This suggests that physical self-worth should be regarded as a mental health indicator in its own right and should be assessed systematically in interventions. Because physical self-perception profiles featuring global physical self-worth subscales have only appeared in the last 10 years, this critical construct has not been assessed in most studies.

About half the studies showed generalized improvement in global self-esteem. This is similar to the conclusions of Leith (1994) and also those from a meta-analysis by Spence and Poon (1997; yet to be published in full), who concluded that a small (.22) but significant effect size exists for the effect of exercise on self-concept or self-esteem. The inconsistency is possibly due to weak instrumentation, because most of the studies have not adopted recent theoretical developments. However, such a finding is also in line with theory, in that we should not expect a construct that is seen to be the weighted outcome of experiences in many life domains, and one that is so critical to human functioning, to be readily changed across all people. Exercise would have to be extremely powerful to cause a significant group change in a matter of a few weeks.

Models of Exercise and Self-Esteem Research

There is much more to learn about the impact of sport and exercise on psychological well-being.

Certainly, more well-designed studies that use the well-validated instruments now available need to be conducted. The past 30 years have yielded little more than one randomized controlled study per year, which is pitifully small for an issue that is so central to human welfare. Furthermore, current theoretical tenets need to be given careful consideration in study design. Sonstroem and Morgan (1989) presented a testable model that captures the multidimensionality and hierarchical organization of the self in the physical domain. They proposed three levels of self-perception. The model suggests that changes may be initiated at the specific self-efficacy level and that these may eventually generalize to broader perceptions of physical competence at a higher level. Also included at this level is the component of physical acceptance, which is seen to work in tandem with perceptions of competence. At the apex is self-esteem. Each of these is reassessed throughout the intervention, on termination, and on follow-up. Three studies have confirmed the model's structure (Baldwin & Courneya, 1997; Sonstroem, Harlow, Gemma, & Osborne, 1991; Sonstroem et al., 1994), and in the latter study, effective modifications were made that accommodated the subscale structure of the PSPP (see figure 4.3). This modification was outlined in more detail by Sonstroem (1998) and Fox (2000). Its combination of comprehensive instrumentation with theoreti-cal underpinnings to intervention design is noteworthy. However, the model is still awaiting use in further intervention research.

SUMMARY AND FUTURE RESEARCH DIRECTIONS

This chapter has outlined the tremendous progress over the last 15 years in the study of the self in sport and exercise contexts. In particular, new instrumentation has been developed that is both comprehensive and diverse and also well founded in self theory and models. We now have a much more complete understanding of the components of the self, and there is increasing agreement on their definition. Self-esteem is a key concept, because it represents a global self-evaluation that is of prime importance to motivation and mental well-being. The physical self often is seen as the public self and plays an important role in human functioning. The main components and its structure have been documented through improved instrumentation that uses a profile approach to assess its various subdomains. Furthermore, we now have a better understanding of how instruments are placed in comparison to each other and how they should be selected and used.

The relationship of the physical self components to behaviors such as sport and exercise can now

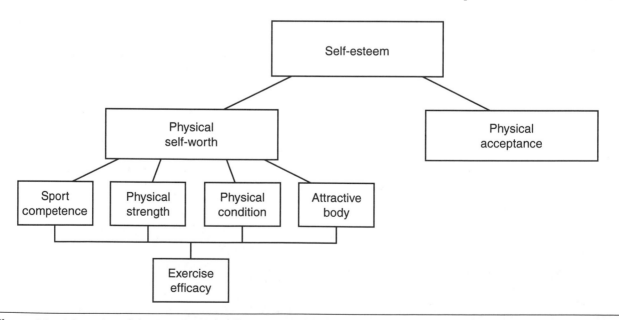

Figure 4.3 Adaptation of the Exercise and Self-Esteem Model (EXSEM) to include the Physical Self-Perception Profile (after Sonstroem et al., 1994).

Reprinted from K.R. Fox, 1998, Advances in measurement of the physical self. In *Advances in sport and exercise psychology measurement*, edited by J.L. Duda (Morgantown, WV: Fitness Information Tech., Inc.), 298. Copyright 1998 by the American Educational Research Association. Reproduced with permission from the publisher.

be studied along with other important elements of the self, such as self-esteem, with more precision.

It is clear that self-perceptions influence choice and persistence in sport and exercise participation from an early age. Less progress has been made concerning the degree to which sport and exercise can improve self-perceptions and self-esteem. There have been few well-designed studies, and little is known about the degree to which the self can be changed or the conditions under which change might occur. Real insight into the self will arise only through a more concerted effort to understand the mechanisms and processes involved in its change and preservation. It could be considered that a positive sense of self is more important to the individual than any other characteristic. We should expect the system that underpins the self to be highly complex, at times subtle, and always intriguing. When the individual is placed in a social context, especially one as powerful and as public as sport or exercise, we can expect a range of mechanisms to be activated. To date, systematic and sequential research into mechanisms involved in change has not been conducted in the physical domain. In particular, we need to know more about the following:

- How sport and exercise involvement creates positive change in individual mental well-being, and the conditions under which that change occurs

- How individuals develop and use self-enhancement strategies including self-presentation in sport and exercise settings

- How sport performance is both driven and hindered by self-referent thought

- How such mechanisms can be harnessed to improve human welfare and well-being

Clearly these are difficult challenges that can be addressed only through a range of research techniques. However, the potential gains are immense in terms of understanding the athlete and the exerciser and their performance and participation.

REFERENCES

Baldwin, M.K., & Courneya, K.S. (1997). Exercise and self-esteem in breast cancer survivors: An application of the Exercise and Self-Esteem Model. *Journal of Sport and Exercise Psychology, 19,* 331–346.

Bandura, A. (1977). Self-efficacy: Toward a unifying theory of behavioral change. *Psychological Review, 84,* 191–215.

Bane, S., & McAuley, E. (1998). Body image and exercise. In J.L. Duda (Ed.), *Advances in sport and exercise psychology measurement* (pp. 311–322). Morgantown, WV: Fitness Information Technology.

Baumeister, R.F. (1987). How the self became a problem: A psychological review of historical research. *Journal of Personality and Social Psychology, 52,* 163–176.

Biddle, S.J.H. (1997). Cognitive theories of motivation and the physical self. In K.R. Fox (Ed.), *The physical self: From motivation to well-being* (pp. 59–82). Champaign, IL: Human Kinetics.

Blaine, B., & Crocker, J. (1993). Self-esteem and self-serving biases in reactions to positive and negative events: An integrative review. In R.F. Baumeister (Ed.), *Self-esteem: The puzzle of low self-regard* (pp. 55–86). New York: Plenum Press.

Brettschneider, W-D., & Heim, R. (1997). Identity, sport and youth development. In K.R. Fox (Ed.), *The physical self: From motivation to well-being* (pp. 205–227). Champaign, IL: Human Kinetics.

Brewer, B.W., Van Raalte, J.L., & Linder, D.E. (1993). Athletic identity: Hercules' muscles or Achilles heel? *International Journal of Sport Psychology, 24,* 237–254.

Brown, J.D. (1993). Motivational conflict and the self: The double bind of low self-esteem. In R.F. Baumeister (Ed.), *Self-esteem: The puzzle of low self-regard* (pp. 117–130). New York: Plenum Press.

Byrne, B.M. (1996). *Measuring self-concept across the lifespan: Issues and instrumentation.* Washington, DC: American Psychological Association.

California Task Force to Promote Self-Esteem and Personal and Social Responsibility. (1990). *Toward a state of self-esteem.* Sacramento: California State Department of Education.

Campbell, R.N. (1984). *The new science: Self-esteem psychology.* Lanham, MD: University Press of America.

Chase, L. (1991). *Physical self-perceptions and activity involvement in the older population.* Unpublished doctoral dissertation, Arizona State University. Tempe, AZ.

Chase, L., & Corbin, C. (1992). Development of the Physical Self-Perception Profile for Older Adults and prediction of activity involvement. *Medicine and Science in Sports and Exercise, 24,* (Supplement) S42.

Cooley, C.H. (1902). *Human nature and the social order.* New York: Scribner's.

Coopersmith, S. (1967). *The antecedents of self-esteem.* San Francisco: Freeman, Cooper.

Deci, E.L., & Ryan, R.M. (1991). A motivational approach to self: Integration in personality. In R. Dienstbier (Ed.), *Nebraska symposium on motivation: Vol. 38: Perspectives on motivation* (pp. 237–288). Lincoln: University of Nebraska.

Deci, E.L., & Ryan, R.M. (1995). Human autonomy: The basis for true self-esteem. In M. Kernis (Ed.), *Efficacy, agency, and self-esteem* (pp. 31–49). New York: Plenum Press.

Diener, E., & Diener, M. (1995). Cross-cultural correlates of life satisfaction and self-esteem. *Journal of Personality and Social Psychology, 68,* 653–663.

Duda, J.L. (Ed.) (1998). *Advances in sport and exercise psychology measurement.* Morgantown, WV: Fitness Information Technology.

Eklund, R.C., & Crawford, S. (1994). Active women, social physique anxiety, and exercise. *Journal of Sport and Exercise Psychology, 16,* 431–448.

Eklund, R.C., Whitehead, J.R., & Welk, G.J. (1997). Validity of the children and youth physical self-perception profile: A confirmatory factor analysis. *Research Quarterly for Exercise and Sport, 68,* 240–256.

Epstein, S. (1973). The self-concept revisited or a theory of a theory. *American Psychologist, 28,* 405–416.

Erikson, E. (1968). *Identity, youth, and crisis.* New York: Norton.

Feltz, D.L., & Brown, E.W. (1984). Perceived competence in soccer skills among youth soccer players. *Journal of Sport Psychology, 6,* 385–394.

Feltz, D.L., & Chase, M. (1998). The measurement of self-efficacy and confidence in sport. In J.L. Duda (Ed.), *Advances in sport and exercise psychology measurement* (pp. 65–80). Morgantown, WV: Fitness Information Technology.

Feltz, D.L., & Petlichkoff, L.M. (1983). Perceived competence among interscholastic sport participants and dropouts. *Canadian Journal of Applied Sports Sciences, 8,* 231–235.

Fitts, W.H. (1965). *Tennessee Self-Concept Scale: Manual.* Los Angeles: Western Psychological Services.

Fox, K.R. (1990). *The Physical Self-Perception Profile Manual.* DeKalb: Office for Health Promotion, Northern Illinois University.

Fox, K.R. (1997). The physical self and processes in self-esteem development. In K.R. Fox (Ed.), *The physical self: From motivation to well-being* (pp. 111–139). Champaign, IL: Human Kinetics.

Fox, K.R. (1998). Advances in the measurement of the physical self. In J.L. Duda (Ed.), *Advances in sport and exercise psychology measurement* (pp. 295–310). Morgantown, WV: Fitness Information Technology.

Fox, K.R. (2000). The effects of exercise on physical self-perceptions and self-esteem. In S.J.H. Biddle, K.R. Fox, & S.H. Boutcher (Eds.), *Physical activity and psychological well-being* (pp. 88–117). London: Routledge & Kegan Paul.

Fox, K.R., & Corbin, C.B. (1989). The Physical Self-Perception Profile: Development and preliminary validation. *Journal of Sport and Exercise Psychology, 11,* 408–430.

Gruber, J.J. (1986). Physical activity and self-esteem development and children: A meta-analysis. *American Academy of Physical Education Papers,* pp. 30–48.

Guidano, V.F. (1986). The self as mediator of cognitive change in psychotherapy. In L.M. Hartman & K.R. Blankstein (Eds.), *Perception of the self in emotional disorder and psychotherapy* (pp. 305–330). New York: Plenum Press.

Hall, H.K., Kerr, A.W., & Matthews, J. (1998). Precompetitive anxiety in sport: The contribution of achievement goals and perfectionism. *Journal of Sport and Exercise Psychology, 20,* 194–217.

Hall, S. (1992). The question of cultural identity. In S. Hall, D. Hell, & T. McGrew (Eds.), *Modernity and its futures* (pp. 374–325). Cambridge: Polity Press.

Hart, E.A., Leary, M.R., & Rejeski, W.A. (1989). The measurement of social physique anxiety. *Journal of Sport and Exercise Psychology, 11,* 94–104.

Harter, S. (1978). Effectance motivation reconsidered: Toward a developmental model. *Human Development, 21,* 34–64.

Harter, S. (1985). *Manual for the Self-Perception Profile for Children.* Denver: University of Denver.

Harter, S. (1988). *Manual for the Self-Perception Profile for Adolescents.* Denver: University of Denver.

Harter, S. (1996). Historical roots of contemporary issues involving self-concept. In B.A. Bracken (Ed.), *Handbook of self-concept* (pp. 1–37). New York: Wiley.

James, W. (1892). *Psychology: The briefer course.* New York: Holt.

Kendzierski, D. (1994). Schema theory: An information processing focus. In R.K. Dishman (Ed.), *Advances in exercise adherence* (pp. 137–159). Champaign, IL: Human Kinetics.

Kendzierski, D., Furr, R.M., & Schiavoni, J. (1998). Physical activity self-definitions: Correlates and perceived criteria. *Journal of Sport and Exercise Psychology, 20,* 176–193.

Leary, M.R. (1992). Self-presentation processes in exercise and sport. *Journal of Sport and Exercise Psychology, 14,* 339–351.

Leary, M.R. (1995). *Self-presentation: Impression management and interpersonal behavior.* Dubuque, IA: Brown & Benchmark.

Leith, L.M. (1994). *Foundations of exercise and mental health.* Morgantown, WV: Fitness Information Technology.

Lintunen, T. (1987). The perceived physical competence scale for children. *Scandinavian Journal of Sports Science, 9,* 57–64.

Lintunen, T., Leskinen, E., Oinonen, M., Salinto, M., & Rahkila, P. (1995). Change, reliability, and stability in self-perceptions in early adolescence: A four-year follow-up study. *International Journal of Behavioral Development, 18,* 351–364.

Maehr, M.L., & Braskamp, L.A. (1986). *The motivation factor: A theory of personal investment.* Lexington, MA: Lexington Books.

Marcia, J. (1980). Identity in adolescence. In J. Adelson (Ed.), *Handbook of adolescent psychology* (pp. 159–187). New York: Wiley.

Markus, H. (1977). Self-schemata and processing information about the self. *Journal of Personality and Social Psychology, 35,* 118–133.

Markus, H., & Wurf, E. (1987). The dynamic self-concept: A social psychological perspective. *Annual Review of Psychology, 38,* 299–337.

Marsh, H.W. (1992). *Self-Description Questionnaire (SDQ) II: A theoretical and empirical basis for the measurement of multiple dimensions of adolescent self-concept. A test manual and research monograph.* Macarthur, New South Wales, Australia: University of Western Sydney, Faculty of Education.

Marsh, H.W. (1997). The measurement of physical self-concept: A construct validation approach. In K.R. Fox (Ed.), *The physical self: From motivation to well-being* (pp. 27–58). Champaign, IL: Human Kinetics.

Marsh, H.W., & Hattie, J. (1996). Theoretical perspectives on the structure of self-concept. In B.A. Bracken (Ed.), *Handbook of self-concept* (pp. 38–90). New York: Wiley.

Marsh, H.W., & Redmayne, R.S. (1994). A multidimensional physical self-concept and its relation to multiple components of physical fitness. *Journal of Sport and Exercise Psychology, 16,* 45–55.

Marsh, H.W., Richards, G., Johnson, S., Roche, L., & Tremayne, P. (1994). Physical Self Description Questionnaire: Psychometric properties and a multitrait-multimethod analysis of relations to existing instruments. *Journal of Sport and Exercise Psychology, 16,* 270–305.

Marsh, H.W., & Sonstroem, R.J. (1995). Importance ratings and specific components of physical self-concept: Relevance to predicting global components of self-concept and exercise. *Journal of Sport and Exercise Psychology, 17,* 84–104.

McAuley, E., Bane, S.M., & Mihalko, S. (1995). Exercise in middle-aged adults: Self-efficacy and self-presentational outcomes. *Preventive Medicine, 24,* 319–328.

McAuley, E., Bane, S.M., Rudolph, D., & Lox, C. (1995). Physique anxiety and exercise in middle-aged adults. *Journal of Gerontology, 50B,* 229–235.

McAuley, E., & Mihalko, S. (1998). Measuring exercise-related self-efficacy. In J.L. Duda (Ed.), *Advances in sport and exercise psychology measurement* (pp. 371–392). Morgantown, WV: Fitness Information Technology.

Messer, B., & Harter, S. (1986). *Manual for the Adult Self-Perception Profile.* Denver: University of Denver.

Murphy, G. (1947). *Personality: A biosocial approach to origins and structure.* New York: Harper & Row.

Neemann, J., & Harter, S. (1986). *Manual for the Self-Perception Profile for College Students.* Denver: University of Denver.

Nicholls, J.G. (1989). *The competitive ethos and democratic education.* Cambridge, MA: Harvard University.

Ostrow, A.C. (1996). *Directory of psychological tests in the sport and exercise sciences* (2nd ed.). Morgantown, WV: Fitness Information Technology.

Papaioannou, A., & Goudas, M. (1999). Motivational climate of the physical education class. In Y. Vanden Auweele, F. Bakker, S. Biddle, M. Durand, & R. Seiler (Eds.), *Psychology for physical educators* (pp. 51–68). Champaign, IL: Human Kinetics.

Petrie, T.A., Diehl, N., Rogers, R.L., & Johnson, C.L. (1996). The Social Physique Anxiety Scale: Reliability and construct validity. *Journal of Sport and Exercise Psychology, 18,* 420–425.

Roberts, G.C., Kleiber, D.A., & Duda, J.L. (1981). An analysis of motivation in children's sport: The role of perceived competence in participation. *Journal of Sport Psychology, 3,* 206–216.

Rogers, C.R. (1951). *Client-centered therapy.* Boston: Houghton Mifflin.

Rosenberg, M. (1965). *Society and the adolescent self-image.* Princeton, NJ: Princeton University Press.

Ryckman, R.M., Robbins, M.A., Thornton, B., & Cantrell, P. (1982). Development and validation of a physical self-efficacy scale. *Journal of Personality and Social Psychology, 42,* 891–900.

Secord, P.F., & Jourard, S.M. (1953). The appraisal of body-cathexis: Body cathexis and the self. *Journal of Consulting Psychology, 17,* 343–347.

Shavelson, R.J., Hubner, J.J., & Stanton, G.C. (1976). Self-concept: Validation of construct interpretations. *Review of Educational Research, 46,* 407–411.

Sonstroem, R.J. (1976). The validity of self-perceptions regarding physical and athletic ability. *Medicine and Science in Sports, 8,* 126–132.

Sonstroem, R.J. (1984). Exercise and self-esteem. *Exercise and Sports Sciences Reviews, 12,* 123–155.

Sonstroem, R.J. (1998). Physical self-concept: Assessment and external validity. *Exercise and Sports Sciences Reviews, 26,* 133–164.

Sonstroem, R.J., Harlow, L.L., Gemma, L.M., & Osborne, S. (1991). Test of structural relationships within a proposed exercise and self-esteem model. *Journal of Personality Assessment, 56,* 348–364.

Sonstroem, R.J., Harlow, L.L., & Josephs, L. (1994). Exercise and self-esteem: Validity of model expansion and exercise associations. *Journal of Sport and Exercise Psychology, 16,* 29–42.

Sonstroem, R.J., Harlow, L.L., & Salisbury, K.S. (1993). Path analysis of a self-esteem model across a competitive swim season. *Research Quarterly for Exercise and Sport, 64,* 335–342.

Sonstroem, R.J., & Kampper, K.P. (1980). Prediction of athletic participation in middle school males. *Research Quarterly for Exercise and Sport, 51,* 685–694.

Sonstroem, R.J., & Morgan, W.P. (1989). Exercise and self-esteem: Rationale and model. *Medicine and Science in Sports and Exercise, 21,* 329–337.

Sonstroem, R.J., & Potts, S.A. (1996). Life adjustment correlates of physical self-concepts. *Medicine and Science in Sports and Exercise, 28,* 619–625.

Sonstroem, R.J., Speliotis, E.D., & Fava, J.L. (1992). Perceived physical competence in adults: An examination of the Physical Self-Perception Profile. *Journal of Sport and Exercise Psychology, 14,* 207–221.

Spence, J.C., & Poon, P. (1997). The effect of physical activity on self-concept: A meta-analysis. *Alberta Centre for Well-Being: Research Update, 4*(3), 4.

Stryker, S. (1987). Identity theory: Developments and extensions. In K. Yardley & T. Holness (Eds.), *Self and identity* (pp. 89–103). New York: Wiley.

Weiss, M.R., & Petlichkoff, L.M. (1989). Children's motivation for participation in and withdrawal from sport: Identifying the missing links. *Pediatric Exercise Science, 1,* 195–211.

White, R.W. (1959). Motivation reconsidered: The concept of competence. *Psychological Review, 66,* 297–333.

Whitehead, J.R. (1995). A study of children's physical self-perceptions using an adapted physical self-perception questionnaire. *Pediatric Exercise Science, 7,* 133–152.

Wilson, P., & Eklund, R.C. (1998). The relationship between competitive anxiety and self-presentational concerns. *Journal of Sport and Exercise Psychology, 20,* 81–97.

Wylie, R.C. (1979). *The self-concept* (Vol. 2). Lincoln: University of Nebraska Press.

Wylie, R.C. (1989). *Measures of self-concept.* Lincoln: University of Nebraska Press.

Motivational Orientations and Sport Behavior

Maureen R. Weiss and Emilio Ferrer-Caja

T he term *motivation* is used so frequently, so casually, and in so many contexts that it appears everybody knows what motivation is. In social psychology, motivation is defined as the direction and intensity of effort (Gill, 1986), but perhaps motivation can best be conceived within a number of *why* questions. Why do individuals participate (or not participate) in physical activity or sport? Why do some individuals participate primarily for the inherent pleasure of the activity, whereas others are influenced more by the external rewards available from participating? Why do some individuals try hard and persist in situations posing adversity, whereas others exert minimal effort and give up easily? Implicit within these questions is an essential understanding of the antecedents or sources of motivation (i.e., what or who influences these variations in motivation?) and the potential consequences of motivation (i.e., what are the physical, psychological, and social benefits?). Given this perspective of motivation, it is easy to understand why this construct is salient to sport psychology researchers and practi-

tioners alike, who strive to maximize physical activity participation and its benefits.

The topic of motivation has been studied from two different but interrelated perspectives in sport psychology. Motivation as an individual difference factor focuses on individuals who vary in certain motivational dispositions or characteristics and on how these variations influence psychological outcomes (e.g., perceived competence, affective responses) and physical activity behavior (e.g., frequency, intensity). For example, Klint and Weiss (1987) found that young gymnasts who reported participation motives higher in affiliation factors (i.e., be with friends, make friends, be part of the team) rated themselves higher in perceived social acceptance than gymnasts who rated affiliation factors as a less important reason for their participation. Alternatively, Duda, Olson, and Templin (1991) found that athletes who subscribed to a higher ego goal orientation (i.e., norm-referenced definition of success) were much more likely to endorse cheating and injuring an opponent in order to win.

We have taken an inclusive approach to motivational orientations and sport behavior in this chapter. We thoroughly reviewed major motivation theories and empirical research testing these theories in the physical domain. This approach resulted in a long but all-encompassing review of motivation in the physical domain. Thus, we recommend that for teaching purposes, the chapter be read and split into units determined by each major section. This would result in six or more lectures on motivation. We believe that such an inclusive approach exposes graduate students to a variety of perspectives and accomplishes the purpose of the text, to review the extant literature from a scholarly perspective.

The other perspective to studying motivation in sport psychology is its role as an outcome variable. From this vantage, motivation is assessed as choice to participate, effort exerted, and sustained effort or persistence. When studied as an outcome variable, the sources of motivation are of central interest. What social environmental and individual difference factors influence motivated behavior directly or indirectly through some mediating variable? Moreover, do moderating variables affect the relationship between antecedents and motivated behavior? For example, Brustad (1993) found that parental enjoyment of physical activity, parental encouragement of their child's participation, and the child's perceived physical competence all contributed to the child's attraction to participating in physical activity. Perceived competence mediated the relationship between parental influence and attraction to physical activity, and gender was a moderating variable—boys reported greater parental encouragement and perceived physical competence than did girls.

The previous examples illuminate two important considerations concerning motivation and sport behavior. First, motivational orientations and social influence factors interact to determine participation outcomes (including motivated behavior). Thus, motivation as an individual difference factor must be studied within the social context in which sport behaviors occur to provide a complete picture of determinants of psychosocial development and outcomes.

Second, although this chapter appears in a part titled "Individual Differences and Sport Behavior" it is nearly impossible to talk about motivation from this perspective without also considering motivation as an outcome variable. We are ultimately interested in the links among motivational orientation (e.g., achievement goals, intrinsic or extrinsic motives), social–environmental factors (e.g., significant others, motivational climate), self-perceptions (e.g., perceived competence), and motivated behavior. Therefore, we examine motivation as an individual difference factor only as it influences change in psychological and behavioral outcomes including self-perceptions, affective responses, and motivation.

Our goal in this chapter is to comprehensively review the literature on motivation and sport behavior. To do this, we describe theories or conceptual models of motivation that have been supported in the physical achievement domain. Second, we synthesize and consolidate relevant sport-related research for each conceptual framework. We critically analyze current issues, controversies, and missing links in the knowledge base for each theory. Finally, we present some ideas for future research that may help explain motivational orientations and behavior from a particular conceptual perspective. We begin the chapter, however, with a review of the early descriptive research on participation motivation and attrition, because these studies significantly affect how we conceptualize motivational orientations and sport behavior today.

PARTICIPATION MOTIVATION AND ATTRITION: FROM DESCRIPTION TO THEORY DEVELOPMENT

The topics of participation motivation and attrition concern themselves with the *reasons why* individuals continue and discontinue participation in sport or physical activity, respectively. In this section we trace the evolution of participation motivation and attrition research by addressing, first, descriptive studies during the early years, and, second, the trend toward more theoretical approaches that have emerged within the last 10 years.

Reasons for Participating in Sport: The Early Years

Research interest in participation motivation emerged in the 1970s with a key study conducted by Alderman and Wood (1976) with Canadian young athletes. These authors found that affiliation (making friends), excellence (doing something very well), arousal (seeking excitement), and esteem (recognition of one's achievements) incentives or motives were valued most strongly. This study seemed to inspire the surge of participation motivation studies that followed.

Sapp and Haubenstricker (1978) conducted a large-scale study of participation motivation as part of a three-phase longitudinal investigation of youth sport programs (State of Michigan, 1976, 1978a, 1978b). A questionnaire tapping reasons for participating in organized nonschool or school sport participation was completed by more than 1,000 boys and girls 11 to 18 years of age. Results revealed that major reasons cited for sport participation were fun, skill development (learn and improve skills), physical fitness, and because their friends played.

A plethora of descriptive studies on participation motivation followed in the 1980s to build on this knowledge base and glean consistent findings that might be used to develop and test theory (see reviews by Gould & Petlichkoff, 1988; Weiss, 1993a; Weiss & Petlichkoff, 1989). Several of these studies targeted participation motives across several sports (Gill, Gross, & Huddleston, 1983; Longhurst & Spink, 1987; Wankel & Kreisel, 1985a; Weingarten, Furst, Tenenbaum, & Schaefer, 1984). Other studies focused on motives within certain sports such as gymnastics (Klint & Weiss, 1986), swimming (Gould, Feltz, & Weiss, 1985), and ice hockey (Ewing, Feltz, Schultz, & Albrecht, 1988).

Several common themes for participating in sport emerged from these studies. Participation motives primarily included (a) developing physical competence (i.e., learn skills, improve skills, achieve goals), (b) gaining social acceptance (i.e., be with and make friends, be part of a group, gain approval from significant adults), (c) enhancing physical fitness and appearance (i.e., get in shape, get stronger), and (d) enjoying one's experiences (i.e., fun, excitement, challenge). In all of these studies respondents rated multiple motives, rather than any single reason, as important for driving their participation.

Across studies, the same reasons for participating cropped up: physical competence, social acceptance, fitness, and fun. However, fun or enjoyment ranked at the top of the list of reasons in a large majority of studies. The prominence of enjoyment led some researchers to study participation motivation from the perspective of factors contributing to enjoyment of sport. For example, Wankel and Pabich (1982) found that improving skills, doing the skills of the game, excitement of a close game, comparing skills against others, and being part of a team were the top-ranked enjoyment factors for 8- to 12-year-old boys participating in baseball, soccer, and ice hockey. These enjoyment sources are recognizable as participation motives in other studies. Subsequent studies by Wankel (Wankel & Kreisel, 1985a, 1985b; Wankel & Sefton, 1989) reinforced his earlier findings that sources of fun are equivalent to participation motives.

Concurrent with the early research on reasons for participating in sport was the troubling finding that a large percentage (35% average) of sport participants drop out each year from a particular program (Gould, 1987). Naturally, researchers and practitioners alike should have been concerned about this statistic, and this concern was evidenced in a survey that identified "why young athletes stop participating in youth sports" as the top-ranked issue of importance by both groups (Gould, 1982). Research on the topic of attrition from sport gained momentum in the 1980s, often in concert with studies of participation motivation in cohort samples (e.g., Gould, Feltz, Horn, & Weiss, 1982; Gould et al., 1985; Klint & Weiss, 1986; McClements, Fry, & Sefton, 1982; Petlichkoff, 1982; Sapp & Haubenstricker, 1978).

Reasons for Discontinuing Sport: The Early Years

Two studies by Orlick (1973, 1974) launched serious interest into why children withdrew from youth sport programs. In the first study, Orlick (1973) classified 32 boys ages 8 and 9 years as either participants or nonparticipants of a particular youth hockey league based on verbal intentions of returning the following season. Three nonparticipants were identified as "dropouts" of the current program, and Orlick pursued their reasons for withdrawal. They cited negative experiences such as lack of playing time and overemphasis on winning as their primary reasons. In his second investigation, Orlick (1974) interviewed 60 former sport participants (ages 7–19 years) who cited primarily negative reasons for their discontinued involvement. A large-scale study of age-group swimmers (N = 1,880) conducted by McPherson, Marteniuk, Tihanyi, and Clark (1980) supported Orlick's negative outlook on youth sport attrition. A majority of respondents identified at least one friend who had quit swimming the previous year, citing reasons such as too much pressure, lack of fun, too time consuming, and conflict with the coach. Moreover, 48% of the swimmers interviewed stated that they wanted to quit at some time during their career. Their reasons included boredom, dislike for the coach, belief that swimming was too time consuming, and interest in other activities.

These discouraging findings were not replicated in the large-scale study conducted by the Youth Sports Institute at Michigan State University (Sapp & Haubenstricker, 1978; State of Michigan, 1978a). Although 24% of 6- to 10-year-olds and 37% of 11- to 18-year-olds indicated a desire to discontinue their particular sport the following year, the types of negative reasons that prevailed in Orlick's study accounted for less than 15% of the reasons cited for sport withdrawal. Instead, the primary reasons cited for discontinuing a particular sport program were interests in other activities and work responsibilities.

Several studies suggested that sport withdrawal may be a temporary phenomenon or may be sport-specific for most athletes. Klint and Weiss (1986) reported that 95% of their former club gymnasts were participating in either another sport or gymnastics at a lower level of intensity, whereas Johns, Lindner, and Wolko (1990) reported that 78% of their former gymnasts had entered another sport activity. Gould et al. (1982) found that 68% of their former youth swimmers were active in other sports and 80% planned to reenter swimming at a later time. Perhaps these athletes found that alternative sports or physical activity environments were better matches for their physical competence, social acceptance, fitness and appearance, and enjoyment motives for participating.

A window through which to view this "mismatch hypothesis" was provided by Klint and Weiss (1986) and McClements et al. (1982), who assessed current and former participants about why they initially participated. Klint and Weiss found that current club gymnasts rated skill development, physical fitness, and competition as their most important participation reasons, whereas former gymnasts rated fun and skill development as their priorities. Interestingly, fun (second highest rating for former gymnasts) was not listed in the top 10 reasons for current gymnasts, and winning (cited as one of the most important reasons by current gymnasts) was not listed in the top 10 reasons for former gymnasts. Similarly, McClements et al. found that boys who remained in ice hockey reported higher achievement-oriented, and less social- and fun-oriented, reasons for their participation than boys who were no longer involved in hockey. These studies suggest that participants who discontinued their sport may have done so because their motives were not being met.

In a thoughtful reality check on the social world of competitive sport, Petlichkoff (1992) cautioned that fun and winning motives, often interpreted as major reasons for continuing and discontinuing, are strongly related to age and competitive level. The structure of sport endorses fun and skill learning at the younger and beginning skill levels but progressively emphasizes winning as participants become older and more skilled. Youth who participate for fun and skill development eventually may select themselves out of sport because they are not good enough or are cut by coaches because of the competitive level of play. Not only is winning equated with success at higher levels

and ages but, because coaching jobs depend on winning, coaches and parents may promote its importance by pressuring athletes to specialize in one sport and devote considerable time to this sport (e.g., sport camps, all-year training). In short, fun and winning motives are intricately linked to the social context surrounding the athlete's involvement at varying ages and competitive levels.

The importance of the social context was nicely demonstrated in a nationwide study by A. White and Coakley (1986; Coakley & White, 1992), who examined young British girls' and boys' decisions about participating in physical activity. Interviews with mostly 13- to 18-year-old participants and nonparticipants revealed that decisions revolved around five common themes: (a) consideration of one's future as an adult; (b) opportunity or desire to demonstrate physical competence and autonomy; (c) social support from parents and same-sex friends; (d) constraints and barriers related to finances, parents, and opposite-sex friends; and (e) past experiences in school sport and physical education. However, the meaning attached to each of these themes depended on gender. Girls reported that parents gave them "conditional permission" to participate in physical activity, that their boyfriends constrained their participation habits, and that they remembered many negative experiences in physical education (e.g., physical appearance concerns, boredom, lack of choice). Boys, in contrast, discussed few constraints from parents or girlfriends and cited less frequent negative experiences in physical education and sport.

In a review and critique of the participation motivation and attrition research through the 1980s, Weiss and Petlichkoff (1989) concluded that attrition from sport should not be viewed necessarily as a negative life event. They also concluded that *dropout* is not an appropriate term for labeling youth who cease participation, because many individuals transfer to other sports, continue in the same sport at a different level of intensity, or make decisions based on developmental transitions. The finding that many youth "drop in and drop out" of sport based on changing interests and opportunities to do other activities suggests a normal developmental phenomenon of sampling activities and choosing ones that allow for current interests, competencies, and goals (i.e., do what friends are doing, demonstrate ability in a sport, try something new, enhance physical appearance). As a result of this review, Weiss and

Petlichkoff (1989) suggested a number of research directions to determine the stability and correlates of participation motives as well as sources and consequences of attrition from sport and physical activity. These included assessments of motives at multiple time periods during participation, developmental differences in participation and attrition motives, and considering the social context surrounding participants' experiences (e.g., culture, gender, school vs. nonschool program).

The 1990s and Beyond: Trends in Participation Motivation and Attrition Research

In contrast to the early studies that primarily described participation and attrition motives in young athletes, research in the 1990s heeded the recommendations for future research (see Petlichkoff, 1994, 1996; Weiss & Petlichkoff, 1989) and proceeded along three different, but interrelated, pathways. First, studies focused on the social context in which sport occurs as a correlate of individuals' participation motives. A second focus considered age-related or developmental differences in participation and attrition motives. Finally, participation motivation research shifted from its focus on describing reasons for participation to grounding within theoretical models that go beyond description to explain and predict cognitive, affective, social, and behavioral sources and outcomes of participation motivation.

Social Contextual Factors

Studies of social contextual or situational factors related to participation motives can be divided into several areas. These include gender (Ebbeck, Gibbons, & Loken-Dahle, 1995; Ryckman & Hamel, 1995), culture (Buonamano, Cei, & Mussino, 1995; Hayashi & Weiss, 1994; Kolt et al., 1999; Wang & Wiese-Bjornstal, 1996), sport or physical activity type (Ebbeck et al., 1995; Hellandsig, 1998), and time of season and player status (Petlichkoff, 1993a, 1993b; Weiss & Frazer, 1995). We embellish on some of these areas in the following paragraphs.

The early research primarily examined participation motives in Western societies (i.e., United States, Canada, Australia, Great Britain). Research on participants from Eastern societies (Japan: Hayashi & Weiss, 1994; China: Wang & Wiese-Bjornstal, 1996) clearly shows that sociocultural factors directly bear on reasons for participating in physical activity and sport. For example, Hayashi and Weiss found that adult Anglo-American and Japanese marathon runners agreed on health and fitness, enjoyment, personal challenge, and achievement motives. However, Anglo-American runners exclusively cited competition and social recognition reasons, whereas only Japanese runners cited having a good experience and being part of a running group.

Another characteristic of early participation motivation research is the "snapshot" nature of assessment, whereby participant motives were assessed at one point during the season. It is conceivable that motives for participation differ depending on the point in the season when measures are completed or that motives change over the course of the season as a result of one's sport experiences. In two studies that integrated the time of season and player status issues, Petlichkoff (1993a, 1993b) found significant differences in participation motives (assessed as achievement motives or goals) among starters, nonstarters, survivors, dropouts, and cuttees of interscholastic sports teams at preseason, early season, and end of season. These results suggest that repeated measurements of participation motives and differentiating individuals who vary in player status are important when assessing motives for participating in sport.

Developmental Differences

More recent studies investigated differences in participation motives across the life span (Brodkin & Weiss, 1990) or focused on the oft-neglected motives and self-perceptions of middle-age and older adults (Ashford, Biddle, & Goudas, 1993; Ebbeck et al., 1995; Gill, Williams, Dowd, Beaudoin, & Martin, 1996; O'Brien-Cousins, 1997; Whaley & Ebbeck, 1997). For example, Ashford et al. compared community sports participants ages 16 to 24, 25 to 44, and 45 or older on reasons for participation and found that the two older groups rated sociopsychological well-being (relaxation, affiliation, aesthetics, excitement) as more important than did the youngest group.

When speaking of developmental differences, most books and journals narrowly define this as infancy through adolescence. However, a lifespan perspective is a more appropriate and inclusive way for examining and understanding age-related differences on psychosocial development and behavioral outcomes. Given that the baby boom generation is entering middle and older adulthood, interest has surged in the determinants and benefits of physical activity participation in these age groups (e.g., O'Brien-Cousins, 1997; Whaley & Ebbeck, 1997). For example, Whaley and Ebbeck uncovered perceived constraints to physical activity in older adults (65–85 years) and found that gender played a key role in the type of constraints identified and strategies for overcoming constraints. These studies of older adults are a good start, but considerable research is needed to understand the developmental factors that influence participation motives and attrition.

From Description to Theory Development

Participation motivation is a good example of an area that proceeded from a descriptive to theory testing stage of research (Landers, 1983). The body of knowledge on participation and attrition naturally led to the development or testing of conceptual frameworks deemed suitable for the nuances of the physical domain (Gould & Petlichkoff, 1988; Petlichkoff, 1994; Weiss, 1993a; Weiss & Chaumeton, 1992).

First, the finding that developing and demonstrating physical competence are consistent motives, whether they involve developing athletic skills or physical fitness and appearance, paved the way for examining participation motivation within theories that highlight perceptions of competence as a key predictor of motivation. These include competence motivation theory (Harter, 1978, 1981a), cognitive evaluation theory (Deci & Ryan, 1985), expectancy-value theory (Eccles et al., 1983), and achievement goal theory (Ames, 1992a; Elliott & Dweck, 1988; Nicholls, 1984, 1989).

The overriding role of fun or enjoyment as a participation motive, the desire to maximize positive and minimize negative experiences, and attractive alternatives (e.g., want to do other sports) cited as a major reason for sport withdrawal are characteristic of the sport commitment model (Scanlan, Carpenter, Schmidt, Simons, & Keeler 1993). Harter's (1978, 1981a) competence motivation theory also features enjoyment or positive affect as central to motivational processes, whereas cognitive evaluation, expectancy-value, and achievement goal theories view enjoyment and other positive affects as important sources or consequences of intrinsic motivation, achievement-related choices, and task-oriented goals, respectively.

Finally, the motive to gain social acceptance, including friendships, peer acceptance, and approval and positive reinforcement by significant adults, implicates the range of theories already mentioned. In each of these theories or conceptual frameworks, reflected appraisals by significant adults, peer evaluation and comparison, and social support and constraints constitute a range of sources whereby individuals derive self-perceptions of competence, affective responses to participation, and motivation to initiate or continue participation in physical activity.

In the sections that follow, we systematically review the major theoretical or conceptual models used to study motivational orientations and sport behavior. These conceptual frameworks of motivation include the following: competence motivation theory (Harter, 1978, 1981a), cognitive evaluation theory (Deci & Ryan, 1985), expectancy-value theory (Eccles et al., 1983), achievement goal theory (Ames, 1992a; Dweck, 1999; Nicholls, 1989), and sport commitment model (Scanlan, Carpenter, Schmidt, et al., 1993).

COMPETENCE MOTIVATION THEORY

Individuals primarily participate in physical activities for intrinsic reasons such as enjoyment of or attraction to the activity and the pleasure and sense of mastery that come from learning and improving skills. Social reasons are also paramount, such as positive support from and interactions with significant adults (i.e., parents, coaches), and the initiation and affirmation of friendships. These concepts are addressed by Harter's (1978, 1981a) competence motivation theory, a conceptually appealing and educationally relevant approach to understanding individuals' motivational patterns and behaviors in specific achievement domains such as sport. Moreover, the model was molded with sensitivity to developmental change and individual differences in key motivational constructs. Since her classic article was published in 1978, Harter's conceptual model and empirical research have been applied widely to the cognitive achievement domain. More importantly, competence motivation theory has been a productive and suitable theory for applications to the physical domain. The following sections review the underpinnings of competence motivation theory, empirical research conducted in the physical domain, and directions for future research.

Theoretical Underpinnings

Imagine a young girl playfully turning cartwheels in the grass or running with abandon on a soccer field. Do you smile as you recall the glee and joy she displayed? What about a young boy mustering the courage to try a new swimming skill? Can you identify with the curiosity and sense of mastery he experienced from his efforts? Researchers would describe these types of behaviors as intrinsic in nature—ones that are motivated by the sense of curiosity, challenge-seeking, self-rewarding quality, and need or urge to have an effect on or master one's environment. The concept of effectance or competence motivation originated by R.W. White (1959) was designed to describe and explain the antecedents and consequences of such an intrinsically motivating desire. His theory was later revised, extended, and operationalized by Harter (1978, 1981a).

White's thesis was that individuals are intrinsically motivated to effectively interact with their social and physical environment and do so by engaging in mastery attempts or behaviors. If these attempts are successful (i.e., competence is demonstrated), feelings of efficacy and inherent pleasure are experienced, which maintain or enhance effectance motivation or the intrinsic desire to master one's environment. A schematic of White's model of effectance motivation (Harter, 1978) is depicted in figure 5.1. White viewed one's motivation to develop mastery, satisfy curiosity, enjoy challenge, and be playful as key behavioral examples of an effectance motivation. White's classic article was embraced as an appealing and intuitive alternative to the reductionist motivation theories of the day (i.e., psychoanalytic, drive theories). Nevertheless, empirical testing of his theory lay dormant for nearly 20 years because constructs such as effectance motivation, feelings of efficacy, and intrinsic pleasure were not operationally defined and could not be measured.

Enter Susan Harter with her conceptual refinements and psychometric developments that allowed empirical testing of predictions stemming from competence motivation theory. Her own classic articles on effectance or competence motivation cast the theory within a developmental perspective (Harter, 1978, 1981a, 1981b) and made a considerable impact in a variety of achievement domains including the physical domain. Basically, Harter viewed competence motivation as a multidimensional construct that influences domain-specific mastery attempts and the development of achievement cognitions, affects, and behaviors such as perceived competence and control, joy and anxiety, and effort and persistence.

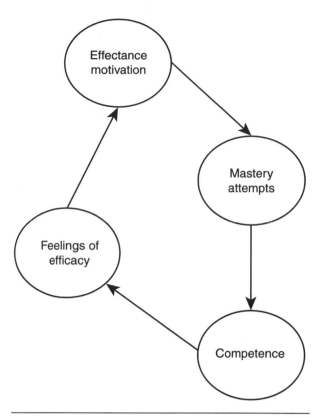

Figure 5.1 Robert White's model of effectance motivation.

Adapted, by permission, from R.W. White, 1959, Motivation reconsidered: The concept of competence. *Psychological Review, 66:* 297–330.

Major Extensions to the Original Effectance Model

Harter (1978, 1981a, 1981b) revised and extended R.W. White's (1959) original model in several ways (see figure 5.2). First, she specified that competence motivation processes will vary depending on the specific achievement domain in which mastery attempts occur (i.e., cognitive, physical, social). That is, children will differ in their level of desire, curiosity, interest, and challenge-seeking (i.e., motivational orientation) to learn and master skills in varying areas such as sports, mathematics, drawing, and computers. Naturally, components or correlates of motivation such as perceived competence, perceived control, and reinforcement and approval by significant others also will vary as a function of the achievement domain in which the child attempts mastery behaviors. Therefore, Harter refined White's global, unitary construct of effectance or competence motivation into a multidimensional construct that considers variations in one's interest to be effective or competent in a particular achievement domain.

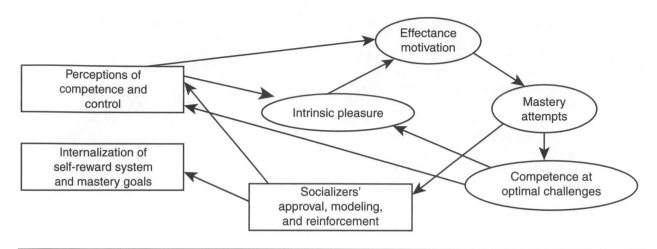

Figure 5.2   Susan Harter's model of competence motivation.

Adapted, by permission, from S. Harter, 1978, Effectance motivation reconsidered. *Human Development, 21:* 34–64.

A second refinement that Harter made to White's original model was related to performance outcomes. Whereas White only addressed the consequences of successful mastery attempts, Harter also considered the consequences of unsuccessful experiences, and the relative balance or interaction between success and failure experiences, on self-perceptions, affective responses, and motivated behaviors. Moreover, Harter demonstrated that success at any type of task or activity is not sufficient to alter competence motivation dimensions; rather, success at optimal challenges, or difficult but realistic goals, provides the greatest feelings of positive affect and, consequently, intrinsic motivation.

Third, Harter added the critical role of socializing agents such as important adults and peers in developing children's perceptions of competence and control, affective responses to mastery attempts and performance outcomes, and intrinsic (e.g., challenge-seeking, curiosity/interest) or extrinsic (i.e., preference for easy tasks, social approval) motivational orientations. Harter delineated the essential need for adult caregivers, in particular, to approve and reinforce independent mastery attempts and not to reserve such responses only for successful performance outcomes. When positive and contingent feedback is given for the process of mastery behaviors, Harter contended, children's perceptions of competence and control, positive affect, and intrinsic motivation are nurtured. Harter also outlined the developmental implications of significant others' affect and behaviors toward the child's efforts.

Fourth, Harter added domain-specific perceptions of competence and control, which she considered to be crucial outcomes as well as mediators of positive affective responses and competence motivation. These self-perception constructs were viewed as consequences of internal or self-referenced criteria (i.e., attraction, improvement), social and norm-referenced criteria (i.e., peer comparison, adult approval), and outcome criteria (i.e., win or lose) that the child may use. Perceived competence has been, by far, the most frequently studied construct within this theory and has been found to be a strong predictor of cognitive (i.e., self-esteem), affective (i.e., enjoyment, anxiety), and behavioral (i.e., achievement) outcomes. Because perceived competence is a strong predictor of achievement outcomes, a significant amount of research has been devoted to understanding the process by which children and adolescents form judgments about how competent they are in the physical domain and how these processes vary developmentally (Horn & Amorose, 1998; Horn & Harris, 1996)

Fifth, Harter positioned White's notion of inherent pleasure as a response to successful mastery within the larger conception of positive affect. Furthermore, Harter strongly urged that affect or emotion be put on center stage as a key variable driving intrinsic motivation and its components. This emphasis placed on affect as a legitimate construct that influences behavior was purposely opposed to the predominant cognitive theories of the 1960s and 1970s such as attribution theory and the overjustification hypothesis within cognitive evaluation theory. Harter's call to "restore affect and emotion to its rightful place, as central to an understanding of behavior" (Harter, 1981b, p. 4) is entirely consistent with the finding of enjoyment or fun as a prime participation motive and lack of enjoyment as a key reason for attrition from sport. Therefore, it is not surprising that competence motivation theory with its inclusion of variables salient to the physical domain—affect, perceived competence, significant others—caught the attention of sport psychology researchers.

Developmental Perspectives of the Model

Motivational processes within the competence motivation model vary developmentally. The developmental component distinguishes this model from the majority of theories that ignore developmental change in structure and content of key constructs. Harter contended that age-related variations exist in the desire to attain mastery in a particular domain, the particular significant other deemed most important in evaluating one's mastery attempts, and perceptions of competence and control (Harter, 1978, 1981a, 1981b, 1981c, 1987, 1990a). The structure of perceived competence, for example, becomes more differentiated with age, with younger children distinguishing between fewer dimensions than do older children. The developmental flair of competence motivation theory is appealing on both theoretical and practical grounds.

A critical developmental component of the competence motivation model concerns the effects of a child's socialization history on motivational processes. Harter contended that, over the childhood years, approval and reinforcement by significant adults for the process, rather than the outcome, of independent mastery attempts should decrease the child's dependence on or need for social reinforcement and externally defined goals to define success. Unconditional support and regard for the child's efforts will help the child develop or internalize a self-reward system (i.e., use of internal criteria for judging personal competence, self-praise for competent performance) and a set of mastery goals (i.e., preference for optimal challenges) by which to deem one's efforts as successful. In contrast, if significant adults disapprove of independent mastery attempts and use inappropriate reinforcement (e.g., lack of reinforcement for attempts, reinforcement only for successful outcome), the child will not progress developmentally but rather will persist in depending on external approval and goals. These developmental changes have implications for other dimensions within the model and, naturally, educational recommendations (Horn & Harris, 1996; Weiss & Ebbeck, 1996).

Relationships Among Constructs in the Model

Putting together all these puzzle pieces results in a picture of antecedents, mediators, and consequences of effectance or competence motivation (refer to figure 5.2). Specifically, the theory posits that intrinsically oriented individuals (effectance motivation oval) are motivated to develop or demonstrate competence in a particular achievement domain (e.g., academic, physical, social), and this urge to be effective leads them to try mastering a task or activity (mastery attempts oval). They prefer challenging rather than easy tasks, ones that will satisfy their curiosity and interest, and they prefer to figure things out on their own rather than rely on an adult for assistance (i.e., independent mastery). If mastery attempts are successful (competence at optimal challenges oval) and significant adults and peers respond with contingent approval and reinforcement (socializers' approval, modeling, reinforcement box), the child will experience increased perceptions of competence and control (perceptions of competence and control box), positive affect (intrinsic pleasure oval), and the urge to continue demonstrating competence in that achievement domain (effectance motivation oval).

From a developmental perspective, children's positive socialization influences and cognitive maturation will pull them away from depending on social reinforcement and externally defined goals and will push them toward reliance on internal criteria (i.e., improvement, effort) and mastery goals to judge physical competence. This process should occur throughout the childhood years so that by early adolescence individuals are capable of using self-rewarding behavior, internal criteria to judge competence, and independent judgments to define success. If this doesn't occur, the opposite scenario unfolds—one in which unsuccessful mastery attempts and inappropriate reinforcement from significant others lead to lowered self-perceptions, increased anxiety, and development of an extrinsic motivational orientation. Harter (1978) acknowledged that the balance between successful and unsuccessful mastery attempts and the pattern of reinforcement over time determines motivational orientation, self-perceptions, affect, and motivated behavior.

Competence motivation theory specifies mastery attempts and performance outcomes in specific achievement domains and explicitly includes constructs that are salient to the physical domain (e.g., significant others, success vs. failure, intrinsic and extrinsic motives, perceived competence, perceived control, affective responses). Moreover, Harter and her colleagues operationalized key constructs such as motivational orientation and perceived competence, allowing for theoretical tenets to be tested. Given these qualitative aspects of competence motivation theory and its attractive and intuitive appeal for educational practice, it is not surprising that empirical testing and support of Harter's theory in the physical domain have flourished in the last 20 years (Weiss & Ebbeck, 1996). This research is presented in the following sections, which have been divided along specific model relationships:

- Perceived competence, participation motives, and attrition from sport
- Developmental trends in perceived competence and motivational orientation
- Influence by significant others on self-perceptions, affect, and motivational orientation
- Perceived competence and achievement-related cognitions, affect, and behavior
- A comprehensive model of global self-worth

Perceived Competence, Participation Motives, and Attrition From Sport

The shift from descriptive to theory-based studies of participation motivation and attrition was launched with competence motivation theory. The theory posits that individuals will strive to demonstrate mastery and continue mastery attempts in particular achievement domains in which they feel competent. Thus, one might hypothesize that continuing sport participants should be higher in perceived physical competence than program nonparticipants or former participants. Roberts, Kleiber, and Duda (1981) found that youth sport participants (ages 9–11), compared with nonparticipants, reported higher perceived physical competence, cognitive competence, and general self-worth. Feltz and Petlichkoff (1983) reported similar physical competence findings for interscholastic participants versus dropouts across a variety of sports, as did Burton and Martens (1986) for current versus former youth wrestlers. Gibbons and Bushakra (1989) found that Special Olympics par-

ticipants were higher on cognitive, physical, and social subscales than nonparticipants. However, Klint (1985) did not find differences in perceived physical competence between continuing and former gymnasts (ages 8–16), nor did Ulrich (1987) on perceived physical competence between 5- to 10-year-old participants and nonparticipants.

These discrepant findings prompted Klint and Weiss (1987) to examine the relationship between perceptions of competence and particular motives for gymnastics participation. It may have been erroneous in previous studies to assume that individuals who are no longer involved in a sport are motivated to demonstrate physical competence and drop out when they have low perceptions of physical competence relative to continuing athletes. Children and youth participate for a multitude of reasons including skill development, enjoyment, social acceptance, and physical fitness. Therefore, Klint and Weiss hypothesized, in accordance with competence motivation predictions, that participants higher in perceived physical competence would cite skill development reasons as more important, whereas those higher in perceived social acceptance would rate friendship and team-oriented reasons as more important compared with low perceived competence cohorts. Results supported these contentions. Ryckman and Hamel (1993) also found that 14-year-old sport participants who were higher in perceived physical ability cited skill development motives as more important than did lower perceived ability peers. These findings may explain, at least in part, the discrepant results previously reported relevant to perceived competence and participant status (i.e., current vs. former participants or nonparticipants).

An alternative approach by some researchers was to investigate the relationship between participant or player status and perceived physical competence. That is, within the larger pool of active participants, players vary in amount of playing time or, stated in competence motivation terms, opportunities to develop and demonstrate mastery. Petlichkoff (1993a, 1993b), in two studies with interscholastic athletic participants, found that starters were consistently higher in perceived physical competence than primary substitutes (i.e., one of the first players into the game) or secondary substitutes (i.e., benchwarmers). Weiss and Frazer (1995) assessed female high school basketball players on key competence motivation variables—perceived success, perceived basketball competence, perceived peer acceptance, and enjoyment—at preseason, midseason, and end of season. No differences existed at preseason, but by midseason and at postseason, starters and primary substitutes were higher on all variables than secondary substitutes. Results from these three studies support the idea that perceptions of competence and positive affect are likely to be stronger in participants who receive more opportunities to develop and demonstrate their competence in a particular achievement domain.

Developmental Trends in Perceived Competence and Motivational Orientation

The developmental perspective of competence motivation theory is especially attractive in light of both theoretical and practical significance. Harter's empirical efforts (1981a, 1981c, 1982, 1990a) clearly delineated developmental trends in dimensions of competence motivation such as perceived competence, perceived control, positive and negative affect, and motivational orientation. Understanding children's conceptions of these motivational components is important to explain variations in achievement behavior and to devise strategies for enhancing positive competence perceptions, affect, and intrinsic motivation. However, a developmental focus does not preclude examining individual variations within developmental level. That is, most but not all young children will depend primarily on parental feedback to determine whether they are physically competent. A developmental approach allows for understanding between—and within—age group differences on key motivational constructs. This section highlights developmental trends in the physical domain: (a) differentiation of competence dimensions, (b) level and accuracy of perceived physical competence, (c) sources of information used to assess physical competence, and (d) changes in motivational orientation.

Differentiation of Competence Dimensions

One of the challenges that developmentalists face in their quest to understand behavioral variations is reliably assessing constructs across a wide age range (Brustad, 1998; Harter, 1981a). How many dimensions of competence are sufficient and necessary to assess, and what age-appropriate content should the items portray for these dimensions? What response format will lend itself to the

least amount of social desirability in children's answers? These are just some of the issues that developmental researchers must grapple with to make sense of age-related differences in the structure and content of motivational constructs.

Much of Harter's early work entailed psychometric efforts to develop valid and reliable measures to assess competence motivation dimensions. By far the most intricate work has been with the construct of perceived competence. Initially, her efforts focused on perceived competence dimensions of 8- to 13-year-old youth (Harter, 1982), after which she addressed the self-perceptions of young children (ages 4–7; Harter & Pike, 1984), adolescents (Harter, 1988), college students (Neeman & Harter, 1986), and adults (Messer & Harter, 1986) in a variety of competence domains as well as general self-worth.

Middle and Late Childhood (Ages 8–13). Harter initiated her efforts with grade-school children who helped her derive specific competence items through responses to individual interviews and group discussions. Stable factor structures were achieved across a number of samples (Harter 1981a, 1982). These findings indicated that children in these age groups were consistent in differentiating among several competence dimensions. Three specific competence domains (cognitive, physical, social) and general self-worth were represented in her Perceived Competence Scale for Children (Harter, 1982). The Cognitive subscale focused on academic performance, the Physical subscale focused on abilities in sports and outdoor games, and the Social Acceptance subscale targeted perceptions of peer relationships. General sense of worth was independent of skill domain and included items such as being a good person, liking oneself, and being happy with the way one is. A later revision of her scale, the Self-Perception Profile for Children (Harter, 1985a) included two additional competence dimensions—physical appearance and behavioral conduct.

A unique aspect of the perceived competence scale is its structured alternative format. Harter conceived this scheme by interviewing children, reviewing the extant literature on assessment, and conducting extensive pilot testing. In response to items, children first decide whether they are more like the child on the left or right side. Children then respond to whether the statement is "sort of" or "really" true for them. This format affords developmental sensitivity and reduces socially desirable answers that are paramount in studies of children's beliefs and attitudes (Brustad, 1998;

Harter, 1981a, 1982; Welk, Corbin, Dowell, & Harris, 1997).

A number of studies conducted in the physical domain have bolstered the versatility of adapting the physical competence subscale to specific sports (e.g., soccer, Feltz & Brown, 1984; swimming, Black & Weiss, 1992; tennis, Ebbeck, 1994). Moreover, studies have shown that children differentiate their competence in physical skills in general and in different sport types (e.g., Klint, 1985; Weiss, Bredemeier, & Shewchuk, 1986), suggesting that assessments should be made at the level of analysis that is most salient to the research question at hand.

Early Childhood (Ages 4–7). Harter and Pike (1984) encountered a much different scenario when they turned their attention to extending the perceived competence scale for middle and late childhood (8–13 years) to young children (4–7 years). For younger children, a pictorial representation of items in the structured alternative format is presented in a one-on-one setting with items representing four dimensions: physical competence, social–peer acceptance, cognitive competence, and maternal acceptance. Harter and Pike consistently found that young children do not differentiate these four competence areas as distinct. Rather, scores from the four dimensions cluster into two categories labeled "general competence" (cognitive and physical competence scores) and "social acceptance" (peer acceptance and maternal acceptance scores). The general competence category depicted items of doing things well, whereas the social acceptance category depicted items that had little to do with competence per se. Children either had friends or they didn't; their mother did things for them or she didn't. Subsequent interviews verified that children believed that they could improve in "general competence" items with practice and trying hard, but that skill or practice had nothing to do with having friends— you "just make friends" if and when you want them (a rather naive yet entertaining thought!).

Harter's physical subscale for young children primarily taps competencies in play rather than sport skills (e.g., swinging, climbing, skipping). She found no gender differences or age-related decline in perceived physical competence from kindergarten to grade 2. To enhance validity of the physical subscale for 4- to 7-year-olds, Beverly Ulrich (1987; Ulrich & Ulrich, 1997) developed picture templates for fundamental motor skills (e.g., throwing, kicking) and sport-specific skills (e.g., batting a base- ball, dribbling a basketball) to accompany Harter's play-oriented items. Ulrich and Ulrich specifically tested whether children in kindergarten, first grade, and second grade (ages 5–8) differentiate their abilities to perform skills at these three levels of difficulty (i.e., play, fundamental skills, sport skills). Results revealed that girls clearly differentiated their competence, with highest perceptions reported for play and lowest perceptions for sport skills. In contrast, boys reported equally high competence perceptions for all levels of skill difficulty.

Adolescence (Ages 14–18). Extending the perceived competence scale for children upward to adolescents (14- to 18-year-olds) also posed challenges for Harter and her colleagues. The dimensionality of perceived competence at this age level further illuminates the differentiation concept as a function of age or development. Specifically, beyond the six dimensions specified for children ages 8 to 13 in the Self-Perception Profile for Children (Harter, 1985a), three additional domains of competence emerge as salient for teenagers: close friendship, romantic appeal, and job competence. The addition of salient, developmentally appropriate competence dimensions allows researchers to test whether the relative importance of and perceived competence in these dimensions change over the adolescent years, as Coakley and White (1992) indicated in their interviews with British teenagers. Harter (1990b) devoted considerable attention to understanding the antecedents of self-concept development and maintenance in adolescents.

In addition to the early childhood, middle to late childhood, and adolescent versions of the self-perception profile, Harter also created developmentally appropriate measures for college students (Neeman & Harter, 1986) and adults (Messer & Harter, 1986) that include yet more distinct domains. Thus, the potential for examining perceived physical competence from a lifespan developmental perspective (Harter, 1990a) awaits attention. In sum, one developmental component of Harter's theory is differentiation of competence domains, which carries practical implications for working with individuals of varying ages in educational settings.

Level and Accuracy of Perceived Physical Competence

Because level of perceived competence (i.e., relative "highness" or "lowness") has been found to be a strong predictor of achievement-related cognitions, affect, and behavior (see Weiss & Ebbeck, 1996), several developmentally oriented questions have been a source of interest among motivation researchers. Does level of perceived competence change with age (i.e., increase or decrease)? Does the relationship between perceived and actual competence become stronger with age (i.e., do individuals become more accurate about their competence)? Do individuals use different information sources to judge physical competence with age, and could this be a reason for observed variations in level and accuracy of perceived competence?

Research examining children's evaluations of their academic competence indicates that levels decline over the early and middle childhood years (see Stipek & MacIver, 1989). Along with this decline is a concomitant increase in accuracy of perceived competence (i.e., higher correlations between actual and perceived competence). However, age trends in perceived physical competence have been mixed. Harter and Pike (1984) found no perceived physical competence changes from ages 4 to 7, but Ulrich and Ulrich (1997) found a significant decline for this age group on perceived motor- and sport-skill competence for girls only. Harter (1982) and Feltz and Brown (1984) found relatively stable perceived physical and soccer competence levels across the childhood ages of 8 to 13 years, but Ulrich (1987) found an age-related decrease in competence perceptions among 5- to 10-year-olds. For the adolescent years, Harter (1988) reported a progressive decline in perceived physical competence for girls in grades 8 to 10 but no change for boys across these age levels. T.E. Duncan and Duncan (1991), using a longitudinal design, showed an increase in boys' perceived physical competence across the adolescent years. In sum, the accumulated data on level of perceived competence as a function of age have been equivocal in the physical domain.

Research on the accuracy of one's competence judgments in the academic domain suggests that young children possess unrealistically high perceptions of competence (i.e., perceived competence is much higher than objective competence assessments). Gradually, perceptions become more accurate across the middle and late childhood years (Harter, 1998; Stipek, 1981; Stipek & Tannatt, 1984). The explanations given for the increase in accuracy of perceived academic competence are children's increasing cognitive sophistication to differentiate ability and effort as causes of success (Nicholls, 1978) as well as systematic changes in the information sources or criteria used to judge personal competence (Stipek & MacIver, 1989). Whereas younger children rely primarily on skill mastery and social reinforcement from adults, the emphasis shifts to peer comparison in older children as a means of judging self-abilities. An alternative hypothesis that is customized for the physical achievement domain is offered by motor developmentalists, who contend that young children's motor abilities and performance are quite variable and thus offer inconsistent information pertaining to their physical competencies for completing a given task (Parker, Larkin, & Ackland, 1993). With experience and maturation, however, motor performance becomes less variable and a more constant source of information by which to judge both possibilities and limitations in mastery attempts (Plumert, 1995).

To determine why children may become more accurate in perceived physical competence with age, Horn and Weiss (1991) tested whether accuracy changes are related to differences in sources of information used to determine physical ability. Children ages 8 to 13 years completed measures of level and sources of perceived competence, while teachers rated each child's actual sport competence. First, correlations between perceived and actual competence revealed a progressive increase with age. Second, 8- to 9-year-old participants cited parental feedback as a more important source than 10- to 13-year-olds, who were significantly higher on peer comparison and evaluation sources. Finally, children were classified as accurate estimators, underestimators, or overestimators and were compared on information sources. Accurate and underestimating children cited peer comparison and evaluation as more important for judging their competence than did overestimating children, who scored higher on self-comparison information. McKiddie and Maynard (1997) replicated and extended Horn and Weiss' (1991) findings on age-related differences in accuracy and criteria for assessing physical competence in 11- to 12- and 14- to 15-year-old youth participating in physical education. These findings support age-related improvements in accuracy of competence judgments that were linked, in part, to variations in the type of information sources used by younger versus older children.

The qualitative feature of accuracy of perceived competence is important to consider because accuracy judgments have been related to a number of achievement-related cognitions, affects, and behaviors such as global self-esteem, anxiety, self-regulatory style, preference for challenge, and motor performance (Connell & Ilardi, 1987; Plumert, 1995; Weiss & Horn, 1990). Thus, we encourage continued exploration of the sources or antecedents of accuracy judgments in the physical domain.

Sources of Information Used to Assess Physical Competence

In all of her perceived competence manuals, Harter (e.g., Harter, 1985a, 1988) recommended delving into why children or adolescents hold the self-perceptions that they reported on the scale. In other words, what criteria are used to help form one's judgments of physical competence? Harter suggested that researchers follow up administering the perceived competence scale by interviewing respondents with such questions as, "How do you know that you are good in sports?" and "How can you tell you are athletic?"

An alternative assessment technique for uncovering competence judgment processes was conceived by Thelma Horn in the form of the Sport Competence Information Scale (SCIS; see Horn & Amorose, 1998, for details concerning scale development). The SCIS contains multiple items for many potential sources of information afforded sport participants. These include evaluation by significant adults (parents, coaches, spectators) and peers (teammates), comparison to peers' ability, speed or ease of learning skills, amount of effort exerted, enjoyment of or attraction to the sport, performance statistics, game outcome (win, lose), skill improvement, achieving self-set goals, and game-related feelings (e.g., confidence, nervousness). The benefit of this questionnaire has been its amenability to sampling large numbers of youth to answer key research questions.

Age and Gender Differences in Competence Sources.

Several studies have investigated the question of which sources are used across the middle and late childhood years (ages 8–14 years). Horn and Hasbrook (1986) assessed girls and boys in an age-group soccer league and divided age groups into 8 to 9, 10 to 11, and 12 to 14 years. The two younger groups (ages 8–9, 10–11) rated evaluative feedback by parents and spectators, as well as winning and losing, as more important sources than did the 12- to 14-year-old group, who scored higher on peer (teammate) comparison. These results supported developmental research that reliance on parental feedback declines with age and the use of peer comparison increases. As

reported earlier, these age- and gender-related findings were replicated and extended by Horn and Weiss (1991) with 8- to 13-year-old youth participating in a variety of sports. Finally, Weiss, Bredemeier, and Shewchuk (1985) found a progressive decline in preference for external criteria (i.e., teacher feedback, grades) to judge performance and an increase in internal criteria (i.e., know on one's own when mistakes are made or when performance is good) among 8- to 13-year-old sport program participants.

Horn, Glenn, and Wentzell (1993) extended the work on children's sources of information by investigating adolescent athletes participating in a variety of sports. Age groups were divided along lines of both age and competitive level, with the younger group (14- to 15-year-olds) comprising athletes who played at the freshman or junior varsity level whereas the older group (16- to 18-year-olds) competed at the highest or varsity level. The younger group rated peer evaluation more importantly as a criterion of ability judgments, whereas the older group scored higher on self-comparison/internal information (i.e., skill improvement, effort exerted), goal achievement, and attraction to their sport. These results lent credence to Harter's (1978, 1981a) claim that dependence on social comparison and evaluation in childhood and early adolescence makes way for reliance on self-referenced sources during adolescence. Gender differences also emerged. Male athletes indicated competitive outcomes (win vs. lose, performance statistics) and speed and ease of learning skills as significantly more important for judging their sport competence than did female athletes, who cited self-comparison, internal information, and evaluation by peers, coaches, and spectators. McKiddie and Maynard (1997) also found that 14- to 15-year-old girls rated adult feedback as more important than did boys of the same age, but no gender differences were found between 11- to 12-year-old boys and girls.

Ebbeck (1990) also uncovered gender differences in sources of performance information among college-age men and women participating in university weight training classes. Women reported using goal setting, learning, effort, improvement, and outside gym changes more frequently than men, who relied more heavily on student feedback. Ebbeck also allowed students to add sources they used to determine their ability that were not represented on the questionnaire. Two categories of sources were mentioned that should be considered in future research: physical and psychological health (e.g., how good I feel, mental and emotional fitness) and self-image (e.g., the way I feel about myself, my self-esteem).

The studies reported so far all used self-report to assess quantitative data on the importance of physical competence information sources. Differences from middle childhood through college-age adults were apparent, as were gender differences in the adolescent and adult groups. Recently, two studies used alternative study designs and measurement techniques to access age-related differences in children's use of self-ability information in the physical domain. Chase (1998), using interview procedures and open-ended questions with 8- to 14-year-old youth ($N = 24$) in physical education classes, found that significant others' feedback, subjective performance success, game statistics, and effort exerted in practice were primary sources used by all age groups. Thus, the sources cited in an open-ended format validated the ones that have been tapped by studies using the SCIS.

In contrast, Amorose and Weiss (1998) used an experimental protocol to determine children's ability judgment processes in response to coaches' feedback. Children 6 to 8 and 12 to 14 years of age watched videotapes of similar age and gender athletes and rated these athletes' ability, effort, and future success expectancy after receiving evaluative, informational, or neutral feedback following successful and unsuccessful performance (hitting a baseball or softball). For both age groups, athletes receiving praise after success were rated as higher in ability than athletes receiving either neutral or informational feedback. For unsuccessful performances, both age groups rated athletes as higher in ability if they received informational feedback and lower in ability if they received criticism. Open-ended questions posed at the experiment's end revealed that older youth relied on form and technique (54% of responses) more than coach's feedback (22%) to make ability judgments, whereas younger children cited both sources equally (35% coach feedback, 32% form/technique). It is conceivable that older youth were more experienced at baseball and softball and drew from their knowledge base to make ability judgments by using cues that were not emphasized in the study design.

The studies reported in this section suggest a rather consistent age-related pattern in use of criteria for judging physical competence. Dependence by younger children (under 10 years) on parental feedback and game outcome declines over the childhood years to make way for peer comparison and evaluation sources in youth ages 11 to 15. With internalization of a self-reward system and adoption of mastery goals, older adolescents (16–18 years) show favorability toward self-referenced criteria such as skill improvement, achievement of goals, and attraction toward activity. Gender differences on sources of competence information do not appear until adolescence, which is consistent with the developmental psychology literature (e.g., Eccles, Wigfield, & Schiefele, 1998; Phillips & Zimmerman, 1990). Readers are also directed to Horn and Harris' (1996) chapter reviewing age-related trends and practical implications concerning perceived physical competence in children and adolescents.

Psychological Characteristics and Sources of Competence Information. According to Harter (1978, 1981a), a socialization history in which significant adults appropriately reinforce independent mastery attempts and show approval toward the process of mastery will help children develop high perceptions of competence and control, positive affect, and an intrinsic motivational orientation. Over time, such children should develop a set of mastery goals and a self-reward system, in which they are capable of self-reinforcing their performance and primarily judge ability by using internal criteria (e.g., improvement, effort). Moreover, this developmental shift is believed to be instrumental in maintaining or enhancing perceptions of competence and performance control, positive affect, and motivated behavior. However, Harter also indicated that some children linger in their dependence on external approval and goals because of noncontingent reinforcement by significant adults, especially parents. Therefore, some researchers have focused on the relation between use of internal versus external criteria and psychological characteristics such as perceived competence, self-esteem, perceptions of control, goal orientations, and anxiety.

Horn and Hasbrook (1987) assessed youth soccer players on physical-domain and soccer-specific perceived competence, perceived performance control (internal, powerful others, unknown), and criteria for assessing soccer competence. No significant relationship was found for the youngest group (8–9 years). However, the 10- to 11-year-olds who scored higher in perceived competence indicated greater importance of peer comparison, internal standards (effort, skill improvement), and positive affect toward soccer as competence sources. Also, children higher in perceived control by powerful others reported higher ratings for game outcome. Similar results were found for 12- to 14-year-old youth. These results partially support Harter's contention of an association between self-perceptions and criteria to judge competence in an achievement domain.

Weiss, Ebbeck, and Horn (1997) extended Horn and Hasbrook's (1987) work by examining the relationships among age, psychological characteristics (perceived competence, self-esteem, anxiety), and sources of information. Profiles of children who represented different patterns of these characteristics emerged from data analysis. A positive profile portrayed children higher in perceived competence and self-esteem and lower in trait anxiety, who primarily used self-referenced criteria and parental evaluation to assess ability. A negative profile consisting of younger children (ages 8–9) lower in perceived competence and higher in trait anxiety indicated primary use of pregame anxiety as an information source and low importance assigned to social comparison and self-referenced criteria. A similar negative profile but with older youth (ages 10–13) highlighted primary use of social comparison and evaluation and low importance assigned to self-referenced criteria. These results identified potential at-risk groups who are characterized by negative personality qualities (i.e., lower self-perceptions, higher trait anxiety) and who depend on pregame nervousness or social comparison and evaluation as performance appraisal sources.

Finally, L. Williams (1994) examined the relationship between goal orientations and criteria for judging physical competence. She hypothesized that adolescent athletes who were higher in task goal orientation would report primary use of internal criteria such as learning and improvement, whereas those higher on ego orientation would assign higher importance to criteria such as social comparison and significant others' evaluations. Results were somewhat mixed: Male athletes higher in task orientation reported that both internal and external criteria were important, whereas those higher in ego orientation subscribed to social comparison as an exclusive source. Female athletes higher in task orientation identified internal criteria and parental feedback; those higher in ego orientation reported both social comparison and goal attainment as important sources.

The findings from all three studies (Horn & Hasbrook, 1987; Weiss et al., 1997; L. Williams, 1994) demonstrate strong relationships among age, psychological characteristics, and informa-

tional criteria to judge physical competence. These findings endorse Harter's (1978, 1981a) conceptualization of a link between self-perceptions (perceived competence, self-esteem, perceived control) and internalization of a self-reward system and set of mastery goals.

Changes in Motivational Orientation

One of Harter's (1978, 1981a) key efforts was to refine and extend R.W. White's (1959) effectance motivation construct into a multidimensional, developmental framework. Because White described the child's urgings toward competence as an inherent or intrinsic desire, Harter set out to define intrinsic motivation in developmentally appropriate and achievement domain–specific terms. Her efforts naturally focused on motivational orientation in the classroom (Harter, 1981c), which was defined as the stance the child adopts toward a specific achievement domain and which provides a measure of the reasons for engaging in particular achievement-related behaviors. The major question addressed is, "To what degree is a child's motivation for classroom learning determined by her or his intrinsic interest in learning and mastery, curiosity, and preference for challenge, in contrast to a more extrinsic orientation in which the child is motivated to obtain teacher approval and/or grades and is dependent on the teacher for guidance" (Harter, 1981c, p. 301)?

To answer these questions, Harter (1981c) developed and validated a classroom motivational orientation scale that included five subscales: (a) preference for challenging versus easy work, (b) curiosity or interest versus pleasing the teacher or getting good grades, (c) preference for independent mastery versus dependence on the teacher, (d) capability of making independent judgments versus reliance on the teacher's judgment, and (e) use of internal criteria versus external criteria. The first three dimensions—challenge, curiosity, and independent mastery—showed moderate to high correlations with one another and were described as a motivational subset. The other two dimensions—independent judgment and criteria—reflected a cognitive–informational component, or what the child knows and on what basis she or he makes decisions.

In the validation process, Harter (1981c) administered the five subscales of motivational orientation to more than 3,000 students in grades 3 through 9. A consistent pattern emerged, whereby the challenge, curiosity/interest, and independent mastery dimensions showed a linear decline with age. Harter explained this trend in terms of school systems increasingly emphasizing extrinsic motives (i.e., good grades, compete favorably with others) with increasing grade level, which then stifles children's intrinsic interest in learning and curiosity about knowledge. The declining scores also suggest that children internalize the reward system available in the public schools, which encourages an extrinsic orientation. An opposite pattern was found for the independent judgment and internal criteria subscales, where a progressive increase in scores was observed with age. Because these subscales characterize cognitive abilities, this pattern makes sense in light of children's increasing cognitive maturity to make independent judgments and use internal criteria to determine performance success. However, the declining scores on motivational subscales indicate that, despite these capabilities, children prefer easier work and pleasing the teacher as they progress up the grade ladder. This prompted Harter (1981c) to exclaim,

> Though it would appear that one's motivation to perform in school is becoming less intrinsic with age, one's motivation in other domains may not show this trend. The child may be channeling intrinsic interest into other areas of his or her life (e.g., social relationships, sports, and other extracurricular activities). Since this particular scale tapped the cognitive domain only, there are no data to bear on this interpretation. (p. 310)

To explore this possibility, Weiss et al. (1985) modified Harter's (1981c) scale and assessed children in grades 3 through 6 on motivational orientation for physical skill learning. They found a similar pattern for the various subscales. The Challenge and Curiosity subscales showed a slight increase from grade 3 to 4, after which a sharp decline was manifested from grades 4 to 6. The Mastery subscale showed a steep decline from grades 3 to 5 with an increase from grades 5 to 6. Moreover, the Mastery subscale revealed lower absolute values than those found by Harter in the classroom setting. For independent judgment and internal criteria, a linear increase in scores was found from grades 3 to 6. Thus, the answer to Harter's musings about age trends in intrinsic motivation in other domains revealed that, in general, children decrease in intrinsic motivation and increase in cognitive abilities in the physical domain.

Weiss et al. (1985) analyzed these results in light of children's socialization through sport and the shift in motivational goals at higher competitive levels. Sport participants learn that if they depend on the coach to judge successful execution of skills and strategies and if they orient their responses toward an emphasis on winning and comparing favorably to others, this is likely to determine their future participation opportunities and performance evaluations from the coach. This scenario was supported in a study by Deci, Schwartz, Sheinman, and Ryan (1981), who found that children whose classroom teachers exhibited more of a controlling rather than an autonomous style of teaching reported higher extrinsic motivation scores. Moreover, both players and coaches show an increase in the goal of "having a winning team" from elementary to high school levels (Chaumeton & Duda, 1988).

Clearly, these developmental trends for intrinsic motivation in the physical domain are cause for concern. However, few studies of age or competitive level differences in intrinsic motivation have been conducted. No doubt, changes in the social context of sport with age and competitive level, much like Harter found with school systems, are likely candidates for the decline in intrinsic motivation in sport. Increased importance placed on winning (Horn & Harris, 1996), a shift in coaches' and parents' goal orientations from task- to ego-involvement (Duda, 1993), emphasis on performance outcomes more than learning (Ames, 1992b), and encouragement toward "game reasoning" (Shields & Bredemeier, 1995) to maximize chances for winning are some examples. Thus, future research should seek to uncover the correlates of change in motivational orientation along with concomitant changes in perceived competence level, accuracy, and sources as youth climb the competitive sport participation ladder.

Influence by Significant Others on Self-Perceptions, Affect, and Motivational Orientation

Harter's (1978, 1981a) competence motivation theory highlighted the role of significant others in shaping children's self-perceptions, affect, and motivational orientation in specific achievement domains. Moreover, she showed that beliefs and behaviors communicated about the process, rather than the product, of mastery attempts are the keys to children's successful adoption of a developmentally appropriate set of internal standards and self-reward system. Harter's inclusion of significant others was inspired by the work of Charles Cooley, who believed that self-esteem was heavily steeped in social origins. His notion of the "looking-glass self" emphasized that individuals use important adults and peers as social mirrors through which they evaluate their competencies and worth as a person. Harter (1990a) showed that social regard or support is a powerful predictor of self-conceptions in children through middle-age adults, but the source of support that is most salient varies developmentally. For young children and adolescents, especially, parental influence is salient and strong, whereas perceived social acceptance and support by general peers (i.e., classmates) and close friends emerge as key determinants of self-perceptions throughout the life span. This section begins with a discussion of research on significant adult influence in the form of parents and coaches and then moves to the individual's peer group as a source of social regard.

Parents

A number of studies in the physical domain illustrate a strong link between parental influence—in the form of attitudes, beliefs, expectancies, and behaviors—and children's self-perceptions, affective responses, self-reported motivation, and levels of activity involvement. According to Harter (1978, 1981a, 1990a), parents are especially important as transmitters of information about the child's competence through the mechanisms of modeling and reinforcement. In youth sport, these behaviors are readily and vividly observed between parents and children in both positive (e.g., unconditional support, encouragement) and negative (e.g., pressure to perform, criticism for errors) ways. Despite the salient role of parents in children's psychological development through sport participation, relatively few studies (compared with the academic domain) have been conducted to more closely examine this link.

Brustad (1988; Brustad & Weiss, 1987) was specifically interested in children's perceptions of parental pressure and evaluation-related worries as potential correlates of positive (enjoyment) and negative (anxiety) affective outcomes in youth sport. Although Brustad and Weiss found no evidence of a link between social evaluation worries and competitive anxiety, Brustad did find a significant relationship for both girls and boys between perceptions of parental pressure and season-long basketball enjoyment. Children who perceived less pressure from parents to perform well reported higher levels of sport enjoyment. Ommundsen and Vaglum (1991) obtained similar results with Norwegian youth soccer players. Brustad also found that children who were higher in competitive anxiety reported more frequent worries about negative evaluation from important others, including parents, than did those lower in anxiety. As well, Weiss, Wiese, and Klint (1989) found that for competitive youth gymnasts, "what my parents will say" and "letting my parents down" were the two most frequently cited worries before competitive events.

Some studies have tapped perceptions of parental support and its relationship to competence perceptions, motivational orientations, and behaviors. For example, Rose, Larkin, and Berger (1994) assessed perceptions of social support among children from physical education classes who were divided into low, moderate, and high motor coordination (i.e., actual physical competence). Highly coordinated boys and girls perceived significantly greater social support from parents than did either the low or moderately coordinated children. Thus, the children who would benefit most from supportive parents reported the least amount of positive responses to their involvement.

Other studies consistent with competence motivation theory focused on highly skilled youth sport competitors. Weiss and Hayashi (1995) sampled high-level competitive gymnasts (ages 7–16) who started at a young age (M = 7.0 years), had participated for an average of five years, and spent on average of 19 hours per week practicing their sport. These intense competitors reported extensive and primarily positive parental influence in the form of parents attending meets, encouraging their children's participation, demonstrating positive affect toward their children's involvement, and holding positive beliefs and realistic expectations about their competence. However, a small percentage (10% to 25%) of gymnasts reported negative interactions with and affective responses from their parents. Leff and Hoyle (1995) examined perceptions of parental support (i.e., involvement, encouragement, positive affect) and pressure (i.e., expectations, concerns about winning, pressure to play well) in high-level competitive tennis players (ages 6–18) who were training at year-round tennis academies. Greater perceived support and lower perceived pressure from fathers and mothers were positively related to greater enjoyment, perceived tennis competence, and global self-esteem.

In a direct test of competence motivation hypotheses, McCullagh, Matzkanin, Shaw, and Maldonado (1993) posited that relationships should be observed between child and parent motives for the child's sport participation, and between child and parent perceptions of the child's competencies. That is, parental modeling, approval, and reinforcement over time should result in the child internalizing motives and competency beliefs that are deemed important by the parents. Parents and children both reported that intrinsic motives (e.g., skill development, fun) were the most important reasons for their sport involvement and that extrinsic motives (e.g., competition, recognition) were least important. Moreover, a significant and moderate relationship was found for parents' and children's perceived social acceptance and athletic competence.

Finally, Babkes and Weiss (1999) comprehensively examined parental influence on children's competence motivation dimensions. Among competitive soccer players (ages 9–12), specific relationships were observed for (a) children's perceptions of parental influence and perceived competence, affect, and motivational orientation, and (b) parent-reported attitudes and behaviors for these same psychosocial outcomes. Categories of parent variables included (a) advocacy (i.e., encouragement to participate), (b) beliefs about athletic competency, (c) positive performance responses (positive and negative reactions), (d) expectations or pressure, (e) involvement (instructing and attending games), and (f) role modeling (i.e., affect toward and participation in regular physical activity). Results for the first study goal indicated a significant and moderately strong relationship between children's perceptions of parental beliefs and behaviors and their soccer experiences. Boys and girls who reported more positive perceptions of their mother's and father's competency beliefs, responses to soccer performance, and role modeling behavior reported higher perceived soccer competence, enjoyment, and intrinsic motivation. However, a nonsignificant relationship emerged between parent-reported beliefs and behaviors and children's self-perceptions, affect, and motivation. The combination of these two results infers that children's perceptions, not parents' report, of parental influence are more important contributors to children's psychological well-being.

The studies just reviewed strongly support the role of parents in children's competence motivation. Specifically, significant relationships were observed between parental support and pressure and children's affective responses to participation (enjoyment, anxiety), perceptions of athletic and sport-specific competence, motivational orientation (i.e., preference for challenge, use of internal criteria), and achievement behaviors (physical activity involvement).

Coaches

The coach has been singled out as a powerful socializing agent in the physical domain (see chapter 10). Coaches, in the way they structure the practice or skill-learning context and respond to participants' mastery behaviors and outcomes, can significantly affect children's and adolescents' competence perceptions, global self-worth, affect, motivational orientation, and actual participation (i.e., continue, discontinue). Coaches' feedback and reinforcement generally comprise informational (i.e., instruction) or evaluative (i.e., praise, criticism) responses to performance attempts and outcomes (successful, unsuccessful). The classic studies by Ron Smith and Frank Smoll (see Smith & Smoll, 1996, for a review) demonstrated that the quantity and quality of coaches' evaluative (i.e., praise for success, less punishment for errors) and informational (i.e., instruction following errors) feedback resulted in higher perceived baseball competence, global self-esteem, enjoyment, and intention to continue playing and lower anxiety and attrition rates in male youth baseball players.

To date, only three studies have examined the role of the coach on children's psychosocial development from the perspective of competence motivation theory. Horn (1985) studied the reinforcement patterns of coaches on players' perceptions of competence and control in practice and competitive contexts. She recorded softball coaches' frequency of evaluative and informational feedback and then determined whether any specific behaviors contributed above and beyond season-long skill improvement to self-perceptions in 13- to 15-year-old female softball players. Results indicated that players who received more frequent praise after successful performances scored lower in perceived physical competence, whereas players who received greater frequencies of criticism in response to errors reported higher competence perceptions. These paradoxical results were explained by Horn in terms of the contingent and appropriate nature of the feedback. Specifically, praise was not given in response to specific and optimally challenging skill accomplishments but instead was offered for mastering easy skills or exhibiting mediocre performance. In contrast, criticism was given based on specific performance levels and usually was combined with valuable information on how to improve on subsequent mastery attempts. To further support this inference, Horn (1984) reported that lower skilled players were given more praise whereas the more talented athletes received more criticism for their efforts.

Black and Weiss (1992) replicated and extended Horn's (1985) study by assessing age-group swimmers' (ages 10–18) perceptions of (rather than observed) contingent coaching praise, information, encouragement, and criticism after successful and unsuccessful swimming performances. Results indicated no relationship between coaching behaviors and perceived competence, enjoyment, and motivation among the youngest group of swimmers (ages 10–11). However, significant and moderately strong correlations were found for the 12- to 14- and 15- to 18-year-old female and male competitive swimmers. Greater perceived praise and praise combined with information after successful swims, and greater encouragement and encouragement combined with information after poor swims, were associated with higher levels of perceived swimming competence, success, challenge motivation, and enjoyment. For 15- to 18-year-olds, more frequent criticism after poor performances was also associated with lower values on these variables. These results not only support Harter's competence motivation predictions but also help to explain the contradictory findings by Horn (1985).

Finally, Allen and Howe (1998) followed up both Horn (1985) and Black and Weiss (1992) by assessing the relationship between contingent coaching behaviors and self-perceptions in high-level adolescent (ages 14–18) female field hockey players. Consistent with Horn's results, skill level was a significant predictor of competence perceptions, but certain coaching behaviors contributed to perceived field hockey competence above and beyond skill level. Specifically, more frequent praise plus instruction was positively associated with perceived competence, whereas more frequent encouragement plus instruction after skill errors was negatively related to perceived competence. The authors explained these latter results in terms of the potential negative cognitive and affective responses that may accompany mistake-contingent encouragement especially if it is given in a team setting. That is, encouragement given in response to a skill error may conspicuously high-light the fact that the athlete just committed a skill error and, in the public appraisal of her teammates, may lower perceptions of competence.

Harter's (1978, 1981a) inclusion of modeling, approval, and reinforcement behaviors by significant adults in children's development of an intrinsic motivational orientation (i.e., high perceived competence and internal control, positive affect, preference for challenge, use of internal criteria) should encourage others to more closely examine the critical role of coaches. Horn and Harris (1996) illustrated through real-world examples how coaches have the choice and power to steer the social context of sport toward a more intrinsic (i.e., mastery-oriented) or extrinsic (i.e., normative-oriented) environment. Coaches' organizational structure of skill learning contexts and philosophy of success communicate loudly what is valued, recognized, and reinforced in the particular achievement setting of sport. As such, the influence of coaching behaviors on individuals' psychological well-being at all ages and skill levels remains a question of theoretical and practical significance.

Peers

One's peers are powerful socializing agents who contribute beyond the influence of adults to children's cognitive, emotional, and social development (see Bukowski, Newcomb, & Hartup, 1996). Harter's (1987, 1990a) study of domain-specific self-conceptions and perceived social regard has consistently shown that both constructs strongly predict global self-worth and emotions in children as well as adults. Specifically, perceived peer acceptance is one of the two most important dimensions related to global self-worth, and general peer and close friend sources of social regard are critical determinants of global self-worth, multiple emotions, and motivational orientation.

Despite the centrality of peers in one's socioemotional development, peer interactions and relationships in the physical domain have been studied much less frequently than the influence of parents, teachers, and coaches (Weiss, Smith, & Theeboom, 1996). This is especially surprising because in areas such as participation motivation, sources of enjoyment and anxiety, sport commitment, and sources of perceived competence, researchers have identified social acceptance from peers, positive team interactions and support, and close friendships as pivotal to children's psychological well-being and motivational orientation. Thus, the influence of peers extends not only to motivation but also to its antecedents (e.g., perceived competence) and consequences (e.g., participation behavior). This points to a need for a renewed interest and focused research efforts on individuals' peer groups as contributors to cognitive, emotional, and psychological well-being in the physical domain.

In the developmental psychology literature, peer acceptance refers to one's popularity (degree to which one is liked or attracted by one's peers) or worthiness within one's peer group. In contrast, friendship refers to aspects of a particular dyadic relationship, such as mutual liking, similarity, and social support functions (e.g., esteem enhancement, loyalty, intimacy, emotional support). Finally, social competence refers to the skills necessary for having successful peer interactions and relationships, such as perspective taking, cooperative problem solving, and interpersonal communication skills (see Rubin, Bukowski, & Parker, 1998). The crucial role afforded to peers in youth psychosocial development is attributed to the early work of Harry Stack Sullivan (1953). He proposed that peer relationships in early and middle childhood were essential for children's sense of belonging in the group, and that close friendships or "chumships" formed during adolescence enabled youth to experience self-validation, overcome loneliness, and develop an overall sense of psychological well-being (Rubin et al., 1998).

To date, a handful of studies have sought to understand peer relationships in the physical domain. Many of these studies are descriptive or atheoretical in nature, but more recent studies have been grounded within theoretical frameworks. Because Harter's (1978, 1981a, 1987, 1990a) theorizing is pertinent to the role of significant adults and peers in multiple domains, studies of peer acceptance, friendship, and social competence have used her model for explaining relationships among peer variables and cognitive, emotional, and motivational consequences in the physical domain.

Peer Acceptance. In her development of self-perception scales for children and adolescents, Harter (1985a, 1988) obtained moderate correlations (r = .30s–.50s) between perceived athletic competence and social acceptance from peers across a number of samples. These correlations suggest that believing one is good in sports is associated with perceptions of popularity and acceptance within one's peer group. Research conducted within organized sport and physical education has shown that children and teenagers identify

"being good at sports" as an important quality for being popular with one's peers, especially among boys (e.g., Chase & Dummer, 1992).

Evans and Roberts (1987), in a clever study of peer status, found that a pecking order of choosing up sides resulted in the most athletically talented boys (grades 3–6) being picked first, who, in turn, held the leadership roles and played the most central positions. This phenomenon also provided these athletically gifted boys with more opportunities to strengthen their friendships and affirm acceptance from the larger peer group. Similarly, the less skilled boys were often "locked out" of games, which signified low peer acceptance and fewer opportunities to affirm social relationships. Glenn and Horn (1993) examined peer status within high school girls soccer teams and found that members were most likely to be identified by teammates as leaders (i.e., afforded peer status) if they were good soccer players, believed they were good in soccer, reported high instrumental behaviors and, to a lesser extent, expressive behaviors. These studies consistently show the strong link between sport ability, certain psychological characteristics, and popularity and status within one's peer group.

Weiss and Duncan (1992) tested the link between physical competence and peer acceptance more directly. They obtained perceived athletic competence and peer acceptance ratings from children (ages 8–13) attending a summer sport camp as well as corresponding ratings from teachers of their actual physical competence and popularity. A significant and strong relationship emerged between the physical competence and peer acceptance variables. Children who perceived themselves as athletically skilled and were rated by their instructors as such also rated themselves as popular with their peer group and were rated by their instructors as high in peer acceptance. Kunesh, Hasbrook, and Lewthwaite (1992), taking a more sociological approach, used interviews, observations, and peer nominations in finding that peer acceptance was strongly related to 11- to 12-year-old girls' positive and negative emotional responses and inclination to continue physical activity and sport participation.

The few studies conducted on peer acceptance in the physical domain consistently point to the powerful influence that one's peer group has on competence perceptions, affective responses, and motivated behavior. Harter (1987, 1990a) found that peers become a more salient reference group than parents starting in late childhood and that perceptions of social adequacy and social support from one's generalized peer group (i.e., classmates, coworkers) are a constant predictor of global self-worth across the life span.

Friendship. Having friends, the identity of one's friends, and the quality of one's friendships are salient and distinct aspects contributing to psychosocial development in youth (Hartup, 1996). Social support from close friends such as esteem enhancement and companionship are crucial features of social adjustment, reduced life stress, and psychological well-being in youth (Rubin et al., 1998). Moreover, a generally accepted notion is that friendship must be studied within the specific social context in which interactions take place (Newcomb & Bagwell, 1995; Zarbatany, Ghesquiere, & Mohr, 1992). That is, findings about friendship in school contexts do not necessarily apply to physical activity contexts. However, only recently have close friendships in sport been studied regarding their significance to children's and adolescents' psychological growth and development.

Bigelow, Lewko, and Salhani (1989) studied children's (ages 9–12) friendship expectations within the sport context. They found that children believed that playing on a sport team contributes to developing new friendships and nurturing particular friendship features such as intimacy, ego reinforcement, loyalty, stimulation value, and acceptance. S.C. Duncan (1993) examined the influence of esteem support and companionship on emotional and motivational outcomes among middle school youth (ages 12–15). Youth who perceived greater friendship quality in these two areas reported greater positive affect during physical education and interest in choosing activities outside of the school setting.

Weiss and Smith (1999, 2001; Weiss et al., 1996) embarked on a series of studies to uncover children's and adolescents' conceptions of friendship in the sport context. In the first study (Weiss et al., 1996), several positive dimensions emerged (e.g., self-esteem enhancement, companionship, pleasant play and association, intimacy, loyalty) as well as some negative dimensions (e.g., conflict, betrayal) of best sport friendships. Importantly, the youth interviewed primarily described their sport friendships in terms of their esteem-enhancing characteristics and positive emotions that were provoked. Next, a sport friendship quality measure was developed and validated consisting of six features: companionship and pleasant play, self-esteem enhancement and supportiveness, things in common, loyalty and intimacy, con-

flict resolution, and conflict (Weiss & Smith, 1999). In the third study (Weiss & Smith, 2001), age and gender variations were found on several friendship quality dimensions, as well as significant relationships between positive friendship qualities and enjoyment and sport commitment. A valid measure of friendship quality should enable researchers to test predictions within competence motivation theory in the future, such as the relative influence of parents and peers at varying age levels and the relationships between friendship quality and self-perceptions, affect, and motivation.

Finally, A.L. Smith (1999) conducted a comprehensive test of the network of relationships among peer variables (acceptance, friendship), self-perceptions (physical self-worth), affective responses, intrinsic motivation, and physical activity behavior within Harter's competence motivation model. Smith studied middle school youth (ages 12–15), finding that both girls' and boys' perceptions of greater peer acceptance and close friendship were related to higher levels of physical self-worth, positive affect, intrinsic motivation, and physical activity levels. These results carry important theoretical implications (support for Harter's model using simultaneous analysis) and practical recommendations for encouraging greater physical activity behavior in early adolescent girls and boys.

It is clear that significant peers who provide acceptance and friendship are critical socializing agents in children's sport experiences. Harter's (1978, 1981a) competence motivation theory and mediational model of global self-worth (Harter, 1987, 1998) provide a logical and appealing roadmap for studying the nature of children's and adolescents' social networks and the pattern of these social relationships with cognitive, emotional, and behavioral outcomes in the physical domain. Moreover, interventions focused on enhancing peer acceptance and friendship quality through structuring of a mastery motivational climate may be the key to maintaining or enhancing feelings of competence, enjoyment, and physical activity levels.

Perceived Competence and Achievement-Related Cognitions, Affect, and Behavior

The pathways in Harter's (1978, 1981a, 1981b) model suggest relationships between perceptions of competence and achievement-related cognitions (e.g., perceived control, self-esteem, motivational orientation), positive and negative affective responses, and behavior (e.g., effort and persistence, physical activity level). To date, studies designed to test these relationships have gleaned strong support for competence motivation theory. As a result, Weiss and Ebbeck (1996) detailed intervention strategies for enhancing perceived physical competence that, in turn, facilitates positive self-evaluations, emotional experiences, and motivated behavior.

Perceived Competence and Achievement Cognitions

Perceptions of physical competence consistently emerge as a strong correlate or predictor of several cognitive variables salient to competence motivation, such as perceptions of control, motivational orientation, and global self-esteem. Few studies have examined the link between perceived competence and control. In Harter's scheme (Connell, 1980; Harter, 1978, 1981a; Harter & Connell, 1984), perceptions of control refer to the degree to which the child understands who or what is responsible for her or his success and failure in a particular achievement domain. Three sources of control have been identified: internal (i.e., "I am responsible for this event"), powerful others (i.e., "Other people are responsible for this event"), and unknown (i.e., "I don't know why an event occurs"). In a handful of studies, perceptions of control were strongly related to perceived competence, motivational orientation, and behavioral consequences (Weigand & Broadhurst, 1998; Weiss et al., 1986; Weiss & Horn, 1990; Weiss, McAuley, Ebbeck, & Wiese, 1990). For example, Weiss et al. (1990) found that children higher in perceived competence (physical or social) made attributions for performance that were more internal and stable, higher in personal control, and lower in external control than their lower perceived competence counterparts. Weiss et al. (1986) reported that participants scoring higher in perceived physical competence and lower in perceived unknown control scored higher in intrinsic motivational orientation.

The results of these studies suggest that children with higher levels of perceived competence are more likely to adopt a functional pattern of cognitions and affect, reflected by perceptions of personal rather than external or unknown control, an intrinsic motivational orientation, and lower anxiety. Because intrinsic pleasure or positive af-

fect has been showcased as central to competence motivation theory, several studies have been designed to investigate the antecedents and consequences of positive, as well as negative, affective responses to physical activity participation.

Perceived Competence and Affective Responses

Several studies have demonstrated that perceptions of physical competence are moderately or strongly related to positive affective experiences, such as enjoyment or attraction to physical activity, and are negatively related to competitive anxiety and stress (Brustad, 1988; Scanlan & Lewthwaite, 1986; Scanlan, Stein, & Ravizza, 1989, 1991; Scanlan & Simons, 1992). Brustad found that higher levels of intrinsic motivational orientation were related to season-long enjoyment, but only general self-esteem was significantly related to competitive trait anxiety for youth sport participants. Ommundsen and Vaglum (1991) replicated Brustad's study with 12- to 16-year-old male competitive soccer players in Norway. Boyd and Yin (1996) also found perceived competence to be the strongest predictor of enjoyment among high school athletes across a number of sports.

Ebbeck and Weiss (1998) used a scale assessing multiple positive (i.e., proud, satisfied, happy) and negative affects (i.e., unhappy, guilty, angry) and found that perceived competence strongly predicted positive affect and, to a lesser degree, negative affect. As well, a model specifying positive and negative affect as predictor variables and perceived competence as the dependent variable also achieved a good fit, with positive (but not negative) affect strongly predicting perceived competence. Finally, A.L. Smith (1999) uncovered a strong relationship between physical self-worth (consisting of sport competence, physical appearance, strength, and conditioning) and attraction to physical activity among female and male middle school youth.

Perceived Competence and Achievement Behaviors

Perceptions of competence are consistently related to motivational orientation, perceived control, self-esteem, and attraction to physical activity. However, ultimately we are most interested in behavioral consequences of changes in perceived competence such as athletic performance, effort and persistence, and physical activity levels. Yet this is an area in which sport psychology has not kept pace with investigations in exercise psychology, where assessments of level, intensity, and duration of physical activity are standard. To date, only a handful of studies have demonstrated the impact that perceived sport competence has on behavioral outcomes.

As part of the Weiss et al. (1986) study discussed earlier, perceptions of competence and control and motivational orientation were examined in relationship to competence in three sport skills (baseball, swimming, gymnastics). Sport program instructors who had interacted with these children (ages 8–12) and observed their activities for 7 weeks rated their sport competence. Perceived competence was either strongly related to its corresponding sport performance (i.e., perceived swimming competence → swimming ability) or generally related to a specific sport ability (i.e., perceived athletic competence → baseball ability). Ulrich (1987) examined young children's (kindergarten to grade 4) perceived and actual motor competence and their relation to choices to participate in organized sport programs. Children higher in perceived physical competence demonstrated superior motor performance in a variety of playground and sport skills (e.g., soccer dribble, playground ball dribble, softball throw, broad jump) compared to those lower in competence perceptions.

Ebbeck (1994) examined the relationship between skill level and several competence motivation variables in tennis participants 10 to 67 years of age. Skill level was objectively determined by using the United States Tennis Association classification rating system, which assigns a score ranging from 1.0 to 7.0 based on standard stroke and game characteristics. Robust findings for male and female participants showed a strong relationship between tennis skill rating and perceptions of tennis competence as well as between tennis skill and preference for optimal challenging activities. Sonstroem, Harlow, and Salisbury (1993) studied the relationship between perceptions of competence, global self-esteem, and swimming performance in adolescent participants. They also demonstrated the strong tie between competence perceptions and sport behavior. Using path analysis procedures and a longitudinal design, these researchers showed not only that actual competence contributes to perceived competence changes but that such variations in self-perceptions also alter swimming performance.

A.L. Smith (1999) focused on physical activity behavior among 12- to 15-year-old boys and girls,

a developmental period marked by reported declines in participation. A model that included several salient competence motivation variables was specified and simultaneously analyzed in relationship to reported frequency and intensity of leisure-time physical activity. Results indicated that peer influence (acceptance and close friendship), physical self-worth, positive affect toward physical activity, and challenge motivation directly or indirectly (through mediating variables) predicted physical activity levels in both girls and boys. This study was important in that it included social, cognitive, affective, and behavioral variables as specified by Harter's (1978, 1981a) competence motivation theory.

A Comprehensive Model of Global Self-Worth

In Harter's (1978, 1981a, 1981b) original competence motivation theory, she implicated not only the important role of domain-specific competence perceptions but also global self-worth or self-esteem. Specifically, successful mastery attempts enhance perceptions of competence and control, positive affect, and global self-worth, which, in turn, directly bear on continued motivation in a particular achievement domain. However, the emphasis on operationalizing constructs and customizing an understanding of relationships among salient variables in specific achievement domains meant that Harter temporarily pushed aside a focus on global self-worth. In Harter's (1985b, 1986, 1987, 1990a, 1998, 1999) later writings, the central role of global self-worth emerged as paramount to her theorizing about determinants of affect and motivation.

Harter's research consistently shows that children ages 8 and older are capable of distinguishing between self-competencies in specific achievement domains as well as making global judgments of self-worth (see Harter, 1998, 1999, for reviews). She introduced a comprehensive model of global self-worth, one in which self-worth mediates the relationship between domain-specific competence perceptions and social support on affect and motivation (see figure 5.3; Harter, 1985b, 1987). Specifically, William James' notion of perceived competence in domains valued as important for success and Charles Cooley's "looking-glass self" in the form of perceived social regard or support from significant adults and peers serve as the two primary antecedents of global self-worth. Affective reactions (e.g., happy, proud, depressed, anx-

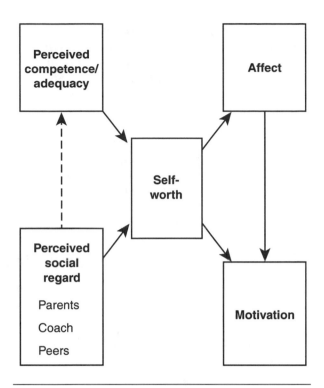

Figure 5.3 Susan Harter's mediational model of global self-worth customized for the physical domain.

Reprinted, by permission, from S. Harter, 1987, The determinants and mediational role of global self-worth in children. In *Contemporary topics in developmental psychology*, edited by N. Eisenberg (New York: Wiley), 219–242.

ious) and motivation to engage in achievement behaviors (e.g., choice, effort, persistence) represent the consequences or outcomes of variations in global self-worth levels. Affect is also posited to directly influence motivated behavior. Moreover, Harter traced the developmental patterns of relationships among antecedents, self-worth, and consequences from young children through late adulthood (see Harter, 1990a, 1998, 1999).

Harter (1990a, 1990b, 1999) uncovered several consistent findings pertaining to the mediational model of global self-worth as it relates to children through older adults. First, perceptions of competence in areas of importance and the influence of significant others are equally strong determinants of self-worth. Second, self-conceptions of physical appearance and social acceptance are the competency/adequacy domains that consistently emerge as the strongest predictors of self-worth. Third, social support from one's general peer group (e.g., classmates, civic group members, co-workers) is the strongest source of social support, with family members (parents, significant other) a close second throughout the life span. Fourth, self-worth and affect are linked strongly beginning

in middle childhood. These robust findings offer considerable support for Harter's comprehensive model of self-worth. Given the consistent and strong findings in the physical domain that perceived competence and socializers' beliefs and behaviors influence achievement-related cognitions, affects, and behaviors, the model carries both theoretical and practical significance in the achievement domain of sport and physical activity. Moreover, because the literature demonstrates that significant adults and peers are salient sources of physical competence information in children and adolescents, we included a link between these two constructs (see dotted line leading from social support to perceived competence in figure 5.3).

Some of the studies previously mentioned provide strong support for Harter's (1985b, 1987) model of self-worth (Ebbeck & Weiss, 1998; Klint, 1988; A.L. Smith, 1999). Ebbeck and Weiss focused on affect as a mediator of the relationship between perceived physical competence and global self-worth (rather than a consequence of global self-worth), a link investigated by Harter (1990a, 1990b) in her research on the influence of depressed mood on self-worth and suicidal thoughts. Ebbeck and Weiss found that positive affect (i.e., proud, happy) mediated the influence of perceived physical competence on global self-esteem in children (ages 8–13) attending an instructional sports program. Smith instead honed in on the competence/adequacy domains of peer acceptance and close friendship as they affect physical self-worth, affect, and motivation in young adolescents. Both forms of peer influence were instrumental contributors to self-worth, affect, and motivation variables.

Ebbeck and Stuart (1993, 1996) examined the relative influence of perceived competence and importance on global self-esteem in two samples of youth sport participants. In the first study, perceived physical competence, individual importance of being successful, and team importance of being successful in combination contributed to explaining variations in global self-worth. However, perceived competence was by far the most meaningful predictor of self-esteem. In the second study, youth sport participants of three age groups (8–9, 10–11, 12–13) completed measures of perceived physical competence and importance of success to self, parents, coach, and team. For each age group, perceived competence was significantly predictive of global self-worth. In addition, parent and team importance were significant contributors to self-esteem for the 8- to 9- and 12- to 13-year-old groups, respectively. These results support Harter's (1987) model in that domain-specific self-conceptions (perceived physical competence) and perceived importance to significant adults and peers of being successful in sport emerged as important determinants of global self-worth.

Harter, Waters, and Whitesell (1998) explored the concept of relational self-worth, or variations in global self-evaluations depending on the social sources of self-evaluation or interpersonal context in which judgments are made. To do so, they contextualized assessment of self-worth by asking high school students (ages 14–18) how they felt about or regarded themselves as a person when they were around parents, teachers, and male and female classmates. Results revealed a stronger relationship between validation support and relational self-worth for corresponding contexts (parent support, self-worth around parents) than for global self-worth. This finding means that adolescents judge themselves as persons differently depending on the social or interpersonal context (i.e., around parents, classmates, teachers) that serves as the frame of reference for self-judgments. These findings also support the comprehensive model of self-worth, specifically in relation to sources of social support and global self-evaluations.

Harter's (1987, 1999) mediational model of global self-worth offers an appealing model from which to design empirical research and educational interventions in the physical domain. These efforts will contribute to our understanding and facilitation of perceived competence, global self-worth, affect, and motivation in sport and physical activity contexts. The large majority of studies reported in this section that are based on competence motivation theory support various links or pathways in the model. Weiss and Ebbeck (1996) reviewed the supporting links and suggested practical implications for enhancing self-esteem and perceptions of competence in youth participating in physical activity.

Summary

The concepts and mechanisms expressed in competence motivation theory and the mediational model of global self-worth are supported across a number of achievement domains and across the life span (see Harter, 1998, 1999, for a review). Moreover, the theoretical links translate directly to applications for teaching and coaching youth as well as adults. More research is needed, especially intervention studies that attempt to enhance multidimensional self-concepts by manipulating the physical and social context of sport. Successful programs have been offered by Marsh and colleagues (Marsh, Richards, & Barnes, 1986a, 1986b; Marsh & Peart, 1988) and Ebbeck and Gibbons (1998), and others should follow suit. Moreover, developmental research that extends beyond level, accuracy, and sources of perceived competence is needed to determine if the pattern of relationships among social, cognitive, affective, and behavioral variables in the mediational model of self-worth holds for groups that vary in age, gender, and competitive level. The productive research to date stemming from Harter's models provides a great deal of optimism for future programs of research.

COGNITIVE EVALUATION THEORY

First formulated by Deci (1975) and subsequently extended by Deci and Ryan (1985), cognitive evaluation theory is one of the major theoretical frameworks concerned with motivational processes. It is one of the theories comprising self-determination theory, a broader framework developed to study motivation of human functioning. According to this broad perspective, motivation is based on a set of innate psychological needs, namely self-determination, competence, and interpersonal relatedness. Cognitive evaluation theory centers primarily on perceptions of self-determination and competence, especially as they mediate the effects of external and internal events on the person's motivation.

The essential idea underlying cognitive evaluation theory is that intrinsic motivation is based on people's need to be competent and self-determining in dealing with their environment. Deci and Ryan (1985) defined intrinsic motivation as the natural tendency to engage in interesting activities to seek and achieve optimal challenges. Extrinsic motivation, in contrast, refers to performing an activity to achieve instrumental outcomes. When an optimal challenge is mastered, the individual experiences an increase in interest and enjoyment that, ultimately, translates into effort and persistence in that activity.

Self-determination can be defined as perceiving choice and allowing those choices to determine one's behaviors. It is, according to Deci (1980), an intrinsic need to experience freedom of choice in initiating one's behavior. Perceived competence refers to beliefs about one's ability in an achievement domain. Cognitive evaluation theory predicts a close relationship between perceived competence and intrinsic motivation in that the more competent individuals feel about performing an activity, the higher their intrinsic motivation levels. However, according to Deci and Ryan, two conditions are needed to maintain this relationship. First, the activity must be optimally challenging; otherwise, it will not provide the individual with sufficient intrinsic interest regardless of how competent the person feels. Second, perceived competence must exist within the context of self-determination. That is, perceived competence will only affect intrinsic motivation when people believe that they have choices in dealing with the situation.

Theoretical Propositions

Deci and Ryan (1985) elaborated on cognitive evaluation theory in four propositions. Proposition 1 refers to people's intrinsic need to be self-determining and suggests that external events can affect intrinsic motivation by influencing perceived locus of causality. Situations promoting an external locus of causality (i.e., behavior is perceived to be controlled by outside factors) will deny self-determination and undermine intrinsic motivation, whereas events that promote an internal locus of causality (i.e., behavior is seen as determined by one's freedom of choice) will facilitate self-determination and intrinsic motivation. This proposition relates to whether events are perceived to be controlling or autonomy-supporting, which foster control-determined beliefs, feelings, and actions. For example, sport programs that allow participants to provide input into or make choices about their participation and goals promote feelings of self-determination. Perceptions of an autocratic or rigid coaching style, in contrast, likely lead to feelings of coercion and decreased self-determination.

Proposition 2 refers to a person's need to be competent by mastering optimal challenges. This proposition posits that external events will affect a person's intrinsic motivation by providing information about her or his competence in a domain or activity. Interpersonal situations that communicate positive information (e.g., contingent and appropriate praise for successful performance) about a person's ability will enhance her or his perceived competence and intrinsic motivation.

In contrast, events that convey negative information (e.g., punishment for skill errors) about the person's abilities should diminish perceived competence and intrinsic motivation.

Proposition 3 states that the informational or controlling aspects that coexist in external situations may hold different salience for individuals. That is, the same event can be perceived as primarily informational or controlling. For example, an individual may perceive an external reward (e.g., money, trophy) as an indicator about his sport competence. In contrast, another person may perceive the same reward as a constraint or coercion to hold her in the activity. The aspect of the situation that is perceived as salient, informational or controlling, will determine the level of self-determination and perceived competence and, ultimately, intrinsic motivation. Finally, an external situation such as a reward also can be perceived as neither informational nor controlling but as amotivating (i.e., absence of motivation). In this last instance, a person's intrinsic motivation is reduced.

Deci and Ryan (1985) extended cognitive evaluation theory by adding a fourth proposition based on R.M. Ryan's (1982) work on intrapersonal events. The terms *internally informational* and *internally controlling* refer to events that occur within the person. These terms imply that intrapersonal events, like external events, can influence perceived competence, self-determination, and intrinsic motivation. Internally informational events (e.g., self-reward, self-regulation) enhance perceived competence and, as a result, maintain or increase intrinsic motivation. In contrast, internally controlling events (e.g., self-imposed pressure, guilt) may decrease self-determination and intrinsic motivation.

Self-Determination and Perceived Competence

According to Deci and Ryan (1985), the physical activity domain can provide individuals with excellent opportunities to satisfy their needs for perceived competence, self-determination, and social relationships. Sports and physical activities portray settings in which competence feedback, optimally challenging activities, and inherently interesting and enjoyable activities are prominent (Koestner & McClelland, 1990; Vallerand, Deci, & Ryan, 1987). Similarly, sport settings also can foster pressures, expectations, outcome goals, and rewards that can undermine intrinsic motivation

(Frederick & Ryan, 1995). Thus, physical achievement is an excellent domain in which to test and apply cognitive evaluation theory.

Rewards and Intrinsic Motivation: The Controlling Aspect

Cognitive evaluation theory originally was developed to examine the effects of external rewards on intrinsic motivation. The initial question that stimulated research in this area was, "If a person is involved in an intrinsically interesting activity and begins to receive an extrinsic reward for doing it, what will happen to his or her intrinsic motivation for the activity?" (Deci & Ryan, 1985, p. 43). Deci (1971, 1972) examined this question in a series of studies in which participants engaged in an interesting activity (i.e., puzzle building). Individuals in the experimental group received monetary rewards for successfully completing the puzzles, but the control group did not. Subsequently, participants were observed during a free-choice activity session to assess their intrinsic interest in the activity as measured by time on task. Results showed that individuals in the reward condition spent less time on the task than their counterparts. Researchers concluded that the reward changed perceived locus of causality from internal to external, thus decreasing participants' intrinsic motivation. Deci's pioneering efforts were replicated in a series of studies by Greene and Lepper (1974; Lepper & Greene, 1975; Lepper, Greene, & Nisbett, 1973). Their research was intended to test the overjustification hypothesis, a notion that expectation of a reward for an intrinsically interesting activity will diminish interest for the activity when the reward is removed. To investigate this presumption, they used paradigms involving different reward conditions (e.g., expected, unexpected, and no-reward). Results revealed that children in the expected reward condition showed less interest in the activity compared with the other groups, thus supporting the overjustification hypothesis. Lepper and Greene suggested that individuals perceived the rewards as controlling their behavior, shifting their focus from the activity itself to the rewards. Thus, when these rewards subsequently were removed, children lost interest in the activity. The authors concluded that external rewards can undermine intrinsic motivation for activities that are perceived as interesting and enjoyable.

Studies examining the controlling aspect of rewards in the physical domain have supported predictions based on cognitive evaluation theory (Orlick & Mosher, 1978; E.D. Ryan, 1977, 1980; Thompson & Wankel, 1980). For example, Orlick and Mosher investigated the influence of external rewards on children's motivation to perform a balance task. After participating in a reward (trophy) or no-reward condition, children were observed during a free-choice activity to determine time spent on the task (i.e., intrinsic motivation). Children who received a trophy showed less interest, whereas those in the control group showed greater interest in the activity. Thus, cognitive evaluation theory was supported in that external rewards given for an interesting activity diminished children's interest. Although results from this study provided empirical evidence for cognitive evaluation predictions, the experiment was conducted in the laboratory, where the conditions could be manipulated easily. However, studies were needed in the field to generalize laboratory findings and to fully support cognitive evaluation theory in ecological settings.

E.D. Ryan (1977, 1980) extended laboratory research to the field to examine theoretical predictions that external rewards given for interesting activities undermine intrinsic motivation. Ryan conducted two studies to investigate the effect of college scholarships on athletes' intrinsic motivation. In the first study, collegiate football players who received or did not receive a scholarship were surveyed on intrinsic motivation as measured by interest, enjoyment, and desire to continue participation in the sport. Scholarship athletes reported more extrinsic reasons for participating in the activity and less enjoyment than athletes who were not on scholarship. Athletes on scholarship may have perceived this reward as the main reason for participating in the activity (i.e., salient aspect), which, in turn, reduced their intrinsic motivation and enjoyment. In the second study, male (football and wrestling) and female (variety of sports) athletes were assessed on intrinsic motivation. Specifically, Ryan wanted to know how athletes perceived the scholarship and how this perception influenced their enjoyment of the activity. Football players on scholarship reported lower intrinsic motivation than those not on scholarship. However, both male wrestlers and female athletes on scholarship reported higher levels of intrinsic motivation than their nonscholarship counterparts. Ryan suggested that wrestlers and female athletes perceived their scholarship as an indicator of high competence because scholarships for both wrestlers and female athletes were

© Human Kinetics

A child's perceived competence influences her intrinsic motivation for performing an activity.

rare (i.e., the informational aspect was more salient). Conversely, football players on scholarship (very common for that sport) may have perceived the reward as controlling their behavior (i.e., pressure to play) and, therefore, developed an external locus of causality that decreased their intrinsic motivation (i.e., the controlling aspect was more salient).

Results from these field studies were consistent with cognitive evaluation theory, specifically the contention that external rewards can have differential salience (i.e., informational, controlling) and influence on intrinsic motivation. Hence, the link between the controlling aspect and self-determination, and the informational aspect and perceived competence, was supported in accordance with cognitive evaluation theory. E.D. Ryan's (1980) second study showed that not all reward types undermine intrinsic motivation. Recent studies suggest a more complex relationship than originally forwarded (see Cameron & Pierce, 1994; Wiersma, 1992; for reviews). The impact of a reward on motivation depends on the meaning of the reward to the recipient rather than the mere reward itself. To determine the salience of the reward, it is important to consider the interpersonal context in which the reward is given. Depending on the context (i.e., emphasis on control and evaluation), the reward can be perceived as controlling or informational. Furthermore, rewards given for uninteresting tasks can increase participation and enjoyment, although enhanced motivation would be extrinsic in nature. Research reviewed so far has focused primarily on the controlling aspect of external rewards. The next section centers on the informational aspect of events such as feedback from external sources or internal sources.

Feedback and Intrinsic Motivation: The Informational Aspect

Information provided by external sources such as significant others and the learning environment has the potential to influence a person's intrinsic motivation. Similarly, internal sources such as goal orientation and self-regulation may also affect intrinsic motivation. In the following sections, such *interpersonal* and *intrapersonal events* influencing intrinsic motivation will be discussed.

Interpersonal Events. According to Deci and Ryan (1985), three factors determine whether an event is informational: namely, experience of choice or absence of unnecessary controls, effectance-relevant information, and absence of conflict with one's needs or feelings. Research in the physical domain has supported this theoretical assumption. In particular, studies have examined the influence of positive and negative information on individuals' perceived competence and intrinsic motivation. Results have shown positive associations among feedback, perceived competence, and intrinsic motivation (Goudas, Biddle, & Fox, 1994b; Rutherford, Corbin, & Chase, 1992; Vallerand, 1983; Vallerand & Reid, 1984; Whitehead & Corbin, 1991).

Vallerand (1983) investigated the relationships among positive feedback, perceived competence, and intrinsic motivation among adolescent ice hockey players. Individuals were assigned to different conditions of amount of positive feedback, ranging from 0 to 24 positive comments (0, 6, 12, 18, 24). Groups who received any amount of positive feedback reported higher levels of perceived competence and intrinsic motivation than players who did not receive positive comments. However, no differences were found among the other feedback groups. Cognitive evaluation predictions were supported in that positive feedback enhanced perceived competence and intrinsic motivation.

In a subsequent study, Vallerand and Reid (1984) examined the effect of feedback type on intrinsic motivation in college men. Participants were randomly assigned to positive feedback, negative feedback, and no-feedback conditions and were asked to perform on a balance task. Results revealed that individuals in the positive feedback condition reported higher levels of intrinsic motivation than did participants in the two other conditions. Moreover, individuals in the no-feedback group scored higher than did cohorts in the negative feedback condition. Consistent with cognitive evaluation theory, intrinsic motivation was influenced by positive feedback via changes in perceived competence.

Whitehead and Corbin (1991) found similar results in a study with children participating in an agility run. Children were given positive, negative, or no feedback about their performance. In line with cognitive evaluation theory, results revealed that participants in the positive feedback group, compared with those receiving negative feedback, reported higher levels of intrinsic motivation. Furthermore, the effect of feedback on intrinsic motivation was mediated by changes in perceived competence. Overall, studies examining the informational aspect of external events have supported Deci and Ryan's (1985) theory by showing a consistent association between perceived competence and intrinsic motivation.

Significant others (i.e., coaches, teachers, parents, peers), who are an important part of the social context, can affect self-determination and perceived competence through controlling versus informational salience. Deci, Schwartz, Sheinman, and Ryan (1981) found that teachers oriented toward providing autonomy in the classroom (grades 4–6) were associated with higher student intrinsic motivation than were teachers oriented toward controlling behavior. Teachers' feelings of pressure also have been related to controlling attitudes toward students (Deci & Ryan, 1982; Deci, Spiegel, Ryan, Koestner, & Kauffman, 1982). Deci et al. (1982) found that teachers who felt responsible for their students' learning were more demanding and controlling and gave students less choice in activities than teachers who were told that their job was to help students to learn. Finally, Grolnick and colleagues (Grolnick & Ryan, 1989; Grolnick, Ryan, & Deci, 1991) found that children who perceived their parents, or whose parents were rated by interviewers, as more autonomy-supporting reported higher perceptions of competence and autonomy than those whose parents were rated as less autonomy-supporting or more controlling.

Research in the physical domain has supported the critical influence of the instructor in participants' motivation. Teachers who allowed participants to engage in decision-making were associated with higher levels of intrinsic motivation among youth in physical education or sport program contexts (Goudas, Biddle, Fox, & Underwood, 1995; Theeboom, De Knop, & Weiss, 1995). More research is needed, however, to examine the effect of coaching styles (i.e., autocratic, democratic), parents' beliefs and behaviors, and teammates' social norms on athletes' intrinsic motivation.

Cognitive evaluation theory suggests that intrinsically motivated learning will be enhanced when the learning environment provides participants with optimally challenging tasks within a context of self-determination (Deci & Ryan, 1985). This contention has been extensively tested and supported within academic settings (see Deci, Vallerand, Pelletier, & Ryan, 1991). Conditions facilitating intrinsic motivation (i.e., the learning process was perceived as self-determining) were related to higher conceptual learning than extrinsically motivated environments among fifth-grade children (Grolnick & Ryan, 1987). In particular, extrinsic learning conditions (i.e., reading a passage to be graded) were associated with inferior conceptual learning when compared with intrinsic conditions (i.e., reading the passage to see what students could learn) or spontaneous conditions (i.e., reading the passage with no prompts for learning). Similarly, Ryan, Connell, Plant, Robinson, and Evans (cited in Deci & Ryan, 1985) found that when students were asked to read a passage and were then free to learn what they wanted, the students' recall of the material was positively related to interest and negatively related to pressure and tension.

Research in the physical domain has consistently supported the influence of the learning environment on intrinsic motivation. An environment emphasizing self-evaluation, improvement, and learning has been positively related to intrinsic motivation (Biddle et al., 1995; Ferrer-Caja & Weiss, 2000; Goudas & Biddle, 1994; Kavussanu & Roberts, 1996). These results support Deci and Ryan's (1985) suggestion that there is a need to create stimulating learning environments in which students can "explore, discover, and learn" (p. 270).

Intrapersonal Events. According to Deci and Ryan (1985), intrapersonal events, like external events, can have varied effects on intrinsic motivation. Internally informational events enhance self-determination and, as a result, maintain or increase intrinsic motivation. In contrast, internally controlling events may be perceived as a source of pressure (i.e., external locus of causality) and may undermine intrinsic motivation. The terms *internally informational* and *internally controlling* refer to events that occur within the person. For example, a player may be extremely worried about her performance in practice even though the coach does not pressure her to perform. In this instance, the player will perceive the practice as internally controlling and will experience high anxiety. In contrast, another player on the same team may be focused on learning and improving during practices. When thinking about a new practice, he will be motivated to meet a challenge or learn a new play. Thus, the regulation of this player's behavior is internally informational. Such behavior is self-determining and, as a consequence, the player is expected to experience high levels of interest and enjoyment.

R.M. Ryan (1982) first introduced the concepts of internally informational and internally controlling in a study examining their effects on intrinsic motivation. Ryan used the ideas of ego and task involvement to define the concepts of internally controlling and internally informational, respectively. College students were assigned to two different conditions in which they had to solve puzzles. In one condition, participants were told that solving the puzzles was an indicator of creative intelligence; they were expected to adopt an ego-involvement. These students' concern about their performance and intelligence was expected to emphasize critical self-evaluation, leading subjects to perform the activity in an internally controlling way, that is, with pressure to perform according to expectations of intelligence. In the other condition, emphasis was placed on the task by stressing the learning process. Participants were expected to be more task-involved and, consequently, to perform the activity in an internally informational way (i.e., focused on task execution and learning). After performing the task, the two groups participated in a free-choice period in which time spent in the activity was used as a measure of intrinsic motivation. Consistent with predictions, results revealed that individuals in the ego-involved or internally controlling group were less intrinsically motivated and reported more pressure and tension than individuals in the task-involved or internally informational group.

The link between goal orientations and intrinsic motivation provides an interesting way to explore intrinsic motivation beyond cognitive evaluation theory boundaries (Butler, 1987, 1989; de Charms, 1968). Butler suggested that distinguishing between task- and ego-involved conceptions of competence would indicate the kinds of competence goals that guide achievement in an activity and would clarify the relation between perceptions of autonomy and competence. Goal orientations also can be useful to examine the motivational sources of behaviors. For example, Ryan, Koestner, and Deci (1991) differentiated persistence in an activity as emanating from intrinsic motivation and internally controlling sources. More recently, Reeve and Deci (1996) found that task involvement predicted intrinsic motivation in a competitive situation, even after they controlled for the effects of self-determination and perceived competence. Research in sport and physical activity settings consistently has supported the link between goal orientations and intrinsic motivation (Biddle et al., 1995; Duda, Chi, Newton, Walling, & Catley, 1995; Ferrer-Caja & Weiss, 2000; Goudas, Biddle, & Fox, 1994a, 1994b; L. Williams & Gill, 1995). In general, task orientation has been positively related to intrinsic motivation, suggesting the importance of including this factor when examining determinants of intrinsic motivation.

A Continuum of Motivational Orientations

In their original formulations, Deci and Ryan (1985) viewed intrinsic and extrinsic motivation as mutually exclusive. Intrinsic motivation referred to doing an activity for its own sake, whereas extrinsic motivation referred to doing an activity to achieve an instrumental goal. This early conceptualization later shifted to a continuum of motivational orientations along which different types of intrinsic and extrinsic motivation, as well as amotivation, can be located (Deci & Ryan, 1985, 1991; Rigby, Deci, Patrick, & Ryan, 1992; Ryan & Connell, 1989; Ryan, Connell, & Deci, 1985). The arrangement of motivational orientations is characterized by their degree of self-determination in the regulation of behavior, and it follows Deci and Ryan's (1985, 1991) contention that individuals internalize and self-regulate behaviors that are important for dealing with their social functioning, even if they are not initially attractive. In ascending order according to self-determination (or autonomy), the continuum of motivational orientations proceeds from amotivation to extrinsic forms of motivation (i.e., external regulation, introjected regulation, identified regulation, and integrated regulation) and finally to intrinsic motivation (see Deci & Ryan, 1985; Vallerand, 1997; for reviews). Several dimensions of intrinsic motivation also have been distinguished (i.e., to know, to accomplish, and to experience stimulation; Vallerand et al., 1992, 1993). Research suggests that types of intrinsic motivation lead to positive outcomes (i.e., interest, enjoyment), whereas extrinsic forms of motivation and amotivation result in negative outcomes (i.e., less effort, higher dropout rates). The self-determined types of motivation (i.e., identified regulation, integrated regulation, and intrinsic motivation) appear to be the critical forms for the individuals' personal development.

The continuum of motivational orientations has prompted abundant research in the physical domain. Some researchers developed measures of motivation in sport (Pelletier et al., 1995) and behavioral regulation in exercise (Mullan, Markland, & Ingledew, 1997), whereas others tested the validity of the continuum (Li & Harmer, 1996). Moreover, diverse investigations have assessed the relationship between motivational dimensions and cognitive and behavioral outcomes. Positive associations were found between self-determined forms of motivation, intentions to exercise, and actual engagement in physical activity (Chatzisarantis & Biddle, 1998; Chatzisarantis, Biddle, & Meek, 1997). A positive relationship also was found between self-determined forms of motivation and participation in a weight loss program, actual weight loss, and weight loss maintenance (G.C. Williams, Grow, Freedman, Ryan, & Deci, 1996).

Vallerand (1997) developed a hierarchical model of intrinsic and extrinsic motivation that is based on the broader self-determination theory and considers the different dimensions of motivation. In this model, he differentiated among social factors, mediators (i.e., autonomy, competence, and relatedness), motivations (i.e., intrinsic, extrinsic, and amotivation), and consequences (i.e., affect, cognition, and behavior) at three different levels (i.e., global, contextual, and situational). Vallerand's model emphasizes the importance of examining these factors simultaneously and provides interesting ideas for research on motivation in physical activity contexts. Recently, Ferrer-Caja and Weiss (2000) examined the influence of social factors (motivational climate, teaching style), mediators (perceived competence, self-determination, goal orientations), intrinsic motivation, and consequences (effort, persistence) in the context of high school physical education classes and found support for such a model.

Competition and Intrinsic Motivation

According to Deci and Ryan (1985), competition is intertwined with intrinsic motivation. The context of sports is particularly salient to examine the effects of competitive outcomes on intrinsic motivation. Competitive contexts involve controlling and informational aspects that influence self-determination and perceived competence (R.M. Ryan, Vallerand, & Deci, 1984). If the person's primary goal is to win, competition may be perceived as a source of pressure and may become a controlling event that will undermine intrinsic motivation. If competition is instead seen as a way to achieve mastery goals based on the learning process, the informational aspect of competition becomes salient, enhancing intrinsic motivation. Despite their relevance, the controlling and informational aspects of competition and their effect on intrinsic motivation scarcely have been examined in the sport domain.

Direct Versus Indirect Competition

The basic paradigm used in studies to examine competition and intrinsic motivation has been to assess direct (i.e., competition with another person) or indirect (i.e., competition with oneself) competition. The underlying idea is that direct competition should decrease intrinsic motivation because competition, by nature, is an extrinsic factor. This does not mean that competition is not a motivating factor, but rather that it is an extrinsic one. In this vein, when a person is involved in direct competition, she or he may need the reward of winning to persist at the activity. As long as participants are successful, they will continue their involvement in the task. With indirect or self-competition, winning should increase intrinsic motivation because success represents positive information about one's competence.

Research has provided empirical support for these contentions. In a pioneering study, Deci, Betley, Kahle, Abrams, and Porac (1981) explored the effects of face-to-face and self-competition

© Human Kinetics

Depending on an individual's goals, competition can either undermine or enhance intrinsic motivation.

conditions in a puzzle-solving activity. Participants in direct competition displayed less intrinsic motivation than participants who competed against themselves, as measured by time on task on a posttest free-choice activity. Lower intrinsic motivation was interpreted as a consequence of perceiving the competition as controlling. Other studies (Epstein & Harackiewicz, 1992; Weinberg & Ragan, 1979) found that competition is positively related to intrinsic motivation. For example, Weinberg and Ragan found that competing against another person or a standard facilitated intrinsic motivation among male participants. Thus, competition can enhance intrinsic motivation under certain conditions.

Objective Versus Subjective Competitive Outcomes

The effects of competition on intrinsic motivation originally were assumed to reside in the objective outcomes of winning and losing. Drawing on this presumption, researchers explored the effect of winning and losing on intrinsic motivation and found that individuals who lost the competitive activity experienced lower levels of intrinsic motivation than individuals who won (Vallerand, Gauvin, & Halliwell, 1986a; Weinberg & Jackson, 1979). However, McAuley and Tammen (1989) revealed that it was not objective outcome (i.e., winning and losing) but rather subjective evaluation of success and failure that influenced perceived

competence and intrinsic motivation in their study of basketball shooting competition. Participants who perceived greater success reported higher competence and intrinsic motivation than those perceiving less success. Interestingly, objective winners and losers were not different on these outcomes.

These findings emphasize the importance of individuals' subjective definitions of success and failure and show how different orientations toward competition (i.e., self- or norm-referenced) influence the salience of one's experiences. Based on these results and in accordance with Deci and Ryan (1985), winning may not be the appropriate focus of youth sport or physical education programs where the main goal is to promote learning, interest, and continuous participation in the activity.

The Competitive Context

According to cognitive evaluation theory, the social context in which an event occurs is critical to how the event is interpreted and, ultimately, how the experience affects intrinsic motivation. The competitive context is one such example, and competition can be structured so as to pressure or coerce participants or to communicate positive competence information. The former situation is likely to undermine whereas the latter facilitates intrinsic motivation.

These theoretical notions have been supported by empirical research in both academic and physical domains (R.M. Ryan, 1982; R.M. Ryan, Mims, & Koestner, 1983; Vallerand, Gauvin, & Halliwell, 1986b). For example, Ryan and colleagues found that controlling contexts (i.e., participants received rewards for doing an activity because that's what they should do) lowered intrinsic motivation compared with informational contexts (i.e., participants received performance-contingent feedback). Vallerand et al. (1986b) examined the effects of competitive structure on intrinsic motivation and perceived competence with middle school age children. They compared an interpersonal competition group (i.e., children were told to perform as best as they could because they were competing against others) with an intrinsic mastery group (i.e., children were encouraged to perform as well as they could by exploring several strategies in the task). Children in the competition condition showed lower intrinsic motivation (less time on task) than did children in the intrinsic mastery condition. Perceived competence, however, was not different between the two groups.

More recently, Reeve and Deci (1996) distinguished elements of the competitive situation and examined their effects on intrinsic motivation. In particular, they examined the influence of competitive set (i.e., competition vs. no competition), competitive outcome (i.e., winning vs. losing), and interpersonal context (i.e., controlling vs. noncontrolling). Undergraduate students participated in a puzzle-solving activity under these different conditions, and their subsequent intrinsic motivation was examined by using indicators of time on task during a free-choice activity and self-reported interest and enjoyment. Individuals who were pressured to win were less intrinsically motivated than those not pressured, and winners were more intrinsically motivated than were losers. Thus, both competitive outcome and the interpersonal context influenced intrinsic motivation, and perceived competence and self-determination mediated these effects. The competitive set, however, did not significantly influence intrinsic motivation. These results suggest that the structure of the competitive context is critical to individuals' interpretations of the controlling or informational aspect of the activity. How individuals experience the context ultimately will influence their intrinsic motivation.

An Interactionist Approach to Intrinsic Motivation

Although the central determinants of intrinsic motivation are perceived competence and self-determination (i.e., individual difference factors), Deci and Ryan (1985) emphasized the importance of the social context for understanding human motivation. Related literature suggests that both individual and contextual factors influence individuals' cognitive and affective responses (Treasure & Roberts, 1995a) and behaviors (Vealey, 1992) in the physical domain. Thus, a thorough understanding of motivational processes requires investigating individual and social contextual factors simultaneously. As a consequence, this approach should lend insight into the relative magnitude and valence of the influence of social and individual factors on intrinsic motivation.

Research in academic settings has supported an interactionist approach to intrinsic motivation. For example, Vallerand, Fortier, and Guay (1997) found that individual factors (i.e., perceived competence and perceived autonomy) and contextual factors (i.e., parents', teachers', and school administrators' autonomy) were positively related to students' self-determined school motivation. In turn, low levels of school motivation were positively associated with intentions to drop out of school and actual dropout behavior.

Research examining the interactive influence of individual and contextual factors in sport settings is relatively scarce and often omits some relevant variables. Nonetheless, the studies that considered this approach concluded that intrinsic motivation is best predicted by some combination of individual differences and contextual factors (Biddle et al., 1995; Cury et al., 1996; Ferrer-Caja & Weiss, 2000; Kavussanu & Roberts, 1996; Mitchell, 1996; Seifriz, Duda, & Chi, 1992). Biddle et al. examined intrinsic interest and intentions to participate in future activities among adolescent students in a physical education context. The authors found that intrinsic interest was positively related to task orientation, perceived autonomy, and perceived competence for activities that were rated as intrinsically interesting by the students (i.e., football, netball). For less interesting activities (i.e., gymnastics), intrinsic interest was associated with perceived autonomy and mastery climate. Cury et al. found that intrinsic interest was most strongly related to perceived competence and perceived mastery climate among adolescent girls; unfortunately, these authors did not assess self-determination. Finally, Ferrer-Caja and Weiss examined individual and social determinants of intrinsic motivation among adolescent students in physical education. Intrinsic motivation was best predicted by task orientation, learning climate, and perceived competence. These variables, in turn, were positively related to motivated behaviors in the form of effort and persistence in the class activities. Contrary to predictions, self-determination was weakly related to intrinsic motivation.

In sum, findings from these studies support the contention that intrinsic motivation is determined by a combination of individual differences and social contextual factors. Thus, an interactive approach that considers both types of factors is needed to understand the psychological mechanisms underlying intrinsic motivation. Such an approach has the ability to strengthen our understanding of intrinsically motivated behavior and its consequences.

Future Research Directions

Although this chapter is not intended to comprehensively critique measurement issues, some aspects are worthy of mention.

Measurement of Intrinsic Motivation

For an extensive review about measurement of intrinsic motivation, readers are referred to Vallerand and Fortier (1998). Here, we briefly address some relevant issues related to the conceptualization and measurement of intrinsic motivation.

Traditionally, intrinsic motivation has been assessed by examining time spent on task, usually during a free-choice activity after an experiment (Deci, 1981). This approach, however, has been criticized for several reasons. First, it fails to distinguish the motivational source originating the behavior (R.M. Ryan et al., 1991). Second, it considers persistence as the measure of motivation, thus confounding motivation with its conceptual consequence (Markland & Hardy, 1997; see Vallerand, 1997; Vallerand & Fortier, 1998; for reviews). This problem of circularity is also apparent in certain measures such as the Intrinsic Motivation Inventory (McAuley, Duncan, & Tammen, 1989), which contains subscales that reflect antecedents (i.e., perceived competence, perceived choice) and consequences (i.e., interest, enjoyment, effort) of intrinsic motivation. This conceptualization of motivation is also inadequate because it fails to distinguish intrinsic motivation from its antecedents and consequences.

Some researchers advocate the use of self-report measures of intrinsic motivation, by assessing participants' reasons for participating in a particular activity and using motivational explanations in the form of *because* statements (Vallerand, 1997). This approach is satisfactory because it allows access to the *why* of behavior and thus focuses on the nature of motivation. Furthermore, some theorists claim that the subjective experience is the crucial aspect when measuring motivation and advocate the use of introspection (Reeve & Deci, 1996). It seems only logical that a thorough understanding of motivation should include both cognitive and behavioral levels of measuring motivation. Although it is relevant to separate both levels of analysis, it is also pertinent to integrate them when examining motivation (Frederick & Ryan, 1995). Despite its apparent advantages to understanding intrinsic motivation and its consequences, this approach has not been used frequently in the physical domain (Ferrer-Caja & Weiss, 2000).

Some of the problems in measuring intrinsic motivation have occurred, in part, from the unclear conceptualization of relevant constructs. Definitions of variables are not consistent across studies, and different terms often are used interchangeably to refer to the same construct. Alternatively, the same term is used to denote different constructs. For example, an ambiguous set of terms is used to designate intrinsic motivation. Some of these terms include *intrinsic motivation, self-determination, autonomy, locus of causality, locus of control, self-regulation,* and, even more confusing, *self-determined motivation, autonomous motivation,* and *self-regulatory motivation.* This disparity is further aggravated when we consider the relationships between intrinsic motivation and its antecedents or consequences. In some instances, researchers have used the terms *perceived autonomy* and *self-determined motivation* (Vallerand et al., 1997), whereas in other studies they have used *perceived self-determination* and *autonomous motivation* (Fortier, Vallerand, & Guay, 1995). Some researchers have examined the relationship between self-determination and intrinsic motivation but used a self-determination measure that also contained an intrinsic motivation subscale (Biddle et al., 1995; Goudas, Biddle, & Fox, 1994b). As a result, it is unclear whether a given correlation is based on empirical processes or mere definitions. Undoubtedly, this inconsistency in terminology has led to confounding findings and ambiguous interpretations across studies. We believe that this is a crucial issue for future work in intrinsic motivation.

Intervention Studies

Longitudinal and intervention studies are needed to extend our understanding of cognitive evaluation theory and the dynamic patterns of motivation. The development of motivation is not a discrete or static phenomenon but rather a continuous process that evolves over time in relation to its sources and outcomes. Studies in the academic domain have revealed interacting patterns of factors that influence intrinsic motivation over time (Gottfried, Fleming, & Gottfried, 1998; Gottfried & Gottfried, 1996). With the exception of a study by Losier and Vallerand (1994) that assessed constructs on two occasions, research in the physical domain has used cross-sectional designs with only one occasion of measurement. Although this type of design allows inferences about associations among the variables at that particular time, it does not provide important information about patterns of change in antecedents, mediators, intrinsic motivation, and behavioral consequences.

This latter point highlights the importance of testing cognitive evaluation theory in the physical domain via intervention studies that use field experimental designs. Although various results have supported, partially supported, or failed to support cognitive evaluation predictions by using correlational designs, we have no data about the efficacy of the theory in altering intrinsic motivation and its antecedents and consequences as a result of manipulating social contextual conditions. Given the research reported in this section, does promotion of a mastery climate within a competitive sport context positively influence perceptions of competence and self-determination and, consequently, intrinsic motivation, effort, and persistence? Are coaches who are perceived as more democratic in their decision-making style associated with athletes who feel better about their ability, autonomy, interest, and enjoyment in relation to the activity? Despite the appeal of cognitive evaluation constructs, the theory's effectiveness in evoking change through teaching interventions is unknown. This point contrasts with studies that use other motivation theories in the physical domain (e.g., competence motivation theory, achievement goal theory).

Multivariate Relationships Among Variables

Another consideration for future research is examining intrinsic motivation simultaneously with its antecedents and consequences. Although inspecting isolated paths can provide information about specific relationships, these findings are sometimes inaccurate and misleading. Incorporating motivational factors within multivariate relationships should not be seen as mere inclusiveness but rather as a response to theoretical contentions. The constructs in cognitive evaluation theory are interdependent and thus should be examined in concert, not as a series of relationships among only certain variables. Adopting a multivariate approach will help determine more accurately what sources contribute most strongly to intrinsic motivation and what consequences stem from variations in intrinsic motivation levels.

A test of theoretically interesting interactions is another direction for examining intrinsic motivation within cognitive evaluation theory. For example, the interaction between perceived competence and self-determination, and their combined effect on intrinsic motivation is a conceptual claim of the original theory (Deci & Ryan, 1985) and a departure from Vallerand's (1997) model of motivation. Markland recently examined this interaction in a series of studies (Markland, 1999; Markland & Hardy, 1997). Interestingly, Markland found that variations in perceived competence positively influenced intrinsic motivation for exercise only under conditions of low self-determination, which is contrary to theoretical predictions.

Relatedness and Self-Determination Constructs

Relatedness is included within self-determination theory as one of the fundamental needs influencing intrinsic motivation (Deci & Ryan, 1985, 1991; R.M. Ryan, 1993; R.M. Ryan & Solky, 1996). Different theorists (e.g., Baumeister & Leary, 1995; Reeve & Sickenius, 1994) also have addressed its relation to motivation. Nevertheless, research examining the dimension of relatedness in the physical domain is virtually nonexistent. It traditionally has been presumed that self-determination, and its key component of personal choice, should invariably enhance intrinsic motivation. Recent findings depart from this assumption and instead emphasize the importance of considering particular social contexts such as one's cultural background or the nature of the activity. For example, individuals from cultures based on interdependence (e.g., Asian) may prefer to have choices made for them by significant others, thus placing greater value on group autonomy than personal autonomy (Iyengar & Lepper, 1999). Similarly, required activities in which individuals have little choice about their participation (i.e., typical physical education class) may obscure the influence of self-determination on intrinsic motivation (Ferrer-Caja & Weiss, 2000). Based on these findings, the relationship between self-determination and motivation deserves closer examination.

Summary

According to cognitive evaluation theory, intrinsic motivation is based on a person's need to be competent and self-determining in dealing with his or her environment. The psychological mechanisms underlying intrinsic motivation may not be as simple as cognitive evaluation theory depicts, and it is necessary to include other factors (e.g., goal orientations, teacher style) to strengthen predictions from this theory and to understand more definitely the underpinnings of intrinsic motivation. More research clearly is needed examining the network of relationships that explain intrinsic motivation if we want to design physical activity and sport programs that facilitate learning and enjoyment that, in turn, maximize the probability of sustained participation.

ECCLES' EXPECTANCY-VALUE MODEL

Inspired primarily by Atkinson's (1964) Expectancy × Incentive Value explanation of achievement behavior, Eccles and her colleagues formulated a model that embraced a multidimensional view of achievement choices (Eccles et al., 1983; Eccles, Adler, & Kaczala, 1982; Eccles, Kaczala, & Meece, 1982; see Eccles et al., 1998, for a review). In particular, Eccles' worldview expresses the relationship between self- and task beliefs with activity choices, effort, persistence, the psychological determinants of self-ability perceptions and subjective task value, and the developmental origins of individual differences in these psychological factors. Eccles primarily was intrigued by variations in achievement behavior in youth who showed similar aptitude and talent in a given domain. That is, given similar competence levels, why do some children definitively feel that they can succeed at just about any skill or activity required of them, whereas others linger in self-

doubt? Why do some children really want to succeed in a particular achievement area, whereas others dismiss or discount the importance of doing well in the same domain?

Eccles' early interest in achievement variations was sparked by rather consistent gender-differentiated patterns in educational and career decisions, especially in mathematics (e.g., Eccles, 1984, 1985, 1987; Eccles, Adler, & Meece, 1984). Despite having similar ability and test scores in elementary school, girls were less likely than boys to choose advanced math courses that would enable them to be eligible and attractive candidates for high-status professions and careers. Eccles contended that girls' lower self-concept of ability in math and lower importance assigned to the value of being good in math were the primary predictors of subsequent motivation (i.e., choice, effort) to take math courses. But what are the correlates and sources of such beliefs and attitudes? And will an understanding of such determinants help in planning interventions to abate such self-fulfilling tendencies?

Eccles and her colleagues sought to design a comprehensive model that would describe and explain behavioral variations (both gender-related and individual differences) in choice, persistence, and performance in children and adolescents across achievement domains. This model is depicted in figure 5.4. Achievement behavior is influenced by two major determinants: expectancies of success and subjective task value. Psychological factors such as self-schemata, goals, perceived task difficulty, and affective experiences are posited to underlie expectancies and value. Sources

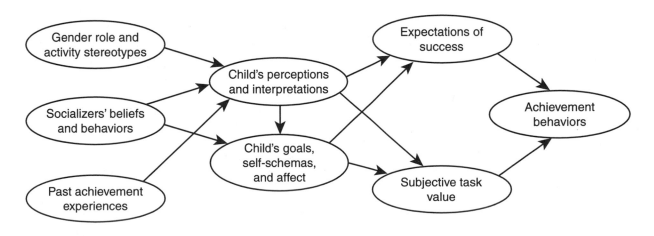

Figure 5.4 Eccles' expectancy-value model of activity choice.

Adapted, by permission, from J.S. Eccles and R.D. Harold, 1991, "Gender differences in sport involvement: Applying the Eccles' expectancy-value model," *Journal of Applied Sport Psychology, 3:* 7–35.

of individual differences in cognitions and affects that predict achievement behavior round out the model. It is important to note that the child's interpretation or perceptions of socializers' beliefs and behaviors, previous achievement experiences, and cultural norms shape the child's competence beliefs, values, and achievement choices, rather than actual ability or past successes and failures. The following sections will overview these key ingredients of the expectancy-value model, review research applying the theory to the physical domain, and offer future research directions.

Theoretical Underpinnings

The expectancy-value model (Eccles et al., 1983, 1998) pictured in figure 5.4 attempts to explain variations in achievement choices among children and adolescents despite similar talent, opportunities to achieve, and history of successes and failures in a particular domain. Achievement choices refer to decisions about whether to participate in an activity, whether to select easy or challenging tasks, how much effort to expend, and whether to persist on a difficult skill or "fold" under the pressure. According to the model, two primary determinants of achievement choices are (a) one's expectancies of success or competence beliefs in a particular domain and (b) the subjective task value or importance placed on being successful in a domain (e.g., math, sports, social interactions). Success expectancies and task value are directly and indirectly influenced by a number of social, cognitive, and affective variables.

According to Eccles, psychological and developmental components make up the model. The psychological component addresses the cognitive and affective variables that influence children's domain-specific achievement behavior, competence beliefs, and value placed on success. These include self- and task beliefs (labeled individual goals and general self-schemata in the model), affective experiences or memories, perceptions of significant adults' and peers' beliefs and behaviors, gender-role stereotypes (e.g., is a domain perceived as masculine?), and past achievement experiences. The developmental component focuses on the sources of children's individual differences in self-concept of ability, achievement goals, expectations of success, task value, and achievement choices. These sources reside in socialization effects (culture, significant others), past successes and failures, and differential aptitudes

in the domain of interest. Each component will be discussed in turn, with supporting research provided by Eccles and her colleagues across achievement domains.

Psychological Determinants of Success Expectancies, Task Value, and Achievement Choices

In Eccles' scheme, expectancies of success are akin to efficacy expectations, or children's confidence in being successful at some specific achievement activity or task. Domain-specific self-conceptions (i.e., perceived competence) are critical determinants of these more task- or activity-specific confidence ratings. Eccles and her colleagues have consistently found expectancies to be strong predictors of achievement choices, especially as a variable differentiating gender-related variations in behavior (Eccles et al., 1983; Eccles & Harold, 1991; Wigfield et al., 1997). For example, Eccles and Harold found that by grade 1, girls reported lower ability perceptions than boys in math and sport, and that among sixth graders, self-concept of ability in sports mediated gender differences in free-time physical activity involvement.

Given the crucial role that success expectations play in achievement choices, it is essential to understand the salient factors that influence the formation of expectancies. The main determinants of success expectancies outlined by Eccles are self-schemata, perceived task difficulty, perceptions of socializers' beliefs and behaviors (i.e., expectations, reinforcement, modeling), causes of past successes and failures, and gender-role stereotypes of achievement activities. Eccles and Harold (1991), for example, reported that children's perceptions of their parents' beliefs about participating and performing well in sport and their parents' importance ratings for boys and girls being good in sports were significantly related to the children's own self-ability ratings in the athletic domain. Perceptions of parents' beliefs were a stronger source of gender differences in children's self-ability ratings than were objective measures of sport ability.

Subjective task value is the second major determinant of achievement choices in Eccles' expectancy-value model. Task value, in general, alludes to the importance an individual attaches to being successful in a particular achievement area. The extent to which an individual perceives that a task meets personal needs or confirms self-beliefs determines the importance or value attached to participating in that activity. Eccles identified four motivational components of subjective task value: attainment value, interest value, utility value, and cost.

Attainment value is defined as personal importance of doing well in a particular achievement domain or activity that will confirm aspects of the self-schema (e.g., athlete, scientist, leader), such as providing opportunities for demonstrating or developing competence. *Interest value* refers to how much enjoyment individuals experience from participating in the activity (i.e., how intrinsically rewarding is the activity?). *Utility value* describes the perceived usefulness of the activity in relation to one's short- or long-term goals such as becoming an adult or investment in a career. Utility value may be high even though interest value is low. For example, a person may experience considerable anxiety and little enjoyment participating in water activities but may choose to take a water safety class because of its anticipated usefulness as a life skill. Finally, *perceived cost* refers to the anticipated time, energy, and opportunities that may be lost if one engages in a particular achievement activity, or the expense of engaging in one activity rather than another more attractive one. Thus, cost is the negative side to the perceived value of the activity. In the water safety example, the individual's perceived costs may include the effort needed to be successful, negative affect in response to peer evaluation, and giving up the chance to spend time in a more desirable activity. Ultimately, individuals weigh the values and costs of engaging in an activity and make their choices accordingly.

As with expectancies, several antecedents of task value are identified in the model. Directly influencing value are the affective memories associated with past achievement experiences. Needless to say, experiences that are associated with positive feelings such as pride, enjoyment, and happiness will positively affect task value, whereas negative memories should be related to valuing the activity less. Valence of emotions and task value, in turn, significantly affect actual behavioral choices and participation intensity. In addition to affective experiences, individuals' goals and self-schemas, their perceptions and interpretations of socializers' beliefs and behaviors, and perceptions of gender roles and activity stereotypes will naturally affect the child's subjective task value.

To demonstrate the interactive relationships among expectancies, task value, and achievement choices, Eccles and her colleagues engaged in several studies that cut across achievement domains such as math, reading, English, music, and sports (Eccles et al., 1983; Eccles & Harold, 1991; Jacobs & Eccles, 1992; Wigfield et al., 1997). Strong support exists for the relationships among salient variables, especially as they relate to gender. Eccles et al. (1983) found that among 5th- through 12th-grade students, boys reported higher success expectancies, lower task difficulty, and greater utility value for mathematics achievement. The researchers also found that self-concept of ability in math was positively related to perceived value, expectancies of success, and plans to continue taking math courses. Finally, results revealed that the effects of gender and history of successes on achievement beliefs and behaviors were mediated by children's perceptions of their parents' expectancy beliefs and subjective value toward math. Specifically, parents held higher competency beliefs and greater attainment value for their sons than for their daughters to achieve in math.

Eccles and Harold (1991) tested the expectancy-value model in elementary (kindergarten through grade 4) and middle school (grade 6) students across English, reading, math, and sport domains. Boys rated themselves as more competent than girls in sport; rated sports as more important, useful, and enjoyable; and reported greater participation rates. Girls reported higher expectancies, value, and participation in reading and English than did boys. Moreover, gender effects on participation rates were not significant when self-concept of ability and task value (attainment, utility) were included as mediating variables. These studies demonstrate that children's interpretations of experiences, rather than the actual experiences themselves, drive their self-conceptions, task beliefs, and achievement behavior in domains that vary in gender stereotyping.

Development of Children's Expectancies of Success, Task Value, and Achievement Behavior

Although the psychological component of the model emphasizes the cognitive and affective variables influencing expectancies, task value, and achievement choices, the developmental component focuses on how children come to adopt or internalize competence beliefs and task value. Of special interest are developmental trends such as changes in these self and task beliefs across the childhood years, or the transition from elementary to middle school. Wigfield et al. (1997), in a 3-year longitudinal study of children's achievement beliefs in math, reading, music, and sports, found that young children were very optimistic about their competencies, but these self-beliefs and attainment and utility value declined in each domain over the elementary years. Interest value, however, depended on the domain of interest: Interest in music and reading decreased whereas interest for math and sports did not. Second, the positive relationship between success expectancies and task value increased over time (i.e., children came to value those domains at which they succeeded). Finally, the authors found that relationships between children's competence beliefs and value about the importance of being successful in a domain and with parents' evaluations of their child's competence became increasingly stronger over the elementary years.

A significant amount of work has been conducted on parents' and teachers' beliefs and behaviors conveyed to children concerning their capability for performing a task, how important it is to be successful in a particular domain, and causal attributions for successes and failures (Eccles et al., 1983; Eccles & Wigfield, 1985). According to Eccles, significant adults such as parents and teachers can shape children's self-evaluations of competence in three ways: as providers of experience, as interpreters of experience, and as role models. For example, parents provide experiences when they sign their children up for sports or for a particular sport based on children's gender. Parents interpret experiences by conveying confidence or lack thereof about their children's probability of success, communicating evaluative feedback, or expressing their beliefs about the importance of being successful in domains such as academics, music, sports, and social activities. Finally, through observation of their parents' behavior, children internalize which achievement domains are important, interesting, and useful at which to strive to excel. As such, parents and teachers model, provide, and interpret salient information and experiences about their expectations and subjective task value for children.

Jacobs and Eccles (1992) explored the influence of mothers' gender-role and competency beliefs of their 11- to 12-year-old children in math, sport, and social domains. Mothers possessed greater ability beliefs for boys in math and sports and for girls in social activities. Consistent with the expectancy-value model, mothers who held stronger gender-stereotypical beliefs were more likely to possess ability estimates that favored boys for

math and sports and girls for social activities. Importantly, gender stereotypes directly influenced mothers' perceptions of their children's abilities in these domains, which, in turn, strongly predicted children's own self-perceptions of ability. Moreover, mothers' perceptions of their children's abilities were stronger determinants of children's self-ratings than were the children's actual abilities in a domain (assessed by teachers' ratings). Thus, mothers' ability estimates for their children mediated the influence of both gender-stereotyped beliefs and actual competence in these domains.

Eccles' expectancy-value model emphasizes cognitive (e.g., competency beliefs, subjective task value), affective (memories of past achievement experiences), and social (adults' and peers' beliefs and behaviors) influences of achievement choices. Moreover, tests of model hypotheses have held up across a variety of domains including sport. Thus, her model is appealing for examining achievement behavior in the physical domain. However, only recently have sport psychologists embraced this theoretical approach in their studies of motivational variations among participants. Although studies testing aspects of the expectancy-value model are gaining momentum, future research can take numerous directions. Therefore, after reviewing the existing sport psychology research that applies Eccles' model to the physical domain, we offer some ideas for extending her model to understand motivational orientations and sport behavior.

Applying Eccles' Model to the Physical Domain

In this section we survey specific studies that have tested Eccles' expectancy-value model with a deliberate interest in achievement in the physical domain, in contrast to studies by Eccles and her colleagues in which sport is but one of several domains to compare model testing findings. Although the studies are sparse, they provide a foundation on which future studies can be designed. To date, studies have examined (a) the suitability of the model to physical activity behavior; (b) gender differences in expectancies, task value, and perceptions of classroom climate; (c) sources of subjective value toward sport involvement; and (d) the influence of parental beliefs and behaviors on children's self-perceptions, subjective value, and physical activity behavior.

Suitability of the Expectancy-Value Model to the Physical Domain

Deeter (1989, 1990) tested Eccles et al.'s (1983) achievement motivation model among university students taking required physical education skills classes. General (trait sport confidence) and task-specific (self-efficacy) measures operationally defined expectancy of success. Task value was assessed through sport achievement orientations (competitiveness, win, goal) that represented attainment and utility value constructs. Achievement behavior was represented by instructors' subjective evaluations of students' class performance and objective performance measures (win percentage in competitions, number of laps run or walked). Results revealed an adequate fit of the model to the data, with expectancy variables emerging as stronger predictors of achievement behavior than task value.

Papaioannou and Theodorakis (1996) synthesized and integrated common constructs from three motivational theories (Eccles' model, theory of planned behavior, achievement goal theory) to determine intention to participate in high school physical education classes. Eccles' model was supported in that perceived competence, interest value, and utility value were all significant predictors of intention to participate. Stephens (1998) also integrated components of Eccles' theory and achievement goal theory and found a positive relationship between task goal orientation and attainment and utility value toward playing youth soccer.

Gender Differences in Expectancies, Value, and Achievement Behavior

Given the rather consistent findings that females report lower self-confidence than males in the sport domain, Lirgg (1991) conducted a meta-analysis to determine the magnitude of such differences and possible moderators of these effects. She reported an overall effect size of 0.40 favoring males, but considerable variability in magnitude of differences was apparent. Using gender-typing of task as a moderator, Lirgg produced an effect size of 0.65 favoring males for masculine-typed tasks and −1.02 favoring females for the only study examining a feminine-typed task (ballet). Lirgg called for more studies on self-confidence in the physical domain that consider gender, gender-stereotyping of activity, age, and situational variables (e.g., competition, evaluative feedback).

Responding to Lirgg's (1991) suggestions, Clifton and Gill (1994) examined self-confidence ratings in the feminine-typed physical activity of cheerleading. This activity was an optimal one in that both females and males participate in the activity and several cheerleading subtasks exist that vary in their perceived gender-appropriateness (e.g., dance, partner stunts, cheers and motions, jumps). Gender main effects revealed that although males rated overall athletic ability higher than females, females were more confident in overall cheerleading ability, cheers and motions, jumps, and dance. These findings support Eccles' model in that individuals' perceptions of activity stereotypes influenced their self-confidence, which, in turn, would be expected to have an effect on activity choice and behavior.

Following research by Eccles and Blumenfeld (1985) implicating classroom context as a predictor of achievement behavior, Lirgg (1993, 1994) examined the influence of same-sex and coed physical education classes on students' self-perceptions, task perceptions, and environmental perceptions. In the first study, self-confidence of learning, utility value, and perceived gender appropriateness of basketball were examined as a function of class context. Middle and high school boys exhibited greater confidence in coed versus same-sex classes, whereas girls in same-sex classes showed a trend toward higher confidence than those in coed classes. Regardless of class context, boys rated basketball as a more masculine activity and as more useful for future leisure time than did girls. These results partially support class context as an important contributor to self-perceptions, value, and gender typing of activities. Environmental perceptions of same-sex versus coed classes (Lirgg, 1994) focused on participants' evaluations of student behavior, involvement, and social interaction tendencies, as well as teacher behavior. Girls in same-sex classes rated their classes as better behaved and more cooperative than did all other groups. These results highlight that classroom climate in the form of same-sex versus coeducational classes is perceived quite differently by gender. These perceptions, according to Eccles, are likely to affect the quantity and quality of opportunities afforded for developing competence, self- and task beliefs, and future activity choices and behavior.

Sources of Subjective Value Toward Sport Involvement

Stuart (1997) was interested in identifying sources of attainment, utility, and interest value toward sport involvement among middle school youth and how these compared to theoretically defined sources in Eccles' model. Eighth-grade (ages 12–14) boys and girls completed questionnaire items pertaining to each component of task value, and then 10 low, 10 medium, and 10 high value scorers were subsequently interviewed about reasons for finding sport interesting, important, and useful (or not). Findings confirmed Eccles et al.'s (1983) origins of subjective task value in that time and energy investment (i.e., perceived cost), affective memories, and significant adult and peer beliefs about the importance of sport participation all played a role in participants' intrinsic, attainment, and utility value ratings.

Parental Influence on Self-Perceptions, Subjective Value, and Physical Activity Behavior

Brustad (1993, 1996) conducted companion studies of the influence of parents' beliefs and behaviors on children's perceived competence and value toward physical activity. In the first study, fourth-grade boys and girls completed measures of perceived athletic competence and attraction toward physical activity, which represented the subjective value construct in Eccles' model. This measure included three dimensions of interest value (e.g., liking of vigorous exercise) and one dimension of utility value (i.e., importance of physical activity to achieving good health). Parents rated their enjoyment of physical activity (interest value), fitness level (modeling), and importance of physical activity (utility value). In addition, they responded to questions about how frequently they encouraged their children to be physically active and how often they participated with their children. A path analysis revealed that parents who reported greater enjoyment of their activity involvement, but not importance or fitness, gave more encouragement to their children to be active. Greater parental enjoyment and encouragement were associated with higher levels of children's perceived competence and attraction to physical activity. Perceived competence was a strong predictor of each of the value dimensions. Finally, findings were moderated by gender: Parents gave more encouragement to their sons than daughters, and girls reported lower perceived physical competence and subjective value toward physical activity than did boys. These results support Eccles' model in that parental beliefs and behaviors influenced children's ability perceptions

and task value. Brustad (1996) replicated these results with a more diverse ethnic and socioeconomic group of children.

Kimiecik and colleagues' systematic series of studies have contributed substantially to our understanding of determinants of children's physical activity from an expectancy-value approach (Dempsey, Kimiecik, & Horn, 1993; Kimiecik & Horn, 1998; Kimiecik, Horn, & Shurin, 1996). Dempsey et al. examined the relationship between parental beliefs and behaviors toward their children's participation and children's moderate-to-vigorous physical activity (MVPA), as well as the relationship between children's self- and activity beliefs and MVPA. Results for the parent–child MVPA link revealed that gender was a significant predictor of children's MVPA, with boys more physically active than girls. However, only parents' perceptions of the child's MVPA competence contributed above and beyond gender to explain MVPA, partially supporting the expectancy-value model. Success expectancies and task goal orientation contributed above and beyond gender for the child's belief system–child MVPA linkage. Children who expressed more confidence in being able to exercise regularly and who defined success in self-referent terms (i.e., effort, mastery) recorded larger MVPA values.

Kimiecik et al. (1996) more extensively examined the relationship between children's fitness-related beliefs, children's perceptions of parental beliefs about them, and MVPA (see figure 5.5). Drawing largely on Eccles et al.'s (1983) model, the authors hypothesized significant relationships for the links between children's beliefs and MVPA and between children's perceptions of parental beliefs and their own beliefs. The association between children's beliefs and MVPA behavior was moderately strong, with significant contributions from perceived competence and task and ego goal orientations. Value of fitness participation did not emerge as a significant contributor to MVPA. A strong relationship emerged between perceptions of parental beliefs and children's self-beliefs about MVPA. Children who perceived that their parents valued fitness, held high competency beliefs for them, and endorsed both task and ego goals reported higher fitness competence and task and ego goals for MVPA.

In the third of the series of studies, Kimiecik and Horn (1998) expanded on previous research by assessing a number of parent influence components within Eccles' model. They examined mothers' and fathers' beliefs about their children's

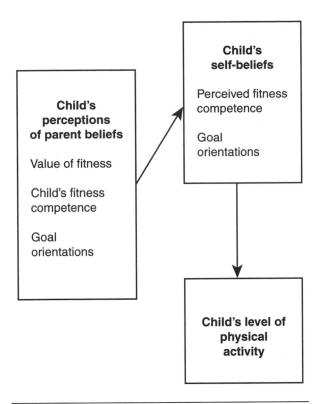

Figure 5.5 Kimiecik et al.'s findings of children's fitness-related beliefs, children's perceptions of parents' beliefs about them, and MVPA behavior.

Adapted, by permission, from J.C. Kimiecik, T.S. Horn, and C.S. Shurin, 1996, "Relationships among children's beliefs, perceptions of their parents' beliefs, and their moderate-to-vigorous physical activity," *Research Quarterly for Exercise and Sport, 67*: 324–336.

MVPA, whether these beliefs were differentiated by their own or their children's gender, the link between parents' and children's MVPA levels as a test of role-modeling effects, and the relationship between parent-reported beliefs and their children's MVPA behavior. Mothers and fathers did not differ on perceived competence, value, or goal orientations for their daughters or sons. Moreover, parent-reported MVPA was not related to children's MVPA (i.e., role-modeling effects were not supported), but parents' competency beliefs for their children, and to a lesser extent mothers' task orientations, were significantly related to children's MVPA.

The studies by Brustad and by Kimiecik and colleagues uncover a rather consistent pattern of findings that strongly support the viability of Eccles' model to the physical domain. First, children's perceived competence is a strong determinant of attraction toward physical activity and actual MVPA. Second, children's perceptions of parental beliefs and behaviors are strongly re-

lated to children's own competency beliefs, goal orientations, and attraction toward physical activity. Third, children's beliefs likely mediate the relationship between perceptions of parental beliefs and children's MVPA. In sum, Eccles' model is supported in highlighting the role of parents as providers and interpreters of experience, children's perceptions being an important influence on their own belief system, and children's expectancies, value, perceived competence, and goal orientations as predictors of activity choices and intensity.

Future Research Directions

Eccles' activity choice model has been tested only recently in sport and exercise psychology. Thus, the door is wide open for testing aspects of the model as they pertain to the specific social context of physical activity, whether it be competitive sport, exercise programs, or physical education classes. Drawing on Eccles et al.'s (1998) review of the current status and future directions of motivation research, we will forward just a few ideas that are salient and timely to the physical achievement domain. However, interested researchers are encouraged to explore these issues further in major theoretical and empirical papers by Eccles and her colleagues (e.g., Eccles & Wigfield, 1995; Eccles, Wigfield, Harold, & Blumenfeld, 1993; Eccles et al., 1998; Wigfield & Eccles, 1992; Wigfield & Karpathian, 1991).

Socializers' Beliefs and Behaviors

Within Eccles' model, significant adults occupy a pivotal source of children's development of self-perceptions, activity value, and motivated behavior in various achievement domains. Parents are models, providers, and interpreters of children's activity experiences. Parental influence, through parents' own self-report or children's perceptions, was consistently implicated in children's psychological and behavioral outcomes (Brustad, 1993, 1996; Dempsey et al., 1993; Kimiecik & Horn, 1998; Kimiecik et al., 1996). Moreover, teachers can have an effect on students' expectancies, value, and achievement through structuring of the classroom climate, through their beliefs and behaviors about students' capabilities, and by using evaluative feedback for performance outcomes (Eccles et al., 1998). Lirgg's (1993, 1994) study of adolescents' perceptions of coeducational versus same-sex classroom contexts supports such differential effects.

Ideas abound for extending the influence of significant adults on children's self- and task beliefs and activity choices. An obvious gap is the role of coaches' beliefs and behaviors concerning children's aptitude for sport achievement. Research within other theoretical frameworks has shown that coaches' use of evaluative and informational feedback bears directly on participants' self- and other evaluations, affective responses, and motivated behavior (e.g., Amorose & Weiss, 1998; Black & Weiss, 1992; Horn, 1985, 1987). Within Eccles' model, one might examine how coaches' beliefs about athletes' competencies relate to coaches' quantity and quality of feedback and, subsequently, athletes' self-ability beliefs, task value, and future involvement choices.

Eccles' model suggests that significant adults influence children's psychosocial development through a combination of role modeling and expectancy beliefs. However, studies in the physical domain have concluded that parent beliefs, but not modeling, are more important sources of children's perceived competence, attraction to physical activity, and MVPA behavior. In these studies, role modeling was defined as parent-reported or child perceptions of parents' fitness or MVPA level. In contrast, parent beliefs such as enjoyment of physical activity and behaviors such as encouragement of and involvement in physical activity emerge as significant predictors of children's attitudes and behavior. We contend that dismissing children's observational learning of parents' influence is not advisable. Modeling is not narrowly defined as extent of involvement in an

achievement domain but also involves the communication of attitudes, values, and beliefs about a particular domain or task (McCullagh & Weiss, 2001). Thus, parents are likely to communicate their attitudes about the value of physical activity by modeling enjoyment and encouragement of physical activity. For example, children who report that their parents enjoy physical activity are aware that their parents like and value exercise; otherwise, why would they express such enjoyment? Parents' expression of enjoyment combined with encouragement of their child to be involved in sport sends a message to the child about the importance, interest, and usefulness of being physically active. Parents' influences as models, interpreters, and providers of experience are difficult to tease apart; thus, we recommend that the observational learning effect of parental beliefs and behaviors continue to be included in studies of sources of children's belief systems.

Recently, Eccles et al. (1998) forwarded a comprehensive model of parental influence on children's motivation and achievement by using a family systems approach (see figure 5.6). In this model, family demographics such as parent characteristics (e.g., single-parent, socioeconomic status), child and sibling characteristics (e.g., birth order, gender), parents' general- and child-specific beliefs and behaviors, and the child's psychosocial outcomes (i.e., self-perceptions, values, goals, activity choices) interact as a reciprocal and dynamic process. Not only do family characteristics and parental beliefs influence the child's achievement-related behavior, but also the child's

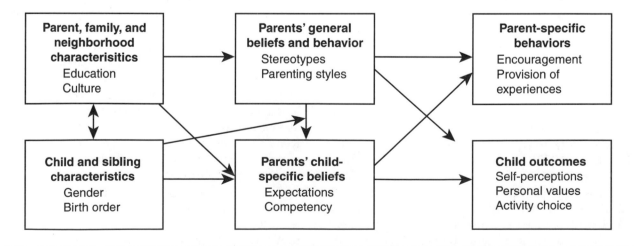

Figure 5.6 Eccles et al.'s (1998) comprehensive model of parental influence on children's motivation and achievement.

Adapted, by permission, from J.S. Eccles, A.W. Wigfield, & U. Schiefele, 1998, Motivation to succeed. In *Handbook of child psychology (5th ed., Vol. 3): Social, emotional, and personality development*, edited by W. Damon (Series Ed.) and N. Eisenberg (Vol. Ed.) (New York: Wiley), 1017-1095.

ability perceptions and personal values certainly may affect subsequent parental beliefs and behaviors. Several aspects of this model are ripe for study within the physical domain. First, the model specifies potential sources of parental beliefs and behaviors such as parent, family, child, sibling, and neighborhood characteristics. Second, parent behaviors are posited to mediate the influence of parental beliefs about the child's competencies and values, and general beliefs about parenting, on children's psychological and achievement outcomes. Third, the model affords importance to siblings as potential moderators of parental beliefs and behaviors toward the target child. How do parents' reactions toward and involvement in an older sibling's sport participation affect the younger child? Is he or she attracted to the same sport? Is he or she attracted to sport at all or instead to a unique achievement domain? Does this differ depending on whether the sibling is male or female? These particular model aspects, and others, are salient considerations of understanding children's achievement behavior in the physical domain.

Finally, we highlight the important role that peers (teammates, close friends) play in children's competency beliefs, value toward activity domains, and behavioral choices. To date, tests of Eccles' model have focused on parents and physical education teachers, but peer acceptance and close friendships are salient relationships sought by children and adolescents. This necessarily means that activity domains that are valued or devalued by one's peer group likely may be endorsed by members to maintain peer status and popularity, and this is likely to enhance or diminish involvement. Peer comparison and evaluation are cited more frequently as sources of physical competence information by early and middle adolescents than by children, and this has implications for competence beliefs, affect toward achievement domains, and motivation to continue involvement. In short, peer influence in the form of acceptance and close friendship is an important source of individuals' self- and activity beliefs and achievement-related choices, and it is an important direction for future tests of Eccles' model in the physical domain.

Contextual Influences

Social context counts. This is a consistent message in all the motivation theories covered in this chapter. The case is no different for Eccles' model. Achievement behaviors occur within social contexts that vary in cultural norms, gender and activity stereotypes, psychological climate, and significant adults' and peers' behaviors. Thus, it is crucial to consider the social context in which children's success expectations, attraction toward the activity, and participatory behaviors occur.

Physical activity contexts usually differ in the degree to which certain practices and values are endorsed. Is learning or performance emphasized? Does the coach allow for autonomy or primarily exert control? Is the process or product of performance more frequently reinforced? Is ability grouping practiced? These are but some of the contextual influences that bear directly on self-judgments of ability, perceptions of what is valued (e.g., effort, learning, outcome) by the teacher or coach, and subsequent desire to continue or discontinue participation. Within Eccles' model, the organization, structure, and teaching practices within particular social contexts are hypothesized to exert important effects on achievement beliefs and behaviors. This is an important area for future research and may include perceptions of the motivational climate, the teacher's management and decision-making styles, and gender and activity stereotypes as they affect self- and task beliefs and achievement-related choices.

A particular focus of some of Eccles' empirical work has been on transitions from one school context to another (e.g., elementary to junior high school, junior high school to senior high school). Eccles and Midgley (1990), for example, documented social contextual changes in the transition from elementary to junior high school that spanned class size, organizational structure for instruction, grading practices, and motivational goals. These changes were deemed "negative motivational effects" because fewer opportunities for autonomy, greater emphasis on competitiveness and social comparison processes, and normative grading and public evaluation practices equated to a poor fit between the needs of early adolescents and their classroom environment. Changes in the social context of achievement were forwarded as one probable explanation for decreased competence perceptions and interest value in many school subjects across older childhood and early adolescence.

The notion of transitioning across social contexts seems particularly relevant to the physical domain. Children often begin their sport careers in programs where skill development and fun are the primary goals. Evaluation and recognition are based on effort and improvement, activities are interesting and varied, and ample playing and practice time is provided. As children climb the athletic skill ladder (e.g., move up to a "select" team), coaches are stricter with rules and criteria for successful performance, drills become less varied and interesting, and performance is emphasized more than effort and improvement. Fewer youth are talented enough to make select or travel squads, resulting in a narrower comparison group by which to judge athletic competence. Thus, competence ratings likely decline and interest in the activity may wane. The pyramid of athletic success is complete when only the "fittest" survive eventual cuts at the higher levels of sport (e.g., regional or state team selections). It would be interesting to conduct a longitudinal study that spans the transition from a skill development- to competitive-oriented league, or from an agency league (e.g., YMCA) to high school competition. Eccles' model suggests that differences in league philosophy, value of the importance of winning, and coaching behaviors will have important effects on participants' expectancies, value, and involvement decisions.

Culture is another important social contextual variable that rarely has been studied in the physical domain. The culture in which one is socialized will affect perceptions of what achievement domains are valued as important, useful, and interesting. Moreover, parents' beliefs and behaviors will communicate expectancies about which activity domains are salient for females and males to be successful at. Again, the physical activity domain appears particularly salient because sport in general and certain sports in particular are represented more or less frequently by certain cultural and ethnic groups than others. Eccles' model is useful in portraying the mechanisms by which cultural norms and values influence participants' perceptions of socializers' beliefs, their own self-beliefs, the value of doing well in an activity, and subsequent achievement behavior.

Conceptualizing and Measuring Subjective Task Value

One of the unique twists of Eccles' expectancy-value model of activity choices is its elaboration on the construct of subjective task value compared with other theories. Not only is value a crucial direct influence of activity choices and involvement intensity, but four distinct components of task value are important to consider independently and in combination (attainment, utility, interest, cost). Eccles and colleagues (e.g., Eccles et al., 1983, 1993, 1998; Eccles & Wigfield, 1995) consider all four components integral to under-

standing and explaining choice, effort, persistence, and performance behaviors in a particular achievement domain.

Subjective value in the physical domain has been conceptualized and measured quite differently across studies. For example, Brustad (1993, 1996) assessed interest in and the importance of physical activity as outcome variables of parental influence and children's perceived competence. In contrast, Dempsey et al. (1993) used one item to assess each of the three value constructs—utility, importance, and interest—but summed the three items to create a composite value construct to be used in analyses. In yet another permutation of the value construct, Kimiecik and colleagues (Kimiecik & Horn, 1998; Kimiecik et al., 1996) assessed children's or parents' ratings of the importance of children participating in a fitness program relative to 16 alternative activities that might be attractive for their age group. Comparing these studies highlights the multitude of ways that subjective task value has been conceptualized and measured. In some studies only certain dimensions of value were assessed (importance, utility, interest), whereas Dempsey et al. assessed all three dimensions but with single-item scales that were summed to form an overall value score.

Eccles and Wigfield and their colleagues have noted the importance of distinguishing different components of task value (see Eccles & Wigfield, 1995; Wigfield & Eccles, 1992; Wigfield et al., 1997). First, in the early elementary years, interest and importance/utility factor into two distinct components, but in 5th through 12th grades they form distinct factors. Moreover, children differentiate task value across achievement domains. Thus, the structure and meaning of subjective value vary developmentally. Second, interest, utility, and importance value differentially predict participation intentions and behavior across achievement domains (Eccles & Harold, 1991; Wigfield & Eccles, 1992). Finally, developmental changes in interest, utility, and attainment value differ from one another and among achievement domains (Wigfield et al., 1997). These results suggest that we need to pay closer attention to conceptualizing and measuring specific components of task value in studies of change over time, sources of task value development, gender differences in subjective value, and value components as predictors of physical achievement–related constructs.

In sum, Eccles' model highlights the role that subjective task value plays in explaining achievement choices, effort, and persistence. As such, it is imperative that we conceptualize task value in the multidimensional way intended by her model, by accounting for importance, utility, interest, and cost. Moreover, valid and reliable multi-item scales such as the ones developed by Eccles and colleagues should be considered (see Eccles & Wigfield, 1995). In considering conceptual and measurement issues, we will be equipped more handily to identify the sources and consequences of subjective task value in the physical domain.

Developmental Issues

Eccles' theoretical model and empirical research have accounted for developmental differences in the level and structure of success expectancies and subjective task value (Eccles et al., 1998; Wigfield, 1994; Wigfield & Eccles, 1992; Wigfield et al., 1997). For example, task value becomes more differentiated with age, and expectancies and value decline over the elementary and secondary years in many academic subjects. Moreover, the relationship between expectancies and value becomes stronger with time, suggesting that children come to value those domains at which they expect to be successful. Although developmental trends in competency beliefs have been explored in the physical domain (see Horn & Amorose, 1998), the trends for subjective value have not been studied. Given consistent gender differences in value and activity choices in sport, and the decline in the number of youth participating in physical activity, longitudinal investigations are desirable for determining whether declines in importance, utility, and interest value occur that may account, at least in part, for these differences and trends.

Determinants of age-related changes in expectancies and value have been of great interest in the academic domain. The key question is whether these changes are a developmental phenomenon (i.e., individual difference) or whether they reflect systematic changes in the social contexts children encounter (e.g., school). Considerable evidence shows that transitions from elementary to middle school include organizational, structural, teacher behavior, and grading practice shifts that produce negative motivational effects in children and teenagers. Do similar trends exist in the domain of sport and, if so, do they reflect age-related changes in cognitive capabilities (e.g., ability is viewed as unchangeable), changes in the structure of sport (i.e., shift from skill development to win-at-all-costs), or an interaction of the two?

Finally, we know that children's competence beliefs and activity value are strongly linked to perceptions of parents' beliefs and values. Do these links between parents' and children's belief systems become stronger or weaker with age as they pertain to the physical domain? Do peer group beliefs and values instead become more salient for older children and adolescents? How do changes in expectancies and importance of sport and physical activity translate to choice, effort, and persistence in physical activity behavior during childhood and adolescence? Is Eccles' expectancy-value model a prime candidate for explaining the dramatic drop-off in participation rates observed from early to later adolescence? These are but some of the developmentally oriented questions awaiting answer via testing within Eccles' model.

Expectancies, Subjective Values, and Achievement Goals

Recently, Eccles and Wigfield (Eccles et al., 1998; Wigfield & Eccles, 1992) integrated aspects of expectancy-value and achievement goal theories to enhance our understanding of motivated behaviors. In particular, they contend that individuals' subjective value (importance, utility, interest) toward a particular domain should influence their goals (task- or ego-involved), which, in turn, affect decisions related to continuing or persisting with the activity in question. For example, if children participate in sport because they find it fun and learn lots of new skills, they are likely to have predominantly task-involved goals. High interest value and task goals are likely to result in continued involvement and high effort so that goals are attained. In contrast, Eccles and Wigfield argue that doing sports for more extrinsic reasons, such as getting a college scholarship (i.e., high utility value), may be conducive to ego-oriented goals that focus on outperforming others so that the end goal can be attained. Thus, they suggest that values and goals work together to produce variations in achievement-related choices and behavior. This integrated idea lends itself nicely as a segue to our last theory of motivational orientations and sport behavior: achievement goal theory.

ACHIEVEMENT GOAL THEORY

Since the first writing of this chapter, the amount of research applying achievement goal theory to the physical domain has grown staggering. In particular, Nicholls' (1989, 1992) and Ames' (1992a, 1992b) writings were enthusiastically embraced by sport motivation researchers and translated into a variety of studies testing the suitability of various hypotheses to sport and physical activity settings. The popularity of the achievement goal perspective in sport resulted in several major review articles in recent years (Duda, 1993; Duda & Whitehead, 1998; Roberts, Treasure, & Kavussanu, 1997). Therefore, our goal is not to rehash these exhaustive reviews but rather to overview key theoretical propositions, synthesize and consolidate empirical research findings, and pose directions for future tests of achievement goal theory.

Achievement Goal Perspective to Motivation

One of the prominent features of sport is variation in individuals' achievement behaviors. Some participants choose challenging activities rather than easy ones, exert appropriate effort while striving for success rather than holding back, and persist through the adversity of learning new skills rather than folding under the pressure. Others choose the alternative route. Why do individuals who possess similar talents and opportunities express these behavioral variations? A number of social cognitive theories based on the central theme of "goals" have been proposed to explain such variations. In particular, Martin Maehr, John Nicholls, Carol Dweck, and Carole Ames formulated theoretical viewpoints based on an achievement goal perspective. Each theorist applies his or her signature to a view of how achievement goals determine motivated behavior, but all are distinguished by a set of common themes.

First, the concept of ability is central to each viewpoint. In fact, achievement situations are identified as those where participants' perceptions of their ability to meet situational demands are the primary concern. However, ability may be construed in several ways. For one individual, ability is demonstrated when she successfully masters a skill that she has been working on for a long time. Her definition of ability is self-referenced in that her focus is on personal mastery and learning. In contrast, another athlete may define ability as outperforming a teammate in practice or an opponent he is guarding in a game. This view of ability is norm-referenced in that performance relative to others is the main criterion for defining success.

Second, each perspective considers achievement motivation as a multidimensional construct,

in which a number of salient individual differences and social environmental factors influence ability perceptions, explanations for success and failure, and motivated behaviors. For example, a child's cognitive developmental level and perceptions of parental beliefs about how she or he should define success and failure can contribute significantly to achievement-related behaviors.

Third, goals are central determinants of motivated behavior, with individuals defining success and failure in terms of how well these goals were attained. In the examples presented earlier, the first athlete will view herself as successful if she attains her goal of mastering the difficult task, whereas the second athlete may only feel successful if he performed better than his opponent, even if objective measures point to a successful performance. Moreover, the type of goals that individuals adopt for achievement striving will influence cognitive and affective responses to success and failure experiences. For example, if our second athlete feels like he failed in his goal attainment, feelings of incompetence and anxiety may set in. These cognitions and affects are thought to mediate the influence of goals on activity choice, effort, persistence, and performance.

Early on, Maehr and Nicholls (1980) contended that achievement motivation takes a variety of forms that are derived from individuals' primary goals or reasons for participatory behavior and the meanings they attach to successful and unsuccessful experiences. Attaining a goal is thought to imply a valued quality about the person, such as being physically competent, socially accepted, or hard working. Moreover, success is defined in terms of attainment or nonattainment of one's personal goals. Maehr and Nicholls' perspective, then, emphasized the qualitative variations in goals rather than quantitative differences in behavior. The aim of their research was to define a comprehensive and universal classification of achievement behaviors based on variations in goals. Three categories of achievement goal orientations were defined as ability-, task-, and social approval–oriented goals. These goals characterize the primary reasons why individuals choose to participate in an achievement domain, how much effort and persistence is directed toward achieving mastery, and how success and failure are defined.

Ability-oriented goals are characterized as the desire to maximize favorable and minimize unfavorable ability perceptions relative to the performance of similar others. Performance outcomes attributed to high ability compared with others will be defined subjectively as success and will result in positive affect and future success expectancies. Conversely, outcomes attributed to low ability will be perceived as failures, resulting in negative affective reactions and little confidence that future mastery attempts will fare any better. Comparing one's performance to others or to normative standards is the overriding source of information used in this goal orientation to judge whether ability and success have been demonstrated.

Task-oriented goals are defined as the desire to demonstrate ability by accomplishing aspects contained within the task or activity itself rather than by achieving normative-based success. Performing a task well is the focal point, such as proper execution of a jump shot, precise follow-through on a round-off dismount, or selecting the advantageous down-the-line shot in tennis. Thus, with a task goal orientation, the process rather than the product of one's mastery attempts is more highly valued. Learning, problem solving, self-improvement, mastery, and enjoyment are examples of task-oriented goals. Self-referent criteria are used to determine whether success was demonstrated, such as comparing performance to previous attempts, using problem-solving strategies, and being satisfied with one's efforts. Successful task mastery should result in sustained high ability perceptions, pride and happiness about one's accomplishment, and the desire to continue participation.

Social approval–oriented goals emphasize the desire to demonstrate virtuous intent (i.e., maximal effort) and thereby gain social approval for these intentions. Effort is seen as a volitional behavior and an indicator of social conformity. Hence, individuals who are motivated to obtain social approval for their actions will demonstrate high levels of effort. Maehr and Nicholls (1980) found support for these universal goals among diverse cultures and ethnic groups, although the degree to which certain goals were promoted or emphasized varied among these groups.

Nicholls' Approach to Achievement Goals

Nicholls (1984, 1989) built on the notion of individuals' ability (renamed ego) and task goals but dropped social approval goals from the earlier repertoire. He offered no explicit reason in his publications for dropping social approval goals. It is possible that Nicholls did not view social approval goals as mutually exclusive from task or ego goals (Urdan & Maehr, 1995). That is, approval

from peers or parents could be gained by demonstrating superior performance or successfully mastering a difficult sport skill. Vealey and Campbell's (1988) findings support this notion by uncovering two goal orientations in a factor analysis: a task goal orientation and a combined social approval and ability orientation. In sum, Nicholls developed his ideas around the two main achievement goals of ego and task.

Nicholls (1978, 1984, 1989) designated several aspects that he considered instrumental for understanding achievement goals. First, he elaborated on developmental variations in conceptions of ability, effort, and task difficulty and how such conceptions relate to one's proneness toward task or ego involvement. Second, he proposed that achievement goals denote worldviews or theories about success in an achievement domain. His notion of a worldview implies that individuals' preferences for a task or ego goal orientation drive their beliefs about the causes of doing well or succeeding in an achievement domain and consequently affect their perceived ability, affective responses, and persistence in achievement situations. Third, Nicholls acknowledged the influence of the social context on achievement goals, such as socialization effects (i.e., culture- and gender-typed beliefs) or situations that emphasize evaluation of abilities by significant others, interpersonal versus intrapersonal competition, distribution of rewards, and classroom structure and teacher behaviors. As such, Nicholls specified both dispositional goals (i.e., goal orientations) and situation-specific goals (i.e., goal involvement).

According to Nicholls, young children do not differentiate between the concepts of ability and effort or ability and task difficulty (Nicholls, 1978; Nicholls & Miller, 1983). Up until about 7 years of age, children tend to use successful task completion as a basis for judging task difficulty. Tasks that children are unsure they are capable of performing are evaluated as difficult. Because difficult tasks require more effort for successful mastery, young children tend to view higher ability as associated with greater effort expenditure. Equating ability with effort, or a positive relationship between the two, is called an undifferentiated conception of ability. Inferences of high ability thus are expected in situations where the child tries hard. Not until about age 11 or 12, Nicholls posits, are difficult tasks evaluated as those that few people are able to perform. At a differentiated conception of ability, ability is viewed as a capacity.

Effort and ability are inversely related; that is, one's ability limits the impact that additional effort can provide to enhance probability of task success. Thus, if two individuals achieve equal performances but one exerts greater effort in the process, he or she is seen as possessing less ability than the individual who required less effort to perform just as well.

Nicholls (1984, 1989) proposed that children who possess an undifferentiated conception of ability and effort tend to be task involved because mastering a task or activity is seen as the primary goal, not demonstrating ability relative to others. Thus, the focus is on self-referent, rather than comparative, information and goals. This does not mean, however, that young children do not use peers as a source of information about how quickly they are learning a skill or to judge their physical competence. The strong, positive relationship between ability and effort instead suggests that effort is the primary cue of ability information. Once a differentiated conception of ability is attained, individuals can view an achievement situation in a task-involved or self-referent way (i.e., the goal is to beat previous performance or achieve a personal best) or in an ego-involved or norm-referent way (i.e., the goal is to win or beat a particular opponent). Nicholls proposed that invoking a task or ego goal depends on individual preferences in goal orientation and situational cues such as emphasis on interpersonal competition or social evaluation. However, Nicholls (1984, 1989; Duda & Nicholls, 1992) demonstrated that the two goals are independent constructs in the academic and physical achievement domains (i.e., task and ego orientations are weakly correlated); thus, variations in both goal orientations are possible (i.e., high–high, low–high, high–low, low–low). Unfortunately, the lingo used in the literature when discussing goal orientations tends to imply an "either/or" quality that may mislead or confuse the possibilities available (Hardy, 1997; Harwood, Hardy, & Swain, 2000; Wigfield & Eccles, 1992).

Nicholls' (1989) notion that one's dispositional goal orientation represents a worldview or theory about success is characterized by studies investigating individuals' perceptions of the purposes of doing well and beliefs about the causes of success in the academic domain. Two goal-belief dimensions have been uncovered: (a) a task goal orientation in combination with the belief that working hard, understanding schoolwork, and collaborating with peers lead to success; and (b) an ego goal orientation together with the belief that success is determined by attempts to outperform others and display superior ability. In a study of cross-domain comparisons, Duda and Nicholls (1992) found that goal-belief dimensions were identical for school and sport. Specifically, one dimension included a task goal orientation and beliefs that motivation or effort and cooperation with peers determine success in both school and sport. A second dimension combined an ego goal orientation with the belief that superior ability leads to success in school and sport. Consequently, Nicholls argued that goal-beliefs will be strongly related to individuals' self-ability perceptions, satisfaction, intrinsic interest, and motivated behaviors after successful and unsuccessful performance outcomes.

Although Nicholls' work has focused mostly on characteristic goal orientations and their relation to motivational consequences, Nicholls (1989) nevertheless acknowledged the important role that the social context plays in individuals' choice of achievement goals in a particular situation. For example, Nicholls argued that situations which promote social comparison processes, invite interpersonal competition, heighten self-awareness of performance, and emphasize social evaluation by significant adults and peers foster an ego-involved stance, even for individuals who prefer a dispositional task goal orientation. Conversely, situations that highlight the importance of learning, self-improvement and mastering optimal challenges, and working hard should elicit a task involvement. For example, Nicholls suggested that observed age-related changes in conceiving ability as a capacity may not only be a function of cognitive development. Rather, shifts in school environments from a focus on effort, learning, and mastery in the elementary schools to a focus on normative grading, social comparison, and ability-grouping in middle and high schools may contribute a great deal to children's conceptions of ability and the causes of success and failure. These beliefs, of course, have ramifications for children's attitudes toward and intensity of effort shown in achievement situations.

Dweck's Approach to Achievement Goals

Dweck, like Nicholls, has investigated variations in achievement behavior in the academic domain. She has proposed that children's conception of intelligence as a stable or changeable characteristic influences cognitions, affective responses, and motivated behaviors (Dweck, 1986, 1999; Dweck & Elliott, 1983; Dweck & Leggett, 1988;

Elliott & Dweck, 1988; Mueller & Dweck, 1998). Children who view intelligence as a global and stable entity are predicted to set goals emphasizing the demonstration of personal adequacy and avoidance of displaying low ability relative to others. Because intelligence is inferred through performance, Dweck terms the goal of demonstrating competence in a norm-referenced way a *performance goal*. In contrast to an entity view, Dweck presents an incremental view of intelligence, whereby intelligence can be enhanced through effort and purposeful strategies. Individuals operating under this conception of intelligence set goals emphasizing improvement of present abilities compared with past achievements, thus the term *learning goal*. In contrast to Nicholls, however, Dweck believes that learning and performance goals lie on a single continuum whereby individuals fall on either the learning or performance side of goals. In Nicholls' scheme, individuals can be low or high on task and ego goals.

Central to Dweck's (1980, 1986, 1999) proposition of learning and performance goals are two distinct behavioral patterns in response to failure. Mastery-oriented individuals align with learning goals and respond to failure as a temporary setback. Instead of internalizing failure as due to low stable ability, they focus on personally controllable factors such as lack of practice, inappropriate strategy selection, and inadequate effort. These factors are under the individual's control or are subject to change in the future as long as more practice, better strategies, and more concerted effort are adopted. In this view, positive affect and expectancies, and most importantly task choice, effort, and persistence, are maintained. Conversely, helpless-oriented children are characterized by performance goals in combination with low ability perceptions, and they attribute their failures to low stable ability, exhibit negative affect, and show deterioration of effort and persistence, resulting in inevitable performance decrements. Dweck argues that the incremental and entity conceptions of intelligence, and their concomitant learning- and performance-oriented goals, are associated with mastery- and helpless-oriented behavioral tendencies, respectively.

Although Dweck and Nicholls use different terms (ego, performance; task, learning) and dimensions (single, dual) for goals, their formulations for the goals–behavior relationship are similar. Dweck's predictions for individuals who embrace learning goals align with Nicholls' predictions for high task–low ego individuals.

Children who are guided by learning or task goals are interested in mastering tasks, learning new skills and strategies, and developing skill, and they have an intrinsic interest in the activity (i.e., mastery-oriented). Self-referenced sources of information are prioritized for defining achievement success such as attainment of self-set goals, attraction toward the activity, degree of skill improvement, and effort expended. Unsuccessful mastery attempts are seen as challenges, not threats, and errors incurred during performance are viewed as an integral part of the learning process. Mastery-oriented individuals are thus likely to prefer optimal challenges and will display the effort and persistence necessary to succeed. Moreover, they will experience positive affect and feelings of satisfaction from their efforts.

In contrast, those who are guided by performance or high ego–low task goals are primarily interested in demonstrating superior performance relative to others. Norm-referenced sources, therefore, define whether success has been attained (e.g., ranking, rating, place of finish). As long as these individuals possess high ability perceptions, they are likely to choose challenging tasks and exert high levels of effort to attain their goal. These behavioral patterns are similar to the learning or task goal–oriented person, regardless of level of perceived ability. The ego or performance goal–oriented person with self-doubts about ability, however, is at risk for low achievement behaviors (i.e., helpless-oriented). In an effort to maximize demonstrating high and minimizing low ability, individuals will choose easy or difficult tasks because they expect to be unsuccessful at optimally challenging tasks. Thus, withholding effort on moderately challenging tasks means that ability cannot be easily judged. Unfortunately, withholding effort and giving up prematurely become a self-fulfilling prophecy in that they reduce the chances for performance improvement and success. It is not surprising that performance- or ego-oriented individuals with low perceived competence are likely to experience feelings of anxiety and other negative affects toward an activity in which they hold low performance expectations.

Ames' Approach to Achievement Goals

Finally, Ames (1984, 1992a, 1992b) has focused her research efforts on the goals emphasized within the classroom environment and on how the task structure, definition and perceived causes of success, and teacher behaviors within classroom contexts influence students' goals, self-perceptions, emotions, and achievement behaviors. Early on, Ames (1984) emphasized the influence of reward structures within educational environments on children's achievement goals and behaviors. A reward structure is defined as an environment in which certain goals are fostered based on criteria for evaluating and recognizing performance. She identified three goal–reward structures: competitive, individualistic, and cooperative. A competitive reward structure is one in which rewards are distributed based on normative achievement; when one person attains a reward, another person is precluded from attaining it. An individualistic reward structure is one where each individual's attainment of a reward is independent of others' performance because rewards are distributed based on personal mastery. A cooperative reward structure is one where rewards are distributed based on group mastery and performance.

Ames argued that competitive, individualistic, and cooperative goal–reward structures involve the use of different motivational processes because success and failure are defined differently under each structure. Specifically, competitive and individualistic goal–reward structures should engender ego- and task-involved goals, respectively, whereas the cooperative structure relates to a moral motivational orientation. Moreover, competitive structures emphasize ability attributions for performance outcome, whereas individualistic and cooperative structures emphasize effort attributions. For example, Ames and Ames (1981) found that previous performance success was a salient source of information used for self-evaluation, and effort attributions were more prevalent in individualized than in competitive classroom settings. Because competitive reward structures encourage individuals to compare personal performance to others' performance, perceptions of individual differences in ability are more likely than in individualistic or cooperative systems, where the performance of others either is not relevant to success perceptions or depends on group rather than individual attainments.

In recent years, goal–reward structures have been referred to more frequently as the motivational or psychological climate in which achievement behaviors take place (Ames, 1992a, 1992b). The individualistic reward structure is akin to a mastery- or task-involving climate, whereas the competitive reward structure translates to a performance- or ego-involving climate. Primary interest is focused on how the structure or climate within the classroom influences the types of goals students are likely to adopt and, subsequently, their achievement beliefs, affects, and behaviors. Ames identified key aspects of the motivational climate: design of tasks and learning activities, distribution of authority or responsibility, use of rewards, and methods of evaluation. She provided considerable evidence from her own work and that of others' of the motivational advantage of classroom tasks that provide students with variety, optimal challenge, and meaningfulness; choices and shared decision-making; and evaluation practices and criteria for recognition that focus on learning, effort, and self-improvement (Ames, 1992a; Ames & Archer, 1988).

Her intervention research in classrooms illuminates the appeal of shaping a mastery motivational climate to ensure students' adoption of task-involved goals, perceptions of ability and success based on effort, adaptive learning strategies, and feelings of enjoyment and satisfaction from engaging in the process of learning (see Ames, 1992a, 1992b). The theoretical dimensions of a mastery climate were defined in terms of how success is defined, what is valued, how mistakes are viewed, how children are evaluated, and what children and teachers are focused on in the classroom. Corresponding organizational and teaching behavior strategies then were developed to align with this definition of a mastery climate, and these included the dimensions of task, authority, recognition, grouping, evaluation, and time (i.e., TARGET; Epstein, 1988). Teachers were trained to use as many of the TARGET strategies as possible and to especially focus their efforts toward at-risk students (i.e., those with low self-esteem or low skills). Results supported a mastery motivational climate in positively influencing self-concept of ability, choice of learning strategies, attitudes, and intrinsic motivation in elementary and secondary school students. Importantly, Ames (1992b) pointed out the structural similarities between classroom and sport environments such as definitions of success, extent of adult control, and type of evaluative practices. Thus, the TARGET intervention should be as applicable and salient in sport as it is in academic settings. We contend that endorsing a mastery motivational climate in sport may be of even greater concern given the emphasis in youth through elite sport on social comparison forms of defining and judging success, use of extrinsic rewards, and coach behaviors that often border on benevolent dictatorship. Moreover, performance in sport, unlike school, is more visible and vulnerable to evaluation by significant adults and peers.

Summary

These theorists have contributed substantially to the literature on understanding and explaining achievement behaviors. More importantly, their ideas and hypotheses make good, logical sense for understanding sport and physical activity motivation. For this reason, it is no wonder that over the last decade a considerable amount of research has applied achievement goal theory to understanding topics that are salient for enhancing children's and adolescents' positive experiences in sport and physical activity. In the following sections we synthesize and consolidate the research on achievement goals in sport. Studies are divided into the following themes: (a) developmental component of achievement goals; (b) achievement goals, perceived purposes of sport, and beliefs about causes of success; (c) goal orientations and participatory behaviors; (d) achievement goals and cognitive, affective, and behavioral outcomes; and (e) the social context and achievement goals.

Developmental Component of Achievement Goals

In a review of Nicholls' (1978, Nicholls & Miller, 1983, 1984) developmental hypotheses of achievement motivation, Duda (1987) advocated the importance of testing these notions in the physical achievement domain. Because ability, effort, and task difficulty are more observable in sport than in academic achievement strivings, the developmental processes for the two domains may be quite different. Thus, children in sport achievement situations would provide an especially salient test of the differentiated–undifferentiated conceptions of ability hypotheses. Watkins and Montgomery (1989) interviewed children and teenagers ages 8, 12, 15, and 18 years concerning their beliefs about contributors to athletic ability. Participants were asked to identify their perceived sources of athletic excellence, and responses were coded according to such categories as effort–experience, natural ability, social support, and emotions–attitudes. Watkins and Montgomery's findings partially supported Nicholls' contentions that children are capable of viewing ability as undifferentiated or differentiated from effort, in that effort as a source of ability declined from age 8 to 18, and natural ability was mentioned most frequently by the two older age groups.

In a more direct test of developmental processes, Fry and Duda (1997) replicated and extended Nicholls' (1978) seminal study. Children ages 5 to 13 were tested on conceptions of ability and effort for both academic (i.e., number of math problems solved) and physical (i.e., throwing a beanbag at a target) tasks. Children were presented two scenarios: one in which two children performed equally successfully with unequal effort, and another that had unequal outcomes, with the "lazier" child performing better. Children were challenged to reason through a series of questions about why the two children performed equally well if one tried harder than the other, or why the child who didn't work hard was more successful than the other. Results were entirely consistent with Nicholls' developmental staging for both the academic and physical tasks. Moreover, a high correlation ($r = .76$) between children's scores for the two domains suggests that the process of differentiating effort and ability is the same. A strong correlation ($r = .67$) between age and conception of ability also demonstrated that younger children were more likely to be undifferentiated and older children differentiated on ability and effort conceptions, although variability within age was also apparent. Whitehead and Smith (1996), using a basketball shooting task with 7- to 13-year-old boys, attained similar findings. Recently, Fry (2000a, 2000b) extended developmental findings to children's differentiation of ability and luck, and ability and task difficulty, respectively, in the physical domain.

Achievement Goals, Perceived Purposes of Sport, and Beliefs About Causes of Success

A person's goal orientation reflects his or her subjective definition of success and the criteria used to determine whether goals and success were attained. Nicholls (1989) believed that achievement goals represent a worldview or personal theory about what is valued and beneficial about education (i.e., an end in itself or a means to an end) and beliefs about the determinants of attaining academic success. He and his colleagues (e.g., Duda & Nicholls, 1992; Nicholls, Patashnick, & Nolen, 1985; Thorkildsen & Nicholls, 1998) consistently found relationships between task and ego orientation, perceived purposes of education, and beliefs about success. A task orientation was aligned with the belief that education provides opportunities for enhanced learning, self-esteem, and mastery experiences, and that effort, learning, hard work, and collaborating with peers determine success. An ego orientation correlated with the belief that educational benefits include opportunities for social status and wealth, and that factors which help students do well in school are demonstrating superior ability, outperforming others, competitiveness, and extrinsic elements such as good behavior, pretending to like the teacher, and luck. The relationship of personal goals with perceived value of involvement in sport and determinants of what helps individuals be successful in sport has followed suit.

Duda (1989a) extended the work of Nicholls and colleagues by examining the correspondence between task and ego goals and perceived purposes of sport participation in high school athletes. Using the stem "A very important thing sport should do . . . ," participants rated 60 items related to beliefs about the value of sport. A moderately strong relationship between goal orientation and perceived value of sport showed that individuals high in task goal orientation and moderately low in ego goal orientation believed that sport is a vehicle for developing mastery and cooperation skills and not for enhancing social status. Athletes high in ego orientation and moderately high in task orientation believed that the purpose of sport was to enhance self-esteem, social status, and competitiveness. S.A. White, Duda, and Keller (1998) found similar results with youth sport participants in that a high task orientation was positively related to the belief that sport promotes self-esteem, good citizenship, mastery and cooperation, and the adoption of a physically active lifestyle.

A host of studies have similarly extended Duda and Nicholls' (1992) findings that task and ego goal orientations relate to beliefs about what causes success in sport (e.g., Hom, Duda, & Miller, 1993; King & Williams, 1997; Lochbaum & Roberts, 1993; Newton & Duda, 1993; Roberts, Treasure, & Kavussanu, 1996). In general, findings revealed that higher task goals are aligned with believing that hard work, effort, and practice are primary determinants of success. Ego task goals were significantly related to superior ability, external factors, and deception or illegal advantage as causes of successful outcomes.

Goal Orientations and Participatory Behaviors

The tenets of achievement goal theory suggest that children who hold predominantly task-oriented goals will choose to remain involved and show adaptive effort and persistence behaviors. The reasoning is that they are motivated to develop and learn skills, master challenges, and value the enjoyable features of sport involvement. The child who adopts strong ego-oriented goals and possesses high ability perceptions will show the same pattern of behaviors as the task-involved child despite definitions of success based on demonstrating superior ability. However, the high ego–low perceived ability child is considered an at-risk candidate for dropping out of sport (Duda, 1987). His or her goal of demonstrating high comparative ability and avoiding demonstrating inability should lead to behaviors that protect self-worth such as easy or difficult task choices, low effort and persistence, and avoidance strategies.

Several studies have applied achievement goal theory to participation motivation and attrition in youth and high school sport (e.g., Burton, 1992; Burton & Martens, 1986; Duda, 1988, 1989b; Ewing, 1981; Petlichkoff, 1993a, 1993b; S.A. White & Duda, 1994; Whitehead, 1995). In the first study to investigate motivational correlates of goal beliefs, Ewing (1981) compared participants, nonparticipants, and dropouts on responses to items following the stem, "I felt successful because . . ." by using a critical incident methodology. She found that dropouts scored higher on ability (ego) goals than the other groups, whereas current participants scored highest on social approval goals. Burton (1992; Burton & Martens, 1986) found support for the utility of achievement goal theory when comparing youth wrestling participants and dropouts. Consistent with predictions, continuing participants scored higher on perceived ability, win/loss record, internal attributions for success, expectancies of success, and value toward the importance of wrestling success.

Duda (1988, 1989b) investigated the relationship between goal perspectives and participatory behaviors in companion studies. In the first study (Duda, 1988), college intramural participants who scored higher on task involvement (either high task–low ego or high task–high ego) reported playing their sport for a longer time period and practicing more frequently in their spare time. Duda (1989b) investigated participant status (participant, nonparticipant, dropout) and preference for task and social comparison (ego) goals. Participants scored higher in both task and ego goals than did nonparticipant and dropout groups. These results were not predicted, and Duda speculated that participants who emphasized ego goals might be candidates for subsequent drop-out.

Collectively, these studies demonstrate the practical utility of applying achievement goal theory to participation motivation and attrition. Our ultimate goal as sport psychology researchers and practitioners is to understand antecedents of continued involvement in sport and physical activity. Therefore, reasons for involvement, achievement goals (i.e., subjective definitions of success), and the criteria used to judge competence and success are important areas to pursue.

Achievement Goals and Cognitive, Affective, and Behavioral Outcomes

Given the differential emphases that task and ego goal orientations place on defining competence and success, it stands to reason that goal orientations will influence a number of thoughts, emotions, and behaviors relevant to sport participation. Specifically, cognitive variables (e.g., beliefs about strategies), affective responses (e.g., enjoyment, satisfaction, and anxiety), and behavioral outcomes (e.g., intensity of effort) have been the focus of several research efforts in the sport domain. Together, these studies garner considerable support for the contention that high task–low ego participants adopt more functional thought patterns, positive affective responses, and motivated behavior than those who are high in ego and low in task orientation. However, few studies have tested achievement goal predictions that a combination of high ego goals and perceived ability will differentiate achievement-related consequences.

Lochbaum and Roberts (1993) found conceptually consistent relationships in a study investigating goal orientations, beliefs about playing strategies, and satisfaction. High school athletes who endorsed high task goals rated practice mastery, coach approval, and effort during competition as important playing strategies. In contrast, those adopting high ego goals indicated social demonstration of ability as most beneficial. Solmon and Boone (1993) conducted a nicely designed study of the role of goals in college students' thoughts, actions, and achievement behaviors during a semester-long physical activity (tennis) class. Task selection (easy, challenging) was assessed through a contract grading system, and achievement behaviors (contract points) subsequently were recorded through observational methods. Cognitive processes included a composite score

denoting anxiety, interest, attitude, attention, use of strategies, and willingness to persist, with higher scores reflecting greater positive and less negative affect, adaptive learning strategies, and task persistence. Results revealed that individuals with higher task goals chose more challenging tasks and recorded higher scores on cognitive processes, whereas higher ego goals were negatively related to these attributes. Moreover, higher task selection and cognitive processes were significant predictors of skill development over the course of the semester.

Several studies have examined the link between goals and emotions (Duda et al., 1995; Hall & Kerr, 1997; Hall, Kerr, & Mathews, 1998; Hom et al., 1993; Roberts et al., 1996; Vlachopoulos, Biddle, & Fox, 1996; Walsh, Crocker, & Bouffard, 1992; L. Williams & Gill, 1995). In general, results across studies ranging from youth sport to college undergraduates showed that higher task goal scores are related to greater positive affect (e.g., enjoyment, intrinsic interest, confidence) and less negative affect (e.g., boredom, anxiety). Fewer coherent relationships were found for ego goals and affective responses.

A few studies concentrated on the relation between goal orientations and effort or persistence (perceived or objective) during achievement task involvement (Duda et al., 1995; Martinek & Williams, 1997; Swain, 1996; Walsh et al., 1992; L. Williams & Gill, 1995). In general, higher scores on task goal orientation related consistently and strongly with higher perceived effort and task persistence. Swain designed a clever study looking at the interaction of goal orientations and situational factors on demonstrated effort and performance—more specifically, the phenomenon of social loafing. He divided high school students into groups varying in task and ego goal orientations (i.e., high–high, high–low, low–high, low–low) and then had them perform a 30-meter sprint under three conditions: individual performance, team performance with individual performance identifiable, and team performance with individual performance not identifiable. Swain hypothesized and results confirmed that high ego–low task individuals would perform worse under nonidentifiable but not identifiable conditions, whereas high task–low ego participants would not show differences across performance conditions. Thus, high ego–low task participants who desire to demonstrate superior ability suffer motivational losses under conditions where ability cannot be demonstrated (i.e., nonidentifiable condition).

The Social Context and Achievement Goals

The majority of research on achievement goals in sport has examined cognitive, affective, and behavioral correlates. However, theorists (Ames, 1992a; Dweck, 1999; Maehr & Nicholls, 1980; Nicholls, 1989; Urdan & Maehr, 1995) acknowledge the important role that the social context can play in one's proneness toward goal orientations and determining goal states (i.e., goal involvement). This section is organized into research focusing on culture, socializers' definitions of success and failure, the motivational or psychological climate, and situation-specific determinants of goal states (e.g., practice vs. competition). Gender variations in achievement behavior are elaborated on by Gill (chapter 11).

Cultural Variations in Achievement Goals

Duda (1985, 1986a, 1986b) found evidence of cultural variations in achievement goals. White males were more ability-oriented than either white females or Navajos and Mexican-Americans of either gender (Duda, 1985, 1986a). White males were higher in social comparison (ability) goals than black and Hispanic males and white females; Hispanic male and female participants defined success in skill mastery terms more frequently than other groups (Duda, 1986b). Other than Duda's systematic early efforts, few empirical studies followed suit, leading Duda and Allison (1990) to dub cross-cultural analysis in sport psychology a void in the field.

Hayashi (1996; Hayashi & Weiss, 1994) responded to Duda and Allison's (1990) plea for more cross-cultural research by focusing on achievement goal variations among physical activity participants from Eastern and Western cultures. In the first study (Hayashi & Weiss, 1994), Anglo and Japanese marathon runners completed measures of achievement goal and competitive orientations. Although results supported the hypothesis that Anglo participants would score higher on competitiveness, Anglos were not higher as predicted on ego or win orientation. In fact, Japanese participants scored significantly higher on win orientation. Results were explained in relation to the uniqueness of the sport (marathon running) and issues related to linguistic and psychometric equivalence (Duda & Hayashi, 1998). To overcome problems of language, translation inaccuracies, and slang terminology that reflect socialization experiences, Hayashi (1996) used qualitative methodology to investigate the relationship between culture and achievement goal orientations. Male adult exercisers from Eastern (native Hawaiians and Anglos who resided in Hawaii) and Western (Anglos who resided in the mainland United States) cultural backgrounds were asked about their definitions of success and failure in the weight room. Hayashi found that social approval and solidarity goals were important to adult exercisers of Hawaiian cultural background. Goals verbalized by participants reflected social ties to their peer group (interdependent goals) and in-group pride and harmony. Few studies have elaborated on social goals and their cognitive, affective, and behavioral outcomes. More recently, Kim and Gill (1997) tested the applicability of achievement goal predictions in Korean adolescent athletes.

The vast numbers of youth participating in sport who represent varying racial, ethnic, and cultural backgrounds merit our concerted attention to understanding both universal and unique motivational aspects of sport behavior (De Knop, Engstrom, Skirstad, & Weiss, 1996). The studies reported here provide an excellent starting point, and contemporary discussion of the conceptual and methodological nuances of conducting cross-cultural research in sport environments is invaluable to researchers interested in pursuing this line of research (Duda & Hayashi, 1998).

Parents' and Coaches' Goal Perspectives and Beliefs About Causes of Success

Socialization of dispositional task and ego orientations is an understudied area in achievement goal theory. Although Ames' work (1992a; Ames & Archer, 1987, 1988) implicated the important role of parents' and teachers' beliefs and behaviors in children's adoption of achievement goals, only a handful of studies have extended these ideas to the physical domain. Studies have addressed the interdependence between parents', coaches', and children's beliefs about what defines and causes success (e.g., Chaumeton & Duda, 1988; Duda & Hom, 1993; Ebbeck & Becker, 1994; Krane, Greenleaf, & Snow, 1997; Roberts, Treasure, & Hall, 1994).

Duda and Hom (1993) assessed parents' and children's (ages 8–15) task and ego goal orientations in basketball. Moderately strong correlations were found between children's task orientation and perceptions of their significant parent's task orientation and between children's ego orientation and perception of their parent's ego orientation. Similarly, Ebbeck and Becker (1994) found a strong correspondence between soccer athletes' (ages 10–14) perceptions of their mother's and father's ego orientation and their self-reported ego goal orientation, as well as between perceived parent task orientation and their own task goal orientation.

Although Ames (see Ames, 1992a) emphasized that teachers' behaviors and structure of classroom environments significantly affect children's goal involvement, perceptions of success, and affective responses, few studies in the sport domain have extended these ideas to coaches' influence on players' goal orientations and psychosocial outcomes. Chaumeton and Duda (1988) examined whether coaches' philosophy and behaviors pertaining to the importance of skill development or winning goals varied by competitive level (elementary, junior, senior high), and whether players perceived that developing skills or having a winning team was emphasized. Results revealed that, across competitive level, coaches' behaviors primarily consisted of praise, instruction, and encouragement, with very few incidences of nonreinforcement and punishment. Although high school players indicated that having a winning team was more important than did junior high or elementary players, players at all levels rated this goal as important (range = 5.29–6.55 on a 7-point scale), as they also did developing skills (range = 6.56–6.94 on a 7-point scale).

Motivational Climate and Cognitive, Affective, and Behavioral Outcomes

An early study that examined goal–reward structure in the physical domain examined the influence of competitive and cooperative physical activity programs on adolescent girls' fitness and self-concepts (Marsh & Peart, 1988). Following a 6-week intervention program, results revealed that both reward structures enhanced physical fitness levels but only the cooperative program enhanced self-concepts of ability and physical appearance, whereas the competitive program lowered them. Marsh's (Marsh et al., 1986a, 1986b) research using Outward Bound activities (i.e., cooperative goal–reward structure) as an intervention has shown good success in improving physical self-conceptions (i.e., ability, appearance). Ebbeck and Gibbons (1998) also implemented a cooperative reward structure intervention and found strong effects on 10- to 12-year-old participants' perceptions of physical ability, appearance, peer acceptance, and global self-worth.

Only a handful of intervention studies have tested the efficacy of a mastery motivational climate on children's achievement-related thoughts, emotions, and behaviors (Goudas et al., 1995; Papaioannou & Kouli, 1999; Theeboom et al., 1995). Theeboom et al. employed mastery and performance climate teaching programs in a children's sports program by using a Chinese martial arts activity (wushu). The programs followed instructional strategies based on the TARGET dimensions, which were implemented for three weeks (14 lessons) with children 8 to 12 years of age. Postintervention comparisons indicated that children in the mastery climate group reported greater enjoyment and demonstrated better motor skills than the performance climate group. Although perceived competence and intrinsic motivation effects were not statistically significant, mastery group participants were unanimous in reporting high ability perceptions and intrinsic motivation, whereas children's responses from the performance group were less pronounced. This study demonstrated the utility and efficacy of deliberately conceiving a mastery motivational climate curriculum in children's sport skill programs. However, this is easier said than done. Implementing such a program in more competitive youth sport programs may be quite difficult because of the entrenched organization in which teams are selected and the emphasis on ability grouping and league standings and championships.

In contrast, the physical education context offers an opportune setting for quality control (i.e., teacher cooperation, focus on skill development) and potentially longer intervention periods than competitive youth sport. Goudas et al. (1995) focused on one dimension, authority, in their study of 12- to 13-year-old girls in a physical education class. Specifically, children participated in a 10-week track-and-field unit in which half the lessons focused on a direct teaching style (the teacher made the majority of instructional decisions) and the other half a differentiated teaching style (students were allowed activity choices). Children responded to the differentiated teaching style lessons with greater intrinsic motivation and task involvement compared to the direct teaching style. Ames (1992a) suggested that the instructional dimensions of task, authority, recognition, grouping, evaluation, and time are multiplicative in nature and should be considered as a whole rather than in parts. Therefore, these results possibly reflect outcomes related to the design of activities, pace of learning, and focus of recognition and evaluation. Despite the attractiveness of conducting interventions in physical education classrooms, a challenge for sport psychology researchers is effecting change in the motivational climate within competitive youth sport and interscholastic programs, where the risk of ego involvement, reductions in enjoyment and intrinsic motivation, and reduced participation looms large.

Papaioannou (1994, 1995a, 1995b, 1998; Papaioannou & Kouli, 1999; Papaioannou & Theodorakis, 1996) has established a programmatic line of research on achievement goals and motivational climate in physical education contexts. Papaioannou (1995a) examined the relationship between perceived motivational climate and differential teacher behavior toward high and low achievers in high school physical education classes. Significant and low–moderate correlations (r = .20–.26) were found between perceived performance climate and favoritism shown toward high achievers and between perceived mastery climate and differential treatment toward low achievers (r = .31–.32). Papaioannou (1998) also found an interesting association between perceived motivational climate and teachers' strategies to keep discipline in classrooms. A mastery climate was associated with students' perceptions that teaching strategies were focused on intrinsic reasons for establishing good behavior in the classroom (e.g., "Attracts our attention by making the lesson more interesting," "Makes us enjoy the lesson"). By contrast a performance climate was related to perceived teaching strategies of an extrinsic nature (e.g., "Makes us feel bad about ourselves if we are not disciplined," "Yells at those who are not disciplined").

The majority of studies have examined relationships among motivational climate, goal orientations, beliefs about the causes of success, and affective responses to sport participation (Ebbeck & Becker, 1994; Goudas & Biddle, 1994; Ommundsen, Roberts, & Kavussanu, 1998; Seifriz et al., 1992; Treasure, 1997; Treasure & Roberts, 1998; Walling, Duda, & Chi, 1993). These studies consistently show positive associations between perceived mastery climate, task goal orientation, and the belief that effort is the cause of success, and between perceived performance climate, ego goal orientation, and the belief that ability causes success. These studies also show that a mastery climate is associated with higher positive affect (e.g., enjoyment, satisfaction, interest) and lower negative affect (e.g., anxiety, boredom), although correlations are often low or moderate at best.

Fewer consistent relationships have been found for perceived performance climate.

More recent studies have investigated models specifying the relationships among motivational climate, goal orientations, and achievement outcomes (Biddle et al., 1995; Ferrer-Caja & Weiss, 2000; Ntoumanis & Biddle, 1997). These studies tested the adequacy of fit between a specified model, obtained data from physical activity participants, and consequently determined the valence and strength of hypothesized relationships among salient variables in the model. For example, Ntoumanis and Biddle simultaneously examined the relationships among motivational climate, goal orientations, self-confidence, and competitive state anxiety in collegiate team sport athletes. The authors found evidence of a reciprocal relationship between goal orientation and climate and an indirect influence of ego goal orientation on cognitive and somatic anxiety through the mediation of self-confidence.

Empirical research on motivational climate in sport contexts is on the verge of explosion. We believe that more experimental studies are needed in which motivational climate is implemented as an intervention strategy and psychosocial and behavioral outcomes are observed in competitive youth and high school sport. Ames' (1992a, 1992b) research and Epstein's (1988, 1989) instructional dimensions lead the way for sport psychology researchers to extend their ideas to a variety of physical activity contexts (Ntoumanis & Biddle, 1999; Treasure & Roberts, 1995b).

Situational Determinants of Goal Involvement

Nicholls (1984, 1989) spoke of individual differences in proneness toward achievement goals (i.e., goal orientation) and situational or state goals (i.e., goal involvement) to differentiate an individual's "usual" versus "right now" goals. This is analogous to other constructs in sport psychology such as trait and state anxiety or perceived competence and self-efficacy. Nicholls and others (Ames, 1992a; Dweck, 1986, Eccles et al., 1998) identified situations that promote interpersonal competition, social evaluation of personal competencies, and normative definitions of success as ones that encourage an ego goal state. In contrast, situations that emphasize self-referenced success and feedback for individual performance and that devalue social and normative evaluation are conducive to task goal states. The achievement goal studies reported in previous sections all used dispositional goals and did not include state goals in their research questions or designs. Recently, a few studies have tackled the distinction between goal orientation and goal involvement by posing research questions that address the perspectives individuals choose based on the situational cues at hand (Hall & Kerr, 1997; Hall et al., 1998; Harwood & Swain, 1998; Swain & Harwood, 1996; L. Williams, 1998).

Swain and Harwood (1996; Harwood & Swain, 1998) conducted two studies, one with swimmers and the other with tennis players, to examine the interactive contributions of goal orientations, swimming trait goals, and situational criteria on state goal involvement. In the first study (Swain & Harwood, 1996), trait goals were assessed as degree of satisfaction with swimming well despite final placing (task goal) or winning even though performance was poor (ego goal). Situational criteria were represented by social and personal ability perceptions, perceived state goal preference of significant others, race outcome value, and mental and physical readiness. State goals were assessed within one hour of the swimmer's heat in his or her main stroke and distance event. The authors found that trait task goal, race outcome value, and perceived goal preference of significant others significantly predicted state task goal, whereas state ego goal, race outcome value, social and personal ability perceptions of ability, and state goal preference of coach and parents predicted state ego goal. Task and ego goal orientations were not significant predictors of task and ego state goals, respectively. The authors replicated and extended their study of antecedents of swimmers' goal states to elite junior tennis players (Harwood & Swain, 1998). Their results demonstrate the importance of considering meaningful situational cues along with race- or match-specific trait goals in explaining state goal involvement.

Future Research Directions

Several review articles have outlined potential directions for future research (e.g., Duda & Whitehead, 1998; Roberts et al., 1997). In light of our synthesis of concepts and studies on achievement goals, we elaborate on three areas that are ripe for further introspection: (a) interaction of goal orientations and perceived ability; (b) goals other than task or ego, especially social goals; and (c) intervention studies.

Goal Orientations and Perceived Ability

According to achievement goal theory (Dweck, 1986, 1999; Nicholls, 1984, 1989), individuals who approach achievement situations with high task involvement will show adaptive learning strategies and behaviors regardless of level of perceived ability. This is justified through their definitions or meanings of success that revolve around self-referent indicators such as personal mastery, skill improvement, and effective problem solving. Because highly task-involved individuals view achievement as a means in itself, and not a means to an end, competence and success are construed by attaining these forms of self-referent goals. Individuals high in ego involvement but who possess high ability perceptions should show the same pattern of behaviors, in the form of choosing optimal challenges, exerting effort, and persisting with difficult skill learning. Although these persons define competence and success in normative terms, their high ability perceptions influence their expectancies of success, and, to demonstrate competence in relation to others, they will embrace challenging tasks and engage in adaptive behaviors to ensure their superiority of skill. The individual high in ego orientation but low in perceived ability, however, has been designated as an at-risk candidate for maladaptive behaviors including dropping out of sport (Duda, 1987). The reasoning is that these individuals do not expect to be successful and thus engage in avoidance strategies, low effort expenditure, and external attributions that help them refrain from demonstrating lack of competence. Because normative goals are salient but they have little faith in achieving better performance than others, these strategies help to protect self-worth and judgments of low ability by others.

Despite these clear formulations, few studies have considered the interaction between goal orientations and perceived ability in the physical domain (Goudas et al., 1994b; Hall & Kerr, 1997; Martinek & Williams, 1997; Walsh et al., 1992; L. Williams & Gill, 1995). Williams and Gill and Goudas et al. specified perceived competence as a mediating variable of the effect of goal orientations on intrinsic motivation. However, predictions based on achievement goal theory would instead specify an *ego goal orientation × perceived competence* interaction term in the model. If the interaction term was significant, then intrinsic motivation scores based on higher or lower ego and higher or lower perceived competence could be graphed and examined in relation to theoretical predictions. One would expect to find individuals who are high in ego goal orientation and perceived competence to be associated with higher intrinsic motivation than those high in ego goal orientation and low in perceived competence.

Martinek and Williams (1997) investigated the link between goal orientation and perceived competence by comparing mastery-oriented and learned-helpless students (grades 6–7) on level of task persistence. By definition (Dweck, 1986), a mastery-oriented person adopts a learning (task) goal orientation, perceives high competence, engages in adaptive motivation behaviors, and responds to failures with lack of effort attributions (i.e., failure is changeable). In contrast, learned-helpless individuals are high in performance goal orientation and low in perceived competence, engage in maladaptive behaviors, and claim lack of ability as a reason for their failures (i.e., failure is stable). Consistent with the hypotheses, mastery-oriented students scored significantly higher on task persistence (attempts per minute on physical education tasks) than learned-helpless students.

Using experimental procedures, Walsh et al. (1992) divided physical education undergraduate students into high and low perceived physical competence and then randomly assigned them to either ego- or task-involving situations. Participants performed on a throwing task and were subjected to several success and failure trials. Positive and negative affect and task persistence were assessed after sets of trials. A goal orientation (task, ego) × perceived competence (low, high) interaction effect did not emerge, failing to support achievement goal predictions. The only difference found was that females in the ego-involving condition demonstrated lower task persistence than the other three groups (male–task, male–ego, female–task).

Besides these studies, we could not locate any others that considered the interaction between goal orientations and perceived competence. Some studies included perceived competence as a dependent variable or as a correlate in nonexperimental studies but not in combination with goal orientation as specified by achievement goal theory. Many of the empirical studies and review articles on the efficacy of the achievement goal perspective concluded by alluding to the detrimental nature of adopting ego goals in sport. However, as several authors have pointed out (e.g., Hardy, 1997, 1998; Harwood et al., 2000; Treasure

& Roberts, 1995a), the achievement domain of sport is a highly ego-involving one, and it is not unreasonable to expect that many athletes will hold both task and ego goals for their competitive performances. Indeed, several studies showed that individuals high in task orientation, whether high or low in ego orientation, were more positive in their thoughts, emotions, and behaviors (e.g., Duda, 1989b; Hom et al., 1993; Roberts et al., 1996). Moreover, Swain (1996) showed that only the high ego–low task individuals socially loafed in a condition where individual ability was not identifiable. Therefore, future studies should consider individuals' level of perceived ability in combination with goal orientation in examining cognitive, affective, and behavioral outcomes in the physical domain.

Whatever Happened to Social Goals?

At the beginning of this section we described the early work of Maehr and Nicholls (1980), which identified three achievement goals: task, ability (ego), and social approval. Subsequent achievement goal research has focused primarily on task and ego goals (Urdan & Maehr, 1995). The disappearance of social approval goals is somewhat of a mystery, and recent articles have called for the inclusion of achievement goals other than task and ego, including a host of social goals (Blumenfeld, 1992; Jarvinen & Nicholls, 1996; Urdan & Maehr, 1995; Wentzel, 1993, 1998). This view is especially salient to the sport domain, because it nicely converges with the original descriptive participation motivation research that found developing and affirming friendships, gaining approval from parents and coaches, and developing a sense of team belonging as important reasons for staying involved in sports.

Urdan and Maehr's (1995) conceptual article on the importance of social goals contributes significantly to the achievement goal literature. We do not know of any published studies in the sport or physical activity domain that have examined social goals within an achievement goal theory perspective. Therefore, an obvious direction for future research on achievement goals is to consider the influence of participants' multiple goals—task, ego, social—on their beliefs, emotions, and motivation in sport contexts. Urdan and Maehr's article is a logical starting point for delving into the role of social goals on achievement attitudes and behaviors. These authors defined social goals as the perceived social purposes for or meaning of achievement in a particular domain. These include, among others, social welfare goals (e.g., to become a productive member of society), social solidarity goals (e.g., to bring honor to one's family or raise esteem within one's in-group), social approval goals (e.g., to please parents, develop friendships, enhance peer acceptance), and social compliance goals (e.g., to become a good person). Hayashi's (1996) findings of in-group pride and harmony goals for participants socialized in the Hawaiian culture are reminiscent of social solidarity goals. The link found between perceptions of peer acceptance and friendship and group affiliation participation motives (Klint & Weiss, 1987) represents an example of social approval goals.

Urdan and Maehr (1995) wrote that the nature and consequences of social goals must be considered in light of a number of variables. These include the type of social goal that is pursued, the values held by the social target, and characteristics of the individual such as age, gender, culture, and the meaning that the person attaches to the social goal. For example, if the importance or value of participating in sport is de-emphasized by a desired peer group, a child may forego opportunities to become involved in sport if social approval goals are a priority. Given the increasing importance that the peer group plays in early adolescence, especially in terms of social conformity and peer pressure, this may be a viable explanation for the dramatic decline in physical activity levels among boys and girls at this age, which continues throughout adolescence. It would be interesting to identify peer groups that assign high and low value to being physically active and to examine concomitant attitudes, goals, and behaviors in its members. A particular social goal also may carry different meaning depending on the individual's age, gender, and cultural background. For example, social approval goals to please one's parents may carry more weight for a 7-year-old than for a 15-year-old; social solidarity goals (e.g., bring honor to one's family or school) may derive greater meaning for individuals from Eastern than from Western societies.

A handful of studies in the achievement goal literature have linked ego goals with unsporting attitudes, legitimacy of hurting an opponent in order to win, and self-ratings of aggression (e.g., Duda et al., 1991; Stephens & Bredemeier, 1996). Interestingly, Stephens and Bredemeier found that perceptions of the team's proaggressive norms and, to a lesser degree, the coach's ego orientation were the strongest predictors of 9- to 14-year-old soccer players' self-reported likelihood to aggress against an opponent. Given Urdan and Maehr's (1995) compelling arguments, it is conceivable that social approval (i.e., from teammates, coach), social solidarity (i.e., maintain social status of the team), or social compliance goals (i.e., be a good member of the team) may be driving the reasons for and perceptions of aggressive play. By assessing multiple goals in our studies of achievement-related attitudes, affective responses, and behaviors, we may gain a deeper understanding of the mechanisms driving these outcomes. Moreover, the socialization mechanisms of social, task, and ego goals in physical activity and sport contexts are not understood well and require considerably more research to untangle the primary antecedents of goals. One such antecedent is the educational setting and practices (e.g., design of activities, teacher behaviors) within the setting (Blumenfeld, 1992), a concept that seems especially salient to the sport domain.

Intervention Studies

Although Ames (1992a, 1992b) outlined the criteria and conditions for promoting a mastery motivational climate, little intervention research has followed suit in the context of the physical domain. Interestingly, most intervention studies have stemmed from a team-building framework not grounded in achievement goal theory, but one that resembles the cooperative reward structure described by Ames (e.g., Ebbeck & Gibbons, 1998; Marsh et al., 1986a, 1986b; Marsh & Peart, 1988). To date, only three published studies have manipulated the dimensions of the classroom climate to observe student beliefs, affects, and motivation over the course of several weeks (Goudas et al., 1995; Solmon, 1996; Theeboom et al., 1995). In contrast, Papaioannou and Kouli (1999) manipulated only the task dimension of the TARGET program by offering task- versus ego-involving activities in two 1-hour lessons in physical education. Ames (1992a, 1992b) cautioned against varying only one dimension of motivational climate because the dimensions of task, authority, recognition, grouping, evaluation, and timing interact in a dynamic way and should be changed systematically and concurrently.

Treasure and Roberts (1995a) suggested that intervening at the level of the significant adults (teachers, coaches, parents) in children's sporting experiences is a far more appealing alternative than focusing on teaching children psychological skills to cope with the negative effects of an ego-involving competitive sport climate. We wholeheartedly agree. Physical education teachers, sport coaches, and parents of young athletes communicate beliefs about competence and success expectancy and about the importance of mastery versus normative success. Moreover, adult behaviors in the form of informational and evaluative feedback and reinforcement for performance processes or outcomes are also powerful communicators of what is valued and recognized in the sport context. The intervention research by Smith and Smoll (1996) has shown that coaches can be trained to reward effort, technique, and other desirable behaviors. A similar approach to motivational climate is needed—teaching coaches of youth sport to design activities during practice that are meaningful and appropriately challenging, allowing for participant choices, and recognizing and evaluating personal improvement alongside the inevitable performance climate that is bound to exist. It is unrealistic to think that we can eliminate the performance-involving nature of competitive sport context, but if a mastery and performance climate can be appropriately balanced, adaptive motivational behaviors should follow.

The situation is a bit different for parents. Although we can talk about teachers and coaches structuring the environment or classroom climate, parents' influence primarily resides in their role as providers and interpreters of experience (Eccles et al., 1983, 1998). For example, parents' goal orientations, beliefs about the educational purposes and causes of success in sport, and attributions given for success and failure speak volumes. Evaluation research of a parent education program that focuses on these elements would empirically validate the numerous anecdotal accounts of parental influence in youth sports. Although S.A. White (1996, 1998) promotes the "parent-initiated motivational climate," we believe that parents do not structure the athletic climate in the same way that teachers and coaches do, such as designing activities, grouping athletes, pacing skill drills, and evaluating effort and ability in a group-oriented context. One might explore a family-systems approach within the home to examine such an idea, but parental influence is more appropriately investigated in terms of parents' communication of beliefs and behaviors concerning children's adoption of goals, beliefs, and affective responses (Ames & Archer, 1988; Eccles et al., 1998; Jacobs & Eccles, 1992).

Although adults are a significant source of so-cial influence for young athletes, the peer group exerts a powerful and meaningful effect starting in childhood and peaking during adolescence (Rubin et al., 1998). In sport, teammates, neighborhood peers, school classmates, and close friends provide important sources of social evaluation, comparison, and support and thus can significantly affect achievement goals, self-ability beliefs, and motivated behaviors. Thus, we extend our target intervention group to peers as a means of positively affecting sport achievement goals and behaviors, as is encouraged by researchers in the academic domain (e.g., Blumenfeld, 1992; Eccles et al., 1998; Jarvinen & Nicholls, 1996; Wentzel, 1998).

Blumenfeld (1992) suggested that a cooperative goal–reward structure, rather than the oft-studied individualistic and competitive structures, may be most appropriate when considering the peer group as an intervention for changing or modifying beliefs about goals and about oneself as well as achievement behaviors. Such educational climates emphasize interdependence among group members, fostering of helping behaviors, and collaborative problem solving to attain desired group goals. Recognition and evaluation are distributed based on group attainment of goals, exerted effort, and performance outcome. These concepts are similar to team-building in competitive sport environments, especially the promotion of task and social group cohesion (e.g., Carron, Spink, & Prapavessis, 1997). Where individuals possess strong social goals or social goals in combination with task or ability goals, peer group interventions may be especially productive agencies of motivational change. We know of no research that has examined the role of the peer group in changing sport participants' achievement beliefs and behaviors. Cooperative or team-building climates that emphasize social support, cohesion, and group-focused goal attainment may hold the key to understanding how to neutralize the competitive goal–reward structure of sport contexts from youth to professional ranks.

SPORT COMMITMENT MODEL

The robust finding that enjoyment or fun is a dominant motive for participating in sport led Scanlan and her colleagues to conduct a series of studies on sources of enjoyment in diverse athletic samples ranging in age, gender, ethnicity, and sport type (Scanlan, Carpenter, Lobel, & Simons,

1993; Scanlan & Lewthwaite, 1986; Scanlan, Ravizza, & Stein, 1989; Scanlan, Stein, & Ravizza, 1989; Stein & Scanlan, 1992). Findings across these samples revealed that positive social interactions (parents, coach, teammates), perceptions of competence, social recognition of competence, effort and mastery, and movement sensations were primary determinants of sport enjoyment. Despite these rather consistent findings of sources of enjoyment, the construct remained largely atheoretical in nature.

In a synthesis of their own and others' empirical work on enjoyment sources, Scanlan and Simons (1992) introduced sport enjoyment as a central construct within a larger conceptual model of motivation that they called the *sport commitment model*. Sport commitment is defined as a psychological construct representing the desire and resolve to continue sport participation (Scanlan, Carpenter, Schmidt, et al., 1993). The focus is on commitment as a psychological state underlying persistence rather than the actual behavior of staying or leaving. The model was primarily adapted from social exchange theory (Kelley & Thibaut, 1978; Thibaut & Kelley, 1959) and models of commitment to interpersonal relationships (Kelley, 1983; Rusbult, 1980, 1988). These models and concomitant research identify three major antecedents of commitment: (a) attraction toward the relationship or activity (e.g., satisfaction, rewards minus costs of being involved), (b) the attractiveness of available alternatives, and (c) constraints or barriers to ceasing activity involvement (e.g., investments, social pressures, feelings of obligation). Attraction and constraints maximize commitment, whereas attractive alternatives minimize commitment to the current activity. Scanlan and her colleagues customized these determinants of commitment to the specific nature of sustained motivation in sport contexts.

The sport commitment model proposed by Scanlan and her colleagues (Scanlan, Carpenter, Schmidt, et al., 1993; Scanlan, Simons, Carpenter, Schmidt, & Keeler, 1993) consists of five determinants that increase or decrease sport commitment (see figure 5.7). Sport enjoyment represents the attraction antecedent and is defined as a positive affective response that reflects feelings of pleasure, liking, and fun. Involvement alternatives reflect attractiveness of other activities that could compete with continued participation in the current activity. Three constructs were identified as representing barriers to discontinuing one's cur-

rent involvement. Personal investments pertain to the time, effort, and financial resources that would be lost if participation in the activity was discontinued. Social constraints refer to perceived pressure from significant adults and peers that instills a sense of obligation to continue involvement. Involvement opportunities are the anticipated or expected benefits afforded from continued participation in sport such as friendships, positive interactions with adults, skill mastery, and physical conditioning. According to predictions stemming from the sport commitment model, perceptions of higher sport enjoyment, personal investments, involvement opportunities, and social constraints should increase sport commitment, whereas the perception that other activities are more attractive is likely to lower commitment. Determinants and level of sport commitment can be investigated at different levels of analysis such as commitment to sport in general, a specific sport program, or a specific sport or physical activity (e.g., swimming or baseball).

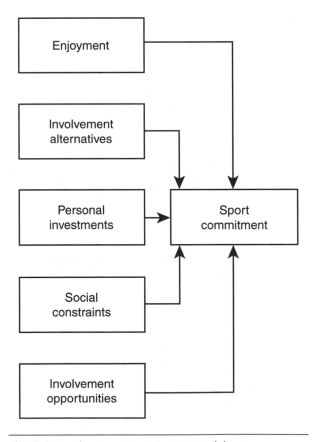

Figure 5.7 The sport commitment model.

Reprinted, by permission, from T.K. Scanlan and J.P. Simons, 1992, The construct of sport enjoyment, in *Motivation in Sport and Exercise*, edited by G.C. Roberts (Champaign, IL: Human Kinetics), 200.

Finally, the behavioral consequences of sport commitment (i.e., whether one actually remains involved or leaves the sport) merit attention to understand the important outcomes of sport commitment. Given the infancy of this conceptual model, however, the determinants and level of sport commitment (i.e., one's expressed desire and resolve to persist) have been the focus of empirical testing in terms of both measurement development and significance of relationships among key constructs defining the model.

Measurement Development and Model Testing

The first steps in validating the sport commitment model involved developing theoretically sound items for key constructs and testing the significance and magnitude of the relationships between determinants and level of sport commitment (Carpenter, Scanlan, Simons, & Lobel, 1993; Scanlan, Carpenter, Schmidt, et al., 1993; Scanlan, Simons, et al., 1993). Multiple items were developed and modified for the six model constructs based on an extant review of both the psychological commitment and youth sport literature, feedback from experts, and evaluation by school teachers and youth athletes to ensure comprehension and readability in children as young as 9 years and of varying sociocultural backgrounds. Validity and reliability testing was conducted with several diverse samples ranging in gender, ethnicity, and age (9–20 years), including youth participating in a variety of agency-sponsored team sports, age-group competitive swimming, and recreational badminton (Scanlan, Carpenter, Schmidt, et al., 1993).

In the first test that examined the relationships predicted by the sport commitment model, only enjoyment and personal investments significantly predicted level of sport commitment in youth baseball and softball players (Scanlan, Carpenter, Schmidt, et al., 1993). Although a nonsignificant predictor, involvement opportunities was moderately correlated with sport commitment ($r = .41$) and sport enjoyment ($r = .55$). Social constraints showed a nonsignificant relationship with sport commitment. A subsequent study with more than 1,300 athletes (ages 10–19) in three different sports revealed that sport enjoyment, personal investments, and involvement opportunities were significant predictors of sport commitment, with social constraints also emerging as a significant but weak contributor (Carpenter et al., 1993). Contrary

to model hypotheses, social constraints were negatively related to commitment to sport.

The consistent finding that sport enjoyment is a strong predictor of sport commitment bolsters Scanlan and her colleagues' efforts to integrate both constructs under a common conceptual umbrella. To further understand the motivational role of the construct of enjoyment, the same sample of diverse youth participants studied by Carpenter et al. (1993) were assessed on their sources of enjoyment (Scanlan, Carpenter, Lobel, & Simons, 1993). A multiple regression analysis indicated that coach support, positive team interactions, and effort and mastery significantly predicted levels of sport enjoyment. The two studies (Carpenter et al., 1993; Scanlan, Carpenter, Lobel, & Simons, 1993) help reveal the antecedents and consequences of sport enjoyment as a construct within the model of sport commitment.

Integrating findings from previous studies, Carpenter (1992) modified and extended the sport commitment model. Several antecedents were added to the model to incorporate contemporary theorizing and increase predictability of sport commitment. These constructs included two additional indexes of attraction: negative sport affect, and satisfaction, rewards, and costs. Other new variables included availability of alternatives, social support, and perceived ability. Carpenter (1992) recruited adolescent female and male sport participants to complete measures at the midpoint of their seasons. Six variables emerged as significant determinants of sport commitment: sport enjoyment, personal investments, recognition opportunities, attractive alternatives, parent support, and coach obligation. Several findings are noteworthy. One is the hypothesized positive relationship found between coach obligation and sport commitment. This variable was assessed through items depicting feelings of pressure from the coach to keep playing and the perception that the coach would be upset and disappointed if the athlete quit playing. Second, consistent with previous studies, sport enjoyment, personal investments, and involvement opportunities were the strongest predictors of sport commitment. Third, the modified attractive alternatives construct, problematic in earlier studies, demonstrated good validity and significantly contributed to level of sport commitment. Finally, although several variables did not emerge as significant predictors of commitment, moderate correlations among determinants (e.g., enjoyment and friend support; enjoyment and perceived ability) suggest that these variables should be considered in further tests of the sport commitment model.

The Dynamic Nature of Sport Commitment

The studies discussed so far have evaluated the nature of relationships between determinants and level of sport commitment at a static point in time. Model predictions also suggest that determinants and commitment are dynamic constructs and that variations over time (e.g., the course of a season) in enjoyment, investments, involvement opportunities, social constraints, and attractive alternatives should correspond with changes in sport commitment. To test this notion, Carpenter and Scanlan (1998) selected a subsample of soccer players to complete measures of commitment constructs at midseason and again near the end of the season (5- to 7-week span). For three constructs—enjoyment, involvement opportunities, and social constraints (the only constructs to achieve adequate reliability)—players were categorized as having increased, having decreased, or showing no change from midseason to the end of season. Soccer athletes who had decreased in enjoyment levels showed a significant decrease in sport commitment over the season, as did athletes who decreased in involvement opportunities. Athletes also showed increased commitment with concomitant increases in involvement opportunities over the season.

Carpenter and Coleman (1998) replicated and extended the previous study with elite young (ages 9–17) British cricket players. Assessments were taken at the beginning and toward the end of the cricket season (about 8 weeks) and included original determinants and ones added by Carpenter (1992). Analyses revealed that fluctuations in sport enjoyment and involvement opportunities were related to associated changes in commitment. Increases in social support and negative affect over the course of the season also were associated with an increase and decrease, respectively, in commitment to cricket. The findings from these two studies investigating change over time in determinants and commitment offer partial support for the dynamic nature of sport commitment.

The sport commitment model is still in its infancy and requires more research to test hypothesized relationships at various levels of analysis (sport in general, program, specific sport) and with diverse groups of participants who vary in talent, age, sport type, and competitive level. In-

deed, in the prologue to their article introducing the model, Scanlan, Carpenter, Schmidt, et al. (1993) acknowledged that the model will no doubt undergo change, and they encouraged readers to join the research effort. With a handful of carefully designed studies launching the research in this area, we can draw on the robust findings pertaining to relationships among variables to further test the sport commitment model.

Are Positive and Negative Affect Possible Mediators in the Sport Commitment Model?

To date, the social constraints determinant has been somewhat baffling. Model predictions posit that social constraints represent perceived social pressure from important others that instill felt obligation to continue playing. Thus, higher social constraints should be related to higher levels of commitment. However, results have shown social constraints to be unrelated (Carpenter, 1992 [friend, parent]; Carpenter & Coleman, 1998; Carpenter & Scanlan, 1998; Scanlan, Carpenter, Schmidt, et al., 1993), weakly and negatively related (Carpenter et al., 1993), or weakly and positively related (Carpenter, 1992 [coach]) to sport commitment. One explanation forwarded by Scanlan and colleagues is based on the youth sport stress literature (e.g., Gould, 1993; Scanlan & Lewthwaite, 1984), in which perceived negative evaluation from significant adults and peers can increase anxiety and stress that, in turn, should lower continued motivation. Carpenter (1992) reported nonsignificant relationships between negative affect and friend, parent, and coach constraints; however, negative affect consisted of items denoting the emotions of unhappy, unpleasant, sad, and bored, none of which denote the negative affective state of anxiety. Therefore, the potential mediating influence of perceived anxiety or stress in the relationship between social constraints and sport commitment remains a question for future research.

Given the research findings to date, it appears conceivable that enjoyment may mediate the influence of several determinants on sport commitment. Sport enjoyment has emerged as a significant predictor, and the strongest predictor ($r = .60-.70$), of sport commitment in each of the studies testing the model. Second, enjoyment is moderately correlated ($r = .27-.55$) with involvement opportunities (e.g., be with friends, interact with coach, improve skills) and personal investments (time and effort put into the sport). Finally, sources of enjoyment consistently include social support and recognition from parents, teammates, and coaches; low perceived pressure from and few negative interactions with parents and coaches (i.e., low social constraints); effort and mastery; perceived competence; and social or life opportunities (Scanlan & Simons, 1992). These constructs are all contained within the sport commitment model. Collectively, these findings suggest that enjoyment may mediate the influence of several constructs on sport commitment. Yet, to date, enjoyment sources have lined up alongside the enjoyment construct to compete for the variance in sport commitment.

These observations led Weiss, Kimmel, and Smith (2001) to propose a mediational model that featured sport enjoyment as the central player explaining junior tennis players' desire to sustain participation. Along with the original model, revised models included ones in which commitment constructs directly or indirectly affected sport commitment through enjoyment. The original sport commitment model, in which all variables directly influenced commitment, showed a good fit of the model. Of the four significant predictors, enjoyment exerted a strong effect, with the others demonstrating relatively weaker effects. The mediational model showed as good a fit as the original model, supporting enjoyment as a filter through which other determinants may influence commitment. Enjoyment emerged as the strongest predictor of tennis commitment and mediated the influence of attractive alternatives and personal investments on commitment. These results suggest that sport enjoyment is key to explaining

variations in the psychological desire and resolve to continue tennis participation. Moreover, the mediational model results are theoretically appealing in that the sources and consequences of the sport enjoyment construct are accounted for within the larger conceptual model of sport commitment. This was one of the main goals targeted by Scanlan and colleagues—the integration of these two constructs within a broader motivational context (Carpenter et al., 1993; Scanlan, Carpenter, Schmidt, et al., 1993; Scanlan & Simons, 1992).

A mediational model suggests that strategies be designed to enhance athletes' enjoyment of or attraction to their sport, which, in turn, increases their desire to sustain motivation. These practical strategies reside in the achievement-related (e.g., skill mastery, perceived competence), intrinsic (e.g., excitement, movement sensations), and social (e.g., friendships, social recognition) sources of enjoyment consistently found in the youth sport literature (Scanlan & Lewthwaite, 1986; Scanlan & Simons, 1992). Figure 5.8 presents a schematic in which the constructs of sport commitment and sport enjoyment are intertwined. Specifically, the antecedents of sport commitment include enjoyment and its sources (achievement, intrinsic, social), which implicitly include the constructs of involvement opportunities, personal investments, social support, social constraints, and involvement alternatives. Consequences of sport commitment include behavioral manifestations of the psychological desire and resolve to maintain involvement, including continuance of or withdrawal from a program or sport, frequency and intensity of involvement, and persistence under adverse conditions.

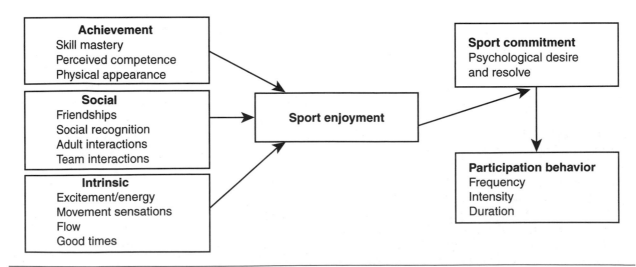

Figure 5.8 Schematic of the sources and consequences of sport enjoyment and sport commitment.

Can the Sport Commitment Model Be Used to Explain Dropout and Burnout?

The studies conducted so far have shown that attraction to an activity (i.e., enjoyment), low alternative options, barriers to ceasing participation (i.e., personal investments, involvement opportunities), and social influence (support and constraints) predict athletes' psychological commitment to an activity. Can some combination of these variables also predict dropout and burnout, which have been linked to commitment (Raedeke, 1997; Schmidt & Stein, 1991)?

According to theory and research on commitment (see Schmidt & Stein, 1991), individuals may be committed to an activity because they want to stay involved based on high satisfaction, low alternatives, and high resources invested (e.g., effort, good experiences). This type of commitment is labeled *attraction-based commitment*. Schmidt and Stein (1991) contended that as long as individuals perceive high rewards and low costs, lack of attractive alternatives, and high investments, they will stay involved in the activity. However, individuals who lose their attraction to a sport program are characterized by low satisfaction or enjoyment, see available alternative activities as more attractive, and decrease their investments in the current activity. These individuals, according to Schmidt and Stein, drawing on social exchange and commitment theories, are candidates for dropout (i.e., leave their current sport for an attractive alternative activity).

In contrast to attraction-based and low attraction commitment, individuals may be committed because they feel they have to stay involved. Although enjoyment of the activity has decreased (i.e., costs exceed rewards), alternative options may not be available or attractive, and the individuals may perceive barriers to ceasing participation (e.g., time and energy invested, lost friendships, obligation to others). This type of commitment is based on dependence rather than attraction and has been labeled *entrapment-based commitment* (Schmidt & Stein, 1991). Schmidt and Stein proposed that individuals who evidence burnout in sport may be experiencing entrapment-based commitment. Similar to athletes who stay for attraction-based reasons, individuals committed out of entrapment perceive low alternatives and high investments but also perceive low rewards, high costs, and low enjoyment or satisfaction. Both types of commitment result in similar behavior, however, in that the individuals remain in the sport but do so for highly different reasons.

Raedeke (1997) tested the notion that commitment and burnout are intricately linked and that burnout reflects entrapment-based commitment. To do so, he assessed adolescent swimmers on benefits, costs, enjoyment, investments, attractive alternatives, and social constraints. Based on Coakley's (1992) sociological perspective of athlete burnout, two other variables were included: personal control and unidimensional athlete identity. Raedeke hypothesized that swimmer profiles would emerge based on a combination of these variables: (a) athletes who show attraction-based commitment, (b) athletes who show entrapment-based commitment, and (c) athletes who show low commitment. In turn, entrapment-based athletes were proposed to show higher burnout levels than either attraction-based or low committed groups. Two different profiles emerged that were similar, but not identical, to entrapment-based characteristics. The strongest entrapment profile (called malcontent swimmers) showed low enjoyment and benefits, high costs and social constraints, and low perceived control. However, these swimmers also showed low investments and high attractive alternatives, contrary to Schmidt and Stein's (1991) hypotheses. Attraction-based and low commitment profiles also were found that were virtually similar to predictions. In support of the proposed link between commitment and burnout, the malcontent swimmers were significantly higher on burnout and lower on attraction-based commitment than both attraction-based and low commitment swimmers. Raedeke's study empirically tested the attraction- and entrapment-based sides of commitment in sport and showed that individuals higher in burnout reflected, in most ways, an entrapment type of commitment.

Future Research Directions

In comparison to the previous section on participation motivation and attrition, where the volume of research necessitated synthesis and consolidation, an inductive approach was more appropriate for the sport commitment research, where only a handful of studies have been conducted. Thus, it goes without saying that the field is wide open for testing and modifying sport commitment model predictions.

Developmental Differences

All the studies conducted thus far combined female and male samples ranging in age from 9 to 19 years. This approach allowed for measurement development and model testing to generalize across diverse populations ranging in age, gender, ethnicity, and sport type. Now that measures have been validated and the nature of relationships is better understood, an important research direction is to determine whether the relationships between determinants and level of sport commitment vary by age, competitive level, and gender.

Gender differences in sport commitment might not be expected in the childhood years but may likely emerge during adolescence. For example, Coakley and White (1992) found that girls reported greater social constraints from parents and opposite-sex friends to continue participating, greater social support from same-sex friends to participate, and more negative affective experiences in school sports and physical education. Social constraints, social support, and affect are prime determinants of sport commitment, so we might expect differences between male and female adolescents on absolute levels of sport commitment as well as the relative influence of determinants.

Behavioral Consequences of Sport Commitment

Sport commitment is defined as the psychological desire and resolve to continue participation in sport. Therefore, a test of the sport commitment model would be incomplete without investigating the actual behavioral consequences of commitment. Are individuals who are higher in psychological resolve to continue involvement more likely to maintain their participation over time, sustain involvement or "stick it out" under adverse conditions, and participate more frequently and intensely than their lower commitment peers? By including the behavioral outcomes of sport commitment in tests of the model, this conceptual framework allows for a comprehensive look at participation motivation and attrition: Do individuals stay in or leave a sport program as a function of determinants and level of psychological commitment? What factors most strongly affect decisions to continue or discontinue involvement? Figure 5.8 gives us some clues; the answers to these questions await empirical attention.

VanYperen (1998) recently conducted a study to determine the major factors related to behavioral commitment (i.e., stay vs. leave) in international, national, and local volleyball referees. Low enjoyment of officiating and high attractive alternatives were significantly related to intention to quit (i.e., one's determination to stop officiating),

which, in turn, was the only direct influence of actual turnover (continue vs. stop officiating). Although one may question the analogy made between "sport commitment" and "intention to quit," this study represents an initial test of the relationships among determinants, a psychological (lack of) commitment construct (intention to stop involvement), and a behavioral consequence (stay vs. leave officiating) that are implied within the sport commitment model.

Prospective or retrospective designs could be used to investigate questions of behavioral commitment. A prospective design would include, throughout a season, at least a baseline measure and preferably multiple measures of determinants and level of commitment. Individuals who drop out of the program voluntarily (i.e., not cut from the team, no season-ending injury) or choose not to return the following season could be compared with players who choose to continue on determinants, level, and the relationship between determinants and level of sport commitment. Barnett, Smoll, and Smith (1992) used this type of design in their study of coaching behaviors and attrition in youth baseball players.

A retrospective design would also be a desirable approach in terms of time investment (one-time assessment), avoidance of participant attrition (in terms of missing data), and the potential for gathering rich data. Athletes could be asked to recall their experiences, cognitions, affective reactions, and decision-making process in weighing the satisfaction, rewards, and costs of a particular activity in relation to alternative options. Because the topic of commitment has the potential to be emotionally charged in either a positive or negative direction, a retrospective approach may allow athletes to tell their stories at a time that is physically removed from being intensely involved in their participation. Scanlan, Stein, and Ravizza's (1989, 1991) in-depth study of former elite figure skaters is an example of retrospective storytelling, with participants who were removed from the throes of their own competitive spotlight able to reflect on the experiences that offered them the most enjoyment and the most stress.

Attraction-Based Versus Obligation-Based Commitment

In an article featuring Anson Dorrance, coach of 15-time national championship women's soccer team at the University of North Carolina, a rival coach was quoted as saying, "Watch them—they run because they want to, not because they have to" (Price, 1998, p. 91). In sport commitment terms, we would say that these players are highly attracted to soccer (i.e., high enjoyment, high perceived benefits and low costs), perceive alternative options as less satisfying, and have invested a considerable amount of time, energy, and emotional involvement in their sport. In contrast, players who continue an activity because they feel they have to participate do so primarily out of obligation or entrapment. Although they are not satisfied and perceive high costs and few benefits of their involvement, they have no or few alternative options and they have already invested so much in the activity. In addition, social norms and pressures may push them to remain in the activity. In either case, the behavioral consequences are the same. Individuals who show high attraction- or entrapment-based commitment stay in, rather than leave, the program or activity. For one group this consequence is positive, but for the other it is negative. The latter group of athletes do not want to participate but feel they must out of obligation. For example, Raedeke's (1997) enthusiastic swimmers manifested characteristics of attraction-based commitment, whereas the malcontent swimmers were characterized by entrapment-based commitment.

Sport commitment, defined as the psychological desire and resolve to continue participation, can be construed as an attraction-based view, and the high correlations with enjoyment across studies support this idea (Raedeke, 1997). Moreover, Raedeke found that malcontent swimmers, representative of entrapment-based commitment, showed significantly lower scores on sport commitment (i.e., attraction-based) than the other groups. However, except for Raedeke, attraction-based commitment and entrapment-based commitment have not been teased apart in the samples studied so far. The majority of studies have examined sport commitment in primarily non-elite youth samples. However, both faces of commitment may not be present in just any youth sample but rather might best be captured in high-level performers who have the potential to experience wide variations in satisfaction, rewards, costs, attractive alternatives, social constraints, and investments into their sport. Moreover, Coakley's (1992) sociological perspective that athletic organizations control high-level performers and encourage them to adopt unidimensional identities would contribute to feelings of entrapment. Therefore, future studies might examine the determinants and consequences of both attraction- and entrapment-based commitment in more elite level samples.

Importantly, however, whether athletes want to or have to continue participation, the behavioral consequence is staying in the activity. For the athletes who are committed because of attraction, persisting in the activity is a positive consequence in that it helps athletes accrue the physical and psychosocial benefits available from participation. However, persistence for the athletes who are committed out of entrapment is a different story. Staying in an activity or situation that is not enjoyable or rewarding and is perceived as costly and pressure-filled may result in other undesirable consequences such as depression, burnout, poor health, and injury. Thus, exploring the antecedents and outcomes of the "have to" type of commitment is important to round out our understanding of the sport commitment construct.

Intervention Studies

The studies to date provide scientific validity as well as intuitive appeal of the model in applying its constructs to maintaining and enhancing motivation in athletes. Moreover, the integration of enjoyment and commitment within a broader framework provides a heuristic model (i.e., figure 5.8) that identifies the antecedents and consequences of both constructs. As such, several possibilities exist for testing the validity of the sport commitment model through intervention research.

Ultimately, coaches, teachers, and parents strive to maintain or enhance attraction-based commitment in their participants. Figure 5.8 suggests that structuring the situation to realize involvement opportunities (e.g., affirm friendships, team spirit, mastery), engage in social support behaviors (e.g., expressing positive beliefs about competencies, encouragement, and positive affective responses), and minimize social constraints (e.g., pressure to perform, controlling behaviors) will result in higher enjoyment and psychological commitment. Higher attraction-based commitment should result in persistence in an activity unless other uncontrollable events such as illness, injury, or a family move preclude this.

These conditions set the stage for intervention programs in which one or more groups are specifically treated in such a way as to maximize determinants of enjoyment and sport commitment while another group is taught "as usual" and serves as a control group. Concomitant changes over the course of the program in enjoyment and commitment sources, enjoyment, and psychological commitment could be assessed, along with behavioral measures of commitment at appropriate times within the study design. The sport commitment model would be validated if corresponding changes in determinants and sport commitment occurred as well as positive associations between psychological and behavioral commitment.

Summary

The sport commitment model is an attractive framework for understanding motivational variations in performers. Its emphasis on the construct of sport enjoyment accounts for major reasons for continuing or withdrawing from sport cited in the participation motivation research. The construct of attractive alternatives emerges consistently as a major reason for dropping out of sport. Personal investments and involvement opportunities encompass the wide range of reasons cited for initiating, continuing, and terminating sport involvement. Finally, social constraints and social support are key to understanding motivational outcomes in sport. Thus, this conceptual model is a parsimonious and comprehensive depiction of participation motivation and attrition that is specific to the sport domain. Research to date strongly supports the sport commitment model, with future research awaiting behavioral validation of its predictions.

CONCLUSION

Motivational orientation in sport is a multidimensional construct that can be approached from a variety of theoretical approaches. Our intent was to provide an extensive overview of several theoretical or conceptual models, empirical research that tested each perspective in the physical domain, current issues and controversies, and directions for future research. We chose six major approaches to the study of motivational orientations and sport behavior that have proven suitable and effective when applied to sport and physical activity contexts. These included participation motivation and attrition, competence motivation theory, cognitive evaluation theory, expectancy-value model, achievement goal theory, and the sport commitment model.

Certain nuances or subtleties characterize each perspective. The participation motivation and at-

trition approach described the reasons why children and adolescents participate in sport and what factors may drive them away. We saw that reasons related to physical competence, social acceptance, and fun and enjoyment pervaded the *why* of behavior in physical activity contexts. This early descriptive research paved the way for subsequent conceptual models that went beyond describing reasons to explaining and predicting activity choices and sustained motivation. Competence motivation theory views positive affect or enjoyment as central to motivational processes. Perceptions of competence and influence by significant adults and peers are important determinants of global self-worth, affect, the desire to seek optimally challenging activities, and an intrinsic interest in mastering these challenges. Developmental differences in perceived competence and motivational orientation are an important feature of this approach. Cognitive evaluation theory considers individuals' interpretations of their experiences as controlling or informational, perceptions of self-determination and competence, and a variety of intrinsic and extrinsic motivational orientations and their consequences. The expectancy-value model highlights the child's success expectations and subjective value toward particular activities as the key predictors of activity choice, and considers the developmental sources of competency beliefs and values. Achievement goal theories feature variations in goals that individuals hold for achievement strivings, which characterize subjective definitions of success and failure, beliefs about the benefits of a domain, and beliefs about what causes success in a particular domain. The sport commitment model is unique in accounting for the crucial construct of sport enjoyment within a broader motivational framework. Sources and consequences of sport enjoyment and commitment are considered within the model, which provides a wealth of opportunities to locate which variables best explain the desire and resolve to continue participation.

Along with their unique twists to understanding motivated behavior, these various approaches have several commonalities. Each theory or model implicates the importance of the social context, including social support and constraints by significant adults and peers, situational factors such as sport type, evaluation potential, culture, gender, and the climate in which learning and performance take place. A number of individual differences make up a common denominator of each approach: self-perceptions (perceived competence, global self-worth), perceived choice or autonomy, goal orientations or goal standards, and subjective task value or the importance of doing well in a domain. Affect is key to all theories whether it be positive affective outcomes (enjoyment, pride, satisfaction) or negative ones (anxiety, boredom). The phenomenon of intrinsic motivation or intrinsic interest, or doing an activity for its own sake, is central to each theory, along with behavioral consequences such as activity choice, intensity of effort, persistence, and continued involvement. Finally, most, but not all, theories contain a developmental component in terms of differentiation of concepts such as ability, task value, and competence; preference or use of particular socializing agents; sources of physical competence information; and trends in intrinsic and extrinsic motivational orientation.

One of the major goals of sport psychology is to determine what factors maximize participation behavior in physical activity contexts. Our research pursuits should focus on identifying factors that promote individuals' sustained physical activity from youth through older adulthood. This kind of sustained physical activity will allow individuals to attain the physical, psychological, and social benefits available from a physically active lifestyle. A critical element affecting whether individuals sustain their involvement and attain these benefits is their motivational orientation. An intrinsic- or mastery-oriented individual embraces optimal challenges, ones in which she or he can learn and improve skills and thereby can enhance perceptions of competence, self-worth, and positive affect toward the value of physical activity. Enhanced self-perceptions and feelings of enjoyment will maintain or enhance intrinsic motivation and consequent choices, level of effort, persistence, and achievement behavior. The extrinsic- or performance-oriented individual who doubts his or her ability, in contrast, will likely select easy or difficult activities, exert minimal effort, and give up if failure appears to be imminent. Perceptions of competence, affect, and motivational consequences are compromised in this case. Thus, focusing our efforts on determinants of an intrinsic motivational orientation will help promote positive outcomes.

Sport psychology scholars and practitioners who face challenges related to program enrollment or persistence must understand the underlying processes that explain motivation in physical achievement settings. A better conceptualization of these processes will lead to research that con-

tributes to sport-specific theory development and asks questions of practical significance. Such an understanding also will inspire the inception of intervention programs that make a difference with our youth when it comes to adopting a physically active lifestyle or choosing to remain involved in sport. We hope that the theoretical and empirical issues presented in this chapter will stimulate researchers and sport educators to pursue these objectives with a desire for mastery, feelings of competence, positive affect, and intrinsic interest.

REFERENCES

Alderman, R.A., & Wood, N.L. (1976). An analysis of incentive motivation in young Canadian athletes. *Canadian Journal of Applied Sport Sciences, 1,* 169–175.

Allen, J.B., & Howe, B. (1998). Player ability, coach feedback, and female adolescent athletes' perceived competence and satisfaction. *Journal of Sport & Exercise Psychology, 20,* 280–299.

Ames, C. (1984). Competitive, cooperative, and individualistic goal structures: A cognitive-motivational analysis. In R. Ames & C. Ames (Eds.), *Research on motivation in education: Vol. 1. Student motivation* (pp. 177–207). Orlando, FL: Academic Press.

Ames, C. (1992a). Classrooms: Goals, structures, and student motivation. *Journal of Educational Psychology, 84,* 261–271.

Ames, C. (1992b). Achievement goals, motivational climate, and motivational processes. In G.C. Roberts (Ed.), *Motivation in sport and exercise* (pp. 161–176). Champaign, IL: Human Kinetics.

Ames, C., & Ames, R. (1981). Competitive versus individualistic goal structures: The salience of past performance information for causal attributions and affect. *Journal of Educational Psychology, 73,* 411–418.

Ames, C., & Archer, J. (1987). Mothers' beliefs about the role of ability and effort in school learning. *Journal of Educational Psychology, 79,* 409–414.

Ames, C., & Archer, J. (1988). Achievement goals in the classroom: Students' learning strategies and motivation processes. *Journal of Educational Psychology, 80,* 260–267.

Amorose, A.J., & Weiss, M.R. (1998). Coaching feedback as a source of information about perceptions of ability: A developmental examination. *Journal of Sport & Exercise Psychology, 20,* 395–420.

Ashford, B., Biddle, S., & Goudas, M. (1993). Participation in community sports centres: Motives and predictors of enjoyment. *Journal of Sports Sciences, 11,* 249–256.

Atkinson, J.W. (1964). *An introduction to motivation.* Princeton, NJ: Van Nostrand.

Babkes, M.L., & Weiss, M.R. (1999). Parental influence on cognitive and affective responses in children's competitive soccer participation. *Pediatric Exercise Science, 11,* 44–62.

Barnett, N.P., Smoll, F.L., & Smith, R.E. (1992). Effects of enhancing coach-athlete relationships on youth sport attrition. *The Sport Psychologist, 6,* 111–127.

Baumeister, R.F., & Leary, M.R. (1995). The need to belong: Desire for interpersonal attachments as a fundamental human motivation. *Psychological Bulletin, 117,* 497–529.

Biddle, S., Cury, F., Goudas, M., Sarrazin, P., Famose, J.P., & Durand, M. (1995). Development of scales to measure perceived physical education class climate: A cross-national project. *British Journal of Educational Psychology, 65,* 341–358.

Bigelow, B.J., Lewko, J.H., & Salhani, L. (1989). Sport-involved children's friendship expectations. *Journal of Sport & Exercise Psychology, 11,* 152–160.

Black, S.J., & Weiss, M.R. (1992). The relationship among perceived coaching behaviors, perceptions of ability, and motivation in competitive age-group swimmers. *Journal of Sport & Exercise Psychology, 14,* 309–325.

Blumenfeld, P.C. (1992). Classroom learning and motivation: Clarifying and expanding goal theory. *Journal of Educational Psychology, 84,* 272–281.

Boyd, M.P., & Yin, Z. (1996). Cognitive-affective sources of sport enjoyment in adolescent sport participants. *Adolescence, 31,* 383–395.

Brodkin, P., & Weiss, M.R. (1990). Developmental differences in motivation for participating in competitive swimming. *Journal of Sport & Exercise Psychology, 12,* 248–263.

Brustad, R.J. (1988). Affective outcomes in competitive youth sport: The influence of intrapersonal and socialization factors. *Journal of Sport & Exercise Psychology, 10,* 307–321.

Brustad, R.J. (1993). Who will go out and play? Parental and psychological influences on children's attraction to physical activity. *Pediatric Exercise Science, 5,* 210–223.

Brustad, R.J. (1996). Attraction to physical activity in urban schoolchildren: Parental socialization and gender influences. *Research Quarterly for Exercise and Sport, 67,* 316–323.

Brustad, R.J. (1998). Developmental considerations in sport and exercise psychology measurement. In J.L. Duda (Ed.), *Advances in sport and exercise psychology measurement* (pp. 461–470). Morgantown, WV: Fitness Information Technology.

Brustad, R.J., & Weiss, M.R. (1987). Competence perceptions and sources of worry in high, medium, and low competitive trait anxious young athletes. *Journal of Sport Psychology, 9,* 97–105.

Bukowski, W.M., Newcomb, A., & Hartup, W.W. (1996). *The company they keep: Friendship in childhood and adolescence.* New York: Cambridge University Press.

Buonamano, R., Cei, A., & Mussino, A. (1995). Participation motivation in Italian youth sport. *The Sport Psychologist, 3,* 265–281.

Burton, D. (1992). Why young wrestlers "hang up" their singlet: An exploratory investigation comparing two models of sport attrition. *Journal of Sport Behavior, 15,* 209–226.

Burton, D., & Martens, R. (1986). Pinned by their own goals: An exploratory investigation into why kids drop out of wrestling. *Journal of Sport Psychology, 8,* 183–197.

Butler, R. (1987). Task-involving and ego-involving properties of evaluation: Effects of different feedback conditions on motivational perceptions, interest, and performance. *Journal of Educational Psychology, 79,* 474–482.

Butler, R. (1989). On the psychological meaning of information about competence: A reply to Ryan and Deci's comment on Butler (1987). *Journal of Educational Psychology, 81,* 269–272.

Cameron, J., & Pierce, W.D. (1994). Reinforcement, reward, and intrinsic motivation: A meta-analysis. *Review of Educational Research, 64,* 363–423.

Carpenter, P.J. (1992). *Staying in sport: Young athletes' motivations for continued involvement.* Unpublished doctoral dissertation, University of California, Los Angeles.

Carpenter, P.J., & Coleman, R. (1998). A longitudinal study of elite youth cricketers' commitment. *International Journal of Sport Psychology, 29,* 195–210.

Carpenter, P.J., & Scanlan, T.K. (1998). Changes over time in the determinants of sport commitment. *Pediatric Exercise Science, 10,* 356–365.

Carpenter, P.J., Scanlan, T.K., Simons, J.P., & Lobel, M. (1993). A test of the sport commitment model using structural equation modeling. *Journal of Sport & Exercise Psychology, 15,* 119–133.

Carron, A.V., Spink, K.S., & Prapavessis, H. (1997). Team building and cohesiveness in the sport and exercise setting: Use of indirect interventions. *Journal of Applied Sport Psychology, 9,* 61–72.

Chase, M.A. (1998). Sources of self-efficacy in physical education and sport. *Journal of Teaching in Physical Education, 18,* 76–89.

Chase, M.A., & Dummer, G.M. (1992). The role of sports as a social status determinant for children. *Research Quarterly for Exercise and Sport, 63,* 418–424.

Chatzisarantis, N.L.D., & Biddle, S.J.H. (1998). Functional significance of psychological variables that are included in the theory of planned behavior: A self-determination theory approach to the study of attitudes, subjective norms, perceptions of control and intentions. *Journal of Social Psychology, 28,* 303–322.

Chatzisarantis, N.L.D., Biddle, S.J.H., & Meek, G.A. (1997). A self-determination theory approach to the study of intentions and the intention-behavior relationship in children's physical activity. *British Journal of Health Psychology, 2,* 343–360.

Chaumeton, N.R., & Duda, J.L. (1988). Is it how you play the game or whether you win or lose? The effect of competitive level and situation on coaching behaviors. *Journal of Sport Behavior, 11,* 157–174.

Clifton, R.T., & Gill, D.L. (1994). Gender differences in self-confidence on a feminine-typed task. *Journal of Sport & Exercise Psychology, 16,* 150–162.

Coakley, J. (1992). Burnout among adolescent athletes: A personal failure or social problem? *Sociology of Sport Journal, 9,* 271–285.

Coakley, J.J., & White, A. (1992). Making decisions: Gender and sport participation among British adolescents. *Sociology of Sport Journal, 9,* 20–35.

Connell, J.P. (1980). *A multidimensional measure of children's perceptions of control.* Denver: University of Denver.

Connell, J.P., & Ilardi, B.C. (1987). Self-system concomitants of discrepancies between children's and teacher's evaluations of academic competence. *Child Development, 58,* 1297–1307.

Cury, F., Biddle, S., Famose, J.P., Goudas, M., Sarrazin, P., & Durand, M. (1996). Personal and situational factors influencing intrinsic interest of adolescent girls in school physical education: A structural equation analysis. *Educational Psychology, 16,* 305–315.

de Charms, R. (1968). *Personal causation: The internal affective determinants of behavior.* New York: Academic Press.

De Knop, P., Engstrom, L.M., Skirstad, B., & Weiss, M.R. (1996). *Worldwide trends in youth sport.* Champaign, IL: Human Kinetics.

Deci, E.L. (1971). Effects of externally mediated rewards on intrinsic motivation. *Journal of Personality and Social Psychology, 18,* 105–115.

Deci, E.L. (1972). Intrinsic motivation, extrinsic reinforcement, and inequity. *Journal of Personality and Social Psychology, 22,* 113–120.

Deci, E.L. (1975). *Intrinsic motivation.* New York: Plenum Press.

Deci, E.L. (1980). *The psychology of self-determination.* Lexington, MA: Heath.

Deci, E.L., Betley, G., Kahle, J., Abrams, L., & Porac, J. (1981). When trying to win: Competition and intrinsic motivation. *Personality and Social Psychology Bulletin, 7,* 79–83.

Deci, E.L., & Ryan, R.M. (1982). Intrinsic motivation to teach: Possibilities and obstacles in our colleges and universities. In J. Bess (Ed.), *New directions for teaching and learning, No. 10: Motivating professors to teach effectively.* San Francisco: Jossey-Bass.

Deci, E.L., & Ryan, R.M. (1985). *Intrinsic motivation and self-determination in human behavior.* New York: Plenum Press.

Deci, E.L., & Ryan, R.M. (1991). A motivational approach to self: Integration in personality. In R. Deinstbier (Ed.), *Nebraska symposium on motivation: Vol. 38. Perspectives on motivation* (pp. 237–288). Lincoln: University of Nebraska Press.

Deci, E.L., Schwartz, A.J., Sheinman, L., & Ryan, R.M. (1981). An instrument to assess adults' orientations toward control versus autonomy with children: Reflections on intrinsic motivation and perceived competence. *Journal of Educational Psychology, 73,* 642–650.

Deci, E.L., Spiegel, N.H., Ryan, R.M., Koestner, R., & Kauffman, M. (1982). The effects of performance standards on teaching styles: The behavior of controlling teachers. *Journal of Educational Psychology, 74,* 852–859.

Deci, E.L., Vallerand, R.J., Pelletier, L.G., & Ryan, R.M. (1991). Motivation and education: The self-determination perspective. *Educational Psychologist, 26,* 325–346.

Deeter, T.E. (1989). Development of a model of achievement behavior for physical activity. *Journal of Sport & Exercise Psychology, 11,* 1–12.

Deeter, T.E. (1990). Re-modeling expectancy and value in physical activity. *Journal of Sport & Exercise Psychology, 12,* 86–91.

Dempsey, J.M., Kimiecik, J.C., & Horn, T.S. (1993). Parental influence on children's moderate to vigorous physical activity participation: An expectancy-value approach. *Pediatric Exercise Science, 5,* 151–167.

Duda, J.L. (1985). Goals and achievement orientations of Anglo- and Mexican-American adolescents in sport and the classroom. *International Journal of Intercultural Relations, 9,* 131–155.

Duda, J.L. (1986a). A cross-cultural analysis of achievement motivation in sport and the classroom. In L.

VanderVelden & J. Humphrey (Eds.), *Current selected research in the psychology and sociology of sport* (pp. 117–131). New York: AMS.

Duda, J.L. (1986b). Perceptions of sport success and failure among white, black and Hispanic adolescents. In J. Watkins, T. Reilly, & L. Burwitz (Eds.), *Sport science* (pp. 214–222). London: Spon.

Duda, J.L. (1987). Toward a developmental theory of motivation in sport. *Journal of Sport Psychology, 9,* 130–145.

Duda, J.L. (1988). The relationship between goal perspectives, persistence and behavioral intensity among male and female recreational sport participants. *Leisure Sciences, 10,* 95–106.

Duda, J.L. (1989a). The relationship between task and ego orientation and the perceived purpose of sport among high school athletes. *Journal of Sport & Exercise Psychology, 11,* 318–335.

Duda, J.L. (1989b). Goal perspectives, participation and persistence in sport. *International Journal of Sport Psychology, 20,* 42–56.

Duda, J.L. (1993). Goals: A social-cognitive approach to the study of achievement motivation in sport. In R.N. Singer, M. Murphey, & L.K. Tennant (Eds.), *Handbook of research on sport psychology* (pp. 421–436). New York: Macmillan.

Duda, J.L., & Allison, M.T. (1990). Cross-cultural analysis in exercise and sport psychology: A void in the field. *Journal of Sport & Exercise Psychology, 12,* 114–131.

Duda, J.L., Chi, L., Newton, M.L., Walling, M.D., & Catley, D. (1995). Task and ego orientation and intrinsic motivation in sport. *International Journal of Sport Psychology, 26,* 40–63.

Duda, J.L., & Hayashi, C.T. (1998). Measurement issues in cross-cultural research within sport and exercise psychology. In J.L. Duda (Ed.), *Advances in sport and exercise psychology measurement* (pp. 471–484). Morgantown: WV: Fitness Information Technology.

Duda, J.L., & Hom, H.L., Jr. (1993). Interdependencies between the perceived and self-reported goal orientations of young athletes and their parents. *Pediatric Exercise Science, 5,* 234–241.

Duda, J.L., & Nicholls, J.G. (1992). Dimensions of achievement motivation in schoolwork and sport. *Journal of Educational Psychology, 84,* 290–299.

Duda, J.L., Olson, L.K., & Templin, T.J. (1991). The relationship of task and ego orientation to sportsmanship attitudes and the perceived legitimacy of injurious acts. *Research Quarterly for Exercise and Sport, 62,* 79–87.

Duda, J.L., & Whitehead, J. (1998). Measurement and goal perspectives in the physical domain. In J.L. Duda (Ed.), *Advances in sport and exercise psychology measurement* (pp. 21–48). Morgantown: WV: Fitness Information Technology.

Duncan, S.C. (1993). The role of cognitive appraisal and friendship provisions in adolescents' affect and motivation toward activity in physical education. *Research Quarterly for Exercise and Sport, 64,* 314–323.

Duncan, T.E., & Duncan, S.C. (1991). A latent growth curve approach to investigating developmental dynamics and correlates of change in children's perceptions of physical competence. *Research Quarterly for Exercise and Sport, 62,* 390–396.

Dweck, C.S. (1980). Learned helplessness in sport. In C. Nadeau, W. Halliwell, K. Newell, & G. Roberts (Eds.), *Psychology of motor behavior and sport—1979* (pp. 1–11). Champaign, IL: Human Kinetics.

Dweck, C.S. (1986). Motivational processes affecting learning. *American Psychologist, 41,* 1040–1048.

Dweck, C.S. (1999). *Self-theories: Their role in motivation, personality, and development.* Philadelphia: Psychology Press.

Dweck, C.S., & Elliott, E.S. (1983). Achievement motivation. In E.M. Hetherington (Ed.), *Socialization, personality, and social development* (pp. 643–691). New York: Wiley.

Dweck, C.S., & Leggett, E.L. (1988). A social–cognitive approach to motivation and personality. *Psychological Review, 95,* 256–273.

Ebbeck, V. (1990). Sources of performance information in the exercise setting. *Journal of Sport & Exercise Psychology, 12,* 56–65.

Ebbeck, V. (1994). Self-perception and motivational characteristics of tennis participants: The influence of age and skill. *Journal of Applied Sport Psychology, 6,* 71–86.

Ebbeck, V., & Becker, S.L. (1994). Psychosocial predictors of goal orientations in youth soccer. *Research Quarterly for Exercise and Sport, 65,* 355–362.

Ebbeck, V., & Gibbons, S.L. (1998). The effect of a team building program on the self-conceptions of grade 6 and 7 physical education students. *Journal of Sport & Exercise Psychology, 20,* 300–310.

Ebbeck, V., Gibbons, S.L., & Loken-Dahle, L.J. (1995). Reasons for adult participation in physical activity: An interactional approach. *International Journal of Sport Psychology, 26,* 262–275.

Ebbeck, V., & Stuart, M.E. (1993). Who determines what's important? Perceptions of competence and importance as predictors of self-esteem in youth football players. *Pediatric Exercise Science, 5,* 253–262.

Ebbeck, V., & Stuart, M.E. (1996). Predictors of self-esteem with youth basketball players. *Pediatric Exercise Science, 8,* 368–378.

Ebbeck, V., & Weiss, M.R. (1998). Determinants of children's self-esteem: An examination of perceived competence and affect in sport. *Pediatric Exercise Science, 10,* 285–298.

Eccles (Parsons), J. (1984). Sex differences in mathematics participation. In M.L. Maehr & W. Steinkamp (Eds.), *Women in science* (pp. 93–137). Greenwich, CT: JAI Press.

Eccles, J.S. (1985). Why doesn't Jane run? Sex differences in educational and occupational patterns. In F.D. Horowitz & M. O'Brien (Eds.), *The gifted and the talented: Developmental perspectives* (pp. 251–295). Washington, DC: American Psychological Association.

Eccles, J.S. (1987). Gender roles and women's achievement-related decisions. *Psychology of Women Quarterly, 11,* 135–172.

Eccles (Parsons), J.S., Adler, T.E., Futterman, R., Goff, S.B., Kaczala, C.M., Meece, J.L., & Midgley, C. (1983). Expectancies, values, and academic behaviors. In J.T. Spence (Ed.), *Achievement and achievement motivation* (pp. 75–146). San Francisco: Freeman.

Eccles (Parsons), J., Adler, T.F., & Kaczala, C.M. (1982). Socialization of achievement attitudes and beliefs: Parental influences. *Child Development, 53,* 310–321.

Eccles (Parsons), J., Adler, T., & Meece, J.L. (1984). Sex differences in achievement: A test of alternate theories. *Journal of Personality and Social Psychology, 46,* 26–43.

Eccles, J.S., & Blumenfeld, P. (1985). Classroom experiences and student gender: Are there differences and do they matter? In L. Wilkison & C. Marrett (Eds.), *Gender influences in classroom interaction* (pp. 79–114). Orlando, FL: Academic Press.

Eccles, J.S., & Harold, R.D. (1991). Gender differences in sport involvement: Applying the Eccles expectancy-value model. *Journal of Applied Sport Psychology, 3,* 7–35.

Eccles (Parsons), J., Kaczala, C.M., & Meece, J.L. (1982). Socialization of achievement attitudes and beliefs: Classroom influences. *Child Development, 53,* 322–339.

Eccles, J.S., & Midgley, C. (1990). Changes in academic motivation and self-perception during early adolescence. In R. Montemayor, G.R. Adams, & T.P. Gullotta (Eds.), *From childhood to adolescence: A transitional period?* (pp. 134–155). Newbury Park, CA: Sage.

Eccles, J., & Wigfield, A. (1985). Teacher expectations and student motivation. In J.B. Dusek (Ed.), *Teacher expectations* (pp. 185–226). Hillsdale, NJ: Erlbaum.

Eccles, J.S., & Wigfield, A. (1995). In the mind of the achiever: The structure of adolescents' academic achievement-related beliefs and self-perceptions. *Personality and Social Psychology Bulletin, 21,* 215–225.

Eccles, J.S., Wigfield, A., Harold, R., & Blumenfeld, P. (1993). Age and gender differences in children's self- and task-perceptions during elementary school. *Child Development, 64,* 830–847.

Eccles, J.S., Wigfield, A.W., & Schiefele, U. (1998). Motivation to succeed. In W. Damon (Series Ed.) & N. Eisenberg (Vol. Ed.), *Handbook of child psychology: Vol. 3. Social, emotional, and personality development* (5th ed., pp. 1017–1095). New York: Wiley.

Elliott, E.S., & Dweck, C.S. (1988). Goals: An approach to motivation and achievement. *Journal of Personality and Social Psychology, 54,* 5–12.

Epstein, J. (1988). Effective schools or effective students? Dealing with diversity. In R. Haskins & D. MacRae (Eds.), *Policies for America's public schools: Teacher equity indicators* (pp. 89–126). Norwood, NJ: Ablex.

Epstein, J. (1989). Family structures and student motivation: A developmental perspective. In C. Ames & R. Ames (Eds.), *Research on motivation in education, Vol. 3* (pp. 259–295). New York: Academic Press.

Epstein, J.A., & Harackiewicz, J.M. (1992). Winning is not enough: The effects of competition and achievement orientation on intrinsic interest. *Personality and Social Psychology Bulletin, 18,* 128–138.

Evans, J., & Roberts, G.C. (1987). Physical competence and the development of children's peer relations. *Quest, 39,* 23–35.

Ewing, M.E. (1981). *Achievement orientations and sport behavior of males and females.* Unpublished doctoral dissertation, University of Illinois at Urbana–Champaign.

Ewing, M.E., Feltz, D.L., Schultz, T.D., & Albrecht, R.R. (1988). Psychological characteristics of competitive young hockey players. In E.W. Brown & C.F. Branta (Eds.), *Competitive sports for children and youth* (pp. 49–61). Champaign, IL: Human Kinetics.

Feltz, D.L., & Brown, E.W. (1984). Perceived competence in soccer skills among youth soccer players. *Journal of Sport Psychology, 6,* 385–394.

Feltz, D.L., & Petlichkoff, L.M. (1983). Perceived competence among interscholastic sport participants and dropouts. *Canadian Journal of Applied Sport Sciences, 8,* 231–235.

Ferrer-Caja, E., & Weiss, M.R. (2000). Predictors of intrinsic motivation among adolescent students in physical education. *Research Quarterly for Exercise and Sport, 71,* 267–279.

Fortier, M.S., Vallerand, R.J., & Guay, F. (1995). Academic motivation and school performance: Toward a structural model. *Contemporary Educational Psychology, 20,* 257–274.

Frederick, C.M., & Ryan, R.M. (1995). Self-determination in sport: A review using cognitive evaluation theory. *International Journal of Sport Psychology, 26,* 5–23.

Fry, M.D. (2000a). A developmental analysis of children's and adolescents' understanding of luck and ability in the physical domain. *Journal of Sport & Exercise Psychology, 22,* 145–166.

Fry, M.D. (2000b). A developmental examination of children's understanding of task difficulty in the physical domain. *Journal of Applied Social Psychology, 12,* 180–202.

Fry, M.D., & Duda, J.L. (1997). A developmental examination of children's understanding of effort and ability in the physical and academic domains. *Research Quarterly for Exercise and Sport, 68,* 331–344.

Gibbons, S.L., & Bushakra, F.B. (1989). Effects of Special Olympics participation on the perceived competence and social acceptance of mentally retarded children. *Adapted Physical Activity Quarterly, 6,* 40–51.

Gill, D.L. (1986). *Psychological dynamics of sport.* Champaign, IL: Human Kinetics.

Gill, D.L., Gross, J.B., & Huddleston, S. (1983). Participation motivation in youth sports. *International Journal of Sport Psychology, 14,* 1–14.

Gill, D.L., Williams, L., Dowd, D.A., Beaudoin, C.M., & Martin, J.J. (1996). Competitive orientations and motives of adult sport and exercise participants. *Journal of Sport Behavior, 19,* 307–318.

Glenn, S.D., & Horn, T.S. (1993). Psychological and personal predictors of leadership behavior in female soccer athletes. *Journal of Applied Sport Psychology, 5,* 17–35.

Gottfried, A.E., Fleming, J.S., & Gottfried, A.W. (1998). Role of cognitively stimulating home environment in children's academic intrinsic motivation: A longitudinal study. *Child Development, 69,* 1448–1460.

Gottfried, A.E., & Gottfried, A.W. (1996). A longitudinal study of academic intrinsic motivation in intellectually gifted children: Childhood through early adolescence. *Gifted Child Quarterly, 40,* 179–183.

Goudas, M., & Biddle, S. (1994). Perceived motivational climate and intrinsic motivation in school physical education classes. *European Journal of Psychology of Education, 9,* 241–250.

Goudas, M., Biddle, S., & Fox, K. (1994a). Achievement goal orientations and intrinsic motivation physical fitness testing with children. *Pediatric Exercise Science, 6,* 159–167.

Goudas, M., Biddle, S., & Fox, K. (1994b). Perceived locus of causality, goal orientations, and perceived competence in school physical education classes. *British Journal of Educational Psychology, 64,* 453–463.

Goudas, M., Biddle, S., Fox, K., & Underwood, M. (1995). It ain't what you do, it's the way that you do it! Teaching style affects children's motivation in track and field lessons. *The Sport Psychologist, 9,* 254–264.

Gould, D. (1982). Sport psychology in the 1980's: Status, direction and challenge in youth sports research. *Journal of Sport Psychology, 4,* 203–218.

Gould, D. (1987). Understanding attrition in youth sport. In D. Gould & M.R. Weiss (Eds.), *Advances in pediatric sport sciences: Vol. 2. Behavioral issues* (pp. 61–85). Champaign, IL: Human Kinetics.

Gould, D. (1993). Intensive sports participation and the prepubescent athlete: Competitive stress and burnout effects. In B. Cahill & A.J. Pearl (Eds.), *Intensive participation in children's sports* (pp. 19–38). Champaign, IL: Human Kinetics.

Gould, D., Feltz, D., Horn, T., & Weiss, M. (1982). Reasons for attrition in competitive youth swimming. *Journal of Sport Behavior, 5,* 155–165.

Gould, D., Feltz, D., & Weiss, M. (1985). Motives for participating in competitive youth swimming. *International Journal of Sport Psychology, 6,* 126–140.

Gould, D., & Petlichkoff, L. (1988). Participation motivation and attrition in young athletes. In F.L. Smoll, R.A. Magill, & M.J. Ash (Eds.), *Children in sport* (3rd ed., pp. 161–178). Champaign, IL: Human Kinetics.

Greene, D., & Lepper, M.R. (1974). Effects of extrinsic rewards on children's subsequent intrinsic interest. *Child Development, 45,* 1141–1145.

Grolnick, W.S., & Ryan, R.M. (1987). Autonomy in children's learning: An experimental and individual difference investigation. *Journal of Personality and Social Psychology, 52,* 890–898.

Grolnick, W.S., & Ryan, R.M. (1989). Parent styles associated with children's self-regulation and competence in school. *Journal of Educational Psychology, 81,* 143–154.

Grolnick, W.S., Ryan, R.M., & Deci, E.L. (1991). Inner resources for school achievement: Motivational mediators of children's perceptions of their parents. *Journal of Educational Psychology, 83,* 508–517.

Hall, H.K., & Kerr, A.W. (1997). Motivational antecedents of precompetitive anxiety in youth sport. *The Sport Psychologist, 11,* 24–42.

Hall, H.K., Kerr, A.W., & Matthews, J. (1998). Precompetitive anxiety in sport: The contribution of achievement goals and perfectionism. *Journal of Sport & Exercise Psychology, 20,* 194–217.

Hardy, L. (1997). Three myths about applied consultancy work. *Journal of Applied Sport Psychology, 9,* 277–294.

Hardy, L. (1998). Responses to the reactants on three myths in applied consultancy work. *Journal of Applied Sport Psychology, 10,* 212–219.

Harter, S. (1978). Effectance motivation reconsidered. *Human Development, 21,* 34–64.

Harter, S. (1981a). A model of intrinsic mastery motivation in children: Individual differences and developmental change. In W.A. Collins (Ed.), *Minnesota Symposium on*

Child Psychology (Vol. 14, pp. 215–255). Hillsdale, NJ: Erlbaum.

Harter, S. (1981b). The development of competence motivation in the mastery of cognitive and physical skills: Is there still a place for joy? In G.C. Roberts & D.M. Landers (Eds.), *Psychology of motor behavior and sport—1980* (pp. 3–29). Champaign, IL: Human Kinetics.

Harter, S. (1981c). A new self-report scale of intrinsic versus extrinsic orientation in the classroom: Motivational and informational components. *Developmental Psychology, 17,* 300–312.

Harter, S. (1982). The perceived competence scale for children. *Child Development, 53,* 87–97.

Harter, S. (1985a). *Manual for the self-perception profile for children.* Denver: University of Denver.

Harter, S. (1985b). Competence as a dimension of self-evaluation: Toward a comprehensive model of self-worth. In R. Leahy (Ed.), *The development of the self* (pp. 55–118). New York: Academic Press.

Harter, S. (1986). Processes underlying the construction, maintenance, and enhancement of the self-concept in children. In J. Suls & A. Greenwald (Eds.), *Psychological perspectives on the self* (Vol. 3, pp. 137–181). Hillsdale, NJ: Erlbaum.

Harter, S. (1987). The determinants and mediational role of global self-worth in children. In N. Eisenberg (Ed.), *Contemporary topics in developmental psychology* (pp. 219–242). New York: Wiley.

Harter, S. (1988). Manual for the self-perception profile for adolescents. Denver: University of Denver.

Harter, S. (1990a). Causes, correlates, and the functional role of global self-worth: A life-span perspective. In R.J. Sternberg & J. Kolligan, Jr. (Eds.), *Competence considered* (pp. 67–97). New Haven, CT: Yale University Press.

Harter, S. (1990b). Processes underlying adolescent self-concept formation. In R. Montemayor, G.R. Adams, & T.P. Gullotta (Eds.), *From childhood to adolescence: A transitional period?* (pp. 205–239). Newbury Park, CA: Sage.

Harter, S. (1998). The development of self-representations. In W. Damon (Series Ed.) & N. Eisenberg (Vol. Ed.), *Handbook of child psychology: Vol. 3. Social, emotional, and personality development* (5th ed., pp. 553–618). New York: Wiley.

Harter, S. (1999). *The construction of the self: A developmental perspective.* New York: Guilford Press.

Harter, S., & Connell, J.P. (1984). A comparison of alternative models of the relationships between academic achievement and children's perceptions of competence, control, and motivational orientation. In J.G. Nicholls (Ed.), *The development of achievement-related cognitions and behaviors* (pp. 219–250). Greenwich, CT: JAI Press.

Harter, S., & Pike, R. (1984). The pictorial scale of perceived competence and social acceptance for young children. *Child Development, 55,* 1962–1982.

Harter, S., Waters, P., & Whitesell, N.R. (1998). Relational self-worth: Differences in perceived worth as a person across interpersonal contexts among adolescents. *Child Development, 69,* 756–766.

Hartup, W.W. (1996). The company they keep: Friendships and their developmental significance. *Child Development, 67,* 1–13.

Harwood, C., Hardy, L., & Swain, A. (2000). Achievement goals in sport: A critique of conceptual and measurement issues. *Journal of Sport & Exercise Psychology, 22,* 235–255.

Harwood, C.G., & Swain, A.B.J. (1998). Antecedents of precompetition achievement goals in elite junior tennis players. *Journal of Sports Sciences, 16,* 357–371.

Hayashi, C.T. (1996). Achievement motivation among Anglo-American and Hawaiian male physical activity participants: Individual differences and social contextual factors. *Journal of Sport & Exercise Psychology, 18,* 194–215.

Hayashi, C.T., & Weiss, M.R. (1994). A cross-cultural analysis of achievement motivation in Anglo and Japanese marathon runners. *International Journal of Sport Psychology, 25,* 187–202.

Hellandsig, E.T. (1998). Motivational predictors of high performance and discontinuation in different types of sports among talented teenage athletes. *International Journal of Sport Psychology, 29,* 27–44.

Hom, H.L., Jr., Duda, J.L., & Miller, A. (1993). Correlates of goal orientations among young athletes. *Pediatric Exercise Science, 5,* 168–176.

Horn, T.S. (1984). Expectancy effects in the interscholastic athletic setting: Methodological considerations. *Journal of Sport Psychology, 6,* 60–76.

Horn, T.S. (1985). Coaches' feedback and changes in children's perceptions of their physical competence. *Journal of Educational Psychology, 77,* 174–186.

Horn, T.S. (1987). The influence of teacher-coach behavior on the psychological development of children. In D. Gould & M.R. Weiss (Eds.), *Advances in pediatric sport sciences: Vol. 2. Behavioral issues* (pp. 121–142). Champaign, IL: Human Kinetics.

Horn, T.S., & Amorose, A.J. (1998). Sources of competence information. In J.L. Duda (Ed.), *Advances in sport and exercise psychology measurement* (pp. 49–64). Morgantown, WV: Fitness Information Technology.

Horn, T.S., Glenn, S.D., & Wentzell, A.B. (1993). Sources of information underlying personal ability judgments in high school athletes. *Pediatric Exercise Science, 5,* 263–274.

Horn, T.S., & Harris, A. (1996). Perceived competence in young athletes: Research findings and recommendations for coaches and parents. In F.L. Smoll & R.E. Smith (Eds.), *Children and youth in sport: A biopsychosocial perspective* (pp. 309–329). Madison, WI: Brown & Benchmark.

Horn, T.S., & Hasbrook, C.A. (1986). Informational components influencing children's perceptions of their physical competence. In M.R. Weiss & D. Gould (Eds.), *Sport for children and youths* (pp. 81–88). Champaign, IL: Human Kinetics.

Horn, T.S., & Hasbrook, C.A. (1987). Psychological characteristics and the criteria children use for self-evaluation. *Journal of Sport Psychology, 9,* 208–221.

Horn, T.S., & Weiss, M.R. (1991). A developmental analysis of children's self-ability judgments. *Pediatric Exercise Science, 3,* 312–328.

Iyengar, S.S., & Lepper, M.R. (1999). Rethinking the value of choice: A cultural perspective on intrinsic motivation. *Journal of Personality and Social Psychology, 76,* 349–366.

Jacobs, J.E., & Eccles, J.S. (1992). The impact of mothers' gender-role stereotypic beliefs on mothers' and children's ability perceptions. *Journal of Personality and Social Psychology, 63,* 932–944.

Jarvinen, D.W., & Nicholls, J.G. (1996). Adolescents' social goals, beliefs about the causes of social success, and satisfaction in peer relations. *Developmental Psychology, 32,* 435–441.

Johns, D.P., Lindner, K.J., & Wolko, K. (1990). Understanding attrition in female competitive gymnastics: Applying social exchange theory. *Sociology of Sport Journal, 7,* 154–171.

Kavussanu, M., & Roberts, G.C. (1996). Motivation in physical activity contexts: The relationship of perceived motivational climate to intrinsic motivation and self-efficacy. *Journal of Sport & Exercise Psychology, 18,* 264–280.

Kelley, H.H. (1983). Love and commitment. In H.H. Kelley, E. Berscheid, A. Christensen, J.H. Harvey, T.L. Huston, G. Levinger, E. McClintock, L.A. Peplau, & D.R. Peterson (Eds.), *Close relationships* (pp. 265–314). New York: W.H. Freeman.

Kelley, H.H., & Thibaut, J.W. (1978). *Interpersonal relations: A theory of interdependence.* New York: Wiley.

Kim, B.J., & Gill, D.L. (1997). A cross-cultural extension of goal perspective theory to Korean youth sport. *Journal of Sport & Exercise Psychology, 19,* 142–155.

Kimiecik, J.C., & Horn, T.S. (1998). Parental beliefs and children's moderate-to-vigorous physical activity. *Research Quarterly for Exercise and Sport, 69,* 163–175.

Kimiecik, J.C., Horn, T.S., & Shurin, C.S. (1996). Relationships among children's beliefs, perceptions of their parents' beliefs, and their moderate-to-vigorous physical activity. *Research Quarterly for Exercise and Sport, 67,* 324–336.

King, L.A., & Williams, T.A. (1997). Goal orientation and performance in martial arts. *Journal of Sport Behavior, 20,* 397–411.

Klint, K.A. (1985). *Participation motives and self-perceptions of current and former athletes in youth gymnastics.* Unpublished master's thesis, University of Oregon, Eugene.

Klint, K.A. (1988). *An analysis of the positivistic and naturalistic paradigms for inquiry: Implications for the field of sport psychology.* Unpublished doctoral dissertation, University of Oregon, Eugene.

Klint, K.A., & Weiss, M.R. (1986). Dropping in and dropping out: Participation motives of current and former youth gymnasts. *Canadian Journal of Applied Sport Sciences, 11,* 106–114.

Klint, K.A., & Weiss, M.R. (1987). Perceived competence and motives for participating in youth sports: A test of Harter's competence motivation theory. *Journal of Sport Psychology, 9,* 55–65.

Koestner, R., & McClelland, D.C. (1990). Perspectives on competence motivation. In L. Pervin (Ed.), *Handbook of personality: Theory and research* (pp. 527–548). New York: Guilford Press.

Kolt, G.S., Kirkby, R.J., Bar-Eli, M., Blumenstein, B., Chadha, N.K., Liu, J., & Kerr, G. (1999). A cross-cultural investigation of reasons for participation in gymnastics. *International Journal of Sport Psychology, 30,* 381–398.

Krane, V., Greenleaf, C.A., & Snow, J. (1997). Reaching for gold and the price of glory: A motivational case study of an elite gymnast. *The Sport Psychologist, 11,* 53–71.

Kunesh, M., Hasbrook, C.A., & Lewthwaite, R. (1992). Physical activity socialization: Peer interactions and affective responses among a sample of sixth grade girls. *Sociology of Sport Journal, 9,* 385–396.

Landers, D.M. (1983). Whatever happened to theory testing in sport psychology? *Journal of Sport Psychology, 5,* 135–151.

Leff, S.S., & Hoyle, R.H. (1995). Young athletes' perceptions of parental support and pressure. *Journal of Youth and Adolescence, 24,* 187–203.

Lepper, M.R., & Greene, D. (1975). Turning play into work: Effects of adult surveillance and extrinsic rewards on children's intrinsic motivation. *Journal of Personality and Social Psychology, 31,* 479–486.

Lepper, M.R., Greene, D., & Nisbett, R.E. (1973). Undermining children's intrinsic interest with extrinsic rewards: A test of the "overjustification" hypothesis. *Journal of Personality and Social Psychology, 28,* 129–137.

Li, F., & Harmer, P. (1996). Testing the simplex assumption underlying the sport motivation scale: A structural equation modeling analysis. *Research Quarterly for Exercise and Sport, 67,* 396–405.

Lirgg, C.D. (1991). Gender differences in self-confidence in physical activity: A meta-analysis of recent studies. *Journal of Sport & Exercise Psychology, 13,* 294–310.

Lirgg, C.D. (1993). Effects of same-sex versus coeducational physical education on the self-perceptions of middle and high school students. *Research Quarterly for Exercise and Sport, 64,* 324–334.

Lirgg, C.D. (1994). Environmental perceptions of students in same-sex and coeducational physical education classes. *Journal of Educational Psychology, 86,* 183–192.

Lochbaum, M.R., & Roberts, G.C. (1993). Goal orientations and perceptions of the sport experience. *Journal of Sport & Exercise Psychology, 15,* 160–171.

Longhurst, K., & Spink, K.S. (1987). Participation motivation of Australian children involved in organized sport. *Canadian Journal of Sport Sciences, 12,* 24–30.

Losier, G.F., & Vallerand, R.J. (1994). The temporal relationship between perceived competence and self-determined motivation. *Journal of Social Psychology, 134,* 793–801.

Maehr, M.L., & Nicholls, J.G. (1980). Culture and achievement motivation: A second look. In N. Warren (Ed.), *Studies in cross-cultural psychology* (pp. 221–267). New York: Academic Press.

Markland, D. (1999). Self-determination moderates the effects of perceived competence on intrinsic motivation in an exercise setting. *Journal of Sport & Exercise Psychology, 21,* 351–352.

Markland, D., & Hardy, L. (1997). On the factorial and construct validity of the Intrinsic Motivation Inventory: Conceptual and operational concerns. *Research Quarterly for Exercise and Sport, 68,* 20–32.

Marsh, H.W., & Peart, N.D. (1988). Competitive and cooperative physical fitness training programs for girls: Effects on physical fitness and multidimensional self-concepts. *Journal of Sport & Exercise Psychology, 10,* 390–407.

Marsh, H.W., Richards, G.E., & Barnes, J. (1986a). Multidimensional self-concepts: The effect of participation in an Outward Bound program. *Journal of Personality and Social Psychology, 50,* 195–204.

Marsh, H.W., Richards, G.E., & Barnes, J. (1986b). Multidimensional self-concepts: A long-term follow-up of the effect of participation in an Outward Bound program. *Personality and Social Psychology Bulletin, 12,* 475–492.

Martinek, T.J., & Williams, L. (1997). Goal orientation and task persistence in learned helpless and mastery oriented students in middle school physical education classes. *International Sports Journal, 1,* 63–76.

McAuley, E., Duncan, T., & Tammen, V.V. (1989). Psychometric properties of the intrinsic motivation inventory in a competitive sport setting: A confirmatory factor analysis. *Research Quarterly for Exercise and Sport, 60,* 48–58.

McAuley, E., & Tammen, V.V. (1989). The effects of subjective and objective competitive outcomes on intrinsic motivation. *Journal of Sport & Exercise Psychology, 11,* 84–93.

McClements, J., Fry, D., & Sefton, J. (1982). A study of hockey participants and drop-outs. In T.D. Orlick, J.T. Partington, & J.H. Salmela (Eds.), *Mental training for coaches and athletes* (pp. 73–74). Ottawa, ON: Coaching Association of Canada.

McCullagh, P., Matzkanin, K.T., Shaw, S.D., & Maldonado, M. (1993). Motivation for participation in physical activity: A comparison of parent child perceived competencies and participation motives. *Pediatric Exercise Science, 5,* 224–233.

McCullagh, P., & Weiss, M.R. (2001). Modeling: Considerations for motor skill performance and psychological responses. In R.N. Singer, H.A. Hausenblas, & C.M. Janelle (Eds.), *Handbook of sport psychology* (2nd ed., pp. 205–238). New York: Wiley.

McKiddie, B., & Maynard, I.W. (1997). Perceived competence of school children in physical education. *Journal of Teaching in Physical Education, 16,* 324–339.

McPherson, B., Marteniuk, R., Tihanyi, J., & Clark, W. (1980). The social system of age group swimmers: The perception of swimmers, parents, and coaches. *Canadian Journal of Applied Sport Sciences, 5,* 142–145.

Messer, B., & Harter, S. (1986). *Manual for the adult self-perception profile.* Denver: University of Denver.

Mitchell, S.A. (1996). Relationships between perceived learning environment and intrinsic motivation in middle school physical education. *Journal of Teaching in Physical Education, 15,* 369–383.

Mueller, C.M., & Dweck, C.S. (1998). Praise for intelligence can undermine children's motivation and performance. *Journal of Personality and Social Psychology, 75,* 33–52.

Mullan, E., Markland, D., & Ingledew, D.K. (1997). A graded conceptualization of self-determination in the regulation of exercise behavior: Development of a measure using confirmatory factor analytic procedures. *Personality and Individual Differences, 23,* 745–752.

Neeman, J., & Harter, S. (1986). *Manual for the self-perception profile for college students.* Denver: University of Denver.

Newcomb, A.F., & Bagwell, C.L. (1995). Children's friendship relations: A meta-analytic review. *Psychological Bulletin, 117,* 306–347.

Newton, M., & Duda, J.L. (1993). Elite adolescent athletes' achievement goals and beliefs concerning success in tennis. *Journal of Sport & Exercise Psychology, 15,* 437–448.

Nicholls, J.G. (1978). The development of the concepts of effort and ability, perceptions of academic attainment, and the understanding that difficult tasks require more ability. *Child Development, 49,* 800–814.

Nicholls, J.G. (1984). Achievement motivation: Conceptions of ability, subjective experience, task choice, and performance. *Psychological Review, 91,* 328–346.

Nicholls, J.G. (1989). *The competitive ethos and democratic education.* Cambridge, MA: Harvard University Press.

Nicholls, J.G. (1992). The general and the specific in the development and expression of achievement motivation. In G.C. Roberts (Ed.), *Motivation in sport and exercise* (pp. 31–56). Champaign, IL: Human Kinetics.

Nicholls, J., & Miller, A.T. (1983). The differentiation of the concepts of ability and difficulty. *Child Development, 54,* 951–959.

Nicholls, J., & Miller, A.T. (1984). Reasoning about the ability of self and others: A developmental study. *Child Development, 55,* 1990–1999.

Nicholls, J.G., Patashnick, M., & Nolen, S.B. (1985). Adolescents' theories of education. *Journal of Educational Psychology, 77,* 683–692.

Ntoumanis, N., & Biddle, S. (1997). The relationship between competitive anxiety, achievement goals, and motivational climates. *Research Quarterly for Exercise and Sport, 69,* 176–187.

Ntoumanis, N., & Biddle, S.J.H. (1999). A review of motivational climate in physical activity. *Journal of Sports Sciences, 17,* 643–665.

O'Brien-Cousins, S. (1997). Elderly tomboys? Sources of self-efficacy for physical activity in late life. *Journal of Aging and Physical Activity, 5,* 229–243.

Ommundsen, Y., Roberts, G.C., & Kavussanu, M. (1998). Perceived motivational climate and cognitive and affective correlates among Norwegian athletes. *Journal of Sports Sciences, 16,* 153–164.

Ommundsen, Y., & Vaglum, P. (1991). Soccer competition anxiety and enjoyment in young boy players: The influence of perceived competence and significant others' emotional involvement. *International Journal of Sport Psychology, 22,* 35–49.

Orlick, T.D. (1973, January/February). Children's sport—A revolution is coming. *Canadian Association for Health, Physical Education and Recreation Journal,* pp. 12–14.

Orlick, T.D. (1974, November/December). The athletic dropout: A high price for inefficiency. *Canadian Association for Health, Physical Education and Recreation Journal,* pp. 21–27.

Orlick, T.D., & Mosher, R. (1978). Extrinsic awards and participant motivation in a sport related task. *International Journal of Sport Psychology, 9,* 27–39.

Papaioannou, A. (1994). Development of a questionnaire to measure achievement orientations in physical education. *Research Quarterly for Exercise and Sport, 65,* 11–20.

Papaioannou, A. (1995a). Differential perceptual and motivational patterns when different goals are adopted. *Journal of Sport & Exercise Psychology, 17,* 18–34.

Papaioannou, A. (1995b). Motivation and goal perspectives in children's physical education. In S. Biddle (Ed.), *European perspectives on sport psychology* (pp. 245–269). Champaign, IL: Human Kinetics.

Papaioannou, A. (1998). Goal perspectives, reasons for being disciplined, and self-reported discipline in physical education lessons. *Journal of Teaching in Physical Education, 17,* 421–441.

Papaioannou, A., & Kouli, O. (1999). The effect of task structure, perceived motivational climate and goal orientation on students' task involvement and anxiety. *Journal of Applied Sport Psychology, 11,* 51–71.

Papaioannou, A., & Theodorakis, Y. (1996). A test of three models for the prediction of intention for participation in physical education lessons. *International Journal of Sport Psychology, 27,* 383–399.

Parker, H.E., Larkin, D., & Ackland, T.R. (1993). Stability and change in children's skill. *Psychological Research, 55,* 182–189.

Pelletier, L.G., Fortier, M.S., Vallerand, R.J., Tuson, K.M., Briere, N.M., & Blais, M.R. (1995). Toward a new measure of intrinsic motivation, extrinsic motivation, and amotivation in sports: The Sport Motivation Scale (SMS). *Journal of Sport & Exercise Psychology, 17,* 35–53.

Petlichkoff, L.M. (1992). Youth sport participation and withdrawal: Is it simply a matter of fun? *Pediatric Exercise Science, 4,* 105–110.

Petlichkoff, L.M. (1993a). Group differences on achievement goal orientations, perceived ability, and level of satisfaction during an athletic season. *Pediatric Exercise Science, 5,* 12–24.

Petlichkoff, L.M. (1993b). Relationship of player status and time of season to achievement goals and perceived ability in interscholastic athletes. *Pediatric Exercise Science, 5,* 242–252.

Petlichkoff, L.M. (1994). Dropping out of sport: Speculation versus reality. In D. Hackfort (Ed.), *Psycho-social issues and interventions in elite sports* (Vol. 1, pp. 60–87). Frankfurt: Sport Sciences International.

Petlichkoff, L.M. (1996). The dropout dilemma in sport. In O. Bar-Or (Ed.), *Encyclopaedia of sports medicine: Vol. VI. The child and adolescent athlete* (pp. 418–430). Oxford, UK: Blackwell Scientific.

Phillips, D.A., & Zimmerman, M. (1990). The developmental course of competence and incompetence among competent children. In R.J. Sternberg & J. Kolligan, Jr. (Eds.), *Competence considered* (pp. 41–66). New Haven, CT: Yale University Press.

Plumert, J.M. (1995). Relations between children's overestimation of their physical abilities and accident proneness. *Developmental Psychology, 31,* 866–876.

Price, S.L. (1998, December 7). Anson Dorrance. *Sports Illustrated, 89*(23), 86–103.

Raedeke, T.D. (1997). Is athlete burnout more than just stress? A sport commitment perspective. *Journal of Sport & Exercise Psychology, 19,* 396–417.

Reeve, J., & Deci, E.L. (1996). Elements of the competitive situation that affect intrinsic motivation. *Personality and Social Psychology Bulletin, 22,* 24–33.

Reeve, J., & Sickenius, B. (1994). Development and validation of a brief measure of the three psychological needs underlying intrinsic motivation: The AFS scales. *Educational & Psychological Measurement, 54,* 506–515.

Rigby, C.S., Deci, E.L., Patrick, B.C., & Ryan, R.M. (1992). Beyond the intrinsic/extrinsic dichotomy: Self-determination in motivation and learning. *Motivation and Emotion, 16,* 165–185.

Roberts, G.C., Kleiber, D., & Duda, J.L. (1981). An analysis of motivation in children's sport: The role of perceived competence in participation. *Journal of Sport Psychology, 3,* 206–216.

Roberts, G.C., Treasure, D.C., & Hall, H.K. (1994). Parental goal orientations and beliefs about the competitive sport experience of their child. *Journal of Applied Social Psychology, 24,* 631–645.

Roberts, G.C., Treasure, D.C., & Kavussanu, M. (1996). Orthogonality of achievement goals and its relationship to beliefs about success and satisfaction in sport. *The Sport Psychologist, 10,* 398–408.

Roberts, G.C., Treasure, D.C., & Kavussanu, M. (1997). Motivation in physical activity contexts: An achievement goal perspective. In M. Maehr & P. Pintrich (Eds.), *Advances in motivation and achievement* (Vol. 10, pp. 413–447). Greenwich, CT: JAI Press.

Rose, B., Larkin, D., & Berger, B.G. (1994). Perceptions of social support in children of low, moderate and high levels of coordination. *ACHPER Healthy Lifestyles Journal, 41*(4), 18–21.

Rubin, K.H., Bukowski, W.M., & Parker, J.G. (1998). Peer interactions, relationships, and groups. In W. Damon (Series Ed.) & N. Eisenberg (Vol. Ed.), *Handbook of child psychology: Vol. 3. Social, emotional, and personality development* (5th ed., pp. 619–700). New York: Wiley.

Rusbult, C. (1980). Satisfaction and commitment in friendships. *Representative Research in Social Psychology, 11,* 96–105.

Rusbult, C. (1988). Commitment in close relationships: The investment model. In L.A. Peplau, D.O. Sears, S.E. Taylor, & J.L. Freedman (Eds.), *Readings in social psychology: Classic and contemporary contributions* (pp. 147–157). Englewood Cliffs, NJ: Prentice Hall.

Rutherford, W.J., Corbin, C.B., & Chase, L.A. (1992). Factors influencing intrinsic motivation towards physical activity. *Health Values, 16,* 19–24.

Ryan, E.D. (1977). Attribution, intrinsic motivation, and athletics. In L.I. Gedvilas & M.E. Kneer (Eds), *Proceedings of the National Association for Physical Education of College Men and National Conference Association for Physical Education of College Women National Conference.* Chicago: University of Illinois at Chicago Circle.

Ryan, E.D. (1980). Attribution, intrinsic motivation, and athletics: A replication and extension. In C.H. Nadeau, W.R. Halliwell, K.M. Newell, & G.C. Roberts (Eds.), *Psychology of motor behavior and sport—1979* (pp. 19–26). Champaign, IL: Human Kinetics.

Ryan, R.M. (1982). Control and information in the intrapersonal sphere: An extension of cognitive evaluation theory. *Journal of Personality and Social Psychology, 45,* 736–750.

Ryan, R.M. (1993). Agency and organization: Intrinsic motivation, autonomy, and the self in psychological development. In R. Dientsbier (Ed.), *Nebraska*

Symposium on Motivation (Vol. 40, pp. 1–56). Lincoln: University of Nebraska Press.

Ryan, R.M., & Connell, J.P. (1989). Perceived locus of causality and internalization: Examining reasons for acting in two domains. *Journal of Personality and Social Psychology, 57,* 749–761.

Ryan, R.M., Connell, J.P., & Deci, E.L. (1985). A motivational analysis of self-determination and self-regulation. In C. Ames & R.E. Ames (Eds.), *Research on motivation in education: The classroom milieu* (pp. 13–51). New York: Academic Press.

Ryan, R.M., Koestner, R., & Deci, E.L. (1991). Ego-involved persistence: When free-choice behavior is not intrinsically motivated. *Motivation and Emotion, 15,* 185–205.

Ryan, R.M., Mims, V., & Koestner, R. (1983). Relation of reward contingency and interpersonal context to intrinsic motivation: A review and test using cognitive evaluation theory. *Journal of Personality and Social Psychology, 45,* 736–750.

Ryan, R.M., & Solky, J.A. (1996). What is supportive about social support? On the psychological needs for autonomy and relatedness. In G.R. Pierce & B.R. Sarason (Eds.), *Handbook of social support and the family* (pp. 249–267). New York: Plenum Press.

Ryan, R.M., Vallerand, R.J., & Deci, E.L. (1984). Intrinsic motivation in sport: A cognitive evaluation theory interpretation. In W.F. Straub & J.M. Williams (Eds.), *Cognitive sport psychology* (pp. 231–242). Lansing, NY: Sport Science Associates.

Ryckman, R.M., & Hamel, J. (1993). Perceived physical ability differences in the sport participation motives of young athletes. *International Journal of Sport Psychology, 24,* 270–283.

Ryckman, R.M., & Hamel, J. (1995). Male and female adolescents' motives related to involvement in organized team sports. *International Journal of Sport Psychology, 26,* 383–397.

Sapp, M., & Haubenstricker, J. (1978, April). *Motivation for joining and reasons for not continuing in youth sport programs in Michigan.* Paper presented at the American Alliance for Health, Physical Education, Recreation and Dance national conference, Kansas City, MO.

Scanlan, T.K., Carpenter, P.J., Lobel, M., & Simons, J.P. (1993). Sources of enjoyment for youth sport athletes. *Pediatric Exercise Science, 5,* 275–285.

Scanlan, T.K., Carpenter, P.J., Schmidt, G.W., Simons, J.P., & Keeler, B. (1993). An introduction to the sport commitment model. *Journal of Sport & Exercise Psychology, 15,* 1–15.

Scanlan, T.K., & Lewthwaite, R. (1984). Social psychological aspects of competition for male youth sport participants: I. Predictors of competitive stress. *Journal of Sport Psychology, 6,* 208–226.

Scanlan, T.K., & Lewthwaite, R. (1986). Social psychological aspects of competition for male youth sport participants: IV. Predictors of enjoyment. *Journal of Sport Psychology, 8,* 25–35.

Scanlan, T.K., Ravizza, K., & Stein, G.L. (1989). An in-depth study of former elite figure skaters: I. Introduction to the project. *Journal of Sport & Exercise Psychology, 11,* 54–64.

Scanlan, T.K., & Simons, J.P. (1992). The construct of sport enjoyment. In G.C. Roberts (Ed.), *Motivation in sport and exercise* (pp. 199–215). Champaign, IL: Human Kinetics.

Scanlan, T.K., Simons, J.P., Carpenter, P.J., Schmidt, G.W., & Keeler, B. (1993). The sport commitment model: Measurement development for the youth-sport domain. *Journal of Sport & Exercise Psychology, 15,* 16–38.

Scanlan, T.K., Stein, G.L., & Ravizza, K. (1989). An in-depth study of former elite figure skaters: II. Sources of enjoyment. *Journal of Sport & Exercise Psychology, 11,* 65–83.

Scanlan, T.K., Stein, G.L., & Ravizza, K. (1991). An in-depth study of former elite figure skaters: III. Sources of stress. *Journal of Sport & Exercise Psychology, 13,* 103–120.

Schmidt, G.W., & Stein, G.L. (1991). Sport commitment: A model integrating enjoyment, dropout, and burnout. *Journal of Sport & Exercise Psychology, 13,* 254–265.

Seifriz, J.J., Duda, J.L., & Chi, L. (1992). The relationship of perceived motivational climate to intrinsic motivation and beliefs about success in basketball. *Journal of Sport & Exercise Psychology, 14,* 375–391.

Shields, D.L., & Bredemeier, B.J. (1995). *Character development and physical activity.* Champaign, IL: Human Kinetics.

Smith, A.L. (1999). Peer relationships and physical activity participation in early adolescence. *Journal of Sport & Exercise Psychology, 21,* 329–350.

Smith, R.E., & Smoll, F.L. (1996). The coach as a focus of research and intervention in youth sports. In F.L. Smoll & R.E. Smith (Eds.), *Children and youth in sport: A biopsychosocial perspective* (pp. 125–141). Madison, WI: Brown & Benchmark.

Solmon, M.A. (1996). Impact of motivational climate on students' behaviors and perceptions in a physical education setting. *Journal of Educational Psychology, 88,* 731–738.

Solmon, M.A., & Boone, J. (1993). The impact of student goal orientation in physical education classes. *Research Quarterly for Exercise and Sport, 64,* 418–424.

Sonstroem, R.J., Harlow, L.L., & Salisbury, K.S. (1993). Path analysis of a self-esteem model across a competitive swim season. *Research Quarterly for Exercise and Sport, 64,* 335–342.

State of Michigan. (1976). *Joint legislative study on youth sports programs, Phase I.* East Lansing: Michigan State University.

State of Michigan (1978a). *Joint legislative study on youth sports programs, Phase II.* East Lansing: Michigan State University.

State of Michigan, (1978b). *Joint legislative study on youth sports programs, Phase III.* East Lansing: Michigan State University.

Stein, G.L., & Scanlan, T.K. (1992). Goal attainment and non-goal occurrences as underlying mechanisms to an athlete's sources of enjoyment. *Pediatric Exercise Science, 4,* 150–165.

Stephens, D.E. (1998). The relationship of goal orientation and perceived ability to enjoyment and value in youth sport. *Pediatric Exercise Science, 10,* 236–247.

Stephens, D.E., & Bredemeier, B.J. (1996). Moral atmosphere and judgments about aggression in girls' soccer:

Relationships among moral and motivational variables. *Journal of Sport & Exercise Psychology, 18,* 158–173.

Stipek, D.J. (1981). Children's perceptions of their own and their classmates' ability. *Journal of Educational Psychology, 73,* 404–410.

Stipek, D., & MacIver, D. (1989). Developmental change in children's assessment of intellectual competence. *Child Development, 60,* 521–538.

Stipek, D.J., & Tannatt, L.M. (1984). Children's judgements of their own and their peers' academic competence. *Journal of Educational Psychology, 76,* 75–84.

Stuart, M.E. (1997). *An examination of adolescents' sources of subjective task value in sport.* Unpublished doctoral dissertation, Oregon State University, Corvallis.

Sullivan, H.S. (1953). *The interpersonal theory of psychiatry.* New York: Norton.

Swain, A. (1996). Social loafing and identifiability: The mediating role of achievement goal orientations. *Research Quarterly for Exercise and Sport, 67,* 337–344.

Swain, A.B.J., & Harwood, C.G. (1996). Antecedents of state goals in age-group swimmers: An interactionist perspective. *Journal of Sports Sciences, 14,* 111–124.

Theeboom, M., De Knop, P., & Weiss, M.R. (1995). Motivational climate, psychosocial responses, and motor skill development in children's sport: A field based-intervention study. *Journal of Sport & Exercise Psychology, 17,* 294–311.

Thibaut, J.W., & Kelley, H.H. (1959). *The social psychology of groups.* New York: Wiley.

Thompson, C.E., & Wankel, L.M. (1980). The effect of perceived activity choice upon frequency of exercise behavior. *Journal of Applied Social Psychology, 10,* 436–443.

Thorkildsen, T.A., & Nicholls, J.G. (1998). Fifth graders' achievement orientations and beliefs: Individual and classroom differences. *Journal of Educational Psychology, 90,* 179–201.

Treasure, D.C. (1997). Perceptions of the motivational climate and elementary school children's cognitive and affective response. *Journal of Sport & Exercise Psychology, 19,* 278–290.

Treasure, D.C., & Roberts, G.C. (1995a). Achievement goals, motivational climate, and achievement strategies and behaviors in sport. *International Journal of Sport Psychology, 26,* 64–80.

Treasure, D.C., & Roberts, G.C. (1995b). Applications of achievement goal theory to physical education: Implications for enhancing motivation. *Quest, 47,* 475–489.

Treasure, D.C., & Roberts, G.C. (1998). Relationship between female adolescents' achievement goal orientations, perceptions of the motivational climate, belief about success and sources of satisfaction in basketball. *International Journal of Sport Psychology, 29,* 211–230.

Ulrich, B.D. (1987). Perceptions of physical competence, motor competence, and participation in organized sport: Their interrelationships in young children. *Research Quarterly for Exercise and Sport, 58,* 57–67.

Ulrich, B.D., & Ulrich, D.A. (1997). Young children's perceptions of their ability to perform simple play and more difficult motor skills. In J.E. Clark & J.H. Humphrey (Eds.), *Motor development: Research and reviews* (Vol. 1, pp. 24–45). Reston, VA: National Association of Sport and Physical Education.

Urdan, T.C., & Maehr, M.L. (1995). Beyond a two-goal theory of motivation and achievement: A case for social goals. *Review of Educational Research, 65,* 213–243.

Vallerand, R.J. (1983). The effect of differential amounts of positive verbal feedback on the intrinsic motivation of male hockey players. *Journal of Sport Psychology, 5,* 100–107.

Vallerand, R.J. (1997). Toward a hierarchical model of intrinsic and extrinsic motivation. In M.P. Zanna (Ed.), *Advances in experimental social psychology* (Vol. 29, pp. 271–360). New York: Academic Press.

Vallerand, R.J., Deci, E.L., & Ryan, R.M. (1987). Intrinsic motivation in sport. In K. Pandolf (Ed.), *Exercise and sport science reviews* (pp. 389–425). New York: MacMillan.

Vallerand, R.J., & Fortier, M.S. (1998). Measures of intrinsic and extrinsic motivation in sport and physical activity: A review and critique. In J.L. Duda (Ed.), *Advances in sport and exercise psychology measurement* (pp. 81–101). Morgantown, WV: Fitness Technology.

Vallerand, R.J., Fortier, M.S., & Guay, M.S. (1997). Self-determination and persistence in a real-life setting: Toward a motivational model of high school dropout. *Journal of Personality and Social Psychology, 72,* 1161–1176.

Vallerand, R.J., Gauvin, L.I., & Halliwell, W.R. (1986a). Negative effects of competition on children's intrinsic motivation. *Journal of Social Psychology, 126,* 649–656.

Vallerand, R.J., Gauvin, L.I., & Halliwell, W.R. (1986b). Effects of zero-sum competition on children's intrinsic motivation and perceived competence. *Journal of Social Psychology, 126,* 465–472.

Vallerand, R.J., Pelletier, L.G., Blais, M.R., Briere, N.M., Senecal, C., & Vallieres, E.F. (1992). The Academic Motivation Scale: A measure of intrinsic, extrinsic, and amotivation in education. *Educational and Psychological Measurement, 52,* 1003–1019.

Vallerand, R.J., Pelletier, L.G., Blais, M.R., Briere, N.M., Senecal, C., & Vallieres, E.F. (1993). On the assessment of intrinsic, extrinsic, and amotivation in education. Evidence on the concurrent and construct validity of the Academic Motivation Scale. *Educational and Psychological Measurement, 53,* 159–172.

Vallerand, R.J., & Reid, G. (1984). On the causal effects of perceived competence on intrinsic motivation: A test of cognitive evaluation theory. *Journal of Sport Psychology, 6,* 94–102.

VanYperen, N.W. (1998). Predicting stay/leave behavior among volleyball referees. *The Sport Psychologist, 12,* 427–439.

Vealey, R.S. (1992). Personality and sport: A comprehensive view. In T.S. Horn (Ed.), *Advances in sport psychology* (pp. 25–59). Champaign, IL: Human Kinetics.

Vealey, R.S., & Campbell, J.L. (1988). Achievement goals of adolescent figure skaters: Impact on self-confidence, anxiety, and performance. *Journal of Adolescent Research, 3,* 227–243.

Vlachopoulos, S., Biddle, S., & Fox, K. (1996). A social-cognitive investigation into the mechanisms of affect generation in children's physical activity. *Journal of Sport & Exercise Psychology, 18,* 174–193.

Walling, M.D., Duda, J.L., & Chi, L. (1993). The perceived motivational climate in sport questionnaire: Construct and predictive validity. *Journal of Sport & Exercise Psychology, 15,* 172–183.

Walsh, J., Crocker, P.R.E., & Bouffard, M. (1992). The effects of perceived competence and goal orientation on affect and task persistence in a physical activity skill. *The Australian Journal of Science and Medicine in Sport, 24,* 86–90.

Wang, J., & Wiese-Bjornstal, D.M. (1996). The relationship of school type and gender to motives for sport participation among youth in the People's Republic of China. *International Journal of Sport Psychology, 28,* 13–24.

Wankel, L.M., & Kreisel, P.S.J. (1985a). Factors underlying enjoyment of youth sports: Sport and age group comparisons. *Journal of Sport Psychology, 7,* 51–64.

Wankel, L.M., & Kreisel, P.S.J. (1985b). Methodological considerations in youth sport motivation research: A comparison of open-ended and paired comparison approaches. *Journal of Sport Psychology, 7,* 65–74.

Wankel, L.M., & Pabich, P. (1982). The minor sport experience: Factors contributing to or detracting from enjoyment. In T. Orlick, J. Partington, & J. Salmela (Eds.), *Mental training for coaches and athletes* (pp. 70–71). Ottawa, ON: Coaching Association of Canada.

Wankel, L.M., & Sefton, J.M. (1989). A season-long investigation of fun in youth sports. *Journal of Sport & Exercise Psychology, 11,* 355–366.

Watkins, B., & Montgomery, A.B. (1989). Conceptions of athletic excellence among children and adolescents. *Child Development, 60,* 1362–1372.

Weigand, D.A., & Broadhurst, C.J. (1998). The relationship among perceived competence, intrinsic motivation, and control perceptions in youth soccer. *International Journal of Sport Psychology, 29,* 324–338.

Weinberg, R.S., & Jackson, A. (1979). Competition and extrinsic rewards: Effect on intrinsic motivation and attribution. *Research Quarterly, 50,* 494–502.

Weinberg, R.S., & Ragan, J. (1979). Effects of competition, success/failure, and sex on intrinsic motivation. *Research Quarterly, 50,* 503–510.

Weingarten, G., Furst, D., Tenenbaum, G., & Schaefer, U. (1984). Motives of Israeli youth for participation in sport. In J.L. Callaghan (Ed.), *Proceedings of the International Symposium, Children to Champions* (pp. 145–153). Los Angeles: University of Southern California.

Weiss, M.R. (1993a). Psychological effects of intensive sport participation on children and youth: Self-esteem and motivation. In B.R. Cahill & A.J. Pearl (Eds.), *Intensive participation in children's sports* (pp. 39–69). Champaign, IL: Human Kinetics.

Weiss, M.R. (1993b). Children's participation in physical activity: Are we having fun yet? *Pediatric Exercise Science, 5,* 205–209.

Weiss, M.R., Bredemeier, B.J., & Shewchuk, R.M. (1985). An intrinsic/extrinsic motivation scale for the youth sport setting: A confirmatory factor analysis. *Journal of Sport Psychology, 7,* 75–91.

Weiss, M.R., Bredemeier, B.J., & Shewchuk, R.M. (1986). The dynamics of perceived competence, perceived control,

and motivational orientation in youth sports. In M.R. Weiss & D. Gould (Eds.), *Sport for children and youths* (pp. 89–101). Champaign, IL: Human Kinetics.

Weiss, M.R., & Chaumeton, N. (1992). Motivational orientations in sport. In T.S. Horn (Eds.), *Advances in sport psychology* (pp. 61–99). Champaign, IL: Human Kinetics.

Weiss, M.R., & Duncan, S.C. (1992). The relation between physical competence and peer acceptance in the context of children's sport participation. *Journal of Sport & Exercise Psychology, 14,* 177–191.

Weiss, M.R., & Ebbeck, V. (1996). Self-esteem and perceptions of competence in youth sport: Theory, research, and enhancement strategies. In O. Bar-Or (Ed.), *The encyclopaedia of sports medicine: Vol. VI. The child and adolescent athlete* (pp. 364–382). Oxford, UK: Blackwell Science.

Weiss, M.R., Ebbeck, V., & Horn, T.S. (1997). Children's self-perceptions and sources of competence information: A cluster analysis. *Journal of Sport & Exercise Psychology, 19,* 52–70.

Weiss, M.R., & Frazer, K.M. (1995). Initial, continued, and sustained motivation in adolescent female athletes: A season-long analysis. *Pediatric Exercise Science, 7,* 314–329.

Weiss, M.R., & Hayashi, C.T. (1995). All in the family: Parent–child socialization influences in competitive youth gymnastics. *Pediatric Exercise Science, 7,* 36–48.

Weiss, M.R., & Horn, T.S. (1990). The relation between children's accuracy estimates of their physical competence and achievement-related characteristics. *Research Quarterly for Exercise and Sport, 61,* 250–258.

Weiss, M.R., Kimmel, L.A., & Smith, A.L. (2001). Determinants of sport commitment among junior tennis players: Enjoyment as a mediating variable. *Pediatric Exercise Science, 13,* 131–144.

Weiss, M.R., McAuley, E., Ebbeck, V., & Wiese, D.M. (1990). Self-esteem and causal attributions for children's physical and social competence in sport. *Journal of Sport & Exercise Psychology, 12,* 21–36.

Weiss, M.R., & Petlichkoff, L.M. (1989). Children's motivation for participation in and withdrawal from sport: Identifying the missing links. *Pediatric Exercise Science, 1,* 195–211.

Weiss, M.R., & Smith, A.L. (1999). Quality of youth sport friendships: Measurement and validation. *Journal of Sport & Exercise Psychology, 21,* 145–166.

Weiss, M.R., & Smith, A.L. (2001). *Friendship quality in youth sport: Relationship to age, gender, and motivation variables.* Manuscript submitted for publication.

Weiss, M.R., Smith, A.L., & Theeboom, M. (1996). "That's what friends are for": Children's and teenagers' perceptions of peer relationships in the sport domain. *Journal of Sport & Exercise Psychology, 18,* 347–379.

Weiss, M.R., Wiese, D.M., & Klint, K.A. (1989). Head over heels with success: The relationship between self-efficacy and performance in competitive youth gymnastics. *Journal of Sport & Exercise Psychology, 11,* 444–451.

Welk, G.J., Corbin, C.B., Dowell, M.N., & Harris, H. (1997). The validity and reliability of two different versions of the children and youth physical self-perception profile.

Measurement in Physical Education and Exercise Science, 1, 163–177.

Wentzel, K. (1993). Motivation and achievement in early adolescence: The role of multiple classroom goals. *Journal of Early Adolescence, 13,* 4–20.

Wentzel, K. (1998). Social relationships and motivation in middle school: The role of parents, teachers, and peers. *Journal of Educational Psychology, 90,* 202–209.

Whaley, D.E., & Ebbeck, V. (1997). Older adults' constraints to participation in structured exercise classes. *Journal of Aging and Physical Activity, 5,* 190–212.

White, A., & Coakley, J. (1986). *Making decisions: The response of young people in the Medway towns to the "Ever thought about sport?" campaign.* London: Sports Council.

White, R.W. (1959). Motivation reconsidered: The concept of competence. *Psychological Review, 66,* 297–330.

White, S.A. (1996). Goal orientation and perceptions of the motivational climate initiated by parents. *Pediatric Exercise Science, 8,* 122–129.

White, S.A. (1998). Adolescent goal profiles, perceptions of the parent-initiated motivational climate, and competitive trait anxiety. *The Sport Psychologist, 12,* 16–28.

White, S.A., & Duda, J.L. (1994). The relationship of gender, level of sport involvement, and participation motivation to task and ego orientations. *International Journal of Sport Psychology, 25,* 4–18.

White, S.A., Duda, J.L., & Keller, M.R. (1998). The relationship between goal orientation and perceived purposes among youth sport participants. *Journal of Sport Behavior, 21,* 474–483.

Whitehead, J. (1995). Multiple achievement orientations and participation in youth sport: A cultural and developmental perspective. *International Journal of Sport Psychology, 26,* 431–452.

Whitehead, J., & Smith, A.G. (1996). Issues in development of a protocol to evaluate children's reasoning about ability and effort in sport. *Perceptual and Motor Skills, 83,* 355–364.

Whitehead, J.R., & Corbin, C.B. (1991). Youth fitness testing: The effect of percentile-based evaluation feedback on intrinsic motivation. *Research Quarterly for Exercise and Sport, 62,* 225–231.

Wiersma, U.J. (1992). The effects of extrinsic rewards in intrinsic motivation: A meta-analysis. *Journal of Occupational & Organizational Psychology, 65,* 101–114.

Wigfield, A. (1994). Expectancy-value theory of achievement motivation: A developmental perspective. *Educational Psychology Review, 6,* 49–78.

Wigfield, A., & Eccles, J.S. (1992). The development of achievement task values: A theoretical analysis. *Developmental Review, 12,* 265–310.

Wigfield, A.W., Eccles, J.S., Yoon, K.S., Harold, R.D., Arbreton, A.J.A., Freedman-Doan, C., & Blumenfeld, P.C. (1997). Change in children's competence beliefs and subjective task values across the elementary school years: A 3-year study. *Journal of Educational Psychology, 89,* 451–469.

Wigfield, A., & Karpathian, M. (1991). Who am I and what can I do? Children's self-concepts and motivation in achievement situations. *Educational Psychologist, 26,* 233–261.

Williams, G.C., Grow, V.M., Freedman, Z.R., Ryan, R.M., & Deci, E.L. (1996). Motivational predictors of weight loss and weight-loss maintenance. *Journal of Personality and Social Psychology, 70,* 115–126.

Williams, L. (1994). Goal orientations and athletes' preferences for competence information sources. *Journal of Sport & Exercise Psychology, 16,* 416–430.

Williams, L. (1998). Contextual influences and goal perspectives among female youth sport participants. *Research Quarterly for Exercise and Sport, 69,* 47–57.

Williams, L., & Gill, D.L. (1995). The role of perceived competence in the motivation of physical activity. *Journal of Sport & Exercise Psychology, 17,* 363–378.

Zarbatany, L., Ghesquiere, K., & Mohr, K. (1992). A context perspective on early adolescents' friendship expectations. *Journal of Early Adolescence, 12,* 111–126.

Self-Efficacy
and Attributional Processes
in Physical Activity

Edward McAuley and Bryan Blissmer

The extent to which people approach or avoid achievement contexts is influenced, in part, by skills and capabilities, previous experiences, and individual characteristics. Clearly, physical activity is a behavioral context that is influenced by such parameters, and individuals use this information to explain why outcomes or events occur and to formulate expectations of personal capabilities. These processes are the focal points of two social cognitive theories that have been applied widely to physical activity research: attribution theory (Weiner, 1985, 1986) and self-efficacy theory (Bandura, 1977, 1986, 1997a). Attribution theory is concerned predominantly with how individuals cognitively appraise the outcomes of achievement situations in terms of causality. Self-efficacy theory focuses on the mediational role played by perceptions of personal agency in affecting diverse aspects of human functioning and behavior. Common to both theories, however, is their foundation in self-referent thought. That is, both theories assume the individual to be capable of controlling thought processes, motivation, and behavior (Bandura, 1986).

In this chapter, we review physical activity research that has its theoretical focus in either self-efficacy or attribution theories and, to a much lesser extent, work that attempts to integrate the two theories with a view to a more thorough understanding of this complex behavior. The chapter is, of course, an updated version of an earlier review (McAuley, 1992b). As with the previous review, we present an overview of each theory, discuss the measurement approaches that have been adopted, and review the pertinent physical activity literature. In addition, we make recommendations about future research in these areas. We then discuss the need to perhaps examine these two theories in tandem rather than in isolation and review some of the scant literature that has attempted to do so.

Preparation of this chapter was supported in part by a grant from the National Institute on Aging (#AG 12113).

ATTRIBUTION THEORY IN SPORT AND PHYSICAL ACTIVITY

The objectives of the following sections are to provide an overview of Weiner's (1972, 1979, 1985) attribution model, discuss methodological concerns when assessing attributions, use sport and exercise research to examine the conceptual links in the model, and discuss future research directions. Because the sport attribution research has been reviewed previously (McAuley, 1992a; McAuley & Duncan, 1990; Rejeski & Brawley, 1983), we have tried to include some contemporary sport attribution research while expanding on research that has been conducted in the exercise domain.

Conceptual Framework

Although other models such as Kelly's (1973) analysis of variance model and Jones and Davis' (1965) correspondent inference theory exist, empirical investigation of attribution theory in sport and exercise has been predominantly driven by Bernard Weiner's (1972, 1979, 1985) attributional model of achievement motivation and emotion. Weiner's model and in particular his more recent reformulation (Weiner, 1985, 1986) represent an elegant and sophisticated attempt to explain the individual's interpretation of achievement outcomes and to understand how that interpretation may influence his or her future behavior.

The foundation of Weiner's model is the premise that after an achievement outcome, individuals will engage in a causal search to determine why a particular outcome occurred. For example, quitting an aerobics program might be attributed to muscle soreness or to an annoying instructor. The reasons used to explain and understand achievement outcomes commonly are referred to as causal attributions. In his original attributional model, Weiner and his colleagues (Weiner et al., 1971) identified ability, effort, task difficulty, and luck as the four causal attributions most commonly ascribed to achievement outcomes. However, subsequent research and theory development have clearly demonstrated that in addition to the four "classic elements," there are numerous other ascriptions to which causality might be

inferred. This is particularly true in the case of such domains as sport and physical activity (see Bukowski & Moore, 1982; Roberts & Pascuzzi, 1979).[1]

Central to Weiner's (1985) reformulated theoretical model is the supposition that causal attributions by and of themselves are largely unimportant. Weiner (1985, 1986) maintained that although causal attributions may influence future behaviors directly, it makes more sense to identify common properties or dimensions that underlie all causal ascriptions. Empirical research consistently has reported the existence of at least three causal dimensions. The three most frequently identified are the locus of causality, stability, and controllability dimensions (e.g., Meyer & Koelbl, 1982; Passer, 1977). The locus of causality refers to whether the cause of the performance or achievement outcome is perceived to reside within or outside of the respondent. The stability dimension concerns the relative variability of the cause over time. Finally, the control dimension determines whether the cause is deemed to be under the control of the attributer or other people. Let us consider how a causal attribution might be translated into dimensional space. Imagine a beginning exerciser who attends several scheduled sessions but then misses the next session. Causality for this event might be ascribed to muscle soreness from the first few sessions, a likely possibility. However, this causal ascription might result in two very distinct dimensional patterns depending on the individual's perspective. It may be ascribed to internal causes, (e.g., "I'm not in good shape," "I exercised too hard"); however, it may be viewed as either stable or unstable (e.g., "exercising will always be painful," "with time I'll get better") and controllable or uncontrollable (e.g., "I can manage my schedule to fit in exercise," "I'm not cut out for exercise").[2] As is discussed later, the dimensional pattern used by the beginning exerciser could have important motivational and behavioral ramifications dependent on whether the attribution is perceived as malleable.

The core of Weiner's (1979, 1985) reformulated model (see figure 6.1) lies in the mediational role played by emotions and expectancy between causal dimensions and future behavior. Weiner proposed that immediately after an achievement

---

1. Weiner (1983) has taken care to point out that he has never theorized the four causal elements of task difficulty, ability, luck, and effort as being the only attributions individuals make for achievement outcomes.
2. Although this $2 \times 2 \times 2$ taxonomy of dimensional structure is well supported, Weiner (1985) conceded that other dimensions (e.g., intention, responsibility) may exist.

outcome, the individual experiences affective responses that are almost "automatic" reactions to the event and are termed *outcome-dependent* affects (Weiner, Russell, & Lerman, 1979). Such affects take the form of feeling good when one is successful and feeling bad when one fails. Subsequently, the individual engages in causal search, in an effort to determine why the outcome occurred (Heider, 1958). Once an attribution has been formulated, it is processed in terms of its relative dimensional placement with respect to locus of causality, stability, and control. Weiner proposed that these dimensions affect future behavior through the mediation of affective reactions and future expectancies. More specifically, Weiner identified the stability dimension as being instrumental in the formation of future expectancies and the locus of causality and control dimensions to be the predominant antecedents of affective reactions. These latter reactions have been termed *attribution-dependent* affects (Weiner et al., 1979). A number of researchers have shown all three causal dimensions to be related to emotions (e.g., Forsyth & McMillan, 1981; McAuley, 1991; McAuley, Russell, & Gross, 1983; Vallerand, 1987), as is depicted in figure 6.1. Additionally, it has been proposed that controllability (in particular, personal control) also may have important implications for future expectancies (Bandura, 1986; McAuley, 1992b).

The following sections review the pertinent literature in sport and exercise and focus on four areas:

- Measurement of causal dimensions
- The attribution–emotion link
- Reviews of contemporary research conducted in sport and exercise
- Future directions

Measurement of Causal Dimensions

Much of the early research on attribution theory relied on measurement systems that required the researcher to code attributional responses along the causal dimensions. In effect, these researchers committed what Russell (1982) referred to as the "fundamental attribution researcher error" by assuming that the investigator can accurately classify subjects' causal attributions in terms of causal structure. Such an approach ignores the individual phenomenology by excluding the subject as an active agent, a factor that is fundamental to the attribution process (McAuley & Gross, 1983;

Rejeski & Brawley, 1983; Russell, 1982). Consider our beginning exerciser from earlier in the chapter. Because the respondent and the researcher may bring very different sets of experiences and knowledge to the generation of the attributions, they are likely to differentially code that attribution along the causal dimensions. Such differences may have important implications for motivation and future behavior.

Russell (1982) developed the Causal Dimension Scale (CDS) to address this basic measurement problem. The CDS and its subsequent modification, the CDSII (McAuley, Duncan, & Russell, 1992), allow the individual to make an open-ended attribution and then classify that attribution along the dimensions of locus of causality, stability, and control (further delineated into personal and external control in the CDSII). Refer to reviews by McAuley (1992b) and Biddle and Hanrahan (1998) for a more thorough discussion of the development and validation of both causal dimension scales.

At this point, the CDSII appears to be a reliable instrument and has been used in many of the contemporary attribution studies in sport and exercise (Biddle & Hanrahan, 1998). Unfortunately, some researchers continue to use attributional measures in which study participants choose from an array of possible attributions for the outcome and then researchers determine which dimensions those responses represent. Biddle and Hill (1992a, 1992b) attempted to examine the link between attributions and emotion in sport by using an attribution measure composed of 12 items intended to represent common outcome attributions in sport. Study participants rated the importance of each item on a 9-point scale. In one study, Biddle and Hill (1992a) assigned the attributions to causal dimensions, whereas in the other study (Biddle & Hill, 1992b) the scores were subjected to a factor analysis. Beyond the obvious problems inherent in supplying subjects with a fixed list of possible attributions, the use of factor analysis is also theoretically flawed. The resultant factor solution treats attributions as dimension independent. Placing an attribution within the "unstable" factor (Biddle & Hill, 1992b) ignores that the attribution also varies along dimensions of causality and control, as indicated by the cross-loading of attributions along factors. The use of researcher-biased measures of the causal dimensions has occurred in other recent physical activity research (e.g., Martinek & Griffith, 1994; Newton & Duda, 1993). Although there are other solutions to the measurement of causal attributions (see Biddle & Hanrahan, 1998), using scales such as the CDSII reduces the likelihood of response bias on the part of the researcher.

Biddle and Hanrahan (1998) suggested that the CDS and CDSII may require validation or modification in various populations because they were initially developed on collegiate samples. Vlachopoulos, Biddle, and Fox (1996) developed a child's version of the CDSII. Unfortunately, they failed to report much of the scale development process, but they did report making modifications such as rewording, rescaling, and reducing the number of items to make the scale more tenable for research with children. More psychometric work needs to be conducted on the modified scale. Research by Blanchard-Fields (1994) and Chipperfield and Segall (1996) raises the intriguing possibility that elderly populations may have a preference to use joint attributions. The directions of the CDSII, which require individuals to select the most important reason for the outcome, may force the elderly to choose between equally important raw attributions. Further research needs to investigate whether the use of joint attributions is merely an artifact of measurement choice stemming from the use of causal chaining or truly indicates a more complex attributional style used by the elderly. Perhaps Fletcher and colleagues' attributional complexity scale (Fletcher, Danilovics, Fernandez, Peterson, & Reeder, 1986), which was designed to examine the complexity of individuals' attributional schemata, may be used to examine the degree to which various demographic groups use different attributional styles. Further research into the examination of measurement systems for population differences in attributional style is highly encouraged. However, at this point, the CDSII appears to be the most applicable measure for physical activity research using Weiner's (1986) model.

The Attribution–Emotion Link

Emotional responses are an integral part of physical activity whether they result as a function of competitive outcomes in sport or as a component of psychological health associated with exercise participation. In the context of Weiner's (1985, 1986) attributional model, emotion is theorized to play an important mediational role between causal dimensions and future behavior. Although the locus of causality historically has been linked with

affective responses (Weiner, 1979), the stability and control dimensions also have been associated with affect generation (McAuley, 1991; McAuley & Duncan, 1989; McAuley et al., 1983; Vallerand, 1987). McAuley and Duncan (1989), in manipulating the outcome of a bicycle ergometer competition, reported that under conditions of perceived failure, locus of causality and stability dimensions resulted in greater negative affect. Courneya and McAuley (1993) reported that personally controllable and stable attributions after performance of a graded exercise test were associated with more positive affect. These findings were replicated by Courneya and McAuley (1996), with greater positive and less negative affect being associated with more stable and personally controllable attributions for perceived success after a 12-week exercise training program. Additionally, Ingledew, Hardy, and Cooper (1996) reported that more negative affect was experienced after personally controllable attributions for perceived failure in meeting health behavior change goals.

It appears that causal dimensions may play an important role in affect generation, but the specific relationships are still unclear. This confusion may well be a function of the rather global approach taken to the measurement of affective responses. Weiner's (1985) attributional model of achievement and emotion makes rather detailed predictions relative to which specific affective responses are influenced by causal dimensions. For example, he suggested that after failure, stable attributions lead to hopelessness, whereas unstable and externally controllable attributions lead to anger (Weiner, 1985). If one considers the exercise–affect literature, there is clearly a move toward isolating affective *dimensions* (e.g., Gauvin & Rejeski, 1993; McAuley & Courneya, 1994). Consequently, focus on specific emotional responses largely has been ignored. If causal attributions are considered to be an important component of the physical activity process, it may be necessary to consider the role of individual affective responses under specific circumstances, rather than the measures of more global affective space.

Thus far, it might be assumed that only causal dimensions are implicated in the attribution–affect relationship. However, attributional influences only represent the reflective process that influences affective responses. Other more objectively influenced processes also appear to be implicated in the generation of affect. These processes have been referred to as *intuitive appraisal* and have been examined in tandem with cogni-

Perceived failure results in negative affect.

tive appraisals in physical activity research (McAuley & Duncan, 1989; Robinson & Howe, 1989; Vallerand, 1987). The consensus findings suggest that both reflective (attributional) appraisal and intuitive appraisal are implicated in the generation of affect. Because most contemporary exercise studies have generally focused on perceptions of outcome, it is unclear to what extent the attribution-independent affect responses confound the relationship between causal dimensions and affect.

Affective responses are an integral part of the physical activity experience, and it appears that reflecting on the causes of these experiences (attributional search) gives rise to specific emotions. Weiner's (1985) model, therefore, provides a useful framework for the study of affect generated in the pursuit of achievement outcomes.

Contemporary Sport Attribution Research

Early studies of causal attributions in physical activity domains (largely sport-related studies) suffered from a host of theoretical and methodological problems (McAuley, 1992b). Much of this literature relied on comparing the differential attributional patterns of winners and losers. These results then typically were interpreted from the perspective of the hedonic or self-serving bias in which success is attributed as internal, stable, and controllable, and failure, in an attempt to protect self-esteem, is attributed externally (Bradley, 1978; Zuckerman, 1979). Contemporary sport research

has indicated that the self-serving bias for success is a relatively robust finding (Hendy & Boyer, 1993; Morgan, Griffin, & Heyward, 1996; White, 1993). Hendy and Boyer (1993), in a study of 624 triathletes, reported success to be attributed to internal and controllable factors, whereas unstable attributional patterns were used to explain an unexpected failure. This pattern generally was replicated in studies by White (1993) and Morgan et al. (1996). Softball players of different ages and genders made internal and controllable attributions after victory (White, 1993), and adolescent (13–18 years) track athletes (N = 755) made more internal, stable, and controllable attributions for success than failure (Morgan, et al., 1996). We need to caution that the differences in these studies reflect gradations of internality, stability, and control, not absolute levels along those dimensions. Therefore, unsuccessful performers may have made internal and stable attributions, but when compared with successful performers, they were less internal and stable.

Little sport research supports a self-protection bias for attributing failure to external causes (McAuley, 1992b). This is not surprising given that external attributions are a rare phenomenon when the subject is an active agent in the attribution process (Russell, McAuley, & Tarico, 1987). In an effort to examine external attributions, McAuley and Shaffer (1993) designed a study in which respondents were asked to place themselves in the role of a star basketball player whose recruitment recently had been questioned by a rival university. This scenario was an actual occurrence that had resulted in the player being forced to "sit out" for a season. Consequently, the methodology generated a large number of externally controllable attributions. These responses were correlated with the anger and outrage directed at the rival coach who was responsible for the allegations. In essence, externally controlled attributions are more likely to occur in situations in which the causal search attempts to place blame, rather than to understand why an outcome occurred (McAuley & Shaffer, 1993). Further study of the

© Human Kinetics

extent to which external attributions occur in the attributional search in natural settings as a means to understanding rather than blaming event outcomes is warranted.

Contemporary attribution research has witnessed an increasing interest in the attribution–affect relationship in sport. In a series of studies, Biddle and Hill (1992a, 1992b) supported Weiner's (1985) hypothesized links between causal dimensions and affect in fencing and squash competitions. Causal attributions and performance satisfaction were related to affect generation in both studies.

Recent work (Hendy & Boyer, 1993; Morgan et al., 1996; White, 1993) has explored differences in attributional patterns by gender and ethnicity. Although previous research indicated that females make more self-defeating attributions after success than males (Bird & Williams, 1980), contemporary research has failed to support this early work. For example, White (1993) reported that female softball players perceived success as more controllable than did males, and Hendy and Boyer (1993) found that female triathletes also perceived more control over success than did males, downplaying the importance of luck and social support. It is possible that this change in attributional patterns over time reflects the increased opportunities and experiences of females in sport. Such opportunities are likely to result in mastery experiences, thereby influencing one's sense of efficacy.

Preliminary work by Morgan et al. (1996) indicated that ethnicity may play a role in attributional patterns. Anglo-American adolescent track athletes perceived success as more internal and controllable than African Americans and Native Americans. Additionally, Anglo-Americans perceived failure as more controllable than African Americans and less stable than Native Americans. Whether such findings can be extended to adult sport participants of diverse ethnic origins remains to be determined.

Contemporary Exercise Attribution Research

Although it has been suggested that causal attributions may be quite useful in understanding exercise adherence (McAuley, 1992a, 1992b), there is still a paucity of research examining attributions for exercise behavior. The self-serving bias appears to operate in exercise settings in much the same way it does in sport settings (Courneya &

McAuley, 1996; Ingledew, et al., 1996; McAuley, 1991; Minifee & McAuley, 1998). That is, exercisers make more internal, stable, and controllable attributions after perceived success for both acute (Courneya & McAuley, 1993) and long-term exercise participation (Courneya & McAuley, 1996; McAuley, 1991).

Although the self-serving bias is recognized as a self-protection mechanism for self-esteem (Bradley, 1978), research by Schoeneman and Curry (1990) suggested that a *personal changeability* pattern of attributions (Anderson, 1983) may be optimal for motivating future behavior change. In this pattern, success is attributed to internal, stable, and controllable causes, whereas failure is attributed to internal, yet changeable (unstable and controllable) factors. Middle-aged adults beginning an exercise program retrospectively reported internal, unstable, and personally controllable attributions for their previous failures at regular exercise (McAuley, Poag, Gleason, & Wraith, 1990). That these individuals currently were enrolled in an exercise program suggests a pattern of behavior that supports a personally changeable profile. Minifee and McAuley (1998) examined attributional patterns made for successful and unsuccessful exercise behavior change among African-American adults. They reported support for the personal changeability tendency with exercise failures that were attributed to unstable but internal and controllable factors, predicting higher expectations for future behavior change. Although these findings, in conjunction with those of Schoeneman and Curry (1990), are quite encouraging, prospective studies are required to determine whether the personal changeability pattern predicts subsequent behavior change.

Research in the exercise domain has supported the proposed link between causal dimensions and affect in both acute and training studies (e.g., Courneya & McAuley, 1993, 1996; Ingledew et al., 1996; McAuley, 1991; McAuley et al., 1990). Despite previous recommendations (McAuley, 1992b), little progress has been made in applying Weiner's (1985) complete attribution–emotion–behavior model to understand exercise behavior. Two exceptions to this are studies by Courneya and McAuley (1996) and Ingledew et al. (1996). Courneya and McAuley (1996) examined attributions, expectations for success, affect, and intentions to continue exercising in 105 adults who had just completed a 12-week aerobic exercise program. Attributions to stable and personally controllable causes resulted in greater positive and lower negative affect, and individuals who perceived the outcome as more favorable reported higher expectations for success in continuing to exercise by themselves. Expectations for future success and affect both predicted unique variance in the intention to continue exercise. Ingledew and colleagues (1996) examined a more diverse set of health behaviors, including exercise, among hospital employees who were attempting to change their behavior. Support was found for the link between the causal dimensions of personal control and stability and attribution-dependent affect (Ingledew et al., 1996). Additionally, the interaction of the dimensions of stability and personal control significantly predicted future behavioral intentions after perceived success. Together, these results demonstrate that attributions and attributional affect can help explain future behavioral intentions. Although these two studies show the promise of attributions in understanding exercise behavior, future exercise research must replicate and expand on these results to include measures and predictions of actual behavior change.

Summary

Causal attributions are at the heart of individuals' search for meaning in events and outcomes, in particular in physical activity outcomes. More often than not, attributions for success and failure are internal and controllable, varying along the stability dimension. Such a pattern of attributions suggests that the individual is responsible for his or her behavior and can change or maintain that behavior, if desired. Attributions for physical activity outcomes have been linked, via causal dimensions, to affective responses and expectations for subsequent behavior, providing a useful expectancy-value model for studying sport and physical activity.

The Future of Attribution Theory in Physical Activity

Understanding the attribution–emotion link has received considerable attention without really resolving the basic question of how such affect is generated. Two strategies may be used in future research to help clarify this crucial conceptual link. First, measurement and prediction of more specific affective reactions, as proposed by Weiner (1985), may be necessary. Investigating the specific affective responses predicted by the interac-

tions of the causal dimensions will necessitate larger sample sizes to obtain individuals within each cell of the 3×3 (or 4×4 if the CDSII is used) dimensional matrix. A second step that may clarify the attribution–emotion link is understanding the link between outcome and attribution-dependent affect. Research has tended to assume that the affective response assessed is the result of the attributional process, but rarely is it clear whether this affect is independent of the outcome. This is demonstrated by the strong correlation between perceived outcome and affect in the Courneya and McAuley (1996) study. Both outcome and attribution-dependent affect must be examined to determine their relationship and the relative importance of the causal dimensions in determining attribution-dependent affect.

Of most importance, however, is examination of the causal process from raw attribution to future behavior (Duncan & McAuley, 1989). Ingledew and colleagues (1996) and Courneya and McAuley (1996) began to address this issue by examining the links between causal dimensions, affect, and intentions for future behavior. However, the step from intention to behavior is clearly influenced by time. Therefore, subsequent research must demonstrate an attribution–behavior link via the components of Weiner's model. To fully test Weiner's (1985, 1986) complete model would involve repeated assessment of the attributional process, possibly in conjunction with measures of other social cognitive variables and behavior. In closing, we argue that attribution theory and, in particular, Weiner's (1985, 1986) model continue to offer a useful theoretical framework for understanding behavior in the physical activity domain. Unfortunately, the tendency has been to test segments of the model to the exclusion of the sequence of events leading from outcome through the attributional process to subsequent behavior. Whether aspects of this model may be more parsimoniously encompassed by other social cognitive frameworks (e.g., Bandura, 1986) remains to be determined.

SELF-EFFICACY AND PHYSICAL ACTIVITY

Our consideration of attribution theory relevant to physical activity embraced both sport and exercise-related research. In the following sections, we review another form of self-referent thought, self-efficacy, but focus on studies that emanate largely from the exercise domain. We do this for a number of reasons. First, exercise has assumed a greater role in preventive approaches to health behavior, and one of the most frequently used approaches to understanding this role has been self-efficacy theory. Second, we believe that self-efficacy is particularly useful as a theoretical approach to understanding exercise behavior because of its influence on choice, effort, persistence, and affective aspects of behavior. Finally, there has been a tremendous increase in exercise-related research that uses self-efficacy as a theoretical orientation. We begin with a brief overview of the theory and its predictions. This is followed by a section dealing with the measurement properties of self-efficacy. Finally, the remaining sections review the contemporary literature dealing with self-efficacy as a determinant and consequence of exercise behavior.

Conceptual Framework

Efficacy expectations are the individual's beliefs in his or her capabilities to execute necessary courses of action to satisfy situational demands and are theorized to influence the activities that individuals choose to approach, the effort expended on such activities, and the degree of persistence demonstrated in the face of failure or aversive stimuli (Bandura, 1986). More recently, Bandura (1995, 1997a) refined the definition of self-efficacy to encompass those beliefs regarding individuals' capabilities to produce performances that will lead to anticipated outcomes. The term *self-regulatory efficacy* is now used, and both the term and definition encompass a social cognitive stance that represents the role that cognitive skills play in behavioral performance above and beyond simply behavioral or skill beliefs. Maddux (1995) suggested that this definitional development has led to the distinction between task self-efficacy, where simple motor skills or capabilities are assessed (e.g., walking a certain distance), and self-regulatory or coping efficacy, where efficacy is assessed relative to impediments or challenges to successful behavioral performance (e.g., carrying out one's walking regimen when tired or stressed or during foul weather).

These judgments of personal efficacy are by definition situation-specific, and efficacy measures are therefore specific to domains of functioning rather than generalized in nature. Efficacy expectations influence human behavior through a variety of processes. Individuals with a strong

sense of personal efficacy approach more challenging tasks, expend greater efforts in these tasks, and persist longer in the face of aversive stimuli. Efficacy beliefs also act as motivational regulators in that they contribute to the formulation of desires and aspirations, as well as to one's degree of commitment to these aspirations (Bandura, 1995). In short, self-efficacy beliefs are theorized to influence motivation, affect, and behavior (Bandura, 1986).

Expectations of personal efficacy are influenced by four major sources of information: past performance accomplishments, social modeling, social or verbal persuasion, and physiological arousal (Bandura, 1997a). Past performance or mastery accomplishments are the most dependable and influential sources of efficacy information. For example, a history of previously successful exercise experiences will facilitate efficacy expectations, whereas previous failures lower perceptions of personal capabilities in that domain. Progress charts, activity logs, and so forth are useful strategies that use mastery experiences. Social modeling or vicarious experiences are sources of efficacy information derived by observing or imagining others engaging in the task to be performed. The proliferation of fitness and exercise videotapes and television shows provide compelling examples of attempts to enhance efficacy expectations and thereby behavior through social modeling. In general, the effects of social modeling are less pronounced than mastery experiences but are particularly useful when one has no personal frame of reference from which to generate efficacy expectations. Social persuasion is a technique commonly used by exercise leaders, significant others, advertising campaigns, and peers to bolster individuals' personal efficacy, but it is less powerful than information based on personal accomplishments. Finally, physiological symptoms are argued to affect behavior through the cognitive evaluation (efficacy expectations) of the information conveyed by such symptoms. For example, muscle soreness, a rapidly beating heart, and shortness of breath in neophyte exercisers can be interpreted as signs that one is incapable of physical activity. Alternatively, if these signs and symptoms are viewed as the body's natural response to stress on the system and they are alleviated with subsequent activity, efficacy is likely to be enhanced.

Self-efficacy theory is a social cognitive approach to behavioral causation in which behavioral, physiological, and cognitive factors and environmental influences all operate as interacting determinants of each other (Bandura, 1986, 1997a). This interacting process, referred to as *reciprocal determinism*, posits that behavior and human functioning are determined by the interrelated influences of individuals' physiological states, behavior, cognition, and the environment. Self-efficacy theory focuses on the role of self-referent thought and provides a common mechanism through which people demonstrate control over their own motivation and behavior. Self-efficacy cognitions have been consistently shown to be important determinants of sport (Feltz, 1992) and exercise behavior (McAuley, 1992a; McAuley, Peña, & Jerome, 2001), as well as social, clinical, and health-related behaviors (Bandura, 1997a). It is important to realize that self-efficacy is not concerned with the skills an individual has but rather with the judgments of what an individual can do with the skills he or she possesses (Bandura, 1986, 1997a).

Measurement of Self-Efficacy

Efficacy cognitions are composed of several dimensions. *Level* of efficacy is concerned with individuals' beliefs in their capability to accomplish a specific task or element of a task. Believing one can walk or jog incremental distances represents a particular level of efficacy. *Strength* of efficacy is concerned with the degree of conviction that a task can be successfully carried out. Therefore, I may indicate that I can walk a block in three minutes (level) but only may be 50% confident in successfully carrying out this task (strength). The final dimension of efficacy is *generality*, which is concerned with the ability of efficacy expectations to predict behavior in related tasks or domains that require parallel skills. For example, efficacy measures that tap individuals' capabilities to engage in strenuous aerobic activity, although developed specifically to predict walking or jogging, also may be useful in predicting aerobic dance or exercise cycling.

McAuley and Mihalko (1998) recently published a comprehensive review of the measurement of exercise-related self-efficacy, which provides a more thorough discussion than can be provided here. They identified several categories of self-efficacy measures used in the exercise literature. *Exercise-specific efficacy* assesses those beliefs regarding individual capabilities to successfully engage in incremental bouts of physical activity relative to frequency and duration at some level

of intensity (e.g., Courneya & McAuley, 1994), exercising over periods of time (e.g., Biddle, Goudas, & Page, 1994), and assessment of particular activities such as walking successive numbers of blocks in incremental periods of time (e.g., Ewart, Taylor, Reese, & DeBusk, 1983). *Barriers efficacy* clearly represents what Bandura (1995, 1997a) more recently referred to as self-regulatory efficacy and assesses beliefs in capabilities to overcome social, personal, and environmental barriers to exercising. Time management, fatigue, weather, family and social demands, and inaccessibility of facilities are typical of the types of barriers assessed (e.g., Marcus, Eaton, Rossi, & Harlow, 1994).

As noted earlier, self-efficacy measures should tap cognitions relative to the domain of interest, and these specific measures consistently are demonstrated to be better predictors of behavior than omnibus assessments of global confidence. Unfortunately, assessment of these global measures persists in the exercise literature. These *general efficacy* measures vary in their content, assessing such beliefs as generalized efficacy (Tipton & Worthington, 1984), trait self-efficacy (Long, 1985), and physical self-efficacy (Kavussanu & McAuley, 1995). The latter measure is typically assessed by the Physical Self-Efficacy (PSE) scale (Ryckman, Robbins, Thornton, & Cantrell, 1982). Although a general measure, the PSE scale may have some utility in the exercise domain because of its generalizing to physical activity. However, such measures are less likely to predict more specific behaviors (e.g., exercise adherence) or to be changed as a function of exposure to acute bouts of exercise than are more specific measures of efficacy (e.g., McAuley, Lox, & Duncan, 1993; Taylor, Bandura, Ewart, Miller, & DeBusk, 1985).

Self-Efficacy and Exercise Behavior

In the following sections, we review what amounts to a rapidly developing literature linking perceptions of personal efficacy to exercise behavior. In a true reciprocally determining fashion, however, efficacy is not simply a determinant of exercise behavior but is also an outcome of exercise behavior. Thus, we have one literature that is largely concerned with using social cognitive theory (Bandura, 1997a, 1986) to predict exercise participation and another literature that details how various aspects of the exercise experience act as sources of efficacy. We review each of these areas separately.

Efficacy As Determinant of Exercise Behavior

Earlier reviews (McAuley 1992a, 1992b) concluded that despite the use of diverse populations, sometimes inadequate operational definitions of exercise behavior, and a variety of methods for assessing self-efficacy expectations, the exercise–physical activity relationship appeared to be remarkably consistent. In essence, self-efficacy was reported to play a significant role in the adoption of, and adherence to, exercise regimens. Studies conducted since these reviews were published were generally more rigorous, included prospective studies, and offered further compelling evidence for the contribution of efficacy expectations to the prediction of physical activity behavior.

Sallis and his colleagues have used social cognitive models in their attempts to understand the behavioral epidemiology of exercise (Hovell, et al., 1991; Sallis, Hovell, Hofstetter, & Barrington, 1992; Sallis et al., 1986, 1989). These researchers have conducted two major community studies of social learning correlates of physical activity in the general population and provide evidence suggesting that self-efficacy plays an important role in the etiology of exercise behavior. Presenting data from the Stanford Community Health Survey, Sallis et al. (1986) reported self-efficacy to be significantly related to exercise behavior at different stages of the natural history of the exercise process. A further study of the correlates of physical activity in a large community sample reported self-efficacy to be the strongest predictor among a host of social learning variables (Sallis et al., 1989). This relationship held true in subset analyses of the sample focusing only on adult Latino participants (Hovell et al., 1991). In the 2-year follow-up study, Sallis et al. (1992) used sets of social, cognitive, and environmental variables, considered to be dynamic or susceptible to change, to predict changes in activity over the 2-year period. In these analyses, changes in self-efficacy were the most consistent predictors of changes in exercise behavior over time.

In our own work, we have been able to demonstrate that exercise-related self-efficacy plays different roles at different stages of the exercise process (McAuley, 1993a, 1993b; McAuley et al., 1993) and that using efficacy-based strategies in training studies enhances adherence (McAuley, Courneya, Rudolph, & Lox, 1994). This work has been conducted largely in the context of initially sedentary, older adults. In the first report (McAuley, 1993a), self-efficacy and body fat were predictive of exercise frequency and intensity at the midpoint of a 5-month program, but exercise participation up to that point was the only predictor of adherence over the remaining period of the program. Such findings are consistent with the perspective that cognitive control systems play their most important role in the acquisition of behavioral proficiencies (Bandura, 1989). When behaviors are less demanding and more easily engaged in (in this case, beyond adoption and adaptation), cognitive control systems (e.g., self-efficacy) give way to lower control systems (e.g., instinctive behavioral patterns; Bandura & Wood, 1989). In a follow-up study (McAuley, 1993b), participants were contacted four months after program completion and were interviewed by telephone and surveyed by mail as to their exercise participation patterns since program termination. Only efficacy was a significant individual predictor of exercise behavior.

Further follow-up data were collected at nine months postprogram, when participants returned for further physiological testing (McAuley et al., 1993). Physiological, behavioral, and cognitive variables were used to predict adherence to activity since program end (frequency of activity) and compliance to the specific exercise prescription given to each participant at program end. Self-efficacy was a unique predictor of adherence, whereas efficacy, aerobic power, and attendance during the program significantly discriminated between compliers and noncompliers. Such findings may have important implications for how exercise programs are structured. For example, if one is interested in having participants continue to be active without necessarily mirroring the content of the formal structured exercise program, then establishing conditions that maximize perceived capabilities appears crucial. Clearly, diverse parameters take on varying degrees of influence at different stages of the exercise process (McAuley, 1993a; Sallis & Hovell, 1990).

McAuley et al. (1994) conducted a randomized controlled trial contrasting an efficacy information-based exercise program with an attention control exercise program in an effort to predict adherence. The efficacy-based group monitored progress in activity and physiological adaptation, viewed videotapes of formerly sedentary adults becoming fitter through physical activity, exercised together in buddy systems, and were provided with appropriate information for interpreting physiological responses to activity. Clear differences in activity patterns were demonstrated over time, with the intervention group adhering at a significantly greater rate than the control group over the 5-month period. Efficacy was also significantly related to patterns of adherence but not to the degree expected. It may well be that in the situation created, where individuals are committed to each other in activity, collective efficacy may play a more crucial role than individual efficacy (Bandura, 1997a). The assessment of collective exercise efficacy has received little attention and should be considered in subsequent research examining determinants of exercise in group settings.

Self-efficacy frequently has been identified as an important determinant of physical activity behavior and function in symptomatic populations. We previously reviewed the work of Ewart and his associates (Ewart, Stewart, Gillilan, & Kelemen, 1986; Ewart, Stewart, Gillilan, Kelemen, Valenti, et al., 1986; Ewart et al., 1983; Taylor et al., 1985), which demonstrated the role played by psychosocial variables in the adoption of, adherence to, and performance of exercise-related activities in this population. Kaplan and his colleagues (Kaplan, Ries, Prewitt, & Eakin, 1994) recently compared standard physiological predictors of remaining life expectancy with a simple measure of exercise self-efficacy in predicting survival rates of patients with chronic obstructive pulmonary disease. In a series of analyses examining both univariate and multivariate models, self-efficacy was a significant predictor of survival ($p < .01$) when compared with all physiological indicators, but when compared with the strongest predictor alone (forced expiratory volume), the influence of self-efficacy was reduced.

Bock et al. (1997) examined the roles of self-efficacy and processes of change in the prediction of exercise behavior during a 12-week cardiac rehabilitation program and at 3-month follow-up. As one would expect in a sample entering a program based on supervised physical conditioning, exercise behavior increased over the course of the program, as did self-efficacy. Lower levels of self-efficacy at program end were related to reductions in activity at follow-up. Unfortunately, the extent to which participants were active during rehabilitation was not controlled statistically, hindering interpretations of the findings.

A growing trend in exercise efficacy research has been to incorporate the self-efficacy construct into other theoretical models (e.g., theory of planned behavior) or to use it as a variable to discrimi-

nate among individuals at various stages of the exercise process (e.g., employing models such as the transtheoretical model of behavior change). Although McAuley, Peña, and Jerome (2001) reviewed this work in some detail, we offer a brief overview here.

Theory of Planned Behavior

Researchers endorsing Ajzen's (1985) theory of planned behavior often have used self-efficacy as a theoretical substitute for the construct of perceived behavioral control. Perceived behavioral control is conceptualized as the perceived ease or difficulty of performing a behavior (Ajzen, 1988) but in many studies has been treated as being synonymous with self-efficacy, a course of action precipitated by Ajzen (1987, 1991). Brawley and his colleagues (DuCharme & Brawley, 1995; Rodgers & Brawley, 1996) reported studies of novice exercisers in which the self-efficacy/perceived behavioral control constructs are predicted exercise intentions (Rodgers & Brawley, 1996) and exercise behavior (DuCharme & Brawley, 1995). Additionally, the planned behavior model has been used to predict exercise behavior over 1-week (Yordy & Lent, 1993) and 2- and 4-week periods (Courneya & McAuley, 1994). In the Yordy and Lent (1993) study, perceived behavioral control and self-efficacy were distinguished from each other, but only self-efficacy (as measured by barriers efficacy) predicted intention to exercise. Courneya and McAuley (1994) treated self-efficacy and perceived behavioral control synonymously in their attempt to determine whether different elements of the planned behavior model acted as differential determinants of intensity, frequency, and duration of activity. Their results suggested that self-efficacy (perceived behavioral control) contributed significant variance to intensity and frequency of exercise behavior beyond that explained by intention.

Self-efficacy has not been accepted universally as a theoretical equivalent of perceived behavioral control (e.g., Biddle, Goudas, & Page, 1994), and attempts have been made to demonstrate the distinction between the two constructs (Terry & O'Leary, 1995). Terry and O'Leary conceptualized perceived behavioral control in the same vein as outcome expectancies yet measured this construct relative to control over exercise behavior. In turn, they measured *self-efficacy* as the relative ease or difficulty of carrying out a 2-week exercise regimen. However, perceived ease or difficulty is not self-efficacy, although it is a related concept. For example, Bandura (1997a) noted that when one measures exercise-related self-efficacy, one is concerned with individual judgments of one's capabilities to exercise regularly in the face of a variety of impediments. Such barriers might be weather, work, fatigue, other commitments, and so forth. Moreover, these barriers most certainly can make regular exercise participation difficult. However, they do not necessarily make one ineffi-cacious!

A number of authors have argued that self-effi-cacy (in addition to perceived behavioral control) should be included in the planned behavior model. However, Bandura (1997a) further argued that all components of the reasoned action and planned behavior models are redundant with constructs already present in his social cognitive model of behavior change. Subsequent research must ex-amine the extent to which such models do indeed overlap and to what extent some constructs may well be independent predictors of exercise and other health behavior change (e.g., Dzewaltowski, 1989). This latter topic, behavioral change over time, has taken on increasing interest among health and exercise psychologists.

Transtheoretical Model

The extent to which individuals pass through clearly defined stages of behavioral change has dominated the recent health behavior change lit-erature. Prochaska and DiClemente's (1983, 1985) transtheoretical model has been used to under-stand such diverse behaviors as smoking cessa-tion, condom use, sunscreen use, cancer self-screening, eating behaviors, and physical activity participation. This model proposes that individu-als pass through the stages of precontemplation, contemplation, preparation, action, and mainte-nance, and it uses an array of process variables (including self-efficacy) to explain, predict, and bring about change at each stage (Prochaska & Velicer, 1997). Despite its legion of followers, the stages of change model was severely criticized by Bandura (1997b), who took the position that the transtheoretical model is not a true stage theory (however, see Prochaska & Velicer, 1997, for a re-joinder to Bandura). Indeed, in the context of ex-ercise behavior, the measurement of stages and process variables such as efficacy is sometimes questionable (see McAuley & Mihalko, 1998; McAuley, Peña, & Jerome, 2001). Be that as it may, in this chapter we confine our statements to briefly reviewing the findings relative to self-efficacy as a correlate of exercise behavior in studies employ-ing the stages of change model.

Much of this work comes from Marcus and her colleagues (Marcus & Owen, 1992; Marcus, Pinto, Simkin, Audrain, & Taylor, 1994; Marcus, Selby, Niaura, & Rossi, 1992; Marcus et al., 1994). In these studies, efficacy is typically measured as confi-dence to participate in exercise in the face of diffi-cult situations (barriers). Participants are drawn from large worksite populations, and the defini-tions and measures used are based on work by Prochaska and his colleagues in smoking cessa-tion (Prochaska & DiClemente, 1983). This work and other applications of the stage model typically show a linear increase in self-efficacy across stages of exercise participation (e.g., Cardinal, 1997; Gorley & Gordon, 1995; Lechner & De Vries, 1995; Wyse, Mercer, Ashford, Buxton, & Gleeson, 1995). Unfortunately, the vast majority of exercise-related research that uses stages of change formulations is cross-sectional, and it is impossible to deter-mine the exact nature of the efficacy–stage rela-tionship. Certainly, social cognitive theory (Bandura, 1986) would propose that increases in exercise behavior can act as a source of efficacy information and that efficacy, in turn, influences subsequent behavior.

Exercise As a Source of Efficacy Information

The majority of efficacy-related physical activity research has focused on efficacy as a determinant (see previous section). However, it is important to remember that efficacy expectations are impor-tant outcome variables in their own right and that exercise experiences can be influential sources of efficacy information. Such exercise experiences can take both acute and chronic forms (e.g., McAuley & Courneya, 1992; McAuley, Courneya, & Lettunich, 1991).

In the case of acute exercise effects on efficacy, exposure to a bout of activity serves as a mastery experience and enhances self-efficacy expecta-tions. For example, McAuley et al. (1991) assessed self-efficacy relative to various activity modes (walking/jogging, stationary cycling, sit-ups) be-fore and after graded maximal exercise testing at baseline and following a 5-month program of walk-ing for middle-aged adults. Both acute exposures enhanced efficacy, but a much more dramatic in-crease occurred over the 5-month period of activ-ity, as expected. However, in a 9-month follow-up study, efficacy had declined significantly from postprogram levels but returned close to original levels after exposure to acute activity (McAuley et al., 1993). In the original study (McAuley et al., 1991) and in a replication study (McAuley, Bane, & Mihalko, 1995), significant gender differences were reported, with men initially being more efficacious than women. Although these differences were not present postprogram in the original study, men and women had statistically different efficacy expectation at five months in the replication study.

It is clear that acute and chronic activity can influence efficacy and that, in turn, physical performance, activity patterns, and adherence might be influenced by efficacy. However, little research has been conducted about the impact that cultural or demographic variables might have in this role. In particular, as the study of physical activity and aging increases, it will be important to take into account that past exposure to exercise opportunities will be less pronounced in older women than in men because of socialization patterns associated with different generations. Additionally, age is likely to have its own independent effect on efficacy. For example, Wilcox and Storandt (1996) reported that age was negatively correlated with self-efficacy in a large cross-sectional sample of women, but that exercisers had significantly higher self-efficacy than nonexercisers. Furthermore, McAuley, Shaffer, and Rudolph (1995) found that older impaired men (mean age = 66.93 years) were less efficacious than their younger counterparts (mean age = 49.18 years) before exercise testing but made significant increases postexercise, whereas the efficacy of the younger adults remained unchanged.

The extent to which physical condition and intensity levels of exercise temper the effects of acute exercise exposures also has been considered. Tate, Petruzzello, and Lox (1995) contrasted efficacy responses under two different exercise intensities and a no-exercise control. Contrasting low- and high-efficacy groups based on a median split, Tate et al. (1995) reported significant increases in efficacy from pre- to postexercise at both 55% and 70% of maximal oxygen uptake. These increases were more marked, as one would expect, in the low-efficacy condition. Similarly, in a contrast of active and less active young adults exercising at 60% of maximal oxygen uptake, Rudolph and McAuley (1995) reported increases in efficacy from pre- to postexercise, with the less active group being less efficacious at both time points but demonstrating proportionally greater increases over time. Clearly, further examination of these potential moderators of the exercise–efficacy relationship is necessary.

As can be seen, examining exercise as a source of efficacy information has typically been conducted in the context of acute exercise bouts. However, an important literature has examined the effects of longer term exercise interventions on self-efficacy and other aspects of psychological function (McAuley & Katula, 1998). A good portion of this work has involved physical activity interventions with clinical samples. In these studies, older individuals suffering from coronary artery disease (e.g., Ewart et al., 1983; Gulanick, 1991; Oldridge & Rogowski, 1990) or chronic obstructive pulmonary disease (e.g., Kaplan, Atkins, & Reinsch, 1984; Toshima, Kaplan, & Ries, 1990) were exposed to an acute bout of exercise, generally a physician-supervised, symptom-limited graded exercise test, followed by an exercise-based intervention. Measures of physical efficacy were taken before and after activity, and in some rare cases during the program and at follow-up.

Kaplan and his colleagues have conducted a longitudinal program of research, part of which has examined exercise–efficacy relationships in a single group of older adults suffering from chronic obstructive pulmonary disease (Kaplan et al., 1984, 1994; Ries, Kaplan, Limberg, & Prewitt, 1995; Toshima et al., 1990). During the study period, subjects completed self-efficacy measures and graded maximal exercise testing at baseline, after a 2-month intervention, and at 6-month intervals for six years. Self-efficacy significantly increased in the experimental group at the end of the intervention and, although these expectations declined at 6-month follow-up, the experimental subjects remained more efficacious than the control group. Further follow-up analyses at 12 and 18 months revealed declines in efficacy in both groups; however, significant group differences remained at the 18-month follow-up, although physical performance differences did not exist beyond 12 months. As noted earlier, self-efficacy was a significant predictor of survival when compared with physiological indicators (Kaplan et al., 1994). In combination, the findings from this series of studies strongly support the role played by exercise interventions in influencing self-efficacy, as well as efficacy being an important correlate of physical health and survival.

A growing body of literature suggests that the effects of exercise on perceptions of personal efficacy are consistent and fairly robust. Such a conclusion appears to hold for studies of both clinical and asymptomatic populations. Although many of these studies adequately measure

© Sally Weigand

Participation in a physically active lifestyle may do much to attenuate age-related declines in physical function.

outcome of acute and chronic exercise participation. Clearly, one of the major quests of exercise and health psychologists is to determine effectively the extent to which the many competing models being used to predict exercise behavior overlap with each other. A number of these models include a self-efficacy component as a key predictor variable. Yet, Bandura (1997b) argued that an overarching social cognitive model effectively subsumes the components of each of these popular approaches to the prediction of exercise and other health-related variables. However, there have been few attempts to pull these social cognitive constructs together in one study, although Dzewaltowski, Noble, and Shaw (1990) compared elements of the planned behavior and social cognitive models. In addition to searching for parsimony in predictive models of exercise behavior, it is imperative that subsequent research adopt longitudinal models to examine the dynamic relationships that exist between efficacy and exercise over time. Additionally, because efficacy appears to be a consistent predictor of physical activity behavior, it will be important to determine which key factors in the exercise environment, prescription, and social milieu might be most effective in enhancing efficacy in the early stages of exercise adoption and adaptation (McAuley et al., 1994).

physical fitness change and self-efficacy, few attempts have been made to examine the extent to which these two important outcome measures are related. Such examination is warranted, because it is not yet clear whether physical activity participation or physical fitness change has a more powerful effect on self-efficacy. For example, many studies reported have focused on older adults. As adults age, there are attendant declines in physical function (flexibility, stamina, mobility, and so forth) that typically are characterized as the natural outcomes of biological aging. However, there is ample evidence to suggest that participation in a physically active lifestyle does much to attenuate these declines. From a social cognitive perspective, these deficits in physical function are theorized to be partially a product of reduced physical efficacy (Bandura, 1997a). Therefore, a more complete examination of the role played by physical activity in the generation of efficacy judgments is warranted.

Beyond the Exercise– Self-Efficacy Relationship

As previously noted, the vast majority of efficacy-related research in the exercise domain has focused on efficacy either as a determinant of physical activity participation over time or as an

EFFICACY AND ATTRIBUTION RELATIONSHIPS

Our review thus far has illustrated how attribution theory and self-efficacy theory have been used as separate theoretical approaches to understanding physical activity behavior. We now review work, albeit limited, that incorporates the broader framework of Bandura's (1986) social cognitive theory in which causal attributions and efficacy cognitions are viewed as reciprocal determinants. From a social cognitive viewpoint, behavior, cognitive and other personal factors, and environmental events interact to determine each other. Central to this conceptualization is the notion that behavior is purposeful and regulated by forethought. This forethought is, in essence, the derivative of self-reflection. Attributional processes are essentially self-reflective processes that attempt to understand the causes of behavioral outcomes. Self-efficacy is also a self-reflective or referent process in that percepts of capabilities often are formed on the basis of information derived from past behaviors. We believe it useful to consider how efficacy and attributional processes might influence each other.

Such a relationship can take two forms. From an attributional perspective (Weiner, 1979, 1985), causal dimensions are theorized to influence affective reactions and expectancies (in this case self-efficacy). Alternatively, Bandura (1986) argued that percepts of efficacy provide information from which causal attributions are formed. For example, highly efficacious children have been shown to attribute failure to lack of effort, whereas less efficacious children ascribe failure to a lack of ability (Collins, 1982). Thus, in a reciprocally determining manner, efficacy is considered to influence the formation of causal attributions and, in turn, these attributions are implicated in the generation of subsequent efficacy expectations. Although these two relationships are not mutually exclusive, they have generally been treated as independent of each other. Indeed, since the last review of this literature (McAuley, 1992a, 1992b), it appears that little progress has been made in empirical attempts to bring together these theoretical models in the physical activity domain. We now review those studies of the attribution–efficacy link followed by those that have considered the effects of efficacy on attributions.

Attributional Influences on Self-Efficacy

In general, very few studies in the physical activity domain have examined this particular relationship in which attributions are the independent variables and self-efficacy is specified distinctly as an outcome of attributional search. In an ambitious recent study, Ingledew et al. (1996) attempted to test an adaptation of Weiner's (1985) model which proposed that attributions influence affective responses and self-efficacy and that these variables would influence subsequent behavior via the mediation of intentions. In a sample of hospital employees ($N = 102$), measures of these constructs were assessed relative to successfully or unsuccessfully carrying out 10 health behaviors, one of which was exercising regularly. This was a longitudinal study assessing current behavior patterns, efficacy, and intention at baseline, then attributions for participants' greatest success or failure, affective responses to this outcome, efficacy, intention, and current behavioral performance one year later. Although a large number of analyses were conducted, we are concerned here with the attribution–efficacy link, and, to some extent, the influence of efficacy on intention and behavior. In the success condition there were no significant relationships between causal dimensions (assessed via the CDSII) and efficacy, and self-efficacy did not predict behavior or intention. In the failure condition, stable and externally controllable attributions were associated with being less efficacious. Once again, efficacy was not related to intention or behavior. However, when each health behavior was considered separately, the authors reported significant associations between efficacy at baseline and intention and behavior one year later, with the efficacy–behavior relationship being attenuated or eliminated when intention was statistically controlled. It is not clear, however, whether these findings were consistent for both failure and success. Additional caution is warranted when interpreting these latter findings because of the single item measurement of efficacy, intention, and behavior; the existence of ceiling effects; and the low number of subjects in analyses of individual behaviors. It is clear from these findings that pooling disparate health behaviors in the testing of theoretical models only reduces our understanding of how model constructs might influence behavior (see also Schoeneman & Curry, 1990).

An additional study in the health behavior domain by Grove (1993) addressed the attribution–efficacy relationship in the context of smoking cessation. Because of the cross-sectional nature of this study, the directionality of the relationship is somewhat blurred. However, Grove (1993) based his arguments in the work of Eiser, van der Pligt, Raw, and Sutton (1985) and viewed efficacy to be predicted by attributions. Smokers ($N = 121$) who had made previous attempts to stop smoking completed attributional measures assessing locus of causality, stability, control, and globality for failure to quit smoking. It appears that all causal dimensions were assessed by single bipolar scales. Self-efficacy was assessed by a barriers efficacy measure (DiClemente, 1981) relative to confidence in abilities to avoid smoking in high-risk situations. Results showed significant but modest correlations between the stability and control dimensions and self-efficacy. More efficacious individuals made less stable and more controllable attributions for previous abstinence failure. Grove (1993) suggested that therapies which focus on changeable and controllable attributions for failure may have important effects on subsequent behavior through their effects on efficacy as a determinant of behavior. Such an approach echoes the "personal changeability" approach to behavior espoused by Anderson (1983) and Schoeneman and Curry (1990) and may have important implications for physical activity behavior.

Self-Efficacy Influences on Attributions

More studies exist that document the effects of efficacy cognitions on causal attributions than the reverse relationship. Early work by Duncan and his colleagues in the physical activity domain (Duncan & McAuley, 1987; McAuley, Duncan, & McElroy, 1989) manipulated self-efficacy prior to cycle ergometry and examined the relationship between self-efficacy and subsequent causal attributions. McAuley et al. (1989) reported that highly self-efficacious children tended to make significantly more controllable and stable attributions for their performance on the ergometer than low-efficacious children. However, Duncan and McAuley (1987) were unable to replicate these findings in an adult sample and suggested that lack of personal involvement and responsibility under laboratory conditions might well alleviate the individual's predisposition to causal search.

McAuley (1991) examined the extent to which past exercise behavior influenced affective responses through the mediation of self-efficacy and causal attributions in middle-aged adults. Path analysis of the temporal relationships indicated that participants who exercised more frequently were more efficacious and made more internal, stable, and controllable attributions for their behavior. Greater self-efficacy was associated with more positive affect and more personally controllable attributions. All three causal dimensions— locus, stability, and personal control—were implicated in the generation of positive affect. These findings support a social cognitive perspective (Bandura, 1986) that causal attributions for events are, in part, structured as a function of the degree of efficacy one has in the domain of interest.

Courneya and McAuley (1993) extended these findings by including another cognitive appraisal process likely to influence affective responses to exercise: perceptions of success. They maintained that self-efficacy and perceived success should influence causal attributions and that efficacy also should be associated with perceived success. More importantly, they argued that perceived success should have a direct effect on affect as well as an indirect effect through causal attributions (Vallerand, 1987). These assumptions were tested in the context of older adults participating in a submaximal graded exercise test after a 5-month walking program. Their results indicated that efficacy had significant positive associations with the dimensions of personal control and stability, both of which influenced affect. Additionally, more efficacious individuals perceived their performance as more successful. Although these findings are in line with social cognitive theory relative to efficacy–attribution relationships, they do not permit inferences relative to behavior or attributional effects on subsequent efficacy. Empirical examination of these processes relative to physical activity behavior is clearly warranted.

These few studies suggest that the self-efficacy–attribution relationship has some support in the physical activity domain. However, further research is needed that explores the complexity of this relationship, the independent and conjoint effects that these variables have on affective responses, and the extent to which these processes are related in the understanding, explanation, and prediction of behavior.

Summary

Although the reciprocal nature of self-efficacy and physical activity is generally well documented, it is clear that the relationship is more complex than would at first appear. Clearly, efficacy does not predict activity patterns at all times, nor do all physical activity stimuli have equal effects on self-efficacy. These relationships can vary according to the action in question, the context under which exposure to activity is experienced, and the temporal nature of the exercise exposure. For example, given the situation-specific nature of self-efficacy, one would expect participation in aerobic exercise and nonaerobic activity to have differential effects on efficacy for walking incremental distances but to have little differential effect on more general measure of physical efficacy. Similarly, efficacy cognitions are more predictive of behavior under challenging circumstances than under habitual demands (McAuley, Lox, & Courneya, 1993). From a contextual standpoint, socially supportive group exercise environments may have markedly different effects on efficacy than would, for example, home-based activity programs. The few studies that have gone beyond the correlational nature of the efficacy–physical activity relationship and have manipulated self-efficacy show promise for furthering our knowledge of how we might structure interventions to maximize efficacy and, in turn, influence both psychosocial and behavioral outcomes associated with exercise.

CONCLUSION

Several studies have been conducted in the last two decades that have embraced attribution and self-efficacy theory, but little effort has been made to examine how these social cognitive perspectives might be related or to help better explain behavior. Attribution theory is at the heart of most cognitive behavioral change theories, and it certainly makes sense that understanding the individual phenomenology relative to *why* people don't exercise or don't comply with exercise prescriptions would be important for maximizing any strategy to change behavior. However, it appears that attribution theory has of late fallen from favor with sport and exercise psychologists. We find this to be particularly disappointing. This apparent fall from grace may have occurred because researchers have not looked beyond simple attributional patterns elicited postevent and, in some cases, empirical forays into the attribution–affect relationship. The extent to which causal attributions influence subsequent behavior through mediating processes such as efficacy and affect generation has largely been ignored (for an exception, see Ingledew et al., 1996). For people to take responsibility for their behavior demands cognitive search relative to why the behavior needs to be changed or why subsequent efforts met with little success (Grove, 1993). Making unstable and personally controllable attributions for previous failures and stable and personally controllable attributions for successes is likely to enhance efficacy and subsequent successful behavior attempts (Anderson, 1983; Schoeneman & Curry, 1990).

In contrast to attribution theory, interest in applying self-efficacy theory to a broad constellation of behaviors, including physical activity, has never been greater. Indeed, the construct has gained such popularity that it is now being inserted into other models of health behavior including the theory of planned behavior (Ajzen, 1985), the health belief model (Rosenstock, 1966), and the transtheoretical model (Prochaska & DiClemente, 1983). However, Bandura (1997b) has criticized such practices, arguing that his social cognitive framework already includes many of the components of these other models, albeit under different rubrics. Human functioning is influenced by numerous mechanisms such as goal mechanisms, self-efficacy mechanisms, and attributional or self-evaluative mechanisms (Bandura & Cervone, 1983). Moreover, social cognitive theory (Bandura, 1986) holds that behavioral, physiological, cognitive, and environmental parameters interact in a reciprocally determining manner. Because a full understanding of behavior as complex as physical activity necessitates an interdisciplinary focus, we believe that social cognitive theory provides a particularly useful theoretical framework for studying such behavior.

REFERENCES

Ajzen, I. (1985). From intentions to actions: A theory of planned behavior. In J. Kuhl & J. Beckmann (Eds.), *Action-control: From cognition to behavior* (pp. 11–39). Heidelberg: Springer.

Ajzen, I. (1987). Attitudes, traits, and actions: Dispositional prediction of behavior in personality and social psychology. In L. Berkowitz (Ed.), *Advances in experimental social psychology* (pp. 1–63). San Diego, CA: Academic Press.

Ajzen, I. (1988). *Attitudes, personality, and behavior*. Chicago: Dorsey Press.

Ajzen, I. (1991). The theory of planned behavior. *Organizational Behavior and Human Decision Processes, 50,* 179–211.

Anderson, C.A. (1983). Motivational and performance deficits in interpersonal settings: The effects of attributional style. *Journal of Personality and Social Psychology, 45,* 1136–1147.

Bandura, A. (1977). Self-efficacy: Towards a unifying theory of behavior change. *Psychological Review, 84,* 191–215.

Bandura, A. (1986). *Social foundations of thought and action: A social cognitive theory*. Englewood Cliffs, NJ: Prentice Hall.

Bandura, A. (1989). Regulation of cognitive processes through perceived self-efficacy. *Developmental Psychology, 25,* 729–735.

Bandura, A. (1995). On rectifying conceptual ecumenism. In J. Maddux (Ed.), *Self-efficacy, adaptation, and adjustment: Theory, research, and application* (pp. 347–375). New York: Plenum Press.

Bandura, A. (1997a). *Self-efficacy: The exercise of control*. New York: Freeman.

Bandura, A. (1997b). The anatomy of stages of change. *American Journal of Health Promotion, 12,* 8–10.

Bandura, A., & Cervone, D. (1983). Self-evaluative and self-efficacy mechanisms governing the motivational effects of goal systems. *Journal of Personality and Social Psychology, 45,* 1017–1028.

Bandura, A., & Wood, R. (1989). Effect of perceived controllability and performance standards on self-regulation of complex decision making. *Journal of Personality and Social Psychology, 56,* 805–814.

Biddle, S., Goudas, M., & Page, A. (1994). Social-psychological predictors of self-reported actual and intended physical activity in a university workforce sample. *British Journal of Sports Medicine, 28,* 160–163.

Biddle, S., & Hanrahan, S. (1998). Attributions and attributional style. In J.L. Duda (Ed.), *Advances in sport and exercise psychology measurement* (pp. 3–19). Morgantown, WV: Fitness Information Technology.

Biddle, S.J.H., & Hill, A.B. (1992a). Attributions for objective outcome and subjective appraisal of performance: Their relationship with emotional reactions in sport. *British Journal of Social Psychology, 31,* 215–226.

Biddle, S.J.H., & Hill, A.B. (1992b). Relationships between attributions and emotions in a laboratory-based sporting contest. *Journal of Sports Sciences, 10,* 65–75.

Bird, A.M., & Williams, J.M. (1980). A developmental-attributional analysis of sex-role stereotypes for sport performance. *Developmental Psychology, 16,* 319–322.

Blanchard-Fields, F. (1994). Age differences in causal attributions from an adult developmental perspective. *Journals of Gerontology: Psychological Sciences, 49,* P43–P51.

Bock, B.C., Albrecht, A.E., Traficante, R.M., Clark, M.M., Pinto, B.M., Tilkemeier, P., & Marcus, B.H. (1997). Predictors of exercise adherence following participation in a cardiac rehabilitation program. *International Journal of Behavioral Medicine, 4,* 60–75.

Bradley, G.W. (1978). Self-serving biases in the attribution process: A reexamination of the fact or fiction question. *Journal of Personality and Social Psychology, 36,* 56–71.

Bukowski, W.M., & Moore, D. (1982). Winners' and losers' attributions for success and failure in a series of athletic events. *Journal of Sport Psychology, 2,* 195–210.

Cardinal, B.J. (1997). Construct validity of stages of change for exercise behavior. *American Journal of Health Promotion, 12,* 68–74.

Chipperfield, J.G., & Segall, A. (1996). Seniors' attributions for task performance difficulties: Implications for feelings of task efficacy. *Journal of Aging and Health, 8,* 489–511.

Collins, J. (1982, March). *Self-efficacy and ability in achievement behavior.* Paper presented at the meeting of The American Educational Research Association, New York.

Courneya, K.S., & McAuley, E. (1993). Efficacy, attributional, and affective responses of older adults following an acute bout of exercise. *Journal of Social Behavior and Personality, 8,* 729–742.

Courneya, K.S., & McAuley, E. (1994). Are there different determinants of the frequency, intensity, and duration of physical activity? *Behavioral Medicine, 20,* 84–90.

Courneya, K.S., & McAuley, E. (1996). Understanding intentions to exercise following a structured exercise program: An attributional perspective. *Journal of Applied Social Psychology, 26,* 670–685.

DiClemente, C.C. (1981). Self-efficacy and smoking cessation maintenance: A preliminary report. *Cognitive Therapy and Research, 5,* 175–187.

DuCharme, K.A., & Brawley, L.R. (1995). Predicting the intentions and behavior of exercise initiates using two forms of self-efficacy. *Journal of Behavioral Medicine, 18,* 479–497.

Duncan, T.E., & McAuley, E. (1987). Efficacy expectations and perceptions of causality in motor performance. *Journal of Sport Psychology, 9,* 385–393.

Duncan, T.E., & McAuley, E. (1989, April). *Cognition and emotion following sport performance: A causal model.* Paper presented at the national meeting of the American Alliance for Health, Physical Education, Recreation and Dance, Boston.

Dzewaltowski, D.A. (1989). Toward a model of exercise motivation. *Journal of Sport & Exercise Psychology, 11,* 251–269.

Dzewaltowski, D.A., Noble, J.M., & Shaw, J.M. (1990). Physical activity participation: Social cognitive theory versus the theories of reasoned action and planned behavior. *Journal of Sport & Exercise Psychology, 12,* 388–405.

Eiser, J.R., van der Pligt, J., Raw, M., & Sutton, S.R. (1985). Trying to stop smoking: Effects of perceived addiction, attributions for failure, and expectancy of success. *Journal of Behavioral Medicine, 8,* 321–341.

Ewart, C.K., Stewart, K.J., Gillilan, R.E., & Kelemen, M.H. (1986). Self-efficacy mediates strength gains during circuit weight training in men with coronary artery disease. *Medicine and Science in Sports and Exercise, 18,* 531–540.

Ewart, C.K., Stewart, K.J., Gillilan, R.E., Kelemen, M.H., Valenti, S.A., Manley, J.D., & Kelemen, M.D. (1986). Usefulness of self-efficacy in predicting overexertion during programmed exercise in coronary artery disease. *American Journal of Cardiology, 57,* 557–561.

Ewart, C.K., Taylor, C.B., Reese, L.B., & DeBusk, R.F. (1983). Effects of early postmyocardial infarction exercise testing on self-perception and subsequent physical activity. *American Journal of Cardiology, 51,* 1076–1080.

Feltz, D.L. (1992). Understanding motivation in sport: A self-efficacy perspective. In G.C. Roberts (Ed.), *Motivation in sport and exercise* (pp. 93–106). Champaign, IL: Human Kinetics.

Fletcher, G.J.O., Danilovics, P., Fernandez, G., Peterson, D., & Reeder, G.D. (1986). Attributional complexity: An individual difference measure. *Journal of Personality and Social Psychology, 51,* 875–884.

Forsyth, D.R., & McMillan, J.H. (1981). Attributions, affect, and expectations: A test of Weiner's three-dimensional model. *Journal of Educational Psychology, 73,* 393–403.

Gauvin, L., & Rejeski, W.J. (1993). The Exercise-Induced Feeling Inventory: Development and initial validation. *Journal of Sport & Exercise Psychology, 15,* 403–423.

Gorley, T., & Gordon, S. (1995). An examination of the transtheoretical model and exercise behavior in older adults. *Journal of Sport & Exercise Psychology, 17,* 312–324.

Grove, J.R. (1993). Attributional correlates of cessation self-efficacy among smokers. *Addictive Behaviors, 18,* 311–320.

Gulanick, M. (1991). Is phase 2 cardiac rehabilitation necessary for early recovery of patients with cardiac disease? A randomized, controlled study. *Heart and Lung, 20,* 9–15.

Heider, F. (1958). *The psychology of interpersonal relations.* New York: Wiley.

Hendy, H.M., & Boyer, B.J. (1993). Gender differences in attributions for triathlon performance. *Sex Roles, 29,* 527–543.

Hovell, M., Sallis, J., Hofstetter, R., Barrington, E., Hackley, M., Elder, J., Castro, F., & Kilbourne, K. (1991). Identification of correlates of physical activity among Latino adults. *Journal of Community Health, 16,* 23–36.

Ingledew, D.K., Hardy, L., & Cooper, C.L. (1996). An attributional model applied to health behavior change. *European Journal of Personality, 10,* 111–132.

Jones, E.E., & Davis, K.E. (1965). From acts to dispositions: The attribution process in person perception. In L. Berkowitz (Ed.), *Advances in experimental social psychology* (Vol. 2, pp. 219–226). New York: Academic Press.

Kaplan, R.M., Atkins, C.J., & Reinsch, S. (1984). Specific efficacy expectations mediate exercise compliance in patients with COPD. *Health Psychology, 3,* 223–242.

Kaplan, R.M., Ries, A.L., Prewitt, L.M., & Eakin, E. (1994). Self-efficacy expectations predict survival for patients with chronic obstructive pulmonary disease. *Health Psychology, 13,* 366–368.

Kavussanu, M., & McAuley, E. (1995). Exercise and optimism: Are highly active individuals more optimistic? *Journal of Sport & Exercise Psychology, 17,* 246–258.

Kelley, H.H. (1973). The process of causal attribution. *American Psychologist, 28,* 107–128.

Lechner, L., & De Vries, H. (1995). Starting participation in an employee fitness program: Attitudes, social influence, and self-efficacy. *Preventive Medicine, 24,* 627–633.

Long, B.C. (1985). Stress-management interventions: A 15-month follow-up of aerobic conditioning and stress inoculation training. *Cognitive Therapy and Research, 9,* 471–478.

Maddux, J. (1995). Looking for common ground: A comment on Bandura and Kirsch. In J. Maddux (Ed.), *Self-efficacy, adaptation, and adjustment: Theory, research, and application* (pp. 377–385). New York: Plenum Press.

Marcus, B.H., Eaton, C.A., Rossi, J.S., & Harlow, L.L. (1994). Self-efficacy, decision-making, and stages of change: An integrative model of physical exercise. *Journal of Applied Social Psychology, 24,* 489–508.

Marcus, B.H., & Owen, N. (1992). Motivational readiness, self-efficacy and decision-making for exercise. *Journal of Applied Social Psychology, 22,* 3–16.

Marcus, B.H., Pinto, B.M., Simkin, L.R., Audrain, J.E., & Taylor, E.R. (1994). Application of theoretical models to exercise behavior among employed women. *American Journal of Health Promotion, 9,* 49–55.

Marcus, B.H., Selby, V.C., Niaura, R.S., & Rossi, J.S. (1992). Self-efficacy and the stages of exercise behavior change. *Research Quarterly for Exercise and Sport, 63,* 60–66.

Martinek, T.J., & Griffith, J.B. (1994). Learned helplessness in physical education: A developmental study of causal attributions and task persistence. *Journal of Teaching in Physical Education, 13,* 108–122.

McAuley, E. (1991). Efficacy, attributional, and affective responses to exercise participation. *Journal of Sport & Exercise Psychology, 13,* 382–393.

McAuley, E. (1992a). Exercise and motivation: A self-efficacy perspective. In G.C. Roberts (Ed.), *Motivation in sport and exercise* (pp. 107–128). Champaign, IL: Human Kinetics.

McAuley, F. (1992b). Self-referent thought in sport and physical activity. In T.S. Horn (Ed.), *Advances in sport psychology* (pp. 101–118). Champaign, IL: Human Kinetics.

McAuley, E. (1993a). The role of efficacy cognitions in the prediction of exercise behavior in middle-aged adults. *Journal of Behavioral Medicine, 15,* 65–88.

McAuley, E. (1993b). Self-efficacy and the maintenance of exercise participation in older adults. *Journal of Behavioral Medicine, 16,* 103–113.

McAuley, E., Bane, S.M., & Milhalko, S.L. (1995). Exercise in middle-aged adults: Self efficacy and self-presentational outcomes. *Preventive Medicine, 24,* 319–328.

McAuley, E., & Courneya, K.S. (1992). Self-efficacy relationships with affective and exertion responses to exercise. *Journal of Applied Social Psychology, 22,* 312–326.

McAuley, E., & Courneya, K.S. (1994). The Subjective Exercise Experience Scale (SEES): Development and preliminary validation. *Journal of Sport & Exercise Psychology, 16,* 67–96.

McAuley, E., Courneya, K.S., & Lettunich, J. (1991). Effects of acute and long-term exercise on self-efficacy responses in sedentary, middle-aged males and females. *The Gerontologist, 31,* 534–542.

McAuley, E., Courneya, K.S., Rudolph, D.L., & Lox, C.L. (1994). Enhancing exercise adherence in middle-aged males and females. *Preventive Medicine, 23,* 498–506.

McAuley, E., & Duncan T.E. (1989). Causal attributions and affective reactions to disconfirming outcomes in motor performance. *Journal of Exercise & Sport Psychology, 11,* 187–200.

McAuley, E., & Duncan, T.E. (1990). The causal attribution process in sport and physical activity. In S. Graham & V. Folkes (Eds.), *Attribution theory: Applications to achievement, mental health, and interpersonal conflict* (pp. 37–52). Hillsdale, NJ: Erlbaum.

McAuley, E., Duncan, T.E., & McElroy, M. (1989). Self-efficacy cognitions and causal attributions for children's motor performance: An exploratory investigation. *Journal of Genetic Psychology, 150,* 65–73.

McAuley, E., Duncan, T.E., & Russell, D. (1992). Measuring causal attributions: The revised Causal Dimension Scale (CDSII). *Personality and Social Psychology Bulletin, 18,* 566–573.

McAuley, E., & Gross, J.B. (1983). Perceptions of causality in sport: An application of the Causal Dimension Scale. *Journal of Sport Psychology, 5,* 72–76.

McAuley, E., & Katula, J. (1998). Physical activity interventions in the elderly: Influence on physical health and psychological function. In R. Schulz, M.P. Lawton, & G. Maddux (Eds.), *Annual review of gerontology and geriatrics* (Vol. 18, pp. 115–154). New York: Springer.

McAuley, E., Lox, D.L., & Duncan, T. (1993). Long-term maintenance of exercise, self-efficacy, and physiological change in older adults. *Journal of Gerontology, 48,* P218–P223.

McAuley, E., & Mihalko, S. (1998). Measuring exercise-related self-efficacy. In J. Duda (Ed.), *Advances in sport and exercise psychology measurement* (pp. 371–390). Morgantown, WV: Fitness Information Technology.

McAuley, E., Peña, M., & Jerome, J.G. (2001). Self-efficacy as a determinant and an outcome of exercise. In G.C. Roberts (Ed.), *Motivation in sport and exercise* (2nd ed., pp. 235–262). Champaign IL: Human Kinetics.

McAuley, E., Poag, K., Gleason, A., & Wraith, S. (1990). Attrition from exercise programs: Attributional and affective processes. *Journal of Social Behavior and Personality, 5,* 591–602.

McAuley, E., Russell, R., & Gross, J.B. (1983). Affective consequences of winning and losing: An attributional analysis. *Journal of Sport Psychology, 5,* 278–287.

McAuley, E., & Shaffer, S. (1993). Affective responses to externally and personally controllable attributions. *Basic and Applied Social Psychology, 14,* 475–485.

McAuley, E., Shaffer, S.M., & Rudolph, D. (1995). Affective responses to acute exercise in elderly impaired males: The moderating effects of self-efficacy and age. *International Journal of Aging and Human Development, 41,* 13–27.

Meyer, J.P., & Koelbl, S.L.M. (1982). Students' test performances: Dimensionality of causal attributions. *Personality and Social Psychology Bulletin, 8,* 31–36.

Minifee, M., & McAuley, E. (1998). An attributional perspective on African American adults' exercise behavior. *Journal of Applied Social Psychology, 28,* 924–936.

Morgan, L.K., Griffin, J., & Heyward, V.H. (1996). Ethnicity, gender, and experience effects on attributional dimensions. *The Sport Psychologist, 10,* 4–16.

Newton, M., & Duda, J.L. (1993). The relationship of task and ego orientation to performance-cognitive content, affect, and attributions in bowling. *Journal of Sport Behavior, 16,* 209–220.

Oldridge, N.B., & Rogowski, B.L. (1990). Self-efficacy and in-patient cardiac rehabilitation. *American Journal of Cardiology, 66,* 362–365.

Passer, M.W. (1977). *Perceiving the causes of success and failure revisited: A multidimensional scaling approach.* Unpublished doctoral dissertation, University of California, Los Angeles.

Prochaska, J.O., & DiClemente, C.C. (1983). Stages and processes of self-change of smoking: Toward an integrative model of change. *Journal of Consulting and Clinical Psychology, 51,* 390–395.

Prochaska, J.O., & DiClemente, C.C. (1985). Common processes of self-change in smoking, weight control, and psychological distress. In S. Shiffman & T. Willis (Eds.),

Coping and substance use (pp. 345–363). New York: Academic Press.

Prochaska, J.O., & Velicer, W.F. (1997). Misinterpretations and misapplications of the transtheoretical model. *American Journal of Health Promotion, 12,* 11–12.

Rejeski, W., & Brawley, L. (1983). Attribution theory in sport: Current status and new perspective. *Journal of Sport Psychology, 5,* 77–99.

Ries, A.L., Kaplan, R.M., Limberg, T.M., & Prewitt, L.M. (1995). Effects of pulmonary rehabilitation on physiologic and psychosocial outcomes in patients with chronic obstructive pulmonary disease. *Annals of Internal Medicine, 122,* 823–832.

Roberts, G.C., & Pascuzzi, D. (1979). Causal attributions in sport: Some theoretical implications. *Journal of Sport Psychology, 1,* 203–211.

Robinson, D.W., & Howe, B.L. (1989). Appraisal variable/affect relationships in youth sports: A test of Weiner's attributional model. *Journal of Sport & Exercise Psychology, 11,* 431–443.

Rodgers, W.M., & Brawley, L.R. (1996). The influence of outcome expectancy and self-efficacy on the behavioral intentions of novice exercisers. *Journal of Applied Social Psychology, 26,* 618–634.

Rosenstock, I.M. (1966). Why people use health services. *Milbank Memorial Fund Quarterly, 44,* 94–124.

Rudolph, D.L., & McAuley, E. (1995). Self-efficacy and salivary cortisol responses to acute exercise in physically active and less active adults. *Journal of Sport & Exercise Psychology, 17,* 206–213.

Russell, D. (1982). The Causal Dimension Scale: A measure of how individuals perceive causes. *Journal of Personality and Social Psychology, 42,* 1137–1145.

Russell, D., McAuley, E., & Tarico, V. (1987). Measuring causal attributions for success and failure: A comparison of methodologies for assessing causal dimensions. *Journal of Personality and Social Psychology, 52,* 1248–1257.

Ryckman, R.M., Robbins, M.A., Thornton, B., & Cantrell, P. (1982). Development and validation of a physical self-efficacy scale. *Journal of Personality and Social Psychology, 42,* 891–900.

Sallis, J.F., Haskell, W.L., Fortmann, S.T., Vranizan, K.M., Taylor, C.B., & Solomon, D.S. (1986). Predictors of adoption and maintenance of physical activity in a community sample. *Preventive Medicine, 15,* 331–341.

Sallis, J.F., & Hovell, M.F. (1990). Determinants of exercise behavior. *Exercise and Sport Sciences Reviews, 18,* 307–330.

Sallis, J.F., Hovell, M.F., Hofstetter, C.R., & Barrington, E. (1992). Explanation of vigorous physical activity during two years using social learning variables. *Social Science and Medicine, 34,* 25–32.

Sallis, J.F., Hovell, M.F., Hofstetter, C.R., Faucher, P., Elder, J.P., Blanchard, J., Casperson, C.J., Powell, K.E., & Christenson, G.M. (1989). A multivariate study of determinants of vigorous exercise in a community sample. *Preventive Medicine, 18,* 20–34.

Schoeneman, T.J., & Curry, S. (1990). Attributions for successful and unsuccessful health behavior change. *Basic and Applied Social Psychology, 11,* 421–431.

Tate, A.K., Petruzzello, S.J., & Lox, C.L. (1995). Examination of the relationship between self-efficacy and affect at varying levels of aerobic exercise intensity. *Journal of Applied Social Psychology, 25,* 1922–1936.

Taylor, C.B., Bandura, A., Ewart, C.K., Miller, N.H., & DeBusk, R.F. (1985). Exercise testing to enhance wives' confidence in their husbands' cardiac capability soon after clinically uncomplicated acute myo-cardial infarction. *American Journal of Cardiology, 55,* 635–638.

Terry, D.J., & O'Leary, J.E. (1995). The theory of planned behaviour: The effects of perceived behavioural control and self-efficacy. *British Journal of Social Psychology, 34,* 199–220.

Tipton, R.M., & Worthington, E.L. (1984). The measurement of generalized self-efficacy: A study of construct validity. *Journal of Personality Assessment, 48,* 545–548.

Toshima, M.T., Kaplan, R.M., & Ries, A.L. (1990). Experimental evaluation of rehabilitation in chronic obstructive pulmonary disease: Short-term effects on exercise endurance and health status. *Health Psychology, 9*(3), 237–252.

Vallerand, R.J. (1987). Antecedents of self-related affects in sport: Preliminary evidence on the intuitive-reflective appraisal model. *Journal of Sport Psychology, 9,* 161–182.

Vlachopoulos, S., Biddle, S., & Fox, K. (1996). A social-cognitive investigation into the mechanisms of affect generation in children's physical activity. *Journal of Sport & Exercise Psychology, 18,* 174–193.

Weiner, B. (1972). *Theories of motivation: From mechanism to cognition.* Chicago: Rand-McNally.

Weiner, B. (1979). A theory of motivation for some classroom experience. *Journal of Educational Psychology, 71,* 3–25.

Weiner, B. (1983). Some methodological pitfalls in attribution research. *Journal of Educational Psychology, 75,* 530–543.

Weiner, B. (1985). An attributional theory of achievement motivation and emotion. *Psychological Review, 92,* 548–573.

Weiner, B. (1986). *An attributional theory of motivation and emotion.* New York: Springer-Verlag.

Weiner, B., Frieze, I., Kukla, A., Reed, L., Rest, S., & Rosenbaum, R.M. (1971*). Perceiving the causes of success and failure.* Morristown, NJ: General Learning Press.

Weiner, B., Russell, D., & Lerman, D. (1979). The cognition-emotion process in achievement-related contexts. *Journal of Personality and Social Psychology, 37,* 1211–1220.

White, S.A. (1993). The effect of gender and age on causal attribution in softball players. *International Journal of Sport Psychology, 24,* 49–58.

Wilcox, S., & Storandt, M. (1996). Relations among age, exercise, and psychological variables in a community sample of women. *Health Psychology, 15,* 110–113.

Wyse, J., Mercer, T., Ashford, B., Buxton, K., & Gleeson, N. (1995). Evidence for the validity and utility of the stages of exercise behaviour change scale in young adults. *Health Education Research, 10,* 365–377.

Yordy, G.A., & Lent, R.W. (1993). Predicting aerobic exercise participation: Social cognitive, reasoned action, and planned behavior models. *Journal of Sport & Exercise Psychology, 15,* 363–374.

Zuckerman, M. (1979). Attribution of success and failure revisited or: The motivational bias is alive and well in attribution theory. *Journal of Personality, 47,* 245–287.

CHAPTER 7

Arousal–Anxiety and Sport Behavior

Daniel Gould, Christy Greenleaf, and Vikki Krane

The relationship between emotional arousal and athletic performance, as well as the related topics of stress and anxiety, has been of central importance throughout the history of sport psychology. As early as 1932, Coleman Griffith, the father of North American sport psychology, referred to the arousal–performance relationship when he discussed the advisability of "keying up teams" and identifying strategies for dealing with athletes' "anxiety and fright" states. In a content analysis of applied sport psychology texts, Vealey (1988) found that arousal control was discussed by 70% of the authors, whereas the method of relaxation training was discussed by 93% of the authors. Finally, virtually every contemporary academic sport psychology text (e.g., Cox, 1998; Gill, 2000; Hardy, Jones, & Gould, 1996; Weinberg & Gould, 1999; Williams, 2001) has devoted considerable attention to the interrelated topics of arousal, anxiety, and stress.

Since the late 1960s, most sport psychology writers (e.g., Cox, 1998; Landers & Boutcher, 1998; Sonstroem, 1984) have emphasized the notion that an optimal level of arousal is associated with best performance, whereas arousal levels above or below optimal level are related to inferior performance. Indeed, the inverted-U hypothesis has become a stable conceptual principle in both the academic and professional sport psychology literature (see Sonstroem, 1984, pp. 108–109). In the last 15 years, however, a number of European sport psychologists (Hardy & Fazey, 1987; Jones & Hardy, 1989; Kerr, 1997) have critically examined the inverted-U hypothesis and have questioned both its conceptual and practical utility. These same criticisms also have begun to emerge in the North American sport psychology literature (Gould & Udry, 1994; Martens, 1987a; Neiss, 1988; Weinberg, 1990). From a different but certainly related perspective, a number of sport psychology investigators (Burton, 1988; Gould, Petlichkoff, Simons, & Vevera, 1987; Hardy et al., 1996; Martens, Vealey, & Burton, 1990) have stated that anxiety is a multidimensional rather than a unitary phenomenon. These researchers have demonstrated that the two different dimensions of anxiety (i.e., somatic and cognitive anxiety states) have differential effects on athletic performance. Finally, important distinctions have begun to be made between anxiety that is seen as facilitative versus debilitative and how such interpretations may influence the arousal–performance relationship (Hanin, 1997; Jones, 1995, 1996; Kerr, 1997).

Given the number of conceptual and methodological changes proposed concerning the arousal–performance relationship, a need exists for an in-depth examination of the current status of research on the topic. The intent of this chapter is to provide such an examination. In addition, in this chapter we examine conceptual systems for providing future research directions, identify central research issues, and recognize methodological refinements and needs.

First, the relationships among anxiety, stress, arousal, activation, and related terms are discussed. This is an important issue, given that major interpretive problems have beset the literature because these terms often are used interchangeably although they are conceptually distinct. Second, we examine and discuss hypotheses and theories about the arousal–performance relationship. These include drive theory, the inverted-U hypothesis, Hanin's (1989) individualized zones of optimal functioning (arousal) hypothesis, multidimensional anxiety theory, Hardy and Fazey's (1987) application of the catastrophe model, Kerr's (1985, 1987) reversal theory interpretation, and Jones and Swain's (1992, 1995) notion of intensity and direction (facilitative vs. debilitative) anxiety. Finally, we present future conceptual and methodological directions for arousal–performance relationship research and identify critical research questions.

DEFINING AROUSAL, STRESS, ANXIETY, AND RELATED TERMS

A long-standing problem in the study of the arousal–performance relationship has been the inconsistent use of terms such as *arousal, stress,* and *anxiety.* These terms have been used interchangeably (e.g., Gould, Petlichkoff, & Weinberg, 1984; Landers, Wang, & Courtet, 1985), although numerous theoretical distinctions have been made among them. The first step in eliminating this semantic confusion is to provide concise operational definitions of the various anxiety-related constructs. Therefore, we next discuss the constructs of arousal, state anxiety, trait anxiety, cognitive anxiety, somatic anxiety, interpersonal state anxiety, and group state anxiety and provide operational definitions for these terms.

Arousal

Arousal typically has been referred to as a unitary construct that embraces both the psychological and physiological energetic systems. Landers defined arousal as "a motivational construct" that represents "the intensity level of behavior" (1980, p. 77). Arousal typically is seen as varying along a continuum from deep sleep to extreme excitement (Malmo, 1959). Landers and Boutcher also view arousal on a continuum and defined it as "an energizing function that is responsible for harnessing of the body's resources for intense and vigorous activity" (1998, p. 198).

Measurements of physiological arousal can be classified as electrophysiological, respiratory and cardiovascular, or biochemical (Hackfort & Schwenkmezger, 1989). Typical measures of arousal include heart rate, blood pressure, respiration rate, electrocortical activity (electroencephalograph), electromyography, biochemical indicants such as epinephrine or adrenaline, and galvanic skin response. Arousal also has been assessed through self-report scales such as the Thayer (1967) Activation–Deactivation Checklist.

As noted earlier, arousal traditionally has been seen as a unitary construct reflecting how activated a performer is at a given moment in time. Contrary to this unitary notion of arousal, Hardy et al. (1996), drawing on the work of Pribram and McGuinness (1975), proposed that arousal and activation are not the same, as has been assumed in the traditional arousal–sport performance research. In contrast, they proposed a more complex and differentiated view of arousal and activation. These authors contend that both activation and arousal involve cognitive and physiological activity of the organism. However, "activation is a complex multidimensional state which reflects the organism's anticipatory readiness to respond, while arousal refers to the organism's immediate response to new stimuli or input" (Hardy et al., 1996, p. 135). Thus, a golfer attempting to make an 8-foot putt tries to achieve some optimal psychological and physiological state before executing the putt. When some other stimulus (e.g., a camera shutter click) becomes evident, however, the performer responds to the new stimulus with arousal. Peak performance, then, comes when one is appropriately activated and arousal does not interfere with this task-specific activation level. Changes in a performer's arousal will improve performance only to the extent they will induce a more, rather than less, appropriate activation pattern.

In this chapter, arousal and activation are differentiated as previously described. However, for simplicity's sake, we refer to arousal-activation implying a complex multifaceted blend of physiological and psychological activity in the organism that varies on a continuum from deep sleep to intense excitement.

Anxiety

Martens (1977) suggested that anxiety reactions result from an objective environmental demand interpreted as threatening (a perceived imbalance between the demand and one's response capabilities) by an individual. Hence, *anxiety* has been viewed as feelings of nervousness and tension associated with activation or arousal of the organism.

Spielberger (1966, 1972) further noted that for a theory of anxiety to be adequate, it must differentiate between anxiety as a mood state and as a personality trait. Additionally, it must differentiate among the stimulus conditions antecedent to these forms of anxiety. Spielberger (1966) proposed the state–trait theory of anxiety, which differentiates between state and trait anxiety. *State anxiety* (A-state) is defined as an emotional state "characterized by subjective, consciously perceived feelings of apprehension and tension, accompanied by or associated with activation or arousal of the autonomic nervous system" (Spielberger, 1966, p. 17). This condition varies from moment to moment and fluctuates proportional to the perceived threat in the immediate situation. *Trait anxiety* (A-trait), on the other hand, is "a motive or acquired behavioral disposition that predisposes an individual to perceive a wide range of objectively nondangerous circumstances as threatening and to respond to these with state anxiety reactions disproportionate in intensity to the magnitude of the objective danger" (Spielberger, 1966, p. 17). The state–trait theory of anxiety predicts that high-trait-anxious individuals will perceive more situations as threatening and react with greater state anxiety in a greater variety of situations than low-trait-anxious individuals.

Anxiety typically has been measured with self-report questionnaires. Although there are many criticisms of self-report measures, especially in regard to their susceptibility to social desirability bias (Hackfort & Schwenkmezger, 1989; Neiss, 1988; Williams & Krane, 1989, 1992), psychological inventories have become the more popular measure of anxiety because of ease of administration, especially in field settings. Martens defended their use by stating that "the assessment of A-state through self-report measures tells us more about the subject's general state (of arousal) than any single or composite index of physiological measures" (1977, p. 115).

Still, as cautioned by Martens et al. (1990) and Williams and Krane (1989, 1992), researchers need to be aware of the potential for social desirability bias and take steps to minimize it. This can be accomplished by developing a good rapport with athletes, using anti–social desirability instructions with questionnaires, and using a social desirability scale to identify athletes likely to repress their true feelings. More recently, R.E. Smith, Schutz, Smoll, and Ptacek (1995) discussed self-deception (or athletes' efforts to unknowingly deceive themselves that they are not anxious, that they are confident, etc.) as another problem with psychological self-report measures. Although this self-deception problem is more difficult to address than social desirability, it should not be overlooked.

Several self-report anxiety inventories commonly are used in sport psychology. Consistent with his state–trait theory of anxiety, Spielberger and his colleagues (Spielberger, Gorsuch, & Lushene, 1970a, 1970b) developed the State–Trait Anxiety Inventory (STAI), which differentiated between state and trait anxiety. This became a popular tool in sport psychology and is still being used by a number of sport and exercise psychology researchers to study anxiety. As the investigation of anxiety in sport psychology progressed, Martens (1977) expressed the need for sport-specific measures of anxiety and developed the Sport Competition Anxiety Test (SCAT) to measure competitive trait anxiety. Competitive trait anxiety was defined as the "tendency to perceive competitive sport situations as threatening and to respond to these situations with feelings of apprehension and tension" (Martens, 1977, p. 23). Martens also noted the need for a sport-specific measure of state anxiety. His modification of the state scale of Spielberger's STAI resulted in the Competitive State Anxiety Inventory (CSAI).

Thus, state anxiety is associated with heightened physiological arousal as a result of increased sympathetic nervous system activity and is defined as a transitory state, or a "right now" feeling of apprehension and tension in a specific situation. Trait anxiety is defined as how one generally feels, or a relatively stable predisposition to perceive a wide range of situations as threatening and to respond to these with state anxiety. Both forms of anxiety are typically assessed via psychological inventories.

Differentiating Between Cognitive and Somatic Anxiety

Considerable sport psychology literature has focused on the multidimensional nature of anxiety (e.g., Burton, 1988; Gould et al., 1987; Krane & Williams, 1987, 1994; Martens et al., 1990). This line of research stems from the work of Borkovec (1976) and Davidson and Schwartz (1976), who differentiated between cognitive and somatic anxiety. Borkovec noted that there are "three separate but interacting" response components of anxiety: cognitive, physiological, and overt behavioral. *Cognitive anxiety* was operationalized as negative concerns about performance, inability to concentrate, and disrupted attention, whereas *somatic anxiety* was operationalized as perceptions of bodily symptoms of autonomic reactivity such as butterflies in the stomach, sweating, shakiness, and increased heart rate (Davidson & Schwartz, 1976; Kauss, 1980; Martens et al., 1990). Behavioral components of anxiety focus on such indicants as facial expressions, changes in communication patterns, and restlessness (Hanson & Gould, 1988).

Although previous research in general psychology and test anxiety had differentiated between cognitive and somatic anxiety, Martens, Burton, Vealey, Bump, and Smith (1990) stimulated this line of research in sport psychology with the development of the CSAI-2, which consisted of separate measures of cognitive and somatic anxiety. (The CSAI-2 also consists of a Self-Confidence subscale, but here we examine the scale only as it directly relates to anxiety research.) Although other multidimensional measures of anxiety have been used by researchers in sport psychology (e.g., Cognitive–Somatic Anxiety Questionnaire; Schwartz, Davidson & Goleman, 1978), the CSAI-2 remains the most commonly used multidimensional anxiety measure.

A multidimensional measure of trait anxiety also was developed by R.E. Smith, Smoll, and Schutz (1990). The Sport Anxiety Scale (SAS) was developed as a sport-specific measure of somatic reactions, cognitive worry, and concentration disruption. Univariate trait anxiety consistently has been found to be highly correlated with both state cognitive and somatic anxiety (Gould et al., 1984; Vealey, 1990). As expected, Krane and Finch (1991) found that trait cognitive and somatic anxiety significantly predicted state cognitive and somatic anxiety, respectively. Krane, Joyce, and Rafeld (1994) further supported the notion that trait cognitive anxiety can predict state cognitive anxiety. However, they also found that state somatic anxiety was most strongly related to concentration disruption, whereas Alexander and Krane (1996) found that trait and state cognitive and somatic anxiety were not significantly related. Additional research is needed to better understand these equivocal results.

Intrapersonal and Group State–Trait Anxiety

Hanin (1989) approached the study of anxiety from a social–psychological perspective. Thus, he incorporated emotional reactions and the social environment into his conceptualization of state anxiety. Like most contemporary anxiety researchers, then, he studied anxiety as an interaction between the person and the environment. The strength of this approach is that it is holistic and does not separate behavior into separate entities; that is, anxiety is examined within the context of relationships with other people and specific qualities of the environment.

Performance anxiety, for Hanin (1989) an emotional reaction experienced while working on a specific task, was further divided into *interpersonal state anxiety* ($S = A_{int}$) and *intragroup state anxiety* ($S = A_{gr}$): "Both constructs refer to the emotional reactions experienced by a person at a given moment in time as a function of *his/her involvement with a particular partner* ($S = A_{int}$) and/or as a member *of a group or team* ($S = A_{gr}$)" (Hanin, 1989, p. 21). Hanin further differentiated between performance anxiety and optimal state anxiety. Optimal *state anxiety* is defined as "the level of performance state anxiety that enables a particular athlete to perform at his/her personal best" (Hanin, 1989, p. 22), whereas *performance anxiety* is his or her specific level of state anxiety in a particular competitive situation.

Interpersonal state anxiety and intragroup state anxiety have been assessed with the Russian adaptation of Spielberger's STAI (STAI-R; Hanin & Spielberger, 1983). The only difference between the English and Russian measures were the instructions. When measuring interpersonal state anxiety, the STAI-R asks the athlete to complete the questionnaire according to "how he/she felt at a particular moment while in actual or anticipated contact with a particular person (partner, coach, trainer, sports administrator, rival, referee, etc.)" (p. 22). When measuring intragroup state anxiety, the athlete is asked "to evaluate how he/she feels at a particular moment as a team member" (p. 22).

Unfortunately, although Hanin's definitions of interpersonal and intergroup anxiety are interesting, little research has been conducted to examine their utility. A need exists for such research.

Metamotivational States and Facilitative Anxiety

To better understand the arousal–performance relationship, Kerr (1985, 1997) advocated the use of Apter's (1976, 1984) theory of psychological reversals, which suggested that high arousal can at times be perceived as either positive or negative. Specifically, Apter's theory of psychological reversals holds that increased arousal may be interpreted as anxiety or excitement depending on one's *metamotivational state*. In a *telic* metamoti-vational state, the subject is goal-directed and serious and high arousal is perceived as negative affect, much like (in our view synonymous with) high state anxiety. In a *paratelic,* high-arousal metamotivational state, however, the subject (in our case, athlete) is in an activity-oriented, playful, positive affect state that is very enjoyable

In a similar vein, Jones and Swain (1992, 1995) and Jones (1995) focused their attention on examining the direction of anxiety (perceptions of facilitative vs. debilitative anxiety) as well as the traditional intensity (amount of anxiety) experienced by athletes. This research, which is reviewed extensively later in this chapter, clearly shows that it is important to examine both the intensity and direction of anxiety when studying the arousal–performance relationship.

Unfortunately, telic metamotivational state and intensity/direction of anxiety measures have not been validated to date. However, in line with reversal theory, which is reviewed later in this chapter, viewing the cognitive component of arousal as more than the negative state anxiety affective response is intuitively appealing and may assist investigators in better unraveling the arousal–athletic performance relationship.

Stress and the Stress Process

The term *stress* often has been used as if it were synonymous with *anxiety*. Martens (1977) noted the inconsistencies in using *stress* in this manner and pointed out that it has at times been defined in three different ways—as a stimulus variable, an intervening variable, or a response variable. Stress also has been described as both an environmental variable and an emotional response to a specific situation (Gould & Petlichkoff, 1988). R.E. Smith and Smoll (1982) suggested that these are two distinct entities and noted that it is important to distinguish between an athlete's perception of stress and potential environmental stressors. Selye (1974) further differentiated among *eustress,* or good stress, and *distress,* or bad stress, suggesting that not all stressors should be perceived as negative.

To address the inconsistencies in the use of the term *stress,* many sport psychologists have used a process definition (e.g., Gould, 1987; Gould & Petlichkoff, 1988; Krane & Greenleaf, 1999; Martens, 1977; Passer, 1982). This type of definition is based on McGrath's (1970) process model of stress (see figure 7.1). In this model, *stress* is defined as "a substantial imbalance between (environmental) demand and response capability, under conditions where failure to meet the demand has important consequences" (p. 20).

McGrath's (1970) model consists of four interrelated stages that can be applied readily to the athletic environment. The first stage consists of an environmental situation or demand placed on an

Intensity and direction of anxiety determine whether arousal is positive or negative.

© Human Kinetics

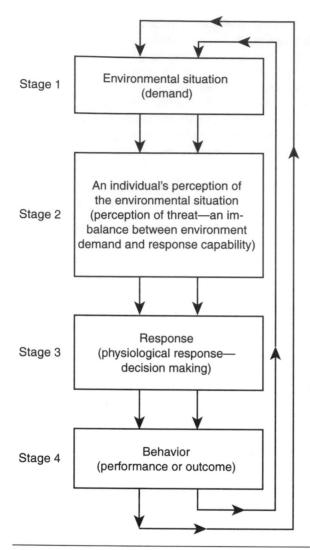

Stage 1 — Environmental situation (demand)

Stage 2 — An individual's perception of the environmental situation (perception of threat—an imbalance between environment demand and response capability)

Stage 3 — Response (physiological response—decision making)

Stage 4 — Behavior (performance or outcome)

Figure 7.1 McGrath's (1970) process model of stress.

Reprinted, by permission, from D. Gould and L. Petlichkoff, 1988, Psychological Stress and the Age-Group Wrestler. In *Competitive Sports for Children and Youth,* edited by E.W. Brown and C.F. Branta (Champaign, IL: Human Kinetics), 65.

athlete that may be perceived differently by different athletes. For example, one tennis player may look forward to a competitive match against a strong opponent, whereas another may perceive the situation as demanding or intimidating. Thus, the second stage is the individual's perception of the environmental demand. Martens (1977) elaborated by indicating that an athlete will feel threatened if he or she perceives an imbalance between the demands of the situation and his or her response capabilities. For instance, the first tennis player in the example may perceive the situation as a challenge (i.e., positive) whereas the second player may perceive it as threatening (i.e., negative) because of the high probability of losing. The

third stage in McGrath's (1970) model is the response of the individual that may consist of increased physiological arousal, as well as increases in state anxiety, telic, and paratelic states. The last stage in the model is the performance or outcome of behavior. Moreover, these four stages are seen as cyclical, continuously influencing one another in a circular fashion.

There are four characteristics of the stress process:

1. Stress is defined as a sequence of events leading to a specific behavior and not in an emotional context.

2. Stress is viewed in a cyclical fashion.

3. Stress may be viewed as positive or negative, as opposed to negative only.

4. The emphasis is placed not merely on the situation but on the athlete's perception of the situation.

Bridging the Gaps Among Stress, Arousal, and Anxiety Terms

Sport psychologists need to resolve the inconsistent use of arousal- and anxiety-related terminology. We have shown in this section that these concepts have distinct meanings. Hence, using them interchangeably or assuming that the measures used to assess one concept (e.g., heart rate, cognitive state anxiety) will adequately reflect the total arousal construct has only clouded the arousal–performance relationship from both theoretical and empirical perspectives. It is imperative that investigators clarify how they are using these terms conceptually and then link their specific arousal and anxiety measures to these conceptual distinctions. Later, we provide a conceptual model for integrating arousal construct terminology. We hope that researchers will use this model in identifying the aspect of arousal or anxiety they wish to examine and in developing appropriate measures of that construct.

AROUSAL–PERFORMANCE HYPOTHESES AND THEORIES

A number of theories and hypotheses have been proposed to account for the relationship between arousal and athletic performance or anxiety and athletic performance. Many of the earlier theories have examined the arousal construct, whereas more recent theories were developed based on the anxiety construct. Two relatively early views that were proposed and tested in the sport and motor performance context were the drive theory and the inverted-U hypothesis. More recently, additional models have been advanced. These include Hanin's optimal zones of arousal hypothesis, multidimensional theory of anxiety, catastrophe model, reversal theory, and the model of facilitative/debilitative anxiety.

The Drive Theory

The drive theory, originally proposed by Hull (1943) and subsequently modified by Spence and Spence (1966), suggested that performance is a product of *drive* and *habit strength*. Drive is considered synonymous with arousal, and habit strength is the dominance of the correct or incorrect response (whether the skill is well learned or novel). Thus, the arousal–performance relationship can be expressed as the linear relationship $P = H \times D$, with increased arousal increasing the frequency of the concomitant response. In the early stages of learning, the dominant response would be the incorrect one. So the theory predicts that increased arousal would be detrimental during skill acquisition. However, later in the learning process (i.e., when a skill is well learned), arousal, or drive, would increase the probability of the dominant "correct" response and performance thus would improve (see figure 7.2).

In an early review of the research on arousal and performance, Taylor (1956) cited a series of studies using a serial verbal maze-learning task that supported the drive theory. In these studies, as anxiety increased, subjects committed more errors during learning of this task. These errors, according to Taylor, were due to interfering response tendencies. A decade later, Spence and Spence (1966) reviewed 25 studies investigating the arousal–performance relationship and found that all but four supported the hypothesis that arousal was positively correlated to performance.

Despite early support for the drive theory, a number of criticisms were leveled against this theory during the 1970s. For example, Martens (1971, 1974) extensively reviewed the drive theory literature and reported that an equal number of studies supported and rejected the predicted relationships between anxiety and performance. It is important to note that early studies supporting the drive theory employed very simple tasks.

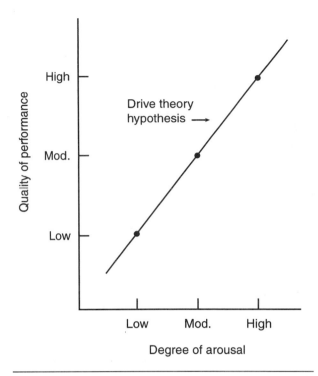

Figure 7.2 The arousal–performance relationship according to drive theory.

Reprinted, by permission, from D. Gill, 1986, *Psychological dynamics of sport* (Champaign, IL: Human Kinetics), 118.

More specifically, the drive theory does not appear to be sufficiently applicable to complex motor tasks (Martens, 1971, 1974; Tobias, 1980; Weinberg, 1979) and thus is considered too simplistic to explain complex athletic performance (Fisher, 1976). Another criticism of the drive theory is that it is very difficult to determine the habit hierarchy of correct and incorrect responses in most motor skill tasks and thus difficult to test the theory adequately. Hence, Martens (1971, 1974) and others (Neiss, 1988; Weinberg, 1990) strongly rejected the use of the drive theory in motor behavior contexts.

The Inverted-U Hypothesis

In 1908, Yerkes and Dodson proposed the inverted-U hypothesis, which also attempted to explain the relationship between arousal and performance. They suggested that heightened arousal enhanced performance to a certain point, after which continued increases in arousal would hinder performance. Thus, the predicted relationship between arousal and performance was curvilinear, taking the shape of an inverted U (see figure 7.3). In support of such a relationship, Duffy (1932) noted that increased muscular tension leads to

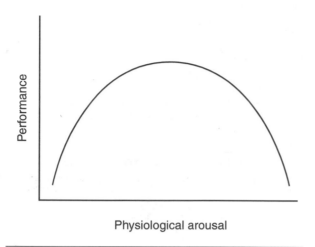

Figure 7.3   Inverted-U model predictions.

Adapted, by permission, from J. Fazey and L. Hardy, 1988, The Inverted-U Hypothesis: A Catastrophe for Sport Psychology. In *Bass Monograph No. 1* (Leeds, U.K.: British Association of Sports Sciences and National Coaching Foundation), 20.

poorer performance of a muscular activity and that high tension would decrease response flexibility. Thus, Duffy concluded that "a moderate degree of tension offers the greatest advantages, since very high tension tends to be disruptive and very low tension involves lack of alertness of effort" (p. 545). Hebb (1955) developed the theory further when he suggested that there was an optimal level of arousal, that is, a level of arousal at which an individual would perform to his or her maximum potential, neither overaroused nor underaroused.

The inverted-U hypothesis has been examined by a number of researchers in sport psychology to study anxiety effects on performance and has received fairly consistent support. Martens and Landers (1970), for example, tested this hypothesis by using a tracing task involving arm steadiness. Subjects who undertook the task in a moderately stressful situation performed the task better than did those in the low-stress or high-stress conditions. Klavora (1977) also found support for the inverted-U hypothesis in his study with male high school basketball players. This study found a range of optimal state anxiety where the best athletic performances were observed. Furthermore, separate inverted-U curves were found for low- and high-trait-anxious athletes. Performance of female collegiate basketball players also was shown to follow an inverted-U pattern (Sonstroem & Bernardo, 1982). Athletes with moderate levels of trait and state anxiety scored the most points and displayed the best

overall performance. The worst performances were exhibited by the high-anxious players. The inverted-U hypothesis also received support in a study of hitting performance in Little League baseball players (Lowe, 1973), with best performances occurring when players were under moderate stress.

Despite receiving some empirical support from sport psychology researchers, the inverted-U hypothesis also has received much criticism. Landers (1980) contended that the inverted-U hypothesis does not explain the relationship between arousal and performance but merely notes that the relationship is curvilinear. Landers suggested that a theory was needed to explain and predict the relationship between arousal and performance. Landers and Boutcher (1998) offered possible attentional explanations (focusing on Easterbrook's, 1959, cue utilization theory and Bacon's, 1974, attentional selectivity notions) for why and how arousal influences performance in an inverted-U fashion. However, a full test of these predictions has never been made. Hence, the inverted-U is merely a general prediction, not a theory that explains how, why, or precisely when arousal affects performance. The inverted-U has also been criticized for "an apparent lack of predictive validity in practical situations" (Hardy & Fazey, 1987, p. 4). Specifically, experiential knowledge suggests that after an athlete's anxiety increases beyond the optimal point (e.g., when an athlete "chokes"), slight decreases in anxiety will not slightly improve performance, as the inverted-U hypothesis predicts it will (Hardy & Fazey, 1987). Rather, performance deteriorates in a drastic and catastrophic fashion. Hardy and Fazey suggest that the relationship between anxiety and performance does not follow the symmetrical inverted-U curve because the two halves of the inverted-U curve match only in theory, not in reality. Landers and Boutcher (1998), however, recently noted that the originators of the inverted-U never expected to see highly symmetrical U relationships—only optimal arousal producing better performance than lower and higher arousal levels.

Other criticisms of the inverted-U hypothesis are based on the methodological, interpretive, conceptual, and statistical problems evident in previous studies purporting to support this hypothesis. Equivocal findings in these studies often are explained by citing individual differences, task characteristics, or imprecise measurement of performance (Weinberg, 1990). Another criticism of the inverted-U hypothesis is the failure to recognize the multidimensional nature of arousal–anxiety (Hardy & Fazey, 1987; Jones & Hardy, 1989). Finally, Neiss (1988) faulted the hypothesis for being by nature not subject to refutation. That is, the proposed variability of optimal arousal and the influence of task complexity allow researchers to fit most data to the inverted-U curve. This is evidenced by the number of studies that apply the inverted-U hypothesis retrospectively (Kerr, 1985). Any evidence contrary to the inverted-U hypothesis can be explained by suggestions that the subjects were not sufficiently aroused or that the task was too simple or complex (Neiss, 1988). These criticisms led Neiss to claim that "the inverted-U hypothesis has not received clear support from a single study" (p. 355).

The Individualized Zones of Optimal Functioning Hypothesis

As an alternative to the inverted-U hypothesis, Russian sport psychologist Yuri Hanin (1980) proposed the zone of optimal functioning (ZOF) state anxiety–performance relationship. Hanin contended that the large variability in state anxiety scores typically found in field studies with different athletic subsamples makes it unlikely that one specific optimal level of state anxiety exists that leads to best performance. Rather, Hanin suggested that through retrospective and systematic multiple observations of athletes' state anxiety and performance levels, a ZOF can be identified. Specifically, this zone consists of an athlete's mean precompetitive state anxiety score on Spielberger and colleagues' (1970a, 1970b) STAI plus or minus four points (approximately one half of a standard deviation). Figure 7.4 compares two swimmers' zones of optimal functioning.

The ZOF hypothesis (in later works labeled the "individualized zones of optimal functioning," or IZOF) was designed as a practical tool that could provide reference points and criteria for diagnosis and evaluation of precompetitive state anxiety in athletes (Hanin, 1980). Athletes whose state anxiety fell within their IZOF would be expected to perform better than athletes whose state anxiety was outside their IZOF. Moreover, some empirical support has been generated for Hanin's contentions. Weightlifters whose state anxiety was outside of their IZOF three days before competition were less successful than weightlifters who remained within their IZOF (Hanin, 1980). A number of additional IZOF model tests have been conducted since its inception. For instance, Morgan

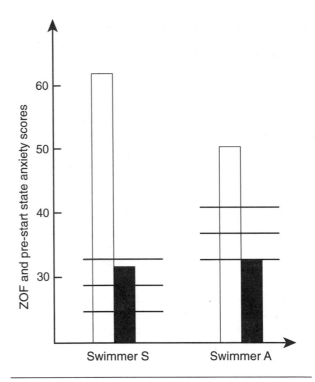

Figure 7.4 Zones of optimal functioning (ZOFs) and state anxiety levels for two swimmers before poor and good performances in competition. Shaded regions refer to successful performance; white regions indicate unsuccessful performance.

Reprinted, by permission, from Speilberger and Diaz-Guerrero, 1986, *Cross-cultural anxiety, vol. 3* (New York: Hemisphere Publishing Corp.).

and his associates (Morgan, O'Connor, Ellickson, & Bradley, 1988; Morgan, O'Connor, Sparling, & Pate, 1987) found that optimal ZOFs existed for elite male and female distance runners even though the Body Awareness Scale (a measure of self-report somatic activation) was used in the investigations, instead of the STAI. Similarly, Turner and Raglin (1993) examined whether track-and-field athletes' precompetitive state anxiety levels were in or out of their previously determined IZOFs over three indoor competitions. Support was found for the IZOF notion, because athletes whose anxiety was within their unique optimal anxiety zone performed better.

Investigators have extended the IZOF model by examining its predictions using multidimensional measures of state anxiety, like the CSAI-2. For example, Krane (1993) examined separate ZOFs for cognitive and somatic anxiety. Partially supporting Hanin's predictions, soccer players' worst performances were when cognitive and somatic anxiety were above their cognitive and somatic anxiety IZOFs, respectively. In another study, Gould, Tuffey, Hardy, and Lochbaum (1993) retrospectively assessed individualized ZOFs and precompetition anxiety by using the CSAI-2. Eleven middle-distance runners served as participants, and anxiety and performance were assessed over the course of the season. Unique to this study, individualized zones were calculated based on a combination or interaction of cognitive and somatic state anxiety levels. Results revealed that the correlation between multidimensional anxiety theory-based IZOF and performance was significant (–.30) and higher than the traditional IZOF, which was only marginally significant. Using multidimensional anxiety measures, then, appears to increase the predictive validity of the ZOF model.

In 1996, Gould and Tuffey conducted a comprehensive review of all the existing IZOF anxiety–performance research. They concluded that although these studies were characterized by some inherent methodological weaknesses (e.g., small sample sizes, failure to take longitudinal assessments, failure to use process measures of performance), overall these studies showed good support for the basic contentions of the IZOF model. However, the percentage of variance accounted for within IZOF model studies generally has not been very high. Furthermore, IZOF contentions have not been verified in all studies.

Several aspects of Hanin's (1980) IZOF make it attractive for researchers in sport psychology. First, it is intuitively appealing and appears to be very realistic. The IZOF also has the strength of precisely predicting the state anxiety levels at which optimal athlete performance will occur. Like the inverted-U hypothesis, it also is conceptually limited to hypothesis status, because no explanation has been forwarded as to why state anxiety influences performance in and out of the IZOF. In fact, Gould and Tuffey (1996) labeled the IZOF model as an "empirical finding in need of theory." They further suggested that possible theoretical constructs to explore include attentional and muscular tension changes associated with in- and out-of-zone performance and anxiety scores. In response to this call, Hanin (1997) suggested that the perceptual or interpretative processes that underlie one's definition of anxiety and the relationships among emotions, motivation, cognitions, and energy/effort be examined in an effort to develop grounded theoretical explanations for the IZOF phenomenon.

Finally, we should note that Hanin (1997) recently expanded his IZOF notion to go beyond the anxiety–performance relationship and explain how a variety of emotions may relate to performance. In essence, a variety of functional or performance-facilitating and dysfunctional or performance-debilitating positive and negative emotions (e.g., lazy, angry, content, furious) have been identified and found to be related to performance within profiles of optimal zones of emotional functioning (see figure 7.5). Initial evidence supports the utility of this expanded approach (see Hanin, 1997, for a review). Also, Prapavessis and Grove (1991) supported this contention when examining mood states in shooters. Competitive mood states specific to each individual were found whereby individualized anger, depression, and confusion ranges were associated with performance. However, further evidence is needed and, as is the case with the original IZOF notion, theoretical explanations need to be developed.

Multidimensional Anxiety Theory

Multidimensional anxiety theory (MAT), an alternative to the inverted-U hypothesis, predicts that cognitive and somatic anxiety will differentially influence athletic performance (Burton, 1988; Martens et al., 1990). Specifically, it predicts a powerful negative linear relationship between cognitive state anxiety and performance and a less powerful, inverted-U relationship between somatic anxiety and performance. Several studies have examined the hypothesized relationships between cognitive anxiety and performance and somatic anxiety and performance (Burton, 1988; Caruso, Dzewaltowski, Gill, & McElroy, 1990; Gould et al., 1987; Hammermeister & Burton, 1995; Karteroliotis & Gill, 1987; Maynard & Howe, 1987; Rodrigo, Lusiardo, & Pereira, 1990). Burton (1988) found a negative linear relationship between cognitive anxiety and performance and a curvilinear relationship between somatic anxiety and swimming performance, thus supporting the predictions of MAT. Krane (1990) found a negative linear relationship between cognitive anxiety and performance in female collegiate soccer players. Contrary to MAT, she also found a negative linear relationship between somatic anxiety and performance.

Other researchers have found only partial support for MAT (Gould et al., 1987; Rodrigo et al., 1990). Gould and colleagues (1987) found somatic anxiety to have a curvilinear relationship with pistol-shooting performance, supporting the inverted-U MAT predictions, whereas contrary to predictions, cognitive anxiety was unrelated to

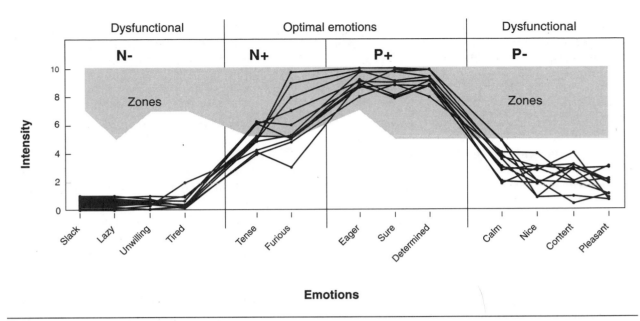

Figure 7.5 Profile of the optimal zone of functioning for a Finnish javelin thrower.

Reprinted, by permission, from Y. Hanin, 1997, "Emotions and athletic performance: Individualized zones of optimal functioning model," *European Yearbook of Sport Psychology, 1:* 29–72. Copyright © Academia Verlag.

performance. Rodrigo et al. (1990), like Gould et al. (1987), supported only the inverse relationship between cognitive anxiety and soccer performance.

Still other researchers have failed to find any support for the anxiety–performance relationships hypothesized by MAT (Caruso et al., 1990; Hammermeister & Burton, 1995; Karteroliotis & Gill, 1987; Maynard & Howe, 1987). Hammermeister and Burton (1995) examined the effect of precompetitive anxiety on the intraindividual performance of endurance athletes. Results suggested that precompetitive anxiety was not debilitative to performance and did not support the MAT anxiety–performance hypotheses. Maynard and Howe (1987) examined the precompetitive anxiety of male rugby players in relation to performance in two rugby games. The only significant finding was a negative correlation between somatic anxiety and performance for those players whom coaches rated as performing below their ability. Thus, both of these studies conducted in a field setting failed to support the negative linear relationship between cognitive anxiety and performance and the inverted-U relationship between somatic anxiety and performance. Laboratory studies also have failed to support the predicted anxiety–performance relationships of MAT. Karteroliotis and Gill (1987) used a competitive pegboard task and failed to find significant relationships between cognitive and somatic anxiety and per-

formance. Caruso et al. (1990) examined anxiety–performance relationships in a laboratory setting involving bicycle competition. Results did not support the predicted relationships between cognitive and somatic anxiety and performance.

Some researchers have examined the relationship between precompetitive state anxiety and components of performance (Davids & Gill, 1995; Parfitt & Hardy, 1993). Parfitt and Hardy (1993), although not specifically testing multidimensional anxiety theory, found differing relationships between subcomponents of state anxiety and types of task. Specifically, a negative linear relationship was found between both cognitive and somatic anxiety and performance on a short-term memory task. Significant positive linear relationships were found between cognitive and somatic anxiety and rebound shooting. Thus, results from the short-term memory task supported the predicted negative linear relationship between anxiety and performance, but no support was found on the rebound shooting task. In another study, Davids and Gill (1995) found a negative relationship between cognitive anxiety and performance on criterion tasks simulating specific aspects of hockey performance.

Little research has attempted to test multidimensional anxiety theory by using intervention research. However, Maynard and colleagues (Maynard & Cotton, 1993; Maynard, Hemmings, & Warwick-Evans, 1995; Maynard, Smith, & Warwick-

Evans, 1995) have conducted a series of intervention studies examining the matching hypothesis in relationship to the predictions of multidimensional anxiety theory. Simply stated, the matching hypothesis predicts that the type of anxiety management technique used—for example, physical relaxation (progressive muscle relaxation) versus cognitive relaxation (negative thought stopping)—depends on the type of state anxiety one experiences. Hence, it is predicted that athletes who experience primarily somatic state anxiety would find a physical relaxation strategy more effective, whereas athletes who primarily experience cognitive state anxiety would find a cognitively based anxiety management technique more effective. Maynard and Cotton (1993) found that intervention techniques aimed at reducing one type of anxiety also reduced the other type. Two follow-up studies examined the effectiveness of anxiety reduction interventions on performance. Specifically, one study used a somatic intervention (Maynard, Hemmings, & Warwick-Evans, 1995) and the second study used a cognitive intervention (Maynard, Smith, & Warwick-Evans, 1995). Neither study found any effect on performance as a result of anxiety-reducing interventions, although some support for the matching hypothesis has been garnered.

Over the last 10 years, multidimensional anxiety theory has been tested in the sport context, with only limited or partial support. Consistent clear support for its contentions has not been found. The strength of the theory lies in its ability to distinguish between anxiety subcomponents and in initial evidence showing that these anxiety components can differentially influence performance. Recent research on the matching hypothesis (an anxiety management intervention based on MAT predictions) has been promising in this regard. Current limitations include a lack of consistent empirical support for its precise predictions (e.g., although somatic and cognitive anxiety often have been found to predict performance differentially, the precise predictions of MAT have seldom been found). Additionally, few investigations have verified that cognitive anxiety negatively influences performance via attentional distraction. Explanations for why and when somatic anxiety influences performance also are needed.

The Catastrophe Model

Another proposed alternative to the inverted-U hypothesis is the behavioral application of catastrophe theory (Hardy & Fazey, 1987). The inverted-U hypothesis and the catastrophe notion are similar in that both predict that increases in arousal will facilitate performance up to an optimal level (figure 7.6). However, the two models differ in what occurs next. The inverted-U hypothesis (see figure 7.3) suggests that with further increases in anxiety, performance will decline in a symmetrical, orderly, curvilinear manner. Thus, slight overanxiousness or excessive arousal will slightly hinder performance. In contrast, the catastrophe model proposes that when an athlete "goes over the top," there will be a large and dramatic decline in performance. Hence, it would be very difficult for athletes to recover from this "catastrophe" even to a mediocre level of performance.

The catastrophe model was derived by Rene Thom (1972/1975) as a mathematical model for describing discontinuities that occur in the physical world. Specifically, Thom believed that few naturally occurring phenomena are symmetrically related in a well-ordered and predictable fashion. Rather, natural phenomena are characterized by sudden transformations and discontinuities. Thus, multivariate mathematical models like catastrophe need to be developed to explain such sudden transformations. Although Thom (1972/1975) developed the catastrophe model, it was popularized by Zeeman (1976) when he demonstrated that

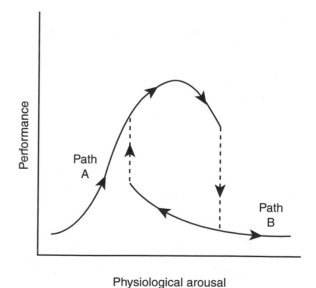

Figure 7.6   Catastrophe model predictions.

Reprinted, by permission, from J. Fazey and L. Hardy, 1988, The Inverted-U Hypothesis: A Catastrophe for Sport Psychology. In *Bass Monograph No. 1* (Leeds, U.K.: British Association of Sports Sciences and National Coaching Foundation), 21.

the model could be applied to a wide range of social science phenomena. Although several catastrophe models have been developed, the most commonly applied model and the one most easily understood is the cusp catastrophe model.

The cusp catastrophe model is three-dimensional and consists of one dependent variable and two independent variables (see Hardy, 1996b, for a detailed explanation). It predicts that the dependent variable can show both unbroken or continuous changes, as well as abrupt discontinuous changes, as a result of changes in the two independent variables. So under some conditions continuous relationships exist, but under other conditions drastic discontinuous changes are predicted to occur.

When used to explain the arousal–performance relationship, the catastrophe model, as described by Hardy and Fazey (1987), holds that the two independent variables affecting athletic performance are cognitive state anxiety and physiological arousal. Hence, as shown in the three-dimensional cusp model in figure 7.7, athletic performance (the dependent variable) is predicted to be associated with increases in physiological arousal. However, the effects of physiological arousal on performance are moderated by cognitive state anxiety (called the *splitting factor*). The key to understanding the model is to recognize that arousal and cognitive state anxiety "interact" and in so doing influence performance in both continuous and discontinuous manners. Thus, the relationship between physiological arousal and performance will differ depending on one's level of cognitive anxiety, with catastrophic performance effects occurring only when cognitive anxiety is high.

Hardy (1996b) indicated that it is helpful to think of a catastrophe performance surface, like the one shown in figure 7.7, as resembling a sheet of paper that is being pushed on with different levels of force (in this case cognitive anxiety and arousal). The back half of the paper or model depicts a continuous or unbroken relationship between the variables. That is, under conditions of low cognitive anxiety or worry, an inverted-U relationship is evident between increases in arousal and performance. The front half of the model, which represents the arousal–performance relationship under conditions of high cognitive anxiety,

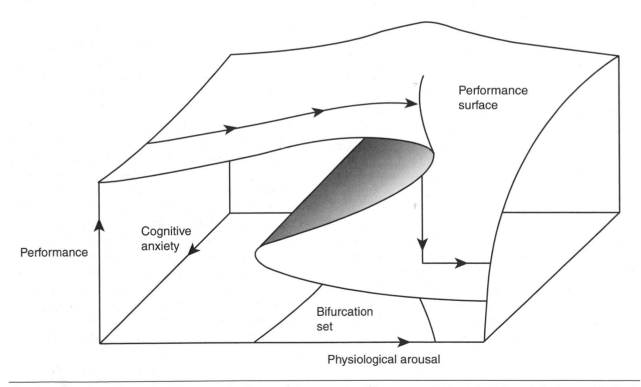

Figure 7.7 A three-dimensional catastrophe theory of the arousal–performance relationship. Although the normal factor is labeled *psychological arousal*, some researchers may label it *somatic anxiety* (e.g., G. Jones, personal communication, May 1989; Krane, 1990).

Reprinted, by permission, from J. Fazey and L. Hardy, 1998, The Inverted-U Hypothesis: A Catastrophe for Sport Psychology. In *Bass Monograph No. 1* (Leeds, U.K.: British Association of Sports Sciences and National Coaching Foundation), 25.

depicts a tear in the performance sheet or paper, which results in two overlapping surfaces between which one's performance can flip or jump. The key, here, is that under conditions of high cognitive state anxiety, increases in physiological arousal continuously improve performance up to some optimal point, after which a drastic or discontinuous shift occurs where performance drops from the upper to lower surface. At times, then, changes in the independent variables (cognitive anxiety and arousal) will result in symmetrical changes in the dependent variable (performance) as depicted in the back half of the model. However, at other times, changes in the independent variables will result in a performance catastrophe—flipping from the upper surface to the lower surface such as depicted in the front of the model.

What is innovative about the catastrophe model is that it is the only arousal–performance model to predict that physiological arousal interacts with an anxiety variable (cognitive state anxiety) to predict athletic performance. Moreover, it does not assume that cognitive anxiety and physiological arousal always interact in a well-ordered fashion when influencing performance. Rather, they interact in a systematic, orderly fashion at times (under conditions of low cognitive anxiety); but when these variables reach certain levels (high physiological arousal combined with high cognitive anxiety), large and drastic catastrophic changes in performance occur.

Because the application of the catastrophe model to the anxiety–performance relationship is a fairly recent development, there are few full or surface fitting tests of the complete catastrophe model in sport psychology. However, Hardy (1996b) delineated several important predictions coming from the model:

- The *interaction* of cognitive state anxiety and physiological arousal will determine performance more than the single effects of either of these variables. Specifically, high cognitive anxiety will enhance performance at low levels of physiological arousal but will hinder performance when physiological arousal is high.

- Cognitive anxiety will not always impair performance (as predicted by MAT). Rather, cognitive state anxiety sometimes can enhance performance. Under conditions of high cognitive anxiety, best performances should be significantly better and worst performances significantly worse than under conditions of low cognitive anxiety.

- When a performer experiences high cognitive anxiety, the graph of performance against physiological arousal follows a different path under conditions of increasing versus decreasing physiological arousal (see figure 7.6). This is known as *hysteresis* and is not expected to occur under conditions of low cognitive anxiety (see Hardy, 1996b, for a more complete discussion of this mathematical catastrophe model concept).

Hardy (1996b) reviewed the evidence supporting these predictions. For example, Edwards and Hardy (1996) and Woodman, Albinson, and Hardy (1997) supported the first prediction. Studying netball players, for instance, Edwards and Hardy (1996) found that a combination of high physiological arousal and high cognitive anxiety led to significantly worse performance than the combination of high physiological arousal and low cognitive anxiety. Moreover, the combination of low physiological arousal with high cognitive state anxiety led to significantly better performance than a combination of low physiological arousal with low cognitive anxiety. Regarding the second prediction, Hardy and Parfitt (1991) and Hardy, Parfitt, and Pates (1994) confirmed that increases in physiological arousal as measured via heart rate were differentially related to performance depending on whether cognitive anxiety was high or low. Best performance, then, was significantly better and worse performance significantly worse when cognitive anxiety was high than when it was low. Finally, hysteresis effects have been supported in several studies (Hardy & Parfitt, 1991; Hardy et al., 1994). Thus, support for the separate catastrophe model predictions has been encouraging.

Full tests of the model have been more difficult to conduct because of the complexity of the statistical surface-fitting analyses involved. Hardy (1996a) recently tested the full model with experienced golfers who self-reported their cognitive state anxiety, somatic state anxiety, and self-confidence while physiological arousal (heart rate) was assessed during a round of golf. Putting performance served as the dependent variable. Although the results appeared to support the superiority of the catastrophe model, Hardy concluded that because of statistical concerns about the method of dynamic differences used to test the model, clear support could not be garnered. This study also investigated predictions based on MAT. Interestingly, however, when self-confidence was integrated into the catastrophe and MAT models, a larger percentage of variance in athletes' performance was explained. This suggests that self-confidence must be considered in arousal–performance models separately from cognitive anxiety and that higher order catastrophe models be considered. (Note: Multiple catastrophe surfaces that can be fitted to data, and the Cusp model used by Hardy and Fazey, 1987, involve the fewest independent variables.)

The strengths of the catastrophe model are that it considers both the effects of physiological arousal and cognitive state anxiety on performance and that it has an intuitive appeal in recognizing that phenomena in real-world athletic settings do not always function in perfectly symmetrical ways. Initial evidence testing its predictions, although far from complete, has been encouraging. Limitations include its complexity and the need to obtain a large number of assessments on the same athletes over time to test the full model. These limitations, however, should not discourage researchers from examining the model, because its potential as a viable explanation for the arousal–performance relationship far outweighs the efforts needed to test it.

Reversal Theory

Another exciting development applicable to the anxiety–performance literature is the reversal theory proposed by K.C.P Smith and Apter (1975) and popularized in the sport psychology literature by Robert Kerr (1985, 1987, 1997). Reversal theory, however, was not originally developed to explain the arousal–performance relationship. Rather, it focused on the relationship between arousal and emotional affect and was forwarded as a general framework for explaining personality and motivation (Apter, 1984). In fact, in his recent book, *Motivation and Emotion in Sport: Reversal Theory,* Kerr (1997) presented reversal theory as a broad theoretical explanation for many psychological processes taking place in sport.

Relative to arousal, the basic contention of reversal theory is that the relationship between arousal and affect depends on one's cognitive interpretation of one's arousal level. High arousal may be interpreted as excitement (pleasant) or anxiety (unpleasant), and low arousal may be interpreted as relaxation (pleasant) or boredom (unpleasant). One's interpretation of affect as pleasant or unpleasant is also known as *hedonic tone.* Furthermore, because both arousal and affect vary on continua, reversal theory predicts that two

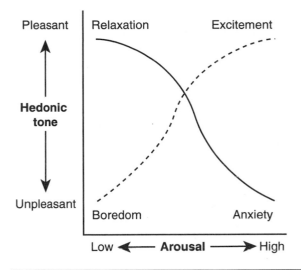

Figure 7.8 The relationship between arousal and affect in the reversal theory.

Reprinted, by permission, from J.H. Kerr, 1985, "The Experience of Arousal: The New Basis for Studying Arousal Effects in Sport," *Journal of Sport Sciences,* 3: 172. Reprinted, by permission of E & FN Spon.

curves depict the relationship between arousal and affective pleasure (figure 7.8).

Because there are two curves on the arousal–pleasure graph, "another dimension of change has been introduced: that of sudden discontinuous switching from one curve to the another. Since these are opposite ways of interpreting arousal the switch can be regarded as constituting a *reversal*" (Apter, 1984, p. 268). Apter also indicated that each curve represents a different meta-motivational state or mode (see figure 7.6). Metamotivational states have been defined as "frames of mind to do with the way a person interprets his or her motives at a given time" (Kerr, 1997, p. 9). Moreover, "metamotivational states go in pairs of opposites, only one member of each pair being operative at a given time" (Kerr, 1985, p. 173). The telic mode is characterized by its seriousness or orientation toward a goal, whereas the paratelic mode is characterized by playfulness or an activity orientation (Apter, 1984; Svebak & Stoyva, 1980). The paratelic mode also can be thought of as arousal-seeking and the telic as arousal-avoiding (see telic and paratelic curves on figure 7.8). More simply, changes from one metamotivational state to the other are reversals (Kerr, 1997). Apter (1984) used the example of risk-taking sports such as rock climbing or parachuting to illustrate his concept of psychological reversals. The danger involved induces a high level of arousal, deemed anxiety in the telic mode, and then when the danger is mastered, the anxiety suddenly reverses and becomes excitement in the paratelic mode. Hence, psychological reversals can take place and result in striking changes in emotional states.

Kerr (1985, 1997), in his application of reversal theory to studying arousal effects in sport, suggested that arousal and stress continua must be viewed jointly and are together related to reversal theory. This results in four quadrants: anxiety, excitement, boredom, and relaxation (figure 7.9). The horizontal arousal continuum and the vertical axis both range from high to low. When arousal and stress (the imbalance between environmental demands and performer response capabilities) are high, anxiety, or overstimulation, results. Boredom, or understimulation, occurs when stress is high and arousal is low. Conversely, when stress is low and arousal is high, excitement occurs. When both arousal and stress are low, the result is sleep. Reversal theory, then, has the potential to integrate both stress and arousal notions nicely into its theoretical framework. A basic interpretation from reversal theory is that arousal is not necessarily pleasant or unpleasant. Rather, depending on one's metamotivational state, it can be perceived as a positive (paratelic) or negative (telic) state.

Kerr and his colleagues (see Kerr, 1997, for a review) have begun to empirically examine reversal theory in sport, including the relationship between telic and paratelic reversals, arousal, and athletic performance. These studies have taken several forms. For example, one line of research has examined the psychological aspects of success or winning and losing in sport. Rugby players, gymnasts, squash competitors, and canoe athletes were studied by having them complete

telic–paratelic state and arousal–stress measures just before and after competition (see Kerr, 1997, for a summary of these studies). Results revealed that successful athletes experienced high levels of arousal as more positive, pleasant, and nonstressful compared with less successful competitors. Successful athletes also exhibited more stable emotional patterns compared with their less successful counterparts.

In the most recent line of research, Males, Kerr, and Gerkovich (1998) conducted season-long interviews with nine elite male slalom canoeists. All paddlers were interviewed within 24 hours after all competitions across a season and were asked what affective responses they felt just before and during competition. The experiences reported by the athletes then were classified into various metamotivational state categories (e.g., telic, paratelic). There were no differences in above- versus below-average performances (as determined by an index for assessing performance using racing results) in the precompetition frequency of telic and paratelic states. However, 30% of the competitors reported paratelic states during above-average performances compared with 14% during below-average performances. Finally, the authors reported that combinations of paratelic conformity and telic mastery metamotivational state—telic-paratelic states combined with "negativist" (tendency to react against prevailing norms) versus "conformist" (tendency to adhere to prescribed norms) metamotivational state—were reported more during above- versus below-average performances. The authors concluded that these results supported reversal theory. Hence, given these findings and those of the previous reversal theory studies conducted by Kerr and his associates (see Kerr, 1997, for a review), some support has been found for reversal theory predictions in sport.

Although reversal theory is intuitively appealing and has received some support in the recent scientific literature, much more research is needed on reversal theory in sport. To date, the theory has been tested predominantly by a single research team, which has focused the bulk of its efforts on supporting various predictions that are derived from the theory. More complete tests of the theory are needed. In addition, greater efforts need to be placed on identifying precise predictions that would fail to support the theory. That is, existing reversal theory studies have not clearly identified the precise conditions under which the theory would and would not be supported and have not discussed findings relative to all such pre-

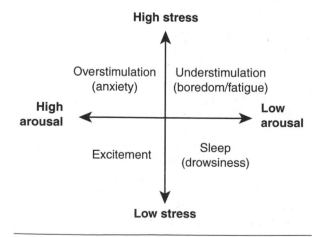

Figure 7.9 Reversal theory arousal–stress continuum.

Reprinted, by permission, from J.H. Kerr, 1985, "The Experience of Arousal: A New Basis for Studying Arousal Effects in Sport," Journal of Sport Sciences, 3: 175. Reprinted by permission of E & FN Spon.

cise predictions. Finally, the testability of the theory needs to be examined in depth, because pre- and postcompetition questionnaires and interviews may not adequately assess moment-to-moment reversals in metamotivational states. Moreover, these metamotivational state "reversals" are what give the theory much of its intuitive appeal.

Thus, reversal theory offers an interesting alternative to other arousal–performance views, because it places considerable emphasis on one's interpretation of felt arousal. The strengths of reversal theory are its intuitive appeal and the important distinction it places on the athlete's interpretation of arousal states. Current limitations include the need for better measures of metamotivational states, the need for additional investigations designed to test its predictions, and the need to show how the theory could be refuted as well as supported. It is certainly a theory that holds potential for increasing our understanding of the arousal–performance relationship.

Intensity and Direction of Multidimensional Competitive Anxiety Symptoms

Historically, most researchers have assumed anxiety to have only negative effects on performance. Hence, the typical approach to anxiety assessment has involved having a participant rate the degree or intensity to which he or she experiences vari-

ous anxiety symptoms (e.g., worry). Several views, such as reversal theory and catastrophe model, suggest that anxiety does not necessarily have negative effects on performance. Additionally, sport psychology researchers have suggested that examining how athletes perceive anxiety (i.e., as facilitative or debilitative) in relationship to their performance readiness may be important in more fully understanding the impact of anxiety on performance (Jones, 1991; Jones & Swain, 1992, 1995; Parfitt, Jones, & Hardy, 1990). The individual's interpretation of anxiety symptoms as either positive and helping performance (i.e., facilitative) or negative and hurting performance (i.e., debilitative) has been defined as the directional dimension of anxiety. Jones and colleagues (Jones, 1991; Jones & Hanton, 1996; Jones, Hanton, & Swain, 1994; Jones & Swain, 1992, 1995; Jones, Swain, & Hardy, 1993; Jones, Swain, & Harwood, 1996) have conducted a series of studies examining directional dimensions of anxiety, as well as the traditional intensity dimensions.

Jones (1991), Jones and Swain (1992), and Swain and Jones (1992) introduced the concept of anxiety "direction" into the sport psychology literature. Drawing on a review of the test anxiety literature, they suggested the importance of considering interpretations of anxiety symptoms or its direction, as well as the traditionally studied intensity of anxiety symptoms, when examining the anxiety–performance relationship. Alpert and Haber, as far back as 1960, demonstrated the relevance of distinguishing between debilitative and facilitative dimensions in examining test anxiety. Academic performance was more strongly predicted by a measure including both facilitative and debilitative anxiety (i.e., the Achievement Anxiety Test) than by a scale measuring only debilitative anxiety. Other test anxiety researchers have supported the importance of distinguishing between

Successful athletes experience high levels of arousal as more positive, pleasant, and nonstressful compared with less successful competitors.

© Human Kinetics

debili-tative and facilitative dimensions of anxiety (e.g., Carrier, Higson, Klimoski, & Peterson, 1984; Hudesman & Wiesner, 1978; Munz, Costello, & Korabek, 1975; Wine, 1980). As in the test anxiety literature, Mahoney and Avener (1977) found that anxiety can be interpreted as facilitative or debilitative. They interviewed gymnasts who were successful or unsuccessful in making the U.S. Olympic team. Their results showed that "the more successful athletes tended to 'use' their anxiety as a stimulant to better performance. The less successful gymnasts seemed to arouse themselves into near panic states" (p. 140). This suggests that successful gymnasts interpreted their anxiety as positive and facilitative for performance, whereas the unsuccessful gymnasts interpreted their anxiety as negative and debilitative for performance.

Jones and his colleagues, in examining directional and intensity dimensions of anxiety, have modified the CSAI-2. The original CSAI-2 was designed to measure the intensity of cognitive anxiety, somatic anxiety, and self-confidence. The questionnaire consists of 27 items, with 9 items in each of the three subscales. Participants rate the intensity of their anxiety symptoms on a 4-point Likert-type scale, ranging from 1 (*not at all*) to 4 (*very much so*). The modified CSAI-2 asks participants to also rate their interpretation of anxiety symptoms on a rating scale from +3 (*very positive*) to –3 (*very negative*). Direction scores, then, can range from –27 to +27. Researchers have used the modified CSAI-2 (Edwards & Hardy, 1996; Jones & Hanton, 1996; Jones & Swain, 1992; Jones et al., 1993, 1994) to measure state anxiety and the CSAI-2 with trait instructions (Jones & Swain, 1995; Jones et al., 1996) to measure trait anxiety.

Jones and colleagues have provided consistent support for differentiating between intensity and direction dimensions of competitive anxiety (Jones & Swain, 1992; Jones et al., 1993, 1994). Correlational analyses of cognitive intensity and direction subscales and somatic intensity and direction subscales have supported the notion that intensity and direction are measures of different constructs (Jones et al., 1993, 1996).

One trend in the research examining both intensity and direction of anxiety symptoms is the importance of the directional dimension. Jones and Swain (1992) examined differences in intensity and direction of competitive state anxiety in high- and low-competitive male athletes from a variety of sports, including rugby, basketball, soccer, and field hockey. The Competitiveness subscale

of the Sport Orientation Questionnaire (Gill & Deeter, 1988) was used as a measure of competitiveness. A median-split divided the participants into high- and low-competitive groups. Cognitive anxiety direction differentiated between the high-competitive group and the low-competitive group. The results indicated that the high-competitive group reported anxiety as more facilitative and less debilitative than the low-competitive group. Jones et al. (1993) also investigated the relationship between intensity and direction of competitive state anxiety and relationships with balance beam performance. Results indicated that gymnasts with "good" beam performances interpreted their cognitive anxiety as more facilitating and less debilitating than gymnasts with "poor" beam performances. Both of these studies found group differences only on the directional dimension of anxiety, indicating the importance of differentiating intensity and direction dimensions of anxiety.

Researchers also have begun to examine individual differences and situational variables. Skill level is one variable that has been examined in relation to intensity and direction of anxiety symptoms. Jones et al. (1994) examined intensity and direction dimensions of anxiety and skill level of competitive swimmers. Similar to previous findings (Jones & Swain, 1992; Jones et al., 1993), no differences were found on the intensity dimension. Elite swimmers reported both cognitive and somatic anxiety as more facilitative and less debilitative than nonelite swimmers. The majority of elite swimmers (85.3%) reported anxiety as facilitative, whereas only 47.7% of nonelite swimmers interpreted anxiety as facilitative. These findings are similar to Jones and Swain's (1992) findings indicating that gymnasts with good performances reported anxiety as more facilitative than those with poor performances.

Jones and Swain (1995) also examined intensity and direction dimensions in relation to skill level. Unlike Jones et al. (1994), Jones and Swain (1995) used trait instructions with the CSAI-2 to assess whether elite cricketers have predispositions to experience anxiety differently than nonelite performers. No differences were found between elite and nonelite players on cognitive or somatic anxiety intensity subscales; however, elite cricketers reported both cognitive and somatic anxiety as more facilitative than did nonelite cricketers. Thus, the studies by Jones et al. (1994) and Jones and Swain (1995) indicate that skill level may be an important moderating factor in an athlete's interpretation of anxiety symptoms.

Positive and negative affect have also been studied in relationship to intensity and direction of anxiety symptoms. Positive and negative affect tends to describe a person's inclination to exhibit adaptive or aversive mood states. Jones et al. (1996) investigated the relationships between intensity and direction dimensions of trait anxiety and positive and negative affect. Previous research findings have indicated that negative affect correlates more strongly to anxiety than positive affect (Tellegen, 1985; Watson & Clarke, 1984; Watson, Clarke, & Tellegen, 1988). According to the proposals of Jones et al. (1994), it was hypothesized that negative affect would correlate more strongly with cognitive and somatic anxiety intensity than would positive affect. The results supported this hypothesis. Specifically, participants who were high or low in negative affect tended to report high or low anxiety intensity despite their levels of positive affect. Additionally, it was hypothesized that performers high in negative affect would interpret their anxiety symptoms as more debilitative, whereas performers high in positive affect would interpret their anxiety symptoms as more facilitative. However, Jones and his colleagues (1996) suggested that positive affect plays a more dominant role in predicting interpretation or direction of both cognitive and somatic anxiety than does negative affect.

Jones (1995) adapted the work of Carver and Scheier (1986, 1988) and presented a control model of debilitative and facilitative competitive state anxiety (figure 7.10). Jones' (1995) model proposes that anxiety is interpreted as facilitative when a person has positive expectancies of coping and achieving the goal. On the other hand, anxiety is proposed to be debilitative when expectancies with regard to coping and goal attainment are negative. Jones and Hanton (1996) tested Jones' (1995) model regarding goal attainment expectancies. The results were interpreted as supporting the hypothesis that swimmers with positive goal attainment expectancies would report anxiety symptoms as more facilitative than swimmers with uncertain or negative goal attainment expectancies. There was no difference in intensity of anxiety symptoms in the positive versus uncertain/negative goal attainment expectancy groups. Thus, both groups had similar ratings of anxiety intensity yet interpreted their anxiety differently based on expectancies of goal attainment. Jones and Hanton concluded that the best support for Jones' (1995) model was found with the perceptions of control over performance goals component.

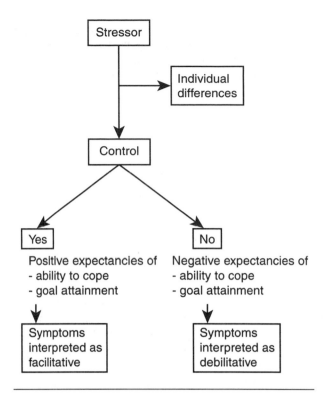

Figure 7.10 Jones' control model of debilitative and facilitative anxiety.

Reprinted, by permission, from G. Jones, 1995, "More than just a game: research developments and issues in competitive anxiety in sport," *British Journal of Psychology*, 86: 449–478. Reproduced with permission from the British Journal of Psychology, © The British Psychological Society.

Edwards and Hardy (1996), contrary to previous research, found that direction of anxiety symptoms did not account for more variance in netball performance than did intensity of anxiety symptoms. Interestingly, Edwards and Hardy (1996) examined their data in relationship to the catastrophe hypothesis and found that high cognitive anxiety can have a facilitative or debilitative performance effect, depending on physiological arousal levels. This finding is significant because it examined interaction effects of cognitive anxiety intensity and physiological arousal. Thus, perhaps this interaction of cognitive anxiety and physiological arousal acts as an underlying mechanism in the interpretation of anxiety symptoms.

Several researchers have suggested that self-confidence may act as a moderator influencing the directional interpretation of competitive anxiety symptoms. Jones and Swain (1992) found that participants high in competitiveness reported self-confidence as more facilitating than did participants low in competitiveness. Jones et al. (1993) found that self-confidence was the only predictor of balance beam performance and accounted for

8.5% of the variance. Jones et al. (1994) found that elite performers had higher self-confidence. Additionally, nonelite participants who interpreted anxiety as debilitative reported lower self-confidence than those who interpreted anxiety as facilitative. Similar to Jones et al. (1994), Jones and Swain (1995) found that both elite and nonelite cricketers interpreting anxiety as facilitating reported higher levels of self-confidence than those interpreting anxiety as debilitating. Edwards and Hardy (1996) found that netball players with higher levels of self-confidence reported anxiety as more facilitative to performance than those with lower levels of self-confidence. Additionally, as self-confidence increased, anxiety intensity scores decreased.

To summarize, then, initial research has been consistent in showing the importance of distinguishing direction of anxiety symptoms, or interpretation of anxiety symptoms as facilitative or debilitative to performance, from intensity of anxiety symptoms (Jones & Hanton, 1996; Jones & Swain, 1992, 1995; Jones et al., 1993, 1994, 1996). Thus, simply measuring anxiety intensity does not provide a complete picture of the anxiety–performance relationship, and anxiety direction must be taken into account. As Swain and Jones (1992) pointed out, individuals may experience the same intensity of anxiety, yet they may interpret the effect on performance differently. One study inconsistent with other research is that of Edwards and Hardy (1996), whose results indicated that anxiety direction did not contribute to the variance in performance any more than anxiety intensity. The authors suggested that differences in the number of teams studied, participant pools, and possible cultural differences may have influenced their findings.

Several individual differences have been examined in relationship to intensity and direction dimensions of anxiety symptoms, including skill level, affect, goal attainment expectancies, and self-confidence. Results from several studies suggest that elite performers interpret anxiety as more facilitating and less debilitating to performance than do nonelite performers (Jones & Swain, 1995; Jones et al., 1994). Performers high in positive affect and low in negative affect report anxiety as more facilitative than performers low in positive affect or high in negative affect (Jones et al., 1996). In relationship to goal expectancies, performers with positive expectancies for goal attainment reported anxiety as more facilitative than performers with uncertain or negative goal attainment expectancies (Jones & Hanton, 1996). Finally, studies have suggested that self-confidence

may protect against negative affects of anxiety (Edwards & Hardy, 1996; Hardy & Jones, 1990; Jones et al., 1993).

Several limitations have been noted in the current line of research examining intensity and direction dimensions of competitive anxiety symptoms. First, the directional component of the modified CSAI-2 has not been fully validated (Jones et al., 1993). However, Burton (1998) suggested that initial research using the modified CSAI-2 has supported the internal consistency and construct validity of the scale. Further validation should be done before researchers pursue lines of research in the area. Second, Edwards and Hardy (1996) suggested that the length of the modified CSAI-2 may be excessive with the addition of the directional component. Third, neither intensity nor direction dimensions have accounted for much variance in performance (Jones et al., 1993). Fourth, on a conceptual level, the question of whether facilitative anxiety is really anxiety is important. Jones and colleagues (Jones, 1995; Jones & Swain, 1992, 1995; Jones et al., 1994) suggested that the positive interpretation of anxiety symptoms (as currently defined on the modified CSAI-2) may be more appropriately labeled as "excitement" or "motivation." Although this issue remains unresolved, it may explain why many anxiety researchers interested in predicting performance have called for examination of, or have begun to examine, other emotions (Gould & Udry, 1994; Hanin, 1997; Hardy et al., 1996; Prapavessis & Grove, 1991). Hence, although the anxiety–performance relationship is a critical topic to examine, efforts to do so will be enhanced if approaches are expanded to simultaneously examine other emotions and affective states.

FUTURE DIRECTIONS IN EXAMINING THE AROUSAL– PERFORMANCE RELATIONSHIP

The time has come to reexamine the relationship between arousal and athletic performance by testing a number of conceptual systems that might better explain this complex phenomenon. To adequately test these theoretical frameworks, however, we will need to make a number of methodological, conceptual, and empirical changes in our research approaches:

• Eradicate ambiguities in the use of arousal terminology

- Develop conditions necessary to test arousal–performance relationship theories adequately

- Incorporate a number of methodological refinements in future investigations

- Consider alternative methodological paradigms, research questions, and approaches when designing future studies

These changes are discussed in some detail in the following sections.

Alleviating Ambiguities in the Use of Arousal Terminology

As noted earlier, there has been considerable inconsistency in the sport psychology literature in the use of arousal-related terminology. This is an extremely important issue because the various terms that pertain to arousal may be related to performance in different ways. Moreover, because many of these concepts and subsequent measures of them have been used interchangeably, it is difficult if not impossible to determine what particular aspects of the arousal construct are being studied, what overlap exists between measures of each construct, and what links exist between specific concepts and performance.

To eliminate the confusion caused by the inconsistent usage of arousal-related terminology, figure 7.11 contains a conceptual model for integrating arousal construct terminology. Arousal/activation is the central construct in this model (Level 1) and is operationally defined as a general physiological and psychological activation of the organism, which varies on a continuum from deep sleep to intense excitement. Activation is the feeling state one achieves in an effort to prepare to perform, whereas arousal is the activity of the organism that results from some unplanned stimulus (Hardy et al., 1996). For years this psychobiological construct has been the focus of study for sport psychologists attempting to link various psychophysiological and emotional states to performance.

Level 2 of the model differentiates between a physiological arousal/activation component (Level 2.A) and a cognitive interpretation-appraisal arousal/activation component (Level 2.B). The physiological component is assessed via measures such as heart rate, respiration, and skin conductance. The cognitive interpretation-appraisal component is further subdivided into three subcomponents including somatic state anxiety (Subcomponent 2.B-1), cognitive state

anxiety or telic state (Subcomponent 2.B-2), and paratelic state (Subcomponent 2.B-3). The somatic state anxiety can be defined as the athlete's perception of his or her level of physiological arousal and is assessed via the CSAI-2 Somatic Anxiety subscale or the Emotionality subscale of the Worry–Emotionality Inventory. The cognitive state anxiety, or telic state, component is the athlete's "negative affect" (worry) appraisal of arousal and can be measured via the CSAI-2 Cognitive Anxiety subscale or the Worry subscale of the Worry–Emotionality Inventory. It is also most likely to relate to Jones' debilitative anxiety notion. The paratelic state, or positive affect appraisal, component of the model is the athlete's positive affect appraisal, which, although hypothesized to exist in reversal theory, has not been operationalized through any valid assessment instrument. Jones, however, used a modified version of the CSAI-2 to measure facilitative state anxiety. Last, Subcomponents 2.B-2.1 and 2.B-2.2 further subdivide the cognitive anxiety, or telic state, subcomponent into interpersonal and intragroup state anxiety according to Hanin's (1980) conceptualization. Finally, the right side of the model depicts trait anxiety, which influences the athlete's cognitive interpretation–appraisal of arousal (Level 2.B) and which, in turn, affects actual physiological arousal (Level 2.A). Sport-specific global trait anxiety is measured by the SCAT, whereas the SAS was developed by R.E. Smith, Smoll, and Schutz (1990) to measure multidimensional trait anxiety.

It is important to note that Level 2 of the model makes a critical distinction between physiological and psychological arousal/activation. Specifically, physiological arousal/activation manifestations are hypothesized to be related to, but conceptually distinct from, one's cognitive interpretation of the arousal/activation construct. This is not to say that physiological arousal/activation and cognitive appraisal of arousal components do not share common variance. In fact, they would be expected to be correlated. We contend, however, that although they are correlated to some degree, they are in many ways unique. Hence, by differentiating between Levels 2.A and 2.B of the model, researchers will not fall prey to the conceptual trap of viewing physiological arousal/activation and state anxiety assessment as synonymous. However, studies should be conducted to identify common variance between these components, while at the same time determining how and/or whether these components differentially relate to performance.

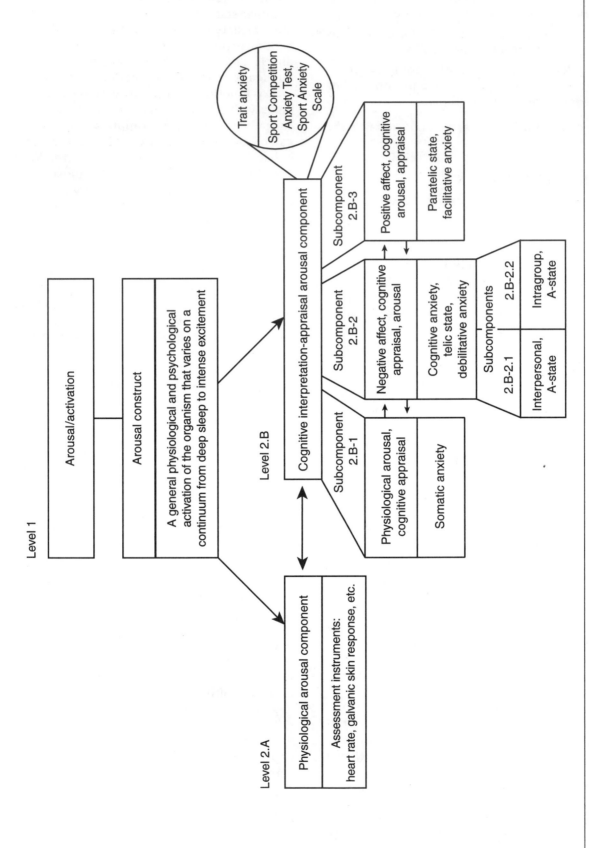

Figure 7.11   A conceptual model for integrating arousal construct terminology.

To further clarify the theoretical distinctions between arousal-related terminology, the conceptual model for integrating arousal/activation terms can be placed easily within current process models of stress (e.g., McGrath, 1970). In particular, figure 7.12 integrates these two models. This figure includes the previously discussed four stages of the stress process. Hence, the athlete is placed under environmental demand (Stage 1), perceives that environment as more or less threatening (Stage 2), and responds to that demand (Stage 3), which leads in turn to specific performance outcomes and various consequences (Stage 4). Furthermore, at Stage 3 in McGrath's model, the conceptual clarification of the arousal terminology has the greatest impact; that is, the athlete has a physi-

ological and psychological response consisting of an arousal/activation component and a cognitive interpretation–appraisal component. These result in varying levels of somatic state anxiety, cognitive state anxiety, and paratelic state responses. These physiological and psychological responses, in turn, influence performance. Stages 3 and 4 of the stress process have been our major focus.

Testing Arousal–Performance Relationship Theories

To adequately test alternative theoretical frameworks for explaining the arousal–performance relationship, investigators must achieve the following:

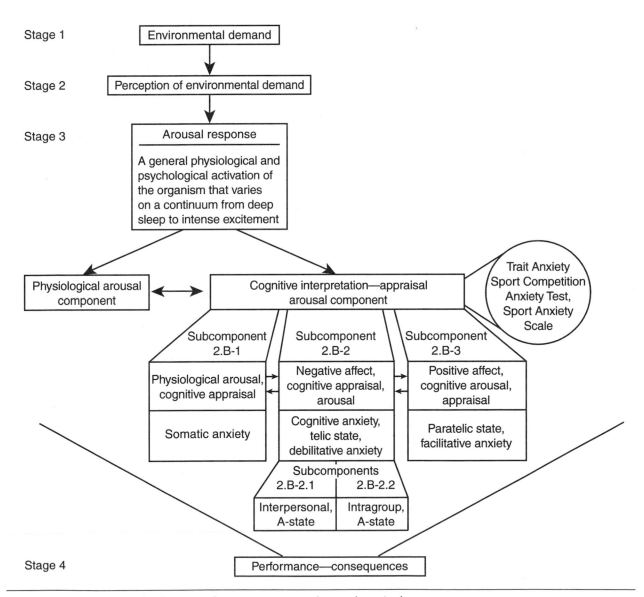

Figure 7.12 The relationship between the stress process and arousal terminology.

- Adequately assess arousal and related states
- Use more sensitive measures of athletic performance
- Employ intraindividual anxiety analyses
- Create at least three distinct levels of arousal when testing nonlinear predictions

These conditional requirements are discussed next.

Assessing Arousal and Related States

If our understanding of the arousal–performance relationship is to improve, we must develop better assessments of the arousal construct. This is required at both the conceptual and empirical levels.

From a conceptual perspective, it has been shown that *arousal, activation, stress, cognitive state anxiety, somatic state anxiety, telic state,* and *paratelic state* have precise meanings. However, researchers (e.g., Gould et al., 1987; Weinberg & Genuchi, 1980) often have used these terms interchangeably. This has caused considerable confusion in the literature because it was assumed that these concepts measured the same underlying construct. However, as previously noted, these concepts may not be related to performance in the same manner. For example, *physiological arousal* and *somatic anxiety* often are viewed as synonymous. However, as Deffenbacher (1980) noted, somatic anxiety is a subject's cognitive interpretation of his or her physiological arousal, not arousal per se. Thus, a portion of the variance between physiological arousal and somatic anxiety may be common and related to performance in the same manner. Alternatively, another portion of the physiological arousal or somatic anxiety variances may be unique and related to performance in a different way.

In a similar vein, reversal theory emphasizes that one's physiological arousal is not directly linked to performance but that the arousal–performance relationship is mediated by one's metamotivational state (i.e., whether one is in a telic or paratelic state). Hence, it is imperative that the link between physiological arousal and cognitive interpretations of physiological arousal be examined.

Finally, some theorists have distinguished between arousal types in the brain itself (Pribram & McGuinness, 1975; Tucker & Williams, 1984). For instance, Pribram and McGuinness hypothesized that three separate neural systems interact: one

regulating input arousal, another regulating response activation, and a third coordinating activation and arousal into effort. Thus, physiological arousal may be more complicated than was once thought.

Unfortunately, no one conceptual system for viewing arousal/activation and related concepts has been accepted by sport psychology researchers. We hope that our model will help rectify this situation. However, even if future investigators do not accept this particular model, they can help alleviate the situation by clearly defining, in both a theoretical and an empirical/operational fashion, the arousal variables that they employ and by using both physiological and psychological measures of arousal/activation whenever possible. This will allow investigators to search for causal links between these concepts and their relationship to performance. Furthermore, researchers must attempt to determine theoretical and empirical differences between physiological and cognitive anxiety/arousal states. For example, although cognitive state anxiety may provide an important measure of negative affect associated with heightened physiological arousal, no adequate measure of paratelic, or positive, psychological arousal states exists. Hence, a need exists to develop a valid measure of the paratelic state. Finally, studies are needed that simultaneously use measures of such states as physiological arousal, somatic anxiety, and cognitive anxiety so that the interrelationships between these states can be compared and contrasted.

Another major measurement issue focuses on the need to use multidimensional arousal/anxiety approaches when examining the arousal–performance relationship. For instance, multidimensional anxiety theory (Wine, 1980) and empirical evidence (Burton, 1988; Gould et al., 1987; Parfitt & Hardy, 1993) suggest that cognitive and somatic state anxiety differentially influence performance. Similarly, Doctor and Altman (1969) and Gould and colleagues (1987) found evidence that somatic anxiety was only related to performance within lower strata of worry, or cognitive anxiety. In a similar vein, Hardy and Parfitt (1991) found initial support for the catastrophe theory prediction that physiological arousal and associated somatic anxiety are negatively related to performance when cognitive anxiety is high but not when it is low. Finally, Svebak and Murgatroyd (1985) reported that telic-dominant subjects showed higher task-irrelevant muscle tension during performance than did paratelic dominant subjects. These results suggest that arousal/anxiety must be viewed and assessed as multidimensional phenomena and that investigators must begin to determine the links between separate arousal–anxiety states and performance, regardless of the theoretical framework used.

Measuring Athletic Performance

Not only must future investigators better conceptualize and assess arousal and arousal-related constructs, but athletic performance must be assessed more accurately and precisely. Too often, researchers attempting to assess the arousal–performance relationship have failed to use standardized performance measures. For example, Gould et al. (1984) assessed performance by outcome (win–loss) across wrestling matches. Because different opponents competed in each match of the tournament, performance was not standardized; rather, it changed as a function of the opponent. Similarly, in golf studies conducted by Martens and colleagues (1990) and McAuley (1985), performance was compared on the front versus the back nine holes of the golf course or across different courses. Thus, in these studies, changing and nonstandardized task demands may have confounded or masked relationships between state anxiety and performance. A better test of the arousal–performance relationship can be obtained when task demands are held constant from one arousal or state anxiety assessment to another. Such was the case with a study conducted by Gould and colleagues (1987), where pistol shooters were required to perform on five separate occasions under identical performance conditions (e.g., identical targets, distance from target, weapon, and range). Hence, only when performance environments are standardized will investigators be able to conduct an accurate and reliable test of the arousal–performance relationship.

Weinberg (1990) suggested that the use of outcome or win–loss performance measures in arousal–performance studies is also a major concern because such measures often lack sensitivity and precision. Specifically, he questioned norm-referenced measures that compare performances of competitors (e.g., 10th-place finish in a road race, lst place in a bowling tournament). For example, a person could win a contest and not approach a personal best or, conversely, could be labeled as an inferior performer (e.g., last-place finish) yet achieve a personal best. Similarly,

Weinberg indicated that comparing game scores may be inaccurate because losing a basketball game 100 to 65 to a top-ranked team might be quite different from losing 100 to 65 to an inferior team. To alleviate these problems, field researchers should use performance measures similar to those used by Burton (1988), where swimmers' best times in an event were assessed relative to their own previous times in that event.

In addition to using standardized and more precise athletic performance measures, the use of process measures of performance also has been advocated (Gould, 1988; Hackfort & Schwenkmezger, 1989; Weinberg, 1990). Instead of focusing attention on the outcome or end result of task performance, process measures focus attention on how the skill is executed or the quality of movement per se. In essence, the process approach "is centrally concerned with how individuals organize and integrate their energies in the execution of motor skills" (Weinberg, 1990, p. 237). Thus, electromyographic or kinematic measures of the movements employed during task performance itself are recommended.

Excellent examples of the utility of using process measures of task performance in arousal–performance relationship studies were provided in several investigations (Beuter & Duda, 1985; Beuter, Duda, & Widule, 1989; Weinberg, 1978; Weinberg & Hunt, 1976). In the Weinberg and Hunt study, electromyographic assessments were used to examine electrical activity in muscles occurring before, during, and after performance on a throwing accuracy task. Results revealed that, compared with low-trait-anxious participants who received failure feedback, high-trait-anxious participants who received failure feedback not only demonstrated inferior performance but displayed more electrical activity in relevant muscles before, during, and after throwing. These individuals also exhibited co-contraction of relevant muscle groups. Similar results were found when the original work was replicated and extended two years later (Weinberg, 1978).

A different but equally useful approach was employed by Beuter and her colleagues (Beuter & Duda, 1985; Beuter et al., 1989). In particular, movement efficiency was assessed via measures of kinematic characteristics of movement (spatial–temporal organization of the ankle, knee, and hip energies as assessed via biomechanical high-speed filming) in children performing a stepping motion under high- and low-arousal conditions. Results reveal a significant increase in the kinetic energy ratios under increased arousal. These results suggest that under high-arousal states, automatic-smooth movements become less smooth and less efficient as a result of volitional control.

Many advantages can be obtained from using more precise and standardized performance measures when examining arousal–performance relationships. In addition, the use of process measures provides investigators with an entirely different perspective on the arousal–performance relationship by identifying what happens during the movement per se. For this reason, process measure studies hold tremendous potential for facilitating arousal–performance relationship theory, because they provide data as to why performance may change under conditions of high arousal or anxiety.

Using Intraindividual Analyses

An important development in arousal–performance relationship methodology has been the use of intraindividual analyses. Intraindividual analyses were first advocated by Sonstroem and Bernardo (1982). Use of intraindividual analyses involves taking multiple state anxiety assessments on the same athlete and then relating the individual's anxiety deviations around his or her own norms to performance. This method differs from previous analyses that compared state anxiety scores between subjects and then linked these scores to performance. For example, in the Sonstroem and Bernardo investigation, female intercollegiate basketball players completed state anxiety assessments before at least three games. State anxiety scores of each subject were standardized relative to that subject's own range and median for the three scores and then were linked to performance.

With this procedure, an inverted-U relationship was found between state anxiety and performance across all subjects. Similarly, investigations by Gould and colleagues (1987), Burton (1988), and Krane et al. (1994) also demonstrated the value of using intraindividual analyses in testing multidimensional state anxiety–performance relationships in pistol shooting, swimming, and softball. Neiss (1988) and Landers (1980) both advocated that arousal researchers who use physiological assessments consider Lacey and Lacey's (1958) notions of interresponse stereotypy and intraresponse stereotypy, which emphasize the identification of specific arousal measures (e.g., heart rate vs. galvanic skin response) that typify specific individuals' stress responses. Neiss and Landers also

suggested that there is a need to look for intraindividual changes in these specific arousal measures when relating them to performance.

Relative to intraindividualizing anxiety and performance data when testing the arousal–performance relationship, Raglin (1992) has been highly critical of the previously mentioned procedures. He correctly identified a flaw in the procedure, that being the assumption that an athlete's median level of anxiety taken across a time span would be moderate. However, his overall conclusion that studies using this procedure should be discounted is incorrect, because if this assumption was false, the likelihood of finding the hypothesized optimal anxiety–performance relationships would be reduced, not increased (Hardy et al., 1996). The key, then, is to use the procedure recommended by Hardy (1996a) to check raw data to ensure that median anxiety scores are indeed moderate.

It is becoming increasingly evident that it is more useful for investigators to examine relative changes in state anxiety/arousal assessments around individual subjects' own previous scores than absolute anxiety/arousal measure changes. The use of between-subjects analyses to test the relationship between anxiety/arousal and performance may not be appropriate. Hence, intraindi-vidual analyses should be conducted in the future.

Testing Nonlinear Arousal–Performance Relationship Predictions

An often overlooked but very important recommendation advocated by Martens (1977) is that when designing tests of the inverted-U hypothesis, investigators must create or assess three distinct levels of arousal. That is, because the inverted-U hypothesis predicts performance differences between low, moderate, and high anxiety levels, to adequately test this hypothesis researchers must obtain at least three significantly different anxiety score measures. Moreover, although these scores must be significantly different, they should be theoretically distinct as well. For example, the scores on the CSAI-2 (Martens et al., 1990) can range from a low of 9 to a high of 36. It is possible and highly probable in laboratory research that an investigator will obtain three significantly different anxiety levels on this scale (e.g., 13, 16, 19). However, from a theoretical perspective, the highest score only approaches the midpoint of the scale, with none of the scores being classified as high anxiety in an absolute sense. Hence, the inverted-U hypothesis cannot be adequately tested with this set of scores, because high anxiety was never assessed or induced. Although the previously discussed intraindividual anxiety analyses may help alleviate this problem (because high anxiety is determined relative to a subject's typical level of state anxiety as opposed to an absolute scale level), it is still imperative that researchers create at least three distinct levels of state anxiety within subjects when testing the inverted-U or other nonlinear models (e.g., catastrophe theory). Moreover, recognizing whether significantly different scores fall within low, moderate, or high scale levels in an absolute sense is important, because multidimensional anxiety investigators (Doctor & Altman, 1969; Gould et al., 1987) have found or predicted that different anxiety–performance relationships occur depending on whether subjects perform under high somatic anxiety or low somatic anxiety.

CRITICAL RESEARCH APPROACHES AND QUESTIONS

Although it is extremely important for investigators to construct conditions to adequately test arousal–performance relationship hypotheses, other paradigmatic issues also must be considered. Chief among these are decisions relative to the types of research approaches to be taken and specific classes of questions to be posed. In particular, investigators need to do the following:

• Conduct idiographic investigations
• Use qualitative methodologies
• Conduct time series analyses
• Move from correlational to causal designs through arousal control investigations
• Broaden their focus of study to other arousal/activation constructs
• Examine complex interactions between arousal-related emotions
• Simultaneously test multiple theories
• Further examine task type influences on the arousal–performance relationship
• Rethink and improve anxiety and arousal-related state assessments

Idiographic Investigations

The traditional sport psychology study of the arousal–performance relationship has used a no-

mothetic approach, in that hypothesized relationships among constructs are examined across large groups of individuals. By its very nature this approach requires that the investigator assume a reductionistic orientation, because it is not logistically possible to study large groups of athletes in a holistic fashion. However, Martens (1987b) argued that sport psychologists also should use such idiographic approaches as case studies, in-depth interviews, and participant observations to make real gains in knowledge about athletes. Given the multivariate nature and complexity of the arousal–performance relationship, using such in-depth approaches would better allow investigators to understand how anxiety affects the athlete as a whole and what systems influence performance over time. It would provide a richness and depth of knowledge about anxiety and performance that has not been generated through the exclusive use of nomothetic methods.

Although we advocate the use of idiographic approaches, we recognize the weakness of such approaches. The gains made in the depth and richness of knowledge are offset by a weakening in the reliability of the knowledge gained. Hence, it would be foolish for investigators to totally abandon the nomothetic approach for an idiographic orientation. Rather, we agree with Hackfort and Schwenkmezger (1989), who recommended that anxiety investigators use both orientations of study. For example, given the need to examine reversal theory predictions, investigators might do well to conduct in-depth case studies to determine if telic and paratelic states exist, whether reversals take place, and under what conditions reversals occur. In fact, Kerr (1997) has already begun using such methods in his own work. Once these concepts are better understood in individual athletes, reliable and valid telic–paratelic state measures could be developed, and large-group studies could be conducted to determine the generalizability and reliability of any identified relationships. Similarly, a better understanding of the catastrophe model could be obtained if investigators studied its predictions across groups of athletes while simultaneously conducting in-depth case studies with specific individuals or subgroups. The nomothetic portion of the investigation would determine whether reliable and stable relationships existed in key variables, whereas the idiographic portion would generate important information about such issues as what cognitions and emotions occur when an athlete "goes over the top" and experiences a catastrophe.

We strongly recommend that future investigators of the arousal–performance relationship use idiographic as well as nomothetic research methodologies in their investigations. Only by combining the two approaches will we maximize our understanding of this complex relationship.

Qualitative Investigations

Closely paralleling the need for more idiographic approaches to the study of the arousal–performance relationship is the need for qualitative investigations. Although only a few qualitative investigations have been conducted in the arousal–performance area, an excellent example of the depth, detail, and richness that can be gained by studying athletes in a qualitative manner was provided by Scanlan and her colleagues (Scanlan, Ravizza, & Stein, 1989; Scanlan, Stein, & Ravizza, 1989, 1990). In this investigation, a variety of very specific sources of enjoyment and stress were identified in former elite figure skaters. More recently, Swain and Jones (1993) followed up a quantitative investigation of intensity and frequency dimensions of competitive state anxiety with structured qualitative interviews and verified the importance of distinguishing between these two anxiety types. These qualitative results, then, demonstrated that not all anxiety experienced was perceived as debilitative to performance.

The strength of the qualitative approach is that it allows the subject to describe in his or her own words the naturally occurring events that surround the phenomenon of interest. The qualitative approach may be especially useful in identifying new variables and relationships in unexplored areas or in obtaining in-depth assessments of athletes' emotions and cognitions. Hence, anxiety–performance investigators would do well to use such an approach.

Time Series Analyses

A third means of advancing our understanding of the anxiety–performance relationship is for investigators to study relationships between anxiety concepts like telic states, somatic anxiety, and arousal over time. Too often in the past, the difficulty of collecting data across time has prevented investigators from conducting such studies. However, time series analyses are essential to test newer anxiety–performance conceptualizations like the catastrophe model. Moreover, many of the difficulties in conducting time series analyses have been alleviated with the advent of highly reliable, portable, psychophysiological testing instruments.

An excellent example of the utility of using time series designs and analyses was a study conducted by Hagtvet and Renmin (1996) in the test anxiety literature. These investigators examined the effects of cognitive, emotional, and motivational parameters on equivalent puzzle performance assessed over time. Findings revealed that state anxiety and the motive to avoid failure were called on at different points in the performance process. Hence, they did not have constant effects; rather, their influence was time dependent.

Finally, investigators must remember that the varied arousal constructs depicted in figure 7.11 are not independent entities. Rather, they are interrelated and most likely will interact with each other over varying sequences of time. For instance, increased physiological arousal may increase perceived threat in an athlete, which increases that athlete's state anxiety and thus hinders performance. This sequence of events, in turn, is perceived as more threatening by the athlete and causes even more physiological arousal. Taking assessments at only one point in time would not reveal the complex interrelationships between these variables. Only through time series analyses will investigators truly understand these time-linked relationships.

Moving From Correlational to Causal Designs

A major interpretive problem inherent in the vast majority of previous studies on the arousal–performance relationship is the correlational nature of their design. That is, arousal or anxiety typically is assessed on a number of occasions and related to performance measures taken on those same occasions. Seldom, however, is the arousal or anxiety level of the athlete manipulated in an effort to assess its hypothesized effects on performance. Although arousal levels have been successfully manipulated in laboratory investigations (e.g., Martens & Landers, 1970), this is very difficult. It is difficult to produce, in laboratory settings, the highly stressful conditions inherent in actual competitive environments. This situation is further compounded by the ethical dilemmas that arise in field settings, where it is often considered unethical to elevate an athlete's arousal level to an extremely high level.

Although it is not possible to manipulate anxiety/arousal in ecologically valid settings, investigators could implement causal designs. For example, Krane and her colleagues (Alexander & Krane, 1996; Krane, Williams, & Feltz, 1992) used path analysis to examine causal relationships among predicted antecedents of anxiety, cognitive and somatic anxiety, and performance. These studies suggest that the impact of performance on subsequent cognitive and somatic anxiety is larger than the impact of anxiety on subsequent performance. The direction of this relationship typically is not examined in studies of the anxiety–performance relationship.

Additionally, researchers could examine functional or causal designs by teaching athletes to use arousal management strategies and then having them employ these strategies systematically. This approach will facilitate our understanding of arousal–performance relationships only if time series analyses are used where relationships are established between arousal concepts and performance. Then, interventions could be introduced to modify these relationships. For instance, investigators might test the efficacy of the catastrophe model by assessing athletes' somatic anxiety, cognitive anxiety, and performance over a period of time. The covariation of these variables then would be measured. Later, a subgroup of these athletes could receive a stress management intervention like R.E. Smith's (1980) stress management training, with other athletes serving as controls. If the intervention athletes were able to prevent catastrophes through their management of cognitive and somatic anxiety levels and the controls experienced catastrophes, some degree of causation would be demonstrated, thus facilitating our understanding of the arousal–performance relationship.

Broaden Focus to Other Arousal/Activation Constructs

One common trend throughout most of the recent arousal/activation theories and hypotheses is the call to broaden the study of emotional states beyond the traditional view of anxiety as negatively effecting performance. It is clear that if one is interested in predicting athletic performance, looking at the traditional negative effects of anxiety is not enough—other arousal-related emotional states must be simultaneously examined. Numerous researchers have supported the notion of examining broader emotional states in an effort to predict performance, including Jones' (1996) and

Jones and Swain's (1992, 1995) call for examining the direction and intensity of anxiety; Hanin's reformulated IZOF positive and negative emotion model; Hardy's (1996a) call to look at higher order catastrophe models that include measures of self-confidence and perceptions of control; and Kerr's (1997) reversal theory explanation for motivation and emotion. Indeed, as Gould and Udry (1994) suggested, peak athletic performance seems to be characterized by an optimal recipe of arousal and emotion-related states.

It is interesting to note that the call for focusing on emotions other than anxiety is not limited to the sport psychology literature. Jones (1996) pointed out that noted psychologist Lazarus (1993) shifted his emphasis from his earlier work on stress to a more encompassing approach including emotions. Hence, anxiety researchers in general are taking a broader focus to the study of anxiety.

This call does not mean that anxiety should be abandoned as a research topic in sport psychology. In fact, anxiety will remain an important component in the arousal–performance relationship and should continue to be studied. What we suggest, however, is that other arousal-related emotions be examined.

Examining Complex Interactions Between Arousal-Related Emotions

Although the catastrophe model has been criticized for being too complex (Gill, 1994) and lacking parsimony (Landers & Boutcher, 1998), one of its most promising features and contributions to the literature is the attention it has brought to the notion that arousal/activation-related emotions such as cognitive state anxiety, physiological arousal, and self-confidence interact to predict athletic performance. Indeed, the catastrophe model research conducted by Hardy and his colleagues (see Hardy, Jones, & Gould, 1996, for a review) has clearly shown that these anxiety components interact to influence performance. And although parsimony is certainly a criterion of a good theory or model, a more important criterion is that the model provide an adequate fit with the data. Arousal–performance researchers, then, must begin to more vigorously examine interactions in arousal/activation emotions.

Multitheory Tests

A problem that has plagued sport psychology research in general and arousal–performance relationship research in particular has been investigators' tendency to rely on one theory. That is, most studies have been designed to test specifically only the inverted-U hypothesis or the multidimensional anxiety theory predictions. However, supporting one theory in isolation of other existing views does not advance science as fast as when two theories are pitted against one another in the same investigation. The need for multitheory tests may be especially appropriate in the arousal–performance area because a number of theories exist and because the various constructs forming the basis of these theories seem to be so interwoven. For this reason, investigators of the arousal–performance relationship should design experiments and studies that simultaneously test multiple theoretical contentions. For instance, an investigator who uses the CSAI-2 to test multidimensional anxiety theory could first examine the predicted linear relationship between cognitive anxiety and performance as well as the predicted curvilinear relationship between somatic anxiety and performance. After those analyses, the researcher then could use the same data to test the catastrophe model by examining the joint effects of these two variables on performance. Such an approach would provide maximum theoretical benefit.

An excellent example of a study that tested multiple theories or models in the anxiety–performance area was conducted by Hardy (1996a). Specifically, the investigation was designed to test multidimensional anxiety theory versus the catastrophe model in predicting golf performance. Golfers' physiological arousal was assessed continually via heart rate as they played a round of golf. Additionally, self-reports of cognitive anxiety, somatic anxiety, and self-confidence were taken. Although neither the catastrophe model nor MAT proved to be a superior predictor of performance, results identified shortcomings of both (the need to include self-confidence and control measures and to examine the anxiety–performance relationship over time). Importantly, this type of research is essential for investigators to determine which models and theories account for the greatest percentage of performance variation and to determine where models potentially may overlap.

Further Examine Task Type Influences on the Arousal–Performance Relationship

One reason consistent support for arousal-performance relationship models may be so elusive is the fact that investigators have focused the bulk of their attention on examining global performance measures. A number of investigators (see Hardy, Jones, & Gould, 1996, for a review of performance measures), however, have focused attention on adopting general psychological research on multidimensional arousal effects on performance processing to sport performance. For example, Hockey and Hamilton (1983) contended that different environmental stressors cause qualitatively different activation states that positively affect some aspects of performance and negatively affect others. Building on this notion, Parfitt et al. (1990) predicted that physiological arousal would enhance some athletic performance processes such as anaerobic power and impair others such as manual dexterity, working memory, and decision-making ability. Some empirical support has been found for this general line of research. For instance, Jones and Cale (1989) found a positive relationship between somatic anxiety and perceptual motor speed in hockey players. Similarly, Parfitt and Hardy (1987) found anxiety had negative effects on cricket batters' ability to rapidly discriminate between stimuli. This line of research appears promising and should be explored further.

Rethink and Improve Anxiety and Arousal-Related State Assessments

Evidence reviewed in this chapter has shown that arousal is a multifaceted construct. Telic/paratelic, intensity/direction, and facilitative/debilitative emotions have been identified as key arousal-related emotional components. With the advent of these new arousal-related constructs, however, comes the need to develop valid measures of them. Jones (1996), in fact, called for renewed efforts to overcome limits of self-report measures by more precisely defining the constructs of interest and developing more precise measures of them. Paralleling the development of better self-report measures is the need to use psychophysiological assessments more often. Measurement models are needed that interrelate cognitive and psychophysiological measures in a multidimensional system (Gill, 1994). Our understanding of the arousal–performance relationship will not be advanced until measurement is improved.

CONCLUSION

When considering future directions, it is easy to focus on what we do not know and forget how much progress has been made. In terms of the arousal–performance relationship, considerable progress has been made through our research efforts. A number of advances have been made in the measurement of state and trait anxiety and in methodological procedures for testing the arousal–performance relationship. We also know that the drive theory has little support, that arousal/activation is multifaceted, and that the relationship between arousal and performance is best described by more complex relationships, many of which are thought to be curvilinear in nature.

Especially exciting are the most recent theories and hypotheses that have been forwarded to take us beyond the inverted-U hypothesis. These theories include reversal and catastrophe models and, more recently, the intensity/direction of anxiety notion. Viewing state anxiety as a multidimensional phenomenon should continue to advance our understanding of the arousal–performance relationship. To maintain this momentum, however, more research is needed, especially systematic studies designed to tackle the complex relationships between various arousal-related constructs and performance. Additionally, investigators must not be afraid to venture into unexplored areas by testing fledgling theories and using new and innovative methodologies such as time series analyses and qualitative assessments. After all, only through innovative, systematic, and well-planned research studies has our current understanding of the arousal–performance relationship evolved. Hence, we challenge future investigators to use the ideas presented here to guide future research efforts and in so doing advance our understanding of the arousal–performance relationship.

REFERENCES

Alexander, V., & Krane, V. (1996). Relationships among performance expectations, anxiety, and performance in collegiate volleyball players. *Journal of Sport Behavior, 19,* 246–269.

Alpert, R., & Haber, N.N. (1960). Anxiety in academic achievement situations. *Journal of Abnormal and Social Psychology, 61,* 207–215.

Apter, M.J. (1976). Some data inconsistent with the optimal arousal theory of motivation. *Perceptual and Motor Skills, 43,* 1209–1210.

Apter, M.J. (1984). Reversal theory and personality: A review. *Journal of Research in Personality, 18,* 265–288.

Bacon, S.J. (1974). Arousal and the range of cue utilization. *Journal of Experimental Psychology, 103,* 81–87.

Beuter, A., & Duda, D.L. (1985). Analysis of the arousal/motor performance relationship in children using movement kinematics. *Journal of Sport Psychology, 7,* 229–243.

Beuter, A., Duda, D.L., & Widule, C.J. (1989). The effect of arousal on joint kinematics and kinetics in children. *Research Quarterly for Exercise and Sport, 60,* 109–116.

Borkovec, T.D. (1976). Physiological and cognitive processes in the regulation of arousal. In G.E. Schwartz & D. Shapiro (Eds.), *Consciousness and self-regulation: Advances in research* (Vol. 1, pp. 261–312). New York: Plenum Press.

Burton, D. (1988). Do anxious swimmers swim slower? Reexamining the elusive anxiety-performance relationship. *Journal of Sport and Exercise Psychology, 10,* 45–61.

Burton, D. (1998). Measuring competitive state anxiety. In J. Duda (Ed.), *Advances in sport and exercise psychology measurement* (pp. 129–148). Morgantown, WV: Fitness Information Technologies.

Carrier, C., Higson, V., Klimoski, V., & Peterson, E. (1984). The effects of facilitative and debilitative achievement anxiety on notetaking. *Journal of Educational Research, 77,* 133–138.

Caruso, C.M., Dzewaltowski, D.A., Gill, D.L., & McElroy, M.A. (1990). Psychological and physiological changes in competitive state anxiety during noncompetition and competition success and failure. *Journal of Sport & Exercise Psychology, 12,* 6–20.

Carver, C.S., & Scheier, M.F. (1986). Functional and dysfunctional responses to anxiety: The interaction between expectancies and self-focused attention. In R. Schwarzer (Ed.), *Self-related cognitions in anxiety and motivation* (pp. 111–141). Hillsdale, NJ: Erlbaum.

Carver, C.S., & Scheier, M.F. (1988). A control-process perspective on anxiety. *Anxiety Research, 1,* 17–22.

Cox, R. (1998). *Sport psychology: Concepts and applications* (4th ed.). Dubuque, IA: Brown.

Davids, D., & Gill, A. (1995). Multidimensional state anxiety prior to different levels of sport competition: Some problems with simulation tasks. *International Journal of Sport Psychology, 26,* 359–382.

Davidson, R.J., & Schwartz, G.E. (1976). The psychobiology of relaxation and related states: A multi-process theory. In D.I. Mostofsky (Ed.), *Behavior control and modification of physiological activity* (pp. 399–442). Englewood Cliffs, NJ: Prentice Hall.

Deffenbacher, J.L. (1980). Worry and emotionality in test anxiety. In I.G. Sarason (Ed.), *Test anxiety: Theory, research, and application* (pp. 111–128). Hillsdale, NJ: Erlbaum.

Doctor, R.M., & Altman, F. (1969). Worry and emotionality as components of test anxiety: Replication and further data. *Psychological Reports, 24,* 563–568.

Duffy, E. (1932). The relationship between muscular tension and quality of performance. *American Journal of Psychology, 44,* 535–546.

Easterbrook, J.A. (1959). The effect of emotion on cue utilization and the organization of behavior. *Psychological Review, 66,* 183–201.

Edwards, T., & Hardy, L. (1996). The interactive effects of intensity and direction of cognitive and somatic anxiety and self-confidence upon performance. *Journal of Sport & Exercise Psychology, 18,* 296–312.

Fisher, A.C. (1976). Psych up, psych out: Relationship of arousal to sport performance. In A.C. Fischer (Ed.), *Psychology of sport: Issues and insights* (pp. 136–144). Mountain View, CA: Mayfield.

Gill, D.L. (1994). A sport and exercise psychology perspective on stress. *Quest, 46,* 20–27.

Gill, D.L. (2000). *Psychological dynamics of sport and exercise* (2nd ed.). Champaign, IL: Human Kinetics.

Gill, D.L., & Deeter, T.E. (1988). Development of the SOQ. *Research Quarterly for Exercise and Sport, 59,* 191–202.

Gould, D. (1987). Promoting-positive sport experiences for children. In J.R. May & M.J. Asken (Eds.), *Sport psychology: The psychological health of the athlete* (pp. 77–98). New York: PMA.

Gould, D. (1988, June). *New directions in theory, research, and measurement in competitive anxiety.* Paper presented at the meeting of the North American Society for the Psychology of Sport and Physical Activity, Knoxville, TN.

Gould, D., & Petlichkoff, L. (1988). Psychological stress and the age-group wrestler. In E.W. Brown & C.F. Branta (Eds.), *Competitive sports for children and youth: An overview of research and issues* (pp. 63–73). Champaign, IL: Human Kinetics.

Gould, D., Petlichkoff, L., Simons, H., & Vevera, M. (1987). The relationship between Competitive State Anxiety Inventory-2 subscale scores and pistol shooting performance. *Journal of Sport & Exercise Psychology, 9,* 33–42.

Gould, D., Petlichkoff, L., & Weinberg, R. S. (1984). Antecedents of, temporal changes in, and relationships between CSAI-2 subcomponents. *Journal of Sport Psychology, 6,* 289–304.

Gould, D., & Tuffey, S. (1996). Zones of optimal functioning research: A review and critique. *Anxiety, Stress, and Coping, 9,* 53–68.

Gould, D., Tuffey, S., Hardy, L., & Lockbaum, M. (1993). Multidimensional state anxiety and middle distance running performance: An exploratory examination of Hanin's (1980) zones of optimal functioning hypothesis. *Journal of Applied Sport Psychology, 5,* 85–95.

Gould, D., & Udry, E. (1994). Psychological skills for enhancing performance: Arousal regulation strategies. *Medicine and Science in Sports and Exercise, 26,* 478–485.

Griffith, C.R. (1932). *Psychology of coaching.* New York: Scribner's.

Hackfort, D., & Schwenkmezger, P. (1989). Measuring anxiety in sports: Perspectives and problems. In D. Hackfort & C.D. Spielberger (Eds.), *Anxiety in sports: An international perspective* (pp. 55–76). New York: Hemisphere.

Hagtvet, K.A., & Renmin, Y. (1996). Anxiety and stress in a time-based performance process. *Anxiety, Stress, and Coping, 9,* 33–51.

Hammermeister, J., & Burton, D. (1995). Anxiety and the Ironman: Investigating the antecedents and consequences of endurance athletes' state anxiety. *The Sport Psychologist, 11,* 29–40.

Hanin, Y.I. (1980). A study of anxiety in sports. In W.F. Straub (Ed.), *Sport psychology: An analysis of athlete behavior* (pp. 236–249). Ithaca, NY: Mouvement.

Hanin, Y.L. (1989). Interpersonal and intragroup anxiety in sports. In D. Hackfort & C.D. Spielberger (Eds.), *Anxiety in sports: An international perspective* (pp. 19–28). New York: Hemisphere.

Hanin, Y. (1997). Emotions and athletic performance: Individual zones of optimal functioning model. *European Yearbook of Sport Psychology, 1,* 29–72.

Hanin, Y.L., & Spielberger, C.D. (1983). The development and validation of the Russian form of the State Trait Anxiety Inventory. In C.D. Spielberger & R. Diaz-Guerrero (Eds.), *Cross-cultural anxiety* (Vol. 2, pp. 15–26). Washington, DC: Hemisphere.

Hanson, T.W., & Gould, D. (1988). Factors affecting the ability of coaches to estimate their athletes' trait and state anxiety levels. *Sport Psychologist, 2,* 298–313.

Hardy, L. (1996a). A test of catastrophe models of anxiety and sports performance against multidimensional anxiety theory models using the method of dynamic differences. *Anxiety, Stress and Coping, 9,* 69–86.

Hardy, L. (1996b). Testing the predictions of the Cusp Catastrophe Model of anxiety and performance. *The Sport Psychologist, 10,* 140–156.

Hardy, L., & Fazey, J. (1987, June). *The inverted-U hypothesis: A catastrophe for sport psychology.* Paper presented at the meeting of the North American Society for the Psychology of Sport and Physical Activity, Vancouver, BC.

Hardy, L., & Jones, G. (1990). Future directions for research into stress in sport. In G. Jones & L. Hardy (Eds.), *Stress and performance in sport* (pp. 281–290). Chichester, UK: Wiley.

Hardy, L., Jones, G., & Gould, D. (1996). *Understanding psychological preparation for sport: Theory and practice of elite performers.* Chichester, UK: Wiley.

Hardy, L., & Parfitt, G. (1991). A catastrophe model of anxiety and performance. *British Journal of Psychology, 82,* 163–178.

Hardy, L., Parfitt, G., & Pates, J. (1994). Performance catastrophes in sport: A test of the hysteresis hypothesis. *Journal of Sport Sciences, 12,* 327–334.

Hebb, D.O. (1955). Drives in the C.N.S. (conceptual nervous system). *Psychological Review, 62,* 243–254.

Hockey, G.R.J., & Hamilton, P. (1983). The cognitive patterning of stress states. In G.R.J. Hockey (Ed.), *Stress and fatigue in human performance* (pp. 331–362). Chichester, UK: Wiley.

Hudesman, J., & Wiesner, E. (1978). Facilitating and debilitating test anxiety among college students and volunteers for desensitization workshops. *Journal of Clinical Psychology, 34,* 485–486.

Hull, C.L. (1943). *Principles of behavior.* New York: Appleton-Century.

Jones, G. (1991). Recent developments and current issues in competitive state anxiety research. *The Psychologist, 4,* 152–155.

Jones, G. (1995). More than just a game: Research developments and issues in competitive anxiety in sport. *British Journal of Psychology, 86,* 499–478.

Jones, G. (1996). Competitive anxiety research: Where to next? In Y. Theodorakis & A. Papaioannou (Eds.), *Sport psychology: New trends and applications* (pp. 353–364). Komotini, Greece: Salto.

Jones, G., & Cale, A. (1989). Relationships between multidimensional competitive state anxiety and cognitive and motor subcomponents of performance. *Journal of Sport Sciences, 7,* 229–240.

Jones, G., & Hanton, S. (1996). Interpretation of competitive anxiety symptoms and goal attainment expectancies. *Journal of Sport & Exercise Psychology, 18,* 144–157.

Jones, G., Hanton, S., & Swain, A. (1994). Intensity and interpretation of anxiety symptoms in elite and non-elite sports performers. *Personality and Individual Differences, 17,* 657–663.

Jones, J.G., & Hardy, L. (1989). Stress and cognitive functioning in sport. *Journal of Sport Sciences, 7,* 41–63.

Jones, G., & Swain, A. (1992). Intensity and direction as dimensions of competitive state anxiety and relationships with competitiveness. *Perceptual and Motor Skills, 74,* 467–472.

Jones, G., & Swain, A. (1995). Predispositions to experience debilitative and facilitative anxiety in elite and non-elite performers. *The Sport Psychologist, 9,* 201–211.

Jones, G., Swain, A., & Hardy, L. (1993). Intensity and direction dimensions of competitive state anxiety and relationships with performance. *Journal of Sport Sciences, 11,* 525–532.

Jones, G., Swain, A., & Harwood, C. (1996). Positive and negative affect as predictors of competitive anxiety. *Personality and Individual Differences, 20,* 109–114.

Karteroliotis, C., & Gill, D.L. (1987). Temporal changes in psychological and physiological components of state anxiety. *Journal of Sport Psychology, 9,* 261–274.

Kauss, D.R. (1980). *Peak performance: Mental game plans for maximizing your athletic potential.* Englewood Cliffs, NJ: Prentice Hall.

Kerr, J.H. (1985). The experience of arousal: A new basis for studying arousal effects in sport. *Journal of Sport Sciences, 3,* 169–179.

Kerr, J.H. (1987). Structural phenomenology and performance. *Journal of Human Movement Studies, 13,* 211–229.

Kerr, J.H. (1997). *Motivation and emotion in sport: Reversal theory.* East Sussex, UK: Psychology Press.

Klavora, P. (1977). An attempt to derive inverted-U curves based on the relationship between anxiety and athletic performance. In D.M. Landers & R.W. Christina (Eds.), *Psychology of motor behavior and sport—1977* (pp. 369–377). Champaign, IL: Human Kinetics.

Krane, V. (1990). *Anxiety and athletic performance: A test of the multidimensional anxiety and catastrophe theories.* Unpublished doctoral dissertation, University of North Carolina at Greensboro.

Krane, V. (1993). A practical method for examining the anxiety-athletic performance relationship: Zone of optimal functioning hypothesis. *The Sport Psychologist, 7,* 113–126.

Krane, V., & Finch, L. (1991, April). *Multidimensional trait anxiety as a predictor of multidimensional state anxiety.* Paper presented at the meeting of the American Alliance for Health, Physical Education, Recreation and Dance, San Francisco.

Krane, V., & Greenleaf, C. (1999). Counseling for the management of stress and anxiety in injured athletes. In D. Wiese-Bjornstahl & R. Ray (Eds.), *Counseling in sports medicine* (pp. 257–274). Champaign, IL: Human Kinetics.

Krane, V., Joyce, D., & Rafeld, J. (1994). Competitive anxiety, situation criticality, and softball performance. *Sport Psychologist, 8,* 58–72.

Krane, V., & Williams, J. (1987). Performance and somatic anxiety, cognitive anxiety, and confidence changes prior to competition. *Journal of Sport Behavior, 10,* 47–56.

Krane, V., & Williams, J. (1994). Cognitive anxiety, somatic anxiety, and confidence in track and field athletes: The impact of gender, competitive level and task characteristics. *International Journal of Sport Psychology, 25,* 205–217.

Krane, V., Williams, J., & Feltz, D.L. (1992). Path analysis examining relationships among cognitive anxiety, somatic anxiety, state confidence, performance expectations, and golf performance. *Journal of Sport Behavior, 15,* 279–295.

Lacey, J., & Lacey, B. (1958). Verification and extension of the principle of autonomic response-stereotypy. *American Journal of Psychology, 71,* 50–73.

Landers, D.M. (1980). The arousal-performance relationship revisited. *Research Quarterly for Exercise and Sport, 51,* 77–90.

Landers, D.M., & Boutcher, S.H. (1998). Arousal performance relationships. In J.M. Williams (Ed.), *Applied sport psychology: Personal growth to peak performance* (3rd ed., pp. 197–218). Mountain View, CA: Mayfield.

Landers, D.M., Wang, M.Q., & Courtet, P. (1985). Peripheral narrowing among experienced and inexperienced rifle shooters under low- and high-stress conditions. *Research Quarterly, 56,* 122–130.

Lazarus, R.S. (1993). From psychological stress to the emotions: A history of changing outlooks. *Annual Review of Psychology, 44,* 1–21.

Lowe, R. (1973). *Stress, arousal, and task performance of Little League baseball players.* Unpublished doctoral dissertation, University of Illinois at Urbana–Champaign.

Mahoney, M.J., & Avener, A. (1977). Psychology of the elite athlete: An exploratory study. *Cognitive Therapy and Research, 1,* 135–141.

Males, J.R., Kerr, J.H., & Gerkovich. M.M. (1998). Metamotivational states during slalom competition: A qualitative analysis using reversal theory. *Journal of Applied Sport Psychology, 10,* 185–200.

Malmo, R.B. (1959). Activation: A neuropsychological dimension. *Psychological Review, 66,* 367–386.

Martens, R. (1971). Anxiety and motor behavior: A review. *Journal of Motor Behavior, 2,* 151–179.

Martens, R. (1974). Arousal and motor performance. In J.H. Wilmore (Ed.), *Exercise and sport science reviews* (Vol. 2, pp. 155–188). New York: Academic Press.

Martens, R. (1977). *Sport competition anxiety test.* Champaign, IL: Human Kinetics.

Martens, R. (1987a). *Coaches guide to sport psychology.* Champaign, IL: Human Kinetics.

Martens, R. (1987b). Science, knowledge and sport psychology. *The Sport Psychologist, 1,* 29–55.

Martens, R., Burton, D., Vealey, R., Bump, L., & Smith, D. (1990). The development of the Competitive State

Anxiety Inventory-2 (CSAI-2). In R. Martens, R.S. Vealey, & D. Burton (Eds.), *Competitive anxiety in sport* (pp. 117–190). Champaign, IL: Human Kinetics.

Martens, R., & Landers, D.M. (1970). Motor performance under stress: A test of the inverted-U hypothesis. *Journal of Personality and Social Psychology, 16,* 29–37.

Martens, R., Vealey, R.S., & Burton, D. (Eds.) (1990). *Competitive anxiety in sport.* Champaign, IL: Human Kinetics.

Maynard, I.W., & Cotton, P.C. (1993). An investigation of two stress-management techniques in a field setting. *The Sport Psychologist, 7,* 375–387.

Maynard, I.W., Hemmings, B., & Warwick-Evans, L. (1995). The effects of a somatic intervention strategy on competitive state anxiety and performance in semiprofessional soccer players. *The Sport Psychologist, 9,* 51–64.

Maynard, I.W., & Howe, B.L. (1987). Interrelations of trait anxiety and state anxiety with game performance of rugby players. *Perceptual and Motor Skills, 64,* 599–602.

Maynard, I.W., Smith, M.J., & Warwick-Evans, L. (1995). The effects of a cognitive intervention strategy on competitive state anxiety and performance in semiprofessional soccer players. *Journal of Sport & Exercise Psychology, 17,* 428–446.

McAuley, E. (1985). State anxiety: Antecedent or result of sport performance. *Journal of Sport Behavior, 8,* 71–77.

McGrath, J.E. (1970). Major methodological issues. In J.E. McGrath (Ed.), *Social and psychological factors in stress* (pp. 19–49). New York: Holt, Rinehart, & Winston.

Morgan, W.P., O'Connor, P.J.O., Ellickson, K.A., & Bradley, P.W. (1988). Personality structure, mood states, and performance in elite male distance runners. *International Journal of Sport Psychology, 19,* 247–263.

Morgan, W.P., O'Connor, P.J.O., Sparling, P., & Pate, R.R. (1987). Psychological characterization of elite female distance runners. *International Journal of Sports Medicine, 8*(Suppl.), 165–182.

Munz, D.C., Costello, C.T., & Korabek, K. (1975). A further test of the inverted-U relating achievement anxiety and academic test performance. *Journal of Psychology, 89,* 39–47.

Neiss, R. (1988). Reconceptualizing arousal: Psychobiological states in motor performance. *Psychological Bulletin, 103,* 345–366.

Parfitt, C.G., & Hardy, L. (1987). Further evidence for the differential effect of competitive anxiety upon a number of cognitive and motor sub-systems. *Journal of Sport Sciences, 5,* 62–63.

Parfitt, G., & Hardy, L. (1993). The effects of competitive anxiety on memory span and rebound shooting tasks in basketball players. *Journal of Sport Sciences, 11,* 517–524.

Parfitt, C.G., Jones, G., & Hardy, L. (1990). Multidimensional anxiety and performance. In G. Jones & L. Hardy (Eds.), *Stress and performance in sports* (pp. 43–80). Chichester, UK: Wiley.

Passer, M.W. (1982). Psychological stress in youth sports. In R.A. Magill, M.J. Ash, & F.L. Small (Eds.), *Children in sport* (2nd ed., pp. 153–177). Champaign, IL: Human Kinetics.

Prapavessis, H., & Grove, R. (1991). Precompetitive emotions and shooting performance: The mental health and zone of optimal function models. *The Sport Psychologist, 5,* 223–234.

Pribram, K.H., & McGuinness, D. (1975). Arousal, activation, and effort in control of attention. *Psychological Review, 82,* 116–149.

Raglin, J.S. (1992). Anxiety and sport performance. *Exercise and Sport Sciences Reviews, 20,* 243–274.

Rodrigo, G., Lusiardo, M., & Pereira, G. (1990). Relationship between anxiety and performance in soccer players. *International Journal of Sport Psychology, 21,* 112–120.

Scanlan, T.K., Ravizza, K., & Stein, G.L. (1989). An in-depth study of former elite figure skaters: Part 1. Introduction to the project. *Journal of Exercise & Sport Psychology, 11,* 54–64.

Scanlan, T.K., Stein, G.L., & Ravizza, K. (1989). An in-depth study of former elite figure skaters: Part 2. Sources of enjoyment. *Journal of Exercise & Sport Psychology, 11,* 65–83.

Scanlan, T.K., Stein, G.L., & Ravizza, K (1990). An in-depth study of former elite figure skaters Part 3. Sources of stress. *Journal of Exercise & Sport Psychology, 13,* 103–120.

Schwartz, G.E., Davidson, R.J., & Goleman, D.J. (1978). Patterning of cognitive and somatic processes in the self-regulation of anxiety: Effects of meditation versus exercise. *Psychosomatic Medicine, 40,* 321–328.

Selye, H. (1974). *Stress without distress.* New York: New American Library.

Smith, K.C.P., & Apter, M.J. (1975). *A theory of psychological reversals.* Chippenham, Wilts, UK: Picton Press.

Smith, R.E. (1980). A cognitive-affective approach to stress management training for athletes. In C. Nadeau, W. Halliwell, K. Newell, & G. Roberts (Eds.), *Psychology of motor behavior and sport—1979* (pp. 54–73). Champaign, IL: Human Kinetics.

Smith, R.E., Schutz, R.W., Smoll, F.L., & Ptacek, J.T. (1995). Development and validation of a multidimensional measure of sport specific psychological skills: The Athletic Coping Skills Inventory—28. *Journal of Sport & Exercise Psychology, 17,* 379–398.

Smith, R.E., & Smoll, F.L. (1982). Psychological stress: A conceptual model and some intervention strategies in youth sports. In R.A. Magill, M.J. Ash, & F.L. Small (Eds.), *Children in sport* (pp. 178–195). Champaign, IL: Human Kinetics.

Smith, R.E., Smoll, F.L., & Schutz, R.W. (1990). Measurement and correlates of sport-specific cognitive and somatic trait anxiety: The sport anxiety scale. *Anxiety Research, 2,* 263–280.

Sonstroem, R.J. (1984). An overview of anxiety and sport. In J.M. Silva & R.S. Weinberg (Eds.), *Psychological foundations of sport* (pp. 104–117). Champaign, IL: Human Kinetics.

Sonstroem, R.J., & Bernardo, P. (1982). Intraindividual pregame state anxiety and basketball performance: A reexamination of the inverted-U curve. *Journal of Sport Psychology, 4,* 235–245.

Spence, J.T., & Spence, K.A. (1966). The motivational components of manifest anxiety: Drive and drive stimuli. In C.D. Spielberger (Ed.), *Anxiety and behavior* (pp. 291–326). New York: Academic Press.

Spielberger, C.D. (1966). Theory and research on anxiety. In C.D. Spielberger (Ed.), *Anxiety and behavior* (pp. 3–22). New York: Academic Press.

Spielberger, C.D. (1972). Anxiety as an emotional state. In C.D. Spielberger (Ed.), *Anxiety: Current trends in theory and research* (Vol. 1, pp. 24–54). New York: Academic Press.

Spielberger, C.D., Gorsuch, R.L., & Lushene, R.E. (1970a). *Manual for the State–Trait Anxiety Inventory*. Palo Alto, CA: Consulting Psychologists Press.

Spielberger, C.D., Gorsuch, R.L., & Lushene, R.E. (1970b). *STAI manual for the state–trait inventory ("self-evaluation questionnaire")*. Palo Alto, CA: Consulting Psychologists Press.

Svebak, S., & Murgatroyd, S. (1985). Metamotivational dominance: A multimethod validation of reversal theory construct. *Journal of Personality and Social Psychology, 48*, 107–116.

Svebak, S., & Stoyva, J. (1980). High arousal can be pleasant and exciting: The theory of psychological reversals. *Biofeedback and Self-Regulation, 5*, 439–444.

Swain, A., & Jones, G. (1992). Relationships between sport achievement orientation and competitive state anxiety. *The Sport Psychologist, 6*, 42–54.

Taylor, J.A. (1956). Drive theory and manifest anxiety. *Psychological Bulletin, 53*, 303–320.

Tellegen, A. (1985). Structures of mood and personality and their relationship to assessing anxiety, with an emphasis on self-report. In A.H. Tuma & J.D. Maser (Eds.), *Anxiety and the anxiety disorders* (pp. 681–706). Hillsdale, NJ: Erlbaum.

Thayer, R.E. (1967). Measurement of activation through self-report. *Psychological Reports, 20*, 663–678.

Thom, R. (1975). *Structural stability and morphogensis* (D.H. Fowler, Trans.). New York: Benjamin-Addison Wesley. (Original work published 1972.)

Tobias, S. (1980). Anxiety and instruction. In I.G. Sarason (Ed.), *Test anxiety: Theory, research, and applications* (pp. 289–310). Hillsdale, NJ: Erlbaum.

Tucker, D.M., & Williams, P.A. (1984). Asymmetric neural control in human self-regulation. *Psychological Review, 91*, 185–215.

Turner, P.E., & Raglin, J.S. (1993). Anxiety and performance in track and field athletes: A comparison of the ZOF and inverted U theories. *Medicine and Science in Sports and Exercise, 23*(Suppl.), S119.

Vealey, R.S. (1988). Future directions in psychological skills training. *The Sport Psychologist, 2*, 318–336.

Vealey, R.S. (1990). Advancements in competitive anxiety research: Use of the Sport Competition Anxiety Test and the Competitive State Anxiety Inventory-2. *Anxiety Research, 2*, 243–261.

Watson, D., & Clarke, L.A. (1984). Negative affectivity: The disposition to experience aversive emotional states. *Psychological Bulletin, 96*, 465–490.

Watson, D., Clarke, L.A., & Tellegen, A. (1988). Development and validation of brief measures of positive and negative affect: The PANAS scales. *Journal of Personality and Social Psychology, 54*, 1063–1070.

Weinberg, R.S. (1978). The effects of success and failure on the patterning of neuromuscular energy. *Journal of Motor Behavior, 10*, 53–61.

Weinberg, R.S. (1979). Anxiety and motor performance: Drive theory vs. cognitive theory. *International Journal of Sport Psychology, 10*, 112–121.

Weinberg, R.S. (1990). Anxiety and motor performance: Where to go from here? *Anxiety Research, 2*, 227–242.

Weinberg, R.S., & Genuchi, M. (1980). Relationship between competitive trait anxiety, state anxiety, and golf performance: A field study. *Journal of Sport Psychology, 2*, 148–154.

Weinberg, R.S., & Gould, D. (1999). *Foundations of sport and exercise psychology* (2nd ed.). Champaign, IL: Human Kinetics.

Weinberg, R.S., & Hunt, V.V. (1976). The interrelationships between anxiety, motor performance, and electromyography. *Journal of Motor Behavior, 8*, 219–224.

Williams, J.M. (Ed.) (2001). *Applied sport psychology: Personal growth to peak performance* (4th ed.). Mountain View, CA: Mayfield.

Williams, J.M., & Krane, V. (1989). Response distortion on self-report questionnaires with female collegiate golfers. *Sport Psychologist, 3*, 212–218.

Williams, J.M., & Krane, V. (1992). Coping styles and self-reported measures of state anxiety and self-confidence. *Journal of Applied Sport Psychology, 4*, 134–143.

Wine, J.D. (1980). Cognitive-attentional theory of test anxiety. In I.G. Sarason (Ed.), *Test anxiety: Theory, research, and application* (pp. 349–385). Hillsdale, NJ: Erlbaum.

Woodman, T., Albinson, J.G., & Hardy, L. (1997). An investigation of the zones of optimal functioning hypothesis within a multidimensional framework. *Journal of Sport & Exercise Psychology, 19*, 131–141.

Yerkes, R.M., & Dodson, J.D. (1908). The relation of strength of stimulus to rapidity of habit formation. *Journal of Comparative Neurology and Psychology, 18*, 459–482.

Zeeman, E.C. (1976, April). Catastrophe theory. *Scientific American, 234*, 65–83.

CHAPTER 8

Moral Development in Sport and Physical Activity: Theory, Research, and Intervention

Maureen R. Weiss and Alan L. Smith

Morality in everyday life and sport is one of the hottest issues in contemporary society. In the last few years, the media have brought to our attention questions about the values of youth, of the biggest software company in the world (Microsoft), of collegiate and professional athletes, and even of the president of the United States. The topic of moral development swings far and wide. Perceptions that values have been neglected in today's society have led to a call for character education in public schools and community youth charters to stem the tide of immoral behavior and instill values toward a genuine concern for human welfare (Damon, 1988, 1995, 1997). This recommendation has raised controversial questions, such as, Which values should be taught, and who should teach them?

This chapter covers moral development in sport and physical activity contexts. Historically, sport has been defended in terms of helping to develop moral virtues (e.g., honesty, respect, fair play) and as a training ground that generalizes to life skills (e.g., learn to compete, cope with stress, cooperate with others). Educators, politicians, businesspersons, and the public have long ex-

tolled the benefits of sport participation for moral and social development. But many critics have countered the adage that "sport builds character" with the argument that sport develops character disorders (see Arnold, 1994, for a discussion of these viewpoints). The trendy adage is that "sport reveals character." If this is so, what do actions in sport reveal?

Media portrayals of sport communicate powerful and visible messages, appearing in highly subscribed magazines such as *Sports Illustrated,* newspaper sports pages, and radio commentaries. First the bad news. Although cavorting with gamblers for self-gain is perhaps best immortalized by the 1919 Chicago Black Sox and Shoeless Joe Jackson, recent stories reveal that dishonesty is alive and well. The International Olympic Committee was implicated in accepting bribes, and university players have been convicted in point-shaving schemes. Violence such as Latrell Sprewell's strangulation of coach P.J. Carlesimo during a basketball practice resulted in a 1-year suspension, followed by the signing of a multimillion dollar contract with another team. Violence in football and ice hockey has been glorified in many media

© Sportschrome East/West

What might Tonya Harding's actions have revealed about her character?

(e.g., University of Notre Dame), verbal abuse (e.g., Atlanta pitcher John Rocker's racist and homophobic comments), and unfair privileges (e.g., University of Minnesota academic cheating) of athletes. Positive role models do appear in the form of individuals such as Arthur Ashe, Bonnie Blair, Cal Ripken, Joe Dumars, Jackie Joyner-Kersee, and Sammy Sosa, to name a few. But the visible moral mentors are much fewer in number than the "bad boys and girls" in sports. Can anything be done to return to the belief that sport builds character? Or is character development in sport dead?

The purpose of our chapter is to review what we know about moral development in sport based on the scientific and educational literature. We begin with a historical perspective on the role of sport in contributing to moral values among youth, followed by definitions, theories, and sport-specific perspectives of moral development. Our most in-depth section is a synthesis and consolidation of the present knowledge base on moral reasoning and behavior in sport and physical activity contexts. A section on moral development intervention describes programs that have translated empirical findings from moral development research to action contexts that are designed to explicitly teach values through physical activity. Finally, we offer suggestions for further research on moral development in sport.

HISTORICAL PERSPECTIVE OF MORAL DEVELOPMENT IN SPORT

The belief that sport participation develops character is long held and emanates from the ancient belief that to be of sound body is to be of sound spirit and mind. Modern conceptions of this relationship can be traced to mid-19th-century Britain, where elite schools promoted sport participation as a means to develop leadership, self-control, honesty, and other virtues (see Shields & Bredemeier, 1995). Sport, in promoting these characteristics, was believed to be a vehicle whereby boys developed into military, industry, and political leaders of the highest caliber. This belief is reflected in the adage made famous by the Duke of Wellington (Arthur Wellesley), who stated that "the Battle of Waterloo was won on the playing fields of Eton."

An amateur model was believed necessary for sport to promote development of character. To link sport with professionalism was to corrupt the character-building process, because material gain

sources. Lest we seem biased toward male athletes in our examples of poor character, we can mention Tonya Harding's involvement in the assault on Nancy Kerrigan before the U.S. Figure Skating Championships in 1994 and Martina Hingis' poor sportsmanship during the 1999 French Open as comparable examples.

These stories have even trickled down to the cartoon pages. Bill Watterson, creator of popular cartoon strip *Calvin and Hobbes,* encapsulated popular opinion of and poked fun at sporting behavior. In one strip, Moe (the school bully) says to Calvin, "You've got two periods to live, Twinky. Then it's gym class, and I turn you into hamburger casserole." As Calvin walks away he mumbles, "I hate gym class. Coach thinks violence is aerobic."

Are there any good news stories? There are, although media tend to highlight the outrageous violence and "juicy" stories of recruiting violations would supplant spiritual gain (Shields & Bredemeier, 1995). The amateur model served as a means of perpetuating and maintaining social strata in English society (see Coakley, 1998) and generally was associated with sport undertaken by the wealthy. Amateurism, therefore, was linked strongly to the pursuit of sport as leisure and as a means to developing gentlemen.

A second key component of character development through sport in mid-19th-century Britain was the self-governing nature of sport. By putting participants in control of the sport experience, leadership, conflict resolution, and other skills were considered more likely to develop. Participants would have to organize and negotiate among themselves, with minimal intervention from adults. The belief in the importance of self-governance is relevant to contemporary concerns about the diminished role of the "sandlot" in youth sport experiences and the shift toward a youth sport model that is adult organized (see Coakley, 1998, and Martens, 1978, for discussions of this issue). Although adult-organized sport activities for youth hold numerous positive benefits, many believe that the rule-bound, adult-officiated nature of such activities removes opportunity for youth to struggle with ethical and other dilemmas and therefore the opportunity to develop character.

As the United States was rapidly industrializing in the mid- to late 19th century, attitudes about the character-building qualities of sport became consonant with those in British society. This was largely the result of the Muscular Christianity movement, where American Protestants promoted sport as a means to develop the spirit (see Wiggins, 1996). The YMCA began to develop competitive sport programs in the late 19th century and was at the forefront of the Muscular Christianity movement. Further perpetuating the belief in the character-building capacity of sport, the playground movement took hold in the early 20th century. This movement fostered the creation of play and sport opportunities for youth of a variety of backgrounds, with particular attention to the waves of immigrant youth entering the country during this time. Combined with inclusion of sport activities in the schools, access to sport was widespread and was believed to be critical to the socialization of the country's youth.

In the 1920s and 1930s, a shift in the emphasis of youth sport dissociated professional educators from the youth sport enterprise. Youth sport was adopting a highly competitive orientation, emphasizing winning and élite-level competition. Physi-cal educators and medical professionals believed that this emphasis placed undue physical and psychological stress on youth and was contrary to the inclusive, character-building emphasis of the playground movement. Physical education and recreation leaders distanced themselves from highly organized sport (see Berryman, 1996). Because Americans had come to believe in the inherent value of sport, agencies outside of the school system easily moved in to fill the void left by the decrease in school-related opportunities for children. This allowed for the development and later success of sport organizations such as Little League Baseball. Thus, despite the concerns of physical educators, youth sport programs proliferated to the degree where today organized sport participation is a ubiquitous feature of childhood in the United States.

Interestingly, although the crafting of resolutions and policy statements regarding youth competitive sport was vigorously pursued from the 1930s to the 1960s, very little empirical research was conducted to explore the character-building or character-endangering nature of sport. McCloy (1930) wrote on the topic of character development through physical education, noting the importance of deliberately designed character development programs as well as the challenges of measurement, issues still discussed by contemporary sport psychology researchers. In later work (e.g., McCloy & Hepp, 1957), he attempted to capture key components of character in physical education through measurement efforts (see also McCloy & Young, 1954). Despite this work, little progress was made in the field until the past two decades. This progress may be attributed in part to the increase in media attention to negative outcomes of sport, the ever-increasing numbers of boys and girls involved in sport, and perceptions that U.S. society has become morally bankrupt, making social institutions such as sport ever critical to the socialization of youth. More than ever before, sport has come under scrutiny of the general public.

Also contributing to the increase in scientific investigations of sport and character development were the production and advancement of theoretical perspectives on moral development. Early research on the topic was not only sporadic but also relatively atheoretical. With the advancement of moral development theory and social psychological training within the sport sciences, a host of researchers in the past two decades have tackled the challenges of this research area. The following section addresses the dominant theoretical perspectives on moral development, namely social learning theory and the structural developmental approaches. These perspectives have allowed sport psychologists to advance the research literature and design intervention strategies for character development in physical education and sport.

DEFINITIONS, THEORIES, AND SPORT-SPECIFIC PERSPECTIVES OF MORAL DEVELOPMENT

Rarely do we refer to the phrase "moral development in sport" in everyday banters about the latest atrocities in professional sport or bending of the rules in the local high school league. Rather we use the term *sportsmanship* (or *sportspersonship)* or talk about developing *character* through sport. As such, everybody knows, or they think they know, what sportsmanship is. This is one of the nagging problems with this area of inquiry—defining sportsmanship or character. *Sportsmanship* is one of those terms that popular magazines, newspapers, and politicians all write or talk about as if everybody knows its universal definition. But depending on the eye of the beholder, sportsmanship, fair play, character, and moral development can mean very different things.

Consider the child's perspective. Nearly 40 years ago, Bovyer (1963) solicited children's (fourth through sixth grades) conceptions of the meaning of sportsmanship by having them write as many ideas as they wanted. The most frequent categorical responses were (a) plays by the rules; (b) respects the decisions, requests, and ideas of other people; (c) is a good loser; (d) is even-tempered; (e) respects the feelings of other people; and, (f) takes turns and lets others play. Thirty years later, Entzion (1991), an elementary physical education teacher, asked his students what sportsmanship meant. Their top 10 responses were remarkably similar to Bovyer's students of a different generation:

- Don't hurt anybody.
- Take turns.
- Don't yell at teammates when they make mistakes.
- Don't cheat.
- Don't cry every time you don't win.
- Don't make excuses when you lose.

- Try for first place.
- Don't tell people they're no good.
- Don't brag.
- Don't kick anyone in the stomach.

Children's definitions of sportsmanship are rather consistent as far as what behaviors are considered fair and unfair play. Their responses include behavioral norms and conventions that are designed to maintain social order (e.g., follow the rules, take turns, be honest) as well as concerns about the physical and psychological well-being of participants (e.g., don't make others feel badly, don't physically hurt anybody, respect others). In a different vein but similar to the children's responses, anecdotes from adults asked to define sportsmanship often allude to "doing the right thing," "acting in an ethical manner," and exemplifying the golden rule ("do unto others as you would have them do unto you").

Given the variety of definitions of sportsmanship by youths and adults, it is no wonder that the scholarly inquiry of moral development in sport has paled in comparison to other topics in sport psychology such as motivation and performance enhancement. We believe that one reason for this is the difficulty with terminology, theoretical underpinnings, and operationally defining such an elusive concept for empirical investigation. Often the reader is bombarded with so many "moral" terms that it becomes as difficult to navigate as the grammar of a foreign language. Thus, our intent in this chapter is to try to make this area of inquiry as user-friendly and accessible as possible. By doing so, we hope that interested readers will accept the challenge to tackle many of the unanswered questions and thus contribute to the knowledge base in moral development.

The following sections contain a nuts-and-bolts overview of the two major theoretical schools of thought that have guided empirical inquiry of moral development in sport, sportsmanship, character, or fair play. The social learning approach represents the viewpoint that people need to comply with norms and conventions of the institution of sport. The structural developmental approaches lean more heavily on the thoughts and judgments underlying behavior in sport (e.g., aggression) and in so doing emphasize concern for one's own and others' physical and emotional welfare. Thus, we can see that children's definitions were very much in line with contemporary theoretical positions. This is not surprising given Kohlberg's (cited in Turiel, 1998) observation of "the child as a moral philosopher," referring to children's use of their social experiences to form judgments about what is just, fair, and right. Detailed descriptions of these theories are found in the mainstream psychology literature (e.g., Eisenberg & Fabes, 1998; Kurtines & Gewirtz, 1991a, 1995; Rest, 1986; Turiel, 1998) and sport psychology books and chapters devoted to moral development (e.g., Bredemeier & Shields, 1993; Shields & Bredemeier, 1995; Weiss & Bredemeier, 1986, 1990).[1]

Social Learning Theory

Social learning theorists (e.g., Bandura, 1986; Burton & Kunce, 1995) contend that moral development occurs as a product of modeling and reinforcement from significant adults and peers within the larger process of socialization. Moral behaviors are defined as actions that conform to social norms and regulations and are learned through interaction with socializing agents. Societally defined moral behaviors such as honesty, altruism, cooperation, and respect exemplify behaviors that are learned by children as a product of socialization within the family, school, and other interpersonal contexts. Children are assumed to internalize the accepted behaviors of their society or culture through the powerful effects of models who are nurturant, warm, and high in status, and through differential reinforcement by significant others such as the giving or withholding of affection, approval, and tangible and vicarious rewards.

Bandura's (1991) more recent social cognitive theory of moral thought and action emphasizes the integration of individual differences and social factors as they govern moral behavior. Bandura contended that personal factors (e.g., moral reasoning, affective reactions), environmental influences (e.g., parental socialization), and moral behavior operate interactively in a reciprocal way. According to Bandura, "The self is not disembodied from social reality" (p. 69). Because Bandura believes that moral conduct is influenced strongly by affective self-reactions aside from environmental effects, self-regulation skills are paramount to instigating change and mobilizing efforts in behaving morally. Self-regulation requires self-monitoring or observation of one's actions, self-judgment of behavior in relation to personal standards and environmental circumstances, and

affective self-reaction. Effective self-regulation of moral behavior not only requires monitoring, judgment, and evaluation but also strong belief in one's capabilities to achieve personal control or self-regulatory efficacy. The stronger the perceived self-regulatory efficacy, the more resilient individuals will be in adhering to their own moral standards and resisting social pressures to transgress.

Eisenberg (1995; Eisenberg & Fabes, 1998) also takes an integrated approach to moral development while primarily working within a social cognitive model. Her focus is on the development of prosocial behavior in children and the factors that affect this development. She developed a heuristic model that proposes how a variety of developmental and social psychological factors influence prosocial behavior. The key factors include (a) moral reasoning and social perspective-taking ability; (b) influence by parents, teachers, and peers; (c) personality correlates (e.g., self-esteem and personal values); (d) affective factors such as empathy, sympathy, and personal distress; and (e) situational factors that play a role in decision-making. Eisenberg claims that all types of personal competencies and environmental influences interact to profoundly affect the development and expression of prosocial behavior.

Structural Developmental Approaches

In contrast to the social learning approach that emphasizes behavioral outcomes, structural developmental theories focus on how individuals reason about or judge values and behavior. As such, individuals are active participants in constructing meaning about moral issues by interacting with adults and peers in a variety of social contexts. The two components of the term *structural developmental* vividly portray this perspective. A moral reasoning structure underlies one's judgments about what are right and wrong behaviors; this structure undergoes developmental change as a result of cognitive maturation and social interactions. Thus, moral development connotes a quantitative increase in content or knowledge and a qualitative change in the way this knowledge is construed. This qualitative change generally proceeds from a focus on self-interest to an other- or rule-oriented focus to a principled stance of mutual interest and welfare in reasoning about legitimacy of behaviors and deciding on

---

1. Some portions of this section were paraphrased from earlier chapters by the first author (Weiss & Bredemeier, 1986, 1990).

a personal course of action. A number of key theorists have made substantive contributions to the structural developmental way of thinking about morality. We now review their major and unique conceptualizations.

Jean Piaget

Piaget (1965) was the first to extensively examine the development of children's moral judgments. His explanation of moral development was tied closely to an understanding of cognitive development, which was an ongoing goal in his attempts to formulate a theory of mental development. Piaget's ideas emanated from his observations of children's interactions while playing the game of marbles. He derived a two-stage model of moral development, one in which children proceed from a morality of constraint to a morality of cooperation.

A morality of constraint reflects unilateral respect for and conformity to adult authority, whereas a morality of cooperation is premised on mutual respect among peers. At the morality of constraint stage, children view rules as rigid and unalterable and as regulations that must be followed. At the morality of cooperation stage, rules are seen as flexible and changeable, subject to negotiation and cooperation with one's peers. These two types of morality form a developmental sequence, with a morality of constraint reflective of children 3 to 8 years of age, whereas a morality of cooperation usually emerges after about age 8.

According to Piaget, objective conceptions of responsibility characterize a morality of constraint, whereas subjective conceptions guide a morality of cooperation. Basically this involves whether behavioral outcome or intent is used in deciding whether an action is moral. A child at a morality of constraint stage will judge a behavior as right or wrong depending on the observable consequences of the action. In contrast, the child at a morality of cooperation stage will use information about intentions as the determining factor for judging legitimacy of behavior. Piaget used forced-choice story formats to assess children's intentionality as a measure of moral reasoning level. For example, Bredemeier, Weiss, Shields, and Shewchuk (1986) customized Piagetian stories to assess moral reasoning in 5- to 7-year-old children. One story entailed a boy who tried to help a man find Main Street so he could meet a friend, but despite the boy's efforts the man got lost (i.e., good intentions, bad outcome). The paired alternative story was one in which a boy tried to play a trick and give the man incorrect directions to Main

Street. However, the man found his way and successfully found his friend (i.e., bad intentions, good outcome). Asking the child, "which child was naughtier" assesses level of intentionality or stage of moral reasoning.

Piaget also suggested that moral growth occurs through social interactions with peers who negotiate and bargain with each other to arrange mutually beneficial experiences. These give-and-take types of interactions among peers, he contended, foster recognition of reciprocity of cooperation and facilitate role-taking and social perspective–taking opportunities that are critical for enhancing moral growth. Robert Selman (1971, 1976) subsequently described the developmental stages that children progress through in acquiring mature social perspective–taking abilities. These stages range from egocentric to reciprocal to societal perspective–taking views. He demonstrated that children's moral judgments are influenced by their ability to understand and take the perspective of others (i.e., "put themselves in another person's shoes").

Lawrence Kohlberg

Kohlberg (1969, 1976) extensively revised Piaget's developmental staging of moral growth. In contrast to Piaget's forced choice stories, Kohlberg instead used open-ended questions to probe individuals' reasoning about how to resolve hypothetical moral dilemmas. Kohlberg formulated his sequence of six stages of moral judgment based on the pattern of responses. Kohlberg's six stages reflect three types of morality that form a developmental sequence: (a) a morality of restraint or preconventional level; (b) a morality of rules, authority, and convention or conventional level; and (c) a morality of justice and principle or post-conventional level. Put simply, these levels represent egocentric, societal, and principled viewpoints on what constitute "the right thing to do."

The preconventional level of moral reasoning, representative of most young children, is associated with the link between morality and sanctions. Judgments of right and wrong depend on the anticipated consequences for engaging in certain actions (i.e., being punished or penalized). The saying "it's cheating only if you get caught" is a perfect example of a preconventional level of moral reasoning. Of course, preconventional reasoning is not reserved for young children, as exemplified by adults who knowingly cut corners on their income tax returns and hope that they will not be audited.

The conventional level of moral reasoning is characterized by the emergence of the concept of being a good person or one who pleases and helps others. This level thus represents an orientation toward social approval by adults and peers and an understanding of how social norms and rules have an effect on moral responsibility. "Playing by the letter of the law" and the "golden rule" represent conventional level forms of moral reasoning.

Finally, a postconventional level of moral reasoning entails recognizing universal values that are not tied to particular societal norms. Athletes who refuse when their coach encourages them to use legal, but potentially harmful, aggressive tactics in a sport because such a practice violates "the spirit of the game" (as opposed to the golden rule) would be using a principled or postconventional level of moral reasoning.

In addition to Kohlberg's six-stage sequence, two important principles guide his understanding of the development of morality. First, cognitive disequilibrium is believed to be a primary mechanism for facilitating moral growth. The notion of cognitive disequilibrium follows from Piaget's conceptions of cognitive development in that all cognitive structures are forms of organizing experiences and actions. When a new experience cannot be assimilated into existing structures, the person is said to be in a state of disequilibrium. Thus, a child who cannot explain his or her interactions in a given situation by using a preconventional level of reasoning searches for a new way of accommodating conceptions about the current dilemma to reestablish equilibrium. The new cognitive structure (i.e., level of moral reasoning) provides a more adequate way of conceptualizing moral experiences. Kohlberg's stages of morality are considered to be sequential and universal based on this perspective. All individuals advance developmentally one stage at a time without skipping any stages (i.e., a staircase analogy). Second, justice is the guiding moral norm from which all others are derived. Each subsequent stage represents a more adequate understanding of the way in which justice can resolve moral conflicts. Thus, Kohlberg's theory of moral development is characterized by an abstract, deductive, and logically consistent way of structuring moral judgments and explaining moral actions.

The world of sport offers numerous examples of moral dilemmas and conflict and thereby opportunities for arguing alternative points of view and playing "devil's advocate" that align with egocentric, societal, and principled levels of moral reasoning. A rare occasion arose in 1998 that resulted in two sport psychologists, Linda Bunker and Shane Murphy, dialoguing about an event from different perspectives in an open forum. The occasion entailed a collegiate basketball player, Nykesha Sales, who was on course to break her school's scoring record. One point away from the record, Sales incurred a season-ending injury forcing her to miss the last game of her college career. Her coach and the coach of the opposing team for the final game mutually agreed to allow Sales to make an uncontested lay-up at the beginning of the game, followed by the opponents being allowed to do the same. Thus, the game would start even at 2–2 and Sales would have her record. Was this action the right thing to do? Box 8.1 documents the contrasting points of view adopted by Bunker and Murphy. Which view do you agree with? Why? What factors are important in driving your point of view? There is, of course, no one right answer, but we believe this is a prime opportunity for thinking about a sport-specific dilemma, discussing the scenario as a group, considering alternative ways of reasoning, and perhaps even reaching agreement (or not) on a course of action.

The significance of Kohlberg's contributions to the field of moral psychology is demonstrated by the fact that his theory of moral stages is taken into account by almost every other theory of moral development (Lickona, 1976). There is no doubt that when Kohlberg died in 1987, the field lost the person who has contributed more to moral development theory than anyone else in the 20th century. His legacy is continued by the many contributions of those he mentored and his colleagues who conduct research related to his conceptions of the development of morality.

Carol Gilligan

Gilligan's (1977, 1982) classic publication *In a Different Voice* challenged Kohlberg's justice orientation of morality. According to interviews with women (ages 15–33) in the 1970s who were struggling with the real-life dilemma of whether to have an abortion, she found a developmental sequence of moral reasoning that paralleled Kohlberg's from egocentric to societal to principled orientations. However, in contrast to Kohlberg's principle of justice, she discovered that women used a principle of responsibility and care to guide their postconventional reasoning. Gilligan argued that personally engaged dilemmas require coordination of autonomy and interdependence and the need to care for both oneself and others. In

Box 8.1
The Case of Nykesha Sales: Two Viewpoints

Linda Bunker

Last week, a wonderful coach decided to give a "gift" to a star player who was one point short of the school record . . . . The basketball player, Nykesha Sales, sustained a season-ending Achilles tendon rupture and would miss the last game. The humanistic coach, Geno Auriemma, decided that the "right thing to do" was to gain the cooperation of the opposing Villanova coach and team and the officials, so the first basket of the game would be scored by the injured player, leg cast and all. The opponents would be allowed to score the next uncontested basket so the score would be 2 to 2 before the real game started. Thus, the injured player would break the school record. All's fair? It was a wonderful gesture by a coach who really cared about his player.

But was it right for the world of sport? The best of sport teaches individuals to strive to do their best; to live with the "bad breaks" and capitalize on opportunities; to savor victories and be gracious in defeat. And to realize that life is not always fair but is always worth living and enjoying the struggles and challenges. As Mariah Burton Nelson, author and former Stanford and professional basketball player,

said about this real-life situation in her sports commentary Friday: One of life's lessons is to learn to sit on the bench and "cheer enthusiastically for your teammates."

Every person must face the "what ifs" in life: What if the injured player had made one more basket in the first game of the season, or not been injured? Then this last game would not be the question. Or what about the person who had the record before? This compassionate coach reportedly consulted the former record holder before executing his plan and asked if it was OK. What were the real options for that former record holder? Say yes, be a good sport and "team player" and show compassion for an injured teammate, or raise legitimate questions about how records are attained and be perceived as unsympathetic, or not caring or look like an egotist.

What is the rest of the story? Isn't sport about life, about the challenges that motivate us, whether we set records or not? Isn't it about dreams? Isn't it about being given credit for our skills, not given gifts that demean sport and the wonderful female athletes who compete?

Shane Murphy

I agree that sport is wonderful. But I think you can take an entirely different look at the above situation if we see it through the lens of what we know about the development of ethics and moral character in sport. This incident created a "firestorm" of controversy in New York, although truthfully much of what transpired was in the minds of the sports reporters. When the general public was surveyed, an over-whelming percentage supported the coach's actions and found the Villanova game memorable. As one of my students put it, "I got chills watching it."

Why are the sports media so out of touch with the public on this issue? If we think back to the research on the development of ethics in sport, we can see the answer. As several studies have demonstrated, a fascinating aspect of sports participation is that the longer one is involved in sports the less sportsmanship one displays or supports. This is especially true by the time an athlete reaches the professional ranks, but the

trend becomes apparent in high school and college. Interestingly, when first surveyed elite female athletes had higher moral standards than their male counterparts. However, over the decade the gap has narrowed and not from the male athletes raising their ethical consciousness. Apparently as female athletes have become more socialized into the sports ethos, their congruence with sportsmanship has lessened.

So we can see why the gap between public perception and sport-involved perception on this issue. The general public still tends to see sport as play, and their recognition of sportsmanship is high. For those with a high level of sports involvement, such as elite athletes and the sports media (who live by promoting an ego oriented approach to sports coverage), there is no room for sportsmanship in their world view.

Several media in NYC commented on the Nykesha Sales play as "threatening the integrity of the sport." But in their rush to "save" the

(continued)

integrity of the game, they failed to realize that the rules of sport are not God-given. Sport is like life. It has meaning because we invest it with meaning. We choose to place importance in the rules because it helps us give our games meaning, significance, structure and history. But they are our rules. And at times we choose to step outside the confines of the game in order to serve higher moral values such as fairness, honesty and integrity. If we place the rules on some higher plane, we become slaves to the rules and lose our own moral compass.

So Linda is right, of course, in one sense, that sport is a wonderful vehicle for teaching about life. I always try to find such situations to point out and discuss with my children. It makes for wonderful learning opportunities. And Nykesha Sales and the UConn and Villanova teams demonstrated, as sports can every so often do, that sometimes we can move beyond the limits of competition and find value in cooperation. And

hopefully we can do the same in our everyday, nonsporting lives. What makes life tough is that often there seems little we can do. And in sports that is perhaps even more true. But in this case, there was an opportunity for a meaningful moment, and the fact that those involved found a way makes it special.

Watching Sales make that basket last week, I was astonished. You just don't see such co-operation or respect between players at the elite levels anymore. Several commentators who said that "women are different from men" that night were dead right. But not because women are more "emotional" or "sensitive," as they argued. But because for one night, the women's teams showed the rest of the sports world that competitive sport still has room for a heart, for a spirit, and for sportsmanship.

Adapted, by permission, from L. Bunker *USA Today*, March 2, 1998; and S. Murphy, Exercise and Sports Psychology listserv, (SPORTPSY@vm.temple.edu, March 2, 1998).

essence, Gilligan argued that a morality of care is linked mainly with females and is qualitatively different from a morality of justice, which is associated mainly with males. These unique moral orientations, Gilligan contended, are driven primarily by differential socialization experiences of boys and girls.

Gilligan's ideas posed considerable controversy among moral development scholars. Although Gilligan criticized Kohlberg for crafting his moral stages of development based primarily on interviews with males, subsequent analysis of Kohlbergian interviews with females and males have shown few gender differences in moral staging. Contrary to Gilligan's contention, scholars generally agree that Kohlberg's advanced moral stages account for judgments about interdependence and concerns with others' welfare, not only concerns about fairness and justice. Other studies show that females and males use both an ethic of care and an ethic of justice to some extent, and few people exclusively use either a care or justice orientation (see Turiel, 1998, for discussion of this issue; and Fisher & Bredemeier, 2000, for a study in the physical domain). Nevertheless, Gilligan's subsequent contributions to understanding girls' and women's psychological and moral development should not be underestimated (e.g., Brown & Gilligan, 1992; Gilligan, Ward, & Taylor, 1988). In a heartfelt piece titled "Remembering Larry," Gilligan (1998) detailed her collegial and personal

relationship with Kohlberg and recounted the course of their divergence in scholarly thinking and roads taken in moral psychology.

Norma Haan

Haan (1977, 1991; Haan, Aerts, & Cooper, 1985) also proposed an alternative structural developmental model to Kohlberg's, wherein morality is best understood by analyzing people's moral reasoning within specific social contexts rather than hypothetical scenarios. Morality involves a decision-making process about any action that has physical or psychological consequences for the well-being of self and others. Moral dialogue and balance are the guiding principles for constructing morality. Thus, social disequilibrium and inductive reasoning are key to moral growth. This contrasts with Kohlberg's notions of cognitive disequilibrium and deductive reasoning based on the principle of justice guiding moral judgments. According to Haan, when individuals are confronted with a situational conflict (i.e., moral dilemma), they need to discuss ("moral dialogue") their corresponding viewpoints and try to reach consensual agreement about a solution to their problem ("moral balance"). Thus, interpersonal communication is key to openly discussing and negotiating needs and rights leading to conflict resolution.

Haan delineated three phases of morality which, like those of Kohlberg and Gilligan, traversed an egocentric to societal to principled level of reasoning. Haan labeled her three "phases" as assimilation, accommodation, and equilibration (similar to Kohlberg's preconventional, conventional, and postconventional). The assimilation phase is characterized by seeking moral balances that give preference to one's own needs and concerns. In the accommodation phase, individuals seek to resolve moral conflict by giving more to the moral exchange than they receive. Finally, recognizing all involved individuals' interests, rights, and needs defines the equilibration phase. Haan also considered the role of coping and defending ego processes in whether an individual interprets a situation as a moral one and in deciding what course of action to implement (see Shields & Bredemeier, 1995).

Table 8.1 summarizes the social learning and structural developmental approaches to moral development. The theories are distinguished based on their definition of moral development, sources or mechanisms of moral growth, and basis for intervention.

James Rest

Rest (1984, 1986, 1994; Narváez & Rest, 1995) argued that there is more to morality than development of moral reasoning or judgment. Thus, he derived a four-component model of morality that attempts to illuminate the factors that impinge on the relationship between moral thoughts and actions. Rather than merely divide these factors into cognitions, affect, and behavior, Rest (1994) asked,

"What must we suppose happens psychologically in order for moral behavior to take place?" And so emerged his four components or processes that influence moral behavior.

The first component, interpreting the situation, involves an awareness of how our actions affect other people. It involves imagining the range of possible courses of action and how each alternative may affect the individuals involved. Rest alternatively labeled this component as moral sensitivity and noted that empathy and role-taking skills are essential for interpreting the situation as a moral one. The second component is judging which action is morally right or wrong. Given that a person accurately interprets the situation (Component 1), she or he judges which course of action is more justifiable. Component 3, deciding what one intends to do, or moral motivation, concerns weighing the importance of and choosing among various competing values. The fourth component, implementing a moral plan of action or moral character, refers to how the individual actually behaves and may be influenced by ego strength, courage, and strength of conviction. Although the four components are presented in a logical sequence, this does not mean that individuals perform them in this order. Rather, these four components are thought to interact with and reciprocally influence one another. The model ultimately was developed as a framework for conducting research and moral education programs.

Narváez and Rest (1995) said that the model depicts an "ensemble of processes" and not a uni-

Table 8.1
Theoretical Approaches to Moral Development

Approach	Definition of morality	Sources of moral development	Basis for intervention
Social learning	Prosocial behaviors in accordance with societal norms	Observational learning, reinforcement, approval by significant others	Role models, moral mentors, tangible and social rewards
Structural—developmental	Concern for physical and emotional welfare of self and others	Cognitive or social disequilibrium when confronted with a moral dilemma; "dialogue and balance" with involved persons	Activities prompting discussion and resolution of moral dilemmas; role-playing; cooperative problem-solving; empowering students to make decisions

dimensional process. That is, failure to act morally may occur because of a weakness in any one skill or component. An individual may possess good moral sensitivity but make ill-advised judgments or may make good judgments but fall down in the translation to actual behavior. As a way of bringing these components down to earth, Narváez and Rest identified real and fictional characters who represented strength and weakness in each of the components. Strong characters include the Tin Man and the Scarecrow from *The Wizard of Oz* for moral sensitivity and moral judgment, respectively, and Don Quixote and Moses for intention and implementation. Weak characters identified for each of the four components are, in order, Bart Simpson, Snow White, Hitler, and Woody Allen characters.

As discussed in later sections of this chapter, moral researchers in the physical domain have enthusiastically embraced Rest's four-component model as applicable for research questions. For example, the components served as dependent variables before and after a moral education program (Gibbons, Ebbeck, & Weiss, 1995) and as correlates of variables such as perceived social approval of antisocial behaviors (Stuart & Ebbeck, 1995) and achievement goal orientations

(Kavussanu & Roberts, 2001). Rest's death in 1999 was a major blow to the field of moral psychology because of his prolific writing and expanse of ideas. In fact, because of his model's thoroughness in considering the range of thoughts, feelings, and behaviors that influence morality, Shields and Bredemeier (1995) used the model as a baseline to shape their 12-component model of moral action in sport.

Shields and Bredemeier's (1995) 12-Component Model of Moral Action

Because of the usefulness of Rest's model of morality for the physical domain, Shields and Bredemeier advocated expanding the model from 4 to 12 components to account for additional factors that may explain variations in moral behavior. Rest actually delineated the factors that were likely to affect each of the four components but did not explicitly include them in the model itself. Shields and Bredemeier specifically embedded three sources of influence (personal competencies, ego processes, and social contextual factors) within the model for each of the four components of morality: interpretation, judgment, choice, and behavior (table 8.2).

Table 8.2
12-Component Model of Moral Action

	Moral interpretation	Moral judgment	Moral choice	Moral behavior
Personal competency influences	Role-taking; social perspective–taking	Moral reasoning; moral beliefs and values	Responsibility judgments; motives; self-concept	Self-regulatory skills; social problem-solving skills
Social contextual influences	Situational ambiguity; goal–reward structure	Moral atmosphere or collective norms	Domain cues; mastery vs. performance climate	Power structure; leadership style
Ego processing influences	Empathy; tolerance of ambiguity	Objectivity, intellectuality, logical analysis as coping; isolation, intellectualizing, rationalization as defending	Sublimation, substitution, suppression as coping; displacement, repression, reaction formation as defending	Concentration as coping; denial as defending

Adapted, by permission, from D.L. Shields and B.J.L. Bredemeier, 1995, *Character development and physical activity* (Champaign, IL: Human Kinetics), 92.

As shown in table 8.2, a host of individual differences (competencies, ego processing) and contextual factors may impinge on specific morality processes or may interact to influence several processes. Personal competencies that may be influential include perspective-taking ability, moral reasoning, legitimacy beliefs, moral motives, achievement goals, moral self-concept, self-regulation skills, and social problem-solving skills. To date, moral reasoning and legitimacy beliefs are the dominant personal competencies studied in relationship to aggressive behavior in sport. Achievement goals are emerging as a variable of interest, but the other competencies and ego-processing variables hardly have been addressed. This is understandable given the recency of this model. Considerable efforts are needed to validate the personal competencies and ego-processing aspects of the 12-component model of moral action in sport.

Shields and Bredemeier also outlined the fundamental contextual factors thought to affect the relationship between moral thought and moral behavior. These are situational ambiguity, goal-reward structure or motivational climate, moral atmosphere or prevailing team norms (e.g., teammates' and coach's beliefs), domain-specific cues, and power structures (e.g., leadership style). Several studies have investigated perceptions of normative reference groups' approval of aggressive behavior in sport and the relationship between collective team norms and tendencies toward aggressive behavior. However, the other factors have barely been considered.

Shields and Bredemeier's (1995) 12-component model offers a useful and appealing way of organizing research on the relationship between moral thought and moral action in physical activity contexts. They described various possibilities for examining personal competencies, ego processing, and social factors as correlates of moral interpretation, judgment, choice, and behavior. With this framework, we hope that sport psychology researchers will accept Shields and Bredemeier's challenge to extend the knowledge base in moral development.

Summary

The history of moral development theory is long and rich. Several theorists have clarified the distinction and relationship between moral judgments and actions. The developmental course of moral growth, and the individual and social factors that impinge on moral judgments and actions, also have been delineated. Shields and Bredemeier's custom model of moral action in sport holds considerable promise for testing the influence of individual and social factors on components of the moral thought–action relationship. Social learning and structural developmental theories have guided moral development in sport research over the last 20 years. Next, we synthesize and consolidate this body of knowledge.

MORAL DEVELOPMENT RESEARCH IN PHYSICAL ACTIVITY SETTINGS

One of the many benefits of theory is that it can be tested through empirical research in specific social contexts such as sport and ultimately can be applied to practical teaching and coaching situations. The two major theoretical orientations previously described that pertain to the physical domain are social learning and structural–developmental schools of thought. Thus, we categorized the data-based research in this section into these two theoretical positions.

Social Learning–Based Studies

Social learning approaches to moral development are focused on the extent to which individuals' behaviors conform to social conventions and norms and thus maintain social organization. Socially accepted values such as responsibility, honesty, altruism, respect, and cooperation are transmitted through observational learning of and reinforcement from significant adults and peers. Social learning methods such as role modeling, explicit teaching of values through character education programs, and approval and disapproval of specific behaviors have been prevalent in both the mainstream (e.g., Damon, 1988) and sport psychology (e.g., Smith, 1988) literature. We have organized the empirical study of sportsmanship based on social learning approaches into four areas: (a) value orientations, (b) socialization of prosocial behaviors, (c) observational learning of sportsmanlike and unsportsmanlike behaviors, and (d) social approval of aggressive and unfair play.

Value Orientations

According to Webb (1969), attitudes toward sport early in one's involvement revolve around a play orientation that consists of a value hierarchy of fairness, skill, and winning. As children mature and gain more competitive sport experience, they move away from a play orientation and adopt a professional orientation, which prioritizes winning first followed by skill and fairness (Blair, 1985; Dubois, 1986; Webb, 1969). This attitude shift is assumed to result from socialization through competitive sport involvement, which tends to emphasize playing and fun at younger ages and lower skill levels versus success and winning among older youth and at higher levels of competition. Moreover, boys scored consistently higher on win orientation than girls at all levels, and female athletes scored higher than female nonathletes (Blair, 1985; Greer & Stewart, 1989; Kane, 1982; Sage, 1980; Webb, 1969).

Knoppers (1985; Knoppers, Schuiteman, & Love, 1986; Knoppers, Zuidema, & Meyer, 1989) questioned the professionalization of attitudes through sport on conceptual and methodological grounds. She contended that the noncontextual nature of Webb's (1969) scale, which is used to assess value orientations, might evoke differential responses among female and male participants who varied in athletic involvement. Knoppers et al. (1989) compared the Webb scale to an alternative that asked respondents to rate the importance of winning, skill, fun, and fairness in a recreational pick-up game and a competitive state championship match. Value toward winning/skill was higher in the competitive than recreational context and was similar for girls and boys when the importance rating scale was used. Neither context nor gender differences were found on value orientations when the Webb scale was used. The authors concluded that value orientations are multidimensional and context-specific, and that empirical attention should be shifted instead toward examining situations that contribute to development of win-at-all-costs attitudes in sport.

Socialization of Prosocial Behaviors

From a social learning perspective, morality is defined in terms of promoting prosocial behaviors, defined as voluntary behavior intended to benefit another (Eisenberg & Fabes, 1998). Prosocial behaviors include altruism, honesty, cooperation, and peer encouragement as well as the demonstration of respect, empathy, responsibility, and equity. Reducing antisocial behaviors such as physical and verbal aggression, selfishness, and lack of responsibility is also a goal of the social learning perspective. Studies indicate that sport experiences influence prosocial and antisocial behaviors. These studies focus on reinforcement and modeling as mechanisms consistent with social learning principles of internalizing moral development.

Kleiber and Roberts (1981) examined the relationship between sport competition and character development in a field experiment involving 10- to 11-year-old children. A 2-week kickball "world series" was constructed to determine effects of win–lose competition versus a control group on altruistic behavior. Results provided little evidence of negative competitive effects on prosocial behavior. Neither treatment group, gender, nor interaction effects emerged, likely because of the short intervention period, small sample size, single measure of morality, and ambiguity of control group activities. Similarly, Orlick (1981) investigated the effects of cooperative games on 5-year-old children's altruistic behavior before and after an 18-week intervention period. Children within two schools were assigned to either a cooperative group that emphasized successful activities completed in partners or a traditional games group that emphasized individual achievement. Equivocal results emerged, in that only one of the two cooperative groups improved, and only one of the two traditional groups declined, in prosocial behavior.

Murphy, Hutchison, and Bailey (1983) used organized games as an intervention for subduing aggressive playground behaviors of kindergarten, first-grade, and second-grade students who arrived at school early and stayed on the playground until classroom instruction started. A design was used in which number of problem behaviors (i.e., aggression, property abuse, rule violations) were recorded during a baseline period (12 days), followed by intervention (7 days), removal of intervention (4 days), and a repeat of intervention conditions (6 days). The games intervention included rope jumping and footrace activities that were instructed and supervised by an aide or college student. The number of aggressive incidents during the games intervention periods was half that of baseline recordings, suggesting that organized activities during typically unsupervised playground times were effective means of curtailing physical and verbal aggression.

Giebink and McKenzie (1985) also used a social learning intervention to enhance social interaction skills during game play in four at-risk boys targeted as demonstrating bad sportsmanship. Intervention strategies included direct instruction, teacher modeling, praise for good sportsmanship, and a contingent reward system (i.e., points for good behavior that counted toward a lottery for gaining tangible rewards). Although the intervention was successful at enhancing good and reducing poor sportsmanship in all four boys, generalization from the physical education to the recreational setting was unsuccessful.

Sharpe (Hastie & Sharpe, 1999; Sharpe, Brown, & Crider, 1995; Sharpe, Crider, Vyhlidal, & Brown, 1996) conducted a series of studies to investigate the effectiveness of a behaviorally based curriculum on students' prosocial skills. Sharpe et al. (1995) targeted third-grade students low in academic achievement and socioeconomic status in an urban school. Two experimental classes and one control class participated within a multiple baseline design. The social curriculum was implemented during team sport activities three times a week for 45 minutes per session for 32 weeks. Specific interventions included the teacher explicitly defining characteristics of good winners and losers, conflict resolution, and peer helping; in addition, students acted as referees and activity captains, resolving conflicts independently of the teacher. In the experimental groups, student leadership and conflict resolution markedly increased and off-task and conflict behaviors decreased. The control group showed no change throughout the study duration on these variables. Moreover, these behaviors from the gymnasium generalized to regular classroom settings. Similar findings emerged for first-, third-, and sixth-grade students of similar characteristics (low socioeconomic status, academic achievement) in urban elementary schools (Sharpe et al., 1996) and for at-risk adolescent boys in their compliance, peer interpersonal behaviors, and self-regulation of social interactions (Hastie & Sharpe, 1999).

Observational Learning of Sportsmanlike and Unsportsmanlike Behaviors

The belief that role models considerably influence children's learning of what is right and wrong in sport has historically been popular (Smith, 1988; Wiggins, 1996). These role models invariably include significant adults such as parents, teachers, coaches, community leaders, and professional athletes, or those more similar in age such as teammates, classmates, and siblings. In an ESPN (1997) special titled, "Sportsmanship in the '90s: Is Winning the Only Thing?" league officials revealed that professional hockey, baseball, basketball, and football were instituting awards and codes of ethics to reward exemplary actions and curtail inappropriate aggressive behaviors. This action is a means

of acknowledging the influential role that athletes play in children's and adolescents' perceptions of right and wrong actions in sport. Aside from the anecdotal accounts of modeling effects, what does the empirical research say about such influence?

Bandura, Ross, and Ross' (1961) classic Bobo doll experiment strongly demonstrated the social learning of aggressive behaviors through modeling. Children ages 3 to 6 years were exposed to aggressive or nonaggressive models or a control group. Children in the aggressive model condition viewed an adult model engage in physically and verbally aggressive behavior toward a 5-foot tall inflated Bobo doll. The behaviors were unlikely to be reproduced by children on their own (e.g., "Sock him in the face," "Pow," striking the toy mallet on the doll's head). Children in the nonaggressive model condition observed the adult assemble tinker toys in a quiet, subdued manner while totally ignoring the Bobo doll. Child observers in the aggressive model condition imitated significantly more general and specific physical and verbal aggressive behaviors than did children in the nonaggressive or control groups.

Michael Smith (1974, 1975, 1978, 1979, 1988) launched a systematic program to scientifically investigate the social learning of aggression and violence in amateur ice hockey. In one study (Smith, 1974), male adolescent ice hockey players rated how violent their favorite professional player and their most admired teammate were on the ice. Players who selected more violent role models tended to receive more assaultive penalties (e.g., fighting, slashing, hooking, high-sticking) than those who chose less violent models. Thus, young ice hockey players' learning and expression of aggressive behavior could be attributed, in part, to the types of adult and peer models they admire.

Smith (1978) surveyed a large number of 12- to 21-year-old hockey players and nonplayers on their consumption of the sport through the mass media. He contended that observers' perceived similarity to professional models and expectations of rewards for expressing similar behaviors were likely to result in approval and modeling of such behaviors. Smith found that 70% and 60% of players and nonplayers, respectively, watched hockey on television at least once a week or more. About 60% of players and nonplayers indicated that they learned how to hit another player illegally from watching professional hockey. Specific examples included spearing, butt-ending, charging, elbowing, tripping, slashing, and high sticking. Among the players who learned illegal tactics, 64% stated that they actually performed these actions at least once or twice during the season. Although this study was descriptive in nature, the results are consistent with observational learning theory and show how mass media portrayals of violence in professional hockey might contribute to attitudes and behaviors of youth and amateur hockey players.

Mugno and Feltz (1985) replicated Smith's (1978) study by investigating the social learning of aggression among football players and nonplayers. They compared youth (ages 12–14) and high school adolescents (ages 15–18) on the extent to which they read about and watched televised college and professional football, whether they learned illegal aggressive actions from watching football and performed such actions, and whether observational learning and aggressive behaviors are related. Players watched (94%) and read (83%) more about football than nonplayers (74% and 55%) and reported learning about 10 illegal aggressive actions compared with about 8.5 actions for nonplayers (e.g., spearing, face-masking, late hits, clipping). Of perhaps greatest importance is that moderately strong correlations emerged between the number of illegal aggressive acts learned through observation and the number of these behaviors that players reported using in their own games ($r = .50$ and $.62$ for youth and high school players, respectively). Finally, 82% of all players reported using at least one of the illegal aggressive behaviors that they had learned through watching high-level football. Thus, similar to Smith's findings for youth ice hockey, Mugno and Feltz demonstrated that young football players may be influenced through observational learning of aggressive behaviors in college and professional football.

White and O'Brien (1999) examined children's role models as a source of social and moral development. Youth ages 5 to 16 years were asked to define, identify characteristics of, and name a hero. Parents were the most frequent response to "Who is your hero?" across all age levels. The 5- to 6- and 8- to 9-year-olds named family members and friends next, whereas 11- to 13-year-olds cited sports figures after parents, followed by family members and political/military figures. The oldest youth (15–16) named sports, political/military, and entertainment figures after parents. When asked why a particular person was their hero, children and adolescents cited helping behaviors (e.g., saving someone, doing good, helping society), caring and protective traits (e.g., helps me when I get in trouble, always there for me), and

unique qualities or talents (e.g., courage, athletic ability). Some act or characteristic beyond talent was essential to being named a hero (e.g., Penny Hardaway, professional basketball player, was named because he helps the homeless). Across age levels, at least one of four characteristics was essential to the definition of a hero: good, courageous, nice, and trustworthy. The authors concluded that children and teenagers identify with their named heroes because they demonstrate moral excellence.

In light of the powerful role of modeling in moral development, Damon (1988) proposed that children be exposed to "moral mentors" or individuals in their community who have distinguished themselves through exemplary moral behavior such as finding shelters for the homeless, fighting discrimination, and saving abused children. Interactive workshops and discussions among moral exemplars and children, Damon contended, would inspire children to develop moral awareness and adopt moral responsibility to perform acts of kindness that are socially relevant.

Social Approval of Aggressive and Unfair Play

Significant adults' and peers' sanctions of aggression in sport make up another set of studies from a social learning perspective. Approval by significant others such as parents, coaches, and teammates signifies a form of reinforcement and justification for demonstrating bad sportsmanship. Indeed, the research strongly supports this stance. Smith (1975) interviewed male adolescent ice hockey players regarding perceptions of their normative reference groups' legitimization of violence during game play. Players responded to questions concerning their father's, mother's, teammates', nonplaying peers', and coach's approval of hard but legal body-checking, fighting back, starting a fight, and penalty-sanctioned boarding and cross-checking. Players perceived that most groups approved or strongly approved of body-checking, with mothers most likely to disapprove of such actions. The large majority of fathers, peers, and teammates favored fighting back if someone else started a fight. A substantial number of teammates and nonplaying peers were viewed as justifying starting a fight and cross-checking, whereas a much smaller number of fathers and mothers were viewed as lauding these actions.

In another study, Smith (1979) documented perceptions of significant others' attitudes toward illegal violence in amateur ice hockey. Select and house league players, ranging in age from 12 to 21 years, were asked about their own and their reference groups' approval of fist-fighting during game play under a variety of situations. Survey data revealed that although greater disapproval toward fist-fighting was perceived for ages 12 to 15 years and house league participants, frequency percentages dramatically shifted for 16- to 21-year-olds and select league participants. For all age groups and levels of competition, rankings were consistent for significant others' approval of violence in hockey: teammates, spectators, self, coach, father, and, last, mother.

Silva (1983) investigated the social learning effects of competitive sport participation on perceptions of aggressive behaviors as legitimate. College-age students were shown a series of slides that depicted rule-violating behavior (e.g., fighting, illegal tackling, tripping) in a number of team sports at the college or professional level. Perceived legitimacy of aggressive game behaviors depended on gender, sport type, and years playing organized sport. Men were much more favorable toward aggressive behaviors than were women. Male participants in collision sports (e.g., football, ice hockey, lacrosse) at youth, high school, and college levels scored higher on legitimacy judgments than those participating in contact sports (e.g., basketball, soccer), who were higher than non–contact sport athletes (e.g., track and field, swimming, baseball). Finally, male high school and college players rated rule-violating behaviors as more legitimate than did male youth sport participants and nonathletes. These results corroborate Smith's (1975, 1979) findings that aggression in sport is viewed as normative behavior among male athletes, especially in contact and collision sports and at higher levels of competition.

Mugno and Feltz (1985) extended Smith's (1975) research to young football players' perceptions of significant others' attitudes toward aggressive behaviors. Youth (ages 12–14) and high school (ages 15–18) players rated whether their father, mother, teammates, nonplaying friends, and spectators viewed aggressive actions as acceptable if they were not called by officials and if they helped the team to win. Frequency percentages revealed that teammates, friends, and spectators were perceived as most approving of such actions. Players also rated the extent to which significant others influenced whether they used aggressive acts in their own games. More than 40% of youth league

players stated that their teammates, coach, and father greatly influenced (highest rating possible) their use of illegal hits, whereas more than 30% of high school players cited teammates and coach. Although young football players learned illegal plays by watching high-level players, and the number of actions they learned correlated highly with their own aggression on the field, they believed that teammates and coach and, to a lesser extent, father, friends, and spectators primarily influenced their aggressive game behaviors.

Stuart and Ebbeck (1995) bridged social learning and structural–developmental theories by considering the influence of significant adults' and peers' approval on the moral thoughts and actions of youth sport participants. Players in fourth to fifth and seventh to eighth grades rated father, mother, coach, and teammate approval for five dilemmas (e.g., whether to injure a player to prevent a basket or push an opponent when the referee isn't looking). For both age groups, teammates were rated as more favorable toward engaging in antisocial behaviors than were coaches and parents. A strong relationship emerged between significant others' approval and moral development variables. For the younger group, approval of antisocial behaviors by mother, father, coach, and teammates was associated with players judging antisocial behaviors as appropriate and stating that they intended to engage in them. For older players, perceived approval of antisocial behaviors by teammates, coach, and parents was associated with lower moral judgment and intent as well as reasoning and behavior. Although all significant others were "significant," mothers for younger players and teammates for older players registered the highest perceived influence on moral variables, lending support to developmental findings (Damon, 1988).

Summary

The studies based primarily on social learning premises support the role of social norms, significant others' approval and modeling, and vicarious reinforcement on players' judgments of right and wrong in sport. The most robust findings include observational learning of illegal and aggressive tactics from high-level competitors, a correlation between actions learned and players' own aggressive tendencies, and perceived approval of aggressive norms in sport by parents, coaches, teammates, nonplaying friends, and spectators. The study by Stuart and Ebbeck (1995) provides a nice segue to structural–developmental approaches in demonstrating the link between perceived social approval and moral thoughts and prosocial behaviors.

Structural Development–Based Studies

In contrast to the social learning definition of moral development, which focuses on behaviors that conform to social norms and conventions, structural–developmental theories emphasize the underlying reasoning or judgment processes associated with behavior. Moral growth can occur through exposure to hypothetical dilemmas that compel participants to think about solutions at more mature reasoning levels, or it can occur as a result of social disequilibrium wherein individuals are personally and emotionally involved in real-life dilemmas that promote the need for "dialogue and balance" among involved parties. Thus, it is not surprising that empirical research embracing structural–developmental approaches to moral development in sport has delved into moral reasoning and a number of cognitive, affective, and behavioral correlates. This body of research is presented in the following sections: (a) moral reasoning in sport and daily life contexts; (b) moral reasoning, perceived legitimacy of aggression, and sport behavior; (c) individual differences and moral development; and (d) social contextual factors and moral development.

Moral Reasoning in Sport and Daily Life Contexts

Jantz (1975) was interested in determining whether Piaget's (1965) developmental stages of morality found among young children playing marbles could be extended to children's moral thinking about the rules of basketball. Boys in grades 1 through 6 (ages 7–12) were questioned individually about the rules of basketball (e.g., What are the rules for playing? Who makes the rules for playing? What happens if you break the rules?), and responses were categorized as a morality of constraint (i.e., unilateral rules imposed by adults) or a morality of cooperation (i.e., mutual agreement of rules). Children in first and second grades (ages 7–8) were higher on morality of constraint than children in third through sixth grades (ages 9–12), who were higher on morality of cooperation. Because Piaget found that children between ages 6 and 8 typically gave morality of constraint responses and children between ages 9 and 12 typically gave morality of cooperation responses, Jantz's findings supported Piaget's

moral development stages in the physical domain.

Rainey, Santilli, and Fallon (1992) also conducted a developmental study but focused on athletes' conceptions of obedience to and legitimacy of authority in two social domains: organized sport (officials) and family (parents). According to Damon (1977, 1983), individuals progress through three stages of conceptions of authority. Level 0 is based on the individual's emotional relationship with or respect for physical attributes of the authority figure. Level 1 is based on perceived social and physical power of the authority figure. Level 2 is based on recognition that the authority figure has prior training or experience that makes him or her more competent. Rainey et al. determined whether Damon's levels of conceptions of authority emerge for both parents and sport officials. Male baseball players of four age groups (6–9, 10–13, 14–17, 18–22) were presented with two conflict scenarios. One depicted a championship game in which an umpire called the participant "out" at home plate but the participant was sure he was safe. The other scenario was one in which parents did not allow the participant to go to an amusement park with a friend because his room was not clean. Participants were asked a series of questions in a structured interview (e.g., "Even when players disagree with umpires they usually obey them. Why do you obey?"). Results revealed a strong relationship between age and conceptions of obedience to ($r = .62, .59$) and legitimacy of ($r = .70, .63$) authority for umpires and parents, respectively. Older players responded with more mature conceptions of authority, supporting Damon's levels.

Bredemeier and her colleagues pioneered efforts toward the scientific understanding of moral development in sport (see Bredemeier & Shields, 1987, 1993; Shields & Bredemeier, 1995, for major reviews). Their early work focused on comparing athletes' and nonathletes' moral reasoning in sport and nonsport domains. Bredemeier and Shields (1984a, 1986a, 1986b) interviewed high school and college basketball players, swimmers, and nonathletes about moral issues in daily life and competitive sport contexts. Several key findings emerged. Moral reasoning for sport was significantly lower than for daily life dilemmas for all subgroups (female, male, high school, college, athlete, nonathlete). For high school participants, athletes and nonathletes did not differ on life or sport moral reasoning. In contrast, college athletes scored significantly lower on life and sport reasoning than did nonathletes. Females scored higher than males on sport moral reasoning at high school and college levels. Finally, basketball players scored significantly lower in sport moral reasoning than swimmers and nonathletes. In contrast, Hall (1986) found that college athletes reasoned at higher moral reasoning levels for sport than for daily life dilemmas. Divergent findings may emanate from the nature of the sport dilemmas used by the researchers.

Bredemeier (1995) further examined the life–sport moral reasoning divergence among fourth-through seventh-grade (ages 9–13) children and youth participating in a summer skill development program. Participants were presented with two life and two sport dilemmas that centered on whether to act honestly or keep a promise to a friend and whether to potentially injure another child who had been perceived to act unfairly. Only the oldest children (sixth to seventh graders) diverged in their reasoning level about daily life and sport contexts. Bredemeier graphed the age-related sport and daily life reasoning scores in this study relative to scores in her earlier studies with high school and college athletes (Bredemeier & Shields, 1984a, 1986b). She concluded that life–sport divergence in moral reasoning appears at about ages 12 to 13 (sixth grade) and continues to broaden as age and sport experience increase. This broadening is attributed to the steeper incline in life reasoning relative to sport reasoning scores.

Beller and Stoll (1995) extended investigation of athlete–nonathlete reasoning differences in sport by asking high school respondents to indicate extent of agreement on a number of commonly occurring sport issues such as retaliation, drug use, fairness, heckling the visiting team, and rule violation when the official isn't looking. They found that high school team sport athletes exhibited lower moral reasoning for sport dilemmas than did nonathletes but not compared with individual sport athletes. However, using a cross-sectional design, Beller and Stoll found a nonsignificant decline in moral reasoning among team and individual sport athletes from 9th through 12th grades.

Priest, Krause, and Beach (1999) used a longitudinal design that included the same methodology as Beller and Stoll (1995) to assess the influence of collegiate sport participation on moral development. Specifically, they followed 631 students over their four years at the U.S. Military Academy, where value development and athletic participation are emphasized strongly. Students are required to participate in intramural or inter-

collegiate sports every year. Students completed the moral development survey early in their first year and toward the end of their fourth year of college life. Moral development scores significantly decreased from pre- to posttest (years 1–4), regardless of sport level (varsity, intramural), sport type (team, individual), and gender. Moreover, varsity athletes were lower in moral reasoning than intramural athletes at the beginning and end of their college years; the same held true for athletes in team sports (basketball, football) compared with individual sports (tennis, golf).

Bredemeier and Shields (Bredemeier & Shields, 1985, 1986b, 1993; Shields & Bredemeier, 1989, 1995) coined the term *game reasoning* to explain the rather consistent findings of life–sport moral reasoning divergence in individuals 12 and older and athlete–nonathlete moral reasoning differences at the high school and college levels. Game reasoning reflects one's viewpoint of sport as a form of bracketed morality, or one that is set apart emotionally from the broader morality of everyday life. Game reasoning involves a moral transformation during athletic contests in which an egocentric or self-interest perspective is considered a legitimate means of pursuing the goal of competition—winning. Features of the sport context help form the "brackets" of sport morality that are embedded within daily life reasoning. These include the formal rules of the game, officials who impose sanctions for breaking rules, the spatial and temporal separation of sport and everyday life experiences, and the insignificant consequences outside game play. Thus, one can temporarily set aside one's usual moral obligation to consider the physical and psychological needs of others to do what it takes to win. However, game reasoning is only legitimate as long as aggressive behavior does not produce negative consequences for the opponent once the game has ended and as long as it occurs within game-defined rules that limit what skills and tactics can be used during the game (Bredemeier & Shields, 1986b, 1986c). Consider the following quote by Bryan Cox, the "NFL's poster child for bad behavior": "When I'm on the field, I think about causing as much pain to the person lined up across from me as possible. During the three hours of the game on Sunday evening, I figure I can commit as many crimes as I want to without going to jail" (ESPN, 1997). His comment clearly communicates the essence of game reasoning, one that is condoned, praised, and even celebrated in professional football.

The notion of game reasoning as a legitimate worldview within sport contexts also suggests that athletes who reason at an egocentric or lower level of moral reasoning will express their thoughts and emotions in ways that differ from individuals who hold higher moral reasoning levels. The *game reasoner* would be more likely to endorse aggressive actions and unfair play in the spirit of winning the game and to express more aggressive behavior or actions that intend to inflict physical or psychological injury to others. In contrast, individuals who express higher levels of moral reasoning would be expected to show more assertive but less aggressive play. Does the empirical research reveal such a coherent pattern in the relationships among moral reasoning, perceived legitimacy of aggression and unfair play, and actual sport behavior?

Moral Reasoning, Perceived Legitimacy of Aggression, and Sport Behavior

The studies reported in this section explore the permutation of relationships among moral thoughts and actions: (a) between moral reasoning and sport behavior (e.g., prosocial, aggressive), (b) between moral reasoning and legitimacy of aggressive actions, and (c) between legitimacy of and tendencies toward aggressive behavior. Thus, the literature on life–sport and athlete–nonathlete moral reasoning differences is extended to the links among moral thoughts, endorsement of unfair play, and behavioral consequences in sport.

Horrocks (1979) conducted one of the first studies to link moral reasoning level and prosocial (sportsmanlike) behaviors. Children in fifth and sixth grades were presented with daily life and sport dilemmas, and teachers rated children on a number of prosocial behaviors including sharing, taking turns, consoling a teammate after a mistake, and abiding by the rules of the game. Relationships between prosocial behavior and moral reasoning were moderately strong ($r = .55$ for daily life, .63 for sport). Children classified as moderate or high in life moral reasoning were higher on prosocial play behavior than low-reasoning children. For sport moral reasoning, children in the high, moderate, and low groups all differed significantly on prosocial behaviors. This study established a strong link between children's moral reasoning and good sportsmanship.

Romance (1984; Romance, Weiss, & Bockoven, 1986) implemented a structural–developmental

moral intervention program with fifth-grade children in a physical education unit. Important to the present discussion are the teachers' observed behavioral changes in the experimental group (higher moral reasoning) compared with the control group over the course of the program. Children became increasingly more active in dialogue sessions that led to more efficient and effective resolutions, fewer reports of misconduct and disciplinary problems occurred, cooperation and sensitivity to less skilled peers were more prevalent, and verbal aggression was curtailed.

Bredemeier and her colleagues extensively tested the assumption that moral reasoning levels should be related to legitimacy of and behavioral tendencies toward aggressive and unfair play (Bredemeier, 1985, 1994; Bredemeier & Shields, 1984b, 1986b, 1986c; Bredemeier, Weiss, Shields, & Cooper, 1986, 1987). Bredemeier and Shields (1984b) correlated college basketball players' moral reasoning scores with coaches' evaluations of player aggression and average number of fouls committed per game. As hypothesized, athletes scoring higher at Kohlberg's Stage 2 (an eye for an eye) and Stage 4 (norms of the game) of moral reasoning were rated and ranked as more aggressive and committed more fouls than athletes scoring lower on these stages. Negative and moderate relationships emerged between moral reasoning and aggressive behavior for Stages 3 (concern for acting good), 5B (right to be free from intentional injury), and 6 (principle of justice) for coaches' evaluations but not for number of fouls committed.

Bredemeier (1985, Bredemeier & Shields, 1986c) randomly selected 20 high school and 20 college basketball players from a larger sample interviewed on life and sport moral dilemmas (Bredemeier & Shields, 1986b). Several weeks after the moral interview, she interviewed these athletes again concerning their judgments about the legitimacy of their own aggressive game behavior and that of a fictional football player. Six increasingly aggressive behaviors were evaluated such as verbally intimidating an opponent, knocking the wind out of an opponent and forcing him to leave the game, throwing an elbow to force the opponent out for the game, and attempting to permanently disable an opponent. Athletes at lower moral reasoning levels endorsed more injurious actions during game play, especially when applied to the hypothetical player's behavior. Interview data revealed that most athletes regarded some degree of hurting an opponent as a legitimate part of sport. However, actions intended to injure an opponent outside of the "game frame" and in violation of game rules were considered illegitimate. These findings support the notion of game reasoning within competitive sport contexts.

In companion studies examining relationships among moral reasoning, legitimacy judgments, and behavioral tendencies in fourth- through seventh-grade (ages 9–13) children, Bredemeier (1994; Bredemeier, Weiss, Shields, & Cooper, 1986, 1987) found that moral reasoning was moderately related to legitimacy judgments of injurious actions ($r = -.25$ for girls, $-.43$ for boys). Children with lower reasoning levels viewed more aggressive play as warranted within the context of sport. Boys' legitimacy judgments, but not girls', were moderately related to self-reported sport aggression; those who saw physically aggressive actions as justified were more likely to report that they too engaged in such behaviors. Boys' participation in high-contact sports and girls' participation in medium-contact sports were moderately related to less mature moral reasoning and greater self-reported aggressive behavior. Sport and life moral reasoning scores were moderately related to self-reported assertiveness ($r = .38, .32$) and aggressiveness ($r = -.28$ to $-.46$) in sport contexts but were weakly related to submissive behavior ($r = .22, .22$).

Solomon and Bredemeier (1999) examined children's moral reasoning and legitimacy judgments about gender-based inequalities in sport (i.e., gender stratification). Children's reasoning about gender stratification is considered to be an important component of social justice thinking, and understanding how children think about gender and justice may help educators address gender inequity in sport more effectively. Boys and girls (ages 6–11) participating in organized youth sport viewed boys as more advantaged in sport contexts because of their higher athletic ability. Most children did not approve of such stratification. However, moral reasoning maturity was unrelated to legitimacy judgments about gender stratification in sport. This means that conceptions about social justice were not associated with conceptions about fairness relative to gender inequality in sport. The non-sport-specific measure of social justice reasoning was implicated as one possible reason for the nonsignificant relationship between moral reasoning and legitimacy.

Ryan, Williams, and Wimer (1990) examined the relationships among college female basketball athletes' legitimacy judgments, behavioral intentions,

and aggressive behaviors over the course of a season. Athletes reported on their own engagement in nonphysical intimidation, physical intimidation, and varying degrees of physical aggression. Preseason legitimacy judgment, but not behavioral intention, was related significantly to season-long aggressive behaviors. The greater number of injurious actions deemed admissible in basketball, the more aggressive players were bound to be. However, legitimacy judgments were quite low, with first-year players scoring about 5.5 and 3.0 at pre- and postseason (possible scores = 0–21). Other players only scored about 2.5 at both time periods. Thus, players on the whole did not accept physically intimidating and other injurious behaviors. Unfortunately, the authors did not report the extent to which players inflicted aggressive behaviors toward opponents during the season, but extrapolation of the data suggests that the number was quite low.

The findings reported in this section, similar to those in the previous section, support the notion of game reasoning. Results establish a relationship between lower sport moral reasoning and greater legitimacy of and expression of aggressive behaviors. More favorable endorsement of aggressive play was related to higher levels of aggression. These relationships especially held for male participants at collegiate, high school, and youth levels. Higher moral reasoning, in contrast, related to more frequent prosocial and assertive, and less aggressive, behaviors. There is always a double-edged sword when considering the nature of sport competition effects. Nevertheless, a substantial amount of the variance in prosocial and aggressive sport behavior is still left unexplained after accounting for moral reasoning and legitimacy judgments. According to Shields and Bredemeier (1995), characteristic individual differences and social contextual factors surrounding competition play a crucial role in participants' moral growth through sport.

Individual Differences and Moral Development

In expanding Rest's (1984, 1986, 1994) four-component model of moral action, Shields and Bredemeier (1995) focused on two major sources of influence—individual and contextual factors—on interpreting the situation, judging what course of action to take, choosing which outcome to pursue, and implementing one's intention. The individual differences that impinge on the process of moral functioning include personal competencies and ego processes, distinguished by one's developmental or dispositional characteristics versus coping and defensive mechanisms used in a given situation. Role-taking and social perspective–taking abilities, moral reasoning, values and beliefs, moral motives, self-conceptions, self-regulation skills, and social problem-solving skills compose the range of individual differences specified by Shields and Bredemeier as instrumental and applicable for understanding moral development in sport.

Values and beliefs (play vs. professional orientation, legitimacy judgments) and moral reasoning level have been discussed as explanations of prosocial and antisocial behaviors. Besides these, self-conceptions are the only individual difference factor investigated empirically to date as a correlate of moral action in sport. Shields and Bredemeier (1995) highlighted achievement goal orientations and the moral self-concept as two primary self-conceptions that affect moral intentions and behaviors. To our knowledge, moral self-concept has not been studied in relation to choice of and implementation of moral actions in sport. However, we believe that this area holds considerable promise based on the work of Harter (1999) in the development of multidimensional self-conceptions and their influence on global self-worth, emotions, and achievement behavior. For example, behavioral conduct and morality are featured as salient domains of the self-concept at every period of the life span, from early childhood to late adulthood.

Research on achievement goal orientations in the physical domain abounds (Weiss & Ferrer-Caja, chapter 5). Characteristic task goal orientation entails conceptions of success in terms of self-referenced information such as improvement, mastery, and learning. An ego goal orientation refers to self-ability evaluations in reference to normative standards such as event outcome and peer comparison. According to Nicholls (1989), achievement goals essentially denote worldviews or theories about success in a particular achievement domain. In support of goal perspective theory, sport-related research shows that task and ego orientations are related to beliefs about the purposes of sport, beliefs about causes of success and failure, positive and negative affect, intrinsic motivation, and participatory behaviors (Weiss & Ferrer-Caja, chapter 5). Given the notion of achievement goals as worldviews about contributors to successful achievement, it is not surprising that recently a handful of studies have explored links among task and ego goal orientations with moral beliefs and behavioral intentions and tendencies.

Duda, Olson, and Templin (1991) reasoned that an egocentric level of moral reasoning that is associated with greater endorsement of aggressive actions in sport is compatible with an ego-oriented goal perspective that focuses on self-interest and demonstrating superior normative ability. They tested their hypothesis by correlating task and ego goal orientations of high school basketball players with sportsmanship attitudes and approval of committing aggressive behaviors to win a game. Higher ego goal involvement was related to approval of unsportsmanlike/cheating behavior and verbal and physical aggression to increase chances of winning. The authors concluded that a motivational interpretation of game reasoning may be viable and that relationships among goal orientation, moral reasoning, and aggression beliefs and behaviors should be explored.

Stephens (2000; Stephens & Bredemeier, 1996; Stephens, Bredemeier, & Shields, 1997) explored the relationship between goal orientations and cheating and aggressive behavior among youth soccer players. In the first study (Stephens & Bredemeier, 1996), players rated their likelihood to play unfairly and aggressively (lie to an official, violate a game rule, hurt an opponent) in a variety of situations (e.g., if the other team had gotten away with same action earlier). The authors found weak relationships between self-reported likelihood to play unfairly/aggressively and task and ego goal orientations. In a replication study, Stephens found that goal orientations were not significant predictors of self-reported likelihood to act aggressively against an opponent. These results do not support a link between goal orientations and tendencies to act in unsportsmanlike ways. However, Kavussanu and Roberts (2001) found a moderate association between ego (but not task) goal orientation, moral functioning, and legitimacy judgments of physically aggressive behavior among female collegiate basketball players.

Dunn and Causgrove Dunn (1999) drew on earlier research that revealed stronger advocacy for aggressive actions in collision or high physical contact sports (Bredemeier et al., 1986; Silva, 1983). They investigated goal orientations, perceived legitimacy of aggressive behaviors, and sportsmanship attitudes among 11- to 14-year-old male competitive ice hockey players. Ego goal orientation, but not task goal orientation, was related to endorsing verbal intimidation, illegal but noninjurious body-checking, and illegal elbowing that caused a player to miss game time, among others. Players higher in task orientation indicated greater acceptance of sportsmanlike behaviors such as respect and concern for social conventions, rules, and officials than did low-scoring peers. Players higher in ego orientation reported lower respect for rules and officials than did low-ego players. These results support the link between goal orientation and sportsmanship attitudes.

The research findings on dispositional goal orientations in relationship to attitudes toward and expressed aggressive behaviors are equivocal. Associations and effect sizes are generally low, suggesting that other individual and social contextual factors have been omitted that may help explain moral judgments, intentions, and behaviors. Recently, some achievement motivation researchers have advocated including social goals rather than limiting goals to just task and ego (e.g., Jarvinen & Nicholls, 1996; Urdan & Maehr, 1995; Wentzel, 1993, 1998). Urdan and Maehr defined social goals as perceived social purposes of domain-specific achievement. Social goals include, among others, social welfare (e.g., become a productive member of society), social solidarity (e.g., bring honor to one's in-group), social approval (e.g., please adults, enhance peer acceptance), and social compliance (e.g., become a good person). It is conceivable that social approval from coach and teammates, social solidarity in the form of maintaining the team's social status, and social compliance by endorsing and upholding team norms may account for variations in self-reported advocacy of and participation in unfair competitive play. The research exploring contextual factors and moral development may help bolster this proposition.

Social Contextual Factors and Moral Development

Shields and Bredemeier (1995) outlined several social contextual factors that may considerably affect moral thoughts and actions in competitive sport contexts. These include the nature of the reward structure (competitive, cooperative) or motivational climate, moral atmosphere (i.e., prevailing team norms), domain-specific reasoning cues, and power structures that may play a role in how gender, race, and social class influence an individual's ability to act according to his or her moral beliefs. Moral atmosphere (i.e., team norms and coaching behaviors) and task- and ego-involving motivational climates are the two contextual factors that have received the most attention in the literature investigating relationships to legitimacy judgments and moral functioning in competitive sport.

The moral atmosphere pertains to characteristics about the sport environment that may mediate or moderate participants' decisions about acting fairly. According to Shields and Bredemeier (1995), central components of the moral atmosphere are the collective norms and conventions guiding appropriate behavior that are adopted, developed, and condoned by team members over time and that are consonant with the image of a particular sport. This notion is reminiscent of Michael Smith's (1974, 1975, 1979, 1988) classic work on young ice hockey players' sources of violence. A salient part of this moral atmosphere is teammates' and coaches' beliefs about what denotes appropriate and inappropriate behavior.

Moral atmosphere was examined as part of Stephens' (2000; Stephens & Bredemeier, 1996) studies of aggression in youth soccer (ages 9–14 years). Perceptions of proaggressive team norms were assessed by players, who indicated the number of teammates who would be likely to lie to an official, hurt an opponent, and violate a critical game rule. Respondents were asked to imagine themselves in the protagonist's position and think about how the protagonist might decide what she should and would do by considering her desire for winning, what her coach and teammates would want, and what would be fair. Coach influence was assessed through players' perceptions of coach ego and task goal orientation. Team norms condoning aggressive behavior were the strongest predictor of players' self-reported aggressive tendencies (for boys and girls), followed by a small contribution from perceptions of coach's ego goal orientation for girls' teams only.

Shields, Bredemeier, Gardner, and Bostrom (1995) investigated coaching behaviors and team cohesion as correlates of collective norms among high school and college athletes. Team norms were tapped by questions pertaining to the number of teammates who would cheat or deliberately hurt an opponent and whether the coach would want players to cheat or injure an opponent for the sake of winning. Shields et al. contended that greater team cohesion must exist for team members to adopt and condone unfair play as an ac-

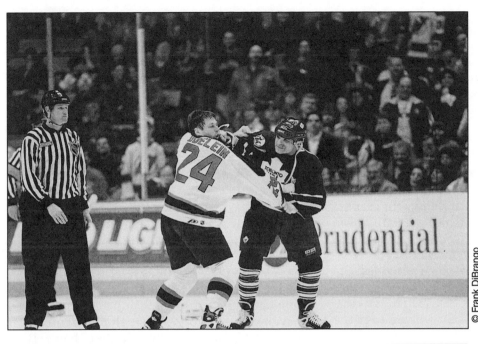

Coach–athlete conflicts included physical abuse (e.g., forced to diet), emotional abuse (e.g., name calling), punishment for errors (e.g., running laps), and favoritism. About half the participants indicated they did not act on their perceived injustice, and they cited the coach's power most frequently for not resisting. To enhance moral sensitivity and an ethic of care among coaches and athletes, the authors urged that sport organizations create opportunities for mediating coach–athlete conflicts in a supportive environment for developing empathy and conflict resolution skills.

© Frank DiBrango

Seeing violence in professional hockey might contribute to youth hockey players developing negative attitudes and behaviors.

ceptable behavioral norm. Instead they found a negative relationship between task cohesion and perceived norms toward unfair play and aggression. Such a relationship suggests that players' perceptions of sticking together and remaining united in pursuing task-related team goals and objectives were higher under conditions where the collective norm was one of not cheating and playing aggressive.

Duquin and Schroeder-Braun (1996) adopted an alternative approach to studying the influence of moral atmosphere on athletes' moral judgments. Sport participants in three age groups (12–14, 15–17, 18 and over) were presented with eight scenarios depicting coach–athlete conflict and rated the degree to which the coach behaved immorally. Scenarios included abusing a teammate in front of the team, showing athletes how to get away with illegal moves, playing a seriously injured athlete, pushing and shoving athletes to make a point, and emotionally abusing team members to make them feel like losers. Male participants and high school students judged scenarios as less morally problematic than did females or other age groups. The groups rated playing an injured athlete, pushing and shoving athletes, and emotionally abusing athletes as most "seriously wrong." Respondents also recalled a time when their coach did something that they felt was unfair or immoral.

Summary

Findings are rather consistent for the divergence between life and sport moral reasoning and for group differences in moral reasoning and legitimacy judgments of aggressive behaviors. Research is less well developed for the link between moral functioning and achievement goal orientations. Personal competencies such as role-taking and social perspective–taking ability, moral self-concept, and self-regulation and social problem-solving skills remain unexamined. Conceptual clarity will need to be maintained by distinguishing moral motives and moral reasoning, moral motives and goal orientations, and their relationships to moral thought and action.

Among contextual factors, a handful of studies reveal that moral atmosphere, defined in terms of collective team norms, is intricately linked to self-ratings of aggression. These results converge nicely with those from social learning–based studies, specifically those on normative reference groups' approval and disapproval of legal and illegal aggression in ice hockey (Smith, 1975, 1979), football (Mugno & Feltz, 1985), and basketball (Stuart & Ebbeck, 1995). Nevertheless, moral atmosphere and motivational climate share common features (e.g., what is recognized, rewarded, and emphasized within the social context) and will need to be distinguished as moral constructs.

Influence of parenting and coaching styles; one's peer group (teammates and nonplaying friends); and situation-specific cues on moral reasoning, beliefs, and behaviors await empirical inquiry. Scientists will need to adopt a variety of research designs and methodologies for studying individual differences, social contextual factors, and moral development in sport.

One of the truly encouraging areas of inquiry and implementation in recent years has been moral development intervention studies and programs. This direction has proliferated since an exhaustive review of moral development in sport 10 years ago (Weiss & Bredemeier, 1990). These studies and programs mix social learning (e.g., modeling, reinforcement) and structural developmental (e.g., dialogue and balance activities) approaches to moral development, or they lean more heavily on one or the other. Because of the richness of this literature that has evolved over the last decade, we highlight these studies and school- and community-based programs in a section of their own.

MORAL DEVELOPMENT INTERVENTIONS IN PHYSICAL ACTIVITY CONTEXTS

The moral character of sport participants has never been under more fire than in recent years. Not only have professional and college sports run amok with incidences of violence on and off the field, gambling, and cheating (e.g., falsifying academic grades, point-shaving, recruiting violations), the effect has also trickled down to high schools and community youth sports. In 1999, the nadir of athletic moral immaturity rocked the nation when investigators of Columbine High School's shooting tragedy uncovered that the perpetrators were instigated in part by being bullied by several of the school's male athletes. This may have explained in part why athletes were the prime targets of their retaliation. National Public Radio carried a story that coaches and athletes at the school were participating in a program designed to raise moral sensitivity and conflict resolution skills. Violence prevention programs increasingly are becoming an essential component of the school curriculum.

Values and moral education, of course, extend far beyond the sport domain to the daily lives of children and teenagers. Given changes in family structure and society in general, educators agree that responsibility for the moral development of youth cannot be left solely to the family environment or to happenstance. Over the last 25 years, school- and community-based programs have sprung up to educate children and youth about moral values and character (Damon, 1988, 1995, 1997; Kurtines & Gewirtz, 1991b, 1995). Although varying results have emerged from programs designed to enhance moral awareness and teach perspective-taking and conflict resolution skills to youth, the key has been the proactive nature of such programs and inclusion of caring and knowledgeable teachers to implement interactive activities.

Theoretical, empirical, and experiential knowledge has inspired socially relevant programs in the last 15 years that are designed to teach young people the difference between right and wrong behaviors in sport and physical activity. Besides differentiating appropriate and inappropriate behaviors, these programs teach children rules of respect for human rights. Rather than rely on chance that children act out of care and concern for others' well-being and not out of self-interest, programs go beyond using social approval, modeling, and reinforcement to impart values such as honesty, responsibility, cooperation, and other altruistic behaviors. They do so by ensuring opportunities for participants to be involved in self-responsibility and responsibility toward others through interactive discussions and group resolutions independent of the teacher or coach. In other words, these programs capitalize on social learning and structural developmental strategies to maximize moral development through physical activity participation.

In this section we introduce and describe ongoing moral and social development programs that are conducted within physical activity contexts. All of these programs are grounded in conceptual models of child development. Some programs document data-based validation of teaching methods and curricular materials. In these cases we report study findings that support the key principles underlying the program philosophy and goals. Other programs are not as intimately tied to empirical findings as much as they are responsive to specific community needs and experiential knowledge of the target population. In either case, these programs' systematic efforts to make a difference in the moral and social development of youth through participation in physical activity are exceptional, and they signal cause for optimism and hope that sport can, in fact, build character.

Fair Play for Kids

In 1986, the Commission for Fair Play was created in response to Canada's concern about violence and erosion of ethics in sport. Members of the commission include educators, administrators, physicians, coaches, officials, media representatives, and former professional and Olympic athletes who volunteer their time to promote the principles of fair play in sport. Their activities include national advertising and promotional campaigns, providing educational support materials, recognizing exemplary citizens who demonstrate fair play through their actions, and proposing fair play initiatives to the Minister of Fitness and Amateur Sport. In 1990, the Commission for Fair Play joined with Sport Canada to develop a teacher's resource manual for grades 4 through 6 (ages 8–11) with the goal of bringing fair play activities into the classroom—language arts, health, art, social studies, science, drama, and physical education classrooms.

The interdisciplinary educational activities focus on developing attitudes and behaviors that exemplify the ideals of fair play identified by the Commission for Fair Play. The five ideals of fair play are (a) respect the rules, (b) respect the officials and accept their decisions, (c) respect your opponent, (d) give everybody an equal chance to participate, and (e) maintain your self-control at all times. These ideals and the processes by which children learn fair play values and attitudes stem from structural developmental and social learning theories and research. The learning processes are specified in the manual as (a) identifying and resolving moral conflicts through discussion and conflict resolution and (b) changing roles and perspectives (e.g., simulation games, social perspective–taking). Although these processes emanate primarily from a structural developmental worldview, social learning theory–based strategies also are emphasized in the curriculum via modeling by former Canadian Olympians, role playing and observational learning, and the rewarding of "fair players." Thus, the Fair Play for Kids curriculum was designed to enhance moral reasoning and behavior, was developed from moral development theory and research, and created curricular activities emphasizing role-taking and social perspective–taking, dialogue and balance, and modeling and reinforcement of fair play behaviors.

The manual's bibliography and appendixes include key theoretical resources, describe levels of moral reasoning, and cite moral intervention studies in the physical domain that bolstered the creation of fair play ideals, learning processes, and specific classroom activities. A review of these contributing studies is noteworthy in light of their precedence to the Fair Play for Kids program.

Intervention Studies Preceding Fair Play for Kids

Bredemeier, Weiss, Shields, and Shewchuk (1986) conducted a field experiment to compare structural development and social learning teaching strategies in improving children's moral reasoning. Participants (ages 5–7) in an instructional sports camp were randomly assigned to social learning, structural developmental, or control groups for the 6-week program. Weekly themes included activities that highlighted fairness, sharing, verbal aggression, physical aggression, distributive justice, and retributive justice. Teacher and peer modeling and verbal and tangible reinforcement comprised social learning strategies for teaching moral themes. Participants in the structural developmental group focused on group discussion and resolution of interpersonal conflicts following naturally occurring or deliberately planned dilemmas. Children in the control group were encouraged to follow game rules and teacher-set class guidelines, with violations leading to direct instruction and time-outs. Within-group analysis showed that both experimental groups significantly increased in moral reasoning from pre- to postintervention, but the control group did not. Between-group differences on moral reasoning at postintervention approached significance ($p < .07$). This study thus established that a moral development intervention could be implemented successfully with children as young as 6 and 7 years old.

Romance et al. (1986) followed with an intervention study in a public school physical education class. They compared structural developmental and control groups consisting of fifth-grade children (ages 10–11) over an 8-week unit. Students in the experimental group were involved in moral dilemmas, discussed issues related to the dilemma within groups, and created moral balances that considered the rights and responsibilities of all students. The experimental group showed significant pre- to postintervention improvement, and the control group a nonsignificant decline, in life and sport moral reasoning. Importantly, the structural development group was significantly higher than the control group at posttest. Students exposed to dilemma, dialogue, and balance strategies showed more prosocial and fewer antisocial behaviors.

Wandzilak, Carroll, and Ansorge (1988) implemented a 9-week moral development program with male junior high school basketball players. A mix of social learning and structural developmental strategies was used, including having players write what they thought sportsmanship meant, offer examples of good and bad sportsmanship, and discuss basketball-specific moral dilemmas daily. The researchers were interested in several aspects of moral development: moral reasoning, perceptions of sportsmanship, and prosocial behaviors. No significant between-group differences emerged, but significant pre- to postintervention improvement occurred in the experimental group, but not the control group. DeBusk and Hellison (1989) also interspersed social learning and structural developmental teaching strategies with 10 delinquency-prone fourth-grade boys in an alternative physical education program lasting six weeks. Interventions included daily teacher talk, student sharing, reflection time, modeling, teacher praise, and dialogue and balance activities. Case study results indicated that the boys' affect, behavior, and knowledge improved during the program.

These four studies conducted in the 1980s, along with the theories driving them, were influential in the creation of Fair Play for Kids in 1990. Moreover, using a target group of children in fourth to sixth grades (ages 8–11) is consistent with findings and recommendations concerning the ages at which competitiveness is fully developed (i.e., social comparison ability) and skills are adequate for moral dialogue and balance. Although the Fair Play for Kids curriculum was carefully based on moral development theory and research, the effectiveness of its specific program of activities and teaching strategies in promoting moral growth had not been tested directly. Sandra Gibbons, a pedagogy researcher at the University of Victoria and a former teacher, was interested in the social and moral development of children through physical education. She set out to test the efficacy of the Fair Play for Kids program with large numbers of children spanning each of the targeted grade levels and across multiple schools.

Intervention Studies
Testing Fair Play for Kids

In the first evaluation of the Fair Play for Kids intervention program, Gibbons et al. (1995) sampled 452 students in 18 fourth-, fifth-, and sixth-grade classrooms in two Canadian provinces. Six classrooms at each grade level were randomly assigned to three groups: (a) control (no fair play curriculum), (b) physical education only (fair play curriculum conducted by physical education teachers only), and (c) all classes (fair play curriculum conducted in physical education and other subjects including health, language arts, social studies, and fine arts). The experimental protocol extended for seven months of the academic year, with at least one fair play activity implemented weekly during the course of the study. Students completed self-reports of moral judgment, reasoning, and intention, and teachers rated each student on frequency of prosocial behaviors before and after the intervention. Strong support emerged for the effectiveness of the Fair Play for Kids curriculum. Children in both experimental groups demonstrated significantly higher posttest scores on all four dependent measures than did controls. Moreover, effect sizes were moderate to large in magnitude, suggesting that the strength of group differences was practically meaningful as well as statistically significant. The two experimental groups did not differ from one another, meaning that moral development can be effectively addressed in the physical education classroom only or in a combination of classes.

Gibbons and Ebbeck (1997) extended the first study in two primary ways. First, given the strong pre- to postintervention changes in moral variables spanning the 7-month program, they wanted to determine if changes can occur more quickly and, if so, which variables are susceptible to such change. Therefore moral judgment, reasoning, intention, and prosocial behavior were assessed at three times during the school year (pre-, mid-, post-intervention). Second, the fair play curriculum includes a mix of social learning and structural developmental teaching strategies and activities. Gibbons and Ebbeck (1997) compared whether strategies unique to social learning (i.e., modeling, reinforcement) or structural development (i.e., dialogue and problem solving) approaches are equally effective for influencing moral growth. Therefore, the experimental groups included a social learning and a structural developmental group. A total of 204 students from nine fourth-, fifth-, and sixth-grade classes (three classes each) participated in a control group or one of two experimental groups during physical education class for seven months. Fair play activities were implemented at least once weekly for the duration of the field experiment. Results indicated that at mid- and postintervention, structural development and social learning participants scored significantly higher than controls on moral judgment, intention, and prosocial behavior. The structural development group scored higher on moral reasoning than did social learning and control group participants at both time periods. These differences were again meaningful (i.e., large effect sizes) as well as statistically significant. In sum, moral growth occurred as early as four months into the intervention and in theoretically consistent ways (i.e., experimental groups were higher than controls on moral judgment, intention, and behavior; structural developmental group was higher than social learning and control groups on moral reasoning).

In sum, the two studies conducted to date on the efficacy of the Fair Play for Kids program strongly supported the strategies and activities promoted within the teacher resource manual. Perhaps the most important aspect of the studies is that the teachers embraced the Fair Play for Kids program and enthusiastically participated in and implemented the program. In the end, the bottom line in effecting a strong intervention is commitment by the social change agents themselves.

Life Skills Development Model[2]

For well over a decade, Steven Danish, a counseling psychologist at Virginia Commonwealth University, has devoted considerable efforts toward using physical activity and sport as a medium through which children and teenagers can develop personal and social competence. He defines competence as "the ability to do life planning, to be self reliant, and to seek the resources of others in coping" (Danish et al., 1990, p. 172). At different developmental levels, these skills naturally relate to a unique set of behaviors. The basic tenet of Danish's model is that psychosocial skills learned on the playing field may transfer to other domains (e.g., school, peer relationships, home, workplace) but only if experiences are specifically designed and implemented with this purpose in mind. These experiences must consider the developmental needs and skills characteristic of various life periods (e.g., need for mastery, autonomy, relationships, identity).

Life skills are defined as essential competencies that must be learned to transfer across domains and be maintained throughout development. Dan-

ish identifies life skills as goal setting, self-regulation skills to attain goals (e.g., positive self-talk, imagery, self-control, decision making), and seeking the social support necessary to maximize achieving goals. For example, a program called Athletes Coaching Teens was developed to reduce health-compromising behaviors in at-risk early adolescents such as substance use, unsafe sex, and violent behavior (Danish et al., 1990). Professional and college athletes spoke at school assemblies about achieving excellence through goal setting and the problems associated with drug involvement, teen pregnancy, and dropping out of school. High school athletes were chosen based on academic, leadership, and athletic qualities to receive training and then implement a program within middle school health classes. Sessions focused on teaching five skills: setting goals, developing plans to attain goals, identifying and overcoming roadblocks to goal attainment, developing problem-solving skills, and learning to rebound from temporary setbacks. These life skills, taught by similar and athlete role models, were believed to help at-risk youth develop the self-knowledge, personal competence, and self-confidence to make informed and healthy decisions as youth and later as older adolescents and adults.

The Going for the Goal (GOAL) program has been implemented in countless cities across the United States and recently in New Zealand (Danish, 1997; Danish & Nellen, 1997). The philosophical basis and action plan for GOAL are similar to Athletes Coaching Teens, with the addition of teaching future-enhancing skills or "what to say yes to" as opposed to "just say no" (Danish & Nellen, 1997, p. 103). GOAL is a 10-hour, 10-session program taught by high school students who are carefully selected based on academic, extracurricular, and leadership skills to inner-city, at-risk youth. Workshop sessions focus on future dreams, setting and reaching goals, understanding and overcoming roadblocks to reaching goals, seeking help from others, rebounding from goal difficulty and learning to self-reward accomplishments, and identifying and building on one's strengths. Informal results regarding GOAL versus control group participants include (a) better school attendance, (b) less substance and alcohol abuse, (c) less violent and other delinquent behaviors, and (d) the belief that GOAL was useful, was important, and would be helpful for their friends (Danish, 1997; Danish & Nellen, 1997).

---

2. Danish, 1997; Danish & Nellen, 1997; Danish, Nellen, & Owens, 1996; Danish, Petitpas, & Hale, 1990, 1992, 1995.

Customized versions of GOAL have been developed to accommodate the specific needs of sports organizations that want to add a life skills component to their traditional sport skills focus (Danish, 1997; Danish & Nellen, 1997). For example, college student-athletes (NCAA Youth Education through Sports) and Junior Olympic divers (U.S. Diving Federation) have collaborated to serve as role models in teaching enrichment sessions. The Black Women in Sports Foundation recruited the Life Skills Center staff to conduct a GOAL clinic in which African-American mentors and mentees worked side by side to learn beginning golf and tennis skills and various aspects of life skills training. Application of GOAL within sport settings continues to emphasize the transferability of life skills in the sport domain to home, school, and workplace settings.

Successful integration of sport and life skills training within sport settings inspired Danish's inception of the Sports United to Promote Education and Recreation (SUPER) program (Danish & Nellen, 1997; Danish et al., 1996). The underlying philosophy of SUPER is that sport and life skills are transferable to other domains. The key is for participants to believe that they have the skills and qualities that are valuable in a variety of social contexts. Workshops focus on the concepts that physical and mental skills are important in both sport and life domains, that it is important to set and attain goals in both domains, and that roadblocks to both life and sport goals can be overcome. Because college student-athletes serve as older peer leaders for teaching adolescent participants sport-specific skills and life skills related to sports, benefits are reciprocal. The peer models gain a sense of empowerment and feeling needed, whereas the adolescent learners are able to interact with similar others who demonstrate the possibilities for achieving sport and life goals. One of the central life skills imparted to participants of the SUPER program is that being competitive and successful in sport and life means learning to compete against themselves and their own potential, not others. Quantitative and qualitative effectiveness of SUPER has not yet been documented, to our knowledge, but given the efficacy of GOAL we expect similar success.

In sum, Danish's life skills intervention programs conducted within sport settings certainly target children's and adolescents' moral and social growth and development. Program philosophy and objectives are grounded in developmental needs and skills; thus, these programs seek to help at-risk youths gain mastery, autonomy, personal identity, and respect for and responsibility toward others. The life skills programs also use important concepts for communicating and for convincing youth to adopt the life skills taught. Strategies such as peer modeling, role-playing, life–sport analogies, and transferability of skills are successful and salient to children and adolescents. Evaluation research of GOAL and SUPER in accomplishing goals and objectives will bolster knowledge about the importance and impact of these programs.

Self- and Social Responsibility Model[3]

Don Hellison, long-time physical educator and advocate for integrating social and motor skill development in youth, developed a physical activity–based responsibility model more than 20 years ago (Hellison, 1978). Reflection on his own, colleagues', and students' experiences teaching urban youth in inner cities such as Portland, Oregon, and Chicago, Illinois, led Hellison to modify and refine the model over time (Hellison, 1985, 1986, 1988, 1995). Today he directs the Physical Education At-Risk Youth Program at the University of Illinois at Chicago. The goals of this program are to serve disadvantaged and at-risk youth, help teachers learn how to teach at-risk youth, conduct and disseminate research on the efficacy of physical activity intervention programs, and raise the consciousness of the physical education profession regarding at-risk youth. His self- and social responsibility model or variations of it are flourishing in physical education, after-school, and organized sport settings in various communities with at-risk populations across the United States and other parts of the world (Hellison, 1989; Hellison et al., 1996).

The responsibility model is a holistic approach designed to balance empowering students with teaching explicit values to maximize development of personal and social skills among inner-city youth who are prone to delinquent activity. A particularly far-reaching goal of the responsibility model is promoting resiliency in youth vulnerable to the risks of poverty and crime (Martinek & Hellison, 1997). Five levels of responsibility are

---

3. Hellison, 1978, 1985, 1986, 1988, 1995; DeBusk & Hellison, 1989; Hellison & Georgiadis, 1992; Hellison, Martinek, & Cutforth, 1996; Martinek & Hellison, 1997.

(a) respecting the rights and feelings of others, (b) being self-motivated (i.e., using effort and persistence), (c) being self-directed (i.e., independent and autonomous), (d) caring about others and working together for the group's welfare, and (e) applying these self- and other responsibilities to domains outside the gym. Each of these responsibilities is designed to build on one another. For example, respecting others defines the foundation for developing social responsibility, because refraining from verbal and physical aggression toward others, resolving conflicts, and including everyone in the activities are minimal requirements for protecting the rights of all program participants (Hellison et al., 1996). Self-motivation and self-direction challenge youth to take responsibility for their effort and goals, which, in turn, stimulate social responsibility in the form of caring about and helping others.

The responsibility levels describe what needs to be learned, but implementation strategies that distribute the power between teacher and students describe how responsibility toward others and self is attained. These strategies include awareness talks, direct instruction, individual decision-making, group evaluation meetings, and reflection time to enable self-evaluation of goal attainment. Awareness talks and direct instruction are teacher-defined to teach students the levels of responsibility and integrate them into the physical activity lessons. Individual decision-making, group meetings, and reflection time shift the onus of responsibility onto the participants themselves. For example, students who "dis" others during the lesson, and thus violate the first responsibility level, may be asked to problem solve together to reach a mutually acceptable solution. Reflection time allows students the opportunity to monitor, evaluate, and reinforce themselves concerning the extent to which they were responsible during the lesson (i.e., respect others' feelings, helping others). Detailed accounts of specific responsibility-based physical activity programs are found in the literature (Cutforth, 1997; Georgiadis, 1990; Hellison et al., 1996).

A prototype program exemplifying the responsibility model was one designed to teach values through basketball to at-risk African-American boys (Hellison & Georgiadis, 1992). Basketball was chosen as the medium to promote personal and social responsibility because it is valued within the subculture of African-American teenage boys. Balance between empowering students and teaching specific values guided the program philosophy, and program success depended on students learning self- and social responsibility skills. Specific values included respecting others' feelings, practicing to improve (self-motivation and self-direction), and being of service to peers (i.e., caring about and helping others to achieve goals). Personal empowerment was accomplished by challenging students to control their behavior when interacting with others, develop appropriate rules for themselves in class, evaluate their own behavior in class, and determine their own motivating activities. Success in attaining responsibility goals was assessed through specific, measurable evaluation. Program evaluation in the form of attendance, students' journal entries, and number of youth achieving higher levels revealed that students accepted the program's goals and worked toward bettering themselves within the context of playing basketball. Data from researchers' field notes and school staff evaluations provided convincing evidence that the program was successful with this vulnerable group of teenage youth.

Overall evaluation of the responsibility model across various projects primarily has been conducted with case study or ethnographic methods. Attendance records, storytelling and interviews, and the unilateral praise of pedagogy scholars in the field support the effectiveness of the responsibility model (Hellison et al., 1996). Although more traditional forms of quantitative or qualitative data are not as ample, Hellison points to the labor-intensive, long-term work required to produce enduring psychosocial effects in youth that would mark success of the self- and social responsibility model. No doubt with time, quantification of these success stories of resilience will be available.

Sport for Peace[4]

The Sport for Peace curriculum is an intervention program recently devised by pedagogy researcher Catherine Ennis to address problems of disruptive and disengaged students in urban high schools. The program was customized to meet the specific needs of urban students, who are often challenged by poverty, single-parent households, and limited educational experiences and

---

4. Ennis, 1999; Ennis et al., 1997, 1999.

opportunities for peer affiliation. Concepts and skills emphasized in the Sport for Peace initiative include personal and social responsibility (e.g., empowerment within the school curriculum, care and concern for others), conflict negotiation skills, nonviolent verbal and physical behavior, and a sense of community. Although Sport for Peace is a new intervention program, extensive data collected over one year document its effectiveness and reveal optimism for future efforts to effect moral and social change within high school systems.

Ennis et al. (1999) detailed their extensive undertaking in implementing the Sport for Peace curriculum in six urban schools with 12 teachers and their students. A three-phase research design included (a) a baseline control period; (b) training, staff development, and experimentation with the curriculum for eight weeks; and (c) application of the Sport for Peace curriculum in a 9-week basketball unit. This last phase consisted of 45 50-minute lessons where teachers were encouraged to select and implement aspects of the Sport for Peace model that were appropriate for their current students. All six teachers and 60 students were interviewed after this phase of the study. As well, field notes and observational data were collected during all three phases of the research design. Qualitative data analysis procedures and interpretation of results were impeccable and impressive.

Results revealed that during Phase 1 (baseline), teachers taught skills briefly and allowed students to organize games for the remainder of the period. Skilled boys were advantaged in this scenario, with few girls participating in the activities. During Phase 2 (training), teachers experimented with modifications to curricular and teaching strategies consistent with the Sport for Peace program. Teachers had the most difficulty with knowing how to incorporate conflict resolution into their classes and avoid the temptation to resolve problems for their students. During this phase, students were able to assume responsibility in discussing problems, expressing their feelings, and negotiating solutions with class members.

In Phase 3 (implementation), students expressed responsibility to their teammates, showed them respect as individuals, and developed a sense of trust as a result of the intervention program. These findings were especially noteworthy for the low-skilled students who enjoyed the program and were more comfortable playing than

during Phase 1 (baseline). Highly skilled students did not like the Sport for Peace program at first because they could not dominate play as they usually did. These students did express satisfaction when they could coach their teammates, organize and run practices, and make game decisions. The authors concluded, "The Sport for Peace curriculum appeared to be instrumental in building the care and concern for others essential to creating mutually trusting and respectful relationships that these students said felt like family" (Ennis et al., 1999, p. 284). Because of the program's impressive results and its sound methodology and design, we believe that the Sport for Peace program represents hope in developing social and moral development among urban youth.

Sociomoral Education Programs[5]

Solomon (1997) has successfully implemented a moral intervention program through physical education with second-grade students identified as at-risk for dysfunctional behavior. The goals of the program were to improve personal and social responsibility by specifically targeting communication skills, cooperation, and sharing among class members. During the 13-week intervention, four moral themes guided the activities during physical education class: trust, helping, problem solving, and body awareness. Lesson plans were carefully structured to ensure explicit teaching of social values and skills. Assessing children's moral reasoning levels and prosocial behaviors before and after the intervention provided a means of evaluating the effectiveness of the program. Children participating in the intervention significantly improved on moral reasoning scores, whereas students in a second-grade class who were not exposed to the themes and activities did not show significant change. Moreover, the classroom teacher of the experimental group reported positive behavior change in her students compared with the start of the program. The curricular elements and teaching strategies of Solomon's (1997) sociomoral education program resemble those used by Romance et al. (1986) and Gibbons (Gibbons & Ebbeck, 1997; Gibbons et al., 1995) and thus offer promise for continued moral growth in elementary-age students.

Miller et al. (1997) described the goals and strategies of a sociomoral education program they have been conducting for several years with fourth- and

---

5. Miller, Bredemeier, & Shields, 1997; Solomon, 1997.

fifth-grade low-income students in an urban elementary school in Northern California. Four moral development goals and concomitant strategies are targeted along with typical motor skill and fitness goals during the three hours per week of physical education over the course of the year. Development of empathy is stimulated through cooperative learning activities, where participants' efforts during interdependent problem solving give them opportunities to understand and appreciate others' needs and feelings. Moral reasoning maturity is targeted through creating a positive moral atmosphere where collective group norms emphasize caring, fairness, and democratic decision-making. A task goal orientation, whereby participants view success and competence in self- rather than norm-referent terms, is emphasized by creating a mastery motivational climate in the classroom. Finally, prosocial behaviors that signify personal and social responsibility are encouraged through a gradual shift from teacher control to student empowerment in line with classmates' willingness to accept responsibility. Anecdotal evidence for the effectiveness of the sociomoral education program is provided through informal examples of group activity, challenges to effecting moral change, and children's testimonial statements. It will be important to document the program's effectiveness in meeting goals through additional data as well as transferability of empathy, moral reasoning, task goals, and responsibility to other physical activity (e.g., organized sport) and social (e.g., home, classroom) domains.

After 20 years at Berkeley, molding their theory of moral action in sport and conducting a plethora of empirical studies, Brenda Bredemeier and David Shields moved to the University of Notre Dame in 1999 to establish and codirect the Center for Sport, Character, and Culture. The mission of the center is to promote character development and ethical behavior in sport and everyday life. To accomplish this mission, specific goals are outlined: (a) conduct research on moral development in sport; (b) coordinate efforts among educators, practitioners, and policymakers to nurture character development through sport; (c) sponsor conferences and workshops; (d) serve as a resource center; and, (e) promote a "sport for all" orientation by encouraging widespread participation in sport and physical activity at all age levels. The advantage of such a center cannot be underestimated in terms of its impact on dissemination, marketing, and funding efforts. There is no doubt that moral development theory, research, and intervention in sport and physical activity contexts will proliferate under Bredemeier and Shields' leadership at the center.

Summary

The intervention programs highlighted in this section offer cause for optimism that physical activity offers an attractive vehicle for effecting moral and social developmental change in children and adolescents. Many of these programs target at-risk youth—individuals characterized by poverty, single-parent families, limited equipment and facilities, and reduced learning experiences in school. These youth are also prone to gang activity, substance abuse, and a pattern of disrespect toward peers. Some programs (Danish's Life Skills, Hellison's Responsibility Model, Ennis' Sport for Peace) have significantly reduced the antisocial behaviors of these youth. Programs such as Fair Play for Kids are implemented successfully during regular physical education classes when teachers accept ownership of the intervention and are committed to achieving its goals. We strongly believe that continued intervention efforts must quantify moral and social gains in participants, so that we can convincingly persuade policymakers to financially and politically endorse our efforts to enhance moral development through sport and physical activity.

FUTURE RESEARCH DIRECTIONS

The sport moral development literature has progressed considerably in the past two decades. The research literature has revealed personal and social contributors to moral functioning in sport as well as means to promote moral development. Theoretical approaches have been adopted in designing research studies and intervention protocols. Although these gains are impressive, there are many more questions to answer. For example, how do significant others effect moral developmental change in athletes? How are team norms relative to moral behavior developed, and what strengthens, weakens, or modifies these norms? What does and does not foster generalization of sport-related intervention effects to other contexts?

To successfully answer these questions, obstacles to the pursuit of moral development research must be addressed. The primary obstacle in this research area is obtaining measures of moral constructs that are simple to use and psychometrically sound. As Bredemeier and Shields (1998) noted in their comprehensive review of moral assessment in sport psychology, the bulk of existing measures in the field need additional psychometric evaluation. Furthermore, researchers need to carefully match use of measures relative to their intended theoretical targets. Measures assessing specific situations or behaviors may not necessarily tap underlying reasoning structures or typical responses of an individual. Conversely, more generalized measures may not accurately predict sport-related moral outcomes because they may not account for experiences, coaching, and other factors that contribute to situation-specific cognition, affect, and behavior.

In addressing how significant others foster moral developmental change in athletes, researchers will need to adopt longitudinal research designs that can target specific moral processes (e.g., reasoning about legitimacy of aggression, translating moral intentions to actions). Although there is a growing intervention literature, this work is characterized by adopting holistic, multimodal approaches to fostering change. That is, interventions typically draw from several theoretical frameworks and employ multiple strategies at one time. This work is extremely valuable but falls short of helping sport psychologists understand the specific variables that produce change at particular phases of the life span, at particular levels of sport experience, or in particular circumstances. For example, an intervention program that promotes positive change in moral reasoning and behavior in fourth- through ninth-grade youth may do so for very different reasons, depending on the age or developmental level (e.g., cognitive age, social perspective taking level) of the target population. Although some longitudinal efforts have been undertaken that target specific variables within controlled research designs (e.g., Gibbons & Ebbeck, 1997), many more such efforts will be required to increase the knowledge base.

Researchers also must address the breadth of what constitutes influence by significant others. If significant others can effect change, what is the mechanism of change? Observational learning appears to be one means by which significant others influence athletes (Mugno & Feltz, 1985; Smith, 1974, 1978), but there are likely others such as persuasion and social interaction. Recent interest in social contextual factors moves us toward better understanding of social influence, in that the social context often is defined in terms that re-

flect attitudes, values, and behaviors of significant others. For example, motivational climate is largely a function of the attitudes and values of significant others in that setting, combined with what they model and reward. By understanding how significant others shape the motivational climate, researchers will come closer to understanding the mechanisms of social influence.

Part of this mission should include attempts to understand group norms, a central component of the moral atmosphere operating in a sport context (Shields et al., 1995). Group norms form over time and, therefore, have to be understood developmentally. In adopting a developmental approach, researchers should emphasize not only what strengthens or contributes to the formation of group norms but also what diminishes or alters them. Also, researchers pursuing this work must keep in mind that linear predictions may not be viable. For example, high team cohesion could lead to a strong norm for cheating and aggression or, alternatively, to respect for the rules and opponents. Furthermore, one might hypothesize that high team cohesion sets the stage for radical shifts or changes in norms, particularly if any of the high-status members of that team voice alternative views. Thus, although group cohesiveness might foster strong, enduring group norms regarding moral behavior, it might also serve as an agent of moral atmosphere change.

Although structural features of the sport environment and a multitude of social agents can affect group norms, we believe that focusing on peer relationships is particularly critical to understanding group norms and their formation. Research examining athlete perceptions of teammates (e.g, Mugno & Feltz, 1985; Smith, 1979; Stuart & Ebbeck, 1995) illustrates the relevance of peers to moral development. Furthermore, our own work on youth sport friendships (Weiss & Smith, 1999; Weiss, Smith, & Theeboom, 1996) has highlighted the relevance of prosocial behavior, conflict, and conflict resolution to youth sport participants, suggesting that relationships among peers can provide a context for moral development. Bukowski and Sippola (1996), in a thoughtful treatment of the philosophical and empirical linkage of morality and friendship, stated that friendships allow children "opportunities to learn about others' needs and feelings and to experience the desire or motivation to be responsive to these needs. Such experiences are likely to form the basis of children's acquisition of concepts such as justice and courage or care" (p. 258). They suggested that studying different types of relationships (e.g., friends vs. acquaintances), how individuals negotiate impartiality (e.g., conflicts between friends and nonfriends), and affective aspects of friendship would reveal how moral development and friendship interconnect.

Research on peer relationships is relatively scant and therefore has not extended well beyond assessing athlete perceptions of their friendships or social acceptance. Rubin, Bukowski, and Parker (1998) indicated that a comprehensive understanding of peer relationships requires examining not only individual perceptions but also peer interactions, the historical context of such interactions (i.e., the relationship), and group processes. Thus, when attempting to understand group norms and their association with peer relationships, an array of research approaches will be necessary, including qualitative methodologies, longitudinal designs, behavioral observation, and social network assessment, as well as the traditional approaches used to date.

Also critical to understanding social influence on moral development in sport is the adoption of an interactionist approach to moral development research. Individual and contextual variables are central to Rest's (1984, 1986, 1994) and Shields and Bredemeier's (1995) models of moral action and should be examined simultaneously. Rather than simultaneously examining individual and social contextual variables in an attempt to understand their respective contributions, researchers have examined individual variables (e.g., legitimacy judgments) across multiple scenarios/dilemmas, which provides only an indirect understanding of how social context might affect moral development. Targeting specific individual and contextual variables simultaneously will substantially advance the knowledge base on moral development in sport, allowing for the development of more parsimonious and effective intervention protocols.

The emerging intervention literature is impressive, showing that we currently have viable programs to promote character. No doubt intervention approaches will benefit from attention to theoretically-based, progressive research on individual and contextual factors related to moral development. However, the intervention literature itself could be enhanced to provide better understanding of pros and cons of the programs developed to date. As noted earlier, some of the intervention programs have not been assessed rigorously from a scientific perspective. Therefore, we strongly encourage researchers to empirically validate existing intervention approaches (see Hastie & Buchanan, 2000, for a recent example). Next, we suggest that intervention studies include longer-term retention assessments to determine if character truly has been developed or is only a temporary change resulting from the intervention program. An example of intervention research that used a retention design is Marsh, Richards, and Barnes' (1986) study, which included an 18-month follow-up assessment of self-conceptions in participants of a 26-day Outward Bound program. Finally, it is important to determine whether intervention programs yield effects that generalize to other contexts. If sport represents a "bracketed" context with regard to moral functioning, then intervention programs exclusive to the sport setting may be bracketed themselves. Research that captures what elements of an intervention program are more or less generalized to other contexts would allow sport psychologists to develop more meaningful interventions and to establish the efficacy of such programs to administrators and policymakers.

In summary, we believe that the moral development literature will continue to move forward with attention to measurement, significant others' influence, collective norms, and the degree to which intervention approaches truly foster development and are generalizable. Adopting a wide range of methodologies and research designs will be critical to this mission, as will mindfulness of multiple levels of social analysis, cognitive–developmental levels of youth research participants, and the simultaneous consideration of individual and contextual variables.

CONCLUSION

In this chapter we tried to communicate knowledge about moral development theory, research, and application in a user-friendly way. In so doing we hope to encourage more readers not only to become interested in the science of moral psychology but also to accept the challenge of exploring untested relationships among moral thoughts and behaviors in the physical domain. Shields and Bredemeier's (1995) model of moral action in sport provides a custom framework for understanding the personal and social factors that may affect the processes of moral sensitivity, judgment, choice, and behavior. The possibilities are wide open for contributing to the validity of the model by studying the interplay of salient variables within a variety of physical activity contexts (e.g., youth sport, school recess). Such work would allow practitioners to develop new and refine existing intervention programs that are designed to enhance character. Intervention research and programs proliferated in the 1990s, but continued intervention work is necessary to quantify change in moral judgment and behavior, determine the short- and long-term effectiveness of programs, and examine whether moral development changes that occur in physical activity contexts generalize to life skills. We look forward to seeing the progress in this content area over the coming years, because there is potential for tremendous theoretical, empirical, and practical advancements.

REFERENCES

Arnold, P.J. (1994). Sport and moral education. *Journal of Moral Education, 23,* 75–89.

Bandura, A. (1986). *Social foundations of thought and action: A social cognitive theory.* Englewood Cliffs, NJ: Prentice Hall.

Bandura, A. (1991). Social-cognitive theory of moral thought and action. In W.M. Kurtines & J.L. Gewirtz, (Eds.), *Handbook of moral behavior and development, Vol. 1: Theory* (pp. 45–103). Hillsdale, NJ: Erlbaum.

Bandura, A., Ross, D., & Ross, S.A. (1961). Transmission of aggression through imitation of aggressive models. *Journal of Abnormal and Social Psychology, 63,* 575–582.

Beller, J.M., & Stoll, S.K. (1995). Moral reasoning of high school student athletes and general students: An empirical study versus personal testimony. *Pediatric Exercise Science, 7,* 352–363.

Berryman, J.W. (1996). The rise of boys' sports in the United States, 1900 to 1970. In F.L. Smoll & R.E. Smith (Eds.), *Children and youth in sport: A biopsychosocial perspective* (pp. 4–14). Madison, WI: Brown & Benchmark.

Blair, S. (1985). The professionalization of attitude toward play in children and adults. *Research Quarterly for Exercise and Sport, 56,* 82–83.

Bovyer, G. (1963). Children's concepts of sportsmanship in the fourth, fifth, and sixth grades. *Research Quarterly, 34,* 282–287.

Bredemeier, B.J. (1985). Moral reasoning and the perceived legitimacy of intentionally injurious sport acts. *Journal of Sport Psychology, 7,* 110–124.

Bredemeier, B.J.L. (1994). Children's moral reasoning and their assertive, aggressive, and submissive tendencies in sport and daily life. *Journal of Sport & Exercise Psychology, 16,* 1–14.

Bredemeier, B.J.L. (1995). Divergence in children's moral reasoning about issues in daily life and sport specific contexts. *International Journal of Sport Psychology, 26,* 453–463.

Bredemeier, B.J., & Shields, D.L. (1984a). Divergence in moral reasoning about sport and everyday life. *Sociology of Sport Journal, 1,* 348–357.

Bredemeier, B.J., & Shields, D.L. (1984b). The utility of moral stage analysis in the investigation of athletic aggression. *Sociology of Sport Journal, 1,* 138–149.

Bredemeier, B.J., & Shields, D.L. (1985). Values and violence in sports today. *Psychology Today, 19*(10), 22–32.

Bredemeier, B.J., & Shields, D.L. (1986a). Moral growth among athletes and nonathletes: A comparative analysis. *Journal of Genetic Psychology, 147,* 7–18.

Bredemeier, B.J., & Shields, D.L. (1986b). Game reasoning and interactional morality. *Journal of Genetic Psychology, 147,* 257–275.

Bredemeier, B.J., & Shields, D.L. (1986c). Athletic aggression: An issue of contextual morality. *Sociology of Sport Journal, 3,* 15–28.

Bredemeier, B.J., & Shields, D.L. (1987). Moral growth through physical activity: A structural/developmental approach. In D. Gould & M.R. Weiss (Eds.), *Advances in pediatric sport sciences, Vol. 2: Behavioral issues* (pp. 143–165). Champaign, IL: Human Kinetics.

Bredemeier, B.J.L., & Shields, D.L.L. (1993). Moral psychology in the context of sport. In R.N. Singer, M. Murphey, & L.K. Tennant (Eds.), *Handbook of research on sport psychology* (pp. 587–599). New York: Macmillan.

Bredemeier, B.J.L., & Shields, D.L.L. (1998). Moral assessment in sport psychology. In J.L. Duda (Ed.), *Advances in sport and exercise psychology measurement* (pp. 257–276). Morgantown, WV: Fitness Information Technology.

Bredemeier, B.J., Weiss, M.R., Shields, D.L., & Cooper, B.A.B. (1986). The relationship of sport involvement with children's moral reasoning and aggression tendencies. *Journal of Sport Psychology, 8,* 304–318.

Bredemeier, B.J., Weiss, M.R., Shields, D.L., & Cooper, B.A.B. (1987). The relationship between children's legitimacy judgments and their moral reasoning, aggression tendencies, and sport involvement. *Sociology of Sport Journal, 4,* 48–60.

Bredemeier, B.J., Weiss, M.R., Shields, D.L., & Shewchuk, R.M. (1986). Promoting moral growth in a summer sport camp: The implementation of theoretically grounded instructional strategies. *Journal of Moral Education, 15,* 212–220.

Brown, L.M., & Gilligan, C. (1992). *Meeting at the crossroads: Women's psychology and girls' development.* Cambridge, MA: Harvard University Press.

Bukowski, W.M., & Sippola, L.K. (1996). Friendship and morality: (How) are they related? In W.M. Bukowski, A.F. Newcomb, & W.W. Hartup (Eds.), *The company they keep: Friendship in childhood and adolescence* (pp. 238–261). New York: Cambridge University Press.

Burton, R.V., & Kunce, L. (1995). Behavioral models of moral development: A brief history and integration. In W.M. Kurtines & J.L. Gewirtz (Eds.), *Moral development: An introduction* (pp. 141–171). Boston: Allyn & Bacon.

Coakley, J.J. (1998). *Sport in society: Issues and controversies.* Boston: WCB McGraw-Hill.

Commission for Fair Play (1990). *Fair Play for Kids.* Ontario, Canada: Commission for Fair Play.

Cutforth, N.J. (1997). What's worth doing? Reflections on an after-school program in a Denver elementary school. *Quest, 49,* 130–139.

Damon, W. (1977). *The social world of the child.* San Francisco: Jossey-Bass.

Damon, W. (1983). The nature of social-cognitive change in the developing child. In W.F. Overton (Ed.), *The relationship between social and cognitive development* (pp. 103–141). Hillsdale, NJ: Erlbaum.

Damon, W. (1988). *The moral child.* New York: Free Press.

Damon, W. (1995). *Greater expectations: Overcoming the culture of indulgence in America's homes and schools.* New York: Free Press.

Damon, W. (1997). *The youth charter: How communities can work together to raise standards for all our children.* New York: Free Press.

Danish, S.J. (1997). Going for the goal: A life skills program for adolescents. In G. Albee & T. Gullotta (Eds.), *Primary preventions work, Vol. 6: Issues in children's and families' lives* (pp. 291–312). Thousand Oaks, CA: Sage.

Danish, S., & Nellen, V.C. (1997). New roles for sport psychologists: Teaching life skills through sport to at-risk youth. *Quest, 49,* 100–113.

Danish, S.J., Nellen, V., & Owens, S. (1996). Community-based programs for adolescents: Using sport to teach life skills. In J.L. Van Raalte & B.W. Brewer (Eds.), *Exploring sport and exercise psychology* (pp. 205–228). Washington, DC: American Psychological Association.

Danish, S.J., Petitpas, A., & Hale, B.D. (1990). Sport as a context for developing competence. In T.P. Gullotta, G.R. Adams, & R. Montemayor (Eds.), *Developing social competency in adolescence* (pp. 169–194). Newbury Park, CA: Sage.

Danish, S.J., Petitpas, A.J., & Hale, B.D. (1992). A developmental-educational intervention model of sport psychology. *The Sport Psychologist, 6,* 403–415.

Danish, S.J., Petitpas, A., & Hale, B.D. (1995). Psychological interventions: A life development model. In S.M. Murphy (Ed.), *Sport psychology interventions* (pp. 19–38). Champaign, IL: Human Kinetics.

DeBusk, M., & Hellison, D. (1989). Implementing a physical education self-responsibility model for delinquency-prone youth. *Journal of Teaching in Physical Education, 8,* 104–112.

Dubois, P.E. (1986). The effect of participation in sport on the value orientations of young athletes. *Sociology of Sport Journal, 3,* 29–42.

Duda, J.L., Olson, L.K., & Templin, T.J. (1991). The relationship of task and ego orientation to sportsmanship attitudes and the perceived legitimacy of injurious acts. *Research Quarterly for Exercise and Sport, 62,* 79–87.

Dunn, J.G.H., & Causgrove Dunn, J. (1999). Goal orientations, perceptions of aggression, and sportspersonship in elite male youth ice hockey players. *The Sport Psychologist, 13,* 183–200.

Duquin, M.E., & Schroeder-Braun, K. (1996). Power, empathy, and moral conflict in sport. *Peace and Conflict: Journal of Peace Psychology, 2,* 351–367.

Eisenberg, N. (1995). Prosocial development: A multifaceted model. In W.M. Kurtines & J.L. Gewirtz (Eds.), *Moral development: An introduction* (pp. 401–429). Boston: Allyn & Bacon.

Eisenberg, N., & Fabes, R.A. (1998). Prosocial development. In N. Eisenberg (Ed.), *Handbook of child psychology, Vol. 3: Social, emotional, and personality development* (pp. 701–778). New York: Wiley.

Ennis, C.D. (1999). Creating a culturally relevant curriculum for disengaged girls. *Sport, Education and Society, 4,* 31–49.

Ennis, C.D., Cothran, D.J., Davidson, K.S., Loftus, S.J., Owens, L., Swanson, L., & Hopsicker, P. (1997). Implementing curriculum within a context of fear and disengagement. *Journal of Teaching in Physical Education, 17,* 58–72.

Ennis, C.D., Solmon, M.A., Satina, B., Loftus, S.J., Mensch, J., & McCauley, M.T. (1999). Creating a sense of family in urban schools using the "Sport for Peace" curriculum. *Research Quarterly for Exercise and Sport, 70,* 273–285.

Entzion, B.J. (1991). A child's view of fairplay. *Strategies, 4,* 16–19.

ESPN (1997). Sportsmanship in the '90's: Is winning the only thing? Originally aired on *Outside the Lines,* November 4.

Fisher, L.A., & Bredemeier, B.J.L. (2000). Caring about injustice: The moral self-perceptions of professional female bodybuilders. *Journal of Sport & Exercise Psychology, 22,* 327–344.

Georgiadis, N. (1990). Does basketball have to be all W's and L's? An alternative program at a residential boys' home. *Journal of Physical Education, Recreation and Dance, 61,* 42–43.

Gibbons, S.L., & Ebbeck, V. (1997). The effect of different teaching strategies on the moral development of physical education students. *Journal of Teaching in Physical Education, 17,* 85–98.

Gibbons, S.L., Ebbeck, V., & Weiss, M.R. (1995). Fair Play for Kids: Effects on the moral development of children in physical education. *Research Quarterly for Exercise and Sport, 66,* 247–255.

Giebink, M.P., & McKenzie, T.C. (1985). Teaching sportsmanship in physical education and recreation: An analysis of intervention and generalization effects. *Journal of Teaching in Physical Education, 4,* 167–177.

Gilligan, C. (1977). In a different voice: Women's conceptions of self and of morality. *Harvard Educational Review, 17,* 481–517.

Gilligan, C. (1982). *In a different voice: Psychological theory and women's development.* Cambridge, MA: Harvard University Press.

Gilligan, C. (1998). Remembering Larry. *Journal of Moral Education, 27,* 125–140.

Gilligan, C., Ward, J., & Taylor, J. (1988). *Mapping the moral domain: A contribution of women's thinking to psychological theory and education.* Cambridge, MA: Harvard University Press.

Greer, D.L., & Stewart, M.J. (1989). Children's attitudes toward play: An investigation of their context specificity and relationship to organized sport experiences. *Journal of Sport & Exercise Psychology, 11,* 336–342.

Haan, N. (1977). *Coping and defending: Processes of self-environment organization.* New York: Academic Press.

Haan, N. (1991). Moral development and action from a social constructivist perspective. In W.M. Kurtines & J.L. Gewirtz, (Eds.), *Handbook of moral behavior and development, Vol. 1: Theory* (pp. 251–273). Hillsdale, NJ: Erlbaum.

Haan, N., Aerts, E., & Cooper, B. (1985). *On moral grounds: The search for practical morality.* New York: New York University Press.

Hall, E. (1986). Moral development levels of athletes in sport-specific and general social situations. In L. Vander Velden & J.H. Humphrey (Eds.), *Psychology and sociology of sport: Current selected research* (pp. 191–204). New York: AMS Press.

Harter, S. (1999). *The construction of the self: A developmental perspective.* New York: Guilford Press.

Hastie, P.A., & Buchanan, A.M. (2000). Teaching responsibility through sport education: Prospects of a coalition. *Research Quarterly for Exercise and Sport, 71,* 25–35.

Hastie, P.A., & Sharpe, T. (1999). Effects of a sport education curriculum on the positive social behavior of at-risk rural adolescent boys. *Journal of Education for Students Placed at Risk, 4,* 417–430.

Hellison, D. (1978). *Beyond balls and bats: Alienated (and other) youth in the gym.* Washington, DC: American Alliance for Health, Physical Education and Recreation.

Hellison, D.R. (1985). *Goals and strategies for teaching physical education.* Champaign, IL: Human Kinetics.

Hellison, D. (1986). Cause of death: Physical education. *Journal of Physical Education, Recreation and Dance, 57,* 27–28.

Hellison, D.R. (1988). Cause of death: Physical education— a sequel. *Journal of Physical Education, Recreation and Dance, 59,* 18–21.

Hellison, D.R. (1995). *Teaching personal and social responsibility through physical activity.* Champaign, IL: Human Kinetics.

Hellison, D., & Georgiadis, N. (1992). Teaching values through basketball. *Strategies, 5,* 5–8.

Hellison, D.R., Martinek, T.J., & Cutforth, N.J. (1996). Beyond violence prevention in inner city physical activity programs. *Peace and Conflict: Journal of Peace Psychology, 2,* 321–337.

Horrocks, R.N. (1979). *The relationship of selected prosocial play behaviors in children to moral reasoning, youth sports participation, and perception of sportsmanship.* Unpublished doctoral dissertation, University of North Carolina at Greensboro.

Jantz, R.K. (1975). Moral thinking in male elementary pupils as reflected by perception of basketball rules. *Research Quarterly, 46,* 414–421.

Jarvinen, D.W., & Nicholls, J.G. (1996). Adolescents' social goals, beliefs about the causes of social success, and satisfaction in peer relations. *Developmental Psychology, 32,* 435–441.

Kane, M.J. (1982). The influence of level of sport participation and sex-role orientation on female professionalization of attitudes toward play. *Journal of Sport Psychology, 4,* 290–294.

Kavussanu, M., & Roberts, G.C. (2001). Moral functioning in sport: An achievement goal perspective. *Journal of Sport & Exercise Psychology, 23,* 37–54.

Kleiber, D.A., & Roberts, G.C. (1981). The effects of sport experience in the development of social character: An exploratory investigation. *Journal of Sport Psychology, 3,* 114–122.

Knoppers, A. (1985). Professionalization of attitudes: A review and critique. *Quest, 37,* 92–102.

Knoppers, A., Schuiteman, J., & Love, B. (1986). Winning is not the only thing. *Sociology of Sport Journal, 3,* 43–56.

Knoppers, A., Zuidema, M., & Meyer, B.B. (1989). Playing to win or playing to play? *Sociology of Sport Journal, 6,* 70–76.

Kohlberg, L. (1969). Stage and sequence: The cognitive-developmental approach to socialization. In D.A. Goslin (Ed.), *Handbook of socialization theory and research* (pp. 347–480). Chicago: Rand McNally.

Kohlberg, L. (1976). Moral stages and moralization: The cognitive-developmental approach. In T. Lickona (Ed.), *Moral development and behavior: Theory, research, and social issues* (pp. 31–53). New York: Holt, Rinehart & Winston.

Kurtines, W.M., & Gewirtz, J.L. (1991a). *Handbook of moral behavior and development, Vol. 1: Theory.* Hillsdale, NJ: Erlbaum.

Kurtines, W.M., & Gewirtz, J.L. (1991b). *Handbook of moral behavior and development, Vol. 3: Application.* Boston: Allyn & Bacon.

Kurtines, W.M., & Gewirtz, J.L. (1995). *Moral development: An introduction.* Hillsdale, NJ: Erlbaum.

Lickona, T. (1976). Critical issues in the study of moral development and behavior. In T. Lickona (Ed.), *Moral development and behavior: Theory, research, and social issues* (pp. 3–27). New York: Holt, Rinehart & Winston.

Marsh, H.W., Richards, G.E., & Barnes, J. (1986). Multidimensional self-concepts: A long-term follow-up of the effect of participation in an Outward Bound program. *Personality and Social Psychology Bulletin, 12,* 475–492.

Martens, R. (1978). *Joy and sadness in children's sports.* Champaign, IL: Human Kinetics.

Martinek, T.J., & Hellison, D.R. (1997). Fostering resiliency in underserved youth through physical activity. *Quest, 49,* 34–49.

McCloy, C.H. (1930). Character building through physical education. *Research Quarterly, 1,* 41–61.

McCloy, C.H., & Hepp, F. (1957). General factors or components of character as related to physical education. *Research Quarterly, 28,* 269–278.

McCloy, C.H., & Young, N.D. (1954). *Tests and measurements in health and physical education* (3rd ed.). New York: Appleton-Century-Crofts.

Miller, S.C., Bredemeier, B.J.L., & Shields, D.L.L. (1997). Sociomoral education through physical education with at-risk children. *Quest, 49,* 114–129.

Mugno, D.A., & Feltz, D.L. (1985). The social learning of aggression in youth football in the United States. *Canadian Journal of Applied Sport Sciences, 10,* 26–35.

Murphy, H.A., Hutchison, J.M., & Bailey, J.S. (1983). Behavioral school psychology goes outdoors: The effect of organized games on playground aggression. *Journal of Applied Behavior Analysis, 16,* 29–35.

Narváez, D., & Rest, J.R. (1995). The four components of acting morally. In W.M. Kurtines & J.L. Gewirtz (Eds.), *Moral development: An introduction* (pp. 385–399). Boston: Allyn & Bacon.

Nicholls, J.G. (1989). *The competitive ethos and democratic education.* Cambridge, MA: Harvard University Press.

Orlick, T.D. (1981). Positive socialization via cooperative games. *Developmental Psychology, 17,* 426–429.

Piaget, J. (1965). *The moral judgement of the child.* New York: Free Press.

Priest, R.F., Krause, J.V., & Beach, J. (1999). Four-year changes in college athletes' ethical value choices in sports situations. *Research Quarterly for Exercise and Sport, 70,* 170–178.

Rainey, D.W., Santilli, N.R., & Fallon, K. (1992). Development of athletes' conceptions of sport officials' authority. *Journal of Sport & Exercise Psychology, 14,* 392–404.

Rest, J.R. (1984). The major components of morality. In W. Kurtines & J. Gewirtz (Eds.), *Morality, moral behavior, and moral development* (pp. 24–40). New York: Wiley.

Rest, J.R. (1986). *Moral development: Advances in research and theory.* New York: Praeger Press.

Rest, J.R. (1994). Background: Theory and research. In J.R. Rest & D. Narvaez (Eds.), *Moral development in the professions: Psychology and applied ethics* (pp. 1–26). Hillsdale, NJ: Erlbaum.

Romance, T.J. (1984). *A program to promote moral development through elementary school physical education.* Unpublished doctoral dissertation, University of Oregon, Eugene.

Romance, T.J., Weiss, M.R., & Bockoven, J. (1986). A program to promote moral development through elementary school physical education. *Journal of Teaching in Physical Education, 5,* 126–136.

Rubin, K.H., Bukowski, W., & Parker, J.G. (1998). Peer interactions, relationships, and groups. In N. Eisenberg (Ed.), *Handbook of child psychology, Vol. 3: Social, emotional, and personality development* (pp. 619–700). New York: Wiley.

Ryan, M.K., Williams, J.M., & Wimer, B. (1990). Athletic aggression: Perceived legitimacy and behavioral intentions in girls' high school basketball. *Journal of Sport & Exercise Psychology, 12,* 48–55.

Sage, G.H. (1980). Orientations toward sport of male and female intercollegiate athletes. *Journal of Sport Psychology, 2,* 355–362.

Selman, R.L. (1971). The relation of role-taking to the development of moral judgment in children. *Child Development, 42,* 79–92.

Selman, R. (1976). Social-cognitive understanding: A guide to educational and clinical practice. In T. Lickona (Ed.), *Moral development and behavior: Theory, research, and social issues* (pp. 299–316). New York: Holt, Rinehart & Winston.

Sharpe, T., Brown, M., & Crider, K. (1995). The effects of sportsmanship curriculum intervention on generalized positive social behavior of urban elementary school students. *Journal of Applied Behavior Analysis, 28,* 401–416.

Sharpe, T., Crider, K., Vyhlidal, T., & Brown, M. (1996). Description and effects of prosocial instruction in an elementary physical education setting. *Education and Treatment of Children, 19,* 435–457.

Shields, D.L., & Bredemeier, B.J. (1989). Moral reasoning, judgment, and action in sport. In J. Goldstein (Ed.),

Sports, games, and play: Social and psychological viewpoints (pp. 59–81). Hillsdale, NJ: Erlbaum.

Shields, D.L.L., & Bredemeier, B.J.L. (1995). *Character development and physical activity.* Champaign, IL: Human Kinetics.

Shields, D.L.L., Bredemeier, B.J.L., Gardner, D.E., & Bostrom, A. (1995). Leadership, cohesion, and team norms regarding cheating and aggression. *Sociology of Sport Journal, 12,* 324–336.

Silva, J.M. (1983). The perceived legitimacy of rule violating behavior in sport. *Journal of Sport Psychology, 5,* 438–448.

Smith, M.D. (1974). Significant others' influence on the assaultive behavior of young hockey players. *International Review of Sport Sociology, 3–4,* 45–56.

Smith, M.D. (1975). The legitimation of violence: Hockey players' perceptions of their reference groups' sanctions for assault. *Canadian Review of Sociology and Anthropology, 12,* 72–80.

Smith, M.D. (1978). Social learning of violence in minor hockey. In F.L. Smoll & R.E. Smith (Eds.), *Psychological perspectives in youth sports* (pp. 91–106). Washington, DC: Hemisphere.

Smith, M.D. (1979). Towards an explanation of hockey violence: A reference other approach. *Canadian Journal of Sociology, 4,* 105–124.

Smith, M.D. (1988). Interpersonal sources of violence in hockey: The influence of parents, coaches, and teammates. In F.L. Smoll, R.A. Magill, & M.J. Ash (Eds.), *Children in sport* (pp. 301–313). Champaign, IL: Human Kinetics.

Solomon, G.B. (1997). Fair play in the gymnasium: Improving social skills among elementary school students. *Journal of Physical Education and Recreation, 68,* 22–25.

Solomon, G.B., & Bredemeier, B.J.L. (1999). Children's moral conceptions of gender stratification in sport. *International Journal of Sport Psychology, 30,* 350–368.

Stephens, D.E. (2000). Predictors of likelihood to aggress in youth soccer: An examination of coed and all-girls teams. *Journal of Sport Behavior, 23,* 311–325.

Stephens, D.E., & Bredemeier, B.J.L. (1996). Moral atmosphere and judgments about aggression in girls' soccer: Relationships among moral and motivational variables. *Journal of Sport & Exercise Psychology, 18,* 158–173.

Stephens, D.E., Bredemeier, B.J.L., & Shields, D.L.L. (1997). Construction of a measure designed to assess players' descriptions and prescriptions for moral behavior in youth sport soccer. *International Journal of Sport Psychology, 28,* 370–390.

Stuart, M.E., & Ebbeck, V. (1995). The influence of perceived social approval on moral development in youth sport. *Pediatric Exercise Science, 7,* 270–280.

Turiel, E. (1998). The development of morality. In N. Eisenberg (Ed.), *Handbook of child psychology, Vol. 3: Social, emotional, and personality development* (pp. 863–932). New York: Wiley.

Urdan, T.C., & Maehr, M.L. (1995). Beyond a two-goal theory of motivation and achievement: A case for social goals. *Review of Educational Research, 65,* 213–243.

Wandzilak, T., Carroll, T., & Ansorge, C.J. (1988). Values development through physical activity: Promoting sportsmanlike behaviors, perceptions, and moral reasoning. *Journal of Teaching in Physical Education, 8,* 13–23.

Webb, H. (1969). Professionalization of attitudes toward play among adolescents. In G. Kenyon (Ed.), *Aspects of contemporary sport sociology* (pp. 161–178). Chicago: The Athletic Institute.

Weiss, M.R., & Bredemeier, B.J. (1986). Moral development. In V. Seefeldt (Ed.), *Physical activity and well-being* (pp. 373–390). Reston, VA: American Alliance for Health, Physical Education, Recreation and Dance.

Weiss, M.R., & Bredemeier, B.J. (1990). Moral development in sport. *Exercise and Sport Sciences Reviews,* 18, 331–378.

Weiss, M.R., & Smith, A.L. (1999). Quality of friendships in youth sport: Measurement development and validation. *Journal of Sport & Exercise Psychology, 21,* 145–166.

Weiss, M.R., Smith, A.L., & Theeboom, M. (1996). "That's what friends are for": Children's and teenagers' perceptions of peer relationships in the sport domain. *Journal of Sport & Exercise Psychology, 18,* 347–379.

Wentzel, K. (1993). Motivation and achievement in early adolescence: The role of multiple classroom goals. *Journal of Early Adolescence, 13,* 4–20.

Wentzel, K. (1998). Social relationships and motivation in middle school: The role of parents, teachers, and peers. *Journal of Educational Psychology, 90,* 202–209.

White, S.H., & O'Brien, J.E. (1999). What is a hero? An exploratory study of students' conceptions of heroes. *Journal of Moral Education, 28,* 81–95.

Wiggins, D.K. (1996). A history of highly competitive sport for American children. In F.L. Smoll & R.E. Smith (Eds.), *Children and youth in sport: A biopsychosocial perspective* (pp. 15–30). Madison, WI: Brown & Benchmark.

PART III

Socioenvironmental Issues, Sociocultural Issues, and Sport Behavior

The six chapters presented in part II identified and discussed the relationship between selected individual difference factors and sport behavior. The collective research and theory reviewed there have shown very clearly that selected characteristics of individual participants can be used to explain and predict how they will behave in sport and physical activity contexts. However, as Fox argues in chapter 4, individual difference factors cannot be understood completely without an accompanying analysis of the cultures to which the individual subscribes, the value systems inherent within those cultures, and the degree to which the individual subscribes to or endorses those cultural values. Thus, sport behavior will be more accurately and completely interpreted if socioenvironmental and sociocultural influences are also taken into account.

The four chapters in part III present a socioenvironmental perspective on individuals' behavior in sport contexts. However, the four chapters differ somewhat in orientation, focus, and format. Chapters 9 and 10 are written from a social psychological perspective in that they focus primarily on factors in the immediate social environment (peer group, coaches' behavior) that may affect athletes' and other physical activity participants' psychological responses and behaviors. Chapters 11 and 12 are written from a sociocultural or sociopolitical perspective in that they focus on the broader social, economic, political, and cultural forces that affect people's behavior in sport and physical activity contexts.

Part III begins with chapter 9, in which W. Neil Widmeyer, Lawrence Brawley, and Albert Carron review current research and theory on group dynamics and identify directions for future research. They begin their chapter with an overview of the major theoretical approaches to the study of sport and exercise groups. They then review the empirical research on three of the most extensively researched aspects or characteristics of groups: size, composition, and cohesion. Finally, they identify a number of problems associated with the study of group dynamics and conclude by outlining two approaches for future research in sport group dynamics.

I wrote chapter 10 to focus on a more specific aspect of the sport group environment—the behavior of the coach. This chapter begins with a discussion of the various conceptual approaches that have been used to design and conduct research oriented toward identifying particular coaching characteristics, leadership styles, and behavioral patterns that will facilitate (or hinder) athletes' performance and psychosocial growth. I describe a composite working model of coaching effectiveness and then use this model as a framework to review the current state of knowledge on coaching effectiveness, to identify gaps in our knowledge base, and to provide recommendations for future researchers interested in identifying how and why coaches behave as they do in practice and competition and how such leader behavior can affect athletes' performance and psychosocial growth.

In the first edition of this text, Diane Gill's chapter on gender issues appeared in part II, "Individual Differences and Sport Behavior." For this second edition, Gill's chapter (chapter 11) has been moved to part III. This change reflects the more contemporary notion that gender should no longer be conceptualized as an individual difference factor (i.e., do males and females differ in motivational orientation, trait anxiety, or competitiveness?) but rather that gender should be approached as a culturally based phenomenon. Gill reflects this perspective by providing a sociohistorical perspective on gender research in sport psychology as well as in physical education and general psychology. Within this context, Gill reviews the existing research and theory that address gender and sport. She concludes by identifying promising directions for researchers interested in gender issues within the sport context. This includes the need to consider gender within the wider context of social diversity. That is, we should no longer consider gender as a single categorical entity but rather should examine the intersections among gender, race, class, and sexual orientation. Gill also outlines how our scholarly understanding of gender within a

cultural and social context can and should be reflected not only in our research but also in our practice with individual athletes.

In chapter 12, Susan Greendorfer examines the broad issue of sport socialization. In contrast to the topical approach used in other chapters in this volume, Greendorfer takes a more inclusive perspective by introducing the socialization process as a general framework that can be used to understand many aspects of sport behavior that are currently of interest to sport psychologists (e.g., achievement motivation, attrition in sport, coaching effectiveness). Greendorfer begins her chapter with a theoretical and conceptual discussion of the socialization process and compares and contrasts the various approaches that researchers across several disciplines have used in studying this area. She then provides an interesting perspective on the nature and manner in which socialization is accomplished. This section includes a critical review of the existing research on socialization into and through sport participation, with particular emphasis on research conducted by sport psychologists. Greendorfer concludes by providing suggestions as to how sport psychologists can use an understanding of the socialization process to examine individuals' sport behavior from a more integrated and holistic perspective.

As I noted in the preface of this text, chapters 11 and 12 in part III discuss issues that are not typically or traditionally perceived to be part of the research literature in sport psychology. The decision to include these chapters is based on the rationale that people's behavior in sport and physical activity situations cannot be completely understood without considering the context within which this behavior occurs. As Brustad states in chapter 2 of this text, "Any account of kinesiology must be rooted in an understanding that human movement activities are cultural practices embedded in the social, economic, political, and cultural contexts in which they are situated." Although sport psychology researchers may choose to focus primarily on the psychological factors affecting sport performance and behavior, we still need to understand, or consider, the role that the social, political, cultural, and economic context may play. Thus, if we truly wish to advance our knowledge base in sport psychology, we must read about, reflect on, and incorporate into our worldview the issues discussed by Greendorfer and Gill in their respective chapters on socialization processes and gender issues. Certainly, these two chapters do not reflect the full range of sociocultural and sociopolitical issues that are important to our study of human behavior in sport contexts, but they do highlight the various contextual factors that we need to consider as we design our research studies and as we interpret our results.

CHAPTER 9

Group Dynamics in Sport

W. Neil Widmeyer, Lawrence R. Brawley, and Albert V. Carron

Since the beginning of social psychology, group dynamics has been recognized as a major branch of the discipline. The term *group dynamics* has been used in two major ways. First, it has been used to depict the vitality and changing nature of groups. Second, it has been seen as the field of study that focuses on the behavior of groups. Although Kurt Lewin (1943) is given credit for coining and popularizing the term, Dorwin Cartwright and Alvin Zander (1968) are two of the most prolific researchers in this area (see Forsyth, 1983). In their classic text, *Group Dynamics,* they stated that this field of inquiry is "dedicated to advancing knowledge about the nature of groups, the laws of their development, and their interrelationships with individuals, other groups, and larger institutions" (Cartwright & Zander, 1968, p. 7). Group dynamics is not normally recognized as a discipline unto itself but, instead, as an area of study within social psychology and sociology. In this chapter, we accept that groups are not static and that group dynamics refers to the scientific study of these changing entities.

The importance of group dynamics stems primarily from the importance of groups. Groups are important because of the large number of groups that each individual encounters and because of the impact that such groups can have on one's life. In addition to a family, most individuals simultaneously belong to a variety of recreational, social, and work groups, all of which can influence and be influenced by the person's thoughts, feelings, and actions. Thus, it is not surprising that group dynamics has been a major interest area

for social psychologists. Because groups can be seen as microcosms of larger societies, they represent a convenient place for sociologists to study broader social systems. In addition, Forsyth (1983) identified anthropology, political science, education, business/industry, speech/communication, social work, criminal justice, and sports/recreation as the other fields that recognize the importance of understanding group dynamics. One consequence of the broad interest in groups (as well as their inherent complexity) has been that theoreticians in various disciplines have advanced a wide variety of definitions.

A GROUP DEFINED

In their recent book, *Group Dynamics in Sport,* Carron and Hausenblas (1998) pointed out that the various approaches which have been taken in defining a group can be classified into five broad categories. One general category, which is illustrated by a definition advanced by Fiedler (1967), emphasizes the *common fate* of members. Thus, Fiedler defined a group as "a set of individuals who share a common fate, that is, who are interdependent in the sense that an event which affects one member is likely to affect all" (p. 6).

In a second general category of definitions, the group is perceived as an avenue through which group members experience *mutual benefit*. The definition forwarded by Bass (1960) provides a good example. Specifically, Bass defined a group as a "collection of individuals whose existence

© Human Kinetics

A group can be as simple as a few friends shooting a basketball around.

other person's basketball), social structure (e.g., a teacher–learner relationship), and group processes (e.g., interaction and communication). Thus, theoreticians have suggested that a fifth component or characteristic, *self-categorization*, be added to the definition of a group. A good example of this fifth component is evident in Brown's (1988) definition: "A group exists when two or more people define themselves as members of it and when its existence is recognized by at least one other" (pp. 2–3).

as a collection is rewarding to the individuals" (p. 39).

Third, groups can be differentiated from collections of individuals in terms of the *social structure* they develop. As a consequence, some theoreticians have capitalized on this characteristic to define a group. The definition advanced by the Sherifs (Sherif & Sherif, 1956) is typical: "Group is a social unit which consists of a number of individuals who stand in (more or less) definite status and role relationships to one another and which possess a set of values or norms of its own regulating the behavior of individual members, at least in matters of consequence to the group" (p. 144).

A fourth approach emphasizes important *group processes* that distinguish a group from a collection of individuals. The definition proposed by Shaw (1981) is typical of this category. He proposed that a group is "two or more persons who are interacting with one another in such a manner that each person influences and is influenced by each other person" (p. 8).

Although these general categories of definition are useful, group dynamics theoreticians realized that the presence of a common fate, mutual benefits, a social structure, and group processes also could be characteristics in a collection of individuals. For example, the relationship between two strangers shooting baskets in a gym could be characterized by a common fate (e.g., eviction if they are caught by the custodians), mutual benefit (e.g., retrieve the

The sport team as a group obviously possesses all of these characteristics. Therefore, drawing on the five general categories of definitions, Carron and Hausenblas (1998) defined a sport team as "a collective of two or more individuals who possess a common identity, have consensus on a shared purpose, share a common fate, exhibit structured patterns of interaction and communication, hold common perceptions about group structure, are personally and instrumentally interdependent, reciprocate interpersonal attraction, and consider themselves to be a group" (pp. 13–14). Sport teams offer a particularly important and interesting environment for the study of group dynamics.

GROUP DYNAMICS IN SPORT TEAMS

In North America today, the team sports of baseball, basketball, football, and, more recently, hockey, soccer, and volleyball attract not only millions of competitors but also countless spectators. Next to the family, the sport team may be the most influential group to which an individual belongs. Teams are organized for children of both sexes as young as age 7 and for adults as old as 90. "Old-timers" leagues in sports such as hockey and softball typically begin at age 30, and individuals often participate into their 60s and 70s.

Team sports are especially prevalent in high school, where students participate in interscholastic, intramural, and recreational groups. As well, many businesses not only adopt a team approach for work but also encourage play on company softball teams. Because the team can be a major social group for the individual for 10 to 30 years, it can have a socializing effect of a similar magnitude to that of the church or school. Despite the prevalence of sport teams and the potential impact such groups may have on individuals, most research conducted within sport has focused on individual participants (i.e., their performance, enjoyment, adherence, etc.). Rarely has the team been studied either as an entity unto itself or as a factor that influences individuals, other teams, or larger organizations.

From an academic perspective, because the sport team is a small group, the sociological and social psychological reasons for studying any group apply. As Loy, McPherson, and Kenyon (1978) pointed out, "Sport groups possess unique structural features that offer special advantages with respect to small group research" (p. 68). Schafer (1966) identified four such advantages. First, because the sport group is a natural, rather than a laboratory, group, it can provide information about group development and group relationships with other groups and the broader social environment. Second, sport research can control a number of confounding variables such as group size and rules of conduct by automatically holding them constant. Third, because sport groups typically pursue zero-sum (i.e., win-or-lose) goals, they provide an ideal context for the study of cooperation, competition, and conflict. Finally, sport offers objective measures of group effectiveness (e.g., number of errors made, points scored, and percentage of games won). Thus, the sport team offers an excellent setting for research on group dynamics.

Group dynamics texts in social psychology, organizational psychology, and sociology show that outside the realm of sport, the following topics are covered most frequently:

- Group formation
- Group tasks
- Group development
- Group composition
- Group size
- Group structure
- Group cohesion
- Group motivation
- Group leadership
- Group conformity
- Intergroup relations
- Group decision-making

For the most part, the same topics that have been studied in nonsport settings have also been investigated in sport. However, the emphasis on specific topics is not the same in both areas. In sport, the topics of cohesion and leadership are overrepresented, whereas size, one of the most examined small-group variables, has hardly been investigated in sport. The paucity of research into certain small-group topics in sport does not necessarily mean that these topics are not important or of interest to sport practitioners and researchers. It may simply be that these topics are difficult to examine in sport or that other topics have been seen as more central to the functioning of athletic teams.

In summary, group dynamics, the scientific study of groups, is a worthwhile endeavor because of the prevalence of groups and the effect they have on people. Likewise, the study of the dynamics of sport groups is equally significant, given the important roles that athletic teams play in the lives of many humans. Although numerous relationships between groups, between groups and individuals, and between groups and larger institutions could be examined, group dynamics research to date has focused primarily on interrelationships within groups. The primary purpose of this chapter is to review current research and theory on group dynamics and identify directions for future research. The chapter is organized into six major sections. In the first section, we outline theoretical approaches to the study of groups. In the second, third, and fourth sections, we present findings from three of the most extensively researched topics within sport groups: group size, group composition, and group cohesion. In the fifth section, general problems associated with the study of group dynamics are delineated. Finally, in the sixth section, we make suggestions for avoiding or minimizing these general problems. Although our primary focus is on group dynamics in sport and exercise, relevant information from other contexts is included.

THEORETICAL APPROACHES FROM OTHER DISCIPLINES

The importance of theoretical perspectives has been espoused by scholars in a wide variety of disciplines. In discussing group dynamics,

McGrath (1984) emphasized that theory is as important as data. Specifically, he stated,

> Theory strengthens a data-based science in several ways: (a) as a means for identifying problems worthy of study; (b) as a means for connecting one problem or one piece of evidence with another, even when they have been given different labels; (c) as a means for estimating (hypothesizing/predicting) the pattern of data likely to be found in a yet-unstudied area; (d) as a means for anticipating what aspects of a problem are most likely to be important. (p. 27)

Thus, theory is necessary to understand previous research findings and to guide future research.

In categorizing theoretical approaches to the study of group dynamics, Shaw (1981) first distinguished between theoretical orientations (e.g., field theory), which apply to a broad range of social contexts, not just groups, and limited theories (e.g., leadership theory), which apply to very specific phenomena within groups. Between these two extremes lie middle-range theories (e.g., exchange theory), which explain more than one aspect of group life, but not all aspects (see Shaw & Costanzo, 1982).

After listing a number of theoretical approaches, most authors conclude that no one theory explains all of group behavior but that each adds something to the understanding of groups. In contrast to such optimistic statements, Zander (1979) proposed,

> There are few well-developed theories about behavior in groups. The theories that do exist, moreover, seldom aid in understanding groups as such, or even the behavior of members on behalf of their groups, because the theories often are based on ideas taken from individual psychology, and these are primarily concerned with the actions of individuals for the good of those individuals. (p. 423)

THEORETICAL APPROACHES TO THE STUDY OF SPORT GROUPS

An extensive review of the research on group dynamics in sport indicates that none of the general theoretical orientations identified by Shaw have been tested or used as a guide in the study of athletic teams. Likewise, rarely have any middle-range

theories been employed in sport. One exception has been Schutz's (1958) fundamental interpersonal relations orientations theory, which has been used to examine coach–athlete compatibility (e.g., Carron & Bennett, 1977). Thus, when theoretical approaches have been used to study athletic teams, they have been what Shaw referred to as limited theories. These theories have focused on such specific aspects of groups as leadership (e.g., Chelladurai, 1978), structure (Grusky, 1963), motivation (Zander, 1971), cohesion (Carron, Widmeyer, & Brawley, 1985), and effectiveness (Steiner, 1972). The reader should also refer to Carron and Hausenblas (1998).

Although the theory and research on cohesion are presented later and leadership is dealt with in chapter 10 in this text, theories of structure and motivation are not discussed. Grusky's theory of formal structure, used primarily by sport sociologists to explain both racial discrimination and ascendancy to leadership, was described in detail by Loy et al. (1978). Although Zander (1971) showed a great interest in athletes, others have not tested his concepts in sport. One limited theory—Steiner's (1972) theory of group productivity—has not been used by sport researchers. This is not surprising given that sport is so performance-oriented. Hence, we outline Steiner's theory in some depth.

Steiner's Theory of Group Productivity

According to Steiner (1972), a group's actual productivity is equal to its potential productivity minus "process losses." Process losses are considered to be the result of either faulty coordination of member resources or less-than-optimal motivation by members. Thus, a group of physical education students might not move a wrestling mat as effectively as they potentially could because they do not all lift and move simultaneously or because some of them do not give a maximum effort. Potential productivity is determined by the amount of relevant resources (e.g., sewing ability is not a relevant resource for moving a wrestling mat). Similarly, communication is more relevant for a football team than for a bowling team because coordination of efforts is more crucial in the former.

According to Steiner's theory, it is predicted that Team A will perform better than Team B if any of the following scenarios is present:

- Team A possesses more relevant resources than Team B while experiencing equal process losses.

- Team A possesses equal relevant resources but experiences fewer process losses than Team B.
- Team A possesses more relevant resources and experiences fewer process losses than Team B.

This prediction suggests that the role of any coach is to increase relevant resources (through instruction, training, and recruiting) and to reduce process losses (through strategies for combining players' contributions and motivating them). Because sport is so performance-oriented, Steiner's theory has innumerable applications. For example, it has been used to determine the relative contributions of ability and cohesion to performance outcome (Gossett & Widmeyer, 1978) and to look at social loafing in rowing performance (Ingham, Levinger, Graves, & Peckham, 1974).

Beginnings to an Overall Theory of Group Dynamics

We have noted that no overall theory explains the dynamics of sport teams or even of groups in general. However, certain models, or conceptual frameworks, have been advanced that identify and organize the categories of variables operating within groups. In one recent framework advanced by McGrath (1984), member interaction was hypothesized to be the central factor in group life. McGrath then identified a number of factors that influence, and are influenced by, interaction processes. Specifically, he proposed that interaction is influenced by member characteristics, group structure, environmental properties, and processes internal to interaction itself. In turn, interaction can influence group members, the environment, and group relationships.

No one researcher has identified all of these relationships within a sport team. However, Carron and Hausenblas (1998) presented a linear model (see figure 9.1) that depicts the majority of inputs, throughputs, and outputs operating within athletic groups. In other generic schematics used to represent sets of relationships about various topics in sport psychology, the term *inputs* refers to antecedents, and the term *throughputs* refers to social psychological processes that link antecedents to the final term, *outputs,* typically called *consequences.* The inputs that Carron and Hausenblas identified are member attributes (social, psychological, and physical characteristics) and group environment (the location and task of the group). Throughputs include group structure (positions, roles, and status of members), group cohesion (group unity), and group processes (e.g., motivation, communication, decision-making). Finally, group outputs are consequences both for the individual members (e.g., satisfaction, adherence) and for the group (e.g., performance, stability). This comprehensive model can be used to determine relationships that could exist, what is actually known to date, and what should be studied in sport groups.

The limited use of theory in group dynamics across all disciplines undoubtedly has restricted the advancement of knowledge in this area. Nevertheless, a considerable amount of research has been conducted. The research from other disciplines has been introduced in such classic works as *Group Dynamics: Research and Theory* (Cartwright & Zander, 1968), *The Sociology of Small Groups* (Mills, 1984), *Group Performance* (Davis, 1969), *Group Process and Productivity* (Steiner, 1972), *Group Dynamics: The Psychology of Small Group Behavior* (Shaw, 1981), and *Groups: Interaction and Performance* (McGrath, 1984).

In contrast, very little has been written about the small group in sport. Brawley (1989) reported that a content analysis of texts (1984–1989) in sport psychology revealed that only 13% of the

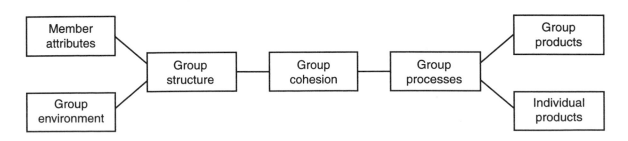

Figure 9.1 A conceptual framework for examining the sport team as a group.

Reprinted, by permission, from A.V. Carron and H.A. Hausenblas, 1998, *Group Dynamics in Sport,* 2nd ed. (Morgantown, WV: FIT Publications), 20.

material was devoted to group dynamics. Similarly, Landers, Boutcher, and Wang (1986) noted that only 9% of the articles appearing in the *Journal of Sport Psychology* from 1979 to 1986 dealt with the sport group. Although some sport psychology texts (e.g., Gill, 1986) contain excellent sections on the sport group, rarely have entire texts been devoted to the topic. One recent exception is Carron and Hausenblas' (1998) *Group Dynamics in Sport*.

The purpose of the next sections is to present research conducted in group dynamics. Although the primary emphasis is on sport or other physical activity settings, relevant research undertaken with other small groups also is discussed. Because the field of group dynamics encompasses many areas of research, we shall restrict ourselves to examining three major topics: group size, group composition, and group cohesion. These topics were selected either because of the amount of research conducted in that area or because of the importance the topic has for sport practitioners. Although we recognize that investigations have been conducted within sport dealing with such topics as group structure and selected group processes (e.g., motivation and attribution), space limitations prohibit discussing such topics here. In addition, other important aspects of groups have been examined extensively but not in conjunction with sport teams. For now, information on such group topics as development, communication, and decision-making must be gleaned from nonsport research.

GROUP SIZE

Historically, one of the most frequently examined variables in nonsport research on group dynamics has been size. Research on this topic has been stimulated by an interest among researchers and practitioners in determining what number of individuals constitute the ideal for group productivity, morale, cohesion, satisfaction, and other outcomes. Specific examples of this research include determining what unit size is optimal for a work group carrying out a manual labor project, for an army platoon entering combat, for a number of friends going on a social outing, and for a secretarial pool within a large corporation.

Popular wisdom says, "The more the merrier," "Two heads are better than one," and "Many hands make the work lighter." However, as Ivan Steiner (1972) pointed out, popular wisdom also says, "Three is a crowd," "Too many cooks spoil the broth," and "A chain is as strong as its weakest link." Scientists, of course, attempt to resolve these conflicting notions.

Theoretical Considerations

Much of the research on group size has been guided by Steiner's theory of group productivity. This conceptual framework can be used to explain the effects of group size on a variety of factors related to group effectiveness. Figure 9.2 illustrates how Steiner's framework explains effects of group size on group productivity. This graph shows that as the number of members in a group increases, the potential for the group to be more productive also increases. The reason for this is quite simple—there are more available resources. It should be apparent, however, that the curve for potential productivity eventually reaches a plateau. This reflects the fact that at some point, all of the expertise necessary for a group to complete its mission is available. Adding new members beyond this point does not increase productivity.

When group size increases beyond the optimal point, it becomes more difficult for each member to interact and communicate in relation to either task or social concerns. It also becomes more difficult to plan and coordinate each group member's activities to ensure minimal duplication and maximal individual involvement. These are examples of group processes. As figure 9.2 illustrates, when group size increases, group processes decrease.

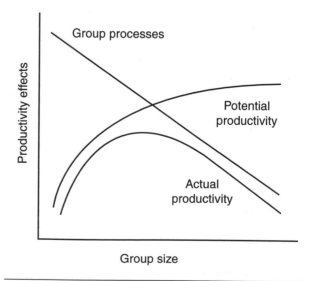

Figure 9.2   The relationship between group size and group productivity.

Adapted, by permission, from A.V. Carron and & H.A. Hausenblas, 1998, *Group dynamics in sport,* 2nd ed. (Morgantown, WV: FIT Publications).

The final relationship depicted in figure 9.2 is between group size and the relative productivity of each member in the group. Relative individual productivity declines with increasing group size. This is considered to be a result of two factors. First, because of the coordination problems already discussed, the efficiency of the group suffers. Also, in larger groups, each individual member does not give his or her maximum effort. This motivation loss, known as social loafing, is discussed later.

Steiner's predictions regarding group size effects are based primarily on research with nonsport groups. Recently, however, several researchers have examined the effects of group size in both sport and exercise contexts.

Group Size in Sport Teams

In 1990, we reported two studies on the impact of group size in sport teams (Widmeyer, Brawley, & Carron, 1990). In designing these studies, we considered and used different functional definitions of group size, including the number of players "carried" on the overall roster of the team and the number on the field of action at one time. In Study 1, the rosters of 3-on-3 recreational basketball teams were manipulated to produce teams that carried 3, 6, and 9 members. Each team played two games per week for 10 weeks.

The results revealed that in the smallest teams, task cohesiveness was highest. That is, it was easiest to obtain consensus and commitment to the group's goals and objectives in the 3-person groups. However, because of the relatively limited number of resources available, it was more difficult for the 3-person teams to compete successfully. As well, social cohesion (i.e., closeness among players) was lowest in these small teams either because athletes were constantly competing or because of the relatively limited number of attractive others with whom to interact. In the largest teams, it was more difficult to obtain consensus and commitment to the group's goals and objectives (i.e., task cohesion was lowest) and still somewhat hard to develop a strong sense of social cohesion. The intermediate-size groups—the 6-person teams—were the highest in social cohesion and also were the most successful in terms of win–loss outcomes.

In Study 2, the number of athletes on the field of action was varied in recreational volleyball teams to produce 3-on-3, 6-on-6, and 12-on-12 competitions. When the participants evaluated these three different situations, they indicated that their sense of enjoyment, their perceptions of cohesiveness, and their feelings of having obtained exercise and being fatigued, of having had influence and responsibility on the team, and of being organized and using strategies were greatest in the 3-on-3 teams and least in the 12-on-12 teams. At the same time, feelings of being crowded increased with increasing team size. The smallest teams were associated with the most positive experiences for the participants. The results from these two studies on sport teams clearly show that group size has an effect on productivity, the nature and amount of cohesiveness that develops, and individual perceptions about the attractiveness of the group.

Group Size in Exercise Groups

In 1990, we also completed two studies that examined the impact of group size in exercise classes (Carron, Brawley, & Widmeyer, 1990). In Study 1, the relationship between the size of fitness classes and the adherence of members was examined. Archival data from 47 fitness classes varying in size from 5 to 46 members were used to form four categories of groups: small (5–17 members), medium (18–26 members), moderately large (27–31), and large (32–46 members). As figure 9.3 shows, both the attendance and retention of participants were highest in the very small and very large fitness

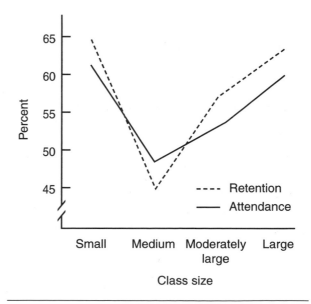

Figure 9.3 Size–adherence relationships in exercise classes.

Reprinted, by permission, from A.V. Carron and H.A. Hausenblas, 1998, *Group dynamics in sport*, 2nd ed. (Morgantown, WV: FIT Publications), 44.

classes and were lowest in the medium and moderately large classes.

The purpose of Study 2 was to examine the nature of the relationship between the size of fitness classes and the social–psychological perceptions of group members. Participants in small classes (6–13 members), medium classes (25–39 members), and a large class (73 members) evaluated their feelings of conspicuousness, the quality and quantity of interactions with their leader, their opportunities for social interaction with other members, the level of crowding and density they experienced, and their feelings of satisfaction. There was a curvilinear relationship between fitness class size and participants' perceptions of the opportunities available for social interaction and also between class size and feelings of crowding and density. Both the small and large classes were perceived more favorably than the medium classes. Perceptions of the instructor and the level of satisfaction experienced varied in a linear way with group size. That is, positive perceptions decreased systematically as class size increased. Finally, there was no difference among the groups in perceptions of conspicuousness.

In three studies, Carron and Spink (1995) examined the impact of class size on perceptions of cohesiveness. The period in which cohesiveness was assessed during the 13-week session varied across the different studies, but the results were consistent nonetheless. Exercisers in smaller classes had stronger perceptions of their class' cohesiveness.

Although it is unwise to overgeneralize from the results of only a few studies, it does seem that smaller is better in fitness class settings. Certainly, further research in the area is recommended.

Group Size and the Phenomenon of Social Loafing

Research on the productivity of groups has identified a phenomenon referred to as social loafing. Social loafing represents a reduction in individual effort that occurs when people work collectively on a problem (Latané, Williams, & Harkins, 1979). One of the earliest studies to report on this phenomenon was conducted by Ringelmann in the late 19th century (cited in Ingham et al., 1974). Using a tug-of-war task, Ringelmann found that the average male exerted 63 kilograms of tension when working by himself (cited in Moede, 1927). Thus, potential productivity for a group could be predicted by multiplying the size of the group by 63

kilograms. However, Ringelmann found that in actuality, for groups of 2, 3, 4, 5, 6, 7, and 8, the average individual in the group produced, respectively, only 93%, 85%, 77%, 70%, 63%, 58%, and 49% of his potential.

Using Steiner's (1972) model of group productivity, Ingham and colleagues (1974) hypothesized that two factors might account for this decrease in individual productivity: poor coordination, resulting from the inability of individuals in groups to exert maximal tension simultaneously, and decreased motivation, resulting from the fact that individual performances cannot be assessed directly in groups. To determine which of these was the more important, Ingham and his colleagues replicated the Ringelmann study. Ringelmann proposed that the major source of the difference between a group's potential productivity and its actual productivity was faulty coordination. Ingham et al. found, rather, that the source was lower motivation (i.e., social loafing).

A considerable amount of research subsequently has verified the presence of social loafing in laboratory and nonlaboratory situations (see Hardy, 1989). In 1993, Karau and Williams undertook a meta-analysis to summarize the results from more than 80 studies. Karau and Williams reported two important findings about social loafing:

- It reliably occurs across a wide cross section of situations including activities involving physical effort or skill (e.g., swimming), cognitive skills (e.g., generating ideas), evaluation (e.g., rating the quality of poems), and perceptual skills (e.g., vigilance on the computer).

- It is not a characteristic of one population (i.e., North Americans) or either gender.

A number of conditions in the situation increase the probability that social loafing will occur. These include the following:

- The individual's output cannot be evaluated independently.
- The task is low in meaningfulness.
- The individual's personal involvement is low.
- The individual's effort cannot be compared against group standards.
- Other individuals contributing to the collective effort are strangers.
- The individual expects that his or her coworkers will do well.

- The individual believes that his or her efforts to the outcome are redundant.

Numerous explanations have been proposed to account for the social loafing phenomenon (Harkins, Latané, & Williams, 1980). The *allocation strategy* proposal is based on the assumption that people are motivated to work hard in groups but save their best efforts for when they work alone because it is personally most beneficial. In the *minimizing strategy* proposal, it is assumed that people are motivated to get by with as little effort as possible. Because there is minimal personal accountability, groups provide an optimal environment in which to loaf. In the *free rider* proposal, it is assumed that people in groups reduce their personal efforts and go for a free ride because they feel their efforts are not essential to the outcome. Finally, the *sucker effect* proposal assumes that individuals in groups reduce their personal efforts because they do not want to provide a free ride to less productive individuals.

Research on the phenomenon of social loafing appears to be on the decline in both the sport sciences and psychology in general. Given that social loafing has important implications for team performance in a variety of sports (e.g., rowing, relays, the scrum in rugby), this is unfortunate. When the description and explanation phases in any area of science have yielded a plethora of information, researchers can proceed to research involving prediction and intervention. Sport science researchers are encouraged to continue their work with these research protocols.

GROUP COMPOSITION

Group composition refers to the properties possessed by group members. These properties include physical characteristics, mental and motor abilities, attitudes, motives, personality traits, and such social identities as age, education, religion, occupation, race, sex, and social status. The effects of group composition can be examined from three perspectives:

- Quantity
- Degree of variation
- Complementarity of properties among members

Although each of these manifestations can influence other group inputs and various group processes, the majority of sport research has focused on the impact of group composition on group productivity.

Quantity of Group Resources

The quantity of a group's resources can be represented by either the average or the sum of member attributes. One intuitively expects that groups possessing more relevant resources will perform better. Examinations of the quantity of resources have sought to determine which resources are relevant and how much of an effect group resources have on group performance. The first area of this research has dealt primarily with psychological and social properties, whereas the second has focused on the abilities of group members.

How does the quantity of social–psychological resources in the group influence its productivity? Cooper and Payne (1967) assessed an aspect of the personality of soccer players and coaches—the extent to which these individuals were task-, self-, and affiliation-oriented when approaching activities. The researchers found that the success of soccer teams was positively related to the task orientations of their coaches/trainers ($r = .72$). Later, the same researchers reported that high task orientation, low self-orientation, and low affiliation orientations of soccer players were positively linked to team success (Cooper & Payne, 1972).

Examining 144 intramural basketball teams, Martens (1970) discovered that teams which were most successful possessed high task and low affiliation motivation. Also, it has been shown that basketball teams that possessed high achievement motivation were very successful (Klein & Christiansen, 1969). In contrast, Widmeyer and Martens (1978) demonstrated that task motivation, affiliation motivation, and self-motivation, considered singly or in combination, did not predict winning in 3-on-3 basketball teams. However, these variables, when combined with group cohesion, increased cohesion's prediction of performance outcome significantly. These results suggest that multivariate approaches should be taken when examining the impact of the quantity of group resources.

Anthropologists Sutton-Smith and Roberts (1964) identified a personality variable known as "action style." They labeled individuals who approached life as if they were playing a game of physical skill as *potents,* those as if playing a game of strategy *strategists,* and those as if playing a game of chance *fortunists*. Members' potent style was positively related to doubles success in men's tennis, whereas negative relationships existed between team success and each of the styles of pure strategy, strategy/fortunism, and pure fortunism (Widmeyer, Loy, & Roberts, 1980).

A subsequent study of 28 female tennis teams (Widmeyer & Loy, 1989) found that members' styles of potent/strategy and pure strategy were significantly related to team success ($r = .70$ and $-.41$, respectively). Although a number of studies have shown that the quantity of psychological variables affects team performance, no attempt has been made to explain why such relationships exist.

Intuitively, it seems that the more resources a group possesses (i.e., in terms of the ability of its members), the better would be the group's performance. In two experiments, Gill (1979) found moderate relationships ($r = .49-.53$) between average member ability and group performance on a motor maze. Jones (1974) reported that the correlation between individual performance and team performance at the professional level was .70 in men's tennis, .80 in women's tennis, .91 in football, .94 in baseball, and .60 in basketball. The different values might reflect differences in the amount of coordination of abilities required in certain sports. For example, basketball requires more coordination than baseball. Therefore, it is possible to have greater productivity losses in basketball because of faulty coordination, and, consequently, there is likely to be a weaker relationship between ability and performance in that sport. Player ability correlated .73 with team performance in men's intramural basketball (Gossett & Widmeyer, 1978), whereas Spense (1980) found the correlation to be .78 in women's intramural teams. The reason why member ability was a better predictor of team success in doubles tennis among women ($r = .77$) than men ($r = .54$) may be that there were greater ability discrepancies among the women (Widmeyer & Loy, 1989). This rationale was extended to explain why women's backhand ability was more closely related to performance ($r = .79$) than forehand ability ($r = .30$). That is, the female players differed little in forehand but greatly in backhand ability.

The studies reported here indicate that only a very few social–psychological variables have been examined when studying the effects of the quantity of member resources. Also, research shows that the strength of the relationship between player ability and team performance varies con-

siderably depending on the sport, the specific skill, and the level of play.

Variability of Group Resources

The variability of group resources focuses on the impact of the heterogeneity of member characteristics and abilities. Klein and Christiansen (1969) reported that 3-person basketball teams whose members were very heterogeneous in achievement motivation were more successful than their homogeneous counterparts. Carron and Hausenblas (1998) suggested a "spillover effect" to explain why heterogeneous groups might perform better than homogeneous groups. According to this hypothesis, a stronger member can positively influence a weaker individual by improving his or her learning and motivation. Nevertheless, in Gill's (1979) experiments, which were introduced earlier, there were no significant relationships between the ability discrepancies of members and group performance on a motor task. In the Widmeyer and Loy (1989) study, which also was introduced earlier, the more homogeneous teams were more successful. Commenting on why women's tennis teams with very homogeneous ability performed better than heterogeneous teams, Widmeyer and Loy (1989) suggested,

> *Many would predict the opposite findings arguing that the heterogeneous teams should do better because they have a high ability person who can play the majority of shots. The results suggest that these female tennis players adopt a very egalitarian strategy when playing with their partners and thus their game was not marked by "poaching" or any other form of overplaying by the better players. It could also be that the homogeneous teams were directing the majority of their shots to the weaker player on heterogeneous teams. Support for these two assumptions lies in the fact that the total ability of the weakest player was more positively related to team performance outcome* ($r = .74$) *than was the total ability of the best player* ($r = .49$). *(p. 27)*

Again, these studies show that only a very limited number of social–psychological variables have been examined when studying the relationship between variability of resources and team performance. Also, the strength of the effect of the variability of players' ability resources on team performance depended on how the game was played.

Complementarity of Group Resources

The relationship between complementarity of group resources and group performance is suggested by the rhyme, "Jack Sprat could eat no fat, his wife could eat no lean; so between the two of them, they licked the platter clean." Complementarity of group members' action styles has been shown to relate to performance in management games (Roberts, Meeker, & Aller, 1972), sport car rallies (Roberts & Kundrat, 1978), deep-sea fishing crews, navy flight crews, and duplicate bridge teams (J. Roberts, personal communication, October 1980). In tennis, serve/volley complementarity was more important for male tennis teams whereas forehand/backhand complementarity was more important for female teams. These differences were considered to be related to differences in the style of play of the two sexes (Widmeyer & Loy, 1989). At the club level studied, the women engaged in lengthy baseline rallies, whereas in men's games, a serve-and-volley style predominated.

When we summarize the research on group composition in sport, we find that researchers have done the following:

- Focused on the effects of either social psychological attributes or ability resources of members on team performance
- Found that ability composition is more strongly related to team performance in coacting than in interacting sports
- Ignored process variables that might explain or mediate composition–performance relationships
- Focused primarily on the quantity or variability of resources but rarely studied the complementarity of resources and, with only one exception, never researched all three of these manifestations simultaneously

GROUP COHESION

Group cohesion is one of the most frequently examined group concepts in sport science. A number of reviews report extensively on the current state of knowledge concerning group cohesion (e.g., Carron, Brawley, & Widmeyer, 1998; Carron & Hausenblas, 1998; Gill, 1988; Widmeyer, Brawley, & Carron, 1985). In this section of the chapter, we summarize the available research captured by these reviews to provide a brief glimpse of the state of knowledge. This summary is necessary to understand the problems associated with the research about cohesion in sport. Major problems are discussed after the summary, and more recent conceptual and measurement approaches are presented.

A summary of the cohesion research in sport is best discussed within the framework presented by Carron and Hausenblas (1998). This framework, which is illustrated in figure 9.4, is a modification of a framework originally proposed by Carron (1982) to help investigators systematically organize the research pertaining to cohesion. As figure 9.4 shows, the correlates of cohesion are categorized within four categories: situational, personal, leadership, and team. The following overview has been taken from Carron and Hausenblas (1998).

Situational Correlates of Cohesion

A number of situational constraints influence the level of cohesiveness present in a team. For example, athletes may cohere in a team because of a wide variety of *contractual* considerations—eligibility rules, geographical restrictions, legal contracts, and so on. Also, there are *normative pressures* against quitting in our society. As a further

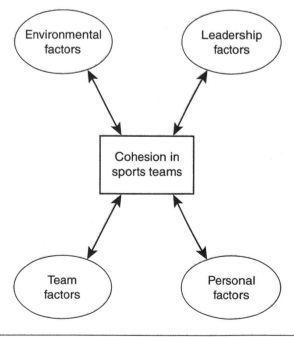

Figure 9.4 A framework to examine the correlates of cohesion.

Adapted, by permission, from A.V. Carron and H.A. Hausenblas, 1998, *Group dynamics in sport*, 2nd ed. (Morgantown, WV: FIT Publications).

example, the *orientation* of the organization can influence the nature and amount of the cohesiveness that is present. In this regard, Spink and Carron (1994) reported that task cohesion was associated with adherence to exercise programs in a university setting, whereas in private fitness clubs it was social cohesion. Also, Granito and Rainey (1988) found that social cohesion was greater in elementary and junior high school basketball teams than in senior high school teams.

Group size is another situational variable that differentially impinges on different aspects of cohesion. For example, as indicated previously, Widmeyer et al. (1990) found that recreational basketball players assigned to teams of varying size playing in a 10-week season expressed greatest task cohesion in small teams, whereas least cohesion was expressed in large teams.

Personal Correlates of Cohesion

A wide cross section of personal factors also are associated with the cohesion present in sport teams. Carron and Hausenblas (1998) found it convenient to organize these personal factors within three categories: demographic attributes, cognitions and motivations, and behaviors.

Demographic Attributes

Member similarity in personal attributes has long been considered a contributor to group cohesion. For example, Eitzen (1975) suggested that cohesion is facilitated when team members are from similar social backgrounds. The view that there are gender differences in cohesion has found some support. For example, Widmeyer et al. (1985) found that male team sport athletes expressed greater social cohesiveness than female team sport athletes. Also, Thompson and Albinson (1991) found greater task cohesiveness in male rowing crews. Conversely, however, Widmeyer and Martens (1978) found no differences in the cohesion of male and female teams. In general, however, there is little evidence indicating that gender differences in cohesion are observed consistently among sport teams.

Cognitions and Motives

The relationship between member cognitions and attitudes is likely reciprocal in nature—member similarity in cognitions and motives contributes to cohesion and, in turn, cohesion contributes to member similarity in cognitions and motives. One

important cognition that is influenced by cohesion is *attributions for responsibility* (Bird, Foster, & Maruyama, 1980; Brawley, Carron, & Widmeyer, 1987; Schlenker & Miller, 1977). On cohesive teams, team-enhancing attributional strategies are used. That is, the members of highly cohesive teams distribute the credit for success and share the responsibility for failure. On the other hand, if the team is low in cohesion, self-enhancing strategies are used—inordinate credit is taken for success and responsibility is denied after failure.

Members experience less anxiety in group situations than when they are alone. Also, members of a cohesive group have less anxiety than a noncohesive group. For example, Martens, Burton, Vealey, Bump, and Smith (1990) noted that individual sport athletes experience greater cognitive and somatic anxiety and lower state self-confidence than do team sport athletes. Also, in a study examining the social anxiety that emanates from self-presentational concerns, Carron and Prapavessis (1997) found that individuals were less anxious in a group or with a best friend than when they were alone. Finally, Prapavessis and Carron (1996) found that athletes in a variety of sports who possessed higher perceptions of task cohesion reported less cognitive state anxiety.

Behavior

Cohesion has been found to be associated with a wide variety of individual behaviors. For example, adherence in exercise classes is positively associated with greater cohesion—whether adherence is operationalized as dropout behavior (Carron, Widmeyer, & Brawley, 1988; Spink & Carron, 1994), absenteeism and lateness (Spink & Carron, 1992), or resistance to disruptive events (Brawley, Carron, & Widmeyer, 1988, Study 2).

Another operational measure of adherence used in business and industry is effort expended. When Prapavessis and Carron (1997) tested athletes from a variety of sports, they found that those athletes who held higher perceptions of their team's task cohesiveness worked in practice at a level that was significantly closer to their maximum.

Social loafing is yet another behavior (and cognition) that is influenced by the team's cohesiveness. Research has shown that athletes on teams higher in cohesion not only are less likely to think that their teammates will socially loaf (Naylor & Brawley, 1992) but are less likely to socially loaf themselves (McKnight, Williams, & Widmeyer, 1991).

Leadership Correlates of Cohesion

The complex interaction between coach and players also appears to influence the development of cohesion. For example, a considerable body of research has examined the association between leader decision style and cohesion (Carron & Chelladurai, 1981; Kozub, 1993; Lee, Kim, & Lim, 1993; Westre & Weiss, 1991). The results from that research have been unequivocal: A participative style of decision-making is related to greater perceptions of cohesiveness.

The type of leadership behavior exhibited by the coach also has been found to be associated with the development of cohesiveness. However, the optimal type of leader behavior is not clear. For example, Westre and Weiss (1991) found that higher levels of training and instruction behavior, social support behavior, and positive feedback with high school football players were associated with higher levels of task cohesion. In a study conducted with high school basketball teams, however, Kozub (1993) found that only higher levels of training and instruction behavior and social support behavior were related to greater task cohesion.

Team Correlates of Cohesion

One group phenomenon that has been examined in a series of investigations by David Paskevich and his colleagues (Dorsch, Widmeyer, Paskevich, & Brawley, 1995; Paskevich, 1995; Paskevich, Brawley, Dorsch, & Widmeyer, 1995) is *collective efficacy*—the sense of shared competence held by team members that they can successfully respond to the demands of the situation (Zaccaro, Blair, Peterson, & Zazanis, 1995). In their research, Paskevich and his colleagues found that the collective efficacy–cohesion relationship is reciprocal; teams that have greater collective efficacy are more cohesive and teams that are more cohesive have greater collective efficacy.

Performance is a second group variable that has been examined extensively for its relationship to cohesion. In the previous edition of this book, we pointed out that the results from that research were equivocal. Some studies reported that teams with more cohesion had more success, whereas other studies reported that cohesion either was unrelated to performance or was even negatively related to performance. More recently, however, Mullen and Copper (1994) summarized the cohesion–performance research by using the statistical protocol of meta-analysis, with the following findings:

- There is a small but significant relationship between cohesion and performance.
- The impact of cohesion on performance increases from artificial (i.e., laboratory) groups to nonsport nonmilitary real groups (e.g., work units), from nonsport nonmilitary real groups to military groups, and from military groups to sport groups.
- The relationship of cohesion to performance is not moderated by task type (i.e., cohesion is as strong a contributor to performance in independent sports such as golf as it is in interdependent sports such as basketball).
- Group success has a stronger relationship to subsequent cohesiveness than cohesiveness has to subsequent group success

Problems With the Research on Cohesion

Historically, a major problem with the cohesion research in sport is the failure to define and measure sport cohesion in more than a unidimensional manner. This problem is not unique to the sport research but is also characteristic of social science in general. In the sport sciences, the practice has been to borrow concepts and measures from the social sciences. Concepts such as fields of forces, resistance to disruption, and attraction to group were borrowed and have guided all but the most contemporary sport studies. However, in a review of the research concerning the definition of group cohesion in general, Mudrack (1989) noted that researchers not only have defined cohesion poorly but also have failed to link cohesion measures to the various definitions of cohesion.

In sport science, little thought has been given to the limitations of borrowing definitions or measures from other fields of study. This same error has been committed by the larger group of social scientists interested in cohesion. All borrowed operational definitions of cohesion do not have universal application to all settings. It may well be inappropriate to use definitions and measures developed in other settings. The overall consequence for social science and sport will be invalid or limited measurement (e.g., unidimensional measure) in many sport investigations.

At the root of the definition problem is one of a still more global dimension, again characteristic of both the social science and sport literature. The global problem is that there is no conceptual or theoretical model that can be used as the basis for defining and measuring cohesion. Without some common foundation to guide research efforts, the variety of cohesion definitions and measures that exist in the literature were inevitable. Subsequent comparisons between studies (e.g., comparing cohesion–performance relationships) may well be inappropriate when the definitions and measures used are not directly comparable. Obviously, the combined problems of lack of a conceptual foundation, poor cohesion definition, and poor link between operational definition and measurement create a kind of research error "domino effect." Research problems of measurement cannot be solved without correcting the more basic problem of lack of a theory or model (Widmeyer et al., 1985). What implications do these problems have for the cohesion research in sport?

A nagging question arises concerning the sport-related cohesion research conducted between 1969 and 1984. If concerns about the definition, theory, and measurement of cohesion went unresolved, can investigators have confidence in previous sport research? Results have been obtained by using cohesion measures that are conceptually and psychometrically inadequate. Results are not comparable because no common measures were used across studies. These deficiencies are of sufficient magnitude that the majority of early studies must be viewed with caution. Much of that research concerns a variety of descriptive and correlational findings.

Carron et al. (1985) subsequently described the related problems of theory, definition, and measurement and developed a conceptual model to address these research problems. The next section describes these developments in response to the problems in sport cohesion research.

Recent Theoretical and Assessment Developments

The dissatisfaction with operational definitions and unidimensional measurement approaches described in the previous section motivated sport scientists to develop new cohesion ideas and related measures. As a consequence, Carron et al. (1985), Gruber and Gray (1981, 1982), and Yukelson, Weinberg, and Jackson (1984) independently developed instruments to measure group cohesion in the sport context. However, the three research approaches to instrument development were quite different. Gruber and Gray and also

Yukelson and his colleagues used a data-driven approach, in which the initial set of items on their instrument were selected by searching the previous literature for items and borrowing items from other instruments. The resultant measure was used to gather data. In turn, these data were explored in search of a statistically understandable measure. In principle, this does not seem like a bad idea until we consider the quality of measures in the previous literature. This data-driven method of developing an instrument fails to account for the possibility that borrowing items from other fields can also result in borrowing research problems. In the case of the Gruber and Gray instrument, items about enjoyment and satisfaction were included in their item pool. These variables are probable consequences of the cohesiveness existing on a team but do not represent the construct itself.

Yukelson and his colleagues (1984) developed the Multidimensional Sport Cohesion Instrument (MSCI) by using the similar approach of initially borrowing items from the previous literature in both the parent discipline and sport (as well as developing their own item pool). However, like Gruber and Gray (1981, 1982), they failed to distinguish antecedent and consequence variables from the construct of cohesion. For example, the MSCI assessed role performance, role clarity, enjoyment, and satisfaction, all of which are possible antecedent or consequence variables but are not indicants of cohesion. Although it is important to study antecedents and consequences of cohesion, using such constructs to operationally define cohesion presents a fundamental problem. Their use obviates the scientific necessity for having a clear conceptual and operational definition that acknowledges cohesion as a unique, group-related psychological variable.

In their data-driven approach to instrument development, Gruber and Gray (1981, 1982) and Yukelson et al. (1984) administered their initial pool of items to different groups of athletes. The resulting data were then factor-analyzed. This procedure reveals the groups of variables (i.e., items) that are most related. The outcome of factor analysis yields factors that the researchers label by using nomenclature that best describes what the items in the factor represent. This data-driven approach amounts to a post hoc analysis of data in search of something that makes sense. Although the product of this analysis yields related factors, the major flaw is that the borrowed items represent constructs that have been confounded with cohesion—the variable that researchers are attempting to identify more clearly. In addition, piecing together the factors post hoc encourages the researcher to label dimensions that "must belong" to cohesion as opposed to discarding the factors if they don't give cohesion an identity unique from other psychological variables.

Although a data-driven approach is systematic, it represents an example of the research error domino effect. This is one reason why the validity of both instruments is unknown. The interested reader is referred to Gruber and Gray (1981, 1982) and to Yukelson et al. (1984) for more detail.

Despite these problems, the measures developed by Gruber and Gray (1981, 1982) and by Yukelson and his colleagues (1984) were the first sport-related instruments to explicitly acknowledge that cohesion was multidimensional. This acknowledgment was an important advance in the sport cohesion literature.

In contrast to the data-driven approach used to develop the previously mentioned instruments, Carron et al. (1985) used a theory-driven approach to develop the Group Environment Questionnaire (GEQ). Our plan was to proceed from Carron's (1982) definition of cohesion—"a dynamic process that is reflected in the tendency for a group to stick together and remain united in pursuit of its goals and objectives" (p. 124)—to the development of a conceptual model of sport group cohesion. The model then would serve as the basis for instrument development and validation.

For the development of the model and the GEQ, the group dynamics literature was reviewed extensively. This review, which focused on the nature of the group and group cohesiveness, resulted in the identification of two major themes that consistently appeared in the literature. These themes centered on the distinction between individual and group aspects of group involvement and the distinction between the task and social aspects of cohesiveness (e.g., Mikalachki, 1969; Van Bergen & Koekebakker, 1959). An example of the former distinction is that group involvement has been examined with respect to the motives of individual members for belonging to their group. By contrast, group involvement also has been considered relative to decisions or perceptions that the entire group has about the group's behavior. Thus, the group as a whole may set goals for performance or goals for a season, or as a group they may decide why they should keep training together at season's end. An example of the latter (i.e., task–social) distinction arises in examining the reasons why groups stay together. Work and competitive sport groups form and pursue task-related activities relative to their goals and objectives and stay together primarily for task reasons. By contrast, leisure and recreational sport groups may form, set social goals and objectives, and stay together primarily to socialize regularly. Historically, cohesion has been considered to be composed of task and social elements (see Carron, 1988).

We proposed a conceptual model of cohesion incorporating the group–individual and the task–social distinctions based on the conclusions and distinctions drawn from the literature review (Carron et al., 1985; see figure 9.5). Our conceptual model and thus our measure derive from three fundamental assumptions. These assumptions are that (a) cohesion is a group property that can be assessed through the perceptions of individual members, (b) the nature of the social cognitions (beliefs) members obtain through group experience

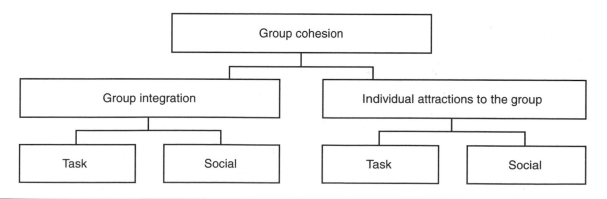

Figure 9.5 A conceptual model of group cohesion.

Reprinted, by permission, from W.N. Widmeyer, L.R. Brawley, and A.V. Carron, 1985, *The measurement of cohesion in sport teams: The group environment questionnaire* (Eastbourne, U.K.), 18. Copyright 1985 by Spodym Publishers.

reflect shared beliefs about the group, and (c) the primary orientation of these group perceptions is multidimensional. These three assumptions are discussed more fully in the following paragraphs.

Assumption 1: Measuring Cohesion Through Group Member Perception

The following points underscore our belief that cohesion can be assessed through the perceptions of individual group members: (a) a group has observable properties to define its stability, (b) members are socialized into their groups and thus develop a set of beliefs about the group and its properties, (c) these beliefs are a product of the selective processing and integration of group-relevant information, (d) the perceptions about one's group that are held by each of its members are a good estimate of characteristic aspects of group unity, and (e) these perceptions can be measured quantitatively.

Assumption 2: The Group and the Individual

Our second assumption arose from the general distinctions apparent from reviewing group dy-

Pregame rituals may help to facilitate group integration.

namics research. Social cognitions that a group member holds about cohesion concern the group and the individual—those about the group as a totality and those about the manner in which the group satisfies an individual member's personal needs and objectives. These social cognitions are labeled (a) group integration—individuals' perceptions about the way their group unites, is close, and is similar as a whole, and (b) individual attraction to the group—an individual's perceptions about (i) personal motives brought by the individual to the group that retain/maintain the member in that group and (ii) perceptions or feelings about what the group provides or gives back to the member. These are learned as a function of being in the group.

Assumption 3: Cohesion Beliefs Have Both Task and Social Orientations

Our third assumption also stems from the general distinctions observed in the group literature—the task and social distinction. Thus, we believe that an individual member's cognitions about the group as a unit and about their attraction to the group have two fundamental orientations: a task orientation that relates to the group's various task objectives for itself and for its members, and a social orientation that relates to developing and maintaining various social relationships and activities within the group.

To summarize, there are four related dimensions in our multidimensional conceptual model of cohesion. These are group integration–task (GI–T), group integration–social (GI–S), individual attractions to the group–task (ATG–T), and individual attractions to the group–social (ATG–S). Group integration is characterized by "us, our, or we" beliefs, whereas individual attractions are characterized by "I, my, or me" beliefs. Each is potentially sufficient to bind people to their group, but depending on the developmental level of the group (i.e., reflected by the stability of various group properties such as organizational structure, role, and status relationships), several dimensions could reflect a group's cohesiveness. The strength of the perceptions that define each dimension is assumed to indicate the nature of the cohesion in the group at a given point in time.

With this reasoning, it is expected that groups at different developmental stages may exhibit different profiles or pictures of their cohesiveness. For example, early in a group's development or early in a season, the task-related aspects of cohesiveness (i.e., ATG–T and GI–T) are more likely to characterize a team's cohesiveness than are social aspects of cohesiveness (i.e., ATG–S and GI–S). The rationale for such a hypothesis comes from group research that has considered the way groups develop (e.g., Moreland & Levine, 1988; Sherif & Sherif, 1969). For example, task-oriented groups like sport teams focus on the motivational basis for their existence—performance and competition. Social relationships and social cohesiveness develop more gradually over time as a function of the interactions that are part of group life and, initially, are of less importance to the group than is the focus on the group's task. Observations of social cohesiveness may be more likely at a later point in the group's development or season after key aspects of the interactions necessary for group task performance become stable. It is conceivable that social cohesiveness could always be weaker than task cohesiveness in groups that must struggle for effective task performance.

Thus, the profile of a group's cohesiveness changes with time, necessitating a measure that examines the multiple dimensions of the construct. Multiple indicators are required to detect the aspects of the construct salient to members at the time of assessment. Each dimension of cohesiveness is not a trait property of a group but is more state-like in that change is a characteristic of the various dimensions—a reflection of change occurring within the group. Accordingly, some aspects of cohesiveness may be more stable than others depending on the group's history, its current state of development, and its motivational base. Also, other forces not yet identified may contribute to a group's cohesiveness. Thus, there is no assumption that the conceptual model is all-encompassing.

The conceptual model that described four dimensions of cohesion and the assumption that group members perceived cohesiveness in multiple ways are the bases for our development of the GEQ, an 18-item, 4-scale instrument that has been shown to be reliable and valid in numerous ways. The validation process for the GEQ has evolved over the 16 years since the instrument was published. The studies that contribute to validation are described in detail elsewhere (e.g., Brawley et al., 1987, 1988; Carron, Widmeyer, & Brawley, 1988; Carron et al., 1985, 1988; Widmeyer et al., 1985, 1990). A recent measurement chapter by Carron et al. (1998) best describes the current thinking on the conceptual model and the research

using the GEQ. Findings from that review are summarized next.

In sport and fitness, the aspects of cohesion assessed by the GEQ (cf. Carron et al., 1998) have been related to several items:

- Group size
- The task interdependence of group members
- Role clarity and acceptance
- The duration of team membership
- Attributions for responsibility
- Leadership style
- Team performance
- Increased adherence and reduced absenteeism
- The team's resistance to disruption
- Social loafing
- Collective efficacy

These relationships are positive, with the exception of reduced absenteeism and social loafing.

When we summarize the results of the sport-related research concerning recent developments in the study of cohesion, five points emerge:

1. Three instruments exist that measure cohesion as more than a unidimensional concept, but only one measure has been extensively validated (i.e., the GEQ).

2. The GEQ is based on a four-dimensional conceptual model and has been validated in numerous studies.

3. The development of a conceptual model of cohesion fills a void in the otherwise atheoretical area of cohesion in sport.

4. Use of the four-dimensional model and the related GEQ instrument avoids the common research error of not linking conceptual operational definitions of cohesion to its measurement.

5. The four aspects of group cohesion specified by the conceptual model are related to both the antecedents and the consequences of cohesiveness in sport. Antecedents are situational characteristics (e.g., size effects), personal characteristics (e.g., gender or social background), leader style, and team (e.g., shared success/failure). Consequences include individual outcomes (e.g., attribution of outcome responsibility, satisfaction with season's performance) and group outcomes (e.g., collective efficacy; greater effort toward group goals).

GROUP DYNAMICS: CURRENT PROBLEMS AND FUTURE DIRECTIONS

It is important to alert future investigators to the problems characteristic of the research in this area. If these problems are identified and remedied, the quality and quantity of research in sport group dynamics will improve. Brawley (1989), Carron (1988), Carron et al. (1998), Carron and Hausenblas (1998), and Widmeyer (1989) have noted that although sport groups represent a major social structure across cultures and are the context within which much of participation and competition occurs, group research is surprisingly limited. We pointed out earlier that a limited amount of research attention has been devoted to groups in the sport science literature. There is little doubt that there is limited knowledge about sport group dynamics. In his book on this topic, Carron (1988) emphasized this point by noting, "Despite the presence of sufficient content to fill eighteen chapters in this book, it is safe to say we know very little about sport groups" (1988, p. 219). Ten years later, Carron and Hausenblas (1998) made this same point, emphasizing that this nagging research deficiency continues to plague sport psychology.

A partial explanation for this problem is that the field of sport psychology has its momentum in the study of individuals and their performance. What sport psychologists often fail to recognize, however, is that the group has a major influence on individual behavior and performance (e.g., motivation, goal setting, performance attributions; Carron, 1988; Carron & Hausenblas, 1998). Ignoring this influence may be a major conceptual and methodological error. The failure to examine the influence of the group on the individual excludes a major source of variance in the prediction of sport behavior. This exclusion has implications for the accuracy of many interpretations in research studies, regarding what influenced behavior. Was it an individual trait or was it the group? Did group cohesion or collective efficacy moderate individual reactions toward success or failure? Kenny and LaVoie (1985) raised this same question with respect to what constitutes appropriate analyses for data collected within a group. If progress is to be made in understanding individual sport behavior, we cannot continue to examine individuals as if they exist in a social vacuum. Both the lack of group research and its impact on individual behavior are major reasons for sport psychologists

to increase their research efforts in this area to a far greater extent than has been attempted in the last 10 years.

The plea for more group-related research in sport may motivate some sport scientists to increase their research efforts. However, a simple increase in research volume will not advance our knowledge. What is needed is a simultaneous attempt to avoid the four global research pitfalls of the past while pursuing strategically chosen research directions.

Global Pitfalls

In sport group research, the scientist can function as an architect or as a laborer. The architect establishes a plan and works toward it, whereas the laborer makes single bricks not necessarily destined for a particular building. Avoiding global research pitfalls prevents the development of an undesirable knowledge base that is simply a collection of unrelated facts about the dynamics of sport groups. What are the four pitfalls to avoid?

The greatest general pitfall in the study of group dynamics in both sport and general social sciences areas is the failure to develop and use theory systematically. Both McGrath (1984) and Zander (1979) noted that group research has been highly fragmented with the collection of many "bricks" or data sets but no theory to systematically guide the collection, ordering, and interpretation of the results. Sport scientists must avoid this pitfall so that they do not perpetuate this problem. With so much atheoretical data collection, consistencies in group behavior are difficult to find. Attending to recent theoretical frameworks advanced by, for example, authors such as Carron (1988), Carron and Hausenblas (1998), or McGrath (1984) will guide research plans and reduce fragmentation of the knowledge base. Also, certain theories about specific phenomena within groups that were mentioned earlier may be useful in developing systematic research.

A second general pitfall for sport scientists is conducting "snapshot" research. This form of investigation, although offering a concise picture of a specific aspect of group life, fails to adequately capture the dynamic nature of groups as they change over time. Most group studies conducted in the sport context are of the snapshot variety, with specific games or seasonal time points as their focus. However, to understand the changing and reciprocal relationships among input and output variables, it will be necessary to conduct prospective, longitudinal studies. A few such attempts have been made in examining group cohesion (e.g., Carron & Ball, 1977; Dorsch, 1998; Paskevich, 1996; Williams & Hacker, 1982). Carron (1988) also described several categories of models concerning the relationships that may occur over time in the development of groups. Although these examples and suggestions exist, sport scientists have yet to take up the challenges they offer in research design. The snapshot design must be coupled with the "video" (longitudinal) approach in future research. It is gratifying to note that more of the latter type of study has been conducted recently.

The third global pitfall to avoid is reliance on a univariate approach in examining groups. The univariate approach often is characterized by simple, bivariate correlations between one independent and one dependent variable. A multivariate approach is required, which involves several independent predictors of one dependent variable or multiple dependent variables (e.g., multiple or multivariate multiple regression). This approach takes into account the complexity of group phenomena and acknowledges interrelationships among group variables that occur simultaneously. For example, Zaccaro et al. (1995) discussed the various interactive processes that occur concurrently within a group whose task demands require member interdependence. Numerous team functions such as offense, defense, coordination, communication, and motivation are hypothesized as contributing factors to the multivariable concept of collective efficacy. Paskevich (1996) examined Zaccaro et al.'s contentions and found that a multifaceted collective efficacy predicted task-related aspects of team cohesion as well as team performance outcome.

A major problem associated with the univariate approach is conducting antecedent-outcome research (e.g., cohesion–performance) while ignoring the group processes that lead to an outcome. A team may be cohesive and, as a result, perform well. However, did their cohesiveness promote the interaction that caused the team to do well? The bivariate correlation between cohesion and performance fails to yield further knowledge in this regard. A multivariate approach that offers hypotheses about process variables affected by cohesion (e.g., communication), which in turn affect performance, would be enlightening.

The fourth global pitfall to avoid is investigating teams alone as the focus of group physical activity research. Teams have unique rules,

properties, and physical structure that are not necessarily comparable to other types of physical activity groups. A variety of other groups in physical activity strongly influence how we exercise (e.g., fitness classes), how we rehabilitate (e.g., cardiac and athlete rehabilitation groups), how we learn motor activities (e.g., physical skill classes, music classes), and how sports are organized (e.g., sport governing bodies, coaching staff, club executive boards, volunteer groups). Furthermore, there is potential to examine group dynamics in physical activity across the life span because there are groups for everyone from the very young (e.g., play groups) to retired and older adults (e.g., master's clubs, fitness for the elderly). The types of groups that influence an individual's physical activity are numerous, complex, and unique. The study of teams alone leads to a narrow view of group dynamics in physical activity.

There are signs that the research is diversifying with respect to the type of group investigated. For example, in a special issue of the *Journal of Applied Sport Psychology*, the concept of team-building was presented. Carron and Spink (1997) provided several examples of the use of team-building strategies to develop cohesion and promote adherence in structured exercise classes for young adults.

In another example that focused on a different age group, Brawley, Rejeski, and Lutes (2000) reported a group-motivated intervention to facilitate the home-based exercise adherence of the elderly. Their intervention was based on principles of social cognitive theory and group dynamics. The group-motivated intervention encouraged the elderly to develop their own independent programs of exercise. The elderly pursued this program beyond a 3-month period of instructed, center-based exercise by steadily increasing their volume of exercise during a subsequent 3-month home-based period (6 months). Finally, these same elders persisted and increased their exercise frequency compared with both a group of elders who had received standard exercise instruction/lifestyle counseling and a control group of apparently healthy but sedentary elderly. The elderly who had received the group-motivated instruction had a much higher rate of exercise adherence than the other two groups, particularly during the months (i.e., months 6–9) where they were completely independent of any support or instruction. Their exercise frequency continued to increase whereas elderly in the other exercise treatment began to adhere less to their independent exercise while elderly in the control condition showed no change. The results have implications for the potential strength of group-motivated procedures in encouraging more enduring behavior change than other individually oriented approaches.

The suggestions detailed in this section are offered in an attempt to increase the research on physical activity groups in a strategic fashion by avoiding the global pitfalls mentioned. Carron (1988), Carron and Hausenblas (1998), Carron, Brawley, and Widmeyer (1998), and McGrath (1984) also offer numerous suggestions about future research directions to pursue in group dynamics.

FUTURE RESEARCH DIRECTIONS

A whole chapter could be devoted to discussing specific future directions. Instead, we suggest two approaches for future research that are intended to increase both the quantity and quality of research in sport group dynamics. The first approach is to move our research beyond description by attempting to answer related research questions of increasingly greater complexity. The second approach is a suggestion for categorizing the functions of sport groups, so that research is directed systematically at these functions. In the following section, the research that could be generated within each approach is discussed.

Moving Beyond Description

Although description is an important aspect of science, it unfortunately has become the main source of information in sport group dynamics. We must move beyond basic description to explanation. To provide a guide for future research in this area, a three-generation hierarchy of research questions is suggested (see Carron, 1988; Zanna & Fazio, 1982) as one approach.

The first-generation (and simplest) question is, Does a relationship exist between variables x and y? For example, does a relationship exist between cohesion and team performance? What are its strength, direction, and reliability? Although the knowledge obtained from investigating this type of question is useful and provokes other research questions, it is unknown whether this relationship occurs for all types of teams or for all types of conditions that might influence the variables studied.

Accordingly, the second-generation question encourages an examination of conditions moder-

ating the relationship: When (i.e., under which conditions) does x relate to y? For example, task cohesion might relate to performance in team sports but not in coactive sports. When these two generations of questions are answered, the boundaries of the phenomenon will be better known and can be placed within some potential theoretical framework (see Carron, 1988).

However, explanations for why these boundaries occur are still tentative unless the third-generation question is answered. Examples of third-generation research questions are, Why does variable x relate to y under some conditions but not others? What are the causes of these relationships? For example, task cohesion may influence team performance because team members perceive coordination interdependence as a requirement for success and as demanded by their task (e.g., basketball). Conversely, no great influence of cohesion on performance may be observed for coactive teams. These athletes may not perceive its necessity, and task completion does not require team member interaction (e.g., bowling). Only by considering the three generations of research questions can we understand the cohesion–performance relationship and make progress toward a theory. This approach to research can operate in tandem with the second approach, which concerns the investigation of group functions. The second approach of investigation of group functions requires us to expand the types of research we conduct with sport groups.

Expanding Existing Research

The sport group research conducted to date primarily has been concerned with cohesion and leadership and their influence on performance. A host of other issues require examination. For example, a considerable amount of group member participation occurs outside of the competitive event (i.e., in preparation for the event). Focusing only on the cohesion–performance relationship, for example, tells us nothing about what conditions moderate or cause the relationship. The impact of other factors such as member resources (e.g., abilities), group structure (e.g., size), processes (e.g., decision-making), and intergroup relationships (e.g., cooperation and conflict) require attention at the level of the group and the level of the individual. In addition to performance, outcomes such as adherence, satisfaction, group efficacy, conformity, group attributions, and motivation require examination.

Although numerous issues require attention, we do not wish to encourage an asystematic approach to their study. Doing so would simply perpetuate the fragmented knowledge base in sport group dynamics. An alternative approach would be to categorize sport groups in some way so that systematic research based on theory could be conducted. There are many ways to attempt this categorization. As one example, McGrath (1984) identified three broad categories of group functions. These functions concern groups as

- task performance systems,
- structures organizing social interaction, and
- mechanisms delivering social influence.

Carrying the example further, the research issues previously identified could be examined, as applicable, within the context of these group functions. Thus, hypotheses about and interpretations of a research issue would be stated relative to the group function. Examining a research issue with respect to a functional theme should lead to more systematic research and a less fragmented knowledge base. To illustrate the research questions associated with these functions, the following examples are provided.

If the team is considered as a task performance system, models such as Steiner's (1972) group productivity formula can be used for the multivariate prediction of team effectiveness as a function of relevant resources, effective coordination due to task cohesion, and increased/decreased motivation to pursue a common team outcome. Some early sport research has already focused on this function.

If the team functions as a means of organizing social interaction, how are team member roles and communication organized for a common understanding of task and social team goals among member athletes? Both the role structure and the communication process among athletes may be influenced by intrateam competition with varying effects on within-team interaction. A study of this organization could reveal whether team processes are effective or ineffective. As well, the degree of social interaction that is promoted or inhibited could provide clues about the eventual level and type of cohesiveness developed. Social satisfaction and motivation would be issues related to this function.

Finally, if the team functions as a powerful social influence over, for example, the efforts of members, do its normative rules bias their thinking (a possible negative effect; Carron, 1988)? The issues of conformity and group attributions obviously are related to this function. Does the degree of team unity influence members in the direction of either a realistic or a false sense of team confidence? The notion of group efficacy would be studied as part of this function.

McGrath's (1984) functions are not the only themes around which thinking about sport groups could be organized. The important point is that a theme or theory be used or tested when investigators attempt to expand the research in sport group dynamics.

The research opportunities in the dynamics of physical activity groups are challenging. Will future investigators attempt to meet the challenge? The worst answer to this question would be if we were forced simply to repeat our concerns in the next edition of this book. Just a few attempts by investigators to follow the suggestions made here would represent a major advancement in the study of group dynamics in physical activity.

REFERENCES

Bass, B.M. (1960). *Leadership, psychology, and organizational behavior*. New York: Harper.

Bird, A.M., Foster, C.D., & Maruyama, G. (1980). Convergent and incremental effects of cohesion on attributions for self and team. *Journal of Sport Psychology, 2*, 181–194.

Brawley, L.R. (1989, June). Theoretical background and intent. In L. Brawley (Chair), *Group size in physical activity: Psychological and behavioral impacts*. Symposium conducted at the meeting of the North American Society of the Psychology of Sport and Physical Activity, Kent, OH.

Brawley, L.R., Carron, A.V., & Widmeyer, W.N. (1987). Assessing the cohesion of teams: Validity of the Group Environment Questionnaire. *Journal of Sport Psychology, 9*, 275–294.

Brawley, L.R., Carron, A.V., & Widmeyer, W.N. (1988). Exploring the relationship between cohesion and resistance to disruption. *Journal of Sport & Exercise Psychology, 10*, 199–213.

Brawley, L.R., Rejeski, W.J., & Lutes, L. (2000). A group-mediated cognitive-behavioral intervention for increasing adherence to physical activity in older adults. *Journal of Applied Biobehavioral Research, 5*, 47–65.

Brown, R. (1988). *Group processes: Dynamics within and between groups*. Oxford, UK: Blackwell.

Carron, A.V. (1982). Cohesiveness in sport groups: Interpretations and considerations. *Journal of Sport Psychology, 4*, 123–128.

Carron, A.V. (1988). *Group dynamics in sport*. London, ON: Spodym.

Carron, A.V., & Ball, J.R. (1977). Cause-effect characteristics of cohesiveness and participation in motivation intercollegiate hockey. *International Review of Sport Sociology, 12,* 49–60.

Carron, A.V., & Bennett, B.B. (1977). Compatibility in the coach-athlete dyad. *Research Quarterly, 48,* 671–679.

Carron, A.V., Brawley, L.R., & Widmeyer, W.N. (1990). The impact of group size in an exercise setting. *Journal of Sport & Exercise Psychology, 12,* 376–387.

Carron, A.V., Brawley, L.R., & Widmeyer, W.N. (1998). The measurement of cohesiveness in sport groups. In J.L. Duda (Ed.), *Advances in sport and exercise psychology measurement* (pp. 213–226). Morgantown, WV: Fitness Information Technology.

Carron, A.V., & Chelladurai, P. (1981). Cohesion as a factor in sport performance. *International Review of Sport Sociology, 16,* 21–41.

Carron, A.V., & Hausenblas, H.A. (1998). *Group dynamics in sport* (2nd ed.). Morgantown, WV: Fitness Information Technology.

Carron, A.V., & Prapavessis, H. (1997). Self-presentation and group influence. *Small Group Research, 28,* 500–516.

Carron, A.V., & Spink, K.S. (1995). The group size-cohesion relationship in minimal groups. *Small Group Research, 26,* 86–105.

Carron, A.V., Widmeyer, W.N., & Brawley, L.R. (1985). The development of an instrument to assess cohesion in sport teams: The Group Environment Questionnaire. *Journal of Sport Psychology, 7,* 244–266.

Carron, A.V., Widmeyer, W.N., & Brawley, L.R. (1988). Group cohesion and individual adherence to physical activity. *Journal of Sport & Exercise Psychology, 10,* 127–138.

Cartwright, D., & Zander, A. (1968). *Group dynamics: Research and theory.* New York: Harper & Row.

Chelladurai, P. (1978). *A contingency model of leadership in athletics.* Unpublished doctoral dissertation, University of Waterloo, Waterloo, ON.

Cooper, R., & Payne, R. (1967). *Personality orientations and performance in football teams: Leaders and subordinates' orientations related to team success* (Report No. 1). Liverpool, UK: Organizational Psychology Group.

Cooper, R., & Payne, R. (1972). Personality orientations and performance in soccer teams. *British Journal of Social and Clinical Psychology, 11,* 2–9.

Davis, J. (1969). *Group performance.* Reading, MA: Addison-Wesley.

Dorsch, K. (1998). *Examining aggressive behaviour from a group perspective.* Unpublished doctoral dissertation, University of Waterloo, Waterloo, ON.

Dorsch, K.D., Widmeyer, W.N., Paskevich, D.M., & Brawley, L.R. (1995). Collective efficacy: Its measurement and relationship to cohesion in ice hockey [Abstract]. *Journal of Applied Sport Psychology, 7,* S56.

Eitzen, D.S. (1975). Group structure and group performance. In D.M. Landers, D.V. Harris, & R.W. Christina (Eds.), *Psychology of sport and motor behavior* (pp. 41–46). University Park: College of Health, Physical Education, and Recreation, Pennsylvania State University.

Fiedler, F.E. (1967). *A theory of leadership effectiveness.* New York: McGraw-Hill.

Forsyth, D.R. (1983). *An introduction to group dynamics.* Belmont, CA: Wadsworth.

Gill, D.L. (1979). The prediction of group motor performance from individual member ability. *Journal of Sport Psychology, 11,* 113–122.

Gill, D.L. (1986). *Psychological dynamics of sport.* Champaign, IL: Human Kinetics.

Gill, D.L. (1988). Cohesion and performance in sport groups. *Exercise and Sport Sciences Reviews, 5.*

Gossett, D., & Widmeyer, W.N. (1978, May). *Improving cohesion's prediction of performance outcome in sport.* Paper presented at the meeting of the North American Society for the Psychology of Sport and Physical Activity, Tallahassee, FL.

Granito, V.J., & Rainey, D.W. (1988). Differences in cohesion between high school and college football teams and starters and nonstarters. *Perceptual and Motor Skills, 66,* 471–477.

Grusky, O. (1963). The effects of formal structure on managerial recruitment: A study of baseball organization. *Sociometry, 26,* 345–353.

Gruber, J.J., & Gray, G.R. (1981). Factor patterns of variables influencing cohesiveness at various levels of basketball competition. *Research Quarterly for Exercise and Sport, 52,* 19–30.

Gruber, J.J., & Gray, G.R. (1982). Responses to forces influencing cohesion as a function of player status and level of male varsity basketball competition. *Research Quarterly for Exercise and Sport, 53,* 27–36.

Hardy, C.J. (1989, June). Social loafing: Economizing individual effort during team performance. In L.R. Brawley (Chair), *Group size in physical activity: Psychological and behavioral impacts.* Symposium conducted at the meeting of the North American Society for the Psychology of Sport and Physical Activity, Kent, OH.

Harkins, S.G., Latané, B., & Williams, K. (1980). Social loafing: Allocating effort or taking it easy? *Journal of Experimental Social Psychology, 16,* 457–465.

Ingham, A.G., Levinger, G., Graves, J., & Peckham, V. (1974). The Ringelmann Effect: Studies of group size and group performance. *Journal of Experimental Social Psychology, 10,* 371–384.

Jones, M.B. (1974). Regressing group on individual effectiveness. *Organizational Behavior and Human Performance, 11,* 426–451.

Karau, S.J., & Williams, K.D. (1993). Social loafing: A meta-analytic review and theoretical integration. *Journal of Personality and Social Psychology, 65,* 681–706.

Kenny, D.A., & LaVoie, L. (1985). Separating individual and group effects. *Journal of Personality and Social Psychology, 48,* 339–348.

Klein, M., & Christiansen, G. (1969). Group composition, group structure and group effectiveness of basketball teams. In J.W. Loy & G.S. Kenyon (Eds.), *Sport, culture, and society* (pp. 397–408). New York: Macmillan.

Kozub, S.A. (1993). *Exploring the relationships among coaching behavior, team cohesion, and player leadership.* Unpublished doctoral dissertation, University of Houston, TX.

Landers, D.M., Boutcher, S.H., & Wang, M.Q. (1986). The history and status of sport psychology: 1979–1985. *Journal of Sport Psychology, 8,* 149–163.

Latané, B., Williams, K., & Harkins, S.J. (1979). Many hands make light the work: The cause and consequences of social loafing. *Journal of Experimental Social Psychology, 37,* 822–832.

Lee, H.K., Kim, B.H., & Lim, B.J. (1993). The influence of structural characteristics on team success in sport groups. *Korean Journal of Sport Science, 5,* 138–154.

Lewin, K. (1943). Forces behind food habits and methods of change. *Bulletin of the National Research Council, 108,* 35–65.

Loy, J.W., McPherson, B.D., & Kenyon, G. (1978). *Sport and social systems: A guide to the analysis, problems, and literature.* Reading, MA: Addison-Wesley.

Martens, R. (1970). Influence of participation motivation on success and satisfaction in team performance. *Research Quarterly, 41,* 510–518.

Martens, R., Burton, D., Vealey, R.S., Bump, L.A., & Smith, D.E. (1990). The Competitive State Anxiety Inventory-2 (CSAI-2). In R. Martens, R.S. Vealey, & D. Burton, *Competitive anxiety in sport* (pp. 117–190). Champaign, IL: Human Kinetics.

McGrath, J.E. (1984). *Groups: Interaction and performance.* Englewood Cliffs, NJ: Prentice Hall.

McKnight, P., Williams, J.M., & Widmeyer, W.N. (1991, October). *The effects of cohesion and identifiability on reducing the likelihood of social loafing.* Paper presented at the Association for the Advancement of Applied Sport Psychology Annual Conference, Savannah, GA.

Mikalachki, A. (1969). *Group cohesion reconsidered.* London: School of Business Administration, University of Western Ontario.

Mills, T.M. (1984). *The sociology of small groups* (2nd ed.). Englewood Cliffs, NJ: Prentice Hall.

Moede, W. (1927). Die Richt linien der Leistungs-Psychologie. *Industrielle Psychotechnik, 4,* 193–207.

Moreland, R.L., & Levine, J.M. (1988). Group dynamics over time: Development and socialization in small groups. In J.E. McGrath (Ed.), *The social psychology of time: New perspectives* (pp. 151–181). Newbury Park, CA: Sage.

Mudrack, P.E. (1989). Defining group cohesiveness: A legacy of confusion? *Small Group Behavior, 20,* 37–49.

Mullen, B., & Copper, C. (1994). The relation between group cohesiveness and performance: An integration. *Psychological Bulletin, 115,* 210–227.

Naylor, K., & Brawley, L.R. (1992, October). *Social loafing: Perceptions and implications.* Paper presented at the Joint Meeting of the Canadian Association of Sport Sciences and the Canadian Psychomotor learning and Sport Psychology Association Conference, Saskatoon, SK.

Paskevich, D.M. (1995). *Conceptual and measurement factors of collective efficacy in its relationship to cohesion and performance outcome.* Unpublished doctoral dissertation, University of Waterloo, Waterloo, ON.

Paskevich, D.M., Brawley, L.R., Dorsch, L.R., & Widmeyer, W.N. (1995). Implications of individual and group level analyses applied to the study of collective efficacy and cohesion [Abstract]. *Journal of Applied Sport Psychology, 7*(Suppl.), S95.

Prapavessis, H., & Carron, A.V. (1996). The effect of group cohesion on competitive state anxiety. *Journal of Sport & Exercise Psychology, 18,* 64–74.

Prapavessis, H., & Carron, A.V. (1997). Cohesion and work output. *Small Group Research, 28,* 294–301.

Roberts, J., & Kundrat, D. (1978). Variation in expressive balance and competence for sports car rally teams. *Urban Life, 7,* 231–251, 276–280.

Roberts, J., Meeker, Q., & Aller, J. (1972). Action style and management game performance: An explanatory consideration. *Naval War College Review, 24,* 65–81.

Schafer, W. (1966, October). *The social structure of sport groups.* Paper presented at the First International Symposium on the Sociology of Sport, Köln, West Germany.

Schlenker, B.R., & Miller, R.S. (1977a). Egocentricism in groups: Self-serving bias or logical information processing. *Journal of Personality and Social Psychology, 35,* 755–764.

Schutz, W.C. (1958). *FIRO: A three-dimensional theory of interpersonal behavior.* New York: Holt, Rinehart, & Winston.

Shaw, M.E. (1981). *Group dynamics: The psychology of small group behavior* (3rd ed.). New York: McGraw-Hill.

Shaw, M.E., & Costanzo, P.R. (1982). *Theories of social psychology* (2nd ed.). New York: McGraw-Hill.

Sherif, M., & Sherif, C.W. (1956). *An outline of social psychology* (rev. ed.). New York: Harper & Row.

Sherif, M., & Sherif, C.W. (1969). *Social psychology* (rev. ed.) New York: Harper & Row.

Spense, E. (1980). *The relative contributions of ability, cohesion, and participation motivation to team performance outcome in women's intramural basketball.* Unpublished manuscript, University of Waterloo, Department of Kinesiology, Waterloo, ON.

Spink, K.S., & Carron, A.V. (1992). Group cohesion and adherence in exercise classes. *Journal of Sport & Exercise Psychology, 14,* 78–86.

Spink, K.S., & Carron, A.V. (1994). Group cohesion effects in exercise groups. *Small Group Research, 25,* 26–42.

Steiner, I.D. (1972). *Group process and productivity.* New York: Academic Press.

Sutton-Smith, B., & Roberts, J. (1964). Rubrics of competitive behavior. *Journal of Genetic Psychology, 105,* 13–37.

Thompson, S.A., & Albinson, J. (1991, October). *An investigation of factors affecting the development of cohesion among intercollegiate rowers.* Paper presented at the Canadian Psychomotor Learning and Sport Psychology conference, London, ON.

Van Bergen, A., & Koekebakker, J. (1959). "Group cohesiveness" in laboratory experiments. *Acta Psychologica, 16,* 81–98.

Westre, K.R., & Weiss, M.R. (1991). The relationship between perceived coaching behaviors and group cohesion in high school football teams. *Sport Psychologist, 5,* 41–54.

Widmeyer, W.N. (1989, June). The study of group size in sport. In L. Brawley (Chair), *Group size in physical activity: Psychological and behavioral impacts.* Symposium conducted at the meeting of the North American Society for the Psychology of Sport and Physical Activity, Kent, OH.

Widmeyer, W.N., Brawley, L.R., & Carron, A.V. (1985). *The measurement of cohesion in sport teams: The Group*

Environment Questionnaire. London, ON: Sports Dynamics.

Widmeyer, W.N., Brawley, L.R., & Carron, A.V. (1990). The effects of group size in sport. *Journal of Sport & Exercise Psychology, 12,* 177–190.

Widmeyer, W.N., & Loy, J.W. (1989). Dynamic duos: An analysis of the relationship between group composition and group performance in women's doubles tennis. In R. Bolton (Ed.), *Studies in honor of J.M. Roberts* (pp. 77–97). New Haven, CT: HRAF.

Widmeyer, W.N., Loy, J.M., & Roberts, J. (1980). The relative contribution of action styles and ability to the performance outcomes of doubles tennis teams. In C. Nadeau, W. Halliwell, K. Newell, & C. Roberts (Eds.), *Psychology of motor behavior and sport—1979* (pp. 209–218). Champaign, IL: Human Kinetics.

Widmeyer, W.N., & Martens, R. (1978). When cohesion predicts performance outcome in sport. *Research Quarterly, 49,* 372–380.

Williams, J.M., & Hacker, C. (1982). Causal relationships among cohesion, satisfaction, and performance in women's intercollegiate field hockey teams. *Journal of Sport Psychology, 4,* 324–337.

Yukelson, D., Weinberg, R., & Jackson, A. (1984). A multidimensional group cohesion instrument for intercollegiate basketball. *Journal of Sport Psychology, 6,* 103–117.

Zaccaro, S.J., Blair, V., Peterson, C., & Zazanis, M. (1995). Collective efficacy. In J. Maddux (1995), *Self-efficacy, adaptation, and adjustment* (pp. 305–328). New York: Plenum Press.

Zander, A. (1971). *Motives and goals in groups.* New York: Academic Press.

Zander, A. (1979). The psychology of group processes. *Annual Review of Psychology, 30,* 417–451.

Zanna, M.P., & Fazio, R.H. (1982). The attitude-behavior relation: Moving toward a third generation of research. In M.P. Zanna, E.T. Higgins, & C.P. Herman (Eds.), *Consistency in social behavior: The Ontario symposium* (Vol. 2, pp. 283–301). Hillsdale, NJ: Erlbaum.

CHAPTER 10

Coaching Effectiveness in the Sport Domain

Thelma S. Horn

Research on coaching effectiveness has been conducted under the general assumption that coaches greatly influence not only the performance and behavior of their athletes but also the athletes' psychological and emotional well-being. In this research context, leadership has been rather generally conceived of as "the behavioral process of influencing individuals and groups toward set goals" (Barrow, 1977, p. 232). Obviously, this is a broad definition that encompasses many dimensions of coaches' leadership behavior, including the processes they use to make decisions, the types of learning activities they use in practice situations, the type and frequency of feedback they give in response to athletes' performances, the techniques they use to motivate individual athletes, and the type of relationships they establish with athletes.

Most of the research that has been conducted on coaching effectiveness within the last three decades has been motivated by a desire to identify the most effective coaching characteristics, leadership styles, or behavioral patterns. Under this research approach, coaching effectiveness typically is operationalized in terms of outcome scores or measures. That is, an effective coaching personality, leadership style, or set of behaviors is defined as that which results in either successful performance outcomes (measured in terms of either win–loss percentages or degree of self-

perceived performance abilities) or positive psychological responses on the part of the athletes (e.g., high perceived ability, high self-esteem, an intrinsic motivational orientation, high levels of sport enjoyment). Because this text as a whole focuses on psychological issues as they are related to sport, the review and analysis of the literature in this chapter are limited primarily to studies that have examined the impact of coaches' behavior on the psychosocial growth and development of athletes. Thus, I do not review the research that has examined the relationship between coaches' behavior and athletes' sport performance and skill learning. Interested readers should examine the literature in sport pedagogy and motor learning.

Despite the number of studies over the last two decades that have examined the effects of coaches' behavior on athletes' psychosocial responses, much remains to be done. Therefore, the purposes of this chapter are to review the available research and theory pertaining to coaching effectiveness in sport settings and provide specific directions for future research in this area.

The first section of this chapter discusses the various conceptual approaches that researchers have used to identify the correlates of coaching effectiveness, and the section ends by specifying a composite working model that can be used not only to review and critique the existing research on coaching effectiveness but also to identify future research directions. The second section of this chapter reviews the current research on coaching effectiveness, and the third section discusses the gaps in our knowledge base and provides recommendations for future research on coaching effectiveness.

CONCEPTUAL APPROACHES TO COACHING EFFECTIVENESS

Although the various research studies conducted to examine coaching effectiveness have shared a common goal (i.e., the identification of effective coaching characteristics, behaviors, and leadership styles), the studies themselves have varied considerably in the methodologies used to measure coaching behavior and in the conceptual basis underlying the study of coaching effectiveness. In this section, I briefly review the various conceptual approaches to coaching or leadership effectiveness.

Early Approaches to Leadership Effectiveness

Many of the initial research studies on coaching effectiveness were linked to, or arose out of, the research and theory on leadership effectiveness in nonsport settings (e.g., in industrial and educational contexts). The early research in these areas used either a trait or a behavioral approach to study leadership effectiveness. Under these conceptual models, effective leadership behavior was assumed to be a function either of the leader's personality or her or his dominant behavior. The typical research design consisted of assessing various aspects of leaders' personalities or behaviors and attempting to identify the particular traits or behaviors that would discriminate successful from unsuccessful leaders. These traits or behaviors were then identified as "effective leadership factors." Although these research approaches were much more commonly used to study effective leadership in industrial, educational, and other formal organizational contexts, a few researchers used the trait or the behavioral approach to study effective leadership in sport. Penman, Hastad, and Cords (1974), for example, measured the degree of authoritarianism in interscholastic male football and basketball head coaches and then tested the degree of correlation between that particular personality characteristic and coaching success.

Penman et al. reported that more successful coaches (i.e., those with highest win–loss percentages) were more authoritarian than less successful coaches. Subsequent sport researchers examined similar aspects of a coach's personality or behavior (e.g., autocratic vs. democratic decision styles, creativity) in an attempt to identify the most effective leadership traits or behaviors (e.g., Hendry, 1969; Lenk, 1977; Pratt & Eitzen, 1989).

Disillusionment arose with the rather simplistic trait and behavioral approaches to the study of leadership effectiveness in nonsport settings, at least partly because this type of research failed to identify a particular set of traits or behaviors that consistently discriminated between effective and noneffective leaders. That is, the set of traits or behaviors identified as effective in one context did not generalize to other contexts. In response to this lack of generalizability, a variety of situationally based theories were proposed. These leadership theories included House's path-goal theory (House, 1971; House & Dessler, 1974), Hersey and Blanchard's (1972) life-cycle theory, and Fiedler's (1967) contingency theory. Although these theoretical models differed from each other considerably in content, all were constructed on the premise that leadership effectiveness cannot be determined solely by assessing the leader's traits or behaviors. Rather, leadership effectiveness is assumed to be a function of both situational and individual factors. More specifically, these situational theories clearly specified that the characteristics and behaviors of the leader and the group members will interact with other aspects of the situation (e.g., task type, work environment) to determine the type of leadership behaviors that will be most effective in attaining the organizational goals. Under this research approach, leadership effectiveness is conceived to be context- or situation-specific. That is, the particular traits, decision styles, and behaviors that are characteristic of an effective leader will vary as a function of factors within the environment.

Although research conducted to test these theories in educational and industrial settings resulted in some support for the situational approach to leadership effectiveness, efforts to apply these same theories to the sport context resulted in minimal success (e.g., Bird, 1977; Chelladurai, 1984; Chelladurai & Carron, 1983; Terry, 1984; Terry & Howe, 1984; VosStrache, 1979). As some writers (e.g., Chelladurai & Carron, 1978; Terry & Howe, 1984) have suggested, sport teams may possess certain unique characteristics that make the general leadership theories inapplicable.

Sport-Oriented Approaches to Leadership Effectiveness

In response to this lack of fit, Chelladurai (1978, 1990, 1993) proposed a theory of leadership effectiveness that was specific to the sport domain. Consistent with the general leadership theories on which his model was based, Chelladurai also posited that leadership effectiveness in the sport domain will be contingent on both situational factors and the characteristics of the group members (i.e., the athletes). Thus, effective leadership behavior can and will vary across specific contexts as the characteristics of the athletes and as the dictates of the situation change.

Chelladurai (1978, 1990, 1993) constructed his Multidimensional Model of Leadership to provide a framework for specifying or identifying effective leadership behavior in specific sport situations. Specifically, Chelladurai proposed that leadership effectiveness can be measured multidimensionally in terms of performance outcomes and member satisfaction. The particular leadership behaviors that will produce such desired outcomes are a function of three interacting aspects of leader behavior: the actual behavior exhibited by the coach/leader, the type of leader behavior preferred by the athletes, and the type of leader behavior appropriate to or required in that situational context. Each construct is driven, in turn, by corresponding antecedent factors or conditions. Specifically, the type of leader behaviors that the athletes prefer their coaches to exhibit will be determined primarily by specific characteristics of the athletes themselves (e.g., age, gender, skill level, psychological characteristics) and by factors within the situation (e.g., organizational expectations, social norms, cultural values). In addition, the actual behavior exhibited by a coach or leader will be a direct function of her or his own personal characteristics (e.g., gender, age, years of experience, psychological characteristics), the situational requirements (e.g., sport competitive level), and individual athletes' preferences. Finally, the behaviors required by the situation will be a function of certain aspects or characteristics of the particular sport situation (e.g., type of sport, program structure, organizational goals, sociocultural environment) and by the characteristics of the team members.

To put the model as a whole into perspective, Chelladurai (1978, 1990, 1993) hypothesized that the positive outcomes of group performance and member (i.e., athlete) satisfaction can be obtained if there is congruence between the three aspects of leader behavior. That is, if the coach exhibits the leadership behaviors that are dictated for the particular situation and that are consistent with members' preferences or desires, then optimal performance and member satisfaction will be achieved. In addition, Chelladurai (1993) recently included a feedback loop, which suggests that a coach's actual behavior may be influenced by his or her athletes' level of satisfaction and performance. Thus, there is a reciprocal relationship between the consequences of coaches' behavior and the type of behaviors they actually exhibit in practice and game contexts.

From a somewhat different perspective, Smoll and Smith (1989) proposed a theoretical model of leadership behavior that emphasizes relationships among situational, cognitive, behavioral, and individual difference variables. Similar to Chelladurai (1978, 1990, 1993), Smoll and Smith incorporated a situational approach to leadership behavior in their argument that the most effective coaching behaviors will vary as a function of situational factors within the athletic context (e.g., nature of the sport, level of competition). However, Smoll and Smith also argued that "a truly comprehensive model of leadership requires that consideration be given not only to situational factors and overt behaviors, but also the cognitive processes and individual difference variables which mediate relationships between antecedents, leader behaviors, and outcomes" (p. 1532). Thus, Smoll and Smith's cognitive–mediational model proposes that the effects of coaches' behaviors on their athletes are mediated not only by situational factors but also by the meaning that the athletes attribute to those coaching behaviors.

As indicated in Smoll and Smith's (1989) cognitive–mediational model, coaches' behavior is influenced by, or is a function of, their own personal characteristics (e.g., coaching goals or motives, behavioral intentions) as well as situational factors (nature of the sport, level of competition). Additionally, the actual behaviors that the coach exhibits in practices and games are interpreted by players in individualized ways. That is, players' interpretations and evaluation of coaches' behaviors are influenced by, or are a function of, their own personal characteristics (e.g., age, gender, competitive trait anxiety), and, again, situational factors (e.g., nature of the sport, level of competition).

In developing their models of leadership effectiveness in the sport domain, Chelladurai (1978, 1990, 1993) and Smoll and Smith (1989) incorporated research and theory from other areas within the field of psychology (e.g., social psychology, cognitive psychology, organizational psychology, educational psychology). Thus, their theoretical models, although rooted in and developed specifically for the sport domain, also were heavily influenced by research and theory on leadership effectiveness in the general psychology field. Given recent advances in the developmental and social cognitive literatures describing the processes by which children's and adolescents' self-perceptions, social perceptions, and motivational orientations are formed (see chapters 4, 5, and 11), new perspectives regarding the influence that coaches may exert on their athletes' psychosocial and emotional development can now be obtained. Specifically, we may need to incorporate other relevant theoretical perspectives, such as those listed in table 10.1, into our investigations of coaching effectiveness. Such perspectives may be combined with components of the existing models on sport leadership effectiveness (e.g., Chelladurai's and Smoll and Smith's models) to create a more comprehensive working model of coaching effectiveness (figure 10.1).

A Working Model of Coaching Effectiveness

Although the working model depicted in figure 10.1 initially may appear somewhat complex, it can be summarized in three major points. First, consistent with both Chelladurai's (1978, 1990, 1993) and Smoll and Smith's (1989) models of leadership effectiveness, the current working model emphasizes that coaches' behavior in athletic contexts (e.g., games, practices) does not occur within a vacuum. Rather, identifiable antecedent factors lead up to, or explain, the types of behaviors coaches will exhibit in sport settings. These antecedent factors are illustrated in the left side of the model (boxes 1–5). Similar to Chelladurai's and Smoll and Smith's models, such factors as the sociocultural context (box 1), the organizational climate (box 2), and the coach's own personal characteristics (box 3) can combine to determine the type of behaviors the coach will exhibit (box 5). However, based on research and theory in the

Table 10.1
Relevant Theoretical Perspectives That May Inform Our Research on Coaching Effectiveness

Theory/model	References
Achievement goal theories	Ames (1984, 1992a, 1992b) Dweck (1986, 1999) Nicholls (1984, 1989)
Attribution theory	Weiner (1986, 1992)
Competence motivation theory	Harter (1978, 1981) White (1959)
Expectancy-value model	Eccles-Parsons et al. (1983) Eccles & Harold (1991)
Self-determination theory	Deci & Ryan (1985, 1991) Deci, Vallerand, Pelletier, & Ryan (1991)
Self-efficacy theory	Bandura (1977, 1986)
Sport commitment model	Scanlan, Carpenter, Schmidt, Simons, & Keeler (1993)

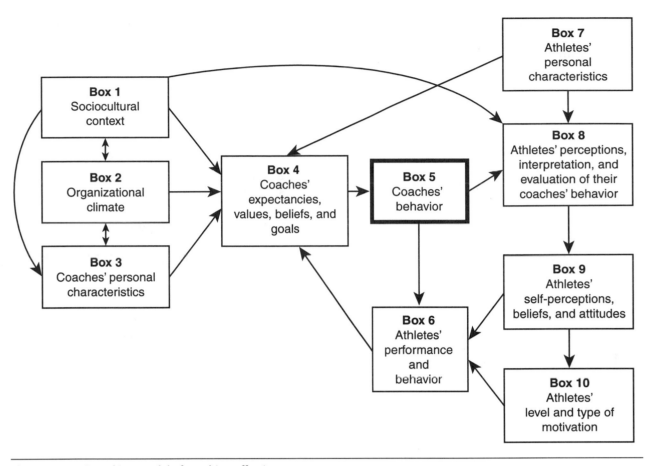

Figure 10.1 A working model of coaching effectiveness.

social cognitive literature (see table 10.1), this working model also proposes that the effects of these three factors (boxes 1–3) on a coach's behavior (box 5) may be mediated, at least in part, through the coach's expectancies, values, beliefs, and goals (box 4).

The second major point with regard to the working model is that the coach's behavior in practices and games affects athletes' performance and behavior (i.e., the hypothesized link between boxes 5 and 6) directly as well as indirectly. This indirect effect is illustrated in the right side of the model (boxes 5 and 7–10). Specifically, consistent with Smoll and Smith's (1989) theoretical model, the current working model also specifies that the indirect effects of a coach's behavior on athletes' performance and behavior are mediated by the meaning the athletes attach to the coach's behavior. That is, this model proposes that athletes may perceive or interpret the coach's behavior in very individualized ways. These individualized perceptions of the coach's behavior affect the athletes' self-perceptions, beliefs, and attitudes (e.g., their

self-confidence, perceptions of competence, self-esteem, and attributional beliefs). In turn, such self-perceptions, beliefs, and attitudes affect athletes' motivation (box 10) as well as their performance and behavior (box 6).

The third point regarding this working model is that, similar to the models of Chelladurai (1978, 1990, 1993) and Smoll and Smith (1989), it clearly specifies that the effectiveness of different types of coaching behaviors will be mediated by both situational and individual difference variables. Specifically, the direct link between a coach's behavior and athletes' performance and behavior is mediated by a variety of sport contextual variables (e.g., competitive level, type of sport) and by a variety of athlete variables (e.g., age, skill level). Similarly, athletes' perceptions and interpretations of their coach's behavior are mediated, or influenced, by their own personal characteristics (e.g., age, gender, psychological traits, and dispositions) and by the sociocultural context. Thus, as these aspects of the working model indicate, we can no longer assume that one set of coaching behaviors will be effective for all athletes and in all sport situations; rather, effective coaching behaviors will vary as a function of the athlete and the sport context.

As noted in the introduction to this chapter, the working model of coaching effectiveness (as diagrammed in figure 10.1) can be used to review and critique the current research on coaching effectiveness but also to identify directions for future research. In the next section, I review the existing research on coaching effectiveness, using the working model as a framework.

EMPIRICAL RESEARCH ON COACHING EFFECTIVENESS

As illustrated in figure 10.1, the cornerstone of the working model on coaching effectiveness is the box labeled "coaches' behavior" (box 5). The primary assumption underlying the research on coaching effectiveness is that a coach's behavior has the capacity to significantly affect athletes' performance as well as their psychological or emotional well-being. This influence can, of course, be positive or negative. This review of the research begins with a discussion of the construct of coaches' behavior.

Coaches' Behavior (Box 5)

Although the term *coaches' behavior* implies a plethora of actions, much of the research in the coaching effectiveness area (at least in regard to the effects of coaching behavior on athletes' psychosocial growth and development) has been limited to an examination of only two dimensions of coaches' behavior: their leadership style and the type of feedback they give to athletes in response to performance successes and failures. This limitation in regard to the way in which coaches' behavior has been conceptualized probably can be attributed to measurement issues. At this point, the majority of the instrumentation that has been developed and tested for reliability and validity has been in one of these two behavioral areas. In the following sections, these two types of instruments are reviewed (see also table 10.2 for a list of these instruments along with relevant references).

Table 10.2
Instrumentation Commonly Used to Assess Coaches' Behavior

Instrument	References
Leadership Scale for Sports (LSS)	Chelladurai (1993) Chelladurai & Riemer (1998) Chelladurai & Saleh (1978, 1980)
Decision-style questionnaires	Chelladurai & Arnott (1985) Chelladurai & Quek (1991) Chelladurai et al. (1989) Gordon (1986)
Perceptions of coaches' interpersonal style	Deci et al. (1981) Pelletier & Vallerand (1985) Vallerand & Pelletier (1985)
Perceived Motivational Climate in Sport Questionnaire-2 (PMCSQ-2)	Duda & Whitehead (1998) Newton & Duda (1993) Seifriz et al. (1992) Walling et al. (1993)
Coaching Behavior Assessment System (CBAS)	Chelladurai & Riemer (1998) Smith et al. (1977) Smith et al. (1978) Smoll et al. (1978)

Coaches' Leadership Style

The most often used instrument to measure coaches' leadership style is the Leadership Scale for Sports (LSS). This instrument was developed by Chelladurai and Saleh (1978, 1980) to measure a broad spectrum of leadership behaviors. The LSS consists of five subscales: two that measure the coach's decision-making style (Democratic and Autocratic), two that measure the coach's motivational tendencies (Social Support and Positive Feedback), and one that measures the coach's instructional behavior (Training and Instruction). Coaches who score high on the Training and Instruction factor exhibit high frequencies of behaviors oriented toward improving the performance of their athletes. These behaviors include (a) emphasizing and facilitating hard and strenuous training; (b) instructing athletes in skills, techniques, and tactics; (c) clarifying the working relationships among team members; and (d) structuring and coordinating the performance activities of the team. Items on the two decision-making style factors describe a coach who allows athletes to participate in decisions about group goals, practice methods, and game tactics and strategies (Democratic Style) and one who is aloof from her or his players and who stresses her or his authority in dealing with them (Autocratic Style). High scores on the Positive Feedback factor describe a coach who consistently responds to good performance by athletes with praise or other rewarding behavior. Finally, items on the Social Support factor measure a coach's tendency to exhibit a concern for individual athletes and to establish a warm, interpersonal relationship with group members. In contrast to the Positive Feedback factor, the behaviors described by the Social Support factor are provided to individual athletes independent of their performance and typically extend outside of the athletic context. Positive Feedback, in turn, is contingent on the athletes' performance and is limited to the athletic context.

The total LSS instrument contains 40 items, each of which is scored on a 5-point scale. Because the LSS was developed specifically to test the tenets of Chelladurai's (1978, 1990, 1993) theoretical model of leadership effectiveness, which specifies the need to measure both the actual leadership behaviors exhibited by a coach as well as the leadership behaviors preferred by athletes, the LSS can be administered in two versions. To measure perceived (actual) coaching behaviors, individual athletes respond to items prefaced with the words, "My coach . . ." (e.g., "My coach expresses appreciation when an athlete performs well"). To measure preferred coaching behaviors, individual items are prefaced with the phrase, "I prefer my coach to . . ." (e.g., "I prefer my coach to ask for the opinion of the athletes on important coaching matters"). In addition, the LSS has been modified to assess coaches' perceptions of their own behavior.

Since its inception, the LSS has been subjected to a number of statistical and methodological procedures to assess its psychometric properties (see concise and complete summary of this work by Chelladurai, 1993, and Chelladurai and Riemer, 1998). In general, these procedures support the reliability and validity of the LSS. However, Chelladurai (1993) and Chelladurai and Riemer (1998) noted some concerns with regard to some of the subscales and made suggestions for future psychometric testing and instrument revision.

As discussed earlier, the LSS provides a general measure of leadership style and thus encompasses a fairly wide range of leadership behaviors. A second type of instrument also has been used with some regularity in the sport leadership research to measure a more specific aspect of the coach's leadership behavior. This type of instrument, typically identified as a decision-style questionnaire, provides a measure of the coach's decision-making style. At least three different forms of the decision-style questionnaire have been developed and used within the past 15 years (Chelladurai & Arnott, 1985; Chelladurai, Haggerty, & Baxter, 1989; Chelladurai & Quek, 1991; Gordon, 1986). These questionnaires were based primarily on a model for decision-making in the athletic domain that was proposed by Chelladurai and Haggerty (1978). This model, identified as the Normative Model of Decision Styles in Coaching, was based in part on Vroom and Yelton's (1973) comprehensive work on leadership and decision-making. Consistent with Vroom and Yelton's theories, Chelladurai and Haggerty proposed that the particular decision-making style used by a coach in any situation can vary on a continuum in which the points are defined in terms of the amount of participation that group members (i.e., athletes) are allowed to have in the decision-making process. The continuum can range from an autocratic decision-making style, where the coach alone makes the decision, to a delegative style, in which the coach delegates the decision to be made by one or more group members (i.e., athletes). Additional points between the two ends can represent a consultative decision-making style, in which the coach consults with one or more team members and then makes the decision, and a participative style, in which the coach and one or more team members jointly make the decision.

Chelladurai and Haggerty (1978) further proposed that the effectiveness of any particular decision-making style can be predicted by assessing certain situational variables. These situational variables include (a) the degree of quality inherent in the problem situation (i.e., how crucial is the decision), (b) the amount of information relevant to the problem solution that is available to the coach (i.e., does the coach possess all relevant information), (c) the complexity of the problem (i.e., the number of factors and their interrelationship), (d) the degree of integration or cohesiveness among group members, (e) the presence or absence of time restrictions in regard to the decision-making process, (f) the degree to which group acceptance of the decision is necessary or crucial, and (g) the amount of status or power the coach holds with regard to team members. The underlying principle of this theoretical approach to decision-making effectiveness is that coaches do not or should not adhere to only one decision-making style. Rather, the particular style that will be most effective will vary as a function of the situation and the characteristics of the group. Subsequent research with this type of instrument has verified that the seven situational factors described earlier explain a significantly greater amount of the variance in preferred and perceived decision styles than do individual difference factors (Chelladurai & Arnott, 1985; Chelladurai & Quek, 1991; Chelladurai et al., 1989).

To assess the decision-making style used by coaches or the decision-making style athletes would prefer their coaches to use, several sets of researchers (Chelladurai & Arnott, 1985; Chelladurai & Quek, 1991; Chelladurai et al., 1989; Gordon, 1986) have developed a decision-style questionnaire that consists of a number of problem cases or situations. Each case describes a common sport situation in which a problem must be solved (e.g., substituting for an injured player, selecting a team quarterback, identifying a team manager, making final "cuts"). The particular cases constituting a questionnaire are chosen specifically to represent possible combinations of the situational factors earlier described (e.g., high in problem complexity, low in group integration). Athletes who complete this questionnaire are variously asked to identify the style they believe their coaches would use in that situation or the style they would prefer their coaches to use. Coaches who complete the questionnaire typically are asked to identify the style they would use in each case or that they think other coaches would use.

Initial estimates of the reliability and validity of these types of questionnaires have been reported (see summaries by Chelladurai, 1993, and Chelladurai & Riemer, 1998). In addition, the content, wording, and format of the questionnaires have been carefully constructed and rather extensively reviewed by knowledgeable experts in the leadership field and by the athletes and coaches themselves. Nevertheless, continued psychometric testing of this type of instrumentation is necessary to ensure that a reliable and valid assessment of decision-making styles can be obtained (see recommendations provided by Chelladurai & Riemer, 1998).

Another tool for assessing a coach's leadership style includes instruments that measure the kind of motivational climate or achievement environment the coach creates in practices and games. Vallerand and Pelletier (Pelletier & Vallerand, 1985; Vallerand & Pelletier, 1985), for example, used a questionnaire that assessed coaches' and athletes' perceptions of the coaches' interpersonal style. This questionnaire was based on (or adapted from) an earlier one developed by Deci, Schwartz, Sheinman, and Ryan (1981) to measure adults' orientations toward control versus autonomy in their interactions with children. The Deci et al. questionnaire, which was titled "Problems in Schools Questionnaire," was administered to classroom teachers to measure the degree to which they attempt to control their students' behavior and performance (a highly controlling interpersonal style) or to encourage the child to assume more responsibility for her or his own performance and behavior (a highly autonomous interpersonal style). This 32-item questionnaire presents eight vignettes describing problems that often occur in school classrooms. Following each vignette are four possible ways by which the teacher could deal with the problems. These four solutions represent four points along a continuum from highly controlling to highly autonomous. The teacher-respondents are asked to read each vignette and then rate each possible response choice (on a scale from 1 to 7) indicating how appropriate they consider that response for handling the depicted situation. The scores from the individual vignettes can be totaled to result in one overall measure of the individual teachers' tendencies to be controlling or autonomous in their interactions with their students. Deci et al. (1981) assessed and reported on the reliability and validity of this scale.

As noted earlier, Vallerand and Pelletier (Pelletier & Vallerand, 1985; Vallerand & Pelletier, 1985) modified the Deci et al. (1981) teacher questionnaire to make it relevant to sport contexts. In their research studies, Vallerand and Pelletier administered two versions of the scale—one to coaches to assess their perceptions of their own interpersonal style and another to athletes to assess their perceptions of their coaches' interpersonal style. The results of these studies in terms of coaching effectiveness are presented and discussed later in this chapter.

From a somewhat different perspective, Duda and her colleagues (Newton & Duda, 1993; Seifriz, Duda, & Chi, 1992; Walling, Duda, & Chi, 1993) also developed an instrument to measure the type of climate coaches create in practices and games. The most recent version of their questionnaire, titled "Perceived Motivational Climate in Sport Questionnaire-2 (PMCSQ-2)" is based on the work of Ames and Archer (1988), who established the importance of considering the subjective motivational climate characterizing classrooms in the academic context. The PMCSQ-2 asks individual respondents to indicate the degree to which their team climate is characterized by a task-involving (mastery-oriented) or an ego-involving (performance-oriented) goal perspective. The items in the scale have been found to be hierarchically ordered into two first-order factors (a task-involving/ mastery-oriented team climate and an ego-involving/performance-oriented team climate) and six subscales (three subsumed under each of the two first-order factors; Newton & Duda, 1997, as cited in Duda & Whitehead, 1998). A task-involving (mastery-oriented) team climate is characterized by perceptions among athletes that trying hard will be rewarded and that all players have an important role to fulfill and thus will be encouraged by the coach. In contrast, in an ego-involving (performance-oriented) climate, athletes perceive that teammates try to outdo each other, players are punished for their mistakes, and individual recognition is limited to only a few stars.

The PMCSQ-2 and its earlier versions were developed on the basis of a strong theoretical and empirical research base and have been subjected to numerous procedures to test their reliability and validity (see summary and analyses of these procedures provided by Duda & Whitehead, 1998).

Furthermore, use of the PMCSQ and the PMCSQ-2 in coaching effectiveness studies has shown support for hypothesized links between perceived team climate and players' cognitions, beliefs, and self-perceptions (see summary of this research provided by Duda & Whitehead, 1988). The results of this research are reviewed later in this chapter. Corresponding instruments have been developed by Papaioannou (1994) and adapted by Biddle et al. (1995) to assess students' perceptions of the motivational climate in physical education classes. These instruments also have been tested for reliability and validity (see summary by Duda & Whitehead, 1988) and have been used recently to examine the relationship between motivational climate and students' self-perceptions, motivation, performance, and affective reactions in physical education contexts.

Coaches' Feedback Patterns

A second major approach to measuring coaching behavior involves assessing the type, frequency, and quality of the feedback coaches give to their athletes in practice and game contexts. The most commonly used instrument in this category is the Coaching Behavior Assessment System (CBAS), which was developed and validated over several years by Smith, Smoll, and Hunt (1977). The CBAS provides a direct, observationally based assessment of 12 categories of coaching behavior. The 12 categories were empirically derived and can be classified broadly into reactive and spontaneous coaching behaviors. Reactive behaviors are those which a coach exhibits in response to a variety of player behaviors. Specifically, the CBAS allows for two coaching responses to a player's desirable or successful performances (reinforcement and nonreinforcement) and five coaching responses to a player's performance errors (mistake-contingent encouragement, mistake-contingent technical instruction, punishment, punitive technical instruction, and ignoring mistakes). In addition, the CBAS specifies one coaching response (keeping control behaviors) to player misbehaviors. In the spontaneous coaching behavior category, the CBAS provides for four types of coaching behaviors: spontaneous general technical instruction (not given in response to a particular player performance attempt), spontaneous general encouragement, team organizational behaviors, and game-irrelevant general communication.

Smith et al. (1977) conducted rather extensive procedures to document the reliability and validity of the CBAS. In addition, the recommended training procedures for data collection are quite extensive and rigorous. An in-depth analysis of the psychometric properties of the CBAS was provided by Chelladurai and Riemer (1998).

As noted before, the CBAS is an observationally based instrument. That is, specially trained observers record the behaviors of the coach in practice or game situations. By summarizing the obtained codings, the user can develop individual coach profiles that show the type and frequency (or relative frequency) of the behaviors that coaches exhibit in sport contexts. Although the CBAS originally was developed as a general measure of a coach's behavioral patterns (i.e., how a coach behaves toward all players on her or his team), the CBAS also has been used by other researchers who were more interested in the variability of coaches' behaviors to individual athletes on their teams (see, e.g., Horn, 1984; Rejeski, Darracott, & Hutslar, 1979; Solomon, Wiegardt, et al., 1996). That is, these researchers recorded the coaches' behaviors toward individual members of their teams and analyzed this data relative to possible coach bias in regard to different categories of athletes. The results of this research are presented later in this chapter.

Although the CBAS originally was developed as an observationally based instrument, it has also been adapted into questionnaire form. Specifically, Smith and Smoll and their colleagues (Smith, Smoll, & Curtis, 1978; Smoll, Smith, Curtis, & Hunt, 1978) developed a corresponding questionnaire to assess both players' and coaches' perceptions and recall of the coaches' behavior. In this questionnaire, players and coaches are provided with a description and example of each of the 12 behaviors from the CBAS. The respondents are then asked to indicate (by using a 7-point scale ranging from *almost never* to *almost always*) the extent to which the coach exhibits each type of behavior. Smith, Smoll, and their colleagues developed the questionnaire version of the CBAS so that they could directly compare the three different measures of a coach's behavior (i.e., the direct, observationally based measure, the athletes' perception/recall of their coach's behavior, and the coach's own perception/recall of her or his behavior). Consistent with their subsequently published mediational model of coaching effectiveness (Smoll & Smith, 1989), the three measures of coaches' behavior were not highly correlated. Thus, Smoll and Smith recommended using both observational and questionnaire measures of coaching behavior.

Other researchers in the coaching effectiveness literature have developed and used questionnaire versions of the CBAS. Horn and colleagues (Amorose & Horn, 2000; Horn & Glenn, 1988) as well as Black and Weiss (1992) and Allen and Howe (1998) modified the questionnaire version of the CBAS to specifically measure athletes' perceptions of the type of feedback coaches give their athletes in response to athletes' performance successes and failures. Thus, these researchers shortened the original CBAS behavior categories to focus only on the reactive category of behaviors (i.e., those that are exhibited only in response to specific player performances). Again, only initial estimates of the reliability and validity of these questionnaire versions of the CBAS have been provided.

Summary: Instrumentation to Assess Coaches' Behavior

Although researchers who study coaching effectiveness may have a number of instruments that they can use to measure coaches' behavior, the choices are still limited to only a few aspects or dimensions of coaches' behavior. Certainly, the measures of coaches' leadership style and their feedback patterns represent significant aspects of coaches' overall behavior and ones that probably have a large impact on athletes' performance, behavior, and psychosocial responses. However, many other dimensions of coaches' behavior have not yet been tapped and may be equally relevant in regard to the mental and emotional well-being of athletes. Initial efforts have been made to develop or adapt different measures of coaching behavior (e.g., Bloom, Crumpton, & Anderson, 1999; Franks, Johnson, & Sinclair, 1988; Goudas, Biddle, Fox, & Underwood, 1995; Kenow & Williams, 1992, 1999; Maclean & Chelladurai, 1995). Use of these instruments in future research studies may well expand our knowledge base regarding the ways in which coaches' behavior can affect the psychosocial growth and development of individual athletes. In the last section of this chapter I discuss these new measurement systems as well as other issues related to measurement of coaching behavior.

As indicated in the working model of coaching effectiveness (see figure 10.1), coaches' behavior does not occur in a vacuum. Rather, there are identifiable antecedents of such behavior. In particular, the working model indicates that coaches' behavior is directly influenced by their expectancies, values, beliefs, and goals. This link between boxes 4 and 5 is explored in the next section.

Direct Antecedents of Coaches' Behavior

The research that supports the hypothesized link between coaches' expectancies, values, beliefs, and goals (box 4) and their subsequent behavior (box 5) comes from a diverse set of research literatures. This includes the research on expectancy (self-fulfilling prophecy) theory; the research on individuals' stereotyped beliefs about gender, race/ethnicity, and sexuality; and the research on goal orientation theory. These issues are discussed in the following paragraphs.

Coaches' Expectations: Effects on Their Behavior

In all likelihood, the best available empirical evidence for the hypothesized link between coaches' expectancies, values, beliefs, and goals and their subsequent behavior in sport contexts comes from the research that has investigated the self-fulfilling prophecy theory as it may occur in sport contexts. This series of research studies (e.g., Horn, 1984; Rejeski et al., 1979; Sinclair & Vealey, 1989; Solomon, Striegel, et al., 1996) was based on a four-step self-fulfilling prophecy model proposed by researchers in educational contexts (Brophy, 1983; Cooper & Tom, 1984; Harris & Rosenthal, 1985) to explain how teachers' expectations can affect the performance of their students. Adapting this four-step process to the athletic setting, researchers have hypothesized that (a) coaches develop, at the beginning of the season, an expectation for each athlete that predicts the level of performance and type of behavior that athlete will exhibit over the season; (b) coaches' expectations affect their behavior toward individual athletes on their team; (c) the differential ways in which individual athletes are treated by the coach affect each athlete's performance and self-perceptions; and (d) athletes' performance and behavior conform to the coaches' original expectations.

The early research studies in sport (e.g., Horn, 1984; Rejeski et al., 1979) examined the second step in this model. Specifically, Rejeski et al. recruited a sample of 14 coaches and 71 male youth league basketball players ranging in age from 8 to 12 years. Using CBAS observational techniques, a team of investigators coded the game and practice behaviors of coaches toward 39 high-expectancy athletes (those athletes identified by the coaches at the end of the data collection period

as the "higher ability" athletes on the team) and 32 low-expectancy athletes (those athletes identified by their coaches as lowest on their team in ability). Comparison of the coaching feedback received by the two groups of athletes indicated that high-expectancy athletes received more reinforcement and that low-expectancy athletes received more general technical instruction and experienced few incidences of nonreinforcement.

In a similar study, Horn (1984) examined the frequency and type of feedback that junior high school softball coaches gave to their high- and low-expectancy athletes in practice and game settings. The results of her study showed no significant differences in the frequency and type of feedback that coaches gave to their high- and low-expectancy athletes in practice contexts. However, some differences were found in game situations. Specifically, coaches tended to initiate more communications with their high-expectancy athletes in game situations than they did with their low-expectancy athletes. In addition, coaches gave their low-expectancy athletes more technical instruction overall and more reinforcement (praise) after their performance successes than they gave to their high-expectancy athletes. Furthermore, the high-expectancy athletes received more punishment after performance errors than did the low-expectancy athletes. Although these latter results appear to contradict the self-fulfilling prophecy theory, which would predict that high-expectancy athletes would receive more reinforcement, less punishment, and more instructional feedback than would their low-expectancy teammates, Horn and her colleagues (Horn, Lox, & Labrador, in press) argued that the higher frequency of reinforcement and praise given by coaches to low-expectancy athletes may actually have been less valuable because it may have been given inappropriately (i.e., given for a mediocre performance or for success at an easy task).

Other expectancy-biased observation studies in sport contexts were conducted by Sinclair and Vealey (1989) and Solomon and colleagues (Solomon, DiMarco, Ohlson, & Reece, 1998; Solomon, Golden, Ciapponi, & Martin, 1998b; Solomon & Kosmitzki, 1996; Solomon, Striegel, et al., 1996; Solomon, Wiegardt, et al., 1996). All of these studies were conducted with older athletes and showed a variety of significant expectancy effects. Solomon, Striegel, et al. (1996) found that collegiate head coaches provided more overall feedback to their high-expectancy players. Sinclair and Vealey (1989) replicated this finding in a sample of elite field hockey coaches and players and also found that high-expectancy athletes received more specific and evaluation feedback whereas low-expectancy players received more prescriptive feedback. In a later study, Solomon, Golden, et al. (1998) found that high-expectancy high school athletes were given greater amounts of instructional feedback whereas their low-expectancy peers were given more management-oriented feedback.

From a somewhat different perspective, Papaioannou (1995) used goal perspective theory (Ames, 1984, 1992a; Dweck, 1986, 1999; Nicholls, 1989) to investigate differential teacher behavior in physical education contexts. Working with a sample of 1,393 junior and senior high students, Papaioannou measured students' perceptions of the achievement (motivational) climate that their teachers created in their classes. He also measured students' perceptions of their teachers' treatment of high and low achievers in the class. The results of this study clearly showed a connection between the type of achievement climate that characterizes individual classrooms and students' perceptions of their teachers' expectancy-biased behavior. Specifically, students who perceived that their teachers created a performance-oriented climate also believed that their teachers favored high achievers in their classes. In contrast, students who perceived that their teachers created a learning-oriented climate perceived that their teachers did not exhibit differential behavior toward the high and low achievers in the class. This study was unique in that it linked expectancy-biased behaviors on the part of the teachers to the overall climate they create in the classroom. Thus, this study provides additional information regarding the ways in which teachers (and probably coaches) allow their expectations to affect their behavior.

Coaches' Stereotyped Beliefs: Effects on Their Behavior

As the studies described in the previous section indicate, coaches' expectancies regarding the athletic abilities or athletic potential of individual athletes on their team affect (or at least are related to) the type of behavior they exhibit toward each athlete. Similarly, it appears likely that other aspects of coaches' attitudes, beliefs, values, and goals might determine how they treat individual athletes on their team. Specifically, it might be hypothesized that coaches who hold strong

gender-stereotyped beliefs (see chapter 11 for discussion of gender stereotypes) would behave very differently toward their male and female athletes. That is, coaches who believe that girls are less physically or psychologically capable than are boys in sport contexts might treat their female players as low-expectancy athletes. On coeducational teams, for example, female athletes may be given less time, attention, and instruction by their coaches in practices and less playing time in games. When they do get playing time, female athletes may be put in positions where they will be most inactive (e.g., right field in baseball) or least likely to touch the ball. Gender-biased coaches who coach all-girls teams may hold lower standards of performance for all of their athletes (based on the belief that girls cannot reach a high standard of performance or proficiency) and thus may reduce the amount and quality of the instruction and feedback they provide for female athletes. As a historical example of such expectancy-biased behavior, one only has to recall the days when girls were not allowed to play full-court basketball (but rather were limited to a half-court game) based on coaches' and physical educators' beliefs that girls were not physiologically capable of such full-court exertion. Thus, it is reasonable to believe that coaches who still hold very gender-stereotyped beliefs regarding sport performance and athletic competence would exhibit different behaviors toward their male and female athletes.

Furthermore, coaches who hold gender-stereotyped beliefs may also hold perceptions of their female athletes that interact or intersect with age. As Horn et al. (in press) explained in their recent chapter on the self-fulfilling prophecy theory in sport contexts, early maturing girls (i.e., those girls who are maturing biologically more quickly than their chronological age would indicate) may be advantaged in sport contexts during the childhood years because they generally tend to be bigger, stronger, and faster than their same chronological age group peers. Thus, coaches may see them as "more athletic" than their peers. However, when these same early maturing girls reach puberty, some of the physical changes that they experience, again at an earlier age than their same-age peers, may cause the coaches to change their expectations and beliefs and thus now see these girls as "less athletic." This age-related change in coaches' perceptions of early maturing girls may occur because the pubertal changes that early maturing girls experience around the age of 10 or 11 (e.g., breast development, menarche, increase in hip width or body fat) typically are not perceived in our society as indicative of athleticism. Thus, the coaches may suddenly see these early maturing girls as less physically competent. This argument is consistent with Malina's (1983, 1994) biosocial hypothesis that there are proportionately more late maturing girls/women in competitive sport after the age of 12 because the linear body build of the late maturer (narrow hips, flat chest, relatively low body fat) is perceived by coaches, parents, and sport administrators to be more conducive to sport proficiency and performance. Thus, early maturing girls may be cut from sport teams or may be socialized out of sport at a relatively early age (i.e., by 12 years) because they are no longer perceived by coaches and sport administrators to be athletic.

It is also reasonable to believe that coaches who hold gender-stereotyped beliefs may hold homophobic views regarding both male and female athletes. Such coaches of male athletes might, for example, act very positively toward the players on their team who fit the masculine stereotype (e.g., have broad shoulders and a muscular body shape, and who act in aggressive ways) but may act much more negatively to the male athletes on their team who do not fit this masculine stereotype (e.g., male athletes who are more slender and who do not consistently act in what the coach believes to be gender-appropriate ways). Similarly, gender-biased and homophobic (i.e., personal attitude or belief characterized by dislike for, or fear of, homosexually identified individuals) coaches of female athletes would act more positively toward female athletes on their team who fit the feminine stereotype (i.e., those athletes who have boyfriends, wear their hair long, and who dress off the court/field in more feminine-typed clothing) than they would to athletes on their team who do not conform to this feminine stereotype. From a different, but certainly related, perspective, we could also hypothesize that a coach who is very homosexually identified may act more positively toward athletes who are similarly identified and more negatively toward athletes who are not. Again, the main point is that coaches' beliefs can affect or determine their behavior toward and with individual athletes. For further discussion of concepts related to gender, sexuality, and sport behavior, see the chapter by Gill in this volume as well as books by Messner (1992) and Lenskyj (1987).

The hypothesized links described in the previous paragraphs between coaches' beliefs concerning gender and sexual orientation and their subsequent behavior toward individual athletes on their team has not been well explored in the sport psychology research literature. Nevertheless, research that measures the degree to which a sample of coaches endorse gender and sexual orientation stereotypes and then examines whether such stereotypical tendencies relate to their behavior would be interesting and would contribute significantly to the research on coaching effectiveness.

Another aspect of coaches' stereotyped beliefs that has begun to be explored relates to race and ethnicity. Coakley (1994) described a number of race-related stereotypes that occur in sport contexts. These include notions that African-American individuals are "naturally" gifted in particular sports or sporting activities (e.g., basketball, sprinting events), and that Euro-American athletes are more competent in mental capabilities (e.g., decision-making) whereas African-American athletes are more competent in physical capabilities (e.g., speed, reaction time). Again, coaches who hold such race-related stereotypes might show greater differences in their behavior toward African-American and Euro-American athletes on their team than would coaches who do not hold such stereotypes. The likelihood of this occurring in the sport context is reinforced by research in educational contexts (e.g., McCormick & Noriega, 1986; Rist, 1970; Rubovits & Maehr, 1973; Wineburg, 1987) that shows differential patterns of teacher behavior to African-American and Euro-American students.

Initial attempts to examine racial biases in regard to coaches' behavior were made by Solomon and her colleagues (Solomon, Wiegardt, et al., 1996), who recorded the frequency and type of feedback given to athletes (male and female) from two college basketball teams. The obtained data were examined to determine if the type of feedback coaches gave to individual athletes on their team varied as a function of the athletes' ethnicity (African-American and Euro-American). Although examination of mean scores indicated that African-American athletes received more instruction and Euro-American athletes received more praise, the statistical analysis revealed no significant differences. Solomon et al. cited the small sample size as one possible explanation for the nonsignificant findings. Obviously, more research on this topic is needed. One suggestion for future researchers would be to actually assess coaches' attitudes and beliefs about race and ethnicity. Assuming that within any particular sample of coaches, there would be variability in endorsement of race-related stereotypes, the obtained observational data of their behavior toward athletes on their team could be examined to determine if the degree to which coaches endorsed stereotypes was reflected in their differential behavioral patterns toward athletes on their team. That is, would coaches who exhibited the strongest race-related stereotyped beliefs also show the greatest differential treatment of their African-American and Euro-American athletes? Such research would test the hypothesized link between coaches' attitudes, values, and beliefs and their subsequent behavior in practice and game context.

The examination of race and ethnicity in regard to coaching behavior should not be limited to comparisons of African-American and Euro-American athletes. As Coakley (1994) noted, very little research has been conducted to examine the experiences of other racial and ethnic groups (e.g., Asian Americans, Hispanic Americans) in sport contexts. Similarly, as Gill notes in her chapter in this volume, race and ethnicity interact with gender, social class, and other diversity characteristics to affect individual athletes' experiences in sport contexts. Thus, for researchers in sport psychology, the examination of the coach–athlete relationship, especially as it concerns ethnicity, race, gender, sexuality, sexual orientation, and social class, will need to be conducted in much more complex ways.

Coaches' Achievement Goal Perspectives: Effects on Their Behavior

As another example of the hypothesized link between boxes 4 and 5 in the working model of coaching effectiveness (see figure 10.1), we can use the tenets of achievement goal orientation theory (Ames, 1984, 1992a; Dweck, 1986; Nicholls, 1984, 1992) to suggest that coaches who hold a predominantly task-oriented perspective regarding their sport program would exhibit behaviors in practices and games that are consistent with such a goal perspective. That is, in contrast to ego-oriented coaches, task-oriented coaches should provide feedback that emphasizes task mastery and individual skill improvement. They should also show persistence in working with all athletes and continually emphasize the important contributions that all athletes make to the team. In contrast, coaches who are predominantly ego-oriented should exhibit behaviors in practices and games that focus attention on peer comparison.

That is, they would be expected to give feedback to individual athletes that is contingent on whether they performed better than teammates rather than giving feedback contingent on individual athletes' demonstration of skill improvement or task mastery (see specific behavioral descriptors provided by Treasure and Roberts, 1995b).

Although a number of research studies have been conducted within the past decade to demonstrate that the type of climate coaches create in practices and games (e.g., a task-oriented or ego-oriented climate) is linked to, or even actually predicts, athletes' performance, perceptions, cognitions, and affective reactions (see recent review by Duda & Whitehead, 1998), these studies have not directly assessed the coaches' own goal orientation, which should, then, determine the type of team climate they would create. Thus, these research studies support the link between boxes 5, 8, 9, and 10 in the working model (figure 10.1). However, additional research is needed to show that coaches' own achievement goal orientation (box 4) is linked to their actual behavior (box 5), which would, in turn, affect athletes' perceptions of the coaches' behavior (box 8) and the athletes' own self-perceptions, beliefs, and attitudes (box 9), as well as their level of motivation (box 10).

As the research and theory cited in this section suggest, there is reason to believe that coaches' behavior during practices and games can be linked to, or predicted by, their expectancies, values, beliefs, and goals. Furthermore, as illustrated in the working model of coaching effectiveness (see figure 10.1), coaches' expectancies, values, beliefs, and goals actually may be determined by three sets of interrelating factors: the sociocultural context, the organizational climate, and the coaches' own personal characteristics. The supporting research and theory for these hypothesized links are discussed in the following sections.

Antecedents of Coaches' Expectancies, Values, Beliefs, and Goals

As noted, at least some empirical evidence shows that coaches' behavior in sport contexts is affected, or even determined, by their expectancies, values, beliefs, and goals. In contrast, very few researchers in the coaching effectiveness area have examined the impact that the sociocultural context (box 1), the organizational climate (box 2), and coaches' own personal characteristics (box

3) can exert on coaches' expectancies, values, beliefs, and goals (box 4) and, ultimately, their behavior (box 5). However, initial research suggests that these are viable links. A brief discussion with regard to each of these antecedents follows.

Sociocultural Context

Although the link between the sociocultural context (box 1) and coaches' expectancies, values, beliefs, and goals (box 4) specified in the working model (figure 10.1) has not been well researched in the sport psychology literature, there is relevant research on the sociocultural context in regard to athletes' perceptions and goals. Specifically, several researchers (e.g., Duda, 1985, 1986a, 1986b; Hayashi, 1996; Hayashi & Weiss, 1994; Kim & Gill, 1997) have investigated cross-cultural variation in athletes' perceptions or interpretations of selected achievement goals. In general, these researchers have found that athletes' achievement goal perspectives vary, at least to a certain extent, as a function of their sociocultural background. Thus, we might expect similar links between coaches' sociocultural background and their expectancies, beliefs, and goals. In addition, the broader sociocultural notions regarding masculinity and femininity may be reflected in coaches' expectancies, values, and goals regarding male and female athletes, which, in turn, may be linked to, or can explain, observed differences in coaches' behavior toward individual athletes on their team. Furthermore, as our colleagues in sociology and sport sociology have pointed out, individual sport groups or teams actually may constitute a subculture that has its own normative expectations, values, and beliefs (see, e.g., articles by Donnelly, 1981; Donnelly & Young, 1988; Johns, 1998; Klein, 1986). By studying these sport subcultures, we may gain a greater understanding of the sociocultural context within which the coach and the athletes live. Thus, we should more completely understand the behaviors they exhibit and the ways in which coaches and athletes interact in specific sport contexts.

Organizational Climate

The second factor identified in the working model (see figure 10.1) as an antecedent of coaches' expectancies, values, beliefs, and goals is organizational climate (see hypothesized link between boxes 2 and 4). This link refers to the impact that the particular sport program structure might have on the coach. Perhaps the most important or relevant example of this hypothesized link comes from the research that has looked at differences in coaches' behavior as a function of sport level. Chaumeton and Duda (1988), for example, found that basketball athletes' perceptions of the behaviors exhibited by their coach in game situations varied as a function of the athletes' age. Specifically, as the players' age increased from elementary school to high school, coaches' behavior was perceived to become more ego-involving. That is, high school coaches, compared with younger age group coaches, were perceived to give reinforcement and punishment to their athletes based on performance outcome rather than performance process. Although Chaumeton and Duda did not directly assess coaches' reasons for giving such differential feedback, it could be hypothesized that the organizational climate of competitive sport changes as players move from youth sport programs to high school programs. That is, at the younger ages, the organizational sport climate may be more oriented toward instruction and skill development. However, as the competitive level increases (i.e., elementary to junior high to high school), greater emphasis may be placed on winning. Such differences in the sport organizational climate may alter coaches' expectancies, values, and goals, which will, in turn, affect their behavior in practices and games (see also discussion on this topic by Horn & Harris, in press).

As the Chaumeton and Duda study (1988) suggests, coaches' expectations, values, and beliefs may change as the emphasis on competitive outcomes increases. However, in their study, level of competition was confounded with athletes' age. Thus, future researchers might separate these two factors by comparing coaches' expectations, values, beliefs, and behavior within specific age levels. This kind of research can be done because in many youth sport programs, children's opportunities for participation can vary as a function of competitive level. At the 11- to 12-year-old age range, for example, children in many soccer programs can play either at the recreational level (no tryouts; all children who want to play are assigned to a team) or at the select level (children have to try out to get assigned to these teams). An interesting comparison at this age level, then, would be to examine the beliefs, expectations, values, and behaviors of the coaches across these two competitive levels. If the two groups of coaches differed, we would have significantly greater information regarding the effects of organizational structure on coaches' behavior in sport contexts and the reasons for such effects.

At the collegiate level as well, organizational structure may be a factor affecting coaches' behavior. Amorose and Horn (1999), for example, collected data that show significant differences in the perceptions of Division I and Division III collegiate male and female athletes regarding their coaches' behavior. Specifically, Division I athletes (compared with Division III athletes) perceived their coaches to exhibit a leadership style that was more autocratic, was less socially supportive, and provided lower frequencies of positive and information-based feedback. These researchers also found significant differences in perceived coaching behavior as a function of the number of athletes on each Division I team who were on scholarship. In particular, coaches of teams in which more than 75% of the athletes on each team were on scholarship were perceived by their athletes to be more autocratic, to be less socially supportive, and to give higher frequencies of punishment-oriented feedback than were coaches of teams that had less athletes on scholarship. According to the working model (and according to work published by Vallerand, Deci, & Ryan, 1987), it can be hypothesized that college coaches who are given relatively more scholarships than other coaches may perceive greater pressure to win. In turn, such a win-oriented goal perspective may cause them to be more autocratic or controlling in their interactions with individual athletes. This interpretation of the data is consistent with research in the educational psychology literature (Deci, Spiegel, Ryan, Koestner, & Kauffman, 1982), which has shown that teachers who were told that they were going to be held responsible for the performance outcomes of their students became more controlling in their interactions with their students than did teachers who were not given such externally set performance standards. Again, by using the working model, it can be hypothesized that the differences in the organizational climate caused differences in the teachers' goals which, in turn, caused differences in their instructional style.

As the research cited in the previous paragraphs indicates, there is at least initial evidence to show that coaches' behavior varies as a function of the organizational climate/program structure. Although it is reasonable to believe that this link between organizational climate and coaches' behavior is mediated by coaches' expectancies, values, beliefs, and goals, there has been relatively little direct research on these links.

Coaches' Personal Characteristics

The third antecedent factor that is hypothesized in the working model of coaching effectiveness (figure 10.1) to affect coaches' expectancies, values, beliefs, and goals, and ultimately their behavior, involves the coaches' own personal characteristics (i.e., hypothesized link between boxes 3 and 4). Although little research has been conducted in the sport psychology literature on this hypothesized link, there are exceptions. Feltz and her colleagues (Feltz, Chase, Moritz, & Sullivan, 1999) recently developed a multidimensional scale to measure coaches' sense of their own efficacy in sport contexts. This scale, titled "Coaching Efficacy Scale (CES)," contains four subscales to measure coaches' perceptions of their ability to affect the learning and performance of their athletes in four areas: game strategy, motivation of athletes, teaching technique, and character building. In testing the validity and reliability of their CES, Feltz et al. collected additional data to test the extent to which coaches' level of coaching efficacy was related to selected aspects of their coaching behavior (as assessed by the CBAS). These results showed that high-self-efficacy coaches provided more praise and encouragement to their athletes in team practices than did low-self-efficacy coaches. In contrast, low-self-efficacy coaches engaged in more instructional and organizational behaviors during practice than did their high-self-efficacy peers. As Feltz et al. noted, these results are consistent with research from the educational psychology literature showing that classroom teachers who possess high levels of self-confidence in regard to their teaching show more commitment to their profession (Coladarci, 1992), display more persistence in the face of failure, and spend more time on teaching than do low-self-confidence teachers (Gibson & Dembo, 1984). Similarly, high-self-efficacy teachers show better student management skills than do low-self-efficacy teachers (Woolfolk, Rosoff, & Hoy, 1990). This research from the educational psychology literature, combined with the initial research by Feltz et al., indicates that additional research on behavioral correlates of coaches' level of self-efficacy or self-confidence would be profitable.

A second example of research in this area is a recent study conducted by Frederick and Morrison (1999). These researchers developed a scale that measured motivational style in coaches. This scale, based on self-determination theory (Deci & Ryan, 1985), distinguishes between coaches who are intrinsically motivated and those who are extrinsically motivated. Frederick and Morrison administered this scale to 137 college coaches and then assessed how well the obtained scores could be related to coaches' decision-making style (autonomous, controlling, and impersonal). Coaches who were high in extrinsic motivation and low in intrinsic motivation were more apt to use an impersonal decision-making style (characterized by indecisiveness in making choices and dependence on past precedents to make decisions), whereas coaches high in intrinsic motivation and low in extrinsic motivation were more apt to use an autonomous decision-making style (i.e., characterized by leadership style in which the coach collects information from others in the social context and then uses such information to make decision). These results, again, support the notion that coaches' personal characteristics can be linked to their actual behavior in sport contexts.

Some other predictors of coaches' expectancies, values, beliefs, goals, and behaviors have been proposed in addition to level of self-efficacy, self-confidence, and intrinsic motivation. Abraham and Collins (1998) and Strean and colleagues (Strean, Senecal, Howlett, & Burgess, 1997) recently published articles in which they argued that such individual difference variables as self-reflectiveness, critical thinking aptitude, decision-making abilities, knowledge bases or structures, and sport or coaching experience may predict coaching behavior and coaching effectiveness. Both of these articles represent new and relatively unique perspectives on coaching behavior that certainly could be explored further.

From the teacher expectancy research literature, initial studies have been conducted to identify the individual difference factors that may explain why some teachers show expectancy-biased behaviors in the classroom and others do not (e.g., Babad, Inbar, & Rosenthal, 1982; Cooper, 1979; Guskey, 1981). Similar research could be conducted in the sport context. As Horn et al. (in press) noted in their chapter on expectancy effects in sport settings, not all coaches are "Pygmalion-prone." That is, although all coaches may form expectations at the beginning of the season concerning the sport competence or sport potential of individual athletes on their team, not all coaches allow such expectations to affect their behavior toward their athletes. Such interindividual variation in the degree to which individual coaches show expectancy-biased behavior suggests that certain characteristics of the

coach would predict her or his tendencies to be expectancy-biased. Consistent with Abraham and Collins (1998) and Strean et al. (1997), we might hypothesize that coaches who are critical thinkers or are very self-reflective would be less apt to show expectancy-biased behavior than would coaches who are lower in these cognitive activities and abilities. Similarly, Smoll and Smith (1989) pointed out that individual differences in self-monitoring may affect coaches' behavior. Specifically, they noted that high self-monitors tend to be more responsive to cues in the sport context and thus are more flexible in their interactions with individual athletes.

Research in the teacher education literature (e.g., Cooper, 1979; Guskey, 1981) indicates that locus of control may influence coaches' expectancy-related tendencies. That is, coaches who have an external locus of control with regard to sport outcomes (i.e., coaches who believe that sport success is not under their own personal control but rather depends on external others) would likely believe that they will have a successful season only if they get good athletes (i.e., "I will be successful if I have good athletes who want to work hard"). In contrast, coaches with internal locus of control should perceive greater control over their sport success. That is, coaches with internal locus of control likely would believe that their teams' success depends largely on things that are under their control (i.e., "If I use the right drills, run my practices efficiently, and train my athletes appropriately, we will be more likely to achieve success"). It could be hypothesized that coaches with an external locus of control would be more apt to exhibit expectancy-biased behaviors in practices and games than would coaches with a more internal locus of control. In addition, because coaches with an internal locus of control believe that they, personally, can affect the learning and performance of their athletes, they should be more apt to persist in the face of failure (i.e., to regroup after a bad loss) and to spend more time outside of practice with lower skilled athletes. In contrast, coaches with an external locus of control, who basically see the athletes as the source of all problems, would give up on individual players who cannot learn new skills or offensive and defensive plays right away. That is, coaches with an external locus of control would be unwilling to persist in teaching individual athletes new skills and techniques and to spend additional time and effort with athletes who are slower learners. Such lack of persistence and willingness to work with all athletes probably could be linked to the coach's locus of control (i.e., her or his belief concerning the cause of performance successes and failures).

Another avenue to explore with regard to the hypothesized links between coaches' own personal characteristics (box 3) and their expectancies, values, beliefs, and goals (box 4) as well as their behavior (box 5) involves the impact of coaches' attentional profiles. Specifically, according to research and theory in the motor learning and sport psychology literatures (see recent reviews by Abernethy, 1993, and Nideffer, 1993), we might develop hypotheses regarding the link between certain attentional skills, abilities, or profiles on the part of coaches and their subsequent ability to identify errors in individual athletes' skill patterns and to their ability to "see" the whole game and to recognize offensive and defensive patterns as they develop.

From a related perspective, it might be interesting to examine the possible link between coaches' own personal level of trait anxiety (box 3) and their subsequent behavior in coaching contexts (box 5). Specifically, according to research and theory concerning the link between athletes' levels of trait anxiety and their performance and behavior in competitive situations (Smith, Smoll, & Wiechman, 1998), we also might hypothesize that coaches' levels of competitive trait anxiety would be related to their ability to attend to relevant cues, to make clear and focused decisions in stressful game situations, and thus to give specific and task-oriented feedback to individual players.

As indicated in the last several paragraphs, there is reason to believe that coaches' personal characteristics actually predict or determine not only their expectancies, values, beliefs, and goals but also their behavior in practices and games. Of course, as the model in figure 10.1 clearly illustrates, coaches' personal characteristics probably work in combination with, and actually interact with, the sociocultural context and the organizational climate to have an effect on coaches' behavior.

As noted earlier in this chapter, the left side of the working model provides a framework to investigate how and why coaches exhibit the types of behaviors they do in practice and game situations. As is evident, relatively little research in sport psychology has been conducted on this side of the model, but the initial studies in this area have provided some support for the specified links.

The right side of the working model (figure 10.1) focuses on the effects of coaches' behavior on athletes' performance, behavior, and psychosocial responses. These links and the supporting research are discussed in the following sections.

Coaches' Behavior: Direct Link With Athletes' Performance and Behavior

As the model (see figure 10.1) illustrates, there is a direct link between coaches' behavior (box 5) and athletes' performance and behavior (box 6). This arrow specifies that certain behaviors which a coach exhibits in practices and games will directly affect her or his athletes' performance and their ability to master the skills. Much of the research conducted in the motor learning and sport pedagogy literatures falls into this category. For example, research shows that the way coaches organize practice sessions, the amount of time they allocate to teaching/learning activities, the types of learning activities and skill progressions that they use, the strategy decisions that they

© Human Kinetics

A coach's ability to change offensive patterns can be critical to the team's performance.

make in competitive situations, the way in which they use skill demonstrations, and the type, frequency, and quality of the feedback that they give to individual athletes can directly affect the skill learning and performance of those athletes (see, e.g., a review by Metzler, 1989). In game situations as well, the coach's ability to identify skill errors and change the offensive and defensive patterns the team is using may be critical to the individual's and the team's performance. Thus, considerable research is available to show that this direct link does exist.

As noted earlier, this direct link between coaches' behavior (box 5) and their athletes' performance and behavior (box 6) is mediated by sport and athlete variables. That is, the types of coaching behaviors that are most effective in facilitating the performance and behavior of athletes will vary as a function of the sport context and the individual athlete. Magill (1994) clearly illustrated this point with regard to the feedback provided by coaches and teachers. As Magill pointed out, the effectiveness and even the necessity of different types of feedback vary as a function of the age and skill level of the student-athlete and of the type of sport skill that the student-athlete is practicing. In addition, several sets of researchers have found that coaches' behavior in practice contexts differs significantly from their behavior in game situations (e.g., Horn, 1985; Wandzilak, Ansorge, & Potter, 1988). Thus, although empirical evidence supports the direct impact that a coach's behavior has on athletes' performance and behavior, this impact needs to be assessed in light of such athlete, sport, or other contextual variables.

Although a significant amount of research has been conducted on the direct link between coaches' behavior and their athletes' performance and behavior (boxes 5–6), that research is not reviewed further in this chapter. As noted in the introductory section, this chapter is limited to reviewing the research that examines the effect of coaches' behavior on the psychosocial growth and development of athletes. Readers who are more interested in the effects of coaches' behavior on athletes' sport performance and motor skill development and learning should examine the motor learning and sport pedagogy literatures.

The effects of coaches' behaviors on athletes' psychosocial growth and development, and ultimately (or indirectly) on the athletes' motor skill learning and performance, are illustrated on the right side of the model (see figure 10.1). In par-

ticular, the right side of the working model hypothesizes that the coach's behavior in practice and game situations (box 5) is interpreted or perceived by athletes (box 8) in ways that affect the athletes' self-perceptions, beliefs, and attitudes (box 9). Such self-perceptions, beliefs, and attitudes, in turn, affect athletes' level or type of motivation (box 10) which, then, affects their performance and behavior in the sport context (box 6). An important cog or point in this process is athletes' perceptions or interpretations of their coaches' behaviors. Thus, this model incorporates the notion that the coach's actual or observable behavior may not be as important as the way the athlete actually perceives or interprets that behavior. Therefore, the review of the research concerning the right side of the working model (the effects of coaches' behavior on athletes' psychosocial responses) begins with a discussion of box 8.

Athletes' Perceptions or Interpretations of Their Coaches' Behavior

As indicated in the working model, the actual behaviors exhibited by coaches in practice and game contexts (box 5) will affect athletes' self-perceptions (box 9) and level of motivation (box 10) only as such coaching behaviors are mediated by athletes' perceptions and interpretations of the coaches' actual behavior (box 8). This notion is also embedded in Smoll and Smith's (1989) cognitive–mediational model. As these authors noted, "The ultimate effects of coaching behaviors are mediated by the meaning that players attribute to them" (p. 1527). In addition, however, individual athletes' perceptions of their coaches' behavior are affected or determined by the athletes' own personal characteristics (i.e., as illustrated in figure 10.1 by the arrow linking boxes 7 and 8). The research to date clearly supports this idea in that individual athletes have been found to differ significantly in their perceptions, interpretations, and evaluations of their coaches' behavior. This research is discussed in the following paragraphs.

Interindividual Variability in Athletes' Perceptions of Their Coaches' Behavior

One characteristic of athletes that may affect their perceptions of their coaches' behavior is age or developmental level. Smith and his colleagues (Smith et al., 1978) found, for example, that children under the age of 10 perceptually differentiated among coaches primarily on the basis of aversive behaviors, such as punishment and punitive, technical instruction. In contrast, children between the ages of 10 and 12 years were more apt to use positive reinforcement and encouragement as the basis for evaluating their coach's behavior. Finally, adolescents (aged 13–15) were more apt to differentiate between coaches on the basis of amount and quality of instruction. These results suggest that children differ in their perception or interpretation of their coaches' feedback as a function of their age.

Further support for such developmental differences in children's perceptions of adult feedback comes from Nicholls' (1989, 1992) goal orientation theory and from research conducted by Whitehead and Smith (1996) and Fry and Duda (1997), showing that younger children (those under the age of 11 or 12) view effort and ability as undifferentiated or only partially differentiated. In other words, younger children believe that a child who exhibits high effort in working on a skill must also be high in ability whereas a child who exhibits low effort on that same skill is low in ability. In contrast, older children (those older than 12) see effort and ability as covarying factors. Thus, they believe that a performer who must exhibit relatively more effort compared with peers to succeed at a task has a lower level of ability. Such age-differential beliefs concerning the relationship of effort and ability can affect children's perceptions of the attributional feedback that their coach gives. If, for example, a coach attributes an athlete's good performance in a soccer game to high effort, the younger child should interpret this feedback as an indicator that he or she has high ability, because to this child, effort and ability are perceived in a similar way. To an older child, however, who sees effort and ability as covarying factors, the coach's attribution of a good performance by the athlete to high effort might actually undermine the athlete's perception of ability. That is, the older child might reason, "If I need to exert high effort to be successful, then I must not be so good at this skill." Similarly, if a coach attributes an athlete's strikeout in a game to lack of effort, the younger child might interpret this as low ability. That is, because the younger child perceives effort and ability to be equal, he or she will interpret the coach's feedback as an indicator that he or she has low ability. In contrast, the older child, who sees effort and ability as covarying factors, may well perceive the coach's attributional feedback for his or her performance failure to lack of effort as an indicator that he or

she has high ability.

Other evidence to support the notion that children of varying ages (or cognitive stages) will differ in their perception or interpretation of adult feedback comes from the educational psychology literature (e.g., Barker & Graham, 1987, and Meyer et al., 1979). Barker and Graham, for example, used laboratory procedures to demonstrate that younger children (less than 11–12 years) interpreted the evaluative feedback (praise, criticism, neutral) given by adults differently than did children older than 11 to 12 years. Furthermore, the obtained differences were consistent with the developmental tenets specified in Nicholls' (1984) achievement goal theory. The practical implications of these developmental differences with regard to the type of feedback coaches should provide children have been delineated by Horn (1987; Horn & Harris, in press).

In regard to attributional feedback, Schunk (1995) recently suggested that children's interpretation of the attributional feedback that adults give to lack of effort may differ as a function of a child's history of successes and failures. If a child has a relatively successful history in a skill such as batting, and the coach attributes one particular strikeout to the athlete's lack of effort, the child will perceive this as a positive indicator of his or her athletic ability. However, if a child has a relatively unsuccessful history in batting, then the coach's attribution of a particular strikeout to lack of effort actually may be interpreted by the child as negative.

In addition to age, developmental level, and skill level, gender also may be a relevant factor affecting athletes' interpretation or perception of their coaches' behavior. Some researchers have found, for example, that the type of perceived coaching behaviors that are most effective in regard to facilitating athletes' self-perceptions (e.g., perceived competence) and level of intrinsic motivation varies as a function of the athletes' gender (Amorose & Horn, in press; Black & Weiss, 1992). Smith and Smoll, in a 1983 study (as cited in Smoll & Smith, 1989), found gender differences in regard to the ways in which male and female elementary school basketball players perceived and evaluated their coaches' behavior (i.e., how much the athletes liked or disliked the behaviors). The results of this gender-differential research, then, support the notion that the effects of coaches' behavior on male and female athletes may differ because the male and female athletes perceive or interpret their coaches' behavior in different ways.

From a different, but certainly related, perspective, it also might be interesting to examine whether the actual behaviors exhibited by coaches in practice and game contexts (box 5) are perceived differently by athletes as a function of the coaches' gender. Given pervasive gender-stereotyped beliefs in regard to sport behaviors (see chapter 11), a male and female coach who exhibited the same actual behavioral style might be perceived or evaluated by athletes, as well as by other individuals in the sport environment (e.g., administrators, spectators, parents), in different ways. Such research has not yet been conducted in the sport psychology field but certainly might provide interesting information concerning the ways in which coaches' behaviors are perceived by athletes and others in the sport context.

At least initial evidence is also available to show that athletes' perceptions or evaluations of their coaches' behavior may vary as a function of the athletes' psychological characteristics. In two studies, Kenow and Williams (1992, 1999) found that collegiate athletes' level of trait and state (especially cognitive) anxiety and state self-confidence affected their perception and evaluation of their coaches' behavior. These researchers also found that the degree to which athletes perceived high or low levels of compatibility with their coach affected their evaluation of their coach's behavior. Similarly, Smoll and Smith (1989) identified other psychological characteristics of athletes that might affect their interpretation of their coaches' behaviors. These characteristics include athletes' achievement-related motives and their level of general and athletic self-esteem.

Interindividual Variability in Athletes' Preferences for Different Types of Coaching Behavior

As further support for the notion that individual athletes differ in their perceptions or interpretation of their coaches' behavior, we can look at the rather extensive research base on athletes' preferences for different types of coaching behavior. This research, which has been based predominantly on Chelladurai's (1978, 1990, 1993) multidimensional model of leadership effectiveness, has examined the extent to which athletes' age, skill, gender, nationality, sport affiliation, and psychological profile may affect the type of leadership styles they prefer their coaches to exhibit. The results of this research were reviewed in considerable detail and clarity by Chelladurai (1993) in his recent chapter on leadership effectiveness in the sport domain. Thus, in the following paragraphs, the results of this research are summarized briefly.

Age, Competitive Level, and Years of Experience as Factors Affecting Athletes' Preferences for Different Types of Coaching Behavior.
Although several sets of researchers (e.g., Chelladurai & Carron, 1983; Terry, 1984; Terry & Howe, 1984; VosStrache, 1979) have used a cross-sectional approach to examine differences between younger and older athletes in preferred leadership styles, the emphasis in these studies has not been on age alone but on age in combination with level of competition or years of sport experience. The studies conducted in this area support the notion that increased age and athletic maturity affect the type of leadership behaviors preferred by athletes. However, these differences may be evident primarily in the earlier age ranges. Specifically, Terry and Howe (1984) administered the LSS to 160 athletes in a variety of sports ranging from 17 to 40 years of age. They found no age differences in regard to preferred coaching behavior. Similarly, Terry (1984) also found no age differences on the five factors of the LSS in a group of 160 athletes ranging in age from 17 to 28 years. In contrast, Chelladurai and Carron (1983), who used the LSS to measure preferred coaching behaviors among four groups of male basketball players (early high school, high school junior, high school senior, and university level), did find some age differences. Specifically, the preference for coaches who show high levels of socially supportive behavior and who exhibit an autocratic leadership style linearly increased across the four age/competitive levels. In regard to coaching behaviors associated with the training and instruction factor, Chelladurai and Carron reported that preference for this set of coaching behaviors decreased for athletes from early to senior high school level but then increased again at the university level.

In an interesting discussion of the research results described in the preceding paragraph, Chelladurai and Carron (1983) suggested that preference for an autocratic coaching style may increase with age and with athletic maturity because sport, as a social system, is generally an autocratic enterprise. Athletes who remain in sport (i.e., those who progress through the various competitive levels) may become "socialized" into preferring less personal responsibility, thus allocating more control to coaches. Similarly, it may be hypothesized that athletes who prefer to retain personal responsibility for their behavior and who do not adapt to the autocratic coaching style may be selectively deleted from participation at the more elite competitive levels. Thus, the finding that preference for an autocratic coaching style increases with age or athletic maturity may not be so much a developmental phenomenon as an environmentally induced outcome. Chelladurai and Carron also speculated that the increased preference with age for a socially supportive coaching style may be because older athletes who compete at more elite levels spend the greater proportion of their time in the sport context and thus need social support from individuals in that environment. In contrast, younger athletes, who may spend more of their time outside of the athletic environment, obtain social support from other non-sport-related individuals and thus have less need for such support from their coaches.

Gender As a Factor Affecting Athletes' Preferences for Different Types of Coaching Behavior.

Although Terry and Howe (1984) did not find gender differences in preferred coaching style in their sample of 17- to 40-year-old athletes, several other researchers have reported quite consistent variation between male and female athletes. Chelladurai and Saleh (1978) found that male physical education majors representing a variety of sports exhibited greater preference than their female peers for an autocratic coaching style, whereas the female participants indicated significantly greater preference than did the males for a democratic coaching style. In addition, the male athletes in this study exceeded their female peers in preference for social support from their coaches. Terry (1984) replicated the finding that male athletes tend to prefer an autocratic coaching style significantly more than do female athletes.

Consistent with the gender differences found in regard to preferred coaching style, two sets of researchers also found similar gender differences in the type of decision-making style athletes prefer their coaches to use in sport contexts. Chelladurai and Arnott (1985) administered a decision style questionnaire to 144 female and male university-level basketball players to identify the type of decision-making style athletes would prefer their coaches to use in example sport situations. Female athletes were significantly more apt than their male peers to prefer a participatory style in which the coach allows the athletes to

participate in the decision-making process. However, these gender differences were not replicated in a later study by Chelladurai et al. (1989) with a similar sample of university level basketball players. The male and female athletes in this study differed in their preferences for particular decision-making styles in only 1 of 32 problem-solving cases.

The results of this research suggest that there are some gender differences in regard to preferred coaching behaviors. Specifically, male and female athletes differ in degree of preference for an autocratic versus a democratic leadership style. Of course, as Chelladurai et al. (1989) and Terry (1984) pointed out, an alternative perspective with regard to this research is that there are considerably more similarities between male and female athletes than differences in preferred coaching behavior. Although gender differences may occur, they typically are found only in regard to the coach's decision-making style. Certainly, further research is necessary to identify the reasons for such observed differences. In addition, future researchers also may benefit from examining gender differences in athletes' preferences for different types of coaching behavior and in their perceptions of such behaviors as a function of the athletes' age. As an example of the value of this research approach, researchers in the developmental and sport psychology literatures have noted that gender differences in regard to various psychological characteristics (e.g., attributional patterns, self-confidence, perceived competence) may not occur until during puberty or even postpuberty (Phillips, 1987; Stevenson & Newman, 1986; Stewart & Corbin, 1988). Thus, few gender differences may be found before the age of 12 or 13 years. In regard to coaching effectiveness, age also may interact with gender to affect preferred and perceived coach behaviors. Such interactional effects may be more interesting to examine and may provide considerably more information about the reasons for observed gender differences than would the examination of age or gender differences separately.

Nationality As a Factor Affecting Athletes' Preferences for Different Types of Coaching Behavior.

According to Chelladurai's (1978, 1990, 1993) model, the sociocultural prescriptions that characterize and differentiate between individual cultures may constitute a situational characteristic that will determine the most effective type of leadership behavior. In testing this aspect of the model, three sets of researchers have compared athletes from different cultures in regard to their preferred coaching style. Terry (1984) administered the LSS to 160 elite athletes from 10 different sports and from several different countries. He reported no differences in preferred coaching style as a function of nationality (United States, Great Britain, and Canada). However, Chelladurai, Malloy, Imamura, and Yamaguchi (1987) and Chelladurai, Imamura, Yamaguchi, Oinuma, and Miyauchi (1988) found significant differences between Japanese and Canadian subjects on several factors from the LSS. Chelladurai et al. (1987) administered the LSS to 156 male physical education students from a Canadian university and 106 male students from a Japanese university. The Japanese sample consisted of students who participated in sports identified as modern (e.g., track and field, rugby, wrestling, volleyball, soccer) and those who participated in more traditional sports (e.g., judo, Kendo, Kyuto). The researchers speculated that the attitudes, beliefs, and values of the two disparate cultures would be reflected in the subjects' preferences for different types of leader behavior. In addition, however, the researchers expected that type of sport (modern vs. traditional) might interact with culture to influence preferred leader behavior. Multivariate and univariate analyses of variance procedures using the five factors of the LSS showed that both groups of Japanese students showed more preference for social support than did the Canadian group. Japanese students who engaged in modern sports showed greater preference than did the Canadian sample for a democratic coaching style. Consistent with the researchers' hypotheses, Japanese students from the traditional sports showed greater preference for an autocratic coaching style than did both the Japanese modern group and the Canadian group. Finally, Canadian students exhibited greater preference for positive feedback than did Japanese athletes from traditional sports. In a follow-up study, Chelladurai et al. (1988) compared 115 Japanese and 100 Canadian university-level male athletes on preferred coaching behaviors. These results showed that the Japanese athletes preferred a more autocratic coaching style and more social support from their coaches, whereas Canadian athletes preferred significantly more training and instruction.

The results of these studies support the hypothesis that sociocultural prescriptions can be identified and used to predict or explain differences between athletes from different cultures in regard to preferred coaching behaviors. However, as Chelladurai et al. (1987) found, the type of sport in which group members are involved may interact with culture to affect preferred coaching styles.

Task Type As a Factor Affecting Athletes' Preferences for Different Types of Coaching Behavior. As noted in the previous section, the type of task in which group members are engaged also may determine which leadership behaviors will be most effective for that team. Based on concepts from both House's (House & Mitchell, 1974) path-goal theory and Chelladurai's (1978, 1990, 1993) multidimensional model of leadership, two particular task attributes have been identified as perhaps the most crucial in determining effective leadership behaviors across sports. These attributes are the degree of task variability inherent in the sport and the extent of cooperation necessary between group members. Task variability describes the environmental conditions under which sport tasks are performed. Sports classified as "open" include those in which the various skills are performed in a constantly changing environment (e.g., soccer, basketball, tennis, volleyball), whereas "closed" sports are performed in a relatively stable, static, and unchanging environment (e.g., gymnastics, swimming, track and field). Sports also can be classified according to the degree of interdependency among group members that is necessary for successful performance. Sports classified as interdependent include those in which successful performance outcomes depend on efficient interaction among teammates (e.g., basketball, soccer, hockey). In contrast, independent sports (e.g., tennis, swimming, gymnastics) do not require interaction among team members.

The sport type characteristics described in the preceding paragraph have been examined with regard to their influence on preferred coaching behavior. Terry and Howe (1984) found no support for the hypothesis that athletes from open sports differ in preferred coaching behaviors from their peers who participate in closed sports. However, they found support for the hypothesis that the degree of interdependency between group members will affect preferred coaching behavior. Specifically, athletes participating in sports that require interaction between group members (i.e., interdependent sports) showed greater preference for an autocratic coaching style and less preference for a democratic coaching style than did their peers who participated in independent (i.e., noninteracting) sports. In a subsequent study with an additional sample of collegiate athletes, Terry (1984) replicated this finding but also found that interdependent sport athletes showed greater preference for high frequencies of training and instruction and rewarding behavior from their coaches and less preference for democratic and social support behavior than did the independent sport athletes.

These results are consistent with the situational approach to leadership effectiveness, which suggests that a highly structured leadership style will be necessary in situations where tasks are varied and interdependency among members is essential. However, in situations where tasks are not varied and where efficient interaction between group members is unnecessary, a highly structured leadership style will be unnecessary and perhaps undesired. Also, as Terry (1984) noted, the greater preference of interdependent sport athletes for high frequencies of rewarding behavior may be a function of within-group competition (i.e., the individual athlete wants to be rewarded in front of her or his peers). Alternatively, because good performance by an individual athlete in interdependent sport contexts is not always immediately visible, such athletes may need rewarding behavior from their coaches more than do athletes from independent sports, where an individual's performance is more easily visible.

More recently, Riemer and Chelladurai (1995) examined the effects of task type on athletes' preferences for different types of coaching behaviors within a single sport. Specifically, these researchers measured the leadership style preferences of college football players and then compared the responses of offensive and defensive players. Their results showed that the two groups of athletes differed in the leadership styles and behaviors they preferred their coaches to exhibit. Defensive players preferred greater amounts of democratic behavior, autocratic behavior, and social support than did offensive players. Again, these results, combined with those that compared coaching leadership style preferences across sports, point to the need to consider context and contextual factors when investigating the correlates of coaching effectiveness.

Athletes' Psychological Characteristics As Factors Affecting Their Preferences for Different Types of Coaching Behavior. Although little research has been conducted to assess the degree to which athletes' psychological characteristics affect their preferences for different types of coaching behaviors, at least one set of researchers has demonstrated support for this notion. Specifically, Horn and Glenn (1988) found that athletes with an internal perception or locus of control showed strong preference for coaches who excelled in training and instruction behaviors. In contrast, athletes with an external perception of control preferred coaches who exhibited an autocratic leadership style. Interestingly, however, gender interacted with these psychological characteristics, because female athletes who were classified as highly competitive trait anxious strongly preferred coaches who provided positive, supportive, and informational feedback. In contrast, male athletes' level of trait anxiety did not affect their preference for particular coaching behaviors. These results provide initial support for the notion that athletes' psychological characteristics may affect the type of leadership behavior they prefer. Further research may identify additional psychological characteristics (e.g., self-confidence, intrinsic/extrinsic motivational orientation, achievement goal orientation) that will affect athletes' preferences for particular leadership behaviors.

In summary, the rather extensive research base on athletes' preferences for particular types of coaching behavior provides additional support for the hypothesized link between boxes 7 and 8 in the working model (see figure 10.1). As the research cited in this section shows, athletes differ from each other in the type of leadership behaviors they prefer their coaches to exhibit. If athletes differ in preferred coaching behavior, then athletes probably also differ in the way in which they perceive, interpret, and evaluate their coaches' behavior. Such interindividual variability in athletes' perceptions, interpretations, and preferences for particular types of coaching behavior supports the need to include box 8 as the mediating factor between boxes 5 and 9. In the next section, I review research that has examined the effects of different types of actual and perceived coaching behaviors on athletes' self-perceptions.

Links Between Coaches' Behavior and Athletes' Self-Perceptions and Level of Motivation

Over the past 25 years, a number of research studies have tested the relationship between coaches' behavior (measured either through observational means or through athletes' perceptions of their coaches' behavior; boxes 5 or 8) and selected dimensions of their athletes' psychosocial responses (e.g., perceived competence, self-esteem; box 9), level of motivation (box 10), or behavior (e.g., sport discontinuation; box 6). In general, this research has supported the hypothesized links. Furthermore, as a review of this research shows, we can now identify particular dimensions of coaches' behavior that appear to be most facilitative of athletes' performance and behavior as well as those that appear to be most detrimental. However, as the research cited in the next sections shows, the effectiveness (or ineffectiveness) of particular types of coaching behavior varies as a function of the athletes themselves and of the sport context.

In the following sections of this chapter, the research studies referred to in the previous paragraph are reviewed. This review is organized into two main sections corresponding to the way in which the coaches' behavior was measured. Specifically, the following literature review begins with the research studies that examined the effects of coaches' leadership styles on athletes' self-perceptions and levels of motivation. The second section focuses on the research studies that examined the effects of coaches' feedback patterns.

Effects of Coaches' Leadership Styles

As noted earlier, the effects of coaches' leadership styles on their athletes' psychosocial growth and development have been measured primarily by using four different instruments. Thus, the review of the research in this section is organized around this measurement component.

Studies Using the LSS. The largest amount of research on the effects of coaches' leadership styles has been conducted with the LSS, which measures five different dimensions of leadership style. In addition, these research studies predominantly have been based on Chelladurai's (1978, 1990, 1993) multidimensional model of leadership effectiveness. According to this model, athletes will experience optimal performance and satisfaction if their coaches' leadership behaviors are congruent with the leadership behaviors that the athletes prefer and with the behaviors required by or appropriate to the particular sport situation. In attempting to test this hypothesized connection between actual, preferred, and required leadership behaviors and the positive outcomes of performance and satisfaction, most researchers

have followed Chelladurai's (1984) lead in conceiving satisfaction to be a multifaceted construct, incorporating satisfaction with a number of aspects of the sport environment including individual personal performance, team performance, type of leadership, and overall team climate. The satisfaction construct typically has been measured by administering a Likert-style questionnaire in which athletes are asked to indicate the degree of satisfaction they feel with regard to each of the previously described facets. Although fewer researchers have attempted to measure performance as a possible outcome of effective leadership, those who have done so have used either team win–loss percentage (e.g., Weiss & Friedrichs, 1986), amount of playing time/starter status (Garland & Barry, 1988), or individualized perceived performance outcomes (e.g., Chelladurai et al., 1988; Horne & Carron, 1985).

The research conducted to test the relationship between satisfaction/performance and leader behavior has provided general support for Chelladurai's (1978, 1990, 1993) model. Chelladurai (1984), for example, who administered both the perceived and preferred versions of the LSS to a sample of 196 university athletes, found that the discrepancy between these two sets of variables (i.e., perceived coaching behaviors subtracted from preferred coaching behaviors) explained a greater percentage of the variance in athletes' satisfaction scores than did either of the two sets of variables alone. In particular, the discrepancy scores indicated that the leadership behaviors of training and instruction and positive feedback were the two dimensions of coaches' behavior that most affected the athletes' level of satisfaction. Subsequent studies conducted by Schliesman (1987) and Horne and Carron (1985) with university-level athletes demonstrated additional support for the relationship between the discrepancy scores representing training and instruction, positive feedback, and social support and measures of athletes' satisfaction with the coaches' leadership. In contrast, Chelladurai and colleagues (1988), who investigated leadership issues with Japanese and Canadian athletes, reported that the perceived (actual) leadership scores explained a greater amount of the variance in athletes' satisfaction scores than did the discrepancy scores. In a more recent study, Riemer and Chelladurai (1995) used hierarchical regression procedures in an attempt to separate out the effects of the three measures of coaches' behavior (preferred, perceived, and the interaction of the two terms) on college football players' level of satisfaction. Their results showed that the relative effects of these three components of coaching behavior varied as a function of the particular leadership subscale. Specifically, the congruence (interaction) of preferred and perceived leadership was most critical to athletes' level of satisfaction in regard to social support from coaches. In contrast, the perceived leadership scores for training and instruction and positive feedback were more significant predictors of athletes' satisfaction than were either the preferred or the congruent scores.

Although Chelladurai and Riemer (1998) recommended further research on the relative contributions of the three measures of coaching behavior to athletes' level of satisfaction and performance, the combined results of these studies support the notion that the discrepancy between actual and preferred leadership behaviors can be used to predict the degree of satisfaction athletes will express about their coach's leadership style. More particularly, it appears that the leadership behaviors associated with training and instruction, positive feedback, and social support are most highly correlated with athlete satisfaction.

As noted, the studies described in the previous paragraph support the interactive effects of actual and preferred leader behaviors on the positive outcome measure of group satisfaction. In addition, however, Chelladurai and colleagues (Chelladurai, 1984; Chelladurai et al., 1988) reported clear evidence that situational factors also must be taken into account in describing the relationship between leader behavior and group satisfaction. Specifically, Chelladurai (1984) found that the relationship between member satisfaction and particular leadership discrepancy scores varied according to sport type (independent vs. interdependent, open vs. closed). That is, the leadership discrepancy scores that were identified as highly predictive for satisfaction among basketball athletes were not necessarily the same as those that predicted satisfaction among wrestlers and track-and-field athletes. In addition, Chelladurai et al. (1988) reported similar differences between Japanese and Canadian athletes in regard to the relationship between leadership variables and athlete satisfaction. Although a significant overall relationship between preferred leader behaviors and satisfaction scores was found for both groups of athletes, the particular leader behaviors that were most predictive differed somewhat across the groups. Although some of the differences obtained in these two studies can be at-

tributed to clearly identifiable aspects of the situation (i.e., characteristics of the sport tasks and varying sociocultural prescriptions), other differences between sport types and cultures cannot be readily explained. Thus, future research in this area is certainly warranted.

More recently, other researchers have used the LSS to examine the more specific relationship between athletes' perceptions of their coaches' leadership style and the athletes' level of satisfaction (Dwyer & Fischer, 1990; McMillin, 1990). The results of these studies also support the value of selected leadership styles. Dwyer and Fischer, for example, found that wrestlers' level of satisfaction with regard to their coaches was high if the wrestlers perceived the coaches to exhibit high levels of positive feedback and training and instructional behaviors and lower levels of autocratic behavior. McMillin, working with university-level soccer players, found that athletes' perceptions of the degree to which their coaches exhibited high frequencies of training and instructional behavior and were democratic in their leadership style were the predictors that contributed the most to athletes' level of satisfaction with their coaches' leadership.

In an expansion of the previous research, Weiss and Friedrichs (1986) incorporated several additional constructs from the Chelladurai (1978, 1990, 1993) model into their study conducted with 251 collegiate male basketball players and their coaches. Specifically, these researchers tested the model's hypothesized connection between coaches' personal characteristics (age at time of hire, previous playing and coaching experience, prior win–loss record), coaches' leadership behaviors (as measured through athletes' perceptions of such behavior), selected situational factors (enrollment size of school, amount of basketball budget, amount of scholarships, prior winning tradition, percentage of coach's appointment), and the positive outcomes of member satisfaction and performance. The outcome variables were measured in terms of seasonal win–loss records and athletes' self-reported satisfaction with various dimensions of their sport environment (e.g., playing conditions, teammates, amount of work, school identification, coaches' leadership). Regression analyses indicated some support for the hypothesis that certain coaching behaviors would be linked to member satisfaction. In particular, high frequencies of rewarding behavior, social support, and a democratic decision-making style on the part of coaches were associated with high satisfaction among their athletes. In contrast, only one leader behavior dimension was associated with team win–loss percentage. Specifically, high frequencies of social support were correlated with poorer performance records. In addition, certain coach attributes including age at time of hire, previous win–loss records, and amount of playing experience were related to athlete satisfaction. That is, coaches hired at younger ages and those with better previous win–loss records but less playing experience received higher satisfaction scores from their athletes than did coaches who did not exhibit such characteristics. These results again support the interacting nature of situational and personal factors in the prediction of leadership effectiveness.

Other studies discussed by Chelladurai (1993) in his recent review of the leadership effectiveness research support the link between athletes' perceptions of their coaches' leadership style and the athletes' level of performance (e.g., see Gordon, 1986, and Serpa, Pataco, & Santos, 1991). Again, these studies were conducted with athletes at a higher level of competition (e.g., university soccer athletes and world-class handball team players). Considerably less research has been conducted with younger athletes or those who play at less competitive levels. Thus, continued research is warranted in this area.

Because the majority of the research studies that have used the LSS as the primary measure of coaches' leadership style have been based on Chelladurai's (1978, 1990, 1993) multidimensional model, the dependent variables in these studies have tended to center on the construct of athletes' satisfaction or on the athletes' level of performance. Only more recently have other researchers used the LSS to examine the impact of particular leadership styles on different aspects of athletes' psychosocial responses.

Amorose and Horn (2000) used the LSS to measure collegiate athletes' ($N = 386$) perceptions of their coaches' leadership style. Drawing on cognitive–evaluation theory (Deci & Ryan, 1980, 1985), these researchers hypothesized that athletes who perceived their coaches to exhibit a more democratic coaching style and to respond to players' performances with high levels of praise, encouragement, and information-based feedback would exhibit higher intrinsic motivation than would athletes who perceived their coaches to be more authoritarian in leadership style. The results of this study support this hypothesized relationship. Specifically, athletes who scored high in intrinsic

motivation perceived their coaches to exhibit a leadership style that was low in autocratic behavior, was high in frequency of positive and information-based feedback, and emphasized a primary orientation toward training and instruction. Amorose and Horn also examined the relationship between perceived coaching style and athletes' intrinsic motivation separately for the male and female athletes. Although the results of the two analyses were generally very similar, it appeared that a democratic coaching style was more important to female athletes' intrinsic motivation than it was to the males. This finding is consistent with the earlier cited research showing that female athletes exhibit greater preference than do their male peers for a democratic coaching style (Chelladurai & Arnott, 1985; Chelladurai & Saleh, 1978).

In a follow-up study, Amorose and Horn (in press) recruited a sample of 72 first-year Division I athletes from a variety of sports. They assessed the intrinsic motivation levels of these athletes at both pre- and postseason and also used the LSS at postseason to assess athletes' perceptions concerning the type of leadership style exhibited by their coaches during the season. Multivariate correlational examination of the data showed that first-year athletes whose level of intrinsic motivation increased over the season perceived that their coaches provided high frequencies of training and instructional behaviors, provided low frequencies of social support, and were low in an autocratic behavioral style. These results, then, linked changes in first-year collegiate athletes' level of intrinsic motivation over a season to their perceptions of their coaches' behavior.

Several studies recently have examined the relationship between coaches' leadership style and athletes' perceptions of team cohesiveness (Gardner, Shields, Bredemeier, & Bostrom, 1996; Pease & Kozub, 1994; Westre & Weiss, 1991). Although the three study samples varied somewhat in age, sport type, and gender, the results were generally very consistent. Specifically, the LSS subscales corresponding to training and instruction, democratic behavior, positive feedback, and social support were positively and significantly related to (or predictive of) high levels of team task cohesion. In addition, Gardner and colleagues found that an autocratic leadership style was negatively related to both team task cohesion and team social cohesion.

In general, then, research examining the relationship between coaches' leadership style (as assessed by using the LSS) and various dimensions of athletes' psychosocial responses has consistently supported the notion that coaches' leadership style is an important factor in affecting athletes' psychosocial well-being. In particular, the type of leadership style the coach exhibits appears to significantly affect athletes' level of satisfaction, the degree to which they will be intrinsically motivated, and their perceptions of their team's cohesiveness.

Studies Using the Decision-Style Questionnaires. As noted earlier in this chapter, another instrument has been developed and used to measure coaches' leadership style. This instrument, based on Chelladurai and Haggerty's (1978) normative model of decision-making styles in coaching, provides a more specific measure of the decision-making styles that individual coaches use in practice and game situations. In a 1988 study, Gordon administered this decision-style questionnaire to 161 male intercollegiate soccer athletes and 18 of their coaches. Athletes were asked to identify which decision style (autocratic, consultative, participative, or delegative) they would prefer their coach to use in 15 different situations and which style they thought their coach would actually use. Coaches were asked to indicate the decision style they would use in each of the 15 situations. Athletes also completed a coaching effectiveness questionnaire that measured their satisfaction with various aspects of their coach's behavior. Correlational analyses of these sets of data revealed strong support for the hypothesis that discrepancy between actual and preferred decision-making styles will decrease satisfaction among athletes. When there was high congruence between a coach's self-reported decision style and that preferred and perceived by athletes, then high ratings of the coach's effectiveness were reported.

Several other studies have used other versions of the decision-style questionnaire (e.g., Chelladurai & Arnott, 1985; Chelladurai & Quek, 1991; Chelladurai et al., 1989). However, these studies did not include a component measuring the effectiveness of coaches' decision styles. That is, these studies only examined the type of decision styles that coaches choose to use or the type of decision styles that athletes perceive or prefer their coaches to use. The effectiveness of these decision styles on athletes' psychosocial growth and development was not assessed. However, based on current research and theory, this aspect of coaches' behavior appears to be an important component to examine in future research studies.

Studies Using the Autonomous/Controlling Leadership Scales. As noted earlier, Vallerand and Pelletier (1985; Pelletier & Vallerand, 1985) conceptualized coaches' leadership style in a different way than did Chelladurai and his colleagues. Vallerand and Pelletier based their conceptualization on research and theory from the educational psychology literature (e.g., Deci, Nezlek, & Sheinman, 1981; Deci, Schwartz, Sheinman, & Ryan, 1981) showing that teachers may exhibit either a controlling pattern of behavior in the classroom (e.g., using rewards to motivate students, promoting ego involvement and competition between students, administering rewards in a controlling fashion) or a more autonomy-oriented pattern of behavior (e.g., encouraging and supporting the transfer of responsibility for student behavior to students themselves). Furthermore, this research has shown that students whose teachers exhibit a more autonomous teaching style score higher on intrinsic motivation than do students whose teachers tend to be more controlling in their classroom behavior. As Vallerand and Losier (1999) argued in a recent review, these results are consistent with self-determination theory (Deci & Ryan, 1985, 1991), which hypothesizes that teachers who act in a controlling manner undermine their students' perceptions of autonomy (i.e., the belief that one is self-initiating in relationship to one's own actions), which, in turn, decreases students' intrinsic motivation. In contrast, teachers who exhibit a more autonomous teaching style facilitate or enhance their students' perceptions of autonomy, thus increasing intrinsic motivation.

To test these theoretical formulations in a more sport-oriented setting, Vallerand and Pelletier (1985; Pelletier & Vallerand, 1985) developed a sport-specific questionnaire to assess coaches' and athletes' perceptions regarding the coaches' tendencies to be either controlling or autonomy-oriented. Vallerand and Pelletier then administered these questionnaires to two samples of teenage swimmers. Swimmers who perceived their coaches to exhibit a more autonomous interpersonal style scored higher on measures of perceived competence and intrinsic motivation than did swimmers who perceived their coaches to be more controlling. Other research studies, based on self-determination theory and conducted to investigate the link between coaches' behavior and athletes' perceptions of competence, autonomy, and relatedness, as well as their levels of intrinsic motivation and persistence in sport, were cited and described by Vallerand and Losier (1999) in their recent review article. The procedures used in these studies included correlational as well as intervention-based methodologies (e.g., Pelletier, Briere, Blais, & Vallerand, 1988). These studies, then, strongly support the notion that the type of leadership style that coaches adopt and exhibit in practice and competitive events can significantly affect their athletes' perceptions of competence, autonomy, and relatedness, which, in turn, can affect their motivational orientation and their persistence in the sport.

Studies Using the PMCSQ and Related Instrumentation. The relatively strong relationship between coaches' leadership style and their athletes' level of motivation and self-perceptions has been demonstrated by researchers who have followed the tenets of Nicholls' (1984, 1989), Dweck's (1986, 1999), and Ames' (1984, 1992a, 1992b) achievement goal orientation theories. This work essentially began with a study conducted by Seifriz et al. (1992) with high school varsity male basketball players. To measure athletes' perceptions of the type of motivational climate created by their coaches during games and practices, these researchers developed the PMCSQ (see earlier discussion of this questionnaire). This questionnaire consists of two subscales: (a) the Mastery Goal (Task-Involving) subscale, which contains items reflecting a team climate that emphasizes hard work and improvement and the importance of all players to the team's goals; and (b) the Performance Goal (Ego-Involving) subscale, which contains items emphasizing between-player rivalry, high frequencies of punishing behavior, and the promotion of individual "stars." Players' scores on the PMCSQ indicated that teams significantly differed from each other in perceived motivational climate. Furthermore, there was a significant relationship between athletes' perceptions of their team's motivational climate and the athletes' achievement-related perceptions and affective responses. Specifically, athletes who perceived that their team's climate was predominantly mastery-oriented reported greater levels of enjoyment and tended to believe that effort leads to success. In contrast, athletes who perceived that their coaches created a performance-oriented (ego-involving) climate exhibited lower levels of enjoyment and tended to believe that basketball success can best be attributed to ability.

Other research with the PMCSQ has resulted in similar findings. Walling et al. (1993) administered the PMCSQ to a sample of male and female adolescent athletes from a variety of sports. Athletes who perceived their coaches to create a mastery-oriented (task-involving) motivational climate scored higher on a satisfaction with team scale and lower on a performance worry scale, whereas athletes who perceived their team climate to be more performance-oriented (ego-involving) scored higher on performance worry and lower on team satisfaction. Treasure and Roberts (1998) also examined the effects of motivational climate on female adolescent athletes' beliefs about the causes of success and sources of satisfaction. Again, athletes' perceptions of a mastery-oriented (task-involving) climate were significantly related to their belief that success follows from one's own efforts and that satisfaction can be obtained from personal mastery experiences. In contrast, athletes perceiving a performance-oriented (ego-involving) climate believed that satisfaction could be derived from outperforming others and that success could be attributed to personal ability and deception.

Other studies have examined the relationship between athletes' perceptions concerning the type of motivational climate that characterizes their team and measures of the athletes' self-perceptions, attitudes, beliefs, values, and behaviors (e.g., Boyd, Yin, Ellis, & French, 1995; Ebbeck & Becker, 1994; Ommundsen, Roberts, & Kavussanu, 1998; Pensgaard & Roberts, 1996; Treasure & Roberts, 1995a). Although these studies differed considerably in participant sample, type of sport, and level of competition, very consistent results were found. Specifically, these studies found that a mastery-oriented (task-involving) climate is positively and significantly related to athletes' level of enjoyment, satisfaction, and interest in the sport as well as their endorsement of a task goal perspective. Some support also has been found for the notion that a performance-oriented (ego-involving) climate is significantly and positively related to perceptions of tension, pressure, and performance anxiety.

Similar results were found by researchers who investigated the effects of motivational climate on students' psychosocial responses in physical education contexts (e.g., Goudas & Biddle, 1994; Kavussanu & Roberts, 1996; Papaioannou, 1994, 1995, 1998; Treasure, 1997). Again, these researchers found support for the value of a mastery-oriented (task-involving) motivational climate in regard to facilitating intrinsic motivation, perceptions of competence, and positive affect on the part of physical education students.

More recently, researchers have begun to conduct more experimentally based studies designed to examine the causal relationship between motivational climate and athletes' psychosocial responses. Theeboom and his colleagues (Theeboom, De Knop, & Weiss, 1995), for example, designed an experimental program in which two groups of children, ages 8 to 12 years, enrolled in a Chinese martial arts activity class were taught by using either a mastery or a performance-oriented teaching style. At the end of the 3-week program, the children in the two groups were compared to determine the effects of the two types of instructional climates. Children in the mastery climate group exhibited greater enjoyment and better motor skills than did the children in the performance climate group. In addition, postprogram interviews with the children suggested that the mastery group children exhibited higher perceptions of personal ability and higher levels of intrinsic motivation than did children in the performance group.

Other researchers also conducted experimentally based studies to examine the effects of motivational climate on individuals' psychosocial responses in other types of physical activity contexts. These contexts have included physical education classes (Goudas et al., 1995; Papaioannou & Kouli, 1999) and exercise settings (Lloyd & Fox, 1992). In general, the results of these studies have consistently supported the link between the motivational climate provided by physical education teachers and exercise leaders and the athletes' (or students') cognitive, affective, and emotional well-being. In particular, a mastery-oriented climate appears to be more facilitative of positive psychosocial responses in children and adults.

In regard to future research in this area, Duda (1996) and Treasure and Roberts (1998) have noted the necessity of adopting an interactional approach. Specifically, these writers argued that athletes' perceptions of the motivational climate will interact with athletes' own dispositional goal orientations to affect their subsequent performance, behavior, and psychosocial responses. In a study designed to assess such hypothesized interactive effects, Treasure and Roberts administered self-report questionnaires to a sample of 274 female adolescent athletes attending a week-long summer basketball camp. These questionnaires assessed the athletes' own personal or dispositional achievement goal orientations (task and ego), their perceptions of the camp's motivational climate (mastery and performance-oriented), and

the athletes' beliefs about the causes of sport success and their sources of satisfaction in regard to the basketball camp experience. Analyses of the data with hierarchical regression techniques showed that athletes' own personal or dispositional achievement goal orientations, as well as their perceptions of the camp's motivational climate, contributed significantly to the prediction of athletes' beliefs concerning sport success and sources of satisfaction. In addition, however, the interaction of these two constructs contributed a significant amount to the regression equations. In particular, athletes' perceptions of a strong mastery motivational climate appeared to complement (or add to) athletes' own high dispositional task orientation in the prediction of mastery experiences as a source of satisfaction. Perhaps more importantly, perception of a mastery motivational climate also buttressed the effects of a low dispositional task orientation in regard to the belief that mastery experiences can be perceived as a source of satisfaction in the sport domain.

These results suggest that the effects of coaches' leadership styles (or the type of motivational climate they create in practices and competitive events) will be moderated, at least in part, by characteristics of the athletes themselves. This notion, again, supports the working model (see figure 10.1) in suggesting that the effectiveness of different types of coaching behaviors will differ as a function of the athletes and the particular sport context (i.e., box 7 appears to be an important component in determining the correlates of coaching effectiveness).

As the research cited in this section has indicated, there is strong and consistent empirical evidence to show that the type of leadership style coaches exhibit in practice and game contexts significantly affects the self-perceptions, level of motivation, and emotional well-being of their athletes. In the next section, I review the research that has examined the effects of coaches' feedback patterns on athletes' psychosocial development.

Effects of Coaches' Feedback Patterns

Much of the research on this topic was stimulated by the series of studies conducted by Smith and Smoll and their colleagues at the University of Washington. They began their work by developing the CBAS, an observational instrument designed to assess the frequency with which individual coaches exhibit 12 behavioral dimensions (Smith et al., 1977; see also earlier section in this chapter). After developing and testing the CBAS, Smith and Smoll and their colleagues (Smith et al., 1978; Smith, Smoll, & Curtis, 1979; Smith, Zane, Smoll, & Coppel, 1983; Smoll et al., 1978) conducted a series of research studies designed to examine the link between coaches' behaviors and young athletes' psychosocial development. In a 1978 descriptive study, Smith et al. used the CBAS to code the behaviors exhibited by 51 male Little League baseball coaches during a total of 202 games. The researchers also asked the coaches at the end of the season to retrospectively rate their own behavior by using a questionnaire version of the CBAS. Finally, the researchers also administered a postseason questionnaire and conducted individual interviews with the 542 boys, ages 8 to 15, who played for the 51 coaches. In these interview sessions, players were asked a series of questions regarding their perceptions of their coaches' behavior (again by using a questionnaire version of the CBAS) and their attitudes toward their coaches, their teammates, and the sport. In addition, the players completed self-report questionnaires selected to assess their general and athletic self-esteem. Athletes who played for coaches who exhibited high frequencies of supportive (reinforcement for player successes and encouragement in response to player errors) and instructional (general technical instruction and mistake-contingent technical instruction) behaviors had more positive postseason attitudes toward their coach, the sport, and their teammates than did players whose coaches exhibited lower frequencies of these supportive and instructional behaviors. In addition, high frequencies of supportive behaviors on the part of the coach were associated with higher levels of postseason self-esteem in the players.

As Smoll and Smith (1989) pointed out in a review of their work, the correlations between coaches' observed behavior (using the CBAS) and coaches' self-ratings regarding their own behavior were generally low and nonsignificant, whereas children's perceptions of the coaches' behavior (as assessed via a CBAS-based questionnaire) correlated much more highly with the actual CBAS scores. Another important finding reported by Smith et al. is that the young athletes' level of self-esteem mediated the coaches' effect on the players' attitudes. Specifically, children low in self-esteem were more affected by the coaches' behavior than were children higher in self-esteem.

In a follow-up study, Smith et al. (1979) used more experimentally based procedures to test for causal links between coaches' behavior and young athletes' psychosocial growth. In the field experiment, 31 Little League baseball coaches were assigned randomly to either an experimental (training) group or a control (no training) group. The coaches in the experimental group participated in a preseason cognitive–behavioral training program that was based on results concerning effective coaching behavior obtained in the earlier study (Smith et al., 1978). The control coaches did not participate in the preseason coaching behavior training program. Observation of the two groups of coaches during the competitive season indicated significant differences in the actual behaviors exhibited by the trained and control groups. That is, the trained coaches differed from the control coaches in ways that were consistent with the behavioral guidelines presented in the preseason training program. At the end of the season, 325 boys (ages 10–15 years) who had played for the two sets of coaches were administered questionnaires and were interviewed in their homes. Significant differences were found between the responses of the young athletes who had played for the trained coaches as opposed to the untrained (control) coaches. Specifically, players of the trained coaches evaluated their coaches more positively and indicated a higher level of attraction for their team than did players of the control coaches. In addition, children who played for the trained coaches exhibited a significant increase in self-esteem compared with their scores from the previous season. In contrast, the children who played for the control coaches showed no significant changes in self-esteem across the same time period. In addition, consistent with the results from their earlier study (Smith et al., 1978), the researchers also found self-esteem to be an important moderator with regard to the effects of coaching behavior on young athletes. In particular, the athletes with the lowest self-esteem showed the greatest differences in attitudes toward the trained and untrained coaches. Thus, again, it appears as if the young athletes who are most affected by their coaches' behavior are those who begin the season with lower levels of self-esteem.

Several years later, Smith and Smoll and their colleagues (Smith et al., 1983) published another observational study regarding coaches' behavior and athletes' postseason attitudes. This study was conducted with 31 youth basketball coaches and 182 of their young male athletes. The researchers again measured coaches' behavior by using the observational version of the CBAS and also assessed players' attitudes in a postseason data collection period. The results of the statistical analysis indicated support for the hypothesized link between coaches' behaviors and their athletes' postseason attitudes. Specifically, the degree to which coaches responded to player errors during games with mistake-contingent technical instruction was positively correlated with players' attraction toward the sport and their evaluation of their coach (e.g., how much they liked the coach, how much they thought their coach knew about basketball, and how good a teacher their coach was). In contrast, high levels of general technical instruction (instruction given in a general manner without reference to a specific player performance), keeping control behaviors (e.g., disciplining or keeping order behaviors), and punishment-oriented feedback (in response to player errors) were negatively related to the players' attitudes toward their coach and the team.

In a somewhat different study examining coaching effectiveness in youth sport, Barnett and her colleagues (Barnett, Smoll, & Smith, 1992) assessed the effects of a coach training program on the frequency with which players discontinued their sport participation. Eight Little League baseball coaches participated in a preseason training workshop designed to encourage them to exhibit the coaching behaviors that had been identified in previous studies as most effective. An additional 10 coaches served as the control group and thus did not participate in the preseason workshop. At the end of the season, boys who played for the experimental group coaches evaluated their coaches, the sport, and their teammates more positively than did the boys who played for the control coaches. Furthermore, the control group boys withdrew from the sport the following baseball season at a significantly greater rate than did boys who had played for the experimental (trained) coaches.

In a follow-up study, Smith, Smoll, and Barnett (1995) examined the effects of a coach training program on sport performance anxiety in young athletes. In this study, 18 male Little League coaches were assigned randomly to either an experimental training group ($n = 8$) or a control (no training) group ($n = 10$). Again, the eight coaches in the experimental group participated in the previously described coaching effectiveness training program, whereas the 10 coaches in the control group received no training. Coaches' behavior during the season was assessed by asking the players to rate their coaches at the end of the season in regard to the frequency with which the coaches exhibited the types of behavior emphasized in the preseason training program. In addition, the players' attitudes toward the sport, the team, and their coach were assessed postseason, and their trait anxiety was measured both preseason and postseason. Athletes who played for the trained coaches showed significantly higher enjoyment of the sport and more positive evaluations of their coach and their teammates than did athletes who played for the untrained coaches. In addition, athletes who played for the trained coaches showed a significant decrease in trait anxiety from pre- to postseason, whereas athletes who played for the untrained coaches showed no such change in anxiety.

In summary, these studies show consistent evidence that the types of behaviors coaches exhibit in practice and game contexts significantly affect the psychosocial growth and development of their players. This significant link between coaches' behavior and players' psychosocial responses has been demonstrated in both correlational and causal studies. However, these research studies were limited predominantly to male athletes and male coaches from such team sports as baseball and basketball. In addition, the athletes across these studies ranged in age from 8 to 15 years, and the dependent variables were limited primarily to self-esteem, player attitudes, and affective reactions. Other researchers subsequently expanded the study participant pool in regard to coaching effectiveness research projects. These studies are described in the following paragraphs.

Horn (1985) used the observational form of the CBAS to assess the frequency and type of behaviors that five softball coaches provided to their junior high female athletes ($n = 72$) in both practice and game contexts. In contrast to Smith and Smoll and their colleagues (Smith et al., 1978, 1979), Horn recorded the type of behaviors coaches gave to individual athletes on their team. In addition, Horn measured selected aspects of athletes' self-perceptions (e.g., perceived competence, perceived performance control, and expectancy for success) at preseason and postseason to test the hypothesis that the type of coaching behaviors individual athletes received over the competitive season would explain a significant amount of the variability between athletes in the changes they experienced over the season in their self-perceptions. Multivariate regression analyses indicated that the types of behaviors coaches exhibited to individual players in practice contexts were related significantly to changes in athletes' perceptions of competence. In particular, higher frequencies of reinforcement and nonreinforcement (coaches giving no reinforcement after a player's success) were negatively related to increases in players' perceptions of competence. That is, players who received high frequencies of either reinforcement or nonreinforcement did not increase in perceptions of competence. In contrast, higher frequencies of critical feedback were associated with increases in players' perceptions of competence. Horn interpreted the results in terms of the contingency and appropriateness of the feedback received by individual athletes. Specifically, she suggested that an important component of coaches' feedback is its contingency to performance. Citing a previous expectancy-based study (Horn, 1984), Horn argued that coaches may not always give positive reinforcement contingent to performance but rather may use it as a motivational technique. In contrast, criticism may be given more

Supportive, information-based feedback can be valuable to an individual's perception of competence.

© Human Kinetics

contingently to performance and thus may serve as a valuable source of information to athletes in terms of their self-assessment of skill competence.

After the publication of these observationally based studies, other researchers also examined the link between coaches' behavior and athletes' psychosocial growth and development. However, these researchers chose to measure players' perceptions of their coaches' behavior (box 8) rather than actual observationally based measures of the coaches' behavior (box 5). Black and Weiss (1992), for example, examined the relationship between athletes' perceptions of their coaches' behavior and the athletes' perceptions of their own ability and their level of intrinsic motivation. The athletes that were sampled included 312 male and female competitive swimmers ranging in age from 10 to 18 years. All study participants completed questionnaires assessing their perceptions of their sport competence and seasonal swimming success and their levels of intrinsic motivation. In addition, they completed a questionnaire version of the CBAS that measured the athletes' perceptions concerning the type of feedback their coaches typically gave in practice and competitive contexts after the swimmers' successful and unsuccessful performances. Multivariate multiple regression procedures were used to test for hypothesized relationships between perceived coaching behavior and the athletes' perceptions of their competence and their motivation. Because preliminary analyses revealed both age and gender differences in the coaching behavior and self-perception variables, separate analyses were conducted for males and females and for athletes from three different age groups. Although there were some rather specific gender and age differences, the results generally indicated that athletes who perceived that their coaches gave them high frequencies of information after successful performances and high frequencies of encouragement and information after unsuccessful performances exhibited higher scores on measures of perceived competence, perceived success, and intrinsic motivation than did athletes whose coaches gave lower frequencies of such positive and information-based feedback.

Similar data collection procedures were used by Allen and Howe (1998), who investigated the relationship between perceived coaching behaviors and athletes' perceptions of their sport competence and their satisfaction with the coach and their team. The study sample consisted of 143 female adolescent field hockey players, aged 14 to

18 years, who were administered a series of self-report questionnaires at an end-of-the-season tournament. The questionnaires assessed (a) the athletes' perceptions of their coaches' feedback patterns (by using a questionnaire version of the CBAS along with additional items designed to assess selected aspects of coaches' nonverbal behavior), (b) the athletes' perceptions of their own sport competence, and (c) their level of satisfaction with the coach and with their own involvement with the team. In addition, the coaches were asked to rate their players' actual field hockey ability by using a 4-point peer comparison-based scale. Multivariate statistical procedures were used to test the extent to which players' actual field hockey ability and their perceptions of their coaches' feedback patterns could explain a significant amount of the variation between the players in their perceptions of competence and level of satisfaction. Players' actual skill ability was a significant predictor of both players' level of perceived competence and satisfaction. In addition, however, selected aspects of coaches' feedback patterns were significantly related to players' perceptions of competence. Specifically, athletes who perceived their coaches to give high frequencies of praise and information-based feedback after successful player performances and low frequencies of encouragement and information-based feedback after player errors scored higher on the perceptions of competence scale than did athletes who perceived their coaches to exhibit the opposite feedback patterns. In addition, players' scores on the measures of satisfaction were significantly and positively related to their level of actual field hockey ability and their perceptions that their coach provided high frequencies of praise and information-based feedback after performance successes and high frequencies of encouragement and information-based feedback after performance errors.

Amorose and Horn (2000) also used a questionnaire version of the CBAS (along with the LSS) to examine the relationship between collegiate athletes' level of intrinsic motivation and their perceptions of their coaches' feedback patterns. Multivariate analysis of this data revealed that athletes (both male and female) who perceived their coaches to provide higher frequencies of positive and information-based feedback, and lower frequencies of punishment-oriented feedback, ignoring players' mistakes, and nonreinforcement of players' successful performances, scored higher on intrinsic motivation than did

players whose coaches exhibited the opposite feedback patterns.

In a more experimentally based research study, Amorose and Weiss (1998) examined how specific types of coaching feedback would affect children's perceptions of athletes' performance. Sixty boys and girls served as the study participants and were specifically selected to represent two age groups (6- to 8-year-olds and 12- to 14-year-olds). All children watched a series of videotape scenarios in which athletes attempted to hit a baseball or softball. After each performance attempt, feedback was provided by a coach whose voice was heard in the background. The videotaped protocol showed three successful performances (i.e., athlete successfully hit the ball) and three unsuccessful performances (i.e., athlete did not hit the ball). After the successful performances, the coach responded with one of three types of feedback: praise, skill-relevant informational feedback, and neutral feedback. Similarly, after the unsuccessful performances, the coach responded with either critical, informational, or neutral feedback. Multivariate analyses indicated that the two age groups did not differ in their reaction to the three types of feedback. Rather, all study participants (regardless of age or gender) rated the successful athletes who received praise from their coach as higher in level of ability, higher in level of effort, and more apt to experience future success than successful athletes who received either neutral or informational feedback. In the unsuccessful condition, the study participants rated the athletes who received informational feedback in response to their performance error as higher in ability and more apt to experience future success than athletes who received either neutral or critical feedback from the coach. Thus, as Amorose and Weiss concluded, it appears as if positive feedback (praise) from coaches in response to players' successes and informational feedback (skill-relevant corrective instruction) in response to player errors may be most facilitative of young athletes' perceptions of ability and expectancies for future success.

Other experimentally based laboratory studies (e.g., Escarti & Guzman, 1999; Fitzsimmons, Landers, Thomas, & van der Marsh, 1991; McAuley, Duncan, Wraith, & Lettunich, 1991) have shown that individual performers who are provided with positive feedback regarding their performance on a physical activity achievement task will subsequently exhibit higher levels of task self-efficacy and significantly better performance than performers who are given negative feedback about their performance. In the most recent of these studies, Escarti and Guzman (1999) used structural equation modeling to demonstrate that positive feedback from the experimenter in response to college students' performance on a hurdling task directly affected both the students' subsequent level of performance and their tendencies to select a more difficult task but also indirectly affected students' performance and task choice as mediated through students' level of task self-efficacy. The results of these more experimentally based laboratory studies support the causal relationship between the feedback individuals receive after their performance attempts and their subsequent perceptions of their ability as well as their performance and behavior.

Summary of Research Linking Coaches' Behavior to Athletes' Psychosocial Growth and Development

The research reviewed here concerning the links between coaches' behaviors in practice and game situations (as measured either directly or indirectly via athletes' perceptions of their coaches' behaviors) and athletes' psychosocial growth and development provides considerable support for these hypothesized connections. In particular, the link between coaches' behaviors (actual or perceived) and athletes' psychosocial growth and development has been supported by correlational as well as experimental research approaches.

Furthermore, this research shows some consistency in regard to the specific coaching leadership styles and feedback patterns that may be most facilitative or detrimental to the psychological well-being of athletes. In particular, a coaching leadership style characterized by high frequencies of training and instructional behavior and high levels of social support and positive feedback appears to be most facilitative of athletes' level of satisfaction, intrinsic motivation, and team cohesion. Similarly, a coaching leadership style that is less autocratic or controlling and more democratic or autonomous in nature has been linked to the development and maintenance of high intrinsic motivation and perceptions of competence in athletes. From a related perspective, coaches who create a mastery-oriented (task-involving) team climate appear more apt to have athletes with higher levels of intrinsic motivation, perceptions of competence, self-efficacy, enjoyment, and interest. Furthermore, a performance-oriented (ego-involving) team climate appears to create higher levels of performance worry and anxiety on the part of athletes.

In regard to feedback patterns, consistent evidence points to the value of coaches providing high frequencies of positive, supportive, and information-based feedback (especially in response to athletes' performance errors) and low frequencies of punishment-oriented feedback. In addition, coaches who frequently provide no feedback in response to players' performance successes (i.e., coach ignores players' successful task attempts) and performance errors (i.e., coach ignores or gives no response to players' unsuccessful task attempts) appear to have athletes with lower perceptions of competence, lower levels of self-esteem and intrinsic motivation, and higher levels of trait anxiety.

The results of the research discussed here concerning the coaching leadership styles, behaviors, and feedback patterns that are most effective (or ineffective) in facilitating athletes' psychosocial growth and development are consistent with the current theoretical literature in the general psychology and sport psychology fields (see table 10.1). For example, according to self-determination theory (Deci & Ryan, 1985, 1991), social or situational factors within the achievement environment that promote a person's feelings of autonomy (i.e., the perception that one is regulating one's own actions), competence (i.e., the perception that one can interact effectively with the environment), and relatedness (i.e., the perception that one is connected with significant others) should increase individuals' level of intrinsic motivation. In contrast, situational factors that "rob" individuals of feelings of autonomy, competence, and relatedness will undermine individuals' intrinsic motivation. It is easy to see, based on these theoretical tenets, how an autocratic or controlling coaching style can undermine athletes' perceptions of autonomy and thus lead to lower intrinsic motivation, whereas an autonomous or democratic coaching style can facilitate athletes' perceptions of autonomy and thus enhance their intrinsic motivation. Furthermore, coaches who provide athletes with significant amounts of social support should promote athletes' perceptions of relatedness and thus facilitate their level of intrinsic motivation.

In regard to feedback patterns, self-determination theory (Deci & Ryan, 1985, 1991) also postulates that events or situational factors that provide the individual with information about her or his competence should facilitate the development of intrinsic motivation in the individual. Conversely, events or situational factors that convey negative information about personal competence should undermine individuals' intrinsic motivation. Drawing on these notions, Ryan, Connell, and Deci (1985) and Horn and colleagues (Amorose & Horn, in press; Horn, 1987; Horn & Harris, in press) have argued that high frequencies of positive and information-based feedback from coaches in response to athletes' performance successes and particularly their performance errors should constitute strong situational sources of information that confirm athletes' perceptions of competence; in turn, these perceptions of competence should increase athletes' levels of intrinsic motivation. In contrast, punishment-oriented feedback can undermine athletes' perceptions of competence, and no feedback (nonreinforcement and ignoring mistakes) from the coaches can serve as a neutral or even negative source of competence information. Again, then, according to self-determination theory, these low perceptions of competence can lead to low levels of intrinsic motivation (see also discussion by Vallerand & Losier, 1999, on the further use of self-determination theory in the study of coaching effectiveness).

Harter's competence motivation theory (1978, 1981) also provides a strong theoretical framework for interpreting the coaching behaviors that appear to be most effective or ineffective. According to Harter, individuals need to receive positive and contingent feedback in response to their mastery attempts in any achievement domain. Receiving such positive and contingent feedback allows children to develop high perceptions of competence and an internal perception of control. Furthermore, this type of feedback during the childhood years is especially important because it helps children internalize achievement goal standards and thus develop a level of independence from external others. Therefore, the research on coaches' feedback patterns—which has rather consistently demonstrated the effectiveness of providing athletes with high frequencies of positive and information-based feedback and the corresponding ineffectiveness of nonreinforcement or ignoring of mistakes—is very much consistent with Harter's competence motivation model.

Obviously, the theoretical models espoused by Nicholls (1984, 1989), Dweck (1986, 1999), and Ames (1984, 1992a, 1992b) also can be used to interpret and support the leadership styles and behaviors that have been found to be most effective or ineffective. Specifically, a mastery-oriented motivational climate, with its emphasis on individual task mastery, self-referenced evaluation, individualized goal structures, and group cooperation rather than competition (see teacher behavior recommendations/guidelines provided by Treasure & Roberts, 1995b), would be expected to facilitate a task goal orientation on the part of athletes. A task goal orientation (in contrast to an ego goal orientation) has been linked to positive affect, high levels of perceived competence and intrinsic motivation, and adaptive achievement beliefs.

Although the other theoretical models listed in table 10.1 have not been used with any consistency in investigating the correlates of coaching effectiveness, they certainly have the potential to do so. The interested reader is referred to Weiss and Ferrer-Caja (chapter 5, this volume) for further discussion of the sport commitment model (Scanlan, Carpenter, Schmidt, Simons, & Keeler, 1993) and the expectancy-value model (Eccles & Harold, 1991) as well as the possible application of these models to the investigation of coaching effectiveness. Furthermore, McAuley and Blissmer (chapter 6, this volume) address issues relating to self-efficacy theory (Bandura, 1977, 1986) and attribution theory (Wiener, 1986, 1992) and thus provide a good source of information about the use of these theories in coaching effectiveness research.

In general, then, the coaching styles, behaviors, and feedback patterns identified earlier as the most effective or ineffective with regard to athletes' psychosocial growth and development have been supported through empirical research but also can be strongly linked to the theoretical literature in the field. Despite the rather significant advances that have occurred over the last two decades in our knowledge base on coaching effectiveness, there is still much to be learned. In the final section of this chapter, I present suggestions and directions for future research.

FUTURE DIRECTIONS IN COACHING EFFECTIVENESS RESEARCH

The preceding review of the empirical research on coaching effectiveness revealed some interesting and fairly consistent results concerning the leadership styles, behaviors, and feedback patterns that are most effective or ineffective. However, considerably more research is needed to provide a clear picture of the impact of coaches' behavior on athletes' psychosocial growth and development. In this section, suggestions for future directions in leadership research are based on the working model of coaching effectiveness (figure 10.1) and have been divided into three major areas. These include the measurement of coaching behavior (box 5), examination of the consequences of coaching behavior (boxes 6–10), and examination of antecedents of coaches' behavior (boxes 1–4).

Measurement of Coaching Behavior

As noted earlier, the majority of the research on coaching effectiveness in the psychosocial area has been conducted by using one or two of a selected set of instruments that were developed to measure coaches' behaviors. These instruments include the LSS, the Decision-Style in Sport Questionnaire, the PMCSQ, and the CBAS. Although these instruments have provided some interesting and valuable information concerning the types of leadership styles, behaviors, and feedback patterns that have a positive or negative effect on athletes' psychosocial growth and development, these instruments have their limitations. Specifically, there still remain concerns about the reliability and validity of all or portions of each instrument. Chelladurai (1993) and Chelladurai and Riemer (1998) recently discussed these concerns relative to the LSS, the CBAS, and the decision-style questionnaires. Similarly, Duda and Whitehead (1998) critically examined the PMCSQ and provided recommendations for instrument revision. Thus, further work is needed to examine the content, format, and structure of these instruments and to incorporate necessary revisions so that we can get a more accurate and valid measure of coaches' behaviors.

Within the last 10 to 15 years, other instruments to measure coaching behavior have been developed or adapted for use in sport contexts (see, e.g., Bloom et al., 1999; Franks et al., 1988; Goudas et al., 1995; Johnson & Franks, 1991; Kenow & Williams, 1992, 1999; Lacy & Goldston, 1990; Maclean & Chelladurai, 1995). Although these instruments have not been used as often as those cited in the previous paragraph, continued work with these instruments to assess the effects of coaching behavior on athletes' psychosocial growth may certainly reveal new information regarding the link between coaches' behaviors and athletes' self-perceptions, level of motivation, and affective reactions.

As noted earlier, our examination of the effects of coaches' behaviors on athletes' psychosocial growth and development primarily has been limited to selected dimensions or aspects of coaches' behaviors. There are certainly many other dimensions to investigate, some of which are highlighted in the following paragraphs.

Nonverbal Coaching Behaviors

In regard to nonverbal behaviors, the research conducted outside of sport psychology (e.g., Heintzman, Leathers, Parrott, & Cairns, 1993) suggests that these types of behaviors as exhibited by coaches in sport contexts might significantly affect athletes' self-perceptions and level of anxiety and motivation. Initial attempts to examine coaches' nonverbal behaviors were conducted by Allen and Howe (1998), Crocker (1990), and Kenow and Williams (1992). These studies indicated that athletes do "see" and interpret the nonverbal behaviors exhibited by their coaches. Furthermore, as Allen and Howe demonstrated, coaches' nonverbal (along with their verbal) behaviors are linked to athletes' perceptions of competence and satisfaction. Thus, as Allen and Howe suggested, it seems reasonable to continue exploring the wide range of nonverbal behaviors that coaches may display and to assess their impact on athletes' psychosocial well-being.

Coaches' Feedback Patterns

In examining coaches' feedback patterns as a factor affecting their athletes' psychosocial growth and development, our research has been limited to looking at only selected types of coaching responses. Specifically, we have typically only measured the frequency (or relative frequency) with which coaches respond to their players' successes and failures with selected types of feedback (e.g., reinforcement, punishment, corrective instruction, encouragement). However, research has shown that the frequency of praise/reinforcement, punishment, or corrective instruction is not necessarily crucial to an individual's performance and psychosocial growth. Rather, the quality (e.g., contingency, specificity, appropriateness) of the praise, punishment, or instruction may have the greatest effect on a performer's physical and psychological responses (Amorose & Weiss, 1998; Brophy, 1981; Chaumeton & Duda, 1988; Horn, 1985, 1987; Magill, 1994; Neapolitan, 1988; Silverman, 1994). For example, does the coach praise and criticize players contingent on the outcome (knowledge of results) of the performance attempt or the process (knowledge of performance) of the skill attempt? Does the coach give general informational feedback (e.g., "Kari, you're not making good choices on your sets out there") or specific informational feedback (e.g., "Kari, on that last play, you should have gone with a back set because there were two blockers on the left side, and . . .")? Does the coach give excessive praise for a mediocre performance (e.g., catching an easy pop-up in baseball/softball) or for success at an easy task (e.g., getting to first base safely on a fielder's error)? Does the coach give excessive criticism for a relatively minor error? Or are the coach's praise and criticism generally appropriate for the level of performance the athlete exhibited? Is the coach consistent across players in the type of feedback and the level of performance that he or she rewards or criticizes? Or does the coach's feedback to individual players reflect differences in her or his level of expectancies for that player? Is the coach's feedback descriptive (e.g., "Joci, your timing on that pass is off") or prescriptive (e.g., "Joci, you need to wait until Nara's forward foot gets beyond her defender before you pass her the ball")? For further information on the distinguishing characteristics of coaches' feedback, see Magill (1994) and Horn (1987).

Another dimension of coaches' feedback that we have not yet consistently measured is its attributional content. Available research and theory in the attributional literature (Weiner, 1986, 1992) certainly indicate that the type of attributions contained in a coach's feedback to her or his players (e.g., "That was a lucky catch you made, Joe" vs. "Great hustle to get to that ball, Joe") could significantly affect the athlete's perception of competence, level of motivation, and affective reactions. For further discussion on the possible effects of attributional feedback in the sport context, see chapters by Horn and colleagues (Horn, 1987; Horn & Harris, in press; Horn et al., in press).

Other Dimensions of Coaching Behavior

In a recent qualitatively based study on coach–athlete interactions in a sport context, d'Arripe-Longueville, Fournier, and Dubois (1998) identified a number of other interesting behaviors of coaches. These behaviors, which differ significantly from previous research in sport psychology, provide a unique perspective on alternative ways to measure the interactions of coaches and athletes. Although the behaviors identified as "ef-

fective" in this study may be limited to athletes at an elite level of competition, it certainly would be interesting to explore the effects of these types of coaching behaviors in other contexts.

As noted earlier, Abraham and Collins (1998), Strean et al. (1997), and Cote, Salmela, Trudel, Baria, and Russell (1995) also have identified other perspectives with regard to coaching effectiveness. As these researchers and authors all argue, our current measures of coaching behavior have limited the range of our research and thus our understanding of the ways in which coaches affect their athletes. We have predominantly used either observationally based instruments (e.g., the CBAS) or self-report questionnaires (e.g., the LSS, the PMCSQ) to assess the coaches' leadership styles, behaviors, and feedback patterns. Recent exceptions to these methodologies are the interview studies conducted by d'Arripe-Longueville et al. (1998), Cote et al. (1995), Bloom, Durand-Bush, and Salmela (1997), and Krane, Greenleaf, and Snow (1997). Continued use of these procedures, as well as others, would quite likely provide different perspectives on coaching effectiveness.

One final point pertaining to the measurement of coaching behavior concerns the relative value of assessing coaches' behaviors directly (e.g., observationally based procedures) or indirectly (e.g., through the perceptions of athletes, coaches, or other individuals in the sport environment). As the empirical research and theory reviewed in this chapter should indicate, both forms of assessment have provided valid and valuable information concerning the effective or ineffective forms of coaching behavior. Furthermore, as portrayed in the working model of coaching effectiveness (see figure 10.1), both constitute important constructs or components in the coaching effectiveness process. Box 5 in figure 10.1 represents the actual behavior exhibited by the coach, and box 8 represents the athletes' perceptions or interpretations of that behavior. Ultimately, both measures of coaching behavior (the direct measure and athletes' perceptions of that behavior) are linked to athletes' psychosocial growth and development as well as their performance and behavior. Thus, researchers have a choice as to which component they wish to assess. However, in our reports of these studies, we need to be clear as to which component (box) we are assessing, and the results of our studies need to be interpreted relative to that component. Of course, it would probably be ideal if both components (both boxes) could be measured in single studies. Such procedures would allow a direct comparison of their relative effects on athletes and also would allow us to test the model as a whole. Nevertheless, both assessment procedures (i.e., measurement of coaches' actual behavior and measurement of players' perceptions of coaches' behavior) should provide valid information about the coaching effectiveness process.

Consequences of Coaches' Behavior

The current research base strongly supports the notion that coaches' behavior significantly affects athletes' psychosocial growth and development. Again, however, this research has been limited to an examination of selected aspects of athletes' psychosocial growth and, ultimately, their performance and behavior. Specifically, in regard to athletes' perceptions, beliefs, attitudes, and level of motivation (boxes 9 and 10), we have concentrated mostly on such constructs as athletes' self-perceptions (e.g., perceived competence, self-esteem, success expectancies), affective reactions (e.g., satisfaction, enjoyment, interest), and level or type (intrinsic or extrinsic) of motivation. Considerably less information is available concerning the coaching styles, behaviors, and feedback patterns that might affect athletes' levels of anxiety (both state and trait), their self-efficacy, their attributional beliefs, their tendencies to experience feelings of learned helplessness (see Martinek, 1996), their perceptions of performance control (locus of control), or their commitment to the sport and the team. In regard to athletes' behaviors, we have little knowledge regarding the effects of different types of coaching behaviors on athletes' work ethic, their willingness to persist in the face of failure, their tendencies to experience athletic burnout, their decisions to discontinue (or continue) sport participation, or their decisions to exhibit aggressive/nonaggressive, moral/immoral, or good/bad sporting behaviors in sport contexts (see also discussion on this type of research by Vallerand & Losier, 1999). Thus, much research needs to be conducted to complete our knowledge base regarding the effects of coaches' behavior on multiple aspects of athletes' psychosocial growth as well as their performance and behavior.

From a somewhat different perspective, we also could examine the consequences or effects of coaches' behavior on the coaches themselves. Although some research has been conducted on this topic (see, e.g., research on the factors lead-ing or contributing to coaching burnout, commitment to coaching, and satisfaction with coaching), these studies were not reviewed in this chapter because my focus here was on examining the effects of coaches' behavior on athletes' psychosocial growth and development. Nevertheless, examining the effects of coaches' behavior on their own psychological responses and reactions and on their performance and behavior remains an interesting research avenue.

As indicated in the working model (figure 10.1), and as pointed out frequently in this chapter, particular coaching styles, behaviors, or feedback patterns that are identified as effective or ineffective will vary as a function of the sport context and as a function of the athletes themselves. Characteristics of the athletes themselves (box 7) will affect their perceptions, interpretation, evaluation, and preferences for different types of coaching behavior. Such interindividual variability within athletes certainly should affect which types of coaching behavior will be most effective. Thus, we cannot generalize the results found in individual studies to all contexts or to all athletes.

Obviously, then, continued research is necessary to investigate and determine the correlates of coaching effectiveness in a variety of contexts and with a variety of athletes. Only then can we identify a general set of coaching behaviors that may be effective across most situations but also a more specific set of coaching behaviors that may characterize coaching effectiveness in specific contexts or with specific types of athletes. Furthermore, studies specifically designed to compare the effects of coaching behaviors across different sport contexts or across different athletes may contribute much to our understanding of these issues. For example, a large-scale research project that attempts to identify and compare the effects of different types of coaching behavior on recreational and elite teams across two or three age levels (e.g., investigating and comparing the effects of coaches' behavior on 16- to 18-year-old, 12- to 14-year-old, and 10- to 11-year-old recreational and elite basketball players) would provide much information concerning the contextual and age-related variables that affect the coach–athlete relationship. Similarly, comparing the effects of different types of coaching behavior on athletes with varying psychological profiles would contribute much to our understanding of interindividual variability in regard to the correlates of coaching effectiveness. Finally, even identifying how athletes' personal characteristics affect their interpretation, evaluation, perception, and preference for different types of coaching behaviors (i.e., see link between boxes 7 and 8) would enhance our understanding of the potential effects of coaches' behavior on athletes' psychosocial growth and development.

Antecedents of Coaches' Behavior

The working model of coaching effectiveness (see figure 10.1) illustrates that coaches' behavior does not occur in isolation or in a vacuum. Rather, there are reasons why coaches exhibit certain leadership styles, behaviors, and feedback patterns. The working model specifies or identifies some possible antecedents. But, as the review of the literature on these antecedents showed, we really have very little research-based information about the hypothesized links between these constructs and coaches' behavior. Thus, this area of research is wide open. Specific suggestions and directions regarding the types of questions that could be addressed in this area were provided earlier in this chapter. Not only should such research studies provide us with theoretical and empirical information regarding the antecedents of coaches' behavior, but this research also should be useful in designing coaching education programs. After all, it is easier to develop intervention programs designed to change or modify individuals' behaviors once we know why such individuals exhibit those behaviors. Thus, examining the antecedents of coaches' behavior should be valuable for both theoretical and practical reasons.

CONCLUSION

The research reviewed in this chapter clearly indicates that athletes' psychosocial growth and development as well as their performance and behavior within sport contexts are significantly influenced by the leadership styles, behaviors, and feedback patterns exhibited by their coaches in practice and game situations. However, it is also evident that our current knowledge base on the correlates of coaching effectiveness has been limited to specific dimensions of coaching behavior and selected measures of the consequences of such behaviors on athletes' psychosocial growth and development. In addition, all of our current knowledge suggests that the particular correlates of effective coaching are context-specific. Thus, the current knowledge base cannot be generalized

to all athletes or to all sport contexts. Contrary, then, to the opinion of some, there is still very much to be learned in this area of study. Given what we already know about the impact that coaches can have on their athletes, further study to identify the effective and ineffective forms of coaching behavior across a wide range of athletic contexts is certainly warranted.

REFERENCES

Abernethy, B. (1993). Attention. In R.N. Singer, M. Murphey, & L.K. Tennant (Eds.), *Handbook of research on sport psychology* (pp. 127–170). New York: Macmillan.

Abraham, A., & Collins, D. (1998). Examining and extending research in coach development. *Quest, 50,* 59–79.

Allen, J.B., & Howe, B. (1998). Player ability, coach feedback, and female adolescent athletes' perceived competence and satisfaction. *Journal of Sport and Exercise Psychology, 20,* 280–299.

Ames, C. (1984). Competitive, cooperative, and individualistic goal structures: A cognitive-motivational analysis. In R. Ames & C. Ames (Eds.), *Research on motivation in education. Vol. 1: Student motivation* (pp. 177–207). Orlando, FL: Academic Press.

Ames, C. (1992a). Classrooms: Goals, structures, and student motivation. *Journal of Educational Psychology, 84,* 261–271.

Ames, C. (1992b). Achievement goals, motivational climate, and motivational processes. In G.C. Roberts (Ed.), *Motivation in sport and exercise* (pp. 161–176). Champaign, IL: Human Kinetics.

Ames, C., & Archer, J. (1988). Achievement goals in the classroom: Students' learning strategies and motivation processes. *Journal of Educational Psychology, 80,* 260–267.

Amorose, A.J., & Horn, T.S. (1999). [An examination of athletes' perceptions of their coaches' behavior as a function of collegiate competitive level and number of available scholarships.] Unpublished raw data.

Amorose, A.J., & Horn, T.S. (2000). Intrinsic motivation: Relationships with collegiate athletes' gender, scholarship status, and perceptions of their coaches' behavior. *Journal of Sport and Exercise Psychology, 22,* 63–84.

Amorose, A.J., & Horn, T.S. (in press). Pre- to post-season changes in the intrinsic motivation of first year college athletes: Relationships with coaching behavior and scholarship status. *Journal of Applied Sport Psychology.*

Amorose, A.J., & Weiss, M.R. (1998). Coaching feedback as a source of information about perceptions of ability: A developmental examination. *Journal of Sport and Exercise Psychology, 20,* 395–420.

Babad, E., Inbar, J., & Rosenthal, R. (1982). Pygmalion, galatea, and the golem: Investigations of biased and unbiased teachers. *Journal of Educational Psychology, 74,* 459–474.

Bandura, A. (1977). Self-efficacy: Toward a unifying theory of behavioral change. *Psychological Review, 84,* 191–215.

Bandura, A. (1986). *Social foundation of thought and action: A social cognitive theory*. Englewood Cliffs, NJ: Prentice Hall.

Barker, G.P., & Graham, S. (1987). Developmental study of praise and blame as attributional cues. *Journal of Educational Psychology, 79,* 62–66.

Barnett, N.P., Smoll, F.L., & Smith, R.E. (1992). Effects of enhancing coach-athlete relationships on youth sport attrition. *The Sport Psychologist, 6,* 111–127.

Barrow, J. (1977). The variables of leadership. A review and conceptual framework. *Academy of Management Review, 2,* 231–251.

Biddle, S., Cury, F., Goudas, M., Sarrazin, P., Famose, J.P., & Durand, M. (1995). Development of scales to measure perceived physical education class climate: A cross-national project. *British Journal of Educational Psychology, 65,* 341–358.

Bird, A.M. (1977). Development of a model for predicting team performance. *Research Quarterly, 48,* 24–32.

Black, S.J., & Weiss, M.R. (1992). The relationship among perceived coaching behaviors, perceptions of ability, and motivation in competitive age-group swimmers. *Journal of Sport and Exercise Psychology, 14,* 309–325.

Bloom, G.A., Crumpton, R., & Anderson, J.E. (1999). A systematic observation study of the teaching behaviors of an expert basketball coach. *The Sport Psychologist, 13,* 157–170.

Bloom, G.A., Durand-Bush, N., & Salmela, J. (1997). Pre- and post-competition routines of expert coaches of team sports. *The Sport Psychologist, 11,* 127–141.

Boyd, M., Yin, Z., Ellis, D., & French, K. (1995). Perceived motivational climate, socialization influences, and affective responses in Little League baseball. *Journal of Sport and Exercise Psychology, 17*(Suppl.), S30.

Brophy, J.E. (1981). Teacher praise: A functional analysis. *Review of Educational Research, 51,* 5–32.

Brophy, J.E. (1983). Research on the self-fulfilling prophecy and teacher expectations. *Journal of Educational Psychology, 75,* 631–661.

Chaumeton, N., & Duda, J. (1988). Is it how you play the game or whether you win or lose? The effect of competitive level and situation on coaching behaviors. *Journal of Sport Behavior, 11,* 157–174.

Chelladurai, P. (1978). *A contingency model of leadership in athletics*. Unpublished doctoral dissertation, University of Waterloo, Canada.

Chelladurai, P. (1984). Discrepancy between preferences and perceptions of leadership behavior and satisfaction of athletes in varying sports. *Journal of Sport Psychology, 6,* 27–41.

Chelladurai, P. (1990). Leadership in sports: A review. *International Journal of Sport Psychology, 21,* 328–354.

Chelladurai, P. (1993). Leadership. In R.N. Singer, M. Murphey, & L.K. Tennant (Eds.), *Handbook of research on sport psychology* (pp. 647–671). New York: Macmillan.

Chelladurai, P., & Arnott, M. (1985). Decision styles in coaching: Preferences of basketball players. *Research Quarterly for Exercise and Sport, 56,* 15–24.

Chelladurai, P., & Carron, A. (1978). *Leadership* (Canadian Association for Health, Physical Education and Recreation Sociology of Sport Monograph Series A). Calgary, AB: University of Calgary.

Chelladurai, P., & Carron, A. (1983). Athletic maturity and preferred leadership. *Journal of Sport Psychology, 5,* 371–380.

Chelladurai, P., & Haggerty, T. (1978). A normative model of decision-making styles in coaching. *Athletic Administration, 13,* 6–9.

Chelladurai, P., Haggerty, T., & Baxter, P. (1989). Decision style choices of university basketball coaches and players. *Journal of Sport and Exercise Psychology, 11,* 201–215.

Chelladurai, P., Imamura, H., Yamaguchi, Y., Oinuma, Y., & Miyauchi, T. (1988). Sport leadership in a cross-national setting: The case of Japanese and Canadian university athletes. *Journal of Sport and Exercise Psychology, 10,* 374–389.

Chelladurai, P., Malloy, D., Imamura, H., & Yamaguchi, Y. (1987). A cross-cultural study of preferred leadership in sports. *Canadian Journal of Sport Sciences, 12,* 106–110.

Chelladurai, P., & Quek, C.B. (1991). Decision style choices of high school basketball coaches: The effects of situational and coach characteristics. *Journal of Sport Behavior, 18,* 91–108.

Chelladurai, P., & Riemer, H.A. (1998). Measurement of leadership in sport. In J.L. Duda (Ed.), *Advances in sport and exercise psychology* (pp. 227–253). Morgantown, WV: Fitness Information Technology.

Chelladurai, P., & Saleh, S. (1978). Preferred leadership in sports. *Canadian Journal of Applied Sport Sciences, 3,* 85–92.

Chelladurai, P., & Saleh, S. (1980). Dimensions of leader behavior in sports: Development of a leadership scale. *Journal of Sport Psychology, 2,* 34–45.

Coakley, J. (1994). Race and ethnicity. In J. Coakley (Ed.), *Sport in society: issues and controversies* (5th ed., pp. 239–273). St. Louis: Mosby-Yearbook.

Coladarci, T. (1992). Teachers' sense of efficacy and commitment to teaching. *Journal of Experimental Education, 60,* 323–337.

Cooper, H.M. (1979). Pygmalion grows up: A model for teacher expectancy communication and performance influence. *Review of Educational Research, 49,* 389–410.

Cooper, H.M., & Tom, D.Y.H. (1984). Teacher expectation research: A review with implications for classroom instruction. *The Elementary School Journal, 85,* 77–89.

Cote, J., Salmela, J., Trudel, P., Baria, A., & Russell, S. (1995). The coaching model: A grounded assessment of expert gymnastic coaches' knowledge. *Journal of Sport and Exercise Psychology, 17,* 1–17.

Crocker, P.R.E. (1990). Facial and verbal congruency: Effects on perceived verbal and emotional feedback. *Canadian Journal of Sport Science, 15,* 17–22.

d'Arripe-Longueville, F., Fournier, J.F., & Dubois, A. (1998). The perceived effectiveness of interactions between expert French judo coaches and elite female athletes. *The Sport Psychologist, 12,* 317–332.

Deci, E.L., & Ryan, R.M. (1980). The empirical exploration of intrinsic motivational processes. In L. Berkowitz (Ed.),

Advances in experimental social psychology (Vol. 13, pp. 39–80). New York: Pergamon Press.

Deci, E.L., & Ryan, R.M. (1985). *Intrinsic motivation and self-determination in human behavior.* New York: Plenum Press.

Deci, E.L., & Ryan, R.M. (1991). A motivational approach to self: Integration in personality. In R. Dientsbier (Ed.), *Nebraska symposium on motivation: Vol. 38. Perspectives on motivation* (pp. 237–288). Lincoln: University of Nebraska Press.

Deci, E.L., Nezlek, J., & Sheinman, L. (1981). Characteristics of the rewarder and intrinsic motivation of the rewardee. *Journal of Personality and Social Psychology, 40,* 1–10.

Deci, E.L., Schwartz, A.J., Sheinman, L., & Ryan, R.M. (1981). An instrument to assess adults' orientation towards control versus autonomy with children: Reflections on intrinsic motivation and perceived competence. *Journal of Educational Psychology, 73,* 642–650.

Deci, E.L., Spiegel, N.H., Ryan, R.M., Koestner, R., & Kauffman, M. (1982). The effects of performance standards on teaching styles: The behavior of controlling teachers. *Journal of Educational Psychology, 74,* 852–859.

Deci, E.L., Vallerand, R.J., Pelletier, L.G., & Ryan, R.M. (1991). Motivation and education: The self-determination perspective. *Educational Psychologist, 26,* 325–346.

Donnelly, P. (1981). Toward a definition of sport subcultures. In M. Hart & S. Birrell (Eds.), *Sport in the sociocultural process* (3rd ed., pp. 565–587). Dubuque, IA: Brown.

Donnelly, P., & Young, K. (1988). The construction and confirmation of identity in sport subcultures. *Sociology of Sport Journal, 5,* 223–240.

Duda, J. (1985). Goals and achievement orientations of Anglo- and Mexican-American adolescents in sport and the classroom. *International Journal of Intercultural Relations, 9,* 131–155.

Duda, J. (1986a). A cross-cultural analysis of achievement motivation in sport and the classroom. In L. VanderVelden & J. Humphrey (Eds.), *Current selected research in the psychology and sociology of sport* (pp. 117–131). New York: AMS.

Duda, J. (1986b). Perceptions of sport success and failure among white, black, and Hispanic adolescents. In J. Watkins, T. Reilly, & L. Burwitz (Eds.), *Sport science* (pp. 214–222). London: Spon.

Duda, J. (1996). Maximizing motivation in sport and physical education among children and adolescents: The case for greater task involvement. *Quest, 48,* 290–302.

Duda, J.L., & Whitehead, J. (1998). Measurement of goal perspectives in the physical domain. In J.L. Duda (Ed.), *Advances in sport and exercise psychology measurement* (pp. 21–48). Morgantown, WV: Fitness Information Technology.

Dweck, C.S. (1986). Motivational processes affecting learning. *American Psychologist, 41,* 1040–1048.

Dweck, C.S. (1999). *Self-theories: Their role in motivation, personality, and development.* Philadelphia: Psychology Press.

Dwyer, J.M., & Fischer, D.G. (1990). Wrestlers' perceptions of coaches' leadership as predictors of satisfaction with leadership. *Perceptual and Motor Skills, 71,* 511–517.

Ebbeck, V., & Becker, S.L. (1994). Psychosocial predictors of goal orientations in youth soccer. *Research Quarterly for Exercise and Sport, 65,* 355–362.

Eccles, J.S., & Harold, R.D. (1991). Gender differences in sport involvement: Applying the Eccles' expectancy-value model. *Journal of Applied Sport Psychology, 3,* 7–35.

Eccles-Parsons, J.S., Adler, T.E., Futterman, R., Goff, S.B., Kaczala, C.M., Meece, J.L., & Midgley, C. (1983). Expectancies, values, and academic behaviors. In J.T. Spence (Ed.), *Achievement and achievement motivation* (pp. 75–146). San Francisco: Freeman.

Escarti, A., & Guzman, J.F. (1999). Effects of feedback on self-efficacy, performance, and choice in an athletic task. *Journal of Applied Sport Psychology, 11,* 83–96.

Feltz, D.L., Chase, M.A., Moritz, S.E., & Sullivan, P.J. (1999). A conceptual model of coaching efficacy: Preliminary investigation and instrument development. *Journal of Educational Psychology, 91,* 765–776.

Fiedler, F. (1967). *A theory of leadership effectiveness.* New York: McGraw-Hill.

Fitzsimmons, P.A., Landers, D.M., Thomas, R.J., & van der Marsh, H. (1991). Does self-efficacy predict performance in experienced weight lifters? *Research Quarterly for Exercise and Sport, 62,* 424–431.

Franks, I.M., Johnson, R.B., & Sinclair, G.D. (1988). The development of a computerized coaching analysis system for recording behavior in sporting environments. *Journal of Teaching in Physical Education, 8,* 23–32.

Frederick, C.M., & Morrison, C.S. (1999). Collegiate coaches: An examination of motivational style and its relationship to decision making and personality. *Journal of Sport Behavior, 22,* 221–233.

Fry, M.D., & Duda, J.L. (1997). A developmental examination of children's understanding of effort and ability in the physical and academic domains. *Research Quarterly for Exercise and Sport, 68,* 331–344.

Gardner, D.E., Shields, D.L.L., Bredemeier, B.J.L., & Bostrom, A. (1996). The relationship between perceived coaching behaviors and team cohesion among baseball and softball players. *The Sport Psychologist, 10,* 367–381.

Garland, D., & Barry, J. (1988). The effects of personality and perceived leader behaviors on performance in collegiate football. *Psychological Record, 38,* 237–247.

Gibson, S., & Dembo, M. (1984). Teacher efficacy: A construct validation. *Journal of Educational Psychology, 76,* 569–582.

Gordon, S. (1986). *Behavioral correlates of coaching effectiveness.* Unpublished doctoral dissertation, University of Alberta, Canada.

Gordon, S. (1988). Decision styles and coaching effectiveness in university soccer. *Canadian Journal of Sport Sciences, 13,* 56–65.

Goudas, M., & Biddle, S. (1994). Perceived motivational climate and intrinsic motivation in school physical education classes. *European Journal of Psychology of Education, 9,* 241–250.

Goudas, M., Biddle, S., Fox, K., & Underwood, M. (1995). It ain't what you do, it's the way that you do it! Teaching style affects children's motivation in track and field lessons. *The Sport Psychologist, 9,* 254–264.

Guskey, T. (1981). Measurement of the responsibility teachers assume for academic successes and failures in the classroom. *Journal of Teacher Education, 32,* 44–51.

Harris, M., & Rosenthal, R. (1985). Mediation of interpersonal expectancy effects: 31 meta-analyses. *Psychological Bulletin, 97,* 363–386.

Harter, S. (1978). Effectance motivation reconsidered. *Human Development, 21,* 34–64.

Harter, S. (1981). A model of intrinsic mastery motivation in children: Individual differences and developmental change. In W.A. Collins (Ed.), *Minnesota Symposium on Child Psychology* (Vol. 14, pp. 215–255). Hillsdale, NJ: Erlbaum.

Hayashi, C.T. (1996). Achievement motivation among Anglo-American and Hawaiian male physical activity participants: Individual differences and social contextual factors. *Journal of Sport and Exercise Psychology, 18,* 194–215.

Hayashi, C.T., & Weiss, M.R. (1994). A cross-cultural analysis of achievement motivation in Anglo and Japanese marathon runners. *International Journal of Sport Psychology, 25,* 187–202.

Heintzman, M., Leathers, D.G., Parrott, R.L., & Cairns, A.B. (1993). Nonverbal rapport building behaviors' effects on perceptions of a supervisor. *Management Communication Quarterly, 7,* 181–208.

Hendry, L. (1969). A personality study of highly successful and "ideal" swimming coaches. *Research Quarterly, 40,* 299–305.

Hersey, P., & Blanchard, K. (1972). *Management of organization behavior.* Englewood Cliffs, NJ: Prentice Hall.

Horn, T.S. (1984). Expectancy effects in the interscholastic athletic setting: Methodological considerations. *Journal of Sport Psychology, 7,* 60–76.

Horn, T.S. (1985). Coaches' feedback and changes in children's perceptions of their physical competence. *Journal of Educational Psychology, 77,* 174–186.

Horn, T.S. (1987). The influence of teacher-coach behavior on the psychological development of children. In D. Gould & M.R. Weiss (Eds.), *Advances in pediatric sport sciences. Vol. 2: Behavioral issues* (pp. 121–142). Champaign, IL: Human Kinetics.

Horn, T.S., & Glenn, S.D. (1988, June). *The relationship between athletes' psychological characteristics and their preference for particular coaching behaviors.* Paper presented at the meeting of the North American Society for the Psychology of Sport and Physical Activity, Knoxville, TN.

Horn, T.S., & Harris, A. (in press). Perceived competence in young athletes: Research findings and recommendations for coaches and parents. In F.L. Smoll & R.E. Smith (Eds.), *Children and youth in sport: A biopsychosocial perspective* (2nd ed.). Dubuque, IA: Kendall/Hunt.

Horn, T.S., Lox, C.L., & Labrador, F. (in press). The self-fulfilling prophecy theory: When coaches' expectations become reality. In J.M. Williams (Ed.), *Applied sport psychology: Personal growth to peak performance* (4th ed.). Mountain View, CA: Mayfield.

Horne, T., & Carron, A. (1985). Compatibility in coach-athlete relationships. *Journal of Sport Psychology, 7,* 137–149.

House, R.J. (1971). A path-goal theory of leader effectiveness. *Administrative Science Quarterly, 16,* 321–338.

House, R.J., & Dessler, G. (1974). A path-goal theory of leadership. In J.G. Hunt & L.L. Larson (Eds.), *Contingency approaches to leadership* (pp. 29–55). Carbondale: Southern Illinois University Press.

House, R., & Mitchell, T. (1974). Path-goal theory of leadership. *Journal of Contemporary Business, 3,* 81–97.

Johns, D. (1998). Fasting and feasting: Paradoxes in the sport ethic. *Sociology of Sport Journal, 15,* 41–63.

Johnson, R.B., & Franks, I.M. (1991). Measuring the reliability of a computer-aided systematic observation instrument. *Canadian Journal of Sport Science, 16,* 45–57.

Kavussanu, M., & Roberts, G.C. (1996). Motivation in physical activity contexts: The relationship of perceived motivational climate to intrinsic motivation and self-efficacy. *Journal of Sport and Exercise Psychology, 18,* 264–280.

Kenow, L.J., & Williams, J.M. (1992). Relationship between anxiety, self-confidence, and evaluation of coaching behaviors. *The Sport Psychologist, 6,* 344–357.

Kenow, L.M., & Williams, J.M. (1999). Coach-athlete compatibility and athletes' perceptions of coaching behaviors. *Journal of Sport Behavior, 22,* 251–259.

Kim, B.J., & Gill, D.L. (1997). A cross-cultural extension of goal perspective theory to Korean youth sport. *Journal of Sport and Exercise Psychology, 19,* 142–155.

Klein, A.M. (1986). Pumping irony: Crisis and contradiction in body building. *Sociology of Sport Journal, 3,* 112–133.

Krane, V., Greenleaf, C.A., & Snow, J. (1997). Reaching for gold and the price of glory: A motivational case study of an elite gymnast. *The Sport Psychologist, 11,* 53–71.

Lacy, A.C., & Goldston, P.O. (1990). Behavioral analysis of male and female coaches in high school girls' basketball. *Journal of Sport Behavior, 13,* 29–39.

Lenk, H. (1977). Authoritarian or democratic styled coaching? In H. Lenk (Ed.), *Team dynamics* (pp. 23–39). Champaign, IL: Stipes.

Lenskyj, H. (1987). *Out of bounds: Women, sport, and sexuality.* Toronto: Women's Press.

Lloyd, J., & Fox, K.R. (1992). Achievement goals and motivation to exercise in adolescent girls: A preliminary study. *British Journal of Physical Education, Research Supplement II,* 12–16.

Maclean, J.C., & Chelladurai, P. (1995). Dimensions of coaching performance: Development of a scale. *Journal of Sport Management, 9,* 194–207.

Magill, R.A. (1994). The influence of augmented feedback on skill learning depends on characteristics of the skill and the learner. *Quest, 46,* 314–327.

Malina, R. (1983). Menarche in athletes: A synthesis and hypothesis. *Annals of Human Biology, 10,* 1–24.

Malina, R. (1994). Physical growth and maturation. In J.R. Thomas (Ed.), *Motor development during childhood and adolescence* (pp. 2–26). Minneapolis, MN: Burgess.

Martinek, T.J. (1996). Fostering hope in youth: A model for explaining learned helplessness in physical activity. *Quest, 48,* 409–421.

McAuley, E., Duncan, T.E., Wraith, S.C., & Lettunich, M. (1991). Self-efficacy, perceptions of success, and intrinsic motivation. *Journal of Applied Social Psychology, 21,* 139–155.

McCormick, T.E., & Noriega, T. (1986). Low versus high expectations: A review of teacher expectation effects on minority students. *Journal of Educational Equity and Leadership, 6,* 224–234.

McMillin, C.J. (1990). *The relationship of athlete self-perceptions and athlete perceptions of leader behaviors to athlete satisfaction.* Unpublished doctoral dissertation, University of Virginia-Charlottesville.

Messner, M.A. (1992). *Power at play: Sports and the problem of masculinity.* Boston: Beacon Press.

Metzler, M. (1989). A review of research on time in sport pedagogy. *Journal of Teaching in Physical Education, 8,* 87–103.

Meyer, W., Bachmann, M., Biermann, U., Hempelmann, M., Ploger, F., & Spiller, H. (1979). The informational value of evaluative behavior: Influences of praise and blame on perceptions of ability. *Journal of Educational Psychology, 71,* 259–268.

Neapolitan, J. (1988). The effects of different types of praise and criticism on performance. *Sociological Focus, 21,* 223–231.

Newton, M.L., & Duda, J.L. (1993). The Perceived Motivational Climate in Sport Questionnaire-2: Construct and predictive validity. *Journal of Sport and Exercise Psychology, 15*(Suppl.), S59.

Nicholls, J.G. (1984). Achievement motivation: Conceptions of ability, subjective experience, task choice, and performance. *Psychological Review, 91,* 328–346.

Nicholls, J.G. (1989). *The competitive ethos and democratic education.* Cambridge, MA: Harvard University Press.

Nicholls, J.G. (1992). The general and the specific in the development and expression of achievement motivation. In G.C. Roberts (Ed.), *Motivation in sport and exercise* (pp. 31–56). Champaign, IL: Human Kinetics.

Nideffer, R.N. (1993). Attention control training. In R.N. Singer, M. Murphey, & L.K. Tennant (Eds.), *Handbook of research on sport psychology* (pp. 542–556). New York: Macmillan.

Ommundsen, Y., Roberts, G.C., & Kavussanu, M. (1998). Perceived motivational climate and cognitive and affective correlates among Norwegian athletes. *Journal of Sports Sciences, 16,* 153–164.

Papaioannou, A. (1994). The development of a questionnaire to measure achievement orientations in physical education. *Research Quarterly for Exercise and Sport, 65,* 11–20.

Papaioannou, A. (1995). Differential perceptual and motivational patterns when different goals are adopted. *Journal of Sport & Exercise Psychology, 17,* 18–34.

Papaioannou, A. (1998). Goal perspectives, reasons for being disciplined, and self-reported discipline in physical education lessons. *Journal of Teaching in Physical Education, 17,* 421–441.

Papaioannou, A., & Kouli, O. (1999). The effect of task structure, perceived motivational climate and goal orientation on students' task involvement and anxiety. *Journal of Applied Sport Psychology, 11,* 51–71.

Pease, D.G., & Kozub, S. (1994). Perceived coaching behaviors and team cohesion in high school girls' basketball teams. *Journal of Sport & Exercise Psychology, 16*(Suppl.), S93.

Pelletier, L.G., Briere, N.M., Blais, M.R., & Vallerand, R.J. (1988). Persisting vs. dropping out: A test of Deci and Ryan's theory. *Canadian Psychology, 29a,* 600.

Pelletier, L.G., & Vallerand, R.J. (1985). *Effects of coaches' interpersonal behavior on athletes' motivational level.* Paper presented at the annual conference of the Canadian Society for Psychomotor Learning and Sport Psychology, Montreal.

Penman, K., Hastad, D., & Cords, W. (1974). Success of the authoritarian coach. *Journal of Social Psychology, 92,* 155–156.

Pensgaard, A.M., & Roberts, G.C. (1996). Perceived motivational climate and sources of stress for Winter Olympic athletes. *Journal of Applied Sport Psychology, 7*(Suppl.), S9.

Phillips, D.A. (1987). Socialization of perceived academic competence among highly competent children. *Child Development, 58,* 1308–1320.

Pratt, S., & Eitzen, D.S. (1989). Contrasting leadership styles and organizational effectiveness: The case of athletic teams. *Social Science Quarterly, 70,* 311–322.

Rejeski, W., Darracott, C., & Hutslar, S. (1979). Pygmalion in youth sports: A field study. *Journal of Sport Psychology, 1,* 311–319.

Riemer, H.A., & Chelladurai, P. (1995). Leadership and satisfaction in athletes. *Journal of Sport and Exercise Psychology, 17,* 276–293.

Rist, R.C. (1970). Student social class and teacher expectations: The self-fulfilling prophecy in ghetto education. *Harvard Educational Review, 40,* 411–451.

Rubovits, P.C., & Maehr, M.L. (1973). Pygmalion black and white. *Journal of Personality and Social Psychology, 25,* 210–218.

Ryan, R.M., Connell, J.P., & Deci, E.L. (1985). A motivational analysis of self-determination and self-regulation in education. In C. Ames & R.E. Ames (Eds.), *Research on motivation in education: The classroom milieu* (pp. 13–51). New York: Academic Press.

Scanlan, T.K., Carpenter, P.J., Schmidt, G.W., Simons, J.P., & Keeler, B. (1993). An introduction to the Sport Commitment Model. *Journal of Sport and Exercise Psychology, 15,* 1–15.

Schliesman, E. (1987). Relationship between the congruence of preferred and actual leader behavior and subordinate satisfaction with leadership. *Journal of Sport Behavior, 10,* 157–166.

Schunk, D.H. (1995). Self-efficacy, motivation, and performance. *Journal of Applied Sport Psychology, 7,* 112–137.

Seifriz, J.J., Duda, J.L., & Chi, L. (1992). The relationship of perceived motivation climate to intrinsic motivation and beliefs about success in basketball. *Journal of Sport & Exercise Psychology, 14,* 375–391.

Serpa, S., Pataco, V., & Santos, F. (1991). Leadership patterns in handball international competition. *International Journal of Sport Psychology, 22,* 78–89.

Silverman, S. (1994). Communication and motor skill learning: What we learn from research in the gymnasium. *Quest, 46,* 345–355.

Sinclair, D.A., & Vealey, R.S. (1989). Effects of coaches' expectations and feedback on the self-perceptions of athletes. *Journal of Sport Behavior, 12,* 77–91.

Smith, R.E., Smoll, F.L., & Barnett, N.P. (1995). Reduction of children's sport anxiety through social support and stress-reduction training for coaches. *Journal of Applied Developmental Psychology, 16,* 125–142.

Smith, R.E., Smoll, F.L., & Curtis, B. (1978). Coaching behaviors in Little League baseball. In F.L. Smoll & R.E. Smith (Eds.), *Psychological perspectives in youth sports* (pp. 173–201). Washington, DC: Hemisphere.

Smith, R.E., Smoll, F.L., & Curtis, B. (1979). Coach effectiveness training: A cognitive-behavioral approach to enhancing relationship skills in youth sport coaches. *Journal of Sport Psychology, 1,* 59–75.

Smith, R., Smoll, F., & Hunt, E. (1977). A system for the behavioral assessment of athletic coaches. *Research Quarterly, 48,* 401–407.

Smith, R.E., Smoll, F.L., & Wiechman, S.A. (1998). Measurement of trait anxiety in sport. In J. Duda (Ed.), *Advances in sport and exercise psychology measurement* (pp. 105–127). Morgantown, WV: Fitness Information Technology.

Smith, R., Zane, N., Smoll, F., & Coppel, D. (1983). Behavioral assessment in youth sports: Coaching behaviors and children's attitudes. *Medicine and Science in Sports and Exercise, 15,* 208–214.

Smoll, F.L., & Smith, R.E. (1989). Leadership behaviors in sport: A theoretical model and research paradigm. *Journal of Applied Social Psychology, 19,* 1522–1551.

Smoll, F., Smith, R., Curtis, B., & Hunt, E. (1978). Towards a mediational model of coach-player relationships. *Research Quarterly for Exercise and Sport, 49,* 528–541.

Solomon, G.B., DiMarco, A.M., Ohlson, C.J., & Reece, S.D. (1998a). Expectations and coaching experience: Is more better? *Journal of Sport Behavior, 21,* 444–455.

Solomon, G.B., Golden, A.J., Ciapponi, T.M., & Martin, A.D. (1998b). Coach expectations and differential feedback: Perceptual flexibility revisited. *Journal of Sport Behavior, 21,* 298–310.

Solomon, G.B., & Kosmitzki, C. (1996). Perceptual flexibility and differential feedback among intercollegiate basketball coaches. *Journal of Sport Behavior, 19,* 163–177.

Solomon, G.B., Striegel, D.A., Eliot, J.F., Heon, S.N., Maas, J.L., & Wayda, V.K. (1996a). The self-fulfilling prophecy in college basketball: Implications for effective coaching. *Journal of Applied Sport Psychology, 8,* 44–59.

Solomon, G.B., Wiegardt, P.A., Yusuf, F.R., Kosmitzki, C., Williams, J., Stevens, C.E., & Wayda, V.K. (1996b). Expectancies and ethnicity: The self-fulfilling prophecy in college basketball. *Journal of Sport & Exercise Psychology, 18,* 83–88.

Stevenson, H., & Newman, R. (1986). Long-term prediction of achievement attitudes in mathematics and reading. *Child Development, 57,* 646–659.

Stewart, M., & Corbin, C. (1988). Feedback dependence among low confidence preadolescent boys and girls. *Research Quarterly for Exercise and Sport, 59,* 160–164.

Strean, W.B., Senecal, K.L., Howlett, S.G., & Burgess, J.M. (1997). Xs and Os and what the coach knows: Improving team strategy through critical thinking. *The Sport Psychologist, 11,* 243–256.

Terry, P. (1984). The coaching preferences of elite athletes competing at Universiade '83. *Canadian Journal of Applied Sport Sciences, 9,* 201–208.

Terry, P., & Howe, B. (1984). Coaching preferences of athletes. *Canadian Journal of Applied Sport Sciences, 9,* 188–193.

Theeboom, M., De Knop, P., & Weiss, M.R. (1995). Motivational climate, psychosocial responses, and motor skill development in children's sport: A field-based intervention study. *Journal of Sport & Exercise Psychology, 17,* 294–311.

Treasure, D.C. (1997). Perceptions of the motivational climate and elementary school children's cognitive and affective response. *Journal of Sport & Exercise Psychology, 19,* 278–290.

Treasure, D.C., & Roberts, G.C. (1995a). Achievement goals, motivational climate, and achievement strategies and behaviors in sport. *International Journal of Sport Psychology, 26,* 64–80.

Treasure, D.C., & Roberts, G.C. (1995b). Applications of achievement goal theory to physical education: Implications for enhancing motivation. *Quest, 47,* 475–489.

Treasure, D.C., & Roberts, G.C. (1998). Relationship between female adolescents' achievement goal orientations, perceptions of the motivational climate, belief about success and sources of satisfaction in basketball. *International Journal of Sport Psychology, 29,* 211–230.

Vallerand, R.J., Deci, E.L., & Ryan, R.M. (1987). Intrinsic motivation in sport. *Exercise and Sport Sciences Reviews, 15,* 389–425.

Vallerand, R.J., & Losier, G.F. (1999). An integrative analysis of intrinsic and extrinsic motivation in sport. *Journal of Applied Sport Psychology, 11,* 142–169.

Vallerand, R.J., & Pelletier, L.G. (1985). *Coaches' interpersonal styles, athletes' perception of their coaches' styles, and athletes' intrinsic motivation and perceived competence: Generalization to the world of swimming.* Paper presented at the annual conference of the Canadian Society for Psychomotor Learning and Sport Psychology, Montreal.

VosStrache, C. (1979). Players' perceptions of leadership qualities for coaches. *Research Quarterly, 50,* 679–686.

Vroom, V., & Yelton, R. (1973). *Leadership and decision-making.* Pittsburgh: University of Pittsburgh Press.

Walling, M.D., Duda, J.L., & Chi, L. (1993). The perceived motivational climate in sport questionnaire: Construct and predictive validity. *Journal of Sport and Exercise Psychology, 15,* 172–183.

Wandzilak, T., Ansorge, C.J., & Potter, G. (1988). Comparison between selected practice and game behaviors of youth sport soccer coaches. *Journal of Sport Behavior, 11,* 78–88.

Weiner, B. (1986). *An attributional theory of motivation and emotion.* New York: Springer-Verlag.

Weiner, B. (1992). *Human motivation: Metaphors, theories, and research.* Newbury Park, CA: Sage.

Weiss, M.R., & Friedrichs, W.D. (1986). The influence of leader behaviors, coach attributes, and institutional variables on performance and satisfaction of collegiate basketball teams. *Journal of Sport Psychology, 8,* 332–346.

Westre, K., & Weiss, M. (1991). The relationship between perceived coaching behaviors and group cohesion in high school football teams. *The Sport Psychologist, 5,* 41–54.

White, R.W. (1959). Motivation reconsidered: The concept of competence. *Psychological Review, 66,* 297–330.

Whitehead, J., & Smith, A.G. (1996). Issues in development of a protocol to evaluate children's reasoning about ability and effort in sport. *Perceptual and Motor Skills, 83,* 355–364.

Wineburg, S. (1987). The self-fulfillment of the self-fulfilling prophecy. *Educational Researcher, 12,* 28–42.

Woolfolk, A.E., Rosoff, B., & Hoy, W.K. (1990). Teachers' sense of efficacy and their beliefs about managing students. *Teaching and Teacher Education, 6,* 137–148.

Gender and Sport Behavior

Diane L. Gill

This chapter covers the scholarship on gender and sport. The topic of gender necessarily crosses into sociological territory, and this chapter, like most gender scholarship, takes a feminist perspective. I do not claim to have the definitive feminist perspective, but this chapter adopts the typical feminist emphasis on women's experiences and views gender as a dynamic, powerful aspect of all our social relations and behaviors. In this chapter, I view gender not simply as an individual difference category (i.e., male vs. female) but as an integral part of our social identity and social environment. Gender is ever present, gender affects all of us, and gender continually intersects with other social identities as part of our continually changing social context.

This chapter, like most gender scholarship, puts women and women's experiences at the center. One could ask, what about men in sport? The quick answer is that men in sport are covered in every other chapter and in nearly all the scholarship that does not explicitly address gender. The longer and more appropriate response is that gender does indeed affect men in sport, and gender scholarship necessarily addresses gender relations for men as well as women. However, we have almost no gender scholarship on men. Some feminist scholars are beginning to address gender issues for men, and some of that work is moving into sport psychology. In particular, Don Sabo and Michael Messner (e.g., Messner & Sabo, 1994) have done wonderful work on gender as it affects men and sport, and I will cover some of that work later in the chapter. We seldom recognize the role of gender in men's lives, and that reflects our limited, dominant societal perspective. That is, we tend to view society from the dominant perspective (male, white, heterosexual, etc.) and do not recognize that gender, race, class, and other social identities affect even those in the dominant position. Feminist analyses, such as the approaches of Messner and Sabo, view gender and culture from the broader relational perspective. Gender is part of everyone's identity, and gender intersects with our many other social identities. Gender exerts a complex, dynamic influence on the sport world and on all our behaviors and relationships within that world. We will begin to explore some of these gender influences in this chapter.

Clearly, girls and women are active participants in the sport world. Ten-year-old girls play in soccer leagues alongside 10-year-old boys. Universities sponsor parallel intercollegiate basketball teams for women and men, and both men and women finish triathlons—in all age categories. Just as clearly, gender makes a difference in our sport behaviors. Gender influences adults' expectations and responses to 10-year-old girl and boy soccer players. Similarly, male and female basketball players face different pressures, and gender influences exercisers' options (such as time and place of exercise), attire, and activities.

Despite the pervasiveness and power of gender in sport and the infinite number of psychological questions we could ask, sport psychology research on gender is limited in all ways. We have little research. Our research questions and methods

How might a child's gender influence adults' expectations?

focus on differences and neglect complex gender issues and relations, and we lack guiding conceptual frameworks to help us understand the complexities of gender in sport and exercise contexts. In some ways, the lack of attention to gender reflects the larger discipline of psychology, which has been slow to move beyond isolated studies of sex differences to more complex issues of gender relations. In other ways, our neglect of gender reflects the place of women in sport and in sport psychology.

From the turn of the century up to the 1970s, when sport psychology emerged as an identifiable area, the term *athlete* meant male athlete. Furthermore, those male athletes were not culturally diverse. Certainly some women engaged in physical activity before the 1970s, as sport historians note (e.g., Spears, 1978), but females entered the modern athletic world in significant numbers only after the passage of Title IX and the related social changes of the early 1970s. Given the short history of women's sport participation, it is not surprising to find that the history of gender in sport psychology is short. Still, the field of sport psychology has lagged behind the issues. This is a particularly striking void when even a moment's

reflection, or a glance at the popular media, reveals many gender issues. The Billie Jean King–Bobby Riggs "Battle of the Sexes" tennis match captured public attention in the early 1970s. Female athletes gained prominence through Olympic coverage in the 1970s, 1980s, and 1990s. The National Collegiate Athletic Association (NCAA) continues to grapple with the issue of "gender equity." Female World Cup soccer team members and Women's National Basketball Association (WNBA) players are featured prominently in the popular media and advertisements, bringing female athletes and gender issues to the attention of the general public. Sport psychologists have contributed little to these discussions, and we seldom consider gender issues and relations in our work.

By definition, psychology focuses on individual behavior, thoughts, and feelings. But we cannot fully understand the individual without considering the larger world—the social context. No behavior takes place in isolation, and social context is especially critical for gender. My emphasis on social context and cultural diversity is intentional and reflects current perspectives on human diversity that are gaining prominence in psychology. Although gender clearly has a biological dimension (as do other diversity issues), the biological markers and correlates are not the keys to the behaviors of interest in sport and exercise psychology.

Trickett, Watts, and Birman (1994), who compiled and integrated works of several noted psychologists, noted that diversity has challenged the foundations of psychology by suggesting that traditional psychology is particularistic rather than universal, and that its theories reflect views, limits, and social contexts of those who created them. They further suggested that psychology's biggest challenge is paradigmatic. We need new ways of thinking to understand diversity. They advocated moving from the dominant psychology view, which emphasizes biology, isolating basic processes, rigorous experimental designs, and a critical-realist philosophy of science, to an emphasis on *people in context*.

In line with Trickett et al.'s (1994) framework, I do not believe we can fully understand the individual without considering the larger world, or people in context. Sport and exercise psychology is explicitly context-dependent, and the context extends far beyond competitive athletics, to encompass diverse participants in all forms of physical activities, in varied exercise and sport settings.

The theme of this chapter is that gender in sport is much like gender and diversity in other domains, and social context is the key. Individuals cannot be isolated from their gender or any other social cultural characteristic. Gender makes a difference, and we must consider people in context to understand their behavior.

While reading the chapter, keep in mind that gender is not synonymous with biological sex. Clearly biological sex is related to gender, as we recognize biological sex, and biological sex elicits our many gender perceptions and makes gender a powerful social identity. But, gender is much more than biology, and it is certainly not a one-dimensional dichotomy. Gender implies gender perceptions and stereotypes, roles and expectations, interpersonal styles, and social relations. Gender, from the view of most gender scholars, is cultural rather than biological.

In this chapter, I first review the historical context of today's gendered sport world. Then I devote most of the chapter to the existing research and theoretical models that address gender and sport. The gender scholarship in sport psychology, like the gender scholarship in psychology, has progressed from research on sex differences and gender roles to more current models that emphasize social processes and context.

THE GENDERED CONTEXT OF SPORT

Before considering the research and professional literature on gender and sport, let's see if gender does make a difference in sport. In other writing (Gill, 1995), I have used the following cases to help readers think about gender. Consider how gender affects your interpretations, responses, and the possible approaches to the following athletes:

- A soccer player who lacks control and is prone to angry outbursts on the field explains by stating, "I really get 'up' for the game, and sometimes I just lose it."

- A basketball player who plays tentatively and lacks confidence explains, "I'm just not a leader and I can't play the way the coach wants."

- The coach thinks a 16-year-old figure skater may have an eating disorder, but the skater explains, "I'm working to keep that 'line,' make it to nationals, and get endorsements."

Does gender influence your responses? Did you identify athletes as male or female? Do you think a coach, sport psychology consultant, trainer, or parent would behave the same with a female and male athlete? If you try to be nonsexist, treat everyone the same, and assume that gender does not matter, you will probably have difficulty. Gender does matter. Trying to treat everyone the same does a disservice to the athletes.

I recently watched *my* (announcer's emphasis) Charlotte Sting play the New York Liberty in a WNBA playoff game. I sat in the arena that the (Men's) National Basketball Association (NBA) also plays in and watched athletes who are taller, faster, stronger, and flashier than I had imagined play in front of a large, enthusiastic crowd with the usual mascot antics and coliseum refreshment stands. Would everything be the same with an NBA game? Is everything the same for Teresa Weather-spoon and the Knicks point guard (e.g., fans, media, coaches)? Does gender make a difference? Female athletic participation has exploded in the last generation, but the numbers of female and male participants are not equal. More important, female athletes are not the same as male athletes. Gender makes a difference, but we must look beyond numbers, biological sex, dichotomous sex differences, and individual differences to the powerful, gendered social context to understand gender issues.

Sport is a physical activity. We call attention to the physical and biological. "Citius, Altius, Fortius"—the Olympic motto—translates as "swifter, higher, stronger." This motto clearly highlights the physical. This motto—swifter, higher, stronger—also inherently implies that sport is competitive and hierarchical, characteristics typically associated with the male gender. Sport seems a likely place to emphasize sex differences, and in some ways, gender in sport differs from gender in other domains. But gender is different in sport not because of the physical emphasis but because the social–historical context is different. The average male may be higher, faster, and stronger than the average female, but sport does not have to be higher, faster, stronger. Sport might be "fun, flair, and friendship." I will note my biases, as warning for the reader—I am not high, fast, or strong, and I am one of the least competitive people I know.

Sport is gendered, and gender is part of social context and social processes in sport. Biological sex is related to gender, but biology does not explain gendered sport. All the meanings, social roles, expectations, standards of appropriate behavior, beauty, power, and status are constructed in the sport culture. We are not born to wear high heels or high-top sneakers.

From the time we are born, our world is shaped by gender. Our parents, teachers, peers, and coaches react to us as girls or boys. Gender is such a pervasive

Pender Socialization

influence in society that it is impossible to pinpoint that influence. Sport is no exception, but the sport world does have unique characteristics.

THE HISTORICAL CONTEXT OF GENDER AND SPORT

To understand gender in sport, we must first understand the social and historical context. Both psychology and physical education have their beginnings in the late 1800s. We can find women and gender issues in both histories, but the histories are quite different. In psychology we find female pioneers facing discriminatory practices and attitudes but persisting to make a place in the academic discipline of psychology, much as women have made a place in many scholarly fields.

In physical education, we find a legacy of strong female leaders who developed women's physical education as an alternative, separate from men's physical education programs. These two separate roots of contemporary gendered sport seldom crossed or interacted. Sport psychology has drawn from psychology theories and research since its emergence in the 1960s, but we have not drawn on the psychology of women scholarship. And, the psychologists (mostly women) working on gender issues largely have ignored sport and physical activity. Gender issues in sport and exercise psychology today have roots in women's physical education and some parallels in psychology, but we have few direct ties and must search to find those roots.

Psychology Roots

Within the last decade, women's early contributions to psychology have been rediscovered. Denmark and Fernandez (1993) cite Mary Putnam Jacobi's (1877) book, *The Question of Rest for Women During Menstruation,* which argued against the belief that women should refrain from physical activity during menstruation, as an early benchmark. Not only is Jacobi's work a benchmark for female psychologists, but it also incorporated women's physical activity long before sport psychology came into its own.

Around the turn of the century, several female pioneers, including Mary Calkins, Christine Ladd-Franklin, Margaret Washburn, Helen Thompson Woolley, and Leta Hollingworth, conducted research, published, and were active in psychology organizations (Denmark & Fernandez, 1993; Furmoto &

Scarborough, 1986). These women took on topics within the realm of the psychology of women or gender issues, and generally they rejected social Darwinism by emphasizing social–cultural influences and refuting myths of male superiority.

Psychology of women came on strong in the 1970s, as women's issues came on strong throughout society. Bardwick's book, *The Psychology of Women,* appeared in 1970, and Sherman's influential handbook, *On the Psychology of Women,* followed in 1971. Although scholars of psychology of women have not embraced sport or physical activity, some have made important contributions. Janet Spence's work and measures of instrumentality/expressiveness and achievement orientation have influenced many sport psychologists. In the introduction to the papers presented at a Festschrift honoring Spence's contributions to gender science, Swann, Langlois, and Gilbert (1999) noted that gender research has charged into the psychological mainstream during the last two decades and that Janet Spence spawned many of the key ideas that shaped the thinking of contemporary researchers.

In my view, the female psychologist with the greatest influence on sport psychology is Carolyn Sherif. Sherif often contributed to sport psychology conferences and scholarship, and she challenged our sport psychology thinking about many issues including competition, group processes, and gender. Sherif posed an early, persuasive feminist challenge that helped turn psychology toward a more social and woman-oriented perspective. Sherif (1982) likened the term *sex roles,* which dominated both sport and psychology gender research, to a "boxcar carrying an assortment of sociological and psychological data along with an explosive mixture of myth and untested assumptions" (p. 392). Sherif's early and persistent advocacy of social psychology, which helped psychologists advance gender scholarship, has had considerable influence on my work, as it has on several others in our field.

Physical Education Roots

Just as women had a place in the beginnings of psychology, women had a place in the early days of physical education. Indeed, women had a highly visible presence. Women's colleges, which offered academic homes to female psychologists, typically promoted physical activity as part of women's education and development. Moreover, physical education for women was separated from men's physical training, and female specialists were needed to plan and conduct such programs. Women's physical education provided a woman-oriented environment long before the women's movement of the 1970s began to encourage such programs.

The legacy of the early female physical educators presents both models and conflicts for today's sport psychologists. No doubt the active, successful women leaders served as role models, and the professional writings of these early leaders are familiar to anyone who has delved into the history of physical education. But early female physical educators focused more on philosophical issues and professional practice than on the science of sport and exercise, and many women had difficulty maintaining a place in the field with the research emphasis in the 1960s.

One other aspect of early women's physical education that seems at odds with today's sport psychology is the approach to competition and athletics. Both men's and women's physical education began in the late 1800s with an emphasis on physical training as part of healthy development and education. As men's programs turned more to competitive athletics, women's physical education turned in other directions. A 1923 conference of key physical education leaders of the day (both men and women) is a benchmark for this anticompetition movement. The guidelines developed by this conference included putting athletes first, preventing exploitation, downplaying competition while emphasizing enjoyment and good sporting behavior, promoting activity for all rather than an elite few, and placing women as leaders for girls' and women's sports. In a clarifying statement, the Women's Division of the National Amateur Athletic Federation (1930) stated that they did believe in competition but disapproved of highly intense, specialized competition. The evil in competition was the emphasis on winning rather than participation, and that statement concluded with the classic line, "A game for every girl and every girl in a game."

THE COMPETITIVE ATHLETICS CONTEXT

The sentiments of the 1923 conference dominated women's physical education and sports programs through the social movements of the 1960s and 1970s. Today's women find a vastly different athletic world than in the 1950s, the 1970s, or even five years ago. In 1967, Kathy Switzer created a stir when she defied the rules barring women to sneak into the Boston marathon. Today (after much prodding) we have an Olympic marathon for women. I grew up as an avid backyard baseball player but was left with few options when most of my teammates moved into Little League. Today girls are star players on youth sport teams. The landmark beginning for this turnaround in women's sports was the 1972 passage of Title IX of the Educational Amendments Act.

Title IX, which emerged from the civil rights and women's movements, is a broad ban on sex discrimination in all educational programs receiving government funds (which is virtually all educational programs), including educational sports programs. Discrimination persists and Title IX challenges continue today, but women and girls have taken giant steps into the sport world. The number of girls in interscholastic athletics and women in intercollegiate athletic programs has increased about 6- to 10-fold from pre–Title IX days (Carpenter & Acosta, 1993; Delpy, 2001; Gill, 1995).

In the United States, women now constitute about one-third of the high school, college, and Olympic athletes in the United States. But, one-third is not one-half, and in other ways women have lost a place. The world of competitive sport is hierarchical with only an elite few reaching the summit, and women are clustered at the bottom. The glass ceiling in sport is lower and more impervious than in other domains, and women have not become coaches, administrators, sports writers, or sports medicine personnel in significant numbers. Before Title IX (1972), nearly all (more than 90%) women's athletic teams were coached by women and had a female athletic director. Today less than half of the women's teams are coached by women, and only 16% have a female director (Carpenter & Acosta, 1993; Delpy, 2001; Gill, 1995). My observations of conferences, journals, and organizations suggests that men (almost definitely white men) dominate research and professional practice in sport and exercise psychology as well as competitive athletics. Sport remains male-dominated with a clear hierarchical structure that is widely accepted and communicated in so many ways that we seldom notice.

GENDER SCHOLARSHIP IN SPORT PSYCHOLOGY

Gender scholarship in sport and exercise psychology largely follows gender scholarship within psychology. Generally, that psychology scholarship has progressed from sex differences (males and females are opposites) to an emphasis on gender role as personality (males = females, if treated alike), to more current social psychology models that emphasize social context and processes. Before reviewing that work, I will clarify my terminology, which follows current terminology in gender scholarship. *Sex differences* refers to biologically based differences between males and females, whereas *gender* refers to social and psychological characteristics and behaviors associated with females and males. Note that I did not refer to gender differences. We may set up research studies to highlight gender differences, and we may speak of differences, but males and females overlap and are more similar than different on gender-related characteristics and behaviors.

As Basow and Rubin (1999) explained in their work on gender influences in adolescence, gender is a psychological and cultural term that refers to the meaning attached to being female or male in a particular culture. Gender roles are based on societal evaluations of behaviors as either masculine or feminine, and these gender expectations vary among societies. Also, we find cultural variations in gender expectations and stereotypes. For example, Binion (1990) found that African-American women were twice as likely as white women to describe themselves as androgynous (having both masculine and feminine characteristics). Gender role expectations also vary with ethnicity, social class, and sexual orientation. Gender role identity describes the degree to which an individual identifies with these socially constructed definitions of masculinity and femininity. Basnow and Rubin noted that although we have strong consensus on gender expectations, most men and women do not conform to the cultural stereotypes of masculinity and femininity. Still, these cultural expectations serve as standards for judging ourselves and others, and these expectations are most salient during the adolescent years. Sport psychologists should be particularly aware of the power of gender roles and expectations, given that so much of our sport activity involves adolescents.

Sex Differences

Although current gender terminology and scholarship have moved beyond sex differences, that work dominated the scholarly literature for some time and still captures public attention. The study and discussion of sex differences have a long and colorful history, often with social–political overtones. Here, I will focus on the psychology research, exemplified by Maccoby and Jacklin's (1974) review of the vast literature on sex differences. Their main finding, which often is ignored, was that few conclusions could be drawn from the diverse literature on sex differences. They did note (and this was definitely not ignored) possible sex differences in four areas: math ability, visual–spatial ability, verbal ability, and aggressive behavior. Subsequent research, particularly meta-analyses, casts doubt even on these differences. The sex difference perspective, which continues to be prominent in media reports and some scholarship, assumed dichotomous biology-based psychological differences—male and female are opposites. In practice, dichotomous sex differences typically are translated to mean that we should treat males one way and females the other way. Today, consensus holds that psychological characteristics associated with females and males are neither dichotomous nor biology-based (e.g., Bem, 1993; Deaux, 1984; Eagley, 1987; Gill, 1995; Hyde & Linn, 1986).

Ashmore (1990) summarized the meta-analyses and research on sex differences and concluded that sex differences are relatively large for certain physical abilities (i.e., throwing velocity) and body use/posturing, more modest for other abilities and social behaviors (e.g., math, aggression), and negligible for all other domains (e.g., leadership, attitudes, some physical abilities such as reaction time and balance). Even the larger sex differences are confounded with nonbiological influences. Ashmore, as well as Maccoby (1990) and Jacklin (1989), advocates abandoning sex differences approaches for more multifaceted and social approaches. Most biological factors are not dichotomously divided but are normally distributed within both females and males. For example, the average college male basketball center is taller than the average female center, but the average female center is taller than most men. For social psychological characteristics such as aggressiveness or confidence, even average differences are elusive, and the evidence does not support biological, dichotomous, sex-linked connections. With criticisms of the sex differences approach, and its failure to shed light on gender-related behavior, psychologists turned to personality and gender roles.

Personality and Gender Role Orientation

Psychologists focused on gender role orientation and, specifically, gender role constructs from

Bem's (1974, 1978) work and the Bem Sex Role Inventory (BSRI). According to Bem, personality is not a function of biology. Instead, both males and females can have masculine or feminine personalities, and androgyny is best. Advocates of androgyny argue that practitioners should treat everyone the same and encourage both masculine and feminine personalities. More recently, the masculine and feminine categories and measures have been widely criticized, and even Bem (1993) has progressed to a more encompassing gender perspective. Still, most sport psychology gender research is based on her early work.

In contrast to earlier approaches, Bem conceived of masculinity and femininity as independent, desirable sets of characteristics rather than opposite extremes of a single dimension. The BSRI contains 60 personality characteristics: 20 are stereotypically feminine (e.g., affectionate, sensitive to the needs of others), 20 are stereotypically masculine (e.g., independent, willing to take risks), and 20 are fillers (e.g., truthful, happy). The person taking the BSRI indicates, on a scale of 1 to 7, how true of herself or himself each characteristic is.

When she developed the BSRI, Bem was interested in assessing androgyny, which is indicated by equal scores on both masculinity and femininity. Bem originally recommended using difference scores (masculinity–femininity scores) to determine androgyny but quickly moved to the four-way classification (figure 11.1), which is used widely in gender role research. Individuals (either females or males) who score high on both are androgynous. Those who score high on masculinity and low on femininity are masculine, and those who score high on femininity and low on masculinity are feminine. Finally, those who score low on both are undifferentiated.

Helmreich and Spence (1977), who developed their own gender role model and measure (Personality Attributes Questionnaire, or PAQ), sampled intercollegiate athletes and reported that most female athletes were either androgynous or masculine, in contrast to their nonathlete college female samples, who were most often classified as feminine. Several subsequent studies with female athletes yielded similar findings. Harris and Jennings (1977) surveyed female distance runners and reported that most were androgynous or masculine. Both Del Rey and Sheppard (1981) and Colker and Widom (1980) used the PAQ and found that most intercollegiate athletes were classified as androgynous or masculine. Myers and Lips (1978), using the BSRI, reported that most female racquetball players were androgynous whereas most males were masculine. Many more studies have surveyed female athletes by using the BSRI or PAQ, but listing more findings would not enlighten us about gender and sport.

Overall, this research suggests that female athletes possess more masculine personality characteristics than do female nonathletes (Gill, 1995). This is not particularly enlightening, and both the methodology and underlying assumptions of this research have been widely criticized. Sport and physical activity, especially competitive athletics, demand instrumental, assertive (certainly competitive) behaviors. Both the BSRI and PAQ include "competitive" as a masculine item, and the higher masculine scores of female athletes probably reflect an overlap with competitiveness. Competitive orientation can be measured directly (e.g., Gill & Deeter, 1988; Gill & Dzewaltowski, 1988), and we do not need to invoke more indirect, controversial measures that do not add any information.

More important, athlete/nonathlete status is an indirect and nonspecific measure of behavior. If instrumental and expressive personality characteristics predict instrumental and expressive behaviors, we should examine those instrumental and expressive behaviors. Even within highly competitive sports, expressive behaviors may be advantageous. Creative, expressive actions may be the key to success for a gymnast. Supportive behaviors of teammates may be critical on a soccer team, and sensitivity to others may help an Olympic

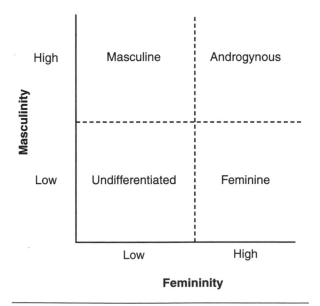

Figure 11.1 The four-way classification used in gender role research.

coach (or a sport psychology consultant) communicate with each athlete. Today, most psychologists recognize the limits of earlier sex differences and gender role approaches and look beyond the male–female and masculine–feminine dichotomies to social development and social cognitive models for explanations.

Gender and Competitive Achievement Orientation

The topic of achievement, and particularly competitive achievement, illustrates the move from sex differences and gender roles to more complex models incorporating social relationships and context. In the early achievement research (McClelland, Atkinson, Clark, & Lowell, 1953) researchers simply took male behavior as the norm until Matina Horner's (1972) doctoral work on fear of success focused attention on gender. Horner's work was publicized widely but quickly dismissed by critics (e.g., Condry & Dyer, 1976; Tresemer, 1977). McElroy and Willis (1979), who specifically considered women's achievement conflicts in sport contexts, concluded that no evidence supports fear of success in female athletes and that female athletes' achievement attitudes are similar to those of male athletes.

We have replaced global achievement motives with multidimensional constructs and an emphasis on achievement cognitions. Spence and Helmreich (1978, 1983) developed a multidimensional measure with separate dimensions of mastery, work, and competitiveness and found that males scored higher than females on mastery and competitiveness, whereas females scored higher than males on work. Gender differences on mastery and work diminished for athletes, but males remained higher than females on competitiveness. Also, masculinity scores related positively to all three achievement dimensions, whereas femininity scores related slightly positively to work and negatively to competitiveness. Generally, gender influence is strongest and most consistent for competitiveness.

My work (Gill, 1988, 1993) on competitive sport orientation also suggests that gender influences vary across dimensions. Several years ago, we developed the Sport Orientation Questionnaire (SOQ; Gill & Deeter, 1988), a sport-specific, multidimensional measure that assesses three dimensions: competitiveness (an achievement orientation to enter and strive for success in competitive sport), win orientation (a desire to win and avoid losing), and goal orientation (an emphasis on

achieving personal goals). With several samples, athletes were more competitive on all SOQ measures, and the competitiveness score was the primary discriminator between athletes and nonathletes (Gill, 1993).

We considered gender throughout our research and found that males typically scored higher than females on competitiveness and win orientation, whereas females typically scored slightly higher than males on goal orientation. With some samples, we also assessed participation in competitive sport, in noncompetitive sport, and in nonsport achievement activities. Overall, males consistently scored higher than females on SOQ competitiveness and win orientation, and males also reported more competitive sport activity and experience. However, females were just as high as males, and sometimes higher, on SOQ goal orientation and general achievement. Also, females were just as likely as males to participate in noncompetitive sport and nonsport achievement activities (Gill, 1993).

Later, when using the SOQ with several varied athlete samples, we found differences among athlete groups on competitive orientations, and especially in win/goal orientation. Moreover, the variation was not simply a gender difference but was related to sport demands. With a sample of international and university athletes and nonathletes from Taiwan, we found strong differences between athletes and nonathletes but minimal gender differences. With one unique sample of ultramarathoners competing in a selective event, we found low win orientations but very high goal orientations and no gender differences (Gill, 1993).

An overview of the SOQ competitiveness scores from several of our samples helps put the gender "differences" into perspective. Generally, males are more competitive than females, but overlap and similarity are the rule. Moreover, differences between athletes and nonathletes, and within athlete samples, typically are stronger than gender differences. In our early university and high school samples (see Gill, 1988, for details), we found a gender difference that was statistically significant, but the difference in means was less than one standard deviation, suggesting considerable overlap.

Table 11.1 depicts the overall results of this research with gender differences (or lack of differences) for athlete and nonathlete samples (see Gill, 1993, for a more detailed review of these studies). The Iowa intercollegiate athletes and nonathletes at the top of the table show a gender difference, but that gender difference is not consistent. Fe-

Table 11.1
SOQ Competitiveness Scores for Male and Female Athletes and Nonathletes

Iowa	Athletes		Nonathletes		Combined			
	Male	Female	Male	Female	Male	Female		
	59.1	57.1	49.4	43.5	54.9	49.4		

Taiwan	International		University		Nonathletes		Combined	
	Male	Female	Male	Female	Male	Female	Male	Female
	56.6	53.3	50.6	49.9	48.2	42.8	50.7	46.9

Ultramarathoners	Male	Female						
	47.5	50.3						

male athletes do not differ significantly from male athletes, and the mean for female athletes is higher than the mean for male nonathletes.

The middle of the table depicts competitiveness scores from a study (Kang, Gill, Acevedo, & Deeter, 1990) comparing international athletes, university athletes, and nonathletes in Taiwan. Overall, females were slightly (but not significantly) lower than males on competitiveness scores. Again, athlete–nonathlete differences were much stronger, and the pattern is similar to the Iowa sample. Female international athletes were more competitive than male university athletes, and female university athletes were more competitive than male nonathletes.

Finally, the bottom of the table depicts the competitiveness scores of our unique sample of ultramarathoners. The gender difference is nonsignificant, and in contrast to all other samples, females were slightly higher than males. Also, the ultramarathoners were similar to the nonathlete samples on competitiveness scores, but they were much higher than nonathletes and other athlete samples on goal orientation (Gill, 1993).

Overall, gender differences in competitiveness are limited and do not seem to reflect either general achievement orientation or interest in sport and exercise activities per se. Instead, competitiveness seems to reflect opportunity and experience in competitive sport, and gender is related to an emphasis on social comparison and winning within sport.

Other researchers reported similar gender influences on reactions to competitive sport. When McNally and Orlick (1975) introduced a coopera-

tive broomball game to children in urban Canada and in the northern territories, they found girls were more receptive to the cooperative rules than were boys. They also noted cultural differences, with northern children more receptive, but the gender influence held in both cultures. Duda (1986) similarly reported both gender and cultural influences on competitiveness with Anglo and Navajo children in the southwestern United States. Male Anglo children were the most win-oriented and placed the most emphasis on athletic ability. Weinberg and Jackson (1979) found that males were more affected by success/failure than were females, and in a related study, Weinberg and Ragan (1979) reported that males were more interested in a competitive activity whereas females preferred a noncompetitive activity.

Although several lines of research suggest gender influences on competitive sport achievement, the research does not point to any unique gender-related personality construct as an explanation. Instead, most investigators are turning to socialization, societal influences, and social cognitive models for explanations.

Jacquelynne Eccles' (1985, 1987; Eccles et al., 1983) model incorporates such sociocultural factors along with achievement cognitions. Eccles recognized that both expectations and importance or value determine achievement choices and behaviors. Gender differences in expectations are common, and gender also influences the value of achievement. Eccles further noted that gender differences in expectations and value develop over time and are influenced by gender role socialization, stereotyped expectations of others, and sociocultural norms, as well as individual characteristics and experiences. Eccles and Harold (1991) summarized existing work and provided evidence that her model holds for sport achievement, that gender influences children's sport achievement perceptions and behaviors at a very young age, and that these gender differences seem to be the product of gender role socialization.

Physical Activity and Self-Perceptions

Before moving away from personality, let us consider self-perceptions, particularly body image and self-esteem. As research, popular media, and our observations suggest, females often lack confidence in their sport and exercise capabilities. As noted in the previous section, Eccles has conducted considerable research on the development of expectations, competence, and self-esteem. In a recent chapter (Eccles, Barber, Jozefowicz, Malenchuk, & Vida, 1999), she noted that gender differences in self-perceptions are usually much larger than one would expect given objective measures of actual performance and competence. Eccles is one of the few developmental psychologists to include sport competence in her work, and she consistently finds larger gender differences in perceptions of sport competence than in other domains. Moreover, even in sport, the gender differences in perceptions are much larger than the gender differences in actual sport-related skills.

Because sport offers the opportunity to develop physical strength and confidence, to strive for excellence, to accomplish a goal through effort and training, and to test oneself in competition, it has tremendous potential to enhance women's sense of competence and control. Diana Nyad, the marathon swimmer, expressed this:

> When asked why, I say that marathon swimming is the most difficult physical, intellectual, and emotional battleground I have encountered, and each time I win, each time I reach the other shore, I feel worthy of any other challenge life has to offer. (Nyad, 1978, p. 152)

Many women who begin activity programs report enhanced self-esteem and a sense of physical competence that often carries over into other aspects of their lives. A few studies support these testimonials. Holloway, Beuter, and Duda (1988), Brown and Harrison (1986), and Trujillo (1983) all report that exercise programs, particularly weight and strength training, enhance the self-concepts

of female participants.

In one particularly exciting report, Erkut, Fields, Sing, and Marx (1996) described their study of experiences (including sport experiences) that influence diverse urban girls. Erkut et al. sampled girls from across the United States representing five ethnic backgrounds (Native American, African American, Anglo-European American, Asian Pacific Islander, Latino) and asked the girls, "What activities make you feel good about yourself?" Athletics was the most common response, mentioned by nearly half (46%) of the girls. When asked what about the activity made them feel good, the most common response was related to mastery or competence (e.g., "I'm good at it") followed by enjoyment. Erkut et al. purposely sampled to consider ethnic and socioeconomic influences, and they found variations in patterns illustrating the power of the social context background. Of most interest for sport psychology, Native American and Asian Pacific Islander girls were most likely to cite athletics. Also, girls of high socioeconomic status were less likely to cite athletics and more likely to cite art activities. In discussing the results, Erkut et al. expressed surprise at the prominence of athletics. They suggested that the findings called attention to the importance of historical context (post–Title IX for these girls). They also noted that sport as a source of mastery and enjoyment is not part of the traditional or contemporary female role. Erkut et al. studied a large, diverse sample and found many variations that highlight the importance of social contexts in the lives of these girls. Although Erkut et al. offered more questions than answers, they suggested exciting directions for sport psychology.

We should note the work on gender and body image within sport and exercise settings (see *The Bodywise Woman*, Melpomene Institute, 1990; Rodin, Silberstein, & Striegel-Moore, 1985, for reviews). Our images of the ideal body, and particularly the ideal female body, have changed through history and across social contexts. As Bordo (1993) convincingly argued, girls learn early how they are supposed to look, dress, and behave in society. Barbie dolls, ballerinas, and supermodels represent the ideal female body—light, fragile, and very feminine (Turkel, 1998). Today's idealized female body is extreme, with very little fat. Although this image is highly visible in advertising and popular culture, it is impossible for most women to achieve. Nevertheless, many women adopt this ideal and struggle to obtain it—less than ideal in terms of physical and mental health.

Boys and men also have concerns about body image, but the literature indicates that girls and women are much more negative about their bodies. Moreover, the concerns are gender-related. Girls are particularly concerned with physical beauty and maintaining the ideal thin shape, whereas boys are more concerned with size, strength, and power. Society shapes body image, and this societal pressure for a body image that is not particularly healthy or attainable for many women likely has a negative influence on self-esteem and psychological well-being as well as on physical health and well-being.

Concerns about body image affect all women, and athletes are just as susceptible as other women to societal pressures toward unrealistic, unhealthy thinness and eating disorders. Such pressures are of particular concern in the "thin body" sports, such as gymnastics, dance, and running. For example, one athlete reported,

At age 14 my cycling coach told me I was "fat" in front of my entire team. . . . At 5'5'', 124 pounds, I was not fat, but my self-esteem was so low that I simply believed him. After all, he was the coach. (Melpomene, 1990, p. 36)

Joan Ryan's (1995) book, *Little Girls in Pretty Boxes,* highlights the pressures and emphasis on childlike bodies for young gymnasts and figure skaters. Research on social physique anxiety (Hart, Leary, & Rejeski, 1989), body image, and disordered eating with athletes and nonathletes (Hausenblaus & Mack, 1998; Petrie, 1996) is equivocal, but clearly athletes are not immune from the pressures and may face specific pressures in certain sport settings. Pressuring an athlete, who already faces tremendous societal pressure to lose weight, is not a desirable approach. Most enlightened coaches and instructors follow nutritional guidelines and emphasize healthy eating and exercise behaviors rather than weight standards. Sport psychology consultants who recognize the pressures and gender influences can help athletes and coaches develop these healthy approaches.

SOCIAL PERSPECTIVES

In the 1980s, gender research moved away from the sex differences and personality approaches to a more social approach, emphasizing gender beliefs and stereotypes. How people think males and females differ is more important than how they actually differ. Although actual differences between females and males on such characteristics as independence or competitiveness are small and inconsistent, we maintain our stereotypes (e.g., Bem, 1985; Deaux, 1984; Deaux & Kite, 1987, 1993; Deaux & Major, 1987; Spence & Helmreich, 1978). These gender stereotypes are pervasive. We exaggerate minimal differences into larger perceived differences through social processes. These perceptions exert a strong influence that may elicit further gender differences. This cycle reflects the feminist position that gender is socially constructed.

Gender stereotypes and gender bias in evaluations certainly exist within sport. Eleanor Metheny (1965) identified gender stereotypes in her classic analysis of the social acceptability of various sports. Metheny concluded that it is not appropriate for women to engage in contests in which

- the resistance of the opponent is overcome by bodily contact,
- the resistance of a heavy object is overcome by direct application of bodily force, or
- the body is projected into or through space over long distances or for extended periods of time.

According to Metheny, acceptable sports for women (e.g., gymnastics, swimming, tennis) emphasize aesthetic qualities and often are individual activities in contrast to direct competition and team sports. Although Metheny offered her analysis more than 30 years ago, our gender stereotypes have not faded away with the implementation of Title IX. Gender stereotypes persist, and they seem more persistent in sport than in other social contexts. For example, Kane and Snyder (1989) confirmed gender stereotyping of sports, as suggested by Metheny, and more explicitly identified physicality and the emphasis on males' physical muscularity, strength, and power as the key feature.

Matteo (1986, 1988) and Csizma, Wittig, and Schurr (1988) confirmed that sports are indeed sex-typed (mostly as masculine). Matteo further reported that sex-typing influenced sport choice and that sex-typed individuals did not participate in gender-inappropriate sports.

Considerable research suggests a gender bias in the evaluation of female and male performance both in and out of sport. Goldberg (1968) reported a bias favoring male authors when women judged articles that were equivalent except for sex of author. Subsequent studies confirmed a male bias but suggested that the bias varies with information and situational characteristics (e.g., Pheterson, Kiesler, & Goldberg, 1971; Wallston & O'Leary, 1981). A series of studies that adopted the Goldberg approach to examine gender bias in attitudes toward hypothetical female and male coaches (Parkhouse & Williams, 1986; Weinberg, Reveles, & Jackson, 1984; Williams & Parkhouse, 1988) revealed a bias favoring male coaches. However, Williams and Parkhouse (1988) reported that female basketball players coached by a successful female did not exhibit the male bias, suggesting more complex influences on gender stereotypes and evaluations.

Gender beliefs and stereotypes are found everywhere. Socialization pressures are pervasive, are strong, and begin early. Parents, teachers, peers, and societal institutions treat girls and boys differently from birth (e.g., American Association of University Women, 1992; Geis, 1993; Sadker, Sadker, & Klein, 1991; Unger & Crawford, 1992). Overall, differential treatment is consistent with producing independence and efficacy in boys and producing emotional sensitivity, nurturance, and helplessness in girls.

Media

One prominent source of differential treatment for sport is the media. Investigations of television, newspaper, and popular magazine coverage of female and male athletes reveal clear gender bias (e.g., Kane, 1989; Kane & Parks, 1992; Messner, Duncan, & Jensen, 1993). First, females receive little coverage (less than 10%) whether considering TV airtime, newspaper space, feature articles, or photographs. Moreover, females and males receive different coverage that reflects gender hierarchy. For example, male athletes typically are featured in uniform and in action, whereas female athletes are typically posed in nonsport, nonactive settings. Generally, athletic ability and accomplishments are emphasized for men, but femininity and physical attractiveness are emphasized for female athletes. Kane (1989) described one graphic example with the 1987–88 Northwest Louisiana State women's basketball media guide cover, which showed the team members in Playboy bunny ears and tails captioned, "These girls can Play, boy!" Gender bias in the sport media usually occurs in more subtle ways. Eitzen and Baca Zinn (1993) reported that a majority of colleges had sexist nicknames or symbols (e.g., adding "-elle," "-ette," or "Lady") that gender-marked the female athletes as different from and less than the male athletes. In a study of 1989 NCAA basketball tournaments and U.S. Open tennis coverage, Messner et al. (1993) noted less stereotyping than in previous studies but still found considerable gender marking (e.g., "women's final four" but "final four" for men) and gendered hierarchy of naming (e.g., women referred to as girls, young ladies, or women; men never referred to as boys).

Gender marking may be appropriate when it is symmetrical or similar for women and men, as it was for most of the tennis coverage, but asymmetrical marking labels females as "other." For example, consider that we have the WNBA, but we don't have the MNBA; what are the gender messages and implications? Gendered language was also apparent in comments. Comments about strength and weakness were ambivalent for women but clearly were about strength for men, and emotional reasons for failure (e.g., nerves, lack of confidence) were cited more often for women. Messner et al. noted that "dominants" in society typically are referred to by last names and subordinates by first names. They found first names used more than 50% of the time to refer to females but only 10% of the time to refer to males. Also, the few male athletes referred to by first names were black male basketball players. No race differences were observed for females, and gender seemed to be the more powerful feature.

My own observations of recent Olympic and NCAA tournaments suggests improvement, with less stereotyping and trivialization of female athletes, but institutional change is slow, and overall, gendered beliefs seem alive and well in the sport world. Activities are gender stereotyped, and the sex-typing of sport activities seems linked with other gender beliefs (e.g., physicality). Gender beliefs influence social processes, and the research on gender bias in evaluation of coaches suggests that influence is at least as likely in sport as in other social interactions. Overt discrimination is unlikely, and participants may not recognize the influence of gendered beliefs in themselves or others. For example, many sport administrators and participants fail to recognize gender beliefs operating when athletic programs developed by and for men, stressing male-linked values and characteristics, are opened to girls and women.

Social Context

The social aspect of gender is more than perceptions and stereotypes; it's the whole context. In *The Female World,* Jesse Bernard (1981) proposed that the social worlds for females and males are different, even when they appear similar. In earlier times we created actual separate worlds for females and males with segregated physical education and sport programs. Although we now have coed activities, the separate worlds have not disappeared. The social world differs for female and male university basketball players, for male and female joggers, and for the girl and boy in a youth soccer game.

Stereotypes are of concern because we act on them; we exaggerate minimal gender differences and restrict opportunities for both females and males. Gender beliefs keep many women out of sport, and gender beliefs restrict the behaviors of both men and women in sport. Both girls and boys can participate in youth gymnastics or baseball, and at early ages physical capabilities are similar. Yet children see female gymnasts and male baseball players as role models; peers gravitate to sex-segregated activities; and most parents, teachers, and coaches support gender-appropriate activities of children.

To illustrate the role of social context, let's consider confidence. Considerable earlier research suggested that females display lower confidence than males across varied settings. Lenney (1977) concluded that the social situation was the primary source of gender differences. Specifically, gender differences emerged with masculine tasks, in competitive settings, when clear, unambiguous feedback was missing. Several studies by Corbin and colleagues within sport psychology (e.g., Corbin, 1981; Corbin, Landers, Feltz, & Senior, 1983; Corbin & Nix, 1979; Corbin, Stewart, & Blair, 1981) confirmed Lenney's propositions. However, these studies were experimental studies with novel motor tasks, conducted in controlled lab settings that purposely strip away social context. We cannot ignore social context in the real world. Sport tasks typically are seen as masculine, competition is the norm, and males and females develop their confidence along with their physical skills through radically different experiences and opportunities.

GENDER RELATIONS AND SOCIAL DIVERSITY: PROMISING DIRECTIONS FOR SPORT PSYCHOLOGY

Feminist and social–cultural perspectives call for consideration of gender within the wider context of social diversity. Gender intersects with race, class, and other aspects of social identity. To understand gender, we also must consider the variations of gender relations as we cross other cultural categories. Sport is not only male, but white, young, middle-class, heterosexual male. And gender affects men as well as women in sport. Sport psychology has progressed from the limited sex differences and gender role approaches, but we have not incorporated diversity or adopted relational analyses that might help us develop a useful gender scholarship. Ann Hall (1996), one of the most insightful and inspiring feminist sport scholars, notes that sport psychologists have relied on categorical research to study gender. We focus on differences, whether we rely on biological or socialization explanations. We focus on individuals and fail to analyze the powerful ways in which gender and race relations are socially and historically constructed. Yevonne Smith (1992), in her review of the research (or lack thereof) on women of color, called for "more relational analyses of and by diverse women of color and to understand how collective personal experiences and processes are informed by race, gender, and class power relations" (p. 224). To date, sport psychology has not heeded the call, but some scholars have at least recognized the shortcomings of our current approaches.

Race and Ethnicity

Ten years ago Duda and Allison (1990) pointed out the striking void in sport psychology on race and ethnicity—and the void persists. Most of the issues raised for gender have parallels in race and ethnicity. That is, stereotypes are pervasive and multifaceted. Racial and ethnic socialization, self-perceptions, and social context influence sport behavior, and a grounding in sociocultural history would enhance our understanding of race and ethnicity in sport. Although parallel issues arise, race and class are qualitatively different from gender, and we do not even have the limited work on stereotypes and individual characteristics to parallel the gender research. Also, gender likely interacts with other diversity characteristics in many complex ways. For example, the experiences of a black, female tennis player are not simply a combination of the experiences of white female and black male players. Althea Gibson's (1979) personal account highlights some of the complex interactions of race and gender and illustrates influences of social history and the immediate social situation in her development as a tennis player and as a person.

Significant numbers of athletes are not white and middle-class, yet power remains solidly white and middle-class. Sport's glass ceiling keeps all but white, middle-class athletes clustered at the bottom. The popular media and some scholars have discussed such practices as "stacking" (e.g., African Americans in positions such as football running back or baseball outfield but not in central quarterback or pitching roles) and the nearly exclusive white male dominance of coaching and management positions. To date, few of these reports have included in-depth or critical analysis of race or class within sport.

Majors (1990) added more critical analysis to the literature with his discussion of the "cool pose" (i.e., a set of expressive lifestyle behaviors) used by black males to counter racism. Majors noted that although a few black males escape limits and express pride, power, and control, the emphasis on the cool pose is self-defeating for the majority because it comes at the expense of education and other opportunities for advancement. Moreover, Majors noted that the cool pose uses sexist oppression to counter racist oppression rather than encouraging more empowering strategies. Majors tied analyses of race and gender, but few others have done so. In her review of the literature on women of color in sport, Smith (1992) reached the primary conclusion that we have a deafening silence on diverse ethnic women in sport.

In 1993, Brooks and Althouse edited a volume on racism in college athletics focusing on the African-American athlete's experience, which included a welcome section on gender and race. (A second edition of this book was published in 2000.) In their chapter, Corbett and Johnson (1993) drew on the limited research and their own insights to focus on African-American women in college sport. They noted that African-American women have a social–historical context of sexual exploitation, low wages, and substandard education and are stereotyped as independent, loud, and dominating. These authors also debunk our popular myth that African-American women gravitate to track. African-American women have had more opportunities in track than some other activities, and talented athletes from Wilma Rudolph to Jackie Joyner-Kersee are widely recognized, but survey data indicate that track is not a particularly popular activity for African-American students, and opportunities likely are limited by social stereotypes and constraints. In another article, Tina

Sloan Green (1993) optimistically discussed Girls Clubs, YWCA, PGM golf (a Philadelphia program for African-American youth), Black Women in Sport Foundation, and the NCAA's National Youth Sport Program as strategies to help overcome barriers and encourage more young African-American women to participate and develop their full potential in sports and athletics.

We can extend considerations further to incorporate other cultural groups and other social categories such as class, age, and physical attributes. The lack of sport psychology research on any category other than gender, and the limits of that gender work, preclude conclusions. Clearly, we should extend our consideration of cultural diversity within our sport psychology research and practice. More important, sport psychology might heed the call of the scholars who advocate critical and relational analyses. Sport studies scholars, including Birrell (1988, 1989), Dewar (1993), and Hargreaves (1994), argue for relational analyses reflected in Hall's (1996) and Smith's (1992) views presented at the beginning of this section. That is, we should move from simple categorical analyses (male vs. female) to analyses of the complex, dynamic ways that gender influences our social environment, behaviors, and interactions. Gender, race, and class relations are power relations, and feminist critiques call for sport psychology to consider the many intersections of gender, race, class, and other power relations.

Gender and Sexuality

Although sport is stereotypically masculine, scholars recognize that gender relations affect men. As discussed by Messner (1992), sport is a powerful force that socializes boys and men into a restricted masculine identity. Messner cited two major forces in sport:

- Competitive hierarchical structure with conditional self-worth that enforces the "must win" style
- Homophobia

Messner described the extent of homophobia, defined as the irrational fear or intolerance of homosexuality, in sport as staggering, and stated that homophobia leads all boys and men (gay or straight) to conform to a narrow definition of masculinity. Real men compete and, above all, avoid anything feminine that might lead one to be branded a sissy. One successful elite athlete interviewed by Messner noted that he was interested in dance as a child but instead threw himself into athletics as a football and track jock. He reflected that he probably would have been a dancer but wanted the macho image of the athlete. Messner tied this masculine identity to sport violence because using violence to achieve a goal is acceptable and encouraged within this identity. Notably, female athletes are less comfortable with aggression in sport. Messner further noted that homophobia in athletics is closely linked with misogyny; sport bonds men together as superior to women.

Messner's linking of homophobia and misogyny reflects Lenskyj's (1987, 1991) analysis citing compulsory heterosexuality as the root of sexist sport practices and Bem's (1993) contention that sexism, heterosexism, and homophobia are all related consequences of the same gender lenses in society. We expect to see men dominate women, and we are uncomfortable with bigger, stronger women who take the active, dominant roles expected of athletes.

Homophobia in sport has been discussed most often as a problem for lesbians, with good reason. Nelson (1991), in her chapter, "A Silence So Loud, It Screams," illustrated restrictions and barriers for lesbians by describing one Ladies' Professional Golf Association tour player who remained closeted to protect her status with friends, family, sponsors, tour personnel, and the general public (prior to Muffin Spencer-Devlin's public and relatively accepted coming out statement in 1997). Not surprisingly, those involved with women's athletics often go out of the way to avoid any appearance of lesbianism. Pat Griffin, who has written and conducted workshops on homophobia in sport and physical education, described this state as, "tip-toeing around a lavender elephant in the locker room and pretending that it's just not there" (1987, p. 3). As Griffin noted (1987, 1992), lesbians are not the problem; homophobia is the problem. Homophobia manifests itself in women's sports in the following ways:

- Silence
- Denial
- Apology
- Promotion of a "heterosexy" image
- Attacks on lesbians
- Preference for male coaches

We stereotypically assume that sport attracts lesbians (of course not gay men), but there is no inherent relationship between sexual orientation

© Human Kinetics

Homophobia in women's sports can manifest itself in a preference for male coaches.

and sport (no gay gene will turn you into a softball player or figure skater). No doubt, homophobia has kept more heterosexual women than lesbians out of sports, and homophobia restricts the behavior of all women in sport. Moreover, as the analyses of Messner (1992) and Ponger (1990) suggest, homophobia probably restricts men in sport even more than it restricts women. As noted earlier, Messner argues that all men, gay or straight, must conform to the male, masculine, heterosexist role to be part of the team and to avoid harassment or physical violence. From a gender relations perspective, homophobia keeps those out of power (women, gay men, and lesbians) out of sport and restricts the behaviors of everyone in the sport environment.

So, the literature does not support dichotomous sex differences; males and females are not opposites. But, women and men are not the same and we cannot ignore gender. Gender is part of a complex, dynamic, ever-changing social context and is a particularly salient, powerful part within sport and exercise settings. Consideration of gender relations and recognition of diversity is critical to effective sport psychology practice.

Toward Feminist Practice in Sport Psychology

Translating gender scholarship into sport practice is a challenge, but the expanding literature on feminist practice in psychology and sociocultural sport studies provide some guidance.

To translate gender scholarship into feminist practice we first must avoid sexist assumptions, standards, and practices. Then, we might follow the lead of psychologists who have moved beyond nonsexist practices to more actively feminist approaches. Feminist practice (Worell & Remer, 1992) incorporates gender scholarship, emphasizes neglected women's experiences (e.g., sexual harassment), and takes a more nonhierarchical, empowering, process-oriented approach that shifts emphasis from personal change to social change.

An aggressive soccer player could be male or female, but a male soccer player is more likely to grow up in a world that reinforces aggressive behavior, and a male athlete is more likely to continue to have such behaviors reinforced. The less aggressive, more tentative approach is more typical of female athletes. Even talented, competitive female athletes are socialized to keep quiet, be good, and let others take the lead. Moreover, most female athletes have a male coach, trainer, athletic director, and professors and deal with males in most other power positions.

Overly aggressive, uncontrolled behavior is not exclusively male, nor are tentative styles exclusively female. Still, we will work more effectively if we recognize gender influences in the athlete's background and situation. Anger control and confidence building have different contexts and likely require different strategies for females and males. Behavior is not just within the athlete but is within a particular sport context and within a larger social context. Both the immediate situation and larger context are gender-related. Moreover, gender relations are mixed with race, class, and other power relations of the athlete's context and background.

Sexual harassment is an issue with clear gender connotations, an issue that is prevalent and likely to emerge in practice, and an issue that has been neglected in sport psychology. Research and writing on violence toward women have expanded greatly, and this is a major contribution of gender

scholarship to the field of psychology. Given the prevalence of sexual harassment and sexual assault, especially for college women, female athletes are much more likely to present problems related to these issues than eating disorders or any other potentially clinical issues. Yet, I have seen virtually nothing in the sport psychology literature on this topic.

Several studies, as well as more public attention, have demonstrated the prevalence of sexual harassment and assault (e.g., Unger & Crawford, 1992; Matlin, 1993). About one-third of college women report being sexually harassed, and when jokes and discriminatory remarks are included, the number increases to more than 50%. Koss (1990; Koss, Gidycz, & Wisniewiski, 1987) has done considerable research on sexual assault, and her findings indicate that 38 of 1,000 college women experience rape or attempted rape in one year, that 85% of sexual assaults are by acquaintances, and that men and women interpret sexual situations and behaviors differently. All women are at risk, and no particular psychological pattern characterizes victims, although college students are at risk and alcohol is often involved. Given that most sport psychology consultants work with college athletes, we should be familiar with this work. Sexual harassment can be a tremendous barrier to educational and athletic achievement, and rape can be a devastating experience. Many victims remain anxious and depressed months later, and some experience severe substance abuse, eating disorders, major depression, or other symptoms years later (e.g., Gordon & Riger, 1989; Koss, 1990; Murphy et al., 1988).

Although I do not know of sport psychology research dealing with these issues, the issues have been raised in more theoretical and popular writing. Nelson (1991), in her aptly titled chapter, "Running Scared," noted that harassment is almost routine and expected by female runners. Women cannot run any time, any place. Lenskyj (1992) recently discussed sexual harassment in sport, drawing ties to power relations and ideology of male sports. Lenskyj noted that sexual harassment raises some unique concerns for female athletes, in addition to the concerns of all women. Specifically, Lenskyj noted that sport (as a nonfeminine activity) may elicit derisive comments; clothes are revealing; female athletes may have spent much time training and less in general social activity; coaches are authoritarian and rule much of athletes' lives; and for some sports merit is equated with heterosexual attractiveness.

Overwhelmingly, sexual harassment involves males harassing females, even in less gender-structured settings than sport. As Lenskyj noted and earlier discussions of homophobia suggest, lesbians and gay men are more likely to be the targets than perpetrators of sexual harassment. Lenskyj notes that allegations of lesbianism may deter female athletes (regardless of sexual orientation) from rejecting male advances or complaining about harassment. A student in my women and sport class interviewed female coaches about lesbianism and, to her surprise, found the married female coach more open and willing to discuss issues than single coaches (lesbian or heterosexual). Given the sport climate, we should not be surprised that female coaches are so worried about charges of lesbianism that they refrain from complaining about harassment or seeking equity for their programs. Sexual harassment (heterosexual or homophobic harassment) intimidates women and maintains traditional power structures.

Sexual harassment and assault recently have been brought to public attention as a concern for male athletes as well as female athletes. Some accounts (e.g., Neimark, 1993) suggest that male athletes are particularly prone to sexual assault. These popular media reports, as well as more theoretical work (e.g., Lenskyj, 1992; Messner, 1992), suggest that male bonding, the privileged status of athletes, and the macho image of sport are contributing factors.

Sexual harassment and assault probably occur much more often that we recognize, and many athletes would not discuss the problem with a sport psychology consultant or anyone else. Consultants who are aware of sport and gender dynamics might be quicker to recognize such issues and help athletes deal with the situation. As well as educating athletes, sport psychologists can take steps to change the situation by educating coaches and administrators. Most universities have counseling and educational programs on sexual harassment and assault as well as established policies and procedures to deal with incidents. Sport consultants can use these resources (e.g., refer victims, incorporate workshops) or develop programs targeted to athletes. Athletes often train in isolated locations during late hours, travel, and may be placed in vulnerable situations more than other students, and female athletes must be aware of sexual harassment and assault concerns.

Male athletes also must be aware of issues, and male administrators can support educational efforts. As Guernsey (1993) reported, several rape prevention programs have been designed for male athletes, such as programs at Cornell and Arkansas, which are supported by coaches and administrators and aim to prevent aggression needed on the field from affecting personal lives. Sport psychologists might use such programs and relevant university resources to educate female and male athletes, coaches, and others, which would go far toward preventing sexual harassment and assault. Again, to take a more feminist approach, we could attempt to change the social situation as well as educate individuals—perhaps by demanding safe lighting, secure facilities, and clear, enforceable policies.

Russell and Fraser's (1999) chapter on lessons learned from self-defense training illustrates a feminist approach for optimizing women's educational experiences and, specifically, for helping women deal with fears of sexual assault and move from victim to an empowered position. They studied participants in the Model Mugging (MM) program, which includes female instructors, male "model muggers" in pads, and participants practicing using full force to "knock out" muggers. Russell and Fraser drew lessons from the MM program and results to suggest guidelines for optimizing women's educational environments. They cited the importance of a safe environment, female instructors as competent models, and inclusion of men as allies but not protectors, allowing participants to demonstrate competence in relation to men. They concluded that programs are most effective if they are structured to ensure success and focus on competencies rather than vulnerabilities.

Russell and Fraser's chapter is included in a text (Davis, Crawford, & Sebrechts, 1999) on ways to optimize the educational experiences of girls and women. These chapters reflect feminist practice in psychology, and specifically in education. Within psychology, several scholars have argued for feminist practice and have taken important steps in those directions. As noted at the beginning of this section, Worell and Remer (1992) advocated feminist psychology practice. More recently, calls for feminist practice have been broadened to include all areas of research, education, and practice in psychology. In July 1993, a National Conference on Education and Training in Feminist Practice was held to explore, integrate, and create a cohesive agenda for training and educating in feminist practice. In the preface to the collective outcome of that conference, Johnson and

Worell (1997) noted that feminist practice is widely defined to include activities related to all areas of psychology—research, teaching, clinical practice and supervision, scholarly writing, leadership, and any other activities in which psychologists participate. The collection includes summaries and consensus statements on feminist practice and directions for specific practice areas, as well as themes that cross all areas. All of the chapters provide guidelines for sport psychologists who wish to be more inclusive, empowering, and effective in their research and practice. In the afterword, Johnson and Worell (1997) listed common themes of feminist practice:

- Includes therapy/intervention, teaching, political action, consultation, writing, scholarship, research, supervision, assessment and diagnosis, administration, and public service

- Promotes transformation and social change

- Assumes the personal is political

- Embraces diversity as a requirement and foundation for practice

- Includes an analysis of power and the multiple ways in which people can be oppressed and oppressing

- Promotes empowerment and the individual woman's voice

- Promotes collaboration

- Promotes the value of diverse methodologies

- Promotes feminist consciousness

- Promotes self-reflection on personal, disciplinary, and other levels as a lifelong process

- Promotes continued evaluation and reflection of our values, ethics, and process, which is an active and reflective feminist process

- Asserts that misogyny and other inequities are damaging

- Encourages demystification of theory and practice

- Views theory and practice as evolving and emerging

The views of the feminist psychologists and the common themes reflect many of the calls for relational analyses and attention to power relations by feminist sport studies scholars. But psychologists also retain concern for the individual. Although the combined focus on the individual and social relations may seem paradoxical at first glance, I see that combination as the essence of a useful sport psychology. Our goal is to understand behavior and help individuals optimize sport experiences and move from the sport settings to enhanced life experiences in the real world. Social context and relations are far more powerful in the real world than in the lab or any research setting.

Gender makes a difference, and human diversity characterizes all of us in all we do. Gender relations are dynamic and vary with the individual, situation, and time. We are just beginning to consider gender relations in our research and practice. We can continue to work on the greater challenge of shaping a sport psychology that incorporates gender relations and values diversity in all forms of practice to enhance sport for all.

REFERENCES

American Association of University Women. (1992). *The AAUW report: How schools shortchange girls. Executive summary*. Washington, DC: American Association of University Women Educational Foundation.

Ashmore, R.D. (1990). Sex, gender, and the individual. In L.A. Pervin (Ed.), *Handbook of personality theory and research* (pp. 486–526). New York: Guilford Press.

Bardwick, J. (1970). *The psychology of women: A study of bio-cultural conflicts*. New York: Harper & Row.

Basow, S.A., & Rubin, L.R. (1999). Gender influences and adolescent development. In N.G. Johnson, M.C. Roberts, & J. Worell (Eds.), *Beyond appearance: A new look at adolescent girls* (pp. 25–52). Washington, DC: American Psychological Association.

Bem, S.L. (1974). The measurement of psychological androgyny. *Journal of Consulting and Clinical Psychology, 42,* 155–162.

Bem, S.L. (1978). Beyond androgyny: Some presumptuous prescriptions for a liberated sexual identity. In J. Sherman & F. Denmark (Eds.), *Psychology of women: Future directions for research* (pp. 1–23). New York: Psychological Dimensions.

Bem, S.L. (1985). Androgyny and gender schema theory: A conceptual and empirical integration. In T.B. Sonderegger (Ed.), *Nebraska symposium on motivation, 1984: Psychology and gender* (pp. 179–226). Lincoln: University of Nebraska Press.

Bem, S.L. (1993). *The lenses of gender*. New Haven, CT: Yale University Press.

Bernard, J. (1981). *The female world*. New York: Free Press.

Binion, V.J. (1990). Psychological androgyny: A black female perspective. *Sex Roles, 22,* 487–507.

Birrell, S.J. (1988). Discourses on the gender/sport relationship: From women in sport to gender relations. *Exercise and Sport Sciences Reviews, 16,* 459–502.

Birrell, S.J. (1989). Racial relations theories and sport: Suggestions for a more critical analysis. *Sociology of Sport Journal, 6,* 212–227.

Bordo, S. (1993). *Unbearable weight: Feminism, western culture, and the body.* Berkeley: University of California.

Brooks, D., & Althouse, R. (1993). *Racism in college athletics: The African-American athlete's experience.* Morgantown, WV: Fitness Information Technology.

Brown, R.D., & Harrison, J.M. (1986). The effects of a strength training program on the strength and self-concept of two female age groups. *Research Quarterly for Exercise and Sport, 57,* 315–320.

Carpenter, L.J., & Acosta, R.V. (1993). Back to the future: Reform with a woman's voice. In D.S. Eitzen (Ed.), *Sport in contemporary society: An anthology* (4th ed., pp. 388–398). New York: St. Martin's Press.

Colker, R., & Widom, C.S. (1980). Correlates of female athletic participation. *Sex Roles, 6,* 47–53.

Condry, J., & Dyer, S. (1976). Fear of success: Attribution of cause to the victim. *Journal of Social Issues, 32,* 63–83.

Corbett, D., & Johnson, W. (1993). The African-American female in collegiate sport: Sexism and racism. In D. Brooks & R. Althouse (Eds.), *Racism in college athletics: The African-American athlete's experience* (pp. 179–204). Morgantown, WV: Fitness Information Technology.

Corbin, C.B. (1981). Sex of subject, sex of opponent, and opponent ability as factors affecting self-confidence in a competitive situation. *Journal of Sport Psychology, 3,* 265–270.

Corbin, C.B., Landers, D.M., Feltz, D.L., & Senior, K. (1983). Sex differences in performance estimates: Female lack of confidence vs. male boastfulness. *Research Quarterly for Exercise and Sport, 54,* 407–410.

Corbin, C.B., & Nix, C. (1979). Sex-typing of physical activities and success predictions of children before and after cross-sex competition. *Journal of Sport Psychology, 1,* 43–52.

Corbin, C.B., Stewart, M.J., & Blair, W.O. (1981). Self-confidence and motor performance of preadolescent boys and girls in different feedback situations. *Journal of Sport Psychology, 3,* 30–34.

Csizma, K.A., Wittig, A.F., & Schurr, K.T. (1988). Sport stereotypes and gender. *Journal of Sport & Exercise Psychology, 10,* 62–74.

Davis, S.N., Crawford, M., & Sebrechts, J. (Eds.) (1999). *Coming into her own: Educational success in girls and women.* San Francisco: Jossey-Bass.

Deaux, K. (1984). From individual differences to social categories: Analysis of a decade's research on gender. *American Psychologist, 39,* 105–116.

Deaux, K., & Kite, M.E. (1987). Thinking about gender. In B.B. Hess & M.M. Ferree (Eds.), *Analyzing gender* (pp. 92–117). Beverly Hills, CA: Sage.

Deaux, K., & Kite, M. (1993). Gender stereotypes. In F.L. Denmark & M.A. Paludi (Eds.), *Psychology of women: A handbook of issues and theories* (pp. 107–139). Westport, CT: Greenwood Press.

Deaux, K., & Major, B. (1987). Putting gender into context: An interactive model of gender-related behavior. *Psychological Review, 94,* 369–389.

Del Rey, P., & Sheppard, S. (1981). Relationship of psychological androgyny in female athletes to self-esteem. *International Journal of Sport Psychology, 12,* 165–175.

Delpy, L. (2001). Management. In K. Christensen, A. Guttmann, & G. Pfister (Eds.), *International encyclopedia of women and sports* (Vol. 2, pp. 690–698). New York: Macmillan.

Denmark, F.L., & Fernandez, L.C. (1993). Historical development of the psychology of women. In F.L. Denmark & M.A. Paludi (Eds.), *Psychology of women: A handbook of issues and theories* (pp. 3–22). Westport, CT: Greenwood Press.

Dewar, A. (1993). Would all the generic women in sport please stand up? Challenges facing feminist sport sociology. *Quest, 45,* 211–229.

Duda, J.L. (1986). A cross-cultural analysis of achievement motivation in sport and the classroom. In L. VanderVelden & J. Humphrey (Eds.), *Current selected research in the psychology and sociology of sport* (pp. 115–132). New York: AMS Press.

Duda, J.L., & Allison, M.T. (1990). Cross-cultural analysis in exercise and sport psychology: A void in the field. *Journal of Sport & Exercise Psychology, 12,* 114–131.

Eagley, A.H. (1987). *Sex differences in social behavior: A social-role interpretation.* Hillsdale, NJ: Erlbaum.

Eccles, J.S. (1985). Sex differences in achievement patterns. In T. Sonderegger (Ed.), *Nebraska Symposium on Motivation, 1984: Psychology and gender* (pp. 97–132). Lincoln: University of Nebraska Press.

Eccles, J.S. (1987). Gender roles and women's achievement-related decisions. *Psychology of Women Quarterly, 11,* 135–172.

Eccles, J.S., Adler, T.F., Futterman, R., Goff, S.B., Kaczala, C.M., Meece, J.L., & Midgley, C. (1983). Expectations, values and academic behaviors. In J. Spence (Ed.), *Achievement and achievement motives* (pp. 75–146). San Francisco: Freeman.

Eccles, J.S., Barber, B., Jozefowicz, D., Malenchuk, O., & Vida, M. (1999). Self-evaluation of competence, task values and self-esteem. In N.G. Johnson, M.C. Roberts, & J. Worell (Eds.), *Beyond appearance: A new look at adolescent girls* (pp. 53–84). Washington, DC: American Psychological Association.

Eccles, J.S., & Harold, R.D. (1991). Gender differences in sport involvement: Applying the Eccles expectancy-value model. *Journal of Applied Sport Psychology, 3,* 7–35.

Eitzen, D.S., & Baca Zinn, M. (1993). The de-athleticization of women: The naming and gender marking of collegiate sports teams. In D.S. Eitzen (Ed.), *Sport in contemporary society: An anthology* (4th ed., pp. 396–405). New York: St. Martin's Press.

Erkut, S., Fields, J.P., Sing, R., & Marx, F. (1996). Diversity in girls' experiences: Feeling good about who you are. In B.J. Ross Leadbeater & N. Way (Eds.), *Urban girls: Resisting stereotypes, creating identities* (pp. 53–64). New York: New York University Press.

Furumoto, L., & Scarborough, E. (1986). Placing women in the history of psychology: The first women psychologists. *American Psychologist, 41,* 35–42.

Geis, F.L. (1993). Self-fulfilling prophecies: A social psychological view of gender. In A.E. Beall & R.J. Sternberg (Eds.), *The psychology of gender* (pp. 9–54). New York: Guilford Press.

Gibson, A. (1979). I always wanted to be somebody. In S.L. Twin (Ed.), *Out of the bleachers* (pp. 130–142). Old Westbury, NY: Feminist Press.

Gill, D.L. (1988). Gender differences in competitive orientation and sport participation. *International Journal of Sport Psychology, 19,* 145–159.

Gill, D.L. (1993). Competitiveness and competitive orientation in sport. In R.N. Singer, M. Murphey, & L.K. Tennant (Eds.), *Handbook of research on sport psychology* (pp. 314–327). New York: Macmillan.

Gill, D.L. (1995). Gender issues: A social-educational perspective. In S.M. Murphy (Ed.), *Sport psychology interventions* (pp. 205–234). Champaign, IL: Human Kinetics.

Gill, D.L., & Deeter, T.E. (1988). Development of the Sport Orientation Questionnaire. *Research Quarterly for Exercise and Sport, 59,* 191–202.

Gill, D.L., & Dzewaltowski, D.A. (1988). Competitive orientations among intercollegiate athletes: Is winning the only thing? *The Sport Psychologist, 2,* 212–221.

Goldberg, P. (1968). Are women prejudiced against women? *Transaction, 5,* 28–30.

Gordon, M.T., & Riger, S. (1989). *The female fear: The social cost of rape.* New York: Free Press.

Green, T.S. (1993). The future of African-American female athletes. In D. Brooks & R. Althouse (Eds.), *Racism in college athletics: The African-American athlete's experience* (pp. 205–223). Morgantown, WV: Fitness Information Technology.

Griffin, P.S. (1987, August). *Homophobia, lesbians, and women's sports: An exploratory analysis.* Paper presented at the American Psychological Association convention, New York.

Griffin, P. (1992). Changing the game: Homophobia, sexism, and lesbians in sport. *Quest, 44,* 251–265.

Guernsey, L. (1993, February 10). More campuses offer rape-prevention programs for male athletes. *Chronicle of Higher Education,* pp. A35, A37.

Hall, M.A. (1996). *Feminism and sporting bodies.* Champaign, IL: Human Kinetics.

Hargreaves, J. (1994). *Sporting females: Critical issues in the history and sociology of women's sports.* New York: Routledge.

Harris, D.V., & Jennings, S.E. (1977). Self-perceptions of female distance runners. *Annals of the New York Academy of Sciences, 301,* 808–815.

Hart, E.A., Leary, M.R., & Rejeski, W.J. (1989). The measurement of social physique anxiety. *Journal of Sport & Exercise Psychology, 11,* 94–104.

Hausenblaus, H.A., & Mack, D.E. (1998). Social physique anxiety and eating disorder correlates among female athletic and nonathletic populations. *Journal of Sport Behavior, 22,* 502–513.

Helmreich, R.L., & Spence, J.T. (1977). Sex roles and achievement. In R.W. Christina & D.M. Landers (Eds.), *Psychology of motor behavior and sport—1976* (Vol. 2, pp. 33–46). Champaign, IL: Human Kinetics.

Holloway, J.B., Beuter, A., & Duda, J.L. (1988). Self-efficacy and training for strength in adolescent girls. *Journal of Applied Social Psychology, 18,* 699–719.

Horner, M.S. (1972). Toward an understanding of achievement-related conflicts in women. *Journal of Social Issues, 28,* 157–176.

Hyde, J.S., & Linn, M.C. (Eds.) (1986). *The psychology of gender: Advances through meta-analysis.* Baltimore, MD: Johns Hopkins University Press.

Jacklin, C.N. (1989). Female and male: Issues of gender. *American Psychologist, 44,* 127–133.

Jacobi, M. (1877). *The question of rest for women during menstruation.* New York: Putnam.

Johnson, N.G., & Worell, J. (1997). Afterword. In J. Worell & N.G. Johnson (Eds.), *Shaping the future of feminist psychology* (pp. 245–249). Washington, DC: American Psychological Association.

Kane, M.J. (1989, March). The post Title IX female athlete in the media. *Journal of Physical Education, Recreation and Dance,* pp. 58–62.

Kane, M.J., & Parks, J.B. (1992). The social construction of gender difference and hierarchy in sport journalism—Few new twists on very old themes. *Women in Sport & Physical Activity Journal, 1,* 49–83.

Kane, M.J., & Snyder, E. (1989). Sport typing: The social "containment" of women. *Arena Review, 13,* 77–96.

Kang, L., Gill, D.L., Acevedo, E.D., & Deeter, T.E. (1990). Competitive orientations among athletes and nonathletes in Taiwan. *International Journal of Sport Psychology, 21,* 146–152.

Koss, M.P. (1990). The women's mental health research agenda. *American Psychologist, 45,* 374–380.

Koss, M.P., Gidycz, C.A., & Wisniewski, N. (1987). The scope of rape: Incidence and prevalence of sexual aggression and victimization in a national sample of higher education students. *Journal of Consulting and Clinical Psychology, 55,* 162–170.

Lenney, E. (1977). Women's self-confidence in achievement settings. *Psychological Bulletin, 84,* 1–13.

Lenskyj, H. (1987). *Out of bounds: Women, sport and sexuality.* Toronto: Women's Press.

Lenskyj, H. (1991). Combating homophobia in sport and physical education. *Sociology of Sport Journal, 8,* 61–69.

Lenskyj, H. (1992). Unsafe at home base: Women's experiences of sexual harassment in university sport and physical education. *Women in Sport & Physical Activity Journal, 1,* 19–33.

Maccoby, E.E. (1990). Gender and relationships. *American Psychologist, 45,* 513–520.

Maccoby, E., & Jacklin, C. (1974). *The psychology of sex differences.* Stanford, CA: Stanford University Press.

Majors, R. (1990). Cool pose: Black masculinity and sports. In M.A. Messner & D.F. Sabo (Eds.), *Sport, men, and the gender order* (pp. 109–114). Champaign, IL: Human Kinetics.

Matlin, M.W. (1993). *The psychology of women* (2nd ed.). Fort Worth, TX: Harcourt Brace Jovanovich.

Matteo, S. (1986). The effect of sex and gender-schematic processing on sport participation. *Sex Roles, 15,* 417–432.

Matteo, S. (1988). The effect of gender-schematic processing on decisions about sex-inappropriate sport behavior. *Sex Roles, 18,* 41–58.

McClelland, D.C., Atkinson, J.W., Clark, R.A., & Lowell, E.C. (1953). *The achievement motive.* New York: Appleton-Century-Crofts.

McElroy, M.A., & Willis, J.D. (1979). Women and the achievement conflict in sport: A preliminary study. *Journal of Sport Psychology, 1,* 241–247.

McNally, J., & Orlick, T. (1975). Cooperative sport structures: A preliminary analysis. *Mouvement, 7,* 267–271.

Melpomene Institute. (1990). *The bodywise woman.* Champaign, IL: Human Kinetics.

Messner, M.A. (1992). *Power at play: Sports and the problem of masculinity.* Boston: Beacon Press.

Messner, M.A., Duncan, M.C., & Jensen, K. (1993). Separating the men from the girls: The gendered language of televised sports. In D.S. Eitzen (Ed.), *Sport in contemporary society: An anthology* (4th ed., pp. 219–233). New York: St. Martin's Press.

Messner, M.A., & Sabo, D.F. (1994). *Sex, violence and power in sports: Rethinking masculinity.* Freedom, CA: The Crossing Press.

Metheny, E. (1965). Symbolic forms of movement: The feminine image in sports. In E. Metheny (Ed.), *Connotations of movement in sport and dance* (pp. 43–56). Dubuque, IA: Brown.

Murphy, S.M., Kilpatrick, D.G., Amick-McMullen, A., Veronen, L., Best, C.L., Villeponteanx, L.A., & Saunders, B.E. (1988). Current psychological functioning of child sexual assault survivors: A community study. *Journal of Interpersonal Violence, 3,* 55–79.

Myers, A.E., & Lips, H.M. (1978). Participation in competitive amateur sports as a function of psychological androgyny. *Sex Roles, 4,* 571–578.

National Amateur Athletic Federation, Women's Division. (1930). *Women and athletics.* New York: Barnes.

Neimark, J. (1993). Out of bounds: The truth about athletes and rape. In D.S. Eitzen (Ed.), *Sport in contemporary society: An anthology* (4th ed., pp. 130–137). New York: St. Martin's Press.

Nelson, M.B. (1991). *Are we winning yet? How women are changing sports and sports are changing women.* New York: Random House.

Nyad, D. (1978). *Other shores.* New York: Random House.

Parkhouse, B.L., & Williams, J.M. (1986). Differential effects of sex and status on evaluation of coaching ability. *Research Quarterly for Exercise and Sport, 57,* 53–59.

Petrie, T.A. (1996). Differences between male and female college lean sport athletes, non-lean sport athletes, and nonathletes on behavioral and psychological indices of eating disorders. *Journal of Applied Sport Psychology, 8,* 218–230.

Pheterson, G.I., Kiesler, S.B., & Goldberg, P.A. (1971). Evaluation of the performance of women as a function of their sex, achievement, and personal history. *Journal of Personality and Social Psychology, 19,* 114–118.

Ponger, B. (1990). Gay jocks: A phenomenology of gay men in athletics. In M.A. Messner & D.F. Sabo (Eds.), *Sport, men and the gender order* (pp. 141–152). Champaign, IL: Human Kinetics.

Rodin, J., Silberstein, L., & Streigel-Moore, R. (1985). Women and weight: A normative discontent. In T. Sonderegger (Ed.), *Nebraska Symposium on Motivation, 1984: Psychology and gender* (pp. 267–307). Lincoln: University of Nebraska Press.

Russell, G.M., & Fraser, K.L. (1999). Lessons learned from self-defense training. In S.N. Davis, M. Crawford, & J. Sebrechts (Eds.), *Coming into her own: Educational success in girls and women* (pp. 260–274). San Francisco: Jossey-Bass.

Ryan, J. (1995). *Little girls in pretty boxes: The making and breaking of elite gymnasts and figure skaters.* New York: Doubleday.

Sadker, M., Sadker, D., & Klein, S. (1991). The issue of gender in elementary and secondary education. *Review of research in education* (pp. 269–334). Washington, DC: American Educational Research Association.

Sherif, C.W. (1982). Needed concepts in the study of gender identity. *Psychology of Women Quarterly, 6,* 375–398.

Sherman, J. (1971). *On the psychology of women.* Springfield, IL: Charles C Thomas.

Smith, Y.R. (1992). Women of color in society and sport. *Quest, 44,* 228–250.

Spears, B. (1978). Prologue: The myth. In C. Oglesby (Ed.), *Women in sport: From myth to reality* (pp. 3–15). Philadelphia: Lea & Febiger.

Spence, J.T., & Helmreich, R.L. (1978). *Masculinity and femininity.* Austin: University of Texas Press.

Spence, J.T., & Helmreich, R.L. (1983). Achievement-related motives and behaviors. In J.T. Spence (Ed.), *Achievement and achievement motives: Psychological and sociological approaches* (pp. 7–74). San Francisco: Freeman.

Swann, W.B., Langlois, J.H., & Gilbert, L.A. (Eds.) (1999). *Sexism and stereotypes in modern society: The gender science of Janet Taylor Spence.* Washington, DC: American Psychological Association.

Tresemer, D.W. (1977). *Fear of success.* New York: Plenum Press.

Trickett, E.J., Watts, R.J., & Birman, D. (Eds.) (1994). *Human diversity: Perspectives on people in context.* San Francisco: Jossey-Bass.

Trujillo, C. (1983). The effect of weight training and running exercise intervention on the self-esteem of college women. *International Journal of Sport Psychology, 14,* 162–173.

Turkel, A.R. (1998). All about Barbie: Distortions of a transitional object. *Journal of the American Academy of Psychoanalysis, 26*(1), 165–177.

Unger, R., & Crawford, M. (1992). *Women and gender: A feminist psychology.* New York: McGraw-Hill.

Wallston, B.S., & O'Leary, V.E. (1981). Sex and gender make a difference: The differential perceptions of women and men. *Review of Personality and Social Psychology, 2,* 9–41.

Weinberg, R.S., & Jackson, A. (1979). Competition and extrinsic rewards: Effect on intrinsic motivation. *Research Quarterly, 50,* 494–502.

Weinberg, R.S., & Ragan, J. (1979). Effects of competition, success/failure, and sex on intrinsic motivation. *Research Quarterly, 50,* 503–510.

Weinberg, R., Reveles, M., & Jackson, A. (1984). Attitudes of male and female athletes toward male and female coaches. *Journal of Sport Psychology, 6,* 448–453.

Williams, J.M., & Parkhouse, B.L. (1988). Social learning theory as a foundation for examining sex bias in evaluation of coaches. *Journal of Sport & Exercise Psychology, 10,* 322–333.

Worell, J., & Remer, P. (1992). *Feminist perspectives in therapy: An empowerment model for women.* Chichester, UK: Wiley.

CHAPTER 12

Socialization Processes and Sport Behavior

Susan L. Greendorfer

The relationship between play, games, sport, and the process of socialization has interested scholars in psychology, anthropology, and sociology for more than a century. Recognizing these activities as a primary medium for teaching children fundamental rules, concepts, and expectations of society (Clausen, 1968; Goslin, 1969; J.M. Roberts & Sutton-Smith, 1962), scholars have been fascinated by the influence that play and games have on social, cognitive, and moral development (Mead, 1934; Piaget, 1965) and the acquisition of cultural values (J.M. Roberts & Sutton-Smith, 1962; Webb, 1969). Until quite recently, however, sport psychologists gave only minimal attention to the process of socialization by simply acknowledging a connection between sport participation, psychosocial development, and the acquisition of social skills, particularly those of responsibility, autonomy, and morality (Barnett, Smoll, & Smith, 1992; Bredemeier & Shields, 1993, 1996; Gould, 1984; Horn & Hasbrook, 1986, 1987; Weiss & Bredemeier, 1990). Essentially, their research pertaining to topics such as competitive stress and teacher–coach influences (Barnett et al., 1992; Horn, 1987; Smith, Smoll, Hunt, Curtis, & Coppel, 1979; Smoll, 1986), perceived competence and achievement motivation (Feltz & Petlichkoff, 1983; G.C. Roberts, 1984, 1986), and attrition (Gould, 1987; Gould, Feltz, Horn, & Weiss, 1982) made no explicit reference to socialization. Connections were simply ignored.

Since the early 1990s, however, sport psychologists have given more serious thought to the relationship between social influence processes and cognitive aspects of sport participation. For example, some researchers have considered the motivational climate for achievement, which by definition orients individuals into achievement (Barnett et al., 1992; Brustad, 1988, 1992; Roberts, Treasure, & Kavussanu, 1997; Weiss & Chaumeton, 1992). Several other researchers have recognized sport as a context for socialization and have focused on modifying coaching behaviors or the sport environment to create a more enjoyable motivational climate (Bakker, DeKoning, Schenau, & DeGroot, 1993; Barnett et al., 1992; G.C. Roberts et al., 1997; Ryckman & Hamel, 1992, 1995; Theeboom, DeKnop, & Weiss, 1995; Weiss & Duncan, 1992; Weiss & Stevens, 1993). In addition, researchers examining the effects of sport participation, most notably psychosocial benefits of continued involvement, have attempted to integrate social with cognitive components of behavior to more completely address socialization influences (Brustad, 1988, 1992; Trew, Kremer, Gallagher, Scully, & Ogle, 1997; Vanreussel et al., 1997). Such efforts to integrate social correlates of children's cognitive processes clearly demonstrate the ways in which formative factors and socialization influences share a reciprocal relationship with youth sport participation (Barnett et al., 1992; Brustad, 1992; Evans & Roberts, 1987; Roberts et al., 1997; Theeboom et al., 1995; Vaughter, Sadh, & Vozzola, 1994).

Noting that motivational factors influencing socialization have been ignored in their research, sport psychologists have acknowledged the relationship between cognitive–developmental and socialization influences in children's acquisition of achievement behaviors, beliefs, and expectations (G.C. Roberts et al., 1997; Ruble, 1987) and in children's sport preferences (Horn & Hasbrook, 1986). Recognition of mutual interactions between socialization and cognitive processes also has influenced research on coaching effectiveness programs, which now include principles of social influence and positive feedback to attenuate athlete attrition (Bakker et al., 1993; Barnett et al., 1992). In addition, the sport environment itself has been recognized as a social as well as cognitive medium for development of peer relations, social skills training, and prosocial behavior (Brustad, 1996; Weiss & Bredemeier, 1990; Weiss & Duncan, 1992).

Although progress toward increased acceptance of socialization parameters has been evident, this process is not complete, particularly with regard to topics related to motivational and attrition research. Some empirical studies continue to limit explanations of persistence or attrition to psychological parameters alone (Weiss & Stevens, 1993), whereas other recent studies narrowly conceptualized motivational models from purely cognitive perspectives (Scanlan, Carpenter, et al., 1993; Scanlan, Simons, Carpenter, Schmidt, & Keeler, 1993). Frequently, studies such as these view research findings simply as decontextualized facts, and their contributions seem limited to very specific "packages of knowledge" about a specific research question or problem. Although such research makes occasional reference to some aspect of sport socialization or social development, these studies tend to be less integrative in nature and have not attempted to synthesize existing research into a coherent body of knowledge about the process of socialization in general or sport socialization in particular.

As previously stated, although increased awareness of the socialization process has led to broader conceptualization in some sport psychology research, progress toward such integration is far from complete. Moreover, the task is not simple. Considerable adaptation of research paradigms is necessary to fully integrate socialization components into existing research in sport psychology. To facilitate such a transition, this chapter offers a general perspective that could be used as a framework for understanding how social and cognitive processes coalesce to influence developmental processes and how such factors fall within the parameters of the process of socialization.

I begin with some basic assumptions about physical activity and cognitive and psychological processes and include social as well as cultural influences. In simple terms, physical activity involvement and performance encompass (a) various *influence* processes; (b) mechanisms and issues related to concepts of *identity;* (c) the nature, quality, and intensity of *interactions;* and (d) *ideological* belief systems—each of which represents a vital component integral to the process of socialization (Greendorfer, Lewko, & Rosengren, in press). In addition, each of these general concepts relates to specific research topics in sport psychology.

As well as reviewing traditional approaches to socialization, I also attempt to broaden possibilities for interpreting existing research from an integrated and more holistic perspective. The first section of this chapter describes socialization in general, in reference to sport and physical activity, and introduces general information about how socialization has been approached theoretically. The second section offers a general description of the nature and manner in which socialization is accomplished, along with general definitions and assumptions that researchers have made about the process. This discussion is followed by a separate look at socialization into and socialization through sport. Although some research findings are summarized in these sections, the focus of discussion is on theoretical issues and conceptual problems that have influenced our understanding of sport socialization. Of course, this chapter would not be complete without some mention of pertinent research in sport psychology that encompasses a socialization paradigm. Major issues and findings from such research are included within the respective sections. Finally, the chapter concludes with suggested paths sport psychologists might follow to pursue this topic, especially considering the separate directions taken by sport psychology and sport sociology.

WHAT IS SOCIALIZATION?

Although socialization encompasses the acquisition of social psychological skills, the process also is a means of integrating individuals into society by transmitting cultural values and traditions (Greendorfer et al., in press). Assumed to be a combination of social learning and social and cognitive development, the process consists of a complex and dynamic constellation of psychological skills, social practices, and cultural (ideological) beliefs (Aberle, 1961; Clausen, 1968; Goslin, 1969).

Historically, the broad process of socialization has been examined systematically by three disciplines: psychology, sociology, and anthropology. In psychology, primary attention has been given to the development of individual characteristics as they are related to social behavior and the basic processes through which these behavioral tendencies are learned (Goslin, 1969). Although several different psychological approaches to socialization can be found in the literature (i.e., genetic, biological), two of the more popular are (a) the psychoanalytic approach—which is interested in the importance that early life experiences have on subsequent personality structure (Freud, 1924; Miller, 1969), and (b) the cognitive approach (Kohlberg, 1966; Piaget, 1951; Zigler & Child, 1969)—which has focused on the development of children's cognitive structures. Regardless of perspective, however, it seems that psychological approaches are behavioristic in nature, focusing on cognitive processes rather than on the nature of the learning experience. Scholars have been more concerned with the fit between the individual and her or his environment (Goslin, 1969), with primary emphasis on personality and cognitive development rather than on identificatory processes and aspects of social or cultural identification. Such considerations clearly focus on the relationship between individual characteristics and attributes of the learner responding to her or his social environment in the process of acquiring behavioral, cognitive, and social skills.

Although sociologists also have been interested in social skills acquired by individuals in varying contexts (Goslin, 1969), their primary interest has concentrated on characteristics of specific groups or structures (institutions) within which the process of socialization occurs. For example, elements of social structure (Inkeles, 1968; Parsons & Bales, 1955), the acquisition of social roles and role negotiation (Biddle & Thomas, 1966; Goffman, 1959; Mead, 1934; Sarbin & Allen, 1968; Stryker, 1959), expectations and interactions that take place between institutionalized settings and individuals and groups (Brim, 1966), theories of learning and social learning (Bandura & Walters, 1963; Mowrer,

1960), and reference group theory (Kemper, 1968) have aroused considerable research attention.

More recently, some scholars have considered socialization from a cultural studies perspective—one that analyzes socialization within the broad context of political economy, history, and theories of social class (Hollands, 1984). This interdisciplinary perspective eschews behaviorism and behaviorist assumptions and attempts to bridge the traditional social sciences with traditional humanities to study cultural aspects of society by using interpretive, historical, and critical modes of inquiry (Hollands, 1984). From this perspective, sport is socially constructed within the context of history, its form and practices a product of antecedent and residual dominant cultural values. Scholars using this perspective conceptualize the process of socialization more broadly, assuming that much of its content emanates from ideological beliefs and cultural practice (Sabo, 1985; Whitson, 1990, 1994). In short, they conceptualize the socialization process as integral to the construction of dominant (hegemonic) culture (Whitson, 1984, 1990, 1994). As such, the process encompasses a broad constellation of values and practices that orient individuals to particular patterns of thinking and feeling that serve particular interests (Whitson, 1984). According to this perspective, the range of human practices and experiences becomes incorporated into a way of thinking or *hegemonic beliefs*, and a social–political system of domination infuses society's institutions and social–cultural practices (one of which is sport) with ideological beliefs that expand and preempt alternative beliefs (Whitson, 1984, 1994). This relatively new way of thinking does not include traditional concepts, assumptions, or methodologies, and instead of being incorporated into the existing socialization literature, this research more typically falls within the realm of gender studies (Greendorfer & Bruce, 1991; Messner, 1988, 1989; Sabo, 1985; Whitson, 1990, 1994). (We find similar trends in cultural studies approaches to African-American, Latino, and lesbian/gay studies, although these topical areas are not nearly as well developed as gender studies.)

The field of anthropology considers socialization from a broad cultural perspective that views the process of socialization as enculturation—the means by which beliefs, values, and customs of society are communicated to individuals so that they become culturally competent. Focus is on the transmission of culture between generations, the interaction between cultural beliefs and social experience, and the maintenance of cultural continuity (Brim, 1957; D'Andrade, 1966; Goslin, 1969).

Although each discipline has developed different concepts and emphases, as suggested by the previous descriptions, the major difference between them (as well as between perspectives within each discipline) lies in how each conceptualizes characteristics of the learner and how each views outcomes of prior experiences. Despite some differences in fundamental assumptions—each discipline views the degree of emphasis that comes from the external environment or from the learner him- or herself differently (Goslin, 1969)—a number of underlying assumptions are remarkably similar. For example, each discipline theoretically assumes that socialization would not be possible without an extraordinary degree of conformity. In this sense, conformity refers to commonly held expectations regarding what constitutes appropriate behaviors, attitudes, expectations and values in a wide range of situations (Goslin, 1969). Second, each discipline assumes that learning takes place in a social setting and takes place in (or is influenced by) the presence of others. Interestingly, although each discipline assumes that socialization is a *two-way interaction* in which both the socializing agent and the learner are influenced in the process of learning roles, the literature in each discipline fails to consider the reciprocal nature of the process. Virtually ignored in the traditional literature or research is the potential for mutual influence, interdependence of interaction, or the bidirectional nature of social learning. In addition, a majority of the socialization literature has not incorporated recent discourses that include the concepts of hegemonic ideology and dominant culture that were previously described.

Although each discipline fundamentally differs in assumptions pertaining to mechanisms or concepts, there are key theoretical points of consensus relative to consequences and global outcomes of socialization. For example, each discipline theoretically agrees that the socialization process plays a key role in social integration—the aim of which is to establish social ties and to teach individuals to behave in accordance with the expectations of others in the social order (Inkeles, 1968) or to orient them into particular patterns of thinking and feeling in accordance with ideological beliefs that permeate institutional structures (Whitson, 1984). As such, each would acknowledge that socialization is a social influence process mediated by individuals, groups, social structures, and cultural practices. Such agreement reflects recognition

that the process involves a complex dynamic between psychological, social, and cultural considerations of learning and development.

Although theoretical concepts from psychoanalytic, developmental, cognitive, genetic, maturational, and learning approaches have been applied to the process of socialization, a *social learning* perspective (Bandura, 1969; Bandura & Walters, 1963; McPherson, 1981) has offered some of the most useful contributions in terms of theoretical development and empirical findings. Based on social psychological concepts of observation, modeling, imitation, and vicarious learning—which assume the presence, as well as the influence, of others—social learning stands in stark contrast to traditional stimulus-response learning. Social learning assumes that behavior, instead of resulting from immediate practice, feedback, or direct reinforcement, is instead observed, assimilated, and exhibited in appropriate situations (McPherson, 1981). Thus, an individual is socialized through the mechanisms of modeling, imitation, and vicarious learning. Although role models represent an important concept in social learning, such models do not necessarily have to be real (e.g., Lindsey Davenport, Tiger Woods); they could be symbolic or imagined characters (e.g., Wonder Woman, Luke Skywalker, Xena). Furthermore, role models need not directly interact with the observer; more often than not, role models are unaware of their impact or influence.

Role theory is another critical component conceptually linked to social learning. This theory attempts to explain how individuals become functioning participants in society by assuming that (a) established patterns of behavior are associated with social positions and social roles, and (b) the content of learning encompasses acquisition of specific role skills that are performed in accordance with expected behaviors associated with social roles (Goslin, 1969; Sarbin & Allen, 1968). Although social learning places primary emphasis on what takes place during childhood, the paradigm assumes that the process is continuous throughout the life cycle. Thus, a social learning orientation views socialization as a continuous process that entails the learning of multiple and prioritized skills, which are to be activated during the performance of specific roles at a specific time or stage of the life cycle (Brim, 1966).

Given this brief description of the content and underlying assumptions of the general socialization process, we can now turn to the ways in which the process relates to sport and physical activity.

WHAT IS SPORT SOCIALIZATION?

Sport socialization research was linked closely with the development of sport sociology during the late 1960s and early 1970s, a period in which considerable effort was made to explain various aspects of sport involvement (Kenyon, 1969; Kenyon & McPherson, 1973). Although this research interest did not extend through the 1980s, the literature is replete with numerous attempts to describe the process by which individuals become involved in sport and physical activity. Included in this research were attempts to explain frequency, duration, and intensity of involvement as well as kind and type of involvement (active vs. passive; actual vs. vicarious; affective vs. behavioral or cognitive involvement). Although most of this research revolved around antecedents of physical activity involvement—how individuals become involved in sport and physical activity (Greendorfer, 1977; Greendorfer & Lewko, 1978a; Kenyon, 1970; Kenyon & McPherson, 1973; Lewko & Greendorfer, 1988; McPherson, 1976, 1981; Snyder & Spreitzer, 1973, 1978; Spreitzer & Snyder, 1976)—some attention was given to consequences or outcomes of physical activity involvement (Duquin, 1977; Kenyon, 1968; Lever, 1976, 1978; Loy & Ingham, 1973; Roberts & Sutton-Smith, 1962; Stevenson, 1975; Watson, 1977).

Researchers examining how individuals become involved in physical activity (i.e., socialization into sport) used a social learning framework to examine factors and influences associated with learning various sport roles. Typically, research focused on active sport participation (the dependent variable) at the elite athlete level. Within this framework, influence by significant others or reference groups (i.e., peers, teachers, family) as well as opportunity structure (i.e., availability of facilities, programs, equipment) took precedence over considerations of motivational, personality, and cognitive influences (independent variables) (Greendorfer, 1977; Greendorfer & Lewko, 1978a, 1978b; Hasbrook, 1986; Hasbrook, Greendorfer, & McMullen, 1981; Kenyon & McPherson, 1973; Lewko, & Greendorfer, 1988; Snyder & Spreitzer, 1973).

Although closely connected, outcomes or socialization effects of sport and games (i.e., socialization through sport) have been treated as if the topic were completely unrelated to the process of becoming involved in physical activity. For the most part, this literature has revolved around attributes and skills that individuals may or may not learn from their participation in play, games, or sport. More significantly, most researchers inferred cause–effect relationships from correlational studies (Dubois, 1986; Duquin, 1977; Greendorfer, 1987b; Lever, 1976, 1978; Loy & Ingham, 1973; Roberts & Sutton-Smith, 1962; Watson, 1977; Webb, 1969). Few, if any, studies were concerned with how skills, values, and outcomes are learned from play, games or sport. Instead of studying when or under what circumstances game playing may change or affect behavior, researchers were content to merely cite differences in behavior after game playing, suggesting by inference that specific types of games lead to or teach specific social behaviors. For example, researchers claimed that, according to observed sex differences in play style and organizational structure of games (e.g., role differentiation, interdependence between player tasks, size of play group, explicitness of goals and number of rules), males are better prepared for leadership and managerial roles (Lever, 1976, 1978) and for participation in the competitive world of business, economics, and politics (Webb, 1969). Despite the intuitively attractive appeal of such notions, researchers have not been concerned with the *mechanisms* by which these specific social, political, or economic skills are learned through game playing.

Some shift in focus and research approach can be observed from recent literature, however (Brandl-Bredenbeck & Brettschneider, 1997), as a few sport psychologists have begun to examine specific skills or developmental outcomes of participation. They have found that moral and cognitive development may be related to activity types (Vaughter et al., 1994) and that different types of toys provide different learning opportunities and teach different kinds of cognitive skills to girls and boys (Etaugh & Liss, 1992; Piaget, 1965; Rheingold & Cook, 1975; Vaughter et al., 1994). In addition, sport psychologists examining cognitive and affective benefits from children's sport participation have suggested that sport is a primary socializing vehicle for teaching children interpersonal skills with adults and peers (Weiss & Duncan, 1992). Moreover, they have suggested that children's peer relations (peer acceptance and social status) in sport might have an effect on perceptions of competence or enjoyment and, as a consequence, might influence decisions to continue or withdraw from sport (Coie, Dodge, & Kupersmidt, 1991; Evans & Roberts, 1987; Weiss & Duncan, 1992). Studies such as these encompass significant aspects of socialization, because they not only demonstrate the viability of sport as a medium for developing beliefs about sport skill competence but also are able to authenticate specific socialization outcomes of physical activity. Consequently, this link between competence (a cognitive skill) and social acceptance, friendship formation, and positive peer relations (social factors that affect social function) is viewed as a very important step in more completely understanding ways in which the socialization process works.

Another topic rarely considered from a perspective of sport socialization is that of *sport withdrawal*—either by attrition (dropping out) or retirement. Before the 1980s, most information on sport retirement was anecdotal and based on journalistic accounts (McPherson, 1980). Recently, however, concepts of socialization have been applied to the process of leaving sport. Disengagement, whether voluntary (i.e., dropping out or retirement) or involuntary (i.e., being cut, participation-ending injury, or retirement), has been considered an aspect of "desocialization" (Brown, 1985; Greendorfer & Blinde, 1985; Hasbrook & Mingesz, 1987). Although such a conceptualization offers promise for future research, very few studies have considered retirement or attrition within the context of socialization.

A popular topic in sport psychology, attrition research falls into two categories. Studies either have been atheoretical, detailing descriptive patterns of dropouts (Sapp & Haubenstricker, 1978) and identifying participation motives of children (Gould, 1987; Gould & Petlichkoff, 1988), or they have used motivational frameworks that focus solely on cognitive and attributional factors (Roberts, Kleiber, & Duda, 1981). Before the 1990s, dropout research ignored a socialization perspective. Some recent studies on motivation and attrition reflect a similar trend, with little inclination to shift focus or to embrace social learning components. Some studies pertaining to reasons for participation tend to highlight dispositional predictors of involvement, thus limiting focus to cognitive variables of enjoyment, interpersonal closeness, and reduction of negative affect (Bakker et al., 1993; Ryckman & Hamel, 1992) or limiting considerations to a social exchange perspective that explains psychological costs, benefits, and satisfaction levels (Weiss & Stevens, 1993). These studies, along with attempts to develop a model for understanding motivation for participation or dropping out of sport, conceptualize constructs narrowly from a social cognition framework

(Scanlan, Carpenter, et al., 1993.). Although this model claims to represent multidimensionality, constructs of enjoyment, investment, and commitment are viewed as and limited to cognitive choice, rather than social learning or cultural influences (Scanlan, Simons, et al., 1993).

Not all studies represent such limited frameworks, however. Some sport psychologists have believed that developmental processes related to specific socialization factors influence motives to continue or withdraw from sport (Barnett et al., 1992; Brustad, 1992; Roberts et al., 1997; Ryckman & Hamel, 1995; Theodorakis, 1994; Weiss & Duncan, 1992). Yet, despite their call to include socialization parameters to more fully accommodate participation motives, enjoyment as a key motivational reason for personal investment, commitment, and identity (Brustad, 1992), it is not clear how many sport psychologists will continue to integrate social correlates with cognitive components of sport participation.

Given the issues raised thus far, then, if sport socialization were viewed along a continuum, the literature could be organized into considerations of *becoming involved, maintaining involvement*, and leaving or *disengaging* from exercise, sport, or physical activity (each phase encompassing social and psychological influences, as well as learning outcomes from physical activity involvement). Moreover, it could be possible for such a perspective to incorporate cultural studies considerations if researchers also would explain how and under what historical and social conditions hegemonic ideology influences socialization practices and beliefs about physical activity. Despite proposals to integrate paradigms more broadly, however, the literature clearly demonstrates that a major portion of existing research embraces behaviorist assumptions, which limits attention to cognitive factors, social learning, and developmental processes. Consistent with this theme, the next section includes a brief outline of general research findings and a theoretical discussion of the two major categories of sport socialization research: *becoming involved* (i.e., socialization into sport) and consequences or outcomes of involvement (i.e., socialization through sport).

SOCIALIZATION INTO SPORT

Recent approaches have criticized the behaviorist or functionalist approach to the study of (sport) socialization and have advocated a paradigm that combines critical and interactionist perspectives (Coakley, 2001). Scholars using such perspectives define socialization in general "as an active process of learning and social development which occurs as we interact with one another and become acquainted with the social world in which we live" (Coakley, 2001, p. 82). Although they agree that sport socialization encompasses becoming involved and staying involved in sport, these scholars advocate qualitative rather than quantitative approaches, and their research concentrates on more full descriptions or "stories" about why people engage in sports. Their research focus is on the meanings associated with sport participation as a cultural experience (Coakley, 2001). Consequently, the most recent sport socialization research uses an interactionist or critical cultural studies approach (Coakley & White, 1992; Donnelly & Young, 1988; Stevenson, 1991, 1997).

In contrast to recent trends, however, the majority of socialization into sport studies have taken an empirical functionalist (behaviorist) perspective. Implicitly or explicitly, these studies used a general social learning paradigm that attempts to explain how individuals acquire essential skills, knowledge, values, and dispositions to become physically active or a sport participant. Theoretically, this paradigm represents three clusters of independent variables that influence the dependent variable, *involvement in a sport role:* (a) personal attributes, (b) socializing agents, and (c) socializing situations. According to the theoretical depiction in figure 12.1, these three clusters are viewed as *determinants* or *causes* of active sport participation (the construct of sport role learning). This dependent variable, which consists of the degree, intensity, and frequency of participation, is the *outcome* of these influences.

Significant Others

Of the three clusters of independent variables, primary attention has been focused on the influence of reference groups and significant others—agents of socialization who, because of their prestige, proximity, and power to distribute love, rewards, and punishment, either consciously or unconsciously influence the sport socialization process (McPherson, 1981). Most studies identify family, peer group, teachers, coaches, and role models as major agents of sport socialization (Borman & Kurdek, 1987; Dubois, 1981; Greendorfer, 1977; Greendorfer & Lewko, 1978a; Higginson, 1985; Lewko & Ewing, 1981).

Personal Attributes

The personal attributes cluster virtually has been ignored, with the exception of a few approaches discussing socialization from a macro perspective. Some studies integrated notions of reward, achievement, competence-based models, and social motivation (Watson, 1976, 1979, 1981, 1984; Watson, Blanksby, & Bloomfield, 1983), and others concentrated on aspects of personality, achievement motivation, perceptions of skill, or the sport experience itself. Regardless of approach, however, researchers made no attempt to link empirical findings to a socialization framework.

During the 1990s, however, a few sport psychologists incorporated an expectancy-value model with socialization and identified a number of socialization factors that could enhance perceived competence (Brustad, 1993b; Coakley & White, 1992; Eccles & Harold, 1991). This research, along with that focusing on motivational climate (Roberts et al., 1997; Theeboom et al., 1995), enjoyment as a key motivational factor (Bakker et al., 1993), and social influences on achievement goals and motivation (Roberts et al., 1997; Ryckman & Hamel, 1995), more fully explored personal attributes of a cognitive–developmental nature. Despite these admirable efforts, however, findings have yet to be placed or understood within a socialization paradigm.

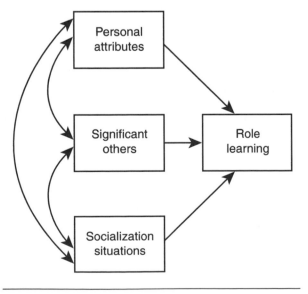

Figure 12.1 The three elements of the social learning paradigm.

Socializing Situations

Similar to personal attributes influences, the cluster represented by socializing situations also has received very little empirical attention (Yamaguchi, 1987). Despite the theoretical significance given to settings and situations, the context in which socialization takes place seems to have been ignored in most empirical studies. When examined, socializing situations seem to have been limited to availability of opportunities (Greendorfer & Lewko, 1978b; Greendorfer, Blinde, & Pellegrini, 1986) instead of conceptually expanding the notion to include access to opportunities or ideological beliefs and value structure (Greendorfer & Ewing, 1981; Greendorfer et al., in press; Yamaguchi, 1987).

As a consequence, the notion of socializing situation has been theoretically and operationally reduced to a collection of specific places, or *opportunity sets,* where participation takes place. In theory, opportunity set should encompass the social and cultural "climate" as well as physical setting and availability of programs or equipment. Unfortunately, most studies have stripped this cluster of variables of its substantive meaning by decontextualizing it and totally ignoring the notion of "lived experience" (i.e., the entire constellation of setting, circumstances, interactions, meanings, and interpretations). Also neglected in the treatment of opportunity set is what happens within a particular time frame and a particular place, with whom, under what circumstances, and with what consequences. In addition to treating opportunity set rather narrowly, both conceptually and methodologically, researchers also have failed to recognize this cluster of variables as a complex and multidimensional construct that consists of ideological values and beliefs as well as such structural influences as social class, race, or geographical location (cf. Greendorfer & Ewing, 1981; Greendorfer & Lewko, 1978b; Greendorfer et al., in press).

Although not a major shift in theoretical perspective, during the mid-1970s researchers began to consider a *social role–social systems approach,* which, similar to the social learning paradigm, also consisted of three main elements: (a) significant others or socializing agents who serve as role models, (b) social situations, and (c) role learners who are characterized by a wide variety of relevant ascribed and achieved personal attributes (e.g., personality traits, motivations, values, attitudes, motor ability, race, ethnicity, gender; McPherson, 1981). Combining psycho-logical with sociological parameters, this approach made a conceptual attempt to deal with complexities of human behavior; namely that significant others exert influence in social settings, and although individuals actively construct their own social reality, they do so within a system of expectations, values, and norms. Despite its attempt to capture the dynamic complexities of the sport socialization process, scholars continued to use an empirical functionalist approach, which created serious methodological questions about the way operational indicators were measured.

CHILDREN'S SPORT SOCIALIZATION

One fundamental assumption underlies sport socialization research: regardless of motor talent, unless individuals are exposed to *social settings* which have *positive influences* that *reward* physical activity or sport, chances are they are not likely to learn physical skills, become involved in physical activity, or adopt a physically active lifestyle (McPherson, 1976; McPherson & Brown, 1988). In general, empirical findings suggest that regardless of sex, individuals become involved during childhood; the strongest predictor of adult involvement is childhood involvement; and physical activity involvement, particularly in competitive sport, is related to sex (Antshel & Anderman, 2000; Colley, Eglinton, & Elliott, 1992; Greendorfer, 1977, 1983; Greendorfer et al., in press; Hoyle & Leff, 1997; Kenyon & McPherson, 1973, 1974; Vihjalmsson & Thorlindsson, 1998). Combining empirical findings from sport sociology with those in sport psychology, Greendorfer et al. (in press) created a heuristic profile that attempted to capture a more complete understanding of sport socialization. Although this profile takes liberties in the use and selection of specific findings, it attempts to describe a developmental progression of the sport socialization process, providing insight into influences more likely to predispose children to learn motor skills and under what circumstances:

- In the early years children spend large amounts of time with close family, including time in physical activities.
- Parents treat infant sons differently than infant daughters, and this differential treatment is reflected in parental interactions in play activities with infants.
- Activities during the early years are more gender similar than gender differentiated.

- Active parents have active children, with boys being more active than girls.
- Parents who enjoy physical activity also encourage their children's involvement in physical activities.
- By grade 1, children hold sport-based perceptions about their ability, enjoyment, and usefulness of sport that carry over time.
- By grade 1, children are monitoring their parents' behavior for cues that reveal the importance that parents attach to participating and doing well in sports.
- During middle childhood, parental participation seems to lose its impact as an influence on children's participation.
- Perceptions of competence that children have are related to perceptions of the child's competence that are held by the parents.

Children's estimations of the importance of sport participation are influenced by their parents' behavior.

© Mary E. Messenger

- Lower parental pressure and lower maternal control in parenting are related to higher enjoyment in sport.
- In middle childhood, time spent on sports is affected by one's ability, one's self-concept, and the value attached to sport competence, with girls most negatively affected (Greendorfer et al., in press).

As previously suggested, this profile offers a better understanding of how sport socialization could be integrated within the context of child development. This profile not only indicates that active participation begins at an early age and that early participation is associated with a great deal of success, but it also suggests that young participants receive positive sanctions and support from family, peers, and teachers (each of whom influences participation within a specific setting; Colley et al., 1992; McPherson, 1981). Supplementary findings in sport psychology demonstrate the following: (a) children positively evaluate coaches who give rewards, technical instruction, and mistake-contingent feedback (Barnett et al., 1992; Smith et al., 1979); (b) decisions relating to future participation and expectancies for future success often are related to the various types of rewards and reinforcements children receive (Roberts, 1984, 1986; Weiss & Stevens, 1993); and (c) continued socialization during the transition from youth to adulthood encompasses development of social identity, learning, and assimilation of skills, values, norms, and self-perceptions (Vanreusel et al., 1997; Yang, Telama, & Laakso, 1996). In short, children who receive positive reinforcement for sport participation in a variety of social and sport settings are more likely to become involved and remain in sport than those who receive neutral or negative messages (DiLorenzo, Stucky-Ropp, Vander Wal, & Gotham, 1998; Greendorfer, 1987a; Greendorfer et al., 1986; McPherson & Brown, 1988).

Sport psychology research related to peer relationships also can be interpreted within the broad context of social development. Researchers have suggested that sport skill and physical competence represent a means of gaining peer acceptance and social status (Brustad, 1996; Coie et al., 1991; Evans & Roberts, 1987). They also have found that sport is a primary socializing vehicle for teaching children interpersonal skills with adults and peers (Weiss & Duncan, 1992). Combined, these findings suggest that reinforcement, reward, feedback, development of peer relationships, acquisition of social skills, and social status are encompassed within the context of sport socialization.

Obviously, integration would require broader conceptual frameworks than have been applied to existing research. Given recent trends in sport sociology, cultural reproduction of dominant belief systems also would need to be included in such conceptualization. Thus, sport sociologists contend that any theoretical conceptualization of social or cognitive developmental aspects of the sport socialization process would be incomplete if cultural and ideological influences were ignored.

Gender Differences in Childhood Sport Socialization

Nowhere is the merging of conceptual paradigms more evident than in the literature related to gender differences in sport socialization. For a number of years, several scholars have argued that the acquisition of game and sport skills has been linked closely to gender role socialization (Greendorfer, 1983; Lever, 1976, 1978; Roberts & Sutton-Smith, 1962). They have argued that motor skill, games, and sport teach males and females how to play their appropriate gender roles. Contending that such activities consist of and convey symbolic meanings about gender in general and gender identity in particular (Dewar, 1987; Griffin, 1988; Messner, 1989; Whitson, 1990), researchers have maintained that perceptions of gender are deeply rooted in ideological beliefs that envelop physical activity participation and performance (Greendorfer et al., in press; Whitson, 1990, 1994).

At a more social–psychological level, researchers have contended that socialization into sport and gender roles can be accomplished primarily through specific social learning mechanisms—differential treatment, stereotyping, and labeling—which individually or collectively perpetuate existing ideologies and social practices. Subtly or overtly, these three mechanisms convey underlying beliefs about what is and what is not appropriate behavior in a physical activity context. Moreover, they are viewed as potent social forces that eventually contribute to the overrepresentation of males and the underrepresentation of females in physical activity. Although chapter 11 represents an in-depth consideration of gender and physical activity, some mention of gender is warranted in this consideration of socialization.

Greendorfer et al. (in press) maintained that family socialization practices in the form of child rearing influence play styles of infants, toddlers, and young children. Arguing that specific ideological beliefs that pertain to gender and have specific implications for sport socialization are embedded in child-rearing practices, the authors cite evidence suggesting that parents *continue to believe* that there are inherent differences between the sexes, and that girls are weaker, more frail, and perhaps less suited for sport and physical activity than boys (Greendorfer, Lewko, & Rosengren,1996; in press; Lewko & Greendorfer, 1980, 1988). Findings suggest that these underlying beliefs shape various practices pertaining to parental interaction and styles of play behavior with sons and daughters (Carson, Burks, & Parke, 1993). Although the link between interaction, physical contact, rough and tumble play, and the development of motor skills and performance is not clear, a number of child development studies have found sex differences (Anastasia, 1981; Schneider, 1993; Sovik, 1993). In contrast, others have suggested few differences between boys and girls before age 4 (Haywood & Getchell, 2001).

Types of toys, which are potent mechanisms of socialization, also have been found to influence childhood play styles (Etaugh & Liss, 1992; Pomerleau, Bolduc, Malcuit, & Cossette, 1990) and motor skill development (Greendorfer et al., in press; Lewko & Greendorfer, 1980). Maintaining that toys emotionally tone children, Greendorfer et al. (in press) argued that toys convey cultural meanings relative to definitions of masculinity and femininity and the appropriateness of activities. Although negligible research attention has been given to the intersection of gender meanings with motor skill development, some scholars have offered a similar argument at the broad cultural level (Dewar, 1987; Messner, 1996; Whitson, 1990). Despite the invisibility of cultural ideology in child-rearing practices, nevertheless, it is evident in socialization outcomes. Table 12.1 outlines various ways in which differential treatment, gender role stereotyping, and labeling of activities have influenced physical activity outcomes.

Close examination of the childhood sport socialization literature suggests that research sheds more light on individuals who remain in sport than on the processes influencing initial involvement. There is a virtual absence of research on younger children and the social and psychological forces that shape their orientations (Greendorfer et al., in press; Lewko & Greendorfer, 1988). Method-

Table 12.1
Toy, Play, and Motor Skill Experiences of Boys and Girls

Early infancy and toddler years:

Child-rearing: Infant girls are touched, handled, and talked to more by 13 months; girls are more dependent and have restricted exploratory range of play environment; independence and exploration are encouraged in boys (Leaper, 2000; Lewko & Greendorfer, 1988; Pomerleau et al., 1990).

Toys: Parents furnish children's rooms with gender-appropriate toys; boys have more toys in number and categories (vehicles, manipulative, instrumental, sports equipment); there is evidence of rigid gender-typing of toys for boys but not for girls (Fisher-Thompson, 1993; Pennell, 1999; Rheingold & Cook, 1975).

Play styles: Girls are less exploratory and play more quietly; boys play with toys requiring gross motor activity, are more vigorous, and are allowed to bang or break toys (Campbell & Eaton, 1999; Etaugh & Liss, 1992; Lewko & Greendorfer, 1980).

Motor skills: Mothers pick up girls for caretaking but tend to play more with boys; fathers swing and play with boys more vigorously (swing or toss overhead), bounce, and roughhouse (Haight, Parke, & Black, 1997; Power & Park, 1982).

Children during first 4 to 5 years of age:

Toys and games: Boys are given more sports equipment and instrumental toys; boys' toys are more complex, are more expensive, have more movable parts, and elicit more motor activity and wider play space; girls are given dolls, dishes, and housekeeping toys that elicit expression and quiet play and more verbal than physical activity; toys acquire more reinforcement value for both sexes; emotional toning and familiarity reinforce requests for similar gender-typed toys (Rheingold & Cook, 1975; Servin, Bohlin, & Berlin, 1999).

Motor skills: Fathers teach gross motor skills to sons, not daughters; neither parent systematically teaches motor skills to daughters; girls sometimes are punished for vigorous physical activity (Carson, Burks, & Parke, 1993; Greendorfer et al., in press; Lewko & Greendorfer, 1980).

Children during middle and late childhood (ages 6–10):

Sport and motor skills: Sport skills are associated with being male and are more highly valued for boys; sport skills are associated with achievement for boys but not for girls; family, peers, and school are important influences of sport socialization for boys; the pattern is more diffuse, less predictable for girls (Cambell & Eaton, 1999; Lewko & Greendorfer, 1988; Posner & Vandell, 1999). Expectancies, rewards, reinforcement, and role models are critical social learning mechanisms (Jambor, 1999); differential mechanisms operate for Blacks and Whites (Blacks are more influenced by values and opportunities; Whites are more influenced by significant others; Greendorfer & Ewing, 1981).

Games: Boys play more complex, active, competitive and team games; girls play less complex, solitary, turn-taking games requiring repetitive tasks (Lever, 1976, 1978; Lewko & Greendorfer, 1980).

ologically, it could be argued that if initial predisposition and entry are shaped before adolescence, much of the existing sport socialization research has been based on *recall of influences* rather than on the actual dynamics of influence processes. Thus, socialization studies tend to identify or explain those influences that *maintain* children's involvement rather than those that explain the process of becoming involved.

Another critical gap in the literature is the absence of research into the nature and extent to which the family socialization process is reciprocal and whether reciprocal interactions differ according to children's sex (Hasbrook, 1982, 1986; McPherson & Brown, 1988). Although very little is known about the way parents differently influence sport behavior of their sons and daughters, even less is known about the way girls and boys who become involved subsequently socialize their parents' sport behavior (Hasbrook, 1982, 1986; McPherson & Brown, 1988). The complex issue of reciprocity and gender influences on reciprocity may be related to degree of social support and nature of interactions with parents, peers, and coaches (Colley et al., 1992; Ryckman & Hamel, 1995; Vanreusel et al., 1997; Weiss & Duncan, 1992), the quality and content of which influence decisions to become involved, remain involved, or leave sport. Inclusion of such considerations suggests the need to shift toward more interactionist or critical perspectives to more fully capture this important dynamic (Coakley, 1998; Nixon, 1990).

A close examination of significant other influence, as related to gender, reveals additional gaps in research, particularly if ability level or skill range is considered. Whereas entry, persistence, or withdrawal could be adapted to an age continuum or temporal component, sport socialization research—especially that on children—has totally ignored the mastery or the skill continuum. Nowhere in the literature do researchers deal with the nature and type of influence from significant others with respect to gender and skill development, pursuit of excellence, development of competence, or striving for achievement. In addition, very little attention has been given to socialization influences on *degree or extent of involvement*. In one study that did take this factor into account, Lewko and Ewing (1981) found no differences in level of involvement due to chronological age. They found that boys and girls highly active in sports by age 9 remained so through age 11, whereas low-active boys and girls at age 9 were low-active at age 11.

Despite these limitations, the information in table 12.1 suggests that as a result of various social learning practices that are influenced by cultural beliefs and values, boys experience a more positively rewarding or supportive set of experiences from early infancy that predispose them toward sport and physical activity. Consequently, they learn basic motor skills, engage in gross physical activity, highly value sport skills and physical ability, and develop a large repertoire of motor skills—all of which are evident by their pervasive participation in competitive team games (Etaugh & Liss, 1992; Lewko & Greendorfer, 1988; Vaughter et al., 1994). In contrast, girls do not receive systematic or consistent encouragement or tutoring in the development of motor skills. Consequently, their engagement in physical activity is problematic. For those who do venture into physical activity, the likelihood is they will gravitate toward sex-typed activities that emphasize qualities associated with being female—rhythmic, graceful movement, emphasizing fluidity of motion (Greendorfer, 1983; Lewko & Greendorfer, 1980, 1988).

Despite the consistency of these patterns, however, recent research on the *changing structure of the family* suggests that increasing levels of maternal employment may significantly influence attitudes toward gender role expectations (Hoffman, 1989; Huston & Alvarez, 1990). Children of working mothers have less stereotyped views of female roles and more positive attitudes toward nontraditional female roles (Greendorfer et al., in press; Lamb 1997). Such shifts may indirectly influence sport socialization influences, resulting in attitudes, beliefs, and practices that ultimately challenge current gender ideology.

ADOLESCENT AND ADULT SPORT SOCIALIZATION

Although research on adolescent sport socialization has been somewhat limited, evidence suggests several things: (a) gender differences persist in activity patterns, with males continuing to be more active and involved in more outdoor activities (Rekers, Sanders, Rasbury, Strauss, & Morey, 1988); (b) low perceived parental pressure is associated with higher levels of participation and enjoyment in sports (Borman & Kurdek, 1987; Brustad, 1988); and (c) participation in sport activities is more likely if it offers opportunities to enhance perceived competence (Brustad, 1993a, 1993b; Coakley & White, 1992) or role identity (Theodorakis, 1994). Another rather interesting pattern has also been observed—the decline of sport participation with increasing age begins to show itself during adolescence (Kirshnit, Ham, & Richards, 1989; Telama & Yang, 2000; Vanreusel et al., 1997).

From a methodological perspective, most research on adolescent and adult sport socialization consists of retrospective data that revolves around significant other influence and opportunity sets. Despite this limitation, however, some clear patterns have emerged. As a child enters adolescence, the influence of the family declines and the peer group becomes more important, particularly in the case of same-sex peers who may function as role models (Brown, 1985; Higginson, 1985; McPherson & Brown, 1988; Patrikkson, 1981). Studies consistently support the emergent role of the peer group, suggesting that along with parents and teachers,

© Human Kinetics

During adolescence, an individual's peer group exerts more influence in the socialization process.

peers provide positive environments toward sport experiences (Greendorfer, 1977; Higginson, 1985; Patrikkson, 1981; Weiss & Duncan, 1992; Yamaguchi, 1984). Additional findings further suggest that siblings may not play a major role in sport socialization of males but may reinforce parental input to female sport socialization (Higginson, 1985; Patrikkson, 1981; Yamaguchi, 1984). Additional studies have indicated that the school system (i.e., teachers and coaches) may play a more important role in stimulating interest in specific sports (McPherson, 1981; McPherson & Brown, 1988; Weiss & Knoppers, 1982). In contrast, parents seem to generate interest in traditional spectator sports, whereas the peer group provides social support and serves as a source of recognition and acknowledgment (Kenyon & McPherson, 1973, 1974; McPherson, 1981). Although schools still appear to provide considerably more sport opportunities for boys (Antshel & Anderman, 2000; Greendorfer, 1983), it does appear that as sport becomes more acceptable as an activity for adolescent females, schools may provide more oppor-

tunities and encouragement for female competitive sport experiences (Curtis, McTeer, & White, 1999; Higginson, 1985; Weiss & Knoppers, 1982).

Although early research on adult sport socialization focused almost exclusively on college-age (Greendorfer, 1977, 1978, 1987a; Kenyon & McPherson, 1973, 1974; McPherson, 1981) or elite male athletes (Kenyon & Knoop, 1978), one study applied the process to older adults (Hasbrook & Mingesz, 1987). This study is an exception, however, as research on the sport socialization process among older age groups seems to have been completely ignored. Consequently, most of what is known about adult sport socialization comes from findings obtained from male and female elite (and college) athletes.

Findings on males suggest that they tend to be first born, to start young, and to experience early success, which is accompanied by recognition and status. Although first influenced by the family (as at least one parent was actively involved in sport during his childhood), from adolescence on, males tend to be influenced more by peers and coaches. There appear to be sport differences in the process, and it is clear that significant other influence differs over time (Kenyon & McPherson, 1973, 1974; McPherson, 1981; Raymore, Barber, Eccles, & Godbey, 1999).

Although there are some differences in female sport socialization, the pattern is quite similar—with two notable exceptions: (a) female athletes are *not* the first born—they tend to be middle or the youngest child; and (b) the school seems *not* to be a major influence in initiating the process but merely reinforces performance and teaches skills previously learned elsewhere. Aside from these differences for the female athlete, one or both parents are actively involved in sport, and sport or physical activity appears to be an important family activity. In addition, the female athlete perceives her skill and ability to be well above average at an early age. Although peer group influence is consistent through the life cycle, it is not clear exactly who in the family influences the female athlete—perhaps because of differences in social class background (Antshel & Anderman, 2000; Greendorfer, 1978, 1987a).

CRITICISMS OF DEFINITIONS, ASSUMPTIONS, AND APPROACHES

Despite the popularity of sport socialization research during the 1970s and early 1980s, interest in the topic began to wane in the mid-1980s. Although specific factors contributing to this malaise are subject to debate, most scholars agree that a growing dissatisfaction with the relatively simple social learning approach (Theberge, 1984), conceptual disenchantment with the theoretical assumptions (Fishwick & Greendorfer, 1987; McPherson, 1986; Nixon, 1990; Theberge, 1984), and failure to develop a coherent body of knowledge (McPherson, 1986) played a significant role in the demise of this research. Although general profiles and patterns provided useful information to some, few researchers used these findings to expand theoretical perspectives. This neglect led some critics to condemn both the social learning and social role–social systems approach because of their technocratic and empiricist roots. As a result of these criticisms, socialization research has become considerably less popular in recent years.

This malaise may be due, *in part,* to criticisms of the theoretical assumptions of socialization theory in general and sport socialization research in particular (Fishwick & Greendorfer, 1987; Greendorfer, 1987a; McPherson, 1986; Theberge, 1984). Essentially, two different types of critiques have appeared in the literature. One asserts that assumptions of structural functionalism are narrow, normatively biased, deterministic, nonreflexive, and overly behavioristic (Coakley, 1998; Giddens, 1979; Theberge, 1984; Wentworth, 1980), whereas the second criticizes theoretical as well as methodological deficiencies specific to sport socialization (Fishwick & Greendorfer, 1987; Greendorfer, 1987a; McPherson, 1986).

As an advocate of the first position, Theberge (1984) challenged the theoretical assumption of social determinism that underlies most behaviorist approaches to socialization. According to this critique, the underlying premise as well as fundamental definition of socialization assumes what the final product of the process ought to be. Such a conceptualization suggests that the individual is a willing recipient of society's prescriptions and norms and is molded into roles. The conceptualization of roles is viewed as deterministic, and it is argued that such a view of social learning fails to deal with notions of reciprocal influence and social agency (i.e., self-determination of individuals who actively make choices during their development and socialization; Coakley, 2001; Giddens, 1979; Hasbrook, 1989; Theberge, 1984; Wentworth, 1980). Proponents of this critique maintain that the focus of existing research is

overly behavioristic, that there has been an overemphasis on micro perspectives (i.e., social psychological variables), and that empiricist assumptions have led to the collection of descriptive social facts without theoretical understanding (Coakley, 2001; McPherson, 1986; Theberge, 1984). They argue that more consideration should be given to such concerns as power, past and present social conditions, residual and prevailing ideological beliefs, social structure, and cultural practices (Coakley, 2001; Greendorfer & Bruce, 1991; Theberge, 1984).

The second criticism is more concerned with methodological issues and research design. This critique argues that (a) the absence of control groups (of nonparticipants), (b) the introduction of gender bias in operational constructs, and (c) the failure to theoretically or methodologically examine normative behavior are more reflective of investigator narrowness than of inherent weaknesses in theoretical structures (Fishwick & Greendorfer, 1987; Greendorfer, 1983; Greendorfer, 1987a; Greendorfer & Bruce, 1991; McPherson, 1986; Nixon, 1990). Proponents of this critique argue that most studies purporting to use the social role–social systems approach failed to create adequate operational indicators of theoretical components. They argue that this failure produced *overly descriptive concrete facts* and stripped social psychological constructs of context and substantive meaning. They further maintain that the research itself failed to capture the complexity and dynamic nature of the sport socialization process (Greendorfer, 1983, 1987a). In short, this criticism is less of underlying theoretical assumptions than it is of depicting the process as overly simplistic and nonanalytical. This criticism claims that too much attention was paid to who or what initiated the process rather than how and under what circumstances, conditions, or cultural (ideological) constraints the process occurs (Greendorfer et al., in press; Lewko & Greendorfer, 1988). From this perspective, critics could argue that *the nature of sport socialization influences* is still not understood and that the lived experiences of socializees as well as socializing agents have not been adequately captured.

Apparently motivated by both the malaise and the existing critiques, recent attempts to rejuvenate sport socialization research have suggested alternative theoretical conceptualizations. Rather than advocating traditional functionalist approaches (e.g., behavioral), researchers have suggested more integrated and holistic (e.g., macro) perspectives. They have turned away from social learning or psychologistic approaches and endorsed one or more of the following approaches:

- Symbolic and other interactionist approaches that recognize personality and individual behavior, social situations, reactions, and reciprocal adjustments that occur within the broader sociocultural context of society (Nixon, 1990)
- More interactive approaches that avoid the dualism between subject and object—focusing more on how personal characteristics (i.e., psychological and physiological) may shape and interact with social–historical factors (Coakley, 2001; Hasbrook, 1989)
- Critical and cultural studies approaches that attempt to capture social totality by examining how science, history, ideology, and expressions of culture influence the process of becoming involved in sport and physical activity (Greendorfer & Bruce, 1991; Whitson, 1984, 1990)

Although each alternative is substantively different, they all share some common features:

- Each places less emphasis on empirical behavior or deterministic causes and effects.
- Each attempts to accommodate macro (social) as well as micro (individual) concepts.
- Each advocates a more integrated or holistic approach.
- Each supports interpretive methodologies.

Although each has its own inherent conceptual difficulties, and only time will tell if one or some combination of all will increase our understanding, these alternatives show great potential for achieving a new level of theoretical, conceptual, and empirical understanding.

SOCIALIZATION THROUGH SPORT

From a broad perspective, this topic focuses on outcomes or consequences of play, games, and sport participation. The assumption that outcomes can be realized depends on whether the individual is socialized into games or sport activities in the first place, and second, whether social learning outcomes are possible from such play activities. Researchers have generated an extensive literature that suggests possible connections between games or sport and social developmen-

tal consequences, implying that such cognitive and affective outcomes as prosocial behavior, cognitive–social–personal growth, cooperation and positive interpersonal relations, moral development, and good citizenship are possible (Brandl-Bredenbeck & Brettschneider, 1997; Bredemeier & Shields, 1993; Coakley, 1993; McPherson & Brown, 1988; Vanreusel et al., 1997; Weiss & Bredemeier, 1990; Weiss & Duncan, 1992).

Despite these assumed connections, however, socialization through sport has been consistently treated as a topic completely unrelated to socialization into sport. A more important consideration is the fact that research on outcomes of sport involvement has not examined the extent to which such outcomes (if they actually occur) may be related to the manner, nature, and type of influences that explain what happens *during* socialization into physical activity. This neglect may have seriously retarded our understanding of *what* as well as *how* individuals learn from physical activity participation.

Underlying the entire topic of socialization through sport is the belief that play and games are an essential component of the overall socialization process and that they are an essential aspect of early-life social experiences. Despite such strong assumptions, however, two important presumptions have never been empirically validated: (a) that sport is a more likely medium than other activities for social learning outcomes, and (b) that learning will be transferred from childhood game experiences or specific sport settings to adult life experiences. Despite these difficulties, however, the majority of research on socialization through sport implicitly, if not explicitly, assumes that participation in physical activity teaches children a variety of skills needed to effectively participate in adult social, political, or economic life.

Although early research focused on the acquisition of *global behavioral patterns* (leadership, character, cooperation), general societal values (achievement, competition, cooperation), or diffuse social roles (good citizen) and skills (Kenyon, 1968), recent studies have focused more on an extensive list of specific behavioral outcomes of participation (i.e., achievement values, personality development, moral behavior, social mobility, and academic achievement; Bredemeier & Shields, 1993, 1996; Gould, 1984; Greendorfer, 1987b). Because the literature on socialization outcomes is extensive, discussion in this section is limited to only three issues, which hardly exhaust the literature on this topic: (a) global values and behavioral outcomes; (b) organizational structure and philosophy of sport programs, and (c) leaving physical activity and sport.

Global Values and General Behavior Outcomes

Three early studies epitomize the way researchers have argued that games and play serve as potent vehicles for the transmission of values, behaviors, or general socialization. In their cross-cultural study of games, J.M. Roberts and Sutton-Smith (1962) suggested that games provide buffered learning experiences that teach societal values. They found that specific values emphasized during child-rearing were linked to specific types of games (i.e., achievement training and games of physical skill, obedience training and games of strategy, and responsibility training and games of chance). These correlational findings were used to propose a conflict-enculturation hypothesis. Conflict-enculturation was based on four premises: (a) games were expressive models of culture and therefore transferred cultural values, (b) game types and cultural complexity were linked, (c) dominant game types were associated with specific child-rearing practices, and (d) sex differences in child-rearing practices were an aspect of sex differences in game playing (Roberts & Sutton-Smith, 1962).

A second study also assumed an association between effective socialization and game playing. Webb (1969) argued that the way games are played in a society reflect the values emphasized and the dominant ideology. Suggesting that sport was a training ground for occupational, social, and political roles of adult life, Webb found that as children grew older they emphasized winning more than fairness. Webb found significant differences in orientations according to age, sex, and religion and concluded that games were vehicles for learning societal values. He argued that this *professionalization of attitudes* was evidence of how effective the socialization process was (i.e., children were adopting appropriate orientations for success in a competitive, achievement-oriented society).

In a slightly different type of study, Lever (1976, 1978) suggested that organizational structure of children's games influenced socialization outcomes. Lever discovered that boys' and girls' games differed in four ways:

- Size and group composition (i.e., boys play in larger, age-heterogeneous groups)

- Types of roles played (i.e., boys' games require more interdependent role skills)
- Goals of games (i.e., boys have a set limit or specific goal)
- Rules (i.e., boys' games have more flexible rules that allow for negotiation)

She maintained that different game types promoted development of very different skills, and because different games produced very different outcomes, Lever concluded that girls learned values which did not prepare them for adult participation in occupational, political, and social life.

Despite the intuitive appeal of this research and the clear parallels drawn between game playing and situations in everyday life, in recent years some harsh criticism has been lodged against this line of research. Three prominent methodological criticisms have challenged the validity of the notion of socialization through sport: (a) that correlational findings have been interpreted as causal relationships, (b) that studies comparing athletes and nonathletes have not controlled for initial differences or selection factors, and (c) that studies fail to explain how transfer occurs (Greendorfer, 1987b; Stevenson 1975). More recently, researchers have claimed that outcomes related to global behaviors such as leadership, character, and moral development, as well as those relating to diffuse roles such a good citizenship and sportspersonship, are not automatic and do not always occur in a positive direction (Bredemeier & Shields, 1993, 1996; Gould, 1984; Greendorfer, 1987b; Hodge, 1988). Consequently, although sport psychologists and sport sociologists have narrowed research focus to specific behaviors by changing their research design, they remain unable to explain why or how social learning occurs with some athletes or participants and not with others (Gould, 1984; Stevenson, 1975).

Organizational Structure and Philosophy of Sport Progress

In recent years, sport psychologists and sport sociologists have expanded socialization through sport research by considering significant others as well as organizational structure as important elements shaping outcomes of the sport experience (Brustad, 1992; Lever, 1978). As a result, more attention has been given to the social environment in which competitive processes occur (Gould, 1984), and socialization through sport considerations have been extended to include coaching behaviors and underlying program philosophy.

Various studies on children and adults have pursued the issue of professionalized orientations, linking such values with sport involvement. In sum, studies have revealed that children, preadolescents, and college students who were involved in sport had more professionalized orientations than those who were not involved in sport (Mantel & VanderVelden, 1974; Nixon, 1980). Such findings suggest that *sport involvement and degree of competition* are related to greater emphasis on success, winning, and individual performance. Results from such studies not only cast serious doubts on notions of building character and encouraging good sportspersonship, but actually contradict the underlying assumption of positive outcomes of physical activity involvement (Bredemeier & Shields, 1993; Gould, 1984; Hodge, 1988).

Additional studies on program philosophy, organizational structure of programs or athletic leagues, and attitudes of coaches have further challenged existing beliefs (cf. Barnett et al., 1992; Theodorakis, 1994). More specifically, Dubois (1986) found that children in educational leagues emphasized participation and sportspersonship over winning, whereas those in competitive leagues valued competition, winning, and improving social status over playing. Harris (1983, 1984) found that relative to behaviors and orientations of coaches, children's conceptualization of their baseball experience was closely related to that of their coaches. What is striking about this finding is that the socialization effect was so powerful that orientations of coaches overrode the children's cultural and ethnic value orientations. Finally, studies on female college athletes suggest that program structure and philosophy, as well as coaches' orientations, may also affect the quality of the sport experience and the value orientations of the participants (Blinde & Greendorfer, 1987; Greendorfer & Blinde, 1990).

Although implications of these research findings still fall within the purview of socialization through sport, it seems that a totally different interpretation or conceptualization of this topic is in order. Sport psychologists would do well to no longer assume that outcomes of participation are automatic or are positive. Also, they would do well to incorporate research findings into more accurate realizations pertaining to cognitive–psychosocial outcomes, such as the following:

- Because competition is a learned social behavior, *any* outcomes from competitive experiences are learned.
- What will be learned most likely will be influenced by the type of experiences an individual has with parents, peers, and coaches.
- Sport experiences are influenced by structural and cultural factors (e.g., program philosophy, organizational structure, program emphasis, and tolerance of external attitudes, pressures, and behaviors of parents, coaches, and fans).

LEAVING SPORT: DROPPING OUT AND RETIREMENT

At some stage after becoming involved, individuals are confronted with the opposite end of the sport socialization continuum—leaving sport or physical activity. *Disengagement* may take several forms. It could be a slow or gradual process of desocialization reflective of declining participation with increasing age (Vanreusel et al., 1997), or it could be an outcome of burnout (Smith, 1986). More than likely, however, leaving sport will involve either a *voluntary choice* (of dropping out or retiring) or an *involuntary choice* that brings about an abrupt and unanticipated termination, such as that caused by injury, being cut from a team, or forced retirement.

Although withdrawal can occur at any age and for a variety of reasons, for most individuals it occurs during adolescence or early adulthood and is the result of *attrition,* a choice made to discontinue involvement (Gould, 1987; McPherson & Brown, 1988). Considering attrition to be the consequence of undesirable psychological experiences for young athletes, until recently sport psychologists have limited their perspective to motivational frameworks that focus on (a) specific reasons for entering and consequently for leaving sport programs (participation motives; Ewing & Seefeldt, 1996; Gould, 1987; Gould et al., 1982; Sapp & Haubenstricker, 1978); (b) task-involved and ego-involved achievement orientations (Nicholls, 1989; G.C. Roberts, 1984); and (c) competence motivation theory (Brustad, 1993a; Feltz & Petlichkoff, 1983; Klint & Weiss, 1986; Roberts et al., 1981).

These and other studies have identified important cognitive and developmental components that may affect the dropout phenomenon. Additional studies have demonstrated that emphasis on competition, lack of fun, not enough playing time, and coaching behavior also contribute to sport attrition. Thus, the decisions to continue or discontinue could be related to interactions and influences from either significant others or the social milieu in which the sport experience takes place (Dubois, 1986, 1990; Gould, 1987). More than a little evidence suggests that negative aspects of the sport environment often are introduced by adults who structure the sport setting in accordance with adult value systems and objectives (Dubois, 1986, 1990; Harris, 1983, 1984). In turn, these values influence program philosophy, suggesting that the organizational structure of youth sport programs often influences the nature and quality of sport experiences (Dubois, 1986, 1990; McPherson & Brown 1988). The recognition that social influences may interact with cognitive–developmental and affective processes may be the reason that sport psychologists have called for a socialization paradigm to enhance understanding of sport attrition (Brustad, 1992; Roberts et al., 1997). Incorporating a broader framework that accommodates antecedent influences—which may socialize children into achievement orientations, affect children's ability to appraise competence, or influence their interpretations and perceptions—represents an important step to more completely understanding this dynamic and complex phenomenon (cf. Brustad, 1992, 1993a, 1993b).

As a consequence, we might expect more theoretically comprehensive explanations for dropping out of sport and more studies similar to that of Brown (1985). In her study of withdrawal from age-group swimming, Brown considered general socialization influences, such as the normative value structure, consideration of personal experience, reinforcement contingencies, and significant other influence. She found that withdrawal occurred over a period during which *individuals gradually divested themselves of commitment, identification, and involvement with their sport role.* Critical in this process was the degree of social support the swimmers received for their participation. These findings demonstrate that attrition can be conceptualized from a socialization perspective and that such a perspective allows for consideration of multiple factors. Ultimately, such paradigms offer a more complex interpretation of empirical findings and a much better cross-disciplinary understanding than currently exists.

Another aspect of leaving sport, *retirement*, also could be better understood if cast within a socialization framework. Unfortunately, interest in sport retirement during the past several decades has been sporadic. Before the 1980s, studies focused on former male athletes in professional spectator sports such as baseball, football, and boxing (Haerle, 1975; Lerch, 1981; Reynolds, 1981; Weinberg & Arond, 1952). These studies viewed retirement as a clinical or psychological event that automatically resulted in adjustment difficulties and life disruption (Ball, 1976; Rosenberg, 1981). Toward the mid-1980s, however, sport sociologists shifted perspectives from adjustment (Lerch, 1981; Reynolds, 1981) and social gerontology (Rosenberg, 1981) to more developmental frameworks (Blinde & Greendorfer, 1985; Coakley, 1983; Greendorfer & Blinde, 1985). In contrast to previous interest in male professional athletes, this shift focused on sport retirement of adolescent and college athletes. Viewing retirement as a process that could be conceptualized as continuity and transition, shifting and reprioritizing interests, mild rather than severe adjustment, and continuing participation rather than termination (Blinde & Greendorfer, 1985; Greendorfer & Blinde, 1985), researchers cast sport retirement as a "rebirth" rather than an ending (Coakley, 1983). Such theoretical perspectives lean more heavily on socialization concepts and have contributed to richer theoretical conceptualizations of sport retirement (Asselin, 1994). Despite such promising inroads, however, sport retirement remains an under-researched topic.

FUTURE RESEARCH DIRECTIONS

Having reviewed issues and underlying assumptions of traditional research approaches to sport socialization, we should ask what the future holds for this topic. Most notably, sport psychology and sport sociology seem to be moving in two distinctly different directions. Those sport sociologists who have not abandoned the topic completely have clearly shifted research paradigms and have moved away from empirical social learning approaches (functionalism; Coakley, 1993, 2001; Donnelly & Young, 1988; Greendorfer & Bruce, 1991; Nixon, 1990). This shift represents a stark contrast in conceptual emphasis as well as methodological approach. One theoretical perspective seems to be toward a socialization-as-interactionist approach (Coakley, 1998; Coakley & White, 1992; Stevenson, 1991) in which *more attention is paid to how people define themselves and their bodies in connection with sport and physical activities, how they make decisions about participation, how their identities related to sport and physical activities are grounded in social relations and social groups, and how the overall process of involvement in these activities is related to control and power relations and characterized by shifting commitments and opportunities. (Coakley, 1993, p. 582)*

Another sociological shift, a critical cultural studies perspective, considers socialization within a broad cultural context of political economy, history, and theories of social class. This perspective focuses more on constellations of values and cultural practices that orient individuals to particular patterns of thinking and feeling about sport, leisure, gender, and the body (Whitson, 1984, 1994). Both perspectives are concerned with concepts of power and ideological belief systems and are specifically interested in how cultural practices and values reproduce dominant orientations, thoughts, and beliefs. These approaches tend to be cross-disciplinary and more macroscopic, and methodological approaches seem to be more qualitative and interpretive in nature (Coakley, 1993; Greendorfer & Bruce, 1991; Nixon, 1990).

Although sport psychology also appears to be shifting in perspective, the proposal to integrate socialization theories with cognitive, developmental, and psychological aspects of sport (Brustad, 1992) does not really represent a paradigmatic shift, nor does it represent an alternative to current methodology. Rather, a topical approach to cognitive and affective processes has simply been broadened in scope to accommodate additional variables that may relate to sport socialization. Research methodologies continue to be empirical behaviorist approaches focusing on variable knowledge. Although including situation with psychological and cognitive constructs might provide some contextual background for understanding, this approach still does not provide the more full contextual information offered by analyses of social, historical, economic, and political contexts.

The direction in sport psychology seems to be similar to that taken by sport sociologists in the 1970s and 1980s—a socialization-as-internalization approach (Coakley, 1993). Although this perspective could capture content and dynamics of interactions between individuals while incorporating such processes with cognitive developmental transitions, it still ignores major components and influences from culture and the social world at large. Although an integration of perspectives that assimilates social influences with psychological and cognitive processes certainly represents a solid foundation on which to build an identifiable knowledge base, it is difficult to see how research findings from different theoretical and methodological approaches could be synthesized coherently into a meaningful body of knowledge without considerable cross-disciplinary enlightenment.

For example, although findings demonstrate that parents are an important "source" of children's perceived competence and a predictor of initial involvement and persistence in achievement-oriented activities such as sport (Brustad, 1996; Horn & Hasbrook, 1986, 1987), current directions suggest that sport psychologists would focus on interactions between parents and children (perhaps examining how parents influence the development of perceived competence and how such influences socialize individuals into or away from physical activity). In contrast, sport sociologists would be more concerned with changing orientations, ideological beliefs, decision-making, commitment and identities, and the meaning of relationships within sport over time (Coakley, 2001).

Despite proposed integration of perspectives in sport psychology, the shift might be only to *how and why significant others are important,* or *how significant others influence and are influenced by the socializee.* Research asking how children are socialized into motivational goal orientations and how such orientations influence participation or withdrawal from physical activity, or how personal characteristics may shape and interact with the social environment and with expectations of significant others (Hasbrook, 1989), still represents decontextualized variable research. In contrast, rather than assessing the nature of normative behavior and expectations or the organizational structure and philosophy of sport programs, sport sociologists will be more interested in perceived meanings or interpretations of the sport experience within the individual's social world. Or, they might focus on sport as a site for ideological formation or resistance to hegemonic practice (Coakley, 2001; Messner, 1988). In short, although sport psychologists are considering the expansion of perspectives within one specific paradigm, sport sociologists are rethinking the entire paradigm of socialization issues and questions.

Thus, sport socialization research seems to be moving in distinctly different directions. A better understanding of this complex process that encompasses cultural, psychological, affective, and developmental processes depends on two critical factors. Scholars interested in this topic must have more than a general familiarity with the existing literature. They need a conceptual working knowledge of theoretical and empirical issues raised over several decades. More importantly, scholars will need to understand the sophisticated distinctions between conceptual issues raised in the various disciplines. They will need to rethink and reinterpret the socialization process from multiple perspectives and as a more *holistic process*. This task will not be easy, because holistic approaches encompass more than an "add and mix" of cognitive, psychological, and developmental processes; the term encompasses more than inclusion of social influences, organizational structure, and behavioral factors within institutional contexts. Moreover, it includes consideration of cultural practices over periods of time in light of dominant ideological belief systems and within a global dynamic that includes power, tension, interactional influences, and interpretation of meaning. To date, neither psychologists nor sociologists of sport have come close to conceptualizing sport socialization within such nested and multiple frameworks.

REFERENCES

Aberle, D.F. (1961). Culture and socialization. In F.L.K. Hsu (Ed.). *Psychological anthropology: Approaches to culture and personality* (pp 381–397). Homewood, IL: The Dorsey Press.

Anastasia, A. (1981). Sex differences: Historical perspectives and methodological implications. *Developmental Review, 1*, 186–206.

Antshel, K., & Anderman, E. (2000). Social influences on sports participation during adolescence. *Journal of Research & Development in Education, 33*, 85–94.

Asselin, M.C. (1994, November). *Transition out of sport: Exploring new theoretical perspectives*. Paper presented at the Annual Conference of the North American Society for the Sociology of Sport, Savannah, GA.

Bakker, F.C., DeKoning, J.J., Schenau, G.J., & De Groot, G. (1993). Motivation of young elite speed skaters. *International Journal of Sport Psychology, 24*, 432–442.

Ball, D. (1976). Failure in sport. *American Sociological Review, 41*, 726–739.

Bandura, A. (1969). A social learning theory of identificatory process. In D.A. Goslin (Ed.), *Handbook of socialization theory and research* (pp. 213–262). Chicago: Rand McNally.

Bandura, A., & Walters, R. (1963). *Social learning and personality development*. New York: Holt, Rinehart & Winston.

Barnett, N.P., Smoll, F.L., & Smith, R.E. (1992). Effects of enhancing coach-athlete relationships on youth sport attrition. *The Sport Psychologist, 6*, 111–127.

Biddle, B.J., & Thomas, E.J. (Eds.) (1966). *Role theory: Concepts and research*. New York: Wiley.

Blinde, E., & Greendorfer, S.L. (1985). A reconceptualization of the process of leaving the role of competitive athlete. *International Review for Sociology of Sport, 20*(1–2), 87–94.

Blinde, E.M., & Greendorfer, S.L. (1987). Structural and philosophical differences in women's intercollegiate sport programs and the sport experience of athletes. *Journal of Sport Behavior, 10*, 59–72.

Borman, K.M., & Kurdek, L.A. (1987). Gender differences associated with playing high school varsity soccer. *Journal of Youth and Adolescence, 16*, 379–399.

Brandl-Bredenbeck, H.P., & Brettschneider, W.D. (1997). Sport involvement and self-concept in German and American adolescents. *International Review for the Sociology of Sport, 32*, 357–371.

Bredemeier, B., & Shields, D. (1993). Moral psychology in the context of sport. In R.N. Singer, M. Murphey, & L.K. Tennant (Eds.), *Handbook of research on sport psychology* (pp. 587–599). New York: Macmillan.

Bredemeier, B., & Shields, D. (1996). Moral development and children's sport. In F.L. Smoll & R.E. Smith (Eds.), *Children and youth in sport: A biopsychosocial perspective* (pp. 381–401). Madison, WI: Brown & Benchmark.

Brim, O.G. (1957). The parent-child relation as a social system: I. Parent and child roles. *Child Development, 28*, 344–364.

Brim, O.G. (1966). Socialization through the life cycle. In O.G. Brim & S. Wheeler (Eds.), *Socialization after childhood: Two essays* (pp. 1–52). New York: Wiley.

Brown, B.A. (1985). Factors influencing the process of withdrawal by female adolescents from the role of competitive age group swimmer. *Sociology of Sport Journal, 2*, 111–129.

Brustad, R.J. (1988). Affective outcomes in competitive youth sport: The influence of intrapersonal and socialization factors. *Journal of Sport & Exercise Psychology, 10*, 307–321.

Brustad, R.J. (1992). Integrating socialization influences into the study of children's motivation in sport. *Journal of Sport & Exercise Psychology, 14*, 59–77.

Brustad, R.J. (1993a). Youth in sport: Psychological considerations. In R.N. Singer, M. Murphey, & L.K. Tennant (Eds.), *Handbook of research on sport psychology* (pp. 695–717). New York: Macmillan.

Brustad, R.J. (1993b). Who will go out and play? Parental and psychological influences on children's attraction to physical activity. *Pediatric Exercise Science, 5*, 210–223.

Brustad, R. (1996). Parental and peer influence on children's psychological development through sport. In F. Smoll & R. Smith (Eds.), *Children and youth in sport* (pp. 112–124). Dubuque, IA: Brown & Benchmark.

Campbell, D., & Eaton, W. (1999). Sex differences in the activity level of infants. *Infant & Child Development, 8*, 1–17.

Carson, J., Burks, V., & Parke, R. (1993). Parent-child physical play: Determinants and consequences. In K.B. MacDonald (Ed.), *Parent-child play* (pp. 197–220). Albany, NY: SUNY Press.

Clausen, J.A. (Ed.). 1968. *Socialization and society*. Boston: Little, Brown & Co.

Coakley, J.J. (1983). Leaving competitive sport: Retirement or rebirth? *Quest, 35,* 1–11.

Coakley, J.J. (1993). Socialization and sport. In R.N. Singer, M. Murphey, & L.K. Tennant (Eds.), *Handbook of research on sport psychology* (pp. 571–586). New York: Macmillan.

Coakley, J.J. (1998). *Sport in society: Issues and controversies* (6th ed.). Boston: McGraw-Hill.

Coakley, J.J. (2001). *Sport in society: Issues and controversies* (7th ed.). Boston: McGraw-Hill.

Coakley, J.J., & White, A. (1992). Making decisions: Gender and sport participation among British adolescents. *Sociology of Sport Journal, 9,* 20–35.

Coie, J.D., Dodge, K.A., & Kupersmidt, J. (1991). Peer group behavior and social status. In S.R. Asher & J.D. Coie (Eds.), *Peer rejection in childhood* (pp. 17–59). New York: Cambridge University Press.

Colley, A., Eglinton, E., & Elliott, E. (1992). Sport participation in middle childhood: Association with styles of play and parental participation. *International Journal of Sport Psychology, 23,* 193–206.

Curtis, J., McTeer, W., & White, P. (1999). Exploring effects of school sport experiences on sport participation in later life. *Sociology of Sport Journal, 16,* 348–365.

D'Andrade, R. (1966). Sex differences and cultural institutions. In E.E. Maccoby (Ed.), *The development of sex differences* (pp. 174–203). Stanford, CA: Stanford University Press.

Dewar, A. (1987). The social construction of gender in physical education. *Women's Studies International Forum, 10,* 453–465.

DiLorenzo, T., Stucky-Ropp, R., Vander Wal, J., & Gotham, H. (1998). Determinants of exercise among children: II. A longitudinal analysis. *Preventive Medicine, 27,* 470–477.

Donnelly, P., & Young, K. (1988). The construction and confirmation of identity in sport subcultures. *Sociology of Sport Journal, 5,* 223–240.

Dubois, P. (1981). The youth sport coach as an agent of socialization: An exploratory study. *Journal of Sport Behavior, 4,* 95–107.

Dubois, P. (1986). The effect of participation in sport on the value orientations of young athletes. *Sociology of Sport Journal, 3,* 29–42.

Dubois, P. (1990). Gender differences in value orientations toward sports: A longitudinal analysis. *Journal of Sport Behavior, 13,* 3–14.

Duquin, M. (1977). Differential sex role socialization toward amplitude appropriation. *Research Quarterly, 48,* 288–292.

Eccles, J.S., & Harold, R.D. (1991). Gender differences in sport involvement: Applying the Eccles expectancy-value model. *Journal of Applied Sport Psychology, 3,* 7–35.

Etaugh, C., & Liss, M.B. (1992). Home, school, and playroom: Training grounds for adult gender roles. *Sex Roles, 26,* 129–147.

Evans, J., & Roberts, G.C. (1987). Physical competence and the development of peer relations. *Quest, 39,* 23–35.

Ewing, M.E., & Seefeldt, V. (1996). Patterns of participation and attrition in American agency-sponsored youth sports. In F.L. Smoll & R.E. Smith (Eds.), *Children and youth in sport: A biopsychosocial perspective* (pp. 31–45). Madison, WI: Brown & Benchmark.

Feltz, D.L., & Petlichkoff, L. (1983). Perceived competence among interscholastic sport participants and dropouts. *Canadian Journal of Applied Sport Sciences, 8,* 231–235.

Fisher-Thompson, D. (1993). Adult toy purchases for children: Factors affecting sex-typed toy selection. *Journal of Applied Developmental Psychology, 14,* 385–406.

Fishwick, L., & Greendorfer, S.L. (1987). Socialization revisited: A critique of the sport related research. *Quest, 39,* 1–8.

Freud, S. (1924). *Character and anal eroticism*. London: Hogarth Press.

Giddens, A. (1979). *Central problems in social theory*. Berkeley: University of California Press.

Goffman, E. (1959). *The presentation of self in everyday life*. New York: Doubleday.

Goslin, D.A. (Ed.) (1969). *Handbook of socialization theory and research*. Chicago: Rand McNally.

Gould, D. (1984). Psychosocial development and children's sport. In J.R. Thomas (Ed.), *Motor development during childhood and adolescence* (pp. 212–237). Minneapolis: Burgess International.

Gould, D. (1987). Understanding attrition in children's sport. In D. Gould & M. Weiss (Eds.), *Advances in pediatric sport sciences: Vol II. Behavioral issues* (pp. 61–85). Champaign, IL: Human Kinetics.

Gould, D., Feltz, D., Horn, T., & Weiss, M. (1982). Reasons for discontinuing involvement in competitive youth swimming. *Journal of Sport Behavior, 5,* 155–165.

Gould, D., & Petlichkoff, L. (1988). Participation motivation and attrition in young athletes. In F.L. Smoll, R.A. Magill, & M.J. Ash (Eds.), *Children in sport* (pp. 161–178). Champaign, IL: Human Kinetics.

Greendorfer, S.L. (1977). The role of socializing agents in female sport involvement. *Research Quarterly, 48,* 304–310.

Greendorfer, S.L. (1978). Social class influence on female sport involvement. *Sex Roles, 4,* 619–625.

Greendorfer, S.L. (1983). Shaping the female athlete: The impact of the family. In M.A. Boutilier & L. San Giovanni (Eds.), *The sporting woman: Feminist and sociological dilemmas* (pp. 135–155). Champaign, IL: Human Kinetics.

Greendorfer, S.L. (1987a). Gender bias in theoretical perspectives: The case of female socialization into sport. *Psychology of Women Quarterly, 11,* 327–340.

Greendorfer, S.L. (1987b). Psycho-social correlates of organized physical activity. *Journal of Physical Education, Recreation and Dance, 58*(7), 59–64.

Greendorfer, S.L., & Blinde, E.M. (1985). "Retirement" from intercollegiate sport: Theoretical and empirical considerations. *Sociology of Sport Journal, 2,* 101–110.

Greendorfer, S.L., & Blinde, E.M. (1990). Structural differences and contrasting organizational models: The female intercollegiate sport experience. In L.

VanderVelden & J. Humphrey (Eds.), *Psychology and sociology of sport: Current selected research* (Vol. 2, pp. 151–164). New York: AMS Press.

Greendorfer, S.L., Blinde, E.M., & Pellegrini, A.M. (1986). Gender differences in Brazilian children's socialization into sport. *International Review of Sociology of Sport, 21,* 51–64.

Greendorfer, S.L., & Bruce, T. (1991). Rejuvenating sport socialization research. *Journal of Sport and Social Issues, 15*(2), 129–144.

Greendorfer, S.L., & Ewing, M.E. (1981). Race and gender differences in children's socialization into sport. *Research Quarterly for Exercise and Sport, 52,* 301–310.

Greendorfer, S.L., & Lewko, J.H. (1978a). Role of family members in sport socialization of children. *Research Quarterly, 49,* 146–152.

Greendorfer, S.L., & Lewko, J.H. (1978b, August). *Children's socialization into sport: A conceptual and empirical analysis.* Paper presented at Ninth World Congress of Sociology, Uppsala, Sweden.

Greendorfer, S.L., Lewko, J.H., & Rosengren, K.S. (1996). Family influence in sport socialization: Sociocultural perspectives. In F. Smoll and R. Smith (Eds.), *Children and youth in sport* (pp. 89–111). Dubuque, IA: Brown and Benchmark..

Greendorfer, S.L., Lewko, J.H., & Rosengren, K.S. (in press). Family influence in sport socialization: Sociocultural perspectives. In F. Smoll & R. Smith (Eds.), *Children and youth in sport* (2nd ed.). Dubuque, IA: Kendall/Hunt.

Griffin, P. (1988). Gender as a socializing agent in physical education. In T.J. Templin & P.G. Schempp (Eds.), *Socialization in physical education: Learning to teach* (pp. 219–233). Champaign, IL: Human Kinetics.

Haerle, R.K. (1975). Career patterns and career contingencies of professional baseball players: An occupational analysis. In D. Ball & J. Loy (Eds.), *Sport and social order* (pp. 461–520). Reading, MA: Addison-Wesley.

Haight, W., Parke, R., & Black, J. (1997). Mothers' and fathers' beliefs about and spontaneous participation in their toddlers' pretend play. *Merrill-Palmer Quarterly, 43,* 271–290.

Harris, J.C. (1983). Interpreting youth baseball: Players' understandings of attention, winning and playing the game. *Research Quarterly for Exercise and Sport, 54,* 330–339.

Harris, J.C. (1984). Interpreting youth baseball: Players' understandings of fun and excitement, danger, and boredom. *Research Quarterly for Exercise and Sport, 55,* 379–382.

Hasbrook, C.A. (1982). The theoretical notion of reciprocity and childhood socialization into sport. In A.O. Dunleavy, A.W. Miracle, & C.R. Rees (Eds.), *Studies in the sociology of sport* (pp. 139–151). Fort Worth: Texas Christian University Press.

Hasbrook, C.A. (1986). Reciprocity and childhood socialization into sport. In L. VanderVelden and J.H. Humphrey (Eds.), *Psychology and sociology of sport: Current selected research* (pp. 135–147). New York: AMS Press.

Hasbrook, C.A. (1989, November). *Reconceptualizing socialization.* Paper presented at Ninth Annual Conference of the North American Society for the Sociology of Sport, Washington, DC.

Hasbrook, C.A., Greendorfer, S.L., & McMullen, J.A. (1981). Implications of social class background on female athletes and nonathletes. In S.L. Greendorfer & A. Yiannakis (Eds.), *Sociology of sport: Diverse perspectives* (pp. 139–152). West Point, NY: Leisure Press.

Hasbrook, C.A., & Mingesz, J.A. (1987, November). *Early socialization into and continuity of involvement in physical activity across the life cycle.* Paper presented at the Eighth Annual North American Society for the Sociology of Sport Conference, Edmonton, AB.

Haywood, K., & Getchell, N. (2001). *Life span motor development* (3rd ed.). Champaign, IL: Human Kinetics.

Higginson, D.C. (1985). The influence of socializing agents in the female sport-participation process. *Adolescence, 20,* 73–82.

Hodge, K.P. (1988). *A conceptual analysis of character development in sport.* Unpublished doctoral dissertation, University of Illinois at Urbana-Champaign.

Hoffman, L.W. (1989). Effects of maternal employment in the two-parent family. *American Psychologist, 44,* 283–292.

Hollands, R.G. (1984). The role of cultural studies and social criticism in the sociological study of sport. *Quest, 36,* 66–79.

Horn, T.S. (1987). The influence of teacher-coach behavior on the psychological development of children. In D. Gould & M.R. Weiss (Eds.), *Advances in pediatric sport sciences* (pp. 121–142). Champaign, IL: Human Kinetics.

Horn, T.S., & Hasbrook, C.A. (1986). Information components influencing children's perception of their physical competence. In M.R. Weiss & D. Gould (Eds.), *Sport for children and youth: Proceedings of the 1984 Olympic Scientific Congress* (pp. 81–88). Champaign, IL: Human Kinetics.

Horn, T.S., & Hasbrook, C.A. (1987). Psychological characteristics and the criteria children use for self-evaluation. *Journal of Sport Psychology, 9,* 208–221.

Hoyle, R., & Leff, S. (1997). The role of parental involvement in youth sport participation and performance. *Adolescence, 32,* 233–243.

Huston, A.C., & Alvarez, M.M. (1990). The socialization context of gender role development in early adolescence. In R. Montemayor, G.R. Adams, & T.P. Gullotta (Eds.), *From childhood to adolescence: A transitional period?* (pp. 156–179). London: Sage.

Inkeles, A. (1968). Society, social structure and child socialization. In J.A. Clausen (Ed.), *Socialization and society* (pp. 73–130). Boston: Little, Brown.

Jambor, E. (1999). Parents as children's socializing agents in youth soccer. *Journal of Sport Behavior, 22,* 350–359.

Kemper, T. (1968). Reference groups, socialization and achievement. *American Sociological Review, 33,* 31–45.

Kenyon, G.S. (1968). Sociological considerations. *Journal of Health, Physical Education and Recreation, 39,* 31–33.

Kenyon, G.S. (1969). Sport involvement: A conceptual go and some consequences thereof. In G.S. Kenyon (Ed.), *Sociology of sport* (pp. 77–84). Chicago: The Athletic Institute.

Kenyon, G.S. (1970). The use of path analysis in sport sociology. *International Review of Sport Sociology, 5*(1), 191–203.

Kenyon, G.S., & Knoop, J.C. (1978, August). *The viability and cross-cultural invariance of a reduced social system model of sport socialization.* Paper presented at the Ninth World Congress of Sociology, Uppsala, Sweden.

Kenyon, G.S., & McPherson, B.D. (1973). Becoming involved in physical activity and sport: A process of socialization. In G.L. Rarick (Ed.), *Physical activity: Human growth and development* (pp. 303–332). New York: Academic Press.

Kenyon, G.S., & McPherson, B.D. (1974). An approach to the study of sport socialization. *International Review of Sport Sociology, 9*, 127–139.

Kirshnit, C.E., Ham, M., & Richards, M.H. (1989). The sporting life: Athletic activities during early adolescence. *Journal of Youth and Adolescence, 18*(6), 601–615.

Klint, K., & Weiss, M.R. (1986). Dropping in and dropping out: Participation motives of current and former youth gymnasts. *Canadian Journal of Applied Sport Sciences, 11*, 106–114.

Kohlberg, L. (1966). A cognitive–developmental analysis of children's sex-role concepts and attitudes. In E.E. Maccoby (Ed.), *The development of sex differences* (pp. 82–173). Stanford, CA: Stanford University Press.

Lamb, M. (1997). *The role of father in child development.* New York: Wiley.

Leaper, C. (2000). Gender, affiliation, assertion and the interactive context of parent-child play. *Developmental Psychology, 36*, 381–393.

Lerch, S.H. (1981). The adjustment to retirement of professional baseball players. In S. Greendorfer & A. Yiannakis (Eds.), *Sociology of sport: Diverse perspectives* (pp. 138–148). West Point, NY: Leisure Press.

Lever, J. (1976). Sex differences in the games children play. *Social Problems, 23*, 478–487.

Lever, J. (1978). Sex differences in the complexity of children's play and games. *American Sociological Review, 43*, 471–482.

Lewko, J.H., & Ewing, M.E. (1981). Sex differences and parental influence in the sport involvement of children. *Journal of Sport Psychology, 2*, 62–68.

Lewko, J.H., & Greendorfer, S.L. (1980). Family influence and sex differences in children's socialization into sport: A review. In R.A. Magill, M.J. Ash, & F.L. Smoll (Eds.), *Children in sport* (2nd ed., pp. 279–293). Champaign, IL: Human Kinetics.

Lewko, J.H., & Greendorfer, S.L. (1988). Family influences in sport socialization of children and adolescents. In F.L. Smoll, R.A. Magill, & M.J. Ash (Eds.), *Children in sport* (3rd ed., pp. 287–300). Champaign, IL: Human Kinetics.

Loy, J.W., & Ingham, A. (1973). Play, games and sport in the psychosocial development of children and youth. In G.L. Rarick (Ed.), *Physical activity: Human growth and development* (pp. 257–302). New York: Academic Press.

Mantel, R., & VanderVelden, L. (1974). The relationship between the professionalization of attitude toward play of preadolescent boys and participation in organized sport. In G. Sage (Ed.), *Sport and American society* (pp. 172–178). Reading, MA: Addison-Wesley.

McPherson, B.D. (1976, April). *The child in competitive sport: Influence of the social milieu.* Paper presented at the Child in Competitive Sport: A symposium on Readiness and Effects, Milwaukee, WI.

McPherson, B.D. (1980). Retirement from professional sport: The process and problems of occupational and psychological adjustment. *Sociological Symposium, 30*, 126–143.

McPherson, B.D. (1981). Socialization into and through sport involvement. In G. Lueschen & G. Sage (Eds.), *Handbook of social science of sport* (pp. 246–273). Champaign, IL: Stipes.

McPherson, B.D. (1986). Socialization theory and research: Toward a "new wave" of scholarly inquiry in a sport context. In C.R. Rees & A.W. Miracle (Eds.), *Sport and social theory* (pp. 111–147). Champaign, IL: Human Kinetics.

McPherson, B.D., & Brown, B.A. (1988) The structure, processes and consequences of sport for children. In F.L. Smoll, R.A. Magill, & M.J. Ash (Eds.), *Children in sport* (3rd ed., pp. 265–286). Champaign, IL: Human Kinetics.

Mead, G.H. (1934). *Mind, self, and society.* Chicago: University of Chicago Press.

Messner, M. (1988). Sport and male domination: The female athlete as contested ideological terrain. *Sociology of Sport Journal, 5*(3), 197–211.

Messner, M.A. (1989). Masculinities and athletic careers. *Gender and Society, 31*, 71–88.

Messner, M.A. (1996). Studying up on sex. *Sociology of Sport Journal, 13*, 221–236.

Miller, D.R. (1969). Psychoanalytic theory of development: A re-evaluation. In D.A. Goslin (Ed.), *Handbook of socialization theory and research* (pp. 481–502). Chicago: Rand McNally.

Mowrer, O.H. (1960). *Learning theory and symbolic process.* New York: Wiley.

Nicholls, J.G. (1989). *Competence and accomplishment: A psychology of achievement motivation.* Cambridge, MA: Harvard University Press.

Nixon, H. (1980). Orientation toward sports participation among college students. *Journal of Sport Behavior, 3*, 29–45.

Nixon, H.L. (1990). Rethinking socialization into sport. *Journal of Sport and Social Issues, 14*, 33–47.

Parsons, T., & Bales, R.F. (1955). *Family, socialization and interaction process.* Glencoe, IL: Free Press.

Patrikkson, G. (1981). Socialization into sports involvement: The influence of family members. *Scandinavian Journal of Sports Sciences, 3*, 27–32.

Pennell, G. (1999). Doing gender with Santa: Gender-typing in children's toy preferences. *Dissertation Abstracts International: Section B: the Science & Engineering, 59*(8-B), 4541.

Piaget, J. (1951). *Play dreams, and imitation in childhood.* London: Routledge & Kegan Paul.

Piaget, J. (1965). *The moral judgment of the child.* New York: Free Press.

Pomerleau, A., Bolduc, D., Malcuit, G., & Cossette, L. (1990). Pink or blue: Environmental gender stereotypes in the first two years of life. *Sex Roles, 22*, 359–367.

Posner, J., & Vandell, D. (1999). After school activities and the development of low-income urban children: A longitudinal study. *Developmental Psychology, 35,* 868–879.

Power, T.G., & Parke, R.D. (1982). Play as a context for early learning: Lab and home analyses. In I.E. Siegel & L.M. Asosa (Eds.), *The family as a learning environment* (pp. 136–147). New York: Plenum Press.

Raymore, L., Barber, B., Eccles, J., & Godbey, G. (1999). Leisure behavior pattern stability during the transition from adolescence to young adulthood. *Journal of Youth & Adolescence, 28,* 79–103.

Rekers, G.A., Sanders, J.A., Rasbury, W.C., Strauss, C.C., & Morey, S.M. (1988). Differentiation of adolescent activity participation. *Journal of Genetic Psychology, 150*(3), 323–335.

Reynolds, M.J. (1981). The effects of sport retirement on the job satisfaction of the former football player. In S.L. Greendorfer & A. Yiannakis (Eds.), *Sociology of sport: Diverse perspectives* (pp. 127–137). West Point, NY: Leisure Press.

Rheingold, H.L., & Cook, K.V. (1975). The contents of boys' and girls' rooms as an index of parents' behavior. *Child Development, 46,* 459–463.

Roberts, G.C. (1984). Toward a new theory of motivation in sport: The role of perceived ability. In J.M. Silva, III, & R.S. Weinberg (Eds.), *Psychological foundations of sport* (pp. 214–228). Champaign, IL: Human Kinetics.

Roberts, G.C. (1986, October). *Motivation in sport: A theory of personal investment.* Paper presented at the American Association for the Advancement of Applied Sport Psychology, Jekyll Island, GA.

Roberts, G.C., Kleiber, D.A., & Duda, J.L. (1981). An analysis of motivation in children's sport: The role of perceived competence in participation. *Journal of Sport Psychology, 3,* 203–211.

Roberts, G.C., Treasure, D.C., & Kavussanu, M. (1997). Motivation in physical activity contexts: An achievement goal perspective. In M. Maehr & P. Pintrich (Eds.), *Advances in motivation and achievement* (Vol. 10, pp. 413–447). Greenwich, CN: JAI Press.

Roberts, J.M., & Sutton-Smith, B. (1962). Child training and game involvement. *Ethnology, 1,* 166–185.

Rosenberg, E. (1981). Gerontological theory and athletic retirement. In S. Greendorfer & A. Yiannakis (Eds.), *Sociology of sport: Diverse perspectives* (pp. 127–137). West Point, NY: Leisure Press.

Ruble, D.N. (1987). The acquisition of self-knowledge: A self-socialization perspective. In N. Eisenberg (Ed.), *Contemporary topics in developmental psychology* (pp. 243–270). New York: Wiley.

Ryckman, R.M., & Hamel, J. (1992). Female adolescents' motives related to involvement in organized team sports. *International Journal of Sport Psychology, 23,* 147–160.

Ryckman, R.M., & Hamel, J. (1995). Male and female adolescents' motives related to involvement in organized team sports. *International Journal of Sport Psychology, 26,* 383–397.

Sabo, D. (1985). Sport, patriarchy, and male identity. *Arena Review, 9*(2), 1–30.

Sapp, M., & Haubenstricker, J. (1978, April). *Motivation for joining and reasons for not continuing in youth sport programs in Michigan.* Paper presented at AAHPERD National Convention, Kansas City, MO.

Sarbin, T.R., & Allen, V. (1968). Role theory. In G. Lindzey & E. Aronson (Eds.), *Handbook of social psychology* (Vol. 1., pp. 488–567). Reading, MA: Addison-Wesley.

Scanlan, T.K., Carpenter, P.J., Schmidt, G.W., Simons, J.P., Schmidt, G.W., & Keeler, B. (1993). An introduction to the sport commitment model. *Journal of Sport & Exercise Psychology, 15,* 1–15.

Scanlan, T.K., Simons, J.P., Carpenter, P.J., Schmidt, G.W., & Keeler, B. (1993). The sport commitment model: Measurement development for the youth-sport domain. *Journal of Sport & Exercise Psychology, 15,* 16–38.

Schneider, W. (1993). The longitudinal study of motor development: Methodological issues. In A.F. Kalverboer, B. Hopkins, & R. Geuze (Eds.), *Motor development in early and later childhood: Longitudinal approaches* (pp. 325–328). Cambridge, UK: Cambridge University Press.

Servin, A., Bohlin, G., & Berlin, L. (1999). Sex differences in 1-, 2-, and 5-year-olds' toy choice in a structured play-session. *Scandinavian Journal of Psychology, 40,* 43–48.

Smith, R. (1986). Toward a cognitive-affective model of athletic burnout. *Journal of Sport Psychology, 8,* 36–50.

Smith, R.E., Smoll, F.L., Hunt, E., Curtis, B., & Coppel, D.B. (1979). Psychology and the bad news bears. In G. Roberts & K.M. Newell (Eds.), *Psychology of motor behavior and sport—1978* (pp. 109–130). Champaign, IL: Human Kinetics.

Smoll, F.L. (1986). Stress reduction strategies in youth sport. In M.R. Weiss & D. Gould (Eds.), *Sport for children and youths* (pp. 127–136). Champaign, IL: Human Kinetics.

Snyder, E.E., & Spreitzer, E. (1973). Family influence and involvement in sports. *Research Quarterly, 44,* 249–255.

Snyder, E.E., & Spreitzer, E. (1978). Socialization comparisons of adolescent female athletes and musicians. *Research Quarterly, 49,* 342–350.

Sovik, N. (1993). Development of children's writing performance: Some educational implications. In A.F. Kalverboer, B. Hopkins, & R. Geuze (Eds.), *Motor development in early and later childhood: Longitudinal approaches* (pp. 243–244). Cambridge, UK: Cambridge University Press.

Spreitzer, E., & Snyder, E.E. (1976). Socialization into sport: An exploratory path analysis. *Research Quarterly, 47,* 238–245.

Stevenson, C.L. (1975). Socialization effects of participation in sport: A critical review of the research. *Research Quarterly, 46,* 287–301.

Stevenson, C.L. (1991). The Christian-athlete: An interactionist-developmental analysis. *Sociology of Sport Journal, 8,* 362–379.

Stevenson, C.L. (1997). Christian-athletes and the culture of elite sport: Dilemmas and solutions. *Sociology of Sport Journal, 14,* 241–262.

Stryker, S. (1959). Symbolic interaction as an approach to family research. *Marriage and Family Living, 21,* 111–119.

Telama, R., & Yang, X. (2000). Decline of physical activity from youth to young adulthood in Finland. *Medicine and Science in Sports and Exercise, 32,* 1617–1622.

Theberge, N. (1984). On the need for a more adequate theory of sport participation. *Sociology of Sport Journal, 1,* 26–35.

Theeboom, M., DeKnop, P., & Weiss, M.R. (1995). Motivational climate, psychological responses and motor skill development in children's sport: A field-based intervention study. *Journal of Sport & Exercise Psychology, 17,* 294–311.

Theodorakis, Y. (1994). Planned behavior, attitude strength, role identity and the prediction of exercise behavior. *The Sport Psychologist, 8,* 149–165.

Trew, K., Kremer, J., Gallagher, A., Scully, D., & Ogle, S. (1997). Young people's participation in sport in Northern Ireland. *International Review for the Sociology of Sport, 32,* 419–431.

Vanreusel, B., Renson, R., Beunen, G., Claessens, A., Lefevre, J., Lysens, R., & Vanden Eynde, B. (1997). A longitudinal study of youth sport participation and adherence to sport in adulthood. *International Review for the Sociology of Sport, 32,* 373–387.

Vaughter, R.M., Sadh, D., & Vozzola, E. (1994). Sex similarities and differences in types of play in games and sports. *Psychology of Women Quarterly, 18,* 85–104.

Vilhjalmsson, R., & Thorlindsson, T. (1998). Factors related to physical activity: A study of adolescents. *Social Science and Medicine, 47,* 665–675.

Watson, G. (1976). Reward systems in children's games. *Review of Sport and Leisure, 1,* 93–121.

Watson, G. (1977). Games, socialization and parental values: Social class differences in parental evaluation of Little League Baseball, *International Review of Sport Sociology, 12,* 17–48.

Watson, G. (1979, January). A competence-based model of children's play and game involvement (pp. 98–116). In J.D. Emmel, D.D. Molyneau, & N.R. Waldrop (Eds.), *Proceedings of ACHPER Conference*, Adelaide, Australia. Kingswood, S.A.: Australian Council for Physical Education & Recreation, South Australian Branch.

Watson, G. (1981). *Introducing children to attractive, competitive situations*. Report to the Department for Youth, Sport and Recreation, Perth, Australia.

Watson, G. (1984). Social motivation in games: Toward a conceptual framework of game attraction. *Journal of Human Movement Studies, 10,* 1–19.

Watson, G., Blanksby, B.A., & Bloomfield, J. (1983, July). *Childhood socialization and competitive swimming: A sociological analysis of Australian elite junior swimmers*. Paper presented at 8th Symposium on Sport and Contemporary Society, International Committee for the Sociology of Sport, Paris.

Webb, H. (1969). Professionalization of attitudes toward play among adolescents. In G.S. Kenyon (Ed.), *Aspects of contemporary sport sociology* (pp. 161–180). Chicago: The Athletic Institute.

Weinberg, S.K., & Arond, H. (1952). The occupational culture of the boxer. *American Journal of Sociology, 57,* 460–469.

Weiss, M., & Bredemeier, B. (1990). Moral development in sport. *Exercise and Sport Science Reviews, 18,* 331–378.

Weiss, M.R., & Chaumeton, N. (1992). Motivational orientation in sport. In T.S. Horn (Ed.), *Advances in sport psychology* (pp. 61–99). Champaign, IL: Human Kinetics.

Weiss, M.R., & Duncan, S.C. (1992). The relationship between physical competence and peer acceptance in the context of children's sport participation. *Journal of Sport & Exercise Psychology, 14,* 177–191.

Weiss, M., & Knoppers, A. (1982). The influence of socializing agents on female collegiate volleyball players. *Journal of Sport Psychology, 4,* 267–279.

Weiss, M.R., & Stevens, C. (1993). Motivation and attrition of female coaches: An application of social exchange theory. *The Sport Psychologist, 7,* 244–261.

Wentworth, W. (1980). *Context and understanding*. New York: Elsevier Science.

Whitson, D. (1984). Sport and hegemony: On the construction of the dominant culture. *Sport Sociology Journal, 1,* 64–78.

Whitson, D. (1990). Sport in the social construction of masculinity. In M. Messner & D. Sabo (Eds.), *Sport, men and the gender order* (pp. 19–29). Champaign, IL: Human Kinetics.

Whitson, D. (1994). The embodiment of gender: Discipline, domination and empowerment. In S. Birrell & C. Cole (Eds.), *Women, sport, and culture* (pp. 353–372). Champaign, IL: Human Kinetics.

Yamaguchi, Y. (1984). A comparative study of adolescent socialization into sport: The case of Japan and Canada. *International Review for Sociology of Sport, 19*(1), 63–82.

Yamaguchi, Y. (1987). A cross-national study of socialization into physical activity in corporate settings: The case of Japan and Canada. *Sociology of Sport Journal, 4,* 61–77.

Yang, X., Telama, R., & Laakso, L. (1996). Parent's physical activity, socio-economic status and education as predictors of physical activity and sport among children and youths: A 12 year follow-up study. *International Review for the Sociology of Sport, 31*(3), 273–294.

Zigler, E., & Child, L.L. (1969). Socialization. In G. Lindzey & E. Aronson (Eds.), *A handbook of social psychology* (Vol. 3, pp. 450–589). Reading, MA: Addison-Wesley.

PART IV

Psychological Skills, Intervention Techniques, and Sport Behavior

As Deborah Feltz and Anthony Kontos noted in chapter 1, there has been increased interest over the last couple of decades in applying sport psychology research to athletes and other physical activity participants. More specifically, within the last two decades, a variety of intervention techniques have been developed and promoted to help athletes develop important psychological skills and thus to enhance their performance or to modify their behavior in sport and physical activity contexts. In line with this more clinical perspective of sport psychology, the five chapters included in part IV examine the extent to which selected psychological skills or intervention techniques can be linked to performance enhancement or behavioral change.

Although there has been considerable controversy in the field concerning the validity of the intervention techniques used by practicing sport psychologists, the chapters in part IV are presented with the assumption that researchers and practitioners can and must work together to understand sport be-

havior. These chapters are therefore written from the perspective that (a) intervention techniques should be based as much as possible on research and theory and (b) applied practices may provide researchers with valuable information that can be used to design research studies and to develop theoretical models of sport behavior. Given this overall perspective, the five chapters in part IV not only discuss the efficacy of selected intervention techniques but also examine potential mechanisms that may explain why and how these intervention strategies affect performance or change behavior.

In chapter 13, Shane Murphy and Kathleen Martin examine imagery as it can be used in sport contexts. The authors begin with a critical discussion of current conceptual perspectives on mental imagery and then propose a multilevel model of analysis indicating that imagery in sport contexts should be investigated on three interrelated but conceptually distinct levels. This model is then used as a framework for examining the current empirical and theoretical state of knowledge on sport imagery and for identifying directions for future researchers.

In chapter 14, Stephen Boutcher examines the complex relationship between attention and sport performance. He begins with a review of the attention/performance link as it has been studied from three different research perspectives including information processing, social psychology, and psychophysiology. Boutcher uses these disparate views of the attentional process to develop an integrated, multidimensional model of attention in sport. He concludes by examining issues related to attentional training in athletes and other physical activity participants.

In chapter 15, Damon Burton and Sarah Naylor review the research and theory on goal setting in sport contexts. They begin with two real-life examples that illustrate the positive and negative effects that goal setting can have on individuals' performance and behavior. Continuing with this Jekyll and Hyde analogy, Burton and Naylor review the theoretical and empirical research on goal setting in physical activity contexts, focusing particularly on the processes and mechanisms that explain why, how, and when goal setting will have positive or negative effects. Burton and Naylor propose a competitive goal-setting model, based on this comprehensive review of the current state of knowledge, that should be used in designing future research studies on goal setting in sport. The authors conclude by highlighting current limitations in our research methodologies and by identifying future research directions.

The last two chapters represent new additions to the second edition of this text. These chapters reflect the rapidly expanding knowledge base on topics related to flow and athletic injury. In chapter 16, Jay Kimiecik and Susan Jackson argue for research examining athletes' subjective experiences as a means to understanding their performance and behavior in sport contexts. Thus, these authors focus on the research that has been conducted on optimal experiences in sport from a flow perspective. They begin by providing a brief history of the scholarly study of optimal experience in sport and other life contexts. This section includes a discussion of two constructs closely related to flow—peak performance and peak experience. Kimiecik and Jackson then describe a theoretical framework for the study of flow and use this model to review and critically analyze the existing research on optimal experiences in sport contexts. They conclude by identifying ideas for future (creative) researchers who wish to explore the role of flow in athletes' sport experiences.

In chapter 17, Eileen Udry and Mark Andersen discuss the research and theory concerning the psychological correlates of athletic injury. In particular, they explore the dual possibilities that psychological factors may serve as antecedents to athletic injuries and that psychological techniques may be used to ameliorate the stress associated with an athletic injury and thus facilitate recovery and rehabilitation. Udry and Andersen begin by discussing measurement issues in this area of research. They then review the empirical and theoretical literature pertaining to the psychological antecedents of sport injury as well as athletes' psychological and behavioral responses to such injuries. This section includes a discussion of four theoretical approaches that researchers and practitioners can use to understand injury rehabilitation adherence in athletes. Udry and Andersen conclude by identifying and discussing future directions for research on the psychological correlates of injury in sport contexts.

CHAPTER 13

The Use of Imagery in Sport

Shane M. Murphy and Kathleen A. Martin

Few mental processes seem to be reported as ubiquitously by athletes as imagery. Athletes of all levels commonly talk of "feeling the shot" and "seeing the shot" before they perform. Sport psychologists have naturally focused a great deal of research attention on the use of imagery in sport. Much of this research has focused heavily on the use of imagery to mentally practice sports skills. Although this is an important research topic, it only addresses one use of imagery in sport. Athletes use imagery for a variety of purposes other than mental practice. In addition, mental practice research has done little to advance our understanding of the cognitive processes that underlie imagery use. In this chapter we propose a three-level model of analysis to guide imagery research and practice in sport. This model addresses the fundamental nature of imagery, the uses of imagery in sport settings, and the meaning of the imagery experience for athletes.

THE MENTAL PRACTICE MODEL OF IMAGERY

The most influential imagery research in sport psychology has investigated the phenomenon whereby athletes practice or rehearse their motor skills in imagination, also known as mental practice (although we argue later that other forms of mental practice are also possible). Comparisons between such "mental practice" and normal "physical practice," that is, the repeated execution of actual motor skills, abound in the sport psychology literature (Denis, 1985; Feltz & Landers, 1983; Grouios, 1992; Richardson, 1967a; Silva, 1983; Suinn, 1997). The assumptions underlying the "mental practice model" have been described elsewhere (Murphy, 1990, 1994), and in the first edition of this book, Murphy and Jowdy (1992) proposed several alternative approaches to the mental practice model of research. In this chapter, we propose a framework for a model of imagery in sport that will provide a more effective guide to research and practice.

Mental practice has a long tradition of research in sport psychology. As early as the 1890s, attention was given to muscular activity during mental operations (Jastrow, 1892). Formal investigations examining the use of mental practice began during the 1930s (Jacobson, 1932; Perry, 1939; Sackett, 1934, 1935). A large majority of the studies conducted before the 1980s were concerned with the effects of mental practice on the learning and performance of motor skills. Nearly all these studies were based in the laboratory, and few used field research methodology. The standard research design involved a between-subjects, pre- to posttest comparison with four groups: physical practice, mental practice, a combination of physical and mental practice, and no practice. To analyze mental practice effects, researchers usually looked at the changes in performance for each

We wish to acknowledge Doug Jowdy, whose scholarship contributed greatly to this chapter.

group from pre- to postintervention. The majority of the studies were not concerned with the mechanisms underlying the "mental practice effect."

MENTAL PRACTICE RESEARCH

A simple review of all published studies indicates mixed findings about the efficacy of mental practice. Although many research studies supported the relationship between mental practice and performance, other studies (Corbin, 1967a; Ryan & Simons, 1981; Shick, 1970; Smyth, 1975; Steel, 1952) failed to find support for the effectiveness of mental practice. However, because different studies used different types of tasks, with different types of subjects and different mental rehearsal strategies, it is difficult to integrate these experiments and draw firm conclusions regarding the effectiveness of mental practice. The use of meta-analytic and narrative reviews has helped to clarify this issue. Meta-analytic reviews are quantitative summaries that describe the average effect size for mental practice, its statistical significance, and variables that moderate its effectiveness (Rosenthal, 1995). Feltz and Landers (1983) conducted the first meta-analysis of the mental practice literature. Their analysis consisted of 60 studies that examined "the effects of some form of mental practice on motor performance" (p. 20). They included studies that employed only mental practice as well as those that combined mental practice with other interventions (such as relaxation, modeling, and psych-up strategies). Feltz and Landers found a statistically significant average effect size of 0.48. This effect size is considered small to medium, but it does indicate that mental practice is better than no practice at all. Task type moderated this effect, with mental practice producing greater effect sizes for cognitive tasks than motor or strength tasks.

Driskell, Copper, and Moran (1994) used more stringent study inclusion criteria in their meta-analysis of 35 mental practice studies. To separate mental practice effects from other intervention effects, they excluded studies in which the mental practice manipulation was combined with other interventions. Driskell and his colleagues reported a significant effect size of 0.53, providing further evidence that mental practice influences performance. In addition, they found greater effect sizes for tasks that required greater cognitive activities, particularly among novice subjects. That is, for novice subjects (those without experience on the performance task), the effects of mental practice were greater for cognitive tasks than physical tasks. For experienced subjects, there was no difference between cognitive and physical tasks. Interestingly, overall, there was no difference in the effect sizes for experienced and novice subjects, indicating that subjects at both skill levels derive equal benefits from mental practice.

Narrative reviews also have been used to synthesize the mental practice literature (Corbin, 1972; Grouios, 1992; Jones & Stuth, 1997; Richardson, 1967a, 1967b; Silva, 1983; Suinn, 1980; Weinberg, 1981). Although the majority of research has supported the effectiveness of mental practice, reviewers have noted the inconsistency of research findings. These mixed findings, it has been argued, may have more to do with the effects of differing methodologies (e.g., the use of different definitions and procedures, inconsistent measurement criteria, manipulation checks) than the effects of mental practice per se (Goginsky & Collins, 1996; Jones & Stuth, 1997). Later in this chapter we propose a different explanation for this inconsistency in the research findings.

Despite the lack of a universal effect of mental practice on performance, reviewers have suggested that mental practice combined and alternated with physical practice is more effective than either type of practice on its own (Jones & Stuth, 1997; Romero & Silvestri, 1990; Weinberg, 1981). This suggests that imagining oneself playing golf, for example, is better than not practicing at all. Imagining playing golf, however, is not as effective as going to the course or driving range and actually practicing. To produce the greatest performance effects, one should use both physical practice and mental practice.

INNOVATIVE MENTAL PRACTICE RESEARCH

In recent years, researchers have begun to study the use of imagery in sports contexts by using novel mental practice research designs that extend our knowledge of how imagery is used by athletes. Garza and Feltz (1998), for example, compared improvement in figure skating performance between athletes who had been assigned to one of three treatment groups:

1. A paper free-skate drawing (PFD) group, where skaters listened to their skating music while drawing their program on a piece

of paper and saying cue words before each jump, spin, and connecting move (Palmer, 1992)

2. A walk-through on floor (WTF) group, where skaters listened to their skating music and walked through their program on the floor while saying cue words before each jump, spin, and connecting move (G. Martin, 1992)

3. A stretching control group that did not engage in any mental training

The interesting methodological addition to this study was the use of drawing (PFD group) and walk-throughs (WTF group) to simulate real-life performance and to facilitate mental practice. Analyses revealed a significant improvement in free-skating performance for both the PFD and WTF groups over the course of the intervention, relative to the control group. Moreover, the effect sizes for the performance improvements were very large, ranging from 1.14 to 1.95. Given these large effect sizes, this study suggests that the use of performance simulation techniques may enhance the mental practice effect.

Beyond the sport domain, simulated performance has demonstrated its effectiveness as an adjunct to mental practice. In the field of dance, Hanrahan, Tetreau, and Sarrazin (1995) reported that subjects can use imagery effectively while moving in dance performance and that imagery is an effective technique for enhancing performance of dance routines. Ross (1985) examined the effects of mental practice to enhance music performance among college trombonists and included a condition in which participants simulated the slide movements that occur while playing their instrument. Musicians were assigned to one of five conditions: physical practice, mental practice, combined physical and mental practice (combined), mental practice with simulated slide movements (simulation), and a no-practice control. Mean improvement scores were calculated for each condition and adjusted for pretest differences in skill level. The order of performance improvement from most to least improved was combined, physical practice, simulation, mental practice, and control. Statistically significant differences existed between the combined and the mental practice and control groups and also between the physical practice and control groups. Together, the Ross (1985), Hanrahan et al. (1995), and Garza and Feltz (1998) studies suggest that it may be possible to increase the effects of mental practice by using body movement rehearsal techniques.

This possibility certainly warrants further investigation.

The use of videotaped modeling also has been examined as a strategy to facilitate mental practice effects (S.W. Gray, 1990; E.G. Hall & Erffmeyer, 1983; Onestak, 1997). When video modeling is used, the athlete watches an expert performer execute the target skill. It is believed that this strategy facilitates correct mental rehearsal of the skill as it should be performed. Gray's (1990) study supported the efficacy of video modeling. Among novice racquetball players, those who received video modeling plus imagery and relaxation training performed better than those who received imagery and relaxation training only. This study replicated earlier findings by E.G. Hall and Erffmeyer (1983) in a study of college basketball players. They found that players who received video modeling plus imagery improved their free throw performance more than players who used imagery and relaxation without video modeling.

Another variable that has been investigated is the rate of the imagery used in mental practice. Andre and Means (1986) hypothesized that the speed of imagery rehearsal will influence the efficacy of mental practice, such that slow motion rehearsal might enhance the effectiveness of the practice by enriching the subject's imagery experience. Contrary to their hypothesis, the regular mental practice group performed better on the posttest than the slow-motion mental practice group.

What is the optimal combination of mental and physical practice time? In a well-designed study, Hird, Landers, Thomas, and Horan (1991) examined the effect of different relative proportions of mental and physical practice on performance of a pegboard (cognitive) and a pursuit rotor (motor) task. Greater performance gains were observed as the relative proportion of physical practice increased. Nonetheless, the group that had 100% mental practice and 0% physical practice still improved significantly compared with the control group. Effect sizes were greater for all treatment groups on the cognitive task than the motor task.

Considerable attention has been paid to the use of mental practice and adjunct techniques (e.g., simulation, videotaped modeling) in facilitating the acquisition and retention of discrete motor skills. Although mental practice also can be used to rehearse entire game plans and strategies (Paivio, 1985), this function virtually has been ignored by researchers. Case study reports have documented the benefits of mental practice for rehearsing plays in football (Fenker & Lambiotte,

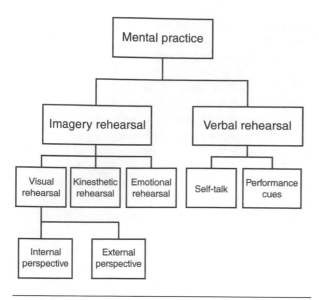

Figure 13.1 Types of mental practice.

1987), and there is anecdotal evidence that athletes engage in mental practice to rehearse the strategy aspects of sports such as soccer and squash (C.R. Hall, Rodgers, & Barr, 1990). We are not aware of any controlled studies that have examined the effects of mental practice on the acquisition or performance of game plans and strategies. Empirical investigations in this area would benefit the field.

The studies reviewed in this section suggest that it is possible to use mental practice research designs, which allow researchers to study some of the ways in which imagery processes are actually used by athletes. Research that studies the natural use of imagery as it is practiced by athletes is to be applauded. But although the mental practice research has helped shape our understanding of imagery use in sport, it is time to move beyond this mental practice research and develop more comprehensive frameworks to guide our research. In the next section we address the fundamental flaws in the mental practice research that render it inadequate as a paradigm for understanding the use of imagery by athletes. Figure 13.1 shows that imagery is but one type of mental practice and that visual imagery is but one type of imagery rehearsal.

PROBLEMS WITH THE MENTAL PRACTICE MODEL OF RESEARCH

Current research into the neurophysiology of imagery suggests that the mental practice model of research is flawed in two key ways. First, there are major problems with the theoretical construct of mental practice. Second, the traditional mental practice versus physical practice research design is inadequate to address the questions being asked. We argue that advances in neuroscience and cognitive psychology in the last two decades represent a major opportunity to advance our knowledge about imagery in sport.

Problems With the Construct of Mental Practice

Central to the mental practice model is the notion that practice can be divided into two kinds—mental and physical. This differentiation is usually taken for granted and rarely examined in the research literature. Physical practice is almost never defined, but we can take it to mean practice that involves movement of the body. Mental practice has been defined as "the symbolic rehearsal of a physical activity in the absence of any gross muscular movements" (Richardson, 1969, p. 95).

Both modern cognitive theories of consciousness (Dennett, 1991) and research findings from the field of neurophysiology (Decety, 1996) suggest that this dichotomy is false. The distinction between the realms of the mental and physical is based on a dualistic philosophy that supposes that the activities of the "mind" are separate from the physical activities of the body (especially the brain). From the perspective of dualism, it makes sense to regard the act of sitting on a bench, closing one's eyes, and imagining making a free throw as very different from actually taking a ball, going on court, and sinking a free throw.

From a cognitive neuroscience viewpoint, however, the realm of the mental is seen to be a direct product of the physical realm, particularly the operations of the brain, central nervous system, and various sensing systems of the body. This approach to cognitive science rejects dualism and seeks to understand the activities of the mind, such as thoughts and images, by understanding the workings of the brain and the body. A dualistic approach divides the world into two levels—mental and physical. The materialistic philosophy underlying the cognitive sciences states that although it is presently not possible to explain all aspects of our phenomenological existence by appealing to what we know about the functions of the brain, there is no reason to suppose that such an understanding is impossible. The goal of cognitive neuroscientists is to fully understand the experience of consciousness by understanding the workings of the body, especially the brain. From this perspective, there is no fundamental difference in nature between imagining making a free throw and moving one's body onto the court, picking up a ball, and throwing it at the basketball hoop. Both involve physical processes located in the body. Both activities can be monitored and assessed. Indeed, the recent availability of brain imaging assessment techniques is partly what enables our current understanding of brain functioning. The differences between these two activities involve only differences in how, and to what extent, the various systems of the brain, central nervous system, and musculature are involved in the activities.

We argue that these conceptual differences between dualism and materialism are not arbitrary, as some might suppose, but are critical to an understanding of imagery in sport. Based on our analysis, it is impossible to completely separate the notion of mental practice from physical practice. By definition, "mental" practice is, in fact, at least partly physical. The converse, that physical practice must always involve mental (cognitive) activity, is also true but rarely considered in the mental practice literature. Obviously there could be no "bodily" (physical) practice without using the systems of the brain and central nervous system.

This analysis implies that research efforts that attempt to show differences in practice effects between mental and physical practice will yield varying results depending on the type of skill being practiced and the appropriateness of the practice strategy for the skill. Both types of practice usually will have some effect, because they involve many of the same systems. As we have seen, this is exactly the overall result of research to date. Our conclusion is that the mental practice research methodology is inadequate to address the use of imagery systems by athletes, a conclusion that is further supported when we examine the rationale of the traditional physical practice, mental practice, and combined group research design.

Problems With the Mental Practice Versus Physical Practice Research Design

The goal of the traditional mental practice research design is to compare the effectiveness of "mental practice" with other types of motor skill practice. As Feltz and Landers (1983) put it, "The specific research question addressed in these studies has been whether a given amount of mental practice or rehearsal prior to performing a motor skill will enhance one's subsequent performance" (p. 25).

Several problems with this research design render the research results very difficult to interpret (Jones & Stuth, 1997; Murphy, 1990, 1994). Consider the analogy that the mental practice research model resembles the "clinical trials" model of medical research. If a new treatment is proposed in medicine, vigorous investigations follow to establish the efficacy of that treatment. For example, a new drug may be discovered to treat hypertension, or a new surgical procedure may be designed to treat tennis elbow. Researchers attempt to establish the efficacy of these treatments and whether they have negative side effects. This is usually done by using the clinical trials methodology whereby the proposed active treatment is compared with no treatment, with a known effective treatment, and with a placebo treatment.

The mental practice model has examined mental practice from a very similar perspective. The basic question that has been asked is, "Does it work?" The "problem" that has been treated by mental practice is improving sports performance (analogous to reducing hypertension or alleviating the tennis elbow). The treatment is mental practice itself (analogous to the drug or the surgical procedure). Mental practice usually is compared with no treatment, with effective treatment (physical practice), and with a placebo treatment.

This research design poses several problems in the case of mental practice. First, mental practice is not a homogeneous, distinct intervention. To say that an athlete is mentally practicing can mean that several activities are going on. As Suinn (1983) pointed out, for example, mentally practicing a tennis serve could involve thinking about serving, talking yourself through the steps in a serve, imagining Pete Sampras hitting a perfect serve, or visualizing a perfect serve you once hit. It is extremely unlikely that these different activities use the same neural substrates or incorporate the same subsystems for processing. Although researchers have acted as if all mental practice studies are examining the same phenomenon, this cannot be the case. Thus, it is likely that no two studies of mental practice actually study the same thing.

Second, the measurement of treatment effects is not well defined in imagery practice research. Most researchers investigating a new hypertension drug will agree on important outcome measures such as various indexes of blood pressure. In the mental practice literature, however, a variety of performance indexes have been used as outcome measures, and many researchers have focused on nonperformance outcomes such as confidence, arousal level, and so on. This again makes comparison across studies difficult.

Finally, assessment of the treatment itself is difficult in the mental practice area. In evaluating a new drug, the drug can be isolated and dosage effects measured. However, imagery is impossible to administer in this way. As researchers have found, most subjects already use imagery in many performance situations, and this can confound the intended experimental effect. When researchers have asked subjects whether their imagery experience actually matched the description given them by the researchers, they often find that subjects have changed the imagery script they were given (Woolfolk, Murphy, Gottesfeld, & Aitken, 1985). Thus, it is vital that researchers carefully check the self-reported mental practice experience of all subjects, although this is rarely done. Only with the recent advent of brain imaging techniques has it been feasible to obtain some external measure of what occurs while participants are using imagery.

Given these problems in research design, it is not surprising that the large number of studies of mental practice have not yielded definitive results. Our review of the literature and our critique of the concept of mental practice and the use of traditional research designs suggest that it is time to move beyond the mental practice model. Instead of thinking of mental practice as a discrete experience, completely different from physical practice, we need to see mental and physical practice on a continuum and investigate the physical and cognitive systems they share, as well as explore any differences that might exist. We suggest that greater conceptual clarity, aided by recent neuropsychological research, together with a multilevel approach to understanding imagery is necessary to further develop imagery research in sport.

DEFINING IMAGERY USE IN SPORT

Imagery is of interest to researchers in many fields. The literature on imagery is truly voluminous and encompasses such fields as cognitive psychology, psychophysiology, the brain sciences, psychotherapy, psychometrics, and more. To focus our investigation, it is useful to define the constructs we are interested in.

We are interested in imagery as it relates to sport. An incomplete list of some of the terms related to imagery use in sport includes *symbolic rehearsal, visualization, modeling, covert practice, cognitive rehearsal, imagery practice, dreams, hallucinations, hypnosis, visuomotor training, introspective rehearsal, implicit practice, ideomotor training, visuomotor behavioral rehearsal* (VMBR; Suinn, 1976), and even *sofa training*. In sport psychology, the terms *imagery* and *mental practice* have been used interchangeably across a variety of contexts. For research purposes, however, imagery and mental practice should be carefully distinguished. As we have seen, mental practice does not always involve imagery processes. Rather, imagery refers to a mental process. Some have called it a "mode of thought" (Heil, 1985). Cognitive psychologists have fiercely debated the nature of this mental process, but there is general agreement that this cognitive function does exist. *Mental practice*, on the other hand, is a descriptive term for a particular technique used by athletes and many other individuals. As Suinn (1983) pointed out, many different kinds of processes can underlie this technique.

For this reason, Suinn (1983) distinguished between mental practice and imagery rehearsal. Only in imagery rehearsal can we definitely conclude that imagery was used to achieve the covert practice. Imagery rehearsal usually involves the subject imagining him- or herself successfully completing the sport skill that is his or her focus of attention. For example, a tennis player learning a new serve may imagine the feel and look of the new skill every night before she goes to bed. Alternatively, an elite diver may pause for a moment on the springboard, imagine himself completing the dive he is about to attempt, and then initiate the dive. In both cases, the sports skill is rehearsed via imagery in the absence of overt movement (although not, as we have argued, in the absence of physical activity).

Imagery processes also have been used in the sports context as components of other interventions, such as relaxation, meditation, pain reduction, and mood control. Thus, imagery is not used only in mental practice situations and is not used by athletes only to rehearse performance. Such alternative uses of imagery have received limited attention in the sport psychology literature (see Heil, 1984, 1985). The model of athletic imagery proposed in this chapter addresses a variety of potential uses of imagery by athletes.

Before initiating the serve, a volleyball player may pause to imagine herself following through the serving motion.

Definitions of imagery tend to vary widely depending on the viewpoint of the researcher. For example, in their review of the use of imagination, Taylor, Pham, Rivkin, and Armor (1998) wrote the following:

The term imagination may be used quite specifically to refer to the mental activities that people engage in when they want to get from a current point in time and place to a subsequent one, having accomplished something in between, such as going on a trip or writing a paper. An activity fundamental to this task is mental simulation. Mental simulation is the imitative representation of some event or series of events. (pp. 429–430)

This definition stresses the utility of imagery and is relevant to sport psychology research because

athletes and coaches are interested in the use of imagery to improve performance or achieve goals.

Another approach toward defining imagery was taken by Richardson (1969), who proposed,

Mental imagery refers to all those quasi-sensory or quasi-perceptual experiences that we are self-consciously aware of and exist for us in the absence of those stimulus conditions that are known to produce their genuine sensory or perceptual counterparts. (pp. 2–3)

This definition addresses several key issues concerning the nature of imagery. First, imagery experiences mimic sensory or perceptual experience. The individual talks of "seeing" an image or "feeling" the movements associated with mental rehearsal. Research in the cognitive sciences suggests that this is because both the sensing and the imagery systems share many cognitive systems (Kosslyn, 1980). Second, the individual is consciously aware of these experiences. Imagery, therefore, is differentiated from dreaming, because individuals are usually unaware that they are dreaming (see J. Singer & Antrobus, 1972). Perry and Morris (1995) suggested that researchers also include the notion of volitional control in their definition of imagery, because this would differentiate imagery from uncontrolled, but conscious, experiences such as daydreaming. Third, imagery takes place without known stimulus antecedents. No mountain or snow need be present, but the skier can close her eyes and imagine skiing. Any experience that satisfies these conditions can be called imagery.

A third aspect of imagery, neglected in many other approaches to understanding this subjective process, is the meaning of the image. This aspect of imagery was emphasized by Ahsen (1984), who argued that imagery can only be fully understood by examining three components of imagery: image (the centrally aroused sensation), the somatic element (the physiological response), and meaning (the interpretation or significance of the image).

A striking feature of attempts to define athletic imagery is that these definitions rely on self-reported experience. There are no immediately observable behavioral correlates of imagery, although the mental practice paradigm was an attempt to measure behavioral changes due to imagery effects. Until recently, it was difficult to ascertain what, if anything, might be happening to an individual who reportedly was engaged in imagery. However, methodologies now exist that allow us to examine some physiological and cognitive correlates of imagery. These methodologies help us understand athletic imagery from new perspectives.

A THREE-LEVEL MODEL OF IMAGERY USE IN SPORT

We propose that by examining imagery from several current perspectives, we will be able to resolve some of the problems in past research and generate an effective guide for future research. In figure 13.2, we present a three-level model of athletic imagery, developed to serve as a research guide.[1] Development of this model began with the proposition that imagery can be understood on several levels. Indeed, the sharply different definitions of imagery examined previously arise from analyzing imagery at different levels.

At the most fundamental level, imagery can be viewed as a physiological and cognitive process. For example, cognitive neuroscientists have proposed that both motor imagery and visual imagery are generated through neuronal processes involving specific brain structures (Kosslyn & Koenig, 1992). Level 1 research attempts to identify the physiological structures involved in a subject's use of imagery and to determine how imagery is incorporated in the visual system or in motor control processes or other self-regulatory

processes. Such research seeks to understand both the physiological substrates underlying imagery as well as the cognitive models that describe the imagery process. Richardson's (1969) is a Level 1 definition of imagery. This level of research was barely addressed within the mental practice model.

Instead, research into mental practice was concerned primarily with the second level of imagery—the use of imagery to achieve performance goals. The fundamental research question addressed by mental practice research was whether it enhances performance. A different way of looking at Level 2 research, however, is to ask how imagery influences performance. For example, at the conclusion of their meta-analytic review of the literature, Feltz and Landers (1983) expressed the hope that their review would "redirect the research efforts of those interested in mental practice away from simply empirical demonstrations of mental practice effects on performance toward an examination of the variables that may moderate or mediate the relations between mental practice and motor performance" (p. 51).

The present analysis suggests, however, that further research of the "mental practice" concept as a basis for Level 2 research is not justified. The three-level model suggests that a more useful research strategy is to use the concepts being studied in Level 1 research as a basis for understanding how athletes use imagery to control and manage their athletic performance. This strategy examines imagery and its relationship to a variety of other psychomotor processes such as perception, decision-making, and feedback as well as to such central psychological processes as motivation, confidence, and concentration. Imagery is studied in a much broader context than simply the rehearsal of motor skills. In this chapter we discuss the development of such a strategy.

Beyond the nature and use of imagery, however, lies another level of analysis. Imagery, as well as being a physiological event, is an experiential event with a variety of associations of meaning for the individual. This suggests that understanding imagery use in sport would be incomplete without understanding the phenomenology of imagery. We propose that this is the third level of imagery research. Theorists such as Ahsen (1984) have stressed the importance of understanding the meaning of imagery to the in-

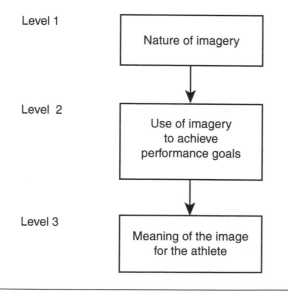

Figure 13.2 A three-level model of imagery in sport.

---

1. The idea for a three-level model of imagery research was stimulated by an article by Susan Drake (1996). However, our model has different levels of analysis than those proposed by Drake.

dividual, but very little Level 3 research has been conducted in sport psychology. Given the growth of descriptive and qualitative research in sport psychology (e.g., Gould, Jackson, & Finch, 1993; Jackson, 1992), this appears to be a most promising research area.

In the remainder of this chapter we examine research that has been conducted at each of the three levels of athletic imagery. We conclude with some proposals for strengthening future research by using the three-level model of athletic imagery.

Level 1: The Nature of the Imagery Process

A fundamental question is, How does the cognitive processing of mental practice take place: through visual imagery, through kinesthetic imagery, or through verbal mediation? As far back as 1939, Perry contended that mental practice was not mediated by imagery processes at all but was mediated primarily by subject verbalizations. This approach suggests that verbal strategies (such as cue labeling) might underlie the mental practice effects found in many studies. A few studies have directly compared imagery strategies and verbal and other strategies. R.N. Singer, Goren, and Risdale (1979) found that an imagery strategy produced more accurate responses and fewer errors on a curvilinear repositioning apparatus than did a labeling, a kinesthetic, and an informed-choice strategy. In another study, R.N. Singer, Risdale, and Korienek (1980) found that imagery and chunking strategies produced more accurate and consistent performances in a movement sequencing task than did a rhythm strategy and a control condition.

This line of research suggests that verbal mediation alone cannot fully account for the mental practice phenomenon. Especially when tasks involving item information or location information are used (Housner, 1984), visual imagery ability seems to be an important determinant of the effectiveness of mental practice. The literature on observational learning (Bandura, 1971) also supports the notion that cognitive processes beyond verbal mediation are involved when modeling is used to acquire motor skills. According to the modeling account of learning, the learner matches executed movement patterns with a conceptual representation or standard. This conceptual representation provides feedback so that corrections can be made on subsequent movement executions. Several studies support the existence of

such a process (Bandura, Jeffery, & Bachicha, 1974; Carroll & Bandura, 1982; Shea, 1977). Although the nature of the conceptual representation is not yet clear, many theorists believe that imagery is involved in this internal representation (cf. Denis, 1985; Richardson, 1985). The literature discussing the mental operations involved in the acquisition of motor movements also refers to the role and function of imagery in mental practice (for more detailed discussions, see Keele, 1982; Magill, 1984; Stelmach & Hughes, 1984).

Interdisciplinary research appears to be moving in the direction of trying to determine the nature of the internal representations generated during imagery rehearsal and how they function. Determining the nature of the encoding of imagery material has been the source of fierce debate in the information-processing literature. A popular view has been that humans encode information in the brain in two ways, pictorially and verbally (Paivio, 1971). Although this approach has been criticized vigorously by theorists who believe that all information is encoded in propositions (or verbally mediated; Pylyshyn, 1973, 1981), newer theories in the information-processing realm have returned to various pictorially or spatially based explanations of imagery (see Pinker & Kosslyn, 1983). Various innovative experimental methodologies have been generated in an attempt to further understand the nature of imagery (Shepard & Metzler, 1971).

The mental practice model generated two major approaches to explaining why mental practice might benefit performance. These approaches are known as the psychoneuromuscular hypothesis and the symbolic learning hypothesis. Both approaches were developed to explain the mental practice phenomenon—why does mentally rehearsing a physical activity improve physical performance?

The major difference between the hypotheses is that the psychoneuromuscular hypothesis locates the effects of imagery in the peripheral musculature and in the feedback loop between muscles and the central nervous system, whereas the symbolic learning hypothesis argues for a centrally mediated learning process, whereby cognitive representations of action are strengthened or organized through repeated activation. The research based on these two approaches has been described extensively in other reviews (Perry & Morris, 1995; Richardson, 1969) and in the previous edition of our chapter, so we will limit our comments on both approaches.

The Psychoneuromuscular Hypothesis and Psychophysiological Explanations of Imagery

The psychoneuromuscular explanation of mental practice is that the muscles involved in the skill being imagined become slightly innervated during mental practice, sufficiently to provide kinesthetic feedback that can be used to make skill adjustments on future trials. Although this explanation has been proposed by a number of researchers (Corbin, 1972; Richardson, 1967b; Schmidt, 1987), it has never been fully developed or stated in sufficient detail to truly deserve being termed a "theory."

Psychoneuromuscular explanations of mental practice effects have a long tradition. As early as the end of the last century, Jastrow (1892) examined and found involuntary movements occurring during various mental operations. According to the ideomotor principle (Carpenter, 1894), an image will produce muscular activity similar to that during actual movement but at a lesser magnitude. Washburn (1916), in *Movement and Mental Imagery*, also suggested that "tentative movements" occur during imagery. Furthermore, the tentative movements during imagery were believed to influence subsequent skilled behavior.

Jacobson (1930a, 1930b, 1930c, 1930d, 1931a, 1931b) extensively researched the area and found that muscle activity while a subject imagined such activities as bending his or her forearm, lifting (curling) a weight, or climbing a rope was generally greater than the muscle activity associated with rest. Furthermore, the muscle activity was located in the specific muscles associated with the movement being studied. Jacobson believed that this research demonstrated that mental practice must be associated with muscle innervation.

From the experimental psychology field, a substantial amount of research has provided evidence that the effects of mental practice cannot be explained by muscular activity during imagery and that mental practice is more a function of operations within the central nervous system (Johnson, 1982; Kohl & Roenker, 1980, 1983). To date, results from studies examining the neuromuscular basis of mental practice in the psychology literature support the contention that the muscular responses, although present (Qualls, 1982), are effects rather than causes of performance changes. Evidence to support a relationship between muscular activity during mental practice and subsequent performance in the sport-related literature has yet to be obtained.

The failure to demonstrate such a relationship is one of the most significant reasons for the current skepticism regarding the psychoneuromuscular hypothesis. Feltz and Landers (1983) in their review of the mental practice literature concluded, "It is doubtful that mental practice effects are produced by low-gain innervation of muscles that will be used during actual performance" (p. 48).

There is little direct evidence to suggest that feedback to the premotor cortex from minute innervations of the peripheral musculature causes mental practice effects. Although the psychoneuromuscular hypothesis fails to explain mental practice effects, it has been a useful heuristic for focusing attention on the psychophysiological mechanisms underlying motor imagery. Our understanding of the relationship between mental activity and physiological responses is still in its infancy, and a more sophisticated, physiologically based theory of mental practice may enhance our understanding of the relationship between imagery and athletic performance.

For example, Mackay (1981) proposed that the use of imagery before performance may "prime" the appropriate muscles, leading to better performance. It is also plausible that the use of imagery affects a variety of physiological systems via its impact on the athlete's cognitive and emotional state. Feltz and Landers (1983) proposed that mental practice may facilitate the development of an "attentional set" for an athlete. Mental practice also may influence performance by facilitating the development of an appropriate "emotional set" for an athlete, enhancing emotions that are critical for effective competitive performance such as confidence and calm.

Urgently needed are investigations of the effects of athletic imagery on the body's physiological responses in preparation for performance. Variables that should be assessed in future research efforts include electromyogram (EMG), electroencephalogram, galvanic skin response, heart rate, and measures of those endocrine products postulated to be involved in effective physical performance, such as endorphins, epinephrine, and cortisol. The impressive and growing body of knowledge in psychoneuroimmunology (Achterberg, Lawlis, Simonton, & Matthews-Simonton, 1977; Lloyd, 1987; Locke, 1982; Marx, 1985; Wechsler, 1987) shows that relationships between cognitive and emotional activity and physiological processes are accessible to empirical investigation, especially with the advanced research technologies available today. The field of sport, with its great emphasis on measuring physical performance, should be especially amenable to testing some of these speculative relationships.

In contrast to psychoneuromuscular explanations, theorists who propose that a symbolic learning explanation of mental practice effects is most compatible with extant research argue that the effects of mental practice are due to operations within the central nervous system. This perspective is reviewed in the next section.

Symbolic Learning Theory and Cognitive Explanations

The symbolic learning hypothesis, sometimes known as the symbolic–perceptual hypothesis (Denis, 1985), holds that mental practice benefits performance because it allows participants to cognitively prepare for and plan performance. Participants can rehearse the sequential aspects of a task, consider the spatial characteristics of the skill, clarify task goals, identify potential problems in performance, and plan effective procedures for task execution. All of these procedures are based in the central nervous system, and, unlike the psychoneuromuscular approach, their execution does not imply the involvement of the peripheral musculature. Symbolic learning approaches to the mental practice phenomenon go back many years, at least to the work of Sackett (1934, 1935) and Perry (1939).

Two main bodies of evidence support the symbolic learning approach. First, a number of studies have shown that mental practice is more effective for tasks that have a high cognitive (as opposed to a motor) component. Second, theoretical accounts of motor learning that argue that the early stages of learning are primarily cognitive (e.g., Fitts, 1962) are compatible with the notion that mental practice will have its greatest effects during the early stages of learning. Several studies have examined whether mental practice is most effective during the early stages of learning. Additionally, recent research that uses sophisticated experimental methodologies has shed light on the symbolic learning explanation controversy. Next we examine these three areas of research.

Effects of Task Characteristics on Mental Practice.
This category of research has examined the nature of the task as a variable influencing mental practice effects. In this approach, tasks

are classified on a continuum ranging from mainly motor tasks to predominantly cognitive tasks. The symbolic learning hypothesis states that the effects of mental practice should be greatest for tasks lying more on the cognitive (symbolic) end of the continuum. For example, a stabilometer task would be classified as mostly a motor task because of the greater involvement of motor components, as opposed to a digit symbol substitution task, which is more symbolic in nature.

Feltz and Landers (1983), in their meta-analysis of research, found that the effects of mental practice on symbolic tasks were greater than the effects on motor or strength tasks. Because this relationship was so clear, even across 60 different studies using many methodologies, Feltz and Landers concluded that the distinction between symbolic and motor aspects of motor skill learning is very robust, therefore strongly supporting the symbolic–perceptual hypothesis. In a replication of the Feltz and Landers study, Oslin (1985) found that the effects of mental practice on symbolic tasks were greater than effects on motor or strength tasks.

Evidence clearly favors the position that mental practice produces the greatest effects on tasks that are high in symbolic (or cognitive) components, supporting the symbolic learning explanation of mental practice. Another research tradition has examined the relative effectiveness of mental practice at different stages of motor skill learning. This research is examined next.

Relationship of Mental Practice to Stages of Learning.
Fitts (1962) identified the first stage of learning as the cognitive phase. In this phase, the learner attends to cognitive (or symbolic) cues regarding the task, spending much time processing information. Mental practice may assist in the organization of such data at the central processing level. In their meta-analytic review of the literature, Feltz and Landers (1983) found that the average mental practice effect size for experienced subjects (at a later learning stage) was larger than that for novice subjects (at an earlier learning stage), although this difference was not significant. This finding runs counter to the hypothesis that mental practice is most effective during early learning. Oslin (1985) found similar results and also showed that experienced subjects tended to use cognitive strategies more often than novice subjects.

More research is necessary before strong conclusions can be drawn about the relationship between the subject's stage of learning and mental practice effects. It is plausible that mental practice serves an organizational and planning role in the early stages of learning of a task and is therefore beneficial to the novice. For imagery rehearsal to be effective, however, it is highly probable that the learner should have a correct internal representation of the task. This could be gained through experience or modeling. Some theorists have questioned the validity of the notion that symbolic factors become less important to learning as it progresses (Adams, 1981). They argue that mental practice should be effective later in learning just as it is early in the learning process, although it might achieve its impact through different processes (motor program strengthening and diversification, e.g., rather than motor program organization). Literature reviews tend to support this position (Feltz & Landers, 1983).

Research on the stages of learning may be more important from a practical viewpoint than a theoretical one. Newer and better methodologies are being found to examine the symbolic learning question. The stage of learning research only indirectly tests the symbolic learning hypothesis. In the next section, we examine more recent research that offers stronger support for the symbolic learning explanation.

Cognitive Research.   Bilateral transfer studies have provided evidence consistent with a central processing account of mental practice effects. Kohl and Roenker (1980) showed that when the task was physically performed with the left hand, subjects who had mentally practiced using their right hand performed as well as or better than subjects who had physically practiced with their right hand. Later studies by the same researchers again showed that performance after mental practice was similar between unilateral and bilateral transfer (Kohl & Roenker, 1983). The authors suggested that the neuromuscular activity concomitant with mental practice is an effect rather than a causal mechanism. They argued that the mechanisms underlying the effects of mental practice are centrally based.

An examination of the type of bias that visual and motor interference would have on the reproduction of movements on a linear positioning task provided further evidence that the effects of mental practice are due to cognitive processes (Johnson, 1982). Research investigating the physiological responses of the brain during imagery also provide interesting results relevant to the symbolic learning explanation. Differences in the

electroencephalographic activity patterns of subjects were found when comparing visual and kinesthetic imagery (Davidson & Schwartz, 1977). A review of recent psychophysiological research into the neuronal processes underlying motor imagery suggests that motor images share the same neural mechanisms that are responsible for preparation and programming of actual movements (Decety, 1996). This relationship has been called "functional equivalence" (Moran, 1996), which also may be applicable to the relationship between visual imagery and the neural substrates for vision (Finke, 1985).

A strong body of research supports centrally based mechanisms in the effectiveness of mental practice. The weakness of symbolic learning explanations is that they describe the location of the effect of mental practice without describing the nature of the imagery processes involved. For example, do the "cognitive" effects of mental practice occur in the encoding, the retrieval, the organization, or the execution of the skill? Without a rigorous explanatory framework, the symbolic learning approach cannot serve as a useful heuristic for researchers. With advances in brain imaging and other assessment techniques, it may be possible to more thoroughly explain symbolic learning in mental practice.

The final model to be examined that addresses the nature of imagery (Level 1 understanding) is a clinical model that draws from an information-processing approach to generate a different way of looking at performance imagery.

An Information-Processing Model

A model of imagery originally developed by Peter Lang to understand research into phobia and anxiety disorders deals specifically with the psychophysiology of imagery. Lang's model uses an information-processing model of imagery (Lang, 1977, 1979) and begins with the assumption that an image is a functionally organized, finite set of propositions stored by the brain. The model further states that a description of an image contains two main types of statements: stimulus propositions and response propositions. Stimulus propositions are statements that describe the content of the scenario to be imagined. Response propositions are statements that describe the individual's response to that imagery scenario.

The image is also believed to incorporate a motor program containing instructions for the individual on how to respond to the image, and it is thus a template for overt responding. Lang's theory assumes that modifying either overt behavior or vivid imagery will change the other. This relationship, it is argued, explains the therapeutic impact of imagery. Lack of identity between the physiological pattern of the perceptual–affective response in overt behavior and in vivid imagery will lead to therapeutic failure.

The crucial point is that response propositions are a fundamental part of the image structure in Lang's theory. The image is not just a stimulus "in the person's head" to which he or she responds. The information-processing model of imagery derives from materialism and a rejection of dualism—the "mental image," in fact, is given a physical presence via its location as a set of propositions in the brain. Imagery does not "trigger" physiological responses in the body but rather incorporates them. Lang and others have demonstrated in a variety of psychophysiological studies that imagery is accompanied by an efferent outflow appropriate to the content of the image (Brady & Levitt, 1966; Brown, 1968; Hale, 1982; Jacobson, 1932; Lang, 1979; Shaw, 1940). Lang's studies of phobic patients have indicated that the greater the magnitude of these physiological responses during imagery, the greater will be the accompanying changes in behavior (Lang, Melamed, & Hart, 1970). Also, imagery instructions that contain response propositions elicit far more physiological responses than do imagery instructions that contain only stimulus propositions (Lang, Kozak, Miller, Levin, & McLean, 1980).

An initial study that used Lang's theory was that of Hecker and Kaczor (1988). Four imagery scenes were used: a neutral scene, an unfamiliar fear scene, a familiar action scene, and a familiar athletic anxiety scene. All scene descriptions contained response propositions except the neutral scene. Heart rate was the only physiological measure. Results showed that physiological response was significantly greater during the familiar action and athletic anxiety scenes (for which subjects presumably had a prototype for overt responding) compared with the fear scene. Physiological response was also significantly greater during the action scene compared with the neutral scene. Although this study somewhat confirms Lang's theory, it was not designed to investigate whether physiological responses during imagery contribute to subsequent behavior (performance) change. This prediction should be investigated by sport psychology researchers.

Although developed independently of Lang's model, Suinn's (1976) visual motor behavior rehearsal (VMBR) model is similar in that he proposed that imagery should be a holistic process that involves a total reintegration of experience, including visual, auditory, tactile, kinesthetic, and emotional cues. Suinn's model provides an excellent example of how the physiological and emotional aspects of imagery can be incorporated into imagery-based interventions by sport psychologists. Indeed, Suinn has demonstrated that physiological responses can be obtained from athletes experiencing athletic imagery (Suinn, 1983), and the VMBR method has received empirical support for its effectiveness (Seabourne, Weinberg, Jackson, & Suinn, 1985).

Summary

Each of the three approaches described here furthers our understanding of the nature of imagery use in sports. The psychoneuromuscular approach, although most likely wrong in predicting that sports performance improves because of low-gain innervation of muscles that will be used during actual performance, focuses attention on the psychophysiological nature of imagery. The symbolic learning hypothesis seems to correctly predict that sports imagery is a centrally located process; now it remains for us to identify the actual brain mechanisms and neural pathways involved. Lang's bioinformational approach is useful because it generates testable hypotheses and relates sports imagery to the field of information processing. However, like the symbolic learning hypothesis, it is not a complete model of imagery use by athletes, and it offers little guidance regarding the many uses of imagery by athletes beyond simple performance rehearsal. Such a complete model must incorporate these other uses of imagery in sport, a task we undertake in the next section.

Level 2: The Use of Imagery to Achieve Goals

The second level on which imagery in sport can be approached involves the instrumental nature of imagery, the various ways in which athletes use imagery to reach specific goals. Imagery interventions have long been popular among applied sport psychologists as a means of helping athletes manage their sports performance. Of the many books that have described psychological interventions in sport, all of them contain at least one chapter on imagery applications (Bennett & Pravitz, 1987; Loehr, 1986; Orlick, 1986, 1990; Porter & Foster, 1986; Williams, 1986; Zaichowsky & Fuchs, 1986). Imagery-based techniques have been used for a wide variety of purposes beyond performance rehearsal, including pain management and arousal regulation. However, few researchers have attempted to systematically describe the ways in which imagery is used in athletic settings.

Recently, an applied model of athletic imagery has been developed (figure 13.3) that conceptualizes the sport situation, the type of imagery used, and imagery ability as factors that determine the outcome of imagery use (K.A. Martin, Moritz, & Hall, 1999). This model proposes that different types of imagery will be used for different athletic goals. Unlike the mental practice model, this model is able to describe athletes' use of imagery to achieve a variety of cognitive, behavioral, and affective changes. Another important feature of this model is that it centers on imagery content (i.e., what the athlete images) as a key determinant of these changes.

The Central Role of Imagery Content

Theorists (e.g., Paivio, 1985) and clinicians (e.g., Suinn, 1996) have linked different types of images with different types of outcomes. For example, Suinn (1996) emphasized that "the content of the imagery is determined by which goals the clinician seeks to achieve: coping, skill acquisition, error analysis, error correction and self-efficacy strengthening . . . altering personal self-image, self-

schemas, or self-perceptions" (p. 31). Yet, despite the theoretical and clinical importance placed on imagery content, this topic has received very little research attention in sport psychology. Until recently, the only studies of imagery content were those that compared the effects of positive and negative imagery. These few studies demonstrated that performance decrements occur when subjects are asked to image themselves failing at a task. For example, studies of both dart-throwing (Powell, 1973) and golf-putting (Woolfolk, Parrish, & Murphy, 1985) showed that imagery of a negative performance outcome (i.e., missing the target or hole) produced poorer performance than imagery of a positive performance outcome (i.e., hitting a bull's-eye, sinking the putt).

In addition to negative outcome imagery, other aspects of imagery content can affect performance-related cognitions and emotions (Murphy, 1990). During the past decade, researchers have begun to identify the various types of images used by athletes (C.R. Hall, Mack, Paivio, & Hausenblas, 1998; C.R. Hall et al., 1990; MacIntyre & Moran, 1996) and their potential effects, such as increased confidence (Moritz, Hall, Martin, & Vadocz, 1996) and decreased anxiety (Vadocz, Hall, & Moritz, 1997). Thus far, five types of imagery have been identified and classified by using a taxonomy developed by Hall and his colleagues (C.R. Hall et al., 1998):

- **Motivational specific (MS).** Paivio (1985) suggested that a crucial function of mental practice for athletes might be to motivate the athlete when

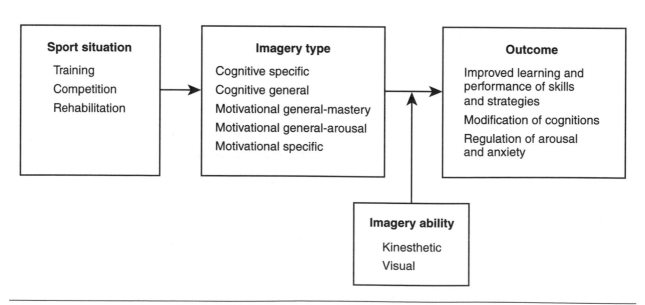

Figure 13.3   An applied model of imagery use in sport.

reinforcers are rare. MS imagery represents specific goals and goal-oriented behaviors such as imagining oneself winning an event, standing on a podium receiving a medal, and being congratulated by other athletes for a good performance.

- **Motivational general–mastery (MG–M).** More general imagery that serves a motivational and mastery perspective function is included in this category. The content of such imagery represents effective coping and mastery of challenging situations, such as imagining being mentally tough, confident, and focused during sport competition.

- **Motivational general–arousal (MG–A).** The athletic imagery in this category focuses on emotional experiences in sport. Imagery that represents feelings of relaxation, stress, arousal, and anxiety in conjunction with sport competition falls in this category.

- **Cognitive specific (CS).** CS imagery is based on imagery rehearsal of specific athletic skills. Images of specific sport skills such as penalty shots in soccer or balance beam dismounts in gymnastics are examples of this category. Most of the mental practice literature deals with imagery of this type.

- **Cognitive general (CG).** Little research attention has been paid to the use of imagery to develop cognitive plans for athletic events. CG imagery refers to the strategies related to a competitive event, such as imaging using full court pressure in basketball or a baseline game in tennis.

The Sport Imagery Questionnaire (SIQ) was developed to measure the extent to which these five imagery types are used (C.R. Hall et al., 1998). The list of SIQ imagery types is probably not exhaustive. It is likely that as researchers further explore athletes' imagery content and its association with sport-related affect and cognition, other types of imagery will be identified. In the meantime, the five SIQ factors represent an attempt to provide a parsimonious taxonomy for athletic imagery content, in the hope that further research will clarify how imagery content affects the athlete and athletic performance.

The Purpose of Imagery Use by Athletes

The five SIQ imagery types form the crux of the model by K.A. Martin et al. (1999). As depicted in figure 13.3, different sport situations (e.g., training vs. competition) are likely to be associated with different types of athletic goals and thus with different types of images. Moreover, imagery abil-

ity is hypothesized to moderate the effectiveness of imagery used by athletes. The next section describes some of the goals, or outcomes, that athletic imagery is used to support. Where possible, evidence is presented that supports the use of a particular type of imagery (i.e., MS, MG–M, MG–A, CS, and CG) to achieve a particular outcome goal (e.g., skill acquisition, arousal regulation).

Skill Acquisition. The mental practice model emphasizes this purpose for athletic imagery, and consequently researchers have devoted considerable attention to studying mental imagery as a tool for facilitating the acquisition of discrete motor skills. Research suggests that the greater the number of cognitive components of the skill, the greater the effects of imagery on learning (Driskell, Copper, & Moran 1994). In fact, some researchers have suggested that "tasks which emphasize kinesthetic cues may not be mentally rehearsable" (Wrisberg & Ragsdale, 1979, p. 207). Although this assertion is challenged by the self-report of many athletes who emphasize the importance of kinesthetic rehearsal, the evidence suggests that primarily motoric tasks require a certain level of familiarity with the skill before imagery can be effective. Presumably, imagery helps the learner develop a conceptual plan for understanding and organizing cognitive tasks.

Some writers (e.g., Gallwey, 1974; Heil, 1985) have suggested that there are two principal ways of learning new motor skills. One way is primarily verbal and analytical, whereas the other is intuitive and global. According to these writers, the second method has much to recommend it, particularly in overcoming the self-critical anxiety that often accompanies the learning of a new skill. Anyone who has learned a sport skill such as a golf swing will certainly remember a time when attention needed to be directed to many subcomponents of the total skill for even a poor approximation of the skill to occur (the molecular approach), and another time, often much later, when a feeling of "gestalt" occurred, and correct skill execution seemed to occur automatically (the molar approach). An interesting research area would be to investigate whether imagery techniques can enhance the transfer of attention from the molecular to the molar level and thus hasten skill acquisition. Another area within the skill acquisition domain that deserves attention is research into the use of imagery by children learning new skills. This appears to be an excellent area of study to further our knowledge of motor skill acquisition.

A few experiments have compared the effects of different types of imagery on the acquisition of motor skills, and all have demonstrated the superiority of CS imagery. For example, in the early stages of a training program for beginner runners (Burhans, Richman, & Bergey, 1988), participants who used CS imagery (imaging perfect performance of all the movements associated with running) showed greater performance improvements than participants who used MS imagery (imaging "crossing the finish line ahead of all the competitors . . . receiving awards, newspaper interviews and being cheered by spectators"). Similarly, Murphy, Woolfolk, and Budney (1988) found that an MG–A strategy was ineffective for improving performance on a strength task. They suggested that arousal imagery may not facilitate performance unless it is accompanied by CS imagery (i.e., imagery of task performance). C. Lee (1990) found that task-relevant imagery (MS) improved performance on a sit-up task significantly more than task-irrelevant imagery (MG–A). These findings suggest that compared with other types of imagery, CS imagery may be the most effective for promoting athletes' acquisition of individual motor skills.

Skill Maintenance. CS imagery is used most often used by athletes to maintain sport skills (K.A. Martin et al., 1999). Despite the wealth of mental imagery studies examining a variety of skills, surprisingly few have looked at the effects of imagery on long-term retention of these skills. Retention tests are much more common in the motor learning area but should be included more frequently in mental practice research. The few studies that have examined retention (e.g., Meacci & Price, 1985) tend to report superior retention for subjects who use an imagery strategy during learning relative to subjects who do not. Yet it would be interesting to examine whether a skill, once learned, could be maintained for long periods of time by imagery alone. It might be possible to establish separate "forgetting" curves for skills not physically practiced but rehearsed with and without mental imagery. Certainly there have been several testimonial accounts of athletes who have maintained their sport skills for long periods by mental practice alone. Empirical verification of these accounts would be extremely relevant for injured athletes, who could use imagery to maintain their skills while rehabilitating.

Developing Athletic Plans and Strategies. Of the five types of imagery measured by the SIQ (C.R. Hall et al., 1998), CG imagery (imagery of game plans and strategies) has received the least empirical attention. However, case study reports have documented the benefits of CG imagery for rehearsing football plays (Fenker & Lambiotte, 1987), wrestling strategies (Rushall, 1988), and entire canoe slalom races (MacIntyre & Moran, 1996). Indeed, CG imagery is commonly used in sport psychology interventions to prepare athletes for upcoming competitions. A good example of this strategy was provided by Rotella, Gansneder, Ojala, and Billing (1980). In their study, successful skiers developed a visual image of the course after previewing it. In the time between inspecting the course and reaching the starting gate, they planned and imaged effective strategies for skiing the course. Less successful skiers, on the other hand, simply tried to maintain positive thoughts before racing.

CG imagery also can be used to plan how an athlete will deal with the entire competition process, from the time she wakes up on competition morning to the time she leaves the competition site. In his book *Psyching for Sport* (1986), Terry Orlick provided a detailed guide for constructing what he called a "competition focus plan," which can be mentally practiced and visualized as often as one wishes before competition. We are not aware of any empirical studies investigating the effectiveness of this imagery intervention. However, mental practice findings regarding the effectiveness of imagery rehearsal in organizing tasks in a conceptual framework suggest that this approach to event planning has merit.

Arousal and Anxiety Regulation. Imagery techniques have long been used in clinical psychology to induce relaxation. This approach has been adopted in sport psychology as a way of calming the anxious and aroused athlete before competition. Sport psychologists (e.g., Harris & Harris, 1984; Orlick, 1990) suggest that various non-sport-specific types of imagery (such as picturing oneself in a peaceful, relaxing place, or imagining muscular tension seeping out of the body and into the air) can relax the athlete. These types of images approximate the MG–A imagery category and can restore a sense of calm when the athlete gets nervous or worried.

Sport psychologists also have suggested that mental imagery can be used to elevate an athlete's level of arousal in preparation for competitive performance. According to bioinformational theory, athletes should use images associated with stress, anxiety, and excitement (i.e., MG–A imagery) to increase arousal. Evidence from anecdotal reports and from research that has examined the use of psych-up strategies in sport indicates that this is, in fact, what athletes do (Caudill et al., 1983; Munroe, Hall, Simms, & Weinberg, 1998; Shelton & Mahoney, 1978). Moreover, MG–A imagery appears to be most effective for increasing arousal. In one study (Hecker & Kaczor, 1988), athletes' heart rates significantly increased above baseline levels when they used an MG–A imagery strategy (i.e., imagery of sport scenes that included response propositions such as "you feel your heart begin to pound" and "you feel butterflies in your stomach"). In contrast, other experiments found that imagery had no effect on arousal when a CS imagery strategy was used (Anshel & Wrisberg, 1993; Weinberg, Seabourne, & Jackson, 1981). In these studies, the preperformance heart rates of participants who imaged successful task performance were no different than the heart rates of participants in a no-imagery control condition. Presumably, unlike MG–A imagery, CS imagery lacks the stimulus characteristics and response propositions required to increase arousal.

Stress Management. In addition to using imagery to manipulate arousal levels at the competition site, athletes also can use imagery to preplan and rehearse their emotional responses before competition. For example, an athlete might sit down with a sport psychologist and list all of the thoughts and feelings she typically experiences in a race situation. Then she identifies the emotions that might interfere with performance or prevent her from giving maximum effort, for example, feelings such as intense fatigue, panic, or depression. Next, the athlete and sport psychologist devise strategies to replace these negative emotions with more appropriate cognitive strategies, perhaps through the use of thought stopping, positive self-talk, or self-affirmations (Porter & Foster, 1986). Finally, the athlete rehearses a race using imagery and sees herself coping successfully by using the techniques she has practiced. The goal of such interventions is for the athlete to develop and become familiar with a set of successful strategies for coping with stress (cf. Lazarus & Folkman, 1984).

There is good support for the effectiveness of these types of imagery-based interventions in teaching athletes to modify their responses to stressful performance. For example, studies have shown stress inoculation training (SIT; Meichenbaum, 1985) to be an effective strategy for con-

trolling anxiety levels before athletic performance (Kerr & Leith, 1993; Mace & Carroll, 1985). SIT is a treatment package that teaches skills for coping with stress and anxiety, and it provides opportunities for rehearsing these skills in imagery. During SIT, athletes are instructed to image the stress and anxiety associated with sport competition and then see themselves dealing with it effectively. The imagery used in SIT is of the MG–A type. This suggests that MG–A may be the most appropriate type of imagery to use when emotional regulation is the athlete's goal.

Imagery combined with relaxation training also can be used to manage stress (Cogan & Petrie, 1995). Consistent with bioinformational theory (Lang, 1977, 1979), it is possible that when athletes pair imagery of their skills with a relaxation response, this response carries over to real-life competitive situations (Lang et al., 1970). In other words, athletes are less stressed and anxious in competitive situations because they have learned, through imagery rehearsal, to feel calm and relaxed in competitive situations (cf. Orlick, 1990). The significant changes in anxiety after SIT and combined imagery–relaxation interventions suggest that imagery rehearsal that includes feelings of relaxation can affect an athlete's level of competitive anxiety. However, further research is needed to tease apart the effects of imagery per se and the effects of other aspects of these interventions (e.g., self-talk in SIT and progressive muscle relaxation in the imagery–relaxation interventions).

Confidence. Imagery's impact on self-confidence has long been recognized by cognitive–behavioral therapists, who have developed a number of imagery strategies that encourage behavior change by asking clients to imagine more successful behaviors than they presently exhibit. These imagery strategies include systematic desensitization (Wolpe, 1958), flooding (Rachman, 1968), coping imagery (Meichenbaum, 1977), implosion (Levis & Hare, 1977), and covert modeling (Cautela & Kearney, 1986).

A case we encountered several years ago illustrates the use of imagery to effect self-confidence in sport. A young athlete sought consultation because she felt she had a problem in defeating opponents who were higher ranked than she. Analysis revealed that she lacked confidence when competing against these individuals, despite possessing the skills necessary to defeat them. This lack of confidence translated into unusually poor performances against good players. An intervention strategy was designed whereby the athlete used MS and MG–M imagery to visualize herself defeating specific higher rated opponents and the consequences of these victories (how others would react, her own emotional response, and so on). Within weeks, she had achieved first-time victories against several ranked opponents. She attributed her success to a newfound confidence generated by her imagery rehearsal.

MG–M imagery may be the most effective type of imagery for enhancing an athlete's self-confidence. The use of images associated with success and competence has been found to be associated with greater self-confidence (Moritz et al., 1996; Vadocz et al., 1997) and self-efficacy (Feltz & Riessinger, 1990). In addition, a recent intervention study examined the effects of an MG–M imagery intervention on the sport confidence of three elite badminton players (Callow, Hardy, & Hall, 1998). A single-subject multiple baseline design was used. Once a week for 20 weeks, players completed Vealey's (1986b) State Sport Confidence Inventory before a match. A baseline for sport confidence was established, and the imagery intervention was implemented for Players 1, 2, and 3 at Weeks 5, 7, and 9, respectively. The 2-week, six-session intervention consisted of imagery associated with confidence, control, and successful management of challenging situations. The intervention increased sport confidence for two of the players and stabilized the other player's level of confidence. It was concluded that an imagery intervention (using MG–M imagery) can improve sport confidence.

Injury Rehabilitation and Pain Management.
Imagery-based techniques have been suggested by several authors for use in injury rehabilitation, healing, and pain management (G. Epstein, 1989; Jaffe, 1980; Levine, 1982). The well-known work of Simonton, Mathews-Simonton, and Creighton (1978) popularized the use of imagery and visualization in assisting the healing process and fighting disease. Some authors have applied this approach to athletes and sports (e.g., Ievleva & Orlick, 1991; Lynch, 1987; Wiese & Weiss, 1987; Yukelson & Murphy, 1993), suggesting the use of visualization for healing sports injuries and coping with athletic pain. Because imagery use after deep relaxation is similar to hypnosis, the extensive literature on hypnosis effects is relevant in this area (Morgan, 1996). These studies have consistently found hypnosis to be effective in treating clinical pain, but only with hypnotic-susceptible patients (Wadden & Anderton, 1982).

A number of authors have described imagery methods that can help injured athletes. For ex-

ample, athletes may use motivational imagery to facilitate adherence to rehabilitation programs, maintain a positive attitude, and manage anxiety and tension (Kerr & Goss, 1996; Wiese, Weiss, & Yukelson, 1991). Athletes also can use imagery to lessen the impact of life- or sport-specific athletic stressors, thus decreasing muscular tension and perhaps the potential for sport injury (Green, 1992). Indeed, gymnasts assigned to a 6-week imagery and relaxation program reported fewer athletic injuries and physical symptoms than gymnasts in a control condition (A. Lee & Hewitt, 1987). Cognitive imagery also can be used to replace physical practice while recuperating. Although mental imagery appears useful for rehabilitating injured athletes, additional research is needed to identify the various types of imagery that are most beneficial to injured athletes (K.S. Martin et al., 1999).

Exercise Behavior.
Given that imagery can enhance athletes' motivation in sports settings (K.S. Martin & Hall, 1995), it is reasonable to suggest that imagery also can enhance participation motivation in exercise contexts (C.R. Hall, 1995). Recent research showed that regular participants in an aerobic dance class frequently used mental imagery to imagine themselves becoming healthier and improving their physical appearance (Hausenblas, Hall, Rodgers, & Munroe, 1997). Envisioning these future "possible selves" could have a potent effect on one's motivation to adhere to a regular exercise program (Gibbons & Gerrard, 1997). In addition, research conducted by physiotherapists (Riccio, Nelson, & Bush, 1990) has shown that imagery can enhance motivation by adding purpose to repetitive or monotonous exercises. Specifically, elderly women performed more repetitions of a reaching-up exercise when they imaged themselves "reaching up to pick up apples" compared with a condition in which no imagery was used. Regular exercisers also use imagery to rehearse the steps and patterns involved in aerobic dance classes (Hausenblas et al., 1997). When used in this way, imagery may facilitate the acquisition of skills required in a fitness program. Research examining the effects of imagery on exercise behavior is still in the preliminary stages, but both MG–M and CS imagery have been shown to be effective for exercisers. Imagery appears to be a viable strategy for enhancing motivation and adherence (C.R. Hall, 1995), and additional studies in this area certainly are warranted.

Concentration and Attention.
Feltz and Landers (1983) proposed that mental practice of

motor skills may facilitate the development of an "attentional set" for the athlete. This idea is an elaboration of the hypothesis that mental practice "primes" the body, especially the muscles, for motor skill execution (e.g., MacKay, 1981). Feltz and Landers argued that mental practice helps focus attention on the relevant aspects of performance, thus occupying attentional capacity and reducing the risk that attention will be directed toward irrelevant or distracting cues.

Borrowing from current concepts in cognitive neuropsychology, it is possible that a well-rehearsed image of a motor skill may be represented centrally by a specific neural network, so that athletes with good imagery skills may be better able to access information critical to successful task execution. This idea was explored in some detail by Moran (1996), who suggested that "researchers in sport psychology can benefit considerably from further collaboration with cognitive psychologists interested in the question of why practice leads to automaticity and improved performance of skills" (p. 229).

Clearly, imagery can be applied in many ways that go beyond the simple rehearsal of sport skills (Jones & Stuth, 1997). In some cases, applications have been developed and used before research has examined their efficacy. We hope that investigators recognize the exciting and rewarding research potential offered by empirical investigation of these interventions. It will be helpful in future research efforts if researchers describe the type of images that they prescribe in their imagery interventions. The model by K.A. Martin et al. (1999) provides a framework to identify the situations and applications associated with a particular type of imagery. The model also may be useful to practitioners who are trying to determine the type of imagery that will result in a particular therapeutic goal (cf. Suinn, 1996).

The model of imagery use in sport proposed by K.A. Martin et al. (1999) and discussed here moves the study of athletic imagery far beyond the confines of the mental practice model. In the next section, we discuss a third level of analysis available to imagery researchers, the analysis of the meaning of athletic imagery.

Level 3: The Meaning of the Image for the Athlete

The final level at which athletic imagery can be analyzed and understood involves the meaning of the imagery for the individual. Images tend to be associational in nature, and even simple images may carry a set of very individualized associations for an athlete. Even if an imagery script is used in an attempt to control the imagery experience across research subjects, individuals in a study will interpret the meaning of the image in a unique way. To date, no sport psychology theory has arrived at a consistent way of incorporating the meaning the image has for the individual within its parameters.

Ahsen's Triple Code Theory

Akhter Ahsen's triple code model of imagery (Ahsen, 1984), referred to as ISM, specifies the three essential parts of imagery that must be described by both theorist and clinician. The first part is the image (I) itself:

> *The image can be defined as a centrally aroused sensation. It possesses all the attributes of a sensation but it is internal at the same time. It represents the outside world and its objects with a degree of sensory realism that enables us to interact with the image as if we were interacting with a real world. (Ahsen, 1984, p. 34)*

The second part is the somatic response (S). That is, as Lang has demonstrated, the act of imagination results in psychophysiological changes in the body. The third aspect of imagery, mostly ignored by the other models, is the meaning (M) of the image. According to Ahsen, every image imparts a definite significance or meaning to the individual. Furthermore, every individual brings his or her unique history into the imagery process, so that the same set of imagery instructions will never produce the same imagery experience for any two individuals.

Ahsen's ISM triple code model reminds researchers to deal with three important aspects of imagery. Adopting the ISM approach suggests that the image script employed should be described completely, and the imagery experience (I component) of the subject should be obtained (e.g., by the content analysis method; M.P. Anderson, 1981b). Psychophysiological measures should be used more frequently, and imagery scripts should contain response propositions in addition to stimulus propositions (assessing the S component of imagery). And finally, the meaning of the image for the subject should be evaluated by the experimenter (measuring the M component of imagery).

Clearly, there has been far less research and theoretical speculation about the third level in our model than the first two levels. However, we have included this third level because we believe that a complete understanding of imagery use in sports is only possible by examining imagery at all three levels, as we demonstrate later in the chapter with some concrete examples. For now, our third level is a signpost, pointing the way to future research efforts.

We have proposed an alternative to the mental practice model of conceptualizing athletic imagery. The three-level analysis of athletic imagery presented here suggests that imagery can be understood and investigated on different levels, including understanding the nature of imagery, its utility in sport, and its meaning to individual athletes. Before concluding the chapter with a cautionary examination of some of the negative effects of imagery and a discussion of some assessment issues, we consider several factors that may have a crucial influence on the outcome of imagery applications with athletes. These factors include the imagery ability of the athlete, the perspective of the imagery, and the use of relaxation in conjunction with imagery.

CONSIDERATIONS IN THE APPLICATION OF ATHLETIC IMAGERY TO SPORTS PERFORMANCE

Several factors have a mediating influence on imagery when applied in sporting situations. In figure 13.3 we illustrate the effect of these variables as influencing the outcome of imagery interventions. The principal factor, which we include in the diagram, is imagery ability, but other factors have been studied and are discussed next.

Imagery Ability

Virtually everyone has the ability to generate and use imagery, but not to the same degree. Several researchers have suggested that mental imagery is most effective for people who are better imagers. Imagery ability typically has been defined by two primary characteristics—*vividness* and *controllability*. Vividness refers to the self-reported clarity and reality of the image, and controllability refers to one's ability to manipulate and direct the image. Controllability is best illustrated by Clark's classic report (1960) of a subject asked to

imagine making a basketball foul shot who reported that the ball would not bounce in his imagination but just stuck to the floor. This is an example of an uncontrolled image.

The major assessment instruments used to measure general imagery ability have been the Vividness of Imagery Scale (Sheehan's 1967 form of Betts's Questionnaire Upon Mental Imagery), the Vividness of Visual Imagery Questionnaire (Marks, 1973), and the Gordon Test of Visual Imagery Control (Richardson, 1969). These scales, however, do not assess one's ability to image movement. Thus, within the motor domain, the most popular imagery assessment tools are the Vividness of Movement Imagery Questionnaire (VMIQ; Isaac, Marks, & Russell, 1986) and the Movement Imagery Questionnaire (MIQ; C.R. Hall & Pongrac, 1983) and revised MIQ (MIQ–R; C.R. Hall & Martin, 1997). The VMIQ assesses only the vividness of visual imagery, whereas the MIQ assesses the ease with which one is able to image both kinesthetically and visually. The MIQ has been praised for directly assessing the kinesthetic component of imagery but also has been criticized for not differentiating between the movement aspect of kinesthetic imagery and the "force" or "effort" dimension of such imagery (Moran & MacIntyre, 1998).

The ability to kinesthetically image (i.e., image the "feel" of a movement) may be particularly relevant in the sport domain, where athletes have reported that they must be able to "feel" themselves doing a movement correctly in imagery before they are able to do it correctly in competition or practice (e.g., Orlick, 1990). Kinesthetic imagery was mentioned more often than visual imagery by high-level athletes in a study of canoe slalom participants (Moran & MacIntyre, 1998), and athletes in that study differentiated between feeling the movement of their limbs and feeling the force and effort involved in performance.

What is the relationship between imagery ability and sports performance? Generally, research indicates that athletes who are better imagers tend to perform better. In one study, superior racquetball players reported better control of their imagery than poorer racquetball players (Meyers, Cooke, Cullen, & Liles, 1979). In another, divers who qualified for the Pan American Games rated their imagery as more vivid and controlled than divers who did not qualify (Highlen & Bennett, 1983). Correlational studies have found significant positive relationships between the controllability of kinesthetic imagery and Olympic performance

Even while practicing, imagery can help the athlete to perform better.

with imagery practice is a significant factor in the improvement of motor skills.

Goss, Hall, Buckolz, and Fishburne (1986) controlled for imagery ability to examine effects on the acquisition and retention of movements. Based on MIQ scores, subjects were classified in one of three groups: high visual, high kinesthetic; high visual, low kinesthetic; and low visual, low kinesthetic. Results revealed a significant difference among all three imagery groups on the acquisition of movement patterns. High visual and high kinesthetic individuals performed best, whereas low visual and low kinesthetic individuals performed worst. However, there was not a significant difference when the groups were tested on retention.

Housner (1984) classified subjects as high or low imagers on the Marks Vividness of Visual Imagery Questionnaire and then had both groups of subjects recall movement patterns after viewing a particular sequence on a video. Subjects with high imagery ability reproduced movements with significantly greater accuracy than those with low imagery ability.

These findings are consistent with other studies that have demonstrated superior learning, retention, and reacquisition of movements for high-ability imagers compared with low-ability imagers. This finding has been demonstrated for a variety of tasks such as the learning of a dial-a-maze task (Ryan & Simons, 1981) and improving performance on a novel balancing task (Ryan & Simons, 1982).

If imagery ability is so crucial to the learning and performance of sports skills, the implication is that athletes should devote time to improving their imagery ability. Most researchers have considered imagery ability to be quite stable and not subject to much change. However, some evidence suggests that imagery abilities indeed improve with practice. Rodgers and her colleagues (Rodgers, Hall, & Buckolz, 1991) administered the MIQ to figure skaters both before and after a 16-week imagery training program. They reported significant improvements in the subjects' visual MIQ scores compared with a control group that did not receive imagery training. These results suggest that like any skill, imagery can be improved through regular, deliberate practice. More research is needed to determine the degree to which "low imagers" can improve their imagery abilities and whether training can improve other types of imagery abilities. It is also unknown whether visual imagery and kinesthetic imagery

for athletes from a variety of sports (Orlick & Partington, 1988), kinesthetic imagery ability (as measured by the MIQ–R) and competition outcome among roller skaters (Vadocz et al., 1997), and imagery controllability and performance rankings for elite canoeists (MacIntyre, Moran, & Jennings, 1997).

In addition to its relationship with athletic performance, imagery ability also seems relevant to the acquisition of motor skills. Isaac (1992) divided novice and skilled trampolinists into two groups: an imagery practice group and a control (no imagery) group. In addition, subjects were classified as having high or low imagery ability on the basis of their VMIQ scores. Over three 6-week periods, both groups attempted to learn or improve three trampoline skills. Subjects in the imagery group, regardless of their trampolining skill level, showed greater performance improvement than the control group. In addition, high-ability imagers improved more than low-ability imagers. Isaac (1992) concluded that high imagery ability combined

© Human Kinetics

develop in similar ways, whether they both can be improved, or indeed whether athletes covary in ability on these two imagery dimensions.

In sum, common sense suggests that imagery ability is one of the most critical variables that might influence mental practice and imagery rehearsal. Yet it has not received the amount of serious attention from researchers that one may expect. Moreover, researchers (C.R. Hall, 1998; Moran, 1993) have lamented the fact that existing measures of imagery are inadequate for assessing various aspects of imagery (e.g., the amount of detail, intensity, kinesthetic qualities) and that these measures may be too general to assess imagery abilities required for specific sports (e.g., team vs. individual sports) or sport situations (e.g., imaging oneself feeling confident and in control). The studies reviewed here suggest that even when imagery abilities are assessed on a few dimensions (i.e., controllability, vividness), their demonstrated effect on learning and performance is significant.

Imagery Perspective

Imagery perspective was formally recognized and identified by Mahoney and Avener (1977), who reported that gymnasts who qualified for the Olympics used more internal images than gymnasts who did not qualify. Mahoney and Avener distinguished between internal and external imagery perspectives in the following way:

In external imagery, a person views himself from the perspective of an external observer (much like in home movies). Internal imagery, on the other hand, requires an approximation of the real life phenomenology such that the person actually imagines being inside his/her body and experiencing those sensations that might be expected in the actual situation. (p. 137)

Mahoney and Avener's findings spurred a line of research that explored whether internal imagery is superior to external imagery. Descriptive studies that compared the imagery of high- versus low-skilled athletes failed to find a reliable effect. No relationship was found between perspective and skill or performance level in a study of racquetball players (Meyers et al., 1979) or among divers and wrestlers (Highlen & Bennett, 1979). However, some research has found that elite athletes use an internal perspective more than nonelite athletes (Mahoney, Gabriel, & Perkins,

1987), and a study of skiers found that higher skilled athletes visualized the course from an internal perspective, whereas the less successful athletes reported visualizing their entire body skiing—an external perspective (Rotella et al., 1980).

Studies that have used experimental designs have consistently failed to find superior performance effects for internal imagery. No difference in performance was found between subjects using internal and external imagery on a dart-throwing task (M.L. Epstein, 1980). Mumford and Hall (1985) compared three different types of imagery (internal kinesthetic, internal visual, and external visual) and found no difference between groups on figure skating performance. Another study compared the effects of internal and external imagery training on cricket performance (Gordon, Weinberg, & Jackson, 1994), finding no significant performance differences between the two imagery groups.

One area in which the internal perspective has regularly produced superior effects involves neuromuscular responses to imagery. Compared with external imagery, internal imagery tends to produce stronger EMG activity in the muscles involved in the imagined activity (for a review, see Hale, 1994). However, research that has examined other psychophysiological responses to imagery has failed to find any difference between internal and external imagery. For example, no differences in oxygen consumption, respiratory rate, respiratory exchange ratio, heart rate, or diastolic blood pressure were found between subjects who imaged a bout of exercise from an internal perspective versus those who used an external perspective (Wang & Morgan, 1992).

In a recent critique of the imagery perspective literature, Hardy (1997) noted that Mahoney and Avener's (1977) explanation of imagery perspectives confounded imagery perspective (internal vs. external) with imagery modality (visual vs. kinesthetic). For example, Mahoney and Avener (1977) used the statement, "when I am preparing to perform, I try to imagine what it will feel like in my muscles" as an indicator of internal perspective imagery, whereas it really indicates kinesthetic imagery. In other words, there has been an assumption that internal and kinesthetic imagery go hand-in-hand and that external imagery precludes a kinesthetic component. Recent evidence suggests that the two are at least somewhat independent (Callow & Hardy, 1997; White & Hardy, 1995). For example, Moran and MacIntyre (1998) found that 25% of the canoe-slalom participants they studied reported experiencing kinesthetic imagery using an external perspective. One athlete stated, "I can feel the same strokes when I'm doing it only the view changes not the sense" (p. 416). Unfortunately, however, virtually all of the imagery perspective research to date has confounded imagery perspective and imagery modality. Any effects that have been seen in imagery perspective studies may have been a consequence of differential uses of kinesthetic imagery rather than of differences in the use of internal and external imagery. Indeed, recent studies that separated imagery perspective and modality showed that kinesthetic imagery improved performance more than visual imagery, regardless of internal or external perspective (Hardy, 1997). This finding is consistent with the predictions of Lang's (1979) model, discussed earlier.

Hardy (1997) also noted that imagery perspective researchers have failed to consider the influence of task and individual difference variables in their studies. Researchers have noted that athletes in different sports prefer different types of imagery. For example, competitive figure skaters (Rodgers et al., 1991) tend to image more from an external perspective, whereas rowers prefer to image from an internal perspective (Barr & Hall, 1992). Drawing on preliminary findings from his research, Hardy (1997) tentatively suggested that if a task strongly emphasizes form or body shape, then kinesthetic imagery from an external perspective might be most beneficial. If a task requires the performer to make relatively simple movements in which form is not particularly important, but the timing of the response relative to external cues is important, then kinesthetic imagery from an internal perspective might be most effective.

Individual differences in imagery ability for a particular perspective or modality also may influence the impact of a particular imagery intervention. Athletes express preferences for certain imagery perspectives and often report switching between perspectives (Jowdy, Murphy, & Durtschi, 1989). Likewise, Gould, Weinberg, and Jackson (1980) reported that most of their subjects spontaneously switched between internal and external perspectives, contrary to instructions. It is feasible that athletes develop an individual imagery style that works best for them. Attempting to change this style may be counterproductive (C.R. Hall, 1997).

These recent critiques suggest that research that attempts to show that internal imagery produces better performance than external imagery is probably fruitless. Instead, researchers might be better advised to investigate whether internal and external imagery perspectives produce differential responses in athletes. For example, internal and external imagery could have different effects on the identification of technical errors (Murphy, 1994), the enhancement of self-efficacy and self-confidence (Hardy, 1997), and so on. There is some evidence that athletes are more likely to experience certain outcomes depending on the perspective adopted. For example, in the Jowdy et al. (1989) survey, 50% of the athletes surveyed reported that their imagery was more clear and vivid when they used internal imagery (only 31% endorsed this outcome for external imagery), and 64% reported that they were more emotionally involved when using internal imagery (vs. 23% of athletes reporting that external imagery was more emotionally involving). Such differential effects on factors such as clarity and emotional involvement in turn may produce different performance outcomes depending on the purpose for which the imagery is used.

Relaxation

Using relaxation in combination with imagery has a long tradition in psychological research, extending back at least to Wolpe's (1958) seminal work on systematic desensitization. In work with athletes, many writers suggest using relaxation inductions before imagery instructions to facilitate imagery control (Suinn, 1985; Vealey, 1986a). Suinn's VMBR method, in fact, requires beginning each imagery session with relaxation induction. However, research results are inconsistent regarding whether combining relaxation with imagery produces effects significantly different from those produced using imagery alone. Several studies have found no significant benefits of combining relaxation with imagery (J.J. Gray, Haring, & Banks, 1984; Hamberger & Lohr, 1980; Weinberg, Seabourne, & Jackson, 1987). Kolonay (1977) found that VMBR significantly improved basketball free-throw shooting over the use of just imagery alone and relaxation alone, although the study has been criticized as being methodologically weak (Perry & Morris, 1995). Several of the studies that demonstrated strong mental practice effects did not use relaxation procedures in combination with the mental practice (e.g., Clark, 1960; Corbin, 1967b; Woolfolk, Parrish, & Murphy, 1985).

If relaxation potentiates the effects of imagery, why? A reasonable hypothesis is that relaxation reduces anxiety and other distracting thoughts and enables subjects to focus more completely on the imagery. Hypnosis has been defined as a "state of focused attention" (Havens, 1985), and it is noteworthy that hypnotic procedures nearly always begin with the induction of a trance state or with deep relaxation. However, even if imagery is enhanced by relaxation, the practical ramifications may be minimal, because few athletic situations, particularly in competition, allow athletes the time necessary to deeply relax. Many of the ways in which athletes use imagery to manage their performance require rapid use of imagery. Relaxation may be most useful as a means of enhancing imagery when used as a vehicle for helping athletes learn and master imagery skills that they can use in applied settings.

In the literature on imagery-related variables, imagery ability has been identified most clearly as influencing the effects of imagery rehearsal on performance. However, athletes use imagery for more than just rehearsing technical aspects of their performance. They also use imagery to rehearse strategies, to motivate themselves, and to regulate their arousal. Additional research is needed to examine the importance of athletes' abilities to image these other types of situations (C.R. Hall, 1998). Negative images seem to exert a powerful and debilitating effect on performance, which confirms anecdotal reports from coaches and athletes regarding the deleterious effects of negative images. Perhaps one function of positive imagery rehearsal is simply to prevent negative imagery, although a study by Beilock, Afremow, Rabe, and Carr (2001) indicated that attempting to replace negative images with corrective ones does not prevent the performance decline due to trying to suppress negative images. Studies about imagery perspective have yielded inconclusive results. Differences in imagery perspectives may be related to the athlete's preferred cognitive style. Perhaps one perspective is better than the other for a particular intervention purpose (e.g., internal perspective and kinesthetic imagery to promote the development of "muscle memory" of a skill, external perspective and visual imagery to detect and analyze errors in task execution). Finally, relaxation may alter the imagery experience for some subjects, but it does not appear to be a prerequisite for producing all imagery rehearsal effects. In the next section we discuss the issue of assessment of imagery in sport.

Assessment Issues

Despite substantial research investigating several imagery-related variables, investigators have not yet identified all of the relevant dimensions of imagery that may influence performance. In reviewing the imagery assessment literature, M.P. Anderson (1981a) concluded, "The number of specific dimensions of imaginal activity that could be assessed is limited only by the number of hypotheses that could be generated linking different aspects of imaginal activity with behaviors of interest to the investigator" (p. 153). Several potentially relevant dimensions of imagery have been suggested but not yet fully explored. For example, individual differences in the ability to become absorbed in the imagery experience (Tellegen & Atkinson, 1974) or one's belief in the performance-enhancing capabilities of imagery (McKenzie & Howe, 1997) could mediate imagery effects. Individual differences in habitual modes of mental processing (i.e., whether one typically responds to cognitive demands with greater visualizing or verbalizing responses) also may influence imagery outcomes (Richardson, 1977). Another possibility is that certain imagery outcomes—such as increased confidence or decreased anxiety—are related to the ability to experience emotions while imaging (Moritz et al., 1996; Vadocz et al., 1997). These examples all suggest that many relevant dimensions of imagery experience have not yet been addressed in sport psychology research.

Research may have lagged in this area because of the lack of a satisfactory approach to assessing and measuring various qualitative dimensions of imagery. This is due, in part, to a paucity of theory development in the mental imagery literature. In their review, Mahoney and Epstein (1981) concluded, "It appears that researchers who are interested in imaginal processes in athletes are left in the unenviable position of facing a potentially important phenomenon that may be elusively dynamic and for which there is no psychometrically adequate assessment" (p. 448). However, some recently proposed approaches to assessing self-reported imagery experiences have demonstrated research potential.

First, Fenker and Cox (1987) showed that a data analysis technique, multidimensional scaling, can be used to describe the emotional experiences of athletes in sporting situations. Because multidimensional scaling allows for both idiographic and nomothetic analyses of self-reported experiences, this strategy may be useful for exploring the variety of emotions associated with specific types of imagery. A second technique, magnitude estimation scaling (Stevens, 1975), was used to assess imagery experiences in a series of studies conducted by Murphy (1985). Magnitude estimation scaling facilitates judgments about an image on a wide variety of dimensions such as reality of the image, sharpness, intensity, level of detail, degree of focus, and degree of attention present. In Murphy's (1985) studies, subjects were able to successfully discriminate among different types of images on many of these dimensions.

In an overview of the use of self-report imagery measures, Vella-Brodrick (1999) criticized most imagery tests for their lack of psychometric development and for the paucity of data on their reliability and validity. Vella-Brodrick undertook a psychometric approach to the development of an imagery assessment instrument. A 133-item draft instrument was administered to 519 athletes and artistic performers, and a factor analysis of the data revealed a three-factor, 21-item best solution. The imagery factors identified by this measure (the Multidimensional Mental Imagery Scale, MMIS) are Sensory Skills (using olfactory, muscular, emotional, gustatory, and auditory dimensions of imagery), Controllability (the ability to hold images over time, prevent distractions, stay focused on task, and change easily from one image to another), and General Factors (items examining the content, purpose, and quality of imagery). A separate vividness scale did not emerge, but Vella-Brodrick believes that the Sensory Skills factor measures both vividness and lifelikeness. A follow-up experiment measuring the psychophysiological responses of subjects during imagery revealed that heightened muscle activation during imagery was positively associated with MMIS scores. The rigorous development of the MMIS is an encouraging sign of progress in assessment, and it is up to researchers to incorporate valid and appropriate assessment of imagery in future studies.

Finally, a major challenge for imagery researchers is to confirm that subjects are actually using imagery and not some other mental practice strategy. To address this issue, Moran (1994) and MacIntyre (1996) have begun to develop sport-imagery validation strategies based on the premises of functional equivalence theory (Kosslyn & Koenig, 1992). According to this theory, imagery is functionally equivalent to perception insofar as it shares the same processing mechanisms and resources and it is able to represent spatial information. Thus, the time taken to image a sport activity should approximate the actual time to perform the activity, and imagery should be disrupted when athletes are asked to perform concurrent tasks involving imagery and perception in the same modality.

A preliminary study involving elite canoeists (MacIntyre, 1996) found that time to image a particular slalom race was highly correlated ($r = .94$) with the actual time to complete the race. In addition, subjects' time to image the race increased significantly (i.e., imagery was disrupted) when they engaged in concurrent tasks (e.g., key tapping, estimating the angle of a line presented on a computer screen) that used the same sensory modalities as their imagery of the race (e.g., kinesthetic and visual modalities). Although research in this area is still in its infancy, it appears that a relatively simple battery of imagery verification tasks can be developed for use with athletes.

Before concluding our analysis with some suggestions for future research directions, we discuss a final important issue in imagery research in sport—understanding adverse outcomes in the research literature.

Adverse Outcomes: Problems With Imagery Use in Sport

The mental practice model directs our attention toward improved performance after rehearsal, but in doing so we overlook the troubling finding that many research subjects experience performance degradation after mental practice. Budney and Woolfolk (1990) pointed out that a reexamination of the Feltz and Landers (1983) meta-analysis revealed that 33 of the 146 effect sizes analyzed were in the negative direction. All of these 33 tasks fell into the motor or strength categories, a finding that suggests that many subjects experience performance deterioration with mental practice.

Can athletic imagery hurt performance? This question was asked directly in Jowdy et al.'s (1989) survey of athletes, coaches, and sport psychologists. In response to the question, "Describe any experience where imagery has inhibited performance," 35% of the athletes, 25% of the coaches, and 87% of the sport psychologists surveyed gave examples of imagery use inhibiting performance. In the real world of sports, imagery can have both beneficial and negative effects on performance.

The mental practice model is not well suited to explaining negative effects of imagery rehearsal.

Practice should improve performance, and greater practice generally should result in greater improvement. But if imagery is conceptualized according to the three-level model, we can see that problems can occur at each level. At the first level, athletes might have trouble with the imagery process. Clark's report (1960) of a subject who could not get the basketball to bounce in his imagination is an example of an uncontrollable image that would give athletes difficulty in rehearsing the desired outcome. Even more fundamentally, many individuals have poor imagery ability, so that they find it difficult to imagine the content described to them. This seems to be especially true of visual imagery.

At the second level, Suinn (1985) pointed out that if athletes imagine incorrect actions in their imagery rehearsal, they may very well program mistakes into their action sequence. This may explain some of the results described earlier regarding the effects of negative imagery on performance. However, it may not explain all such findings. As Murphy (1986) pointed out, in several of the negative imagery studies (Woolfolk, Parrish, & Murphy, 1985; Woolfolk, Murphy, et al., 1985), the subjects in the negative imagery group were actually instructed to imagine a correct putting stroke but were told to imagine a negative outcome (the ball missing the cup). In such cases, it seems less likely that the subject's motor program was interfered with and more likely that some other factor, such as decreased confidence, caused the performance degradation.

The model by K.A. Martin et al. (1999) also suggests that at the second level, athletes might experience poor outcomes with imagery use if the type of imagery used is not suitable for the performance outcome desired. This proposal has received some research support. For example, White and Hardy (1995) found that internal visual imagery was more effective for a simulated canoe slalom task but that external visual imagery was more helpful for a simulated gymnastics task emphasizing technical execution.

Finally, at the third level, the individual's interpretation of and associations with the imagery used may have a major impact on the effect of the imagery. This was forcefully illustrated when one of us (Murphy) was working with a group of elite young figure skaters as part of a mental training program. Work with another skater had indicated that a powerful image the athlete used to relax and concentrate before beginning his program involved imagining "a bright ball of energy, glow-ing golden, floating in front of me, which I inhale and take down to the center of my body. There I feel the energy radiate to all parts of my body, golden and warm, bringing me a peaceful attitude and providing me with the energy I will need for my program." Almost the same imagery description was used with the group of young skaters, followed by a description of a perfect skating program.

The skaters then were asked to describe their imagery experience. The results were surprising. One skater reported that he had imagined the glowing energy ball "exploding in my stomach, leaving a gaping hole in my body, so that I was crippled and unable to compete." Another skater said that the image of the ball of energy "blinded me, so that when I began skating I could not see where I was going, and I crashed into the wall of the rink and lay there, unmoving." A third athlete reported imagining inhaling a helium-filled balloon, leaving her speaking in a squeaky voice, at which point she began giggling uncontrollably and was unable to skate. And so it went, with every athlete reporting a different experience. Clearly, these young skaters were bringing their own fears, anxieties, and preconceptions into the imagery process, with the result that they brought their own meanings to the imagery, different from the meaning intended by the sport psychologist. Such a phenomenon might affect any athlete. For example, an athlete might experience good results by using imagery rehearsal to focus attention and build confidence before several competitions but subsequently may experience a poor result because of outside factors. The athlete might be surprised to find that the next time he uses his imagery rehearsal, it makes him feel anxious because of its association with the previous poor performance. We emphasize again that imagery and mental practice are not a benign panacea for performance woes but that imagery is a dynamic process that is part of the athlete's motor control system and also involves the athlete's cognitive, attentional, and emotional processes.

Are there any times when athletes and coaches should be especially wary of imagery rehearsal producing an adverse outcome? Experience suggests that the following situations might contribute to adverse outcomes for imagery use.

• **Increasing anxiety.** Athletes who tend to become overexcited before competition may find that imagery of an upcoming event increases their anxiety beyond manageable levels. An athlete in the Jowdy et al. (1989) study reported, "[The imagery] got me so pumped up and excited that I couldn't do anything."

- **Distraction.** Athletes who have a difficult time controlling their attention at competitions may find that the content of the imagery is critical in helping or hurting their efforts to focus. Imagery that directs an athlete to irrelevant factors may hurt performance. A coach in the Jowdy et al. (1989) study mentioned, "The only time where it has not enhanced performance is when the swimmer became distracted and not totally focused."

- **Lack of control.** Athletes who often report control problems with their imagery may be prone to experiencing either unwanted images (e.g., of failure) or imagery rehearsals that contain undesired content. Athletes and coaches should use care in employing imagery rehearsals if the athlete lacks confidence in her imagery.

- **Overconfidence.** Athletes often are advised to imagine a perfect performance before competition. However, in some cases this might lead an athlete to overlook small details of preparation, which might be necessary for superior performance. Another athlete in the Jowdy et al. (1989) study said, "Sometimes when I see myself being too good then things don't go well. It's a cocky attitude that overcomes me."

We now conclude with a summary of suggestions meant to guide future research efforts. In this final section, we offer some proposals for researchers interested in the relationships between imagery and sporting performance.

FUTURE RESEARCH DIRECTIONS

Although a great deal of interesting and informative research into imagery use in sport has been conducted, a number of weaknesses in the current research base emerged during this literature review. These weaknesses have been noted throughout the chapter, and in this final section we provide some concrete suggestions for improving research efforts.

Provide Complete Descriptions of Imagery Variables Used in Research

A problem for investigators wishing to replicate research in this area is that published studies rarely describe in detail what subjects were instructed to imagine in the study. Until more information is collected concerning the effects of various imagery variables (e.g., imagery ability, imagery perspective, presence of response propositions, length of time used for imagery, whether imagery practice was allowed, subjects' prior use of imagery, and use of relaxation), it seems wise to describe in detail all relevant variables within the study. This will be a great boon in allowing comparisons among studies. Some recent studies have done just this, providing much more detail about the imagery interventions used (Carter & Kelley, 1997; Hanrahan et al., 1995).

We suggest that imagery instructions be classified as an independent variable in research. If the actual instructions given by the experimenter as to what to imagine and how to imagine it are always classified as an independent variable, a database will quickly be established concerning the effects of the instructions themselves.

Use Manipulation Checks in All Imagery Interventions

How do researchers know what subjects are really imagining? This question raises a fundamental concern in imagery research, which is always complicated by the inherently subjective nature of the object of study. New means of addressing this issue have included the use of psychophysiological measures during imagery and creative task requirements and assessment approaches (e.g., MacIntyre, 1996; Shepard & Metzler, 1971). However, there is no substitute for asking the subject to describe his or her imagery experience. Many of the studies that included such a check found that the imagery experience reported by some subjects was different from that described by the experimenter (Harris & Robinson, 1986; Jowdy, 1987; Smyth, 1975; Woolfolk, Murphy, et al., 1985).

Use Psychophysiological Approaches to the Study of Imagery

To further our understanding of imagery processes, researchers should use new biotechnology techniques to explore the many systemic changes (neural, endocrine, and immunological) that are thought to accompany imagery experiences (e.g., Rider & Achterberg, 1989). This will require greater interdisciplinary research among sport and exercise scientists. Presently, it is difficult to find studies in the sport psychology literature that include physiological measures other than EMG and heart rate. This situation is lamentable, given the variety of technologies available to assess the body's responses to cognitive and emotional stimuli (Lloyd, 1987).

Develop of Better Assessment Methods in Athletic Imagery Research

The mental practice literature has been characterized by a lack of adequate assessment of potential imagery dimensions. Development of better assessment methods will accompany increased theory testing in the imagery area. Researchers must design assessment approaches that better test the theory being investigated. The development of instruments such as the MIQ, the Exercise Imagery Questionnaire, the MMIS (Vella-Brodrick, 1999), and the SIQ is an important step in this process (C.R. Hall, 1998).

Use High-Level Athletes in Research

Much of the mental practice literature has relied on analog research designs, which presents a critical generalizability problem for researchers. Most published studies of mental practice, for example, use nonathletic samples, expose them briefly to imagery rehearsal techniques, and proceed to measure mental practice effects in noncompetitive situations (Greenspan & Feltz, 1989). It is difficult to generalize from such studies to the athletic population, because this is not how imagery rehearsal techniques typically are used (cf. the critique of mental practice designs by Silva, 1983). Elite athletes are highly motivated to achieve excellent performance and are often diligent in practicing the cognitive strategies they use to manage their performance (Orlick & Partington, 1988).

There is no research to indicate whether there are large differences between how elite athletes use imagery strategies compared with recreational-level athletes. Differences among elite athletes at the national level are likely to be much smaller than differences between elite and nonelite athletes. Very few studies have examined psychological differences between elite athletes and appropriate nonelite controls (Morgan, O'Connor, Sparling, & Pate, 1987). Both descriptive and explanatory research studies need to be conducted to reveal the types of cognitive processes used by athletes at all levels.

Examine the Acquisition and Development of Imagery Skills

Few athletic imagery studies have been conducted with children (Li-Wei, Qi-Wei, Orlick, & Zitzelsberger, 1992), and we lack basic descriptive research of how and in what context young athletes acquire and develop their imagery skills. Evidence suggests that athletes have been using imagery processes for centuries, and experience suggests that most athletes do not learn how to use imagery from a sport psychologist. Athletes naturally begin to use imagery as they develop motor control. Very little is known about how basic imagery skills are learned and then applied to more complex situations such as problem-solving.

Examine Training in Imagery Use

Researchers should focus on three critical questions about imagery training. First, if subjects are trained in imagery use (George, 1986) and allowed sufficient time to practice imagery techniques, will this affect the magnitude of mental practice and other imagery effects? Second, will imagery effects on performance be greater if subjects are taught how to apply the techniques to manage their performance, as has been suggested by some writers (e.g., C. Lee, 1990; Murphy et al., 1988)? Third, what is the impact of teaching imagery skills to serious athletes? It is apparent that applied sport psychologists have begun to offer imagery training programs to a variety of elite and junior athletes (Gould, Tammen, Murphy, & May, 1989; Orlick, 1989), but few evaluations of the effectiveness of such interventions have been published.

CONCLUSION

Many myths and misconceptions have gathered around the use of imagery in sport. The mental practice model has tended to focus attention on the question, Does imagery rehearsal work? This is like asking, Does breathing work? As demonstrated in this chapter, imagery is a basic cognitive function in humans and is central to motor skill acquisition and execution. But imagery also is used in many ways that go beyond the mental practice of sport skills. Athletes use imagery to manage their performance in competitive situations, to solve problems, and to maintain motivation during training. Athletes' self-reports indicate that they routinely use imagery to master skills and achieve consistently superior performances (C.R. Hall et al., 1990; Orlick & Partington, 1988). This chapter provides a multilevel analysis of athletic imagery, which suggests that imagery should be investigated on three levels: understanding the nature of imagery, its utility in sport, and its meaning to individual athletes. The use of rigorous imagery models in sport psychology will bring many benefits to researchers and practitioners. As theory development becomes a more integral part of the research process, the study of imagery in sport psychology will enter its most productive and exciting stage.

REFERENCES

Achterberg, J., Lawlis, G.F., Simonton, O.C., & Mathews-Simonton, S. (1977). Psychological factors and blood chemistries as disease outcome predictors for cancer patients. *Multivariate Experimental Clinical Research, 3,* 107–122.

Adams, J.A. (1981). Do cognitive factors in motor performance become nonfunctional with practice? *Journal of Motor Behavior, 13,* 262–273.

Ahsen, A. (1984). ISM: The triple code model for imagery and psychophysiology. *Journal of Mental Imagery, 8,* 15–42.

Anderson, M.P. (1981a). Assessment of imaginal processes: Approaches and issues. In T.V. Merluzzi, C.R. Glass, & M. Genest (Eds.), *Cognitive assessment* (pp. 149–187). New York: Guilford Press.

Anderson, M.P. (1981b). Imagery assessment through content analysis. In E. Klinge (Ed.), *Imagery: Vol. 2. Concepts, results, and applications.* New York: Plenum Press.

Andre, J.C., & Means, J.R. (1986). Rate of imagery in mental practice: An experimental investigation. *Journal of Sport Psychology, 8,* 124–128.

Anshel, M.H., & Wrisberg, C.A. (1993). Reducing warm-up decrement in the performance of a tennis serve. *Journal of Sport and Exercise Psychology, 15,* 290–303.

Bandura, A. (Ed.) (1971). *Psychological modeling: Conflicting theories.* Chicago: Aldine-Atherton.

Bandura, A., Jeffery, R., & Bachicha, D.L. (1974). Analysis of memory codes and cumulative rehearsal in observational learning. *Journal of Research in Personality, 17,* 295–305.

Barr, K., & Hall, C. (1992). The use of imagery by rowers. *International Journal of Sport Psychology, 23,* 243–261.

Beilock, S.L., Afremow, J.A., Rabe, A.L., & Carr, T.H. (2001). "Don't miss!" The debilitating effects of suppressive imagery on golf putting performance. *Journal of Sport and Exercise Psychology, 23,* 200–221.

Bennett, J.G., & Pravitz, J.E. (1987). *Profile of a winner: Advanced mental training for athletes.* Ithaca, NY: Sport Science International.

Brady, J.P., & Levitt, E.E. (1966). Hypnotically induced visual hallucinations. *Psychosomatic Medicine, 28,* 351–353.

Brown, B.B. (1968). Visual recall ability and eye movements. *Psychophysiology, 4,* 300–306.

Budney, A.J., & Woolfolk, R.L. (1990). Using the wrong image: An exploration of the adverse effects of imagery on performance. *Journal of Mental Imagery, 14,* 75–86.

Burhans, R.S., Richman, C.L., & Bergey, D.B. (1988). Mental imagery training: Effects on running speed performance. *International Journal of Sport Psychology, 19,* 26–37.

Callow, N., & Hardy, L. (1997). Kinaesthetic imagery and its interaction with visual imagery perspectives during the acquisition of a short gymnastics sequence. *Journal of Sport Sciences, 15,* 75.

Callow, N., Hardy, L., & Hall, C. (1998). The effect of a motivational-mastery imagery intervention on the sport performance of three elite badminton players. *Journal of Applied Sport Psychology, 10,* S135.

Carpenter, W.B. (1894). *Principles of mental physiology.* New York: Appleton.

Carroll, W.R., & Bandura, A. (1982). The role of visual monitoring in observational learning of action patterns: Making the unobservable observable. *Journal of Behavior, 14,* 153–167.

Carter, J.E., & Kelly, A.E. (1997). Using traditional and paradoxical imagery interventions with reactant intramural athletes. *The Sport Psychologist, 11,* 175–189.

Caudill, D., Weinberg, R., & Jackson, A. (1983). Psyching-up and track athletes: A preliminary investigation. *Journal of Sport Psychology, 5,* 231–235.

Cautela, J.R., & Kearney, A.J. (1986). *The correct conditioning handbook.* New York: Springer.

Clark, L.V. (1960). Effect of mental practice on the development of a certain motor skill. *Research Quarterly, 31,* 560–569.

Cogan, K.D., & Petrie, T.A. (1995). Sport consultation: An evaluation of a season-long intervention with female collegiate gymnasts. *The Sport Psychologist, 9,* 282–296.

Corbin, C.B. (1967a). Effects of mental practice on skill development after controlled practice. *Research Quarterly, 38,* 534–538.

Corbin, C.B. (1967b). The effects of covert rehearsal on the development of a complex motor skill. *Journal of General Psychology, 76,* 143–150.

Corbin, C. (1972). Mental practice. In W.P. Morgan (Ed.), *Ergogenic aids and muscular performance* (pp. 94–118). New York: Academic Press.

Davidson, R.J., & Schwartz G.E. (1977). Brain mechanisms subserving self-generated imagery: Electrophysiological specificity and patterning. *Psychophysiology, 14,* 598–602.

Decety, J. (1996). The neurophysiological basis of motor imagery. *Behavioural Brain Research, 77,* 45–52.

Denis, M. (1985). Visual imagery and the use of mental practice in the development of motor skills. *Canadian Journal of Applied Sport Science, 10,* 4S–16S.

Dennett, D.C. (1991). *Consciousness explained.* Boston: Little, Brown.

Drake, S.M. (1996). Guided imagery and education: Theory, practice and experience. *Journal of Mental Imagery, 20,* 1–58.

Driskell, J.E., Copper, C., & Moran, A. (1994). Does mental practice enhance performance? *Journal of Applied Psychology, 79,* 481–491.

Epstein, G. (1989). *Healing visualizations: Creating health through imagery.* New York: Bantam Books.

Epstein, M.L. (1980). The relationships of mental imagery and mental practice to performance of a motor task. *Journal of Sport Psychology, 2,* 211–220.

Feltz, D.L., & Landers, D.M. (1983). The effects of mental practice on motor skill learning and performance: A meta-analysis. *Journal of Sport Psychology, 5,* 25–57.

Feltz, D.L., & Riessinger, C.A. (1990). Effects of in vivo emotive imagery and performance feedback on self-efficacy and muscular endurance. *Journal of Sport & Exercise Psychology, 12,* 132–143.

Fenker, R.M., & Cox, C. (1987, June). *The measurement of peak performance states for athletes in four sports: A problem-oriented cognitive mapping technique.* Paper presented at the meeting of the North American Society for the Psychology of Sport and Physical Activity, Vancouver, BC.

Fenker, R.M., & Lambiotte, J.G. (1987). A performance enhancement program for a college football team: One incredible season. *The Sport Psychologist, 1,* 224–236.

Finke, R.A. (1985). Theories relating mental imagery to perception. *Psychological Bulletin, 98,* 236–259.

Fitts, D.M. (1962). Skill training. In R. Glaser (Ed.), *Training research and education* (pp. 177–199). Pittsburgh: University of Pittsburgh Press.

Gallwey, W.T. (1974). *The inner game of tennis.* New York: Random House.

Garza, D.L., & Feltz, D.L. (1998). Effects of selected mental practice techniques on performance ratings, self-efficacy, and state anxiety of competitive figure skaters. *The Sport Psychologist, 12,* 1–15.

George, L. (1986). Mental imagery enhancement training in behavior theory: Current status and future prospects. *Psychotherapy, 23,* 81–92.

Gibbons, F.X., & Gerrard, M. (1997). Health images and their effects on health behavior. In B.P. Buunk & F.X. Gibbons (Eds.), *Health, coping, and well-being: Perspectives from social comparison theory* (pp. 63–94). Mahwah, NJ: Erlbaum.

Goginsky, A.M., & Collins, D. (1996). Research design and mental practice. *Journal of Sport Sciences, 14,* 381–392.

Gordon, S., Weinberg, R., & Jackson, A. (1994). Effect of internal and external imagery on cricket performance. *Journal of Sport Behavior, 17,* 60–75.

Goss, S., Hall, C., Buckolz, E., & Fishburne, G. (1986). Imagery ability and the acquisition and retention of movements. *Memory and Cognition, 14,* 469–477.

Gould, D., Jackson, S.A., & Finch, L.M. (1993). Life at the top: The experiences of U.S. national champion figure skaters. *The Sport Psychologist, 7,* 354–374.

Gould, D., Tammen, V., Murphy, S.M., & May, J. (1989). An examination of U.S. Olympic sport psychology consultants and the services they provide. *The Sport Psychologist, 3,* 300–312.

Gould, D., Weinberg, R., & Jackson, A. (1980). Mental preparation strategies, cognitions and strength performance. *Journal of Sport Psychology, 2,* 329–339.

Gray, J.J., Haring, M.J., & Banks, N.M. (1984). Mental rehearsal for sport performance: Exploring the relaxation-imagery paradigm. *Journal of Sport Behavior, 7,* 68–78.

Gray, S.W. (1990). Effect of visuomotor rehearsal with videotaped modeling on racquetball performance of beginning players. *Perceptual and Motor Skills, 70,* 379–385.

Green, L.B. (1992). The use of imagery in the rehabilitation of injured athletes. *The Sport Psychologist, 6,* 416–428.

Greenspan, M.J., & Feltz, D.L. (1989). Psychological interventions with athletes in competitive situations: A review. *The Sport Psychologist, 3,* 219–236.

Grouios, G. (1992). Mental practice: A review. *Journal of Sport Behavior, 15,* 42–59.

Hale, B.D. (1982). The effects of internal and external imagery on muscular and ocular concomitants. *Journal of Sport Psychology, 4,* 379–387.

Hale, B.D. (1994). Imagery perspectives and learning in sports performance. In A. Sheikh & E. Korn (Eds.), *Imagery in sports and physical performance* (pp. 75–96). Farmingdale, NY: Baywood.

Hall, C.R. (1995). The motivational function of mental imagery for participation in sport and exercise. In J. Annett, B. Cripps, & H. Steinberg (Eds.), *Exercise addiction: Motivation for participation in sport and exercise* (pp. 17–23). Leicester, UK: BPS.

Hall, C.R. (1997). Lew Hardy's third myth: A matter of perspective. *Journal of Applied Sport Psychology, 9,* 310–313.

Hall, C.R. (1998). Measuring imagery abilities and imagery use. In J. Duda (Ed.), *Advances in sport and exercise psychology measurement* (pp. 165–172). Morgantown, WV: Fitness Information Technology.

Hall, C.R., Mack, D., Paivio, A., & Hausenblas, H. A. (1998). Imagery use by athletes: Development of the Sport Imagery Questionnaire. *International Journal of Sport Psychology, 29,* 73–89.

Hall, C.R., & Martin, K.A. (1997). Measuring movement imagery abilities: A revision of the movement imagery questionnaire. *Journal of Mental Imagery, 21,* 143–154.

Hall, C.R., & Pongrac, J. (1983). *Movement imagery questionnaire.* London: University of Western Ontario.

Hall, C.R., Rodgers, W.M., & Barr, K.A. (1990). The use of imagery by athletes in selected sports. *The Sport Psychologist, 4,* 1–10.

Hall, E.G., & Erffmeyer, E.S. (1983). The effect of visuo-motor behavior rehearsal with videotaped modeling on free throw accuracy of intercollegiate female basketball players. *Journal of Sport Psychology, 5,* 343–346.

Hamberger, K., & Lohr, J. (1980). Relationship of relaxation training to the controllability of imagery. *Perceptual and Motor Skills, 51,* 103–110.

Hanrahan, C., Tetreau, B., & Sarrazin, C. (1995). Use of imagery while performing dance movement. *International Journal of Sport Psychology, 26,* 413–430.

Hardy, L. (1997). Three myths about applied consultancy work. *Journal of Applied Sport Psychology, 9,* 277–294.

Harris, D.V., & Harris, B.L. (1984). *The athlete's guide to sports psychology: Mental skills for physical people.* New York: Leisure Press.

Harris, D.V., & Robinson, W.J. (1986). The effects of skill level on EMG activity during internal and external imagery. *Journal of Sport Psychology, 8,* 105–111.

Hausenblas, H.A., Hall, C.R., Rodgers, W.M., & Munroe, K. (1997). *Imagery use by exercise participants: Preliminary investigation and scale development.* Manuscript submitted for publication.

Havens, R. (1985). *The wisdom of Milton H. Erickson.* New York: Irvington.

Hecker, J.E., & Kaczor, L.M. (1988). Application of imagery theory to sport psychology: Some preliminary findings. *Journal of Sport Psychology, 10,* 363–373.

Heil, J. (1984). Imagery for sport: Theory, research and practice. In W.F. Straub & J.M. Williams (Eds.), *Cognitive sport psychology* (pp. 245–252). Lansing, NY: Sport Science Associates.

Heil, J. (1985, June). *The role of imagery in sport: As a "training tool" and as a "mode of thought."* Paper presented at the Sixth World Congress in Sport Psychology, Copenhagen, Denmark.

Highlen, P.S., & Bennett, B.B. (1979). Psychological characteristics of successful and non-successful elite wrestlers: An exploratory study. *Journal of Sport Psychology, 1,* 123–137.

Highlen, P.S., & Bennett, B.B. (1983). Elite divers and wrestlers: A comparison between open and closed-skill athletes. *Journal of Sport Psychology, 5,* 390–409.

Hird, J.S., Landers, D.M., Thomas, J.R., & Horan, J.J. (1991). Physical practice is superior to mental practice in enhancing cognitive and motor task performance. *Journal of Sport and Exercise Psychology, 13,* 281–293.

Housner, L.D. (1984). The role of visual imagery in recall of modeled motoric stimuli. *Journal of Sport Psychology, 6,* 148–158.

Ievleva, L., & Orlick, T. (1991). Mental links to enhanced healing: An exploratory study. *The Sport Psychologist, 5,* 25–40.

Isaac, A.R. (1992). Mental practice: Does it work in the field? *The Sport Psychologist, 6,* 192–198.

Isaac, A., Marks, D., & Russell, E. (1986). An instrument for assessing imagery of movement: The vividness of movement imagery questionnaire (VMIQ). *Journal of Mental Imagery, 10,* 23–30.

Jackson, S. (1992). Examining flow experiences in sport contexts: Conceptual issues and methodological concerns. *Journal of Applied Sport Psychology, 4,* 161–180.

Jacobson, E. (1930a). Electrical measures of neuromuscular states during mental activities I. *American Journal of Physiology, 91,* 567–608.

Jacobson, E. (1930b). Electrical measures of neuromuscular states during mental activities II. *American Journal of Physiology, 94,* 22–34.

Jacobson, E. (1930c). Electrical measures of neuromuscular states during mental activities III. *American Journal of Physiology, 95,* 694–702.

Jacobson, E. (1930d). Electrical measures of neuromuscular states during mental activities IV. *American Journal of Physiology, 95,* 703–712.

Jacobson, E. (1931a). Electrical measures of neuromuscular states during mental activities V. *American Journal of Physiology, 96,* 115–121.

Jacobson, E. (1931b). Electrical measures of neuromuscular states during mental activities VI. *American Journal of Physiology, 96,* 122–125.

Jacobson, E. (1932). Electrophysiology of mental activities. *American Journal of Psychology, 44,* 677–694.

Jaffe, D.T. (1980). *Healing from within.* New York: Knopf.

Jastrow, J.A. (1892). Study of involuntary movements. *American Journal of Psychology, 4,* 398–407.

Johnson, R. (1982). The functional equivalence of imagery and movement. *Quarterly Journal of Experimental Psychology, 34A,* 349–365.

Jones, L., & Stuth, G. (1997). The uses of mental imagery in athletics: An overview. *Applied and Preventive Psychology, 6,* 101–115.

Jowdy, D.P. (1987). *Muscular responses during imagery as a function of motor skill level.* Unpublished master's thesis, The Pennsylvania State University, University Park.

Jowdy, D.P., Murphy, S.M., & Durtschi, S. (1989). *An assessment of the use of imagery by elite athletes: Athlete, coach and psychologist perspectives.* Unpublished report to the United States Olympic Committee, Colorado Springs.

Keele, S.W. (1982). Learning and control of coordinated motor patterns: The programming perspective. In J.A. Scott-Kelso (Ed.), *Human motor behavior: An introduction* (pp. 161–188). Hillsdale: Erlbaum.

Kerr, G., & Goss, J. (1996). The effects of a stress management program on injuries and stress levels. *Journal of Applied Sport Psychology, 8,* 109–117.

Kerr, G., & Leith, L. (1993). Stress management and athletic performance. *The Sport Psychologist, 7,* 221–231.

Kohl, R.M., & Roenker, D.L. (1980). Bilateral transfer as a function of mental imagery. *Journal of Motor Behavior, 12,* 197–206.

Kohl, R.M., & Roenker, D.L. (1983). Mechanism involvement during skill imagery. *Journal of Motor Behavior, 15,* 179–190.

Kolonay, B.J. (1977). *The effects of visuo-motor behavior rehearsal on athletic performance.* Unpublished master's thesis, City University of New York, Hunter College.

Kosslyn, S.M. (1980). *Image and mind.* Cambridge, MA: Harvard University Press.

Kosslyn, S.M., & Koenig, O. (1992). *Wet mind: The new cognitive neuroscience.* New York: Free Press.

Lang, P.J. (1977). Imagery in therapy: An information-processing analysis of fear. *Behavior Therapy, 8,* 862–886.

Lang, P.J. (1979). A bio-informational theory of emotional imagery. *Psychophysiology, 16,* 495–512.

Lang, P.J., Kozak, M., Miller, G.A., Levin, D.N., & McLean, A. (1980). Emotional imagery: Conceptual structure and pattern of somato-visceral response. *Psychophysiology, 17,* 179–192.

Lang, P.J., Melamed, B.G., & Hart, J.A. (1970). A psychophysiological analysis of fear modification using an automated desensitization procedure. *Journal of Abnormal Psychology, 76,* 229–234.

Lazarus, A.S., & Folkman, S. (1984). *Stress, appraisal, and coping.* New York: Springer.

Lee, A., & Hewitt, J. (1987). Using visual imagery in a flotation tank to improve gymnastic performance and reduce physical symptoms. *International Journal of Sport Psychology, 18,* 223–230.

Lee, C. (1990). Psyching up for a muscular endurance task: Effects of image content on performance and mood state. *Journal of Sport & Exercise Psychology, 12,* 66–73.

Levine, S. (1982). *Who dies*. New York: Anchor Books.

Levis, D.J., & Hare, N. (1977). A review of the theoretical rationale and empirical support for the extinction approach of implosive (flooding) therapy. In M. Hersen, R.M. Eisler, & P.M. Miller (Eds.), *Progress in behavior modification* (Vol. 5, pp. 299–376). New York: Academic Press.

Li-Wei, Z., Qi-Wei, M., Orlick, T., & Zitzelsberger, L. (1992). The effect of mental-imagery training on performance enhancement with 7–10 year old children. *The Sport Psychologist, 6*, 230–241.

Lloyd, R. (1987). *Explorations in psychoneuroimmunology*. Orlando, FL: Crewe & Stratton.

Locke, S.E. (1982). Stress, adaptation, and immunity: Studies in humans. *General Hospital Psychiatry, 4*, 49–58.

Loehr, J. (1986). *Mental toughness training for sports*. Lexington, MA: Stephen Greene Press.

Lynch, G. (1987). *The total runner: A complete mind-body guide to optimal performance*. Englewood Cliffs, NJ: Prentice Hall.

Mace, R.D., & Carroll, D. (1985). The control of anxiety in sport: Stress inoculation training prior to abseiling. *International Journal of Sport Psychology, 16*, 165–175.

MacIntyre, T. (1996). Imagery validation: How do we know athletes are imaging during mental practice? *Pages, 3*, 57–72.

MacIntyre, T., & Moran, A. (1996). Imagery use among canoeists: A worldwide survey of novice, intermediate, and elite slalomists. *Journal of Applied Sport Psychology, 8*, S132.

MacIntyre, T., Moran, A., & Jennings, D. J. (1997). *Are mental imagery abilities related to canoe-slalom performance?* Unpublished manuscript, University College Dublin.

MacKay, D.G. (1981). The problem of rehearsal or mental practice. *Journal of Motor Behavior, 13*, 274–285.

Magill, R.A. (1984). Influences on remembering movement information. In W.F. Straub & J.M. Williams (Eds.), *Cognitive sport psychology* (pp. 175–188). New York: Sport Science Associates.

Mahoney, M.J., & Avener, M. (1977). Psychology of the elite athlete: An exploratory study. *Cognitive Therapy and Research, 3*, 361–366.

Mahoney, M.J., & Epstein, M. (1981). The assessment of cognition in athletes. In T.V. Merluzzi, C.R. Glass, & M. Genest (Eds.), *Cognitive assessment* (pp. 439–451). New York: Guilford Press.

Mahoney, M.J., Gabriel, T.J., & Perkins, T.S. (1987). Psychological skills and exceptional athletic performance. *The Sport Psychologist, 1*, 181–199.

Marks, D.F. (1973). Visual imagery differences in the recall of pictures. *British Journal of Psychology, 64*, 17–24.

Martin, G. (1992). *Sport psychology for figure skaters with audio cassette*. Winnipeg: Manitoba section of the Canadian Figure Skating Association.

Martin, K.A., & Hall, C.R. (1995). Using mental imagery to enhance intrinsic motivation. *Journal of Sport & Exercise Psychology, 17*, 54–69.

Martin, K.A., Moritz, S.E., & Hall, C.R. (1999). Imagery use in sport: A literature review and applied model. *The Sport Psychologist, 13*, 245–268.

Marx, J.L. (1985). The immune system "belongs in the body." *Science, 227*, 1198–1192.

McKenzie, A.D., & Howe, B.L. (1997). The effect of imagery on self-efficacy for a motor skill. *International Journal of Sport Psychology, 28*, 196–210.

Meacci, W.G., & Price, E.E. (1985). Acquisition and retention of golf putting skill through the relaxation, visualization and body rehearsal intervention. *Research Quarterly for Exercise and Sport, 56*, 176–179.

Meichenbaum, D. (1977). *Cognitive-behavior modification: An integrative approach*. New York: Plenum Press.

Meichenbaum, D. (1985). *Stress inoculation training*. New York: Pergamon Press.

Meyers, A.W., Cooke, C.J., Cullen, J., & Liles, L. (1979). Psychological aspects of athletic competitors: A replication across sports. *Cognitive Therapy and Research, 3*, 361–366.

Moran, A. (1993). Conceptual and methodological issues in the measurement of mental imagery skills in athletes. *Journal of Sport Behavior, 16*, 156–170.

Moran, A. (1994, June). *Mental rehearsal in sport: From practice to theory*. Paper presented at the Annual Conference of the North American Society for the Psychology of Sport and Physical Activity, Clearwater, FL.

Moran, A. (1996). *The psychology of concentration in sport performers: A cognitive analysis*. East Sussex, UK: Psychology Press.

Moran, A., & MacIntyre, T. (1998). "There's more to an image than meets the eye": A qualitative study of kinesthetic imagery among elite canoe-slalomists. *The Irish Journal of Psychology, 19*, 406–423.

Morgan, W. (1996). Hypnosis in sport and exercise psychology. In J. Van Raalte & B. Brewer (Eds.), *Exploring sport and exercise psychology* (pp. 107–132). Washington, DC: American Psychological Association.

Morgan, W.P., O'Connor, P.J., Sparling, P.B., & Pate, R.R. (1987). Psychological characterization of the elite female distance runner. *International Journal of Sports Medicine, 8*, 124–131.

Moritz, S.E., Hall, C.R., Martin, K.A., & Vadocz, E. (1996). What are confident athletes imaging? An examination of image content. *The Sport Psychologist, 10*, 171–179.

Mumford, P., & Hall, C. (1985). The effects of internal and external imagery on performing figures in figure skating. *Canadian Journal of Applied Sport Sciences, 10*, 171–177.

Munroe, K., Hall, C., Simms, S., & Weinberg, R. (1998) The influence of type of sport and time of season on athletes' use of imagery. *The Sport Psychologist, 12*, 440–449.

Murphy, S.M. (1985). *Emotional imagery and its effects on strength and fine motor skill performance*. Unpublished doctoral dissertation, Rutgers University, NJ.

Murphy, S.M. (1986). Re: Sports psychology. *The Behavior Therapist, 9*, 60.

Murphy, S.M. (1990). Models of imagery in sport psychology: A review. *Journal of Mental Imagery, 14*, 153–172.

Murphy, S.M. (1994). Imagery interventions in sport. *Medicine and Science in Sports and Exercise, 26*, 486–494.

Murphy, S.M., & Jowdy, D. (1992). Imagery and mental practice. In T. Horn (Ed.), *Advances in sport psychology* (pp. 221–250). Champaign, IL: Human Kinetics.

Murphy, S.M., Woolfolk, R.L., & Budney, A.J. (1988). The effects of emotive imagery on strength performance. *Journal of Sport & Exercise Psychology, 10,* 334–345.

Onestak, D.M. (1997). The effect of visuo-motor behavior rehearsal and videotaped modeling on the free-throw performance of intercollegiate athletes. *Journal of Sport Behavior, 20,* 185–198.

Orlick, T. (1986). *Psyching for sport: Mental training for athletes.* Champaign, IL: Human Kinetics.

Orlick, T. (1989). Reflections on SportPsych consulting with individual and team sport athletes at Summer and Winter Olympic Games. *The Sport Psychologist, 3,* 358–365.

Orlick, T. (1990). *In pursuit of excellence* (2nd ed.). Champaign, IL: Human Kinetics.

Orlick, T., & Partington, J. (1988) Mental links to excellence. *The Sport Psychologist, 2,* 105–130.

Oslin, J.L. (1985). *A meta-analysis of mental practice research: Differentiation between intent and type of cognitive activity utilized.* Unpublished master's thesis, Kent State University, Kent, OH.

Paivio, A. (1971). *Imagery and verbal processes.* New York: Holt, Rinehart and Winston.

Paivio, A. (1985). Cognitive and motivational functions of imagery in human performance. *Canadian Journal of Applied Sport Sciences, 10,* 22–28.

Palmer, S. (1992). A comparison of mental practice techniques as applied to the developing competitive figure skater. *The Sport Psychologist, 6,* 148–155.

Perry, H.M. (1939). The relative efficiency of actual and imaginary practice in five selected tasks. *Archives of Psychology, 34,* 5–75.

Perry, C., & Morris, T. (1995). Mental imagery in sport. In T. Morris & J. Summers (Eds.), *Sport psychology: Theory, applications and issues* (pp. 339–385). Brisbane, Australia: Wiley.

Pinker, S., & Kosslyn, S.M. (1983). Theories of mental imagery. In A.A. Sheikh (Ed.), *Imagery: Current theory research and application* (pp. 43–71). New York: Wiley.

Porter, K., & Foster, J. (1986). *The mental athlete: Inner training for peak performance.* Dubuque, IA: Brown.

Powell, G.E. (1973). Negative and positive mental practice in motor skill acquisition. *Perceptual and Motor Skills, 37,* 312.

Pylyshyn, Z.W. (1973). What the mind's eye tells the mind's brain: A critique of mental imagery. *Psychological Bulletin, 80,* 1–23.

Pylyshyn, Z. (1981). The imagery debate: Analog media versus tacit knowledge. In N. Block (Ed.), *Imagery* (pp. 151–205). Cambridge, MA: MIT Press.

Qualls, P.J. (1982). The physiological measurement of imagery: An overview. *Imagination, Cognition and Personality, 2,* 89–101.

Rachman, S. (1968). *Phobias: Their nature and control.* Springfield, IL: Charles C Thomas.

Riccio, C.M., Nelson, D.L., & Bush, M.A. (1990). Adding purpose to the repetitive exercise of elderly women through imagery. *American Journal of Occupational Therapy, 44,* 714–719.

Richardson, A. (1967a). Mental practice: A review and discussion: Part I. *Research Quarterly, 38,* 95–107.

Richardson, A. (1967b). Mental practice: A review and discussion: Part II. *Research Quarterly, 38,* 263–273.

Richardson, A. (1969). *Mental imagery.* New York: Springer.

Richardson, A. (1977). Verbalizer-visualizer: A cognitive style dimension. *Journal of Mental Imagery, 1,* 109–126.

Richardson, A. (1985). Imagery: Definition and types. In A.A. Sheikh (Ed.), *Imagery: Current theory research and application* (pp. 3–42). New York: Wiley.

Rider, M.S., & Achterberg, J. (1989). Effect of music-assisted imagery on neutrophils and lymphocytes. *Biofeedback and Self-Regulation, 14,* 247–257.

Rodgers, W., Hall, C., & Buckolz, E. (1991). The effect of an imagery training program on imagery ability, imagery use, and figure skating performance. *Journal of Applied Sport Psychology, 3,* 109–125.

Romero, K., & Silvestri, L. (1990). The role of mental practice in the acquisition and performance of motor skills. *Journal of Instructional Psychology, 17,* 218–221.

Rosenthal, R. (1995). Writing meta-analytic reviews. *Psychological Bulletin, 188,* 183–192.

Ross, S.L. (1985). The effectiveness of mental practice in improving the performance of college trombonists. *Journal of Research in Music Education, 33,* 221–230.

Rotella, R.J., Gansneder, B., Ojala, D., & Billing, J. (1980). Cognitions and coping strategies of elite skiers: An exploratory study of young developing athletes. *Journal of Sport Psychology, 2,* 350–354.

Rushall, B.S. (1988). Covert modeling as a procedure for altering an athlete's psychological state. *The Sport Psychologist, 2,* 131–140.

Ryan, E.D., & Simons, J. (1981). Cognitive demand imagery, and frequency of mental practice as factors influencing the acquisition of mental skills. *Journal of Sport Psychology, 3,* 35–45.

Ryan, E.D., & Simons, J. (1982). Efficacy of mental imagery in enhancing mental practice of motor skills. *Journal of Sport Psychology, 4,* 41–51.

Sackett, R.S. (1934). The influences of symbolic rehearsal upon the retention of a maze habit. *Journal of General Psychology, 10,* 376–395.

Sackett, R.S. (1935). The relationship between amount of symbolic rehearsal and retention of a maze habit. *Journal of General Psychology, 13,* 113–128.

Schmidt, R.A. (1987). *Motor control and learning* (2nd ed.). Champaign: Human Kinetics.

Seabourne, T.G., Weinberg, R.S., Jackson, A., & Suinn, R.M. (1985). Effect of individualized, nonindividualized, and package intervention strategies on karate performance. *Journal of Sport Psychology, 7,* 40–50.

Shaw, W.A. (1940). The relation of muscular action potentials to imaginal weightlifting. *Archives of Psychology, 247,* 50.

Shea, J.B. (1977). Effects of labelling on motor short-term memory. *Journal of Experimental Psychology: Human Learning and Memory, 3,* 92–99.

Sheehan, P. (1967). A shortened form of Bett's Questionnaire upon mental imagery. *Journal of Clinical Psychology, 23,* 386–389.

Shepard, R.N., & Metzler, J. (1971). Mental rotation of three-dimensional objects. *Science, 171,* 701–703.

Shick, J. (1970). Effects of mental practice on selected volleyball skills for college women. *Research Quarterly, 41,* 88–94.

Shelton, T.O., & Mahoney, M.J. (1978). The content and effect of "psyching-up" strategies in weightlifters. *Cognitive Therapy and Research, 2,* 275–284.

Silva, J.M., III. (1983). Covert rehearsal strategies. In M.W. Williams (Ed.), *Ergogenic aids in sport* (pp. 253–274). Champaign, IL: Human Kinetics.

Simonton, O.C., Mathews-Simonton, S., & Creighton, J. (1978). *Getting well again.* Los Angeles, CA: Tarcher.

Singer, J., & Antrobus, J.S. (1972). Daydreaming, imaginal processes and personality: A normative study. In P. Sheehan (Ed.), *The function and nature of imagery* (pp. 175-202). New York: Academic Press.

Singer, R.N., Goren, R.F., & Risdale, S. (1979, July). The effect of various strategies on the acquisition, retention, and transfer of a serial positioning task. *U.S. Army Research Institute for the Behavioral and Social Sciences, Tr. 399,* p. 52.

Singer, R.N., Risdale, S., & Korienek, G.G. (1980). Achievement in a serial positioning task and the role of the learner's strategies. *Perceptual and Motor Skills, 50,* 735–747.

Smyth, M.M. (1975). The role of mental practice in skill acquisition. *Journal of Motor Behavior, 7,* 199–206.

Steel, W.I. (1952). The effect of mental practice on the acquisition of a motor skill. *Journal of Physical Education, 44,* 101–208.

Stelmach, G.E., & Hughes, B. (1984). Memory cognition and motor behavior. In W.F. Straub & J.M. Williams (Eds.), *Cognitive sport psychology* (pp. 163–174). New York: Sport Science Associates.

Stevens, S.S. (1975). *Psychophysics: Introduction to its perceptual, neural, and social aspects.* New York: Wiley.

Suinn, R.M. (1976). Visual motor behavior rehearsal for adaptive behavior. In J. Krumboltz & C. Thoresen (Eds.), *Counseling methods* (pp. 360–366). New York: Holt.

Suinn, R.M. (1980). Psychology and sports performance: Principles and applications. In R. Suinn (Ed.), *Psychology in sports: Methods and applications* (pp. 26–36). Minneapolis: Burgess International.

Suinn, R.M. (1983). Imagery and sports. In A.A. Sheikh (Ed.). *Imagery: Current theory research and application* (pp. 507–534). New York: Wiley.

Suinn, R.M. (1985). Imagery rehearsal applications to performance enhancement. *The Behavior Therapist, 8,* 155–159.

Suinn, R.M. (1996). Imagery rehearsal: A tool for clinical practice. *Psychotherapy in Private Practice, 15,* 27–31.

Suinn, R.M. (1997). Mental practice in sport psychology: Where have we been, where do we go? *Clinical Psychology, 4,* 189–207.

Taylor, S.E., Pham, L.B., Rivkin, I.D., & Armor, D.A. (1998). Harnessing the imagination: Mental simulation, self-regulation, and coping. *American Psychologist, 53,* 429–439.

Tellegen, A., & Atkinson, G. (1974). Openess to absorbing and self-altering experiences ("absorption"), a trait related to hypnotic susceptibility. *Journal of Abnormal Psychology, 83,* 268–277.

Vadocz, E., Hall, C.R., & Moritz, S.E. (1997). The relationship between competitive anxiety and imagery use. *Journal of Applied Sport Psychology, 9,* 241–253.

Vealey, R. (1986a). Imagery training for performance enhancement. In J.M. Williams (Ed.), *Applied sport psychology: Personal growth to peak performance* (pp. 209–234). Mountain View, CA: Mayfield.

Vealey, R. (1986b). Conceptualization of sport confidence and competitive orientation: Preliminary investigation and instrument development. *Journal of Sport Psychology, 8,* 221–246.

Vella-Brodrick, D.A. (1999). *Development and psychometric evaluation of the Multidimensional Mental Imagery Scale.* Unpublished doctoral dissertation, Monash University, Melbourne, Australia.

Wadden, T.A., & Anderton, C.H. (1982). The clinical use of hypnosis. *Psychological Bulletin, 91,* 215–243.

Wang, Y., & Morgan, W. P. (1992). The effect of imagery perspectives on the psychophysiological responses to imagined exercise. *Behavioural Brain Research, 52,* 167–174.

Washburn, M.F. (1916). *Movement and mental imagery.* Boston: Houghton Mifflin.

Wechsler, R. (1987, August). A new prescription: Mind over malady. *Science Periodical on Research in Technology and Sport,* pp. 1–11.

Weinberg, R.S. (1981). The relationship between mental preparation strategies and motor performance: A review and critique. *Quest, 33,* 195–213.

Weinberg, R.S., Seabourne, T.G., & Jackson, A. (1981). Effects of visuo-motor behavior rehearsal, relaxation, and imagery on karate performance. *Journal of Sport Psychology, 3,* 228–238.

Weinberg, R.S., Seabourne, T.G., & Jackson, A. (1987). Arousal and relaxation instructions prior to the use of imagery. *International Journal of Sport Psychology, 18,* 205–214.

White, A., & Hardy, L. (1995). Use of different imagery perspectives on learning and performance of different motor skills. *British Journal of Psychology, 86,* 169–180.

Wiese, D.M., & Weiss, M.R. (1987). Psychological rehabilitation and physical injury: Implications for the sportsmedicine team. *The Sport Psychologist, 1,* 318–330.

Wiese, D.M., Weiss, M.R., & Yukelson, D.P. (1991). Sport psychology in the training room: A survey of athletic trainers. *The Sport Psychologist, 5,* 15–24.

Williams, J. (Ed.) (1986). *Applied sport psychology.* Palo Alto, CA: Mayfield.

Wolpe, J. (1958). *Psychotherapy by reciprocal inhibition.* Stanford, CA: Stanford University Press.

Woolfolk, R.L., Murphy, S.M., Gottesfeld, D., & Aitken, D. (1985). The effects of mental practice of task and mental depiction of task outcome on motor performance. *Journal of Sport Psychology, 7,* 191–197.

Woolfolk, R., Parrish, W., & Murphy, S.M. (1985). The effects of positive and negative imagery on motor skill performance. *Cognitive Therapy and Research, 9,* 235–341.

Wrisberg, C.A., & Ragsdale, M.R. (1979). Cognitive demand and practice level: Factors in the mental practice of motor skills. *Journal of Human Movement Studies, 5,* 201–208.

Yukelson, D., & Murphy, S.M. (1993). Psychological considerations in the prevention of sports injuries. In P. Renstrom (Ed.), *Sports injuries: Basic principles of prevention and care*, pp. 321–333. Oxford: Blackwell Scientific.

Zaichowsky, L.D., & Fuchs, C.Z. (1986). *The psychology of motor behavior: Development, control, learning, and performance*. Ithaca, NY: Mouvement.

CHAPTER 14

Attentional Processes and Sport Performance

Stephen H. Boutcher

The study of attention has had a rich and varied history. In the late 1800s and early 1900s, the laboratories of Wundt, Titchener, and Helmholtz carried out many experiments examining different aspects of attention. Surprisingly, however, interest in attention waned over the next 25 years and was not rekindled until the advent of World War II, which challenged psychologists with many applied problems concerning attention (e.g., how long could a radar operator watch a screen without a decline in attention). Presently, attention is one of the core themes in psychology and is viewed as a complex multidisciplinary field of study. According to Parasuraman (1984), research in attention is being conducted in many areas of the psychological sciences including cognitive psychology, psychophysiology, neuropsychology, and developmental psychology.

In the sport context, several authors have suggested that attention is a vital aspect of athletic performance (Boutcher, 1990; Moran, 1996; Nideffer, 1976a). However, the research examining the role of attention in sport is underdeveloped. Furthermore, few studies have examined the attentional mechanisms underpinning athletic performance. Thus, a suitable framework to study the influence of attention on sport skills has not been established.

In this chapter I review the research and theory pertaining to attention with a view toward synthe-sizing various perspectives to develop a better understanding of the relationship between attention and performance. The first part of this chapter focuses on a review of the attention/ performance literature as it has been studied from three different perspectives: information processing, social psychology, and psychophysiology. At the conclusion of this section I present a synthesis of the three perspectives and an integrated model of attention in sport. The last part of this chapter focuses on a more applied perspective, discussing several issues related to attentional training in athletes.

THEORETICAL AND EMPIRICAL PERSPECTIVES OF ATTENTION

Attention in sport has been studied from three perspectives: information processing, social psychology, and psychophysiology. Each of these research thrusts has emphasized a different but related perspective of the attentional process. Research in information processing has established the existence of two related forms of processing: Control processing requires effort and is slow and cumbersome, whereas automatic processing is effortless, quick, and efficient. Social psychologists have focused on individual differences and environmental influences on attentional processes and have documented the ability of extraneous, inappropriate cues to disrupt performance. Sport psychophysiologists have attempted to examine the underlying mechanisms of attention by monitoring cortical and cardiac activity; both cortical and autonomic indicants of attention have been used successfully to assess attentional style in athletes during performance. The following three sections discuss the relevant aspects of these approaches necessary to develop an integrated model of attention and sport performance.

INFORMATION-PROCESSING PERSPECTIVE

Cognitive psychologists consider humans to be processors of information. The information-processing approach attempts to understand the stimulus–response relationship, stimulus being some kind of information entering the body through the sensory system and response being the resulting behavior. This approach assumes that a number of processing stages occur between the stimulus and response initiation. Although the names of the different stages vary, most information-processing models include perceptual, short-term memory, and long-term memory stages. For overviews of different information-processing models, see Marteniuk (1976) and Schmidt (1988).

Information-processing models provide a framework for examining the characteristics of perception, memory, decision-making, and attention. Attention is conceptualized as the ability to switch focus from one source of information to another and as the amount of information that can be attended to at any one time. Thus, attention is a central concept in the information-processing approach. Researchers working from this perspective have focused primarily on three aspects of attention—the three interacting processes of selective attention, capacity, and alertness (Posner & Bois, 1971). Because the literature examining these processes is extensive, only those aspects pertinent to the theme of this chapter are examined here (for more complete overviews, see Abernethy, 1993; Parasuraman, 1984; Schmidt, 1988).

Attentional Selectivity

Selective attention refers to the process by which certain information from the internal or external environment enters the information-processing system while other information is screened out or ignored. In any situation, the organism is constantly bombarded with a mass of information from both the internal and external environments and can only assimilate a certain amount at a particular moment. Therefore, selection is necessary so that only a few stimuli are processed. The organism focuses on certain aspects that directly affect behavior, whereas the remaining stimuli serve as background. Selection can be "voluntary" or "involuntary" depending on whether the selection is due to the organism or to the actual stimuli itself. Selection can take place in a large variety of behavioral situations. That is, an individual may choose to focus "inwardly" on certain strategies and past experiences or "outwardly" on a wide range of environmental cues. Thus, selection is multifaceted and appears to be an essential condition for sport performance. William James expressed this quite succinctly in his classical statement that "without selective interest, experience is an utter chaos" (James, 1890).

Selective attention is believed to play a central role in both the learning and performing of sport skills. However, the stimuli that are essential for a particular performance change as a function of practice and skill improvement. For example, neophytes first learning to dribble a basketball must devote much attention to watching the ball and are unable to lift their heads to focus on the players around them. With practice, however, players can dribble without watching the ball, and the skill becomes more synchronized and automatic. Eventually, after many years of practice, players can dribble with either hand while simultaneously defending the ball from an opposition point guard and monitoring the positions of fellow players. In this latter situation, most of the performer's attention is focused externally on surrounding players rather than on the process of dribbling. In contrast, the player sent to the foul line does not have to attend to the same amount of external information. However, because the foul shot is typically well learned, attention that was previously available to focus on teammates and opponents now has the potential to focus on task-irrelevant cues and internal information such as worry about missing, spectators, and so forth.

This basketball example shows that with practice, attention can be changed from a cumbersome, conscious process to a smooth unconscious process. These two aspects of attention have been called *control* and *automatic processing* (Schneider, Dumais, & Shiffrin, 1984). Control processing is used to process novel or inconsistent information and is slow, effortful, capacity limited, and controlled by the individual. In sport, control processing is involved when decisions are required. For example, a golfer who is considering distance, wind conditions, and the position of hazards to determine club selection would use control processing. In contrast, automatic processing, which is responsible for the performance of well-learned skills, is fast, effortless, and not under direct conscious control. In sport, automatic processing is found when athletes have developed skills after many years of practice. Thus, the professional golfer swinging the club uses automatic processing. The major differences between automatic and control processing are that automatic processing requires little effort, attention, or awareness, whereas control processing requires high awareness, much attention, and intensive effort. All sports require a combination of automatic and control processing, because athletes need to perform many skills in a reflexive, automatic manner yet also must make decisions and process inconsistent cues and new information. Closed-skill sports such as golf, archery, and shooting probably require more automatic processing, whereas open-skill sports involve a combination of the two. Thus, control processing (slow, effortful, capacity limited, and controlled by the individual) and automatic processing (fast, effortless, and not under direct conscious control) have the potential to play important roles in sport performance.

Attentional Capacity

A second aspect of attention that has been examined relative to performance is *attentional capacity*. This term refers to the fact that control processing is limited in the amount of information that can be processed at one time. Specifically, an individual is limited to performing one complex task at a time and, thus, would have difficulty focusing attention on two sources of information simultaneously. Consequently, control processing can be viewed as having a limited capacity for processing information from either the internal or external environments. Thus, performing multiple tasks or attempting to focus on more than one source of information may impair performance. An example of control processing overload in the sport context would be two coaches simultaneously giving a basketball player a stream of instructions during a time-out.

The restrictions on attentional capacity are due to both structural and central capacity limitations. Structural interference involves two tasks performed at the same time using the same receptor or effector systems. For example, listening for the sound of a starter's gun while at the same time listening to a voice in the crowd could provoke auditory structural interference. Capacity interference occurs when two tasks compete for limited central information-processing capacity simultaneously. Fixed-capacity and undifferentiated theories represent two different views for explaining how task performance will be affected if capacity for processing is exceeded. Fixed-capacity theories (e.g., Broadbent, 1958; Keele, 1973; Kerr, 1973; Norman, 1969) assume that capacity is fixed in size and remains the same for different tasks. In contrast, theories of undifferentiated capacity (e.g., Kahneman, 1973) view attention as a resource that can be channeled to various processing operations. This approach is a more flexible view of attention and suggests that capacity changes as task requirements change. Multiple resource theory (Navon & Gopher, 1979; Wickens, 1984) is a recent extension of flexible attentional capacity

© Photo Network/Chad Ehlers

Trap shooting probably requires more automatic processing than control processing.

and suggests that attention may consist of a set of pools of resources, each with its own capacity to handle information processing. This view suggests that processes requiring attention may be able to handle more than one stimulus at any one time (parallel processing). The ability of the human information-processing system to process multiple sources of information simultaneously would depend on the importance of the tasks involved, task difficulty, and structural considerations. Resource theory generally is viewed as an attractive framework for understanding attention. Critics of the theory, however, have focused on issues regarding practice and divided attention and the number of resources necessary to cover all aspects of attention (see Hirst, 1986).

Whereas control processing is fragmentized, requires much attention, effort, and awareness, and can only handle relatively simple tasks, automatic processing is just the opposite. Automatic processing requires little attention, effort, or awareness, is not serial dependent, and is holistic rather than fragmentized in nature. The capacity limitations of automatic processing are less restrictive compared with those of control processing. For instance, performing a golf swing involves a variety of muscles initiated by millions of efferent neural impulses. Presumably, if this process had to be consciously monitored by an individual, the task would be overwhelming. Thus, control processing, which may be dominant in the early stages of learning (Shiffrin, 1976), eventually will give way to automatic processing if the skill is to be performed in an effortless, efficient manner. For skill performance, then, the greater attentional capacity limitation of control processing compared with that of automatic processing is an important factor.

Attentional Alertness

The third aspect of attention that has been examined in information-processing research concerns the effects of alertness and arousal on the breadth of the attentional field. Easterbrook (1959), in a comprehensive review of the available literature, cited numerous research studies supporting the hypothesis that increases in emotional arousal narrow the attentional field because of systematic reduction in the range of cue utilization. More recently, Landers (1980a,b; 1981) used the work of Easterbrook (1959) to examine the effects of emotional arousal on athletes' visual field during performance. Numerous studies have indicated that

in stressful situations, performance on a central visual task decreases the ability to respond to peripheral stimuli (Bacon, 1974; Hockey, 1970; Landers, Qi, & Courtet, 1985). Thus, it appears that arousal can bring about sensitivity loss to cues that are in the peripheral visual field. In sport, point guard play in basketball provides an example of how overarousal can affect the visual attentional field. If a point guard is looking for teammates outside the key (scanning the periphery of his or her attentional field), overarousal may bring about perceptual narrowing. This narrow focus may prevent the point guard from detecting open players in the periphery. Because many sport skills are performed in aroused states, the phenomenon of attentional field narrowing may be an important determinant of sport performance.

Summary

Researchers using the information perspective have focused primarily on selection, alertness, and capacity aspects of attention. Important aspects of selective attention are control and automatic processing. Control processing is slow, requires effort, and is controlled by the individual. In contrast, automatic processing is fast, effortless, and not under conscious individual control. Control processing is important in the early stages of learning and for dealing with novel and inconsistent information, whereas automatic processing is responsible for skills that are so well learned they require little attention or effort. Regarding alertness, it has been demonstrated that increases in emotional arousal can narrow the attentional field because of systematic reduction in the range of cue utilization. It also has been shown that the capacity limitation of control processing is more restrictive compared with that of automatic processing.

SOCIAL PSYCHOLOGICAL PERSPECTIVES

Because sport typically requires performance of well-learned skills, automatic processing appears to be an important aspect of athletic performance. However, successful sport performance also requires the use of control processing. For instance, receivers and quarterbacks have to constantly monitor the environment through control processing to attend to vital cues. In these performance situations, focusing attention on task-irrelevant information while attempting to perform well-learned skills may impair performance. This aspect of control processing (i.e., the possibility that task-irrelevant rather than relevant stimuli may enter the information-processing system, thus disrupting performance) has been studied largely by social psychologists. Most theories and explanations concerning this phenomenon have evolved from research in test anxiety, self-awareness, and pain. Three areas of this attentional research are pertinent to the role of attentional control and performance of well-learned skills: distraction theories, automatic functioning, and attentional style.

Distraction Theories

Distraction theories focus on the loss of attention caused by factors that attract attention to task-irrelevant cues. Thus, if task-irrelevant cues attract an athlete's attention, performance may suffer. If an archer focuses solely on thoughts of missing the target, attention might be disrupted and performance degraded. Similarly, if a baseball batter does not focus visual attention on the pitcher, he or she probably will not make contact with the ball. Thus, even momentary loss of concentration during the initial flight of the ball may have devastating results.

One factor that may divert attention to irrelevant stimuli is worry. Sarason (1972) and Wine (1971) suggested that worry as an emotional state distracts attention and thus can explain the negative effects of test anxiety on performance. According to Sarason and Wine, anxious individuals typically focus their attention on task-irrelevant thoughts and ignore critical task cues during testing. Thus, individuals who dwell on thoughts such as, "I know I'll fail because I'm not as good as the others" are not focusing their attention on task-relevant cues and will not produce performance results that reflect their ability. Acute anxiety, in the form of self-debilitating thoughts, has been associated with competitive athletic situations (Kroll, 1982). Thus, this research on distraction seems to be especially relevant to the study of sport. Processing task-irrelevant information can explain performance decrements in a wide range of athletic settings. In highly competitive situations, for example, performance could be hampered because the individual athlete focuses on self-defeating thoughts. In contrast, in nonstimulating, low-arousal environments (e.g., competitions that occur over hours or days), a lack of intensity in

attention may cause the athlete to miss important task-relevant cues.

Another source of distraction information is self-awareness. Carver and Scheier (1981) suggested that attending to oneself while performing may take attention away from task cues, thus degrading performance. Other authors (Duval & Wicklund, 1972; Scheier, Fenigstein, & Buss, 1974) have suggested that it is impossible to attend to oneself and to the environment at the same time. Because social facilitation generally tends to increase self-awareness (Carver & Scheier, 1978), the presence of spectators and cameras at sporting events has the potential to increase focus on the self, thus distracting the athlete. Thus, distraction in the form of worry or self-awareness is another attentional factor that can affect skill performance.

Automatic Functioning

The second area of study in the social psychology research literature that is relevant to the disruptive effects of inappropriate attentional focus concerns the automatic execution of sport skills. This concept relates to the automatic processing idea that was discussed in the section on information processing. Baumeister (1984) suggested that competitive pressure makes individuals want to do so well that they tend to focus on the process of performance. In competitive situations, when individuals realize the importance of correct skill execution, they attempt to ensure success by consciously monitoring the process of performance. That is, they attempt to put the execution of a skill, which is typically under automatic processing control, under the control processing mechanism. Unfortunately, consciousness (control processing) does not contain the necessary information regarding the muscle movement and coordination that is essential for effective performance. Thus, attempting to actively or consciously control the process involved in a skill can degrade performance (Kimble & Perlmuter, 1970). An example of the effect of consciously controlling well-learned skills was provided by Langer and Imber (1979), who demonstrated that attempting to ensure accuracy by consciously monitoring finger movements during typing was detrimental to performance. Also, focusing attention on hand movements during piano playing has been found to detract from performance (Keele, 1973). Baumeister (1984) also demonstrated this effect by using laboratory tasks when he found that increasing subjects' attention to the process of performing debilitated performance. Thus, attempting to ensure success by consciously monitoring performance during competition is another inefficient use of attention.

Attentional Style

It is feasible that there are individual differences regarding the distraction and automatic processing concepts discussed in the previous sections. Thus, in competitive situations, certain athletes might use an attentional style that hinders performance. Variations in attentional style and their effect on sport performance have formed the focus of much of the attentional research in sport psychology. For instance, Nideffer (1976b), using concepts developed by Easterbrook (1959), Wachtel (1967), and Bacon (1974), suggested that the attentional demands of any sporting situation will vary along two dimensions: width (broad or narrow) and direction (internal or external). A broad-external focus requires individuals to focus on a wide area of the external environment (e.g., a quarterback scanning the width of the field), whereas with a broad-internal focus attention is focused internally on a variety of strategies and past experience. A narrow-external focus is appropriate for activities that require the individual to focus on a narrow aspect of the external environment, such as a golf ball or the ring in foul shooting. A narrow-internal attentional focus is most suited to attending to specific images or cognitive cues.

The challenge for the athlete, according to Nideffer, is to match the attentional demands of the sporting environment with the appropriate attentional style. Therefore, performance may be impaired when an individual uses an inappropriate style for a particular activity (e.g., a baseball batter who broadly focuses his attention on players and spectators rather than using a narrow focus on the pitcher). Nideffer (1976b) also used Easterbrook's notion of attentional narrowing to explain the effects of anxiety and arousal on attentional processes. As discussed previously, the suggestion is that arousal produces an involuntary narrowing in attention and may interfere with the individual's ability to shift attentional focus.

Nideffer (1976b) proposed that individuals may possess a particular attentional style. These styles, which are relatively stable across situations and over time, may affect performance in certain situations if the athlete's style is incompatible with the attentional requirements of that situation. For example, a basketball player may consistently focus on thoughts of missing when shooting foul shots. In contrast, the aspects of attention that are state-dependent are situation-specific and thus are amenable to change. Nideffer (1976b) developed the Test of Attentional and Interpersonal Style (TAIS) to assess the strengths and weaknesses of an individual's attentional style. The subscales of the TAIS are Broad-External, External Overload, Broad-Internal, Internal Overload, Narrow Effective Focus, and Errors of Underinclusion. Although Nideffer provided preliminary support for the reliability and validity of the TAIS (Nideffer, 1976c), more recent research has suggested that the TAIS has limited validity and predictive properties for sport performance. Landers (1981, 1985a), who reviewed research examining the TAIS and sport performance, concluded that the scale seems to measure the narrow–broad dimension but not the internal–external dimension. Furthermore, he found no evidence that the TAIS is a good predictor of sport performance. Other researchers have developed sport-specific versions of the TAIS for tennis (Van Schoyck & Grasha, 1981) and baseball (Albrecht & Feltz, 1987) in an attempt to increase the reliability and validity of questionnaire assessment of attentional style. Although these versions of the TAIS increased internal consistency and were better predictors of performance, the prediction–performance relationship was still weak.

It appears that any questionnaire assessment of attention is inherently limited in at least two ways. For instance, the assumption underlying questionnaire assessment is that athletes are able to accurately assess their attentional focus across varying situations. The veracity of this assumption has not been established. Second, there are problems with the assumption that attention can be accurately described through self-analysis and language. As discussed earlier, the automatic processing aspect of attention appears to be free of conscious monitoring (Schneider et al., 1984). Thus, a paradox may exist when athletes are asked to assess nonconscious attentional states by way of conscious processing.

A related aspect of attentional style is the association/dissociation attentional strategies used by elite and nonelite marathon runners. Exploratory interviews with such athletes (Morgan & Pollack, 1977) have revealed that elite runners compared with nonelite runners were less likely to use dissociative strategies when running (focusing on distractive thoughts to divert attention from physical discomfort). Rather, elite marathoners reported that they used associative strategies (focusing on bodily sensations such as breathing and feelings in legs) more often than did nonelite runners.

More recently, Schomer (1986) suggested that postinterview data, post-race questionnaires, and anecdotal reports do not accurately assess the continuous thought flow of runners while running. To test this suggestion, Schomer (1986) used a tape recorder to record runners' thoughts while they ran on a treadmill. The tapes were then content analyzed by coding thoughts into mental strategies. From this analysis, 10 categories emerged as mental strategy subclassifications. Comparison of elite and nonelite runners' use of the 10 categories did not support the results of Morgan and Pollack (1977), who found that elite marathoners used associative mental strategies, whereas non-world-class runners preferred to dissociate. In contrast, the results of the Schomer study suggest that regardless of the marathon runners' status, increased running pace was accompanied by a predominately associative mental strategy.

In a second study, Schomer (1987) trained marathon runners to use associative thinking. A 5-week mental strategy training program taught nonelite marathon runners to use associative thought processes similar to those of superior marathon runners. Eight of the 10 marathon runners undergoing the program exhibited increased associative thought processes and an increase in perceived training effort. Schomer concluded that the use of associative mental strategies during marathon running and training might enable athletes to achieve an optimum running threshold. Overall, these results suggest that an associative attentional focus may be most beneficial for long-distance sporting events such as marathon running.

Social psychologists' interest in attention has focused primarily on the disruptive influence of nonrelevant task stimuli such as worry and self-consciousness. In well-learned tasks, inappropriate use of control processing appears to have the potential to hamper the performance of well-learned skills that are typically under the control of automatic processing. In sport, where many skills are well learned, there is potential for athletes to interfere with automatic nonconscious performance by focusing on distracting information such as worry and fear of failure and by consciously attempting to control movement.

Social psychologists also have been interested in potential individual differences in attentional capabilities. These differences in attentional style of different athletic groups have been assessed through questionnaires. The rationale behind such questionnaires is that assessment of an athlete's attentional style can predict future performance. Unfortunately, no evidence exists that attentional questionnaires are good predictors of sport performance. Also, because of the nature of automatic processing, the validity of assessing attentional states by retrospective recall may be questioned. Other ways of assessing attentional style include interviews and thought sampling techniques. The latter strategy may have greater potential for attentional assessment, because it does not rely on retrospective recall.

PSYCHOPHYSIOLOGICAL PERSPECTIVES

In contrast to cognitive psychologists who have attempted to understand attention by studying the whole process (receptor, information processing, and motor output), psychophysiologists have attempted to identify the mechanisms of attention by examining its component parts. In psychophysiological research, electroencephalogram (EEG), evoked response potentials (ERPs), and heart rate primarily have been used to examine attention and its relationship to performance. For instance, EEG (obtained by monitoring general cortical activity through scalp electrodes) has been studied in relation to a variety of cognitive tasks including vigilance detection, perceptual structuring, and object recognition and discrimination. ERPs, which are averaged brain responses to a series of stimuli, also have been examined as indicants of attention and have been found to be sensitive to the level of concentration on a task.

Psychophysiological indicants of attention also have been used in sport research. Hatfield, Landers, and Ray (1984), for example, examined left and right brain alpha EEG activity of elite rifle shooters while subjects were shooting and while they performed a series of mental tasks. Results indicated that progressive electrocortical lateralization occurred toward right hemispheric dominance before the trigger pull. Thus, seconds before pulling the trigger, shooters exhibited more alpha activity in their left hemisphere compared with their right. The authors suggested that elite shooters may possess such a high degree of attentional focus that they can effectively reduce conscious mental activities of the left hemisphere, thus reducing cognitions unnecessary to performance of the task.

Crews and Landers (1992) found similar decreases in left hemispheric alpha EEG activity immediately before striking the ball in golf putting. Unlike shooters, however, golfers showed decreased right hemispheric alpha activity before putting. The authors suggested that the different EEG responses during putting may be caused by the need for both hands to be actively involved in putting.

Importantly, Landers et al. (1994) showed that as novice archers improve performance, their EEG asymmetries change to resemble those of elite archers. These authors found that left hemisphere alpha activity of novice archers before releasing the arrow increased as archers improved performance. However, too much of an increase was associated with poorer performance. Also, after the 15-week archery class, heart rates of the novice archers were observed to decelerate seconds before shooting. The authors concluded that EEG asymmetries and heart rate deceleration are markers of attention that change with learning.

Other sport scientists have examined ERPs before and during shooting. In this research, multiple ERPs are recorded and then separated from other electrocortical noise by signal averaging techniques. For example, Konttinen and Lyytinen (1992) and Konttinen, Lyytinen, and Konttinen (1995) examined an ERP known as slow wave. They found that increases in frontal negative shifts were associated with successful performance if central-right slow waves were more positive than central-left slow waves. The authors suggested that the results reflected the ability of elite shooters to eradicate irrelevant motor activity while concentrating on visuospatial processing.

These data support the notion that there are general processing differences between the left and right cerebral hemispheres of the brain. For example, studies of split-brain patients' performance (LeDoux, Wilson, & Gazzaniga, 1977; Sperry, 1968) and EEG patterns (McKee, Humphrey, & McAdam, 1973) and lateral eye movements (Schwartz, Davidson, & Maer, 1975; Tucker, Shearer, & Murray, 1977) have demonstrated that for most people, verbal and linguistic processing occurs in the left cerebral hemisphere, whereas spatial cognitive processing occurs in the right hemisphere. Also, the left hemisphere appears to process information analytically, breaking down

a concept into discrete parts, whereas the right hemisphere processes holistically in a gestaltic fashion (Tucker et al., 1977).

Another variable that has been used to explore attentional states in athletes is cardiac deceleration. For example, a number of studies have found heart rate deceleration with elite rifle shooters just before the trigger pull (Helin, Sihvonen, & Hanninen, 1987; Konttinen & Lyytinen, 1992; Landers, Christina, Hatfield, Doyle, & Daniels, 1980). Similar results have been found with archers who exhibited a progressive deceleration in heart rate seconds before the release of the arrow (Landers et al., 1994). Interestingly, another study examining heart rate deceleration of elite archers did not find heart rate deceleration before arrow release (Salazar et al., 1990). The authors explained the absence of heart rate deceleration in their elite archers because of the physiological strain imposed when drawing a 14- to 22-kilogram bow. They concluded that cardiac deceleration can be used as an attentional index

© Human Kinetics

Elite golfers, such as Tiger Woods, experience significant cardiac deceleration while putting.

only when the preparatory state is not physiologically demanding.

Boutcher and Zinsser (1990) also found similar deceleration effects with elite and beginning golfers on a putting task. Both groups displayed heart rate deceleration during the performance of 4- and 12-foot putts, although the elite golfers showed significantly greater deceleration. The elite golfers also possessed significantly less variable preshot routines. The authors suggested that the different heart rate deceleration patterns may reflect the more efficient attentional control of the elite golfers. Other researchers examining old and young golfers have found similar results (Molander & Backman, 1989).

Sport psychophysiologists have studied attention by monitoring cortical and autonomic responses during athletic performance. EEG studies have indicated that elite shooters display cortical lateral asymmetry during shooting performance. Also, cardiac deceleration has been associated with attentional states in archery, shooting, and putting.

SUMMARY AND SYNTHESIS OF THEORETICAL PERSPECTIVES

The review of the research and theory presented in the first half of this chapter has revealed that the attention–performance relationship has been studied from three different viewpoints. Despite the relatively diverse nature of these three perspectives, they actually represent complementary approaches and together provide a unique, integrated perspective on the relationship between attention and sport performance. Therefore, I recommend that future research into the attentional processes underlying athletic performance take into account the principles outlined in the previous sections on information processing, social psychology, and sport psychophysiological research. Thus, attention should be viewed as a multifaceted, multilevel phenomenon that can be assessed through questionnaires, thought sampling, observation analysis, performance, and psychophysiological measures. The appropriateness of the measure would depend on whether skill performance is carried out in either the control or automatic processing mode. In addition, other factors that need to be considered when investigating the attention–performance relationship include individual differences, environmental influences, and changes in the performer's level of arousal. A preliminary framework based on this multidimensional approach is illustrated in figure 14.1. This proposed model integrates relevant aspects of the research and theory on attention from all three perspectives. As shown in figure 14.1, enduring disposition (e.g., high trait anxiety), demands of the activity (e.g., putting vs. sprinting), and environmental factors (e.g., spectators and television cameras) initially will determine the level of physiological arousal of the individual. During task performance, this arousal could be channeled into control processing, automatic

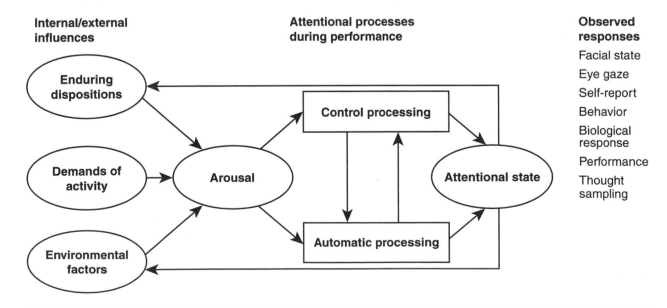

Figure 14.1 Interactions between internal and external factors and attentional processing.

processing, or a combination of both. The appropriateness of using either control or automatic processing would be determined by the nature of the task. An optimal attentional state, then, would be achieved if the individual reached or attained the exact balance of control and automatic processing essential for that particular task. Obviously, disruption in attentional processes would occur if internal or external factors caused the individual to reach a level of arousal that would cause an imbalance in control and automatic processing.

The arrows linking the ellipses and boxes in figure 14.1 indicate feedback mechanisms that would allow for factors to interact and influence attention both during and after performance. An example of the interaction of these factors is a golfer attempting to hole an important putt. The perceived importance of the putt (e.g., a putt to win a tournament) could increase physiological arousal and anxiety, which, in turn, could reduce the golfer's attentional capacity. This anxiety could generate thoughts of missing the putt, which could direct attention away from task-relevant cues. Thus, the golfer's attention may be focused mostly on irrelevant information and may be primarily in the control-processing mode. This may be detrimental to putting performance, which probably should be performed in the automatic processing mode.

Possible ways to measure either control or automatic processing are illustrated in the end column. Self-report may be most useful for individuals engaging in control processing, although this does not preclude the use of retrospective recall to assess feelings and emotions associated with automatic processing. Variables such as facial state, eye gaze (discussed further in the next section), and psychophysiological variables also appear to have potential for measuring attention during athletic performance.

In summary, researchers who study the relationship between attention and performance need to consider integrated models of attention. Viewing attention from a multidimensional perspective may generate more systematic research and provide a more reliable and valid research paradigm.

APPLIED PERSPECTIVES ON ATTENTIONAL CONTROL

As shown in this review, attentional theories of sport performance are not well developed. In addition, the empirical research that has been conducted on attention in sport has lacked a unifying model. Consequently, techniques to improve athletes' attentional capabilities have not been developed within a theoretical framework and largely have proceeded by trial and error. Certainly, applied research needs to be conducted to better understand how athletes' attentional capabilities can be improved. Specifically, qualitative strategies (e.g., single-subject research) should be wedded to the idiographic framework suggested earlier.

Given the lack of empirical research on attentional training, sport psychologists who want to provide attentional training for individual athletes will need to develop programs that are based on the research and theory discussed previously. The purpose of this last section is to outline a preliminary attentional training program. This proposed training program is based on the research and theory described in the previous sections. These recommendations are consistent with the principles outlined in the integrated model illustrated in figure 14.1. However, considerably more field research is needed to test the suitability and efficacy of these proposed techniques. This final section is divided into three parts: assessment of athletes' attentional strengths and weaknesses, basic attentional training, and advanced attentional training.

Assessment of Attentional Strengths and Weaknesses

Before an attentional training program can be designed and conducted with individual athletes, it will be necessary to assess the athlete's attentional strengths and weaknesses. Given the multifaceted nature of attention, it follows that assessment strategies should be most effective if they are also multifaceted. Some possible ways to assess an individual's attentional capabilities include questionnaires, interviews, thought sampling techniques, observational analysis, performance tests, and psychophysiological measurement. These assessment strategies are examined further in the following paragraphs.

Sport-specific questionnaires seem to be more reliable and predict more variance associated with performance than general measures of attention (Zaichkowsky, 1984). As discussed previously, sport-specific forms of the TAIS have been developed for tennis (Van Schoyck & Grasha, 1982) and baseball (Albrecht & Feltz, 1987). However, these questionnaires should be used with caution and only as one part of a multidimensional assessment of attention because of their inherent limitations, which were discussed previously. The thought sampling technique (Klinger, 1984; Schomer, 1986) appears to be a more valid way of assessing what athletes focus their thoughts on during performance. This technique involves recording individuals' thoughts during actual activity (usually by tape recorder); it seems to be especially appropriate for continuous activities such as running but also could be adapted to other sports. For instance, golfers could record on a tape or write on a scorecard (see Boutcher & Rotella, 1987) their thoughts and feelings after shots. The researchers could then perform content analysis and estimate attentional foci during task performance.

Athletes' attentional strengths also could be measured through laboratory tasks such as choice reaction time tasks, the Stroop test, and the grid test. For instance, in research with elite and nonelite archers, Landers, Boutcher, and Wang (1986) found that the better archers recorded lower reaction times when performing a reaction/anticipation time task than did their lesser skilled counterparts. Better archers' lower reaction times were due to greater consistency across performance trials and were not because the better archers were innately faster. Thus, it is feasible that these elite athletes' responses were more consistent because they could concentrate more effectively in this testing situation. Whether this difference in concentrational capabilities is linked to actual performance differences between elite and nonelite archers has not been established.

Another laboratory task that could be used to assess attentional capabilities is the Stroop test (Stroop, 1935). This test involves watching a series of slides flashed on a screen at the rate of one per second. On each slide is a word of a color in a contrasting color. For example, the word *red* may appear in green letters. Participants are required to report the color of the letters rather than the word. This task has been used extensively in a variety of research areas and usually produces heart rate increases of approximately 10 to 20 beats per minute. The task requires individuals to learn to focus attention on the color aspect of the slide while ignoring the letters. Stroop performance could be collected and used both to assess the efficacy of the Stroop as a training strategy and to assess the efficacy of other attentional techniques. The grid test is another task that has been used with athletes (Harris, 1984). This test involves checking off random numbers on a sheet as quickly as possible in a 1-minute period. This test is administered easily and requires little equipment. As discussed in the section on advanced attentional training, other more sport-specific attentional strategies involving computers and videos could be used after initial experience with these laboratory tasks.

Another form of attentional assessment involves the use of observational behavioral analysis. Crews and Boutcher (1987) developed an observational analysis technique, which they have used to assess the consistency of professional golfers' preshot routines. In a series of studies, they found that elite golfers possessed more consistent preshot routines than collegiate or beginning golfers (Boutcher & Crews, 1987; Crews & Boutcher, 1986). Thus, behavioral analysis through observation or videotaping appears to be an effective way of examining the behavioral concomitants of attention during actual performance.

Another potential indicant of attention is the assessment of facial or eye states. A well-developed body of literature has examined facial reactions as an indicant of affective states (Ekman & Friesan, 1975; Izard, 1977; Tomkins, 1983; Tourangeau & Ellsworth, 1979), although facial reactions associated with attentive states do not appear to have been examined. Similarly, the direction and characteristics of eye gaze have not been tested with regard to athletic performance. However, it is feasible that facial responses and eye gaze may reflect the general control and automatic processing styles discussed earlier. For instance, Tucker et al. (1977) characterized an individual's hemispheric usage by observing lateral eye movements. As discussed previously, research has established that for most individuals, verbal and linguistic processing occurs in the left hemisphere of the brain, whereas spatial cognition and perception generally are processed in the right hemisphere. Kocel, Galin, Ornstein, and Merrin (1972) suggested that individuals who are responding to a question will tend to look left if the response requires spatial thinking and right if the question requires verbal thought. Thus, lateral eye movement to different types of questions may indicate primary activation of the contralateral hemisphere. Although this lateral eye movement assessment has not been used in sport, research in cognitive behavioral therapy suggested that cognitive behavioral methods were most effective if they employed cognition of the participants' nonpreferred hemisphere (Tucker et al., 1977). Consequently, it may be possible to characterize athletes as to their primary patterns of hemispheric usage based on the frequency of leftward and rightward eye movement when responding to different types of sport-related questions.

Psychophysiological indicants of attention also could be used to assess attention. Equipment to collect indicants of attentional style is becoming cheaper, more portable, and easier to use. Several companies offer relatively inexpensive, user-friendly biofeedback systems that can collect a host of physiological variables. Thus, EEG, heart rate, pulse amplitude, respiration, EMG, skin temperature, and other physiological variables can be either used in a biofeedback setting or stored for research or applied purposes. Autonomic indicants of attention such as heart rate are less affected by movement and, therefore, lend themselves to collection during actual performance. For example, wrist telemetry monitors (Polar Heart Watches) can record up to 24 hours of heart rate during actual athletic performance and then can be downloaded to a computer and displayed graphically. Because cardiac patterns seem to be associated with attentional style (Boutcher & Zinsser, 1990; Crews & Landers, 1992), this variable seems to have potential for assessing cognitive activity during performance.

Finally, techniques to assess the attentional demands of sporting situations also need to be developed. As Nideffer (1976a) pointed out, athletes need to match the attentional demands of the sporting environment with the appropriate attentional style. Thus, it seems important that the athlete's attentional strengths and weaknesses should be assessed and compared with the attentional demands of the particular sport. Table 14.1 illustrates some of the factors that need to be considered when analyzing the attentional demands of an individual position in a particular sport. Open-skill activities involve continuous and repetitive movement patterns (e.g., swimming or basketball), whereas closed-skill activities are of a stop-and-start nature (e.g., golf or archery). Fine skills require accuracy and generally involve more delicate movements (e.g., putting or dart throwing), whereas gross skills are more dynamic and involve larger muscle groups (e.g., sprinting). Generally, fast, gross, open-skill sports are less prone to sources of distraction because of more limited attentional capacity when performing. In contrast, closed-skill activities may be more susceptible to disruption of attention because of the extra time and capacity available.

This section has described possible ways to assess an individual's attentional capabilities. These include questionnaires, interviews, thought-sampling techniques, observational analysis, performance tests, and psychophysiological measurement. A method to categorize the attentional demands of different sports was also described.

Basic Attentional Training

Based on the multidimensional profile that can be obtained from the assessment of an athlete's attentional capabilities, a training program could be designed around the athlete's attentional strengths and weaknesses. If basic attentional training is required, the program would start at a basic level and gradually progress to more complex, sophisticated attentional skills. However, it is not clear if attentional training on laboratory or nonsport tasks actually will transfer to athletic performance. Considerably more research needs to be conducted to assess the generalizability of attentional training as well as that of other forms of training (e.g., relaxation and imagery). Nevertheless, there appears to be potential in viewing attentional skills in a similar fashion to motor skills where the learning environment is most productive if structured in a graduated fashion (Adler, 1981). Thus, attentional training on laboratory

Table 14.1
Nature of Sport Skills and External Demands

Nature of the task	External factors	Attentional processing
1. Slow/fast	1. Game demands	1. Control processing
2. Open/closed	2. Environmental demands	2. Automatic processing
3. Fine/gross	3. —	3. Combination of above

tasks such as the Stroop, reaction time, and grid tests could form the first phase of the attention-training program, with training on more sport-specific skills conducted in later phases.

In addition to the laboratory training tasks already identified, biofeedback is another technique that can be used to develop basic attentional skills. Biofeedback requires individuals to be able to self-monitor and eventually control autonomic and somatic responses by interacting with some form of feedback loop (usually a computer). Thus, athletes can practice basic attentional control by learning to focus their attention on a variety of biofeedback cues. When athletes are directed to watch the screen or listen to an auditory cue, their attentional efficiency could be assessed by monitoring the resultant effects on the physiological variables being used. Because biofeedback reinforces the subject, this type of training task gives instant feedback to the individual regarding his or her ability to focus and adjust to the appropriate cue.

Thus, basic attentional training programs could be structured around a variety of laboratory tasks and organized so that attentional tasks become progressively more difficult. Through these types of training activities, athletes could attempt to acquire basic control of variables such as heart rate, respiration, and attentional focus.

Advanced Attentional Training

An extension of basic attentional training may take the form of a sport-individualized program. At this advanced phase, it first should be verified that the athlete has acquired basic attentional control and is ready to develop sport-specific attentional skills. Also for closed-skill athletes, much of the initial work at the advanced attentional training level needs to focus on the development of sound, effective preperformance routines (Boutcher, 1990; Moran, 1996). Thus, the precursor to successful attentional control during actual performance may be the establishment of a series of behavioral, physiological, and cognitive cues, which optimally prime both body and mind for the ensuing skill.

Although an increasing number of researchers are examining preperformance states, little research has explored attentional states during actual athletic performance. This lack of inquiry is probably due to the general reluctance of cognitive psychologists to examine processes that are not readily available to conscious processing.

Consequently, unconscious or subconscious processing largely has been confined to psychodynamic theory and has remained relatively unexplored in cognitive psychology (Kissin, 1986). In sport, optimal attentional states have been labeled peak performance (Privette, 1982; 1983) or flow states (Csikszentmihalyi, 1975). Unfortunately, these states have been assessed through retrospective self-report of athletes (Ravizza, 1984). This approach views optimal attentional functioning as an outcome rather than a process and does not tell us much about the underlying process (Hatfield & Landers, 1983). Thus, an outcome approach may not be helpful in designing programs to improve attentional flow during performance.

A tentative hypothesis based on the concepts of control versus automatic processing and left versus right brain functioning, which were discussed earlier, may help stimulate research into the process of attentional flow. As noted earlier, previous research has demonstrated that elite shooters exhibit different patterns of left and right brain cortical activity than less elite shooters (Hatfield & Landers, 1983). Specifically, the elite shooters showed suppressed left hemisphere and enhanced right brain activity. This particular pattern may represent the optimal attentional state during automatic skill execution. Furthermore, because performing in competitive environments is likely to generate physiological arousal (Moran, 1996; Nideffer, 1976a), it is possible that attentional flow may be achieved when physiological arousal is channeled into automatic processing rather than control processing. Thus, focusing attention on the task at hand when physiologically aroused may increase attentional flow. Because arousal tends to focus and narrow attention (Easterbrook, 1959), it is plausible that increased arousal and task-appropriate processing may generate the positive emotion, focused attention, and oneness with the task that are associated with attentional flow states (Ravizza, 1984). Thus, optimal attentional flow may be created by the athlete who directs arousal away from task-irrelevant information and into the task itself. This relationship is diagrammed in figure 14.1. Consequently, the challenge for the athlete or any other performer may be to learn how to direct competition-generated arousal into automatic processing of the task at hand while suppressing analytical processing. Thus, actively thinking of "nothing" while allowing skills to be performed reflexively and automatically may be the most efficient attentional style for those athletes who typically perform in competitive, challenging situations.

Because a large body of research indicates that brain-wave activity can be self-regulated, sport-specific EEG biofeedback seems to be of value in teaching athletes appropriate attentional focus during performance. For instance, research has established that individuals can learn to suppress cortical activity by learning to enhance alpha waves (Bauer, 1976; Elder et al., 1985; Jackson & Eberly, 1982). Furthermore, other studies have demonstrated that participants can self-regulate EEG activity. For example, Schwartz, Davidson, and Pugwash (1976) trained participants to develop both symmetrical and asymmetrical EEG patterns. Suter, Griffin, Smallhouse, and Whitlach (1981) also showed biofeedback control of EEG asymmetries.

In the sport context, one study has examined the effect of brain-wave biofeedback on archery performance. Landers et al. (1991) administered right hemispheric alpha feedback, left hemispheric alpha feedback, or no feedback to three groups of archers. The left hemisphere group improved performance, whereas the right hemisphere group exhibited significantly worse performance.

Although the efficacy of these EEG biofeedback techniques has yet to be established in sport, the increasing use of biofeedback in a variety of athletic situations (Landers, 1985b) suggests that this technique has potential. For example, it is possible that biofeedback techniques could be combined with sport-specific videos. Thus, the athlete could be trained to produce the appropriate attentional focus while participating in a video experience of the actual sport. Progressing from the video to actual sporting situations on the practice ground and then eventually to the actual competitive setting appears to be logical. However, the efficacy of these techniques relative to the sport domain clearly needs to be established through research.

Applied aspects of attentional control in sport are only beginning to be explored. Many of the ideas and suggestions expressed in this section are speculative and unsubstantiated by empirical research. It was not my intent to provide the reader with untried techniques but rather to provide a broad review of potential strategies that need to be investigated. I hope that this attempt to synthesize related research in attention to applied interests in sport will generate both basic and applied investigations into the attention phenomenon.

CONCLUSION

In this chapter I have attempted to integrate research examining different aspects of attention from the areas of information processing, social psychology, and psychophysiology. Each of these research thrusts has emphasized a different but related perspective of the attentional process. Research in information processing has established the existence of two related forms of processing. Control processing requires effort and is slow and cumbersome, whereas automatic processing is effortless, quick, and efficient. Social psychologists have focused on individual differences and environmental influences on attentional processes. The ability of extraneous, inappropriate cues to disrupt performance has been established. Sport psychophysiologists have attempted to examine the underlying mechanisms of attention by monitoring cortical and cardiac activity. Both cortical and autonomic indicants of attention have been used successfully to assess attentional style in athletes during performance. A preliminary model encapsulating these principles was outlined. This multilevel, multifaceted nature of attention was developed further in the applied section, and I described a variety of assessment and training strategies. Assessment strategies included questionnaire, performance, thought-sampling techniques, behavioral analysis, and psychophysiological indicants. A preliminary model of attentional flow during peak performance was outlined. I then described training strategies to enhance attentional abilities including performance tests, computer and video tasks, and biofeedback strategies.

REFERENCES

Abernethy, B. (1993). Attention. In R.N. Singer, M. Murphey, & L.K. Tennant (Eds.), *Handbook of research on sport psychology* (pp. 127–170). New York: Macmillan.

Adler, J.D. (1981). Strategies of skill acquisition: A guide for teachers. *Motor Skill: Theory Into Practice, 5,* 75–80.

Albrecht, R.A., & Feltz, D.L. (1987). Generality and specificity of attention related to competitive anxiety and sport performance. *Journal of Sport & Exercise Psychology, 9,* 231–248.

Bacon, S. (1974). Arousal and the range of cue utilization. *Journal of Experimental Psychology, 102,* 81–87.

Bauer, R.H. (1976). Short-term memory: EEG alpha correlates and the effect of increased alpha. *Behavioral Biology, 17,* 425–433.

Baumeister, R.F. (1984). Choking under pressure: Self-consciousness and paradoxical effects of incentives on skillful performance. *Journal of Personality and Social Psychology, 46,* 610–620.

Boutcher, S.H. (1990). The role of performance routines in sport. In G. Jones & L. Hardy (Eds.), *Stress and performance in sport* (pp. 231–245). London: Wiley.

Boutcher, S.H., & Crews, D.J. (1987). The effect of a preshot routine on a well-learned skill. *International Journal of Sport Psychology, 18,* 30–39.

Boutcher, S.H., & Rotella, R.J. (1987). A psychological skills educational program for closed-skill performance enhancement. *The Sport Psychologist, 1,* 127–137.

Boutcher, S.H., & Zinsser, N. (1990). Cardiac deceleration of elite and beginning golfers during putting. *Journal of Sport Psychology, 12,* 37–47.

Broadbent, D.E. (1958). *Perception and communication.* London: Pergamon Press.

Carver, C.S., & Scheier, M.F. (1978). Self-focusing effects of dispositional self-consciousness, mirror presence, and audience presence. *Journal of Personality and Social Psychology, 36,* 324–332.

Carver, C.S., & Scheier, M.F. (1981). *Attention and self-regulation.* New York: Springer-Verlag.

Crews, D.J., & Boutcher, S.H. (1986). The effects of structured preshot behaviors on beginning golf performance. *Perceptual and Motor Skills, 62,* 291–294.

Crews, D.J., & Boutcher, S.H. (1987). An observational analysis of professional female golfers during tournament play. *Journal of Sport Behavior, 9,* 51–58.

Crews, D.J., & Landers, D.L. (1992). Electroencephalographic measures of attentional patterns prior to the golf putt. *Medicine and Science in Sports and Exercise, 25,* 116–126.

Csikszentmihalyi, M. (1975). Play and intrinsic rewards. *Journal of Humanistic Psychology, 15,* 41–63.

Duval, S., & Wicklund, R.A. (1972). *A theory of objective self-awareness.* New York: Academic Press.

Easterbrook, J.A. (1959). The effect of emotion on cue utilization and the organization of behavior. *Psychological Review, 66,* 183–201.

Ekman, P., & Friesan, M.V. (1975). *Unmasking the face.* Englewood Cliffs, NJ: Prentice Hall.

Elder, S.T., Grenier, C., Lashley, J., Martyn, S., Regenbogen, D., & Roundtree, G. (1985). Can subjects be trained to communicate through the use of EEG biofeedback? *Biofeedback and Self-Regulation, 10,* 88–89.

Harris, D. (1984). *Sports psychology.* New York: Leisure Press.

Hatfield, B.D., & Landers, D.M. (1983). Psychophysiology— A new direction for sport psychology. *Journal of Sport Psychology, 5,* 243–259.

Hatfield, B.D., Landers, D.M., & Ray, W.J. (1984). Cognitive processes during self-paced motor performance: An electroencephalographic profile of skilled marksmen. *Journal of Sport Psychology, 6,* 42–59.

Helin, P., Sihvonen, R., & Hanninen, O. (1987). Timing of the triggering action of shooting in relation to the cardiac cycle. *British Journal of Sports Medicine, 21,* 33–36.

Hirst, W. (1986). The psychology of attention. In J. LeDoux & W. Hirst (Eds.), *Mind and brain* (pp. 105–141). Cambridge, UK: Cambridge University Press.

Hockey, G. (1970). Effects of loud noise on attentional selectivity. *Quarterly Journal of Experimental Psychology, 22,* 28–36.

Izard, C.E. (1977). *Human emotions.* New York: Plenum Press.

Jackson, G.M., & Eberly, D.A. (1982). Facilitation of performance on an arithmetic task as a result of the application of a biofeedback procedure to suppress alpha wave activity. *Biofeedback and Self-Regulation, 7,* 211–221.

James, W. (1890). *Principles of psychology* (Vol. 1). New York: Holt.

Kahneman, D. (1973). *Attention and effort.* Englewood Cliffs, NJ: Prentice Hall.

Keele, S.W. (1973). *Attention and human performance.* Pacific Palisades, CA: Goodyear.

Kerr, B. (1973). Processing demands during mental operations. *Memory and Cognition, 1,* 401–412.

Kimble, G., & Perlmuter, L. (1970). The problem of volition. *Psychological Review, 77,* 361–384.

Kissin, B. (1986). *Conscious and unconscious programs in the brain.* New York: Plenum Press.

Klinger, E. (1984). A consciousness-sampling analysis of test anxiety and performance. *Journal of Personality and Social Psychology, 47,* 1376–1390.

Kocel, K., Galin, D., Ornstein, R., & Merrin, E.L. (1972). Lateral eye movements and cognitive mode. *Psychonomic Science, 27,* 223–224.

Konttinen, N., & Lyytinen, K. (1992). Physiology of preparation: Brain slow waves, heart rate, and respiration preceding triggering in rifle shooting. *International Journal of Sports Psychology, 23,* 110–127.

Konttinen, N., Lyytinen, K., & Konttinen, R. (1995). Brain slow potentials reflecting successful shooting performance. *Research Quarterly for Exercise and Sport, 66,* 64–72.

Kroll, W. (1982). Competitive athletic stress factors in athletes and coaches. In L.D. Zaichowsky & W.E. Sime (Eds), *Stress management for sport* (pp. 1–10). Reston, VA: American Alliance for Health, Physical Education, Recreation and Dance.

Landers, D.M. (1980a). Arousal, attention, and skilled performance: Further considerations. *Quest, 33,* 271–283.

Landers, D.M. (1980b). Motivation and performance: The role of arousal and attentional factors. In W.F. Straub (Ed.), *Sport psychology. An analysis of athlete behavior* (pp. 91–125). New York: Mouvement.

Landers, D.M. (1981). Arousal, attention, and skilled performance: Further considerations. *Quest, 33,* 271–283.

Landers, D.M. (1985a, May). *Beyond the TAIS: Alternative behavioral and psychophysiological measures for determining an internal vs. external focus of attention.* Paper presented at the North American Society for the Psychology of Sport and Physical Activity Conference, Gulfport, MS.

Landers, D.M. (1985b). Psychophysiological assessment and biofeedback: Application for athletes in closed-skill sports. In J. Sandweiss & S. Wolf (Eds.), *Biofeedback and sports science* (pp. 65–105). New York: Plenum Press.

Landers, D.M., Boutcher, S.H., & Wang, M.Q. (1986). A psychobiological study of archery performance. *Research Quarterly for Exercise and Sport, 57,* 236–244.

Landers, D.M., Christina, R., Hatfield, B.D., Doyle, L.A., & Daniels, F.S. (1980). Moving competitive shooting into the scientists' lab. *American Rifleman, 128,* 36–37, 76–77.

Landers, D.M., Han, M., Salazar, W., Petruzzello, S.J., Kubitz, K.A., & Gannon, T.L. (1994). Effects of learning on electroencephalographic and electrocardiographic patterns in novice archers. *International Journal of Sport Psychology, 25,* 313–330.

Landers, D.M., Petruzzello, S.J., Salazar, W., Kubitz, C.A., Crews, D.J., Kubitz, K.A., Gannon, T.L., & Han, M. (1991). The influence of electrocortical biofeedback on performance in pre-elite archers. *Medicine and Science in Sports and Exercise, 23,* 123–129.

Landers, D.M., Qi, W.M., & Courtet, P. (1985). Peripheral narrowing among experienced and inexperienced rifle-shooters under low- and high-stress conditions. *Research Quarterly for Exercise and Sport, 56,* 122–130.

Langer, E.J., & Imber, L.G. (1979). When practice makes imperfect: Debilitating effects of overlearning. *Journal of Personality and Social Psychology, 37,* 2014–2024.

LeDoux, J.E., Wilson, D.H., & Gazzaniga, M.S. (1977). Manipulo-spatial aspects of cerebral lateralization: Clues to the origin of lateralization. *Neuropsychologica, 15,* 743–750.

Marteniuk, R.G. (1976). *Information processing in motor skills.* New York: Holt, Reinhart, and Winston.

McKee, G., Humphrey, B., & McAdam, N.W. (1973). Scaled lateralization of alpha activity during linguistic and musical tasks. *Psychophysiology, 10,* 441–443.

Molander, B., & Backman, L. (1989). Age differences in heart rate patterns during concentration in a precision sport: Implications for attentional functioning. *Journal of Gerontology: Psychological Sciences, 44,* 80–87.

Moran, A. (1996). *The psychology of concentration in sport performers.* Hove, UK: Psychology Press.

Morgan, W.P., & Pollack, M.L. (1977). Psychologic characterization of the elite distance runner. *Annals of the New York Academy of Sciences, 301,* 382–403.

Navon, D., & Gopher, D. (1979). On the economy of the human processing system. *Psychological Review, 86,* 214–255.

Nideffer, R. (1976a). *The inner athlete: Mind plus muscle for winning.* San Diego, CA: Enhanced Performance Associates.

Nideffer, R. (1976b). Test of attentional and interpersonal style. *Journal of Personality and Social Psychology, 34,* 394–404.

Nideffer, R. (1976c). *An interpreters' manual for the test of attentional and interpersonal style.* Rochester, New York: Behavioral Research Applications Group.

Norman, D. (1969). Toward a theory of memory and attention. *Psychological Review, 75,* 522–536.

Parasuraman, R. (1984). Preface. In R. Parasuraman & D. Davies (Eds.), *Varieties of attention* (pp. xi–xvi). Orlando, FL: Academic Press.

Parasuraman, R., & Davies, D. (1984). *Varieties of attention.* Orlando, FL: Academic Press.

Posner, M.I., & Bois, S.J. (1971). Components of attention. *Psychological Review, 78,* 391–408.

Privette, G. (1982). Peak performance in sports: A factorial topology. *International Journal of Sport Psychology, 13,* 242–249.

Privette, G. (1983). Peak experience, peak performance, and flow: A comparative analysis of positive human experiences. *Journal of Personality and Social Psychology, 43,* 1361–1367.

Ravizza, K. (1984). Qualities of the peak experience in sport. In J. Silva & R. Weinberg (Eds.), *Psychological foundations of sport* (pp. 452–461). Champaign, IL: Human Kinetics.

Salazar, W., Landers, D.M., Petruzzello, S.J., Han, M., Crews, D.J., & Kubitz, K.A. (1990). Hemispheric asymmetry, cardiac response, and performance in elite archers. *Research Quarterly for Exercise and Sports, 61,* 351–359.

Sarason, I.G. (1972). Experimental approaches to test anxiety: Attention and the uses of information. In C.D. Spielberger (Ed.), *Anxiety: Current trends in theory and research* (Vol. 2, pp. 380–403). New York: Academic Press.

Scheier, M.S., Fenigstein, A., & Buss, A.H. (1974). Self-awareness and physical aggression. *Journal of Experimental Social Psychology, 10,* 264–273.

Schomer, H. H. (1986). Mental strategies and the perception of effort of marathon runners. *International Journal of Sport Psychology, 17,* 41–59.

Schomer, H. H. (1987). Mental strategy training programme for marathon runners. *International Journal of Sport Psychology, 18,* 133–151.

Schmidt, R.A. (1988). *Motor control and learning.* Champaign, IL: Human Kinetics.

Schneider, W., Dumais, S.T., & Shiffrin, R.M. (1984). Automatic and control processing and attention. In R. Parasuraman & R. Davies (Eds.), *Varieties of attention* (pp. 1–27). Orlando, FL: Academic Press.

Schwartz, G.E., Davidson, R.J., & Maer, F. (1975). Right hemispheric specialization for emotion: Interactions with cognitions. *Science, 190,* 286–290.

Schwartz, G.E., Davidson, R.J., & Pugwash, E. (1976). Voluntary control of patterns of EEG parietal asymmetry: Cognitive concomitants. *Psychophysiology, 13,* 498–504.

Shiffrin, R.M. (1976). Capacity limitations in information processing, attention, and memory. In W.K. Estes (Ed.), *Handbook of learning and cognitive processes* (Vol. 4, pp. 117–136). Hillsdale, NJ: Erlbaum.

Sperry, R.W. (1968). Hemisphere deconnection and unity in conscious awareness. *American Psychologist, 23,* 723–733.

Stroop, J.P. (1935). Studies of interference in serial verbal reactions. *Journal of Experimental Psychology, 18,* 643–662.

Suter, S., Griffin, G., Smallhouse, P., & Whitlach, S. (1981). Biofeedback regulation of temporal EEG alpha asymmetries. *Biofeedback and Self-Regulation, 6,* 45–56.

Tomkins, S. (1983). Affect theory. In P. Eckman (Ed.), *Emotion in the human face* (2nd ed., pp. 353–395). New York: Cambridge University Press.

Tourangeau, R., & Ellsworth, P. C. (1979). The role of facial response in the experience of emotion. *Journal of Personality and Social Psychology, 37,* 1519–1531.

Tucker, D.M., Shearer, S.L., & Murray, J.D. (1977). Hemispheric specialization and cognitive behavior therapy. *Cognitive Therapy and Research, 1,* 263–273.

Van Schoyck, S.R., & Grasha, A.F. (1981). Attentional style variations and athletic ability: The advantage of a sports-specific test. *Journal of Sport Psychology, 3,* 149–165.

Wachtel, P.L. (1967). Conceptions of broad or narrow attention. *Psychological Bulletin, 68,* 417–429.

Wickens, C.D. (1984). Processing resources in attention. In R. Parasuraman & R. Davies (Eds.), *Varieties of attention* (pp. 63–102). Orlando, FL: Academic Press.

Wine, J. (1971). Test anxiety and direction of attention. *Psychological Bulletin, 76,* 92–104.

Zaichkowsky, L.D. (1984). Attentional styles. In W. Straub & J. Williams (Eds.), *Cognitive sport psychology* (pp. 140–150). New York: Sports Science Associates.

The Jekyll/Hyde Nature of Goals: Revisiting and Updating Goal-Setting in Sport

Damon Burton and Sarah Naylor

R esearch on goal-setting in sport has exploded in the nine years since the first edition of this text was published. A quick perusal of the burgeoning goal literature prompts two inescapable conclusions. First, goals work. Second, goal-setting is somewhat more complicated than it looks—at least if we hope to maximize the effectiveness of setting goals to enhance competitive performance. Recent studies of the goal-setting patterns of adolescent, collegiate, and Olympic athletes (Burton, Weinberg, Yukelson, & Weigand, 1998, 2001; Weinberg, Burke, & Jackson, 1997; Weinberg, Burton, Yukelson, & Weigand, 1993, 2000) have confirmed that almost all athletes set goals, but on average, most athletes rate goals as only moderately effective. Thus, athletes intuitively know goals can help, but they have trouble figuring out how to best set goals to maximize their effectiveness. The nature of the deceptively complex goal-setting process is perhaps best illustrated in two real-life examples.

First, here is an example of goal-setting at its best. Dick Vermeil was the 1999 NFL Coach of the Year, resurrecting the St. Louis Rams from one of the NFL's worst teams to Super Bowl champion.

This was Vermeil's second coaching career, coming 15 years after retiring as one of the game's most successful coaches, a career that was built around setting and achieving a series of goals. When Dick Vermeil first decided to become a football coach during his senior year in high school, he vowed to his high school coach Bill Wood, "If I'm going to do it, I'm going to do it right" (B. Smith, 1983, p. 63). To Vermeil, "right" meant setting a series of realistic goals, developing systematic action plans to make those goals reality, and then working long hours to ensure that all goals were achieved.

Vermeil's goals provided a road map for his coaching career, complete with seven intermediate markers to help ensure that his career was making systematic progress toward his dream of taking a team to the Super Bowl (B. Smith, 1983). Goal 1 was to earn undergraduate and master's degrees and become a high school head football coach. Subgoals were to win the league title and become Coach of the Year. Vermeil quickly accomplished these goals at Hillsdale High in San Mateo, California, and he then moved on to his second goal, becoming a junior college head coach while again winning Coach of the Year honors. This goal was accomplished by age 27 in his only season coaching Napa Junior College in Northern California to a 7–2 record. Not surprisingly, Vermeil's reputation quickly spread. Goals 3 to 5 were to become a major college assistant coach, to become an NFL assistant coach, and then to return to collegiate football as a head coach, with subgoals of winning the Rose Bowl and becoming the PAC 10 Coach of the Year. These three goals were accomplished on schedule, with the final goal attained by age 37 when Vermeil returned to UCLA as its head coach, taking the Bruins to 6–3–2 and 9–2 records in two seasons. The second year at UCLA included a PAC 10 title, conference Coach of the Year honors, and a 23–10 upset of Ohio State in the Rose Bowl. The sixth goal was the inevitable next step of becoming an NFL head coach, and Vermeil accomplished that goal soon after the Rose Bowl victory when he was hired as head coach of the Philadelphia Eagles. Finally, Goal 7 was to get the lowly Eagles into the Super Bowl, a feat he accomplished by his fifth season in 1982.

In Dick Vermeil's case, his goals proved extremely successful in helping him accomplish his career objectives. However, Vermeil's goals were not accomplished by accident. He understood the goal-setting process and the importance of developing action plans, working hard to implement those plans effectively, and frequently evaluating to keep goals on track and enhance motivation. Vermeil broke his long-term goals down into short-term goals. Each morning of his football coaching career, Vermeil made "to do" lists on a yellow legal pad, listing the many daily and weekly goals that must be accomplished for those long-term goals to become reality. Lists were made for his wife, his administrative assistant, his personnel director, but most of all himself. "Doing it right" meant that the lists included all the minute details that were important for eventual success, and normally the lists required 16- to 20-hour days to ensure that they were fully accomplished. Such was the systematic approach to goal-setting that helped Dick Vermeil become a successful coach at the high school, junior college, major college, and professional levels.

Goals don't always work so effectively, particularly if the individuals setting those goals don't understand the goal-setting process and the importance of using key process variables such as action plans and goal evaluation to ensure success. For example, here's a case study from the first author's coaching experience that typifies the flip side of setting goals—the insidious problems

© Human Kinetics

When set correctly, goals can lead to a major payoff.

that can arise when coaches and athletes use goals incorrectly, prompting diffidence and anxiety that undermine performance.

My initial revelation of the complexity of goal-setting came in my final year as a high school basketball coach. Going into the season, expectations for the team were high in our community. "Best basketball team since the state championship club 5 years ago," the regulars at the drug store told me repeatedly. Not surprisingly, conference coaches made us preseason favorites to win the league title, and I caught the fever too, fully expecting this team to bring our community another state title. However, because I was concerned that these lofty expectations would breed overconfidence and complacency, our team set only one goal for the season—to win the Central Prairie League Championship.

During the first four weeks of the season, the team played superbly, better than any team I had ever coached. Although this team was somewhat undersized, the players were talented, played well together, understood what we wanted to do offensively and defensively, and executed with tremendous confidence and aggressiveness. Our record at Christmas break was 6–1, with our only loss coming on the road in double overtime to the third-ranked team in the state.

Then a funny thing happened on the way to our "dream" season. Our community was hit by a particularly nasty flu strain, decimating the team for more than three weeks. During this stretch we had at least two starters out of every game, and although the kids confronted this adversity head on, seemingly practicing harder and competing more intensely than ever; we still lost six of the next seven games. Suddenly, the single goal we had established for the season was now unrealistic, and the players fixated on this failure. For several weeks, my assistant coach and I did nothing but put out "brush fires," spending many hours talking to players individually and as a team about putting our problems behind us and making the best of the remaining season. We also instituted a substitute goal—qualifying for the state tournament—but for some unexplained reason, commitment to that new goal was moderate at best.

Although we lost only four more games the rest of the year—all by small margins—and nearly qualified for the state tournament, we were just not the same team. We recovered physically and continued to improve our offensive and defensive execution over that final 6 weeks of the season, but psychologically, the damage was irreparable. We had lost that great confidence and mental toughness that had allowed us to play with such poise, aggressiveness, and composure. Now our play was punctuated by timidity, indecision, and mental lapses. The close losses were particularly frustrating because the team that played with such great confidence before Christmas almost assuredly would have won those games. Above all, everyone seemed to understand intuitively that like Humpty Dumpty, once our self-confidence was shattered, it was virtually impossible to put our collective efficacy back together.

These two stories demonstrate the complex nature of goal-setting. The two faces of goals can be as different as Dr. Jekyll and Mr. Hyde, and this Jekyll and Hyde nature of goals is an important reason why we must strive to better understand the goal-setting process. The extensive research on goal-setting, both within (Burton, 1992, 1993; Kyllo & Landers, 1995; Weinberg, 1994) and out-

side of sport (Locke & Latham, 1990), has confirmed that setting goals can be an effective performance enhancement strategy. However, the challenge to both researchers and practitioners is to better understand the goal-setting process to maximize the motivational and self-confidence benefits that goals can provide, thereby enhancing performance.

Therefore, the primary purpose of this chapter is to review existing theory and research on goal-setting with the intent of better understanding the goal-setting process and how to maximize the effectiveness of setting goals in sport. In the first section we define goal-setting, clarifying what goals are, their primary psychological functions, and the role of goals in such divergent constructs as motivation and stress. In the second section we review theory and research on goal-setting, highlighting the role that goal attributes such as focus, specificity, difficulty, valence, proximity, and collectivity play in goal effectiveness. The third section focuses on why goals work less effectively in sport. In the fourth section we describe a revised competitive goal-setting model and briefly review both model predictions and research testing model predictions in sport. The fifth section outlines several important measurement issues that currently limit goal research and practical implementation. Finally, in the last section we address future directions in goal-setting research, highlighting five important issues that seemingly have an impact on goal effectiveness.

WHAT ARE GOALS?

William James's classic definition of attention is prefaced by the statement, "Everyone knows what attention is" (1890, p. 455). It is tempting to define goal-setting in a similar way, because it is one of the most commonly used performance enhancement strategies in the behavioral sciences that both researchers and practitioners assume has a straightforward meaning. Webster's New World Dictionary defines a goal as "an object or end that one strives to attain; an aim." The world's most preeminent goal-setting researcher, Edwin Locke, defined a goal simply as "what an individual is trying to accomplish; it is the object or aim of an action" (Locke, Shaw, Saari, & Latham, 1981, p. 126).

Locke took an objective approach to conceptualizing goal-setting that emphasizes behavior as purposeful and human beings as rational creatures who survive by using their intellect to govern their behavior. Although goal-setting has gone by a number of terms including "level of aspiration" in the 1930s and "management by objectives" in business contexts, the term *goal* is commonly used today in a vast array of disciplines and contexts to refer to these cognitive regulators of behavior. As easy as it might be to accept goals as the tools to pursue goal-directed behavior, goals don't necessarily work at a conscious level all the time. Locke and Latham (1990) emphasized that goals go in and out of conscious awareness at different times. For example, focusing on winning a game may disrupt performance because it interferes with actions needed to reach the goal. Particularly with habitual actions such as automated sport skills (e.g., jump shots in basketball or drop volleys in tennis) goals help to initiate action, but once initiated, little conscious control is needed to pursue those goals effectively.

Locke and Latham (1990) also emphasized that every goal includes two basic components: direction and product quantity or quality. Direction implies choice, specifically the choice about how to direct or focus one's behavior, whereas product quantity or quality suggests a minimal standard of performance that must be attained. For example, when a high school athlete sets a goal to make the varsity basketball team, a choice is involved to pursue basketball instead of competing in other winter sports or extracurricular activities. Moreover, that choice also constitutes a commitment by the athlete to work on developing his or her basketball skills to a high enough level to be selected for the high school varsity team.

Goal Mechanisms: How Goals Work

Another basic goal-setting question is, How do goals work? Goal theorists (e.g., Locke, 1968; Locke & Latham, 1990) have identified four important mechanisms that underlie the goal-setting process. According to Locke and his colleagues, goals prompt us to do the following:

- Direct action by focusing attention
- Increase effort and intensity
- Encourage persistence in the face of failure or adversity
- Promote the development of new task or problem-solving strategies

The direct, short-term motivational function of goals is most readily apparent with the first three

goal mechanisms, whereas developing new task strategies is an indirect, long-term process that may be necessary with complex tasks or when confronting failure or adversity. That is, as long as the task is relatively straightforward and athletes can perform the skill effectively, the motivational benefits of goals should improve the quantity and/or quality of performance. However, for highly complex tasks or when the athlete has problems learning or executing proper skill mechanics, direct motivational goal mechanisms may not be enough to ensure goal attainment. Developing new task strategies involves working smarter as well as longer and harder. For example, a basketball coach with a team who shoots free throws poorly may set a goal to increase the team free throw percentage from 54% to 62%, and to accomplish this goal, he may develop an action plan that calls for players to shoot 500 free throws each day in practice. Regrettably, the motivational benefits of such a goal will probably be ineffective if the players have major flaws in their free throw mechanics, don't use the same routine shooting free throws in practice that they use in competition, or become distracted during stressful competitive free throw situations. Thus, developing new task strategies would first focus on making desirable changes in shooting form, developing a consistent routine that is used in both practice and competition, and teaching players how to remain focused on positive performance cues during pressure-packed free throw situations; then, the motivational benefits of goals could be used to automate those new shooting fundamentals.

State and Trait Conceptions of Goals

Several subdisciplines within psychology use the term *goal* as a major component in both motivational and stress theories, prompting confusion about the exact meaning of the term in specific contexts. The notion of goals is currently used in two major ways. First, business psychologists such as Edwin Locke and his colleagues (Locke & Latham, 1990; Locke et al., 1981) view goals as a direct motivational strategy. In this context, goals function primarily like a psychological state, providing a specific standard that motivates individuals to focus their attention and improve efforts at attaining a particular quantity or quality of performance. Similarly, stress researchers such as Richard Lazarus (1991; Lazarus & Folkman, 1984) use goals as an important component of stress models, conceptualizing that stress will occur when individuals become challenged or threatened about their ability to attain important goals. In both cases, this state conception of goals focuses on attaining a goal in a particular situation for a specific purpose—in one case the prospect of success should engender personal motivation, and in the other the threat of failure should promote stress.

Several motivation theorists (Dweck, 1980, 1999; Elliott & Dweck, 1988; Maehr & Braskamp, 1986; Maehr & Nicholls, 1980; Nicholls, 1984a, 1984b) used the notion of goals to suggest a more global purpose for involvement in particular activities. Goals in this context are more like personality traits, implying predispositions for participation based on underlying motives for how individuals view ability and what they want to attain or accomplish. Motivation theorists often label these more global goals *goal orientations* (e.g., Dweck, 1999; Elliott & Dweck, 1988; Maehr & Braskamp, 1986; Maehr & Nicholls, 1980; Nicholls, 1984a, 1984b). Inherent in the idea of goal orientations is the premise that success and failure are subjective perceptions, not objective events. Thus, success can be attained in any situation in which individuals are able to either infer personally desirable characteristics, qualities, or attributes about themselves or attain personally meaningful objectives (Maehr & Braskamp, 1986). Dweck (1999) emphasized that goal orientations reflect underlying theories of ability, both what ability means and how it develops. In attempting to integrate these two notions of goals, we believe that these two conceptions are highly complementary, with discrete goals serving as the tools for achieving more global goal orientations.

REVIEWING GOAL-SETTING THEORY AND RESEARCH

The acid test of any intervention strategy is, Does it work? Goal-setting has been a topic of great interest to researchers and practitioners, and research testing the efficacy of goals for enhancing performance has been the primary focus of both the general (Locke & Latham, 1990) and sport goal-setting literatures (Burton, 1992, 1993; Kyllo & Landers, 1995; Weinberg, 1994). Four specific questions have guided this research:

- How consistently do goals enhance performance?

- What is the magnitude of performance enhancement effects from setting goals?
- How well do goal-setting effects generalize across tasks, populations, and time spans?
- What types of goals promote the greatest performance enhancement effects?

Overall Goal-Setting Effectiveness

The consensus of more than 500 goal-setting studies (Burton, 1992, 1993; Chidester & Grigsby, 1984; Hunter & Schmidt, 1983; Kyllo & Landers, 1995; Locke & Latham, 1990; Locke et al., 1981; Mento, Steel, & Karren, 1987; Tubbs, 1986; Weinberg, 1994; Wood, Mento, & Locke, 1987) is that specific, difficult goals prompt higher levels of performance than vague, do-your-best, or no goals. Of the 201 studies reviewed by Locke and Latham (1990), goal-setting effects were demonstrated totally or contingently in 183 studies, a 91% success rate. Moreover, five meta-analyses of general goal-setting research (Chidester & Grigsby, 1984; Hunter & Schmidt, 1983; Mento et al., 1987; Tubbs, 1986; Wood et al., 1987), each containing from 17 to 53 goal-setting studies and including from 1,278 to 6,635 subjects, demonstrated mean effect sizes ranging from .42 to .80, representing performance increases of 8.4% to 16%.

A comprehensive review of the goal-setting literature convincingly demonstrates the generalizability of goal-setting findings (Burton, 1992, 1993; Chidester & Grigsby, 1984; Hunter & Schmidt, 1983; Kyllo & Landers, 1995; Locke & Latham, 1990; Locke et al., 1981; Mento et al., 1987; Tubbs, 1986; Weinberg, 1994; Wood et al., 1987). Locke and Latham's (1990) review of nearly 500 goal-setting studies confirmed tremendous consistency for the frequency and magnitude of goal-setting effects across different tasks, settings, performance criteria, and types of participants. Locke and Latham documented goal-setting effects across 90 different tasks, ranging from simple laboratory experiments (e.g., listing nouns, computation) to complex tasks such as prose learning and management simulation, as well as across a great diversity of subject populations that varied in gender, age, race, socioeconomic status, and type of employment (e.g., loggers, factory workers, engineers and scientists, and college professors). Finally, goal-setting effects have been demonstrated for time spans as short as 1 minute and as long as 36 months (Ivancevich, 1974). Clearly, these data confirm that goal-setting is both a highly consistent and a robust performance enhancement strategy that works almost universally for most participants across a variety of tasks and settings. Overall, these results strongly indicate that goal-setting is one of the most effective performance enhancement techniques available in the behavioral sciences.

Goal-Setting Research in Sport

A perusal of sport-specific goal research (Burton, 1992, 1993; Kyllo & Landers, 1995; Weinberg, 1994) confirms that setting goals is also an effective performance enhancement technique in the physical activity domain. In the only meta-analysis of goal research in sport, Kyllo and Landers (1995) examined 49 goal-setting studies in sport and physical activity, using 36 of them in their analysis. When compared to no goals or do-your-best goals, goal-setting yielded an effect size of .34, a slightly smaller value than the effect sizes of .42 to .80 found in the general goal literature. Our review that summarized findings from only published research found 67 goal-setting manuscripts published with sport samples, 56 of which met our inclusion criteria. Of those 56 goal-setting studies in sport and physical activity, 44 demonstrated moderate to strong goal-setting effects, a 79% effectiveness rate (table 15.1). The review for the initial version of this chapter completed nine years ago found only 14 studies, two-thirds of which revealed significant goal-setting effects. Thus, as the number of goal-setting studies in sport increase, goal-setting results in sport gradually look more like general goal-setting results.

Goal Attribute Research

Although the overall effectiveness of goals is clearly the most extensively researched goal-setting topic, goal attribute research has been a close second (Locke & Latham, 1990). Goal attribute research focuses on determining what types of goals are most effective in enhancing performance, and this section highlights research assessing the efficacy of six goal types that are frequently used in sport: goal focus, goal specificity, goal difficulty, goal valence, goal proximity, and goal collectivity.

Goal Focus

Goal focus, a term coined by sport goal researchers (Burton, 1989b, 1992, 1993; Kingston & Hardy, 1997; Kingston, Hardy, & Markland, 1992), refers to what the goal is designed to accomplish—either a specific performance objective (e.g., run the 100 meters in less than 10 seconds or collect 10 rebounds per game) or a desired outcome (e.g., win a match or place in the top five in this race). Originally, goal focus dealt primarily with performance versus outcome goals (Burton, 1989b). Performance goals were defined in terms of their "process" focus, emphasizing form, technique, improvement, and attaining specific performance standards, whereas outcome goals were more "product" oriented, focusing on social comparison and object outcome (i.e., place in a race, winning or losing; Burton, 1989b). Burton (1989b, 1992, 1993) argued that the superiority of performance goals is due to their greater flexibility and controllability compared with outcome goals. The flexibility of performance goals allows athletes of all ability levels to raise and lower goal difficulty levels to maintain an optimal level of challenge that is demanding but realistic for their current performance capabilities, thus prompting higher motivation and more consistent success. Moreover, the controllability of performance goals means that performers have a higher degree of control over their own success, thus allowing them to internalize credit for that success as indicative of high or improved ability. Sport goal research (Burton, 1989b; L. Hardy, Jones, & Gould, 1996; Kingston & Hardy, 1997; Kingston et al., 1992; Schunk & Swartz, 1993; Zimmerman, 1989) generally has found performance goals to be more effective than outcome goals. Further support for the superiority of performance goals has come from the goal orientation literature (e.g., Duda & Hall, 2001) and from anecdotal reports of sport psychology consultants (Gould, 1998; L. Hardy et al., 1996; Orlick, 1986). In their meta-analysis, Kyllo and Landers (1995) questioned the superiority of performance goals, although they did not directly test this prediction. The superior performance enhancement effects of performance compared with outcome goals have been attributed to several factors besides flexibility and controllability, including (a) increased attentional focus (Kingston & Hardy, 1994, 1997), (b) enhanced concentration (Beggs, 1990; Boutcher, 1990; L. Hardy & Nelson, 1988), (c) automation of key skills (L. Hardy et al., 1996), and (d) improved self-efficacy due to higher levels of perceived control (Burton, 1989b; Hall & Byrne, 1988).

Kingston and Hardy (1994, 1997) recently clarified and broadened the goal focus distinction by separating performance goals into two goal categories termed *performance* and *process* goals. In this refined goal focus categorization, process

Table 15.1

Summary of Goal Research in Sport and Physical Activity

Study	Participants	Results	Level of support
General goal effectiveness (goal versus no-goal/control conditions: 11 out of 15 studies strongly or partially supported general goal effectiveness)			
Anshel, Weinberg, & Jackson (1992)	54 undergraduate students	All goal conditions (easy, difficult, and self-set) performed better than a no-goal condition on a juggling task	Strong
Bar-Eli, Levy-Kolker, Tenenbaum, & Weinberg (1993)	184 army trainees	No difference between five goal setting conditions and no-goal condition on physical fitness tasks	Weak
Barnett (1977)	93 female high school students	No difference in juggling performance between two student-set goal conditions and three no-goal conditions	Weak
Barnett & Stanicek (1979)	30 university archery undergraduates	Goal condition resulted in superior archery performance compared to no goal condition	Strong
Boyce & Wayda (1994)	252 female university weight training students	Self-set and assigned goal condition performed better than no goal condition	Strong
Hollingsworth (1975)	90 junior high school students	No difference between performance goal condition, "do your best" condition, and no goal condition on a juggling task	Weak
Humphries, Thomas, & Nelson (1991)	60 college males	Goal conditions led to superior mirror tracing performance compared to no goal condition	Strong
Lerner, Ostrow, & Etzel (1996)	12 female basketball players	Goal setting condition resulted in superior free throw shooting improvement compared with goal setting + imagery condition and imagery condition	Moderate
Nelson (1978)	100 college males	Assigned goal condition performed better on a muscular endurance task compared to no goal condition	Strong
Shoenfelt (1996)	12 female collegiate basketball players	Goals and feedback condition increased free throw accuracy more than did control condition	Strong
Tenenbaum, Pinchas, Elbaz, Bar-Elik, & Weinberg (1991)	214 9th grade white Israeli students	Short-term, long-term, and short-term + long-term goal conditions performed better on sit-up task compared to no goal or "do your best" goal condition	Strong
Theodorakis (1996)	48 undergraduate physical education students	Self efficacy and goal setting were found to be predictors of performance on a tennis service task	Moderate
Tzetzis, Kioumourtzoglou, & Mavromalis (1997)	78 boys associated with a basketball academy	Goal setting coupled with performance feedback on simple and complex basketball tasks improved performance more than feedback alone	Strong
Weinberg, Burton, Yukelson, & Weigand (1993)	678 intercollegiate male and female athletes	Nearly all subjects reported setting goals and perceived goals to be moderately to highly effective	Strong
Weinberg, Garland, Bruya, & Jackson (1990)	87 undergraduate students in fitness courses	No difference between realistic, unrealistic, "do your best," and no-goal conditions on a sit-up task	Weak

(continued)

Table 15.1 (continued)

Goal difficulty (7 out of 16 studies supported or partially supported goal difficulty predictions)

Study	Participants	Results	Level of support
Anshel, Weinberg, & Jackson (1992)	54 undergraduate students	Difficult goals increased intrinsic motivation while easy goals decreased intrinsic motivation on a juggling task	Strong for goal difficulty
Bar-Eli, Levy-Kolker, Tenenbaum, & Weinberg (1993)	184 army trainees	No difference between easy, moderate, hard, very hard, "do your best," and control goal setting conditions on physical fitness tasks	Weak for goal difficulty
Bar-Eli, Tenenbaum, Pie, Blesh, & Almog (1997)	364 male high school students	Difficult/realistic group exhibited the greatest increase in sit-up performance compared to the easy goal, "do your best," and no-goal groups	Strong for difficult, yet realistic goals
Boyce (1990)	90 students in a rifle shooting contest	Only the specific/difficult condition was superior to the "do your best" condition on shooting task	Strong for goal difficulty
Boyce (1990)	135 university riflery class participants	Specific and difficult goal conditions performed better than "do your best" condition during a rifle shooting task	Strong for goal difficulty
Frieman, Weinberg, & Jackson (1990)	45 novice and 27 intermediate bowlers	Long-term, specific, and difficult goal conditions performed better than "do your best" condition	Strong for goal difficulty
Hall, Weinberg, & Jackson (1987)	94 college males	No difference in hand dynamometer performance between "improve by 40 seconds" goal condition and "improve by 70 seconds" goal condition	Weak for goal difficulty
Humphries, Thomas, & Nelson (1991)	60 college males	No difference in mirror tracing performance between attainable and unattainable goal conditions	Weak for goal difficulty
Nelson (1978)	100 college males	Students in the fictitious goal/norm group (highly difficult suggested goal/norm) performed best, compared to two realistic norm/goal groups and a control group	Moderate for goal difficulty
Weinberg, Burke, & Jackson (1997)	224 youth tennis players	Athletes preferred setting moderately difficult goals	Moderate for goal difficulty
Weinberg, Bruya, Jackson, & Garland (1986)	123 students enrolled in university courses	No difference between extremely hard goals, highly improbable goals, and "do your best" goals on a sit-up task	Weak for goal difficulty
	30 students enrolled in university courses	No difference between easy, moderate, and extremely hard goal conditions on a sit-up task	Weak for goal difficulty
Weinberg, Fowler, Jackson, Bagnall, & Bruya (1991)	114 boys and 135 girls from 3rd through 5th grades	No difference between easy, difficult, improbable, and "do your best" goal conditions on a sit-up task	Weak for goal difficulty
	50 college males and 50 college females	No difference between easy, moderately difficult, very difficult, highly improbable, and "do your best" goal conditions on a basketball shooting performance	Weak for goal difficulty
Weinberg, Garland, Bruya, & Jackson (1990)	87 undergraduate students in fitness courses	No difference between realistic, unrealistic, "do your best," and no-goal conditions on a sit-up task	Weak for goal difficulty
	120 participants	No difference between moderately difficult, difficult, unrealistic, and "do your best" goal conditions on a hand dynamometer task	Weak for goal difficulty

Goal focus (6 out of 7 studies directly or indirectly supported the use of multiple goal-focus strategies)

Burton (1989)	29 collegiate swimmers	Setting performance goals more effectively enhanced both competitive cognitions and performance compared to a control condition	Strong for performance goals
Filby, Maynard, & Graydon (1999)	40 adult participants	Multiple-goal strategies (outcome + performance + process goals) more effectively improved soccer performance compared to single-goal strategies	Strong for multiple goal-focus strategies
Giannini, Weinberg, & Jackson (1988)	100 college male recreational basketball players	No difference between competitive, cooperative, and mastery goal conditions on a basketball task	Weak for goal focus differential effects
Kingston & Hardy (1997)	37 club golfers	Both process goal and performance goal groups showed improvement in golf handicap, the process goal condition showed significant improvement more quickly	Strong for process and performance goals
Weinberg, Burke, & Jackson (1997)	224 youth tennis players	Descriptive study findings identify three most important goals: To improve performance, to have fun, and to win	Moderate for process, performance, and outcome goals
Weinberg, Burton, Yukelson, & Weigand (1993)	678 intercollegiate male and female athletes	Males set more outcome goals and less performance goals compared to females, and both groups reported goals to be effective	Moderate for performance and outcome goals
Zimmerman & Kitsantas (1996)	50 female high school physical education students	Process goals led to improved dart throwing performance compared to product goals	Strong for process goals

Goal proximity (3 out of 8 studies supported or partially supported setting both short- and long-term goals)

Bar-Eli, Hartman, & Levy-Kolker (1994)	80 adolescents with behavior disorders	Although both conditions improved, the short- + long-term goal condition showed greatest increase in sit-up performance compared to the long-term only goal condition	Strong for setting both short- and long-term goals
Boyce (1992)	181 university students	No difference between short-term, long-term, and short-term + long-term conditions on shooting task performance	Weak for setting both short- and long-term goals
Frierman, Weinberg, & Jackson (1990)	45 novice and 27 intermediate bowlers	Of the four goal conditions (short-term, long-term, short- + long-term, and "do your best"), only the long-term goal condition improved more than "do your best" condition	Weak for setting both short- and long-term goals
Hall & Byrne (1988)	43 male and 11 female university weight training students	The two long-term + intermediate goal conditions performed better than long-term only goal condition on an endurance task	Moderate for setting both short- and long-term goals
Howe & Poole (1992)	115 male undergraduate physical education students	No difference between short-term, and short- + long-term goal conditions or basketball shooting performance	Weak for setting both short- and long-term goals
Tenenbaum, Pinchas, Ebaz, Bar-Eli, & Weinberg (1991)	214 9th grade white Israeli students	Short-term + long-term goal condition performed best on sit-up task compared to short-term only or long-term only goal conditions	Strong for setting both short- and long-term goals
Weinberg, Bruya, & Jackson (1985)	96 students enrolled in university fitness courses	No difference between short-term, long-term, short-term + long-term, and "do your best" conditions on sit-up task	Weak for setting both short- and long-term goals
Weinberg, Bruya, Longino, & Jackson (1988)	130 boys and 125 girls from grades 4-6	No difference between short-term, long-term, and short-term + long-term conditions on sit-up endurance task	Weak for setting both short- and long-term goals

(continued)

467

Table 15.1
(continued)

Goal specificity (13 out of 22 studies strongly or partially supported goal specificity predictions)

Study	Participants	Results	Level of support
Bar-Eli, Levy-Kolker, Tenenbaum, & Weinberg (1993)	184 army trainees	No differences between four specific goal conditions (easy, moderate, hard, very hard), "do your best" goal condition, and control condition on physical fitness tests	Weak for goal specificity
Bar-Eli, Tenenbaum, Pie, Btesh, & Almog (1997)	364 high school students	All specific goal groups (easy, difficult/realistic, and improbably/unrealistic) performed better than non-specific goal groups on sit-up task	Strong for goal specificity
Boyce (1990)	90 students in a rifle shooting contest	Of three goal conditions (specific/difficult, specific/moderate, and "do your best"), specific/difficult condition was superior to "do your best" condition	Moderate for specificity
Boyce (1990)	135 university riflery class participants	Specific and difficult goal conditions performed better than "do your best" condition during a rifle shooting task	Strong for goal specificity
Boyce (1992)	181 university students	Short-term goal, long-term goal, and short- + long-term goal conditions performed better on shooting task compared to "do your best" condition	Strong for goal specificity
Boyce (1992)	138 university riflery class participants	Both self-set and assigned goal conditions performed better than "do your best" condition during a rifle shooting task	Moderate for goal specificity
Boyce (1994)	30 experienced pistol shooters	No difference between instructor-set and "do your best" goal conditions on a pistol shooting task	Weak for goal specificity
Boyce & Bingham (1997)	288 college students performing a bowling task	No difference between self-set, assigned, and "do your best" goal conditions on bowling performance	Weak for goal specificity
Burton (1989)	16 male and 7 female under-graduate basketball students	Specific-goal condition performed better on most basketball skills compared to general-goal condition	Moderate for goal specificity
Erbaugh & Barnett (1988)	52 elementary school children	Both goal conditions (goals, goals/modeling) enhanced rope jumping performance compared to "do your best" condition	Strong for goal specificity
Frierman, Weinberg, & Jackson (1990)	45 novice and 27 intermediate bowlers	Of the four goal conditions (short-term, long-term, short- + long-term, and "do your best"), only the long-term goal condition improved more than the "do your best" condition	Moderate for goal specificity
Giannini, Weinberg, & Jackson (1988)	100 college male recreational basketball players	Only competitive goal condition performed better than "do your best"–without-feedback condition on a basketball task	Weak for goal specificity
Hall & Byrne (1988)	43 male and 11 female university weight training students	The two long-term + intermediate goal conditions performed better than a "do your best" condition on an endurance task	Moderate for goal specificity
Hall, Weinberg, & Jackson (1987)	94 college males	The two specific goal conditions performed better than the "do your best" condition on a hand dynamometer endurance task	Strong for goal specificity
Hollingsworth (1975)	90 junior high school students	No difference between performance goal condition, "do your best" condition, and no goal condition on a juggling task	Weak for goal specificity
Lee & Edwards (1984)	93 5th grade physical education students	Specific goals (self-set and assigned) enhanced performance to a greater extent than did "do your best" goals on motor tasks	Strong for goal specificity
Tenenbaum, Pinchas, Elbaz, Bar-Eli, & Weinberg (1991)	214 9th grade white Israeli students	Short-term + long-term goal condition performed better on sit-up task compared to "do your best" goal condition	Strong for goal specificity

Study	Participants	Findings	Conclusion
Weinberg, Bruya, & Jackson (1985)	96 students enrolled in university fitness courses	No difference between short-term, long-term, short-term + long-term, and "do your best" conditions on a sit-up task	Weak for goal specificity
Weinberg, Bruya, Jackson, & Garland (1986)	123 students enrolled in university fitness courses	No difference between extremely hard goals, highly improbable goals, and "do your best" goals on a sit-up task	Weak for goal specificity
Weinberg, Bruya, Longino, & Jackson (1988)	130 boys and 125 girls from grades 4-6	Specific goals led to better performance on a sit-up endurance task compared to "do your best" goals	Moderate for goal specificity
Weinberg, Garland, Bruya, & Jackson (1990)	87 undergraduate students in fitness courses	No difference between realistic, unrealistic, "do your best," and no-goal conditions on a sit-up task	Weak for goal specificity
	120 participants	No difference between moderately difficult, difficult, unrealistic, and "do your best" goal conditions on a hand dynamometer task	Weak for goal specificity

Goal collectivity (2 studies support or partially supported the setting of group goals)

Study	Participants	Findings	Conclusion
Brawley, Carron, & Widmeyer (1992)	167 college and recreational athletes	Group goals were general rather than specific, and while process goals predominated during practice, groups set both outcome and process goals during competition	Group goals exploratory study
Johnson, Ostrow, Perma, & Etzel (1997)	36 male undergraduate bowling students	Of the three conditions (group goals, individual goals, and "do your best" goals), only the group goals condition improved bowling performance	Strong for group goals
Widmeyer & DuCharme (1997)	Not applicable	Position paper on enhancing team cohesion through team goal setting	Not applicable

Goal participation (1 out of 7 studies partially supported self-set goals as superior to assigned goals)

Study	Participants	Findings	Conclusion
Boyce (1992)	138 university riflery class participants	No difference between self-set and assigned goal conditions on the rifle shooting performance	Weak for goal setting participation
Boyce & Bingham (1997)	288 college students performing a bowling task	No difference between self-set, assigned, and "do your best" goal conditions on bowling performance	Weak for goal setting participation
Boyce & Wayda (1994)	252 female university weight training students	Assigned goal condition performed better than self-set goal condition	Weak for goal setting participation
Fairall & Rodgers (1997)	67 track and field athletes	No difference between participative, assigned, and self-set goal conditions	Weak for goal setting participation
Hall & Byrne (1988)	43 male and 11 female university weight training students	No difference between long term + instructor-set and long term + self-set intermediate goal condition on an endurance task	Weak for goal setting participation
Lambert, Moore, & Dixon (1999)	4 female gymnasts	Gymnasts with a more internal locus of control benefited from self-set goals, while external locus of control gymnasts benefited from coach-set goals	Moderate for goal setting participation
Lee & Edwards (1984)	93 5th grade physical education students	Assigned goals enhanced performance to a greater extent than did self-set goals on two out of three motor tasks	Weak for goal setting participation

Task complexity (1 of 2 studies partially supported task complexity as a moderating variable of goal-setting effectiveness)

Study	Participants	Findings	Conclusion
Anshel, Weinberg, & Jackson (1992)	54 undergraduate students	All goal conditions (easy, difficult, and self-set) improved for both simple and difficult juggling tasks	Strong for simple and difficult tasks
Burton (1989)	16 male and 7 female under-graduate basketball students	Specific-goal condition outperformed general-goal condition on low but not on moderate or high complexity basketball tasks	Moderate support for task complexity distinction

(continued)

469

Table 15.1
(continued)

Study	Participants	Results	Level of support
Goal interventions (4 out of 5 studies supported or partially supported goal-setting as an effective intervention technique)			
Anderson, Crowell, Doman, & Howard (1988)	17 male intercollegiate hockey players	Goal setting intervention increased hitting performance during hockey games	Strong for goal setting as an intervention strategy
Galvan & Ward (1988)	5 collegiate tennis players	Goal setting, in part, reduced the number of inappropriate on-court behaviors immediately following the goal setting intervention	Strong for goal setting as an intervention strategy
Miller & McAuley (1987)	18 undergraduate students	No difference in free throw performance between goal-training and no-goal-training conditions	Weak for goal setting as an intervention strategy
Swain & Jones (1995)	4 male collegiate basketball players	Goal setting intervention enhanced basketball skills for three out of four participants	Moderate for goal setting as an intervention strategy
Wanlin, Hrycaiko, Martin, & Mahon (1997)	4 female speed skaters	Goal setting intervention enhanced skating performance	Strong for goal setting as an intervention strategy
Goals and self-efficacy			
Miller & McAuley (1987)	18 undergraduate students	Goal-training condition reported higher free throw self-efficacy compared to no-goal-training condition	Strong for enhancing self-efficacy
Poag & McAuley (1992)	76 adult female community conditioning participants	Goal efficacy predicted perceived goal achievement at the end of the program	Strong for efficacy as a goal moderator
Theodorakis (1996)	48 undergraduate physical education students	Self efficacy and goal setting were found to be predictors of performance on a tennis service task	Strong for efficacy as a predictor of performance
Meta-analyses and reviews			
Burton (1992)			
Burton (1993)			
Burton, Naylor, & Holliday (2001)			
Kyllo & Landers (1995)			
Weinberg (1994)			

goals refer to improving form, technique, and strategy, whereas performance goals are limited to improving overall performance (e.g., running a faster time, throwing farther, or shooting a lower score). Kingston and Hardy's rationale for this reconceptualization is that performance goals still focus on the end products of performance, although success is based on the attainment of absolute or self-referenced performance standards (e.g., shooting a 74 in a round of golf, running the 100 meters in 10.22 seconds, or scoring 25 points in a basketball game). Their new conceptualization of goal focus places these types of goals on a continuum, with outcome goals on the product end of the continuum, process goals on the opposite end of the continuum, and performance goals in between. Clearly, this revised goal focus model makes a valuable addition to both the empirical and applied sport psychology literatures because process goals are definitely more flexible and controllable than performance goals. In sport, where many behaviors are highly complex and take much practice to master, process goals should function as the stepping stones to achieving required performance levels that will ultimately lead to desired outcomes. Moreover, some complex tasks require that performers first develop new or more effective task strategies for performing skills before the motivational benefits of goals can promote enhanced performance. Thus, process goals obviously could provide the framework for developing these new or improved task strategies which, over time, can be automated to raise performance to the levels necessary to attain projected outcomes.

Preliminary work by Kingston, Hardy, and their colleagues (Kingston et al., 1992; Kingston & Hardy, 1994, 1997) have supported the validity of their reconceptualization of goal focus, demonstrating several important benefits of process compared with performance goals. These benefits include (a) helping athletes improve concentration because of more effective allocation of attentional resources (L. Hardy & Nelson, 1988; Kingston & Hardy, 1997), (b) enhancing self-efficacy because success at attaining process goals is more controllable (Kingston & Hardy, 1997), and (c) improving control of cognitive anxiety because process goals allow greater flexibility to set performance standards that are optimal for current performance capabilities, thus reducing stress prompted by unrealistically high goals (Kingston & Hardy, 1997; Kingston et al., 1992). Kingston and Hardy's (1997) preliminary research found no difference in over-

all improvement in golf performance between golfers setting process versus performance goals, although both goal-setting groups improved significantly more than did a control group. However, the process goal group demonstrated their performance improvement more quickly than did their performance goal counterparts, suggesting some possible benefit in terms of speed of improvement. Our review of goal focus research revealed that 9 of 10 studies supported the efficacy of using a combination of process, performance, and outcome goals rather than using any of these goals individually (see table 15.1).

Most experts (Burton, 1989b; Gould, 1998) agree that outcome goals seem to be more popular or more emphasized in our modern sport culture, primarily because of the tremendous rewards available for winning (i.e., trophies, medals, recognition, fame, money, etc.). The popular sport literature offers numerous examples of how winning is glorified and attainment of performance or process goals trivialized. However, recent research on goal practices in sport (Burton et al., 1998, 2001; Weinberg et al., 1993, 1997, 2000) has confirmed that athletes don't necessarily buy into this traditional goal-setting wisdom. Surveys with collegiate athletes and youth tennis players (Burton et al., 1998; Weinberg et al., 1993, 1997) revealed that both age groups of athletes set performance and outcome goals with virtually equal frequency and effectiveness. Moreover, the research on the goal practices of Olympic athletes (Weinberg et al., 2000; Burton et al., 2001) demonstrated that elite performers set performance goals slightly more often and more effectively than outcome goals, although these differences were nonsignificant. However, Olympic performers reported more frequently making outcome goals slightly more important than performance goals in competition. Thus, athletes value outcome goals, but they have become more sophisticated about using process and performance goals as means to achieve desired outcomes.

Goal Specificity

Early reviews of the general goal-specificity literature (Chidester & Grigsby, 1984; Latham & Lee, 1986; Locke et al., 1981; Mento et al., 1987; Tubbs, 1986) concluded that goal specificity, or precision, enhances performance. Locke and his colleagues (1981) found that 51 of 53 goal specificity studies partially or completely supported the premise that specific goals promote better performance than general or do-your-best goals or no goals, whereas several meta-analytic reviews (Chidester & Grigsby, 1984; Latham & Lee, 1986; Mento et al., 1987) confirmed that goal specificity consistently improved performance.

However, Locke and Latham's (1990) more recent revision of goal-setting theory predicts that goal specificity is a less important goal attribute than goal difficulty and will contribute primarily to enhancing performance consistency rather than performance quality. Locke and Latham hypothesized that making difficult goals specific will further enhance performance because specific goals make it more difficult to feel successful with performance that is lower than one's goal. They further argued that when goals are vague, it is easier for individuals to give themselves the "benefit of the doubt" in evaluating performance and rate a relatively lower level of performance as acceptable. For example, Kernan and Lord (1989) found that individuals with no specific goals generally evaluated their performance more positively than participants with specific, difficult goals when provided with varying types of negative feedback.

Locke and Latham (1990) concluded that goal specificity does not have a direct performance enhancement effect; rather goal specificity interacts with goal difficulty to influence performance. Thus, specific, easy goals may actually be less effective than vague, hard goals (Locke, Chah, Harrison, & Lustgarten, 1989). Locke and Latham (1990) hypothesized that when goal difficulty is controlled, the major effect of goal specificity is to reduce performance variance by reducing interpretative leeway in evaluating success. In support of this prediction, Locke et al. (1989) separated the effects of goal difficulty and goal specificity and found that the more specific the goal, the lower the performance variance. Therefore, goal specificity seems to be an important attribute of effective goals, but its impact is most prominent when combined with goal difficulty to maintain more stringent standards for success, thereby reducing performance variability.

Interestingly, goal specificity research in sport has not looked at the effects of specificity independent of goal difficulty. Although approximately 15 of 25 studies in sport (i.e., 60%) have documented that athletes who set specific goals performed significantly better than performers who set general, do-your-best goals or no goals, significant goal-setting effects were not found for the remaining 10 studies. However, it is unclear whether these effects would remain if goal difficulty effects were partialled out.

Goal Difficulty

Locke and Latham's (1990) goal-setting theory postulates a positive linear relationship between goal difficulty and performance, primarily because difficult goals prompt greater effort and persistence than do easy goals. However, goal-setting theory acknowledges that as individuals reach the upper limits of their ability at high goal difficulty levels, performance plateaus. Nevertheless, the consensus of nearly 200 general goal-setting studies strongly supported this "goal difficulty hypothesis." Locke and Latham found that 91% of the 192 goal difficulty studies they reviewed demonstrated positive (140 studies) or contingently positive (35 studies) relationships between difficult goals and performance. Moreover, four meta-analyses of goal difficulty research (Chidester & Grigsby, 1984; Mento et al., 1987; Tubbs, 1986; Wood et al., 1987), each reviewing up to 72 studies and containing as many as 7,500 participants, demonstrated mean effect sizes ranging from .52 to .82, representing performance increments from 10.4% to 16.4%. Thus, general goal reviews strongly support the goal difficulty hypothesis, and a number of more recent studies (Chesney & Locke, 1991; Ruth, 1996; White, Kjelgaard, & Harkins, 1995; Wood & Locke, 1990) have further supported this prediction, although research has shown that as goals exceed individuals' performance capability, excessively difficult goals will be abandoned in favor of more realistic self-set goals. For example, Wright, Hollenbeck, Wolf, and McMahan (1995) found that when goals were operationalized in terms of absolute performance level, the traditional linear relationship between goal difficulty and performance resulted. However, when goals were operationalized in terms of performance improvement, an inverted-U relationship emerged between goal difficulty and performance. Clearly, perceived ability seems to mediate the relationship between goal difficulty and performance.

Surprisingly, sport goal research generally contradicts the goal difficulty hypothesis (see table 15.1). Initial goal difficulty research by Weinberg and his colleagues (Hall, Weinberg, & Jackson, 1987; Weinberg, Bruya, Jackson, & Garland, 1986) was the first to question the goal difficulty hypothesis. Hall et al. (1987) compared hand dynamometer endurance performance of performers randomly assigned to three goal conditions: do your best, improve by 40 seconds, and improve by 70 seconds. Although the researchers confirmed that participants who were assigned to the two specific-goal conditions performed better than their do-your-best counterparts, the authors found no goal difficulty effects for the specific goal conditions. Similarly, Weinberg et al. (1986) found no goal difficulty effects for participants assigned to easy, moderate, and extremely hard goal conditions who performed a sit-up task for five weeks.

Our review found that only 10 of 19 studies (i.e., 53%) supported goal difficulty predictions (see table 15.1). Not only have a number of studies failed to demonstrate hypothesized goal difficulty effects, but they also contradicted the prediction that unrealistically high goals will impair performance (see table 15.1).

Recent research surveying goal practices in sport (Weinberg et al., 1993, 2000) has demonstrated that moderately difficult, rather than difficult, goals are preferred by the majority of collegiate and Olympic athletes, and that more effective goal-setters (Burton et al., 1998, 2001) set moderately difficult goals more frequently than difficult ones. Moreover, reviews of sport goal research (Kyllo & Landers, 1995; Weinberg, 1994) have revealed that moderately difficult goals are more effective than difficult goals in sport, accounting for an effect size of .53.

Several explanations are offered for the contradictory findings for goal difficulty between the sport and general goal literatures. First, researchers' operationalization of goal difficulty may differ between general and sport domains. Locke (1991) suggested that a difficult goal is one that no more than 10% of participants can achieve, although there is little evidence that this criterion has been used consistently by researchers in either general or sport goal research. However, a goal that can be accomplished by only 5% to 10% of performers may be too difficult, prompting low goal acceptance and motivating individuals to set more realistic goals on their own (i.e., spontaneous goal-setting; Kyllo & Landers, 1995). Second, Campbell and Furrer (1995) suggested that the effects of goal difficulty can be mediated by competition. Results investigating the effects of competition on goal-setting performance in a math class demonstrated that across three goal conditions (i.e., easy, moderate, and difficult), participants performing in the noncompetitive environment significantly outperformed their counterparts in the competitive environment. Although there was no difference in the mean number of problems attempted across conditions, competitive students made significantly more mistakes than did noncompetitive classmates, suggesting that com-

petition may reduce goal effects by increasing anxiety or reducing concentration. Interestingly, Lerner and Locke (1995) found that competition did not mediate goal effects on sport performance. Because of the competitive nature of athletics and the degree to which athletes compete in most situations, further investigation of the role of competition as a mediator of goal difficulty results seems warranted.

Goal Valence

Sport practitioners often encourage athletes to set goals in positive terms, focusing on what they want to accomplish (e.g., two hits in four at-bats) rather than what they hope to avoid (e.g., striking out or going 0 for 4; Gould, 1998). However, Kirschenbaum (1984) argued against the conventional wisdom of this goal-setting strategy. Based on extensive self-regulation research, Kirschenbaum (1984) concluded that positively focused goals are most effective for new or difficult skills (e.g., Johnston-O'Connor & Kirschenbaum, 1984; Kirschenbaum, Ordman, Tomarken, & Holtzbauer, 1982), whereas negatively focused goals that emphasize minimizing mistakes are more effective for well-learned skills (e.g., Kirschenbaum, Wittrock, Smith, & Monson, 1984). We were unable to find any sport research on goal valence, suggesting that additional research is definitely needed to clarify goal valence effects in sport domains.

Goal Proximity

Burton (1992) defined long-term goals as any objective 6 or more weeks into the future, whereas any goal of shorter duration is considered a short-term goal. Locke and Latham's (1990) goal-setting theory makes no specific predictions about the efficacy of short-term versus long-term goals, and existing reviews of goal proximity research (Kirschenbaum, 1985; Locke & Latham, 1990) have revealed equivocal results, prompting confusion about what specific goal proximity recommendations to make to practitioners. Here is a brief review of the divergent conceptual perspectives on goal proximity.

Clinical researchers (e.g., Bandura, 1986) believe that short-term goals are more effective because they provide more frequent evaluation of success, which stimulates development of self-confidence when goals are attained and motivation regardless of the outcome, thus preventing procrastination and premature discouragement. Burton (1989b) emphasized other positive attributes of short-term goals, contending that short-term goals are more flexible and controllable. Because short-term goals are more flexible, they can be readily raised or lowered to maintain optimal challenge levels. Moreover, the controllability of short-term goals makes it easier for performers to take credit for success as indicative of high ability and a strong work ethic.

Proponents of long-term goals (e.g., Kirschenbaum, 1985) theorize that long-term goals facilitate greater performance improvement than short-term goals because they foster "protracted choice." These authors argue that too frequent goal assessment may prompt excessive evaluation, making it difficult to remain focused on performance because social comparison concerns become more salient (Nicholls, 1984a, 1992). Performers should feel like "pawns" because goals are perceived as controlling rather than informational (e.g., deCharms, 1976; Deci & Ryan, 1985). Thus, long-term goals would allow short-term flexibility that prevents discouragement if individuals should fail to attain daily performance goals.

Locke and Latham's (1990) review suggests that goal proximity has not been a popular topic for goal-setting research, perhaps because of the limited impact of this goal attribute on goal-setting efficacy or the difficulty that researchers have had in identifying the optimal time span for short-term and long-term goals. In the latter case, goals that are set too often may become intrusive, distracting, and annoying, thus prompting their rejection. Conversely, goals set too infrequently may be viewed as unreal and not worthy of attention, thus failing to generate the effort and persistence needed to enhance performance.

Although research conducted in both sport and nonsport settings (Bandura & Simon, 1977; Bar-Eli, Hartman, & Levy-Kolker, 1994; Borrelli & Mermelstein, 1994; Hall & Byrne, 1988; Kirschenbaum, 1985; Latham & Locke, 1991) suggests that long-term goals are important to provide individuals with direction for their achievement strivings, these findings also confirm that the motivational impact of long-term goals depends on establishing short-term goals to serve as intermediate steps in the achievement process (Bandura & Simon, 1977; Hall & Byrne, 1988; Locke, Cartledge, & Knerr, 1970). In sport, goal proximity findings are similarly equivocal, with the number of studies investigating long- versus short-term goals limited. The consensus of sport goal proximity research (Kyllo & Landers, 1995; Tenenbaum, Weinberg, Pinchas, Elbaz, & Bar-Eli, 1991) is that long-term goals en-

hance performance most effectively when short-term goals are used to mark progress. Kyllo and Landers's (1995) meta-analysis of the sport goal research demonstrated an effect size of .48 for the combined effect of short- and long-term goals on performance. Our review found that three of eight sport studies (i.e., 38%) revealed that a combination of short- and long-term goals was superior to either type of goals individually. Extensive future goal proximity research seems needed not only to confirm the superiority of a combination of short-term and long-term goals but to also identify the most effective time frames for short-term and long-term goals and to verify the relationship between these two goal proximity types.

Goal Collectivity

Group/team goals are objectives established for the collective performance of two or more individuals. According to Brawley, Carron, and Widmeyer (1992), team goals tend to be more general rather than specific, and the focus of team goals often varies considerably between practice and competition. In practice, these authors found that team goals were process (89.9%) rather than outcome oriented (10.1%), focusing on skill/strategy (66.1%), effort (29.3%), and fitness (4.6%). Conversely, competitive goals were evenly split between outcome (53.1%) and process (46.9%), focusing on skill/strategy (43.5%), outcomes (41.5%), and effort (15%). Team goals have been found to affect psychological variables such as team satisfaction, cohesion, and motivation as well as performance (Brawley, Carron, & Widmeyer, 1993).

Locke and Latham's (1990) goal-setting theory makes no predictions about the effectiveness of group/team versus individual goals, but available reviews of group goal-setting research (Carroll, 1986; Kondrasuk, 1981; Locke & Latham, 1990; Rodgers & Hunter, 1989) revealed that team goals enhance performance as effectively as do individual goals. Locke and Latham's review revealed that 38 of 41 group goal-setting studies (93%) demonstrated positive or contingently positive performance enhancement effects, virtually the same success rate as individual goal-setting findings. Locke and Latham concluded that team goals, in addition to or instead of individual goals, are necessary or at least facilitative when the task is a group/team task rather than an individual one.

Although the efficacy of group/team goals has been confirmed, direct comparisons of the effectiveness of group/team versus individual goals have been relatively limited, both in sport and nonsport settings (Hinsz, 1995; Larey & Paulus, 1995; Shalley, 1995). Larey and Paulus (1995) assigned participants to no-goal, individual-goal, and interactive-goal conditions for a brainstorming task, and their results demonstrated that individual-goal performers set more difficult goals (i.e., number of ideas generated) than did their counterparts in the interactive-goal condition. Low perceptions of other team members' ability were believed to lower the difficulty of team goals. In two additional studies (Hinsz, 1995; Shalley, 1995), similar decrements in performance were evident for team- compared with individual-goal conditions, with group performance decrements explained by (a) reduced goal difficulty due to an averaging of goal difficulty levels across performers and (b) the distraction effect of other team members on the creative process.

A lone goal collectivity study in sport (Johnson, Ostrow, Perna, & Etzel, 1997) contradicts general goal research on the efficacy of group/team versus individual goals. Johnson and his colleagues (1997) examined the impact of do-your-best, individual, and team goal-setting conditions on bowling performance. Contrary to general goal collectivity results, they found that team goals increased bowling performance more than either do-your-best or individual-goal groups, in part because they were significantly harder goals than were set in either of the other two conditions. Goal collectivity is probably not an either/or proposition. Team goals offer direction for establishing appropriate types and levels of individual goals that are then responsible for the specific motivational benefits to individual performers. In fact, social loafing research (e.g., C.J. Hardy & Latane, 1988; Jackson & Williams, 1985; Latane, 1986; Latane, Williams, & Harkins, 1979) predicts that group/team goals, without accompanying individual goals, may reduce performance by prompting social loafing. Social loafing is a group performance phenomenon in which individuals working together on a task tend to exert less individual effort than when they perform the same task alone (Jackson & Williams, 1985). Although not extensively studied in sport settings, social loafing has been shown to occur for a variety of physically effortful tasks (e.g., Ingham, Levinger, Graves, & Peckham, 1974; Kerr & Brunn, 1981; Latane et al., 1979).

Interestingly, research has confirmed that social loafing is reduced or eliminated when individual performance is identifiable (Williams, Harkins & Latane, 1981) and when individuals perceive that they have made a unique contribution to the group effort or have performed difficult tasks (Harkins & Petty, 1982). Thus, the implication of social loafing research for goal collectivity is that individuals who set group/team goals should be prone to loaf and perform below their capabilities unless they also set individual goals that hold each team member responsible for a specific level of performance and these individual goals are perceived as indispensable for team success. Teams need to use the "role" concept for setting individual goals to maximize identifiability and accountability. Thus, individual goals are set based on the role that each player needs to fulfill to maximize team effectiveness. Regrettably, goal collectivity predictions that a combination of group/team and individual goals should maximize performance have not been tested adequately to allow firm conclusions about team goals.

Based on the consensus of goal attribute research, the following recommendations can be made for the types of goals that practitioners should set in sport. First, performers should set a combination of process, performance, and outcome goals. Outcome goals should be focused primarily on increasing practice motivation, whereas athletes should concentrate on process and performance goals during competition. Second, goals should be constructed that are specific, measurable, and moderately difficult to improve both the quality and consistency of performance. Third, goals should be positive and focused on attaining desirable performance outcomes rather than focused on eliminating performance problems or avoiding potential pitfalls. Finally, although research on goal proximity and collectivity remains equivocal, practitioners should use a combination of short- and long-term goals and individual and team goals to promote maximal performance gains.

WHY GOALS WORK LESS EFFECTIVELY IN SPORT

Nine years ago, when the original version of this chapter was published, goal setting in sport enhanced performance in two-thirds of 14 studies compared with the 91% success rate in the general goal literature. The consistency of goal setting in sport has jumped to 79% as an additional 40 studies have been completed, significantly reducing the gap in effectiveness between the two domains. If this trend continues over another 50 studies, there may eventually be only a 5% to 7% difference in goal-setting efficacy between sport and business contexts. However, we believe that several major differences between sport and business domains will continue to suppress goal-setting effectiveness in sport (Locke, 1991, 1994; Weinberg & Weigand, 1993, 1996). Although Locke conducted an interesting debate with Weinberg and Weigand, their discussion was largely methodological, highlighting the following five issues: participants' motivation levels, goal setting in do-your-best conditions, feedback in do-your-best conditions, personal goals, and goal difficulty. Because of space limitations, the interested reader is encouraged to review the original commentary (Locke, 1991, 1994; Weinberg & Weigand, 1993, 1996) or our more detailed analysis elsewhere (Burton, Naylor, & Holliday, 2001).

Although this methodological debate has proved entertaining, it failed to explain why goals are less effective in sport compared with business settings. We agree with Weinberg and Weigand (1993, 1996) that if goal setting is a robust phenomenon that has a significant and practical impact on sport performance, then systematic goal-setting programs should demonstrate superior performance to spontaneously set goals, despite these minor methodological problems. The fact that most collegiate and Olympic athletes (Burton et al., 1998, 2001; Weinberg et al., 1993, 2000) rate goals as only moderately effective, and that reviews of goal-setting research (Kyllo & Landers, 1995; Weinberg, 1994) document less robust goal effects in sport and exercise, suggests that other, more influential, factors may account for this discrepancy. In the previous edition of this chapter, five factors were posited as more plausible explanations for the less consistent goal-setting effects in sport: (a) small sample sizes of sport studies, (b) athletes operating closer to their performance potential, (c) highly complex skills being performed in sport, (d) failure to use appropriate goal implementation strategies, and (e) individual differences that influence goal-setting effectiveness. We now look at the viability of these five explanations.

Small Sample Size

One concern about the less consistent and robust goal-setting effects in sport is that these findings reflect a lack of statistical power because of small sample size (Cohen, 1992). Kyllo and Landers (1995) argued that this is a viable reason for the divergent goal-setting results across the two do-

mains. They drew a random sample of 22 studies from the published studies in both sport and business domains and generated mean cell sample sizes, reporting that sport research typically tested 26 subjects per cell compared with 43 subjects per cell in the general goal literature. Kyllo and Landers also performed a follow-up power analysis (Cohen, 1992) on a sample of eight studies from the sport goal literature and calculated a mean power of .53 for this sample, a value well below the .80 Cohen recommended as minimal to reduce the risk of Type II error. Thus, Kyllo and Landers concluded that small sample size is a possible reason for reduced goal-setting effects in sport and exercise.

About 20% to 25% of the goal-setting studies in sport have used samples of 30 or fewer subjects, and sample sizes in competitive goal-setting studies generally have increased significantly in the past nine years (see table 15.1). Because of the sensitivity of many inferential statistics to sample size, small samples may be responsible for the less consistent goal-setting effects in sport. However, careful scrutiny of goal-setting research in sport reveals that the average sample size across all goal attributes research except goal collectivity was more than 100 participants, and most goal conditions had a minimum of 20 participants (see table 15.1). Both sample parameters appear large enough to adequately demonstrate differences in goal-setting effects, thus somewhat discounting sample size as a prime explanation of the less consistent goal-setting effects in sport.

Athletes Operating Closer to Their Performance Potential

The argument that athletes are operating closer to their performance potential in sport is consistent with Locke and Latham's (1990) predictions for the moderating effects of ability on goal-setting effectiveness. Locke and Latham present convincing evidence that the goal effectiveness curve flattens out as individuals approach the limits of their ability, in part because ability factors restrict the amount of improvement that can be made through goal setting. This explanation seems plausible for most of the nonsignificant goal-setting research in sport.

Task Complexity

The task complexity argument is consistent with Locke and Latham's prediction that task complexity will mediate goal-setting effectiveness, particularly that simple tasks will demonstrate quicker and larger goal-setting effects than more complex tasks. Wood and his coworkers (1987) performed a meta-analysis on 125 goal-setting studies to assess the influence of task complexity as a moderator of goal-setting effectiveness. Multiple regression analyses revealed that task complexity predicted 6% of the variance in goal difficulty-performance effects and 95% of the variance in goal difficulty/specificity-performance results. Moreover, when separate meta-analyses were computed for studies with low, moderate, and high task complexity ratings, the effect sizes for both goal difficulty and goal difficulty/specificity were larger for simpler compared with more complex tasks. These findings confirm that task complexity does moderate goal-setting effects, although the exact mechanism behind complexity results remains speculative.

In sport, one of two studies supported task complexity predictions (see table 15.1). Burton (1989a) confirmed that complex tasks involve a greater time lag to demonstrate goal-setting effects because new task strategies often have to be developed to perform the skill more effectively, although Anshel, Weinberg, and Jackson (1992) found no task complexity effects. Only when individuals have developed effective task strategies can the motivational effects of goals stimulate performance increments by prompting greater effort and persistence. Because most sports involve the development of many individual and team skills and strategies and because of the relatively short treatment length of most sport studies, this explanation again seems plausible for most of the nonsignificant goal-setting studies in sport.

Failure to Use Appropriate Goal-Implementation Strategies

Locke and Latham (1990) emphasized in their goal-setting theory that setting goals is only one component of the goal-setting process. Although research on goal process variables has not received extensive empirical attention, the consensus of research (Kyllo & Landers, 1995; Locke & Latham, 1990) is that strategies such as writing down and posting goals, developing action plans, and evaluating goal attainment enhance overall goal-setting effectiveness. Recent collegiate and Olympic goal-setting surveys (Burton et al., 1998, 2001) confirmed that more effective goal-setters use all goal implementation strategies more frequently and

with greater effectiveness than do less effective goal-setters. Although details are sketchy for some studies, making it difficult to assess the degree to which appropriate goal implementation strategies were used, many of the nonsignificant goal-setting studies in sport have failed to use one or more of these key goal implementation strategies necessary to maximize goal effectiveness (see Burton et al., 2001, for a more detailed explanation).

Individual Differences

Locke and Latham's (1990) goal-setting theory suggests that individual differences, particularly self-efficacy, should significantly affect how people respond to goal setting, particularly for complex tasks and goal difficulty levels in the upper ranges of performers' ability. Specifically, these authors predict that when confronted with temporary failure on complex tasks, performers with high self-efficacy will increase the quality of their task strategies and will increase effort and persistence to make those strategies work. Conversely, competitors with low self-efficacy normally will display less functional task strategies and reduced effort and persistence. Although self-efficacy has been shown to influence goal effectiveness, individual differences largely have been overlooked in sport and nonsport goal-setting research, and they remain a viable explanation for nonsignificant findings in goal-setting research.

In summary, the somewhat less consistent and robust goal-setting results in sport may be attributable to five primary factors: small sample sizes, performers operating closer to their performance potential, athletes performing highly complex skills that make the demonstration of goal-setting effects a more lengthy and difficult process, failure to use key goal-implementation strategies, and individual differences that prompt specific types of athletes to respond to goal-setting programs in idiosyncratic ways. Although each of these explanations is intriguing, the role of individual differences in the goal-setting process seems to have received little attention in goal-setting research and thus appears particularly appropriate for further conceptual and empirical study.

REVISED COMPETITIVE GOAL-SETTING MODEL

In the first edition of this text 9 years ago, a competitive goal-setting (CGS) model was proposed that attempted to integrate discrete and global conceptions of goals and account for personality influences on the goal-setting process. The model elicited a number of provocative comments from other goal-setting researchers, both pro and con, but a paucity of research testing model predictions. The major reason for the limited research testing the CGS model is probably the difficulty of empirically classifying individuals into appropriate goal-setting styles, an important prerequisite to testing model predictions. Nevertheless, several studies conducted by Burton and his colleagues and students (e.g., Burton, 1989b; Burton et al., 2001; Pierce & Burton, 1998; Burton & Sharples, 2001) generally have supported model predictions, prompting us to believe that the model still has something to offer researchers attempting to better understand the goal-setting process and how to make it work more effectively. Thus, we present here a modified version of the model with some specific suggestions for research to test key model predictions in the hope that it may promote independent research to better assess the viability of this conceptual framework. In this section we first describe the revised CGS model (RCGS) and briefly review important model predictions. Next, we review the limited research that directly tests model predictions in sport and draw tentative conclusions. Individuals who are interested in the related research that provided the empirical rationale for the model and its specific predictions are referred to the original edition of this text (see Burton, 1992).

The CGS model was originally advanced not to put forth a new theory of goal setting but simply to provide a heuristic tool to better understand two important issues about goal setting. First, the model attempts to integrate state and trait conceptions of goals into a single more comprehensive model that considers both the motivational and stress-related functions of goals. Second, the comprehensive model makes specific predictions that can aid our understanding and investigation of the goal-setting process in sport (figure 15.1). The RCGS model offers a slightly expanded version of the original model that is consistent with these two purposes, maintains consistency with the huge influx of recent goal-setting research, and emphasizes key "process" variables that affect goal-setting effectiveness.

Consistent with the large body of cognitive motivation research (Dweck, 1999; Elliott & Dweck, 1988; Locke, 1968; Locke et al., 1981; Maehr, 1984; Nicholls, 1984a, 1984b), the RCGS model shown in figure 15.1 predicts that the motivational function of goals is most evident in the top portion of the model between links 1 through 6. First, goal orientations interact with perceived ability to prompt the development of three distinct goal-setting styles: performance-oriented (see link 1), success-oriented (see link 2), and failure-oriented (see link 3). These goal-setting styles, along with key situational variables such as situation type (i.e., practice vs. competition), activity importance, task complexity, and performance expectancies, then dictate the specific goals set (i.e., process, performance, and/or outcome; see link 4). Next, these discrete goals interact with key process variables such as perceived goal commitment and identification of obstacles and roadblocks to prompt specific goal responses—task choice, effort/intensity, strategy development, and persistence/continuing motivation (link 5). These goal responses significantly determine how athletes will perform and their competitive outcome (link 6).

Based on perceived ability theory and research (e.g., Dweck, 1999; Elliott & Dweck, 1988; Harter, 1981; Nicholls, 1984a, 1984b), the RCGS model further predicts that goals have an important self-evaluation function because they become the standards against which process, performance, and outcome are weighed to determine perceived success and failure and to assess specific success/failure attributions (link 7), the two primary antecedents of perceived competence or ability (link 8). Finally, the RCGS model predicts that perceived ability directly influences motivational consequent variables such as future expectancies, affect, and activity importance (link 9). Feedback loops then allow motivational consequent variables to subsequently influence goal orientations, specific goals, goal process variables, and goal responses (link 10).

The RCGS model is depicted as a sequential process to facilitate understanding of the separate motivation and self-evaluation functions of goals. In reality, the process is probably much more complex and feedback loops are much more extensive. Moreover, the model does not attempt to resolve the dispute about the primacy of cognition versus affect, but it emphasizes that these variables are related, probably in some reciprocal fashion. The RCGS model makes specific predictions about the types of practice and competitive goals set by athletes who adopt different goal-setting styles and how these goal patterns will affect competitors' cognition and performance. In the next section, we briefly review each goal-setting style and

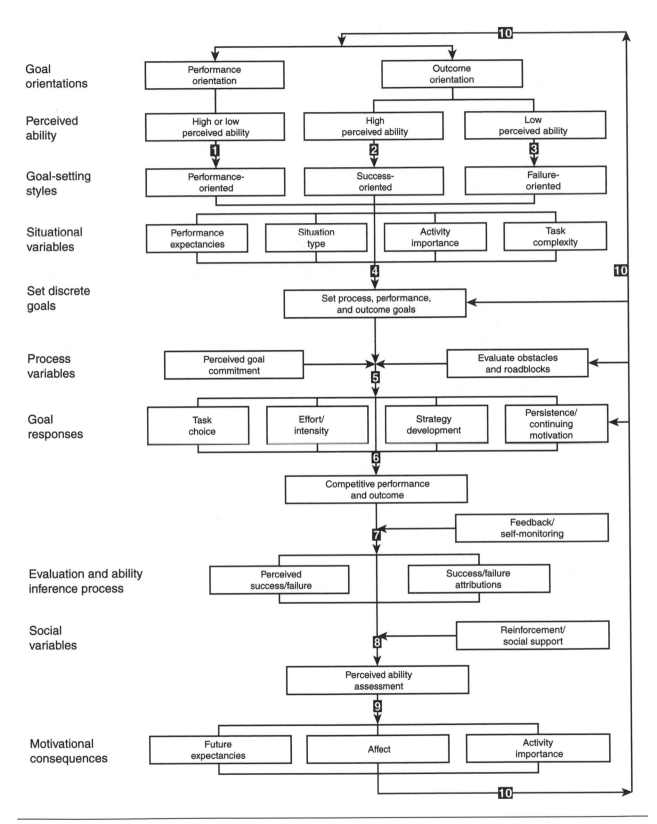

Figure 15.1 Revised competitive goal-setting model.

479

make specific predictions about their preferred goal-setting patterns.

Goal-Setting Styles

The notion of goal-setting styles is based on motivation theory and research that combines the concept of global goal orientations with personal perceptions of ability. Contemporary conceptions of goal orientations are based on two primary theoretical premises (e.g., Dweck, 1999; Elliott & Dweck, 1988; Nicholls, 1984a, 1984b). First, perceived competence or ability is conceived as the critical underlying construct responsible for mediating motivational behaviors. Second, individuals' goal orientations are hypothesized to mediate how perceived ability develops and its impact on achievement behavior, primarily because they dictate how success and failure are assessed.

Motivation researchers (Diener & Dweck, 1978; Dweck, 1980, 1999; Elliott & Dweck, 1988; Nicholls, 1984a, 1984b) have postulated two primary goal orientations in achievement situations. Although

goal orientation terminology differs among researchers, they define these goal orientations quite similarly. In this chapter, the two goal orientations are labeled *performance* and *outcome* because these are terms that practitioners can relate to readily.

Athletes adopting a performance orientation define success and failure in sport and related achievement domains predominantly according to whether they are able to learn and master new tasks or improve skills and performance. These performers believe that ability and skill can continue to be refined throughout their careers, and they define success in terms of self-referent standards, striving for learning, skill improvement, goal attainment, and/or task mastery. Perceived ability doesn't seem to mediate motivation for performance-oriented individuals, and athletes high or low in perceived ability demonstrate similar motivational patterns. Performance-oriented competitors assume they have the ability to learn and improve if they put forth sufficient effort. Thus, such a process focus frees them from worrying

Table 15.2
Characteristics of Performance-, Success-, and Failure-Oriented Goal-Setting Styles

	1. How athletes define success and failure	2. Level of perceived ability	3. Normal goal priority	4. Competitive outlook	5. Attributions	
					Success	Failure
Performance-oriented	Learning, improvement and increasing self-referent ability	High or low as long as can learn and improve	1. Process 2. Performance 3. Outcome	Positive and optimistic	High effort (ability assumed)	• Often don't perceive failure • Effort
Success-oriented	Competitive outcome and positive social comparison as a means of demonstrating high ability	High ability—socially compares well (i.e., wins often)	1. Outcome 2. Performance 3. Process	Positive and optimistic	High ability	Internal, unstable, controllable factors (i.e., low effort or poor mental preparation)
Failure-oriented	Avoid competition and social comparison for fear of demonstrating low ability	Low ability—poor social comparison (i.e., loses often)	1. Outcome 2. Performance 3. Process	Negative and pessimistic	External or uncontrollable factors (i.e., luck or easy tasks)	Low ability

about demonstrating their competence and allows them to concentrate on ways of learning and enhancing their performance. Although these athletes certainly care about outcome, particularly winning, their top priority and the focus of their attention is process more than the final product.

Individuals who adopt an outcome goal orientation seek to "maintain positive judgments of their ability and avoid negative judgments by seeking to prove, validate, or document their ability and not discredit it" (Elliott & Dweck, 1988, p. 5). Outcome goal orientations define success or failure predominantly based on social comparison processes, thus making winning or positive social comparison essential to maintain high perceived ability. For outcome-oriented performers, improvement and task mastery are important, but primarily as a means (i.e., process) to the desired end of achieving positive social comparison (i.e., product).

The RCGS model hypothesizes that goal orientation and level of perceived ability interact to create three distinct goal-setting styles: performance-oriented, success-oriented, and failure-oriented. The general focus of each of these goal-setting styles is outlined in table 15.2 along with specific characteristics of each style.

Performance-Oriented Goal-Setting Style

As noted in columns 1 through 3 of table 15.2, performance-oriented (PO) athletes adopt a learning model of ability that defines success predominantly in terms of learning and improvement, rather than demonstrating ability to others. Thus, high- and low-skilled PO performers should demonstrate similar motivational patterns in practice and competition. Ability comparison is a secondary issue for PO competitors because they are primarily interested in raising perceived ability through learning and skill development. PO athletes should view most situations as opportunities to learn and improve their skills, thus prompting high levels of intrinsic motivation.

Based on learned helplessness and perceived ability research (e.g., Diener & Dweck, 1978; Dweck, 1980, 1999; Elliott & Dweck, 1988; Nicholls, 1984a), the RCGS model predicts that PO athletes

6. Effort expenditure	7. Task choice preferences	8. Response to failure	9. Performance	10. Goal attribute preferences	11. Response to goal-setting program
Consistently high to maximize learning and improvement	• Prefer very hard tasks • Embrace all opportunities to learn and improve at risk of making numerous mistakes	Dramatically increased effort and improved problem solving	• Perform extremely well • Long-term athletes will closely approach performance potential	• Self-referenced • Specific • Difficult • Positive • Individual/team • Long-term/short-term	Improve performance significantly
Effort only as high as necessary to win and demonstrate positive social comparison	• Prefer moderately difficult tasks • Will sacrifice learning if risks extensive failure	Increased effort and improved problem solving	• Generally will perform good enough to win • Long-term potential depends on situational factors that prompt development of full capabilities	• Social comparative • Specific • Moderately difficult • Positive/negative • Individual/team • Long-term/short-term	Improve performance moderately
• Low effort on moderate tasks to confuse ability evaluation • High effort on easy tasks to avoid failure	• Prefer very hard or very easy tasks • Sacrifice learning to avoid failure and displaying low ability	Give up easily, reduce effort and will drop out if can	Poor performance, which deteriorates with continued failure	• Social comparative • General • Moderately easy • Positive • Team • Long-term	Decrease performance slightly

assume the ability to learn and improve, prompting them to attribute success primarily to effort (see column 5). Moreover, PO competitors are predicted to view lack of success in a positive, constructive way, seldom making failure attributions (see column 5). Because of their learning focus, PO competitors deal with lack of success by increasing effort or developing new problem-solving strategies (see column 8).

Performers adopting a PO goal-setting style are predicted to select challenging or difficult goals even at the risk of making mistakes because their primary objective is to increase competence (see column 7). PO athletes also should exert high effort in most situations to maximize learning and performance improvement regardless of the level of task difficulty (see column 6). Moreover, the model predicts that PO competitors should confront failure constructively, remain focused on the task, and develop more effective problem-solving strategies, thus demonstrating high persistence and continuing motivation for their sport (see column 8).

The RCGS model predicts that PO athletes should perform consistently better than failure-oriented (FO) performers in all situations (see column 9). Success-oriented (SO) and PO competitors should demonstrate similar levels of performance over the short run and in success situations, but PO athletes should respond better to failure and come closer to reaching their performance potential over the course of their careers because they set more challenging goals, give consistently higher effort, use more effective problem-solving strategies, and persist longer in the face of failure (see column 9). Moreover, because athletes maximize their chances of winning by performing their best, PO competitors also should win more over their careers than SO or FO performers of similar ability.

Finally, the RCGS model predicts that PO athletes should experience positive motivational consequences from goal setting. Their learning focus allows PO competitors to remain optimistic about their ability to learn and improve despite temporary plateaus or failure. In fact, low current ability in a valued area may actually make skill acquisition more desirable for them, enhancing motivation (Diener & Dweck, 1978; Dweck, 1999). The model also predicts that PO athletes should experience satisfaction and pride from success, and although they should perceive negative affect when unsuccessful, these mild negative emotions should prompt PO competitors to demonstrate even higher future motivation. Finally, PO athletes

are predicted to increase their commitment to challenging tasks that help them learn and improve.

Success-Oriented Goal-Setting Style

Competitors with SO goal-setting styles adopt a capacity model of ability that views skill or competence as fixed and limited so success is defined based on social comparison and competitive outcome. However, because they win consistently and socially compare well, they perceive they have high ability (see columns 1–3 of table 15.2). An SO performer's primary objective is to win in order to demonstrate competence (columns 1 and 3). Although they view most situations as opportunities to demonstrate competence, SO competitors are optimally motivated and confident and play their best only when matched against an opponent of similar ability (i.e., moderate task difficulty; see column 7). SO athletes are predicted to attribute success to ability, an internal, stable, controllable factor that creates a positive and optimistic outlook toward competition, whereas failure normally is attributed to internal, unstable, controllable factors such as low effort, poor mental preparation, and the need to further develop skills (see column 5). Although SO competitors still worry about failure, they normally respond to failure in a constructive way (see column 8).

The RCGS model hypothesizes that competitors with SO goal-setting styles will avoid challenging goals if they perceive a risk of significant public failure or numerous mistakes (see column 7). Instead, they are predicted to prefer to set moderately difficult goals on tasks at which they are already reasonably proficient to ensure that low ability is not revealed. SO competitors' effort expenditure is predicted to fluctuate, depending on task difficulty (see column 6). For moderately difficult tasks, SO performers should put forth high effort to reach their goals. However, when the task is easy, SO competitors will expend as little effort as necessary to win, a strategy that allows them to demonstrate even higher ability. Finally, for very difficult tasks where the probability of failure is high, SO athletes will exert high effort until they become convinced that successful social comparison is not possible; then they will concentrate their effort on other tasks at which they are more likely to be successful (see column 6).

The RCGS model predicts that the relatively high perceived ability of SO athletes should help them approach failure in a positive way and allow them to manifest high confidence, remain task-focused, and develop effective problem-solving strategies (see column 8). However, because of their need to continue to demonstrate high ability, the continuing motivation of SO performers eventually should deteriorate with extensive failure. The model also predicts that SO athletes generally will perform well (see column 9). However, SO performers are not expected to perform as close to their performance potential over the long run as PO competitors because their concern about demonstrating high ability to others reduces performance in two ways. First, the importance of positive social comparison reduces the level of challenge of the goals set and limits how long SO athletes will persist in the face of failure. Second, the desire to maximize demonstration of ability prompts SO competitors to give low effort against weaker opponents and not look for ways to learn and improve unless pushed to do so to win. Such motivational patterns ultimately prevent SO performers from developing to the full extent of their performance potential across their careers.

According to the RCGS model, SO athletes should experience positive motivational consequences from the goal-setting process. SO performers are predicted to maintain optimistic future expectancies because past experience has told them that their normatively "high ability" will allow them to continue to socially compare well. The model also predicts that SO competitors should experience satisfaction and pride from success, whereas dissatisfaction over failure coupled with functional attributional patterns should prompt even higher motivation when they fail. Finally, SO athletes are predicted to increase activity importance for tasks at which they socially compare well to enhance their perceptions of ability.

Failure-Oriented Goal-Setting Style

Performers with FO goal-setting styles are outcome-oriented and adopt a capacity model of ability that views competence as fixed and limited, thus prompting them to define success in terms of social comparison. However, FO competitors have low perceived ability because of their inability to socially compare well (see columns 1–3 of table 15.2). An FO competitor's primary objective is to prevent others from finding out he or she has low ability, and competitive situations become sources of fear because of the risk of publicly revealing incompetence. Thus, FO athletes approach competition with diffidence and anxiety and often perform well below their capabilities. The

RCGS model hypothesizes that FO competitors typically attribute failure to lack of ability, thus reinforcing their negative perceptions of competence (column 5). Success, however, is normally attributed to external or uncontrollable factors such as luck or an easy task, thus doing little to increase feelings of competence (column 5). Regrettably, goals that foster increased success will not necessarily increase motivation for FO performers unless they also take responsibility for their success or perceive they can do something to turn failure into future success.

According to the RCGS model, FO performers have little interest in learning and normally demonstrate extreme task choice preferences (see column 7). Because they are concerned with concealing their low ability from others, they should set easy goals for tasks at which they are already experienced or proficient or else adopt extremely difficult goals so they have an excuse for failure. The RCGS model predicts that the effort expenditure of FO competitors will fluctuate with the level of task difficulty (see column 6). FO athletes who have not completely given up hope of demonstrating high ability should choose very difficult tasks. Despite the high probability of failure, FO performers will exert high effort trying to "get lucky" and demonstrate high ability, while secure in the knowledge that they have a good excuse for almost certain failure. However, once FO athletes become resigned to having low ability, they should prefer easy tasks and put forth high effort to ensure that they will not fail (see column 6). Moderately difficult tasks are predicted to be highly threatening to FO competitors, prompting them to respond by putting forth low effort as an ego-defense mechanism. Thus, this "token effort" strategy helps FO performers to hide their low ability from others by creating confusion about whether failure was due to lack of ability or simply low effort (see column 6).

The RCGS model hypothesizes that FO performers should demonstrate a significant deterioration in problem-solving skills when confronted with failure, probably because of the negative effects of diffidence and anxiety that prompt attentional distraction (see column 8). Finally, FO athletes are predicted to demonstrate a sharp deterioration in persistence and continuing motivation, even with minimal failure. Fear of revealing low ability to others should prompt FO competitors to respond to failure by developing high levels of anxiety and self-doubt, focusing internally on their own arousal and self-rumination, and demonstrating severe deterioration in their problem-solving skills (see column 8).

Conceptual arguments derived from the RCGS model predict that FO athletes normally should perform poorly (see column 9). Fear of failure due to inability to socially compare well should elicit high levels of anxiety that significantly impair FO competitors' performance. Moreover, negative competitive cognitions coupled with the most dysfunctional types of goal responses—including easy goal difficulty, low effort expenditure, poor strategy development (particularly under failure), and low persistence—should ensure that performance deteriorates even further over time (see column 9).

Finally, the model predicts that FO athletes should experience generally negative motivational consequences from the goal-setting process. FO performers are predicted to demonstrate negative future expectancies because of previous unsuccessful social comparison that they attributed to low ability. The model also predicts that FO competitors will experience minimal satisfaction from success, which they attribute to external, uncontrollable factors, whereas failure should promote extensive negative affect such as anxiety and shame that should impair performance and prompt a desire to drop out of sport. Finally, FO athletes are predicted to devalue activities that force them to risk demonstrating low ability as a precursor to dropping out or changing activities.

Goal Attribute Preferences

Based on the general descriptions for each goal-setting style just reviewed, the next section specifies RCGS model predictions for the goal attribute preferences of each goal-setting style, including goal specificity, goal difficulty, goal proximity, goal collectivity, and goal valence (see column 10).

Preferred Goal Attributes of PO Athletes

The RCGS model hypothesizes that PO athletes' learning orientation should prompt them to prefer self-referenced goals that are specific, difficult, and positive as well as set both individual and team and long-term and short-term goals (see column 10). Performers adopting PO goal-setting styles are predicted to prefer goals with these attributes because such goals provide maximum information for developing new strategies to facilitate learning and performance improvement. PO competitors also are predicted to set long-term goals to provide direction for their efforts, but they

achieve these goals by developing action plans that focus on reaching specific short-term goals as realistic steps to obtaining these long-term objectives. However, because PO performers are interested in learning as a long-term and ongoing process, they should focus more on long-term goals than either SO or FO competitors, delaying gratification and accepting temporary setbacks as the price that must be paid to maximize learning and skill development (see column 10).

Preferred Goal Attributes of SO Athletes

Because SO competitors adopt a capacity model of ability and define success in terms of positive social comparison, the RCGS model predicts that they should prefer goals that are specific and moderately difficult and that are both positive and negative, individual and team, and short- and long-term (see column 10). SO performers should prefer specific and moderately difficult goals that maximize their chances of positive social comparison and ensure that SO performers consistently demonstrate high ability. They also should benefit from positively focused goals for new or difficult skills but prefer more negatively focused goals that emphasize minimizing mistakes for well-learned skills. Model predictions suggest that both individual and team goals should facilitate social comparison, thus allowing SO competitors to demonstrate high ability. Athletes with SO goal-setting styles also should set a combination of short- and long-term goals (e.g., "I want to win the race this week as an important step toward my long-term goal of being an Olympic champion"). However, because of their concern with demonstrating high ability to others, SO performers should place more emphasis on short-term goals, sometimes retarding long-term skill development because it would cause a temporary decrease in performance that might hurt immediate social comparison (see column 10).

Preferred Goal Attributes of FO Athletes

Finally, the RCGS model predicts that FO athletes should dislike competition because it threatens to reveal their low ability, thus prompting them to prefer goals that are general, team-oriented, extremely difficult or easy, long-term, and positively focused (see column 10). General and team-oriented goals make social comparison more difficult, thus lessening its threat. Extremely difficult goals retain a small chance of demonstrating high ability while providing a built-in excuse for failure, whereas easy goals maximize the chances of success. Finally, long-term goals delay the threatening evaluation process as long as possible, and because FO performers have a strong fear of failure, they are also predicted to prefer positively focused goals that lessen concern about revealing low ability (see column 10).

Moderating Variables

Two important moderating variables have an impact on goal-setting effects in the RCGS model: commitment and feedback. This section briefly describes the role that these variables play in influencing the goal–performance relationship.

Goal Commitment

For goals to have motivational value, individuals must develop a high degree of commitment to goal achievement. Goal commitment is an important component of Locke's (1968) goal-setting model, and he emphasized that without commitment, individuals probably will not do what it takes to achieve goals. Moreover, Locke postulated that factors such as participation in setting the goal, incentives available for goal achievement, and the level of trust and supportiveness of others in the organization including coaches, teammates, and parents are important to the development of high commitment. In several meta-analyses, Locke and his colleagues (Locke, 1996; Locke, Latham, & Erez, 1988) emphasized that goal commitment is most important when goals are specific and difficult, and

commitment is enhanced when goals are perceived to be important yet attainable.

Interestingly, the mechanism by which commitment influences goals is somewhat complicated. For example, Locke and Latham (1990) identified an interesting interaction between level of commitment and goal difficulty, in which under low goal difficulty, low-commitment individuals perform better than their high-commitment counterparts, whereas under high goal difficulty, the opposite occurs. These predictions suggest that highly committed performers will attempt to make their performance conform to their goals, whether they are easy or difficult, more than less committed performers, thus highlighting the importance of setting difficult goals to enhance performance. General goal-setting research has confirmed that a number of factors can improve commitment, including the authority of the individual assigning the goals (e.g., Latham, Erez, & Locke, 1988; Latham & Lee, 1986; Latham & Yukl, 1975; Oldham, 1975), peer influences (e.g., Matsui, Kakuyama, & Onglatco, 1987; Rakestraw & Weiss, 1981), competition (e.g., Locke & Shaw, 1984; Mitchell, Rothman, & Liden, 1985; Shalley, Oldham, & Porac, 1987), public disclosure of goals (e.g., Hayes et al., 1985; Hollenbeck, Williams, & Klein, 1989), incentives and rewards (e.g., Huber, 1985; Riedel, Nebeker, & Cooper, 1988; Terborg, 1976), and goal participation (e.g., Earley, 1985; Earley & Kanfer, 1985; Erez, 1986; Erez, Earley, & Hulin, 1985).

Interestingly, Locke and Latham's (1990) review of the goal participation literature confirmed that participation has a negligible impact on enhancing goal effectiveness through increased commitment. A number of studies (e.g., Boyce & Wayda, 1994; Earley & Kanfer, 1985; Erbaugh & Barnett, 1986; Hollenbeck et al., 1989; A.M. Lee & Edwards, 1984; Racicot, Day, & Lord, 1991) have demonstrated that assigned goals are more difficult and inspire higher levels of effort and commitment than do self-set goals. Interestingly, Hinsz (1995) found that despite the higher performance in the assigned goal condition,

© Sally Weigand

Highly committed individuals perform better when pursuing difficult goals.

participants in the self-set goal condition had more positive affect toward setting goals. However, these results were far from unanimous, because three studies (Ludwig & Geller, 1997; Madden, 1996; Yearta, Maitlis, & Briner, 1995) demonstrated contradictory results.

Sport goal research (Fairall & Rodgers, 1997; Kyllo & Landers, 1995; Racicot et al., 1991; Theodorakis, 1996) strongly supports the view that participation in goal setting enhances commitment. Although Boyce's (1992a) research provided a lone contradictory result, a meta-analysis by Kyllo and Landers (1995) demonstrated an effect size of .62 for goal participation enhancing performance, suggesting that athletes who were involved in the goal-setting process were more likely to be committed to their goals, were more likely to have more input in developing effective goal strategies, and subsequently were more likely to attain their goals than athletes with assigned goals. Recent research with Olympic athletes (Weinberg et al., 2000) demonstrated that commitment can be enhanced by a variety of factors, particularly intrinsic (e.g., participation in setting goals and/or telling others), extrinsic (e.g., making national teams or winning rewards, sponsorship, endorsements, or international medals), and social support (e.g., support from others, help shaping goals) factors. Their research also confirmed that writing goals down and posting them enhanced commitment. Moreover, more effective goal-setters could be distinguished from less effective goal-setters based on their commitment in two areas: social support from significant others and extrinsic rewards (Burton et al., 2001).

Feedback

Locke and Latham's (1990) goal theory contends that feedback is an essential part of the goal-setting process and is necessary for enhancing performance. In the most comprehensive review to date of the role that feedback plays in goal setting, Locke and Latham (1990) reviewed 33 studies comparing the effectiveness of goals plus feedback with either goals or feedback individually. They found that 17 of 18 studies demonstrated that the combination of goals and feedback was significantly better than goals alone, and 21 of 22 studies revealed that the combination was superior to feedback alone. Moreover, Mento et al. (1987) demonstrated through their meta-analysis of goal-setting research that when feedback was added to goal setting, productivity increased an additional 17%. Thus, the consensus of the general goal-set-

ting literature is that feedback is an important and necessary moderator of goal-setting effects. Subsequent self-monitoring research (Earley, Northcraft, Lee, & Lituchy, 1990; Hutchison & Garstka, 1996; Locke, 1996; Martens, Hiralall, & Bradley, 1997; Mesch, Farh, & Podsakoff, 1994; Roberts & Reed, 1996; Shoenfelt, 1996; Tzetzis, Kioumourtzoglou, & Mavromatis, 1997; Vance & Colella, 1990; Zagumny & Johnson, 1992; Zimmerman & Kitsantas, 1996) further confirmed the importance of feedback on goal attainment. Locke's (1996) meta-analysis revealed that goal setting is most effective when progress feedback is given. However, he cautioned that feedback is only effective when taken constructively, because if feedback is viewed negatively, self-efficacy and effort expenditure toward the goal may be compromised. Similarly, Vance and Colella (1990) compared two types of feedback and concluded that when goal discrepancy feedback became too negative (i.e., the individual was far from reaching his or her goal), goals were abandoned. Interestingly, when performers were given past performance and negative goal discrepancy feedback, they shifted their goal to exceeding past performance rather than achieving the more difficult current goal. Thus, it appears that individuals revert to a more idiographic forms of comparison when objective goal difficulty is too high.

Research Testing the Revised Goal-Setting Model

As mentioned earlier, the original CGS model elicited a lot of discussion but a paucity of research that tested model predictions. Based on initial justification for the development of the CGS model (Burton, 1992, 1993) and subsequent research that tested specific model predictions, we conclude that there is solid preliminary support for the efficacy of the model as a conceptual framework for guiding goal-setting research and application. The model has been tested primarily by Burton and his colleagues and students (e.g., Burton, 1989b; Burton & Sharples, 2001; Burton et al., 2001; Pierce & Burton, 1998), whose research generally has supported model predictions, as well as Kingston and Hardy's (1997) performance versus process goal research, which indirectly supports model predictions. The major contradictory findings were provided by Kyllo and Landers (1995) in a meta-analysis of goal-setting research in sport and exercise, in which they concluded that "absolute goals" in which everyone is working toward the same goals (i.e., equated to outcome goals) are superior to "relative goals" in which goals focus on individual performance targets and performance levels (i.e., equated to performance goals). This section briefly reviews the sport research testing the RCGS model.

Burton (1989b) did not test goal-setting styles or even compare performance versus outcome goals directly. Pilot testing suggested that most collegiate athletes adopted outcome goals as their top priority, primarily because of the attractive extrinsic rewards attached to positive social comparison (e.g., medals, trophies, recognition, and fame). Thus, Burton (1989b) instituted a season-long Goal-Setting Training (GST) Program designed to teach members of a collegiate swim team to set performance goals as their highest priority. Burton then compared these swimmers' competitive cognitions and performance to another conference team that received no GST intervention and was assumed to set predominantly outcome goals. Across the 5-month intervention, Burton found that with training, GST swimmers became more performance-oriented and more skilled at setting challenging but realistic goals. By the Big 10 Championships at the end of the season, GST swimmers demonstrated more positive competitive cognitions, particularly reduced cognitive anxiety and increased self-confidence, and greater performance improvement than did non-GST swimmers.

Kingston and Hardy (1997) also failed to directly test goal-setting styles or even specifically compare performance versus outcome goals. However, if we can assume that the control group in this study focused on outcome to evaluate performance in the absence of any process or performance standards, then Kingston and Hardy demonstrated that performance-related goals are superior to their outcome-related counterparts in the development of positive competitive cognitions and performance improvement. Moreover, results revealed that golfing performance significantly improved for the process-goal group from the beginning to the middle of the intervention and for the performance-goal group from the beginning to the end of the intervention, whereas the control group did not significantly improve its golfing performance across the year-long intervention. Competitive cognition data also confirmed that the two performance treatment groups reported lower cognitive anxiety than did the control group, whereas the process-goal group reported significantly higher self-efficacy, cognitive anxiety control, and concentration than did the performance-goal or control groups. Thus, even

though the researchers expanded the notion of performance goals, their data provide partial support for the RCGS model.

Pierce and Burton (1998) designed a study to test model predictions directly in conjunction with an 8-week GST intervention program developed for female junior high school gymnasts. Gymnasts were categorized into goal-setting-style groups by both clinical and empirical procedures (i.e., 84% agreement on group assignment between methods), and SO, FO, and PO gymnasts were compared on competitive cognitions and performance across five meets. Consistent with model predictions, none of the FO gymnasts competed in even one event for all five meets, and most succeeded in avoiding social comparison by refusing to take part in weekly tryouts to win a spot in the competitive lineup. Results comparing gymnasts' performance for their most important event revealed a significant group by time interaction that was consistent with model predictions, whereas similar analyses for competitive cognitions demonstrated trends in the predicted directions, although greater variability in scores prevented these findings from reaching statistical significance for this relatively small sample. As predicted, PO gymnasts significantly improved their performance across meets, whereas somewhat surprisingly, SO performers experienced a slight decrease in their performance over the course of the season. Finally, results of postseason GST program evaluations revealed significant group differences, with PO gymnasts rating the GST program more favorably than did SO or FO performers.

Similarly, Burton and Sharples (2001) conducted a GST intervention with three female collegiate cross country runners: one PO, the second SO, and the third an SO athlete who became much more PO across the season. Idiographic results generally confirmed model predictions. First, the PO runner developed the most positive and productive competitive cognitions and improved her performance (i.e., both time and place) most across the 13-week season and compared with the previous season. Second, the SO runner had the most anxiety and confidence problems throughout the season, particularly at big meets such as the conference championships, and her performance made little improvement across the season or compared with the previous season. Finally, the competitive cognitions and performance of the third runner, who started out SO but made a transition to PO by the end of the season, were intermediary to those of her PO and SO teammates. Her performance at the conference championships was significantly faster than the previous season, in part because of her lowest anxiety and highest self-confidence levels of the season.

As part of a larger study on the goal patterns of Olympic athletes, Burton et al. (2001) generally supported theoretical predictions about the impact of goal-setting styles on athletes' goal patterns. The RCGS model predicts that SO and PO athletes will respond similarly over the short run and during success experiences, whereas differences between these two goal-setting styles will only emerge slowly over time or under failure conditions. Burton and his colleagues tested these predictions by first assessing the goal-setting styles of 338 Olympic athletes in 12 sports based on empirical procedures that used a combination of self-confidence and competitive orientation scores. Results investigating differences in the goal patterns of these goal-setting style groups revealed that the majority of athletes were empirically categorized as SO (58%), followed by PO (29%) and FO (13%). Moreover, goal pattern results demonstrated little difference between the goal patterns of SO and PO athletes, although FO athletes were significantly lower on almost all goal frequency, effectiveness, commitment, and barrier subscales. Interestingly, comparisons of goal-setting style groups for the most experienced 20% of the sample revealed that PO athletes used significantly more effective goal practices than SO-oriented performers, who were still superior to FO competitors. Overall, this survey investigation provides moderate support for the RCGS model, although it points to some of the primary methodological problems of accurately measuring goal-setting styles.

Support for the RCGS model is not unanimous. Kyllo and Landers's (1995) meta-analysis of goal-setting research in sport and exercise offers the major contradictory finding, their review concluding that outcome goals are superior to performance goals in stimulating performance improvement. Kyllo and Landers drew this conclusion based on several questionable assumptions. First, they concluded that "absolute goals" in which everyone is working toward the same standards are superior to "relative goals" in which goals target individual performance objectives and performance levels. Kyllo and Landers argued that absolute goals are equivalent to outcome goals because of the common goal, and relative goals are similar to performance goals because they focus on individual performance. However, their logic

seems flawed. They defined absolute goals as "a standard shared or common to all athletes," but performers may have both performance and outcome goals in common, making this argument shaky at best. Relative goals that focus on individual performance obviously may focus on both performance and outcome targets, again suggesting that the performance-outcome distinction doesn't seem to be consistent with Kyllo and Landers's absolute-relative dimension. Second, their performance-outcome conclusion is based on an interaction between goal difficulty and goal type, so that moderately difficult goals specified in absolute terms have significantly higher mean effect sizes (.91) than do moderately difficult goals specified in relative terms (effect size = .36). Finally, Kyllo and Landers excluded the Burton (1989b) study from their analyses for methodological reasons (i.e., couldn't compute an effect size), even though it was the one study that most directly tested the performance versus outcome predictions of interest.

In a final major test of the RCGS model, Lerner and Locke (1995) attempted to test the mediating effects of self-efficacy and goal orientation on the goal–performance relationship. Interestingly, consistent with Locke's (1991) predictions, they found that personal goals and self-efficacy completely mediated the effects of motivational orientation on performance, suggesting that self-efficacy has a greater impact on performance than does motivational orientation. However, several methodological problems seem to confound their results. First, they used the total SOQ score rather than individual subscale scores, so the effects of performance, outcome, and competitiveness were assessed in combination rather than individually. Second, goals were assigned to subjects in this study, but to accurately assess the role of motivational orientation, performers would need to be free to set their own goals. Finally, the effects of goal orientation are most likely to affect performance for an ego-involving task whose success is highly important rather than the simple sit-up task that was used. Despite these methodology problems, Lerner and Locke (1995) confirmed that both goal orientation and self-efficacy were significantly related to performance, providing partial support for the RCGS model.

Two conclusions are inescapable from this review of research testing the RCGS model. First, a great deal more research testing RCGS model predictions is needed. Second, the limited research to date provides moderate support for model predictions, although independent model tests using larger sample sizes in ecologically valid settings are needed to evaluate its true efficacy.

MEASUREMENT ISSUES IN GOAL SETTING

As with most research in the behavioral sciences, measurement issues seem to dictate the quantity and quality of goal-setting research produced. The current status of goal-setting research suggests that at least three major measurement issues currently limit goal research and consequently limit our conceptual and practical understanding of how goals can be used most effectively. These issues include identifying the role of goal hierarchies in the goal-setting process, accurately measuring goal discrepancy and goal importance, and using measurement techniques to more accurately assess athletes' goal-setting styles.

Investigating Goal Hierarchies

A goal hierarchy is a systematic way of arranging and using goals based on a structured prioritization system. Most individuals generally set multiple goals for different areas of their lives and various time periods, which focus on differential performance objectives. For example, athletes might concurrently have sport, academic, social, and career goals that are all highly valued and worked on simultaneously. Similarly, athletes often set goals for a variety of time periods, including dream, long-term, moderate-term, and short-term goals. Finally, athletes may set different types of goals that focus on different aspects of performance. These could include outcome goals (to win the next competition); performance goals (to score 12 points, grab 10 rebounds, and make four assists); and process goals to accomplish these performance goals (e.g., being prepared to shoot when they receive the pass, blocking their opponent out as far from the basket as possible, and turning and facing the basket whenever they receive a pass).

The problem with multiple goals is developing a system to keep them straight and knowing when and how to focus on each type of goal at the appropriate time. For example, Hardy and his colleagues (L. Hardy, 1997; Kingston & Hardy, 1997) suggested that elite performers may focus outcome goals on long-term objectives such as winning a World Championships or Olympic Games

to sustain their motivation over long, difficult training periods or to increase motivation during a monotonous practice. In contrast, performance and process goals are both used to help athletes enhance short-term skill development and improvement, perform their best for a specific competition, or focus during critical moments of important competitions. These issues regarding goal focus and proximity are further complicated by athletes' needs to set goals in other domains to enhance their quality of life.

From a research standpoint, measurement strategies need to be developed to reliably and validly assess athletes' goal hierarchies, including goal focus and proximity factors across different achievement domains. Moreover, measurement techniques are needed to better understand goal priorities, including how personal priorities are developed for different types of goals, how priorities might change across situations, and what situational factors prompt a change in priorities to athletes' goal hierarchies. From a practical standpoint, athletes need help understanding how to organize and prioritize their goals most effectively. Specific guidelines also are needed to help athletes prevent goal overload and to determine what types of goals they should focus on in specific situations to maximize motivation, self-confidence, and performance.

Measuring Goal Discrepancy and Goal Importance

In Lazarus's (1991) stress model, goals play an important role in stress and motivation perceptions, with goal relevance or importance and goal discrepancy two primary components of primary appraisal. Lazarus defined goal importance as the sum total of the factors that enhance the value of a particular goal, whereas goal discrepancy is the difference between the goal individuals set and the actual performance that they expect to achieve. Lazarus believes that threat appraisal occurs when goal discrepancy is negative (i.e., stress/anxiety), whereas challenge appraisal reflects a positive goal discrepancy (i.e., motivation). Goal importance then magnifies challenge or threat appraisal based on the value placed on goal attainment, thereby inflating stress and motivation levels.

According to Lazarus's (1991) model, goal importance amplifies or suppresses the impact of goal discrepancy on overall appraisal. However, research has had minimal success illuminating the relationship of goal discrepancy and goal importance to overall appraisal and, through it, their impact on stress/anxiety, motivation, and performance. Measurement issues clearly have prompted some of this confusion, and a number of issues need attention if the conceptual role of goal discrepancy and importance is to be better understood. First, should we measure goal importance as a state, trait, or both? Obviously, goal importance is both a state and a trait. As a trait, athletes have a general level of importance that they place on attainment of their goals, although goal importance may vary across different achievement domains in athletes' lives. As a state, goal importance may vary somewhat from situation to situation, although there is probably an interaction effect with athletes' changing goal hierarchies.

Second, should goal importance be measured objectively or subjectively? Goal importance can be measured subjectively by having athletes rate the relative importance of all their goals at the moment taken in totality. Such a strategy is relatively simple and focuses on allowing athletes to consider all their goals and provide an overall rating on how important it is to attain all of them. A more objective measure of goal importance also can be developed that requires athletes to identify their three or four most important goals and then rate each specific goal on importance of goal attainment, summing all item totals. Clearly, subjective goal importance assessment is easier, but as yet, little information is available to assess which approach is more psychometrically appropriate.

Third, how can we reliably and validly measure goal importance? In sport and exercise, goal importance traditionally has been measured by using single-item Likert-type scales. Although this strategy is quick and easy to implement, it does not provide the researcher with a reliable measure of state goal importance, and its validity is also somewhat questionable. Graham (1999) recently developed a state Goal Importance Scale (GIS), a five-item instrument designed to provide a reliable and valid measure of state goal importance in sport. The GIS has not been used extensively in the sport goal literature, but it does offer a promising measurement tool for assessing subjective goal importance in specific situations.

Goal discrepancy seems to have fewer dimensions because it appears to be a state and not a trait measure. However, should goal discrepancy be measured objectively or subjectively? If goal discrepancy is measured subjectively, athletes would rate how well they expect to attain all their important goals at the moment. Again, this simpler strategy allows athletes to simultaneously consider all their goals and provide an overall rating on how likely they are to attain those goals. Objective measures of goal discrepancy would involve athletes identifying their three or four most important goals and then separately rating each one on expected goal attainment. These goal attainment scores then would be summed to create an overall goal discrepancy score. Hoar, Burton, and Crocker (2000) used the objective goal discrepancy strategy with moderate effectiveness, but extensive work is needed to develop psychometrically sound measures of goal importance and goal discrepancy.

Measuring Goal-Setting Styles

The ultimate utility of goal-setting styles will hinge, in part, on researchers' ability to develop effective instruments to measure them. One approach to testing goal-setting styles is to conduct a lab study by using a learned helplessness paradigm (Elliott & Dweck, 1988). In such a study, goal orientation and perceived ability are experimentally manipulated to investigate their impact on motivation and performance variables. However, it also seems desirable to develop instruments that can measure existing goal-setting styles in real sport situations so goal-setting styles can be investigated in ecologically valid settings. Regrettably, the task of developing reliable and valid instruments to measure PO, SO, and FO goal-setting styles has proved challenging for three reasons. First, reliable and valid instruments must be identified or developed to measure both goal orientation and perceived ability. Second, joint scores for goal orientation and perceived ability must be identified that accurately bound each goal-setting style. Finally, because goal-setting styles seem to be influenced by powerful situational factors, both state and trait versions of goal-setting style instrumentation must be developed.

Several reliable and valid instruments have been developed to measure goal orientation in sport, including Duda and Nicholls's (1992) Task and Ego Orientation in Sport Questionnaire, Gill and Deeter's (1988) Sport Orientation Questionnaire, Roberts and Balague's (1991) Perceptions of Success Questionnaire, and Vealey's (1986) Competitive Orientation Inventory. Duda and Whitehead (1998) provide a complete description of these goal perspective measures and their relative strengths and weaknesses. Both the Task and Ego Orientation in Sport Questionnaire and Competitive

Orientation Inventory have been used to empirically assess goal-setting styles, and both measures have similar problems with accurately categorizing athletes who are on the borderline between the two goal orientations. Further research is needed to determine which existing measure is most strongly related to goal setting as well as which best categorizes goal-setting styles.

At least two reliable and valid instruments have been developed to measure perceived ability-related constructs in sport, including Fox and Corbin's (1989) Physical Self-Perception Profile and Vealey's (1986, 1988) State–Trait Sport Confidence Inventory. Feltz and Chase (1998) and Fox (1998) provide more complete descriptions of competence measures and their relative strengths and weaknesses. Both these instruments have been used to assess goal-setting styles in sport, but results have been equivocal and the decision on which instruments provide the most valid measure of goal-setting styles must await future research. In the meantime, researchers will have to select instruments to measure goal-setting styles in sport based on theoretical rationale and personal preferences.

Not only do researchers need reliable and valid instruments to assess goal orientation and perceived ability in sport, they also need to identify the specific score profiles on each instrument that can be used to define each goal-setting style. Moreover, the RCGS model views goal-setting styles as both (a) a general predisposition to set certain kinds of goals across most situations (i.e., psychological trait) and (b) momentary goal-setting behavior reflecting the influence of particular situational factors (i.e., psychological states). Thus, athletes who typically adopt a PO goal-setting style may be constrained by powerful situational factors to adopt an FO style in a particularly important competition. To assess the influence of goal-setting styles on motivation and performance accurately, researchers need to develop measurement instruments that assess both trait and state goal-setting styles so that research can assess the stability of these styles across situations.

FUTURE DIRECTIONS IN GOAL-SETTING RESEARCH IN SPORT

Although goal setting is one of the most heavily researched areas in sport psychology, a number of important issues await future research. Five areas of research seem to be critical to obtaining a better understanding of goal setting and how to best use goals to enhance performance in sport and exercise. First, we need to better understand the optimal level of goal difficulty for specific individuals and particular situations as well as how to help practitioners adjust goal difficulty to more optimal levels. Second, the role that goals play in the periodization of mental training needs to be elucidated, and strategies to use goals to enhance periodization need to be developed. Third, we need to know the impact of self-monitoring and evaluation on goal-setting effectiveness and the optimal amount and type of self-monitoring or evaluation. Fourth, we need to know the role that action plans play in goal-setting effectiveness and how action plans can be developed most successfully. Finally, we need to know how to maximize goal-setting generalization effects across subjects, tasks, and domains.

Identify Optimal Goal Difficulty

The RCGS model predicts that the establishment of goals that are too difficult for SO and FO athletes can prompt diffidence, anxiety, and attentional distraction that impair performance. This prediction suggests that goal-setting styles have an optimal goal difficulty range for best performance. Several researchers have attempted to provide strategies to determine appropriate levels of goal difficulty (e.g., O'Block & Evans, 1984), but few goal-setting studies have attempted to operationalize the goal difficulty level that will foster best performance. Although Burton and his colleagues (Burton, Daw, Williams-Rice, & Phillips, 1989) attempted to assess typical goal difficulty levels for different goal-setting styles in a basketball class, little is known about how well these goal difficulty ranges generalize to more competitive situations or other sports. Additional questions concerning how to optimize goal difficulty need to be addressed, including the following: How should goal difficulty be adjusted as key situational factors, such as importance of the competition, change? How does personal goal difficulty influence performance? Is the relationship between goal difficulty and performance linear or curvilinear?

Understand How to Best Periodize Goal Setting

Periodization is an approach to training originally developed by physiologists to maximize performance gains by systematically varying the volume and intensity of physical training (Bompa, 1999). Although exercise physiologists debate the value of periodization, its principles are used extensively to guide strength and conditioning training worldwide (Bompa, 1999). Currently, applications of periodization principles to mental training have had little empirical examination, but anecdotal evidence suggests that a periodized approach to mental training may be more enjoyable, may promote greater mental training effectiveness, and may enhance performance compared with standard, nonperiodized mental training approaches.

Most of periodization theory focuses on Selye's general adaptation syndrome as its underlying conceptual rationale, and training is then broken up into macro, meso, and micro training cycles. Season-long macrocycles are broken down into intermediate length mesocycles that typically last 4 to 8 weeks. Within each mesocycle, several distinct microcycles are identified such as preparation, competition, and peaking, and the frequency and intensity of physical and mental training are adjusted to maximize positive adaptation. Thus, basketball players may start the season shooting 100 to 150 free throws per day and shooting large blocks of free throws at one time. By the end of the season, they may be shooting only 35 to 50 free throws per day, but each shot is taken as if shooting in a realistic competitive situation (i.e., shooting no more than two free throws at a time while distracting aspects of important competitive situations are simulated).

Although periodization requires clear, long-term goals that are broken down into realistic daily, weekly, and monthly subgoals, many issues related to periodizing goal setting remain equivocal. For example, how frequently should goals be changed and evaluated in periodized mental training programs? How should goals change through the different cycles of periodization, and what factors determine how to adjust goals according to situational demands?

Quantify the Frequency of and Strategies for Goal Monitoring and Evaluation

Kirschenbaum (1984) concluded that self-monitoring and self-evaluation are necessary but not sufficient to maintain effective self-regulation. Drawing on Carver and Scheier's (1981) self-focused attention model, Kirschenbaum and Tomarken (1982) argued that increasing self-

awareness through self-monitoring typically increases attempts to match behavior to goals. However, there seems to be a trade-off inherent in self-monitoring and evaluation. If monitoring and evaluation are too infrequent, athletes will have difficulty perceiving improvement in competence, which is necessary to enhance intrinsic motivation (e.g., Deci & Ryan, 1985; Vallerand, Gauvin, & Halliwell, 1986). However, if monitoring and evaluation are too frequent, it may be difficult to maintain a performance orientation because extensive evaluation makes outcome concerns more salient (e.g., Nicholls, 1984a) and may prompt individuals to feel like "pawns" because goals are perceived as controlling rather than informational (e.g., deCharms, 1976; Deci & Ryan, 1985; Vallerand et al., 1986). In fact, some self-regulation research (Kirschenbaum & Tomarken, 1982) suggests that moderately specific and longer term plans may facilitate self-control to a greater degree than specific, short-term plans. Indeed, anecdotal evidence from a dozen years of practical goal-setting work with athletes confirms that maintaining the same goals for weekly intervals seems to facilitate improvement more than changing goals daily. Additional goal monitoring and evaluation questions need further research: Does excessive self-evaluation lower perceived ability? If so, how? What is the most effective way to provide feedback to encourage development of both self-confidence and motivation? Can social support (e.g., the buddy system) be used to facilitate self-monitoring?

Environmental Engineering/ Developing Action Plans

Goal-setting research assessing the moderating effects of task complexity (Mento et al., 1987) suggested that the motivational benefits of goals only work when athletes are practicing skills correctly and have good action plans for long-term skill development (e.g., Hall & Byrne, 1988). Thus, optimal skill development requires first developing sound technique and then practicing that skill until it becomes highly automated. For complex skills, athletes must find competent coaches who can help them develop correct technique. Moreover, coaches must understand the basic principles of periodization of training so they can develop accurate action plans that help athletes adjust goals appropriately during different portions of training or skill development (Bompa, 1999). Heckhausen and Strang (1988) demonstrated that performers who were more effective at developing action plans to modify exertion performed better on a simulated basketball task, particularly under stressful conditions, than did less action-oriented performers. One of the most difficult aspects of skill development is understanding when a learning strategy is appropriate and needs only systematic practice to automate skills and when it is limited or ineffectual and a new strategy must be developed to reach one's performance potential. Abandoning an effective strategy too soon is undesirable and will only lengthen the time necessary to automate skills. However, practicing an ineffective technique will prevent optimal skill development. Perhaps one of the talents that separates effective from ineffective coaches is the ability to know which approach is needed in a particular situation. Future research is needed on a number of environmental engineering/action plan questions: Would formal problem-solving training facilitate the development of new strategies necessary to enhance complex skills? How does the coach know when to encourage athletes to practice existing strategies more diligently versus modifying task strategies to maximize skill development?

Generalization of Goal-Setting Effects

Kirschenbaum (1984) suggested that self-regulatory failure typically occurs because of the inability to generalize relevant behaviors to other settings, times, or conditions. Kirschenbaum (1984) emphasized that circumventing generalization problems requires an obsessive–compulsive behavior style in which vigilant self-monitoring and self-evaluation lead to appropriate changes in goals or goal levels. Not only do goals need to be set in sport that help athletes develop new skills and strategies, but goals also need to be established that focus on how skills and strategies must be adjusted in different competitions, at different times of the competitive season, and against different opponents. Some goal generalization questions needing further research include the following:

- What situational cues typically prompt athletes to adopt a particular goal-setting style?
- How can athletes be trained to maintain a particular perspective in the face of highly contradictory situational factors?
- How can goal-setting strategies best help FO athletes become PO athletes?

SUMMARY AND CONCLUSION

This chapter introduced the mental training tool of goal setting and described the primary functions of goals. Goal-setting theory and research were reviewed, including goal attribute research on goal focus, goal specificity, goal difficulty, goal valence, goal proximity, and goal collectivity. Four explanations were offered for why goals are less effective in sport than in other achievement domains. Next, a revised competitive goal setting (RCGS) model was presented as a heuristic tool that integrates the motivational and stress management functions of goals into an overall conceptual framework that hypothesizes three distinct goal-setting styles; this tool also makes specific predictions for the attributes of each goal-setting style and their impact on goal responses and motivational consequences. Research supporting the RCGS model was reviewed, with these findings moderately supportive of the RCGS model and the notion of goal-setting styles. Three important measurement issues inherent in the model and goal-setting implementation were discussed. Finally, five future directions for goal-setting research were proposed that highlight the role of individual differences and goal implementation strategies in goal-setting effectiveness.

REFERENCES

Anderson, D.C., Crowell, C.R., Doman, M., & Howard, G.S. (1988). Performance posting, goal setting, and activity-contingent praise as applied to a university hockey team. *Journal of Applied Psychology, 73,* 87–95.

Anshel, M.H., Weinberg, R.S., & Jackson, A. (1992). The effect of goal difficulty and task complexity on intrinsic motivation and motor performance. *Journal of Sport Behavior, 15,* 159–176.

Bandura, A. (1986). *Social foundations of thought and actions: A social cognitive theory.* Englewood Cliffs, NJ: Prentice Hall.

Bandura, A., & Simon, K.M. (1977). The role of proximal intentions in self-regulation of refractory behavior. *Cognitive Therapy and Research, 1,* 177–193.

Bar-Eli, M., Hartman, I., & Levy-Kolker, N. (1994). Using goal setting to improve physical performance of adolescents with behavior disorders: The effect of goal proximity. *Adapted Physical Activity Quarterly, 11,* 86–97.

Bar-Eli, M., Levy-Kolker, N., Tenenbaum, G., & Weinberg, R.S. (1993). Effect of goal difficulty on performance of aerobic, anaerobic and power tasks in laboratory and field settings. *Journal of Sport Behavior, 16,* 17–32.

Bar-Eli, M., Tenenbaum, G., Pie, J., Btesh, Y., & Almog, A. (1997). Effect of goal difficulty, goal specificity and duration of practice time intervals on muscular endurance performance. *Journal of Sport Sciences, 15,* 125–135.

Barnett, M.L. (1977). Effects of two methods of goal setting on learning a gross motor task. *Research Quarterly, 48,* 19–23.

Barnett, M.L., & Stanicek, J.A. (1979). Effects of goal-setting on achievement in archery. *Research Quarterly, 50,* 328–332.

Beggs, A. (1990). Goal setting in sport. In G. Jones & L. Hardy (Eds.), *Stress and performance in sport* (135–170). Chichester, UK: Wiley.

Bompa, T.O. (1999). *Periodization training for sports.* Champaign, IL: Human Kinetics.

Borrelli, B., & Mermelstein, R. (1994). Goal setting and behavior change in a smoking cessation program. *Cognitive Therapy and Research, 18,* 69–83.

Boutcher, S. (1990). The role of performance routines in sport. In G. Jones & L. Hardy (Eds.), *Stress and performance in sport* (pp. 231–245). Chichester, UK: Wiley.

Boyce, B.A. (1990a). Effects of goal specificity and goal difficulty upon skill acquisition of a selected shooting task. *Perceptual and Motor Skills, 70,* 1031–1039.

Boyce, B.A. (1990b). The effect of instructor-set goals upon skill acquisition and retention of a selected shooting task. *Journal of Teaching in Physical Education, 9,* 115–122.

Boyce, B.A. (1992a). Effects of assigned versus participant-set goals on skill acquisition and retention of a selected shooting task. *Journal of Teaching in Physical Education, 11,* 220–234.

Boyce, B.A. (1992b). The effects of goal proximity on skill acquisition and retention of a shooting task in a field-based setting. *Journal of Sport & Exercise Psychology, 14,* 298–308.

Boyce, B.A. (1994). The effects of goal setting on performance and spontaneous goal-setting behavior of experienced pistol shooters. *The Sport Psychologist, 8,* 87–93.

Boyce, B.A., & Bingham, S.M. (1997). The effects of self-efficacy and goal setting on bowling performance. *Journal of Teaching in Physical Education, 16,* 312–323.

Boyce, B.A., & Wayda, V.K. (1994). The effects of assigned and self-set goals on task performance. *Journal of Sport & Exercise Psychology, 16,* 258–269.

Brawley, L.R., Carron, A.V., & Widmeyer, W.N. (1992). The nature of group goals in sport teams: A phenomenological analysis. *The Sport Psychologist, 6,* 323–333.

Brawley, L.R., Carron, A.V., & Widmeyer, W.N. (1993). The influence of the group and its cohesiveness on perceptions of group goal-related variables. *Journal of Sport & Exercise Psychology, 15,* 245–260.

Burton, D. (1989a). The impact of goal specificity and task complexity on basketball skill development. *The Sport Psychologist, 3,* 34–47.

Burton, D. (1989b). Winning isn't everything: Examining the impact of performance goals on collegiate swimmers' cognitions and performance. *The Sport Psychologist, 3,* 105–132.

Burton, D. (1992). The Jekyll/Hyde nature of goals: Reconceptualizing goal setting in sport. In T. Horn (Ed.), *Advances in sport psychology* (pp. 267–297). Champaign, IL: Human Kinetics.

Burton, D. (1993). Goal setting in sport. In R.N. Singer, M. Murphey, & L.K. Tennant (Eds.), *Handbook of research on sport psychology* (pp. 467–491). New York: Macmillan.

Burton, D., Daw, J., Williams-Rice, B.T., & Phillips, D. (1989, October). *Goal setting styles: The influence of self-esteem on goal difficulty preferences.* Paper presented at the meeting of the Canadian Society for Psychomotor Learning and Sport Psychology, Victoria, BC.

Burton, D., Naylor, S., & Holliday, B. (2001). Goal setting in sport: Investigating the goal effectiveness paradox. In R.N. Singer, H.A. Hausenblas, & C.M. Janelle (Eds.), *Handbook of sport psychology* (2nd ed., pp. 497–528). New York: Wiley.

Burton, D., & Sharples, P. (2001). *The impact of goal setting styles on the effectiveness of a goal setting training program for women's collegiate cross country runners.* Manuscript in preparation.

Burton, D., Weinberg, R.S., Yukelson, D., & Weigand, D. (1998). The goal effectiveness paradox in sport: Examining the goal practices of collegiate athletes. *The Sport Psychologist, 12,* 404–418.

Burton, D., Weinberg, R.S., Yukelson, D., & Weigand, D. (2001). *An elite perspective on the goal effectiveness paradox in sport: Surveying the goal practices of Olympic athletes.* Manuscript in preparation.

Campbell, D.J., & Furrer, D.M. (1995). Goal setting and competition as determinants of task performance. *Journal of Organizational Behavior, 16,* 377–389.

Carroll, S.J. (1986). Management by objectives: Three decades of research and experience. In S.L. Rynes & G.T. Milkovich (Eds.), *Current issues in human resource management.* Plato, TX: Business Publications.

Carver, C.S., & Scheier, M.F. (1981). *Attention and self-regulation: A control-theory approach to human behavior.* New York: Springer-Verlag.

Chesney, A., & Locke, E. (1991). Relationships among goal difficulty, business strategies, and performance on a complex management simulation task. *Academy of Management Journal, 34,* 400–424.

Chidester, T.R., & Grigsby, W.C. (1984). A meta-analysis of the goal setting-performance literature. In J.A. Pearce & R.B. Robinson (Eds.), *Academy of management proceedings* (pp. 202–206). Ada, OH: Academy of Management.

Cohen, J. (1992). A power primer. *Psychological Bulletin, 112,* 155–159.

deCharms, R. (1976). *Enhancing motivation: Change in the classroom.* New York: Irvington.

Deci, E.L., & Ryan, R.M. (1985). *Intrinsic motivation and self-determination in human behavior.* New York: Plenum Press.

DeShon, R.P., & Alexander, R.A. (1996). Goal setting effects on implicit and explicit learning of complex tasks. *Organizational Behavior and Human Decision Processes, 65,* 18–36.

Diener, C.I., & Dweck, C.S. (1978). An analysis of learned helplessness: Continuous changes in performance, strategy, and achievement cognitions following failure. *Journal of Personality and Social Psychology, 36,* 451–462.

Duda, J.L., & Hall, H. (2001). Achievement goal theory in sport: Recent extensions and future directions. In R.N. Singer, H.A. Hausenblas, & C.M. Janelle (Eds.), *Handbook of sport psychology* (2nd ed., pp. 417–443). New York: Wiley.

Duda, J.L., & Nicholls, J.G. (1992). Dimensions of achievement motivation in schoolwork and sport. *Journal of Educational Psychology, 84,* 1–10.

Duda, J.L., & Whitehead, J. (1998). Measurement of goal perspectives in the physical domain. In J.L. Duda (Ed.), *Advances in sport and exercise psychology measurement* (pp. 21–48). Morgantown, WV: Fitness Information Technology.

Dweck, C.S. (1980). Learned helplessness in sport. In C.H. Nadeau, W.R. Halliwell, K.M. Newell, & G.C. Roberts (Eds.), *Psychology of motor behavior and sport—1979* (pp. 1–12). Champaign, IL: Human Kinetics.

Dweck, C. (1999). *Self theories: Their role in motivation, personality, and development.* Philadelphia: Psychology Press/Taylor and Francis.

Earley, P.C. (1985). Influence of information, choice, and task complexity upon goal acceptance, performance, and personal goals. *Journal of Applied Psychology, 70,* 481–491.

Earley, P.C., Connolly, T., & Ekegren, G. (1989). Goals, strategy development, and task performance: Some limits on the efficacy of goal setting. *Journal of Applied Psychology, 74,* 24–33.

Earley, P., & Kanfer, R. (1985). The influence of component participation and role models on goal acceptance, goal satisfaction, and performance. *Organizational Behavior and Human Decision Processes, 36,* 378–390.

Earley, P., Northcraft, G., Lee, C., & Lituchy, T. (1990). Impact of process and outcome feedback on the relation of goal setting to task performance. *Academy of Management Journal, 33,* 87–105.

Elliott, E.S., & Dweck, C.S. (1988). Goals: An approach to motivation and achievement. *Journal of Personality and Social Psychology, 54,* 5–12.

Erbaugh, S.J., & Barnett, M.L. (1986). Effects of modeling and goal-setting on the jumping performance of primary-grade children. *Perceptual and Motor Skills, 63,* 1287–1293.

Erez, M. (1986). The congruence of goal setting strategies with socio-cultural values, and its effect on performance. *Journal of Management, 12,* 585–592.

Erez, M., Earley, P.C., & Hulin, C.L. (1985). The impact of participation on goal acceptance and performance: A two-step model. *Academy of Management Journal, 28,* 50–66.

Erez, M., & Zidon, I. (1984). Effect of goal acceptance on the relationship of goal difficulty to performance. *Journal of Applied Psychology, 69,* 69–78.

Fairall, D.G., & Rodgers, W.M. (1997). The effects of goal-setting method on goal attributes in athletes: A field experiment. *Journal of Sport & Exercise Psychology, 19,* 1–16.

Feltz, D.L., & Chase, M.A. (1998). The measurement of self-efficacy and confidence in sport. In J.L. Duda (Ed.), *Advances in sport and exercise psychology measurement* (pp. 65–80). Morgantown, WV: Fitness Information Technology.

Filby, W.C.D., Maynard, I.W., & Graydon, J.K. (1999). The effect of multiple-goal strategies on performance outcomes in training and competition. *Journal of Applied Sport Psychology, 11,* 230–246.

Fox, K.R. (1998). Advances in the measurement of the physical self. In J.L. Duda (Ed.), *Advances in sport and exercise psychology measurement* (pp. 295–310). Morgantown, WV: Fitness Information Technology.

Fox, K.R., & Corbin, C.B. (1989). The physical self-perception profile: Development and preliminary validation. *Journal of Sport & Exercise Psychology, 11,* 408–430.

Frierman, S.H., Weinberg, R.S., & Jackson, A. (1990). The relationship between goal proximity and specificity in bowling: A field experiment. *The Sport Psychologist, 4,* 145–154.

Galvan, Z.J., & Ward, P. (1998). Effects of public posting on inappropriate on-court behaviors by collegiate tennis players. *The Sport Psychologist, 12,* 419–426.

Giannini, J.M., Weinberg, R.S., & Jackson, A.J. (1988). The effects of mastery, competitive, and cooperative goals on the performance of simple and complex basketball skills. *Journal of Sport & Exercise Psychology, 10,* 408–417.

Gill, D.L., & Deeter, T.E. (1988). Development of the sport orientation questionnaire. *Research Quarterly for Exercise and Sport, 59,* 191–202.

Gould, D. (1998). Goal setting for peak performance. In J.M. Williams (Ed.), *Applied sport psychology: Personal growth to peak performance* (3rd ed., pp. 182–196). Mountain View, CA: Mayfield.

Graham, T. (1999). *The contribution of goal characteristics and causal attributions to emotional experience in youth sport participants.* Unpublished doctoral dissertation, University of Saskatchewan, Saskatoon, SK.

Hall, H.K., & Byrne, A.T.J. (1988). Goal setting in sport: Clarifying recent anomalies. *Journal of Sport & Exercise Psychology, 10,* 184–198.

Hall, H.K., Weinberg, R.S., & Jackson, A. (1987). Effects of goal specificity, goal difficulty, and information feedback on endurance performance. *Journal of Sport Psychology, 9,* 43–54.

Hardy, C.J., & Latane, B. (1988). Social loafing in cheerleaders: Effects of team membership and competition. *Journal of Sport & Exercise Psychology, 10,* 109–114.

Hardy, L. (1997). The Coleman Roberts Griffith address: Three myths about applied consultancy work. *Journal of Applied Sport Psychology, 9,* 277–294.

Hardy, L., Jones, J.G., & Gould, D. (1996). *Understanding psychological preparation for sport: Theory and practice of elite performers.* Chichester, UK: Wiley.

Hardy, L., & Nelson, D. (1988). Self-control training in sport and work. *Ergonomics, 31,* 1573–1585.

Harkins, S.G., & Petty, R.E. (1982). Effects of task difficulty and task uniqueness on social loafing. *Journal of Personality and Social Psychology, 43,* 1214–1229.

Harter, S. (1981). The development of competence motivation in the mastery of cognitive and physical skills: Is there still a place for joy? In G.C. Roberts & D.M. Landers (Eds.), *Psychology of motor behavior and sport—1980* (pp. 3–29). Champaign, IL: Human Kinetics.

Hayes, S.C., Rosenfarb, I., Wulfert, E., Munt, E.D., Korn, Z., & Kettle, R.D. (1985). Self-reinforcement effects: An artifact of social standard setting? *Journal of Applied Behavior Analysis, 18,* 201–214.

Heckhausen, H., & Strang, H. (1988). Efficiency under record performance demands: Exertion control—An individual difference variable? *Journal of Personality and Social Psychology, 55,* 489–498.

Hinsz, V. (1995). Goal setting by groups performing an additive task: A comparison with individual goal setting. *Journal of Applied Social Psychology, 25,* 965–990.

Hoar, S., Burton, D., & Crocker, P.R.E. (2000). *Takedowns and reversals: An examination of coping consistency within and across competitive wrestling transactions.* Manuscript submitted for publication.

Hollenbeck, J.R., Williams, C.R., & Klein, H.J. (1989). An empirical examination of the antecedents of commitment to difficult goals. *Journal of Applied Psychology, 74,* 18–23.

Hollingsworth, B. (1975). Effects of performance goals and anxiety on learning a gross motor task. *Research Quarterly, 46,* 162–168.

Howe, B., & Poole, R. (1992). Goal proximity and achievement motivation of high school boys in a basketball shooting task. *Journal of Teaching in Physical Education, 11,* 248–255.

Huber, V.L. (1985). Comparison of monetary reinforcers and goal setting as learning incentives. *Psychological Reports, 56,* 223–235.

Humphries, C.A., Thomas, J.R., & Nelson, J.K. (1991). Effects of attainable and unattainable goals on mirror-tracing performance and retention of a motor task. *Perceptual and Motor Skills, 72,* 1231–1237.

Hunter, J.E., & Schmidt, F.L. (1983). Quantifying the effects of psychological interventions on employee job performance and work force productivity. *American Psychologist, 38,* 473–478.

Hutchison, S., & Garstka, M.L. (1996). Sources of perceived organizational support: Goal setting and feedback. *Journal of Applied Social Psychology, 26,* 1351–1366.

Ingham, A., Levinger, G., Graves, J., & Peckham, V. (1974). The Ringlemann effect: Studies of group size and group performance. *Journal of Experimental Social Psychology, 10,* 371–384.

Ivancevich, J.M. (1974). Changes in performance in a management by objectives program. *Administrative Science Quarterly, 19,* 563–574.

Jackson, J.M., & Williams, K.D. (1985). Social loafing on difficult tasks: Working collectively can improve performance. *Journal of Personality and Social Psychology, 49,* 937–942.

James, W. (1890). *The principles of psychology* (Vol. 1). New York: Holt.

Johnson, S.R., Ostrow, A.C., Perna, F.M., & Etzel, E.F. (1997). The effects of group versus individual goal setting on bowling performance. *The Sport Psychologist, 11,* 190–200.

Johnston-O'Connor, E.J., & Kirschenbaum, D.S. (1984). Something succeeds like success: Positive self-monitoring for unskilled golfers. *Cognitive Therapy and Research, 10,* 123–136.

Jones, G., & Cale, A. (1997). Goal difficulty, anxiety and performance. *Ergonomics, 40,* 319–333.

Jones, G., & Hanton, S. (1996). Interpretation of competitive anxiety symptoms and goal attainment expectancies. *Journal of Sport & Exercise Psychology, 18,* 144–157.

Kane, T.D., Marks, M.A., Zaccaro, S.J., & Blair, V. (1996). Self-efficacy, personal goals, and wrestlers' self-regulation. *Journal of Sport & Exercise Psychology, 18,* 36–48.

Kernan, M.G., & Lord, R.G. (1989). The effects of explicit goals and specific feedback on escalation processes. *Journal of Applied Social Psychology, 19,* 1125–1143.

Kerr, N.L., & Brunn, S.E. (1981). Ringlemann revisited: Alternative explanations for the social loafing effect. *Personality and Social Psychology Bulletin, 7,* 224–231.

Kingston, K.M., & Hardy, L. (1994). Factors affecting the salience of outcome, performance, and process goals in golf. In A. Cochran & M. Farrally (Eds.), *Science and golf 2* (pp. 144–149). London: Chapman-Hill.

Kingston, K.M., & Hardy, L. (1997). Effects of different types of goals on processes that support performance. *The Sport Psychologist, 11,* 277–293.

Kingston, K.M., Hardy, L., & Markland, D. (1992). Study to compare the effect of two different goal orientations and stress levels on a number of situationally relevant performance subcomponents. *Journal of Sport Sciences, 10,* 610–611.

Kirschenbaum, D.S. (1984). Self-regulation and sport psychology: Nurturing an emerging symbiosis. *Journal of Sport Psychology, 6,* 159–183.

Kirschenbaum, D.S. (1985). Proximity and specificity of planning: A position paper. *Cognitive Therapy and Research, 9,* 489–506.

Kirschenbaum, D.S., Ordman, A.M., Tomarken, A.J., & Holtzbauer, R. (1982). Effects of differential self-monitoring and level of mastery on sport performance: Brain power bowling. *Cognitive Therapy and Research, 6,* 335–342.

Kirschenbaum, D.S., & Tomarken, A.J. (1982). On facing the generalization problem: The study of self-regulatory failure. In P.C. Kendall (Ed.), *Advances in cognitive-behavioral research and therapy* (Vol. 1, pp. 121–200). New York: Academic Press.

Kirschenbaum, D.S., Wittrock, D.A., Smith, R.J., & Monson, W. (1984). Criticism inoculation training: Concept in search of a strategy. *Journal of Sport Psychology, 6,* 77–93.

Kondrasuk, J.N. (1981). Studies in MBO effectiveness. *Academy of Management Review, 6,* 419–430.

Kyllo, L.B., & Landers, D.M. (1995). Goal-setting in sport and exercise: A research synthesis to resolve the controversy. *Journal of Sport & Exercise Psychology, 17,* 117–137.

Lambert, S.N., Moore, D.W., & Dixon, R.S. (1999). Gymnasts in training: The differential effects of self- and coach-set goals as a function of locus of control. *Journal of Applied Sport Psychology, 11,* 72–82.

Larey, T.S., & Paulus, P.B. (1995). Social comparison and goal setting in brainstorming groups. *Journal of Applied Social Psychology, 25,* 1579–1596.

Latane, B. (1986). Responsibility and effort in organizations. In P. Goodman (Ed.), *Groups and organizations* (pp. 277–303). San Francisco: Josey-Bass.

Latane, B., Williams, K.D., & Harkins, S.G. (1979). Many hands make light the work: The causes and consequences of social loafing. *Journal of Personality and Social Psychology, 37,* 823–832.

Latham, G.P., Erez, M., & Locke, E.A. (1988). Resolving scientific disputes by the joint design of crucial experiments by the antagonists: Application to the Erez-Latham dispute regarding participation in goal setting. *Journal of Applied Psychology, 73,* 753–772.

Latham, G.P., & Lee, T.W. (1986). Goal setting. In E.A. Locke (Ed.), *Generalizing from laboratory to field settings: Research findings from industrial-organizational psychology, organizational behavior, and human resource management* (pp. 101–117). Lexington, MA: Heath.

Latham, G.P., & Locke, E.A. (1991). Self-regulation through goal setting. *Organizational Behavior and Human Decision Processes, 50,* 212–247.

Latham, G.P., & Yukl, G.A. (1975). Assigned versus participative goal setting with educated and uneducated woods workers. *Journal of Applied Psychology, 60,* 299–302.

Lazarus, R.S. (1991). *Emotion and adaptation.* New York: Oxford University Press.

Lazarus, R.S., & Folkman, S. (1984). *Stress, appraisal and coping.* New York: Springer.

Lee, A.M., & Edwards, R.V. (1984). Assigned and self-selected goals as determinants of motor skill performance. *Education, 105,* 87–91.

Lee, C. (1988). The relationship between goal setting, self-efficacy and female field hockey team performance. *International Journal of Sport Psychology, 20,* 147–161.

Lerner, B.S., & Locke, E.A. (1995). The effects of goal setting, self-efficacy, competition and personal traits on the performance of an endurance task. *Journal of Sport & Exercise Psychology, 17,* 138–152.

Lerner, B.S., Ostrow, A.C., Yura, M.T., & Etzel, E.F. (1996). The effects of goal-setting and imagery training programs on the free-throw performance of female collegiate basketball players. *The Sport Psychologist, 10,* 382–397.

Locke, E.A. (1968). Toward a theory of task motivation and incentives. *Organizational Behavior and Human Performance, 3,* 157–189.

Locke, E.A. (1991). Problems with goal-setting research in sports—and their solution. *Journal of Sport & Exercise Psychology, 8,* 311–316.

Locke, E.A. (1994). Comments on Weinberg and Weigand. *Journal of Sport & Exercise Psychology, 16,* 212–215.

Locke, E.A. (1996). Motivation through conscious goal setting. *Applied and Preventative Psychology, 5,* 117–124.

Locke, E.A., Cartledge, N., & Knerr, C.S. (1970). Studies of the relationship between satisfaction, goal setting, and performance. *Organizational Behavior and Human Performance, 5,* 135–158.

Locke, E.A., Chah, D.O., Harrison, S., & Lustgarten, N. (1989). Separating the effects of goal specificity from goal level. *Organizational Behavior and Human Decision Processes, 43,* 270–287.

Locke, E.A., & Latham, G.P. (1990). *A theory of goal setting and task performance.* Englewood Cliffs, NJ: Prentice Hall.

Locke, E.A., Latham, G.P., & Erez, M. (1988). The determinants of goal commitment. *Academy of Management Review, 13,* 23–39.

Locke, E.A., & Shaw, K.N. (1984). Atkinson's inverse-U curve and missing cognitive variables. *Psychological Reports, 55,* 403–412.

Locke, E.A., Shaw, K.N., Saari, L.M., & Latham, G.P. (1981). Goal setting and task performance: 1969–1980. *Psychological Bulletin, 90,* 125–152.

Ludwig, T.D., & Geller, E.S. (1997). Assigned versus participative goal setting and response generalization: Managing injury control among professional pizza deliverers. *Journal of Applied Psychology, 82,* 253–261.

Madden, L.E. (1996). Motivating students to learn better through own goal-setting. *Education, 117,* 411–414.

Maehr, M.L. (1984). Meaning and motivation. In R. Ames & C. Ames (Eds.), *Research on motivation in education: Student motivation* (Vol. 1, 115–144). New York: Academic Press.

Maehr, M.L., & Braskamp, L. (1986). *The motivation factor: A theory of personal investment.* Lexington, MA: Heath.

Maehr, M.L., & Nicholls, J.G. (1980). Culture and achievement motivation: A second look. In N. Warren (Ed.), *Studies in cross-cultural psychology* (pp. 341–363). New York: Academic Press.

Martens, B.K., Hiralall, A.S., & Bradley, T.A. (1997). A note to teacher: Improving student behavior through goal setting and feedback. *School Psychology Quarterly, 12,* 33–41.

Matsui, T., Kakuyama, T., & Onglatco, M.L. (1987). Effects of goals and feedback on performance in groups. *Journal of Applied Psychology, 72,* 407–415.

Mento, A.J., Steel, R.P., & Karren, R.J. (1987). A meta-analytic study of the effects of goal setting on task performance: 1966–1984. *Organization Behavior and Human Decision Processes, 39,* 52–83.

Mesch, D., Farh, J., & Podsakoff, P. (1994). Effects of feedback sign on group goal setting, strategies, and performance. *Group and Organizational Management, 19,* 309–333.

Miller, J.T., & McAuley, E. (1987). Effects of a goal-setting training program on basketball free-throw self-efficacy and performance. *The Sport Psychologist, 1,* 103–113.

Mitchell, T.R., Rothman, M., & Liden, R.C. (1985). Effects of normative information on task performance. *Journal of Applied Psychology, 70,* 48–55.

Nelson, J.K. (1978). Motivating effects of the use of norms and goals with endurance testing. *Research Quarterly, 49,* 317–321.

Nicholls, J.G. (1984a). Conceptions of ability and achievement motivation. In R. Ames & C. Ames (Eds.), *Research on motivation in education: Student motivation* (Vol. 1, pp. 39–73). New York: Academic Press.

Nicholls, J.G. (1984b). Achievement motivation: Conceptions of ability, subjective experience, task choice, and performance. *Psychological Review, 91,* 328–346.

Nicholls, J.G. (1992). The general and the specific in the development and expression of achievement motivation. In G.C. Roberts (Ed.), *Motivation in sport and exercise* (pp. 31–56). Champaign, IL: Human Kinetics.

O'Block, F.R., & Evans, F.H. (1984). Goal setting as a motivational technique. In J.M. Silva & R.S. Weinberg (Eds.), *Psychological foundations of sport* (pp. 188–196). Champaign, IL: Human Kinetics.

Oldham, G.R. (1975). The impact of supervisory characteristics on goal acceptance. *Academy of Management Journal, 18*, 461–475.

Orlick, T. (1986). *Psyching for sport: Mental training for athletes*. Champaign, IL: Human Kinetics.

Pierce, B.E., & Burton, D. (1998). Scoring the perfect 10: Investigating the impact of goal-setting styles on a goal-setting program for female gymnasts. *The Sport Psychologist, 12*, 156–168.

Poag, K., & McAuley, E. (1992). Goal setting, self-efficacy and exercise behavior. *Journal of Sport & Exercise Psychology, 14*, 352–360.

Poag-DuCharme, K.A., & Brawley, L.R. (1994). Perceptions of the behavioral influence of goals: A mediational relationship to exercise. *Journal of Applied Sport Psychology, 6*, 32–50.

Racicot, B., Day, D., & Lord, R. (1991). Type A behavior pattern and goal setting under different conditions of choice. *Motivation and Emotion, 15*, 67–79.

Rakestraw, T.L., & Weiss, H.M. (1981). The interaction of social influences and task experience on goals, performance, and performance satisfaction. *Organizational Behavior and Human Performance, 27*, 326–344.

Riedel, J.A., Nebeker, D.M., & Cooper, B.L. (1988). The influence of monetary incentives on goal choice, goal commitment, and task performance. *Organizational Behavior and Human Decision Processes, 42*, 155–180.

Roberts, G., & Reed, T. (1996, Fall). Performance appraisal participation, goal setting and feedback. *Review of Public Personnel Administration*, pp. 29–61.

Roberts, G.C., & Balague, G. (1991). *The development and validation of the Perception of Success Questionnaire*. Paper presented at the FEPSAC Congress, Cologne, Germany.

Rodgers, R.C., & Hunter, J.E. (1989). *The impact of management by objectives on organizational productivity*. Unpublished manuscript, School of Public Administration, University of Kentucky, Lexington, KY.

Ruth, W. (1996). Goal setting and behavior contracting for students with emotional and behavioral difficulties: Analysis of daily, weekly, and total goal attainment. *Psychology in the Schools, 33*, 153–158.

Schunk, D., & Swartz, C. (1993). Goals and process feedback: Effects on self-efficacy and writing achievement. *Contemporary Educational Psychology, 18*, 337–354.

Shalley, C. (1995). Effects of coaction, expected evaluation, and goal setting on creativity and productivity. *Academy of Management Journal, 38*, 483–503.

Shalley, C.E., Oldham, G.R., & Porac, J.F. (1987). Effects of goal difficulty, goal-setting method, and expected external evaluation on intrinsic motivation. *Academy of Management Journal, 30*, 553–563.

Shoenfelt, E.L. (1996). Goal setting and feedback as a posttraining strategy to increase the transfer of training. *Perceptual and Motor Skills, 83*, 176–178.

Smith, B. (1983, March 28). A new life. *Sports Illustrated, 58*, 62–74.

Smith, M., & Lee, C. (1992). Goal setting and performance in a novel coordination task: Mediating mechanisms. *Journal of Sport & Exercise Psychology, 14*, 169–176.

Swain, A., & Jones, G. (1995). Effects of goal-setting interventions on selected basketball skills: A single-subject design. *Research Quarterly for Exercise and Sport, 66*, 51–63.

Tenenbaum, G., Weinberg, R.S., Pinchas, S., Elbaz, G., & Bar-Eli, M. (1991). Effect of goal proximity and goal specificity on muscular endurance performance: A replication and extension. *Journal of Sport & Exercise Psychology, 13*, 174–187.

Terborg, J.R. (1976). The motivational components of goal setting. *Journal of Applied Psychology, 61*, 613–621.

Theodorakis, Y. (1995). Effects of self-efficacy, satisfaction, and personal goals on swimming performance. *The Sport Psychologist, 9*, 245–253.

Theodorakis, Y. (1996). The influence of goals, commitment, self-efficacy and self-satisfaction on motor performance. *Journal of Applied Sport Psychology, 8*, 171–182.

Tubbs, M.E. (1986). Goal setting: A meta-analytic examination of the empirical evidence. *Journal of Applied Psychology, 71*, 474–483.

Tzetzis, G., Kioumourtzoglou, E., & Mavromatis, G. (1997). Goal setting and feedback for the development of instructional strategies. *Perceptual and Motor Skills, 84*, 1411–1427.

Vallerand, R.J., Gauvin, L.I., & Halliwell, W.R. (1986). Effects of zero-sum competition on children's intrinsic motivation and perceived competence. *Journal of Social Psychology, 126*, 465–472.

Vance, R., & Colella, A. (1990). Effects of two types of feedback on goal acceptance and personal goals. *Journal of Applied Psychology, 75*, 68–76.

Vealey, R.S. (1986). Conceptualization of sport-confidence and competitive orientation: Preliminary investigation and instrument development. *Journal of Sport Psychology, 8*, 221–246.

Vealey, R.S. (1988). Sport-confidence and competitive orientation: An addendum on scoring procedures and gender differences. *Journal of Sport & Exercise Psychology, 10*, 471–478.

Wanlin, C.M., Hrycaiko, D.W., Martin, G.L., & Mahon, M. (1997). The effects of a goal-setting package on the performance of speed skaters. *Journal of Applied Sport Psychology, 9*, 212–228.

Weinberg, R.S. (1994). Goal setting and performance in sport and exercise settings: A synthesis and critique. *Medicine and Science in Sports and Exercise, 26*, 469–477.

Weinberg, R.S., Bruya, L.D., & Jackson, A. (1985). The effects of goal proximity and goal specificity on endurance performance. *Journal of Sport Psychology, 7*, 296–305.

Weinberg, R.S., Bruya, L.D., Jackson, A., & Garland, H. (1986). Goal difficulty and endurance performance: A challenge to the goal attainability assumption. *Journal of Sport Behavior, 10*, 82–92.

Weinberg, R.S., Bruya, L.D., Longino, J., & Jackson, A. (1988). Effect of goal proximity and specificity on endurance performance of primary-grade children. *Journal of Sport & Exercise Psychology, 10*, 81–91.

Weinberg, R.S., Burke, K.L., & Jackson, A. (1997). Coaches' and players' perceptions of goal setting in junior tennis: An exploratory investigation. *The Sport Psychologist, 11,* 426–439.

Weinberg, R.S., Burton, D., Yukelson, D., & Weigand, D. (1993). Goal setting in competitive sport: An exploratory investigation of practices of collegiate athletes. *The Sport Psychologist, 7,* 275–289.

Weinberg, R.S., Burton, D., Yukelson, D., & Weigand, D. (2000). Perceived goal setting practices of Olympic athletes: An exploratory investigation. *The Sport Psychologist, 14,* 279–295.

Weinberg, R.S., Fowler, C., Jackson, A., Bagnall, J., & Bruya, L. (1991). Effect of goal difficulty on motor performance: A replication across tasks and subjects. *Journal of Sport & Exercise Psychology, 13,* 160–173.

Weinberg, R.S., Garland, H., Bruya, L., & Jackson, A. (1990). Effect of goal difficulty and positive reinforcement on endurance performance. *Journal of Sport & Exercise Psychology, 12,* 144–156.

Weinberg, R.S., Stitcher, T., & Richardson, P. (1994). Effects of seasonal goal setting on lacrosse performance. *The Sport Psychologist, 8,* 166–175.

Weinberg, R.S., & Weigand, D. (1993). Goal setting in sport and exercise: A reaction to Locke. *Journal of Sport & Exercise Psychology, 15,* 88–96.

Weinberg, R.S., & Weigand, D.A. (1996). Let the discussions continue: A reaction to Locke's comments on Weinberg and Weigand. *Journal of Sport & Exercise Psychology, 18,* 89–93.

Weldon, E., Jehn, K., & Pradham, P. (1991). Processes that mediate the relationship between a group goal and improved group performance. *Journal of Personality and Social Psychology, 61,* 555–569.

White, P.H., Kjelgaard, M.M., & Harkins, S.G. (1995). Testing the contribution of self-evaluation to goal-setting effects. *Journal of Personality and Social Psychology, 69,* 69–79.

Widmeyer, W.N., & Ducharme, K. (1997). Team building through team goal setting. *Journal of Applied Sport Psychology, 9,* 97–113.

Williams, K.D., Harkins, S.G., & Latane, B. (1981). Identifiability as a deterrent to social loafing: Two cheering experiments. *Journal of Personality and Social Psychology, 40,* 303–311.

Wood, R.E., & Locke, E.A. (1990). Goal setting and strategy effects on complex tasks. *Research in Organizational Behavior, 12,* 73–109.

Wood, R.E., Mento, A.J., & Locke, E.A. (1987). Task complexity as a moderator of goal effects: A meta-analysis. *Journal of Applied Psychology, 72,* 416–425.

Wright, P.M., Hollenbeck, J.R., Wolf, S., & McMahan, G.C. (1995). The effects of varying goal difficulty operationalizations on goal setting outcomes and processes. *Organizational Behavior and Human Decision Processes, 61,* 28–43.

Yearta, S., Maitlis, S., & Briner, R. (1995). An exploratory study of goal setting in theory and practice: A motivational technique that works? *Journal of Occupational and Organizational Psychology, 68,* 237–252.

Zagumny, M., & Johnson, C. (1992). Using reinforcement and goal setting to increase proof reading accuracy. *Perceptual and Motor Skills, 75,* 1330.

Zimmerman, B. (1989). A social cognitive view of self-regulated academic learning. *Journal of Educational Psychology, 81,* 329–339.

Zimmerman, B.J., & Kitsantas, A. (1996). Self-regulated learning of a motoric skill: The role of goal setting and self-monitoring. *Journal of Applied Sport Psychology, 8,* 60–75.

Optimal Experience in Sport: A Flow Perspective

Jay C. Kimiecik and Susan A. Jackson

*The secret of life
is enjoying the passage of time.*

—James Taylor

Much of the sport psychology research over the past 25 years has attempted to understand how cognitive processes are related to athletes' behavior and performance, which are then linked in a variety of ways to different kinds of outcomes (e.g., winning vs. losing, attaining medals). Certainly, this type of research is essential to understanding—and helping athletes and coaches to understand—issues surrounding performance enhancement. However, this research focus tends to ignore the core element of what it means to be human: subjective experience. For instance, understanding the relationship between an athlete's perception of confidence and his or her performance in a specific sporting event is quite different from understanding the meaning, or lived experience, of that event for the athlete.

One way to view this distinction is to conceptualize our humanness as a triad of behavior, cognition, and affect that focuses on the periphery of experience (figure 16.1). Subjective experience forms the core and connects these three areas to create meaning in our lives. Subjective experience is the bottom line of existence (Csikszentmihalyi, 1982). If we are interested in understanding ath-

letes in a sport context, we must describe and understand the quality of their experience. As deCharms and Muir (1978) observed more than 20 years ago,

> *Theories and data abound. Are we making major advances in understanding motivation? Let us suggest that they are minor. We continually overlook our major source of knowledge— a personal, nonobjective source which is at the heart of each minitheory but not acknowledged. Our methodologies fall short because they lead us into more and more detailed specification of external conditions for producing behavioral effects and ignore the critical variable, namely the way the person experiences (not perceives) the conditions that we so elaborately contrive. (p. 107)*

Subjective experience, or states of consciousness, can be conceptualized along a continuum that extends from psychic entropy (disorder in consciousness) to psychic negentropy (contents of consciousness are in harmony with each other; Csikszentmihalyi, 1990). When the subjective experiences of sport participants have been studied, investigation has focused more on the negative pole, addressing such areas as stress and anxiety (see work by Scanlan, Stein, & Ravizza, 1989, and Wankel & Kreisel, 1985, for exceptions).

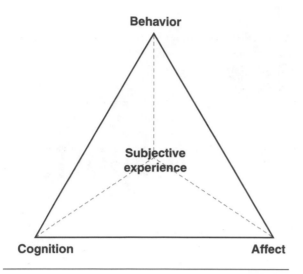

Figure 16.1 Subjective experience as the core of human experience.

Hence, we know much less about athletes' positive or optimal experiences than their negative or stressful ones. If subjective experience is the essence of what it means to be human, then it makes sense to study all kinds of experience, positive as well as negative. Sport contexts provide a rich laboratory for such exploration because athletes' states of consciousness cover the entire gamut of the subjective experience continuum. As an athlete, the first author can remember crying after making four errors in one inning of the finals of a state fast-pitch softball tournament and crying for joy when his high school baseball team won a sectional championship. The range of consciousness that sport elicits is truly remarkable, which makes it an ideal context in which to study subjective experience.

For a number of years both of us have been interested in learning more about the optimal experiences of sport participants, with the perhaps naive goal that we might optimize our own as well as others' physical activity experiences. Although we have barely scratched the surface of understanding optimal experience in sport, a growing body of research may add to the knowledge base in sport psychology and could catalyze exciting research. The primary purpose of this chapter is to examine the research that has been conducted on optimal experience in sport from a *flow* perspective. Certainly flow is not the only way to operationalize or examine optimal experience in sport. However, flow is the optimal experience perspective with which we are most familiar, and it is probably the approach to studying optimal

experience that has received the most attention in recent years.

We have divided the chapter into four main sections. The first section provides a brief history of the study of optimal experience as well as an overview of peak performance and peak experience—two terms that parallel or overlap with flow. In the second section we describe the flow model and its relevance to life. The third section presents a critical analysis of the research that has examined optimal experience in sport from a flow perspective. Within this analysis and synthesis of the research on flow, we present our views and analysis of some theoretical, paradigmatic, and measurement issues that researchers need to consider when studying flow in sport. Last, we provide some ideas and possible directions for future research examining optimal experience in sport and other physical activity contexts (e.g., exercise).

BRIEF HISTORY AND OVERVIEW OF OPTIMAL EXPERIENCE IN SPORT

Over 25 years ago, Csikszentmihalyi (1975) first published *Beyond Boredom and Anxiety*. This seminal work focusing on flow, which built on Maslow's (1964, 1968) pioneering efforts in the area of peak experience and self-actualization (Csikszentmihalyi, 1988), led to the development of optimal experience as an important area of study. It was also around this time that Ravizza (1975, 1977) was studying aspects of peak experience in sport. In the mid-1980s, Garfield and Bennett (1984) and Loehr (1986) examined the characteristics of peak performance states in sport. There has been much overlap, and considerable confusion, pertaining to the definition and operationalization of flow, peak performance, and peak experience in sport, not to mention joy, enjoyment, and fun. As Jackson (2000a) and Wankel (1997) pointed out, some ambiguity and overlap with these kinds of constructs can aid in understanding the sport experience, because they open possibilities for synthesis and integration of different kinds of work.

Optimal experience is a useful umbrella term for classifying positive states of consciousness in sport. Underneath this umbrella term are concepts such as peak experience, peak performance, flow, enjoyment, and fun. Because of space constraints, we do not discuss these terms at length in this chapter. For those interested in definitional conundrums pertaining to optimal experience, a number of articles, chapters, and books do exist (see

Jackson, 2000a; Kimiecik & Harris, 1996; McInman & Grove, 1991; Podilchak, 1991; Privette & Bundrick, 1991; Wankel, 1997; Warner, 1987). Because peak performance and peak experience are so closely aligned with flow states (Jackson, 1993), we first present our views on these two forms of optimal experience as well as their potential link with flow before delving into the specifics on flow in sport.

Peak Performance

Peak performance is not inherently an optimal experience because the term typically has been defined as superior functioning exceeding an individual's probable performance quality, or full use of potential in any activity (Forbes, 1989; Privette, 1983). In athletics, this refers to the release of latent powers to perform optimally within a specific sport competition. Peak performance is very idiosyncratic. An athlete may not win the gold medal but may still have a peak performance because she may have the performance of a lifetime. An athlete who goes well beyond any prior performance standard is likely to describe it as a peak performance. An interesting question is, What kinds of psychological states underlie a peak performance? Is a peak performance also an optimal experience? Studies typically show that athletes' thoughts and feelings are extremely positive when they perform at their peak (see review by Williams & Krane, 1998). We have not found any evidence in the sport psychology research where an athlete stated that he or she had a best performance and did not experience a variety of very positive psychological and emotional states. In fact, a number of studies support the notion that peak performances are characterized by underlying optimal, subjective experience.

In a nonsport study, Privette and Bundrick (1991) found that full focus and sense of self in clear process were the two primary elements of peak performance. In an interview study by Garfield and Bennett (1984), elite athletes reported such factors as physical and mental relaxation, confidence, a present-centered focus, being highly energized, extraordinary awareness, feeling in control, and "in the cocoon" to describe their mental state during outstanding performances. In addition, these athletes had a sense that they were detached from the external environment and its distractions during their best performances. Loehr (1982) interviewed athletes about their experiences when performing at their best and cited a

similar set of positive factors: high energy, fun and enjoyment, no pressure, optimism and positiveness, mental calmness, confidence, focus, and in control. In a qualitative study, Cohn (1991) found a set of peak performance factors reported by elite golfers that closely resembled those of Garfield and Bennett (1984) and Loehr (1982). A narrow focus of attention, being immersed in the present, feelings of control and confidence, having no fear, and feeling physically and mentally relaxed were key characteristics of peak golfing performance. Eklund (1994), interviewing collegiate wrestlers, found that best performances were accompanied by an intense competitive focus and high confidence, which mirrors the findings of Gould, Eklund, and Jackson (1992) based on their interviews with successful Olympic wrestlers.

We believe that flow serves as a useful concept for integrating the findings from studies that have examined the optimal psychological states or strategies typically associated with peak performances in sport contexts. As Jackson (2000a) pointed out, flow states reflect optimal mental functioning, total focus, and complete absorption in a task. The notion that athletes perform their best when in flow is supported by findings from Jackson and Roberts (1992), who found correlational support for a link between flow and peak performance, operationally defined as one's best-ever performance. Qualitative analyses also supported a link between flow and peak performance, with best performances being associated with flow state characteristics. In a more recent study that used the Flow State Scale (FSS; Jackson & Marsh, 1996), Jackson, Thomas, Marsh, and Smethurst (2001) found correlational support for relationships between flow and performance. Both an objective performance measure, finishing position, and a subjective measure of success correlated with flow scores on the FSS. The subjective performance measure was more strongly related to flow scores than to finishing position, no doubt because of the closer association between two self-report measures than one self-report measure and one general objective performance measure.

There appears to be a close relationship between flow and peak performance. This link is supported by the similarity between the characteristics used by athletes to describe flow and peak performance. Athletes' descriptions of their peak performances in studies by Cohn (1991), Garfield and Bennett (1984), and Loehr (1986) closely resemble flow characteristics. More research is needed to examine the specifics of the flow–peak performance link. For example, surely there must be times when athletes in flow do not perform at their peak. When does this occur? What are the conditions when optimal mental states do not lead to peak performances? In addition, can an athlete perform at her peak without optimal mental states, such as flow? These are questions that optimal experience research could address. However, the empirical findings to date along with an intuitive relatedness between flow and peak performance suggest that one important consequence of experiencing flow in sport is performing optimally. Although we are intrigued by this relationship from a performance-enhancement perspective, we are hesitant in making too much of it. As Csikszentmihalyi (1988) suggested, it may be best to downplay the connection between flow and peak performance because "as soon as the emphasis shifts from the experience per se to what you can accomplish with it, we are back in the realm of everyday life ruled by extrinsic considerations" (p. 375).

Peak Experience

Maslow (1968) was one of the first researchers to systematically examine peak experiences across a variety of life dimensions. Maslow's work led him to define a peak experience as a moment of highest happiness in one's life. Although peak experiences are infrequent in the lives of most people, Maslow argued for their importance because they can lead to growth or actualization of the individual. Maslow developed an extensive list of peak experience factors, some of which included total attention, rich perceptions, time–space disorientation, perceptions of unity, and feelings of wonder and awe. One of the first attempts to examine the specific nature of athletes' peak experiences was conducted by Ravizza (1977, 1984), who examined Maslow's concept of peak experience by asking athletes to describe their one most joyful, blissful moment while participating in their primary sport. Three common characteristics of sport peak experience emerged from Ravizza's analysis of the interview data: focused awareness leading to total absorption in the task, feelings of total control of self and the environment, and a sense of self-transcendence, where the athlete described a complete merging of action and awareness. It is evident that these three descriptors of peak experience in sport blend with those outlined earlier by Maslow.

Privette and Bundrick (1991) have been specifically interested in delineating the concepts peak performance, peak experience, and flow. They define peak experience as intense joy, or a moment of highest happiness, that is not necessarily performance related. The distinguishing characteristics of peak experience that Privette and Bundrick have uncovered are fulfillment, significance, and spirituality. In essence, it seems that peak experience is aligned more closely with a positive emotions focus, whereas peak performance has more of a behavioral or an outcome focus. Both may be considered as very positive events that share some psychological and emotional commonalities. It is interesting to note that studies which have examined peak experience in sport (e.g., Cohn, 1986; Ravizza, 1977) have focused on performance. We are not aware of any studies that found athletes' peak experiences to be unrelated to a peak performance. In addition, athletes' descriptions of their peak experiences (Ravizza, 1984) resemble very closely the descriptions that athletes give of peak performances (Cohn, 1991).

In sum, peak performance is an episode of superior functioning, whereas peak experience is a moment of highest happiness and ecstasy. For example, for a basketball player, a peak performance might be scoring 30 points in a game when he has been averaging 10 (superior functioning), and a peak experience might be winning the conference championship (ecstasy, highest happiness). Importantly, the player's peak experience may not be linked with his personal performance during the game. That is, the player may have performed poorly but because the outcome was so positive, a peak experience could still occur. Also, because peak experience is a subjective experience, winning the conference championship may or may not lead to a peak experience for every member of the team.

The Relationships Among Flow, Peak Performance, and Peak Experience

As is evident, the relationships among flow, peak performance, and peak experience can be complex. What do athletes think? Only one study (Jackson, 1993) has asked athletes about the relationships among these three forms of optimal experience. Jackson defined these three constructs for elite athletes as (a) flow—a totally absorbing and rewarding experience, one which stood out from average; (b) peak performance—performing at an optimal level; and (c) peak experience—a time of highest happiness and fulfillment. She then asked the athletes how they viewed the relationship among these three experiences in their own sport participation. Predictably, participants expressed a range of ideas about how these experiences were related. However, the athletes provided little support for the independence of these constructs. Rather, support was found for the idea that there are flexible boundaries between the three phenomena and that often one and the same event may be a flow experience, a peak performance, and a peak experience. Seventy-five percent of the athletes said flow was always part of their peak performances, and 71% said flow was always involved in their peak experiences. The athletes viewed flow as an optimal mental state that led to their peak performances. When an athlete was able to achieve a peak performance without flow, it was through working very hard, being very fit, being able to control the performance, or luck.

Jackson (1993) also found that the athletes perceived both flow and peak experience to involve enjoyment, and this is where the athletes perceived the link between these two experiences to be strongest. The enjoyable aspect of flow was the most salient dimension in the analyses of athletes' flow experiences, so it is not surprising that there was a perceived relationship between flow and peak experience. When peak experience occurred without flow, it was through achievement of a valued goal, particularly through working hard, winning, exceeding expectations, or overcoming great odds. In these cases it seems that athletes identified a peak experience after the fact, on reflection. For an experience to be enjoyed during its occurrence, it seems that a state involving flow is more likely to be present than absent.

The findings with elite athletes, along with the other work examining peak experience and peak performance, indicate that understanding the role of optimal experience in sport is a complex task. Knowing to what extent these terms describe the same or different experiences would help to build a common understanding of optimal experiences. From a flow perspective, optimal psychological states probably underlie most peak performances, but we would be less certain in making such a connection between flow and peak experience. Peak experience may not necessarily involve flow (Jackson, 1993). As you will see shortly, flow states occur when perceived challenges and skills are in balance and above average. Based on this operationalization of flow, the intensity of a flow state can be much less than that of a peak experi-

ence. In addition, a peak performance may not lead to a peak experience, and an athlete can probably have a peak experience without having a peak performance. This can get confusing, which means it is a good area for further research. It seems important to know if athletes' peak performances can occur without flow states. How important is individual performance to peak experiences in sport? What are the conditions under which peak experiences occur? Is flow a lower level form of peak experience, or is it something different? Much of the research in this area has focused on retrospective interviews of athletes. Hence, much of what is known is based on association of certain psychological factors or states with peak performance or peak experience. That means we do not really know if these psychological states are merely associated with these experiences or are actual precursors to optimal experience.

Although peak performance and peak experience are very relevant to sport, these two concepts are not strongly grounded in psychosocial theory, which somewhat limits their usefulness for understanding athletes' experiences. That is why Csikszentmihalyi's work in the area of flow is so appealing from a research perspective. Flow provides a theoretical framework with a substantive history of evidence—both qualitative and quantitative—supporting its contentions. We believe that flow is the essence of a positive performance state of mind and should become more integral to the research examining the positive subjective experience of sport and physical activity participants. Next we present an overview of flow and its dimensions.

THE DEFINITION AND DIMENSIONS OF FLOW

Flow is a very positive psychological state that typically occurs when a person perceives a balance between the challenges associated with a situation and her capabilities to accomplish or meet these demands (Csikszentmihalyi, 1990). Flow is predicted to occur when this balance occurs and is above a person's average skills–challenge balance. Several flow characteristics, or dimensions, have been described by Csikszentmihalyi (1990, 1993) and supported in the sport environment through qualitative and quantitative research (e.g., Jackson, 1996; Jackson & Marsh, 1996). These dimensions of flow are a challenge–skill balance, merging of action and awareness, clear goals and feedback, total concentration on the task at hand, sense of control, loss of self-consciousness, time transformation, and an autotelic (intrinsically rewarding) experience. Because these dimensions are described in depth elsewhere (see Csikszentmihalyi, 1990; Jackson & Csikszentmihalyi, 1999), we provide only a brief sketch of each.

Challenge-Skill Balance

According to Csikszentmihalyi's operationalization of flow, individuals will experience flow when they perceive that the challenges of the situation and their skills are in balance and are above their average subjective experience (Csikszentmihalyi & Csikszentmihalyi, 1988). If there is an imbalance between skills and challenges, it is highly unlikely that individuals will experience flow. More likely, they will experience anxiety, relaxation, boredom, or apathy. Anxiety occurs when a person perceives the challenges of the situation to be higher than perceived skills; relaxation or boredom results from the skills outweighing the challenges; and apathy occurs when both perceived challenges and skills are balanced and less than an individual's average experiences. Typically, the quality of an individual's experience is most optimal in flow, least optimal in apathy, and less than optimal in boredom or anxiety.

Merging of Action and Awareness

Merging of action and awareness suggests that involvement is so deep that it becomes spontaneous or seemingly automatic (Csikszentmihalyi, 1990). Individuals are no longer aware that they are separate from their actions. Simply, an individual becomes one with the activity. Jackson (1992) found that many elite athletes described this flow dimension as "being in the groove"; others said, "I am not thinking about anything . . . it just happens automatically."

Clear Goals and Feedback

These two flow dimensions are frequently discussed concurrently (see Csikszentmihalyi, 1990). When a person is in flow, goals are either clearly defined by planning ahead or are developed while engaging in the activity. When a person knows and understands the goals for an activity, it is more likely for him or her to become totally immersed or engaged. In addition, a clear goal makes it easier

to process feedback, which provides messages that the actor is progressing with the goal. The powerful symbiosis between goals and feedback creates order in consciousness, which is at the core of the flow experience.

Total Concentration

According to Csikszentmihalyi (1997, p. 31), "When goals are clear, feedback relevant, and challenges and skills are in balance, attention becomes ordered and fully invested. Because of the total demand on psychic energy, a person in flow is completely focused." The complete focus on the task at hand stands out as the clearest indication of flow. All distractions are kept at a minimum or are nonexistent, and only a select range of information is allowed into awareness.

Sense of Control

When in flow, a person feels in control of the situation without worrying about losing control. An athlete interviewed by Jackson (19929) stated, "It feels like I can do anything in that (flow) state" (p. 19). The key to this dimension is the perception of control that one feels. Another athlete said, "As strange as it sounds, I don't feel like I am in control of anything at all . . . my body just takes over. On the other hand, though, I feel like I am totally in control of everything" (Jackson, 1992, p. 19). It is not just the sense of being in control that is important. For flow to occur, the individual must have a sense of "exercising control in difficult situations" (Csikszentmihalyi, 1990, p. 61).

Loss of Self-Consciousness

When a person is in flow, there is no room for distractions or worry about how one is perceived by others. There is no self-consciousness; a sense of separateness from the world is overcome, which results in a feeling of oneness with the environment. The absence of self-consciousness does not mean that the individual is unaware of his thoughts and bodily movements. Rather, it is a keen awareness that is not threatening. In essence, the self is fully functioning but is not aware of itself doing so.

Time Transformation

The perception of time may either speed up or slow down when a person is in flow. In flow, time is distorted by the experience. For example, a distance runner in flow may not even recall what hap-

A distance runner in flow may experience a distorted perception of time.

© Sally Weigand

Positive Outcomes of Flow

Results of studies examining flow states in a variety of contexts suggest that people consider flow to be an optimal and thoroughly enjoyable experience (e.g., Csikszentmihalyi & LeFevre, 1989; Jackson, 1992, 1996; Scanlan, Stein, & Ravizza, 1989). For instance, Scanlan and colleagues (1989), in a qualitative study of elite figure skaters, found that one source of positive affect for the skaters was the act of skating, which included flowlike experiences. A recent study that examined children's physical activity experiences at a summer sports camp indicated that their flow experiences were positively related to "feeling good" and "perceived success" (Mandigo, Thompson, & Couture, 1998). In a nonsport setting, Csikszentmihalyi and LeFevre (1989) found that people in flow at work had greater positive affect and potency than workers not in flow. Data from a variety of sources indicate a strong, positive relationship between flow and positive affective experiences, which are important because "emotions focus attention by mobilizing the entire organism in an approach or avoidance mode" (Csikszentmihalyi, 1997, p. 25). By having many flow experiences in a specific activity, which are intimately linked to positive affect, an individual is likely to want to approach that activity again and again. Kimiecik and Harris (1996) suggested a positive motivational cycle, whereby flow leads to positive affective experiences, which then enhance intrinsic motivation (i.e., the desire to do something for its own sake). That is, the activity becomes autotelic over time (Csikszentmihalyi, 1975, 1990). The positive affect and potency tied to flow states typically occur after the activity, not during the activity (Csikszentmihalyi, 1997), and these affective experiences can vary in intensity.

Csikszentmihalyi (1997) suggested that the positive affective experiences related to flow states do more than enhance individuals' intrinsic motivation and transform a specific activity to one autotelic in nature. This process also leads to complexity

pened during a race and may perceive that it ended more quickly than it actually did. Time transformation is generally the least mentioned flow dimension in qualitative research (Jackson, 1996), and in psychometric scale work, time transformation has not been found to relate strongly to other flow dimensions (Jackson & Marsh, 1996; Marsh & Jackson, 1999). In addition, Csikszentmihalyi (1990) acknowledged that there are situations in sport where being aware of the time is paramount, which could make it difficult to experience transcendence of time. Further research in sport is necessary to better understand the role of the time transformation dimension of flow.

Autotelic Experience

Csikszentmihalyi (1990) described an autotelic experience as the end result of flow, one that is intrinsically rewarding. Statements such as "I was on a high" and "I really had a great experience" illustrate the end product of a flow experience. Importantly, a flow state is such a positive subjective state that the individual desires to perform the activity for its own sake. When an individual stretches her capacity to the fullest extent, integrates mind and body, and is fully immersed in an activity, the outcome is likely to be autotelic, an activity done for its own sake because it provides powerful intrinsic rewards.

and growth in consciousness. Csikszentmihalyi (1993) proposed that after a flow experience, the organization of the self becomes more complex, through the opposing processes of *differentiation* and *integration*. Although space constrains us from delving into the intricacies of complexity, the basic notion is that flow contributes to the growth of the self through the process of "complexification." Simply, flow increases potential for personal growth because this state involves the simultaneous interaction of differentiation and integration, which Csikszentmihalyi (1993) defined as follows:

> *Differentiation refers to the degree to which a system (i.e., an organ such as the brain, or an individual, a family, a corporation, a culture, or humanity as a whole) is composed of parts that differ in structure or function from one another. Integration refers to the extent to which the different parts communicate and enhance one another's goals. A system that is more differentiated and integrated than another is said to be more complex. (p. 156)*

According to Csikszentmihalyi (1993), differentiation occurs as one seeks out new and greater challenges, which provide greater opportunities for an individual to become more unique and to explore limits and potential; integration occurs when an individual increases skills to master these new challenges. These skills then become part of the self, leaving one feeling more in tune with oneself and with the world in general. The optimal development of both integration and differentiation, through flow states, leads to a more harmonious self. By becoming more complex through flow, people experience personal growth. They develop new skills and meet new challenges, which enhances feelings about the self, produces positive emotions, and elevates an individual above his daily, humdrum existence.

In sum, flow is a very positive experience that increases the desire to perform an activity for the intrinsic rewards it provides. Flow enhances quality of life and leads to personal growth through the process of complexification. Some of the questions that we and other sport psychology researchers have been interested in are, Do athletes experience flow in ways similar to those that Csikszentmihalyi identified? Is flow relevant to the experiences of athletes? Can athletes control flow experiences? Can the factors influencing flow experiences in athletes be identified? In the next section we present research that has examined some of these questions.

REVIEW AND ANALYSIS OF RESEARCH ON FLOW IN SPORT

Flow research in sport is in an emergent stage, and there are many more questions than answers. Much of the work has been conducted with elite athletes, and that is where we start. However, in this section we also review flow studies on nonelite sport participants, examine the notion of an autotelic personality in sport, and discuss paradigmatic and measurement issues pertaining to research on flow in sport.

Flow in Elite Sport Contexts

When researchers have studied peak performance and optimal experience in sport, elite athletes have been the population of primary interest. Operationally, we define elite athletes as those who participate in U.S. Division I collegiate sport or higher, and the focal group mostly will have competed at an international level. From a flow perspective, the interest in elite athletes is based primarily on the assumption that athletes participating at a high skill level are more likely to be familiar with peak performance and flow experiences (Jackson, 1996). Csikszentmihalyi and Nakamura (1989) suggested that ability needs to be relatively high before anything resembling flow can occur. As discussed later, a number of researchers have been interested in examining that assumption more closely.

Jackson (1992, 1996) has been interested in establishing the relevance of Csikszentmihalyi's (1990) flow framework to elite athletes' flow experiences. The underlying question addressed in these two qualitative studies was, How is the experience of flow understood, interpreted, and given meaning by athletes? Specifically, how do athletes' descriptions of flow experiences compare with the dimensions of flow outlined in Csikszentmihalyi's (1990) flow model?

In Jackson's (1992) study, she interviewed 16 former U.S. National Champion figure skaters, and the 1996 study involved 28 elite athletes from Australia and New Zealand. All athletes were asked to describe an optimal sport experience, one that stood out as being better than average. For the skaters, many of their descriptions of optimal experience included feelings such as clarity, awareness, and perceived control of the situation. It was apparent from the skaters' clear and concise accounts of their flow experiences that they were describing very memorable and valued times. The "unique" state that the skaters recounted closely resembled the description of flow by Csikszentmihalyi (1990). Therefore, the results indicated that "there was a close agreement between the skater's perceptions of flow and the theoretical descriptions of the flow construct" (Jackson, 1992, p. 177).

Jackson (1996) found a consistency of responses about elite athletes' experiences of flow. For example, in describing flow experiences, these elite athletes used terms and phrases such as *awareness*, *automaticity*, *narrow focus*, *things happening in slow motion*, and *feeling in control*, which were characteristics of flow also described by the skaters. Of the 295 flow state descriptors, 97% could be classified into one of Csiksentmihalyi's nine flow dimensions. In addition, both groups of elite athletes provided very rich descriptions of flow states, which clearly show that flow is an experience that elite athletes are familiar with and value highly.

These two studies strongly support the relevancy of flow and its dimensions for elite athletes in a variety of sports. However, both groups of athletes minimally endorsed the loss of self-consciousness and time transformation dimensions of flow. This issue is addressed to a greater extent in the measurement section, but studies using sport-specific measures of flow also showed that time transformation and, to a lesser extent, loss of self-consciousness were weaker dimensions of a global flow construct from a psychometric perspective (Jackson, Kimiecik, Ford, & Marsh, 1998; Jackson & Marsh, 1996; Kowal & Fortier, 1999).

Facilitators of Flow for Elite Athletes

The results of the studies by Jackson (1992, 1996) support the notion that elite athletes experience flow at least some of the time in practice or competition and in ways that correspond with Csikszentmihalyi's theoretical formulations of flow. These athletes also believe that the experience of flow motivates them to participate in their sport regularly. This work on the essence and relevance of the flow experience for athletes has been paralleled by a search for the factors that may facilitate such experiences. We have gone down this path cautiously, not wanting to destroy the magic and allure of flow states, which are partly due to the uncertainty of when such states occur. Knowing that flow occurs for an athlete, but not knowing when it will occur, is part of the joy of being a performer. However, Jackson (1992, 1995) has shown that many of the elite athletes in her research believe that flow is controllable. An elite figure skater commented on the perceived controllability of flow:

I think you can increase it. . . . It's not a conscious effort. If you try to do it, it's not going to work. I think maybe through trying you turn off the switch so it can't happen. . . . I think there are things, factors you can lessen, to make it happen more often. I don't think it is something you can turn on and off like a light switch. (Jackson, 1992, p. 174)

If elite athletes believe flow to be controllable, it makes sense to examine the factors that may facilitate this optimal state. In both of Jackson's (1992, 1995) studies, she asked athletes what they perceived to be the most important factors for getting into flow and then developed categories of themes from inductive analysis of interview transcripts. As summarized by Jackson (2000a), confidence, or positive mental attitude, was perceived by the athletes to be an important flow facilitator. This finding follows from flow theory, which states that flow will occur only when a person perceives that his skills match the challenge of the situation. For any athlete to experience flow, he must be confident in his abilities to meet the challenge of the situation. Another relevant flow facilitator from the 1995 study was the extent to which the athlete had prepared for the event and had a good plan for how she would perform. The importance of mental plans to optimal performance are well recognized in the applied sport performance literature (e.g., Orlick, 1998). Being well prepared and knowing clearly what you are going to do in an event allows for a complete focus on the task at hand, and this ability to tune in to the event facilitates the occurrence of flow. As found in qualitative analyses, other factors perceived by athletes to increase the chances of flow included optimal arousal levels, high motivation, feeling good during the performance, maintaining an appropriate focus, having optimal environmental and situational conditions, and positive team play and interaction (Jackson, 1992, 1995).

In addition to asking athletes what factors they perceived helped them get into flow, Jackson (1992, 1995) asked them about factors that prevented or disrupted flow. One of the most frequent responses to this question focused on nonoptimal environmental or situational conditions. This category included factors such as undesirable weather conditions, uncontrollable event influences, and distracting interactions with others before or during the event. Lack of physical preparation or readiness was also an obstacle to flow, as were physical problems such as injury or fatigue. As expected, lacking confidence or having a negative mental attitude was perceived to make flow difficult to experience. Similarly, if motivation was lacking for the event, flow was less likely. Inappropriate focus, whether it was thinking too much, not being focused enough, or worrying about the competition, was an impediment to flow. Problems relating to performing as a team were also obstacles to flow.

This qualitative research by Jackson (1992, 1995) provides some interesting information about factors that elite athletes perceive to affect their experience of flow during performance. In a quantitative approach to examining facilitators or correlates of flow, Jackson and Roberts (1992) studied positive performance states of 200 Division I college athletes. This study examined a possible link between athletes' goal orientations and their flow experiences. The authors hypothesized that athletes high in a task orientation would report experiencing flow more often than those low in a task orientation and that an ego orientation would be unrelated to flow states. An additional hypothesis was that athletes high in perceived ability would report experiencing flow more than athletes low in perceived ability. As defined by Duda (1992), task orientation is a focus on the task at hand while relying on a self-referenced concept of ability. Conversely, ego involvement invokes normative comparison and concern with outcomes; success is based on doing better than others. Research in education (Deci & Ryan, 1987; Nicholls, 1984) and sport settings (Duda, 1988; Duda & Nicholls, 1992) indicates that task-involved individuals typically experience greater intrinsic interest in tasks, persist longer, and are more likely to perform the task for its own sake.

In flow terms, being task-involved should enable athletes to focus more on the task at hand, leading to task absorption, higher levels of concentration, and feelings of control, all characteristics of the flow state. Although it is certainly feasible that ego-involved athletes also experience flow, it may be more difficult because ego-involvement is more likely to produce counter states of flow, such as anxiety and boredom. For example, athletes who continually compare their ability to others are more likely to perceive more competitive situations as overly challenging, which could lead to

higher levels of anxiety. The flow literature and research on competitive anxiety (Martens, Vealey, & Burton, 1990) suggest that this state is not associated with positive performances. Boredom is also a greater possibility for ego-involved athletes, because these athletes may perceive opponents as less challenging than they really are to protect perceptions of competence. That is, they may underestimate the challenge, feign disinterest, and act as if the whole thing is rather boring and unworthy of their talent. In contrast, no matter what the level of ability (within reason) of a task-involved athlete's opponent, he or she will attempt to match challenges with skills, sometimes creatively, to learn the most from the situation and, perhaps, get into flow. It seems that there may be many "flowlike" advantages to being task-involved versus ego-involved. This relationship has been identified in a very practical way by Orlick (1990):

> The ideal performance focus is total concentration to your performance . . . focusing on distracting thoughts (about final placing, others' expectations, the weather) interfere with an effective task focus . . . stay in the moment, which is the only one that you can influence anyway. (p. 16)

The findings of Jackson and Roberts (1992) support the hypothesized relationships among goal orientations, perceived ability, and flow. Athletes high in task involvement reported experiencing flow more frequently than athletes low in task involvement, whereas ego orientation was unrelated to flow. These findings support the work and observations of applied sport psychology consultants (e.g., Loehr, 1986; Orlick, 1986) who suggest that focusing solely on outcome and comparisons of one's ability with other athletes—an ego orientation—does not lend itself to positive performance. As Orlick (1986, p. 10) pointed out, "The problem with thinking about winning or losing the event is that you lose focus of what you need to do in order to win." Jackson and Roberts (1992) also found perceived ability to be associated with experiencing flow. It is important to focus on perceived, rather than actual, ability because within the flow model, "it is not the skills we actually have that determine how we feel, but the ones we think we have" (Csikszentmihalyi, 1990, p. 75).

Although a number of studies have focused on the use of psychological skills training to enhance elite athlete performance (see review by Murphy & Martin, this volume), we are aware of only one study that attempted to link psychological skills training with flow states in elite athletes (Straub, 1996). In a time series design, five college wrestlers underwent a mental imagery program for a 5- to 10-week period after baselines were established for each participant. Four of the five wrestlers increased significantly in the self-reported frequency of flow states as measured by the balance between challenge and skill. For example, one wrestler reported increasing his frequency of flow states from 33.3% of his matches during baseline to 76.9% of the matches during treatment. In poststudy interviews, one wrestler explained how mental imagery helped him focus and increase flow states:

> Last year, some matches, I'd say I was in flow. I mean, but, what I went through this year of having a specific competition and pre-competition plan, it allowed me to focus more on what I was going to do than in the past. Because when it is general your mind goes every different way. But with this, once you get used to it, you know exactly what you are going to do. So it takes a lot of that thinking and cognitive skills which you'd be using, and you're able to take that energy and direct it to a different area during the match. (Straub, 1996, p. 121)

Certainly this study has limitations (e.g., small sample size), but it demonstrates some of the exciting, and creative, possibilities of integrating psychological skills training with some of the findings on flow facilitators to build a foundation for optimal experience. We would certainly like to see more of this kind of applied research as it relates to flow states and elite athletes.

The research with elite athletes demonstrates the relevance, centrality, and perceived controllability of flow experiences for this unique group of sport participants. In addition, both qualitative and quantitative studies have identified a set of factors that may facilitate flow experiences. In the qualitative work, such dimensions as confidence or positive mental attitude, competitive plans or preparation, maintaining appropriate focus, and optimal physical preparation or readiness were perceived by a significant number of elite athletes to be important for getting into flow. In the quantitative work, high task orientation and high perceived ability were associated with elite athletes' flow states. We can make connections between the findings of the qualitative and quantitative studies. A task orientation would be linked intimately with the dimension of maintaining appropriate focus, whereas perceived ability and the dimension of confidence or positive mental attitude share some commonality. These kinds of connections pertaining to flow facilitators demonstrate the usefulness of using multiple research approaches to study flow experiences in sport.

The Challenge of Experiencing Flow for Elite Athletes

Although we know that elite athletes experience flow, we also know that they experience it relatively infrequently. In fact, 81% of the U.S. National Champion figure skaters interviewed by Jackson (1992) said that they did not experience flow very often. It is possible that nonelite athletes have the opportunity to experience flow to a greater extent than elite athletes, even though their actual ability is at a much lower level. Mitchell (1988) hypothesized that the highly competitive nature of elite sport and a competitive goal orientation can make it difficult to achieve a flow state. In other words, as sport participants move into more competitive environments with a greater emphasis on the outcomes, a shift occurs in the many forms of play to the "earning of success, from means to an end" (Mitchell, 1988, p. 55). Competition then becomes the dominant form of play and winning the primary goal. Intrinsic satisfaction is replaced by extrinsic rewards such as profit and prestige. As a result of this shift, the likelihood of flow may be decreased because the sport environment is no longer conducive to positive psychological states of experience. The flow dynamics have changed. More value is placed on external rewards, such as scholarships and bonuses. For example, an athlete may focus more on winning the prize money in a race than on his experience in running the race. This focus on the future rather than the present may diminish the likelihood of flow experiences.

Work that has examined the intrinsic versus extrinsic motivation of scholarship athletes partially supports the view that an emphasis on the extrinsic aspects of competition potentially can minimize the quality of the sport experience. Ryan (1977) surveyed male scholarship and nonscholarship athletes at two institutions to examine the link between external rewards (i.e., scholarship) and type of motivation emphasized by the athletes. He found that scholarship athletes cited more extrinsic reasons for participation and lower enjoyment levels than the nonscholarship athletes. In a follow-up investigation with a larger sample, including male football players and wrestlers and female athletes in a variety of sports, Ryan (1980) found that football players on scholarship scored lower on intrinsic motivation than nonscholarship football players. However, the wrestlers and female athletes on scholarship scored higher on intrinsic motivation than their nonscholarship teammates. These findings suggest that because the extrinsic orientation of collegiate football is heavily emphasized (i.e., win at all costs), scholarship football players are more likely to view their experience as controlling, whereas scholarship athletes in "minor" sports, such as wrestling, are more likely to view their sport experience from an intrinsic perspective.

Although no causality could be established, Ryan's research on scholarships and motivation is particularly relevant to this discussion of the sport context and flow. According to Deci and Ryan (1985, p. 29), "When highly intrinsically motivated, organisms will be extremely interested in what they are doing and experience a sense of flow." Flow theory suggests that a focus on extrinsic aspects of the experience is a major barrier to facilitating optimal experience.

Furthermore, although participants may be good judges of their own enjoyment, they are quickly stripped of this responsibility as judges and referees supervise the game. As Mitchell (1988, p. 55) stated, "Making decisions about the conduct of play becomes too critical to remain in the hands of the players themselves." As this shift from play to sport to highly competitive sport occurs, there is the potential for many of the precursors of the flow experience to be diminished or replaced. Therefore, the flow experience for elite athletes in highly competitive, extrinsically-focused environments may not occur as frequently as one might think, precisely because of the motivational processes identified by intrinsic motivation and flow theory.

This does not suggest that elite athletes do not experience flow. Clearly, the work by Jackson (1992, 1995) shows that they do. What this discussion on the link between competition and subjective experience suggests is that people who participate in less externally controlled sport environments also experience flow, perhaps even to a greater extent than elite athletes. The nonelite participant may not be as immersed in the extrinsically oriented aspects of the competitive environment as is the elite athlete. If nonscholarship athletes are likely to focus on the intrinsic aspects of competition, isn't it possible that nonelite sport

participants might also focus on intrinsic aspects of the experience? This intrinsic orientation could enhance the possibility of their experiencing flow.

Jackson (1996) pointed out that flow research in sport needs to go beyond the elite athlete to ascertain how generalizable the flow experiences described by elite athletes are to other types of sport participants. Do nonelite sport participants experience flow? Do they experience flow to a greater or lesser extent than elite athletes? Can facilitators or determinants of flow be identified in sport participants who are less skilled? Are flow states a motivating factor to participate in sport for nonelite athletes? In the next section, we discuss some interesting issues pertaining to the flow experience of nonelite sport participants and present the empirical work that has been conducted on flow in nonelite sport contexts.

Flow in Nonelite Sport Contexts

Nonelite sport participants are typically individuals who are less skilled than elite athletes and who do not compete for medals in national or international competitions. The majority of sport participants are of nonelite status, and so it makes sense to study the quality of their experience because it could have long-term implications for understanding motivation, participation, and quality of life. As Wankel and Berger (1990) pointed out, very little is known about the subjective quality of people's participation in leisure activities such as sport.

Interestingly, Csikszentmihalyi's (1975) original work on flow is relevant to a discussion of the propensity of different types of physical activity participants to experience flow. In examining the flow states of rock climbers, composers, modern dancers, chess players, and basketball players, Csikszentmihalyi (p. 18) found that the basketball players demonstrated a "deviant pattern." They were the only group that ranked "competition, measuring self against others" as most important. All of the other groups studied ranked "enjoyment of the experience and use of skills" as most important, whereas the basketball players ranked this item fifth out of seven choices. Csikszentmihalyi explained this pattern in the following way:

Possibly, however, the pattern reflects the activity [basketball], rather than the players' background. In other words, basketball, or other competitive sports, may provide a reward structure in which enjoyment comes from mea-

suring oneself against others and from developing one's skills, rather than from experiencing the activity itself. (p. 18)

This quote suggests that the very nature of competition could move its participants away from the intrinsic aspects (e.g., flow) of the sport experience. In addition, this leaves open the possibility that nonelite sport participants in less competitive environments certainly could experience flow. A spattering of extant research supports this notion, which is briefly reviewed next.

Using the flow framework, Chalip, Csikszentmihalyi, Kleiber, and Larson (1984) examined the subjective experiences of adolescents participating in organized sport, informal sport, and physical education classes as well as in other life activities. The study examined subjective experience by means of the experience sampling method (ESM), where each participant carried an electronic pager and a pad of self-report forms for one week. At random times the pager would go off, which signaled the participant to fill out the report. This method has been found to produce valid and reliable data in previous studies of varied populations (Csikszentmihalyi & Graef, 1980; Csikszentmihalyi, Larson, & Prescott, 1977). Participants were 75 male and female students from a Chicago suburb. The results indicated that organized sport provided substantially more positive experience than the rest of everyday life. The sense of control was highest in physical education class and lowest in informal sport. The perception of skill was highest in informal sport and lowest in physical education class, and more was perceived to be at stake in organized sport compared with informal sport and physical education class. Interestingly, the relationship between motivation and the perception of skill varied significantly across all three groups. In physical education classes, the more students felt skilled, the more they wanted to do. However, the opposite was found for organized sport, and in informal sport no relationship was found between motivation and the perception of skill.

Furthermore, only in informal sports were challenges and skills positively related to enjoyment, whereas in organized sport and physical education class the relationship was negative. During organized sport, most participants regarded their challenges to outweigh their skills. A similar pattern was found in physical education class. Only in informal sport did perceived skill and perceived challenge match. These results suggest that the informal sport context, when no adults were present, provided the best environment conceivable for adolescents to experience flow. In the informal sport context, the participants had more control of the challenge–skill balance, which is typically how flow is operationalized and measured (see Csikszentmihalyi, 1990). This provides some evidence that nonelite sport participants may have an advantage over elite athletes in being more able to control and structure their environment to optimize the skill–challenge balance and, in turn, the quality of their experience.

In sum, some data from Csikszentmihalyi and colleagues suggest that sport for the nonelite, ranging from adolescent to adult, elicits a variety of flow experiences. Certainly more research is needed that uses an ESM-type approach on adult, nonelite sport participants to determine the

© Human Kinetics

Informal physical activity provides one of the best environments for adolescents to experience flow.

quality of their experiences. Comparing samples of athletes according to skill level and across a variety of competitive contexts also would provide much-needed information about the role of flow for elite versus nonelite participants. Similar to flow studies on the elite athlete, there has been some recent interest in examining the facilitators of flow for nonelite sport participants, and we review some of that work next.

Facilitators of Flow for Nonelite Sport Participants

Two general questions guide the work that has examined facilitators of flow for nonelite sport participants: Might psychological factors facilitate nonelite sport participants' flow states? How significant a role do these "determinants" play in participants' optimal experience?

Unlike Jackson's (1992, 1995) qualitative work examining facilitators of flow for elite athletes, the studies that have addressed this topic with nonelite sport participants have been grounded in the traditional, positivistic, quantitative approach. As shown in a later section, the scientific paradigm one adopts to study flow influences the type of studies conducted and the subsequent findings and interpretations of the flow experience.

Stein, Kimiecik, Daniels, and Jackson (1995) conducted three studies investigating possible antecedents of flow in a variety of nonelite physical activity contexts—tennis, basketball, and golf. The initial tennis study focused on adults of varying ability participating in a parks and recreation weekend tournament. The next two studies used an ESM approach as recommended by Csikszentmihalyi (1988). The basketball study targeted college students enrolled in a physical activity course, and the golf study focused on older adult golfers of average ability. Although the link between psychological antecedents of flow, such as goals, competence, and confidence, was weak, the results showed that optimal experience occurs for these kinds of participants. Most importantly, a difference seemed to exist between contexts that emphasized competition, where above-average skill levels (regardless of challenge) produced high quality of experience and a context that emphasized learning, and where above-average skills and challenges (flow) were linked to a high quality of experience.

These findings support, in part, the argument in the previous section that as performance and outcome become more important in sport environments, the role of flow becomes less clear. For example, the golfers experienced nearly as much satisfaction, control, and concentration when in a bored state (skills above average and challenges below average) as when in a flow state (skills and challenges above average), and their performance was better in the bored state. These golfers were part of a league, and the good-natured competition involved small bets per hole, small bets per round, bragging rights for the day, and so forth. It is interesting in that other studies looking at flow relative to daily life experience found that high school students interpreted the boredom context as more optimal than flow during productive and outcome-oriented situations (e.g., Carli, Fave, & Massimini, 1988).

From a quality of experience perspective, the findings of these studies suggest that in competitive environments, where performance and winning versus losing are highlighted, rating skill to be above average optimizes the experience to a greater extent than perceiving a balance between challenge and skill. A study by Jackson, Kimiecik, Ford, and Marsh (1998) on masters athletes' flow experiences supports the important role of perceived skill, and the ambiguous role of challenge, in influencing quality of experience. Using the FSS, which assesses flow on nine dimensions, Jackson and colleagues examined the relationships between flow and ratings of performance via measures of perceived success and perceived skills and challenges after participation in one competitive event. Perceived success and perceived skills were correlated significantly with a number of the nine flow dimensions, whereas the perceived challenges variable was not correlated with any of the flow dimensions. Moneta and Csikszentmihalyi (1996) also found differential patterns between perceived skills and challenges and quality of experience variables in a variety of life contexts outside of sport. In their study, they found that concentration and involvement were positively related to ratings of challenge, whereas wishing to do the activity and happiness were negatively related.

The role of flow in sport as it relates to the quality of one's experience is complex. Outside of sport, flow is almost always a more positive experience than boredom, anxiety, or apathy (Csikszentmihalyi, 1997). However, when competition and an emphasis on performance are introduced, high skill is perceived by some participants to be more desirable than high challenge because high skill, with minimal challenge, leads to desired outcomes (e.g., winning). At some point, however, one must wonder about the long-term effects of basing positive experience on the relationship between high skill/low challenge and desired outcome, which an overemphasis on the outcomes of sport can promote. Csikszentmihalyi (1988, p. 369) suggested that when "the flow experience is split, its motivational force is bound to be reduced." For example, an athlete who perceives high skill/low challenge as optimal compared with high skill/high challenge may experience happiness and a desire to perform the activity but not optimal concentration or involvement in the activity. In the short term, this kind of experience may produce a victory, but in the long term splitting the flow experience may not be in her best interest. Can an athlete learn, grow, and develop without increasing the challenge? As Moneta and Csikszentmihalyi (1996) pointed out, however, individuals face a perplexing problem when they desire high challenge/high skill conditions, even though from an experience perspective these conditions produce the most optimal psychological states. Increasing the challenge may mean a loss of happiness and a wishing to be there, which could override the positive concentration and involvement that come from high skill/high challenge experiences.

Results from the Stein et al. (1995) and Jackson, Kimiecik, Ford, and Marsh (1998) studies in sport, along with the Moneta and Csikszentmihalyi (1996) findings, suggest that the flow model may not be able to account for what is perceived as positive quality of experience in some situations. To an athlete, perceived high skill/low challenge may not always be boring. In a learning environment, perceived high challenge/low skill may make the learner not anxious but aroused and excited about the prospect of learning something new. Research on flow in sport should begin to address some of these issues. Perhaps individual differences, such as an autotelic personality, can account for some of the findings discussed here. The studies that have examined this possibility in sport are presented next.

The Autotelic Personality and Flow in Sport

For years Csikszentmihalyi (1975, 1990, 1997) has hinted at the existence of an autotelic personality to partially explain the large individual differences in people's flow experiences. For example, Wells (1988), studying mothers, found that some mothers were in flow only 4% of the time, whereas others were in flow more than 40% of the time. In our interpretation, Csikszentmihalyi views the autotelic personality as part of the individual that is influenced by both genetics and learning.

In essence, the autotelic personality notion refers to an individual who generally does things for their own sake, rather than to achieve some later external goal. That is, certain types of people may be better equipped psychologically, regardless of the situation, to experience flow. Hypotheses have been forwarded to account for individual differences in the ability to experience flow. For example, one possibility involves differences in how people process information, with some people better able to concentrate more efficiently (Hamilton, 1981). Another suggestion is that some people are better able to turn obstacles into challenges and thus realize their potential, without being self-conscious (Logan, 1988). Logan described the non-self-conscious individual as one who is able to become engrossed in an activity because of the lack of preoccupation with the self. Relatedly, Moneta and Csikszentmihalyi (1996) suggested a possible link between hardiness and flow. This makes sense, because Kobasa's (1979) conceptualization of hardiness includes a composite of perceptions of control, commitment, and challenge, which parallel the dimensions of flow outlined earlier in this chapter. In support of this possibility, Perritt (1999) demonstrated a significant relationship between the control and commitment hardiness subscales and dispositional flow for collegiate track-and-field athletes.

Ellis, Voelkl, and Morris (1994) proposed self-affirmation as another personality variable that may differentiate people's flow experiences. Work in the area of intrinsic motivation (e.g., Deci & Ryan, 1985) suggests that those who feel more in control of their own actions (i.e., self-determined) are more likely to be intrinsically motivated, and there are associations between flow and intrinsic motivation. Csikszentmihalyi (1988) suggested that we need to learn more about the configuration of traits associated with the large variability in people's flow states and to then determine how much of this configuration can be learned or developed over time.

We have been intrigued by the possibility of the autotelic personality involved in people's flow experiences in sport. We take a general interactionist perspective (see Vealey, this volume) following the framework presented by Kimiecik and Stein (1992). This framework suggests that certain dispositional (e.g., attentional style) and state (e.g., anxiety) psychological factors interact with various factors in the sport context (e.g., type of sport) to determine whether an athlete is likely to experience flow. In revisiting this framework, we would probably add intrinsic motivation to the list of dispositional factors because of the suggested link between intrinsic motivation and flow (Csikszentmihalyi, 1997; Deci & Ryan, 1985).

Little empirical work has been conducted on the situational factors and their role in flow states, although one can see how the previous discussion on the importance of competition and the competitive context could be very relevant to optimal experience in sport. In addition, Jackson's (1995) work on elite athletes' beliefs about flow disrupters showed that nonoptimal environmental or situational conditions were the primary factors for getting athletes out of flow. These findings demonstrate the necessity for flow research in sport to examine the dynamic interaction of person and situational factors and their influence on flow states.

Deciding which psychological factors might be associated with flow states in sport is a difficult task because there are few empirical data to direct such an endeavor. The few studies that have been conducted have focused primarily on dispositional factors (Jackson, Kimiecik, Ford, & Marsh, 1998; Jackson & Roberts, 1992; Kowal & Fortier, 1999). In the next few sections, we present a number of dispositional factors that could constitute an autotelic personality in sport, and we discuss findings from studies that have examined the association of these person factors with flow states.

Goal Orientation

Goal orientation is a much studied concept in sport and exercise psychology, one that has been shown to be important to understanding individuals' motivations to engage in certain activities (e.g., Duda, 1992; Nicholls, 1992). Within the sport context, task and ego orientations seem to be particularly relevant, because they relate to perceptions of ability, which are highly valued in athletic environments (Duda, 1992). Although it is possible to be high or low on either one or both factors, individuals are thought to have a preference for a particular frame of reference within achievement situations. As reported earlier, Jackson and Roberts (1992) found correlational support for a positive association between task orientation and flow in college athletes. Athletes with a task orientation

may be more likely to experience flow than athletes with an ego orientation because of the individual's focus on the task rather than on anticipated outcomes. Task orientation thus would be expected to be positively associated with flow.

Perceived Sport Ability

Perceived ability has been related positively to flow in both quantitative (Jackson & Roberts, 1992) and qualitative (Jackson, 1995) research. Csikszentmihalyi and Nakamura (1989) suggested that both challenges and skills must be relatively high before anything resembling a flow experience comes about. We focus on "perceived" sport ability because within the flow model, "it is not the skills we actually have that determine how we feel, but the ones we think we have" (Csikszentmihalyi, 1990, p. 75). We expect that perceived ability would have a positive relationship with flow.

Competitive Trait Anxiety

Competitive trait anxiety is the "tendency to perceive competitive situations as threatening and to respond to these situations with feelings of apprehension or tension" (Martens, 1977, p. 23). From a flow perspective, high trait anxiety would be expected to prevent flow because the athlete's psychic energy is too fluid or erratic. One cannot totally immerse oneself in an activity when worry or tension is the primary focus. Anxiety is the antithesis of flow in Csikszentmihalyi's (1975, 1990) flow model. An athlete cannot be in flow while experiencing high anxiety. Jackson (1995), in her qualitative research with athletes, found that athletes recognized the importance of optimal arousal to achieving flow states. Hence, we would expect competitive trait anxiety to be negatively related to athletes' flow states.

Intrinsic Motivation

Intrinsic motivation involves "innate, organismic needs for competence and self-determination. The intrinsic needs for competence and self-determination motivate an ongoing process of seeking and attempting to conquer optimal challenges" (Deci & Ryan, 1985, p. 32). Self-determination is intimately linked to the concept of autonomy, a person's sense that intentional behavior is choicefully self-regulated, is flexible, and occurs in the absence of pressure. In contrast, the concept of control refers to intentional behavior that is perceived by the actor to be coerced by intrapsychic and environmental forces. Theoretically, an individual who perceives autonomy should be more likely to experience flow than an individual who feels pressure toward particular outcomes because she will be extremely interested in the task at hand (Deci & Ryan, 1985). Jackson (1995) found that high motivation to engage in the activity was an important flow facilitator for elite athletes. Intrinsic motivation and autotelic experience (Csikszentmihalyi, 1990) are theoretically similar constructs, with autotelic activities being done for their own sake without expectation of future reward. Thus, a positive relationship would be expected between intrinsic motivation and flow.

In a recent study, we examined the role of these dispositional factors—task and ego orientation, perceived sport ability, competitive trait anxiety, and intrinsic motivation—in masters athletes' flow states at both the dispositional and state level (Jackson, Kimiecik, Ford, & Marsh, 1998). We used these potential autotelic personality factors as correlates of flow and expected that perceived ability, task goal orientation, and intrinsic motivation would be positively associated with flow and competitive trait anxiety negatively related to flow. We expected that these dispositional factors would be more associated with a dispositional flow measure, the Trait Flow Scale[1] (Jackson, Kimiecik, Ford, & Marsh, 1998; Marsh & Jackson, 1999) than a state flow measure, the FSS (Jackson & Marsh, 1996) but that there still would be significant associations at the state level. Results indicated that perceived sport ability, an intrinsic motivation factor, and competitive trait anxiety were related in the predicted way to dispositional and state flow, but task and ego goal orientation were unrelated to flow. These findings lend credence to the notion that something akin to autotelic personality may exist. We have a long way to go, however, in figuring out the role of personality factors in understanding optimal experience in sport. We are uncertain as to why task orientation did not relate to either dispositional or state flow in this study.

Perceptions of sport ability seem to be crucial for flow states, and findings of Jackson et al. (2001) add even further support. These researchers assessed relationships between flow, as measured by both the DFS and the FSS, and psychological skills/strategies and athletic self-concept. Components of athletic self concept, as assessed by the Elite Athlete Self Description Questionnaire

(Marsh, Hey, Johnson, & Perry, 1997), that were positively related to flow were mental and physical skills and perception of self as an overall skilled performer in one's event.

Measurement Issues in the Study of Flow in Sport

The two major challenges to measurement in the study of flow in sport pertain to (a) the difficulty of examining and measuring potential correlates of flow and (b) measuring flow itself. We examine these two challenges in more detail in the next two sections.

Measuring Correlates of Flow in Sport

To highlight the measurement challenge inherent in examining correlates of flow, we next analyze three flow-in-sport studies—Jackson, Kimiecik, Ford, and Marsh (1998), Stein et al. (1995), and Kowal and Fortier (1999).

Kowal and Fortier (1999) were interested in examining the relationships among intrinsic motivation, extrinsic motivation, amotivation, and flow at a situational level with a group of masters swimmers. This work was based on Vallerand's (1997) hierarchical model of intrinsic and extrinsic motivation, which posits three levels of motivation: global, contextual, and situational. These researchers hypothesized that both intrinsic motivation and self-determined extrinsic motivation, assessed at the situational level, would be positively related to swimmers' flow experiences—as measured by the FSS—in a practice. They were particularly interested in examining these relationships at the situational or state level because Stein et al. (1995) found very weak or no relationships between measures of confidence and competence and flow states in recreational sport contexts. Kowal and Fortier also measured athletes' perceptions of autonomy, competence, and relatedness pertaining to swim practice to determine if these intrinsically oriented factors were related to flow. Results indicated that swimmers who reported a high incidence of flow had significantly higher levels of intrinsic motivation and self-determined extrinsic motivation than swimmers reporting a low incidence of flow. No differences were found in non-self-determined extrinsic motivation and amotivation. In addition, participants in the high-flow

---

1. The Trait Flow Scale was renamed the Dispositional Flow Scale (DFS; Jackson et al., 2001) to better reflect what it was designed to measure.

groups reported significantly greater levels of perceived competence and relatedness than participants in the low-flow groups.

At first glance, the results of Jackson and colleagues and Stein et al. seem to conflict with the findings of Kowal and Fortier. The Jackson study did not find extrinsic motivation to be related to flow, whereas the masters swimming study did. Also, Kowal and Fortier found perception of swimming competence associated with flow states, whereas Stein and colleagues did not find a measure of competence to be related to flow states in tennis players or golfers. In fact, Kowal and Fortier stated,

> *This basic finding runs contrary to the results of Stein et al. (1995) who questioned whether situational motivational antecedents are associated with flow states, and whether antecedents of flow could, in fact, be identified. The results here clearly suggest that situational motivation is linked with flow and that motivational antecedents of the flow state may indeed be identifiable. (p. 134)*

The findings of these two studies are a classic example of why caution is warranted when studying correlates of flow states in sport as well as comparing findings across studies. Because of the different ways in which these two studies measured the independent and dependent variables, the findings may not be in conflict at all. In fact, the studies were really examining different sides of the same coin. Kowal and Fortier suggested that their findings conflicted with those of Stein and colleagues because Kowal and Fortier found perceptions of competence to be significantly related to flow, whereas Stein and colleagues did not. Why might this be the case?

First, the measures of competence were different in the two studies. For instance, in the golf study, players were asked to rate their competence right before the hole they were about to play. In the study of masters swimmers, a three-item measure of practice competence was used, which the researchers adapted from Harter's Perceived Competence Scale for Children (1982). Hence, the two measures of competence are quite different and could account for the disparate findings.

Second, the time pertaining to subject completion of the competence measures may be a factor in explaining different findings. Stein et al. (1995) assessed perceived competence for a particular hole immediately before playing the hole and then assessed quality of the experience immediately

after completion of the hole. Kowal and Fortier had the masters swimmers complete all study measures immediately after a practice session—determinants (e.g., competence), motivation (e.g., intrinsic), and experience (flow states). Hence, Kowal and Fortier really were examining competence as a correlate of flow, and we wonder if the stronger relationship between perceived competence and flow in the swimming study emerged because these two variables were assessed together immediately after the practice. It is much easier to assess one's competence accurately after having experienced an event (i.e., swimming practice) than to gauge one's competence before playing a golf hole. How often has the reader stood on the tee of an "easy" 120-yard par three hole and said, "I've got the flag covered on this one," only to walk away with a double-bogey? Do you think your perceptions of competence would be different before and after the hole? Hence, the time that the measures were completed in the Kowal and Fortier study may have enhanced the probability of finding positive relationships between competence and flow, whereas the Stein et al. pre–post approach may have reduced the chances of a significant relationship.

Third, the type of sport examined could be another factor in explaining the disparate findings. As outlined by Kimiecik and Stein (1992), the type of sport cannot be ignored when examining flow states. Swimming, especially practice or lap swimming, is a relatively continuous, self-paced physical activity with little disruption. Golf has more stops and starts, and it is more difficult to get an accurate measure of flow. How do you measure flow in golf? Flow for a complete 18 holes? Nine holes? Each shot? Certainly the different types of sport could account for the different findings in the two studies.

Fourth, similar to the competence measures in both studies, flow was measured differently in each study. Stein et al. used the ESM approach and obtained golfers' assessments of challenges and skills (i.e., flow) after 14 or more holes during seven rounds of golf. Flow was operationalized as when challenges and skills were balanced and were above one's average. Kowal and Fortier measured flow immediately after one practice by using the FSS (Jackson & Marsh, 1996). For analyses, they used the overall score on the FSS to categorize swimmers below the 33rd percentile as low flow and swimmers above the 66th percentile as high flow. High-flow swimmers were more likely to perceive high competence than low-flow swimmers. As you can see, the two flow measures are quite different.

These two studies are so different in terms of measures of competence and flow, type of sport, and timing of measures that to say the findings conflict is misleading. The findings are different, not conflicting, because the studies are different, and future work on antecedents of flow in sport will need to address issues such as these if we are to obtain a more complete picture of psychological and situational factors that may promote or inhibit flow states.

A similar analysis can be conducted to explain different findings between Kowal and Fortier (1999) and Jackson, Kimiecik, Ford, and Marsh (1998) with respect to motivational correlates and flow states. As reported earlier, Kowal and Fortier found intrinsic motivation and self-determined extrinsic motivation to be significantly related to flow, whereas Jackson et al. only found an intrinsic motivation factor to be related to flow states. Interestingly, the approaches of these two studies are similar in that both used masters athletes and a one-time measure of flow, either the FSS or the DFS. However, the measures of motivation were different. Jackson et al. measured motivation with the Sport Motivation Scale (SMS; Pelletier et al., 1995), which assesses different dimensions of motivation at a contextual level (see Vallerand, 1997) by asking the athlete, "Why do you practice your sport?" The SMS consists of seven subscales that measure three types of intrinsic motivation (to know, to accomplish, to experience stimulation), three forms of regulation for extrinsic motivation (external, introjection, and identification), and amotivation. Identification is the closest measure to what Deci and Ryan (1991) labeled self-determined extrinsic motivation. The results indicated that only the intrinsic motivation to experience stimulation measure was significantly related to flow, as measured by the DFS (more strongly) or the FSS (weaker relationship). Kowal and Fortier used an adapted version of the Situational Motivational Scale (Guay & Vallerand, 1995) and asked swimmers to respond to each item according to, "Why did you participate in this swim practice?" This measure corresponds to Vallerand's (1997) situational level outlined in his motivational taxonomy. Thus, although each study assessed intrinsic motivation, extrinsic motivation, and amotivation, the level of motivation of interest was different. These findings demonstrate the need for studies that examine the relationship between different levels of motivation

and quality of experience in varied sport situations.

As you can see, examining correlates of flow is replete with measurement challenges and opportunities, not the least of which is how researchers operationalize and measure flow states. We discuss this measurement challenge next.

Measuring Flow in Sport

One of the greatest challenges in flow research, or any research involving subjective experiences, is finding ways to accurately and reliably assess the experience itself (see Jackson, 2000 for further discussion about this measurement issue). As with most other sport psychology constructs, there is no one way to measure flow in sport. Flow is an optimal experience, a state of consciousness. Like all experiential phenomena, flow cannot easily be quantified by psychometrics or illuminated through investigative interviewing. No single measurement approach will be able to provide trouble-free assessments of the flow experience. The second author has attempted to use and develop multiple ways of researching flow—both quantitative and qualitative—in sport that may help make flow a more accessible concept to both researchers and practitioners.

Qualitative methods can provide rich accounts of flow, and this was the first approach to understanding this phenomenon used by Csikszentmihalyi (1975). Jackson (2000a) first used a primarily quantitative, questionnaire-based approach (Jackson & Roberts, 1992) to study flow and interviewed a small subsample of athletes about their flow experiences. This led to two larger scale interview-based studies of flow with elite athletes (Jackson, 1992, 1995, 1996). As reviewed earlier, these studies showed that elite athletes have a good grasp of flow experientially, if not theoretically. Certainly there are limitations to qualitative approaches, including the retrospective element of interviews, the small samples conducive to this type of research, and the interpretive biases of the researchers, which all influence an understanding of the flow experience. However, the fact that flow is amenable to understanding through open-ended interviews makes this approach an important means for studying flow in sport.

Wanting to examine associations between flow and other psychological constructs, Jackson developed the FSS and a corresponding dispositional version of the instrument, the DFS. The DFS is a dispositional assessment of the frequency with which people experience flow. The DFS was designed to assess the dispositional component of flow, whereas the FSS was designed to assess the state component. The FSS is designed to be administered after a specific sport event, to assess the experience of flow in that event. The DFS is designed to assess the frequency with which respondents report experiencing flow in general during participation in sport. The assumptions underlying this measurement approach are that flow is a specific psychological state amenable to state-based assessments (using the FSS) and also that people differ in their propensity to experience flow on a regular basis (using the DFS).

Both the FSS and DFS instruments have undergone psychometric analyses and were found to have an acceptable factor structure and reliability (Jackson & Marsh, 1996; Marsh & Jackson, 1999). Nine factors, corresponding to the nine flow dimensions, have been validated through confirmatory factor analyses of the instruments. One of the factors, time transformation, has shown little relation to the global flow factor in the research with the scale to date. This may be partly due to the items used to assess this factor, but there is also a possibility that time transformation is not a central dimension to athletes' flow experiences. An additional factor, loss of self-consciousness, has not demonstrated as strong a relationship with global flow as the other flow factors. Recently, Jackson and Eklund (in press) analyzed new versions of the flow scales, the DFS-2 and the FSS-2. These revised scales developed by Jackson (2000b) include several new items that replace poorer performing items in the original versions. Research with the DFS-2 and FSS-2 should help to clarify the relationship of time transformation and loss of self-consciousness to the global flow construct as well as clarify the relative relevance of the nine flow factors to athletes' flow experiences.

The ESM (Csikszentmihalyi & Larson, 1987) is the primary means of assessing flow used by Csikszentmihalyi and colleagues (e.g., Csikszentmihalyi, Rathunde, & Whalen, 1993). Study participants wear a beeper or watch that is programmed to signal at eight random times during a day for one week. ESM participants use self-report booklets to record measurements of mood, flow characteristics, and other factors such as motivation to be engaged in the activity at the time of each signal. By using an operational definition of flow based on equivalence of challenges and skills, this method assesses quality of experience when the individual is in flow as well as when not in flow.

The ESM approach rarely has been used in sport psychological research. As described earlier, Stein et al. (1995), using modified ESM procedures, found that on average basketball students, tennis players, and golfers enjoyed better quality of experiences in flow than when in other states assessed by the ESM: apathy, boredom, and anxiety. Predicted relationships with other psychological factors assessed in the study were not supported. The assessments of experience were not based on a true ESM approach but on preplanned and structured incidents. The idea of random beeping of athletes during performance is understandably greeted with skepticism. However, the usefulness of the ESM approach, as evidenced in research with this method by Csikszentmihalyi and colleagues, suggests it should not be bypassed as an approach to assessing flow in sport. Creative ways of applying ESM may result in fruitful investigations of flow in sport. The ESM can be used to study a range of experiential states and cognitions and provides a tool for assessing experience as it occurs.

Jackson (2000a) suggested that to understand positive experiential states in sport, a multi-method approach to measurement (i.e., both quantitative and qualitative) will yield the greatest amount and types of information. As the tools of measurement are refined, the possibilities for gathering important information about these experiences will increase significantly. As the research reviewed in this chapter indicates, both qualitative and quantitative approaches provide a unique understanding of factors that may be associated with flow experiences in sport. Any empirical approach used to study flow has limitations, but each has potential to provide some useful information about flow and the factors associated with this state. There is a need for more research, using a variety of methodologies, to examine flow and what influences this positive experience in sport. However, the next section provides a cautionary note from a scientific paradigmatic perspective for any researcher interested in studying flow in sport.

Scientific Paradigms and the Study of Flow in Sport

Flow as an area of scientific study serves as a rich metaphor for examining some of the paradigmatic issues that have been addressed by others in sport psychology (e.g., Dewar & Horn, 1992; Feltz, 1987; Martens, 1987) and by those who have examined the epistemology and paradigms of science

(Fahlberg & Fahlberg, 1994; Lincoln & Guba, 1985; Valle, King, & Halling, 1989). We have many more questions than answers on these issues as they pertain to studying flow, but we believe that they are issues worth addressing.

Recent research on flow in sport has attempted to examine correlates of flow, a subjective experience, with variables that could be categorized as cognitions or perceptions (e.g., perceived ability). The variables that have been used are important as demonstrated by the significant findings to date (e.g., Jackson, Kimiecik, Ford, & Marsh, 1998; Jackson et al., 2001; Kowal & Fortier, 1999), but they are removed from the phenomenology or lived experience of the individual.

According to Valle et al. (1989), mainstream psychology, based on the positivistic, hypothetico-deductive philosophy of science, is designed to deal with only one half of the behavior–experience polarity: behavior. The major emphasis is on asking *why* questions through a cause–effect analysis. Hence, most of the psychological factors of interest to sport psychologists, such as self-efficacy and anxiety, have been developed and studied within this scientific paradigm. More importantly, they are used to explain, understand, and predict behavior.

The existential phenomenological approach, similar to interpretivistic philosophy of science espoused by Lincoln and Guba (1985), seeks to "explicate the essence, structure, or form of both human *experience* and human behavior as revealed through essentially descriptive techniques including disciplined reflection" (Valle et al., 1989, p. 6). In this approach, linear causality (cause–effect) thinking, hypothesis generation, and asking *why* questions are nonexistent. Rather, the emphasis is on elucidating lived experience by asking, "What?"

This is a relevant issue for those who study flow. The quantitative research that has begun to appear on assessing flow and variables related to its occurrence in sport comes from an interest in addressing what factors might affect the occurrence of flow in sport. This is an interesting question from both a conceptual and an applied level. However, because of the uniqueness of the flow experience, it is also important to continue to explore the phenomenology of this experience. Different methodological approaches are suited to addressing these different types of questions about flow. Although a quantitative approach can provide information about the relationships among different psychological variables with flow,

qualitative methods fare much better when we attempt to understand lived experience. Combining quantitative and qualitative perspectives is not without its problems from a philosophy of science perspective (Buchanan, 1992). However, a pragmatic approach suggests that it is useful to use whatever approaches can answer the questions of interest (Patton, 1990). At this point, we certainly encourage multiple approaches and multiple methods to study flow. Although we have provided some research possibilities throughout this chapter, we end this review with some possible directions for those who want to investigate flow in sport.

FUTURE DIRECTIONS IN FLOW IN SPORT RESEARCH

A number of possibilities exist for creative researchers who are willing to deal with the ambiguity and challenge of studying flow in sport. Here we present some ideas for continuing to explore the role of flow in athletes' sport experiences.

We suggest that research would be interesting and fruitful if it were to examine the dynamic interaction between potential personal and situational antecedents of flow experiences in sport. What types of personal factors (e.g., attentional style) interact with what kinds of contexts (e.g., type of sport situation) to produce the most optimal sport experiences? Much of the research has examined either personal factors or situational factors and their association with flow, but not both together. This interactive type of research may be more complex and difficult but could provide new knowledge about flow states in sport. Jackson and colleagues (Jackson, Kimiecik, Ford, & Marsh, 1998; Jackson et al., 2001) recently have begun to look at both types of factors, by using dispositional and state flow measures and examining associations with personal and situational factors in sport.

More research on the different quadrants of experience in the flow model, such as flow, anxiety, boredom, and apathy, and the quality of experience associated with each in sport would be very beneficial. For instance, a number of studies (Ellis et al., 1994; Mandigo, Thompson, & Couture, 1998; Moneta & Csikszentmihalyi, 1996; Stein et al., 1995) have found high skill/low challenge (boredom) to be as optimal, if not more so, than high skill/high challenge (flow). Is perceived high skill/low challenge really boredom for individuals? This is where sport, with its varying degrees of competition, could provide an interesting environment to assess these relationships. Only future work can tell us if high skill/low challenge is really as optimal a state as flow and if that quadrant needs to be renamed. In Csikszentmihalyi's (1997) more recent writings, the relaxation and boredom quadrants were switched, indicating that the former precedes the latter.

Taking an interdisciplinary approach, it would be useful to examine the link between flow states, hemispheric functioning, and sport performance. Integrating the psychosocial approach to studying flow with sport psychophysiology (Hatfield & Landers, 1983) seems to be an ideal way to examine the role of optimal experience and its connection to psychophysiological phenomena. As Csikszentmihalyi (1988, p. 371) pointed out, early neurophysiological studies by Hamilton (1976, 1981) showed that individuals who can turn boring situations into flowlike states process information in a peculiar way:

> It seems that when they concentrate on a task, their cortical activation level—measuring the mental effort they are expending—actually decreases from baseline, instead of increasing, as it normally should. This could be a neurological indication of one of the central components of the phenomenology of flow, a measure of deep concentration on a limited stimulus field that excludes everything else from consciousness. (p. 371)

Researchers who study psychophysiology of sport (e.g., Crews & Landers, 1990; Salazar et al., 1990) have been interested in using hemispheric asymmetries in EEG activity to examine attentional focus in a variety of sport tasks. The left hemisphere appears to process information analytically and is more involved in language, whereas the right hemisphere processes holistically and is more adept at spatial cognitive processing and pattern recognition. In general, results from hemispheric studies in sport show that elite athletes (e.g., archers, shooters) have a higher degree of alpha activity in the left hemisphere than in their right seconds before performing their task. Alpha waves are indications of relaxation, which is considered useful for sport performance because this would mean that the left hemisphere is less active, thus reducing cognitions unnecessary to task performance (Boutcher, 1992).

Is there a connection between flow and brain wave patterns? Is the result of increased alpha activity in the left hemisphere an optimal state of mind? What comes first? Does flow lead to differential brain wave patterns? Psychophysiologists argue that retrospective self-report of optimal states such as flow (e.g., the ESM) views attentional functioning as an outcome rather than a process and does not tell us much about the underlying process (see Boutcher, 1992; Hatfield & Landers, 1983). Certainly, there are limitations of using self-report to assess optimal attentional patterns, but we have several questions: What is the cause of the differential brain wave patterns that the sport psychophysiological research has identified? How do elite archers, for example, suppress left-brain involvement in performance through an increase in alpha waves? How is the brain wave activity self-regulated? Boutcher (1992) suggested that this optimal brain wave pattern may be created by "the athlete who directs arousal away from task-irrelevant information and into the task itself" (p. 262). This seems to indicate that an optimally conscious thought process (i.e., flow) is needed to direct the athlete to the automatic processing aspect of attention, which some consider to be free of conscious monitoring (Schneider, Dumais, & Shiffrin, 1984). To address these issues, some creative and innovative research could be conducted that integrates the psychosocial with the psychophysiological perspective on optimal attentional processes and experiences in sport.

More optimal experience research is needed on nonelite sport participants. As asked earlier, do they experience flow in similar ways as elite athletes with respect to intensity and frequency? Elite athletes suggest that flow is very important to their participation in their sport (Jackson, 1995). Do nonelite sport participants have similar views? This question becomes even more relevant as our perspective shifts from sport performance to physical activity and long-term health. What motivates people who do not have high athletic ability to exercise regularly? As the Surgeon General's report on physical activity and health suggested (U.S. Department of Health and Human Services, 1996), answering this question is a high public health priority. Does optimal experience play a role in people's continued participation in exercise?

Wankel (1985) interviewed exercise program adherers and dropouts to examine the role of quality of experience factors, such as curiosity, social relationships, and developing skills in their exercise participation. Results show that both adherers and dropouts joined the program for health-related reasons such as losing weight and preventing disease. These factors did not differentiate between the adherers and the dropouts. Rather, the non-health-related, quality of experience variables were cited as the primary reasons for adherers' continued involvement in the program. Although this study did not examine flow states directly, the results indirectly suggest that optimal experience could be very important to continued exercise participation.

In another interview study, Szabo and Kimiecik (1997) asked runners of varying ability and competitive orientation about their flow experiences. Findings suggest that the runners who rarely entered races and considered themselves to have "average" running ability experienced flow and viewed it as reason for running. A 32-year-old female runner in this category said:

> I guess I'm thinking, well the potential for flow keeps you out there, whether or not, I mean I could have zero percent flow or very low percentage of flow experiences or opportunities for them, but the potential for them, because they are a good place to be, is enough to keep me going.

Last, Jackson, Kimiecik, and Attridge (1998) interviewed a group of nonelite masters athletes. One of the goals of the interviews was to ascertain reasons for their continued participation. Through inductive analyses, the authors labeled a category "enjoy the sport," which refers to optimal states of mind the participants experience when doing their sport. A 49-year-old female triathlete talked about this enjoyment:

> I love activity. I think I just love the feeling you get from it. I know that I love watching a person playing a sport just to see the energy that goes into it. It's like a dance for me. It's the same creativity that you find in a dance. So, I love it, I love it.

The findings from these qualitative studies suggest that regular physical activity participants experience—and value—their optimal experiences in ways similar to elite athletes. These studies are a good beginning, and more research is needed to understand the role of flow in people's physical activity experiences outside of elite sport.

Along these same lines, work on flow could be integrated with some of the exciting work being done on the role of emotions in exercise contexts (e.g., Gauvin, Rejeski, & Norris, 1996). Flow theory suggests that quality of experience is optimal when people experience flow. That is, individuals in flow typically experience greater postexperience positive affect and potency than individuals in states of boredom, anxiety, or apathy (e.g., Csikszentmihalyi & LeFevre, 1989). In a study with women, Gauvin and colleagues (1996) found that acute bouts of vigorous physical activity were associated with significant improvements in affect and feeling states over a 6-week period. Could positive experience during exercise be a mediating variable between exercise and people's feeling states? That is, do people who experience flow during exercise have greater positive affect than people who do not experience flow? Petruzzello and Landers (1994) suggested that individual differences may play a role in the relationship between exercise and affective change, but this possibility has not been examined. In addition, what is the role of flow in continued physical activity participation for different types of participants? Addressing these questions would be a useful way of determining the role of flow in exercise contexts.

Research with the newly revised flow scales (Jackson, 2000b; Jackson & Eklund, in press) and the ESM (e.g., Csikszentmihalyi & Larson, 1987) should provide useful information on the role of flow in various physical activity contexts. The ESM would be particularly useful for understanding how quality of experience in physical activity relates to quality of experience in other areas of people's lives. In addition, the DFS-2, the FSS-2, and the ESM provide opportunities to examine possible antecedents and consequences of flow as they occur in sport and exercise. This type of research could provide a better understanding of the personal and situational factors underlying flow states in physical activity.

CONCLUSION

We began this chapter by suggesting that optimal experiences in sport provide a rich and valuable source for understanding athletes' participation. Flow, one form of optimal subjective experience, has been shown to play a central role in athletes' sport experiences. We need to know more about how personal factors and the physical activity context shape and influence flow states. Measurement and scientific paradigmatic issues are relevant and influence the approach to studying flow as well as interpretation of findings.

From a measurement perspective, an experiential state such as flow is difficult to measure. As

Jackson (2000a) pointed out, measuring flow is certainly not as straightforward as measuring heart rate or flexibility, but most of the constructs in sport and exercise psychology that we are interested in do not present straightforward measurement options. Confidence, attributions, motivation, and anxiety have all had a period of development where measures have progressed from their infancy to being quite robust. Anxiety, for example, now has several self-report options that have spurred a good deal of research. As measurement options for flow expand and mature, the potential for researching this construct will also increase.

In the end, the importance and relevance of flow in sport and other physical activity contexts are a matter of belief. Is there a state of mind where one is totally absorbed in the task with focused concentration, an optimal psychological state that stands out from everyday life? Are there moments where everything is just right with the world, when an athlete, worker, or mother experiences magic? The empirical and anecdotal evidence seems to suggest that there is and that this state of mind has important implications for human development, evolution, quality of life, and performance. We believe that this optimal state of mind exists, is worthy of further study in sport and other physical activity contexts, and, as Csikszentmihalyi (1982) stated, is the "bottom line of existence." Flow is a way of getting at the meaning, or lived experience, of living. As Fahlberg and Fahlberg (1994) stated:

When we realize, finally, that human beings are more than mere objects to be manipulated and controlled, then we can truly understand the necessity of recognizing this human world through the described epistemologies. Meaning in life and the freedom to live that life then become concerns for reflection and inquiry. When human consciousness and meaning are recognized, a human science for movement is possible. (p. 108)

Flow should be at the core of any human science interested in knowing more about the links among consciousness, movement, and what it means to live a life.

REFERENCES

Boutcher, S. (1992). Attention and athletic performance: An integrated approach. In T. Horn (Ed.), *Advances in sport psychology* (1st ed., pp. 251–265). Champaign, IL: Human Kinetics.

Buchanan, D. (1992). An uneasy alliance: Combining qualitative and quantitative research methods. *Health Education Quarterly, 19,* 117–135.

Carli, M., Fave, A.C., & Massimini, F. (1988). The quality of experience in the flow channels: Comparison of Italian and U.S. students. In M. Csikszentmihalyi & I. Csikszentmihalyi (Eds.), *Optimal experience: Psychological studies of flow in consciousness* (pp. 288–306). New York: Cambridge University Press.

Chalip, L., Csikszentmihalyi, M., Kleiber, D., & Larson, R. (1984). Variations of experience in formal and informal sport. *Research Quarterly for Exercise and Sport, 55,* 109–116.

Cohn, P. (1986). *An exploration of the golfer's peak-experience.* Unpublished manuscript, California State University, Fullerton.

Cohn, P. (1991). An exploratory study of peak performance in golf. *The Sport Psychologist, 5,* 1–14.

Crews, D., & Landers, D. (1990). Electroencephalographic measures of attentional patterns prior to the golf putt. *Medicine and Science in Sports and Exercise, 25,* 116–126.

Csikszentmihalyi, M. (1975). *Beyond boredom and anxiety.* San Francisco: Jossey-Bass.

Csikszentmihalyi, M. (1982). Toward a psychology of optimal experience. In L. Wheeler (Ed.), *Review of personality and social psychology* (pp. 13–36). Beverly Hills, CA: Sage.

Csikszentmihalyi, M. (1988). The future of flow. In M. Csikszentmihalyi & I. Csikszentmihalyi (Eds.). *Optimal experience: Psychological studies of flow in consciousness* (pp. 364–383). New York: Cambridge University Press.

Csikszentmihalyi, M. (1990). *Flow: The psychology of optimal experience.* New York: Harper & Row.

Csikszentmihalyi, M. (1993). *The evolving self.* New York: Harper & Row.

Csikszentmihalyi, M. (1997). *Finding flow.* New York: Harper Collins.

Csikszentmihalyi, M., & Csikszentmihalyi, I. (1988). Measurement of flow in everyday life: Introduction to Part IV. In M. Csikszentmihalyi & I. Csikszentmihalyi (Eds.), *Optimal experience: Psychological studies of flow in consciousness* (pp. 251–265). New York: Cambridge University Press.

Csikszentmihalyi, M., & Graef, R. (1980). The experience of freedom in daily life. *American Journal of Community Psychology, 8,* 401–414.

Csikszentmihalyi, M., & Larson, R. (1987). Validity and reliability of the experience-sampling method. *Journal of Nervous and Mental Disease, 175,* 526–536.

Csikszentmihalyi, M., Larson, R., & Prescott, S. (1977). The ecology of adolescent activity and experience. *Journal of Youth and Adolescence, 6,* 281–294.

Csikszentmihalyi, M., & LeFevre, J. (1989). Optimal experience in work and leisure. *Journal of Personality and Social Psychology, 56,* 815–822.

Csikszentmihalyi, M., & Nakamura, J. (1989). The dynamics of intrinsic motivation: A study of adolescents. In C. Ames & R. Ames (Eds.), *Research on motivation in education: Vol. 3. Goals and cognitions* (pp. 45–71). New York: Academic Press.

Csikszentmihalyi, M., Rathunde, K., & Whalen, S. (1993). *Talented teenagers: The roots of success and failure.* New York: Cambridge University Press.

DeCharms, R., & Muir, M. (1978). Motivation: Social approaches. *Annual Reviews in Psychology, 29,* 91–113.

Deci, E.L., & Ryan, R.M. (1985). *Intrinsic motivation and self-determination in human behavior.* New York: Plenum Press.

Deci, E., & Ryan, R. (1987). The support of autonomy and the control of behavior. *Journal of Personality and Social Psychology, 53,* 1024–1037.

Deci, E., & Ryan, R. (1991). A motivational approach to self: Integration in personality. In R. Dienstbier (Ed.), *Nebraska symposium on motivation: Vol 38. Perspectives on motivation* (pp. 237–288). Lincoln: University of Nebraska Press.

Dewar, A., & Horn, T. (1992). A critical analysis of knowledge construction in sport psychology. In T. Horn (Ed.), *Advances in sport psychology* (1st ed., pp. 13–22). Champaign, IL: Human Kinetics.

Duda, J.L. (1988). The relationship between goal perspectives and persistence and intensity among recreational sport participants. *Leisure Sciences, 10,* 95–106.

Duda, J.L. (1992). Motivation in sport settings: A goal perspective approach. In G. Roberts (Ed.), *Motivation in sport and exercise* (pp. 57–92). Champaign, IL: Human Kinetics.

Duda, J.L., & Nicholls, J.G. (1992). Dimensions of achievement motivation in schoolwork and sport. *Journal of Educational Psychology, 84,* 290–299.

Eklund, R. (1994). A season long investigation of competitive cognition in collegiate wrestlers. *Research Quarterly for Exercise and Sport, 65,* 169–183.

Ellis, G., Voelkl, J., & Morris, C. (1994). Measurement and analysis issues with explanation of variance in daily experience using the flow model. *Journal of Leisure Research, 26,* 337–356.

Fahlberg, L.L., & Fahlberg, L.A. (1994). A human science for the study of movement: An integration of multiple ways of knowing. *Research Quarterly for Exercise and Sport, 65,* 100–109.

Feltz, D. (1987). Advancing knowledge in sport psychology: Strategies for expanding our conceptual framework. *Quest, 39,* 243–254.

Forbes, J. (1989). The cognitive psychobiology of performance regulation. *Journal of Sports Medicine and Physical Fitness, 29,* 202–207.

Garfield, C., & Bennett, Z. (1984). *Peak performance.* New York: Warner Books.

Gauvin, L., & Rejeski, W., & Norris (1996). A naturalistic study of the impact of acute physical activity on feeling states and affect in women. *Health Psychology, 15,* 391–397.

Gould, D., Eklund, R., & Jackson, S. (1992). 1988 USA Olympic Wrestling Excellence II: Competitive cognition and affect. *The Sport Psychologist, 6,* 383–402.

Guay, F., & Vallerand, R. (1995, June). *The situational motivational scale.* Paper presented at the Annual Convention of the American Psychological Society, New York.

Hamilton, J. (1976). Attention and intrinsic rewards in the control of psychophysiological states. *Psychotherapy and Psychosomatics, 27,* 54–61.

Hamilton, J.A. (1981). Attention, personality, and self-regulation of mood: Absorbing interest and boredom. In B.A. Maher (Ed.), *Progress in experimental personality research* (Vol. 10, pp. 282–315). New York: Academic Press.

Harter, S. (1982). The perceived competence scale for children. *Child Development, 53,* 87–97.

Hatfield, B., & Landers, D. (1983). Psychophysiology: A new direction for sport psychology. *Journal of Sport Psychology, 5,* 243–259.

Jackson, S.A. (1992). Athletes in flow: A qualitative investigation of flow states in elite figure skaters. *Journal of Applied Sport Psychology, 4,* 161–180.

Jackson, S.A. (1993). Elite athletes in flow: The psychology of optimal experience in sport. (Doctoral Dissertation, University of North Carolina at Greensboro, 1992). *Dissertation Abstracts International, 54,* 124A.

Jackson, S.A. (1995). Factors influencing the occurrence of flow states in elite athletes. *Journal of Applied Sport Psychology, 7,* 135–163.

Jackson, S.A. (1996). Toward a conceptual understanding of the flow experience in elite athletes. *Research Quarterly for Exercise and Sport, 67,* 76–90.

Jackson, S.A. (2000a). Joy, fun, and flow state in sport. In Y. Hanin (Ed.), *Emotions in sport* (pp. 135–156). Champaign, IL: Human Kinetics.

Jackson, S.A. (2000b). The Dispositional Flow Scale-2 and the Flow State Scale-2. In J. Maltby, C.A. Lewis, & A. Hill (Eds.), *Commissioned reviews of 250 psychological tests* (pp. 50–52, 61–63). Lampter, UK: Edwin Mellen.

Jackson, S.A., & Csikszentmihalyi, M. (1999). *Flow in sports: The keys to optimal experiences and performances.* Champaign, IL: Human Kinetics.

Jackson, S.A., & Eklund, R.C. (in press). Assessing flow in physical activity: The Flow State Scale-2 (FSS-2) and Dispositional Flow Scale-2 (DFS-2). *Journal of Sport & Exercise Psychology.*

Jackson, S.A., Kimiecik, J., & Attridge, T. (1998). *Interviews with masters athletes.* Unpublished data.

Jackson, S.A., Kimiecik, J., Ford, S., & Marsh, H.W. (1998). Psychological correlates of flow in sport. *Journal of Sport & Exercise Psychology, 20,* 358–378.

Jackson, S.A., & Marsh, H.W. (1996). Development and validation of a scale to measure optimal experience: The flow state scale. *Journal of Sport & Exercise Psychology, 18,* 17–35.

Jackson, S.A., & Roberts, G.C. (1992). Positive performance states of athletes: Toward a conceptual understanding of peak performance. *The Sport Psychologist, 6,* 156–171.

Jackson, S.A., Thomas, P.R., Marsh, H.W., & Smethurst, C.J. (2001). Relationships between flow, self-concept, psychological skills, and performance. *Journal of Applied Sport Psychology, 13,* 154–178.

Kimiecik, J., & Harris, A. (1996). What is enjoyment? A conceptual/definitional analysis with implications for sport and exercise psychology. *Journal of Sport & Exercise Psychology, 18,* 247–263.

Kimiecik, J., & Stein, G. (1992). Examining flow experiences in sport contexts: Conceptual issues and methodological concerns. *Journal of Applied Sport Psychology, 4,* 144–160.

Kobasa, S. (1979). Stressful life events, personality, and health: An inquiry into hardiness. *Journal of Personality and Social Psychology, 37,* 1–11.

Kowal, J., & Fortier, M. (1999). Motivational determinants of flow: Contributions from self-determination theory. *Journal of Social Psychology, 139,* 355–368.

Lincoln, Y.S., & Guba, E.G. (1985). *Naturalistic inquiry.* Newbury Park, CA: Sage.

Loehr, J. (1982). *Mental toughness for sports: Achieving athletic excellence.* New York: Forum.

Loehr, J. (1986). *Mental toughness training for sports.* Lexington, MA: Stephen Green.

Logan, R.D. (1988). Flow in solitary ordeals. In M. Csikszentmihalyi & I. Csikszentmihalyi (Eds.), *Optimal experience: Psychological studies of flow in consciousness* (pp. 172–180). New York: Cambridge University Press.

Mandigo, J., Thompson, L., & Couture, R. (1998, June). *Equating flow theory with the quality of children's physical activity experiences.* Presented at the annual North American Psychology of Sport and Physical Activity Conference, St. Charles, IL.

Marsh, H.W., Hey, J., Johnson, S., & Perry, C. (1997). Elite Athlete Self Description Questionnaire: Hierarchical confirmatory factor analysis of responses by two distinct groups of elite athletes. *International Journal of Sport Psychology, 28,* 237–258.

Marsh, H.W., & Jackson, S.A. (1999). Flow experience in sport: Construct validation of multidimensional hierarchical state and trait responses. *Structural Equation Modeling, 6,* 343–371.

Martens, R. (1977). *Sport Competition Anxiety Test.* Champaign, IL: Human Kinetics.

Martens, R. (1987). Science, knowledge, and sport psychology. *The Sport Psychologist, 1,* 29–55.

Martens, R., Vealey, R.S., & Burton, D. (1990). *Competitive anxiety in sport.* Champaign, IL: Human Kinetics.

Maslow, A. (1964). *Religion, values, and peak experiences.* New York: Viking Press.

Maslow, A. (1968). *Toward a psychology of being.* New York: Van Nostrand.

McInman, A., & Grove, J. (1991). Peak moments in sport: A literature review. *Quest, 43,* 333–351.

Mitchell, R.G. (1988). Sociological implications of the flow experience. In M. Csikszentmihalyi & I. Csikszentmihalyi (Eds.) *Optimal experience: Psychological studies of flow in consciousness* (pp. 36–59). New York: Cambridge University Press.

Moneta, G., & Csikszentmihalyi, M. (1996). The effect of perceived challenges and skills on the quality of subjective experience. *Journal of Personality, 64,* 275–310.

Nicholls, J. (1984). Achievement motivation: Conceptions of ability, subjective experience, task choice, and performance. *Psychological Review, 91,* 328–346.

Nicholls, J.G. (1992). The general and the specific in the development and expression of achievement motivation. In G. Roberts (Ed.), *Motivation in sport and exercise* (pp. 31–56). Champaign, IL: Human Kinetics.

Orlick, T. (1986). *Psyching for sport.* Champaign, IL: Human Kinetics

Orlick, T. (1990). *In pursuit of excellence.* Champaign, IL: Human Kinetics.

Orlick, T. (1998). *Embracing your potential.* Champaign, IL: Human Kinetics.

Patton, M.Q. (1990). *Qualitative evaluation and research methods* (2nd ed.). Newbury Park, CA: Sage.

Pelletier, L.G., Fortier, M.S., Vallerand, R.J., Tuson, K.M., Briere, N.M., & Blais, M.R. (1995). Toward a new measure of intrinsic motivation, extrinsic motivation, and amotivation in sports: The Sport Motivation Scale (SMS). *Journal of Sport & Exercise Psychology, 17,* 35–53.

Perritt, N. (1999). *Hardiness and optimism as predictors of the frequency of flow athletes experience in sport.* Unpublished master's thesis, Miami University, Oxford, OH.

Petruzzello, S., & Landers, D. (1994). State anxiety reduction and exercise: Does hemispheric activation reflect such changes? *Medicine and Science in Sports and Exercise, 26,* 1028–1035.

Podilchak, W. (1991). Establishing the fun in leisure. *Leisure Sciences, 13,* 123–136.

Privette, G. (1983). Peak experience, peak performance, and flow: A comparative analysis of positive human experiences. *Journal of Personality and Social Psychology, 45,* 1361–1368.

Privette, G., & Bundrick, C.M. (1991). Peak experience, peak performance, and flow. *Journal of Social Behavior and Personality, 6,* 169–188.

Ravizza, K. (1975). A subjective study of the athlete's greatest moment in sport. *Proceedings of the 7th Canadian Psychomotor Learning and Sport Psychology Symposium* (pp. 399–404). Toronto: Coaching Association of Canada.

Ravizza, K. (1977). Peak experiences in sport. *Journal of Humanistic Psychology, 17,* 35–40.

Ravizza, K. (1984). Qualities of the peak-experience in sport. In J. Silva & R. Weinberg (Eds.), *Psychological foundations of sport* (pp. 452–461). Champaign, IL: Human Kinetics.

Ryan, E. (1977). Attribution, intrinsic motivation, and athletics. In L. Gedvilas & M. Kneer (Eds.), *Proceedings of the National Association for Physical Education of College Men National Conference Association for Physical Education of College Women National Conference.* Chicago: University of Illinois at Chicago Circle.

Ryan, E. (1980). Attribution, intrinsic motivation, and athletics: A replication and extension. In C. Nadeau, W. Halliwell, K. Newell, & G. Roberts (Eds.), *Psychology of motor behavior and sport—1979* (pp. 19–26). Champaign, IL: Human Kinetics.

Salazar, W., Landers, D., Petruzello, S., Myungwoo, H., Crews, D., & Kubitz, K. (1990). Hemispheric asymmetry, cardiac response, and performance in elite archers. *Research Quarterly for Exercise and Sport, 61,* 351–359.

Scanlan, T.K., Stein, G.L., & Ravizza, K. (1989). An in-depth study of former elite figure skaters: II. Sources of enjoyment. *Journal of Sport & Exercise Psychology, 11,* 65–83.

Schneider, W., Dumais, S., & Shiffrin, R. (1984). Automatic and control processing and attention. In R. Parasuraman & R. Davies (Eds.), *Varieties of attention* (pp. 1–27). Orlando, FL: Academic Press.

Stein, G., Kimiecik, J., Daniels, J., & Jackson, S.A. (1995). Psychological antecedents of flow in recreational sport. *Personality and Social Psychology Bulletin, 21,* 125–135.

Straub, C. (1996). *Effects of a mental imagery program on psychological skills and perceived flow states of collegiate wrestlers.* Unpublished master's thesis, Miami University, Oxford, OH.

Szabo, C., & Kimiecik, J. (1997, February). *Flow and running.* Paper presented at the Midwest Sport and Exercise Psychology Conference, Ball State University, Muncie, IN.

U.S. Department of Health and Human Services. (1996). *Physical activity and health: A report of the Surgeon General.* Atlanta, GA: U.S. Department of Health and Human Services, Centers for Disease Control and Prevention, National Center for Chronic Disease Prevention and Health Promotion.

Valle, R.S., King, M., & Halling, S. (1989). An introduction to existential-phenomenological thought in psychology. In R.S. Valle & S. Halling (Eds.), *Existential-phenomenological perspectives in psychology* (pp. 3–16). New York: Plenum Press.

Vallerand, R.J. (1997). Toward a hierarchical model of intrinsic and extrinsic motivation. In M. Zanna (Ed.), *Advances in experimental social psychology* (Vol. 29, pp. 271–360). New York: Academic Press.

Wankel, L. (1985). Personal and situational factors affecting exercise involvement: The importance of enjoyment. *Research Quarterly for Exercise and Sport, 56,* 275–282.

Wankel, L. (1997). "Strawpersons," selective reporting, and inconsistent logic: A response to Kimiecik and Harris's analysis of enjoyment. *Journal of Sport & Exercise Psychology, 19,* 98–109.

Wankel, L.M., & Berger, B.G. (1990). The psychological and social benefits of sport and physical activity. *Journal of Leisure Research, 22,* 167–182.

Wankel, L.M., & Kreisel, P.J. (1985). Factors underlying enjoyment of youth sports: Sport and age group comparisons. *Journal of Sport Psychology, 7,* 51–64.

Warner, R. (1987). *Freedom, enjoyment, and happiness.* Ithaca, NY: Cornell University Press.

Wells, A. (1988). Self-esteem and optimal experience. In M. Csikszentmihalyi & I. Csikszentmihalyi (Eds.), *Optimal experience: Psychological studies of flow in consciousness* (pp. 327–341). New York: Cambridge University Press.

Williams, J., & Krane, V. (1998). Psychological characteristics of peak performance. In J. Williams (Ed.), *Applied sport psychology* (3rd ed., pp. 158–170). Mountain View, CA: Mayfield.

CHAPTER 17

Athletic Injury and Sport Behavior

Eileen Udry and Mark B. Andersen

Many individuals in today's society lead sedentary lives. Accordingly, health professionals from a variety of realms spend considerable time and resources attempting—often with limited success—to increase activity levels among sedentary people. Thus, it is somewhat ironic that for another group of individuals, namely athletes, being forced into physical inactivity because of injuries often constitutes a significant form of stress. Although the epidemiological evidence suggests that injury rates tend to vary by the type of sport and level of participation (Uitenbroek, 1996), injuries are endemic to sport. Recognizing that no athlete is immune to injuries, Richard Steadman, a prominent orthopedic surgeon, termed sport injuries "the greatest equalizers" (Steadman, 1993).

Despite the best efforts to prevent injuries, it is unlikely that injuries will be completely eradicated. However, it is of both theoretical and practical interest to ask whether there are ways to reduce the risk of injury by exploiting what is known about the psychological factors associated with injuries. Additionally, once injuries have occurred, it is also of interest to examine ways to ameliorate the stress associated with athletic injuries and

to facilitate recovery and rehabilitation adherence. The purpose of this chapter is to explore these issues. The chapter is organized into four major sections. We begin with a discussion of measurement issues that are germane to understanding the psychological aspects of athletic injuries. This is an important starting point, because the way that injury-related terms have been operationally defined in previous research has varied considerably, and the use of inconsistent definitions has been confusing. Second, we review the literature pertaining to the psychological antecedents, or precursors, to athletic injuries. Third, we examine athletes' responses—both psychological and behavioral—to injuries. In the fourth section we provide directions for future research relative to both the antecedents and responses to injuries.

DEFINITIONAL AND MEASUREMENT ISSUES

What is an athletic injury? And how would one measure injury? These are two extremely basic questions that we need to answer before research can progress. Unfortunately, these questions tend

We are grateful to Diane Wiese-Bjornstal, PhD, for the very thorough review and comments she provided for a draft of this chapter.

to be asked infrequently and are much less satisfactorily answered in the psychologically based injury literature. Athletic injuries have been perfunctorily defined as any injury that results in missed practice or competition or alters participation (e.g., Blackwell & McCullagh, 1990). Athletes, however, become injured from factors other than sport participation. Is it an athletic injury if an athlete slips in the shower and splits his chin open? Is it an athletic injury if a softball player on the way to practice has a bicycle accident and jams her knee? One would hardly consider these athletic injuries, yet these injuries would cause missed or modified practice. When we examined the literature, some studies apparently included any injury that occurred during a certain amount of time (e.g., Hanson, McCullagh, & Tonymon, 1992), whereas others used athletic training reports and identified the situation of injury (e.g., game or practice; Petrie, 1993a). The former study presumably included nonathletic injuries, whereas the latter study did not mention what was done with data from nonathletic injuries.

Would an operational definition of *athletic injury* such as "those injuries occurring only in an athletic context that require missing or modifying practice or competition for one day or more" be valuable and more precise than the various definitions in the literature? We do not believe this definition is particularly helpful. The objective of all the studies on athletic injury, and the ultimate goal of injury research, is improved health and welfare of athletes in and outside of their sports. Thus, instead of looking at "athletic" injury, it seems that we would be better served by examining "athlete" injuries. A more thorough discussion of measurement and definitional issues is provided by Petrie and Falkstein (1998) and Andersen and Williams (1999).

Once an injury has occurred, athletes typically are involved in some type of rehabilitation program. It is frequently of interest to know the degree to which athletes maintain their rehabilitation programs. *Compliance* and *adherence* often are used interchangeably to describe rehabilitation-related behaviors. However, using these terms in this manner also has been a source of confusion. Agris (1989) contended that the term *compliance* should be used when referring to individuals following a regimen prescribed by a health care provider and that this term implies a relatively passive role on the part of the patient. In contrast, the term *adherence* suggests a more equitable role in which individuals participate in establishing the

regimen and determining how various rehabilitation goals will be reached. In general, it is thought that the more complex and long-term the health problem, the more desirable it is to use an adherence rather than compliance approach. Brewer (1998) noted that athletic rehabilitation programs are often relatively complex and may include instructions for restricting physical activity (e.g., workout limitations), completing home exercises, performing cryotherapy, attending physical therapy sessions, and taking the appropriate medications in the proper dosages. Thus, sport injury rehabilitation may encompass a multitude of behaviors and take place in a number of settings (Brewer, 1998). Thus, the term *adherence* as opposed to *compliance* is thought to be more appropriate.

INJURY ANTECEDENTS

Understanding the factors that might predispose athletes to an increased risk of injury has been the focus of considerable research, and injury antecedents have been examined from a variety of perspectives. These include physiological (e.g., body composition), anatomical (e.g., biomechanical factors), and environmental (e.g., training surfaces) perspectives. Although the influence of these factors is not disputed, the scope of this chapter is limited to examining the role psychological factors may play in increasing the risk of injuries among athletes.

Research into the psychosocial antecedents of athletic injury has its roots in the landmark work of Holmes and Rahe (1967). Their work on the relationship between major life events stress and illness outcome sparked a revolution in behavioral medicine. They found that individuals who had experienced many major life events (e.g., death of a loved one, divorce, moving to a new place) over the previous year were much more likely to fall ill in the near future than those who experienced lower levels of life events stress. They believed the stress of adjusting to major life events left one more susceptible to disease. In support of Holmes and Rahe, there is now overwhelming evidence to show that stress has negative effects on immune system function (O'Leary, 1990).

In 1970, Holmes used the Social and Readjustment Rating Scale (Holmes & Rahe, 1967) as a predictor, not of illness, but of American football injuries. Holmes found that football players who had experienced many major life events were more likely to incur an athletic injury than those who had experienced few life events. Later, Bramwell, Masuda, Wagner, and Holmes (1975) modified the Social and Readjustment Rating Scale to fit American university athletes. Using the Social and Athletic Readjustment Rating Scale, they found similar results among football players, as the high life events group appeared to experience the most injuries. Cryan and Alles (1983), using the Social and Athletic Readjustment Rating Scale, replicated the findings of Bramwell et al. (1975) with another university football team.

Sarason, Johnson, and Siegel (1978) refined the measurement of life events by distinguishing between negative events and positive ones. Their Life Experiences Survey was modified by Passer and Seese (1983) for an athletic population, and they found that positive life events were not linked to football injury, but negative life events were. Again, football players with more negative life events stress were more likely to be injured. Passer and Seese were also the first researchers to test for the influence of personality moderator variables (e.g., locus of control) on the effects of life events stress on injury outcome. They did not, however, find any significant connections between personality variables and likelihood of injury.

The available research suggests that the association between life events stress and sport injuries appears quite robust. In a comprehensive review of the research literature, Williams and Roepke (1993) examined 20 studies (Blackwell & McCullagh, 1990; Bramwell et al., 1975; Coddington & Troxell, 1980; Cryan & Alles, 1983; Hanson et al., 1992; Hardy, O'Connor, & Geisler, 1990; Hardy, Prentice, Kirsanoff, Richman, & Rosenfeld, 1987; Hardy, Richman, & Rosenfeld, 1991; Hardy & Riehl, 1988; Holmes, 1970; Kerr & Minden, 1988; Lysens, Vanden Auweele, & Ostyn, 1986; J.R. May, Veach, Reed, & Griffey, 1985; J.R. May, Veach, Southard, & Herring, 1985; Passer & Seese, 1983; Petrie, 1992; R.E. Smith, Ptacek, & Smoll, 1992; R.E. Smith, Smoll, & Ptacek, 1990) and found that there were significant positive associations between life events, stress, and athlete injuries in 18 of the studies. More recently, Williams and Andersen (1998) reported that of the 10 athletic injury and life events stress studies conducted since the Williams and Roepke review, 9 found similar associations (Andersen & Williams, 1999; Byrd, 1993; Fawkner, 1995; Kolt & Kirkby, 1996; Meyer, 1995; Perna & McDowell, 1993; Petrie, 1993a, 1993b; Thompson & Morris, 1994). Given that life events stress and injury relationships occurred across many differ-

ent sports and came from studies that measured the variables in a variety of ways, these consistent results are convincing. However, the relationship between life events stress and sport injuries is complex, because at least one study (Petrie, 1993b) showed that even positive life events can be related to injury.

As noted previously, the early studies (e.g., Bramwell et al., 1975; Holmes, 1970) testing the relationship between psychosocial variables and athletic injury produced findings that paralleled those from the field of psychoneuroimmunology, whereby an increased risk of life events stress was associated with an increased risk of illness or injury. One difference, however, was that in the area of psychoneuroimmunology, the immune system was clearly identified as the mediating link between life events stress and an increased risk of illness. The connections between athletic injuries and life events did not have the same clear evidence of association between life events stress and immune system suppression; thus, a sport-specific model for injury antecedents was needed. A comprehensive theoretical framework for the relationship between stress and athletic injury, along with proposed mechanisms behind that relationship, appeared in the literature in 1988 (Andersen & Williams, 1988). We now turn to a more complete description of this model and the related research.

A Stress-Based Model of Athletic Injury

By examining the stress–injury (see previously cited references), stress–accident, and stress–illness literatures (e.g., Stuart & Brown, 1981), Andersen and Williams (1988) developed a model that proposed possible factors and underlying mechanisms for the relationship between stress and athletic injury. The proposed model is the most comprehensive and influential model concerning antecedents to athletic injury that has been developed, and for this reason we limit our discussion to this framework. More specifically, this model includes three broad categories of psychosocial factors (personality, history of stressors, and coping resources) along with two major categories of interventions aimed at reducing injury risk through addressing either the cognitive appraisal or the physiological/attentional aspects of the stress response. In 1998, Williams and Andersen reviewed the evidence for the model's viability and made some minor revisions in the model's structure. Figure 17.1 represents a schematic of the model in its updated form. In the following

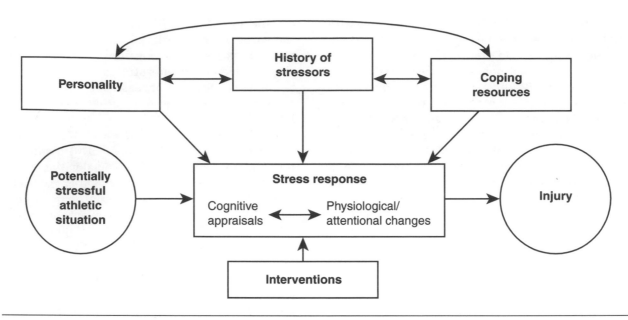

Figure 17.1   Williams and Andersen's (1998) model of injury antecedents.

Copyright 1998. From "Psychological antecedents of sport injury: Review and critique of the stress-injury model" by J. Williams and M. Andersen. Reproduced by permission of Taylor & Francis, Inc., **www.routledge-ny.com**.

sections, we discuss the component parts of the model and their links with each other.

The Stress Response

The core of the model of stress and athletic injury is the stress response. The model suggests that when athletes confront potentially stressful athletic situations, they will make cognitive appraisals of the demands of the situation, their abilities to meet the demands, and the consequences of meeting (or not meeting) these demands. If athletes perceive that the demands of the situations are greater than their resources and that the consequences of failing to meet the demands are dire (e.g., being cut from the team), then their stress responses, and the accompanying physiological and attentional disruptions, may be substantial. Many physiological responses occur during stress (e.g., sympathetic nervous system activation), but one response that is most likely to influence injury outcome is peripheral narrowing, such as not detecting important peripheral visual (or auditory) cues that would alert one to being in harm's way (e.g., a tackler coming in from the side in football).

Most of the research involving stress responsivity and perceptual/attentional changes has been laboratory based. Williams, Tonymon, and Andersen (1990, 1991) found that individuals who had recently experienced substantial life events stress and daily hassles exhibited greater

peripheral narrowing during laboratory stress than did participants with opposite profiles, suggesting that those with more stressors in their lives have greater stress responses. Williams and Andersen (1997) also found that individuals with greater life events stress had more perceptual deficits in the central field of vision (greater distractibility). Additionally, they found that males with high life events stress, low coping resources, and low social support had the lowest perceptual sensitivity. Most recently, Andersen and Williams (1999) examined athletes' stress responses in the laboratory and then linked these responses to injuries recorded over the competitive season. The researchers found that peripheral narrowing during laboratory stress and major negative life events together accounted for 26% of subsequent injury incidence variance for athletes low in social support. Thus, the connection between life events, perceptual deficits, social support, and injury outcome was finally demonstrated.

The most recent laboratory research on life events stress and perceptual deficits during stress has produced some interesting results. Bum, Morris, and Andersen (1996) attempted to make laboratory conditions more ecologically valid by adding physiological and auditory stress to perceptual detection tasks. They found that as stress increased (noise only, physical activity only, noise and physical activity together), perceptual deficits also increased, and the deficits increased more for those with high negative life events. Even more interesting, Bum, Morris, and Andersen (1998) found that a simple program of relaxation (autogenic training) for an experimental group resulted in better peripheral detection and response to central vision targets than a control group. These results suggest that simple interventions may help reduce stress responsivity and thus, possibly, injury risk.

Generalized muscle tension during stress is another obvious response that may predispose athletes to injury. Generalized muscle tension is thought to lead to stiff movements, awkward landings, and increased fatigue, especially in prolonged performance (e.g., a soccer match). Performing with antagonistic and agonistic muscles fighting each other can easily lead to a variety of musculoskeletal strains and sprains. Only one study (Andersen, 1989) examined muscle tension (i.e., via EMG) and stress under laboratory conditions, but it did not find a significant connection between life events stress and generalized muscle tension. EMG data, however, are notoriously labile as a variable, warranting further research in this area.

The laboratory research described in this section strongly suggests why people with high stress and low buffering factors have greater perceptual deficits during stress. Furthermore, Andersen and Williams (1999) established the connections between life events stress in laboratory situations, perceptual changes during stress, and subsequent injury in actual athletic contexts. Bum et al. (1996, 1998) attempted to make laboratory conditions closer to real competitive conditions, but the stress of competition is difficult to replicate. The work of Bum et al., however, needs to be expanded to include season-long injury data on athletes tested under laboratory conditions. In the future, with telemetry technology, researchers may be able to examine stress responsivity (but probably not perceptual deficits) and athletic injury as they occur in the field. Such research may provide more real-life information on the usefulness of the stress–injury model.

History of Stressors

In the previous section we discussed the center of figure 17.1—the stress response. We now discuss the history of stressors, which is shown at the top middle portion of figure 17.1. The category of history of stressors includes three factors: life events stress, daily hassles, and previous injuries. The role of major life events stress and athletic injury was discussed extensively in the previous

section. Kanner, Coyne, Schaefer, and Lazarus (1981) originally suggested that major life events may cause stress and disrupt lives because such events increase minor problems and hassles. For example, the death of a spouse may result in a wide range of demands being placed on the survivor (e.g., paying bills, transportation, settling an estate) that may be relatively minor but are chronic hassles. These chronic stressors may exert daily wear and tear on an individual.

Several research studies have examined the hypothesized connection between daily hassles and athletic injuries. Research into daily hassles and athletic injury, except for one study, has not produced a solid connection (e.g., Blackwell & McCullagh, 1990; Hanson et al., 1992; Meyer, 1995; R.E. Smith et al., 1990). The problem with the previous studies, however, is that daily hassles were measured at only one time or over monthly periods (e.g., Byrd, 1993; Meyer, 1995). Daily hassles are dynamic and need to be measured more frequently over the course of an athletic season. For university athletes, for example, one would expect an increase in hassles before each major competition and during both the end-of-season playoffs and the end-of-semester final exams. Measuring daily hassles only once, or monthly, over the course of an injury study seems to miss the point of examining this variable.

The value of measuring the construct of daily hassles more frequently was demonstrated in a study conducted by Fawkner, McMurray, and Summers (1999). In this work, Fawkner et al. measured hassles every week during athletes' competitive seasons. They found a dramatic increase in hassles the week before, and the week of, athletic injuries. These results provide a strong rationale for the continued examination of this stress variable in athletic injury research. However, Bringer and Udry (1998) did not find a connection with biweekly measures of daily hassles and injury outcome. Thus, the role of daily hassles in injury research is still not firmly established.

In the model of stress and athletic injury (Andersen & Williams, 1988), previous injury was included as the "history of stressors." This variable has not been examined extensively, but Lysens et al. (1984) found that if physical education students had a history of injury, then they also had a greater likelihood of a future injury. Increased likelihood of injury because of previous injury may stem from returning to full physical activity while not being completely recovered physically or returning to physical activity but not being psychologically ready. For example, athletes may be physically recovered but may still have anxieties about returning to activities and possible reinjury. Those anxieties may lead to a substantial stress response and, thus, may set athletes up for reinjury. Thus, researchers may wish to examine previous injury and the related variable of psychological readiness to return to full activity as predictors of future injury, because these variables may have substantial relationships to who becomes injured again.

Personality

The personality section of figure 17.1 (upper left) has received considerably less attention from researchers than the history of stressors. Andersen and Williams (1988, 1993) hypothesized that the presence of certain personality traits, such as hardiness, would predispose athletes to view athletic situations as less threatening and more challenging, resulting in a lower stress response and, thus, lower injury risk. Other traits, such as competitive anxiety, would be hypothesized to predispose athletes to exhibit more pronounced stress responses in competitive situations and, consequently, injury risk would be greater. Research into personality and athletic injury has produced mixed results. Some studies have shown relationships between self-concept, locus of control, or trait anxiety and injury (e.g., Kolt & Kirkby, 1996; Pargman & Lunt, 1989), whereas others have shown no relationship between these variables (Hanson et al., 1992; Kerr & Minden, 1988; McLeod & Kirkby, 1995).

Although Andersen and Williams (1988) did not propose Type A personality as a predisposing factor for athletic injuries, research by K.B. Fields, Delaney, and Hinkle (1990) indicated that runners who scored higher on a Type A personality scale were more likely to become injured. Recently, the personality trait and personality-related variables of sensation seeking, positive states of mind, and mood states have emerged as predictors of injury outcome. R.E. Smith et al. (1992), in a study of 425 male and female high school athletes from a variety of teams, found a positive relationship between sport-related stressors and injury time-loss only for athletes who tested low on the personality variable of sensation seeking. A secondary hypothesis, that high sensation seekers would incur more injuries because of greater risk-taking behavior, was not supported.

Positive states of mind, the ability to experience positive states such as maintaining focus, sharing with others, and staying relaxed, are also related to injury risk. Williams et al. (1993) showed that athletes who were able to experience more positive states of mind were less likely to become injured. Fawkner (1995) measured the mood states of athletes weekly over the course of a season with the Profile of Mood States (McNair, Lorr, & Droppelman, 1971) and found that as mood shifted negatively, the likelihood of injury increased. Meyer (1995) examined the personality traits of perfectionism and denial and found that athletes high in both personality variables also had the strongest relationships to negative life events and injury. The athletes in the Meyer study were long-distance runners, and many of their injuries were chronic. As Williams and Andersen (1998) suggested, overuse or chronic injuries may be influenced by personality variables, such as perfectionism, and may not necessarily be the product of an acute stress response. The studies mentioned here are provocative and suggest that personality and personality-related variables need more attention in psychosocial factors and athletic injury research.

As mentioned previously, the personality–injury research is a mixed bag. The equivocality of the personality results likely stems from measurement and methodological problems (e.g., sport vs. general measures of personality, issues of statistical power, and definitions and measurements of injury). Because of space limitations, the complex problems of personality and injury research are not discussed in detail here. The interested reader is referred to Williams and Andersen (1998) for an overview of the difficulties of personality, sport, and injury research and to Vealey's chapter on personality in this volume.

Coping Resources

The third set of factors in the Williams and Andersen (1998) model that is proposed to have an effect on athletic injury is coping resources. This category, shown in the upper right portion of figure 17.1, includes such resources as general coping skills and strategies, stress management, and social support. Several studies have supported the link between general coping and athletic injuries. Specifically, in the Williams, Tonymon, and Wadsworth (1986) study with volleyball players, coping resources were the only significant predictor of athletic injury, with those low in coping resources having more injuries. Hanson et al. (1992) also found that coping resources were the best discriminator for both severity and number of injuries.

Athletes who have a high amount of social support may not be injured as often as those with a low amount of support.

The research on the influence of social support on athletic injuries has not provided clear results. Some studies have shown a direct effect of social support on injury, with athletes who were low in social support exhibiting more injuries (e.g., Byrd, 1993; Hardy et al., 1987, 1990). Other studies have found that the relationship between social support and injury may occur only in extreme groups (Andersen & Williams, 1999; Petrie, 1992; R.E. Smith et al., 1990). Smith et al., for example, found a strong relationship between negative life events and injury outcome only for athletes who had both low social support and low coping resources. Hence, Smith et al. showed that the relationship between life events and injury is not simple. One of the goals of athletic injury research is to identify those at risk, and Smith et al. suggested that not only those with many major life events are vulnerable. Rather, this work suggests that athletes who are also low in psychosocial variables that operate in conjunction (i.e., low social support and low coping resources) are at risk. These findings should be carefully considered in any research on antecedent psychosocial factors and athletic injury.

In their stress-based models of athletic injury, Andersen and Williams (1988) and Williams and Andersen (1998) suggested that social support could have either a direct effect on stress responsivity and, thus, injury outcome or an indirect (buffering) effect by serving as a moderator of the history of stressors. These two paths of influence reflect current models of social support in the general health literature (Cohen & Wills, 1985). More support for the buffering model has appeared in the athletic injury research. Along with R.E. Smith et al. (1990), Petrie (1992) found a relationship between life stress and injury only for gymnasts who were low in social support. It appeared that for gymnasts with high life stress but also high social support, the social support buffered the negative effects of life stress. In a later study, Petrie (1993a) supported his 1992 findings but also found something not predicted. Starters on teams under conditions of low stress and high social support were more likely to be injured than those with low levels of support. Petric suggested that under low levels of stress and high social support, greater risk-taking behaviors may occur, placing athletes at higher risk of injury. Similarly, Hardy et al. (1991) also found some unexpected results. For example, high levels of social support among male athletes with object losses or high positive life events were associated with negative well-being.

To summarize, the influence of social support in particular, and coping more generally, is an important facet of understanding athletic injury outcomes. The relationship of social support to injury outcome, however, has produced some unexpected findings. One reason that the link between social support and injuries has been associated with unexpected findings may be related to the multidimensional nature of social support. That is, different types of social support (e.g., emotional challenge vs. listening support) may have differential relationships to injury risk.

Intervention/Prevention Research

The final component of the Williams and Andersen (1998) model, shown in the bottom portion of figure 17.1, focuses on intervention, or prevention, research as it relates to athletic injuries. Unfortunately, only a limited number of studies have examined the effectiveness of injury prevention intervention efforts. DeWitt (1980) noted anecdotally that the basketball players in her study complained less about minor injuries after some cognitive and biofeedback training, but no injury data were actually gathered.

Three more recent empirically based studies examined the effectiveness of interventions on reducing the incidence of athletic injury. Davis (1991) introduced swimmers and football players to a relaxation intervention and found 52% and 33% reductions, respectively, in injury over the previous year. Using a more rigorous design, Kerr and Goss (1996) offered a 16-session stress management program to gymnasts (delivered over eight months). The program was essentially Meichenbaum's (1985) stress inoculation training (SIT). Although the injury incidence reduction indexes for the control group and the experimental group receiving the training were not statistically significantly different from each other, there was an apparent reduction in injury (the effect size, Cohen's *d*, was .67, which was in the medium to large range). Andersen and Stoové (1998) suggested that Kerr and Goss's nonsignificant findings were more a problem of power and Type II error and that, given the effect size, there was substantial evidence that the stress management program was effective in reducing injury incidence. More powerful studies need to be conducted. More recently, Perna, Antoni, and Schneiderman (1998) found that a 4-week cognitive behavioral stress management intervention was effective in reduced injury and illness among collegiate rowers. See Durso-Cupal (1998) for further suggestions on psychosocial interventions for athletic injury reduction.

Conclusions Regarding Psychological Antecedents to Injury

There appears to be substantial overall support for the current version of the Williams and Andersen (1998) model of stress and athletic injury. In regard to the personality category, the variables in the personality section of the model were originally posited as "educated guesses." Some of those variables (e.g., hardiness, achievement motivation) have not yet been tested. Other variables, such as positive states of mind (Williams, Hogan, & Andersen, 1993) and mood (Fawkner, 1995), which are related to personality, have shown associations to injury outcome. It is clear, however, that the personality section of the model is the least explored facet of the model and needs further examination.

In their revision of the model, Williams and Andersen (1998) suggested that bidirectional arrows be placed between personality and history of stressors, personality and coping resources, and coping resources and history of stressors. These arrows would indicate that these three categories of variables interact with one another to influence athletes' stress responses and ultimately, their susceptibility to athletic injury. For example, the ability to experience positive states of mind may help an athlete cope better with major life events stress and daily hassles and be less vulnerable to athletic injury. Also, major life events stress may profoundly affect personality. Posttraumatic stress disorder (American Psychiatric Association, 1994) is an obvious example, and changes in personality after trauma often are observed (e.g., Kishi, Robinson, & Forrester, 1994). Traumatic events can also influence coping, such as having a loved one with cancer (e.g., Compas, Worsham, Ey, & Howell, 1996).

In the original version of their model, Andersen and Williams (1988) included self-prescribed medication as a variable within the coping resources category. In their revised work, Williams and Andersen (1998) proposed removing this variable because the ability to measure it is severely limited by the clandestine nature of some of the self-medications and the illegality of some drug use in sport.

In the stress response section, Williams and Andersen suggested that perceptual changes in audition during stress also be investigated. Landers, Wang, and Courtet (1985) found peripheral auditory narrowing in high stress conditions. Athletes who do not hear well or who are slow to respond to auditory cues, especially of danger approaching, may be at greater risk of injury. Thus, the examination of perceptual changes during stress should be expanded to include audition. Finally, Williams and Andersen suggested that the model was probably most appropriate for acute injury etiology with its emphasis on acute stress responsivity. Chronic or overuse injuries probably occur through pathways other than an acute stress response (cf. Meyer, 1995).

The past decade has produced considerable support for the Andersen and Williams (1988) model. The recent review of the athletic injury literature and the revision of the model (Williams & Andersen, 1998) suggest that the framework postulated is a solid one. Nevertheless, several aspects of the model need further testing. For example, research on the stress response and mechanisms behind injury vulnerability is needed. Under coping resources, the social support of athletes is still a construct without adequate measurement, and more comprehensive model testing through methods such as structural equation modeling have yet to be seriously undertaken. Finally, although the Andersen and Williams model has been the dominant framework used by researchers to examine antecedents to injuries, there may be alternative, viable explanations.

INJURY RESPONSES

The previous section summarized the current literature relating to antecedents of athletic injuries and intervention strategies to reduce injury risk. As noted earlier, however, it is likely that injuries will continue to occur despite our best efforts at prevention. The descriptive literature relative to injuries among athletes contains a number of interesting findings. First, perhaps not surprisingly, it has been documented repeatedly that injuries are a significant form of stress for athletes (Brewer & Petrie, 1995; Gould, Jackson, & Finch, 1993; Roh, Newcomer, Perna, & Etzel, 1998; Udry, 1997; Udry, Gould, Bridges, & Beck, 1997; Udry, Gould, Bridges, & Tuffey, 1997). For instance, injured athletes reported more depressed mood than their injured counterparts at 1-week postinjury, although there were no differences in mood between these two groups at 1-month follow-up (Roh et al., 1998). Interestingly, qualitative interviews with injured athletes have revealed that the psychological and interpersonal sources of stress tend to be more salient to an athlete than are the physical and/or medical concerns stemming from injuries (Gould, Udry, Bridges, & Beck, 1997).

Second, although psychological distress among athletes after injuries is relatively common, it appears that a subset of athletes, usually estimated at 5% to 19%, report psychological distress levels comparable to those seen among individuals seeking mental health treatment (Brewer, Linder, & Phelps, 1995; Brewer, Petitpas, Van Raalte, Sklar, & Ditmar, 1995; Leddy, Lambert, & Ogles, 1994). The rates at which injured athletes tend to experience high levels of psychological distress after injuries appear to be comparable to those found among patients who have been hospitalized for acute myocardial infarction (C.B. Taylor, Miller, Smith, & DeBusk, 1997).

Finally, research has demonstrated that those who play an important role in athletes' rehabilitation (e.g., sports medicine providers) often do not share athletes' perceptions regarding the severity of injuries or the amount of psychological distress injured athletes typically experience (Brewer, Linder, & Phelps, 1995; Brewer, Petitpas, et al., 1995; Crossman & Jamieson, 1985). These findings are especially interesting in light of recent research suggesting that negative emotional responses to injury can be moderated by social support. Green and Weinberg (2001) found that athletes who were more satisfied with their social support networks displayed less mood disturbances after an injury than those who were less satisfied with their social support.

It is clear that researchers and practitioners need to understand athletic injuries not only from a physical (medical) viewpoint but also from a psychological perspective. To this end, the remainder of this chapter focuses on the psychological and behavioral responses associated with athlete injuries. We start by discussing the psychological responses (e.g., cognitive and emotional) to injuries. We then examine the behavioral responses related to injuries among athletes, namely the relationship between psychological processes and rehabilitation behaviors.

Psychological Responses to Injuries

Understanding the complex and often bewildering nature of responses to a loss of health among physically active individuals has proven to be a challenge for researchers. In the main, two types of theoretical perspectives have been used to understand and conceptually organize injured athletes' psychological (cognitive and emotional) responses to injuries. These theoretical models include stage models and cognitive appraisal models, both of which are discussed in the following sections.

Stage Models

Although a variety of stage models (sometimes referred to as phase or grief models) have been forwarded (see Evans & Hardy, 1995, for a review), a conceptual similarity across various stage models is the assumption that when athletes become injured, they experience a somewhat predictable sequence of psychological responses. Most notably, Kübler-Ross (1969) developed a stage model based on her clinical experiences with terminally ill patients; this model subsequently has been adapted and applied to the area of sport injury response (e.g., Lynch, 1988). Specifically,

Kübler-Ross suggested that when faced with a loss of health, individuals experience the following reactions: denial, anger, bargaining, depression, and acceptance. Although some have interpreted these stages as highly sequential and invariant, Kübler-Ross herself indicated that individuals may skip stages as well as pass through stages more than once (Evans & Hardy, 1995).

Some researchers and theorists (e.g., Morrey, Stuart, Smith, & Wiese-Bjornstal, 1999; Rose & Jevne, 1993; A. Smith, 1996) have argued that there may be significant differences in the experiences of terminally ill patients and injured athletes and have questioned the validity of the Kübler-Ross model for athletic injury. Accordingly, McDonald and Hardy (1990) and Heil (1993) posited stage models that were generated from work with injured athletes. McDonald and Hardy's model, the most parsimonious, suggests a two-stage model of recovery that includes reactive and adaptive phases. Heil's (1993) affective cycle model suggests that athletes' injury recovery includes three processes: distress (shock, anger, bargaining, anxiety, depression, isolation, guilt, humiliation, helplessness); denial (viewed as both an ordinary process of selective attention and a more clinical defense mechanism); and determined coping (varying degrees of acceptance of the injury and its influence on short- and long-term goals). Interestingly, Heil referred to his model as being one of "cycles" or "phases" rather than "stages" to account for the possibility that individuals may regress between phases based on the progress in rehabilitation and other factors. A shared feature of this model and other stage approaches, however, is its emphasis on the general tendency toward adaptation as rehabilitation proceeds (Evans & Hardy, 1995).

To summarize, numerous stage models have been proposed to explain injured athletes' responses to injury. These models differ relative to the number of stages that an injured athlete might be expected to experience and the specific stages that might occur. When stage models are tested, various components of the model can be scrutinized (Evans & Hardy, 1995). First, researchers can test the sequence of reactions; for example, does anger typically follow denial, as suggested by the Kübler-Ross (1969) model? Alternatively, researchers can test the range of emotional, cognitive, and behavioral responses; for example, does a model that has two dimensions adequately capture the range of injured athletes' experiences?

Udry and colleagues (1997) have examined the range of emotions and cognitive responses reported by athletes who experienced season-ending injuries. The qualitative approach used in their study allowed participants to describe their psychological reactions to their injuries in their own words (i.e., free from the constraints imposed by existing models of injury response). The authors then compared the injured athletes' responses to three existing stage models of recovery, namely, the models of Kübler-Ross (1969), McDonald and Hardy (1990), and Heil (1993). Although retrospective interviews were used, injured athletes reported relatively few instances of denial—a psychological process encompassed by both Kübler-Ross's and Heil's models. This finding is consistent with research in health psychology by Carver et al. (1993), who found that denial was used relatively infrequently among a sample of cancer patients. However, the construct of denial has proved to be both controversial and elusive for a variety of reasons. First, denial may not be a psychological process that is readily measurable through typical self-report instruments. Second, researchers and theorists have not always used uniform definitions of the construct and have disagreed over whether denial is an adaptive or maladaptive process. Finally, certain behaviors (e.g., continuing to compete when injured) may labeled as "denial" by others but may result from athletes' lack of understanding about their injuries (Wiese-Bjornstal, Smith, & LaMott, 1995) or their ability to generally tolerate higher levels of pain than nonathletes (Jaremko, Silbert, & Mann, 1981). The construct of denial as it relates to stage models warrants continued refinement and exploration, but it is possible that denial plays a limited role in most athletes' responses to injury.

As part of a larger quantitative investigation examining the emotional impact of injuries, Pearson and Jones (1992) also conducted retrospective qualitative interviews with injured athletes. Although the interviews were conducted with a limited number of athletes ($N = 6$) and the severity of the injuries was not specified, there was a tendency for the athletes to vacillate between emotional highs and lows. This oscillation of responses has been interpreted as characteristic of support for stage or phase approaches (Evans & Hardy, 1995), in that it speaks to the dynamic nature of emotional responses following injuries.

One criticism of stage models is that there is some assumption that the stages are discrete. For example, the Kübler-Ross model would predict that the third stage of the process would be distinguished by bargaining and would precede the fourth stage, which would be characterized by depression. Some evidence, however, suggests that athletes' mood responses to injuries may not be as specific or discrete as is implied by stage models (e.g., injured athletes may have both more anger and depressed mood at the same time). Specifically, A. Smith, Scott, O'Fallon, and Young (1990) and McDonald and Hardy (1990) found that the subscales of the mood disturbance inventories used tended to be highly intercorrelated (i.e., mood disturbances tend to be more global in nature). It is tempting to conclude from these findings that there is little evidence that the stages are discrete. It also may be possible that the assessment tools used to measure mood states are not sensitive enough to detect changes or that assessments need to be taken more frequently to pick up subtle changes in athletes' emotional states (Evans & Hardy, 1995).

It is difficult to make firm conclusions regarding the utility of stage models because they have not been adequately tested and a variety of measurement issues may need to be addressed before these models can be subjected to scientific scrutiny. As Evans and Hardy (1995) noted, "In general, contemporary theorists have spent more time and effort criticizing and inconsistently conceptualizing classical approaches to grief (in particular stage approaches) than in proposing models of grief that can be empirically tested and verified" (p. 233). Thus, continued exploration of the viability of stage models is warranted.

Cognitive Appraisal Models

Some researchers and theorists who study sport injury response have examined psychological responses to injuries from what have been termed *cognitive appraisal* or *stress and coping* perspectives. Similar to stage models, a variety of cognitive appraisal models have been forwarded in the literature (e.g., Brewer, 1994; Grove, 1993; Udry, 1997; Weiss & Troxel, 1986; Wiese-Bjornstal, Smith, Shaffer, & Morrey, 1998). Most of these models are rooted in the stress and coping literature of general psychology (Cohen & Wills, 1985; Lazarus & Folkman, 1984). Space limitations preclude a detailed discussion of each model in this chapter. Wiese-Bjornstal and colleagues are responsible for the most enduring line of theory development and model construction related to the application of cognitive appraisal models among injured athletes

(Wiese-Bjornstal & Smith, 1993; Wiese-Bjornstal et al., 1995, 1998). For this reason, the most recent cognitive appraisal model of Wiese-Bjornstal and colleagues (1998) will serve as the basis for this discussion (see figure 17.2).

Several aspects of figure 17.2 bear mentioning. First, one can observe similarities between figure 17.2, which focuses on postinjury factors, and figure 17.1, which focuses on athletic injury antecedents. Indeed, Wiese-Bjornstal and colleagues (1993) indicated that their model was developed as an extension of the Andersen and Williams (1988) antecedents to injury model. Specifically, Wiese-Bjornstal and colleagues thought that the factors which might predispose athletes to an increased risk of injury (e.g., low coping resources, personality dispositions) also might play a role in postinjury adjustment.

In addition, as shown in figure 17.2, Wiese-Bjornstal and colleagues (1998) suggested that a variety of personal (e.g., personality, injury severity) and situational factors (e.g., time of season, accessibility to rehabilitation, sport ethic) influence the way injured athletes cognitively appraise their injuries (e.g., threatening vs. nonthreatening). In turn, how athletes cognitively appraise their injuries appears to influence their emotional (e.g., anger vs. positive outlook) and behavioral responses (e.g., rehabilitation adherence). The potential behavioral responses to injuries as predicted by cognitive appraisal models are discussed later in this chapter. For now we wish only to point out that the model encompasses cognitive, emotional, and behavioral responses. Finally, injured athletes' cognitive, emotional, and behavioral responses may, in turn, have implications for both psychological and physical recovery outcomes.

Another aspect of the model shown in figure 17.2 that is worth noting is that it is recursive. That is, the model captures the dynamic nature of injury responses and rehabilitation. For instance, if an athlete experiences a setback in rehabilitation (e.g., reinjures a previously repaired knee), the individual may cognitively reappraise the injury in terms of its severity and consequences. Historically, cognitive appraisal models tended not to include this dynamic component (e.g., Brewer, 1994), and this was one of the ways in which cognitive appraisal models were thought to be distinct from stage approaches. The recent work of Wiese-Bjornstal and colleagues (1998) provides a more comprehensive model that allows stage and cognitive appraisal models to be viewed as complementary rather than competing approaches.

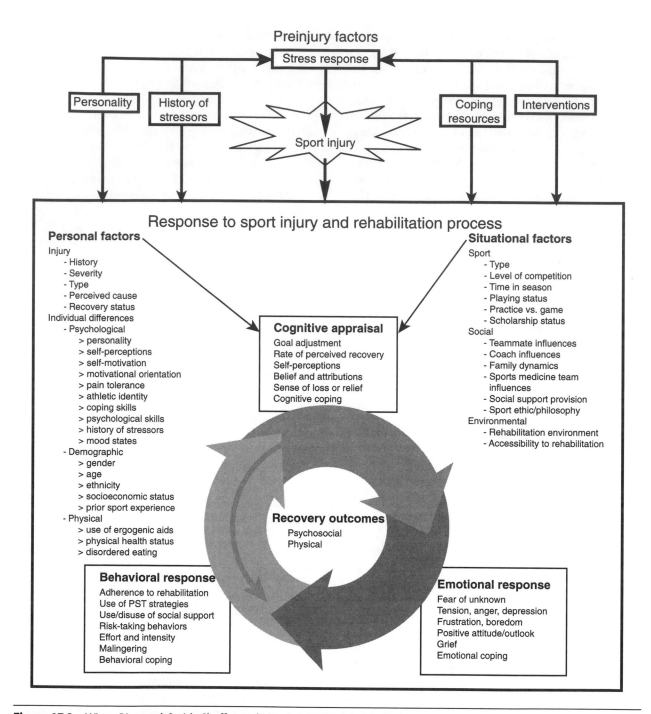

Preinjury factors

Figure 17.2   Wiese-Bjornstal, Smith, Shaffer, and Morrey's (1998) model of injury response.

Copyright 1998. From "An integrated model of response to sport injury: Psychological and sociological" by D. Weise-Bjornstal and A. Smith et al. Reproduced by permission of Taylor & Francis, Inc., **www.routledge-ny.com**.

The conceptual framework presented by Wiese-Bjornstal and colleagues (1998) is important for a variety of reasons. First, compared with the traditional stages approaches, it has been subjected to more extensive empirical testing. (For a thorough review, see Wiese-Bjornstal et al., 1995, 1998.) Second, it is a sport-specific model that attempts to account for the distinct contextual factors that are associated with injuries in the athletic realm. For instance, in their most recent work, Wiese-Bjornstal and colleagues (1998) reviewed research examining how the social networks and norms of certain sports may increase the likelihood that athletes will continue to practice and compete when injured (e.g., Nixon, 1992; 1993). Given that the literature contains numerous appeals for sport psychology researchers and practitioners to consider the social context of sport-related phenomena (Brustad & Ritter-Taylor, 1997; Dewar & Horn, 1992), this recent addition to the Wiese-Bjornstal model is both timely and meaningful.

Intervention Research

A consistent, although not uniform, finding in the psychologically based injury literature is that, after an injury, athletes will experience some form of psychological distress (Brewer, Petitpas, Van Raalte, Sklar, & Ditmar, 1995; Udry, 1997). Given that some psychological distress after injuries is relatively common, the question then becomes whether there are ways to ameliorate distress by using theoretically based interventions. Although the number of interventions is limited, the available evidence from the few investigations that have been conducted is encouraging (Durso-Cupal, 1998). Specifically, Ross and Berger (1996) examined whether Meichenbaum's (1985) SIT program was successful in reducing postsurgery distress among injured athletes. Related health psychology research with SIT has demonstrated its usefulness with burn patients (Wernick, Jaremko, & Taylor, 1981), presurgical patients (Wells, Howard, Nowlin, & Vargas, 1986), and athletes coping with exertional pain (Whitmarsh & Alderman, 1993) as well as with reducing the risk of injuries among athletes (Kerr & Goss, 1996). Consistent with the previous research demonstrating the efficacy of SIT, Ross and Berger found that injured athletes who received the SIT intervention experienced lower levels of postsurgical anxiety and pain and took fewer days to recover knee strength. Cupal and Brewer (2001) also examined the effectiveness of intervention efforts targeting injured athletes recovering from knee surgery. The intervention they used was multifaceted but included imagery and relaxation training. The researchers found that injured athletes who received the intervention reported less reinjury anxiety, greater control over their recovery, and a faster return to their desired levels of physical activities.

Although the use of postinjury interventions seems warranted given the current state of literature, several caveats are in order. In the general health psychology literature, several large-scale randomized intervention studies, using both group and home-based interventions, have attempted to reduce anxiety and depression among cardiac patients (Oldridge, Streiner, Hoffman, & Guyatt, 1995; C.B. Taylor et al., 1997). But it has not been uniformly demonstrated that patients who received the multifaceted stress reduction (via coping and social support) interventions fared better psychologically than those who received the customary care program. More specifically, in studies by both Oldridge and colleagues and Taylor and colleagues, both intervention and control groups showed similar patterns of psychological recovery from baseline to 12-month follow-up. There are, however, several problematic aspects related to how some of the intervention efforts have been delivered. First, researchers have not verified the extent to which participants actually used the intervention. In addition, a lack of placebo control groups has been noted (Levitt, Deisinger, Wall, Ford, & Cassisi, 1995). These shortcomings stand as reminders for researchers working with injured athletes to carefully plan, evaluate, and monitor their interventions.

Conclusions Regarding Psychological Responses to Injury

Until recently, the psychologically based injury response literature largely consisted of anecdotal and clinical accounts. This trend has changed dramatically in the last decade with the rapid increase in research and theory development relating to athletes' psychological response to injuries. Two theoretical approaches—stage and cognitive appraisal approaches—have been forwarded as a means of understanding psychological responses to injuries. Although stage approaches and cognitive approaches historically have been presented as competing explanations, it is not necessary to look at these two approaches in an "either/or" light. That is, both perspectives may help us understand athletes' responses to injury. For example, the information provided by stage models may shed light on *what* and *when* responses are experienced and, thus, compel researchers to heed the dynamic nature of injuries. Alternatively, classic cognitive appraisal approaches may be better suited to answering *why* certain emotions are experienced. Thus, rather than choosing or deciding which type of theory is best, a more productive approach may be to recognize the contributions of the various theoretical postinjury response models.

Additionally, although a number of authors (e.g., Heil, 1993; Williams & Roepke, 1993) have advocated the use of intervention strategies (e.g., imagery, relaxation training), the number of well-controlled, theoretically grounded interventions aimed at reducing the psychological distress that often accompanies injuries has been limited. Considerably more research is needed in this area.

Behavioral Responses to Injuries: Rehabilitation Adherence

The previous section discussed the psychological ramifications of athletic injuries. Given the apparent complexity of athletes' psychological responses to injuries, it is not surprising that this topic has dominated the research. Once athletes are injured, however, not only psychological but also behavioral responses are of interest. Specifically, behavioral responses of interest include, but are not limited to, adherence issues, malingering, and the extent to which athletes engage in risk-taking behaviors (Wiese-Bjornstal et al., 1998). Because of space limitations, our discussion will focus only on adherence-related issues.

It is generally thought that individuals who do not adhere to their rehabilitation programs are at greater risk of reinjury (Heil, 1993), but the prevalence of nonadherence to rehabilitation programs is not well established. In a review article on sport injury adherence, Brewer (1998) cited evidence that adherence levels among injured athletes have ranged from 40% to 91% depending on how adherence is measured. Udry (1995), working with a sample of severely injured athletes, found that the majority demonstrated relatively high levels of adherence. However, a subset of athletes had very low adherence levels (i.e., attended less than 40% of their rehabilitation sessions) and, overall, rehabilitation adherence levels declined during the course of lengthy rehabilitation programs. A.H. Taylor and May (1996) noted that as rehabilitation programs (outside of university settings) are increasingly becoming more home-based, there may be a trend for adherence levels to diminish. Finally, a number of surveys of sports medicine providers have found a lack of adherence to established rehabilitation protocols (which may include overadherence as well as underadherence), indicating that adherence issues are a significant concern among injured athletes (Ford & Gordon, 1997; Larson, Starkey, & Zaichkowsky, 1996). Thus, we clearly need to further our understanding of the processes associated with rehabilitation adherence and rehabilitation outcomes stemming from adherence among injured athletes.

As noted previously, relatively few studies have examined the psychological processes associated with injury rehabilitation adherence, and theoretically based studies have been particularly scarce. More than a decade ago, Duda, Smart, and Tappe (1989) called for more theoretically based injury rehabilitation research. There was not much change in the character of the research in the ensuing decade, and this call was echoed recently by Brewer (1998). In this section, we review the literature on injury rehabilitation adherence. More specifically, because of the paucity of theoretically based adherence studies, we outline several theoretical models that appear to hold promise for future researchers. We discuss cognitive appraisal models, value expectancy models, goal perspective theory, and the transtheoretical model.

Cognitive Appraisal Models

Earlier we introduced the rudiments of various cognitive appraisal models as they pertain to the psychological responses to injuries. We noted that cognitive appraisal models (see figure 17.2) also have been forwarded as a means of understanding rehabilitation adherence (Brewer, 1998). At this juncture, we review some of the research on athletic injury rehabilitation adherence from a cognitive appraisal perspective.

A number of studies have examined the relationship between emotional responses to injuries and rehabilitation adherence. Daly, Brewer, Van Raalte, Petitpas, and Sklar (1995) found that individuals' cognitive appraisals of the difficulty of coping with injuries and their mood disturbances were negatively correlated with rehabilitation adherence in a sports medicine clinic. These findings were buttressed by findings from Brickner's (1997) investigation, which also reported an inverse relationship with mood disturbance levels and rehabilitation adherence. In contrast, however, Brewer et al. (2000) found no correlation between psychological distress and adherence.

Udry (1997) examined rehabilitation adherence levels among a sample of recreational athletes using a cognitive appraisal perspective. This study examined the effect on adherence levels of various types of coping: negative emotion (i.e., preoccupation with negative consequences of an injury), instrumental coping (i.e., problem-focused coping), distraction (i.e., thinking about other things or engaging in unrelated activities), and palliative coping (i.e., activities or responses that are soothing or alleviate the unpleasantness of an injury). Instrumental coping was positively linked to adherence levels although this was only true in the later phases of rehabilitation. Alternatively, palliative coping was negatively linked to rehabilitation adherence, although this too was not apparent until the later phases of rehabilitation.

In short, a number of investigators have used cognitive appraisal models to understand rehabilitation adherence behavior. The interested reader is referred to Brewer (2001) for a more comprehensive review.

Value Expectancy Approaches: Protection Motivation Theory

Another approach that has been used to examine adherence-related issues of injured athletes can be classified as a "value expectancy approach." Numerous value expectancy models exist, including protection motivation theory (Maddux & Rogers, 1983; Rogers, 1975), the health belief model (Rosenstock, Strecher, & Becker, 1988), and the theory of planned behavior (Ajzen, 1988). A commonality of value expectancy models is the premise that behavior can be predicted based on the value that individuals place on outcomes and their expectations that given behaviors will lead to those outcomes (Prentice-Dunn & Rogers, 1986). Value expectancy theories have a well-established tradition in the social–psychological and health-related realms, having been applied to a wide variety of health behaviors including cardiac rehabilitation (Oldridge & Streiner, 1990), exercise behavior (Slenker, Price, Roberts, & Jurs, 1984), emergency room care and follow-up appointments (Jones, Jones, & Katz, 1991), dental care, and seatbelt use (Rosenstock, 1990). Our discussion of value expectancy models will be limited to a discussion of protection motivation theory (PMT; Prentice-Dunn & Rogers, 1986; Rogers, 1975). We limit our discussion to PMT because of space considerations and because it is one of the few value expectancy models that have been applied to athletic injury rehabilita-

tion adherence. A more comprehensive description of value expectancy models is provided by Carter (1990) and Rosenstock (1990).

PMT was originally formulated by Rogers (1975) and subsequently modified by Maddux and Rogers (1983) and Prentice-Dunn and Rogers (1986). The revised version of PMT is the focus of this discussion, with a schematic of PMT provided in figure 17.3.

As shown in the left part of figure 17.3, environmental (e.g., verbal persuasion, modeling) and intrapersonal (e.g., personality variables, prior experience) information about a health threat is thought to initiate two cognitive processes: *threat appraisal* and *coping appraisal*. Threat appraisal accounts for factors that decrease or increase the probability of individuals making maladaptive responses (e.g., responses that place individuals at risk, such as not attending rehabilitation). Factors that increase the chances of maladaptive responses are intrinsic (e.g., bodily pleasure) and extrinsic rewards (e.g., social approval). Factors that decrease the probability of maladaptive responses are *perceived severity*, or the perceived degree of harm, discomfort, or damage that will result from health hazards, and *vulnerability to threat*, or the degree to which individuals perceive risks if they continue their unhealthy behavior (Prentice-Dunn & Rogers, 1986). Thus, intrinsic and extrinsic rewards minus perceived severity and vulnerability are thought to influence individuals' threat appraisal.

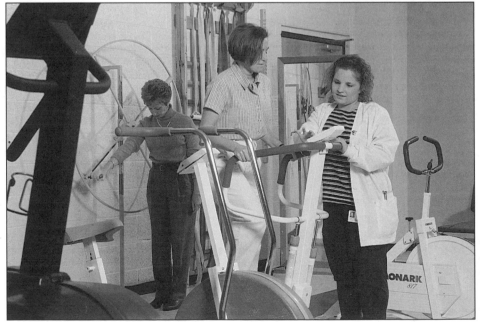

© Terry Wild Studio

Individuals who adhere to their rehabilitation programs could face a lower risk of reinjury than those who do not.

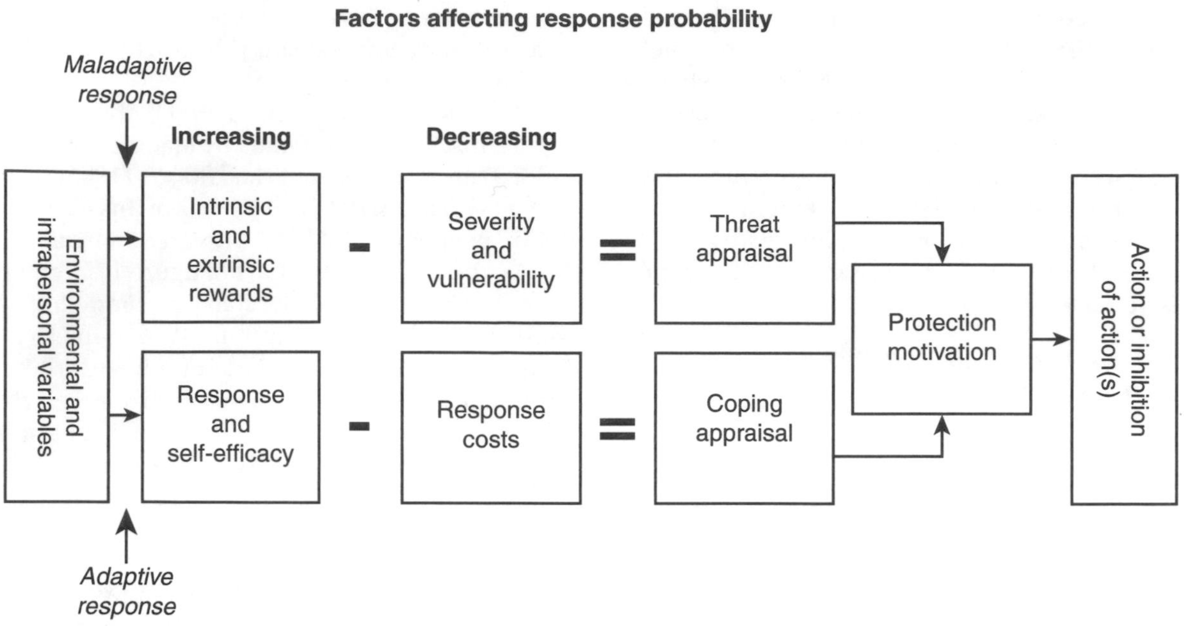

Factors affecting response probability

Figure 17.3 Adapted from Prentice-Dunn and Rogers's (1986) model of protection motivation theory.

Adapted, by permission, from S. Prentice-Dunn and R. Rogers, 1986, "Protection motivation theory and preventative health: Beyond the health belief model," *Health Education Research, 1(3):* 153–161. Reproduced by permission of Oxford University Press.

The second process individuals engage in is coping appraisal (Maddux, 1993). Coping appraisal accounts for those factors that decrease or increase the probability of individuals making adaptive responses. Coping appraisal is thought to be primarily influenced by *response efficacy*, or individuals' perception of the effectiveness of a given coping strategy in preventing a negative health condition (e.g., attending rehabilitation will prevent scar tissue buildup) or encouraging positive health status (e.g., attending rehabilitation will speed recovery), and *self-efficacy*, or the belief that one can successfully execute the behavior required to produce the desired outcome (Bandura, 1977; e.g., the belief that it is possible to consistently attend rehabilitation sessions). Thus, as response efficacy and self-efficacy increase, there should be a concomitant increase in the probability of adherence. The probability of engaging in the behavior, however, should decrease in proportion to the perceived response costs (e.g., inconvenience, complexity, loss of social support; Maddux, 1993). Therefore, response efficacy and self-efficacy minus response cost are thought to influence individuals' coping appraisal.

As indicated by the right side of figure 17.3, threat appraisal and coping appraisal combine to form individuals' protection motivation. Thus,

protection motivation is viewed as an intervening variable that initiates, sustains, and directs behavior. In turn, the behavioral responses produced by protection motivation are thought to encompass both explicit behavior (e.g., completing rehabilitation exercises) and the inhibition of actions (e.g., refraining from activities that are likely to increase the risk of reinjury; Prentice-Dunn & Rogers, 1986).

A.H. Taylor and May (1996) conducted one of the few investigations applying PMT to injury adherence behaviors. Using a questionnaire that had been developed to tap the constructs of PMT (i.e., the Sports Injury Rehabilitation Beliefs Survey, or SIRBS; S. May, 1995), 62 British university athletes completed self-assessments at various times during their rehabilitation. Athletes' responses on the SIRBS were compared with adherence levels that were assessed through both self-report measures and observations by sports medicine providers. The results partially supported the tenets of PMT, although the contribution of the constructs of PMT (e.g., severity, self-efficacy, etc.) varied with respect to whether the target behavior was adherence to an active rehabilitation program or to a regimen of rest or modified activity.

The strengths of A.H. Taylor and May's (1996) investigation included adherence being measured through multiple methods (i.e., athlete self-reports and sports medicine providers' assessments) and being assessed as a multidimensional construct (i.e., active rehabilitation, rest). Unfortunately, the results of this investigation must be viewed cautiously because of measurement problems. Specifically, the subscale of the SIRBS that taps individuals' perception of severity had a reported internal consistency of only .52. Because other injury adherence–related investigations have been plagued by similar measurement issues (J. Fields, Murphey, Horodyski, & Stopka, 1995; Fisher, Domm, & Wuest, 1988), there is clearly a need for researchers to use psychometrically sound assessment measures (Brewer, 1998).

To summarize, PMT was developed for the purpose of understanding health-related behaviors. Research with injured athletes using this theoretical framework is currently limited. Despite such limitations, this theory and other value expectancy theories may further our understanding of rehabilitation adherence among injured athletes.

Goal Perspective Theory

Based within a social cognitive framework, goal perspective theory addresses the different types of behaviors that can be observed in various achievement settings (see Weiss in this volume for a more comprehensive review). According to Nicholls (1984), individuals select and pursue goals in a way that will allow them to demonstrate competence, or at least their perception of competence. One way that individuals can view their ability is through the adoption of what is termed a *task orientation*. A task orientation involves the use of self-referenced strategies to define perceptions of ability and success. Another way that individuals can define ability is through the adoption of an *ego orientation*. An ego orientation makes greater use of normative-based assessments to interpret ability and success. In keeping with a social cognitive perspective, situational factors also are hypothesized to influence the goal perspectives that individuals adopt. For instance, if the environment emphasizes competition, individuals will tend to use normative strategies to interpret their ability and success (Nicholls, 1984). In turn, these differential motivational orientations and situational factors may influence individuals' expectations about tasks, the amount of effort they will invest in tasks, and their persistence.

Several studies have incorporated goal perspective theory to examine rehabilitation adherence levels among athletic populations. Duda et al.

(1989) found that injured athletes who believed in the efficacy of their treatment, perceived greater social support for their rehabilitation, were more self-motivated or goal directed, and emphasized a task-orientation demonstrated higher rehabilitation adherence levels. More recently, Lampton, Lambert, and Yost (1993) found that injured athletes low in self-esteem and high in ego orientation tended to have lower rehabilitation adherence levels. In contrast to the work of Duda et al., task orientation was not found to be related to treatment adherence. Given these preliminary findings, it may be worthwhile for researchers to consider the potential contribution that goal perspective might make relative to injury rehabilitation adherence.

Transtheoretical Model

The transtheoretical model (TM), which is sometimes referred to as the "stages of change" model or "readiness for change" model, is a process-organized model that addresses the psychological changes individuals engage in when making changes in health-related behaviors (Prochaska & Marcus, 1994). Thus, the TM is not viewed as a competing model to the previous perspectives as much as one that integrates elements from various existing theoretical frameworks.

A central assertion of the TM is that individuals progress through distinct stages as they initiate and maintain health behaviors (Prochaska & Marcus, 1994). More specifically, there are thought to be five stages of behavior change:

- Precontemplation: The individual is currently not involved in making behavioral change and has no intention of beginning to make a change.
- Contemplation: The individual is not currently engaged in making a behavioral change but is thinking about starting to in the future.
- Preparation: The individual has started to engage in the behavioral change but does so on a limited or inconsistent level.
- Action: The individual demonstrates less than 6 months of sustained behavioral change.
- Maintenance: The individual demonstrates more than 6 months of regular participation in the behavior.

Research has shown that individuals who are in different stages of behavior change engage in different psychological processes regarding the behavior of interest (Marcus, Rossi, Selby, Niaura, & Abrams, 1992). For instance, individuals who are in the earliest stage of making a behavioral change have the lowest self-efficacy relative to their ability to engage in the behavior. Additionally, these individuals tend to perceive the greatest number of barriers and the fewest number of benefits resulting from behavioral changes.

The TM has been applied successfully to a diverse range of health-related behaviors including smoking, sunscreen use, high-fat diets, alcohol consumption, mammography screening, condom use (Prochaska et al., 1994), exercise behavior (Marcus, Rossi et al., 1992), and cardiac rehabilitation adherence among older adults (Hellman, 1997). Research using the TM as it relates to sport injury rehabilitation is not well developed. In one of the initial studies in this area, Wong (1998) modified the questionnaires used to test the TM in the exercise domain for use in the sports injury domain and reported that the modified assessments appeared to be applicable. Udry, Shelbourne and Gray (2001) used Wong's modified TM measures to examine athletes' psychological processes shortly before undergoing major knee surgery. Participants in the Udry et al. investigation reported relatively high levels of patient readiness for surgery (e.g., high levels of self-efficacy, more pros than cons associated with surgery) and an overall pattern of results that were somewhat different than those reported by Wong. With several initial studies completed, additional research is needed to determine whether injured athletes' self-reported readiness for change is linked to adherence and recovery outcomes.

A rather compelling implication of the TM is that it suggests that intervention efforts are most effective when they are stage matched (Marcus, Rakowski, & Rossi, 1992). Specifically, Marcus and colleagues showed that, relative to exercise behavior, individuals who are in the precontemplation stage may benefit from educational efforts focusing on the benefits of exercise. In contrast, individuals who are in the action stage may benefit more from goal setting and incentive programs. Adopting this approach in the realm of injury rehabilitation could assist sports medicine providers in screening injured athletes before surgery. Specifically, injured athletes who perceive more barriers than benefits to injury rehabilitation and who are low in self-efficacy may benefit from postponing their surgery.

Brewer (1998) suggested that the value of the TM may be restricted because of the "time-limited" nature of injury rehabilitation. The TM, however, has been used to predict rehabilitation adherence among older adults after cardiac surgery—a condition that might also be presumed to be time limited (Hellman, 1997). Alternatively, the TM approach may prove to be more useful relative to working on adherence behaviors with athletes who have experienced chronic rather than acute injuries, where the time-limited nature of injures is not as salient.

We have attempted to highlight the potential applications of the TM. Additionally, several studies suggest there may be some utility in using the TM to understand sport injuries. However, further research in this area is needed before the usefulness of the TM can be accurately assessed.

Conclusions Regarding Behavioral Responses to Injury: Rehabilitation Adherence

As has been mentioned, relatively little attention has been given to the issues surrounding injury rehabilitation adherence, and even fewer studies have been conducted within sound theoretical frameworks. Although we have provided an overview of several theoretical models and their corresponding research, several caveats are in order. First, the models that have been presented should not be viewed as constituting an exhaustive list. Certainly, other models exist (e.g., self-efficacy theory; Bandura, 1977) that ultimately may prove to be more useful than the ones we have outlined. Thus, perhaps the most important message is the call for researchers to ground their research on rehabilitation adherence within a theoretical framework.

Second, although we have underscored the need for theory-based research, it is likely that some classes of theories will be more productive than others in terms of their predictive capabilities. Behaviors in the health domain are often classified as (but are not limited to) *preventive health behavior* and *sick-role behavior* (Glanz, Lewis, & Rimer, 1990). Preventive health behaviors encompass those activities undertaken by individuals who believe themselves to be healthy, or asymptomatic, for the purpose of preventing illness. In contrast, sick-role behavior entails those activities undertaken by individuals who consider themselves to be ill or injured for the purposes of getting well. Sick-role behavior includes receiving treatment from medical providers, and there is typically some level of exemption from individuals' ordinary responsibilities. Exercise adherence among apparently healthy individuals is more of a preventive health behavior, whereas athletic injury rehabilitation adherence behavior seems to fall closer to the category of sick-role behavior. A.H. Taylor and May's (1996) work with PMT in injury rehabilitation adherence found a different pattern of results compared with the pattern of results reported when PMT has been applied to exercise adherence. This differential pattern of results may have occurred because Taylor and May examined sick-role behavior rather than preventive health behavior. Thus, we agree with Duda et al. (1989), who suggested that it may not be wise to simply generalize the results from exercise adherence and the medical realm to athletic injury rehabilitation.

Third, although we have presented a number of theories pertaining to adherence that have been used in other domains, we do not mean to imply that sport-specific models of adherence should not be developed or that the existing theories should not be modified. The work of Scanlan and colleagues (Scanlan, Carpenter, Schmidt, Simons, & Keeler, 1993; Scanlan, Stein, & Ravizza, 1991), who have developed a model of sport commitment, is an excellent example of sport-specific model building. This type of theory building may be useful for researchers who study injury rehabilitation. Alternatively, in examining the exercise adherence theory and research, Maddux (1993) provided an integrated model of exercise behavior that captures many of the common elements of existing models of exercise behavior (e.g., theory of planned behavior, self-efficacy theory). Although it appears to be premature to forward a comprehensive model of injury rehabilitation adherence given the nascent character of the literature, the strengths of different models may be maximized when researchers can examine and test the conceptual similarities across various theoretical models.

FUTURE RESEARCH DIRECTIONS

We have discussed the psychology of athlete injuries from both antecedents and responses perspectives. These two areas of research have evolved in relatively distinct ways. Thus, as we conclude with recommendations for future research, we have organized our suggestions relative to these areas.

Injury Antecedents

First, although the early studies on the stress–injury relationship may have led researchers to conclude that there was a simple and direct relationship between stress and injury, recent research has revealed that this is not the case. It seems that the stress and athletic injury relationship is a complex one, with numerous variables influencing outcome (e.g., R.E. Smith et al., 1990). Research designs that can capture the complexities of the interrelationships between psychosocial factors are sorely needed. In addition, although a large body of research implicates psychosocial factors as antecedents to injuries, injuries clearly result from physiological, biomechanical, equipment, and field condition factors. Thus, multidisciplinary research is needed that allows researchers to explore how psychological and physical factors interact.

Second, we are still in the initial stages of understanding the underlying mechanisms of athletic injuries. At this point, generalized muscle tension seems to be an intuitively appealing explanation. Unfortunately, only one study (Andersen, 1989) examined muscle tension during stress, and that study was inconclusive. Limitations of the Andersen study included laboratory stressors (probably much lower than real-life stress) and drawing participants from a general, not athletic, population. However, measuring muscle tension in the field would be quite difficult. Laboratory methods with greater ecological validity such as those of Bum et al. (1996, 1998), using physiological and auditory stressors, may help in examining the role that generalized muscle tension may play in stress responses and injury outcome.

Related to this issue, researchers may wish to attempt to make laboratory stress conditions even more ecologically valid than the Bum et al. (1996, 1998) studies by adding other environmental variables such as high ambient heat and humidity. Bursill (1958) reported greater peripheral vision narrowing under such conditions. Many athletic competitions are held in stressful environmental conditions of high heat and humidity (e.g., the 1996 Olympics in Atlanta, the 1998 Commonwealth Games in Kuala Lumpur, Malaysia).

Additionally, studies with repeated measures of stressors are still needed. For example, as cited previously, Fawkner et al.'s (1999) study—whereby daily hassles were measured on numerous occasions throughout the competitive season—is commendable and revealed that hassles tended to increase before injuries occurred. The potential for using daily hassles as a means of monitoring injury risk needs further exploration.

Finally, the ultimate goal of research into the antecedents of athletic injury has to be the development and implementation of interventions aimed at reducing injury risk. This reduction is the outcome of most interest to coaches, athletes, administrators, and investors (in professional sport). It is surprising that only three studies (which were rather weakly designed but highly suggestive) indicate injury risk can be reduced. We hope that more intervention studies will be performed.

Injury Responses

There has been a growing sophistication in the type of methodologies used to investigate the psychological and behavioral responses to injuries. More recently, researchers examining injury responses by using quantitative methods have been prone to use prospective and repeated-measures designs (e.g., Morrey et al., 1999; Udry, 1997) with control or comparison groups (e.g., Cupal & Brewer, 2001; Leddy et al., 1994; Ross & Berger, 1996). The use of these more rigorous designs should be continued. The availability and use of psychometrically questionable instruments, however, continue to be problematic.

We maintain that qualitative methodologies also stand to make significant contributions to our knowledge base regarding the responses to athletic injury. But this approach is not immune to the need to demonstrate rigor and should be used judiciously. For instance, qualitative approaches may be well suited for assessing psychological processes that might not be accessible given the current state of measurement (e.g., denial, bargaining). As Evans and Hardy (1995) noted, however, retrospective interviews may not be as useful in helping researchers understand the precise sequencing of emotions that injured athletes experience. Peterson (1997) provided an excellent example of how qualitative interviews can be used in a prospective manner. This work entailed prolonged and persistent (i.e., 6–10) interviews with injured athletes over the course of their injury recovery, and the results were subjected to rigorous and detailed data analytic procedures.

We previously identified the need for researchers to explore the antecedents of injuries by making laboratory-based studies more ecologically valid. Along similar lines, investigations examining the responses to injuries often fail to account for the way injury rehabilitation actually occurs. For example, once an injury has occurred, researchers typically assess mood disturbances at some predetermined postinjury time (e.g., 1 week, 2 weeks). Often, however, no mention is made of whether any of the athletes experienced setbacks or additional injuries—factors that might significantly affect subsequent psychological distress levels. Although various conceptual models of injury response now encompass the dynamic nature of injuries, researchers have been slow to incorporate this facet into research designs and data analytic procedures.

As with the injury prevention literature, relatively few sound studies have examined the efficacy of interventions aimed at the postinjury time period. Evans and Hardy (1995) raised an intriguing point relative to the use of intervention work. Specifically, they suggested that researchers "explore theory driven interventions for use with injured athletes when they are in different grief/injury phases" (p. 243). This is a compelling point in its own right but is also consistent with the transtheoretical approach. Simply put, if the psychological and behavioral responses to injuries are viewed as processes, then it makes sense to use intervention strategies that match the athlete's readiness to receive the intervention.

Finally, we did not discuss in any detail the possible influence of psychological factors (e.g., disposition, use of coping strategies, imagery) on recovery outcomes (e.g., confidence, regaining range of motion of an injured joint) among injured athletes. Some preliminary work in this domain has been completed (e.g., Cupal & Brewer, 2001; Ievleva & Orlick, 1991; Ross & Berger, 1996; Scott & Jarrett, 1998). It is often not clear, however, whether the link between psychological factors and recovery rates is direct or if recovery rates are influenced by mediating variables such as adherence levels. In the future, researchers should attempt to use research designs that address these critical questions.

SUMMARY

Research and theory development related to the psychology of athlete injuries can be categorized as relating to either the antecedents or the responses to injuries. The research on antecedents to injury has largely been organized around the conceptual model presented by Andersen and Williams (1988) and subsequently modified by Williams and Andersen (1998). Overall, this model has received consistent support, and a number of areas within the model have been identified as particularly ripe for further research. Specifically, additional research is needed on the role of social support as it relates to the stress–injury relationship, the mechanisms underlying stress–injury relationships, and interventions aimed at reducing injury risk.

Regarding the responses to injuries, stage approaches and cognitive appraisal approaches have been used to understand how athletes psychologically respond to their injuries. Cognitive appraisal approaches have received consistent support in the literature, but there have been so few empirical tests of stage approaches that it is not possible to draw firm conclusions regarding their utility. Four theoretical approaches were forwarded relative to understanding injury rehabilitation adherence or the behavioral responses of athletes to injuries. The theoretical approaches discussed included cognitive appraisal, value expectancy, goal perspective, and the transtheoretical model. Given that relatively few studies on the behavioral responses to athlete injuries have been conducted, it is not yet known which, if any, of these adherence models will be the most useful in predicting adherence to injury rehabilitation.

REFERENCES

Agris, W.S. (1989). Understanding compliance with the medical regimen: The scope of the problem and a theoretical perspective. *Arthritis Care Research, 2 (Suppl.),* 2–7.

Ajzen, I. (1988). *Attitudes, personality, and behavior.* Chicago: Dorsey Press.

American Psychiatric Association. (1994). *Diagnostic and statistical manual of mental disorders* (4th ed.). Washington, DC: Author.

Andersen, M.B. (1989). Psychosocial factors and changes in peripheral vision, muscle tension, and fine motor skills during stress. *Dissertation Abstracts International, 49*(10-B), 4580.

Andersen, M.B., & Stoove, M.A. (1998). The sanctity of $p < .05$ obfuscates good stuff: A comment on Kerr and Goss. *Journal of Applied Sport Psychology, 10,* 168–173.

Andersen, M.B., & Williams, J.M. (1988). A model of stress and athletic injury: Prediction and prevention. *Journal of Sport & Exercise Psychology, 10,* 294–306.

Andersen, M.B., & Williams, J.M. (1993). Psychological risk factors and injury prevention. In J. Heil (Ed.), *Psychology of sport injury* (pp. 49–57). Champaign, IL: Human Kinetics.

Andersen, M.B., & Williams, J.M. (1999). Athletic injury, psychosocial factors, and perceptual changes during stress. *Journal of Sports Sciences, 17,* 735–741.

Bandura, A. (1977). Self-efficacy: Toward a unifying theory of personality change. *Psychological Review, 84,* 191–215.

Blackwell, B., & McCullagh, P. (1990). The relationship of athletic injury to life stress, competitive anxiety, and coping resources. *Athletic Training, 25,* 23–27.

Bramwell, S.T., Masuda, M., Wagner, N.H., & Holmes, T.H. (1975). Psychological factors in athletic injuries: Development and application of the Social and Athletic Readjustment Rating Scale (SARRS). *Journal of Human Stress, 1,* 6–20.

Brewer, B.W. (1994). Review and critique of models of psychological adjustment to athletic injury. *Journal of Applied Sport Psychology, 6,* 87–100.

Brewer, B.W. (1998). Adherence to sport injury rehabilitation programs. *Journal of Applied Sport Psychology, 10,* 70–82.

Brewer, B.W. (2001). Psychology of sport injury rehabilitation. In R.N. Singer, H.A. Hausenblas, & C.M. Janelle (Eds.), *Handbook of sport psychology* (2nd ed., pp. 787–809). New York: Wiley.

Brewer, B.W., Linder, D.E., & Phelps, C.M. (1995). Situational correlates of emotional adjustment to athletic injury. *Clinical Journal of Sports Medicine, 5,* 241–245.

Brewer, B.W., Petitpas, A.J., Van Raalte, J.L., Sklar, J.H., & Ditmar, T.D. (1995). Prevalence of psychological distress among patients at a physical therapy clinic specializing in sports medicine. *Sports Medicine Training and Rehabilitation, 6,* 139–145.

Brewer, B.W., & Petrie, T.A. (1995). A comparison between injured and uninjured football players on selected psychosocial variables. *Academic Athletic Journal, 9,* 11–18.

Brewer, B.W., Van Raalte, J.L., Cornelius, A.E., Petitpas, A.J., Sklar, J.H., Pohlman, M.H., Krushell, R.J., & Ditmar, T.D. (2000). Psychological factors, rehabilitation, adherence, and rehabilitation outcome after anterior cruciate ligament reconstruction. *Rehabilitation Psychology, 45,* 20–37.

Brickner, J.C. (1997). *Mood states and compliance of patients with orthopedic rehabilitation.* Unpublished master's thesis, Springfield College, Springfield, MA.

Bringer, J.D., & Udry, E. (1998). Psychosocial precursors to athletic injury in adolescent competitive athletes [Abstract]. *Journal of Applied Sport Psychology, 10* (Suppl.), 126.

Brustad, R.J., & Ritter-Taylor, M. (1997). Applying social psychological perspectives to the sport psychology consulting process. *The Sport Psychologist, 11,* 107–119.

Bum, D., Morris, T., & Andersen, M.B. (1996). Stress, life stress, and visual attention. In D. Kenny (Ed.), *Proceedings (edited abstracts): International congress on stress and health* (p. 37). Sydney, Australia: University of Sydney.

Bum, D., Morris, T., & Andersen, M.B. (1998, August). *Stress, stress management, and visual attention.* Paper presented at the International Congress of Applied Psychology, San Francisco.

Bursill, A.E. (1958). The restriction of peripheral vision during exposure to hot and humid conditions. *Quarterly Journal of Experimental Psychology, 10,* 113–129.

Byrd, B.J. (1993). *The relationship of history of stressors, personality, and coping resources with the incidence of athletic injuries.* Unpublished master's thesis, University of Colorado, Boulder.

Carter, W.B. (1990). Health behavior as a rational process: Theory of reasoned action and multiattribute utility theory. In K. Glanz, F.M. Lewis, & B.K. Rimer (Eds.), *Health behavior and health education* (pp. 63–91). San Francisco: Jossey-Bass.

Carver, C.S., Pozo, C., Harris, S.D., Noriega, V., Scheier, M.F., Robinson, D.S., Ketcham, A.S., Moffat, F.L., & Clark, K.C. (1993). How coping mediates the effect of optimism on distress: A study of women with early stage breast cancer. *Journal of Personality and Social Psychology, 65,* 375–390.

Coddington, R.D., & Troxell, J.R. (1980). The effect of emotional factors on football injury rates: A pilot study. *Journal of Human Stress, 6,* 3–5.

Cohen, S., & Wills, T.A. (1985). Stress, social support, and the buffering hypothesis. *Psychological Bulletin, 98,* 310–357.

Compas, B.E., Worsham, N.L., Ey, S., & Howell, D.C. (1996). When Mom or Dad has cancer: II. Coping, cognitive appraisals, and psychological distress in children of cancer patients. *Health Psychology, 15,* 167–175.

Crossman, J., & Jamieson, J. (1985). Differences in perceptions of seriousness of disrupting effects of athletic injury as viewed by athletes and their trainer. *Perceptual and Motor Skills, 61,* 1131–1134.

Cryan, P.O., & Alles, E.F. (1983). The relationship between stress and football injuries. *Journal of Sports Medicine and Physical Fitness, 23,* 52–58.

Cupal, D. D., & Brewer, B. W. (2001). Effects of relaxation and guided imagery on knee strength, reinjury anxiety, and pain following anterior cruciate ligament reconstruction. *Rehabilitation Psychology, 46,* 28–43.

Daly, J.M., Brewer, B.W., Van Raalte, J.L., Petitpas, A.J., & Sklar, J.H. (1995). Cognitive appraisal, emotional adjustment, and adherence to rehabilitation following knee surgery. *Journal of Sport Rehabilitation, 4,* 23–30.

Davis, J.O. (1991). Sports injuries and stress management: An opportunity for research. *The Sport Psychologist, 5,* 175–182.

Dewar, A., & Horn, T.S. (1992). A critical analysis of knowledge construction in sport psychology. In T.S. Horn (Ed.), *Advances in sport psychology* (pp. 13–24). Champaign, IL: Human Kinetics.

DeWitt, D.J. (1980). Cognitive and biofeedback training for stress reduction with university athletes. *Journal of Sport Psychology, 2,* 288–294.

Duda, J.L., Smart, A.E., & Tappe, M.K. (1989). Predictors of adherence in the rehabilitation of athletic injuries: An application of personal investment theory. *Journal of Sport & Exercise Psychology, 11,* 367–381.

Durso-Cupal, D. (1998). Psychological interventions in sport injury prevention and rehabilitation. *Journal of Applied Sport Psychology, 10,* 103–123.

Evans, L., & Hardy, L. (1995). Sport injury and grief responses: A review. *Journal of Sport and Exercise Psychology, 17,* 227–245.

Fawkner, H.J. (1995). *Predisposition to injury in athletes: The role of psychosocial factors.* Unpublished master's thesis, University of Melbourne, Australia.

Fawkner, H.J., McMurray, N.E., & Summers, J.J. (1999). Athletic injury and minor life events: A prospective study. *Journal of Science and Medicine in Sports, 2,* 117–124.

Fields, J., Murphey, M., Horodyski, M., & Stopka, C. (1995). Factors associated with adherence to sport injury rehabilitation in college-age recreational athletes. *Journal of Sport Rehabilitation, 4,* 172–180.

Fields, K.B., Delaney, M., & Hinkle, S. (1990). A prospective study of type A behavior and running injuries. *Journal of Family Practice, 30,* 425–429.

Fisher, A.C., Domm, M.A., & Wuest, D.A. (1988). Adherence to sports-related rehabilitation programs. *The Physician and Sportsmedicine, 16*(7), 47–52.

Ford, I.W., & Gordon, S. (1997). Perspectives of sport physiotherapists on the frequency and significance of psychological factors in professional practice: Implications for curriculum design in professional training. *Australian Journal of Science and Medicine in Sports, 29*(2), 34–40.

Glanz, K., Lewis, F., & Rimer, B. (1990). Health education and health behavior: The foundations. In K. Glanz, F. Lewis, & B. Rimer (Eds.), *Health behavior and health education* (pp. 3–32). San Francisco: Jossey-Bass.

Gould, D., Jackson, S., & Finch, L. (1993). Sources of stress in national champion figure skaters. *Journal of Sport & Exercise Psychology, 15,* 134–159.

Gould, D., Udry, E., Bridges, D., & Beck, L. (1997). Stress sources encountered when rehabilitating from season-ending ski injuries. *The Sport Psychologist, 11,* 381–403.

Green, S.L., & Weinberg, R.S. (2001). Relationships among athletic identity, coping skills, social support, and the psychological impact of injury in recreational athletes. *Journal of Applied Sport Psychology, 13,*(1), 40–59.

Grove, J.R. (1993). Personality and injury rehabilitation among sport performers. In D. Pargman (Ed.), *Psychological basis of sport injuries* (pp. 99–120). Morgantown, WV: Fitness Information Technology.

Hanson, S.J., McCullagh, P., & Tonymon, P. (1992). The relationship of personality characteristics, life stress, and coping resources to athletic injury. *Journal of Sport & Exercise Psychology, 14,* 262–272.

Hardy, C.J., O'Connor, K.A., & Geisler, P.R. (1990). The role of gender and social support in the life stress injury relationship. Paper presented at the Annual Conference of the Association for the Advancement of Applied Sport Psychology, San Antonio, TX.

Hardy, C.J., Prentice, W.E., Kirsanoff, M.T., Richman, J.M., & Rosenfeld, L.B. (1987, June). Life stress, social support, and athletic injury: In search of relationships. In J. M. Williams (Chair), *Psychological factors in injury occurrence.* Symposium conducted at the annual meeting of the North American Society for the Psychology of Sport and Physical Activity, Vancouver, BC.

Hardy, C.J., Richman, J.M., & Rosenfeld, L.B. (1991). The role of social support in the life stress/injury relationship. *The Sport Psychologist, 5,* 128–139.

Hardy, C.J., & Riehl, M. A. (1988). An examination of the life stress-injury relationship among noncontact sport participants. *Behavioral Medicine, 14,* 113–118.

Heil, J. (1993). *Psychology of sport injury.* Champaign, IL: Human Kinetics.

Hellman, E.A. (1997). Use of the stages of change in exercise adherence model among older adults with a cardiac diagnosis. *Journal of Cardiopulmonary Rehabilitation, 17,* 145–155.

Holmes, T. (1970). Psychological screening. In *Football injuries: Paper presented at a workshop*. Sponsored by Subcommittee on Athletic Injuries, Committee on the Skeletal System, Division of Medical Sciences, National Research Council, February 1969 (pp. 211–214). Washington, DC: National Academy of Sciences.

Holmes, T., & Rahe, R. J. (1967). The Social and Readjustment Rating Scale. *Journal of Psychosomatic Research, 11*, 213–218.

Ievleva, L., & Orlick, T. (1991). Mental links to enhanced healing: An exploratory study. *The Sport Psychologist, 5*, 25–40.

Jaremko, M.E., Silbert, L., & Mann, T. (1981). The differential ability of athletes and nonathletes to cope with two types of pain: A radical behavioral model. *Psychological Record, 31*, 265–275.

Jones, S.L., Jones, P.K., & Katz, J. (1991). Compliance in acute and chronic patients receiving a health belief model intervention in the emergency department. *Social Science in Medicine, 32*, 1183–1189.

Kanner, A.D., Coyne, J.C., Schaefer, C., & Lazarus, R.S. (1981). Comparison of two modes of stress management: Daily hassles and uplifts versus major life events. *Journal of Behavioral Medicine, 4*, 1–39.

Kerr, G., & Goss, J. (1996). The effects of a stress management program on injuries and stress levels. *Journal of Applied Sport Psychology, 8*, 109–117.

Kerr, G., & Minden, H. (1988). Psychological factors related to the occurrence of athletic injuries. *Journal of Sport & Exercise Psychology, 10*, 167–173.

Kishi, Y., Robinson, R.G., & Forrester, A.W. (1994). Prospective longitudinal study of depression following spinal cord injury. *Journal of Neuropsychiatry and Clinical Neurosciences, 6*, 237–244.

Kolt, G., & Kirkby, R. (1996). Injury in Australian female competitive gymnasts: A psychological perspective. *Australian Physiotherapy, 42*, 121–126.

Kübler-Ross, E. (1969). *On death and dying*. New York: Macmillan.

Lampton, C.C., Lambert, M.E., & Yost, R. (1993). The effects of psychological factors in sports medicine rehabilitation adherence. *Journal of Sports Medicine and Physical Fitness, 33*, 292–299.

Landers, D.M., Wang, M.Q., & Courtet, P. (1985). Peripheral narrowing among experienced and inexperienced rifle shooters under low- and high-stress conditions. *Research Quarterly for Exercise and Sport, 56*, 122–130.

Larson, G.A., Starkey, C., & Zaichkowsky, L.D. (1996). Psychological aspects of athletic injuries as perceived by athletic trainers. *The Sport Psychologist, 10*, 37–47.

Lazarus, R.S., & Folkman, S. (1984). *Stress, appraisal, and coping*. New York: Springer-Verlag.

Leddy, M.H., Lambert, M.J., & Ogles, B.M. (1994). Psychological consequences of athletic injury among high level competitors. *Research Quarterly for Exercise and Sport, 65*, 347–354.

Levitt, R., Deisinger, J.A., Wall, J.R., Ford, L., & Cassisi, J.E. (1995). EMG feedback-assisted postoperative rehabilitation of minor arthroscopic knee surgeries. *Journal of Sports Medicine and Physical Fitness, 35*, 218–223.

Lynch, G.P. (1988). Athletic injuries and the practicing sport psychologist: Practical guidelines for assisting athletes. *The Sport Psychologist, 2*, 161–167.

Lysens, R., Steverlynck, A., Vanden Auweele, Y., Lefevre, J., Renson, L., Claessens, A., & Ostyn, M. (1984). The predictability of sports injuries. *Sports Medicine, 1*, 6–10.

Lysens, R., Vanden Auweele, Y., & Ostyn, M. (1986). The relationship between psychosocial factors and sports injuries. *Journal of Sports Medicine and Physical Fitness, 26*, 77–84.

Maddux, J.E. (1993). Social cognitive models of health and exercise behavior: An introduction and review of conceptual issues. *Journal of Applied Sport Psychology, 5*, 116–140.

Maddux, J.E., & Rogers, R.W. (1983). Protection motivation and self-efficacy: A revised theory of fear of appeals and attitude change. *Journal of Experimental Social Psychology, 19*, 469–479.

Marcus, B.H., Rakowski, W., & Rossi, J.S. (1992). Assessing motivational readiness and decision making for exercise. *Health Psychology, 11*, 257–261.

Marcus, B.H., Rossi, J.S., Selby, V.C., Niaura, R.S., & Abrams, D.B. (1992). The stages and processes of exercise adoption and maintenance in a worksite sample. *Health Psychology, 11*, 386–395.

May, J.R., Veach, T.L., Reed, M.W., & Griffey, M.S. (1985). A psychological study of health, injury, and performance in athletes on the U.S. alpine ski team. *The Physician and Sportsmedicine, 13*, 111–115.

May, J.R., Veach, T.L., Southard, S.W., & Herring, K. (1985). The effects of life change on injuries, illness, and performance. In N.K. Butts, T.G. Gushkin, & B. Zarins (Eds.), *The elite athlete* (pp. 171–179). Jamaica, NY: Spectrum Books.

May, S. (1995). *An investigation into compliance with sports injury rehabilitation regimens*. Unpublished doctoral dissertation, University of Brighton, Eastbourne, UK.

McDonald, S.A., & Hardy, C.J. (1990). Affective response patterns of the injured athlete: An exploratory analysis. *The Sport Psychologist, 4*, 261–274.

McLeod, S., & Kirkby, R.J. (1995). Locus of control as a predictor of injury in elite basketball players. *Sports Medicine, Training, and Rehabilitation, 6*, 201–206.

McNair, D., Lorr, M., & Droppelman, L. (1971). *Manual for the Profile of Mood States*. San Diego: Educational and Industrial Testing Service.

Meichenbaum, D. (1985). *Stress inoculation training*. New York: Pergamon Press.

Meyer, K.N. (1995). *The influence of personality factors, life stress, and coping strategies on the incidence of injury in long-distance runners*. Unpublished master's thesis, University of Colorado, Boulder.

Morrey, M.A., Stuart, M.J., Smith, A.M., & Wiese-Bjornstal, D.M. (1999). A longitudinal examination of athletes' emotional and cognitive responses to anterior cruciate ligament injury. *Clinical Journal of Sports Medicine, 9*, 63–60.

Nicholls, J.G. (1984). Achievement motivation: Conceptions of ability, subjective experience, task choice, and performance. *Psychological Review, 91*, 328–346.

Nixon, H.L. (1992). A social network analysis of influences on athletes to play with pain and injuries. *Journal of Sport and Social Issues, 16*, 127–135.

Nixon, H.L. (1993). Accepting the risks of pain and injury in sport: Mediated cultural influences on playing hurt. *Sociology of Sport Journal, 10*, 183–196.

Oldridge, N.B., & Streiner, D.L. (1990). The health belief model: Predicting compliance and dropout in cardiac rehabilitation. *Medicine and Science in Sports and Exercise, 22*, 678–683.

Oldridge, N., Streiner, D., Hoffman, R., & Guyatt, G. (1995). Profile of mood states and cardiac rehabilitation after acute myocardial infarction. *Medicine and Science in Sports and Exercise, 27*, 900–905.

O'Leary, A. (1990). Stress, emotion, and human immune function. *Psychological Bulletin, 108*, 363–382.

Pargman, D., & Lunt, S. D. (1989). The relationship of self-concept and locus of control to the severity of injury in freshman collegiate football players. *Sports Medicine, Training, and Rehabilitation, 1*, 201–208.

Passer, M.W., & Seese, M.D. (1983). Life stress and athletic injury: Examination of positive versus negative events and three moderator variables. *Journal of Human Stress, 9*, 11–16.

Pearson, L., & Jones, G. (1992). Emotional effects of sports injuries: Implications for physiotherapists. *Physiotherapy, 78*, 762–770.

Perna, F.M., Antoni, M., & Schneiderman, N. (1998). Psychological intervention prevents injury/illness among athletes [Abstract]. *Journal of Applied Sport Psychology, 10* (Suppl.), 53–54.

Perna, F., & McDowell, S. (1993, October). *The association of stress and coping with illness and injury among elite athletes.* Paper presented at the annual meeting of the Association for the Advancement of Applied Sport Psychology, Montreal, PQ.

Peterson, K.M. (1997). Role of social support in coping with athletic injury rehabilitation: A longitudinal qualitative investigation [Abstract]. *Journal of Applied Sport Psychology, 9* (Suppl.), 33.

Petrie, T.A. (1992). Psychosocial antecedents of athletic injury: The effects of life stress and social support on female collegiate gymnasts. *Behavioral Medicine, 18*, 127–138.

Petrie, T.A. (1993a). The moderating effects of social support and playing status on the life stress-injury relationship. *Journal of Applied Sport Psychology, 5*, 1–16.

Petrie, T.A. (1993b). Coping skills, competitive trait anxiety, and playing status: Moderating effects of the life stress-injury relationship. *Journal of Sport & Exercise Psychology, 15*, 261–274.

Petrie, T.A., & Falkstein, D.L. (1998). Methodological, measurement, and statistical issues in research on sport injury prediction. *Journal of Applied Sport Psychology, 10*, 26–45.

Prentice-Dunn, S., & Rogers, R.W. (1986). Protection motivation theory and preventive health: Beyond the health belief model. *Health Education Research, 1*, 153–161.

Prochaska, J.O., & Marcus, B.H. (1994). The transtheoretical model. In R.K. Dishman (Ed.), *Advances in exercise adherence* (2nd ed., pp. 161–180). Champaign, IL: Human Kinetics.

Prochaska, J.O., Velicer, W.F., Rossi, J.S., Goldstein, M.G., Marcus, B.H., Rakowski, W., Fiore, C., Harlow, L.L.,

Redding, C.A., Rosenbloom, D., & Rossi, S.R. (1994). Stages of change and decisional balance for 12 problem behaviors. *Health Psychology, 13*, 39–46.

Roh, J.L., Newcomer, R.R., Perna, F.M., & Etzel, E.F. (1998). Depressive mood states among college athletes: Pre- and post-injury [Abstract]. *Journal of Applied Sport Psychology, 10* (Suppl.), 54.

Rogers, R.W. (1975). A protection motivation theory of fear appeals and attitude change. *Journal of Psychology, 91*, 93–114.

Rose, J., & Jevne, R.F. (1993). Psychological processes associated with athletic injuries. *The Sport Psychologist, 7*, 309–328.

Rosenstock, I.M. (1990). The health belief model: Explaining health behavior through expectancies. In K. Glanz, F.M. Lewis, & B.K. Rimer (Eds.), *Health behavior and health education* (pp. 39–62). San Francisco: Jossey-Bass.

Rosenstock, I.M., Strecher, V.J., & Becker, M.H. (1988). Social learning theory and the health belief model. *Health Education Quarterly, 15*, 175–183.

Ross, M.J., & Berger, R.S. (1996). Effects of stress inoculation training on athletes' postsurgical pain and rehabilitation after orthopedic injury. *Journal of Consulting and Clinical Psychology, 64*, 406–410.

Sarason, I.G., Johnson, J.H., & Siegel, J.M. (1978). Assessing the impact of life changes: Development of the Life Experiences Survey. *Journal of Consulting and Clinical Psychology, 46*, 932–946.

Scanlan, T.K., Carpenter, P.J., Schmidt, G.W., Simons, J.P., & Keeler, B. (1993). An introduction to the sport commitment model. *Journal of Sport & Exercise Psychology, 15*, 1–15.

Scanlan, T.K., Stein, G.L., & Ravizza, K. (1991). An in-depth study of former elite figure skaters: III. Sources of stress. *Journal of Sport & Exercise Psychology, 13*, 103–120.

Scott, D., & Jarrett, C. (1998). A psychophysiological intervention in athletic injury rehabilitation: A case study [Abstract]. *Journal of Applied Sport Psychology, 10* (Suppl.), 139.

Slenker, S.E., Price, J.H., Roberts, S.M., & Jurs, S.G. (1984). Joggers versus nonexercisers: An analysis of knowledge, attitudes, and beliefs about jogging. *Research Quarterly for Exercise and Sport, 55*, 371–378.

Smith, A. (1996). Psychological impact of injuries in athletes. *Sports Medicine, 22*, 391–405.

Smith, A., Scott, S., O'Fallon, W., & Young, M. (1990). Emotional responses of athletes to injury. *Mayo Clinic Proceedings, 65*, 38–50.

Smith, R.E., Ptacek, J.T., & Smoll, F.L. (1992). Sensation seeking, stress, and adolescent injuries: A test of stress-buffering, risk-taking, and coping skills hypotheses. *Journal of Personality and Social Psychology, 62*, 1016–1024.

Smith, R.E., Smoll, F.L., & Ptacek, J.T. (1990). Conjunctive moderator variables in vulnerability and resiliency research: Life stress, social support, and coping skills, and adolescent sport injuries. *Journal of Personality and Social Psychology, 58*, 360–369.

Steadman, R. (1993). A physician's approach to the psychology of injury. In J. Heil (Ed.), *Psychology of sport injury* (pp. 25–31). Champaign, IL: Human Kinetics.

Stuart, J.C., & Brown, B.M. (1981). The relationship of stress and coping ability to incidence of diseases and accidents. *Journal of Psychosomatic Research, 25,* 255–260.

Taylor, A.H., & May, S. (1996). Threat and coping appraisal as determinants of compliance with sports injury rehabilitation: An application of protection motivation theory. *Journal of Sports Sciences, 14,* 471–482.

Taylor, C.B., Miller, N.H., Smith, P.M., & DeBusk, R. (1997). The effect of a home-based, case-managed, multifactorial risk-reduction program on reducing psychological distress in patients with cardiovascular disease. *Journal of Cardiopulmonary Rehabilitation, 17,* 157–162.

Thompson, N.J., & Morris, R.D. (1994). Predicting injury risk in adolescent football players: The importance of psychological variables. *Journal of Pediatric Psychology, 19,* 415–429.

Udry, E. (1995). *Examining mood, coping, and social support in the context of athletic injuries.* Unpublished doctoral dissertation, University of North Carolina–Greensboro.

Udry, E. (1997). Coping and social support among injured athletes following surgery. *Journal of Sport & Exercise Psychology, 19,* 71–90.

Udry, E., Gould, D., Bridges, D., & Beck, L. (1997). Down but not out: Athlete responses to season-ending injuries. *Journal of Sport & Exercise Psychology, 19,* 229–248.

Udry, E., Gould, D., Bridges, D., & Tuffey, S. (1997). People helping people? Examining the social ties of athletes coping with burnout and injury stress. *Journal of Sport & Exercise Psychology, 19,* 369–395.

Udry, E., Shelbourne, K.D., & Gray, T. (2001, October). Recreational athletes' readiness for ACL surgery: Describing and comparing the adolescent and adult experience. In B.W. Brewer (Chair), Adolescent issues in sport injury rehabilitation. Symposium conducted at the Annual Conference of the Association for the Advancement of Applied Sport Psychology, Orlando, FL.

Uitenbroek, D.G. (1996). Sports, exercise, and other causes of injuries: Results of a population survey. *Research Quarterly for Exercise and Sport, 67,* 380–385.

Weiss, M.R., & Troxel, R.K. (1986). Psychology of the injured athlete. *Athletic Training, 21,* 104–109.

Wells, J.K., Howard, G.S., Nowlin, W.F., & Vargas, M.J. (1986). Presurgical anxiety and postsurgical pain and adjustment: Effects of a stress inoculation procedure. *Journal of Consulting and Clinical Psychology, 54,* 831–835.

Wernick, R.L., Jaremko, M.E., & Taylor, P.W. (1981). Pain management in severely burned adults: A test of stress inoculation. *Journal of Behavioral Medicine, 4,* 103–109.

Whitmarsh, B.G., & Alderman, R.B. (1993). Role of psychological skills training in increasing athletic pain tolerance. *The Sport Psychologist, 7,* 388–399.

Wiese-Bjornstal, D.M., & Smith, A.M. (1993). Counseling strategies for enhanced recovery of injured athletes within a team approach. In D. Pargman (Ed.), *Psychological bases of sport injuries* (pp. 149–182). Morgantown, WV: Fitness Information Technology.

Wiese-Bjornstal, D.M., Smith, A.M., & LaMott, E.E. (1995). A model of psychologic response to athletic injury and rehabilitation. *Athletic Training, 1,* 17–30.

Wiese-Bjornstal, D.M., Smith, A.M., Shaffer, S.M., & Morrey, M.A. (1998). An integrated model of response to sport injury: Psychological and sociological dynamics. *Journal of Applied Sport Psychology, 10,* 46–69.

Williams, J.M., & Andersen, M.B. (1997). Psychosocial influences on central and peripheral vision and reaction time during demanding tasks. *Behavioral Medicine, 26,* 160–167.

Williams, J.M., & Andersen, M.B. (1998). Psychosocial antecedents of sport injury: Review and critique of the stress and injury model. *Journal of Applied Sport Psychology, 10,* 5–25.

Williams, J.M., Hogan, T.D., & Andersen, M.B. (1993). Positive states of mind and athletic injury risk. *Psychosomatic Medicine, 55,* 468–472.

Williams, J.M., & Roepke, N. (1993). Psychology of injury and injury rehabilitation. In R.N. Singer, M. Murphey, & L.K. Tennant (Eds.), *Handbook of research on sport psychology* (pp. 815–839). New York: Macmillan.

Williams, J.M., Tonymon, P., & Andersen, M.B. (1990). Effects of life-event stress on anxiety and peripheral narrowing. *Behavioral Medicine, 16,* 174–181.

Williams, J.M., Tonymon, P., & Andersen, M.B. (1991). Effects of stressors and coping resources on anxiety and peripheral narrowing in recreational athletes. *Journal of Applied Sport Psychology, 3,* 126–141.

Williams, J.M., Tonymon, P., & Wadsworth, W.A. (1986). Relationship of stress to injury in intercollegiate volleyball. *Journal of Human Stress, 12,* 38–43.

Wong, I. (1998). *Injury rehabilitation behavior: An investigation of stages and processes of change in the athlete-therapist relationship.* Unpublished master's thesis, University of Oregon, Eugene.

Index

About the Editor

Thelma S. Horn, PhD, is an associate professor and member of the graduate faculty at Miami University of Ohio. Horn is the former editor and a current editorial board member of the *Journal of Sport and Exercise Psychology;* associate editor of the *Journal of Applied Sport Psychology;* and an editorial board member for *Measurement in Physical Education and Exercise Science.*

Horn received her PhD in psychology of sport and physical activity from Michigan State University. She earned a master of arts degree in coaching behavior from Western Michigan University at Kalamazoo and a bachelor of science degree in psychology from Calvin College in Grand Rapids, Michigan.

Editor of the first edition of *Advances in Sport Psychology,* Horn has also contributed chapters to several other books and has published many articles and proceedings on sport psychology. In 1999, she was co-winner of the research writing award from *Research Quarterly for Exercise and Sport;* and in 1993, Miami University honored her with the Richard T. Delp Outstanding Faculty Award. In her free time, Horn enjoys reading, running, and watching amateur athletic contests.

About the Contributors

Mark B. Andersen, PhD, is a registered and licensed psychologist in Australia and the United States. He is the first and current Section Editor of the Professional Practice section of *The Sport Psychologist*. Dr. Andersen lives in St. Kilda, Victoria, and actively supports many restaurants in his neighborhood.

Bryan Blissmer, PhD, is an assistant professor in the Department of Physical Education and Exercise Science at the University of Rhode Island. He was awarded the 2001 Society of Behavioral Medicine Outstanding Dissertation award. Dr. Blissmer is currently working with the University of Rhode Island's Cancer Prevention Center.

Stephen H. Boutcher, PhD, is an associate professor in the Department of Physiology and Pharmacology at the University of New South Wales' School of Medical Science. He is a keen golfer and jogger, and he lives in Sydney with his wife, Yati.

Lawrence Brawley, PhD, is a professor in the Department of Kinesiology at the University of Waterloo.

Robert Brustad, PhD, is Professor of Kinesiology and Physical Education at the University of Northern Colorado in Greeley. His major research focus has been in the social psychology of sport and physical activity with primary attention dedicated to parental socialization influences upon children's physical activity and sport involvement. He is former editor and associate editor for the *Journal of Sport and Exercise Psychology* and also served as the Social Psychology chair of the Association for the Advancement of Applied Sport Psychology (AAASP). His hobbies include running, music, and trying to teach his dogs new tricks.

Damon Burton, PhD, is a coauthor of *Competitive Anxiety in Sport*. Dr. Burton uses goal-setting extensively in mental skills consulting with high school, college, and Olympic athletes. He enjoys the outdoors of Idaho and watching and coaching his three sons.

Albert V. Carron, EdD, is coauthor of *The Psychology of Physical Activity* with H. Hausenblas and P. Estabrooks. Dr. Carron also coauthored *The Group Environment Questionnaire: Test Manual* with Lawrence Brawley and Neil Widmeyer. He is a recipient of the International Olympic Committee's "Sport Science Award of the IOC President for 1996."

Deborah L. Feltz, PhD, is currently President and a fellow of the American Academy of Kinesiology and Physical Education. She is also a fellow in the American Psychological Association and served on the sport psychology advisory committee to the U.S. Olympic Committee. Dr. Feltz's research has included studies of modeling influences on motor performance, the influence of self-efficacy on anxiety and sport performance, gender influences on self-efficacy in sport, and the influence of collective efficacy in sport terms. Her most recent scholarship has focused on the development of a model of coaching efficacy and testing its antecedents and consequences.

Emilio Ferrer-Caja, MS, is a doctoral candidate in quantitative psychology at the University of Virginia. Emilio is interested in methods to analyze change and dynamics, intrinsic motivation, and intellectual development and academic achievement.

Kenneth R. Fox, PhD, is an International Fellow of the American Academy of Kinesiology and Physical Education. Dr. Fox is also a Fellow of the British Association of Sport and Exercise Sciences. He is editor of *The Physical Self: From Motivation to Well Being* and coeditor of *Physical Activity and Psychological Well Being*.

Diane Gill, PhD, is past president of Division 47 (Exercise and Sport Psychology) of the American Psychological Association, former president of NASPSPA and of the Research Consortium of AAHPERD, and former editor of the *Journal of Sport and Exercise Psychology*. Her research interests focus on physical activity and well being across the lifespan, with an emphasis on social psychology, particularly gender and cultural diversity. Dr. Gill is author of *Psychological Dynamics of Sport and Exercise.*

Daniel Gould, PhD, is a professor in the Department of Exercise and Sport Science at the University of North Carolina, Greensboro. Dr. Gould is the former president of the Association for the Advancement of Applied Sport Psychology (1988–89) and the American Alliance for Health, Physical Education, Recreation and Dance Sport Psychology Academy (1986). Daniel, his wife, Deb, and his two sons, Kevin and Brian, live in Greensboro, NC. In his leisure time, Dr. Gould enjoys swimming, fitness activities, and spending time with his children.

Susan L. Greendorfer, PhD, was a faculty member in the Department of Kinesiology at the University of Illinois at Urbana-Champaign for 25 years. Her research focused on gender, socialization and physical activity, sport retirement, and mass media portrayals of women in physical activity. Now retired, Dr. Greendorfer's interests are concerned with socialization and leisure.

Christy A. Greenleaf, PhD, is an assistant professor in the Department of Kinesiology, Health Promotion and Recreation at the University of North Texas. She enjoys figure skating.

Sue Jackson, PhD, recently coauthored Flow in Sports: The Keys to Optimal Experiences and Performances with Mihaly Csikszentmihalyi. Since being awarded two doctoral dissertation awards for her study of flow in elite athletes, Dr. Jackson has developed a program of research focusing on investigating the flow phenomenon in physical activity. Sue lives in NSW, Australia with her husband and two sons.

Jay Kimiecik, PhD, is an associate professor in health studies at Miami University in Oxford, Ohio. He is coauthor of *The Intrinsic Exerciser: Discovering the Joy of Exercise* and host of FitTalk, a talk radio show on exercise and fitness. Jay's writing has appeared in such magazines as *Runner's World* and *Psychology Today.* He is also author of the *Y Personal Fitness Program,* an exercise behavior change program that is used in over 500 YMCAs in North America. Dr. Kimiecik lives in Oxford, Ohio with his wife and two children.

Anthony P. Kontos, PhD, received the 2000–2001 Dissertation of the Year Award from the Sport and Exercise Psychology Academy of the National As-

sociation for Sport and Physical Education. Dr. Kontos currently directs research and applied activities at the Behavioral Performance Lab and provides sport psychology consulting to collegiate athletes as part of the Sports Medicine staff at the University of New Orleans. His research interests include perceived risk and risk taking, psychology of injury, sport concussion, youth sports, and applied sport psychology issues.

Vikki Krane, PhD, is a professor in the School of Human Movement, Sport, and Leisure Studies at Bowling Green State University in Ohio.

Kathleen Martin, PhD, is a professor in the Department of Kinesiology at McMaster University. Dr. Martin researches the psychosocial aspects of exercise and other health-related behaviors, with a particular interest in studying the psychological mechanism (e.g., increased self-efficacy, reduced pain) by which exercise improves various aspects of health-related quality of life (HRQL).

Edward McAuley, PhD, is widely published in kinesiology, psychology, and gerontology. He is an Associate of the University of Illinois' Beckman Institute for Advanced Science and Technology. Dr. McAuley is also Associate Editor of the Journal of Aging and Physical Activity and a member of the editorial boards of *Health Psychology* and the *Journal of Behavioral Medicine.*

Shane Murphy, PhD, was the U.S. team sport psychologist at the Olympic Games in Seoul and Albertville and a consultant to the U.S. Olympic Committee on mental preparation for the 2000 Summer Games in Sydney and the 2002 Winter Games in Salt Lake City. Dr. Murphy was given the Distinguished professional Practice Award by the Association for the Advancement of Applied Sport Psychology in 2000. He teaches sport, health, and exercise psychology at Western Connecticut State University.

Sarah Naylor received her PhD in Education from the University of Idaho. Dr. Naylor is currently a Performance Enhancement Instructor at the United States Military Academy.

Alan L. Smith, PhD, teaches undergraduate and graduate courses in social psychology of sport and exercise. His research focuses on friendships and other social relationships of youth in sport and physical activity contexts. Dr. Smith is a Certified Consultant, AAASP and is Director of the Purdue University Mental Skills Training Program, which provides sport psychology services to Purdue intercollegiate athletes and coaches. Dr. Smith is also a member of the USA Swimming Sport Science Committee.

Eileen Udry, PhD, is an assistant professor in the Department of Physical Education at Indiana University-Purdue University Indianapolis. Dr. Udry's research focuses on examining psychosocial aspects of sport injuries. She lives in Indiana where she enjoys working out and trying to remain injury free.

Robin S. Vealey, PhD, is a professor in the Department of Physical Education, Health, and Sport Studies at Miami University in Oxford, Ohio.

Maureen R. Weiss, PhD, served as Director of the Children's Summer Sports Program at the University of Oregon from 1982 to 1997. She also served as President for the Association for the Advancement of Applied Sport Psychology (AAASP) from 1996 to 1998. Dr. Weiss has also served as Editor of *Research Quarterly for Exercise and Sport* (1993–1996) and as Associate Editor of the *Journal of Sport and Exercise Psychology* (1998–2000). She is currently serving as President-elect of the Research Consortium of AAHPERD.

W. Neil Widmeyer, PhD, taught and coached at the University of Waterloo for 25 years. He presently teaches sessionals at McMaster, Wilfrid Laurier, and York universities. During the past seven years, Dr. Widmeyer has done extensive consulting with numerous skiers, skaters, and golfers, as well as the highly successful Guelph Storm hockey team.